# Baker's Concise
# Dictionary
# of Religion

# Baker's Concise Dictionary of Religion

### Donald T. Kauffman,
### *Editor*

**BAKER BOOK HOUSE**
Grand Rapids, Michigan 49506

Formerly published under the title,
*The Dictionary of Religious Terms*
and
*Baker's Pocket Dictionary of Religious Terms*

© 1967 by Donald T. Kauffman

Reprinted by Baker Book House
with permission of copyright owner

ISBN: 0-8010-5467-2

First printing, July 1985

*For Jeanne*

# PREFACE

This book seeks to present as much information about significant religious terms, symbols, rites, faiths, movements, orders, sites, ideas, and people as could be put within these pages. The scope is as broad as the questing spirit of man; the entries range from the major faiths to the smallest religious groups, from religious art and architecture to music and literature with spiritual overtones, from ancient animism through church history to such diverse contemporary phenomena as the cargo cults, the theology of the death of God, and the Second Vatican Council.

Living persons have not been included except as they relate inseparably to some contemporary religious movement or fact. On the other hand, revisions and additions were continued up to the latest practicable point before publication.

In many cases the meaning of an entry follows it immediately in italics. The use of SMALL CAPITALS throughout indicates a related entry under that or a similar heading. Few abbreviations are included except for c. for "approximately."

I have tried to indicate merely the religious meanings of the terms herein; many of these have other meanings which this volume does not attempt to list. And at the risk of oversimplifying, I have sought to include only the most significant information under the various entries. Yet no one can be more conscious than myself of the limitations of any attempt to pinpoint in a few words the nature of a faith, the dimensions of a life, or the meaning of a great religious idea or movement. Obviously, many volumes could be (and of course have been) written about each of hundreds of the entries. In addition, I have often had to choose between imposing authorities in seeking to establish all manner of facts (especially dates). Material herein, therefore, may not always agree with other "standard references." For the non-expert who wants a concise guide to the central facts and terms in the worlds of religion, however, this book will, I trust, be of service.

It would be impossible to give proper acknowledgment to all those to whom I am indebted for the completion of this dictionary. Certainly no one could prepare such a work without help from a great many individuals, living and dead; inevitably he must stand on the shoulders of Titans. A special debt of gratitude is owed by the undersigned for the counsel and help of Monsignor Henry G. J. Beck, Rabbi Solomon S. Bernards, Mr. Irving Bussel, Mr. Belden Menkus, and Dr. Frank S. Mead. And the book is much the better for the heroic editorial labors of Miss Lois Balcom. It goes without saying that all its inadequacies are my own.

Working on a book like this becomes an incredible journey. On it one meets gallant and saintly souls across the ages, and is continually amazed at the glory and the shame, the love and cruelty and faith and hope all woven together in the fabric of the history of religion.

All of it I have tried to present as accurately, fairly, and objectively as possible. Yet no one is without presuppositions, and I would not attempt to conceal my own Christian conviction. Writing this book has increased my appreciation for the many fascinating facets of man's religious quest—and has enlarged my confidence in the God beyond all human comprehension, the God in whom we live and move and have our being, to whom be glory forever.

DONALD T. KAUFFMAN

# A

**A** 1. Greek letter Alpha, *beginning.* 2. Symbol for CODEX ALEXANDRINUS.

**A.A.** Abbreviation for ALCOHOLICS ANONYMOUS.

**AAH-TE-HUTI** Egyptian moon god and manifestation of THOTH.

**AARON** First high priest in JUDAISM; brother and assistant of MOSES.

**AARON BEN MOSES BEN ASHER (eleventh century)** Rabbi who collected various readings of the OLD TESTAMENT. His system of vowel and accent markings is still used.

**AARON BEN ELIJAH OF NICOMEDIA (fourteenth century)** Jewish theologian and Bible interpreter.

**AARONIC** 1. Related to AARON, or to the Jewish AARONITES. 2. Belonging to the second order of MORMON priests.

**AARONITES** Jewish priests descended from AARON.

**AB** 1. Fifth month in the Jewish ecclesiastical year. The ninth day of Ab marks the Fast of Ab, commemorating the destruction of Jerusalem and the temple. 2. In ancient Egyptian religion, the will and emotion symbolized by the heart.

**ABACUC** HABAKKUK.

**ABADDON** *destruction* 1. OLD TESTAMENT realm of the dead. 2. Hebrew counterpart of Greek Apollyon, angel who reigns over the bottomless pit (REVELATION 9:11).

**AB AETERNO** *forever.*

**ABAILARD** See ABELARD.

**ABANA, ABANAH, or AMANA** River of Syria (II KINGS 5:12) identified with the modern Nahr Barada which flows from the Anti-Lebanon to Damascus.

**ABARBANEL** See ABRAVANEL.

**ABARIM** *places beyond* 1. Mountain in Moab near the Dead Sea (NUMBERS 27:12). 2. The whole land east of the Jordan River.

**ABBA** *father* 1. ARAMAIC word for father or Father (God). 2. In JUDAISM, teacher or sage. 3. In EASTERN churches, title of BISHOP or PATRIARCH.

**ABBA ARIKA (160–247)** Babylonian Jewish teacher whose studies led to the compilation of the TALMUD.

**ABBACY** The office, term, jurisdiction, or privileges of an ABBOT.

**ABBAHU (279–320)** Palestinian RABBI, praised by Roman officials, who encouraged the study of Greek by the Jewish people.

**ABBA MARI (13th–14th century)** French RABBI whose defense of orthodox JUDAISM against philosophic rationalism led to a schism among the Jews.

**ABBAS EFFENDI ABDU-L-BAHA (1844–1921)** Early leader of BAHAISM; son of the founder.

**ABBAYE (273–339)** Outstanding Jewish teacher of Babylonia.

**ABBÉ** French title of ABBOT or ecclesiastic.

**ABBESS** Superior or leader of a CONVENT or community of NUNS.

**ABBEY** 1. A MONASTERY. 2. A church connected with a monastery.

**ABBO OF FLEURY (c.945–1004)** French monk who defended his monastery from domination by the bishops. He was a prolific writer.

**ABBOT** 1. Head of an abbey for men. 2. Clerical or lay head of a guild in the Middle Ages.

**ABBOT, EZRA (1819–1884)** NEW TESTAMENT scholar, professor at Harvard Divinity School.

**ABBOT, GEORGE (1562–1633)** Archbishop of Canterbury who had PURITAN sympathies and contributed translations to the KING JAMES BIBLE.

**ABBOTT, EDWIN ABBOTT (1838–1926)**

ANGLICAN clergyman, biographer, student of the GOSPELS, and popular religious writer.

**ABBOTT, LYMAN (1835–1922)** CONGREGATIONAL writer, editor, and pastor of Plymouth Church in Brooklyn, New York. He advocated humane theology and social reform.

**ABBREVIATOR** An official who drafted the pope's ecclesiastical writings. The college of abbreviators was abolished in 1908.

**ABDA** See OBADIAH.

**ABD AR-RAZZAQ (?–1329)** Persian mystic and pantheistic philosopher; author of a SUFI dictionary.

**ABDIAS** See OBADIAH.

**ABDU-L-BAHA** BAHAIST title.

**ABDULLAH IBN YASIN (?–c.1059)** MOSLEM founder of the sect of the ALMORAVIDES.

**ABECEDARIANS** Sixteenth-century German followers of Nicolas STORCH, who held that human knowledge hinders religious understanding and that knowledge even of the alphabet is unnecessary.

**À BECKET** See THOMAS À BECKET.

**ABEDNEGO** One of the three companions of Daniel cast into a furnace by Nebuchadnezzar during the Jewish captivity in Babylon (DANIEL 3:1–30; I MACCABEES 2: 59).

**ABEKEN, HEINRICH (1809–1872)** German theologian and diplomat.

**ABEL** Second son of Adam and Eve, killed by his brother Cain (GENESIS 4:1–5).

**ABELARD, PIERRE or PETER (1079–1142)** SCHOLASTIC theologian and philosopher. Emphasizing the place of reason in theology, he influenced the rationalism of the thirteenth century. Famous for his romance with his pupil Héloïse. Also spelled Abailard.

**ABELIANS or ABELITES** Christian sect which arose about 370 in North Africa, practiced continence in marriage, and was extinct by the year 400.

**ABELL or ABEL, THOMAS (?–1540)** Chaplain to Catherine of Aragon. Opposing her divorce by Henry VIII, he was executed for treason but was later beatified.

**ABEN-EZRA (c.1092–1167)** Full name Abraham ben Meir Ibn Ezra. Celebrated Spanish rabbi, commentator, philosopher, and theologian. He wrote prodigiously,

emphasizing history and grammar in his OLD TESTAMENT commentaries.

**ABERNETHY, JOHN (1680–1740)** Irish PRESBYTERIAN clergyman who, though EVANGELICAL in belief, opposed tests of ORTHODOXY and stood for freedom of conscience.

**ABGAR V** Mesopotamian king who, according to tradition, sent a letter to Jesus asking relief from his leprosy and received a reply promising to send him one of the disciples. These Epistles of Abgar were pronounced apocryphal by the Council of Rome in 494.

**ABHAYAGIRI** Famous BUDDHIST monastery at Anuradhapura.

**ABHIDHAMMA or ABHIDHAMMAPITAKA** (one of the three PITAKAS) Division of BUDDHIST scriptures, largely a commentary on Buddha's sermons.

**ABHISEKA** 1. HINDU ceremonial bathing. 2. Highest state of BUDDHIST perfection. 3. Buddhist baptism or consecration. 4. Rite in vedic religion involving anointing of king or officials.

**ABIATHAR** Jewish priest who defended David but rebelled against Solomon (I SAMUEL 22:9–23; II SAMUEL 15:17, 29).

**ABIB** See NISAN.

**ABIBAS** Martyr of Edessa burned in 322, commemorated as a saint in the Greek Church.

**ABIGAIL** 1. Wife of NABAL; later became the wife of DAVID, King of Israel. 2. A sister of David.

**ABIMELECH** *father of the king* 1. The name of several Philistine kings mentioned in the OLD TESTAMENT; possibly a title. 2. A son of Gideon who murdered his 70 brothers (JUDGES 9).

**ABISHAG** Beautiful Shunammite girl who cherished King David in his old age (I KINGS 1, 2).

**ABJURATION** Formal renunciation of APOSTASY, HERESY, or SCHISM.

**ABLUTION** Cleansing as a religious rite. The cleansing agent is usually water, but oil, blood, sulphur, and other materials are used in some religions for ritual washing. ROMAN CATHOLIC ablution means: *a.* washing of the celebrant's fingers and the chalice during mass; *b.* the mixture of water and wine with which the ablution is performed.

**ABNER** *father of light* Commander of

King Saul's army. Killed by Joab, he was mourned by David (II SAMUEL 2, 3).

**ABODAH** *divine service* Worship in the Jewish sanctuary.

**ABODE OF LOVE** AGAPEMONE. Religious community founded by Henry James Prince at Spaxton, England, c.1850. The group held all things in common and believed in the imminent return of Christ. Although the members enjoyed a reputation for righteousness, a scandal and lawsuit erupted c.1860.

**ABOLITIONISM** Belief in the abolition of slavery. Adherents of this belief in the United States formed a movement c.1830–1861 with strong religious foundations.

**ABOMINATION** Bible term for something horrible, particularly, wrong ritual or belief.

**ABOMINATION OF DESOLATION** Desecration of the Jerusalem temple or a similar profanation (MATTHEW 24:15; MARK 13:14).

**ABRACADABRA** Magical word or diagram, perhaps of Syrian origin. An abracadabra of the second century was a GNOSTIC formula for protection from evil powers.

**ABRAHAM** Father of the Jewish people, regarded by Christians as spiritual father of all who believe (GALATIANS 3:7). His titles Father of the Faithful and Friend of God (II CHRONICLES 20:7) are also used by MOHAMMEDANS who deem him ancestor of the Arabs. Abraham traveled from Ur of the Chaldees to Canaan where God entered into a COVENANT with him and his faith was tested (GENESIS 11:27–25:10).

**ABRAHAM, APOCALYPSE OF** See APOCALYPSE OF ABRAHAM.

**ABRAHAM, USQUE** (sixteenth century) Portuguese Jew who translated the Spanish Bible.

**ABRAHAM ABELE BEN CHAIM HA-LEVI** (1635–1683) Polish authority on Jewish law.

**ABRAHAM A SANCTA CLARA** (1644–1709) Popular but eccentric AUGUSTINIAN monk and preacher of Vienna.

**ABRAHAM BEN DAVID OF POSQUIERES** (1125–1198) Author of important opinions on Jewish law.

**ABRAHAM BEN MEIR IBN EZRA** See ABENEZRA.

**ABRAHAM IBN DAUD** (c.1110–1180) Spanish Jewish historian and philosopher who espoused ARISTOTELIANISM and influenced MAIMONIDES.

**ABRAHAMITES** 1. Ninth-century followers of Abraham of Antioch who were accused of idolatry, licentiousness, and heresy. 2. Eighteenth-century Bohemian group who professed the religion of Abraham but rejected all Scripture except the Ten Commandments (see DECALOGUE) and the LORD'S PRAYER.

**ABRAHAMS, ISRAEL** (1858–1925) Liberal Jewish leader and rabbinic scholar.

**ABRAM** See ABRAHAM.

**ABRAVANEL or ABARBANEL, ISAAC** (1437–1508) Spanish Jewish philosopher, theologian, statesman, and Biblical exegete. He emphasized importance of original setting for understanding of the Bible.

**ABRAVANEL, JUDAH** (c.1460–1530) Jewish physician and philosopher who said that happiness is "union of human intellect with divine intelligence."

**ABRAXAS** Name applied by GNOSTIC leader to God or to the 365 spirits emanating from Him. An Abraxas stone is a jewel engraved with the word Abraxas in Greek, whose letters number 365.

**ABSALOM** *father of peace* Handsome third son of David who killed his brother Amnon for violating their sister Tamar, led a rebellion against his father, and was slain when his long hair caught in a tree (II SAMUEL 3:3; 13–19).

**ABSALON** (c.1128–1201) Danish general who became Archbishop of Lund. Victorious in war, intellectually brilliant, he introduced religious orders into Denmark and built schools and churches.

**ABSOLUTE, THE** In philosophy, the ultimate or unknowable; in theology, ultimate Reality or God.

**ABSOLUTE IDEALISM** Hegelian philosophical system viewing all reality as an expression of the Absolute Intelligence. (See HEGEL, GEORG WILHELM FRIEDRICH.)

**ABSOLUTION** Remission of the guilt or penalty of sin. CATHOLIC absolution must be through a priest or bishop following contrition, confession, and promise of satisfaction.

**ABSTEMII** Persons who abstain from drinking wine at the EUCHARIST.

**ABSTINENCE** 1. Refraining from any-

thing, such as marriage, food, or drink.
2. Fasting. 3. Refraining from alcoholic beverages.

**ABSTINENTS** Third-century sect in France and Spain whose members condemned marriage, meat, and wine. They claimed that these were made not by God but by the devil.

**ABU** Mountain in Rajputana, India, sacred to JAINS and HINDUS. More than a mile high, it is famous for its shrines.

**ABU BAKR (c.573–634)** *father of the camel's foal* One of the first converts and a close friend of MOHAMMED. Known as al-Siddik, "the Faithful," he succeeded Mohammed as leader of ISLAM. During his two years as KHALIF, the religion became firmly entrenched in Arabia.

**ABU HANIFA (699–767)** Mohammedan jurist and theologian of Persia who founded the HANAFITE legal system of ISLAM.

**ABULAFIA, ABRAHAM BEN SAMUEL (1240–1292)** Spanish Jew who attempted to convert the pope to JUDAISM.

**ABU-L-FARAJ** See BAR HEBRAEUS, GREGORIUS.

**ABUNA** *our father* METROPOLITAN of the ABYSSINIAN CHURCH.

**ABUNDANTIA** *abundance* Roman goddess of good luck and prosperity.

**ABU SAID IBN ABI-L-KHAIR (976–1049)** First Persian DERVISH to write a rubaiyat in the SUFI tradition.

**ABYDOS** Center of OSIRIS worship in ancient Egypt.

**ABYSS** 1. In the OLD TESTAMENT Scriptures, the place of departed spirits. 2. In the NEW TESTAMENT, the abode of Satan and the demons. 3. In GNOSTICISM, the supreme deity.

**ABYSSINIAN CHURCH** The Church of Ethiopia, dating from the fourth century, requiring CIRCUMCISION and SABBATH worship. Traditionally MONOPHYSITE, it was connected with the COPTIC CHURCH of Egypt until 1936.

**A.C.** 1. *Ante Christum,* before Christ. 2. *Anno Christi,* in the year of Christ.

**ACACIA** Durable wood used in the furniture of the Jewish tabernacle and burned on BUDDHIST altars. It is considered a symbol of immortality.

**ACACIAN SCHISM** 1. Fourth-century division over ARIANISM, named for ACACIUS

OF CAESAREA. 2. Fifth-century division between the Eastern and Western churches caused in part by publication of the HENOTIKON, a formula for union between MONOPHYSITES and the orthodox.

**ACACIAN SECT** Disciples of ACACIUS OF CAESAREA.

**ACACIUS (c.322–436)** Bishop of Berea who helped depose CHRYSOSTOM.

**ACACIUS OF CAESAREA (?–366)** Arian bishop who opposed the NICENE CREED and was deposed by the Synod of LAMPSACUS.

**ACACIUS OF CONSTANTINOPLE (?–488)** PATRIARCH who persuaded the Emperor ZENO to issue the HENOTIKON which led to schism in the church.

**ACADEMIES, EVANGELICAL** German PROTESTANT retreats for Christian study.

**ACADEMIES, PONTIFICAL** CATHOLIC societies for the study of art, science, etc.

**ACADEMIES, TALMUDIC** Jewish schools for the study of TALMUDIC law.

**A CAPELLA** *in church* Singing without instrumental accompaniment.

**ACARIE, SISTER MARIA (1566–1618)** CARMELITE nun and mystical leader.

**ACATHISTUS** *not sitting* Hymn of the GREEK CATHOLIC CHURCH in honor of MARY.

**ACATHOLIC** *not Catholic.*

**ACCAD** See AKKAD.

**ACCA LARENTIA** Roman goddess of fertility, guardian of the city.

**ACCEPTANCE** Favorable acceptance of man by God. In many religions this is accomplished by ritual or ethical deeds. In CHRISTIANITY man is accepted by God through Christ's redemption, which is accepted by faith and produces good works.

**ACCEPTANTS** Eighteenth-century French clergymen who accepted the Bull UNIGENITUS without reservation during the debate over JANSENISM.

**ACCESS, PRAYER OF** Prayer before the EUCHARIST.

**ACCIDENT** Philosophically, the quality of something not essential to its nature, like color or shape. Theologically, CATHOLICISM holds that the bread and wine consecrated in the mass retain their "accidents"—their outward appearance—but in essence are transubstantiated into the very body and blood of Christ.

**ACCIDIA or ACCIDIE** Capital sin of spiritual indifference or laziness.

**ACCOMMODATION** 1. Adaptation of religious truth to the comprehension of the learner. 2. Application of one reference to a different one, as is done in Matthew 2:15 in quoting Hosea 11:1.

**ACELDAMA, HACELDAMA, or AKELDAMA** Potter's field where Judas hanged himself (MATTHEW 27:3–10; ACTS 1:16–19).

**ACHAB** See AHAB.

**ACHAIA** Province of Greece whose capital was Corinth and whose Christian converts aided the poor in Jerusalem (ROMANS 15:26).

**ACHAN** Member of the tribe of Judah who hid part of the spoil from Jericho and who was stoned to death in punishment (JOSHUA 7).

**ACHAZ** See AHAZ (MATTHEW 1:9).

**ACHELOUS** Greek river god.

**ACHERON** In Greek mythology, river bounding HADES.

**ACHIACHARUS** Adviser of SENNACHERIB whose moralizing fables and wise sayings have been found in various eastern cultures, including the Jewish colony of ELEPHANTINE.

**ACHILLES** Outstanding hero of the Trojan War in Greek mythology. Dipped in the River Styx to be made invulnerable, he could be wounded only in the heel which the water did not cover.

**ACHIOR** Sheikh of the AMMONITES in the book of Judith.

**ACHISH** King of Gath who aided David when fleeing from Saul (I SAMUEL 21; 27—29).

**ACHTERFELDT, JOHANN HEINRICH (1788–1864)** German theologian, adept in dogmatic and systematic theology, who upheld the Hermesian School.

**ACKERMANN, PETER FOURER (1771–1831)** ROMAN CATHOLIC theologian and professor of Old Testament language, literature, and theology.

**ACOEMETI or STUDITES** Order of monks founded early in the fifth century by the Syrian monk Alexander. Divided into three groups who worked in continuous relays, they performed divine service without interruption day and night. They were condemned by a synod in Rome in 534 for holding that MARY was not the mother of God.

**ACOLYTE** An assistant in worship. In CATHOLICISM, *a.* an assistant at mass, or *b.* a member of the highest of the four minor orders.

**ACOMINATUS, MICHAEL (c.1140–1220)** Clergyman, writer, and Archbishop of Athens.

**ACONCIO, GIACOMO (1492–c.1566)** Italian engineer who left the ROMAN CATHOLIC CHURCH for the DUTCH REFORMED CHURCH in London and was refused the sacrament by the Bishop of London. A pioneer in religious toleration, he sought a common denominator, calling the different creeds "stratagems of Satan" to divide the church.

**ACOSMISM** Philosophical view that denies the reality of the world and holds that only God is real.

**ACOSTA, JOSE DE (c.1539–1600)** Spanish author and member of the SOCIETY OF JESUS who became a missionary to Peru and an astute historian of Peru and Mexico.

**ACOSTA, URIEL (c.1590–1647)** Portuguese CATHOLIC who converted to JUDAISM but was excommunicated for the bitterness of his attacks on Christianity. Apparently disillusioned by both faiths, he finally committed suicide.

**ACRE** Harbor on seacoast of Palestine; also called Ptolemais. It was the center of many struggles, religious and secular, particularly during the CRUSADES.

**ACRELIUS, ISRAEL (1714–1800)** Swedish missionary in Delaware, Pennsylvania, and New Jersey.

**ACRES OF DIAMONDS** Lecture by Russell CONWELL, later a book, the proceeds from which helped educate thousands of American youths. Its thesis is that treasure is often found close at hand.

**ACROSTIC** Arrangement of words in which the first letter of each line ordinarily combines with others to form a word or words, or the alphabet. The first eight verses of Psalm 119 all begin with the letter aleph, the next eight with the letter beth, and so on through all the letters of the Hebrew alphabet. The Greek word for fish, *ichthus,* had a special meaning for early Christians because of the following acrostic:

> Iesous (Jesus)
> CHristos (Christ)
> THeou (of God)
> Uiou (the Son)
> Soter (the Saviour)

**ACT** What a person does freely and purposefully. In moral theology, such action merits praise or blame unless an act becomes less than human through such factors as ignorance, force, or mere habit. Metaphysically, act is a state of real as opposed to possible existence.

**ACTA APOSTOLICAE SEDIS** Official publication of the VATICAN.

**ACTA MARTYRUM** *Acts of the Martyrs* A record of the acts and lives of the early Christians who died for their faith. EUSEBIUS OF CAESAREA was an early compiler of such a record. Many such accounts were collected.

**ACTA SANCTORUM** *Acts of the Saints* A collection of saints' lives begun in the seventeenth century by BOLLANDISTS, Jesuit scholars. It is arranged according to the days of the calendar but has not yet reached the month of December.

**ACTION** Ancient name for the mass.

**ACTION SERMON** In Scottish PRESBYTERIANISM, a sermon before the LORD'S SUPPER.

**ACTIVISM** Philosophy of ultimate reality as activity, or of ultimate truth as pragmatic utility.

**ACT OF GOD** Legal conception of an unavoidable event.

**ACTON, JOHN E.E.D. (1834–1902)** Liberal ROMAN CATHOLIC historian and editor in England who chafed at the church's hierarchy and opposed the doctrine of papal infallibility until its official promulgation. He was a Lord, a Member of Parliament, and a brilliant professor of modern history at Cambridge; famous for the aphorism, "Power tends to corrupt; absolute power corrupts absolutely."

**ACTS OF JOHN** Apocryphal account, dating from the second or third century, of the life and death of the Apostle JOHN.

**ACTS OF PILATE** Apocryphal story, probably dating from the fourth century, of the trial, execution, and resurrection of CHRIST.

**ACTS OF ST. PAUL** Apocryphal, romantic account of the works of the Apostle PAUL, dating from the second century.

**ACTS OF ST. PETER** Apocryphal account, dating from the second century, of the miracles and martyrdom of the Apostle PETER. It includes both the "Quo Vadis?" story and that of Peter being crucified head downward.

**ACTS OF STS. PAUL AND THECLA** Apocryphal account of events in the lives of the Apostle Paul and a virgin named Thecla. It was taken from the ACTS OF ST. PAUL.

**ACTS OF THE APOSTLES** Fifth book of the NEW TESTAMENT, written by LUKE (a companion and probably the physician of PAUL) as a sequel to the Gospel of Luke. It records the history of the church from the ascension of CHRIST to the imprisonment of Paul in Rome.

**ACTS OF THE MARTYRS** See ACTA MARTYRUM.

**ACTS OF THE SAINTS** See ACTA SANCTORUM.

**ACTUAL GRACE** The gracious impulsion of God inclining a person toward good.

**ACTUAL SIN** Personal, voluntary rebellion against, or lack of conformity to, the will of God.

**ACUÑA, CRISTÓBAL DE (1597–c.1676)** Spanish JESUIT missionary and explorer of the Amazon.

**A.D.** See "ANNO DOMINI."

**AD** According to the KORAN and Arabian tradition, son of Uz and ancestor of the Adites, a powerful tribe of giants who worshiped four idols: Sakia, Hafedha, Razeka, and Salema.

**ADAB** Ancient city of Mesopotamia containing a temple of the goddess ARURU and a ZIGGURAT (a temple in the shape of a square tower with a ramp spiraling up the sides).

**ADAD or HADAD** God of storms in Canaan, Syria, and Babylonia; also known as Ramman, "The Thunderer." A temple to him and to the sky god ANU has been found at Assur.

**ADAH** 1. Wife of Lamech (GENESIS 4:19 ff.). 2. Wife of Esau who was also called Bashemath (GENESIS 26:34; 36:2, 4).

**ADALBERT, ST. (?–741)** English saint who built a church in Egmont, Holland, and became Utrecht's first archbishop.

**ADALBERT, ST. (c.950–997)** "Apostle of the Prussians" who became Bishop of Prague and later missionary in Germany and Poland.

**ADALBERT or ADELBERT (c.1000–1072)** Saxon nobleman appointed Archbishop of Hamburg and Bremen, which he tried to make the center of a unified church of Northern Europe with himself as PATRI-

ARCH. Although he was a capable church-man and statesman, this plan failed.

**ADALDAGUS (tenth century)** Archbishop of Hamburg and Bremen who established three EPISCOPAL sees in Jutland and sent missionaries among the northern nations.

**ADALHARD (c.753–826)** Abbot of Corbie; one of the first to proclaim openly that the laws must be obeyed equally by patricians and by commoners.

**ADAM** 1. The Hebrew word for man. 2. The first man, created by God in His image to have dominion over the earth. Placed in the garden of Eden, he was expelled when he ate the fruit of the forbidden tree of the knowledge of good and evil (GENESIS 1—3).

**ADAM, MELCHIOR (?–1622)** German scholar and churchman whose writings provide much information about the history, churchmen, and philosophers of the sixteenth century.

**ADAM, THE LAST** In the Apostle Paul's doctrine, Jesus Christ as head of a new race. As Adam's sin brought death to mankind, Paul states, Christ's work of salvation brought men eternal life (ROMANS 5:12–21; I CORINTHIANS 15:22, 45–49).

**ADAMITES** 1. A sect of the second and third centuries in North Africa whose adherents worshiped without clothing to indicate a return to the purity of Adam before the fall. 2. A group which appeared in Europe in the thirteenth century whose members had communistic ideas and a belief in cleansing from sin and the coming of a Savior named Marokan. They were suppressed and persecuted for centuries.

**ADAM KADMON** Jewish name for primeval man, closer to God than Adam.

**ADAMNAN (c.624–704)** Irish historian and saint whose *Life of St. Columba* and *Concerning Holy Places* are valuable antiquities.

**ADAM OF ST. VICTOR (?–1177 or 1192)** Author of a BIBLE dictionary and of sequences (hymn-like rhythms sung in medieval times). Some consider him to be one of the greatest poets of the Middle Ages.

**ADAMS, HANNAH (1755–1831)** New England author who wrote the first study of the Jews in America and also a dictionary of religions.

**ADAM'S BRIDGE** A chain of shoals between Ceylon and India originating, according to SANSKRIT legend, with RAMA. He built the chain as a causeway to rescue his wife Sita who had been kidnaped by a monkey.

**ADAM SCOTUS (twelfth century)** Scottish MYSTIC and BISHOP.

**ADAMSON, PATRICK (1537–1592)** Scottish CALVINIST who became Archbishop of St. Andrews but was twice excommunicated by the PRESBYTERIAN Church. He translated Job, Lamentations, and Jeremiah into Latin and was considered one of the most learned writers of the sixteenth century.

**ADAM'S PEAK** Mountain in Ceylon considered sacred by BUDDHISTS, HINDUS, and MOHAMMEDANS. The latter believe that an apparent footprint on the summit, more than five feet long, was left by Adam.

**ADAPA** Sage and king of Babylonia. According to Babylonian legend, it was through him mankind lost its immortality.

**ADAR** 1. Babylonian god of the summer sun. 2. Sixth month in the Hebrew civil calendar.

**ADAR SHENI** Second month of ADAR, occurring in the Jewish leap year.

**ADDAMS, JANE (1860–1935)** American social worker who founded Hull House in Chicago, brought about many social reforms, and advocated peace and women's suffrage. She desired "to make social progress . . . express the spirit of Christ."

**ADDER** Venomous serpent symbolizing evil, temptation, or the devil.

**ADDIR HU** Jewish hymn for PASSOVER Eve.

**ADDISON, JOSEPH (1672–1719)** English essayist who wrote *Evidences of the Christian Religion* and paraphrased the Psalms. "The Spacious Firmament on High," based on Psalm 19, is still sung.

**ADDRESS TO THE ROMAN CATHOLICS OF THE UNITED STATES** First ROMAN CATHOLIC publication in the United States, made in 1784 by Bishop John CARROLL.

**ADELBERT** See ADALBERT (c.1000–1072).

**ADEODATUS (fourth century)** Illegitimate son of St. AUGUSTINE.

**ADEODATUS (?–676)** Roman monk who became pope and suppressed the MONOTHELITE belief.

**ADEPTS** MAHATMAS in THEOSOPHY.

**ADHEMAR DE MONTEIL (?–1098)** Bishop and crusader who led the first CRUSADE and sought amicable relationships with Christians of the East.

**ADIAPHORA** *indifferent things* Theological term for things or actions which in themselves are neither moral nor immoral.

**ADIAPHORISTS** Sixteenth-century group which favored the plan of Charles V to reunite CATHOLICS and LUTHERANS by tolerating such things as candles and the Latin MASS while holding to the doctrine of JUSTIFICATION BY FAITH.

**ADIBUDDHA** The eternal BUDDHA from whom the five Dhyani Buddhas have come to earth.

**ADIBUDDHISM** Form of BUDDHISM in Nepal.

**ADI GRANTH** Scripture of SIKHISM.

**AD INFINITUM** Latin phrase meaning "limitless."

**ADITES** See AD.

**ADITI** Name of "The Infinite One" in VEDIC RELIGION.

**ADITYA** 1. HINDU mother of the creator-gods. 2. One of the twelve gods of the months in Hindu myth, sometimes identified with the planets.

**ADJURE** To swear under sacred penalty of a curse.

**ADLER, CYRUS (1863–1940)** Jewish CONSERVATIVE scholar and leader. Founder of the Jewish Historical Society of America, he wrote and edited a number of books and was president of Dropsie College and the Jewish Theological Seminary.

**ADLER, FELIX (1851–1933)** Founder of the Society for ETHICAL CULTURE and the American Ethical Union. He opposed child labor and worked for many other reforms in society, believing that ethical relationships are more important than ritual or belief.

**ADLER, HERMANN (1839–1911)** Chief RABBI in London who worked for various social reforms.

**ADLER, NATHAN MARCUS (1803–1890)** British chief RABBI who originated the United Synagogue of England.

**AD LIMINA APOSTOLORUM** Visits to the tombs of the Apostles Peter and Paul in Rome.

**ADMAD, MIRZA GHULAM** See ADMADIYA.

**ADMADIYA** MOSLEM sect in India founded by Mirza Ghulam Admad. It aggressively seeks members throughout the world.

**AD MAIOREM DEI GLORIAM** *to the greater glory of God* Theistic motto particularly favored by the SOCIETY OF JESUS.

**ADMONITION** Disciplinary action once widely used by churches in considering the expulsion or readmission of delinquent members.

**ADMONITION TO PARLIAMENT** Widely influential PURITAN manifesto, published in 1572, demanding CHURCH OF ENGLAND reforms such as restriction of bishops' power and of "papist" elements in worship, and greater direct reliance upon authority of Scripture.

**ADO (c.800–874)** Archbishop of Vienne in France who compiled a MARTYROLOGY and wrote other books. He had great zeal for morality and church discipline.

**ADONAI** 1. A name for the Lord used by the Jews as a substitute for JEHOVAH, which they considered it sacrilegious to pronounce. 2. Name for one of the AEONS in GNOSTICISM.

**ADONIS** 1. Beautiful youth in Greek mythology whose annual death and resurrection suggests that he was god of vegetation or corn. 2. Greek counterpart of Babylonian TAMMUZ.

**ADONIST** A worshiper of ADONIS.

**ADON OLAM** *Lord of the universe* Jewish hymn chanted at morning worship services.

**ADOPTION** In theology and the NEW TESTAMENT, adoption is God's action in accepting humans into His family as His children, through their faith in Jesus Christ.

**ADOPTIONISM** 1. A HERESY of the second and third centuries that JESUS was purely human until He became divine by adoption at His baptism. 2. Eighth–century Spanish heresy that CHRIST is the Son of God only by adoption.

**ADORATION** 1. Veneration of religious objects or holy persons. 2. Worship of God.

**ADORO TE DEVOTE** *Thee I Adore* Medieval eucharistic hymn, sometimes attributed to THOMAS AQUINAS.

**ADRAMMELECH** Samaritan god to whom children were sacrificed (II KINGS 17:31).

**ADRET, SOLOMON BEN (1235–1310)** Spanish scholar and philosopher who defended JUDAISM against various attacks.

**ADRIAN, ST. (?–303)** Praetorian guard who became a Christian martyr—he was executed and dismembered. Considered a patron saint of soldiers, he is honored on September 8.

**ADRIAN I (?–795)** Pope who put an end to the iconoclastic persecution, supporting the Empress Irene in her battle against ICONOCLASM.

**ADRIAN IV (c.1100–1159)** The only Englishman to be pope. He caused Frederick I and William I to recognize the pope's superiority to the emperor.

**ADRIAN VI (1459–1523)** Pope who had studied under the BRETHREN OF THE COMMON LIFE and been Inquisitor of Aragon and Navarre. Initially welcoming reform, he later opposed doctrinal changes and demanded that Martin LUTHER be punished for heresy.

**ADSULLATA** Celtic river goddess, perhaps a priestess of hot springs.

**ADULTERY** Unfaithfulness to the marriage vow, recognized by most religions as sinful. In the BIBLE, adultery is sometimes a symbolic term for the unfaithfulness of the people of God to Him.

**ADULT SCHOOLS** British nondenominational study groups which seek to enrich life through Bible study, religious and cultural discussion, service projects, and friendship.

**ADVAITA** HINDU term for the denial of dualism, as of spirit and matter.

**ADVENT** 1. The birth of JESUS Christ. 2. The return of CHRIST. 3. The season before Christmas honoring the coming of Christ, beginning with the Sunday nearest November 30.

**ADVENT CHRISTIAN CHURCH** ADVENTIST denomination originally known as the Advent Christian Association; organized in 1860.

**ADVENTISTS** Those who emphasize the SECOND COMING of Christ as an imminent physical return.

**ADVENT SUNDAY** First day of ADVENT and the Sunday nearest St. Andrew's Day on November 30.

**ADVERSARY** In SCRIPTURE, sometimes the devil (I PETER 5:8).

**ADVOCATE** Legal defender of a person or cause. In the New Testament, Christ is the believer's advocate at the judgment (I JOHN 2:1), and the Holy Spirit is an Advocate (*paraclete,* translated "Comforter" in the KING JAMES BIBLE). Beatifi-

cation in the ROMAN CATHOLIC CHURCH involves a DEVIL'S ADVOCATE who seeks arguments against the action and God's advocate who answers such arguments.

**ADVOCATUS DEI** *advocate of God* See ADVOCATE.

**ADVOCATUS DIABOLI** *advocate of the devil* See ADVOCATE; DEVIL'S ADVOCATE.

**ADVOCATUS ECCLESIAE** *advocate of the church* Medieval caretaker of a church or abbey.

**ADVOWSON** ANGLICAN right of appointment to a vacant parish or other ecclesiastical office. In English law the advowson is a right of property which can be sold or transferred.

**ADYTUM** Holiest portion of a temple or church.

**AEACUS** Greek god who was judge of the world of HADES.

**AEDESIUS (?–355)** NEOPLATONIST philosopher who taught EUSEBIUS OF NICOMEDIA.

**AEGEAN RELIGION** Nature worship, controlled by the Aegean kings, of the sun, moon, stars, and other natural objects. It included fetishes, sacrifice, and worship of the dead.

**AEGEAN SEA** Portion of the Mediterranean Sea east of Greece, crossed by the Apostle PAUL in his missionary travels.

**AEGIR** Norse god of the ocean.

**AEGIS** Shield of ZEUS.

**AELFRIC (c.955–1021)** English abbot who taught Christian doctrine and history through HOMILIES. He is said to have denied the immaculate birth of MARY and the doctrine of TRANSUBSTANTIATION.

**AELIA CAPITOLINA** Name of Jerusalem after its destruction in A.D. 70 and its rebuilding by Hadrian with a temple to Jupiter Capitolinus where the Jewish temple had stood.

**AELRED (c.1110–1167)** British abbot, theologian, and church leader.

**AENEAS** A favorite of the gods in Homeric legend.

**AEOLUS** Greek god of the wind.

**AEON or EON** 1. Age or period of time. 2. Emanation from God in GNOSTIC religion.

**AESCULAPIUS or ASKLEPIOS** Greek god of medicine whose staff had a serpent entwined around it. His symbols were the cock and snake, and serpents were kept in the Greek temples of healing.

**AESIR** The greater gods forming the entourage of ODIN in Nordic mythology.

**AESMA** Spirit of vengeance and wrath in ZOROASTRIAN religion.

**AETERNI PATRIS** Encyclical of LEO XIII commending the study of St. THOMAS AQUINAS.

**AETHER or ETHER** 1. Greek element. 2. In STOICISM, God.

**AETIANS** See ANOMOIANS.

**AFFINITY** Theological term for relationship resulting from marriage.

**AFFIRMATION** Solemn declaration, or statement of principles.

**AFFIRMATION OF FAITH** Personal profession of faith.

**AFFLATUS** Supernatural revelation or impulse.

**AFFRE, DENIS AUGUSTE (1793–1848)** Archbishop of Paris who was killed while attempting to bring about peace during the riots of June, 1848.

**AFFUSION** BAPTISM by pouring water over the candidate's head.

**AFIKOMEN** Last thing eaten at the Jewish SEDER.

**AFRICA INLAND MISSION** Largest mission in East Africa, founded in Philadelphia, Pennsylvania, in 1895.

**AFRICAN METHODIST EPISCOPAL CHURCH** Negro denomination which withdrew from the METHODIST EPISCOPAL CHURCH in Philadelphia, Pennsylvania, in 1787.

**AFRICAN METHODIST EPISCOPAL ZION CHURCH** Negro denomination which withdrew from John Street Methodist Church in New York in 1796.

**AFRICAN ORTHODOX CHURCH** Negro denomination which withdrew from the PROTESTANT EPISCOPAL CHURCH in 1919 and maintains EPISCOPAL standards and structure.

**AFRICAN UNION FIRST COLORED METHODIST PROTESTANT CHURCH, INC.** Negro denomination resulting from union of two American denominations in 1866.

**AFRICANUS, SEXTUS JULIUS (fl. 221)** Christian traveler and historian who wrote a history of the world from the creation to his own day.

**AFZELIUS, ARVID AUGUST (1785–1871)** Swedish poet, priest, and translator of mythological poetry.

**AGABUS** Christian prophet of Jerusalem who foretold a famine (ACTS 11:27, 28)

and Paul's imprisonment (ACTS 21:10, 11).

**AGAG** Amalekite king who was cut to pieces by the prophet Samuel (I SAMUEL 15).

**AGA KHAN I (1800–1881)** Persian ruler who became leader of the ISMAILI Mohammedans in India and in many other countries.

**AGA KHAN III (1877–1957)** Grandson of AGA KHAN I who succeeded as spiritual leader of the ISMAILI Mohammedans, founding the All-India Moslem League and contributing lavishly to MOSLEM causes. He became president of the League of Nations in 1937.

**AGAMAS** Religious writings of JAINISM.

**AGANIPPE** Greek nymph whose spring was sacred to the MUSES.

**AGANJU** A god of the West African Yoruba tribe who was the father of seventeen gods including the sun and moon.

**AGAPE** 1. Greek word for self-giving love (see I CORINTHIANS 13). 2. Love-feast or fellowship meal among the early Christians. 3. By about the fourth century A.D., a charity supper no longer connected with the LORD'S SUPPER.

**AGAPEMONE** See ABODE OF LOVE.

**AGAPEMONITES** Members of the Agapemone community who believed that Christ would soon return. They termed themselves "children of the resurrection," and later accepted J. H. Smyth-Pigott as Christ reincarnated.

**AGAPETAE, AGAPETI** 1. Nuns and monks of the early church and the early Middle Ages who lived together ascetically. 2. Fourth-century group of GNOSTICS.

**AGAPETUS I** Pope (535–536), Defender of ORTHODOXY and founder of an ecclesiastical library at Rome.

**AGAPETUS II** Pope (946–955) who sought to regain the former discipline and power of the church.

**AGAR** See HAGAR.

**AGASSIZ, LOUIS (1807–1883)** Brilliant Swiss-American naturalist who believed every specie of life was a thought of God.

**AGASSOU** Panther god of Dahomey, West Africa.

**AGATHA** Sicilian virgin martyred in 251 by torture, fire, and imprisonment. Patron saint of Catania, Sicily.

**AGATHANGELOS (fourth century?) messenger of good tidings** Armenian historian who chronicled the life of St. GREGORY THE ILLUMINATOR and the conversion of Armenia.

**AGATHO (c.575–681)** Pope (678–681) who opposed MONOTHELITISM and secular domination of the church.

**AGATHOLOGY** Theological study of that which is good.

**AGATI** 1. BUDDHIST term for the right spiritual pathway. 2. Buddhist term for regeneration.

**AGDE, COUNCIL OF (506)** Church council which regulated obligations of members and various other matters; though favoring celibacy in the priesthood, it restricted MONASTICISM.

**AGE** In Scripture, often a long indeterminate period of time; frequently the present age is contrasted with the future age in which God reigns supreme.

**AGE, CANONICAL** Ecclesiastical determination of the age at which a person enters a special status.

**AGE OF FAITH** Period of the Middle Ages (c.1000–1500) during which the church deeply affected European society and life.

**AGE OF INNOCENCE** Period before the Fall when man lived in a special relationship to God of neither sin nor salvation (GENESIS 1:28—3:13).

**AGE OF REASON** 1. The eighteenth century in which rationalism and DEISM permeated England and France. 2. The age when an individual is held to be morally responsible, as at the age of seven. 3. Title of Thomas PAINE's Deistic attack on atheism, Christianity, and monarchy.

**AGGEUS** See HAGGAI.

**AGGIORNAMENTO** Pope JOHN XIII's phrase describing his aim "to bring the Church up to date."

**AGHORAPANTHIS** HINDU sect whose members are said to practice cannibalism and to wear little but necklaces of human skulls.

**AGIOS O THEOS Holy God** Anthem originating in Eastern LITURGIES of the church.

**AGLIPAY, GREGORIO (1860–1940)** Founder of the powerful Philippine Independent Church.

**AGNELLUS OF PISA (c.1190–1236)** CATHOLIC founder of the FRANCISCAN Province in England.

**AGNES, ST. (c.291–304)** Roman virgin believed beheaded for her chastity. Her sym-

bol is a lamb, the Latin word for which is *agnus*.

**AGNI** HINDU god of fire; mediator between the gods and men, he forgives and punishes sin.

**AGNOETAE** 1. Fourth-century sect which held that God's omniscience extends only to the present, and to the past only through memory. 2. Sixth-century MONOPHYSITE sect founded by a deacon of Alexandria named Themistius. It held that Christ as a man was not omniscient, on the basis of such Scriptures as MARK 13:32.

**AGNOSTICISM** Philosophy that the truth concerning God and the spiritual world can be neither proved nor disproved.

**AGNUS DEI Lamb of God** 1. Anthem beginning "O Lamb of God." 2. Symbolic representation of Christ as a lamb. 3. A triple invocation in the MASS.

**AGOBARD (c.779–840)** Scholar, prelate, and reformer who opposed image worship, prayer to saints, and many superstitions.

**AGONIZANTS** CATHOLIC fraternity which aids the sick and dying.

**AGONOTHETES** Supervisor of the sacred games in classical Greece.

**AGONY** CHRISTIAN representation of the sufferings of Jesus as He faced the prospect of the cross and prayed that the cup might pass from Him.

**AGRAPHA** The sayings of JESUS not recorded in the four GOSPELS. Very few such sayings are considered authentic.

**AGREDA, MARIA (1602–1665)** Spanish ABBESS who from childhood experienced visions; she wrote *The Mystic City of God.*

**AGRICOLA, JOHANNES (c.1494–1566)** German PROTESTANT reformer who was early associated with LUTHER but who differed from him in the contention that Christians are wholly free from the MOSAIC LAW.

**AGRICOLA, RUDOLPH (1443–1485)** Dutch HUMANIST who opposed SCHOLASTIC THEOLOGY.

**AGRIONIA** Sacred Greek festival celebrated at night in honor of DIONYSUS the Wild.

**AGUDAT ISRAEL** Orthodox Jewish organization founded 1912. (See ORTHODOX JUDAISM.)

**AGUNAH** Jewish term for woman whose husband has disappeared.

**A.H.** MOSLEM symbol of chronology,

marking Mohammed's HEGIRA as the beginning of the MOHAMMEDAN era.

**AHA or AHAI OF SHABHA (eighth century)** Jewish anthologist and TALMUDIST.

**AHAB or ACHAB** King of Israel in the ninth century B.C. A powerful ruler, he is famous for his notorious pagan wife JEZEBEL.

**AHABAH RABBAH** *overflowing love* Ancient Jewish prayer recited twice daily.

**AHAI OF SHABHA** See AHA.

**AHALYA** First woman created by BRAHMA.

**AHASUERUS** 1. The king mentioned in the books of Ezra and Esther who is apparently to be identified with the Persian monarch Xerxes I. Also spelled Assuerus. 2. The WANDERING JEW of medieval legend.

**AHAZ or ACHAZ** King of Judah in the eighth century B.C. During his weak reign the prophets ISAIAH, HOSEA, and MICAH ministered.

**AHI** HINDU serpent god.

**AHIKAR LEGEND** A legend about the Eastern vizier Ahikar the Wise, which appears to have influenced the Book of TOBIT.

**AHIMSA** BUDDHIST and JAIN term for compassion and nonviolence toward every living creature.

**AHITHOPHEL** Adviser to King David who defected to Absalom during the latter's rebellion and hanged himself (II SAMUEL 15 —17).

**AHMAD IBN HANBAL (780–855)** MOSLEM theologian, ascetic, and saint. Founder of the literalistic HANBALITE school of canon law, he collected many Moslem proverbs and traditions, and firmly defended traditional orthodoxy.

**AHMADIYA** Modern reform movement among MOSLEMS; originated in India and marked by evangelistic drive.

**AHRIMAN** Also called Angra Mainyu and Anra Mainyu. The evil principle or leader of evil spirits in ZOROASTRIANISM, "the Destructive Spirit." As the source of evil in the universe, Ahriman is destined to defeat by AHURA MAZDA or Ormazd.

**AHSONNUTLI** Male-female creator in Navajo Indian myth.

**AHURA** See ASURA.

**AHURA MAZDA** *The Wise Lord* Supreme beneficent being in ZOROASTRIANISM, also called Ormazd or Ormuzd. See also AMESHAS.

**AI or HAI** Canaanite city destroyed by JOSHUA.

**AIDAN (?–651)** Irish monk sent from the Iona monastery to evangelize northern England. He established a church, a monastery, and a bishopric in Northumbria, and was praised by the chronicler BEDE.

**AILLY, PIERRE D' (1350–1420)** French cardinal and theologian. He sought to end the GREAT SCHISM of 1378–1417 and took part in the condemnation of John HUSS.

**AILRED (1109–1167)** British MYSTIC, theologian, and ABBOT.

**AIN** See AYIN.

**AINSWORTH, HENRY (1571–c.1622)** English PROTESTANT pastor and scholar; of CONGREGATIONAL, NONCONFORMIST leanings.

**AINU RELIGION** Animistic religion of the aboriginal Ainus of Japan. Central in it is the raising and eating of a bear to whom prayers are made.

**AIRAY, HENRY (c.1560–1616)** Cultured PURITAN pastor, preacher, teacher, and theologian.

**AIR GODS** Gods of the clouds, wind, lightning, etc., common to various religions.

**AISLE** 1. Passage between groups of seats in a church. 2. Properly, a side passage in a church, usually leading off from the NAVE.

**AIYANAR** Popular HINDU god, son of Siva and Vishnu.

**AIZEN MYO-O** Japanese love god.

**AJANTA** Site in Hyderabad, India, of 30 caves containing magnificent BUDDHIST paintings and sculpture.

**AJIVIKA** Humanistic HINDU sect of medieval India similar to JAINISM. Established by GOSALA in the fifth century B.C., its doctrines were deterministic and pessimistic.

**AKA-KANET** Araucanian Indian harvest god.

**AKALIS** Militant ascetic SIKH group.

**AKASHA** BUDDHIST term for ultimate substance of the universe.

**AKBAR, JALAL (1542–1605)** Mogul emperor of India known for his interest in and tolerance of religions other than his native ISLAM. He founded a short-lived eclectic religion called Din Illahi, "The Divine Faith."

**AKEDAH** Jewish term for the binding of a sacrifice.

**AKELDAMA** See ACELDAMA.

**À KEMPIS** See THOMAS À KEMPIS.

**AKHENATON** See IKHNATON.

**AKHMIM FRAGMENT** Greek fragment containing portions of apocryphal writings; discovered in Egypt in 1886.

**AKHNATON** See IKHNATON.

**AKIBA (or AKIVA) BEN JOSEPH (c.50–132)** Great Palestinian RABBI martyred by the Romans in the revolt of BAR KOKBA. He systematized the HALAKAH, carefully compiling the oral laws of JUDAISM.

**AKKAD or ACCAD** Ancient name for north Babylonia, center of Semitic culture.

**AKKUM** Jewish term for star worshipers, pagans.

**AKRA** Persian bird of immortality.

**AKSHOBHYA** The imperturbable BUDDHA.

**AKSUM** See AXUM.

**AKUA** Polynesian name for Hawaiian gods.

**AKUPERA** HINDU name for the turtle which supports the earth.

**ALABARCH** Chief magistrate of JUDAISM in Alexandria under the Ptolemies.

**ALABASTER** Marble, symbol of heaven, often used in temples and tombs.

**ALABASTER, WILLIAM (1567–1640)** English mystical poet and commentator.

**ALACOQUE, MARGARET MARY, ST. (1647–1690)** French nun who had a vision of Christ and founded the devotion to the Sacred Heart of Jesus; canonized in 1920.

**ALAGHOM NAUM** Supreme deity and creator worshiped by the Mayan Tzental tribe.

**ALAIN DE LILLE (c.1128–1202)** French scholastic theologian, poet, and philosopher. Although he emphasized the importance of faith in Christianity, he sought to undergird faith with logic.

**ALAPA** Light blow on the cheek of a person being confirmed, symbolizing his entrance into spiritual warfare.

**ALASCO, JOHANNES** See LASKI, JOHN.

**ALB** Long white linen liturgical vestment with long sleeves, worn by priests celebrating the eucharist. It symbolizes innocence or purity.

**ALBAN, ST. (third or fourth century)** First British martyr, probably slain by Diocletian, Decius, or Valerian. About 793 a church was built where Alban was martyred, and later a MONASTERY.

**ALBANEL, CHARLES (1616–1696)** Jesuit missionary who came from France to Canada in 1649 and explored much new land.

**ALBANIAN ORTHODOX CHURCH** The Albanian branch of the EASTERN ORTHODOX CHURCH, descending from the ancient Western Illyricum. The Albanian Orthodox Diocese in America includes about half the Albanians in the United States.

**ALBERONI, GIULIO (1664–1752)** Spanish-Italian CARDINAL and political figure.

**ALBERT OF PRUSSIA (1490–1568)** PROTESTANT duke who secularized his duchy and supported OSIANDER in his quarrel with MELANCHTHON over JUSTIFICATION by faith.

**ALBERTUS MAGNUS (c.1206–1280)** Outstanding SCHOLASTIC philosopher. A scientific observer, he tried to square the ideas of ARISTOTLE with the doctrines of Christianity. His *Summa Theologiae* influenced THOMAS AQUINAS, but he said of theology: "It is taught by demons, it teaches about demons, and it leads to demons."

**ALBIGENSES** Medieval "heretics" concentrated in southern France. Accused of asceticism, mysticism, and MANICHAEAN dualism, they were suppressed by the ALBIGENSIAN CRUSADE.

**ALBIGENSIAN CRUSADE** Crusade ordered by INNOCENT III against the ALBIGENSES. At Montsegur in 1245, 200 were burned in a day.

**ALBIGENSIANS** See ALBIGENSES.

**ALBIORIX** Celtic war god.

**ALBO, JOSEPH (c.1380–1444)** Medieval Jewish apologist who found three fundamental principles in religion: faith in God, revelation, and justice.

**ALBORNOZ, GIL ALVAREZ DE (c.1310–1367)** Spanish statesman and CARDINAL who sought to restore papal authority.

**ALBRIGHT, JACOB (1759–1808)** Founder of the Evangelical Association, now merged into the EVANGELICAL UNITED BRETHREN CHURCH. He was born in Pennsylvania, became a successful businessman, and experienced conversion which led him to enter the clergy and found the Association.

**ALBRIGHT BRETHREN** An early name for

the Evangelical Association founded by Jacob ALBRIGHT.

**ALCESTIS** In Greek mythology, wife of Admetus; she offered her life to save his.

**AL-CHARIZI, JUDAH (1165–1235)** Jewish poet and philosopher of medieval Spain.

**ALCHEMY** Medieval art which attempted to change the lower metals into the more valuable ones. Egyptian and Semitic legends credit it with religious origins.

**AL CHET** Jewish term for a confession of sins on the Day of ATONEMENT.

**ALCIMUS** Jewish appointee to the priesthood opposed by the MACCABEES (1 MACCABEES 7, 9).

**ALCINOUS** Platonic philosopher who mixed the ideas of ARISTOTLE and PLATO with Eastern mysticism. His god was unknown.

**ALCOHOLICS ANONYMOUS** Group founded in 1934 to help alcoholics. Although not a religious organization, it has a distinctly religious emphasis, including faith in a higher power, confession, and restitution.

**ALCORAN** See KORAN.

**ALCOTT, BRONSON (1799–1888)** Educator, transcendentalist philosopher, and social reformer; father of Louisa May Alcott.

**ALCUIN (c.735–804)** English scholar and churchman who directed an educational program for Charlemagne. He defended orthodox Christianity against ADOPTIANISM.

**ALCUIN CLUB** English group which promotes the study and use of the BOOK OF COMMON PRAYER.

**ALDERSGATE** The street in London where the heart of John WESLEY was "strangely warmed" and his religious career given a unique impetus.

**ALDHELM (c.640–709)** English bishop, scholar, and musician. He founded several monasteries and extended Christianity in southern England.

**ALDRED (?–1069)** English churchman and archbishop at the time of William the Conqueror.

**ALDRICH, BESS STREETER (1881–1954)** American religious novelist. Her books include *A Lantern in Her Hand* and *Journey into Christmas*.

**ALEANDRO, GIROLAMO (1480–1542)** Italian churchman and scholar who opposed LUTHER at the DIET OF WORMS. His resistance to the REFORMATION was unsuccessful.

**ALEION BAAL** Son of BAAL in ancient Canaanite mythology; god of air, wind, and rain.

**ALENIO, GIULIO (1582–1649)** JESUIT missionary from Italy to China. He wrote a life of Christ in Chinese.

**ALENU** Prayer ending Jewish prayer service.

**ALEPH** 1. First letter in the Hebrew alphabet. 2. Symbol for CODEX SINAITICUS.

**ALEPH-BET** The Hebrew alphabet, which begins with the letters "aleph" and "beth."

**ALESIUS, ALEXANDER (1500–1565)** Scottish Protestant reformer and theologian; friend of LUTHER, MELANCHTHON, and CRANMER.

**ALETHIOLOGY** Philosophic term for the doctrine of truth.

**ALEXANDER** The name of eight popes.

**ALEXANDER, ST. (c.273–326)** Bishop of Alexandria who censured ARIUS and figured in the Arian controversy.

**ALEXANDER II (?–1073)** Anselmo Baggio, pope who strengthened ecclesiastical discipline and the power of the papacy.

**ALEXANDER III (?–1181)** Orlando Bandinelli, pope who strengthened church courts and helped centralize church power. He backed THOMAS À BECKET and imposed penance on Henry II for Becket's murder. He convened the Third LATERAN COUNCIL and is considered one of the great medieval popes.

**ALEXANDER IV (?–1261)** Rinaldo Conti, pope who sought to unite the Eastern and Western churches and brought the INQUISITION into northern France.

**ALEXANDER VI (1431–1503)** Rodriga Borgia, Spanish pope notorious for bribery, murder, and irreligion. He executed SAVONAROLA. Among his children were Giovanni, Cesare, and Lucrezia Borgia. He patronized the arts, and artists Michelangelo and Raphael. Some acclaim his political and administrative ability.

**ALEXANDER, ARCHIBALD (1772–1851)** American PRESBYTERIAN theologian. Some eighteen hundred candidates for the ministry studied under him during his forty years as professor of didactic and polemic theology at Princeton Theological Seminary.

**ALEXANDER, CALEB (1755–1828)** A founder of Hamilton College and Auburn Theological Seminary in New York State.

**ALEXANDER, JOSEPH ADDISON (1809–1860)** PRESBYTERIAN exegete and scholar in Oriental literature.

**ALEXANDER, SAMUEL (1859–1938)** British philosopher who conceived of God as the result of cosmic evolution.

**ALEXANDER, WILLIAM LINDSAY (1808–1884)** Scottish divine and scholar.

**ALEXANDER OF HALES (c.1175–1245)** English theologian and scholar who won his reputation in France as "the Unanswerable Doctor." A FRANCISCAN who influenced THOMAS AQUINAS, Alexander sought to harmonize the ideas of AUGUSTINE, ARISTOTLE, NEOPLATONISM, and Arabian philosophy.

**ALEXANDER THE PAPHLAGONIAN (second century)** Religious imposter of Asia Minor. He made money through false oracles and celebrated his own marriage to the moon.

**ALEXANDRE, NOEL (1639–1724)** Church historian and theologian of France.

**ALEXANDRIA** Egyptian city where St. Mark is reputed to have founded a church. Site of COPTIC, EASTERN, and ROMAN CATHOLIC churches.

**ALEXANDRIAN LIBRARY** Famous library founded in Alexandria, Egypt, by Ptolemy I. Jewish tradition holds that the SEPTUAGINT was made for the Alexandrian Library.

**ALEXANDRIAN RITE** Liturgical and canonical system of the patriarchate of Alexandria.

**ALEXANDRIAN SCHOOL** Philosophical school combining Greek and Oriental thought, and emphasizing the allegorical interpretation of Scripture.

**ALEXANDRISTS** Renaissance philosophers who believed that the soul is material and therefore not immortal.

**ALEXIANS** Lay fraternal order whose patron is St. ALEXIUS.

**ALEXIUS, ST. (?–417)** Chosen to be the patron, though apparently not the founder, of the Alexians.

**AL-FARABI (?–950)** Arabian Moslem philosopher who sought to harmonize ISLAM and Greek philosophy.

**AL-FASI, ISAAC BEN JACOB (1013–1103)** Jewish scholar who codified and simplified the exposition of the TALMUD. He founded an academy in Spain.

**ALFATIN** Messianic type of deliverer in Moorish myth. Now sleeping, he is expected to arise eventually to avenge the faithful.

**ALFONSI, PETRUS (1062–1110)** Jewish convert to CHRISTIANITY who then wrote dialogues against the Jews.

**ALFONSO II (1185–1223)** King of Portugal whose struggles with the church over property resulted in his excommunication.

**ALFORD, HENRY (1810–1871)** English scholar and churchman. Dean of Canterbury, he is famed for his Greek NEW TESTAMENT and his Biblical commentary.

**ALFRED THE GREAT (849–899)** Saxon king who helped unify England, strengthened justice, aided the church, and revived learning in his realm. He translated into English such Latin works as Augustine's *Soliloquies*, Bede's *Ecclesiastical History*, and Gregory the Great's *Pastoral Care*.

**ALGARDI, ALESSANDRO (1595–1654)** Italian sculptor who made a statue in bronze of Pope Innocent X, and designed a monument for Leo XI.

**AL-GAZALI (c.1058–1111)** Arabian philosopher and MOSLEM mystic and theologian. Preferring asceticism to rationalism, he has been called "the Thomas Aquinas of Islam."

**AL-GAZEL** See AL-GAZALI.

**ALGER OF LIEGE (?–c.1131)** French monk who wrote several important ecclesiastical works.

**AL-GHAZALI** See AL-GAZALI.

**ALGUM** See ALMUG.

**AL-HALLAJ** See HALLAJ.

**ALI (c.600–661)** Fourth KHALIF of ISLAM. The husband of Fatima, Mohammed's daughter, Ali was one of the first and most faithful of the Prophet's followers. From his Khalifate dates the Moslem division into SUNNITES and SHIITES.

**ALI, MIRZA HUSAYN** See BAHA ULLAH.

**ALIENATION** Doctrine that church property may be conveyed only as canon law provides.

**ALITURGICAL** 1. Referring to a time when the EUCHARIST may not be celebrated. 2. Nonliturgical.

**ALIYAH** 1. Participation in reading from the PENTATEUCH by men in the synagogue. 2. Migrations to Israel.

**ALJAMA** Quarters for either Moors or Jews in Mediterranean lands.

**AL-KINDI** See KINDI.

**AL-KORAN** The KORAN.

**ALLACCI, LEONE (1586–1669)** Greek theologian, writer, and VATICAN librarian.

**ALLAH** Syriac, Arabic, and Moslem name for God. A contraction of al-Ilah ("The God," "The One Worthy of Worship"), the name Allah was given world renown by MOHAMMED, his Prophet (see ISLAM).

**ALLAHABAD** City of India located at the junction of the sacred Ganges and Jumna rivers. HINDU shrine.

**ALLAN, CHARLES HENRY** See ANANDA METTEYA.

**ALLAT** Nabatean mother of the gods.

**ALLATU** Babylonian queen of the world of the dead.

**ALLEGIANCE, OATH OF** Pledge to the King required of CHURCH OF ENGLAND clergymen by an act in 1868.

**ALLEGORY** Symbolic representation of truth. An allegory is usually longer and more involved than a fable or parable. The allegorical interpretation of Scripture has often supplanted the literal or historical meaning. The ALEXANDRIAN theologians favored this type of interpretation.

**ALLEGRI, GREGORIO (1582–1652)** Italian priest, singer, and composer of the MISERERE.

**ALLEINE, JOSEPH (1634–1668)** English PURITAN preacher and scholar. He was often imprisoned and an outcast.

**ALLELUIA** See HALLELUJAH.

**ALLEN, RICHARD (1760–1831)** American clergyman who bought his freedom from slavery. In 1787 in Philadelphia, he organized the first Negro church in the United States. The first Negro minister to be ordained in the METHODIST CHURCH, he became a BISHOP of the African Methodist Episcopal Church.

**ALLENBY, EDMUND H. H. (1861–1936)** Bible-reading British field marshal who drove the Turks from Palestine and captured Jerusalem in 1918.

**ALLESTREE, RICHARD (1619–1681)** A British clergyman who was a controversial but excellent preacher.

**ALLEY** Correct ecclesiastical term for a passage between rows of pews.

**ALL HALLOWS' or HALLOWMAS** See ALL SAINTS' DAY.

**ALLIANCE ISRAELITE UNIVERSELLE** World Jewish organization formed to aid victims of anti-Semitism.

**ALLIANCE OF REFORMED CHURCHES** World alliance of REFORMED and PRESBYTERIAN churches, formed in 1875.

**ALLISON, FRANCIS (1705–1779)** Presbyterian scholar active in precipitating the Great Schism in the PRESBYTERIAN CHURCH IN THE U.S.A. in 1744.

**ALLIX, PETER (1641–1717)** Churchman who wrote voluminously in the fields of church history and theology.

**ALLOCUTION** 1. Solemn address by the pope in secret consistory. 2. The pope's remarks to a public audience, as in his regular afternoon audiences.

**ALLOUEZ, CLAUDE JEAN (1622–1689)** JESUIT missionary from France to Canada. Becoming Bishop of Quebec, he founded several missions in the Great Lakes area.

**ALL SAINTS' DAY** Feast day held November 1 in commemoration of all the saints of God.

**ALL SOULS' DAY** Feast held November 2 (occasionally November 3) for prayer for the faithful suffering in PURGATORY.

**ALMA MATER** *bounteous mother* The name of such Roman goddesses as CYBELE and CERES.

**ALMANAC** 1. A calendar which might include various additional data. The first almanacs usually indicated religious holidays. Those which followed the invention of printing often contained astrological and other predictions of the future. 2. A listing of ecclesiastical festivals and special days.

**ALMIGHTY** Designation of God as allpowerful, unlimited.

**ALMOHADES** 1. Puritanical MOSLEM religious confederation founded about 1120 by MOHAMMED IBN TUMART. 2. The resultant Berber Moslem dynasty which drove out the ALMORAVIDES and controlled Spain and Morocco throughout the twelfth and thirteenth centuries.

**ALMOND** Small tree with nutlike fruit symbolizing beauty, divine favor, and rebirth.

**ALMONER** One who distributes alms,

often in a religious order, to aid the poor or afflicted.

**ALMONRY**  Place for the distribution of alms.

**ALMORAVIDES**  Militant confederation of Berber Moslems, organized by Yahya ibn Omar, which ruled Spain and Morocco until displaced by the ALMOHADES about 1174.

**ALMS**  Provision of relief for the poor or needy. JUDAISM, CHRISTIANITY, and ISLAM all enjoin almsgiving as an important duty.

**ALMS BASON**  Large plate for the presentation of a congregation's offering before the altar.

**ALMS BOX**  Church receptacle for gifts for the poor.

**ALMUCE**  Hooded fur or fur-lined cape used as a choir vestment. It symbolizes dignity.

**ALMUG or ALGUM**  Precious wood, possibly red sandalwood, used in Solomon's palace and temple (I KINGS 10:11). It was also used for musical instruments.

**ALOADAE**  Two giants in Greek mythology who were condemned to endless torment in Tartarus for trying to overthrow the gods.

**ALOE**  African plant of the lily family whose juice has medicinal properties. The aloe has religious value in ISLAM. In CHRISTENDOM it may symbolize the PASSION or the VIRGIN MARY.

**ALOGI**  Heretics of the second century who refused the teaching in the Gospel of John that Jesus is the eternal Word or LOGOS. Their leader was GAIUS.

**ALOIDAE**  See ALOADAE.

**ALOMBRADOS or ALUMBRADOS**  Mystic sixteenth-century Spanish sect which, according to their opponents, rejected the sacraments, the ministry, and good works. Most of them were exterminated in 1623 in the Spanish INQUISITION.

**ALOYSIUS, ST. (1568–1591)**  Italian JESUIT who died of the plague; patron of young people.

**ALPHA**  First letter in the Greek alphabet.

**ALPHA and OMEGA**  First and last letters of the Greek alphabet, designating God and Christ as the Beginning and the End (REVELATION 1:8; 21:6; 22:13).

**ALPHASI, ISAAC (1013–1103)**  Jewish

RABBI of Spain who condensed and simplified the TALMUD.

**ALPHEGE (954–1012)**  English archbishop who was murdered after he was captured by the Danes and refused to ask his parishioners to ransom him.

**ALPHITOMANCY**  Ancient means of divination using loaves of barley and honey.

**ALPHONSUS LIGUORI, ST. (1696–1787)**  Italian musician and ecclesiastic who founded the REDEMPTORIST order to help the poor. He developed the viewpoint in casuistry known as EQUIPROBABILISM. He favored majority opinion of the theologians on moral questions.

**ALROY, DAVID (twelfth century)**  Self-styled "Jewish Messiah," slain by his father-in-law.

**ALTAR**  A base used for religious sacrifice and/or worship. The form may be a mound, a block, a table, or a platform. Altars are as old as religion. Christian altars commemorate the death of Christ and may be used for the EUCHARIST, or Lord's Supper.

**ALTAR BREAD**  Bread or wafers used in holy communion or EUCHARIST.

**ALTAR CROSS**  A cross, usually metal, standing on the altar to symbolize the CRUCIFIXION.

**ALTAR CURTAINS**  Curtains hanging above each end of the altar.

**ALTAR-FELLOWSHIP**  LUTHERAN term for participation in COMMUNION.

**ALTAR GUILD**  Women's association organized to care for the ALTAR and CHANCEL furnishings.

**ALTAR LIGHTS**  The candles at either side of the cross on the ALTAR.

**ALTAR LINEN**  Cloth covering the ALTAR during worship.

**ALTAR OF INCENSE**  The golden ALTAR on which incense was burned in the Jewish tabernacle and temple.

**ALTAR OF REPOSE**  Elevation on which the COMMUNION sacrament is placed from MAUNDAY THURSDAY to GOOD FRIDAY.

**ALTICHIERO DA ZEVIO (c.1330–c.1395)**  Italian painter whose frescoes in the churches of St. Antonio and St. Giorgio are notable examples of ecclesiastical art.

**ALTRUISM**  Ethical system based on the ultimate good of others as the basis of moral conduct.

**ALTUM DOMINIUM** *supreme power* CATHOLIC term for the supreme control of ecclesiastical property by the pope.

**ALUMBRADOES** See ALOMBRADOES.

**ALUMNUS** 1. A child reared in a MONAS-TERY. 2. An ecclesiastical student.

**A.M.** See "AVE MARIA."

**AMAHASPANDS** The six spirits attending AHURA MAZDAH in ZOROASTRIAN religion.

**AMAITE-RANGI** Sky demon of Polynesian myth.

**AMALEKITES** Native Canaanites at war with the Hebrews until driven out by King SAUL.

**AMALRICIANS** Pantheistic mystics, followers of AMALRIC OF BENA, also known as BRETHREN OF THE FREE SPIRIT. Accused of indulgence in enormities, they were subjected to the INQUISITION. Meister Eckhart was a noted Amalrician (see ECKHART, JOHANNES).

**AMALRIC OF BENA** (?-c.1207) French philosopher-theologian who held that the TRINITY was revealed in successive historical epochs, that God is everything, and that those in the love of God cannot sin no matter what they do. He and his followers acknowledged no control but that of the Spirit.

**AMALTHEIA** Female goat who nursed ZEUS. Her horn became a mythological horn of plenty.

**AMAN** See HAMAN.

**AMANA** See ABANA.

**AMANA COMMUNITY** Group which came from Germany to the United States and founded a communal religious society in Iowa. It is now the Amana Church Society.

**AMARAVATI** 1. Capital of Swarga, the HINDU paradise. 2. City of India, once capital of the BUDDHIST Andhra kingdom which was then a SIVA center. A famous archaeological site, it contains a well-known Buddhist sepulchral monument and carvings depicting the life of BUDDHA.

**AMARITES** German pietists who ultimately became the AMANA COMMUNITY.

**AMARNA** See TEL-EL-AMARNA.

**AMATERASU-OMIKAMI** *heaven-shining great one* Japanese sun goddess, origin of the Japanese nation.

**AMATHAON** 1. Celtic wizard. 2. Aegean sea goddess.

**AMATUS LUSITANUS** (1510–1568) Jewish physician and philosopher of Greece.

**AMAZIAH** King of Judah in the eighth century B.C.

**AMAZON** A warlike female of Greek mythology.

**AMBARVALIA** Roman springtime fertility rite.

**AMBISAGRUS** Jove-like Celtic god.

**AMBO** In the early church, a reading desk. Later, in the Christian basilicas, this was a lectern or platform for the singing of liturgical portions of the service.

**AMBOISE, GEORGES D'** (1460–1510) Cardinal and first minister of the crown in France. A great tomb honors him at Rouen.

**AMBROSE, ST.** (c.340–397) Early champion of orthodox Christianity against both paganism and ARIANISM. Born in Trier, he became Bishop of Milan and his eloquent preaching led to the conversion of AUGUSTINE. He wrote a number of hymns and homilies, his interpretation of Scripture being largely allegorical. Ambrose is one of the outstanding church fathers (see FATHERS OF THE CHURCH).

**AMBROSE** (1708–1771) Russian ARCHBISHOP who, though concerned for the poor, was strangled by a mob he tried to help in time of plague.

**AMBROSE, AUTPERT** (?–778) BENEDICTINE monk of early France who wrote several works including commentaries.

**AMBROSE, ISAAC** (1604–1664) English PURITAN whose book *Looking to Jesus* has been compared with *Pilgrim's Progress*.

**AMBROSE THE CAMALDULIAN** (1386–1439) Ambrogio Traversari, Italian churchman who translated Greek theology and sermons, including those of CHRYSOSTOM. (See also CAMALDOLESE.)

**AMBROSIA** Food which gave the Greek gods immortal life.

**AMBROSIAN CHANT** Liturgical music of the Milanese rite, attributed to St. Ambrose of Milan.

**AMBROSIANS** 1. Catholic order of Milan (fourteenth century) whose members followed the Ambrosian rite and preached. 2. ANABAPTIST sect of the sixteenth century which by-passed the clergy and claimed direct communication with God through the HOLY SPIRIT.

**AMBROSIASTER** A name for the unknown author of a commentary on the Pauline Epistles, long attributed to St. AMBROSE. The commentary was written in the fourth century and AUGUSTINE ascribed it, in part at least, to HILARY OF POITIERS.

**AMBRY**  See AUMBRY.

**AMBULATORY**  A covered walkway outside of a church or a processional aisle within it.

**A.M.D.G.**  Abbreviation for Latin motto "AD MAIOREM DEI GLORIAM."

**AMEMAIT or AMMAIT**  Monster in Egyptian mythology which devoured those who failed the test for immortality.

**AMEN**  1. The cauldron of Ceridwen, an early British fertility goddess. 2. Egyptian god; see AMON. 3. Affirmation in Hebrew, often concluding Jewish or Christian prayer, meaning "So may it be" or "So it is" or "So it must be." Derived from a Hebrew word for sureness or trust, "Amen" has rich Biblical meaning. Jesus used it in the sense of "Truly" (cf. JOHN 3:3). In Revelation 3:14, Christ is called "the Amen" who is faithful and true.

**AMENEMOPE (c.1,000 B.C.)**  Egyptian book of wisdom.

**AMENHOTEP III or AMENOPHIS III (?–c.1372 B.C.)**  Egyptian king during whose reign worship of the god ATON began. Amenhotep III was father of IKHNATON.

**AMENOPHIS III**  See AMENHOTEP III.

**AMEN-RA**  See AMON-RA.

**AMENT**  Egyptian mother goddess, wife of AMON or Amen.

**AMENTI**  Egyptian realm of the dead.

**AMERETAT**  ZOROASTRIAN spirit of immortality, one of the six attendants of AHURA MAZDA.

**AMERICAN BAPTIST ASSOCIATION**  Group of conservative BAPTIST churches, sometimes called Missionary Baptist Churches, descending from the Land Mark Baptists, with headquarters in Texarkana in the United States. See LANDMARKISM.

**AMERICAN BAPTIST CONVENTION**  One of the larger BAPTIST groups in the United States, formerly known as the Northern Baptist Convention.

**AMERICAN BIBLE SOCIETY**  Nondenominational organization dedicated to the translation of the Bible and its widest possible distribution. Headquarters are in New York City.

**AMERICAN BOARD OF COMMISSIONERS FOR FOREIGN MISSIONS**  First foreign missions society organized in the United States (1810). It resulted from the "hay-stack prayer meeting" of five young men at Williams College. It is now the UNITED CHURCH BOARD FOR WORLD MINISTRIES of the UNITED CHURCH OF CHRIST.

**AMERICAN CARPATHO-RUSSIAN ORTHODOX GREEK CATHOLIC CHURCH**  A self-governing diocese in the United States, originating in the RUSSIAN ORTHODOX CHURCH.

**AMERICAN CATHOLIC CHURCH, ARCHDIOCESE OF NEW YORK**  An OLD CATHOLIC church whose orders derive from the SYRIAN ORTHODOX CHURCH OF ANTIOCH.

**AMERICAN CATHOLIC CHURCH (SYRO-ANTIOCHEAN)**  American division of the Jacobite Apostolic Church.

**AMERICAN CHURCH**  Native American Indian religious group, incorporated in California. Members rely on the hallucinatory drug PEYOTE for contact with God.

**AMERICAN COUNCIL OF CHRISTIAN CHURCHES**  Small right-wing organization which opposes most other religious organizations and their programs.

**AMERICAN ETHICAL UNION**  Organization of ETHICAL CULTURE societies in the United States; it upholds ultraliberal religious philosophy and social application.

**AMERICAN EVANGELICAL LUTHERAN CHURCH**  Danish Lutheran church now merged into the LUTHERAN CHURCH IN AMERICA.

**AMERICAN FRIENDS SERVICE COMMITTEE**  QUAKER agency which has aided refugees and needy persons throughout the world and seeks to promote justice and peace in all lands.

**AMERICAN HOLY ORTHODOX CATHOLIC APOSTOLIC EASTERN CHURCH**  An independent Orthodox Eastern church affiliated with The Orthodox Catholic Patriarchate of America.

**AMERICANISM**  Theologically, an American movement begun in the nineteenth century to adapt the ROMAN CATHOLIC CHURCH to democratic and other humanitarian values. It was condemned in 1899 by LEO XIII.

**AMERICAN JEWISH COMMITTEE**  Jewish organization founded in 1906 for the aid and defense of Jews throughout the world.

**AMERICAN JEWISH CONGRESS**  Group organized in 1917 which was the source of the WORLD JEWISH CONGRESS.

**AMERICAN LUTHERAN CHURCH**  Lutheran

denomination in the United States, formed through a merger of German, Norwegian, and Danish Lutherans in 1963.

**AMERICAN ORTHODOX CHURCH** American denomination in full sympathy with the RUSSIAN ORTHODOX CHURCH, holding to the Western rite as authorized by the Moscow Synod of 1870.

**AMERICAN REFORM** Term for American Jewish modernization, including worship in the vernacular, symbolic interpretation of sacrifice and Torah, and rejection of the idea of a personal Messiah.

**AMERICAN RELIGION** Term for the distinctive character of much religion in the United States—in general more activist, more wealthy, more popular, and less traditional than in other countries.

**AMERICAN REVISED VERSION** See REVISED STANDARD VERSION.

**AMERICAN SCHOOLS OF ORIENTAL RESEARCH** Archaeological organization with schools in Bagdad and Jerusalem and headquarters at Yale University. Millar Burrows and Carl Hermann Kraeling have been among the presidents of the Schools.

**AMERICAN STANDARD VERSION** American version of a new interdenominational translation of the Bible published in 1901, soon after the similar English REVISED VERSION, 1880–1890. See also REVISED STANDARD VERSION.

**AMES, WILLIAM (1576–1633)** Eloquent English Puritan minister whose outspokenness brought about many controversies. A CALVINIST, he opposed ARMINIAN theology and ANGLICAN "debauchery."

**AMESHAS or AMESHA SPENTAS** The six immortal spirits attending AHURA MAZDA, personifying health, harmony, righteousness, wisdom, saving health, and immortality. Also called AMSHASPANDS.

**AM HA-ARETZ** Jewish term for the common people, the peasants, or the ignorant (as used in the TALMUD).

**AMIATINUS, CODEX** See CODEX AMIATINUS.

**AMICE** Collar-like cloth worn by a priest under the ALB.

**AMIDA** Japanese BUDDHIST term for the "Buddha of Infinite Light."

**AMIDAH** See SHEMONEH ESREH.

**AMILLENNIALISM** Eschatological system of thought in which the millennium and other future events are interpreted symbolically.

**AMIR ALI, SEYYID (1849–1928)** A descendant of MOHAMMED, born in India, who became a distinguished magistrate and judge. He constantly sought to advance the lot of Indian MOSLEMS and wrote a life of Mohammed and other books interpreting ISLAM.

**AMIRINI** A goddess of the West African Yoruba tribe.

**AMIS DU BUDDHISME, LES** Paris Buddhist Society, headquarters of BUDDHISM in France.

**AMISH** A name for strict MENNONITES, deriving from the Swiss Mennonite bishop Jacob Amman, whose literal interpretation of the Mennonite confession of faith divided the Mennonite world for two centuries. Several Mennonite bodies still include the word Amish in their names.

**AMITA, AMITABHA** Sanskrit form of Amida, "Buddha of Infinite Light." A very popular deity, he has many names and interpretations.

**AMITAYUS** Deity of immortal life in Tibetan BUDDHISM.

**AMMAIT** See AMEMAIT.

**AMMAN** Modern capital of Jordan.

**AMMAN, JACOB** See AMISH.

**AMMI** *my people* God's name for Israel in Hosea 2:1, 23. "Lo-ammi" in 1:9 means "Not My People."

**AMMON** Egyptian god; see AMON. 2. Lot's son; see BEN-AMMI. 3. Egyptian hermit, a famous ascetic of the fourth century.

**AMMONITES** Desert people, descendants of AMMON or BEN-AMMI, who lived east of the Jordan and were continually at war with the Israelites, to whom they were historically related (GENESIS 19:37–38). Their god was Milcom and their capital the modern Amman.

**AMNON** Oldest son of King David, killed by his half-brother ABSALOM for violating his half-sister Tamar (II SAMUEL 13).

**AMOGHASIDDHI** *He whose accomplishment is not meaningless* A Tibetan personification of Buddha.

**AMON or AMEN, AMMON, AMUN** Egyptian god of Thebes, often pictured as a man with head of a ram. See also AMON-RA.

**AMON-RA** As the Egyptian god AMON, or

Amen, became identified with the sun god RA, or Re, he was known as Amon-Ra or Amen-Re. He was then the supreme deity, with a shrine and oracle at Siwa in the desert of Libya.

**AMOR**   Amorite god.

**AMORA** *speaker*   An interpreter of the MISHNA, the Jewish oral law. The views of the Amoraim are found in the GEMARA and the TALMUD.

**AMORAL**   Term for that which is neither good nor bad. The amoral person has no sense of moral responsibility.

**AMORITES**   Aboriginal people of ancient Canaan conquered by the invading children of Israel. They had blue eyes and straight noses.

**AMOS**   1. A prophet of the eighth century B.C. with a powerful message of the Lordship of God, the self-destruction of evil, and the necessity of personal and social righteousness. Originally a shepherd, Amos preached in the Northern Kingdom of Israel during the reign of Jeroboam II, with vivid pastoral imagery and intense conviction. 2. The book of the MINOR PROPHETS which bears Amos' name and message.

**AMPHIBALUS**   1. A chasuble-like garment once worn by Gallican priests. 2. A CHASUBLE.

**AMPHICTYONY**   A complex of Greek tribes or communities whose purpose was the maintenance of a temple or shrine, religious legislation, etc. The most important amphictyony was at Delphi.

**AMPHILOCUS**   A famous prophet of Greek myth.

**AMPHION**   In Greek mythology, one of the twin sons of ZEUS. The other twin was ZETHUS.

**AMPHITRITE**   Greek queen of the sea, daughter of Oceanus and wife of Poseidon.

**AMPULLA**   A narrow-necked vase used in ancient times to hold holy oil and to anoint corpses. It symbolizes consecration. Ampullae have been found in catacombs; in medieval times travelers used them to bring oil from sacred shrines. The modern ampulla holds oil consecrated by a bishop.

**AMRAM**   1. The father of Moses (NUMBERS 26:59). 2. A "son of Bani" who took a Gentile wife (EZRA 10:19, 34).

**AMRAM BEN SCHESCHNA (?–874)**   Famous Hebrew scholar who headed the Academy of Sura in Persia. His liturgical work was extensive and still influences Jewish religion.

**AMRITA**   HINDU water of life or nectar of the gods.

**AMRITANANDA, THERA (twentieth century)**   Leading BUDDHIST of Nepal who in 1956 organized the fourth Congress of World Fellowship of Buddhists.

**AMRITSAR**   City in India which is the center of the SIKH religion, founded in 1577 by the guru Ram Das. In it are the Pool of Immortality, the Temple of the Gods, and the holy book GRANTH.

**AMRU-L-KAIS (sixth century)**   Arabian poet considered by Mohammed as the greatest poet before the advent of ISLAM.

**AMSDORF, NIKOLAUS VON (1483–1565)**   German reformer and backer of Martin LUTHER. From him much of our knowledge of Luther comes.

**AMSHASPANDS**   See AMESHAS.

**AMSTERDAM ASSEMBLY**   The gathering in Holland in 1948 at which the WORLD COUNCIL OF CHURCHES was constituted.

**AMULET**   Small object or formula used to ward off evil or danger.

**AMUN**   See AMON.

**AMYOT, JOSEPH (1718–c.1795)**   French JESUIT missionary to China.

**AMYRALDIANS**   Followers of the theological system of Moses AMYRALDUS.

**AMYRALDUS, MOSES (1596–1664)**   French Protestant theologian who tempered his belief in CALVINISM with the doctrine that all men are predestined to salvation, but on the condition that each one possesses saving faith. This faith is placed by God in His elect. Apart from his theology, Amyraldus wrote several popular devotional works.

**AMYRAUT, MOISE**   See AMYRALDUS, MOSES.

**AN**   Egyptian god of the sun or moon.

**ANABAPTISTS or ANTIPAEDOBAPTISTS**   Original names of those who insisted on baptizing only adults, and on rebaptizing those who had received that sacrament in infancy; later called Baptists. Both Catholics and Protestants persecuted the Anabaptists of the sixteenth century in various parts of Europe.

**ANACLETUS or CLETUS**   Roman pope (76–88) and martyr.

**ANAGAMIN**   In Buddhism, one who after

death is born again, not on earth but in heaven.

**ANAGOGICAL** Reference to a type of allegorical interpretation of Scripture in which the literal words hide secret truth.

**ANAHITA** 1. ZOROASTRIAN water spirit. 2. Persian fertility goddess.

**ANAITIS** See ANAHITA.

**ANAKIM** Giants inhabiting Canaan before its conquest by the Hebrews.

**ANALECTS** Collected miscellaneous passages, as the Analects of Confucius.

**ANALOGY** Theological term for proportion or likeness in relating one thing or person to another. THOMAS AQUINAS taught that the same qualities could be ascribed to both God and finite creatures only analogically.

**ANALOGY OF RELIGION (1736)** Famous apologetic work of Joseph BUTLER, showing the reasonableness of the Christian faith.

**ANALYSIS** Short for psychoanalysis, which claims some transformations of personality as startling as religious conversions.

**ANAMNESIS** Liturgical term for the commemoration of the passion, resurrection, and ascension of Christ.

**ANAN BEN DAVID (eighth century)** Persian Jew who founded the Jewish sect of the KARAITES about 765.

**ANANDA** *bliss* First cousin and "beloved disciple" of BUDDHA. He persuaded Buddha to permit women to be nuns. He attained enlightenment; later his relics were the objects of worship.

**ANANDA METTEYA** Buddhist name of Charles Henry Allan, who sought to establish BUDDHISM in Great Britain in the early twentieth century.

**ANANIAS** 1. One of the Three Holy Children of the APOCRYPHA. 2. High priest in Jerusalem, killed about 65 A.D. 3. A member of the New Testament church who lied about his gift to the church and upon Peter's rebuke fell dead (ACTS 5:1–11).

**ANANKE** Greek personification of Fate, worshiped at Corinth.

**ANAPHORA** *offering up* Central prayer in the eucharistic liturgy.

**ANARCHISM, CHRISTIAN** Religious-political views of TOLSTOY and his followers, based on Tolstoy's interpretation of the teachings of Jesus. Basically, anarchism holds that government is inherently evil.

**ANASTASIA (fourth century)** A Christian martyr of Sirmium, said to have been a Roman noblewoman who was generous to the needy.

**ANASTASIUS** The name of four popes.

**ANASTASIUS I (?–401)** Pope (399–401) who condemned the writings of ORIGEN.

**ANATHEMA** *something set up above* In Hebrew worship that which was devoted to God was, anathema and must be destroyed (LEVITICUS 27:29; JOSHUA 6:17). In Greek religion anathema meant devoting something irrevocably to a god in a temple. In the New Testament anathema means "accursed" (I CORINTHIANS 16:22). In medieval times a person anathematized was both excommunicated and subjected to damnation.

**ANATHEMA MARANATHA** This expression in I Corinthians actually is a transliteration of one Greek word and two Aramaic words. The meaning is, "Let him be accursed. Our Lord, come."

**ANATIWA** According to the Karaya Indians of Brazil, an evil spirit which caused the deluge.

**ANATU** Spouse of ANU who was the supreme Babylonian god.

**ANAXAGORAS (c.500–c.430 B.C.)** Greek philosopher, the first to posit infinite mind as the source of activity and order in the universe. For such heresies as the belief that the sun is an enormous white-hot mass, he was banished from Athens.

**ANCESTOR WORSHIP** Widespread religious phenomenon dating from ancient times. It is found in HINDUISM, CONFUCIANISM, and many other nonmonotheistic religions.

**ANCHIETA, JOSE DE (1530–1597)** Spanish JESUIT missionary; the first Brazilian writer, he composed religious, philosophical, and historical works.

**ANCHOR** CHRISTIAN symbol of hope (HEBREWS 6:19).

**ANCHORESS** A woman who lives in a cell apart from the world for meditation and prayer.

**ANCHORITE** One who lives alone, usually in a cell, for purposes of spiritual discipline, silence, and prayer.

**ANCIENT AND MYSTICAL ORDER OF PO-AHTUN** Chief administrative agency of the Mayan Temple, a North American group which seeks to preserve certain American Indian religious values.

**ANCIENT CHRISTIAN FELLOWSHIP** Group belonging to the APOSTOLIC EPISCOPAL CHURCH, with doctrines similar to other Eastern Orthodox churches but using English in its services.

**ANCIENT OF DAYS** Old Testament term for the Lord (DANIEL 7:9, 13, 22), indicating His supratemporal nature.

**ANCILLON, CHARLES (1659–1715)** French PROTESTANT educator.

**ANCREN RIWLE** Anonymously written treatise from about 1200 giving guidance to three young English ladies living in a hermitage.

**ANDAMANESE RELIGION** The religion of the Mongoloid pigmy natives of the Andaman Islands in the Bay of Bengal. It has no specific ritual, but is closely related to changes in the seasons, particularly the monsoons. There is a deep belief in the spirit world, and in visions and dreams.

**ANDJETI** Ancient name for the Egyptian god OSIRIS.

**ANDOVER CONTROVERSY** A late-nineteenth-century dispute between certain CONGREGATIONALISTS, at Andover Theological Seminary in Massachusetts and elsewhere, who believed that persons who die without hearing the gospel have a second chance after death, and others who insisted that no salvation is possible for those who reject the gospel in this life.

**ANDRÉ, BROTHER (1845–1937)** Catholic mystic of Montreal to whom are attributed a number of miraculous healings.

**ANDREAE LAURENTIUS (c.1470–1552)** Churchman who helped translate the Swedish Bible and strengthened the ecclesiastical independence of the Swedish king Gustavus I.

**ANDREW** One of Christ's Twelve Apostles, brother of Peter and John. Originally a fisherman, he brought Peter and several others to Jesus. He is known as the patron saint of Scotland and of Russia. According to tradition he traveled into Russia and was martyred in Greece on a cross in the form of the letter X.

**ANDREWES, LANCELOT (1555–1626)** Outstanding English churchman whose book *Private Devotions* had wide influence. Famous as a theologian and preacher, he

held a middle-ground stance in the development of the English reformation of religion, and took part in producing the "Authorized Version" of the Bible sponsored by James I. (See KING JAMES VERSION.)

**ANDREW OF CRETE (c.660–c.720)** Greek theologian and hymn writer. He opposed MONOTHELITISM. His hymn beginning "Christian! dost thou see them" is still in use.

**ANDREW OF LONGJUMEAU (thirteenth century)** French DOMINICAN churchman who served as messenger from Pope Innocent IV to the Mongols and wrote an account of Mongol Christianity.

**ANDREWS, LORRIN (1795–1868)** American PROTESTANT missionary to Hawaii who became a Hawaiian educator and judge.

**ANDREW'S CROSS, ST.** A cross in the form of the letter X, symbol of the Apostle Andrew, although the tradition that he died on such a cross is fourteenth-century or later.

**ANDRONICUS** A Jewish convert to Christianity at Rome (ROMANS 16:7).

**ANEMONE** A variety of the buttercup flower. A Chinese symbol of death, in early Christian art the anemone with its triple leaves symbolized the TRINITY, and also became a symbol of sorrow, sickness, and death.

**ANET** Sacred fish which swam before the Egyptian god RA to warn him of danger.

**ANGEL** *messenger* Spirit being of JUDAISM and CHRISTIANITY, often a messenger from God to man. Angels are prominent both in the Old Testament and in the New Testament. They were mentioned in Persian religion, and are not unknown in the teachings of ISLAM.

**ANGELA DEI MERICI, ST. (1470–1540)** Italian nun who founded the order of the URSULINES for women and was canonized in 1807.

**ANGELA OF FOLIGNO (c.1248–1309)** Italian nun who had many visions and was beatified in 1693.

**ANGELIC BROTHERS** Community founded by J. G. GICHTEL in the seventeenth century. Members believed they had already achieved the angelic state.

**ANGELIC DOCTOR** A name for St. THOMAS AQUINAS.

**ANGELIC HYMN** The hymn "Gloria in

Excelsis" which is based on the angels' song at the birth of Christ (LUKE 2:14).

**ANGELICO, FRA (c.1400–1455)** DOMINI-CAN monk, born in Tuscany, who became one of the greatest painters of his time. An excusively religious painter, he is admired for many treatments of Christ, the Virgin, prophets, saints, and events in the life of Christ and the church. His first work was the illumination of manuscripts. He is known for his brilliant color, bold inventiveness, and deep spirituality.

**ANGEL OF THE LORD** Old Testament reference to a messenger of Jehovah who sometimes seems identical with Him (cf. GENESIS 16:7–12; EXODUS 3:2; JUDGES 13:3 ff.). The angel of the Lord in the New Testament is identified as Gabriel (LUKE 1:19) or another heavenly messenger.

**ANGELOLOGY** Study of angels.

**ANGELS OF THE CHURCHES** The "messengers" of seven churches in Asia Minor (REVELATION 1—3).

**ANGELUS** Thrice-daily time of prayer in memory of the ANNUNCIATION.

**ANGELUS SILESIUS (1624–1677)** Pseudonym of German mystic Johannes Scheffler. His many poems and hymns were influenced by Jacob BOEHME and influenced later PIETISM.

**ANGELUS TEMPLE** Headquarters of the INTERNATIONAL CHURCH OF THE FOUR-SQUARE GOSPEL, founded by Aimee Semple McPherson.

**ANGERONA** Roman goddess of healing and protection.

**ANGIRAS** Father of the preceptor of the gods in HINDUISM.

**ANGKOR THOM** Ancient Cambodian capital at whose center lay a temple, the BAYON, used in BUDDHIST and HINDU worship. It is beautifully and elaborately decorated, inside and out.

**ANGKOR WAT** Enormous Cambodian temple with impressive architecture and sculpture, probably connected with the worship of BUDDHA.

**ANGLICAN CHANT** Music in the ANGLI-CAN churches based on the ancient Psalm tunes.

**ANGLICAN CHURCH OF CANADA** Canadian denomination which is similar to and in communion with the CHURCH OF ENG-LAND. Its former name was the Church of England in Canada.

**ANGLICAN COMMUNION** The CHURCH OF ENGLAND in fellowship with Anglican churches throughout the world.

**ANGLICAN EVANGELICAL GROUP MOVEMENT** British association of those with liberal evangelical sympathies which aims to free the EVANGELICAL movement within the CHURCH OF ENGLAND from obscurantism and ultraconservatism.

**ANGLICANISM** The distinctive organization and teachings of the CHURCH OF ENGLAND and related ecclesiastical bodies. Claiming to be CATHOLIC, Scriptural, and REFORMED, Anglicanism seeks to maintain the best elements of both Protestantism and Catholicism. Its standards are the BIBLE, the CREEDS, and the BOOK OF COMMON PRAYER.

**ANGLO-CATHOLICISM** Movement in the Church of England which stresses the Catholic and universal aspects of ANGLICANISM. It holds Catholicity to be inherent in a church whose officials are in direct spiritual descent from the Apostles and whose doctrines have not changed since earliest times.

**ANGLO-ISRAEL** See BRITISH ISRAELISM.

**ANGLO-SAXON MISSIONARIES** Early British Christians, usually of outstanding zeal and ability, such as PATRICK, COLUMBA, and COLUMBANUS.

**ANGLO-SAXON RELIGION** Christianity came early to the British Isles. The See of Canterbury was organized by St. AUGUSTINE in 597, and the Anglo-Saxon church may be said to have progressed from that date until the Norman Conquest. Even after 1066, its best traditions were perpetuated through the life of St. WULSTAN, a great native churchman.

**ANGRA MAINYU** See AHRIMAN.

**ANGUS** Celtic love god.

**ANHUR** Egyptian god of war.

**ANIIM ZEMIROT** *I will chant sweet songs* Responsive hymn chanted in the synagogue; "Hymn of Glory."

**ANIMA CHRISTI** *soul of Christ* EUCHARISTIC prayer beginning, "Soul of Christ, sanctify me. . . ."

**ANIMALISM** Belief that human beings have basically no spiritual qualities other than those of mammals in general.

**ANIMAL MAGNETISM** "Voluntary or involuntary action of error," according to CHRISTIAN SCIENCE.

**ANIMAL WORSHIP** Ancient and widespread primitive religious practice. Many kinds of animals, birds, fish, and serpents have been the objects of worship.

**ANIMATISM** The personification, but not necessarily the deification, of plants, animals, etc.

**ANIMISM** "Belief in spiritual beings" (E. B. Tylor). Generally, denotes belief that every object in the universe has its own individual spirit. Philosophically, animism is the doctrine that life is distinct from the physical or mechanical.

**ANIT** Mother of Horus, a god in Egyptian religion.

**ANKH** A cross below a loop, symbolizing life and immortality in Egyptian religion.

**ANNA** 1. The old woman who prophesied when Jesus was presented in the Temple (LUKE 2:36–38). 2. Anna or Anne, according to tradition, is the mother of the Virgin MARY and is venerated in the EASTERN CHURCH.

**ANNA PERENNA** Ancient Roman goddess of the new year, worshiped at the full moon of the first month (March).

**ANNA-PURNA** *filled with food* Wife of SIVA in HINDUISM.

**ANNAS** Jewish high priest, father-in-law of Caiaphas, before whom Jesus appeared when on trial.

**ANNATES** Tax on an ecclesiastical appointment, originally (in the Middle Ages) consisting of the first year's profits from a BENEFICE. These were paid to the pope, a bishop, or (in England) to the king.

**ANNE** See ANNA.

**ANNEXED BOOK** Original manuscript of the BOOK OF COMMON PRAYER of England. This was annexed to the Act of Uniformity in 1662.

**ANNIHILATIONISM** The doctrine that the souls of the wicked are not immortal but are destroyed at death or afterward.

**ANNIHILATIONISTS** Those who hold to annihilationism.

**ANNO, ST.** (c. 1010–1075) Archbishop of Cologne who succeeded in having Alexander II made pope in place of his rival Honorius.

**ANNO DOMINI** *in the year of the Lord* Abbreviated "A.D." System of dating events from the traditionally accepted year of the birth of Christ (which may actually have been between 8 and 4 B.C.).

**ANNONA** Roman goddess or personification of the year's harvest, often symbolized by a horn of plenty.

**ANNUAL CONFERENCE** 1. The annual assembly of an ecclesiastical body. 2. The annual convocation of the METHODIST CHURCH and its basic governing body.

**ANNUIT COEPTIS** *He [God] has smiled on our undertaking* Motto on the reverse of the Great Seal of the United States.

**ANNUNCIATION** The announcement of the angel Gabriel to the Virgin Mary that she was to be the mother of Jesus (LUKE 1:26–38). The Feast of the Annunciation is observed March 25. A great number of paintings depict this theme.

**ANNWN** Celtic name for the place of the dead.

**ANOINT** 1. To consecrate with holy oil. 2. To consecrate spiritually, as in the anointing of the HOLY SPIRIT.

**ANOMOIANS** Extreme Arians of the fourth century. ARIUS had taught that Jesus Christ had been created by God and was neither fully human nor fully divine. The Anomoians taught that Christ bore no resemblance to God, was totally unlike (Greek *anamoios*) Him. They were also known as Aetians, Eunomians, and Exoucontians. Anomoianism was condemned in 381. (See also EUNOMIUS.)

**ANOMY** That which cannot be explained naturalistically; a miracle.

**ANOSH or ENOSH** MANDAEAN word for man as a divine being temporarily exiled in the material world.

**ANOUKIS** Greek form of the name of the Egyptian goddess ANQUET.

**ANPU** See ANUBIS.

**ANQUET** Egyptian goddess of the first cataract of the Nile.

**ANQUETIL-DUPERRON, ABRAHAM HYACINTHE (1731–1805)** French orientalist who translated the *Zend Avesta* of ZOROASTRIANISM, the *Vendidad Sade*, the *Upanishads*, and a life of Zoroaster.

**ANRA MAINYU** See AHRIMAN.

**ANSELM, ST.** (c. 1033–1109) Italian-born churchman who became Archbishop of Canterbury and a unique Schoolman (see

SCHOLASTICS). He devised the ontological argument for the existence of God, based on the thought that man conceives of a perfect Being, that one attribute of perfection is existence, and that the very idea of a perfect Being therefore implies the existence of God. Anselm's *Cur Deus Homo?* (*Why Did God Become Man?*), his greatest work, is a logical analysis of the necessity of the ATONEMENT of Christ. Herman Hausheer says Anselm "created the doctrine of atonement." Anselm based theology on faith: "I believe that I may understand."

**ANSGAR, ST. (801–865)** Missionary to Sweden and Denmark; "Apostle of the North." The first archbishop of Hamburg, he died regretting that he could not be a martyr for Christ.

**ANSGARII SYNOD** Swedish denomination which merged with the Mission Synod in 1885 to form the Swedish Evangelical Mission Covenant of America.

**ANSHAR AND KISHAR** Two Babylonian gods who arose out of chaos together.

**ANSHE KNESSET HAGEDOLAH** Men of the GREAT ASSEMBLY, organized in JUDAISM at the time of Ezra.

**ANTAEUS** Giant in Greek mythology who became stronger by touching Earth, his mother. Hercules defeated him by lifting him up so that he could not renew his strength, and then crushing him.

**ANTECHAPEL** The part of a chapel on the western side of the choir screen (i.e., ornamental wood or iron work separating the space to the east, occupied by the choir, from the space to the west, occupied by the congregation).

**ANTE-COMMUNION** Early part of the COMMUNION service.

**ANTEDILUVIAN** Before the flood which, according to Genesis and many ancient legends, covered a great part or all of the earth.

**ANTELAPSARIANISM** See SUPRALAPSARIANISM.

**ANTE-NICENE FATHERS** Those church fathers who preceded the First Council of NICAEA (A.D. 325). See FATHERS OF THE CHURCH.

**ANTEPENDIUM** Ecclesiastical hanging which adorns the front of the altar.

**ANTHAT** Ugarit goddess of war and love.

**ANTHEM** Sacred choral composition with words from Scripture.

**ANTHEMIUS OF TRALLES (sixth century)** Greek builder of the Church of HAGIA SOPHIA in Constantinople.

**ANTHESTERIA** A DIONYSIAC festival of Greece held in February. Originally it was a ceremony relating to the souls of the dead.

**ANTHIM THE IBERIAN (?–1716)** Learned Rumanian churchman who helped bring the Rumanian language into the church.

**ANTHONY, ST. (c.250–350)** Egyptian hermit and father of MONASTICISM. In the deserts he experienced many temptations, often seeing Satan as a wild beast or an alluring woman.

**ANTHONY OF PADUA, ST. (1195–1231)** Eloquent FRANCISCAN monk, preacher, theologian, and saint. Called "Hammer of Heretics," he preached in France, Italy, and Sicily. He was canonized in 1232.

**ANTHONY, ST., ORDERS OF** There are several of these: the Disciples of St. Anthony, the Hospitalers of St. Anthony, the Antonians founded by Abram Poresigh, the Congregation of St. Anthony, and the Chaldean Antonians.

**ANTHRATHI** Egyptian name of ANTHAT.

**ANTHROPOCENTRISM** The making of man rather than God the center of thought.

**ANTHROPOLATRY** The worship of man, or the conception of God as human.

**ANTHROPOLOGY** Theologically, the doctrine of man in relation to God.

**ANTHROPOMORPHISM** The ascription of human characteristics to God. Classic Christian theology holds that God has "neither parts nor passions."

**ANTHROPOPATHISM** The ascription of human emotions or passions to God, or to the nonhuman.

**ANTHROPOSOPHY** A religious philosophy based on THEOSOPHY but centered in man rather than in God; derived largely from the philosophy of Rudolf STEINER.

**ANTIBURGHERS** Opponents of the Burghers in Scottish church history. They seceded from the Church of Scotland, refusing to take an oath called the "Burgess Oath" which certified that church as "the true religion."

**ANTICHRIST** *against Christ* The enemy and opposite of Jesus Christ (I JOHN 2:18, 22; 4:3; II JOHN 7). In the Middle Ages church leaders sometimes called one another Antichrist, while the reformers saw the papacy as fulfilling the term. Nero, Mohammed, and many others have been accused of being Antichrist.

**ANTICHRISTIAN** Opposed to the CHRISTIAN faith or world-view.

**ANTICLERICALISM** Opposition to clerical influence in political matters. This movement was important in the French Revolution. Anticlericalism has been strong in Europe during the nineteenth and twentieth centuries, and has been a feature of political communism.

**ANTI-DEFAMATION LEAGUE** Division of the B'NAI B'RITH for the protection of Jewish rights.

**ANTIDORON** In the GREEK CATHOLIC CHURCH, the bread distributed after the mass.

**ANTIGONUS** 1. Grandson of Simon Hasmonai or Maccabee, killed by his brother ARISTOBULUS I c.105 B.C. 2. Son of Aristobulus II, made high priest and king in Judea c.40 B.C. The last of the Hasmonean kings, Antigonus was put to death by Antony at Antioch c.37 B.C.

**ANTILEGOMENA** Term for New Testament books not considered canonical or genuine.

**ANTIMASONIC MOVEMENT** American political movement of the early nineteenth century with religious overtones. Overtly opposed to the supposed evils of FREEMASONRY and championed by the National Republicans, antimasonry achieved the proportions of a religious crusade and was supported by many churches.

**ANTIMINSION** Portable altar in the GREEK CATHOLIC CHURCH consisting of a cloth containing relics.

**ANTIMISSIONARY MOVEMENT** A reaction against the growing centralization in missions, temperance, Sunday school, and other projects among religious groups—both denominationally and interdenominationally—in the early nineteenth century in the United States.

**ANTINOMIANISM** Rejection of the authority of the moral law on the grounds that Christian grace and freedom supersede the law.

**ANTINOMISTIC CONTROVERSY** A dispute about law and grace within the LUTHERAN churches during the last half of the six-

teenth century. Against AGRICOLA and others, who maintained that the Ten Commandments belonged to the courts rather than to the churches, LUTHER held that both the Law and the Gospel should be proclaimed by ministers of Christ.

**ANTINOMY** In metaphysics, opposition between *a*. two principles both of which seem true, or *b*. inferences drawn from such paradoxical principles. Immanuel KANT argued, from antinomies concerning the nature of the universe, that time and space are subjective.

**ANTIOCH** 1. City in Pisidia, Asia Minor, with a large Jewish population, visited several times by St. Paul (ACTS 13:14, 14:21). 2. City in Syria about 300 miles north of Jerusalem, made capital of Syria about 64 B.C. At Antioch the disciples of Jesus were first called Christians (ACTS 11:26).

**ANTIOCH, SYNODS OF** More than 30 synods were held in Syrian Antioch during the early centuries of the church. The first three condemned the heresies of PAUL OF SAMOSATA. Two synods about 341 deposed ATHANASIUS and attempted to replace the NICENE CREED with other creeds less strong against ARIANISM.

**ANTIOCHENE RITE** The system of laws and rites of the patriarchate of Antioch in Syria.

**ANTIOCHIAN SCHOOL** Theological point of view associated with Syrian Antioch during the early centuries of the church. It opposed the allegorical interpretations of Scripture fostered by the ALEXANDRIAN SCHOOL, emphasizing rationalism, the grammatico-historical method of exegesis, and free moral agency in man.

**ANTIOCHUS** 1. (?–c.408) Bishop of Ptolemais in Palestine, known for his eloquent preaching. 2. (6th–7th century) Monk at St. Saba, near Jerusalem, at the time of the capture of Jerusalem by the Persians in 614.

**ANTIOCHUS EPIPHANES (?–163 B.C.)** Antiochus IV, king of Syria 175–163 B.C. About 167 B.C., attempting to Hellenize the Jews, he prohibited worship in the temple and defiled it with an idol. Passages in the book of Daniel appear to refer to him, as do the Books of the Maccabees.

**ANTIOCHUS EUPATOR (c.173–162 B.C.)** Antiochus V, son of Antiochus Epiphanes and boy king of Syria who made peace with the Jews before being overthrown by Demetrius I.

**ANTIOPE** 1. Greek beauty raped by ZEUS and visited with madness by DIONYSUS. 2. Queen of the Amazons.

**ANTIPAEDOBAPTISTS** See ANABAPTISTS.

**ANTIPAS** 1. One of the Herods, son of HEROD THE GREAT. 2. A martyr of Pergamum and according to tradition the first bishop of that city (REVELATION 2:13).

**ANTIPATER** One of the Herods, father of HEROD THE GREAT.

**ANTIPHON** 1. Short phrase sung before and after a psalm or canticle in Christian worship. 2. Festival chant preparatory for mass. 3. Psalm or anthem sung antiphonally by alternating choirs.

**ANTIPHONAL MUSIC** Music sung by alternating or facing choirs.

**ANTIPHONARY** Book of antiphons.

**ANTIPHONY** Alternative singing by two parts of a congregation or choir. The Psalms were probably sung in part antiphonally, and Christian worship has made much use of this form.

**ANTIPOPE** One claiming or elected to the highest position in the ROMAN CATHOLIC CHURCH but whose position has been declared invalid.

**ANTIQUITIES, SACRED** Whatever relates to the ancient Jews, to the early Christians, or to those connected with them.

**ANTIREMONSTRANTS** 1. Those opposed to those who protest, particularly in ecclesiastical matters. 2. Dutch CALVINISTS of the early seventeenth century who were opposed to the ARMINIANS of Holland.

**ANTI-ROMANISM** 1. Opposition to the ROMAN CATHOLIC CHURCH. 2. Stance of the Protestant evangelical groups in France, particularly following the REFORMATION.

**ANTI-SABBATARIANS** 1. Those who reject the observance of the Jewish SABBATH. 2. Those who oppose laws prohibiting various activities on Sunday.

**ANTI-SALOON LEAGUE** Temperance organization founded in 1893 at Oberlin, Ohio, to exterminate "the beverage liquor traffic." Backed by many PROTESTANT churches, the League succeeded in securing passage of the Eighteenth Amendment which prohibited the sale of alcoholic beverages.

**ANTI-SEMITISM** Opposition to or hatred of the Jews, often highly organized. It existed as anciently as in the Eighteenth Dynasty of Egypt when Jews were harassed by the Pharaohs, it flourished sporadically throughout the Middle Ages, and it climaxed in the horrors of NAZISM before and during World War II. Often colored by religious propaganda, the anti-Semitic movement desecrates all true religion.

**ANTISTHENES (c.445–c.365 B.C.)** Founder of the CYNIC school of philosophy. For him there was only one God, who was totally unknown; happiness resulted from being good; and the good life must be sought for its own sake.

**ANTITHESIS** In philosophy, the opposite of a dialectical concept or thesis which is followed by a new concept or synthesis. (This is the basis of HEGEL's absolute idealism.)

**ANTI-TRINITARIANISM** Opposition to the orthodox Christian belief in the Holy TRINITY, often applied to UNITARIANISM and SOCINIANISM.

**ANTITYPE** The correlative of a figure or symbol. In theology many Old Testament objects, rites, or personages have been considered types of Christ or of New Testament truths, these being the realities or antitypes.

**ANTOINE, NICOLE (1600–1632)** French REFORMED preacher, alleged to hold strange opinions about Jesus, who embraced JUDAISM and was burned at Geneva.

**ANTOINE, PÉRE (1748–1829)** Spanish CAPUCHIN priest in the United States. A controversial figure, he appears to have been empowered to begin the INQUISITION in the United States, although he never did so.

**ANTONELLI, GIACOMO (1806–1876)** Italian statesman and cardinal thought to have influenced Pope PIUS IX. He championed the papacy against the unification of Italy.

**ANTONELLO DA MESSINA (c.1430–1479)** Italian painter whose studies of JEROME, JESUS, the MADONNA, and other subjects blend simplicity with detail.

**ANTONIANS** 1. See ANTHONY, ST., ORDERS OF. 2. Name of several monastic orders. 3. Followers of Anton Unternäher in Switzerland. ANTINOMIANS, they believed in unrestrained sexual love and regarded their founder as Son of Man and Redeemer.

**ANTONINUS, ST.** (1389–1459) Italian DOMINICAN theologian and archbishop. He did pioneer work in moral theology and helped his people during disasters from plague and earthquake.

**ANTONINUS LIBERALIS (second century)** Greek author of *Collected Metamorphoses,* 41 mythological stories.

**ANTONINUS PIUS (86–161)** Roman emperor known for his integrity and good works, yet during whose reign POLYCARP was burned at the stake.

**ANTU** See BORNEO, RELIGION IN.

**ANU** 1. Supreme god of Babylonian religion, god of the sky and ruler of earthly and heavenly events. See also ADAD. 2. Celtic fertility goddess.

**ANUBIS or ANUP** Jackal-headed god of the dead in Egyptian religion; one of its most ancient gods.

**ANUNAKI** Babylonian earth gods or earth spirits.

**ANUNITUM** See ISHTAR.

**ANUP** See ANUBIS.

**ANUSIM** Jews forced to convert to Christianity but who secretly held to their faith.

**ANVIL** Symbol of martyrdom.

**APADANA** BUDDHIST book containing biographies of many of Buddha's first disciples.

**A PARTE ANTE** SCHOLASTIC term for the eternal past of God.

**A PARTE POST** SCHOLASTIC term for the eternal future of God.

**APASON** See APSU.

**APATHY** Stoic and early Christian term for the extinction of lust and sin, or the control of evil passions.

**APATURIA** Autumn festival of Athenians and Ionians in which the gods were worshiped, the clans met, and oxen were sacrificed to ZEUS and ATHENA.

**APAYA** The lower worlds, including hell, according to BUDDHISM.

**APE** Symbol of sloth, sin, lust, or Satan in religious art.

**APELLES (fourth century B.C.)** Greek painter of APHRODITE rising from the sea, Alexander holding the thunderbolts of ZEUS, the procession of the high priest of ARTEMIS, and other pagan religious subjects.

**APEP** Egyptian serpent god who opposed RA and the sun gods.

**APET** Egyptian hippopotamus goddess.

**APHRAATES (fourth century)** First strong writer and first Church Father of the early Christian church in Syria. A monk and probably a bishop, he composed 23 treatises on various phases of Christian life and theology.

**APHRODITE** Greek goddess of love and beauty, corresponding to the Roman love-goddess VENUS and the Semitic ASTARTE.

**APIS** Egyptian bull-god worshiped at Memphis; in him OSIRIS was thought to be incarnate.

**APISIRAHTS** Morning god of the Blackfoot Indians.

**APO** ZOROASTRIAN water-being.

**APOCALYPSE** *unveiling or revelation* 1. A religious writing about the end of the world. 2. The Book of Revelation in the New Testament.

**APOCALYPSE OF ABRAHAM** Apocryphal Jewish writing from about the first century A.D., recounting Abraham's conversion and visions.

**APOCALYPSE OF BARUCH** 1. A Jewish apocryphal work in Greek telling of Baruch's visions of seven heavens. 2. A Syriac book similar to IV Ezra.

**APOCALYPSE OF MOSES** See BOOK OF JUBILEES.

**APOCALYPSE OF PETER** Regarded as the most important of the apocryphal apocalypses. A second-century work similar in some respects to the New Testament II Peter, containing a vision of Christians in heaven.

**APOCALYPTICISM** Religious preoccupation with the end of the world and concomitant events.

**APOCALYPTIC LITERATURE** Writings such as Daniel and Revelation dealing with future events, the destruction of evil, and the triumph of God.

**APOCATASTASIS** *reestablishment* Greek word for return to a former place or condition. Theologically, indicates the doctrine that all free moral agents will eventually achieve salvation. ORIGEN construed this word in Acts 3:21 to mean that finally even Satan will be reconciled to God.

**APOCATEQUIL** Inca god of lightning.

**APOCRYPHA** *hidden things* 1. Books in the Western canon of the OLD TESTAMENT accepted by ROMAN CATHOLICS but not considered canonical by JEWS and PROTESTANTS. They are: I and II Esdras; Tobit; Judith; Esther 10:4—16:24; Wisdom; Ecclesiasticus; Baruch; Daniel 3:24—90, 13—14; The Prayer of Manasses; and I and II Maccabees. 2. This term sometimes refers to what is technically called PSEUDEPIGRAPHA, or to epistles, gospels and the like not considered part of the canon of Scripture.

**APOLLINARIANISM** Theological doctrine of APOLLINARIS OF LAODICEA, condemned by the First Council of CONSTANTINOPLE in 381. It held that Christ's human nature was replaced by the divine LOGOS and therefore that Christ was not completely human.

**APOLLINARIS OF LAODICEA (c.315–c.390)** Also known as Apollinaris the Younger, he collaborated with his father, Apollinaris the Elder, in paraphrasing the Bible along classical Greek lines, and fathered the heretical theological system of APOLLINARIANISM. He became Bishop of Laodicea in Syria.

**APOLLINARIS SIDONIUS (c.430–c.488)** Christian writer, politician, and bishop, canonized as St. Sidonius.

**APOLLINARIUS** See APOLLINARIS.

**APOLLO** Youthful and handsome Greek god of healing, prophecy, flocks, and the arts. He was one of the most important gods of Olympus.

**APOLLODORUS (second century B.C.)** Greek author of a book about the gods.

**APOLLONIUS OF TYANA (c.4 B.C.–A.D. c.100)** Greek philosopher who claimed he could foresee the future. According to his biographer Philostratus, he performed many miracles.

**APOLLOS** An Alexandrian Jew who became a Christian teacher and preached the gospel at Ephesus and Corinth (ACTS 18; 19; I CORINTHIANS 1:10–12; 3:4–6; 16:12).

**APOLLYON** See ABADDON.

**APOLOGETICS** The systematic, logical defense of Christianity, Judaism, or another coherent faith. Courses in this subject are a tradition in theological seminaries.

**APOLOGIA PRO VITA SUA Defense of His Life** Famous book by John Henry NEWMAN, tracing his spiritual development and explaining why he left the CHURCH OF ENG-

LAND for the ROMAN CATHOLIC CHURCH in which he became a cardinal.

**APOLOGISTS** Defenders of the Christian faith. Famous apologists are PAUL, JUSTIN MARTYR, TERTULLIAN, ORIGEN, EUSEBIUS, ATHANASIUS, AUGUSTINE, and THOMAS AQUINAS.

**APOLOGUE** A short fable or story with a moral. LUTHER considered apologues to be excellent aids to virtue.

**APOLYSIS** A prayer of dismissal in the EASTERN CHURCH.

**APOPHTHEGMATA PATRUM** Anthology of the sayings of Egyptian monks, dating from the fourth century.

**APOSTASY** Leaving the faith. A problem in both Judaism and Christianity, apostasy was regarded very seriously during the centuries of persecution. ROMAN CATHOLICISM recognizes departure from MONASTIC or clerical vows as apostasy.

**APOSTATE** One who has completely abandoned the Christian faith.

**A POSTERIORI** In philosophy and theology, reasoning from facts or experience, as opposed to the a priori building of a system by reasoning from given principles.

**APOSTIL** An explanatory note on a text of Scripture, or a commentary on a Scripture lesson.

**APOSTLE one sent** 1. One of The Twelve chosen by JESUS to oversee and carry on His work: PETER, JAMES, JOHN, ANDREW, THOMAS, JAMES THE LESS, JUDE, PHILIP, BARTHOLOMEW, MATTHEW, SIMON, and JUDAS (who was replaced by MATTHIAS). 2. A New Testament missionary such as PAUL or BARNABAS; in Christian literature "The Apostle" often means Paul. 3. In Christian history such missionaries as AUGUSTINE and PATRICK have been called apostles.

**APOSTLE OF ENGLAND** See AUGUSTINE OF CANTERBURY.

**APOSTLE OF THE GENTILES** The Apostle Paul, who was called to evangelize the Gentiles as Peter was the Jews. Compare Galatians 2:7.

**APOSTLES' CREED** One of the shortest and oldest statements of Christian faith. Although some of its phrases may be traced to the second century, this creed was not connected with the apostolic period until the fourth century. Its present form dates from the sixteenth century.

**APOSTOLATE** The office or the mission of an apostle.

**APOSTOLIC AGE** The first century of Christian history, covering the New Testament period.

**APOSTOLIC BRETHREN or APOSTOLICI** The name of several Christian sects whose members sought to emulate the Twelve APOSTLES, particularly: 1. Celibate communists of the fourth and fifth centuries in Asia Minor. 2. European twelfth-century groups with MANICHAEAN ideas. 3. Christian communists of northern Italy who followed the teachings of Gerhard Sagarelli (or Gerard Segerelli or Segalelli) from about the year 1260. Taking vows of poverty, chastity, and idleness, they preached repentance and the males often took spiritual sisters as companions. Sagarelli was burned at the stake and his successor, Dolcino of Novara, was torn to pieces with red-hot pincers. Nevertheless the movement continued in Europe throughout the fourteenth century.

**APOSTOLIC CANONS** Anonymously written rules for the clerical life, dating from the fourth century; included is a list of the books of the Bible.

**APOSTOLIC CHRISTIAN CHURCH** An association of Holiness churches in Germany and Switzerland. See HOLINESS CHURCH.

**APOSTOLIC CHRISTIAN CHURCH (NAZARENE)** Holiness group, possibly originating in Hungary, which developed among German and Swiss immigrants in the United States.

**APOSTOLIC CHRISTIAN CHURCHES OF AMERICA** Pacifistic association of Holiness churches in the United States; Swiss-German origins.

**APOSTOLIC CHRISTIANITY** A term for the Christian faith and life of the first century.

**APOSTOLIC CHURCH DIRECTORY** Collection of moral and ecclesiastical precepts from the third century of Egyptian Christianity.

**APOSTOLIC CONSTITUTIONS** A fourth-century collection of rules of Christian faith, life, and worship, for both laymen and clergy. Possibly of Syrian origin, this work, arranged in eight books, concludes with the 85 rules of the APOSTOLIC CANONS. It contains much important information about the early church.

**APOSTOLIC COUNCIL** The first council in the Christian church, described in Acts 15. It made the important decision that GENTILES may be admitted to the church on condition of faith, without keeping all the regulations of JUDAISM.

**APOSTOLIC DECREE** The decision of the APOSTOLIC COUNCIL, granting Gentile Christians liberty in all but minimal moral requirements.

**APOSTOLIC DELEGATE** A representative of the pope to a country that has no other diplomatic relationship with the VATICAN.

**APOSTOLIC EPISCOPAL CHURCH** Autonomous American CATHOLIC denomination claiming apostolic orders through Chaldean succession.

**APOSTOLIC FAITH MISSION** Group in the western United States which emphasizes holiness, FAITH HEALING, speaking in tongues (see GLOSSOLALIA), and FOOT WASHING.

**APOSTOLIC FATHERS** Early church leaders contemporary with the apostles, such as CLEMENT, BARNABAS, HERMAS, IGNATIUS, and POLYCARP.

**APOSTOLICI** See APOSTOLIC BRETHREN.

**APOSTOLIC LETTERS** 1. The NEW TESTAMENT epistles of Paul, Peter, John, etc. 2. Messages from the VATICAN.

**APOSTOLIC MAJESTY** A title conferred on Stephen, first Christian king of Hungary, in 1001, and held by later Hungarian kings into the twentieth century.

**APOSTOLIC METHODIST CHURCH** The smallest METHODIST denomination in the United States, with three churches and ultraconservative teachings.

**APOSTOLIC NUNCIO** The permanent ambassador from the pope to a foreign capital.

**APOSTOLIC OVERCOMING HOLY CHURCH OF GOD** Small denomination in southern United States, founded by the Rev. W. T. Phillips.

**APOSTOLIC SEE** 1. The DIOCESE of the pope (who is also Bishop of Rome). 2. A church founded by an apostle such as the church at Jerusalem or Ephesus.

**APOSTOLIC SUCCESSION** The doctrine that properly ordained bishops convey the grace of God through an unbroken chain of the laying on of hands going back to the first apostles of Christ. The ROMAN, EASTERN, and ANGLICAN churches hold that such unbroken physical succession is essential to a valid Christian ministry. Other Christians reject this theory.

**APOSTOLICUM** Continental term for the APOSTLES' CREED.

**APOSTOLIUS, MICHAEL (fifteenth century)** A Christian Greek theologian who copied many manuscripts and helped preserve much classical and Christian literature.

**APOSTOOL, SAMUEL (1638–c.1695)** MENNONITE preacher who insisted on the importance of right doctrine in the Christian life, in opposition to the emphasis on practical living made by Hans Galenus. Apostool's followers were called Apostoolians.

**APOTACTICI, or APOTACTITES** Variant of Apostolici. See APOSTOLIC BRETHREN.

**APOTHEOSIS** Deification, as of the Roman emperors, who were considered to be gods upon their death.

**APPAREL** Ecclesiastical term for embroidery on a priest's ALB or AMICE.

**APPARITION** Preternatural appearance of a ghost or spirit. ISLAM and other religions often emphasize apparitions of this kind.

**APPARITIONS OF THE VIRGIN** Appearances of the Virgin MARY, as at Lourdes in France, where eighteen such manifestations have been attested to.

**APPARITOR or APPARATOR** Ecclesiastical official who summons people to appear before a church court and carries out court decrees.

**APPELLANTS** Priests who appeal from an ecclesiastical decision or a papal bull.

**APPHIA** A Christian woman of Colosse (PHILEMON 2) who, according to tradition, was martyred with Philemon in the first century A.D.

**APPIAN WAY** The famous Roman highroad from Rome to Capua along which Paul walked (ACTS 28:15). On it near Rome are catacombs and tombs.

**APPIUS FORUM or MARKET** A point on the Appian Way about 40 miles east of Rome where Paul was encouraged by meeting some Christian brothers (ACTS 28:15).

**APPLE** Symbol of temptation, sin, man's fall, or salvation. Although the apple has traditionally been thought to have been the fruit forbidden in the garden of Eden, there is no Biblical basis for this.

**APPLESEED, JOHNNY** See CHAPMAN, JOHN.

**APPROPRIATION** 1. In the Christian faith, appropriation is the acceptance of salvation and making it one's own. 2. In ecclesiastical law, appropriation is the annexation of a BENEFICE, as in the assignment of parish funds to a MONASTERY.

**APPROVED SUPPLY PASTOR** A METHODIST term for a ministerial candidate who fills a pulpit in a church on a temporary basis.

**APRIES (sixth century B.C.)** Egyptian king who tried to offset Nebuchadnezzar's siege of Jerusalem in 586 B.C. Jeremiah refers to him as Pharaoh-Hophra (JEREMIAH 44: 30).

**A PRIORI** Philosophical or theological term for knowledge independent of experience.

**APRON** A short cassock used in the CHURCH OF ENGLAND.

**APSARAS** HINDU wind spirits or heavenly nymphs who may wed mortals.

**APSE** The termination of a sanctuary, originally and usually in the shape of a semicircle covered by a half dome. It was universally used in early Christian BASILICAS.

**APSU or APASON** The abyss from which all things came, according to Babylonian mythology.

**APU-HAU** Polynesian god of storms.

**APULEIUS, LUCIUS (c.125–?)** Roman writer and Platonist philosopher. Celebrated author of *The Golden Ass,* Apuleius also wrote about magic, God, and DAEMONS.

**APU-MATANGI** *whirlwind* A Polynesian storm god.

**AQUARIANS** 1. A third-century sect who refused wine and used only water in the EUCHARIST. 2. A fifth-century group who abstained from drinking anything alcoholic.

**AQUAVIVA, CLAUDIO (1543–1615)** An Italian Jesuit who was fifth general of the SOCIETY OF JESUS. He founded the Society's system of education.

**AQUILA** A Jewish Christian who with his wife Priscilla helped the Apostle Paul (ACTS 18:2–3; ROMANS 16:3–4).

**AQUILA, VERSION OF** A Greek version of the OLD TESTAMENT translated by AQUILA OF PONTUS. Very popular in the synagogues, this version was considered very accurate and was quite literal.

**AQUILA OF PONTUS (second century)** A native of Sinope in Pontus on the coast of the Black Sea; his translation of the Old Testament, though criticized by many

Christians, was praised by the Church Fathers ORIGEN and JEROME, and displaced the SEPTUAGINT in many synagogues. He is said to have been a disciple of Rabbi AKIBA and may have been converted to JUDAISM from CHRISTIANITY.

**AQUINAS, THOMAS** See THOMAS AQUINAS.

**AR** Old Testament word for city.

**ARA** Latin word for ALTAR.

**ARABAH** The desert between the Dead Sea and the Gulf of Aqaba.

**ARACHNE** Greek weaving woman who, because her tapestries so perfectly portrayed the love affairs of the gods, was changed into a spider by ATHENA.

**ARAF** Mohammedan name for PURGATORY.

**ARAHAT or ARHAT** A BUDDHIST "Worthy One" who has attained NIRVANA.

**ARALU** The Babylonian abode of the dead, with seven doors of entrance and none of exit.

**ARAM** 1. The ancient name for Syria. 2. The Aramean people of Aram, who were among the chief enemies of Israel in the ninth and eighth centuries B.C. 3. The son of Shem and grandson of Noah (GENESIS 10:22–23), from whom the Arameans are considered to have descended.

**ARAMAIC** The language of the Arameans (see ARAM), which became the *lingua franca* of the Middle East in late Old Testament and New Testament times. Most of the TALMUD and parts of the OLD TESTAMENT are written in Aramaic and reflect its influences. Jesus and the early disciples all apparently spoke in Aramaic.

**ARAMAITI** One of the six Holy Ones attending AHURA MAZDA, the special spirit of the earth.

**ARAMEANS** See ARAM.

**ARANDA, PEDRO PABLA ABARCA, COUNT OF (1719–1798)** Spanish general and civil minister during whose reign the SOCIETY OF JESUS was expelled from Spain.

**ARANYAKA** A part of the sacred Hindu VEDAS designed for study by forest dwellers.

**ARARAT** 1. An ancient name for ancient Armenia. 2. Two mountains in Turkey or Armenia bear this name. Ararat is the traditional site of the landing of Noah's ARK.

**ARASON, JON (1484–1551)** Poet and bishop of Iceland who brought printing into that country.

**ARATOR (sixth century)** Christian poet, writer, and cleric.

**ARATUS (third century B.C.)** Greek poet quoted by St. Paul in his sermon on Mars Hill (ACTS 17:28).

**ARAUCANIAN RELIGION** Religion of the Araucanian Indians of Chile, involving ancestor worship, puberty rites, human sacrifice, and cannibalism.

**ARBAAH MINIM** Four kinds of branches used in the Jewish celebration of Sukkoth (see BOOTHS, FEAST OF).

**ARBA KOSOT** The four cups of wine drunk by each person at PASSOVER.

**ARCANA COELESTIA** *Heavenly Secrets* An important work of the religious innovator Emanuel SWEDENBORG.

**ARCANI DISCIPLINA** *secret teaching* Secret instruction about the SACRAMENTS, the TRINITY, etc., given in early Christian times only to those who had been baptized into the church.

**ARCHAEOLOGY** The study of human tools, records, and remains from the past. This science has greatly added to religious knowledge, particularly in the BIBLE LANDS where it has often corroborated Biblical data.

**ARCHANGEL** A chief angel (DANIEL 12:1). Michael and Gabriel are among the archangels in CHRISTIAN, JEWISH, and MOSLEM tradition.

**ARCHBISHOP** The chief BISHOP of an area in the church.

**ARCHCHAPLAIN** The chief CHAPLAIN.

**ARCHDEACON** A chief DEACON or priest, ranking only below a BISHOP. In Anglican churches an archdeacon may administer part of a bishop's diocese.

**ARCHDIOCESE** The territory governed by an ARCHBISHOP.

**ARCHELAUS** The son of HEROD THE GREAT who ruled Judea and Samaria 4 B.C. to A.D. 6, during the infancy of Jesus.

**ARCHETYPE** An original pattern. Christian theology sometimes refers to Christ, for example, as the archetype of all Christians.

**ARCHFIEND** The chief demon, or Satan.

**ARCHIMANDRITE** The head of a large monastery or of several monasteries in the EASTERN CHURCH.

**ARCHIPPUS** A Christian at Colosse in Greece, possibly leader of the church there (COLOSSIANS 4:17).

**ARCHON** The official responsible for the

conduct of an ecclesiastical function in the EASTERN CHURCH.

**ARCHONS** Manichaean sons of darkness. See MANICHAEISM.

**ARCHPRIEST** A chief priest. In the early church the archpriest was chief assistant to a BISHOP.

**ARCOSOLIUM** An arched cell or recess in a catacomb, particularly for use as a tomb. Many martyrs were buried in arcosolia.

**AREOPAGUS** "Mars Hill," sacred meeting place in Athens where the Apostle Paul preached to the Athenians (ACTS 17:19).

**ARES** Greek god of war, similar to the Roman god Mars.

**ARESSON, JON (c.1484–1550)** A CATHOLIC bishop of Iceland who wrote Christian poetry and was executed for resisting the influence of the REFORMATION.

**ARETHAS (c.860–940)** Byzantine scholar and theologian who wrote a commentary on the book of Revelation.

**ARHAT** See ARAHAT.

**ARIADNE** Ancient Greek goddess of vegetation. In Greek mythology, Ariadne helped Theseus kill the Minotaur.

**ARIAN** Relating to ARIUS or ARIANISM.

**ARIANISM** The theological position that Christ is subordinate to the Father, created or begotten but not eternal. It was condemned at the First Council of NICAEA in 325. Several shades of Arianism have appeared in church history, and its influence has been widespread.

**ARIDITY** A term among ancient mystics for the dryness of the soul which makes worship and communion with God difficult.

**ARIEL** 1. A symbolic name of Jerusalem (ISAIAH 29:1). 2. A prankish spirit in Shakespeare's play *The Tempest*.

**ARIMATHEA** The home of Joseph of Arimathea, who secured the body of the crucified Saviour and laid it in his own tomb (MATTHEW 27:57). It may have been Ramathaim-Zophim or Rama northwest of Jerusalem.

**ARIMINUM AND SELEUCIA, SYNODS OF** Two synods summoned by the Emperor CONSTANTINE to bring together the bishops of the Eastern and Western churches in 359 for the purpose of settling the ARIAN dispute concerning the deity of Christ.

**ARISTAEUS** A benevolent Greek god of healing whose worship was widespread; he was often represented as a young shepherd carrying a sheep on his shoulders.

**ARISTEAS** The pen name of an unknown writer of the second century B.C. He wrote a *Letter* giving a fanciful story of how the Old Testament was translated from Hebrew into the Greek SEPTUAGINT.

**ARISTIDES, ST. (second century)** Christian Greek philosopher whose *Apology* protested harassment of Christians.

**ARISTIDES, APOLOGY OF** See ARISTIDES. A Syriac manuscript of the *Apology* was found on Mt. Sinai in 1889. It seeks to puncture the heathen religions and to show the superiority of Christianity.

**ARISTION (first century)** One of the principal authorities for the traditions about Jesus, according to PAPIAS.

**ARISTIPPUS (c.435–356 B.C.)** The founder of the Cyrenaic school of Greek philosophy. He saw pleasure as the supreme good, and made goodness and enjoyment practically synonymous.

**ARISTOBULUS I (c.140 B.C.–103 B.C.)** First Hasmonean King of Judea.

**ARISTOBULUS OF PANEAS (second century B.C.)** Jewish philosopher of Alexandria who tried to reconcile Greek philosophy with JUDAISM and to prove that the early Greek philosophers had taken material from Scripture.

**ARISTOTELIAN ETHICS** Aristotle greatly influenced Christianity, especially through DANTE, LAUD, and THOMAS AQUINAS, as well as ISLAM and JUDAISM in the Middle Ages. Aristotelianism emphasizes facts and substances above underlying principles, and lends itself to an ethics of self-interest.

**ARISTOTELIAN PHILOSOPHY** Beginning with Plato's emphasis on the unity of reality and the primacy of ideas or principles, Aristotle's view of the world as a complex of different substances led to a philosophy geared to actual scientific observation, to a respect for facts, and to an appreciation of the potentiality of matter and of causation. Aristotelianism sees four causes for everything: material, formal, efficient, and final.

**ARISTOTELIAN THEOLOGY** Aristotle's theory of causation led to the concept of a Prime Mover or Uncaused Cause. Although his God was not personal but was pure form, Aristotle believed in "laying hold on immortality" and held that the soul is important and that man must be like the gods.

**ARISTOTLE (384–322 B.C.)** One of the world's greatest thinkers, philosophers, and moralists. He built on the work of Socrates and PLATO, was a tutor of Alexander the Great, and greatly influenced religious thought long after his death.

**ARIUS (c.256–336)** A presbyter of the church of Alexandria who developed views of Christ as subordinate to God which were declared heretical at the First Council of NICAEA. He was excommunicated in 321 but later ordered readmitted to the church by the emperor.

**ARK** A vessel or chest. 1. Noah's ark was a large boat which carried NOAH and his immediate family and many animals through the Flood. The ark sometimes symbolizes salvation or the church. 2. An ark held the infant MOSES until the pharaoh's daughter rescued him from the Nile during the official extermination of male Jewish babies. 3. The ark of the covenant was a chest of acacia wood overlaid with gold which held the tablets of the law. Placed in the HOLY OF HOLIES, first in the tabernacle and then in the temple at Jerusalem, the ark of the covenant was never seen again after NEBUCHADNEZZAR's destruction of Jerusalem.

**ARLES** A city in southeastern France which was an archiepiscopal see from the fourth through the eighteenth centuries and where fifteen church councils were held between 314 and 1275. These dealt with such matters as DONATISM, persecutions, doctrines, and church organization.

**ARLES, SYNOD OF** The first general council in the Western Church. Convoked by CONSTANTINE I in 314, in order to settle a dispute between the DONATISTS and the CATHOLICS of North Africa, it condemned the principal positions of the Donatists.

**ARMAGEDDON** A mountain of Megiddo near Mount Carmel in Palestine on the plain of Esdraelon. Here a number of violent battles have been fought and here, according to Revelation 16:16, the kings of the earth engage in what appears to be a final struggle before the Kingdom of God is fully established. Thus Armageddon indicates both a violent battle and the final war of the ages.

**ARMAGH** A town of Northern Ireland where St. PATRICK founded his church about 445 and where there are both PROTESTANT and CATHOLIC archbishoprics and two cathedrals.

**ARMAGH, BOOK OF** A collection of documents from the eighth or ninth centuries including lives of PATRICK and MARTIN OF TOURS.

**ARMENIAN CHURCH** Comprising the Asia Minor of New Testament times, Armenia is the oldest Christian country. Because GREGORY THE ILLUMINATOR converted King Tiridates to Christianity about 301, the Armenian Church is sometimes termed the Gregorian Church. Many of its members died for their faith when the Persians tried to make them worship ZOROASTER in the fifth century. Armenian Christians are sometimes termed MONOPHYSITE, although many of their theologians claim the orthodox view of Christ. Priests in the church may marry and there are seven sacraments. Armenian Christians have often been persecuted and since 1893 vast numbers have been massacred by the Turks and the Soviets.

**ARMENIAN CHURCH, NORTH AMERICAN DIOCESE** This body joined the NATIONAL COUNCIL OF CHURCHES in 1957. An American hierarchy directs its work, although its headquarters are in Armenia near Mount Ararat.

**ARMENIAN RITE** The system and forms of worship of the ARMENIAN CHURCH.

**ARMENIAN VERSION** A translation of the Bible from Syriac and Greek into Armenian, by Sahak and Mesrob, possibly in the early part of the fifth century.

**ARMINIANISM** A Christian theological system emphasizing the freedom of man and opposing strict Calvinistic views of unconditional election and irresistible grace. Its influence has been strong on modern Protestantism, especially METHODISM.

**ARMINIUS, JACOBUS (1560–1609)** Mild-mannered DUTCH REFORMED pastor who reacted against the dogmatic CALVINISM of his time with views which developed into "Arminianism," stressing man's part in salvation. He felt that there was good as well as evil in Rome and that all Protestants should live in brotherly love. Though continually attacked, he held his position as a theological professor at Leiden until his death.

**ARMOR** In religious art, a symbol of chivalry or of salvation.

**ARMORIUM** In Catholic churches, a recess over the altar containing the PYX.

**ARMOR OF GOD** The spiritual equipment —faith, Scripture, and the like—with which the Christian fights off the powers of evil (EPHESIANS 6:11–18).

**ARNAKNAGSAK** The Eskimo goddess of food.

**ARNAUD, HENRI (1641–1721)** WALDENSIAN leader who served his people as both pastor and general. For two years he successfully directed their defense in the Swiss mountains against the armies of France.

**ARNAULD, ANTOINE (1612–1694)** French Catholic JANSENIST priest and theologian. A friend of PASCAL, he spent most of his life in controversy with Jesuits, Calvinists, freethinkers, and others. He was the first noted theologian to accept the philosophy of DESCARTES.

**ARNAULD, MARIE ANGELIQUE (1591–1661)** Cistercian ABBESS of France with strong JANSENIST leanings; she reformed her convent and was an able writer and ecclesiastical leader. Also spelled Arnault, Arnaut.

**ARNAULD, ROBERT ARNAULD D'ANDILLY (1588–1674)** A brother of Antoine and Marie Arnauld; he wrote Christian poetry and translated the works of JOSEPHUS, the *Confessions of St. Augustine,* and the NEW TESTAMENT into delicate French. The latter popularized the Scriptures in France although it was severely criticized.

**ARNDT, JOHANN (1555–1621)** LUTHERAN theologian and MYSTIC of Germany who sided with MELANCHTHON and the CALVINISTS in the controversies of his time. His devotional writings had great influence.

**ARNOBIUS (fourth century)** Christian teacher of northern Africa whose defense of Christianity against charges that it was the cause of various disasters ranks him with the better apologists. He believed that the truth of Christianity is demonstrable from the evidence.

**ARNOBIUS THE YOUNGER (fifth century)** An African monk who held SEMI-PELAGIAN views, wrote an allegorical commentary on the Psalms, and attacked St. AUGUSTINE's doctrine of grace.

**ARNOLD, GOTTFRIED (1666–1714)** German professor of church history and PROTESTANT theologian who was also a pastor and a devotional writer. He wrote several hymns, edited the works of Angelus Silesius, and wrote the first church history in German—actually an important history of Protestant mysticism.

**ARNOLD, MATTHEW (1822–1888)** English writer, author of several important studies of religion which popularized his spiritual outlook and moral purpose. He defined religion as "morality touched with emotion."

**ARNOLD, THOMAS (1795–1842)** English clergyman and educator who sought to give his pupils Christian principles and who often embraced liberal political and religious views.

**ARNOLD OF BRESCIA (c.1090–1155)** Italian priest who sought to reform the church and was exiled, excommunicated, and eventually executed. He said: "Clerks who have estates, bishops who hold fiefs, monks who possess property, cannot be saved."

**ARNON** A river in Jordan about 50 miles long which once formed the boundary between the Moabites and the Amorites, and later that between Moab and Israel. It empties into the Dead Sea and its waters are always clear.

**ARON HA-KODESH** *the holy ark* A closet in the synagogue containing the scrolls of the TORAH.

**ARRIAN (second century)** Also known as Flavius Arrianus, Arrian was a Greek philosopher and historian whose notes on the lectures of EPICTETUS outline Stoic ethics and whose publication of Epictetus' *Enchiridion* prepared the way for its Christian adaptation. Nevertheless, he considered Christianity "mad fanaticism and custom."

**ARROW** Symbol of spiritual weaponry, death, plague; also of St. SEBASTIAN (martyred with arrows).

**ARS MORIENDI** A clergyman's guide in ministering to the dying.

**ARTAXERXES I (?–425 B.C.)** King of Persia (464–425 B.C.) who permitted Ezra and Nehemiah to restore Jerusalem and its defenses.

**ARTAXERXES II (?–358 B.C.)** Good-natured but weak king of Persia (404–358

B.C.) during whose reign MITHRAISM was revived.

**ARTEMIS** Greek goddess of chastity, of wildlife, of sea travelers, and of the hunt. She was also considered to be a moon goddess and is identified with DIANA.

**ARTEMON (third century)** Christian teacher at Rome with ADOPTIONIST or Sabellian views. He is said to have held that Christ, superior to the prophets, was merely a man.

**ARTEMONITES** Followers of ARTEMON, a small group of whom existed in the third century.

**ARTHA** One of the four great aims of HINDUISM: material possession.

**ARTHUR** Legendary king of early Britain whose story may rest upon Celtic mythology but who is remembered as a Christian champion of justice.

**ARTICLE OF FAITH** A statement of Christian belief.

**ARTICLES, FORTY-TWO** Anglican confession of 1553 which all clergy, teachers, and members of universities had to accept. Drafted by Thomas CRANMER, they formed the basis of the Thirty-Nine Articles of the Church of England (see ARTICLES, THIRTY-NINE).

**ARTICLES, SIX** An English law of 1539 intended to slow down the REFORMATION. Pro-Catholic, it was largely ignored.

**ARTICLES, TEN** The first articles of faith adopted by the CHURCH OF ENGLAND in the REFORMATION. They mention three sacraments, favor prayers for the dead, and indicate that justification is the result not only of faith but also of charity and contrition.

**ARTICLES, THIRTEEN** A statement, drawn up in 1538, of the articles of faith held in common between the LUTHERANS and ANGLICANS of the sixteenth century, modeled on the AUGSBURG CONFESSION and a basis for the later Forty-Two ARTICLES.

**ARTICLES, THIRTY-NINE** The doctrinal confession of the CHURCH OF ENGLAND and the PROTESTANT EPISCOPAL CHURCH, along with the APOSTLES' CREED, the NICENE CREED, the ATHANASIAN CREED, the BOOK OF COMMON PRAYER, the CATECHISM, and the Scriptures. Adopted in 1563 on the basis of the Forty-Two Articles, the Thirty-Nine Articles have a Calvinistic, non-Roman emphasis.

**ARTICLES, THIRTY-SEVEN** See BELGIC CONFESSION.

**ARTICLES, TWELVE** A statement of the German workers' and farmers' demands for justice at the time of the PEASANTS' REVOLT in 1525. LUTHER agreed with the demands although he opposed the revolt.

**ARTICLES, TWENTY-FIVE** The articles of faith drawn up by John WESLEY for the METHODISTS (see ARTICLES OF RELIGION).

**ARTICLES OF RELIGION** 1. The doctrinal articles of the METHODIST CHURCH prepared by John WESLEY on the basis of the Thirty-Nine Articles of the Church of England. 2. The Thirty-Nine Articles of the CHURCH OF ENGLAND (see ARTICLES, THIRTY-NINE).

**ARTICLES OF WAR** The declaration of faith of the SALVATION ARMY, used as a manual in that organization's onslaught on evil.

**ARTIFACT** A product of man as distinguished from a natural object, as defined by the science of ARCHAEOLOGY.

**ARTIO** Celtic goddess, possibly worshiped in connection with the rites of a bear clan.

**ARUNDEL, THOMAS (1353–1414)** Archbishop of Canterbury who sought to defend the church against heresy by severely suppressing the LOLLARDS. In 1408 he established an inquisition against heresy. He prohibited the circulation of the Scriptures in English.

**ARURU** Babylonian creator-goddess.

**ARVAL BROTHERS** Ancient Roman priesthood of twelve brothers who offered an annual sacrifice for the fertility of the fields. Their deity was the earth goddess Dea Dia.

**ARYA SAMAJ** HINDU reformation movement begun by DAYANANDA SARASWATI. Opposing Christianity, it holds to monotheism and a high ethic, and seeks to reconcile the VEDAS (the Hindu Scriptures) with modern culture and science.

**ARYMAN** One of the twelve HINDU guardians of the months of the year.

**ASA** A king of Judah in the ninth century B.C. who used the temple funds to bribe the king of Damascus to attack the kingdom of Israel, and who was zealous in destroying idols.

**ASANGA (fourth century)** Indian BRAHMAN converted to BUDDHISM who, with his brother Vasubandhu, founded the Yoga-cara School of MAHAYANA Buddhism.

**ASAPH**  Leader of the choir of King David whose name appears with many of the Psalms (50; 73—83). He may have written some of them.

**ASAR-HAP**  Sacred bull of Memphis in ancient Egyptian religion.

**ASARI**  Syrian god of harvest.

**ASBURY, FRANCIS (1745–1816)**  English-born leader in early American METHODISM. Developing evangelism by the use of circuit riders, he himself traveled thousands of miles on horseback every year. He personally controlled much of the government of the Methodist churches in the United States and was their first bishop.

**ASCENSION**  The rising of Christ from earth into heaven (ACTS 1:9).

**ASCENSION DAY**  CHRISTIAN feast, observed since the fourth century, honoring the ascension of Christ. It is celebrated 40 days after EASTER.

**ASCENSION OF ISAIAH**  A second-century document relating how Isaiah was sawn asunder (compare HEBREWS 11:37) and traveled through the seven heavens. The authorship is both Jewish and Christian.

**ASCETICISM**  A philosophy of self-denial and self-discipline. It has ancient roots and has been found in many religions, usually with the aim of elevating the soul by denying the body. Occasionally ascetic groups such as the Essenes and Nazarites were found in JUDAISM, but a considerable number have flourished in Christianity. With spiritual intentions, Christian ascetics have abstained from all kinds of pleasure—from food and drink to sex—particularly in MONASTICISM but also in many of the sects. However, the New Testament and contemporary Christianity in general accept the natural and pleasant things of life as gifts for which to thank God, and regard the material world not as an enemy but as a place for the exercise of the spiritual life.

**ASCH, SHOLEM (1880–1957)**  Jewish writer whose plays, stories, and novels reveal unusual spiritual depth. Asch wrote *The God of Vengeance, The Nazarene, The Apostle, Mary,* and many other widely acclaimed works.

**ASCLEPIUS**  See AESCULAPIUS.

**ASCRIPTION**  The offering of praise, particularly in prayer, or following a sermon.

**ASEITY**  Philosophical term for existence derived from itself, as of the self-sustained existence of God.

**ASENATH**  The Egyptian wife of Joseph and daughter of Potipherah.

**ASER**  See ASHER.

**ASERAH**  Phoenician wife of the high god, EL.

**ASGARD**  Norse home of the gods, containing the hall of Valhalla where warriors slain in battle continually feast.

**ASGAYA-GIGAGEI**  Thunder god of the Cherokee Indians.

**ASHA**  The spirit of fire and righteousness who attends AHURA MAZDAH in ZOROASTRIAN myth.

**ASHAMNU**  Jewish term for the confession of sin.

**ASH ARI (873–935)**  Arabian MOSLEM theologian, author of more than a hundred works. He sought to square theology with philosophy.

**ASHER or ASER**  Jacob's eighth son from whom one of the twelve tribes was named.

**ASHERAH**  Old Testament "grove"—a hewn tree trunk which may have been a symbol, as the term was a variation of the name of the goddess Ashtoreth or ASTARTE, who was a Canaanite goddess of fertility. Also called ISHTAR.

**ASHERATIAN**  Ancient Semite sea goddess.

**ASHER BEN YEHIEL (thirteenth century)**  Pious Jewish rabbi who fled to Spain from German persecution. He opposed philosophy and codified Jewish law, becoming an outstanding authority on the latter.

**ASHES**  In the Old Testament a sign of mourning (ESTHER 4:1), ashes are a universal symbol of penitence and mortality, as on ASH WEDNESDAY.

**ASHI, RAB (352–427)**  Head of the Sura Academy at Babylon and first editor of the TALMUD. His pupil Rabina completed the work.

**ASHIMA**  God of the people of Hamath in Samaria (II KINGS 17:30).

**ASHIPU**  Babylonian priests whose special duty it was to ward off such jinn, or evil spirits, as LILITH.

**ASHIRAT**  Canaanite sun goddess.

**ASHKELON, ASKALON, or ASKELON**  Ancient city on the Mediterranean 12 miles north of Gaza. There the goddess ASTARTE was worshiped by the Canaanites. It was one of the five main cities of the Philistines.

In it HEROD THE GREAT was born and his sister SALOME lived. Ashkelon was a strategic city in the CRUSADES.

**ASHKENAZ** 1. Son of Gomer (GENESIS 10:3). 2. A people who lived in Armenia (JEREMIAH 51:27).

**ASHKENAZIM** German or central European Jews, as distinguished from the SEPHARDIM of Portugal and Spain.

**ASHLAND BRETHREN** A group in the BRETHREN CHURCH OF PROGRESSIVE DUNKERS which has its annual conference at Ashland, Ohio. Its theology is ARMINIAN.

**ASHLEY, ANTHONY ASHLEY COOPER** See SHAFTESBURY.

**ASHMUN, JEHUDI (1794–1828)** New York-born CONGREGATIONAL missionary to Liberia who helped save freed Negroes there from extinction. He spent his life strengthening the colony.

**ASHRAM** 1. A community in India whose members live together in monastery fashion for spiritual exercise and service to others. 2. In the United States, a retreat for spiritual meditation organized under the inspiration of Dr. E. Stanley Jones.

**ASH-SHAFII (ninth century)** Founder of the SHAFIITE RITE in MOSLEM law.

**ASHTAROTH, ASHTORETH** Hebrew forms of the name of ASTARTE.

**ASHUR, ASSHUR, or ASSUR** Chief Assyrian god, specializing in war and victory; often represented drawing a bow or as a winged sun.

**ASHUSHU-NAMIR** Babylonian messenger of the gods; condemned to eat garbage.

**ASHVAGHOSHA** See ASVAGHOSA.

**ASH WEDNESDAY** First day of LENT, forty days before EASTER. In CATHOLIC churches, Ash Wednesday worshipers receive a mark on their foreheads from the ashes of the palm leaves from the past year's PALM SUNDAY. They are reminded that "thou art dust and unto dust thou shalt return."

**ASIA MINOR** The main part of modern Turkey. Across its hills and mountains the Apostle PAUL traveled in establishing the church throughout the Roman Empire. Many churches resulted there.

**"AS IF" PHILOSOPHY** The doctrine that religion and philosophy are "fictions," i.e., elements of knowledge that cannot be proved in the sense of conforming to reality, but that one should live in accordance with them "as if" they are true.

**ASINARII** A contemptuous term for Jews and Christians on the grounds that they worship an ass. A third-century drawing of an ass-headed man being crucified may reflect this feeling toward the early Christians.

**ASK** The first man in Nordic mythology. His wife, the first woman, was named Embla, and was made from a tree.

**ASKALON or ASKELON** See ASHKELON.

**ASKE, ROBERT (?–1537)** Yorkshire lawyer who led the "Pilgrimage of Grace" when English Catholics rebelled against the governmental confiscation of monasteries, abolition of papal supremacy, and increase in taxation under Henry VIII. The beloved leader of some 40,000 men, he and others were hanged for treason.

**ASKEW, ANNE (1521–1546)** An English girl from Lincoln whose acquaintance with PROTESTANTS and reading of the Bible led to her conversion. Turned out of the house by her husband, she was apprehended by the Bishop of London and asked whether "the priests cannot make the body of Christ." For her answer, "I have read that God made man, but that man can make God I never yet read," she was stretched on the rack and burned.

**ASKLEPIOS** See AESCULAPIUS.

**ASMODEUS** An evil demon in JEWISH and ZOROASTRIAN literature. Compare Tobit 3:6.

**ASNAPPER** See ASSUR-BANI-PAL.

**ASOKA (?–232 B.C.)** Great ruler of ancient India who after his ruthless conquest of the state of Kalinga was converted from BRAHMANISM to BUDDHISM. He then inscribed great ethical edicts on pillars throughout his kingdom and preached nonviolence, building hospitals, prohibiting warfare and animal sacrifice, and protecting animal life. Under his rule India became Buddhist, Buddhist missionaries were sent as far as Greece, the Pali Scriptures were codified, and Buddhism became a world religion. Asoka became a Buddhist lay brother.

**ASOPUS** Greek river god.

**ASP** Bible name for a venomous snake, particularly the Egyptian cobra which may be as long as six feet.

**ASPERGES** The sprinkling of holy water over altar and people before mass. Its name derives from Psalm 51:7.

**ASPERGILLUM** The brush or instrument used to sprinkle holy water.

**ASPERSION** BAPTISM by sprinkling water on the head.

**ASPIRANT** A person who plans or trains to enter an ecclesiastical vocation.

**ASPIRATION** A short prayer.

**ASS** The donkey, the beast of burden and transportation in the Bible. A religious symbol of humility, the ass was made a symbol of the Apostle Thomas by West-phalian Germans in the Middle Ages because of Thomas' slowness in believing.

**ASS, FEAST OF THE** A medieval French festival held on January 14, commemorating the flight of the Holy Family into Egypt, which presumably involved an ass. The festival so degenerated that it was finally prohibited.

**ASSASSINS** Members of a secret MOSLEM order of the ISMAILI sect. Originally SHIITES, they murdered their enemies to gain political power and were at their peak during the CRUSADES. Their name derives from their use of hashish, a marijuana-like narcotic.

**ASSEMBLIES** 1. In the New Testament, gatherings of Christians. 2. In various churches, large gatherings for ecclesiastical business. 3. Among BRETHREN groups, congregations.

**ASSEMBLIES OF GOD** International Protestant group which holds to FUNDAMENTALIST beliefs and emphasizes SPIRITUAL HEALING and, often, the BAPTISM OF THE HOLY SPIRIT.

**ASSEMBLIES OF GOD, GENERAL COUNCIL** Largest Pentecostal denomination in the United States, with fundamentalist ARMINIAN doctrines and emphasis on BAPTISM OF THE HOLY SPIRIT and tongue-speaking (see GLOSSOLALIA).

**ASSEMBLIES OF THE FRENCH CLERGY** Meetings of the CATHOLIC clergy of France at five-year intervals from the sixteenth through the eighteenth centuries to consider taxation and other ecclesiastical matters.

**ASSEMBLY, GENERAL** The central power of the PRESBYTERIAN system, being a Presbyterian denomination's annual representative gathering for ecclesiastical business.

**ASSEMBLY, WESTMINSTER** See WESTMINSTER ASSEMBLY.

**ASSENT** Agreement with a proposition or doctrine, as a religious belief.

**ASSENT, DECLARATION OF** Formal subscription by clergymen of the CHURCH OF ENGLAND expressing assent to its standards of belief.

**ASSER (?–909)** Welsh monk who taught Latin to King Alfred, became a bishop, and wrote a biography of Alfred.

**ASSERET-HA-DIBROT** Jewish term for the Ten Commandments (see DECALOGUE).

**ASSESSOR** An assistant advising a judge in an ecclesiastical case.

**ASSHUR** See ASHUR.

**ASSIMILATIONISTS** Jews who advocate absorption into the national cultural majority, thus losing their Jewish identity. There are many shades of opinion respecting this problem.

**ASSISI** The central Italian city where St. FRANCIS was born. Now an episcopal see, it contains Francis' tomb and other imposing churches and points of historical interest.

**ASSIZE OF CLARENDON** English council called by Henry II in an attempt to gain control of various church affairs. It failed in its purpose because of the opposition of the English bishops.

**ASSOCIATE PRESBYTERIAN CHURCH OF NORTH AMERICA** The remnant of a Scottish secession from the established church, carried to the United States and surviving several unions of churches.

**ASSOCIATE REFORMED PRESBYTERIAN CHURCH (GENERAL SYNOD)** Small American Presbyterian group with Scottish Covenanter origins.

**ASSOCIATION OF PENTECOSTAL CHURCHES IN AMERICA** A New England Pentecostal group which merged into the Pentecostal Church of the Nazarene.

**ASSOS** See ASSUS.

**ASSUERUS** See AHASUERUS.

**ASSUMPTION** CATHOLIC doctrine that the Saviour's mother MARY went bodily into heaven. Similar assumptions are recorded of ENOCH and ELIJAH.

**ASSUMPTION, FEAST OF** Commemoration on August 15 in ROMAN CATHOLIC and EASTERN ORTHODOX churches of the ASSUMPTION of the Virgin Mary.

**ASSUMPTIONISTS** Also called Augustinians of the Assumption, this is a Catholic educational and missionary order founded at Nîmes, France, in 1843. In 1900 it was suppressed.

**ASSUMPTION OF MOSES** A Jewish work from the first century A.D. in which Moses predicts the history of the Israelites.

**ASSUR** See ASHUR.

**ASSURANCE** Theologically, conviction of salvation. Christians with assurance of salvation know that they know God and that they are His.

**ASSUR-BANI-PAL (seventh century B.C.)** King of Assyria whose library held 22,000 tablets including the Babylonian stories of the creation and the flood. He is probably the Asnapper of Ezra 4:10.

**ASSUS or ASSOS** A Greek city in northwestern Asia Minor on whose summit was a temple of ATHENA. PAUL visited Assus in his travels (ACTS 20:13, 14).

**ASSYRIAN CHURCH** One name for the NESTORIAN CHURCH of Iran, Iraq, and Malabar, India.

**ASSYRIAN JACOBITE APOSTOLIC CHURCH** Church group which fled Turkish persecution and came to the United States in 1907 to establish congregations. Its doctrine is based on the NICENE CREED.

**ASSYRIAN ORTHODOX CHURCH** A church with roots in Syria and with seven sacraments. It accepts only the first three ECUMENICAL COUNCILS.

**ASTAR** See ISHTAR.

**ASTARTE** Ancient Semitic goddess of fertility and sexual love. She was worshiped by the Phoenicians and Canaanites with BAAL, the male god of reproduction, in ecstatic sex rites. She was prominent in a number of ancient religions and was known as ISHTAR to the Babylonians, APHRODITE to the Greeks, and Ashtoreth or Ashtaroth to the Hebrews. The Old Testament condemns her worship as well as that of BAAL.

**ASTERISK** A vessel used in the EASTERN CHURCH to protect the eucharistic bread.

**ASTRAEA** Greek goddess of justice, the last deity to leave earth at the end of the Golden Age.

**ASTRAL SPIRITS** Beings who inhabited the heavenly bodies, according to ancient notion.

**ASTROLOGY** Ancient method of predicting future events from the motions of the stars and planets, and of analyzing the influences of these on human life. It was important in Babylonian, Greek, and Roman religion, and a factor in the development of the science of astronomy. It is still of interest to many today.

**ASTRUC, JEAN (1684–1766)** French CATHOLIC physician whose study of skin diseases led him to an analysis of the PENTATEUCH and to the discovery of two apparently different documents behind it, the Yahwistic (see "J") and the Elohistic (see "E"). The modern documentary study of Scripture dates largely from Astruc's findings.

**ASURA or AHURA** 1. Ancient Aryan name for god in India and Iran. 2. In HINDUISM, "elder brothers of the gods" whose demonic powers oppose those of the other deities. The Hindu Scriptures, the VEDAS, contrast *asura* (evil) with *deva* (good).

**ASV** Abbreviation for the AMERICAN STANDARD VERSION of the Bible, published in 1901.

**ASVAGHOSA (first century A.D.)** A BRAHMAN scholar who was converted to BUDDHISM and became a founder of MAHAYANA Buddhism. A poet and writer, he wrote a life of BUDDHA in verse which is important in the Mahayana movement.

**ASVAMEDHA** The sacrifice of one or more horses by kings in ancient India.

**ASVINS** Twin gods of light and healing in ancient VEDIC RELIGION. They brought the dawn, and are sometimes identified with the morning and evening stars.

**ASYNIUR** Ancient Scandinavian goddesses attending FREYA or FRIGGA.

**ATAGUCHU** Inca god of obscure purpose.

**ATARGATIS** Ancient Syrian "fish goddess," a nature deity connected with water, and wife of Hadad.

**ATEN** See ATONISM.

**ATHALIAH** Wicked queen of Judah, daughter of AHAB, who tried to kill all the male children in the royal family.

**ATHANARIC (?–381)** Visigoth ruler famed principally for his fierce persecution of the Christians in his realm.

**ATHANASIA** Term for deathlessness or immortality.

**ATHANASIAN CREED** One of the great Christian creeds spelling out the doctrines of the TRINITY and the INCARNATION, dating from the sixth century. It was once thought to have been written by ATHANASIUS.

**ATHANASIUS (c.297–373)** Churchman of Alexandria in Egypt who became the city's patriarch and a staunch defender of orthodoxy. Against the ARIANS he held that Christ was of the same substance with the Father, eternally divine and fully God. Exiled five times, he fought for a gospel of complete redemption until his views won over the Western world. He is known as father of orthodoxy.

**ATHARVA-VEDA** The Veda of popular Hinduism, the fourth and latest of the Hindu scriptures. It contains charms, hymns, and prayers.

**ATHEISM** Denial of the existence of any supreme being, or of God; or disbelief in theism or Christianity.

**ATHENA** Important Greek goddess of wisdom. She was patroness of cities and the arts, goddess of victory in war, and patron of Athens which honored her with the majestic Parthenon. She was known by several names, especially Pallas Athena, in her various aspects.

**ATHENAGORAS (second century)** Christian writer who defended the Christians against charges of incest and cannibalism, and was the first Christian to make a philosophical defense of the TRINITY. He also wrote a treatise on the resurrection, holding that marriage is indissoluble even by death. He was a powerful Christian apologist.

**ATHENOGENES (second century)** Christian martyr who composed the "Hymn for the Lighting of the Lamps."

**ATHENS** Resplendent city of ancient Greece, noted as a center of culture and religion. Named for its patron goddess Athena, it was famous for its temples and statues. The Apostle Paul noted that the Athenians were uncommonly religious, with an altar even to an unknown god (ACTS 17:22–23).

**ATHIAS, JOSEPH (seventeenth century)** Spanish-born Jewish printer whose editions of the Bible are outstanding for their accuracy and beauty.

**ATHLETICS** In the New Testament such athletic contests as racing and wrestling symbolize the Christian contest for eternal life.

**ATHOS** Greek peninsula containing 20 BASILIAN monasteries of the EASTERN ORTHODOX CHURCH. They are rich in ancient documents and examples of Byzantine art. No woman and no female animal is allowed on Athos.

**ATISA (982–1054)** Indian-born scholar who reformed Tibetan BUDDHISM. He founded the "Virtuous Way" school of Buddhism.

**ATLANTIS** In Greek legend, island with advanced culture which sank below the sea.

**ATLAS** In Greek mythology, strong man who holds up the heavens on his mighty shoulders.

**ATMAN** Wind, breath, or soul in the religions of India. The atman might be either the individual consciousness or the World Soul to whom all return.

**ATMIYA SABHA** See RAM MOHAN ROY.

**ATMU** Egyptian god of the heavens, at one time identified with the setting sun.

**ATON** Egyptian sun god popularized by IKHNATON.

**ATONEMENT** "At-one-ment" or reconciliation between man and God. Various ancient religions recognized an estrangement between Deity and humanity, and sacrifices were often made to end the rift. In JUDAISM different offerings and sacrifices were specified for different sins. CHRISTIANITY recognizes the fallenness and lostness of all mankind and the work of Christ as the means of bringing about atonement for sin and reconciliation with God. When Christ is received by faith, the objective sacrifice of the Saviour and the subjective change in the believer make the atonement effective.

**ATONEMENT, DAY OF** The Jewish Day of Atonement is Yom Kippur, the holiest day in the Jewish year. It is held on the tenth day of Tishri (approximately October) as the conclusion of ten days of penitence and is observed with fasting, rest, worship, and prayer for the forgiveness of sins.

**ATONEMENT, FRIARS OF THE** A FRANCISCAN group founded at Graymoor, Garrison, New York in 1899 as a PROTESTANT EPISCOPAL organization. In 1909 it was received into the ROMAN CATHOLIC CHURCH. It is an evangelistic society whose members take vows of poverty, chastity, and obedience.

**ATONISM** The religion of Aton or Aten, the Egyptian sun god. Aton's worship was established by Pharaoh Amenhotep IV, who preferred the name IKHNATON, in the fourteenth century B.C., as a venture in monotheism. Aton was regarded as supreme and the other deities were down-graded. But on Amenhotep's death Atonism ended and the old forms of religion returned.

**ATRIUM** An entrance court in ancient churches.

**ATROPOS** One of the FATES of ancient Greece.

**ATTAR** Arabian love goddess.

**ATTER** God of war among the ancient Semites.

**ATTILA (?–453)** King of the Huns, sometimes called "The Scourge of God." He overran Europe and attacked the Roman Empire, before finally dying of a hemorrhage.

**ATTIS** Phrygian tree spirit or god of vegetation.

**ATTRIBUTES, DIVINE** The characteristics of God such as omnipotence, omniscience, omnipresence, eternity, holiness, and perfect love.

**ATTRITION** Imperfect repentance, as opposed to contrition motivated by love for God.

**AUBURN AFFIRMATION** An affirmation circulated in 1924 in the PRESBYTERIAN CHURCH, U.S.A., rejecting the attempt to define Christianity in terms of the "five points" of fundamentalism (see "The FUNDAMENTALS"). About 1300 ministers signed the affirmation.

**AUBURN DECLARATION** An American Presbyterian statement of doctrine issued in 1837. It led toward the eventual reunion of Old School and New School Presbyterians.

**AUDIENTES** In the early church, persons in the initial stages of catechetical instruction.

**AUDITOR** An official in an ecclesiastical case who listens to the evidence and records it for his superior.

**AUFKLÄRUNG** German for the ENLIGHTENMENT.

**AUGEAS** Son of Helios, the Greek sun god.

**AUGSBURG, CONFESSION OF** The great creed of the Protestant REFORMATION and of LUTHERANISM. Compiled by MELANCHTHON and presented at the Diet of Augsburg in 1530, the 21 articles in the first part define Lutheran doctrine. The second part sets forth seven abuses LUTHER saw in the ROMAN CATHOLIC CHURCH.

**AUGSBURG, INTERIM OF** The period in which the formula prepared at the Diet of Augsburg held in 1548 brought a measure of religious agreement between LUTHERANS and CATHOLICS. It lasted only until 1552.

**AUGSBURG, PEACE OF** The settlement of religious conflicts at the Diet of Augsburg held in 1555. The prince of each area was permitted to decide whether his land was to be LUTHERAN or CATHOLIC. Objectors in an area could choose a country of their faith. Although other religions were ignored, the coexistence of Catholicism and Lutheranism was recognized.

**AUGSBURG FRIENDS** A group in the United States which seceded from the United Norwegian Lutheran Church over differences of opinion on church government and education. In 1897 it was organized as the Lutheran Free Church.

**AUGURS** In ancient Rome, trained priests from the patrician class who interpreted such natural signs as eclipses or the flight of birds as significant omens. Sometimes lots were cast or the entrails of animals examined to determine the will of the gods.

**AUGURY** 1. The science or practice of foretelling the future or interpreting omens. 2. An omen or portent divined by augurs.

**AUGUSTA, JOHN (1500–1575)** A minister of the BOHEMIAN BRETHREN who studied under LUTHER and MELANCHTHON and tried to bring about an understanding among the various Protestants. He was forbidden to preach or teach.

**AUGUSTANA** Latin name for the AUGSBURG CONFESSION.

**AUGUSTANA EVANGELICAL LUTHERAN CHURCH** Denomination organized in the United States by Swedish immigrants in 1860. Its roots were in seventeenth-century Swedish Lutheranism and eighteenth-century Swedish PIETISM. In 1962 it merged into The LUTHERAN CHURCH IN AMERICA.

**AUGUSTANA SYNOD** Organization of Swedish and Norwegian Lutherans which later (1860) became the Augustana Evangelical Lutheran Church.

**AUGUSTINE, ST. (354–430)** Aurelius Augustinus, to give his name its Latin form, was one of the strongest minds and influences in church history. Wayward in his youth, he became a MANICHEE, but in 387 was converted to thoroughgoing Christianity. In the church he became bishop of

Hippo in northern Africa and a powerful theologian and apologist. His *City of God* defended Christianity against the charge that it had produced the fall of the Roman Empire. His *On the Trinity* systematized Christian theology. His battles with the DONATISTS and PELAGIANS produced a clearcut exposition of salvation by grace through faith—and of the authority and supremacy of the church. Thus his writings produced both the church that swept triumphantly through the Middle Ages and the REFORMATION that ushered in the Protestant era.

**AUGUSTINE, RULE OF** The basis of the constitutions of the AUGUSTINIAN CANONS, the DOMINICANS, and various other CATHOLIC orders, based on St. Augustine's writings on community life. Its regulations are relatively few and emphasize common prayer, individual poverty, charity, and unity.

**AUGUSTINE OF CANTERBURY, ST. (?–604)** BENEDICTINE monk of Rome who led a mission of 40 monks to England in 597. Augustine baptized King Ethelbert and many of his subjects; Queen Bertha had already become a Christian. He brought many books to England, probably influencing its culture thereby, became first Archbishop of Canterbury, and built a monastery. But the Celtic monks of Britain never accepted him and his efforts to unite the Celtic and Roman churches failed. Augustine (also written "Austin") is sometimes called "Apostle of the English."

**AUGUSTINIAN CANONS** Members of a ROMAN CATHOLIC order dating from the eleventh century and following the Rule of St. AUGUSTINE, emphasizing prayer, poverty, unity, and charity.

**AUGUSTINIAN FRIARS or HERMITS** CATHOLIC order founded when various groups of Italian hermits were formed in 1256 into a single organization governed by the Rule of St. AUGUSTINE. They are also called Augustinians. They have three branches: The CALCED, the DISCALCED, and the Recollects. Their garb is a black tunic with hood, cowl, and girdle.

**AUGUSTINIANISM** Theological term for AUGUSTINE of Hippo's doctrines of sin, salvation, predestination, man's will, God's grace, the church, and the like. Reformed theologians see in Augustine the same doctrines as in PAUL and CALVIN, while CATHO-

LIC theologians find him a bulwark of their doctrines concerning the church, the sacraments, and divine grace.

**AUGUSTINIAN NUNS** Female religious affiliated with the Order of Hermits of St. Augustine, or other Augustinian Sisters.

**AUGUSTINIANS** 1. Followers of Augustine's doctrines. 2. AUGUSTINIAN FRIARS. 3. Members of orders governed by the Rule of St. AUGUSTINE.

**AUGUSTINIANS OF THE ASSUMPTION** See ASSUMPTIONISTS.

**AUGUSTUS (63 B.C.–A.D. 14)** The first Roman emperor who decreed "that all the world should be taxed" (LUKE 2:1) when Jesus was born. A just and beneficent ruler, he worked in the interest of peace, morality, and religion.

**AUGUSTUS I (1526–1586)** LUTHERAN elector of Saxony who helped bring about religious peace and sought to unite the Protestants in his district. However, he enforced Lutheranism and tortured the CALVINISTIC followers of MELANCHTHON.

**AULIC COUNCIL** Judicial organ of the Holy Roman Empire.

**AUM or OM** BUDDHIST prayer with complex symbolic meanings.

**AUMBRY or AMBRY** Receptacle in the wall of a church in which holy oils or objects were kept in the Middle Ages. In ANGLICAN churches the RESERVED SACRAMENT may be kept in the aumbry.

**AUREOLE** Golden radiance or luminous cloud surrounding the whole figure of a saint, angel, or divine being in CHRISTIAN art. The halo, in contrast, surrounds only the head.

**AURICULAR CONFESSION** Confession of one's sins in the presence of a priest in the confessional.

**AURORA** Roman goddess of the dawn.

**AUSCULTA FILI** *listen, my son* Papal encyclical of BONIFACE VIII in 1301 affirming the pope's authority over temporal powers.

**AUST** See ISIS.

**AUSTERITY** Severe physical discipline or mortification from sincere motives—the welfare of the soul or love for God.

**AUSTIN** Contraction of Augustine, used especially for St. AUGUSTINE OF CANTERBURY.

**AUTHORITY** The supreme authority is the right of God to rule the universe He created—His power over the world and over mankind. Christians find God's authority centralized in Jesus Christ and made known through the Scriptures, the church, and the conviction of the Holy Spirit. PROTESTANTS emphasize the authority of Scripture, CATHOLICS that of the church, and QUAKERS that of the Spirit's "inner light."

**AUTHORIZED VERSION** See KING JAMES BIBLE.

**AUTOCEPHALOUS** Term for early Christian bishops who were independent and autonomous—particularly in the EASTERN CHURCH.

**AUTO DA FE** *act of faith* Ceremonial procession accompanying final judgment during the INQUISITION. After mass, those judged heretical were handed over to the secular government to be burned.

**AUTONOMY** Self-government or independence. Absolute autonomy in Christianity is impossible because God is sovereign and man's true freedom consists in submission to His will.

**AUTO SACRAMENTAL** A Spanish play similar to the medieval morality plays. The auto sacramental was based on a religious theme and might be preceded by a procession.

**AUTOSUGGESTION** Self-suggestion which may influence mind and body. The idea that prayer and faith are merely forms of autosuggestion has never been taken seriously by Christianity.

**AUXENTIUS (fourth century)** An Arian theologian of Milan who was one of the strongest opponents of Nicene Christology in the WESTERN CHURCH during his lifetime.

**AUXILIARY BISHOP** A bishop who assists another in the same diocese.

**AUXILIARY SAINTS** A specific group of fourteen saints venerated because of the power attributed to their prayers.

**AV** Abbreviation for Authorized Version (see KING JAMES BIBLE).

**AVADANA** Sanskrit stories supposedly told by Buddha, illustrating the BUDDHIST doctrine of "KARMA."

**AVALOKITESVARA** A candidate for Buddhahood who becomes the saviour of his generation. Incarnating suffering and love, an Avalokitesvara may exist in male or female form and is often the object of BUDDHIST worship.

**AVALON** The realm of the dead in Celtic myth, the ocean paradise where Arthur and other heroes reigned forever.

**AVATAR** HINDU term for the INCARNATION of a deity. VISHNU, the Preserver, is held to have been incarnated nine times, the ninth as BUDDHA; the last time he will appear as Kalki to judge the world. Hindu deities SIVA and KRISHNA are also believed to become flesh. Vishnu's eighth avatar was as Krishna.

**AVATARA** Plural form of avatar.

**AV BET DIN** Jewish term for court president.

**AVE** *hail* 1. A salutation. 2. A Roman Catholic prayer. See AVE MARIA.

**AVEL** Jewish term for mourner.

**AVELE ZION** *Mourners of Zion* Jewish mourners, particularly a group in Jerusalem.

**AVELOKITA** See AVALOKITESVARA.

**AVE MARIA** *Hail, Mary* A salutation to the Virgin Mary based originally on that of the angel Gabriel in Luke 1:28, 42. The complete prayer used in Catholic devotion is: "Hail Mary, full of grace, the Lord is with thee; blessed art thou among women, and blessed is the fruit of thy womb, Jesus. Holy Mary, Mother of God, pray for us sinners now and at the hour of our death. Amen."

**AVENCIBROL** See IBN GABIROL, SOLOMON BEN JUDAH.

**AVENGER** 1. God is sometimes termed "the Great Avenger." 2. In Judaism's earlier stages, one who had wronged another received vengeance from a kinsman of the victim—often blood revenge. Later, cities of refuge protected the object of vengeance from injustice.

**AVE REGINA COELORUM** *Hail, Queen of the Heavens* Second antiphon of the Virgin used in CATHOLIC services from the Feast of the Purification until Maundy Thursday.

**AVERROES (1126–1198)** Arabian MOSLEM philosopher and commentator on ARISTOTLE. Admired by the Catholic Schoolmen, he has been called the greatest Arabian philosopher in the West, and he long influenced Western thought. Averroes held that faith and reason did not conflict, that the soul dies with the brain, but that reason is eternal.

**AVERROISTS** Disciples of AVERROES who adopted his doctrines and admired his writings. The leader of the Averroist school in Paris was SIGER DE BRABANT, whose teachings were condemned about 1270. Averroism lived on in France and Italy until the fifteenth century.

**AVESTA** 1. The scripture of ZOROASTRIAN-ISM, also called Zend Avesta. It is held to have consisted originally of 20 books written by Zoroaster but it is now limited to five surviving parts. 2. An ancient Iranian language in which the Avesta is written.

**AV HA-RACHAMIN** *Father of Mercies* An ancient prayer for Jews who have been killed for their faith.

**AVICEBRON** See IBN GABIROL, SOLOMON BEN JUDAH.

**AVICENNA (980–1037)** Arabian mystic, physician, and philosopher. A student of MOSLEM theology, he interpreted Aristotle along Neoplatonist lines and was something of a pantheist.

**AVIDYA** HINDU term for ignorance.

**AVIGNON** French city where several popes and antipopes lived during the Middle Ages. Here were papal headquarters during the BABYLONIAN CAPTIVITY, 1309–1378.

**AVILA, JUAN DE (1500–1569)** "Apostle of Andalusia," Avila was a Spanish priest among whose followers was St. THERESA. He was beatified in 1893.

**AVINU MALKENU** *Our Father, Our King* Opening words of a Jewish invocation.

**AVODAH** *service* 1. A consecrated life. 2. A Jewish service.

**AVVAKUM (c.1620–1681)** Conservative leader in the RUSSIAN ORTHODOX CHURCH. An "old believer" who refused to accept the revised Greek form of the Russian ritual, he was exiled to Siberia in 1653 and finally burned at the stake.

**AWAKENING** Term for religious renewal or revival.

**AWAKENING, GREAT** Christian revival which swept the American Colonies during the eighteenth century. Jonathan EDWARDS and George WHITEFIELD were prominent preachers in the Awakening.

**AWHIOWHIO** Ancient Australian god of whirlwinds.

**AWONAWILONA** Zuni creator.

**AX** The symbol of St. BONIFACE and of Thomas of Canterbury.

**AXUM or AKSUM** Ethiopian city to which St. Frumentius brought Christianity in the fourth century. It is still dear to Ethiopian Christianity as a religious center.

**AYACUCHO** Peruvian city famous for its churches and convents.

**AYESHA (c.610–678)** Mohammed's favorite wife. MOSLEMS honor her as the Prophetess and the Mother of Believers.

**AYIN** 1. Sixteenth letter in the Hebrew alphabet. 2. Ayin is also the name of two towns mentioned in the Old Testament.

**AYIN HA-RA** Jewish term for the Evil Eye which is supposed to produce a harmful effect on its object.

**AYLMER, JOHN (1521–1594)** Bishop of London who tutored Lady Jane Grey, opposed the doctrine of TRANSUBSTANTIATION, and helped John FOXE translate his *Book of Martyrs* into Latin. After being made bishop he treated his opponents harshly.

**AZAN** Moslem call to prayer.

**AZARIAH** 1. A king of Judah also known as UZZIAH. 2. One of the four Jewish youths cast into a furnace for refusing to worship a golden statue of Nebuchadnezzar. 3. The name of a number of other Old Testament figures.

**AZARIAH, V. S. (1874–1945)** First Anglican bishop in India.

**AZAZEL** Hebrew word for "the scapegoat" (LEVITICUS 16:10) released on the Day of ATONEMENT to bear away sins. Later the name was used to refer to a fallen angel or to the devil.

**AZAZIL** MOSLEM term for the devil.

**AZIDAHAKA** ZOROASTRIAN serpent-devil.

**AZRAEL** MOSLEM death angel.

**AZTEC RELIGION** The religion of the Aztecs of Mexico, like their culture, was complex. Their myths tell of a great flood and of several humans who survived by building a ship. They practiced human sacrifice and had many gods, chief among them HUITZILOPOCHTLI, TEZCATLIPOCA, and QUETZALCOATL.

**AZULAI, HAYIM JOSEPH DAVID (1724–1806)** Student of rabbinical lore and literature, and renowned bibliographer.

**AZYMITES** *not leavened* A contemptuous name given by members of the EASTERN ORTHODOX CHURCH to those in the ROMAN CATHOLIC CHURCH because of the latter's use of unleavened bread in the EUCHARIST.

# B

**B** 1. Greek letter Beta, second letter in the Greek alphabet. 2. Symbol for CODEX VATICANUS, a fourth-century manuscript of the Old and New Testaments in Greek.

**BA** 1. Ancient Egyptian word for the human soul, considered immortal; often represented as a hawk with human head and arms. 2. Sacred goat worshiped in ancient Egypt.

**BAADER, FRANZ XAVER VON (1765–1841)** German CATHOLIC engineer, philosopher, and MYSTIC. Greatly influenced by Jakob BOEHME and Friedrich Schelling, Baader often wrote symbolically or vaguely. His system of thought found a place for both faith and reason. He viewed God as an evolving dynamic process, and history as the history of God's saving love.

**BAAL** 1. Semitic name for lord or master. 2. The name of various local gods in ancient Canaan and Phoenicia. 3. By the fourteenth century B.C. in Canaan, Baal was the name given the son of the high god EL and was the god of virility and fertility. 4. Baal occurs in many forms and combinations in the Old Testament, and is thought by some scholars to have been an early name of Yahweh, or Jehovah, although the Jewish prophets continually denounced Baalism.

**BAALAT, BAALATH, or BELTIS** Semitic fertility goddess, counterpart of Baal.

**BAALAT BEER** Canaanite goddess of the well.

**BAALAT GEBEL** Canaanite goddess of Byblos.

**BAALBEK** Lebanese city, once a center of Baal worship and later a site of temples of JUPITER and BACCHUS.

**BAAL BERITH** Canaanite god of oaths.

**BAAL GAD** Canaanite god of pleasure.

**BAAL GEBEL** Canaanite god of BYBLOS.

**BAALI** *my Lord* A name by which God was once called in Israel (HOSEA 2:16, 17).

**BAALIM** Plural of BAAL. Various Canaanite cities had separate Baal cults.

**BAALISM** The nature-fertility religion of ancient Canaan, linked to the return of spring and celebrated with sexual abandon.

**BAAL LEBANON** Canaanite god of Lebanon.

**BAAL MARGOD** Canaanite god of the dance.

**BAAL MARPE** Canaanite god of healing.

**BAAL PEOR** Canaanite god of Peor, worshiped in orgiastic ceremonies.

**BAAL PERIZIM** Canaanite god of wells.

**BAAL SHAMAIN** Babylonian god of the heavens.

**BAAL-SHEM-TOV (1700–1760)** Russian-born Jewish mystic who founded HASIDISM. Known as a healer, he made the way to God simple and joyous and was loved by the common people. He was originally Israel ben Eliezer; his popular name means "Master of the Good Name."

**BAAL TAMAR** Canaanite god of the palm tree.

**BAALZEBUB** See BEELZEBUB.

**BAASHA** Wicked king of Israel who fought Asa, king of Judah.

**BAB, THE** Title assumed by Mirza Ali Mohammed ibn Radhik, or Sayyid Ali Mohammed, also called Bab ed-Din ("The Gate of the Faith"). He founded BABISM in 1844.

**BABA BOOK or BABA-MAASEH** Fantastic Jewish story or Yiddish romance.

**BABASTIS** See BAST.

**BABBAR** Sumerian sun god.

**BAB ED-DIN** See BAB, THE.

**BABEL** Ancient name for the city of BABYLON where men tried to build a tower as high as heaven, and were punished with "a babble of tongues" and scattered (GEN-ESIS 11:1–9).

**BABEL, ISAAC E. (1894–1941)** Brilliant Russian Jewish fiction writer who probably died in a Soviet concentration camp.

**BABI** 1. Babism. 2. A Babist. 3. Related to Babism.

**BABISM** A religion that grew out of IS-LAM in Persia. There in 1844 Sayyid Ali Mohammed of Shiraz, the BAB, was recognized as a great prophet succeeding MO-HAMMED and CHRIST. He did away with the religious laws of the KORAN and wrote a new revelation, the *Beyan*. He gathered eighteen disciples and foretold the coming of one greater than himself. In 1850 Sayyid Ali Mohammed and his disciples were tortured and killed, together with more than 20,000 followers—the Bab in triumphant martyrdom. In 1863 many accepted BAHA ULLAH as the Messiah who the Bab had announced would follow him. Thus BAHAISM began. Babism proclaimed the absolute unity of God and the sacredness of the number nineteen. (Nineteen years separated the manifestations of the Bab and Baha Ullah.)

**BABYLAS (third century)** Bishop of Antioch who refused to let the Emperor Philip take part in worship until he had confessed and done penance for a murder. Under the Emperor Decius, Babylas died in prison. JOHN CHRYSOSTOM extolled him.

**BABYLON** 1. Ancient capital of Babylonia and one of the most important cities of the East in the preclassical era. Located on the Euphrates River north of the Persian Gulf, its patron god was MARDUK or Bel and it added to the renown of Hammurabi, Nebuchadnezzar, Sennacherib, Cyrus, and Darius I. 2. Biblical name for Babylonia. 3. A symbolic name for worldly paganism and sensualism.

**BABYLONIA** Mesopotamia, the land between the Tigris and Euphrates rivers. Here the Garden of Eden may have been (GENESIS 2:14), and the cradle of civilization.

**BABYLONIAN CAPTIVITY** 1. The time between the fall of Jerusalem in 586 B.C. and the rebuilding of its temple in 538 B.C. During that period the Jewish people were exiles in Mesopotamia or Babylonia. 2. The period when the popes were exiled from Rome at Avignon in France, 1309–1377.

**BABYLONIAN CAPTIVITY OF THE CHURCH** A work by Martin LUTHER attacking the papacy, the authority of the priests, and the inherent efficacy of the sacraments.

**BABYLONIAN RELIGION** Babylonian gods included the moon god Sin, the sun god Shamash, the storm god Adad, the earth god Enlil, the water god Ea, the vegetation god Dumuzi, the love goddess Inanna, and the lord of heaven, Anu. Babylonia's temples were the tiered ZIGGURATS; its worship included sacrifices, prayers, and psalms; and its myths contained accounts of the Creation and the Flood similar to those in Genesis.

**BACA** *weeping or balsam* Palestinian valley with a reputation for drought (PSALM 84:6).

**BACABS** Mayan agricultural gods of the four corners of the earth.

**BACCHANALIA** Wild Roman festivals honoring BACCHUS. Originally religious rites for women only, they were later attended by men and became so licentious they were prohibited in 186 B.C.

**BACCHANTE** A female worshiper or attendant of BACCHUS.

**BACCHUS** Later name of DIONYSUS. Greek and Roman god of wine, vineyards, and fertility; worshiped in the uninhibited BAC-CHANALIA.

**BACH, JOHANN SEBASTIAN (1685–1750)** One of the greatest Western composers. A LUTHERAN, he wrote most of his work for church services: magnificats, motets, passions, oratorios, 300 cantatas, and nearly 400 chorales. His *Mass in B Minor, Christmas Oratorio, Saint Matthew Passion,* and *Saint John Passion* are incomparably profound.

**BACHARACH, YAIR (1639–1702)** German rabbi and Talmudist.

**BACHMAN, JOHN (1790–1874)** American naturalist and LUTHERAN minister. He wrote books on both nature and religion, and assisted John James Audubon. He also founded the Lutheran Synod and the Lutheran Theological Seminary of South Carolina.

**BACKSLIDE** Religious term indicating spiritual regression.

**BACKUS, ISAAC (1724–1806)** New England minister and evangelist. He was converted in the GREAT AWAKENING and became a Separatist and "NEW LIGHT," then a CONGREGATIONALIST, and finally a BAPTIST. He wrote voluminously and defended religious freedom.

**BACON, BENJAMIN W. (1860–1932)** American CONGREGATIONALIST and Biblical scholar, particularly outstanding in the criticism of the Gospels.

**BACON, FRANCIS (1561–1626)** ANGLICAN statesman and philosopher who substituted the inductive approach of modern science for the a priori methods of scholastic philosophy. He denied the authority of absolute rules of ethics and the philosophy of "the highest good."

**BACON, LEONARD (1802–1881)** American CONGREGATIONAL minister and anti-slavery leader. Author of the "Pilgrim Hymn," he had a liberal mind and was devoted to the welfare of his community and nation. His essays on slavery influenced Abraham Lincoln.

**BACON, ROGER (c.1214–c.1294)** English FRANCISCAN scientist and philosopher. He is believed to have been imprisoned and his works condemned on some occasions although the facts are in doubt. He extolled the church, sought to improve the condition of the Greek and Hebrew texts of the Bible, and had such scientific and philosophical insight that he was called "Doctor Mirabilis."

**BADB** A Celtic war goddess.

**BADBY, JOHN (?–1410)** English LOLLARD mechanic or tailor who was burned for denying that the EUCHARIST bread became Christ. He said that if this were so, there would be 20,000 gods in England.

**BADCHAN** Master of ceremonies at a Jewish marriage.

**BADER, JESSE M. (1886–1963)** American clergyman and author. He served the World Convention of Churches of Christ as general secretary, and was secretary of evangelism for the DISCIPLES OF CHRIST, the FEDERAL COUNCIL OF CHURCHES, and the NATIONAL COUNCIL OF CHURCHES.

**BAD FAITH** Catholic term identifying those who remain outside the church even though convinced of its authority.

**BADGE** Emblem of identification. Both the Fourth LATERAN COUNCIL (1215) and Nazism (1930's) required Jews to wear a distinguishing badge.

**BADRINATH** A site of holy pilgrimages, a monastery, and a temple of SIVA in the Himalayas, India.

**BADUH** An Eastern spirit invoked to speed messages by writing the Arabic numerals 8, 6, 4, and 2.

**BAECK, LEO (1873–1956)** German Jewish theologian and rabbi who resisted NAZISM.

**BAER, DOB (1710–1772)** Jewish Hasidic leader who succeeded BAAL-SHEM-TOV.

**BAETYL** Sacred pillar or stone, the latter sometimes a meteorite, attached to worship in ancient Greece and Aegea.

**BAHAISM** A religious movement dedicated to religious unity, world peace, and humanitarian service. It was founded by BAHA ULLAH who was considered the Promised One of BABISM. It sees revelation and human evolution as progressive, and Baha Ullah as a prophet succeeding ABRAHAM, MOSES, CHRIST, MOHAMMED, and the BAB. Its center is in Haifa, Israel.

**BAHAMUT** MOSLEM name of the fish which supports the bull which ultimately supports the earth.

**BAHA ULLAH (1817–1892)** *Glory of God* Founder of BAHAISM; originally Mirza Hussein Ali Nuri. A Persian, he became a disciple of BAB and in 1863 he announced that he was "the one who was to come," foretold by the Bab. He spent most of his life in prison and wrote *The Book of Certitude, Hidden Words,* and *Seven Valleys.* He wrote many letters to world leaders pleading for peace, international law, and humanitarian concern.

**BAHIR** Ancient Jewish cabalistic work.

**BAHMAN** ZOROASTRIAN spirit of good thought.

**BAHREICH** A town in India with a MOSLEM monastery and the tomb of Saiyud Salar Masud, a famous Moslem leader. This tomb is a popular place of pilgrimage for both Moslems and Hindus.

**BAHYA BEN JOSEPH or BAHYA IBN PAQUDA (eleventh century)** Spanish Jewish philosopher who wrote *Duties of the Heart,* an ethical guide emphasizing the law and the love of God.

**BAIDAWI (thirteenth century)** MOSLEM critic and author of a commentary on the KORAN, *The Secrets of Revelation.*

**BAILLIE, ROBERT (1599–1662)** A Scottish theologian, delegate to the WESTMINSTER ASSEMBLY, and principal of Glasgow University. He refused a bishopric and is said to have known twelve languages. His letters give a vivid picture of his era.

**BAINI, GIUSEPPE (1775–1844)** Italian composer of ecclesiastical music—his *Miserere* is still used in the Sistine chapel —and musical director and critic.

**BAIRAM** *festival* One of the two leading festivals in ISLAM. The Lesser Bairam is held for three days after Ramadan. The Greater Bairam is held for about three days beginning on the tenth of the last month and is a time of animal sacrifice. At both festivals, presents are exchanged, friends visited, and graves honored.

**BAITULOS** Phoenician heaven.

**BAIUS, MICHAEL (1513–1589)** Belgian CATHOLIC theologian who emphasized sin in his theological system. For his adherence to the doctrines of AUGUSTINE, he was opposed and some of his writings condemned. He was a forerunner of Cornelius JANSEN.

**BAKER, HENRY WILLIAMS (1821–1877)** A writer and compiler of hymns who supported the HIGH CHURCH movement in the CHURCH OF ENGLAND. He wrote "The King of Love My Shepherd Is" and "Lord, Thy Word Abideth."

**BAKHCHISARAI** A city of Crimea with many mosques; once the center of KARAITE Judaism.

**BAKIS** A term for Greek prophets and transmitters of oracles.

**BAKOCZ, THOMAS (1442–1521)** A Hungarian leader in church and state whose whole life seemed to be marked by ambition and treachery.

**BALAAM** A Gentile prophet hired by the Moabite king Balak to curse the Jews. Instead of a curse he invoked blessings upon the Jews, including a prophecy of the Messiah (NUMBERS 22—24). Later he led the Jews into sin, and he is a New Testament example of apostasy (cf. NUMBERS 31; II PETER 2:15, 16; JUDE 11).

**BALAK** The king of Moab who tried to buy Balaam's curses (NUMBERS 22—24).

**BALANCE** A weighing instrument using a balancing beam. In the Bible the balance is a symbol of justice, righteousness, and judgment.

**BALDACHINO** A canopy over an altar or tomb.

**BALDER** Norse god of light, joy, purity, and peace. Though greatly loved, he was killed by Loki, spirit of evil. A spear of mistletoe was used to kill him, according to legend, because nothing else would harm him.

**BALDOVINETTI, ALESSO (c.1425–1499)** Italian painter of many altarpieces and frescoes for churches.

**BALE, JOHN (1495–1563)** English bishop and dramatist whose plays attacked monasticism and promoted the Protestant REFORMATION.

**BALEN, HENDRIK VAN (1575–1632)** Dutch painter of many Biblical and mythological scenes.

**BALFOUR, ARTHUR JAMES (1848–1930)** British statesman whose Balfour Declaration in 1917 supported ZIONIST hopes of a Jewish state in Palestine. He sought world peace and wrote books on theism, humanism, and modern belief.

**BALFOUR DECLARATION** See BALFOUR.

**BALGUY, JOHN (1686–1748)** A theologian of the CHURCH OF ENGLAND who taught that goodness conforms to reason and that God acts according to the order and harmony in the universe.

**BALKIS** The name of the Queen of Sheba in the KORAN.

**BALL, JOHN (?–1381)** English priest who preached the teachings of John WYCLIF, proclaimed social equality, and was executed after encouraging the peasant rebellion of 1381. He had been excommunicated for preaching "errors and schisms and scandals."

**BALL, JOHN (1585–1640)** PURITAN divine whose views of the covenants of works and of grace are enshrined in the Westminster standards of Presbyterian churches. He wrote two catechisms and has been hailed as one of the English fathers of PRESBYTERIANISM.

**BALLANCHE, PIERRE SIMON (1776–1847)** French scholar and theocrat who sought to explain history and society in terms of Christianity.

**BALLOU, ADIN (1803–1890)** American UNIVERSALIST clergyman and writer, prominent in communal and socialistic enterprises.

**BALLOU, HOSEA (1771–1852)** A clergyman sometimes termed "father of American Universalism." He wrote a number of hymns and theological works and edited two UNIVERSALIST periodicals. He was the first president of Tufts College, and a lucid advocate of his faith.

**BALM**  1. In the Bible, the resin or gum of an Arabian plant used for healing and embalming. 2. Today, balsam gum mixed with oil for CHRISM on Holy Thursday.

**BALTHAZAR**  Legendary name of one of the wise men who came from the East to worship the infant Jesus. The Bible does not name or number the wise men.

**BALTIMORE, COUNCILS OF**  The councils of the ROMAN CATHOLIC CHURCH in the United States. Three PLENARY COUNCILS and ten provincial synods have been held in Baltimore. Their decrees, binding on all Catholics in the United States, have concerned education, the sacraments, books, secret societies, and many other topics. At the Third Plenary Council in 1884 the Baltimore Catechism was inaugurated and the Catholic University of America was begun.

**BAMBINO**  An artistic representation of the baby Jesus, particularly the doll-like figure used in churches at Christmas.

**BAMPTON LECTURES**  Lectures delivered annually in the university church at Oxford for the exposition and defense of the Christian faith. They have sometimes been criticized as not fulfilling this original purpose. They result from the will of John Bampton (1689–1751).

**BAN**  1. Excommunication or interdict. 2. An ecclesiastical fine. 3. A curse or malediction.

**BANCROFT, RICHARD (1544–1610)**  Archbishop of Canterbury who superintended the KING JAMES VERSION of the Bible and was prominent in the Hampton Court conference of ANGLICAN and PRESBYTERIAN clergy in 1604. He was a rigid HIGH CHURCHMAN, believed in the divine right of bishops, and was bitterly opposed to the PURITANS.

**BANDS**  1. Small groups originated by WESLEY to promote personal holiness and good works. 2. White collar pendants worn by some clergymen.

**BANEZ, DOMINGO (1528–1604)**  Spanish theologian who counseled THERESA OF AVILA and staunchly defended THOMISM.

**BANGKOK**  The capital of Thailand, a religious center with some 400 BUDDHIST monasteries. Its pagoda, Wat Arun, contains sculptures of angels, giants, INDRA, and BUDDHA. The Chapel of the Emerald Buddha is resplendent.

**BANGORIAN CONTROVERSY**  A widespread dispute in the CHURCH OF ENGLAND between those who took the traditional view that Christ had delegated His authority to the church, and those—led by Benjamin HOADLY, Bishop of Bangor—who took an Erastian position and contended that Christ's Kingdom is not of this world and that His authority has not been thus delegated. The controversy ended in the cessation of convocation in 1717; it was not resumed until 1852.

**BANGOR USE**  An ancient ritual used in Bangor and elsewhere in Wales before the REFORMATION and probably rich in Celtic influence.

**BANIAN**  A member of a HINDU merchant caste who eats no meat.

**BANKERS**  Church curtains or coverings of various types.

**BANNER**  1. A symbol of victory. 2. A flag adorned with sacred or ecclesiastical symbols, such as crosses. 3. One who bans or curses his neighbors.

**BANNERJEA, KRISHNA MOHUN (1813–1885)**  A prominent HINDU scholar of India converted to Christianity and ordained in the ANGLICAN COMMUNION.

**BANNS**  Public announcement in church of a forthcoming marriage. The purpose is to prevent secret or improper marriages.

**BANSHEE**  A Celtic specter whose nocturnal wailing foretells a death in the family.

**BANTU RELIGION**  A loose term for the religious milieu of the Zulus and other tribes south of the Congo. It is characterized on the whole by totemism, animism, and worship of ancestors.

**BANYAN**  A sacred tree of India with many auxiliary trunks covering a wide area.

**BAPHOMET**  A sacred figure—apparently with two faces, male and female—which the Knights TEMPLAR were accused in the fourteenth century of possessing and worshiping in OPHIAN rites.

**BAPTISM**  Essential initiatory rite in most churches. BAPTISTS consider it an ordinance for adults in which the candidate, upon profession of faith, is totally immersed in water. In most other churches baptism is a sacrament for the children of Christian parents as well as for adult converts, and may be performed by sprinkling or pouring water as well as by immersion. FRIENDS and some other groups reject all such external rites. Baptism has an ancient history; in some religions the subject has been baptized in oil, wine, blood, or some other liquid.

**BAPTISM, BELIEVERS'** BAPTISM administered only to adults or those who have reached "the age of accountability" on personal confession of faith in Christ.

**BAPTISM, INFANT** Baptism of children with Christian parents or sponsors, usually by sprinkling water on the head. See also CHRISTENING.

**BAPTISMAL BOWL or FONT** A vessel holding water for BAPTISM.

**BAPTISMAL GARMENT** Special clothing worn by one being baptized.

**BAPTISMAL NAME** "Christian name" given at BAPTISM.

**BAPTISMAL REGENERATION** The doctrine that a person is born again at baptism, based on such Scriptures as Titus 3:5 and John 3:3.

**BAPTISMAL SHELL** A natural or metal shell from which baptismal water is poured on the candidate's head.

**BAPTISMAL VOW** The promise made at baptism by the candidate or his sponsors, usually involving allegiance to Christ or renunciation of the world, the flesh, and the devil.

**BAPTISM FOR THE DEAD** A practice alluded to in I Corinthians 15:29 by which, apparently, a living Christian was baptized on behalf of a dead one. The practice was continued by the MARCIONITES, MONTANISTS, and CERINTHIANS, and is now practiced by MORMONS.

**BAPTISM OF THE HOLY SPIRIT** The outpouring of the HOLY SPIRIT or Holy Ghost upon Christian believers in a special way. This took place on the Day of PENTECOST early in the history of the church. Many Christians consider that every believer is baptized with the Spirit. Others hold that such baptism is a special work of the Spirit following regeneration and involving special spiritual endowments.

**BAPTIST ANTI-MISSION MOVEMENT** A trend against cooperative support of missions and other work in some Baptist churches.

**BAPTIST ASSOCIATION** An interchurch association of BAPTISTS in a particular area for common denominational purposes.

**BAPTIST BROTHERHOOD** An organization of men, particularly among Southern Baptists, for such purposes as evangelism and work with boys.

**BAPTIST CHURCH** See BAPTISTS.

**BAPTIST CONVENTION** A state or national grouping of BAPTISTS for common denominational purposes.

**BAPTISTERY** A special part of the church for baptisms. In the early ages of the church, the baptistery was often a special building. Among modern BAPTISTS it is a receptacle large enough for immersion, usually at the front of the church.

**BAPTIST GENERAL CONFERENCE OF AMERICA** A conservative group of Baptists with Swedish origins, active as a general conference in the United States since 1879.

**BAPTISTRY** See BAPTISTERY.

**BAPTISTS** Christians, once called ANABAPTISTS or Antipaedobaptists, who emphasize baptism by immersion in water upon the personal profession of faith of the candidate. One of the early Protestant divisions opposing infant baptism and upholding personal and ecclesiastical freedom, Baptists have historically emphasized the sole authority of the Bible, personal Christian experience, and the primary authority of the local church. Many early Baptists were martyred in the cause of religious freedom. Today Baptists constitute one of the largest groups of Christians in the world, with more than 40 million members. See also names of individual Baptist groups.

**BAPTIST UNION OF GREAT BRITAIN AND IRELAND** An advisory organization of 27 British Baptist Associations.

**BAPTIST WORLD ALLIANCE** An international fellowship of Baptists organized in 1905. It holds a world congress every five years and seeks to strengthen Baptist interests throughout the world. Nonlegislative, the Alliance has headquarters in Washington, D.C.

**BAR** Aramaic word for son, common in many Biblical names.

**BARABBAS** The robber and murderer

chosen for release by the people when Pilate offered them a choice between Barabbas and Jesus (MATTHEW 27:16). His name apparently means "son of the father," "son of the master," or "son of Abba."

**BARACA-PHILATHEA BIBLE CLASSES** A movement featuring Bible classes for men (Baraca, "Blessing") and women (Philathea, "Lover of the truth"); very popular in the early twentieth century in many parts of the world.

**BARAGA, FREDERIC (1797–1868)** A CATHOLIC missionary to Indians in upper Michigan, made bishop of that area.

**BARAITA** A Jewish term for teachings of the Tannaim (talmudic teachers) not included in the MISHNAH.

**BARAK** The general who helped the prophetess Deborah drive the Canaanites out of the land (JUDGES 4—5).

**BARAKA** African Berber term for sanctity in someone or something. It is often associated with MOHAMMED and with Moslem saints.

**BARAT, MADELEINE SOPHIE, ST. (1779–1865)** A talented French nun who founded the Society of the Sacred Heart and was canonized.

**BARBARA** A young woman martyred for her Christian faith in the third or fourth century, and considered the patron saint of lightning, fireworks, guns, gunners, and miners.

**BARBAULD, ANNA LETITIA (1743–1825)** English wife of a UNITARIAN preacher; author of many Christian poems and hymns.

**BARBARIAN** In the New Testament, one outside Greek or Roman civilization (ROMANS 1:14; I CORINTHIANS 14:11).

**BARBE** WALDENSIAN title for pastor or preacher.

**BARBERINI, FRANCESCO (1597–1679)** Italian cardinal who founded a library of rare manuscripts in Rome.

**BARBIER, LOUIS (1593–1670)** French bishop of great wit who gained wealth from gambling.

**BARBON, PRAISE-GOD** See BAREBONE, PRAISE-GOD.

**BARBOUR, CLARENCE A. (1867–1937)** American clergyman, Y.M.C.A. secretary, educator, and author. He was an able professor of homiletics and president of the Rochester Theological Seminary. He was also president of Brown University.

**BARCLAY, ALEXANDER (c.1475–1552)** British monk and poet whose *Ship of Fools* satirized the priests, judges, and others of his era.

**BARCLAY, JOHN (1734–1798)** A minister of the CHURCH OF SCOTLAND whose followers became known as BARCLAYITES or Bereans.

**BARCLAY, ROBERT (1648–1690)** Powerful Scottish QUAKER leader, often imprisoned. His *Apology for the True Christian Religion* lucidly expounded the Friends' doctrine of the INNER LIGHT. He became British governor of East New Jersey in America. His *Catechism and Confession of Faith* became very popular among the Friends. He traveled in Europe with George FOX and William PENN, and aided Penn in the establishment of Pennsylvania.

**BARCLAYITES** Mild Calvinists who followed John Barclay in the eighteenth century after his presbytery prohibited him from preaching. They later merged into CONGREGATIONALISM.

**BAR COCHBA** See BAR KOKBA, SIMON.

**BARDESANES (c.154–c.222)** Syrian Christian poet, hymn writer, and missionary to Armenia. Although he has been called "the last of the GNOSTICS," Bardesanes seems to have held to essentially orthodox notions. On the other hand, his theology was dualistic and he tried to relieve God of responsibility for evil by denying that He created the world. He saw Christians as a new race and emphasized faith and monotheism.

**BAREBONE, PRAISE-GOD (c.1596–1679)** Wealthy English leather merchant and lay preacher who left the BAPTISTS to join the sect of FIFTH MONARCHY MEN. A controversial figure, he defended infant baptism and supported Cromwell's republic.

**BAREBONE'S PARLIAMENT** A satirical name for the parliament of 140 "godly men" nominated by Oliver Cromwell in 1653 of which Praise-God Barebone was a member. It accomplished little in spite of its members' zeal.

**BARGHEST** A monstrous spectral dog regarded in northern England as a portent of death.

**BAR-HEBRAEUS, GREGORIUS (1226–1286)** A Syrian JACOBITE scholar who wrote books of science, history, philosophy, and theology. Originally named Abu-l-Faraj, he wrote a history of the world, a commentary on ARISTOTLE, and a commentary on the text of the Scriptures.

**BAR-ILAN UNIVERSITY** First Orthodox-sponsored university in Israel, located near Tel Aviv.

**BARING-GOULD, SABINE (1834–1924)** English rector and author of books in many areas. He is known for his novels, his studies of religion and mythology, and the hymn "Onward Christian Soldiers."

**BARIS** Babylonian word for: 1. a ship; 2. the place where the ark landed in the Babylonian story of the Flood.

**BAR-JESUS** The sorcerer and false prophet who was stricken with blindness for interfering with Paul's evangelistic labors (ACTS 13:6–12). Also called Elymas.

**BAR-JONA son of Jona** A name for Peter (MATTHEW 16:17).

**BAR KOKBA, SIMON (?–135) son of the star** Jewish leader killed in a revolt against the Roman government during the reign of Hadrian. He was called "Simeon, Prince of Israel" and many Jews believed he was the MESSIAH. Also written Cochba, Kochba, Kokhba.

**BARLAAM AND JOSAPHAT** A popular medieval romance about the conversion of the prince Josaphat by the monk Barlaam, and their ascetic seclusion in the wilderness. It appears in many translations and seems to be based on the story of BUDDHA.

**BARMEN DECLARATION** A statement of German churches in 1934, under the influence of Karl Barth and Martin Niemoeller, declaring the allegiance of the church to Jesus Christ rather than to NAZISM. While acknowledging the state's divine appointment to provide justice and peace, the Declaration of Barmen rejected the claim that the state "should and could become the single and totalitarian order of human life." Thus began the CONFESSING CHURCH which opposed anti-Semitism and state supremacy.

**BAR MITZVAH son of the commandment or son of duty** 1. The Jewish ritual at which a boy becomes eligible to take part in public worship. It is solemnized on the first Sabbath after the boy's thirteenth birthday and is an important social as well as religious event. 2. A Jewish boy who becomes thirteen, becoming morally responsible for his actions and eligible to take part in Jewish worship.

**BARNABAS, ST.** The companion of Paul on several missionary journeys. According to tradition he was bishop of Milan, and martyred at Rome or in Cyprus. He is honored by a feast day on June 11.

**BARNABAS, EPISTLE OF** An epistle from the first century ascribed to Barnabas. It found hidden meanings in the Old Testament upholding the Christian faith over against JUDAISM.

**BARNABAS, GOSPEL OF** A fifteenth-century work in Italian ascribed to Barnabas but with a MOSLEM slant and a GNOSTIC background.

**BARNABITES** The Clerics Regular of St. Paul, founded at Milan in 1530 by Antonio Maria Zaccaria, for education, relief of the sick, mission work, and study of the epistles of Paul.

**BARNES, ALBERT (1798–1870)** American PRESBYTERIAN minister whose sermon "The Way of Salvation" led to a heresy trial and whose *Notes* were popular commentaries on the Bible. In the division between strict CALVINISTS and NEW SCHOOL Presbyterians, he sided with the latter. He preached total abstinence from alcohol, the abolition of slavery, and an unlimited atonement.

**BARNES, ERNEST WILLIAM (1874–1953)** Bishop and leader of the modernist movement in the CHURCH OF ENGLAND. Accepting Darwinian evolution and a scientific approach to religion, he disturbed both EVANGELICALS and ANGLO-CATHOLICS because of his views. He was a consistent pacifist and opposed atomic weapons

**BARNES, ROBERT (c.1495–1540)** English reformer who denounced the worldliness of the clergy, became a friend of Martin LUTHER, and was burned without trial. He helped bring about the Protestant aspects of the CHURCH OF ENGLAND.

**BARNETT, SAMUEL AUGUSTUS (1849–1913)** English cleric and social reformer who opened Toynbee Hall, the first settlement house in 1884. With his wife Henrietta he started adult evening schools, improved the payment of relief, and wrote *Practicable Socialism*.

**BARONIUS, CAESAR (1538–1607)** Italian

cardinal and authority in church history. He was taught by St. Philip NERI and revised the errors from the Roman Martyrology. He was an honest historian, and almost became a pope.

**BARRIER ACT** An action in the CHURCH OF SCOTLAND in 1697 to prevent hasty legislation by causing an amendment to the constitution, offered at one assembly, to be referred to a future assembly of the church.

**BARRINGTON, JOHN SHUTE (1678–1734)** English lawyer and writer of theology who championed the civil rights of PROTESTANT dissenters.

**BARRIOS, DANIEL LEVI (1626–1701)** Spanish Jewish mystic, poet, and historian.

**BARROW, HENRY (c.1550–1593)** English PURITAN whose defense of separation from the established church led to his being hanged for sedition.

**BARROW, ISAAC (1630–1677)** English theologian and mathematician who wrote *A Treatise on the Pope's Supremacy.*

**BARROWS, JOHN HENRY (1847–1902)** American CONGREGATIONAL and PRESBYTERIAN minister who organized the World's Parliament of Religions in 1893 and became president of Oberlin College in 1899.

**BARROWS, SAMUEL JUNE (1845–1909)** American UNITARIAN clergyman and representative in Congress. He helped to advance prison reform.

**BAR-SALIBI, JACOB (twelfth century)** Bishop in the Syrian Jacobite Church (see JACOBITES) and prolific writer.

**BARSOM** 1. A bundle of twigs used in ZOROASTRIAN worship. 2. A bundle of metal rods employed in PARSEE worship.

**BARTHOLOMEW, ST.** One of Jesus' Twelve Apostles, also called Nathanael. According to tradition, he traveled as a missionary to India and was flayed alive in Armenia. A feast day honors him on August 24. He is sometimes represented by three flaying knives.

**BARTHOLOMEW, GOSPEL OF** An apocryphal gospel with a GNOSTIC viewpoint erroneously attributed to St. Bartholomew.

**BARTHOLOMEW'S DAY MASSACRE, ST.** The slaughter of thousands of HUGUENOTS, in France, on the nights of August 23 and 24, 1572. Some estimate as many as 100,-000 deaths. The event was celebrated in Rome with a TE DEUM and a medal of commemoration.

**BARTIMAEUS** A blind man healed by Christ near Jericho (MARK 10:46–52).

**BARUCH** *blessed* Amanuensis of the Prophet Jeremiah, imprisoned with him (JEREMIAH 36:4).

**BARUCH** The name of four different noncanonical books relating to the scribe Baruch and probably all dating from the first or second century A.D.

**BASCOM, HENRY B. (1796–1850)** American METHODIST clergyman and circuit rider who became president of Madison College and of Transylvania University. He also helped organize the METHODIST EPISCOPAL CHURCH and became one of its first bishops.

**BASEL, CONFESSION OF** A REFORMATION statement promulgated at Basel, Switzerland, in 1531. Its position is midway between those of ZWINGLI and LUTHER. It states that Christ is present in the LORD's SUPPER as the food of the soul.

**BASEL, COUNCIL OF** A reforming council of the ROMAN CATHOLIC CHURCH, 1431–1449. It declared its supremacy over the pope and was itself denounced by the pope as heretical. Thus the power of the papacy, which the council had sought to curb, remained unshaken.

**BASHO (1643–1694)** Japanese poet who founded the Haiku school of ZEN Buddhism.

**BASIL, ST.** See BASIL THE GREAT.

**BASILEA, SOLOMON (1680–1743)** Jewish commentator and cabalist.

**BASILIAN MONKS** CENOBITES of the EASTERN ORTHODOX CHURCH from whose ranks the hierarchs in that church are chosen. They are governed by the Rule of St. BASIL THE GREAT. They have monasteries on Mt. Sinai, Mt. Athos, and elsewhere.

**BASILICA** 1. A large Roman building often built in the form of a rectangular hall. 2. A church built like a Roman basilica, as many churches have been since the fourth century.

**BASILIDEANS** Followers of BASILIDES, numerous in Egypt and Europe until the end of the fourth century. They held many GNOSTIC views and believed that God the Father sent His Emanation into Jesus to save the world from the Creator-God Jehovah. Jesus, they held, only seemed to suffer and did not actually die on the cross.

**BASILIDES (second century)** Famous GNOS-TIC leader in Alexandria during the reign of Hadrian (117–138).

**BASILISK** A dangerous monster, part serpent and part cock, symbolizing the devil or AntiChrist in medieval art.

**BASIL THE GREAT (c.330–379)** A bishop of Caesarea, brother of St. GREGORY OF NYSSA, and friend of St. GREGORY of Nazianzus. He established the Rule of the BASILIAN MONKS. Zealous for orthodox Christianity, he led the fight against ARIANISM and revised the liturgy of the GREEK ORTHODOX CHURCH. He was an ascetic and a famed writer and preacher.

**BASIN** A vessel for holding water or offerings.

**BASLE** See BASEL.

**BAS MITZVAH** See BAT MITZVAH.

**BASNAGE, JACQUES (1653–1723)** French Protestant pastor, theologian, and church historian. He was a firm CALVINIST.

**BASON** An ecclesiastical basin, particularly a receptacle for offering plates.

**BASSANO, JACOPO (c.1515–1592)** Venetian painter of many religious scenes.

**BASSENDYNE BIBLE** The earliest English Bible published in Scotland, in 1579.

**BASSETT, JAMES (1834–1906)** American PRESBYTERIAN missionary who founded the first mission in Teheran and later supervised other mission stations, as head of the Eastern Mission of Persia.

**BASSO-JAUN** A Basque forest god.

**BAST** Egyptian cat goddess, symbolizing the sun and sex, also known as Ubastet and BUBASTIS.

**BATHIA** Traditional name of the princess who saved the infant MOSES when she found him in the Nile bulrushes.

**BATHING** A religious rite among HINDUS, Old Testament Jews, and the monastic community at Qumran on the Dead Sea.

**BATH-SHEBA** The wife of Uriah the Hittite, taken by King David who married her after having Uriah killed by being placed on the front line of battle. From David's union with her came the son Solomon (II SAMUEL 11—12).

**BAT KOL** *daughter of the voice* Jewish term for a divine revelation or prophetic pronouncement.

**BAT or BAS MITZVAH** Jewish ceremony for girls similar to the BAR MITZVAH for boys.

**BATTLE-AXE EXPERIMENT** A religious experiment by Theophilus GATES near Philadelphia, Pennsylvania, similar to that of the ONEIDA COMMUNITY. In 1837 Gates announced a new order in which all rules had passed away and every man was to love the woman of his choice—regardless of marital relationship—according to "the principle of holiness." A community of such lovers and their soul mates, practicing free love and nudism in spiritual abandon, shocked the world for a number of years.

**BA'U** Babylonian harvest goddess.

**BAUER, BRUNO (1809–1882)** German historian, theologian, and Biblical critic. He believed the New Testament was the result of imagination dating from the second century—a combination of ideas from PHILO, Seneca, and JOSEPHUS. Considering his criticism destructive, the government revoked his license to teach.

**BAUR, FERDINAND CHRISTIAN (1792–1860)** German PROTESTANT theologian and critic; leader of the TÜBINGEN SCHOOL of theology. He interpreted the Bible from the standpoint of Hegelian philosophy and rejected the New Testament books which did not reflect a Pauline–Petrine conflict. As a result he found little genuine in the New Testament except Romans, Corinthians, and Galatians.

**BAUTAIN, LOUIS (1796–1867)** French priest and philosopher who held that God is known through faith, feeling, and spiritual insight.

**BAVINCK, J. H. (c.1896–1964)** A conservative professor of missions at the Free University of Amsterdam.

**BAXTER, RICHARD (1615–1691)** English NONCONFORMIST leader and pastor who wrote 168 works including *A Call to the Unconverted, The Reformed Pastor,* and *The Saints' Everlasting Rest.* A man of liberal and irenic mind, he served as a chaplain in Oliver Cromwell's army but spoke in his presence in favor of the monarchy. Although a moderate PRESBYTERIAN, he accepted modified EPISCOPALIANISM and felt that all Christians should be able to unite on the basis of the Ten Commandments (see DECALOGUE), the LORD'S PRAYER, and the APOSTLES' CREED. During his ministry at Kidderminster, the whole community spirit changed from irreligious brutality to Christian devotion.

**65**

There a statue in his honor was erected in 1875.

**BAY** The laurel tree, source of the Grecian victor's crown.

**BAYADERE** The devadasis or dancing girls of HINDU temples.

**BAYEUX TAPESTRY** A beautifully embroidered strip of linen preserved in Normandy, depicting the Norman invasion of England and the ecclesiastical garb of that time.

**BAYLE, PIERRE (1647–1706)** French philosopher of HUGUENOT background who espoused religious toleration, held that faith and reason are mutually exclusive, and influenced the deists and rationalists of his age.

**BAYON** Cambodian temple. See ANGKOR THOM.

**BAY PEOPLE** Term for the early PURITANS of Massachusetts.

**BAY PSALM BOOK** A book of the Psalms, the first book printed in the British Colonies.

**B.C.** Abbreviation for "Before Christ." Cf. A.D.

**BDELLIUM** A gum like myrrh mentioned in Genesis 2:12 and Numbers 11:7.

**BEACHY AMISH MENNONITE CHURCHES** Churches in the United States which separated from the Old Order Mennonites and are less strict, refusing to shun members who enter other churches.

**BEADLE** A church officer appointed by the vestry to keep order in the parish, or a sexton in a synagogue. In the CHURCH OF SCOTLAND, the beadle has such tasks as caring for the church building. In ecclesiastical processions, the beadle may carry the mace.

**BEADROLL** A roll of deceased persons for whom prayers are to be said.

**BEADS** A device for counting prayers used by BUDDHISTS, HINDUS, and MOHAMMEDANS. Beads in CATHOLICISM are the ROSARY. The word *pray* in Middle English was "bede."

**BEADSMAN or BEDESMAN** An almsman who prays for his benefactor.

**BEAR** The bear was often involved in primitive cave religion. In many cases its flesh appears to have been eaten and its head raised on a pole and worshiped. In religious art, the bear often symbolizes solitude, martyrdom, or the devil.

**BEAST** Beasts appear in the apocalyptic visions of Daniel and John, in the books of Daniel and Revelation. In Scripture a beast often appears to represent human government. In Islamic and other religious literature, a monstrous beast often symbolizes the evil powers opposed to God.

**BEATIFICATION** The ecclesiastical act of formally declaring a person "Blessed," often a step toward canonization, or enrolling him as a saint.

**BEATIFIC VISION** The full knowledge of God accompanied by indescribable joy and bliss. This is the reward of the redeemed in heaven (I CORINTHIANS 13:12; I JOHN 3:2) but is sometimes realized on earth in mystic vision or communion.

**BEATING THE BOUNDS** The practice of defining parish boundaries in ancient England by beating the circumference with willows.

**BEATITUDE** Blessedness.

**BEATITUDES** A term for the first part of the SERMON ON THE MOUNT, indicating the blessedness of Christian meekness, purity, etc. The Beatitudes are found in Matthew 5:3–11 and Luke 6:20–22.

**BEATON, DAVID (1494–1546)** Scottish cardinal and Archbishop of St. Andrews who ruthlessly persecuted the Scottish Reformers and caused George WISHART to be executed. The same year Wishart was killed (1546), Beaton was murdered by conspirators.

**BEATUS** *Blessed* The title of one beatified in the process of canonization.

**BEAUFORT, LEO J. C. (1890–1965)** FRANCISCAN priest and spokesman for foreign affairs in the Netherlands. A member of the European Commission on Human Rights, he was a delegate to the United Nations from the year it was founded until his death.

**BEC** BENEDICTINE abbey in Normandy, France. Founded by LANFRANC and directed at one time by ANSELM, it influenced churchmen and theologians for centuries.

**BECK, JOHANN TOBIAS** PROTESTANT theologian of Tübingen, Germany, who stressed the creative life of the Holy Spirit in the history of the Jewish people and in the growth of the Scriptures. He influenced Adolph SCHLATTER and other later theologians.

**BECKET, THOMAS À**    See THOMAS À BECKET.

**BECKX, PIERRE JEAN (1795–1887)**  Belgian churchman who became general of the SOCIETY OF JESUS and wrote the *Month of May.*

**BECON, THOMAS (c.1513–1567)**  English PROTESTANT reformer influenced by LUTHER and ZWINGLI. He wrote several books and enjoyed a number of ecclesiastical benefices.

**BEDARESI,    YEDAYAH    (1270–1340)** French-born Jewish poet and philosopher who wrote MIDRASHIM on Scripture and the long poem *The Test of the World.*

**BEDE, ST. or THE VENERABLE (c.672–735)** English historian, BENEDICTINE monk, and theologian. He is famous for his hymns, his Scripture commentaries, and his *Ecclesiastical History of the English Nation* which relates the course of British Christianity from 597 to 731. His biographer Plummer called him "the Christian thinker and student." His title "Venerable" may merely indicate that he was a priest, although he was esteemed during his life both for his saintliness and for his scholarship. His feast day is May 27.

**BEDESMAN**    See BEADSMAN.

**BEE**  Symbol of eloquence, industry, and virtue in Christian art.

**BEECHER, HENRY WARD (1813–1887)**  Popular American CONGREGATIONAL preacher, brother of Harriet Beecher Stowe, whose championing of the abolition of slavery and of women's suffrage influenced American history. His favorite theme in preaching was love.

**BEECHER, LYMAN (1775–1863)**  American PRESBYTERIAN preacher, the father of Harriet Beecher Stowe and Henry Ward Beecher. A foe of intemperance, dueling, and UNITARIAN inroads among the faithful, he was a founder of the American Bible Society and a president of Lane Theological Seminary. He was an eloquent preacher. At various times he was charged with holding heretical views, but was tried and acquitted in 1835.

**BEEHIVE**  Religious symbol of eloquence, and of St. AMBROSE.

**BEELZEBUB, BEELZEBUL, or BAALZEBUB** This was an ancient Canaanite god whose name is a form of BAAL and who was the Philistine deity of Ekron (II KINGS 1:2).

The name may have originally meant "heavenly lord" or "lord of evil intrigue"; the translation "lord of the flies" may have been a satiric alteration. In the New Testament Beelzebub is another name for Satan (cf. MATTHEW 10:25).

**BEER-HOFMANN,    RICHARD    (1866–1945)** Austrian writer of fiction, drama, and poetry with a strong Jewish insight.

**BEERSHEBA** *seven wells*  In the Bible, the city which marked the southern boundary of Palestine, mentioned in connection with ABRAHAM, ELIJAH, and others. It is now capital of the Negev. The Battle of Beersheba in 1917 led to the capture of Jerusalem by the British.

**BEGBIE,    HAROLD    (1871–1929)**  English writer of books with social and religious themes, including *Twice-born Men* and *The Life of William Booth.*

**BEGHARDS**  European laymen, often artisans, weavers, and the like, who led a communal life with mystical and philanthropic aims. Confused with Franciscans and beggars, and accused of perfectionism (i.e., belief that after attaining a certain state, nothing one might do could be regarded as sin) and immorality, they were condemned, persecuted, and apparently exterminated by the end of the fifteenth century.

**BEGOCHIDDI**  Supreme Navajo god.

**BEGUINES**  Members of lay sisterhoods corresponding to the male BEGHARDS. Becoming prominent in Europe in the twelfth century, they were harried and suspected of heresy and immorality by both PROTESTANTS and CATHOLICS. A few of their communities still exist in Holland, Germany, and Belgium.

**BEHEMOTH**  Old Testament animal (cf. JOB 40:15), apparently a hippopotamus.

**BEHISTUN** *place of the gods*  Village in Persia below a steep rock which contains inscriptions and a striking carving showing how Darius I defeated his enemies with the help of AHURA MAZDA. Sir Henry Rawlinson's deciphering of the inscriptions unlocked the mystery of other cuneiform writings.

**BEHMENITES**    See BOEHME, JAKOB.

**BEING**  What exists, actually or potentially. Theologically, God is necessary and supreme Being while all other existence is contingent being. The Lord defined Himself to Moses as "I am that I am" (EXODUS 3:14). Ontology is the science or study of being.

**BEISSEL, JOHANN CONRAD (1690–1768)** German-American hymn writer and religious leader who founded the SEVENTH-DAY BAPTIST CHURCH and religious community in Ephrata, Pennsylvania. The latter stressed celibacy and communal life.

**BEKKER, BALTHASAR (1634–1698)** Dutch pastor and author who was defrocked for denying sorcery and possession by demons.

**BEL or BELUS** 1. Another form of BAAL. 2. In the Old Testament, the Babylonian god also known as Marduk or Enlil (cf. ISAIAH 46:1).

**BEL AND THE DRAGON** Apocryphal work attached to the Old Testament book of Daniel narrating how Daniel was saved from the lions' den after opposing the worship of the idol Bel and of a dragon.

**BELET** Ancient Semitic fertility goddess.

**BELFRY** Bell tower, particularly for a church.

**BELGIC CONFESSION** A Calvinistic creed with 37 articles prepared in 1561 and adopted by the Synod of DORT in 1619. It has been adopted as a symbol by many REFORMED denominations.

**BELIAL** 1. In the Old Testament, someone or something worthless. 2. In the New Testament, a name for Satan. In Milton's *Paradise Lost*, Belial and Beelzebub were fallen angels.

**BELIEF** Faith, trust, or assent to doctrine. According to the New Testament, salvation is through believing in Christ. Belief, however, today often connotes intellectual assent or creedal doctrine, while faith has a more personal and spiritual meaning in common parlance.

**BELIEVERS' BAPTISM** See BAPTISM, BELIEVERS'.

**BELILI** Sumerian goddess of the moon and love.

**BELIT the lady** Supreme Babylonian goddess, perhaps the same as Baalat.

**BELL** Bells have often summoned Christians to public worship in recent generations, and have done so in Europe for centuries. Small bells are rung at mass, funerals, and the ANGELUS, in CATHOLIC usage. On occasion bells have been baptized.

**BELLARMINE, ST. (1542–1621)** Full name

Roberto Francesco Romolo Bellarmino. Italian cardinal and theologian who defended CATHOLIC institutions and doctrines with great learning and skill. He was a popular devotional writer, admired and welcomed Galileo despite the latter's supposed scientific heresy, and was canonized in 1930. His feast day is May 13.

**BELL, BOOK AND CANDLE** Ancient ceremony of excommunication or anathema. When the accursed person was so declared, the book containing the anathema was clapped shut, the 13 candles of the officiating bishop and priests were extinguished, and bells were rung.

**BELL COTE or BELL COT** A turret, gable, or group of arches where bells are hung—apart from the church tower, if there is one.

**BELLOC, HILAIRE (1870–1953)** English author who skillfully upheld woman suffrage, nationalism, and his CATHOLIC faith. He defended medievalism and Catholic economic liberalism.

**BELLONA** Roman war goddess.

**BELLOWS, HENRY W. (1814–1882)** American UNITARIAN pastor who organized the U.S. Sanitary Commission which aided wounded soldiers of the Civil War.

**BELMONTE, JACOB (1570–1629)** Founder of the Jewish community of Amsterdam, Holland.

**BELOMANCY** Term for ancient Semitic divination by using arrows or darts (cf. EZEKIEL 21:21).

**BELOT, GUSTAVE (1859–1930)** French philosopher who believed that the science of morals was impossible on the basis of metaphysics and that morality is a natural growth rather than a code or system.

**BELOVED DISCIPLE** The Apostle John.

**BELOVED PHYSICIAN** The Apostle Luke, a Greek physician who wrote the Gospel of Luke and the Acts of the Apostles.

**BELOVED SON** The Father's identification of Christ the Son at the latter's baptism (MATTHEW 3:17).

**BELSHAZZAR** King of Babylon at whose last dinner writing appeared on the wall announcing his doom and conquest by the Persians (DANIEL 5).

**BELTANE** Celtic festival of May Day, at the beginning of summer, and of early November at summer's end. It was marked by Beltane fires or "needfires"—bonfires—and its name may have been connected with worship of Bel or BAAL.

**BELTESHAZZAR** Babylonian name of Daniel (DANIEL 1:7; 2:26).

**BELTIS** See BAALAT.

**BELUS** See BEL.

**BELVEDERE** Famous museum at the VATICAN containing important classical art and statuary.

**BEMA** 1. Sanctuary in an EASTERN ORTHODOX CHURCH. 2. Reading desk in a Jewish synagogue. See BIMAH. 3. Christian altar.

**BEMBO, PIETRO (1470–1547)** Italian cardinal and humanistic theologian.

**BEMIDBAR** Jewish term for the Book of Numbers in the Old Testament.

**BEN** Hebrew word for "son" or "son of."

**BEN-AMMI or BENAMMI** *son of my people* Lot's son, also called Ammon; ancestor of the AMMONITES.

**BENARES** City on the Ganges in India where BUDDHA once preached; a shrine of HINDUISM, with a Hindu university, visited by more than a million Hindu pilgrims each year. Many BRAHMANS live there.

**BEN ASHER, AARON** See AARON BEN MOSES BEN ASHER.

**BEN-AVRUOM** *son of Abraham* A Jew.

**BENCH RENT** Church pew rent.

**BENEDICAMUS DOMINO** *let us bless the Lord* Priestly conclusion of mass, at ADVENT and other special times.

**BENEDIC, ANIMA MEA** *bless the Lord, O my soul* Beginning of a Psalm and of an anthem based on it.

**BENEDICITE** *bless ye* A canticle based on Psalm 148 sung in many churches during LENT instead of the TE DEUM.

**BENEDICT, ST. (c.480–c.547)** Italian monk who as a youth of fourteen began to live as a hermit in a cave, and later gathered several cells with thirteen monks in each one. After becoming abbot of a monastery, he founded a monastery at Monte Cassino where began the order of BENEDICTINE monks. Benedict's rule required the monks in the order to copy manuscripts and study as well as to work physically and to attend to the things of the soul. His feast day is March 21, the day of his death.

**BENEDICT I** Pope (575–579) during a period of famine and of inroads on Rome by the Lombards.

**BENEDICT III** Pope (855–858) who

sought to raise the moral standards of both single and married persons.

**BENEDICT V** Pope, known as "the Grammarian" because of his scholarly ability, who held the office from May to June, 964, and was removed by Emperor Otto I.

**BENEDICT XI (1240–1304)** Scholarly pope who wrote commentaries on the Psalms and Matthew, secured peace between the Vatican and France, encouraged mission work in Persia and Mongolia, bettered Vatican finances, and was beatified by Pope Clement XII.

**BENEDICT XII (?–1342)** Pope (1334–1342) who sought the reunion of the Greek and Roman churches, improved the training of ecclesiastical novices, and enlarged the papal treasury. He proclaimed that the faithful without sins to expiate enter into the BEATIFIC VISION as soon as they die.

**BENEDICT XIII** This is the title of both Pietro Francesco Orsini, pope 1724–1730, and Pedro de Luna, antipope 1394–1422.

**BENEDICT XIV (1675–1758)** Gifted pope (1740–1758) who advanced education, suppressed usury, wrote a number of important ecclesiastical works, and restored Roman relationships with the MELCHITES and MARONITES.

**BENEDICT XV (1854–1922)** Churchman made pope at the beginning of World War I who aided war victims and sought peace throughout the war and afterwards. While he was pope, official relations were resumed between the Vatican and both England and France. He promulgated encyclicals commemorating the death of St. Jerome, instituting the Oriental Institute, and promoting Biblical studies.

**BENEDICT BISCOP, ST. (c.628–690)** English ecclesiastic who taught Bede and erected several monasteries.

**BENEDICTINE** Liqueur originally made by French Benedictine monks, each bottle of which is initialed with the letters D.O.M. for the dedication *Deo Optimo Maximo:* "To God most good, most great."

**BENEDICTINES** Most ancient monastic order in the West, founded by St. Benedict at Monte Cassino, Italy, in the sixth century. The Benedictine monks wear black habits and follow the Rule of St. Benedict. Each monk is attached for life to one monastery. Since their inception the Benedictines have fostered scholarship and culture; they led the restoration of the Gregorian plain chant to the church service. Out of their order grew the CELESTINE, CISTERCIAN, OLIVETAN, and other orders.

**BENEDICTION** Blessing. In Protestant worship a benediction by the minister usually concludes the service, often with a verse from Scripture such as II Corinthians 13:14. Among CATHOLICS, the benediction indicates various forms of liturgical blessings. When written with capital B, it refers to a blessing with the RESERVED SACRAMENT.

**BENEDICTIONALE** A collection of blessings in various forms.

**BENEDICTION OF THE BLESSED SACRAMENT** A blessing by a ROMAN CATHOLIC priest during which the HOST is either placed in the CIBORIUM or exposed in a MONSTRANCE.

**BENEDICT OF ANIANE, ST. (751–821)** Founder of the monastery of Aniane in 779.

**BENEDICT OF MONTE CASSINO or NURSIA** See BENEDICT, ST.

**BENEDICTORY** Relating to a benediction or a blessing.

**BENEDICT THE BLACK, ST. (?–1589)** Negro slave of Sicily who became a FRANCISCAN superior and was canonized in 1807. His feast day is April 4.

**BENEDICTUS** 1. Thanksgiving hymn of Zacharias over the birth of his son who became John the Baptist (LUKE 1:68–79). 2. Christian hymn based on Zacharias' hymn. 3. Choral statement in the mass based on Matthew 21:9.

**BENEDICTUS ABBAS (?–1194)** Abbot of Peterborough, England, who wrote two works about THOMAS À BECKET.

**BENEDICTUS ES** ANGLICAN canticle based on "Song of the Three Holy Children."

**BENEDICTUS QUI VENIT** Anthem based on Matthew 21:9.

**BENEFICE** Ecclesiastical income, or a church office to which is attached property or income therefrom. In the CHURCH OF ENGLAND the benefice is a pastorate, bishopric, or the like.

**BENEFICIATUS** One who holds a BENEFICE.

**BENEFIT OF CLERGY** The medieval privilege, given clergymen and persons who could read, of being tried in an ecclesiastical rather than in a secular court. The result was sometimes a miscarriage of justice in the form of a lighter penalty or an acquittal. This "benefit" has been abolished in the United States and England.

**BENE ISRAEL** *sons of Israel* Community of dark-skinned Jews, principally in the area of Bombay, in India. Their origin there has been estimated variously as the eighteenth century A.D., the second century A.D., the sixth century B.C., or earlier. Their knowledge of conventional JUDAISM appears to date in the main from recent history.

**BENEVOLENCE** 1. In philosophy and theology, desire for the good of others; ethical aim of altruism or self-giving love. Jonathan EDWARDS termed benevolence the supreme Christian virtue. Rabbi HILLEL summed up the law thus: "What you would not have done to yourself, do not do to your neighbor." 2. Financial aid for religious or other charitable purposes.

**BENFEY, THEODOR (1809–1881)** German scholar noted for his work in Sanskrit and primitive mythology.

**BENGAL** City of India once predominantly BUDDHIST but whose citizens are now about half HINDU and half MOSLEM.

**BENGEL, JOHANN ALBRECHT (1687–1752)** German LUTHERAN churchman, New Testament scholar, and theological professor. He embraced PIETISM and PREMILLENNIALISM. He prepared an important Greek text of the New Testament and an exegetical New Testament commentary. He originated the theory of manuscript recensions, and endorsed grammatico-historical interpretation of Scripture.

**BENHADAD** Three kings of Damascus by this name are mentioned in the Old Testament (I KINGS 15:17–20; I KINGS 20:1–21; II KINGS 13:3–25).

**BENI ISRAEL** See BENE ISRAEL.

**BENJAMIN** *son of the right hand* 1. Last son of Jacob and Rachel, father of the Jewish tribe of Benjamin. He was dearly loved by his parents and brothers. 2. Members of the tribe of Benjamin were loyal to Judah and fierce fighters. King Saul and the Apostle Paul were both of the tribe of Benjamin. 3. Several Old Testament figures have the name of Benjamin.

**BENJAMIN OF TUDELA (?–1173)** Jewish RABBI who traveled east as far as China and wrote an impotrant *Itinerary* of his journeys, describing Jewish communities and customs as he found them.

**BENNO, ST. (1010–1106)** German bishop who upheld the pope against Emperor Henry IV and was deposed but later restored to his prelacy. His canonization in 1523 drew a blast from Martin LUTHER against him as "new false god and old devil," although he had labored for the conversion of the heathen Selavonians. His feast day is June 16.

**BENNU** Egyptian phoenix which was said to die periodically and be reborn in fire.

**BENOIT, PETER LEONARD (1834–1901)** Belgian composer of a number of sacred works and an opera *Drama Christi.*

**BENSON, EDWARD WHITE (1829–1896)** Archbishop of Canterbury in England who brought about closer relationships between the CHURCH OF ENGLAND and the Eastern churches, Assyrian and Russian. He wrote a book on the APOCALYPSE and some hymns, and combined statesmanship with churchmanship.

**BENTEN** Japanese goddess of luck and of the sea.

**BENTHAM, JEREMY (1748–1832)** English moralist and philosopher who developed the system of UTILITARIANISM, with its ethos of the greatest happiness of the greatest number of people. He helped bring about reforms in the penal system, criminal law, and other areas.

**BENTHAMISM** Ethical and philosophical system of Jeremy BENTHAM.

**BEN YEHUDAH, ELIEZER (1858–1922)** Lithuanian-born Jewish scholar who founded the Hebrew Language Council and prepared a 16-volume *Dictionary of Ancient and Modern Hebrew.*

**BENZOZIA** Basque mother-goddess.

**BERACHAH** *blessing* 1. Follower of King David (I CHRONICLES 12:3). 2. Valley north of Hebron where Jehoshaphat blessed the people after a victory (II CHRONICLES 20:26).

**BERACHYAH** See BEREKHIAH BEN NATRONAI HA-NAKDAN.

**BERAKAH** *blessing* Jewish prayer of blessing or thanksgiving.

**BERAT** Town in Albania, seven-eights of whose residents are MOSLEM but which has a bishopric of the ALBANIAN ORTHODOX CHURCH as well as a mosque dating from the fifteenth century. The Albanian Orthodox Church announced its independent status at Berat in 1922.

**BERCEO, GONZALO DE (c.1180–c.1265)** Earliest poet known in Spain. A BENEDICTINE deacon and priest, he wrote more than 13,000 devotional verses. Berceo composed lives of St. Oria, St. Dominic, and many other saints and ecclesiastics. He wrote 25 poems about the miracles of MARY.

**BERCHTA** German goddess of spinners.

**BERDYAEV, NICHOLAS (1874–1948)** RUSSIAN ORTHODOX theologian and philosopher whose work has sharply influenced contemporary theology. Sympathetic to the mystics, he criticized various political and philosophical ideas and was especially concerned with the ethical implications of religion and the dehumanization of modern man. Berdyaev believed that God and man are correlated perfectly in the God-Man Christ, and that man fulfills himself in creativity.

**BEREANS** 1. Citizens of Berea in Macedonia commended for their zeal in searching the Scriptures (ACTS 17:10). 2. Eighteenth-century followers of John BARCLAY.

**BEREKHIAH BEN NATRONAI HA-NAKDAN (12th or 13th century)** Jewish philosopher and scholar famous for his prose *Fox Fables,* somewhat similar to Aesop's *Fables,* though original and drawn from many sources. Also called Berachyah.

**BERENGAR OF TOURS (c.998–c.1088)** French churchman and theologian who was declared a heretic for stating his belief that the elements of the EUCHARIST become the body and blood of Christ only in the partaker's mind. He appreciated the doctrines of AUGUSTINE and felt that the latter's doctrine was in harmony with his own attack on TRANSUBSTANTIATION.

**BERESHITH** *in the beginning* Hebrew name of the book of Genesis.

**BERGAMO** Episcopal see in northern Italy, site of several beautiful church buildings.

**BERGDAMAN RELIGION** The Bergdama

natives of southwestern Africa worship a god called Gamab and give special prominence to fire in their worship.

**BERGGRAV, EIVIND (1884–1959)** Norwegian LUTHERAN bishop and ecumenical leader who heroically resisted the Quisling government during World War II.

**BERGSON, HENRI (1859–1941)** French Jewish philosopher who found a dynamic personal God in concrete situations, a God who evolves and grows. He set intuition over against reason, and held that only intuition perceives the life force which the material world resists. He hailed religion as an aid to man's progress.

**BERITH** *covenant* Concept important in JUDAISM and Scripture. God entered into covenant with Noah, Abraham, and Moses. Christians find a final covenant of salvation, superseding the old covenant of law, in Christ.

**BERITH HACHDOSO** See BRIT HACHDOSO.

**BERITH MILAH** See BRIT MILAH.

**BERKELEIANISM** Subjective idealism: the theory propounded by George BERKELEY that the only knowledge of which we can be sure is that of our own ideas.

**BERKELEY, GEORGE (1685–1753)** Irish bishop and philosopher. At 43 he went to Rhode Island in the interest of converting American Indians. Developing the theory of subjective idealism, Berkeley tried to refute atheism and held that people perceive only qualities, not things. All data, he said, are signs from God; nothing exists apart from our perception, and all things are perceived in the mind of God, who is the center of the universe.

**BERNADETTE, ST. (1844–1879)** French girl, originally Marie Bernarde Soubirous, who claimed to have seen the Virgin Mary 18 times near her home in Lourdes. Criticized and abused, she finally joined the Sisters of Notre Dame and died in their convent at Nevers. She was canonized in 1933. Her feast day is April 16 (February 18 in France).

**BERNANOS, GEORGES (1888–1948)** French CATHOLIC author whose novels mirror his concern with materialism and his mysticism and faith in the ROMAN CATHOLIC CHURCH.

**BERNARD, JOHN HENRY (1860–1927)** Archbishop of Dublin, Ireland, who prepared an anthology of Irish hymns and a commentary on the pastoral Epistles; he strove for the unity of Ireland.

**BERNARDINES** The Reformed Congregation of St. Bernard; the Italian division of the Feuillants, reformed CISTERCIANS.

**BERNARDIN OF SIENA (1380–1444)** Popular Franciscan preacher of Italy who aroused devotion to the name of Jesus and helped bring about a religious revival. He was an early member of the OBSERVANTS, a reform group within the FRANCISCANS.

**BERNARD OF CLAIRVAUX, ST. (c.1090–1153)** French mystic, abbot of a CISTERCIAN monastery at Clairvaux, who has been called "most powerful churchman of twelfth-century Europe." He was counselor to kings and popes, preacher of the Second CRUSADE, and agent of the condemnation of ABELARD and ARNOLD OF BRESCIA. A man of holy reputation and an eloquent tongue, he was tireless in good works and brought about new devotion to Jesus and Mary in his church. He wrote many religious treatises and hymns, including "O Sacred Head Now Wounded." He was canonized in 1174. His feast day is August 20.

**BERNARD OF CLUNY (twelfth century)** French monk of Cluny, once famous for his sermons and writings, who wrote a long poem "On Contempt of the World" which is the source of many hymns, including "Jerusalem the Golden." Also known as Bernard of Morlaix.

**BERNARD OF MENTHON (?–c.1081)** Italian ecclesiastic who founded the hospices of St. Bernard in the Alps.

**BERNARD OF MORLAIX** See BERNARD OF CLUNY.

**BERNARD OF TOURS (twelfth century)** Medieval scholar who interpreted Genesis along Christian Platonist lines.

**BERNAYS, JAKOB (1824–1881)** German Jewish philologist who taught at the Jewish Theological Seminary at Breslau and wrote a number of books about Greek philosophers.

**BERNE, THESES OF** Ten statements of faith, drawn up by two Swiss pastors and revised by ZWINGLI, which led to the REFORMATION in Switzerland.

**BERNICE** Sister of Herod Agrippa II and mistress of Titus before whom Paul preached at Caesarea. She declared Paul worthy of death (ACTS 25; 26).

**BERNWARD or BERWARD, ST.** (?–1022) German bishop who promoted ecclesiastical craftsmanship. He was canonized in 1193. His feast day is November 20.

**BEROSSUS (third century B.C.)** Babylonian priest of BEL who translated a work on astrology and astronomy into Greek and wrote down accounts of the Flood and other ancient events. Only fragments of his *History of Babylonia* are still extant.

**BEROUTH** Phoenician god who fathered heaven and earth.

**BERSERK** Reckless fighter in Scandinavian myth.

**BERTHOLD OF REGENSBURG (c.1220–1272)** FRANCISCAN monk and powerful preacher who has been called "the Chrysostom of the Middle Ages." He made missionary journeys throughout a large part of Europe and denounced the preachers who sold indulgences.

**BERTINORO, OBADIAH (fifteenth century)** Jewish rabbi and commentator on the MISHNAH who aided the Jews in Palestine.

**BERTOLD VON REGENSBURG** See BERTHOLD OF REGENSBURG.

**BERULLE, PIERRE DE (1575–1629)** French cardinal who founded the Congregation of the French Oratory and wrote *The Majesty of Jesus*. He also established the reformed CARMELITES in France. URBAN VIII called him "Apostle of the Incarnate Word."

**BERWARD** See BERNWARD, ST.

**BERYL** Very hard gem, transparent or of various colors, used in the breastplate of the high priest (EXODUS 28:20) and in the foundations of the new Jerusalem (REVELATION 21:20).

**BES** Egyptian god of pleasure, recreation, and music, represented as a grotesque dwarf. He protected children and drove away evil spirits.

**BESAMIM** Spices used at the Jewish service of HAVDALAH.

**BESANT, ANNIE (1847–1933)** Leading THEOSOPHIST who founded the Central Hindu College in Benares, India, and was president of the Theosophical Society. She wrote many books and believed that Jiddu Krishnamurti was the new Messiah.

**BESSARION (c.1395–1472)** Greek scholar and CATHOLIC cardinal who spent much of his life in Italy, later becoming patriarch of Constantinople. He patronized scholars and promoted learning, bringing NEOPLATONISM into Italy.

**BESTIARY** Popular medieval book describing many real and imaginary animals, and drawing "morals" from them theoretically applicable to human conduct.

**BETA** Second letter in the Greek alphabet.

**BET AM** *house of the people* Jewish term for synagogue.

**BET DIN** *house of judgment* Jewish court.

**BETH** Second letter in the Hebrew alphabet, meaning "house." The word *beth* is incorporated into many Biblical and Jewish names.

**BETHABARA** *house of the ford* Point on the east bank of the Jordan River near the Dead Sea where John the Baptist baptized (JOHN 1:28).

**BET HA-KNESSET** *house of meeting* Synagogue.

**BET HA-MIDRASH** *house of study* Jewish term for the synagogue as a center of learning, or for a sort of Jewish high school where the MIDRASH is taught.

**BETHANY** *house of figs* Village at the foot of the Mount of Olives, two miles from Jerusalem, where Mary, Martha, and Lazarus lived. Here many outstanding events in the life of Jesus occurred (MATTHEW 21:17; 26:6; MARK 11:1, 11; JOHN 11; 12:1–3).

**BETHEL** *house of God* Village 11 miles north of Jerusalem where Abraham built an altar and Jacob dreamed of angels. In later times it became a center of heathen worship.

**BETHEL BAPTIST ASSEMBLY** Association of Baptist ministers in midwestern United States.

**BETHESDA** *house of grace* Pool in Jerusalem where Jesus told an invalid of 38 years to take up his bed and walk (JOHN 5:2 ff.). It may be the pool beneath the Church of St. Anne.

**BETHLEHEM** *house of bread* Town close to Jerusalem where Benjamin, David, and Jesus were born. Here CONSTANTINE erected a church in whose court St. JEROME lived for thirty years. One of the chief activities in Bethlehem today is the manufacture and sale of religious mementoes.

**BETHLEHEMITES** 1. Thirteenth-century

English friars with a garb like that of the Dominicans. 2. Knights and Hospitalers of the Blessed Mary. 3. Bethlehemite Order of Guatemala, a nursing order active in South America through the seventeenth, eighteenth, and early nineteenth centuries.

**BETH-PEOR**   Town on or near Mt. Nebo where the Canaanite god Baal Peor was worshiped (DEUTERONOMY 3:29).

**BETHPHAGE** *house of unripe figs*   Village near the Mount of Olives where Jesus' disciples found the ass for the Triumphal Entry (MATTHEW 21:1–11).

**BETHSABEE**   See BATH-SHEBA.

**BETHSAIDA** *house of fishermen*   Town on the Sea of Galilee where Philip, Andrew, and Peter were born, and where many things happened in the life of Christ (MATTHEW 11:21; JOHN 12:21).

**BETH-SHAN**   Town in the Valley of Jezreel where Saul and his sons were killed in battle. It is a richly rewarding archaeological site.

**BETH-SHEMETH**   See HELIOPOLIS.

**BETROTHAL**   Promise to marry a certain person, sometimes accompanied by religious ceremonies, and often, as in marriage, considered by the church to have far-reaching ethical and spiritual implications.

**BEULAH** *married*   Name given Palestine or Israel to mean married to the Lord and enjoying His favor (ISAIAH 62:4).

**BEVERLEY MINSTER**   English church whose centuries-old building is an outstanding example of Gothic architecture.

**BEWER, JULIUS A. (1877–1953)**   German-born CONGREGATIONALIST Old Testament scholar who taught in the United States at Oberlin College, Columbia University, and Union Theological Seminary, and was a "liberal evangelical" critic of Scripture.

**BEYSCHLAG, WILLIBALD (1823–1900)**   German EVANGELICAL theologian of the mediating school who disagreed with both the Chalcedonian Christology and the rationalism of such men as RENAN. One of his strongest desires was for the unity of the church.

**BEZA, THEODORE (1519–1605)**   French theologian who defended John Calvin's burning of SERVETUS and was known as spokesman for the REFORMED churches of France. He also helped prepare Greek and Latin versions of the New Testament,

wrote a biography of CALVIN, and succeeded him as head of the Genevan government.

**BEZALEEL** *in the shadow of God*   1. Craftsman and artist who designed the tabernacle for Jewish worship in the wilderness (EXODUS 31:1–5). 2. Hebrew who married a Gentile wife (EZRA 10:30).

**B.F.B.S.**   Abbreviation for BRITISH AND FOREIGN BIBLE SOCIETY.

**BHADRA VIRA**   Vedic name for SIVA.

**BHAGA**   Vedic guardian of a month of the year.

**BHAGAVAD-GITA** *song of the Master*   Popular HINDU devotional book, in the form of a dialogue between Arjuna and KRISHNA, setting forth ideas about immortality and salvation. The latter is viewed as achieved through selfless duty, knowledge of the supreme God, and faith in a personal god such as Krishna.

**BHAGAVAT** *the Master or the blessed Lord*   HINDU term in a prayer to VISHNU.

**BHAKTA**   Hindu who places emphasis on BHAKTI-MARGA rather than on some other way of salvation. Bhaktas have unmarried ascetic priests.

**BHAKTAMALA**   Bhakta textbook.

**BHAKTI** *attachment to an ideal*   BUDDHIST term for attachment to and love for a deity.

**BHAKTI-MARGA**   HINDU term for the way of salvation through love for or trust in a personal god such as KRISHNA.

**BHAKTI-YOGA**   HINDU term for salvation, similar to BHAKTI-MARGA.

**BHAIRAVA** *the terrible one*   Name of the Hindu god SIVA.

**BHAIRAVI**   Siva's wife, sometimes called DEVI.

**BHAVANI**   Form of Parvati, wife of HINDU god Siva, adorned with corpses and skeletons.

**BHIKKU or BHIKSHU**   Ascetic disciple of BUDDHA who keeps the 10 Precepts and 227 Rules of his religion.

**BHIMA**   Gigantic prince in HINDU myth.

**B-IAME**   Supreme deity in primitive Australian religion.

**BIARD, PIERRE (c.1567–1622)**   French Catholic Jesuit teacher of theology who became a missionary to Acadia in Nova Scotia and what is now Bar Harbor, Maine.

**BIBAGO, ABRAHAM (?–1489)**   Spanish Hebrew philosopher and commentator.

**BIBLE** *books*   Name of Christianity's sacred Scriptures, composed of the books of the Old and New Testaments, beginning with Genesis and ending with Revelation. There have been many versions and translations of the Bible.

**BIBLE BELT**  Rather derisive term for the southern United States where the Bible is emphasized and often interpreted very literally.

**BIBLE BIGOTS or BIBLE MOTHS**  Name given the students who gathered around John and Charles WESLEY, for Bible reading and prayer, at Oxford University about 1729.

**BIBLE CHRISTIANS**  Group founded by the Methodist lay preacher, William O'Bryan or Bryant, in 1815 in Devonshire, England. Sometimes called Bryanites, they merged with the United Methodist Church in 1907.

**BIBLE COMMUNISM**  Term for the kind of communal life practiced in the ONEIDA COMMUNITY (New York) under the direction of the community's founder, John Humphrey NOYES.

**BIBLE LANDS**  Countries prominent in the Bible: Palestine, Egypt, Arabia, Syria, Turkey, Greece, Assyria, and Babylonia.

**BIBLE MOTHS**  See BIBLE BIGOTS.

**BIBLE PRESBYTERIAN CHURCH**  Denomination in the United States which withdrew from the Orthodox Presbyterian Church in 1936 under Carl McIntyre, emphasizing FUNDAMENTALISM and PREMILLENNIALISM.

**BIBLE PROTESTANT CHURCH**  American denomination which withdrew from the Methodist Protestant Church in 1939 and emphasizes FUNDAMENTALIST beliefs.

**BIBLE SCHOOL**  A school, particularly in the United States, which specializes in teaching the English Bible and in training pastors and missionaries.

**BIBLE SOCIETY**  Organization for translating and disseminating the Bible. Two of the earliest Bible Societies were formed in New England in 1649 and in Germany in 1710. Four large organizations of this kind today are the AMERICAN BIBLE SOCIETY, the BRITISH AND FOREIGN BIBLE SOCIETY, the National Bible Society of Scotland, and the Netherlands Bible Society. These distribute 17 million volumes of Scripture a year, and other societies distribute 8 million more.

**BIBLIANDER, THEODOR**  (c.1504–1564) Swiss theologian who followed Ulrich ZWINGLI at Zurich University as professor of theology and Biblical literature. Somewhat humanistic, he was dismissed in 1560 for opposing CALVINISM.

**BIBLICAL ARCHAEOLOGY**  Study of human artifacts in the lands of the Bible—Palestine, Egypt, Syria, etc. This modern science has shown the historical accuracy of many Old Testament data.

**BIBLICAL COMMISSION**  Committee of cardinals appointed in 1902 by Pope LEO XIII to publish Biblical studies, safeguard the authority of Scripture, decide points of critical dispute, and defend CATHOLIC exegesis.

**BIBLICAL CRITICISM**  Science or art of studying the text, authorship, date, and meaning of various parts of the Bible. Lower criticism deals primarily with the text while higher criticism concerns itself with questions of authorship and the like.

**BIBLICAL INTRODUCTION**  Formally, the historical and literary study and criticism of the Bible.

**BIBLICAL THEOLOGY**  The study of God on the basis of the teachings of Scripture rather than on a priori theological or philosophical considerations.

**BIBLICISM**  Term for strict adherence to the literal interpretation of the Bible.

**BIBLIOLATRY**  Worship of a book, particularly of the Bible.

**BIBLIOMANCY**  Finding guidance by opening a book—especially the Bible—at random and taking one's directions from the words that first meet the eye.

**BIBLION**  Greek term for a scroll long enough to contain one of the Gospels or a similar amount of material. From the plural, *biblia*, "books," our word for Bible is derived.

**BICKERSTETH, EDWARD (1786–1850)**  English rector and secretary of the CHURCH MISSIONARY SOCIETY who wrote and compiled a number of hymns.

**BICKERTONITES**  See CHURCH OF JESUS CHRIST.

**BIDDING PRAYER**  1. Among LUTHERANS, a prayer in which the people are bidden to pray for certain specific things. 2. In ANGLICAN churches, prayer before the sermon, or the exhortation to pray for certain causes. 3. In medieval churches, a list of causes or persons for which the people were bidden to pray.

**BIDDLE, JOHN (1615–1662)** English teacher and theologian who founded English UNITARIANISM. For his denial of the TRINITY he was imprisoned a number of times. He died of fever while in prison.

**BIEDERMANN, ALOIS EMMANUEL (1819–1885)** Swiss professor of theology who took Hegel's monism as the basis of his belief. For him God is spiritual but not personal.

**BIEL, GABRIEL (c.1420–1495)** German churchman and professor of theology who systematized the nominalistic theology of WILLIAM OF OCCAM and was one of the great SCHOLASTIC philosophers. His writings introduced Martin LUTHER to theology.

**BIELBOG** Good white god of ancient central European religion.

**BIERMANN, GOTTLIEB PETER (1758–1844)** German artist whose masterpiece "The Ascension" is well known.

**BIFROST** Ancient Norse name for the rainbow which bridged heaven and earth. It was guarded by HEIMDALLR, the god of light.

**BIGAMY** 1. Marriage to two mates at the same time, condemned by many religions. 2. Term in canon law for marriage after the death of the first wife, considered to mar the marriage symbolism of Christ and the church.

**BIGG, CHARLES (1840–1908)** English rector and professor of church history.

**BIGOT** Person intolerant of other—particularly religious—ideas. Originally a bigot was a religious hypocrite.

**BIHARI-LAL (seventeenth century)** Writer of India, about whom little is known; he composed the popular and amorous verses of the Hindi *Sat-sai*, which has been translated into Sanskrit twice.

**BIKKU or BIKSHU** Elementary grade of BUDDHIST discipleship.

**BIKKUR CHOLIM *visiting the ill*** Jewish term for self-giving care of others as enjoined by the TORAH.

**BIKOL** Malayan Christian of Luzon or a nearby island.

**BIKSHU** See BIKKU.

**BIL** Norse goddess, possibly also a heavenly body that followed the moon sometime in the past.

**BILBUL** Hebrew term for confusion or anarchy.

**BILDAD** One of the three men who sought to comfort Job in his afflictions (JOB 2:11; 8; 18).

**BILE** Celtic name for the lord of hell and death.

**BILGRAMI, SAYYID HUSAIN (1843–1926)** Indian politician who did much for ISLAM in India.

**BILLING, EINAR MAGNUS (1871–1939)** Swedish bishop and professor of theology who contributed to religious education and religious freedom.

**BILNEY, THOMAS (c.1495–1531)** English preacher whose study of the New Testament led to his questioning of the worship and mediation of the saints. Influencing such men as Hugh LATIMER and Matthew PARKER, he was charged with LOLLARDISM, arrested, and burned at the stake. Since he proved orthodox on many points of Catholicism, Bishop Richard Nix who caused his arrest was later condemned for his handling of the matter.

**BILOCATION** Belief that a being may be in more than one place at once. Anthony of Padua and other saints are held to have accomplished this. The doctrine is sometimes cited in connection with the real presence of Christ's body and blood wherever the EUCHARIST is celebrated.

**BIMAH or BEMA** Synagogue lectern.

**BIMBO-GAMI** Japanese god of the poor and poverty.

**BIMELER, JOSEPH MICHAEL (1778–1853)** German separatist who helped the disciples of Barbara Grubermann found the communal religious settlement of Zoar, in Ohio. He has been called a religious genius.

**BINATION** Conducting mass twice on the same day. Although bination (or duplication) is legally restricted except with special permission, for all practical purposes it is permissible whenever necessary.

**BINCHOIS, GILLES DE (c.1400–1460)** Flemish composer of masses and other ecclesiastical music.

**BINDING AND LOOSING** "Power of the keys" referred to in Matthew 16:19 and 18:18. Christ's representatives are given the power to exercise ecclesiastical and spiritual discipline.

**BINGHAM, HIRAM (1789–1869)** CONGRE-

GATIONALIST clergyman from New England who founded the first PROTESTANT mission in Hawaii.

**BINGHAM, HIRAM (1831–1908)** Hiram Bingham's son, also a CONGREGATIONALIST missionary. He established a Christian mission in the Gilbert Islands, translated the Bible into the natives' language, and prepared other aids to worship.

**BINGHAM, JOSEPH (1668–1723)** English clergyman and theologian who favored lay baptism and prepared a ten-volume work on Christian antiquities, *Origines Ecclesiasticae.*

**BINNEY, THOMAS (1798–1874)** English CONGREGATIONALIST ecclesiastic and popular preacher who furthered church psalmody and wrote devotional poems and hymns.

**BINZUKU** Japanese BUDDHIST who was deified after healing the sick with apparently miraculous power.

**BIOGENESIS** Theory that life can come only from life, originating in opposition to the theory of the spontaneous generation of life.

**BION (third century B.C.)** Greek philosopher and moralist who satirized religion, the gods, and astrology. (Not to be confused with the bucolic poet Bion of the second century B.C.)

**BIOSOPHY** Religious system of education originated by Frederick KETTNER.

**BIRAN, MAINE DE (1766–1824)** French psychologist and philosopher who saw religion as primarily feeling.

**BIRD** Religious symbol of the soul or spirituality.

**BIRETTA** Square cap with several ridges worn by CATHOLIC and ANGLICAN clergy: black for priests, purple for bishops, and red for Roman Catholic cardinals.

**BIRGITTA** See BRIDGET OF SWEDEN, ST.

**BIRKAT HA-MAZON** Jewish term for prayer at mealtime.

**BIRTHRIGHT** In the Bible, the rights of the first-born male child. Esau sold his birthright to his brother Jacob for a dish of lentils (GENESIS 25:34).

**BIRTHRIGHT CHURCH MEMBERSHIP** In late seventeenth-century New England, church membership for children of believers, based on the HALF-WAY COVENANT.

**BISHAMON** Japanese god of war and luck.

**BISHOP** The New Testament bishop was the *episkopos* or overseer who superintended a church; in some cases the bishop seems to have been synonymous with apostle or elder. Through the generations the bishop's power grew until it became one of the highest offices in the church. The powers and duties of the bishop vary in different churches.

**BISHOP COADJUTOR** Assistant to the bishop in a diocese.

**BISHOP HILL** Village in Illinois founded by Swedish immigrants on the basis of religious communism. The original community went out of existence after the murder of its leader, Eric Janson, in 1850.

**BISHOP-IN-ORDINARY** Residential or diocesan bishop.

**BISHOP IN PARTIBUS** A bishop who has no actual diocese but who has been named bishop of a city far away "in partibus infidelium" (in heathen parts) for nominal superintendence.

**BISHOP OF THE JEWS** In medieval Europe, the name of a converted Jew.

**BISHOPRIC** A bishop's office or diocese.

**BISHOPS' BIBLE** Official English version of the Bible from 1568 to 1611, when the Authorized Version replaced it (see KING JAMES VERSION). Many of the translators were bishops of the Church of England.

**BISHOPS' BOOK** Book explaining the Ten Commandments, the Lord's Prayer, the Ave Maria, and the like, compiled by English ecclesiastics in 1537.

**BISHOP SUFFRAGAN** A bishop whose office is similar to that of BISHOP COADJUTOR.

**BISHOPS' WARS** Two short wars in 1639 and 1640 between Charles I and the Scots. The latter wanted to do away with the episcopal system while the king tried to impose on them the BOOK OF COMMON PRAYER of England and other ANGLICAN observances. The wars led to the loss of Charles' throne and head.

**BISMILLAH** *in the name of God* Arabic expression enjoined upon MOSLEMS for use on important occasions.

**BITH AND BIRREN** Celtic Adam and Eve.

**BITHYNIA** Province near the Black Sea to whose Christian residents the First Epistle of Peter is addressed (1:1). The Councils of Nicaea and Chalcedon were held in Bithynia.

**BLACK** Religious symbol of mourning, death, sin, sickness, and evil. Used at funerals and on Good Friday and All Souls' Day.

**BLACK, HUGH (1868–1953)** Scottish pastor who became professor of practical theology at Union Theological Seminary, New York, and wrote several books.

**BLACK ART or BLACK MAGIC** Magic attributed to intercourse with the devil or evil spirits.

**BLACK BOOK** One of the two sacred books of the Yezidis ("Worshipers of God") of Kurdistan, whose religion seems a mixture of many elements.

**BLACK BOOKS** Term for Bibles, missals, etc. sold in religious book stores. Such books, usually bound in black, are distinguished from other religious books in this way.

**BLACK CANONS** Medieval name for the Augustinian Order of Canons Regular of England.

**BLACK DEATH** Violent fourteenth-century plague which killed nearly half the population of some European countries and changed the social and ecclesiastical structure for many years. Thereafter, many improperly trained priests took orders, the working classes began to rise, and large church properties began to be confiscated.

**BLACK FAST** Very austere type of fasting practiced in the medieval period in LENT and before ordination.

**BLACK FATHERS** A name for the Fathers of the Holy Ghost and the Immaculate Heart of Mary.

**BLACK FRIARS** English DOMINICAN monks, who wear black.

**BLACK JEWS** In India, term applied to brown-skinned Jews to distinguish them from a group known as "White Jews." Sometimes used also for Negro Jewish groups. See CHURCH OF GOD AND SAINTS OF CHRIST.

**BLACK LETTER DAYS** Minor holy days in the ecclesiastical calendar, printed there in black in contrast to the major days which are printed in red.

**BLACK MAGIC** See BLACK ART.

**BLACK MASS** 1. Anti-Christian parody of mass involving worship of Satan. 2. ROMAN CATHOLIC requiem mass at which black vestments garb the officiants.

**BLACK MONASTERY** AUGUSTINIAN monastery in Wittenberg, Germany, in which the monks wore black. Martin LUTHER had a cell there.

**BLACK MONKS** Benedictine monks of medieval England.

**BLACK MUSLIMS** Negro religious group in the United States similar in some respects to ISLAM. It advocates a type of reverse segregation, aiming at "our own Black State," and appears to be more social and political than religious.

**BLACK POPE** Name sometimes given the Jesuits' superior general, because of the black garb of members of the SOCIETY OF JESUS.

**BLACK RUBRIC** Statement inserted into King Edward's Second Prayer Book in England about 1552, explaining that kneeling at COMMUNION did not imply belief in TRANSUBSTANTIATION. This "Declaration on Kneeling" was printed in black.

**BLACK SISTERS** Alexian nuns.

**BLACK STONE** The Moslems' sacred stone, housed in the "KAABA" at Mecca, believed given to Abraham by the angel Gabriel.

**BLACK SUNDAY** Term for PASSION SUNDAY, the second before Easter.

**BLACKWELL, ANTOINETTE (1825–1921)** First ordained woman minister in the United States; originally CONGREGATIONAL, she became a UNITARIAN. She advocated women's rights and the abolition of Negro slavery.

**BLAESILLA (fourth century)** Female acquaintance of St. JEROME at whose request he wrote a commentary on Ecclesiastes.

**BLAIR, JAMES (1656–1743)** Scottish-born missionary to Virginia from the CHURCH OF ENGLAND; he founded the College of William and Mary.

**BLAISE, ST. (?–c.316)** Armenian bishop said to have been martyred under Licinius. He is invoked to cure sore throats and cattle diseases; his feast day is February 3 (February 11 in the East).

**BLAKE, WILLIAM (1757–1827)** English visionary, poet, and painter of mystical scenes. Various religions influenced his reaction against the strict rationalism of his era. He wrote *Songs of Innocence, The Marriage of Heaven and Hell, Jerusalem,* and much else. Religious symbolism filled his poetry, engravings, and water colors.

**BLASPHEMY** Speaking or writing anything insulting God. Blasphemy brought the death penalty in ancient JUDAISM (LEVITICUS 24:16). In some religions blasphemy includes speaking against saints or sacred figures. In the West it is an ecclesiastical and civil offense.

**BLAVATSKY, HELENA PETROVNA (1831–1891)** Russian cofounder, with H. S. Alcott, of the Theosophical Society (see THEOSOPHY). It has been said that she visited Tibet and performed miracles. Her disciples observe May 8 as White Lotus Day in memory of her death on that day in 1891. She wrote *Isis Unveiled* and other works.

**BLESS** To bless is to praise God, to pray for another, to consecrate, to wish one well, or to convey God's favor. Christ often blessed people. Since the Middle Ages, Christian worship has often concluded with a blessing by the presiding official.

**BLESSED** CATHOLIC term for a person who has been beatified or pronounced blessed.

**BLESSED LITTLE SIMON OF TRENT** See SIMON OF TRENT, BLESSED LITTLE.

**BLESSED SACRAMENT** EUCHARIST or communion.

**BLESSING OF THE NEW MOON** Synagogue prayers on the SABBATH preceding or upon the first rising of the new moon.

**BLICKLING HOMILIES** Sermons and homilies from the time of Aelfred and Aelfric, the manuscript of which is at Blickling Hall in Norfolk, England.

**BLINDNESS** Symbol of spiritual lack of perception.

**BLISS** Highest possible happiness.

**BLISS, DANIEL (1823–1916)** American missionary to Syria who founded what is now the American University there.

**BLISS, P. P. (1838–1876)** American gospel singer and song writer who led the singing at the D. L. Moody revivals. He wrote "Jesus Loves Me" and "Hold the Fort."

**BLOMFIELD, CHARLES J. (1786–1857)** Genial bishop of the CHURCH OF ENGLAND who sought church reform and balance. He consecrated 200 new churches during his tenure.

**BLONDEL, MAURICE (1861–1949)** French CATHOLIC philosopher who followed PLATO and AUGUSTINE in their philosophical approach to God. He based the argument for God on volition, and saw Him as "first principle and last term." He believed that intellection leads to the BEATIFIC VISION.

**BLOOD** Religious symbol of life, sacrifice, martyrdom, and redemption. Ancient religions often utilized blood sacrifices; the Old Testament declares that "without the shedding of blood is no remission of sin." The blood of Christ atones for the sin of man (I JOHN 1:7; LUKE 22:20; HEBREWS 9:11–14).

**BLOOMGARDEN, SOLOMON (1870–1927)** American Jewish writer who translated the Old Testament into Yiddish and with Charles Spivak compiled a Hebrew-Yiddish dictionary.

**BLUE** Symbol of truth and heaven. The Scottish Covenanters made blue their color in opposition to the royal red of the king, and thus blue became identified with PRESBYTERIANISM. In liturgical churches blue is the color for Advent, the pre-Lenten season, the Nativity of St. John Baptist, All Souls' Day, funerals, and requiems. In some countries blue is the special color of the Virgin Mary.

**BLUE LAWS** Laws radically restricting private conduct. The name comes from the blue paper on which the New Haven PURITAN community printed its laws governing dress, the Sabbath, and other matters. Fundamentalist attitudes have produced many so-called blue laws concerning the sale of tobacco and alcohol, the Sunday closing of businesses, birth control, etc.

**BLUE NUNS** Term for the Sisters of the Temple and other Catholic sisterhoods with blue in their garb.

**BLUMHARDT, CHRISTOPH (1842–1919)** Son of Johann Christoph BLUMHARDT who promoted social ideals, seeing in them fulfillment of New Testament Christianity.

**BLUMHARDT, JOHANN CHRISTOPH (1805–1880)** Swiss pastor in Germany who founded an institute for SPIRITUAL HEALING at Bad Boll and brought about a religious revival in his community.

**B'NAI AKIBA** Orthodox Jewish youth organization.

**B'NAI B'RITH *sons of the covenant*** Jewish service organization which interests itself in human rights, Jewish needs, intercultural relationships, and various social projects.

**BO**   God of war in Dahomey, West Africa.
**BOANERGES** *sons of thunder*   Name by which Jesus designated James and John (MARK 3:17), possibly because of their fiery dispositions as young men.
**BOAT**   1. Boat-shaped vessel for incense in some churches. 2. As a sea vessel, an ancient Christian symbol of salvation.
**BOAZ**   Wealthy Hebrew who married Ruth the Moabitess and became an ancestor of King David and of Jesus (RUTH 2:1; 4:21; LUKE 3:32).
**BOBECHE**   Receptacle around a candle to catch wax drippings.
**BOCOR**   VOODOO priest or sorcerer of Haiti, thought to be able to bottle up the soul of a dying person.
**BOCSKAY, STEPHEN (1557–1606)**   Hungarian prince who led a revolt in Transylvania against the attempts of Emperor Rudolf II to make Hungary exclusively Catholic. Through his efforts, the Peace of Vienna (1606) guaranteed religious rights in Hungary and Transylvania.
**BODH GAYA**   See BUDDH GAYA.
**BODHI**   BUDDHIST term for enlightenment.
**BODHIDHARMA (sixth century)**   BUDDHIST missionary from India to China, where he became the first Eastern patriarch. After meditating in silence for nine years in a temple at Lo-yang, Honan, he founded ZEN Buddhism.
**BODHISATTVA**   One destined for enlightenment and Buddhahood. He must pass through ten stages to accomplish this and may have to live many lives, practicing the six Perfections in the process.
**BODHNATH**   Temple in Nepal considered the most important BUDDHIST shrine outside the borders of India.
**BODY**   The physical dwelling of the immortal soul and spirit. Scripture speaks of the body as one's house or tent or outward garment. God made man's body of the dust of the earth; when He breathed upon him, man became a living soul (GENESIS 2).
**BOECE**   See BOETHIUS.
**BOEHLER, PETER (1712–1775)**   Moravian missionary from Germany to Georgia who founded the cities of Bethlehem and Nazareth in Pennsylvania. He became a bishop of the MORAVIAN CHURCH.
**BOEHM, MARTIN (1725–1812)**   American MENNONITE bishop who became a founder

and bishop of the CHURCH OF THE UNITED BRETHREN IN CHRIST (now the EVANGELICAL UNITED BRETHREN CHURCH).
**BOEHME, JAKOB (1575–1624)**   German shoemaker who became one of the most important and influential mystics in the history of religion. He saw God as both All and Nothing, the Abyss and Ground of all being and all opposites. He is sometimes termed a Christian theosophist. His followers, the Behmenites or Boehmenists, tended eventually to become Quakers. See FRIENDS, SOCIETY OF.
**BOEHMENISTS**   See BOEHME, JAKOB.
**BOETHIUS (c.475–525)**   Roman senator, philosopher, and NEOPLATONIST who wrote *The Consolation of Philosophy*, influential through the Middle Ages, which indicates how the soul finds the vision of God through philosophy.
**BOETHUSIANS**   Ancient Jewish sect similar to that of the SADUCEES, which questioned the continuance of life after death.
**BOG**   Slavonic word for God.
**BOGOMILS**   Heretical Christian group originating in the Balkans during the seventh, eighth, and ninth centuries. Their beliefs reflected GNOSTIC and MANICHAEAN elements; they rejected the sacraments and the miracles ascribed to Mary and the saints and images. The Bogomils were saved from Christian persecution in Bosnia through its conquest by the Turks.
**BOHEMIAN BRETHREN** or **MORAVIAN BRETHREN**   Czechoslovakian Christians banded together in the fifteenth century in the interests of simple, ascetic, pacifistic Christianity. Their spiritual descendants constitute the MORAVIAN CHURCH.
**BÖHM, DOMINIKUS (1880–1955)**   Influential German church architect.
**BOLLANDISTS**   Belgian Jesuit editors of the *Acta Sanctorum*, the lives of the saints, which they constantly revise. Their name derives from their seventeenth-century leader, John Bolland.
**BOLOGNA, CONCORDAT OF**   Agreement in 1516 between Pope LEO X and Francis I of France which gave the latter virtual control of the Catholic Church in France.
**BOMBERG, DANIEL (?–1549)**   Dutch Christian printer of the first complete edition of the TALMUD and of a rabbinical Bible.
**BON**   Ancient animistic religion of Tibet.

**BONA DEA** *good goddess* Ancient Roman fertility goddess and protectress of herds and crops, among whose worshipers wine and myrtle were forbidden. She was worshiped only by women; men were not permitted even to hear her name. She was also known as Fauna, Fatua, or Damia.

**BONALD, LOUIS (1754–1840)** French philosopher who founded "traditionalist" Catholic theology. He held that the first language came from God, and that from it may be deduced the existence of God and the infallible authority of the church.

**BONAR, HORATIUS (1808–1889)** Scottish PRESBYTERIAN minister whose independence led to the formation of the FREE CHURCH. A religious writer and editor, he published several hymnals and wrote such hymns as "What a Friend We Have in Jesus" and "I Heard the Voice of Jesus Say."

**BONAVENTURA** or **BONAVENTURE, ST. (1221–1274)** FRANCISCAN theologian, cardinal, and saint. Known as "the Seraphic Doctor," because of his religious zeal, he was nevertheless of a peaceful temperament; he harmonized the teachings of ARISTOTLE and AUGUSTINE, wrote mystical devotional guides, and found the chief end of man to be the contemplation of God, upon whom all things depend. He was canonized in 1482; his feast day is July 14.

**BONDAGE** Scriptural term for slavery, particularly to sin, from which the Christian finds freedom.

**BONHOEFFER, DIETRICH (1906–1945)** German Christian thinker and theologian hanged by the Nazis during World War II. Famous for his *Ethics* and *Cost of Discipleship*. He wrote: "When Christ calls a man, He bids him come and die."

**BONIFACE, ST. (c.675–754)** English-born "Apostle of Germany." A BENEDICTINE priest, he was sent by Pope Gregory II as a missionary to the pagan Germans beyond the Rhine. At Geismar he chopped down the sacred oak of Thor. He became Metropolitan of Germany and formed bishoprics and monasteries there. After reforming the Frankish church and becoming archbishop of Mainz he was martyred by savages in the Netherlands. His feast day is June 5.

**BONIFACE V (seventh century)** Pope (619–625) who decreed that churches are

places of sanctuary for hunted criminals; he worked to evangelize England.

**BONIFACE VIII (1235–1303)** Pope (1294–1303) who issued the bull *Unam Sanctam* to reestablish the supremacy of the papacy. He was a skillful canon lawyer but was often involved in conflicts with European countries and was imprisoned in 1303 by Philip of France. The people rescued him but he died within a month.

**BONIFACE IX (c.1345–1404)** Pope (1389–1404) during the GREAT SCHISM when Clement VII and Benedict XIII also claimed to be head of the Catholic Church. He brought about order in the papal states but was the object of much criticism.

**BONIFACE OF QUERFURT, ST. (?–1009)** German missionary, "Apostle of the Prussians," who preached the gospel among the peoples on the eastern coast of the Baltic. He was martyred by the pagans on the borders of Lithuania. Later canonized, he is remembered in a feast day on June 19. He was also known as Bruno of Querfurt.

**BONIFATIUS-VEREIN** Organization to protect CATHOLIC interests in Germany and support Catholics in Protestant areas there.

**BONN CONFERENCES** Conferences in Bonn, Germany, in 1874 and 1875 to promote reunion between OLD CATHOLICS and other groups holding to historical Christian systems of theology and organization.

**BONNER, EDMUND (c.1500–1569)** Bishop of London who superintended the printing of the GREAT BIBLE in Paris, served Cromwell, and opposed papal supremacy. Later, he opposed the rule of boyish King Edward VI and proclaimed the papal supremacy he had fought, causing 125 Protestants to be burned in his diocese.

**BONOSIANS** Followers of BONOSUS in France and Spain from the fifth to the seventh centuries. They may have been ARIANS.

**BONOSUS (fourth century)** Bishop of Naissus condemned for denying the perpetual virginity of the Virgin Mary.

**BONZE** BUDDHIST monk or priest in China and Japan.

**BOOK** Symbol of authorship or learning in religious art. A book may also symbolize the Bible, the Old Testament, the New Testament, or the teaching profession.

**BOOK OF COMMON DISCIPLINE** Sixteenth-century Scottish PRESBYTERIAN book of church organization.

**BOOK OF COMMON ORDER** Worship directory prepared by John KNOX in 1556 for the English Protestant congregations in Geneva, Switzerland.

**BOOK OF COMMON PRAYER** ANGLICAN service book produced under Edward VI in 1549. It has had a strong influence on Christian worship in all communions.

**BOOK OF CONCORD** The collective LUTHERAN confessions of faith, published in 1580 together with such creeds as the APOSTLES' and NICENE.

**BOOK OF DEER** Irish manuscript of the four GOSPELS written in Gaelic, dating from the ninth century.

**BOOK OF DOCTRINES AND COVENANTS** Volume written by Joseph SMITH concerning MORMON doctrines.

**BOOK OF HISTORY** CONFUCIAN work relating ancient history of China.

**BOOK OF JUBILEES** First-century B.C. apocryphal Jewish book which dates the events of Genesis and interprets their meaning, i.e., the history of the world from the Creation to the giving of the Law at Sinai. Also called Apocalypse of Moses.

**BOOK OF LIFE** 1. Jewish term for the heavenly record of the just. 2. New Testament term for the register of the redeemed.

**BOOK OF MORMON** Scriptures of the Latter-Day Saints (see CHURCH OF JESUS CHRIST OF LATTER-DAY SAINTS) written on golden tablets, discovered and translated by Joseph SMITH in the early nineteenth century. Mormons say the Book of Mormon "supports but does not supplant" the Bible.

**BOOK OF REMEMBRANCE** Memorial book, recording various gifts and donors, often kept in a church narthex or vestibule.

**BOOK OF SECRETS** Second-century collection of charms, prayers, etc. used by GNOSTIC Jews for such varied purposes as to become invisible, succeed in love, and win horse races.

**BOOK OF SPORTS** Definition of activities permitted on Sunday in Great Britain, issued by King James I but later withdrawn.

**BOOK OF THE DEAD** Sacred book of ancient Egyptian religion containing prayers, exorcisms, charms, and literature, for the guidance of those journeying through the regions of the dead.

**BOOK OF THE RIGHTEOUS** Twelfth-century Spanish work retelling Jewish history from Adam to Joshua.

**BOOKS, THE** Scriptures of Confucianism. There are four Books: *The Great Learning, The Golden Mean, The Analects,* and *The Works of Mencius.* The Four Books together with the FIVE CLASSICS are the written foundation of CONFUCIANISM.

**BOOS, MARTIN (1762–1825)** German pietist leader who preached "Christ for us and in us" and proclaimed the doctrines of JUSTIFICATION by faith. A ROMAN CATHOLIC priest and teacher, he was often criticized and imprisoned, but he produced a widespread revival of faith.

**BOOTH, BALLINGTON (1859–1940)** A son of William BOOTH, Commander of the SALVATION ARMY in Australia and the United States, and founder of the VOLUNTEERS OF AMERICA.

**BOOTH, CATHERINE MUMFORD (1829–1890)** English welfare worker and wife of William Booth who founded the SALVATION ARMY. She has been called "mother of the Salvation Army." Excommunicated with William from the Wesleyan Methodist Church, she helped her husband establish the Army and developed its "Female Ministry." She preached much and improved the welfare of women and children in England.

**BOOTH, EVANGELINE CORY (1865–1950)** Daughter of William BOOTH, she began preaching at 17, wrote many songs and books, and became general of the SALVATION ARMY.

**BOOTH, WILLIAM (1829–1912)** Wesleyan Methodist preacher in England who was excommunicated, became pastor of a dissident group called the Reformers, and established the East London Revival Society which became the SALVATION ARMY. At first much criticized, Booth lived to receive great honor for his pioneer work among the outcasts of the world.

**BOOTH, WILLIAM BRAMWELL (1856–1929)** Oldest son of William BOOTH and general of the SALVATION ARMY after his father's death. He opposed and stamped out the trade in young girls which was prevalent in his time.

**BOOTHS, FEAST OF, FEAST OF TABER-NACLES, or SUKKOTH** Jewish seven-day autumn festival in which leafy booths are erected commemorating the Jewish sojourn in the wilderness before the entrance into the Promised Land. The seven days prescribed in the Old Testament are followed by two more today, and the whole period is one of joy and thanksgiving (cf. LEVITICUS 23:42; NUMBERS 29:12–40).

**BORBORIANS or BORBORITES** Dualistic and libertine GNOSTICS of the second through the fifth centuries. They denied the resurrection and the last judgment.

**BOREAS** Greek personification of the north wind, one of the sons of EOS, goddess of the dawn.

**BORGIA, CESARE (c. 1475–1507)** Opportunistic Italian politician, illegitimate younger son of Pope Alexander VI, who put his own candidates in the College of Cardinals and tried to manipulate the papacy but succeeded only in strengthening it, and in bringing greater unity to the papal states.

**BORIS I (?–907)** Tsar of Bulgaria who was baptized into the EASTERN ORTHODOX CHURCH and brought that faith into Bulgaria, despite the attempts of Pope NICHOLAS I to make that country ROMAN CATHOLIC. In 889 Boris abdicated and entered a monastery. He is a saint of the Orthodox Church.

**BORMANUS** Ancient Celtic god.

**BORNEO, RELIGION IN** The Dayak natives of Borneo worship more than 300 gods and goddesses along with spirits of disease, souls of plants, and the peculiar earth-dwelling *antu*. They present gifts to good spirits and try to ward off the malevolence of evil ones. All their feasts appear to have religious aspects. Mediums seek to heal their diseases through finding the wandering souls of the sick ones.

**BORNHOLMERS or BORNHOLMIANS** Danish pietistic group who followed P. C. Trandberg in the late nineteenth century, emphasizing the new birth and the free grace of God. The group originated on the island of Bornholm. The name was also used of other revivalist groups in Denmark and Sweden.

**BORROMEO, CHARLES or CARL** See CHARLES BORROMEO.

**BORROW, GEORGE HENRY (1803–1881)** English writer and traveler in Europe, particularly among the gypsies. An agent of the BRITISH AND FOREIGN BIBLE SOCIETY, Borrow translated the Gospel of Luke and other English works into European languages.

**BORVO** Celtic god of hot springs.

**BO-SAN** Monk in a BUDDHIST temple.

**BOSANQUET, BERNARD (1848–1923)** English philosopher who sought to base the unity of the world on the Christian doctrine of the Holy Spirit. He believed that the Absolute is individual rather than personal, and that it is unworthy for a person to desire immortality for himself because the greatest values continue in the Absolute.

**BOSCH, HIERONYMUS (c. 1450–1516)** Dutch painter whose works were often bizarre and symbolic, representing religious and mythological themes. He painted "The Last Judgment," "The Mocking of Christ," "St. Jerome in the Desert," "The Temptation of St. Anthony," and many other scenes in his imponderable style.

**BOSCI** Fifth-century ascetics, also called "Grazers," who lived in the fields to get away from the world and civilization.

**BOSCO, JOHN** See JOHN BOSCO.

**BOSSUET, JACQUES BENIGNE (1627–1704)** French churchman and preacher who bitterly attacked FENELON, the QUIETISTS, the JESUITS, and the PROTESTANTS. A brilliant man, he seems to have fallen most open to criticism in his violent spirit of controversy.

**BOSTANAI BEN CHANINAI (602–660)** First Prince of the Captivity (Exilarch) of the Jews of Mesopotamia after the Arabs' Moslem conquest. Many legends have been told about him.

**BOSTON, THOMAS (1677–1732)** Scottish PRESBYTERIAN churchman and author of a number of books popular in his time. His *Marrow of Modern Divinity* held to a strict CALVINISM of special grace and limited atonement. The General Assembly of the Presbyterian Church of Scotland condemned the book in 1720.

**BOSTON COUNCIL** Congregational assembly in Boston in 1865 which resulted in a spurt in mission work in the United States.

**BOSTRÖM, CHRISTOFFER JAKOB (1797–1866)** Swedish idealist philosopher who felt that certain Christian doctrines falsely

-epresent God as less than pure Spirit. He held that the state exists only in God.

**BO TREE** Pipal or wild fig tree of India, sacred to Buddhists because the Buddha is believed to have attained enlightenment underneath one. A bo tree is still worshiped at Anuradhapura in Ceylon. It was planted in the third century B.C. from a slip from the tree made famous by Buddha at Buddh Gaya.

**BOTTICELLI, SANDRO (c.1444–1510)** Superb Italian painter whose works decorated a number of churches and many of whose paintings depicted mythological or Christian religious scenes. His patrons, the Medici, were represented among the figures in his "Adoration of the Magi."

**BOUDINOT, ELIAS (1740–1821)** American revolutionist who was first president of the Continental Congress and first president of the AMERICAN BIBLE SOCIETY, which he helped found. He was also a philanthropist to the Indians, who he believed might have been the ten lost tribes of Israel.

**BOURDALOUE, LOUIS (1632–1704)** Eloquent French JESUIT preacher whose sermons combined perceptive insight with the authority of his gentle saintliness. Voltaire praised his preaching.

**BOURGEOISIE** In the Middle Ages the bourgeois were the lower class while in more recent centuries in Europe the bourgeois have been the money-making middle class, supposed to be essentially uncultured and materialistic. Protestantism has been called a bourgeois religion.

**BOURIGNIANISM** Term for those who followed the teachings of Antoinette BOURIGNON in Scotland, France, and Holland in the seventeenth and eighteenth centuries. The PRESBYTERIAN CHURCH in Scotland denounced it as a heresy in 1701 and 1711.

**BOURIGNON, ANTOINETTE (1616–1680)** Dutch MYSTIC, at first a ROMAN CATHOLIC, who left a convent to attack religions of all kinds. She saw the spirit of the gospel as emotion rather than cult, doctrine, or good works, and denied the ATONEMENT and the necessity of Scripture.

**BOURNE, HUGH (1772–1852)** English Methodist preacher whose outdoor revivals led to his founding of the PRIMITIVE METHODISTS. He was a teetotaler.

**BOUSSET, JOHANN FRANZ WILHELM (1865–1920)** German professor of New Testament theology whose research has added to the knowledge of the early centuries of the church.

**BOUYAN** Slavonic paradise.

**BOW** 1. Religious symbol of power and war. 2. The rainbow is associated in the Old Testament with God's promise to NOAH, after the flood, that water would never again destroy the earth.

**BOWING** Ancient and widespread form of reverence. Christians usually bow in prayer; CATHOLICS and HIGH CHURCHMEN bow to the cross and at specified times in the service.

**BOWNE, BORDEN PARKER (1847–1910)** American philosopher, head of the department of philosophy at Boston University, who developed the philosophy of PERSONALISM or transcendental empiricism. A student of Christianity, he influenced theology and philosophy in a liberal direction, emphasizing personality and personal freedom.

**BOXER REBELLION** Anti-Western Chinese insurrection in 1899 and 1900 during which many foreigners and Christian missionaries were killed. It was ended by an international police force. An indemnity of $333 million was forced upon China, which was thus made poorer and more dependent than ever.

**BOXING DAY** Day after Christmas in Great Britain.

**BOY BISHOP** Boy elected in the Middle Ages to execute most of the duties of a bishop. The election took place during the festival of Holy Innocents, or, in England, at the feast of St. Nicholas, the children's patron. The boy bishop blessed the people and performed all the cathedral offices except mass.

**BOYLE, ROBERT (1627–1691)** British scientist and philosopher who held that the order, beauty, design, etc. in the universe reveal a wise Creator. He sought to harmonize science and Christianity.

**BOYLE LECTURES** Lectures founded by the will of Robert Boyle to prove the Christian religion true "against notorious infidels, viz. atheists, theists, pagans, Jews and Mohammedans." Eight lectures are delivered annually; Christian controversies are forbidden in them.

**BOYS' BRIGADE** Organization for Sunday-school boys founded in 1883 in Glasgow, Scotland. It sought to combine Bible study with drill parade, discipline, sports, first aid, education, and other objectives spiritual and physical. The movement was honored by several kings of England. An organization with the same name in the United States lays more stress on Bible study and conversion.

**BRABOURNE, THEOPHILUS (1590–c.1661)** English PURITAN who was imprisoned for advocating the keeping of Saturday rather than Sunday as the Christian Sabbath.

**BRACHIUM SAECULARE** *secular arm* Canon-law term for the power of the civil government to intervene in cases dealing with the church. This power was invoked in the Middle Ages when the ecclesiastical power turned heretics over to the state to be killed.

**BRADBURY, WILLIAM BATCHELDER (1816– 1868)** American musician who composed such hymns as "Just As I Am," "He Leadeth Me," and "Savior, Like a Shepherd Lead Us."

**BRADFORD, JOHN (c.1510–1555)** Popular English preacher who was chaplain to King Edward VI and burned for sedition under Queen Mary. He wrote *The Hurt of Hearing Mass* and other works, most of them of a devotional nature.

**BRADFORD, WILLIAM (1590–1657)** PILGRIM leader who governed Plymouth Colony with such ability that he was reelected 30 times. He was relatively tolerant of deviations from PURITANISM, and preserved friendship with the Indians.

**BRADLEY, FRANCIS HERBERT (1846–1924)** English philosopher who proclaimed objective idealism and held that God is finite and unsatisfying—necessarily—to religious seekers.

**BRADWARDINE, THOMAS (c.1290–1349)** Archbishop of Canterbury in England who attacked PELAGIANISM so enthusiastically that he formulated a rigid PREDESTINARIANISM. Known as "Doctor Profundus," he influenced WYCLIF and others.

**BRAFMAN, JACOB (1825–1879)** Jewish writer of fraudulent pamphlets revealing an alleged Jewish plot to conquer the world.

**BRAGI or BRAGE** Norse god of poetry and eloquence who welcomed heroes to Valhalla.

**BRAGI-CUP** Beverage drunk at feasts and funerals in honor of BRAGI.

**BRAHMA** 1. Creator-god in HINDUISM; with VISHNU and SIVA, one of its three supreme deities. A remote god, his popularity has declined in proportion to that of Vishnu and Siva, and he now has only one temple, near Ajmer, India. He is considered the Lord and Father of all things; from time to time he is reborn from a lotus. 2. In BUDDHISM, term for "godlike" or "sacred."

**BRAHMA AAMAJ** See BRAHMA SAMAJ.

**BRAHMA-CARIYA** BUDDHIST term for a chaste life or person.

**BRAHMA, DAY OF** See KALPA.

**BRAHMAN** 1. Priest caste in HINDUISM, highest of its four castes. 2. Term for power in Indian religions. 3. The power or soul of the universe. 4. Indian prayer or hymn.

**BRAHMANAS** Commentaries on the vedic texts of India. (See VEDAS.)

**BRAHMANASPATI** Vedic lord of prayer.

**BRAHMANISM** 1. Ancient pantheistic religion of India which followed the VEDIC RELIGION and preceded modern HINDUISM. Brahmanism began the trend toward monotheism and solidified the caste system of India. 2. Term for the more intellectual aspects of Hinduism.

**BRAHMAPUTRA** River of India whose headwaters are in Tibet and whose lower region is sacred to HINDUS.

**BRAHMA SAMAJ** Reformed, monotheistic form of Hinduism initiated in 1828 by RAM MOHAN ROY or Rammohun Roy. It opposes idolatry and emphasizes congregational worship and reform, including women's rights. With a tiny membership, its influence has been great.

**BRAHMA VIHARA** *holy state of mind* One of the four states of meditation in BUDDHISM.

**BRAINERD, DAVID (1718–1747)** American missionary to the Indians, sent by the Scottish Society for the Propagation of Christian Knowledge to the Indians of New York, New Jersey, and Pennsylvania. His selfless devotion and life of prayer inspired Henry MARTYN and other missionaries. He died of tuberculosis in his thirtieth year.

**BRAMBLE** In religious art, symbol of the purity of MARY.

**BRAMHALL, JOHN (1594–1663)** English

ecclesiastic who led the Church of Ireland to accept the Thirty-Nine ARTICLES of the Church of England.

**BRANCH THEORY** A theory of the church, growing out of the OXFORD MOVEMENT, that the Roman, Anglican, and Eastern churches are but three branches of the one Church of Christ, providing that each branch holds the apostolic faith and practices APOSTOLIC SUCCESSION.

**BRANT, JOSEPH (1742–1807)** "Thayendanegea," American Indian (Mohawk) war chief and Christian missionary. He translated the Gospel of Mark and the Book of Common Prayer into the Mohawk language, did mission work in upstate New York and upper Canada, and built the first Episcopal church in the Dominion.

**BRANT, SEBASTIAN (1457–1521)** German satirist and humanist whose allegorical *Ship of Fools* lashed the foibles of his time —including those of the church—and helped pave the way for the REFORMATION.

**BRAY, THOMAS (1656–1730)** English churchman who organized the Anglican Church in Maryland, helped found the Society for the Propagation of the Gospel, and founded the Society for Promoting Christian Knowledge. He sent missionaries and libraries to North America and was active in a number of projects with religious or philanthropic purposes.

**BRAZEN LAVER** Circular brass washbowl in the Jewish tabernacle and temple.

**BRAZEN SERPENT** Image of a brass snake erected by Moses during a plague of serpents in the wilderness. Whoever looked at the uplifted brazen serpent was saved (NUMBERS 21:9).

**BREAD** "Staff of life" among ancient peoples. As the Bread of Life, Jesus represented Himself as essential to real life. Friends broke bread together; this kind of brotherly fellowship is symbolized in the Christian EUCHARIST. In religious symbolism, bread represents life or providential care.

**BREAD BOX** Container for the wafer in the EUCHARIST.

**BREAD PLATE** Plate for distribution of bread or wafers in the EUCHARIST.

**BREAKING OF BREAD** Sharing food, particularly in the fellowship of the LORD'S SUPPER (LUKE 24:35; ACTS 2:42).

**BREAKSPEAR, NICHOLAS** English name of Pope ADRIAN IV.

**BREAST, STRIKING THE** Symbol of mourning among ancient Hebrews and modern HINDUS. In the CATHOLIC liturgy it indicates penitence.

**BREASTED, JAMES HENRY (1865–1935)** American archaeologist and orientalist who did important research at sites in Egypt and Mesopotamia. He was director of the Oriental Institute and president of the American Oriental Society.

**BREASTPLATE OF RIGHTEOUSNESS** Vestment worn over the EPHOD of the Jewish high priest. It contained twelve jewels symbolizing the twelve tribes of Israel.

**BREASTPLATE OF ST. PATRICK** Ancient Irish hymn calling on the angels, the prophets, the powers of heaven and earth, the Father, the Holy Spirit, and Christ for protection from evil.

**BREBEUF, JEAN DE, ST. (1593–1649)** French JESUIT missionary and martyr of North America. After evangelizing the Huron Indians of Quebec, he was tortured to death by the Iroquois Indians at the height of the war between the two groups. He was canonized in 1930; his feast day is September 26 or March 16.

**BRECK, JAMES LLOYD (1818–1876)** American EPISCOPAL churchman and missionary to the Chippewa Indians.

**BREDA, DECLARATION OF** Declaration of religious toleration announced by Charles II at Breda in the Netherlands in 1660.

**BREECHES BIBLE** Bible printed in Geneva in 1560 in which the "aprons" made for Adam and Eve were translated "breeches."

**BRENDAN, ST. (c.484–578)** Irish abbot of a BENEDICTINE monastery and saint whose feast day is May 16. A medieval tale recounts his marvelous adventures during a voyage across the Atlantic.

**BRENT, CHARLES H. (1862–1929)** Canadian-born ANGLICAN churchman, Chief of Chaplains of the American Expeditionary Force in Europe in World War I. An energetic fighter of trade in opium and narcotics, Bishop Brent was a leader in the ecumenical movement and president of WORLD CONFERENCE ON FAITH AND ORDER.

**BRENZ, JOHANN (1499–1570)** German priest who adopted Luther's views and advocated toleration of heretics.

**BRES, GUIDO DE (1522–1567)** Belgian

preacher, reformer, and author of the BEL-GIC CONFESSION. Holding Protestant theological views, he attempted to quell sedition in his country but was caught with the seditionists and hanged.

**BRETHREN** Name of various Christian groups. Although the New Testament Christians were called "brethren" (ACTS 28:15), the name was not prevalent until the Middle Ages, when various communities of brethren were formed. A number of present-day Brethren groups have grown out of eighteenth-century origins in Germany. These were often former LUTHERANS who accepted the Bible literally, emphasizing TRINE IMMERSION, JUSTIFICATION by faith, holiness of life, FAITH HEALING, FOOT WASHING, and pacifism. The Brethren were also called DUNKERS, Tunkers, and Dunkards.

**BRETHREN, PLYMOUTH** See PLYMOUTH BRETHREN.

**BRETHREN, RIVER** See RIVER BRETHREN.

**BRETHREN CHURCH (PROGRESSIVE DUNK-ERS)** Denomination founded in the United States in 1882, emphasizing TRINE IMMERSION, FOOT WASHING, and other typically Brethren doctrines.

**BRETHREN IN CHRIST** Branch of the RIVER BRETHREN which chose the name Brethren in Christ in 1862 in Pennsylvania. Governed by bishops, ministers, and deacons, the church has an annual conference and sponsors three colleges.

**BRETHREN OF THE COMMON LIFE** Communal organization of devout CATHOLICS founded in Holland by Gerard GROOTE and Florentius Radewyn about 1380. Taking vows of poverty, chastity, and obedience, the members sought to live the Gospel in the world. THOMAS À KEMPIS reflects the spirituality of the Brethren, whose order apparently died out in the seventeenth century. Thomas was a member of the Canons of Windesheim, a similar group originated by Radewyn.

**BRETHREN OF THE FREE SPIRIT** One or more mystical pantheistic sects of medieval Europe dating from the thirteenth century. See also AMALRICIANS, AMALRIC OF BENA.

**BREVIARY** Liturgical book containing services and prayers for the day's CANONICAL HOURS. Its use is obligatory for priests and members of certain religious communities. The breviary originated in the eleventh century.

**BREWSTER, WILLIAM (1567–1644)** PILGRIM leader who printed separatist tracts in Europe and led the Plymouth Colony from 1620 to 1629. He was a ruling elder, lay teacher and preacher, and able administrator.

**BRIDAL FAST** Jewish couples traditionally fast on their wedding day until the ceremony is complete.

**BRIDE** Symbolic term for the people of God in the intimacy of their relationship to the Lord, the divine Bridegroom.

**BRIDEGROOM OF THE TORAH and BRIDE-GROOM OF BERESHITH** Orthodox Jewish term for the two men who participate in the service of the Rejoicing of the Law, at the completion of the public reading of the Pentateuch.

**BRIDES OF THE GODS** Young women attached to HINDU temples.

**BRIDGET, ST. (c.453–c.523)** A patron saint and holy woman of Ireland who founded a church and monastery at Kildare. She was also a favorite saint of Scotland and England. She is famed for her generosity and justice. Her feast day is February 1.

**BRIDGET OF SWEDEN, ST. (c.1303–1373)** Swedish noblewoman who founded the Bridgettines, or Order of the Most Holy Saviour. She had visions and revelations from Jesus and Mary, and sought to reform the church. Her feast day is October 8. She is sometimes called Birgitta.

**BRIDGETTINES** Catholic order of Augustinian canonesses formed by St. BRIDGET OF SWEDEN about 1350. Members, in five countries, devote themselves to meditation, prayer, and literary pursuits.

**BRIDGMAN, ELIJAH C. (1801–1861)** First American PROTESTANT missionary to China. He translated the Bible into Chinese.

**BRIEF** Epistle from the pope signed by his secretary and less formal than a papal BULL. It is sealed with the pope's so-called Fisherman's Ring.

**BRIGANTA** Ancient British goddess.

**BRIGGS, CHARLES AUGUSTUS (1841–1913)** American theologian, Bible scholar, and professor at Union Theological Seminary. His views on the authority of Scripture and his advocacy of higher criticism led to his suspension from the PRESBYTERIAN ministry, after which he became a priest of the PROTESTANT EPISCOPAL CHURCH.

**BRIGHT, JOHN (1811–1889)** English QUAKER politician who fought capital punishment and war, advocated land reforms and church disestablishment in Ireland, and sought to reduce the size of the British Army.

**BRIGHTMAN, EDGAR S. (1884–1953)** American philosopher who held to empirical PERSONALISM. His God was finite, limited by the "Given."

**BRIGIT** Celtic goddess of Ireland who was deity of fire, fertility, medicine, poetry, and learning. She is thought to have been metamorphosed into St. Bridget.

**BRIGITTINES** See BRIDGETTINES.

**BRIHASPATI** VEDIC lord of prayer. Possessing a hundred wings, he inspires prayer and protects the faithful.

**BRILL, MATTYS (1550–1583)** Dutch painter who did frescoes in the Vatican for Pope GREGORY XIII.

**BRINDABAN** Town in India with a thousand shrines and temples. Many legends of KRISHNA involve Brindaban.

**BRINSERS** Popular name of the UNITED ZION CHURCH of the River Brethren. The name refers to the church's founder, Matthias Brinser.

**BRIT HACHDOSO or BERITH HACHDOSO** Hebrew term for the new covenant.

**BRITISH AND FOREIGN BIBLE SOCIETY** Largest and oldest Bible society, formed in 1804. An independent organization founded for the publication and distribution of the Scriptures, it has translated them into most of the known languages.

**BRITISH COUNCIL OF CHRISTIANS AND JEWS** Organization formed by Archbishop William TEMPLE in 1942 to (in his words) "resist intolerance and promote mutual understanding between Jews and Christians."

**BRITISH COUNCIL OF CHURCHES** Federation of various churches and interdenominational bodies of the British Isles for cooperative purposes. Its creedal basis is belief in Jesus Christ as God and Saviour; it accepts the doctrinal statement of the WORLD COUNCIL OF CHURCHES.

**BRITISH ISRAELISM or ANGLO-ISRAELISM** Religious movement based on the hypothesis that the British people are descendants of the ten lost tribes of Israel, and that the United States and the nations of the British Commonwealth fulfill prophecies concerning the Jews. Measurements of the Great Pyramid of Gizeh are sometimes cited to further this belief.

**BRITISH MADHA BODHI SOCIETY** BUDDHIST organization founded in 1926 in England.

**BRITISH MORALISTS** Anthony Ashley Cooper, William Paley, Joseph Butler, and other thinkers whose approach to ethics was independent of religion.

**BRIT MILAH or BERITH MILAH** Jewish term for the covenant of CIRCUMCISION begun by Abraham. Circumcision of Jewish males takes place on the eighth day after their birth.

**BRIZO** Greek goddess, worshiped in Delos, who delivered oracles in dreams and protected sailors and fishermen.

**BROAD CHURCH** Term for those in the CHURCH OF ENGLAND who interpret its creeds in a broad, liberal manner. They are theologically between High and Low Churchmen. At present the Broad Church position is at least partially modernist.

**BROADUS, JOHN A. (1827–1895)** SOUTHERN BAPTIST churchman, New Testament scholar, and homiletic expert.

**BROOKE, STOPFORD AUGUSTUS (1832–1916)** Learned preacher of the CHURCH OF ENGLAND who lost his faith in miracles and became a UNITARIAN clergyman.

**BROOKS, PHILLIPS (1835–1893)** American EPISCOPAL preacher and bishop who wrote the hymn "O Little Town of Bethlehem."

**BRORSON, HANS A. (1694–1764)** Danish bishop and writer of several outstanding Christmas hymns.

**BROTHER** 1. Christian term for another Christian. 2. CATHOLIC term for members of various orders or congregations.

**BROTHERHOOD** Fraternal unity based on spiritual ties.

**BROTHERHOOD BY THE RIVER** Early name of the BRETHREN IN CHRIST.

**BROTHERHOOD IN DAUPHIN** Term for RIVER BRETHREN who settled in Dauphin County, Pennsylvania.

**BROTHERHOOD MOVEMENT** English organization founded by John Blackham in 1875 as a Sunday Bible class for young men. Motto: "One is your Master, even Christ, and all ye are brethren."

**BROTHERHOOD OF MAN** Concept of human fraternity based on such insights as that of the prophet Malachi: "Have we not all one Father? Hath not one God created us?" (2:10).

**BROTHERHOOD OF ST. ANDREW** EPISCOPAL organization in the United States.

**BROTHERHOOD OF THE NEW LIFE** Communal religious group founded in New York State in the nineteenth century by the mystic Thomas Lake HARRIS.

**BROTHERHOOD OF THE POOR** See KHALSA.

**BROTHERHOOD WEEK** Week ending February 22, widely observed to promote understanding among differing groups, inaugurated by the NATIONAL CONFERENCE OF CHRISTIANS AND JEWS.

**BROTHER LAWRENCE (c.1605 – 1691)** French MYSTIC and CARMELITE lay brother, once a soldier, converted by meditating on a tree. In charge of the monastery kitchen, he gave much thought to spiritual communion with God and is known for the devotion indicated in the book *The Practice of the Presence of God*. His maxims and prayers were published after his death.

**BROTHERS, RICHARD (1757–1824)** British fanatic who announced himself as "nephew of the Almighty, and prince of the Hebrews, appointed to lead them to the land of Canaan." He planned to lead his followers to the New Jerusalem which was to be built on the Jordan River. He is thought by some to be an originator of BRITISH ISRAELISM, although this is denied by others.

**BROTHERS AND SISTERS OF THE FREE SPIRIT** Unpopular religious groups of the Middle Ages in Europe, emphasizing freedom from church control.

**BROTHERS HOSPITALERS** AUGUSTINIAN order of laymen founded in the sixth century in Spain by St. JOHN OF GOD. Members vow to serve those ill in hospitals for life; the order maintains more than a hundred hospitals.

**BROTHERS OF CHARITY** CATHOLIC order founded in the nineteenth century in Belgium to care for orphans and others in need.

**BROTHERS OF JESUS** James, Joses, Simon, and Judas (MATTHEW 13:55). In general

Protestants consider these four to have been children of Joseph and Mary while Catholics believe they were cousins of Jesus.

**BROTHERS OF THE COMMON LIFE** See BRETHREN OF THE COMMON LIFE.

**BROTHERS PENITENT or PENITENTES** Group found in southwestern United States, particularly New Mexico, whose members carry heavy crosses and carts and flog and "crucify" one of their number on Good Friday, after which he is "resurrected." Although the group originated in the FRANCISCAN flagellants, its practices were condemned by the ROMAN CATHOLIC CHURCH in 1889.

**BROWN** Religious symbol of degradation or renunciation.

**BROWN, ARTHUR JUDSON (1856–1963)** American PRESBYTERIAN missionary to China and denominational secretary of foreign missions. Author of *The Foreign Missionary*.

**BROWN, JOHN (1800–1859)** American abolitionist leader, educated at one time for the CONGREGATIONAL ministry, who planned to defeat slavery with force. His execution after raiding the Federal arsenal at Harpers Ferry, Virginia, was considered martyrdom by other abolitionists. He strongly felt he was led by God and died in peaceful confidence.

**BROWN, OLYMPIA (1835–1926)** Suffragist leader and one of the first American women to be ordained to the ministry. She served in the UNIVERSALIST Church and was president of the Wisconsin Woman's Suffrage Association.

**BROWN, SAMUEL ROBBINS (1810–1880)** American missionary to China (1839–1847) and Japan (1859–1879). He brought to America the first Chinese students to be educated in the United States.

**BROWN, WILLIAM ADAMS (1865–1943)** American PRESBYTERIAN churchman and theologian. He led liberal causes and social reform, and was acitve in the FEDERAL COUNCIL OF CHURCHES and the ecumenical movement.

**BROWNE, GEORGE (?–1556)** AUGUSTINIAN friar and Archbishop of Dublin who suppressed Irish monasteries, led in the union of the Irish Church with the Church of England, and opposed the worship of images. Although he sided with the REFOR-

MATION, he was harsh and unpopular with many.

**BROWNE, LEWIS (1897–1949)** Jewish rabbi who wrote such books as *This Believing World, How Odd of God,* and *The World's Great Scriptures.*

**BROWNE, ROBERT (c.1550–1633)** English preacher who attacked the CHURCH OF ENGLAND and led a group called Brownists. A separatist, he denounced "ungodlie communion with wicked persons" and set forth CONGREGATIONAL principles of church government. In 1591 he received ordination in the Church of England and at 83 he went from a fight with his parish constable to jail where he died.

**BROWNE, THOMAS (1605–1682)** English doctor and writer whose *Religio Medici* sought to reconcile scientific advance and Christian belief, and whose *Urn Burial* discussed death and immortality.

**BROWNIE** Good spirit or elf originating in Scottish folklore.

**BROWNING, ROBERT (1812–1889)** English poet with strong religious interests. His religious poems include "Christmas Day," "Easter Eve," "A Death in the Desert," "Cleon," "A Strange Epistle," and "Rabbi Ben Ezra." He interpreted the Christian faith through poetry and was intensely interested in the growth and triumph of the human soul.

**BROWNISTS** Early British CONGREGATION-ALISTS or separatists named for ROBERT BROWNE.

**BRUCE, A. B. (1831–1899)** Scottish FREE CHURCH ecclesiastic and professor, famous for his *Training of the Twelve.* He was interested in church music and in allegedly novel principles of criticism of Scripture.

**BRUCH, MAX (1838–1920)** German musician famous, among other things, for his variations on the *Kol Nidre.*

**BRUDERHOF** Communal group founded by Mennonite Jacob Hutter in the sixteenth century. A branch of present-day followers, sometimes called HUTTERIAN BRETHREN or Hutterites, is to be found in the United States.

**BRUGGLERS** Eighteenth-century Swiss sect originated by Christian and Jerome Kohler and Elizabeth Kissling, who considered themselves the three Persons of the Trinity and foresaw the end of the world in 1748.

**BRUNHILD** In Scandinavian myth, Brunhild is a VALKYRIE and daughter of WODEN, and is loved by Siegfried.

**BRUNO, ST. (c.925–965)** German archbishop who advanced education, particularly for the clergy, and reformed many of the monasteries in his area. His feast day is October 11.

**BRUNO, ST. (c.1030–1101)** German monk who founded the CARTHUSIAN ORDER at Chartreuse in the Alps. He wrote commentaries on the Psalms and the Epistles of Paul. His feast day is October 6.

**BRUNO, GIORDANO (1548–1600)** Italian freethinking philosopher, often regarded as "first of the modern philosophers." He became a DOMINICAN monk at 15. Disillusioned and skeptical, he fled from Rome in 1576. He won the opposition of CATHOLICS because of his views on TRANSUBSTANTIATION, the IMMACULATE CONCEPTION, and the monastic life; of PROTESTANTS because he was skeptical of miracles and Scripture; and of the philosophers and scientists of the time because he opposed ARISTOTELIANISM, accepted COPERNICUS' heretical views, and went on record that "he who promotes science increases the sources of grief." He held that there are as many points of view as there are worlds, that knowledge cannot be limited, that God is the soul of the universe, and that the human soul is immortal because it is a part of God. The church imprisoned him for seven years and when he refused to recant he was burned at the stake. In 1889 a statue was erected to his memory on the spot where he had been burned.

**BRUNO OF QUERFURT** See BONIFACE OF QUERFURT.

**BRYAN, WILLIAM JENNINGS (1860–1925)** American political leader. A Democrat and PRESBYTERIAN, Bryan early gained fame by attacking the gold standard as a "cross of gold" on which labor was crucified. After many years of effort on behalf of peace, woman suffrage, and prohibition, he fought the teaching of evolution in the schools, becoming Chief Counsel for the prosecution of J. T. Scopes, who was tried in 1925 by the State of Tennessee for so doing. Scopes was represented by Clarence DARROW.

**BUBASTIS** Greek form of the Egyptian goddess BAST or Ubasti, represented as a woman with the head of a lioness or cat.

**BUBER, MARTIN (1878–1965)** Viennese Jewish philosopher and religious leader who translated the Old Testament into German. A ZIONIST, he sought understanding between Jews and Arabs. He saw genuine religion as a personal dialogue, an "I-Thou" relationship between God and man. Reinhold Niebuhr called him "the greatest living Jewish philosopher."

**BUCER, MARTIN (1491–1551)** German reformer. He became a DOMINICAN monk at 14. Hearing LUTHER speak at Wittenberg, he accepted Protestant views, although he appears to have been more of a CALVINIST than a LUTHERAN. He sought earnestly to reconcile the two opposing views, particularly as regards the LORD'S SUPPER. Failing to accept the AUGSBURG INTERIM compromise, he went to England where he influenced Cranmer and Edward VI.

**BUCHAN, ELSPETH** See BUCHANITES.

**BUCHANAN, GEORGE (1506–1582)** Scottish PROTESTANT and humanist who held that government derives from those governed and that if a monarch does not rule for the good of his people he may justly be dethroned. He also made a Latin verse translation of the Psalms, and satirized the FRANCISCAN friars.

**BUCHANITES** Eighteenth-century Scottish religious community founded by Elspeth Buchan. A divorcée, she and others, including Hugh White, a minister, lived in a barn where they were accused of promiscuity and infanticide. Elspeth believed herself to be the woman clothed with the sun of Revelation 12, and the Rev. Mr. White was thought to be the manchild, mentioned in the same passage, who was to rule with a rod of iron. The Buchanites expected to be translated rather than to die.

**BUCHMAN, FRANK (1878–1961)** American LUTHERAN evangelist who founded the OXFORD GROUP and a later campaign called MORAL RE-ARMAMENT.

**BUCKFAST ABBEY** BENEDICTINE abbey at Devon, England, dating from premedieval times. The CISTERCIANS reorganized it about 1135 and the BENEDICTINES rebuilt it between 1906 and 1932.

**BUDDE, KARL (1850–1935)** German Old Testament scholar and theologian who advanced Old Testament criticism.

**BUDDHA Enlightened One (c.563–483 B.C.)** 1. Philosopher of India who founded BUDDHISM. Originally Siddhartha Gautama, he lived in luxury until he was 29 when he left his wife and child to seek for truth. He found it under a bo tree and went forth to proclaim Buddhism's NOBLE EIGHTFOLD PATH. 2. A deified religious teacher in Buddhism.

**BUDDHACARITA** Poetic life of Buddha by ASVAGHOSA.

**BUDDHA DAY** Day of full moon in the month Vaisakha (April or May) set by World Fellowship of Buddhists to honor Buddha.

**BUDDHA-DHAMMA** Southeast Asian term for BUDDHISM.

**BUDDHA GAYA** See BUDDH GAYA.

**BUDDHAGHOSA (fifth century)** Buddhist scholar of India. He wrote *The Path of Purity* and commentaries on PITAKAS, translated many Buddhist works into Pali, and is said to have brought BUDDHISM to Burma.

**BUDDHAHOOD** The "enlightenment" of perfect wisdom and omniscience. It is marked by such physical characteristics as a golden skin and a ten-foot halo.

**BUDDHA JAYANTI** Celebrations of the year 2,500 in the BUDDHIST era (1956–7).

**BUDDHA RIPA** Image of BUDDHA.

**BUDDH GAYA or BODH GAYA** Village in India where Prince Gautama, according to tradition, received enlightenment under a sacred bo tree and became BUDDHA. Hence Buddh Gaya is a sacred shrine of Buddhism.

**BUDDHI** Buddhist term for supreme understanding.

**BUDDHISM** Doctrine or way of Buddha. The world's first international religion, it now has over 350 million adherents. It proclaims four noble truths relating to sorrow and desire, and the NOBLE EIGHTFOLD PATH or Middle Way of right views, right resolutions, right speech, right conduct, right occupation, right endeavor, right contemplation, and right meditation. Its goal is nirvana and immortality. An outstanding contemporary Buddhist is U Thant, third secretary general of the United Nations.

**BUDDHIST CHURCHES OF AMERICA** Buddhist group in the United States representing the JODO Shinsu Sect. It maintains a home for the elderly in California. Most of its members are Japanese in origin.

**BUDDHIST COUNCILS** Six great councils of Buddhism have been held since the time of Gautama BUDDHA. The third council, about 240 B.C., fixed the canon of Buddhist Scripture. The sixth great council was held in 1954.

**BUDDHIST SOCIETY** European Buddhist association.

**BUDDHIST SOCIETY OF GREAT BRITAIN AND IRELAND** British Buddhist organization, founded in 1907. It has a VIHARA at Knightsbridge, London.

**BUGENHAVEN, JOHANN (1485–1558)** German reformer and friend of Martin LUTHER who carried the REFORMATION into northern Germany and Denmark. A skillful organizer, he helped Luther translate the Bible.

**BUGIA** Portable candlestick used in CATHOLIC liturgy.

**BUJI** Japanese term for the ZEN Buddhist attitude of seeing and accepting things as they actually are.

**BUKHARI (810–870)** Arabic MOSLEM scholar whose collection of more than 7,000 of Mohammed's sayings is revered next to the KORAN. He is said to have gathered 300,000 traditions from 1,000 men in making this collection. Moslems make pilgrimages to his grave.

**BULGAKOV, SERGIUS (1870–1944)** Russian theologian of the EASTERN ORTHODOX CHURCH who warmly supported the ecumenical movement. He propounded a theology in which WISDOM relates God to the world.

**BULGARIAN EASTERN ORTHODOX CHURCH** Division of the Bulgarian Orthodox Church in the United States, its members having immigrated from the Balkans.

**BULGARIAN ORTHODOX CHURCH** State church of Bulgaria.

**BULL** Bulls figure in many ancient religions. The Canaanites' god Baal was sometimes represented riding a bull. Many Egyptian gods had the form of a bull. Bulls were sacrificed in JUDAISM, and in the mystery religions of Greece.

**BULL, PAPAL** Apostolic letter of the pope announcing the canonization of a saint, a pronouncement on doctrine, or some other important matter. It bears the papal seal. Papal bulls proclaimed the INFALLIBILITY

OF THE POPE in 1871 and the ASSUMPTION of the Virgin in 1950.

**BULLARIUM** Collection of papal BULLS, or of similar documents.

**BULLETIN** Term for printed order of service in many churces.

**BULLETIN BOARD** Announcement board within or outside of a church.

**BULLINGER, HEINRICH (1504–1575)** Swiss PROTESTANT churchman and reformer who led Swiss Protestantism after Zwingli died and wrote a biography of Zwingli. He drafted the Second HELVETIC CONFESSION. He married a nun by whom he had eleven children. He corresponded with HENRY VIII, EDWARD VI, and ELIZABETH of England.

**BULLOCK** Symbol of sacrifice, atonement, and St. Luke.

**BULL-ROARER** Thin piece of wood or stone attached to a string. When whirled it produces a roar like thunder. Dating from the Stone Age, it has been found in all parts of the world and was important in primitive religions—perhaps representing the voice of a god.

**BULRUSH** Reed of Palestine and Egypt from which Egyptian papyrus was made. The baby Moses was hidden among bulrushes in the Nile (EXODUS 2:3). In religious art the bulrush symbolizes humility, and faithfulness to the Saviour.

**BUN-JIL** Aboriginal Australians' creator-god, who made men from clay.

**BUNYAN, JOHN (1628–1688)** English tinker who became a BAPTIST and was imprisoned for twelve years for preaching without a license. In jail he wrote a number of books. His *Pilgrim's Progress* and *Holy War* are remarkable allegories of Christian truth.

**BURGHERS** Members of the Secession Church of Scotland who construed the burgess oath upholding the "true religion presently professed within this realm" to be the Protestant faith. Their opponents, the ANTIBURGHERS, interpreted the oath to mean the Established Church, and refused to take it.

**BURI or BUR** First man, according to Scandinavian myth; the grandfather of Odin (see WODEN).

**BURIAL** Interment of a corpse, often the occasion of religious rites. Burial has Biblical precedent; Abraham and Jesus were buried in tombs. CATHOLIC burial is not granted to non- or nominal Catholics. In American burial the undertaker often supplies much of the religious atmosphere.

**BURIASH** Storm god of the Kassites of Iran.

**BURLAMAQUI, JEAN JACQUES (1694–1748)** Swiss moralist and jurist who based all law on natural law, which he saw originating in the law of God and the human mind.

**BURMA, RELIGION IN** BUDDHISM is the predominant faith in Burma; monks from its ubiquitous monasteries teach in its public schools, and Buddhist temples serve as a focus for community life. The ancient capital of Pagan—now in ruins—had thousands of Buddhist shrines. Some of the hill tribes of Burma are animistic. There are BAPTIST and ROMAN CATHOLIC churches here and there, as well as those of other denominations.

**BURNAND, EUGENE (1850–1921)** Swiss artist who painted such Biblical scenes as "Peter and John Running to the Tomb," "Come Unto Me," and "The Talents."

**BURNE-JONES, EDWARD (1833–1898)** English painter who executed stained-glass designs for many churches and painted "The Star of Bethlehem" and "The Morning of the Resurrection."

**BURNING** Fire has had immemorial religious significance. Ancient altars smoked with burned sacrifices; the Canaanites burned children for Molech. Throughout the Middle Ages and for a while afterward, heretics and other religious offenders were burned at the stake.

**BURNING BUSH** At Mount Horeb in Egypt, Moses found a bush burning but not being consumed. There the Lord spoke to him, and he was called to lead his people forth from Egyptian oppression (EXODUS 3). Christian symbolists see the burning bush as a type or sign of the Virgin to come.

**BURNT OFFERINGS** Ancient Jewish burnt offerings were of animals entirely consumed on altars to the Lord.

**BURSAR** Treasurer of a cathedral or religious community.

**BURSARY** Funds of a cathedral, college, or religious order.

**BURSE** Stiff square case for the linen corporal for the eucharist. Its color is changed with the liturgical season.

**BURSFIELD UNION** German BENEDICTINE order of monasteries which flourished from the fifteenth to the eighteenth century.

**BUSHIDO** Japanese code of chivalry which drew elements from CONFUCIANISM and ZEN Buddhism. It fostered loyalty, courage, benevolence, honor, justice, and similar virtues.

**BUSHMAN RELIGION** The religion of the Bushmen of southern Africa combines animism and totemism. The moon is worshiped and the family unit plays a large part in religious ceremonies.

**BUSHNELL, HORACE (1802–1876)** American CONGREGATIONAL churchman prominent in the movement to modify traditional CALVINISM toward a more humane and liberal form. He wrote the book *Christian Nurture* (see). He set forth the moral view of the ATONEMENT, sought to "lift the natural into the supernatural," and centered theology in Christ and Christian experience.

**BUSIRI (1211–1294)** MOSLEM Arabian poet whose works were largely religious. His "Poem of the Mantle" praised MOHAMMED for curing him of paralysis; the poem has long been considered sacred.

**BUSKINS** Elegant stockings worn by a BISHOP or mitred ABBOT at pontifical mass.

**BUSSUMARUS** *big-lipped* A supreme Celtic god.

**BU-STON (1290–1364)** Tibetan BUDDHIST scholar who systematized and wrote commentaries on the Buddhist Scriptures.

**BUTLER, ALBAN (1710–1773)** English CATHOLIC churchman, famous for his *Lives of the Saints* which occupied him for 30 years.

**BUTLER, JOSEPH (1692–1752)** Theologian and apologist of the CHURCH OF ENGLAND, famous for his *Analogy of Religion* which attacked DEISM and tried to find a rational foundation for Christianity in the world of nature.

**BUTSUDEN** Sacred shrine of a Japanese BUDDHIST monastery, holding the main image of BUDDHA.

**BUTTERFLY** Religious symbol of resurrection.

**BUTTRESS** Mass of masonry supporting a wall. Mesopotamian temples employed them. They made the Gothic cathedrals of the Middle Ages possible by counterbalancing the great groined vaults and arches of those inimitable buildings.

**BUTZER, MARTIN**   See BUCER, MARTIN.

**BUXTORF, JOHANN (1564–1629)** German rabbinical scholar.

**BUXTORF, JOHANN (1599–1664)** "Buxtorf the Younger," son of the above, who completed a Hebrew concordance and a rabbinic lexicon begun by his father. He tried to prove that the Hebrew vowel points were divinely inspired.

**B.V.M.**   Abbreviation for the Blessed Virgin Mary.

**BYBLOS**   Important Phoenician city where ADONIS was worshiped. Also called Jebail or Gebal (EZEKIEL 27:9), Byblos has preserved its name in the word Bible. (Many papyrus "books" were housed in Byblos.)

**BYELUN** *the white one*   Beneficent god of the Slavs.

**BYZANTINE CHURCH**   Term for the Eastern Orthodox Church.

**BYZANTINE MUSIC**   Music peculiar to the Greek Orthodox Church. With no fixed rhythm, it fused song with accompaniment, and sometimes threaded a hymn among the verses of a psalm. John of Damascus and Coamas of Jerusalem contributed some of its greatest hymns.

**BYZANTINE RITE**   Liturgy of the Eastern Orthodox Church. Originating in the church at Constantinople, its original language was old Greek.

**BYZANTINE TEXT**   Term for the standard New Testament text of the Greek-speaking churches.

**BYZANTIUM**   Ancient Thrace, chosen by Emperor Constantine in 325 as the Roman Empire's new capital. It became Constantinople in 330 and was to become the capital of the Byzantine Empire and of Eastern Christianity.

# C

C Symbol for CODEX EPHRAEMI RESCRIPTUS (see).

CAABA See KAABA.

CABALA heritage Mystical, esoteric method of interpreting Scripture, popular among Jews and to some extent among Christians in the Middle Ages. Claiming descent by oral tradition from Abraham, it is a THEOSOPHIC system based on finding occult meanings in every letter and word of Scripture. It is accompanied by such writings as The Book of Creation and The Book of Brightness and seems to show NEOPLATONIC influence. HASIDIC Jews still accept it to some extent.

CABASILAS, NICOLAUS (?-1371) Byzantine churchman and mystic who wrote a number of treatises opposing union between the Greek and Roman churches. He believed that union with Christ is achieved through BAPTISM, CONFIRMATION, and the EUCHARIST.

CABIRI Ancient nature deities, or underworld demons, worshiped on the shores of the Mediterranean.

CABRINI, FRANCES XAVIER, ST. (1850–1917) Italian-born nun who founded the Missionary Sisters of the Sacred Heart of Jesus, established many hospitals and welfare institutions in the United States, and was the first American citizen to be canonized a ROMAN CATHOLIC saint. Her feast day is December 22.

CADBURY, ELIZABETH MARY (1858–1935) Englishwoman who worked for peace and social reforms, and was president of England's National Council of Evangelical Free Churches in 1925.

CADI Judge in a Moslem court. He must be versed in the KORAN and render judgments according to the canon law of ISLAM.

CADMAN, S. PARKES (1864–1936) American CONGREGATIONAL churchman and ecumenical leader.

CAEDMON, ST. (seventh century) The earliest English Christian poet. In vigorous verse he retold various Bible stories. His feast day is February 11.

CAESAR Name of a family of Roman emperors. Jesus was born during the reign of Caesar Augustus and crucified during that of Tiberius Caesar.

CAESAREA Important harbor city of Palestine during the reign of HEROD THE GREAT. Here Pontius Pilate lived, Peter preached, and Paul was imprisoned.

CAESAREA PHILIPPI City near Mt. Hermon, north of the Sea of Galilee, near which Peter confessed that Jesus was the Christ or MESSIAH (MATTHEW 16:13–16). In this region Canaanite fertility gods had been worshiped and a Roman cult had centered around the god Pan.

CAESARIUS OF ARLES (c.470–543) Monk of Lerins, France, who founded a monastery for women and wrote monastic rules for both monks and nuns. He emphasized prayer, Scripture, and discipline.

CAESARIUS OF HEISTERBACH (c.1170–c.1240) German CISTERCIAN monk who tried to improve social conditions in his order. He wrote lives of St. Elizabeth and St. Engelbert. His Dialogue on Visions and Miracles, an anthology of religious anecdotes, is an important source of information on medieval religious events and beliefs.

CAESAROPAPISM Control of the church by the state.

CAGLIOSTRO, ALESSANDRO (1743–1795) Italian alchemist and FREEMASON condemned to death for heresy by the INQUISITION but permitted to die in prison.

CAIAPHAS Jewish high priest who presided over the council at which Jesus was condemned to die (JOHN 18:24).

**CAIN** First child of Adam and Eve and first murderer because he killed his brother Abel (GENESIS 4:1–15).

**CAINITES** Second-century GNOSTICS who honored CAIN, KORAH, the SODOMITES, and JUDAS ISCARIOT. They believed the Creator of this world was an evil "Demiurge" who must be disobeyed.

**CAIS** Ancient god of the Semites.

**CAJETAN, ST. (1468–1534)** Italian cardinal who presided when Martin LUTHER appeared at the Diet of Augsburg, and aided in drawing up the bull which excommunicated Luther. He also founded a congregation of priests called THEATINES, and wrote commentaries on the works of ARISTOTLE and Aquinas (see THOMAS AQUINAS). Cajetan's feast day is August 7.

**CALCED** *shod* Term to distinguish members of religious orders who wear shoes or boots from those who are barefoot or sandaled.

**CALDERON DE LA BARCA, PEDRO (1600–1681)** Spanish writer of profound religious and philosophical drama and poetry. His famous plays include *Life Is a Dream* and *To God for Reasons of State*.

**CALDRON** In Christian art, symbol of the Apostle JOHN.

**CALEB** Faithful and courageous spy who investigated the promised land of Canaan and recommended that the Hebrews enter it (NUMBERS 13–14).

**CALEFACTORY** Monastery room with heat, or living room.

**CALENDAR, CHURCH** Often, a printed announcement of the order of service and of coming events of importance to the congregation.

**CALENDAR, ECCLESIASTICAL** Listing of the events of the church year, usually beginning with the ADVENT season.

**CALF, GOLDEN** 1. Idol made by Aaron while Moses was receiving the Ten Commandments (EXODUS 32:1–6). 2. Idol erected by Jeroboam I at Bethel (another was at Dan) when the kingdom of Israel separated from the kingdom of Judah (I KINGS 12:26–32).

**CALF, WINGED** Symbol of St. LUKE.

**CALIPH** See KHALIF.

**CALIPHATE** See KHALIFATE.

**CALIXTINES** Moderate HUSSITES or UTRA-QUISTS of Moravia and Bohemia. They held

that the people should receive both the wine and the bread during mass.

**CALIXTUS, GEORGIUS (1586–1656)** German LUTHERAN theologian who sought to unite Christendom on the basis of such symbols as the APOSTLES' CREED, emphasizing what the different bodies hold in common. The result was that all groups tended to reject his efforts.

**CALL** 1. Divine summons to a special work, as to the ministry of the gospel. 2. Invitation from a church to a minister to become its pastor.

**CALOVIUS (1612–1686)** German LUTHERAN churchman and theologian who attacked the teachings of GEORGIUS CALIXTUS and was an able champion of Lutheran orthodoxy in the seventeenth century.

**CALOYER** *venerable* An Eastern monk, particularly BASILIAN.

**CALVARY** *skull* From the Latin *calvaria*, the Greek *kranion*, and the Aramaic *golgotha*—all meaning "skull." 1. Place of Christ's crucifixion, outside Jerusalem. The name may have derived from the shape of the hill where the crucifixion took place, from skulls scattered there, or from a tradition that Adam's skull had been buried at that site. 2. Sculptural depiction of the Crucifixion. 3. Experience of suffering to an intense degree.

**CALVARY, GORDON'S** Place near Jerusalem's Damascus Gate suggested by Charles G. Gordon and Otto Thenius as possible site of the Crucifixion. This skull-shaped mound with eye-like caves, sometimes called the Garden Tomb, is not accepted by many investigators as the actual Calvary.

**CALVARY CROSS** Ecclesiastical cross with a three-step base symbolizing faith, hope, and love. Also known as the Graded Cross, it has the general form of the Latin Cross.

**CALVARY PENTECOSTAL CHURCH, INC.** American denomination founded in 1931 at Olympia, Washington.

**CALVERT, GEORGE (c.1580–1632)** "Lord Baltimore," English politician who converted to CATHOLICISM and was granted the American territory which became Maryland in the United States.

**CALVIN, JOHN (1509–1564)** French-Swiss Protestant reformer and theologian. Originally trained for the ROMAN CATHOLIC CHURCH, Calvin turned to law and literature but was converted to the newly promulgated Protestant faith about 1533. He is famous for his monumental theological treatise, *The Institutes of the Christian Religion,* his influence on the new Protestant movement, his leadership in GENEVA, Switzerland, and his historic role as theologian of PROTESTANTISM and father of PRESBYTERIANISM. He is credited with massive influence on both Puritanism and the newly developing capitalism of the times.

**CALVINISM** System of theology and church polity attributed to the systematization of John CALVIN but believed by its adherents to be rooted squarely in the teachings of PAUL and AUGUSTINE. It emphasizes the sovereignty of the grace of God, divine predestination of all events, election to eternal life, eternal security of the believer, total depravity of the unbeliever, the supreme authority of Scripture, the necessity of the church and the sacraments of baptism and the Lord's Supper, church unity and government by elders or presbyters, and the Christian's duty to glorify God in every sphere.

**CALVINISTIC METHODISTS** British denomination which grew out of revivals in England and Wales in the eighteenth century, METHODIST in outlook but CALVINISTIC in theology. A branch established in the United States, the Calvinistic Methodist Church, united with the Presbyterian Church in 1920.

**CAMALDOLESE or CAMALDULIANS** Order of monks, nuns, and hermits founded by St. Romuald early in the eleventh century. Its members wear white garments and live under austere discipline.

**CAMAXTLI** Aztec god of war.

**CAMAZOTZ** Mayan bat god.

**CAMBRIDGE PLATFORM** Congregationalist declaration of doctrine and discipline adopted at Cambridge, Massachusetts, in 1648 and normative for American CONGREGATIONALISM.

**CAMBRIDGE PLATONISTS** Semimystic philosophers and Christian apologists centering in Cambridge University in the seventeenth century. Influenced by Platonism (see PLATO) and NEOPLATONISM, they advocated humanistic tendencies in ethics, tolerance in religion, and reason in philosophy.

**CAMEL** Symbol of something difficult to accept (MATTHEW 23:24).

**CAMELOT** Mythical site of King Arthur's court.

**CAMENAE** Roman nymphs of springs or fountains, identified with Greek MUSES.

**CAMERA** Ecclesiastical treasury department, as the papal Camera Apostolica.

**CAMERARIUS, JOACHIM (1500 – 1574)** German scholar who assisted MELANCHTHON in preparing the AUGSBURG CONFESSION and aided the REFORMATION in Europe.

**CAMERON, JOHN (c.1579–1625)** Scottish Protestant theologian who originated the semi-Arminian variety of French Calvinism sometimes known as AMYRALDIANISM. He also upheld the divine right of kings.

**CAMERON, RICHARD (c.1648–1680)** Scottish Covenanter preacher, slain while fighting state control of religion in attempted war against Charles II. Before battle he prayed, "Lord, spare the green and take the ripe."

**CAMERONIANS** Covenanter Presbyterians of Scotland who followed the extreme principles of Richard Cameron. Most of them finally united with the Free Church of Scotland.

**CAMERONITES** Another name for the Scottish Amyraldians who followed the theology of John CAMERON. They held that man's will is inclined toward good or evil by his own knowledge, and that Christ died for all.

**CAMILLA** Girl who attended a Roman priest or priestess.

**CAMILLUS** Boy who attended a Roman priest or priestess.

**CAMISARDS** French HUGUENOTS who fought the attempt to make them Catholics after the EDICT OF NANTES was revoked. Their name came from the white shirt or *camise* often worn by them as a disguise in night attacks. Their leaders were Roland Laporte and Jean CAVALIER.

**CAMPAGUS** Ancient type of boot worn by popes and others.

**CAMPANILE** Italian belfry and watch tower connected with churches or town halls but usually detached from the building proper.

**CAMPANIUS, JOHN (1601–1683)** Swedish LUTHERAN missionary to Indians on the Delaware in the United States.

**CAMPBELL, ALEXANDER (1788 – 1866)** Irish-born PRESBYTERIAN minister who founded the DISCIPLES OF CHRIST—or Christians or CAMPBELLITES—in West Virginia about 1827. He was the founder and first president of Bethany College in that state.

**CAMPBELL, THOMAS (1763–1854)** Father of Alexander CAMPBELL (above) and organizer in the United States of the Christian Association. He and his views aided the beginning of the DISCIPLES OF CHRIST.

**CAMPBELLITES** Term for the DISCIPLES OF CHRIST who followed Alexander and Thomas CAMPBELL. They practiced immersion and emphasized the Second Coming and New Testament Christianity.

**CAMPION, EDMUND (c.1540–1581)** ANGLICAN divine who became a Jesuit (see SOCIETY OF JESUS), converted a number of Englishmen to CATHOLICISM, and printed the pamphlet *Ten Reasons* against PROTESTANTISM. He was racked, hanged, drawn, and quartered. In 1886 he was beatified.

**CAMP MEETING** Distinctively American religious institution which originated in nineteenth-century frontier life in connection with religious revivals. James MC-GREADY is credited with holding the first camp meeting in Kentucky about 1800. Usually held in tents or the open, camp meetings often generated emotional disturbance as well as spiritual aid.

**CAMPUS CRUSADE FOR CHRIST** Conservative interdenominational Christian organization for the evangelization of college students. It was founded by Bill Bright at the University of California in 1951.

**CAMUS, ALBERT (1913–1960)** French author whose drama, essays, and novels reflect the human situation and man's spiritual dilemma in EXISTENTIALIST and HUMANISTIC overtones. He wrote *The Plague, The Fall,* and *The Myth of Sisyphus.*

**CANA** Village in Galilee where Jesus performed His first miracles (JOHN 2; 4). Here He turned water into wine at a wedding and healed a nobleman's son.

**CANAAN** 1. Noah's grandson, Ham's son, father of the Canaanites (GENESIS 9; 10). 2. Palestine, the land of promise to which Moses led the children of Israel. It is roughly the area between the Jordan River and the Mediterranean Sea.

**CANACHUS (sixth century B.C.)** Greek sculptor of two great statues of Apollo.

**CANADIAN COUNCIL OF CHURCHES** Cooperative association of the PROTESTANT churches of Canada, organized in 1944. It is the Canadian arm of the WORLD COUNCIL OF CHURCHES. It honors Jesus Christ "as God and Saviour."

**CANCELLI** Latticed screen before the CHANCEL of a church.

**CANDIDATE** 1. One ready for ordination, as for the priesthood. 2. Clergyman who makes himself available for a pastorate.

**CANDLE** Religious symbol of light, truth, prayer, and possibly sacrifice, prominent in many churches. Candles are essential to MASS and many other ceremonies.

**CANDLELIGHT SERVICE** Popular Christian service at ADVENT and EPIPHANY symbolizing the coming of Christ as Light of the World.

**CANDLEMAS** Christian festival held February 2 commemorating the presentation of the infant Jesus in the temple (LUKE 2). Western churches honor Christ at Candelmas while Eastern churches make it a festival of the Virgin Mother. In this service candles are often blessed.

**CANDLISH, ROBERT SMITH (1806–1873)** Eloquent Scottish preacher and FREE CHURCH leader.

**CANISIUS, PETER** See PETER CANISIUS.

**CANNIBALISM** Among primitive people cannibalism was sometimes practiced for such religious purposes as human sacrifice and protective magic.

**CANNON, GEORGE QUAYLE (1827–1901)** English-born MORMON apostle and missionary to Hawaii. In 1888 he was imprisoned for polygamy.

**CANNON, JAMES, JR. (1864–1944)** American METHODIST bishop and prohibitionist. He was head of the World League Against Alcoholism.

**CANO, MELCHIOR (1509–1560)** Spanish DOMINICAN theologian and bishop who sought greater Spanish independence of the VATICAN and more scientifically based theology.

**CANON** 1. Person holding a particular ecclesiastical office. 2. Ecclesiastical decree. 3. List of saints. 4. List of sacred books. 5. Term for ecclesiastical legislation, as in canon law. 6. Central portion of the mass. 7. In the Eastern Church, nine hymns of the orthros (morning office of worship).

**CANON, BUDDHIST**   MAHAYANA Buddhism has no canon of sacred writings. HINAYANA Buddhism has accepted, since the third century B.C., the PALI CANON of the Three Baskets.

**CANON, JEWISH**   The Scriptures considered inspired and authoritative, as set forth about 100 A.D. by a rabbinical assembly at Jamnia. They are the 39 books commonly accepted as constituting the Old Testament.

**CANONESS**   Member of a religious order for women, pledged to poverty and chastity.

**CANONICAL HOURS**   The seven periods of the Divine Office: MATINS (which includes NOCTURN and LAUDS), PRIME, TERCE, SEXT, NONES, VESPERS, and COMPLINE.

**CANONICAL MARRIAGE**   Marriage in accord with church law.

**CANONICITY**   Meeting the standard of the biblical canon. For example, the canonicity of the four Gospels is seldom questioned.

**CANONIZATION**   Enrollment of a beatified person as a saint of the church. BEATIFICATION is a preliminary step.

**CANON LAW**   Law regulating the church.

**CANON OF THE MASS**   Prayer of consecration in the MASS.

**CANON OF SCRIPTURE**   Term for the books of the Christian Bible. Protestants accept the 39 books of the Old Testament and the 27 books of the New Testament as divinely inspired and authoritative for faith and life. Catholics accept also the books known to Protestants as APOCRYPHA.

**CANOPY**   Ornamental covering, as above a pulpit.

**CANTATA**   Choral composition with varied parts; either sacred on secular. Bach developed it as an integral part of the LUTHERAN church service, usually ending with a chorale in which the congregation joins.

**CANTATE DOMINO** *Sing unto the Lord* Title of Psalm 98, a CANTICLE for evening prayer in the CHURCH OF ENGLAND.

**CANTERBURY**   Borough in Kent, long a spiritual center of English Christianity. Here AUGUSTINE built an abbey; here THOMAS À BECKET was murdered, and thenceforward Canterbury became the center of pilgrimages to Becket's shrine. Here Mary I burned 41 of her enemies. And here, in accordance with ancient tradition, the Archbishop of Canterbury presides as primate of all England.

**CANTICLE**   Song or prayer, usually based on Scripture, chanted in church.

**CANTICLE OF THE BLESSED VIRGIN**   Name for the MAGNIFICAT, the Song of Mary in the Gospel of Luke (1:46–55).

**CANTICLE OF THE SUN**   Hymn of FRANCIS OF ASSISI beginning, "Be Thou praised, my Lord, with all Thy creatures, above all Brother Sun." It is praise of all things made by God.

**CANTICLES**   See SONG OF SONGS.

**CANTIQUE**   Popular hymn in folk vein, similar to a Negro spiritual.

**CANTOR**   1. Church singer or choir leader. 2. Synagogue singer of liturgical music and leader of worship.

**CANTORIS**   Term for choir members who sit on the north side of the choir with the cantor in antiphonal singing.

**CAODAISTS**   Adherents of a monotheistic, syncretistic religion of French Indo-China, synthesizing BUDDHISM, CONFUCIANISM, and CHRISTIANITY. They emphasize human affection and seek to communicate with spirits.

**CAPA ROTUNDA**   Jewish cloak.

**CAPERNAUM**   Town on the northern side of the Sea of Galilee. Here Jesus once dwelt and preached.

**CAPGRAVE, JOHN (1393–1464)**   English AUGUSTINIAN friar who wrote a chronicle of English history and a book of lives of English saints, besides sermons and commentaries.

**CAPH**   Eleventh letter of the Hebrew alphabet.

**CAPISTRANO**   See JOHN CAPISTRAN.

**CAPITALISM**   Capitalism, which places the ownership and management of goods in private hands, is sometimes associated with "the Protestant ethic" because of the reliance of both Protestantism and capitalism on thrift, industry, individual responsibility, and the like.

**CAPITAL PUNISHMENT**   The right of the state to pronounce the death penalty has the sanction of the Apostle Paul (ROMANS 13:1–5), and of many religious groups. There is nevertheless a growing feeling that Christianity—and, indeed, any religion at its best—is irreconcilable with capital punishment.

**CAPITOL**  Temple of JUPITER at Rome.

**CAPITULAR**  Belonging to an ecclesiastical chapter.

**CAPITULAR MASS**  Principal daily MASS.

**CAPITULARY**  1. Collection of laws compiled for a DIOCESE. 2. Summary of contents of a book of the Bible.

**CAPITULATIONS**  1. Agreements with a BISHOP or POPE by which he is to do certain things after his election. 2. Treaties granting privileges by recent Turkish sultans to citizens of other states.

**CAPPA**  Ecclesiastical cape.

**CAPPADOCIA**  Region north of Cilicia in Asia Minor (cf. I PETER 1:1). In ancient times Cappadocia had temples to Venasa and Comana. King Solomon's horses may have come from that country. Three great theologians of the fourth century hailed from it (see CAPPADOCIAN FATHERS).

**CAPPADOCIAN FATHERS**  BASIL THE GREAT, GREGORY OF NYSSA, and GREGORY OF NAZIANZUS were Cappadocia's gift to fourth-century theology. The three upheld orthodoxy and helped defeat ARIANISM at the Council of CONSTANTINOPLE.

**CAPPA MAGNA**  Cloak with a long train for CARDINALS, BISHOPS, and other high-level dignitaries.

**CAPSALI, MOSES (1420–1495)**  Chief rabbi of Turkey.

**CAPTAIN OF OUR SALVATION**  Jesus Christ (HEBREWS 2:10).

**CAPTIVITY EPISTLES**  Letters thought to have been written by the Apostle Paul while imprisoned in Rome: Philippians, Colossians, Ephesians, and Philemon.

**CAPUCHINS**  Order of FRANCISCAN friars instituted about 1525 in Italy. They have specialized in missions and preaching. Their name derives from their pointed hood (*capuche*) and they are distinguished for their poverty, beards, and brown robes. During the seventeenth century they made many converts and helped advance the Counter Reformation.

**CARAITES**  See KARAITES.

**CARBUNCLE**  Symbol of martyrdom, or of the suffering of Christ.

**CARDINAL**  Highest ecclesiastic in the RO-MAN CATHOLIC CHURCH, next to the pope. As a council the cardinals have an important part in church government; as a college they elect a pope when there is a vacancy.

**CARDINALATE**  1. Cardinal's office or rank. 2. The CARDINALS of the church collectively.

**CARDINAL BISHOP**  Official of highest rank in the college of cardinals (see also CARDINAL PRIESTS and CARDINAL DEACONS). The cardinal bishops have seven sees near Rome.

**CARDINAL DEACON**  Lowest rank among the cardinals.

**CARDINAL PRIEST**  Center rank in the college of CARDINALS is held by the cardinal priests, who are usually ARCHBISHOPS outside the Roman province.

**CARDINAL VIRTUES**  According to PLATO, the qualities of character on which human conduct hinges are prudence, justice, self-control, and courage. To these "natural" virtues certain medieval scholars added the three "theological" virtues of faith, hope, and love. Although the first four are generally considered the cardinal virtues, all seven are sometimes so listed.

**CARE**  Cooperative for American Relief Everywhere, the full name of CARE, is the arm of several churches, religious agencies, and national organizations in the United States for providing food, books, tools, and other supplies to those in need in various parts of the world.

**CAREY, WILLIAM (1761–1834)**  English shoemaker who became a BAPTIST minister and one of the first Protestant missionaries to India. Talented in linguistics, he wrote grammars and dictionaries in various languages of India, translated the New Testament, and established a school and a printing press. Through the latter, Carey published more than 200,000 Bibles and portions of Scripture. He was also Oriental professor for thirty years in a Calcutta college. Carey's example has spurred the entire movement of modern missions.

**CARGILL, DONALD (c.1610–1681)**  Scottish COVENANTER minister who resisted ANGLICAN control of the Scottish church, helped publish the Sanquhar Declaration, and excommunicated Charles II. He was executed.

**CARGO CULTS**  Contemporary Melanesian cults whose members believe that the white men enjoy plenty of good things, from radios to canned food, by writing magic symbols on paper. They also believe that white rule will soon end, at which time they will have an abundance of "cargo": radios, machines, etc.

**CARILLON** Set of fixed bells played with hammers, usually operated from a keyboard. Many carillons are in towers of churches, particularly in the United States.

**CARITAS** 1. Latin for "love," translated "charity" in the KING JAMES BIBLE. 2. Catholic European social welfare organization aiding social security, cooperative housing, and child welfare.

**CARLISLE, WILSON (1847–1942)** English businessman who became a curate and founded the CHURCH ARMY. This is an ANGLICAN counterpart of the SALVATION ARMY, seeking to give spiritual and social aid to prisoners, poor people, and soldiers and sailors.

**CARLSON, PAUL (1928–1964)** Member of the Evangelical Covenant Church of America who went as medical missionary to the Congo. Accused of spying, he was shot and killed at the age of 36 amid a massacre of a number of whites.

**CARLSTADT (1480–1541)** German Protestant reformer, originally Andreas Bodenstein; he was known by the name of his birthplace (Carlstadt, Bavaria). At first a THOMIST professor of theology, he was converted to AUGUSTINIAN doctrines of grace about 1515 while at Rome. Thereafter he became the most extreme among the reformers. He celebrated the EUCHARIST without VESTMENTS, announced his engagement to be married, attacked MONASTICISM, and finally declared the SACRAMENTS unnecessary. In 1524 LUTHER called him a new Judas, and Carlstadt fled to Switzerland where he remained the rest of his life.

**CARLYLE, THOMAS (1795–1881)** British writer and philosopher. Though opposing all churches and creeds, he saw a spiritual world beneath the physical, and proclaimed an immanent and beneficent God. The "Everlasting Yea," he said, is to love God; the universe is orderly and "the Religious Principle lies unseen in the hearts of all good men." Yet religion must outgrow its old garments and find new forms. Believing in the divinity of man, Carlyle held that the world's heroes and leaders must shape its destiny. His influence was great in both Europe and America.

**CARMATHIANS** See KARMATHIANS.

**CARMEL** 1. Town near Hebron in Palestine where Saul commemorated his conquest of the Amalekites (I SAMUEL 15:12). 2. Twelve-mile-long mountain of Palestine extending from Esdraelon to the Mediterannean Sea. Here Elijah challenged the priests of Baal (I KINGS 18:19–46); here were shrines of Jupiter and Baal, and sacred oracles; here, through the Christian era, dwelt many eremites, or hermits. On it today are a BAHAI shrine and a CARMELITE monastery.

**CARMELITES** CATHOLIC order of friars founded on Mt. Carmel about 1150. Their origin is said to have been a community of hermits established by Elijah. The Carmelites have Calced (shod) and Discalced (barefoot or sandaled) branches. In Britain they are called White Friars from their white mantles over brown cloaks. Their objectives are meditation, intercession, missions, and theology. Among their famous members have been St. THERESA OF AVILA and St. JOHN OF THE CROSS, who together renewed the order when it was declining in the sixteenth century.

**CARMICHAEL, AMY WILSON (?–1951)** British missionary to India and founder of the DOHNAVUR FELLOWSHIP.

**CARNAC** French town, site of many megalithic monuments. These great upright stones, similar to those at Stonehenge in England, may have been associated with an oriental theosophical cult. Fertility rites and the worship of HERMES may well have been involved.

**CARNAL** New Testament word for "of the flesh" or sinful—as contrasted with spiritual and God-related. Scripture never condemns physical or material things as such.

**CARNATION** Religious symbol of love.

**CARNEIA** Greek festival in which a priest directed four youths to pursue another covered with garlands. It appears to have been a ceremony of fertility or harvest. The name comes from the month Karneios, occurring in midsummer.

**CARNIVAL** In the Middle Ages, the days before LENT. The name indicates "Farewell, flesh"; the festivities go back to pre-

Christian festivities of early spring. Egypt, Greece, Rome, and Teutonic Europe knew such seasons of merrymaking, which were carried over into pre-Lenten periods of license and masquerade.

**CARO or KARO, JOSEPH BEN EPHRAIM (1488–1575)** Spanish-born mystic; codifier and interpreter of Jewish law. He wrote *Shulhan Aruk* and *Bet Yosef;* the former has long been regarded as authoritative in connection with disagreements on law and ritual. Caro worked principally in Palestine.

**CAROL** Popular and joyous hymn, or devotional song or ballad, akin to folk-song in that a great body of traditional carols, originating in the Middle Ages, are of unknown authorship. While some have been associated with other seasons, such as Easter or May Day, the carol is most closely linked with Christmas. The first Christmas carol may be said to have been the angels' song at Christ's birth (LUKE 2:14). Although true carols adhere to a distinct musical and literary form, the popular contemporary revival uses the term for many other types of religious song.

**CAROLINE BOOKS** Document attributed to CHARLEMAGNE, in four books, attacking the Iconoclastic Council which forbade all images and the Second Council of NICAEA which permitted excessive reverence to images. Thus the Caroline Books approved the use of images for decorative purposes but prohibited their worship.

**CARPOCRATES (second century)** Alexandrian founder of a communal sect which despised material things and honored Jesus as but one of several saviours. Carpocrates' son, who died at the age of 17, was worshiped by the sect as a god.

**CARRANZA, BARTOLOME (1503–1576)** Learned Spanish DOMINICAN ecclesiastic who was imprisoned for a number of years for his theological errors. He was accused of wishing to limit the power of the pope, accepting ideas of ERASMUS, and destroying the faith of Charles V. He attended the Council of TRENT and was Archbishop of Toledo.

**CARREL** "Monk's study"; a niche in a cloister where one person may study. Today the term is also used in some libraries.

**CARREL, ALEXIS (1873–1944)** French-born biologist who became a medical researcher in the United States and won a Nobel Prize in physiology and medicine. His book *Man, the Unknown* explores the relationships of medicine, life, faith, and God.

**CARROLL, JOHN (1735–1815)** CATHOLIC ecclesiastic and educator. The first American bishop, he became Archbishop of Baltimore. He defended Roman Catholics against the charge that they were not loyal to the interests of the United States.

**CARTESIANISM** Philosophy of René DES-CARTES and his followers. Building on an existential foundation, he reasoned, "I think, therefore I am." He reasoned from self to God, saw the physical and mental worlds as entirely distinct, and held that the only connection between the two worlds was the activity of God. Cartesianism considers the content of one's conscious thought to depend upon the existence of God.

**CARTHAGE** Ancient city of northern Africa. Its religion was originally Phoenician, worshiping Molech, Eshmun, Tanit, and a host of lesser deities. Children were burned in worship of Molech or Baal-Ammon. Greek and Roman elements mixed with the older religion; Apollo and Dido invaded the city's army of gods. Christianity came early to Carthage. Its bishops included Aggripinus, TERTULLIAN, and CYPRIAN. FELICITY and PERPETUA were martyred and DONATISM and PELA-GIANISM flourished there.

**CARTHAGE, SYNODS OF** At least twelve important ecclesiastical synods were held at Carthage during the period from the third through the sixth centuries. They included the Conference of Carthage in 411 and the Council of Africa in 418.

**CARTHUSIANS** CATHOLIC monastic order founded in France in 1084 by St. BRUNO. This is the most severe order in the church; the members live in separate cells, live in prayer and silence, and speak to one another only once a week, except for daily services. They wear white and make Chartreuse liqueur. There are some nuns in the order.

**CARTOUCHE** 1. Wall tablet popular in seventeenth-century English churches for commemoration of the dead. 2. Oval Egyptian amulet worn for protection against the loss of one's name and soul.

**CARTWRIGHT, PETER (1785–1872)** American METHODIST preacher and circuit rider. Ordained by Bishops ASBURY and McKendree, he ran for Congress against Abraham Lincoln and lost to him. He baptized 12,000 converts, preached over 14,000 times, and founded Illinois Wesleyan University.

**CARVER, GEORGE WASHINGTON (c.1864–1943)** American Negro chemist and inventor. He asked God why He had made the peanut and proceeded to make 300 products from it, ranging from cheese and coffee to ink and soap. He was a man of brilliant mind and profound Christian faith.

**CARY, PHOEBE (1824–1871)** Christian poet of the United States, famous for the hymn "Nearer Home."

**CASE, SHIRLEY JACKSON (1872–1947)** American church historian and New Testament scholar. A BAPTIST and a liberal theologian, he emphasized the influence of its surroundings on the ancient church.

**CASSANDER, GEORGE (1513–1566)** Dutch theologian who opposed the claims of the pope but interpreted Protestant doctrines along Catholic lines, winning attacks from both Protestants and Catholics.

**CASSIAN, JOHN, ST. (c.360–435)** Hermit of the Middle East who helped found MONASTICISM in the West. Theologically a Semi-Pelagian, he wrote two works on monasticism. The Eastern Church considers him a saint. His feast day is July 23.

**CASSIODORUS (c.487–c.583)** Roman writer who founded two monasteries at Squillace, encouraged the copying of manuscripts, and wrote several religious books. The latter included a commentary on the Psalms, notes on other Scriptures, an encyclopedia for monks, and a discussion of *The Soul.*

**CASSOCK** Tight long-sleeved robe, usually black, worn by priests. It symbolizes devotion. The pope's cassock is white, a cardinal's red, a bishop's purple.

**CASTAGNO, ANDREA DEL (c.1423–1457)** Italian Renaissance religious painter. He painted "The Last Supper" and "David" and decorated a number of churches.

**CASTALIA** Spring on Mt. Parnassus near Delhi in Greece, sacred to APOLLO and the MUSES. Long considered a source of inspiration, it is now known as the Fountain of St. John.

**CASTALION or CASTELLIO, SÉBASTIEN (1515–1563)** French Protestant reformer who defended religious toleration, denounced the burning of Servetus, translated the Bible into Latin and French. He held that deeds are more important than creeds and that God requires sincerity. Also written Châtillon, Sébastian.

**CASTANETS** Concave percussion instruments clapped together to accompany the dancing in the rites of BACCHUS and DIONYSUS.

**CASTE** 1. Social system of hereditary divisions between groups. The caste system in India appears to have been imported by the conquering Aryans, who gave the lowlier occupations to the native dark-skinned Dravidians. BUDDHISM divides people into *a.* priests, *b.* warriors, *c.* farmers, merchants, and artisans and *d.* the menial laboring class. Lowest of all are the untouchable Pariahs. 2. Class, division, or position created by the caste system.

**CASTEL GANDOLFO** Town near Rome where the pope makes his summer residence.

**CASTELLIO** See CASTALION, SÉBASTIEN.

**CASTOR AND POLLUX** In classical myth, twin sons of Zeus and Leda who brought comfort to sailors by appearing to them in the form of St. Elmo's fire.

**CASTRATI** 1. Male sopranos, emasculated to preserve their high voices, who sang in papal and ecclesiastical choirs. The production of castrati was condemned by Popes BENEDICT XIV and CLEMENT XIV. 2. Eighteenth-century Russian cult of men who mutilated themselves to carry out literally the thought of Matthew 19:12.

**CASUISTRY** 1. Application of moral standards and principles to concrete questions of right and wrong in human conduct. 2. Because of the legalistic or hypocritical form such casuistry sometimes took, casuistry often means ethical sophistry, equivocation, quibbling, or evasion.

**CASWALL, EDWARD (1814–1878)** ANGLICAN curate who became a CATHOLIC priest and poet. He published devotional books and translated several Latin hymns, including "Jesus, the Very Thought of Thee."

**CAT** Animal considered by the ancient Egyptians and Norsemen to be divine; its life was protected in Egypt, and it was often embalmed after death. In religious art the cat is a symbol of lust or laziness.

**CATABAPTISTS** Term for those opposing BAPTISM.

**CATACOMBS** Subterranean burial places for Christians at Rome and other ancient cities. Some of these may have served as underground churches or as places of refuge from persecution.

**CATAFALQUE** Funeral stand, stage, framework, or hearse.

**CATECHESIS** Oral teaching of CATECHUMENS.

**CATECHETICS** Science or theology of teaching children or converts the Christian faith.

**CATECHISM** Summary or manual of doctrine for the instruction of those learning about Christianity; often arranged in the form of questions and answers.

**CATECHISM, LARGER** See LARGER CATECHISM.

**CATECHISM, SHORTER** See SHORTER CATECHISM.

**CATECHISM, SMALLER** Luther's catechism for laymen and children (1529).

**CATECHUMEN** One receiving Christian instruction while preparing for BAPTISM or CONFIRMATION.

**CATECHUMENS, MASS OF THE** First part of the EUCHARIST or communion service.

**CATEGORICAL IMPERATIVE** Immanuel KANT'S term for absolute moral law of which he suggested that there were two forms, one being the treatment of persons as ends and not means.

**CATENA** *chain* Series of excerpts from patristic and other early ecclesiastical authorities, combined for interpretation of Scripture or doctrine.

**CATENA, VINCENZIO (c.1470–1531)** Italian painter of many religious themes.

**CATENA AUREA** Group of commentaries on the GOSPELS compiled by St. AUGUSTINE.

**CATHARI** *the pure*. Also called Cathars, BOGOMILS, and ALBIGENSES, the Cathari were members of a medieval heretical group with MANICHAEAN and GNOSTIC teachings. Like the Gnostics, the Cathari held that physical things are intrinsically evil and are ruled over by Satan. They

were completely ascetic and saw salvation not as something accomplished by Christ but as a baptism with the Spirit and a denial of the flesh. They fasted thrice a week, observed LENT thrice a year, and forbade various foods (meat, cheese, eggs, and milk) and sex. Members renounced the church and the cross. Beginning as Believers, they went on to become, through BAPTISM OF THE HOLY SPIRIT, the Perfect. By the end of the fifteenth century they had been wiped out by persecution and the INQUISITION.

**CATHEDRA** *chair* 1. Official church teaching promulgated by a BISHOP or POPE. 2. Bishop's chair or throne.

**CATHEDRA, EX** *from the throne* Term for a formal pronouncement by the POPE infallibly defining a doctrine defending faith or morals.

**CATHEDRAL** 1. Church where a BISHOP has his *cathedra* as center of his DIOCESE. Cathedrals are usually large structures and often have several clergymen. 2. Relating to a bishop or POPE; official or authoritative.

**CATHEDRAL PRIORY** Building attached to a CATHEDRAL, for residential and religious purposes.

**CATHEDRAL SCHOOL** Diocesan parochial school.

**CATHERINE** Seven Catholic saints bear this name; see below.

**CATHERINE DE MEDICI (1519–1589)** French queen who plotted the Massacre of St. BARTHOLOMEW'S DAY in 1572.

**CATHERINE OF ALEXANDRIA, ST. (c. early fourth century)** Greek virgin martyr, tortured on a spiked wheel and beheaded. She is said to have been very learned. Among her symbols are the wheel and the book; her feast day is November 25.

**CATHERINE OF GENOA, ST. (1447–1510)** Italian mystic who gave her life to caring for the ill and wrote *Dialogues of the Soul and Body*. Canonized in 1737, she is remembered on July 22, her feast day.

**CATHERINE OF SIENA, ST. (1347–1380)** Italian dyer's daughter who whipped herself as a child and vowed perpetual virginity as a young girl. At the age of 28, the STIGMATA appeared on her. She had mystic visions in response to which she devoted herself to caring for the sick and poor. She also had great influence with the pope and helped end the GREAT SCHISM dividing the church. Vida Scudder called her "the most remarkable woman of the fourteenth century"; many acknowledge her to have been one of the greatest medieval religious persons. Although unable to write, she dictated *The Book of Divine Doctrine* and about 400 letters. She was declared a saint in 1461; her feast day is April 30.

**CATHERINE TEKAKWITHA (1656–1680)** American Indian of the Mohawk tribe, baptized as a girl of seven. Stoned for her faith, she became a Canadian ascetic and missionary and is said to have worked miracles.

**CATHOLIC** *universal* 1. Worldwide, unrestricted, well rounded. 2. Belonging to the one true "Holy Catholic Church" whose members love and serve Christ. 3. Related to the ROMAN CATHOLIC CHURCH.

**CATHOLIC ACTION** Lay ROMAN CATHOLIC activity carrying out cultural, moral, educational, or ecclesiastical purposes. It was defined in a letter of Pope PIUS XI in 1928, and has allied organizations in several countries.

**CATHOLIC APOSTOLIC CHURCH** Group formed under the inspiration of the Rev. Edward IRVING in London in the early nineteenth century, although the members regard Irving as the forerunner rather than the founder. Sometimes called IRVINGITES, the community was originally governed by twelve apostles. It practices the use of prophecy, unknown tongues, and other spiritual gifts. The liturgy is elaborate and there is believed to be a real presence of Christ in the EUCHARIST. Each congregation has an angel, 24 priests, and deacons, acolytes, and other officers. The Second Coming is emphasized.

**CATHOLIC CHURCH** 1. The whole Christian church, consisting of all believers. 2. The orthodox church, contrasted with groups considered heretical or divisive. 3. The ROMAN CATHOLIC CHURCH.

**CATHOLIC EMANCIPATION** British removal of anti-Catholic penal laws. Beginning in the eighteenth century, this emancipation movement is now fairly well complete in Great Britain, although laws still exclude Catholics from certain positions.

**CATHOLIC EPISTLES** "General" or "universal" letters of the New Testament: James; I, II, and III John; I and II Peter; and Jude. The name derives from the fact that these letters are not addressed to any specific individual or church—unlike the other New Testament epistles.

**CATHOLIC EVIDENCE GUILD** Lay Catholic movement emphasizing outdoor witnessing to beliefs of the ROMAN CATHOLIC CHURCH.

**CATHOLICITY** 1. Faith or system of the whole professing church. 2. Faith or doctrine of the ROMAN CATHOLIC CHURCH. 3. Breadth of belief or outlook.

**CATHOLIC LEAGUE or HOLY LEAGUE** Organization in France, originally headed by King Henry III, 1576–1598, which tried to suppress PROTESTANT belief and influence.

**CATHOLIC REFORMATION** See COUNTER REFORMATION.

**CATHOLIKOS or CATHOLICOS** 1. Patriarch of the ARMENIAN CHURCH. 2. Patriarch of the NESTORIAN CHURCH. 3. Head of several monasteries in the same city.

**CATO, DIONYSIUS (c. third century)** Author considered to have written *Dionysii Catonis Disticha de Moribus ad Filium*, a monotheistic moral treatise popular in the Middle Ages.

**CAUAC** Red Mayan god of the south.

**CAUCHON, PIERRE (?–1442)** French bishop who presided over the trial of JOAN OF ARC in 1431. He was posthumously excommunicated.

**CAUL** Membrane sometimes found around a newly born child's head. In Scotland such a caul was considered a sign of good luck or holiness.

**CAUSE** 1. Reason for something. In the older forms of theology and philosophy, God was considered the uncaused First Cause. 2. Ecclesiastical case, or a case before a church court.

**CAUTEL** Direction for correctly administering the SACRAMENTS.

**CAVALIER, JEAN (1681–1740)** Skillful leader of the CAMISARDS in eighteenth-century France. Finally abandoned by most of the Camisards, who thought he had been "bought off" with a pension, he fled to Spain and Great Britain. He was finally made lieutenant-governor of Jersey.

**CAVALIERS** English supporters of Charles I in the seventeenth century. The Cavaliers were in general of ANGLICAN persuasion while their opponents, the ROUNDHEADS, tended to have PURITAN and parliamentary (democratic) sympathies.

**CAVASILAS, NICKALAOS (?–1371)** Greek mystic, philosopher, and ecclesiastic. He supported the Greek against the Roman Church and wrote *Life in Christ* and other works. According to Dr. George Zachariades, "He is considered one of the greatest representatives of the Greek Church in mysticism."

**CECILIA, ST. (second century)** Martyr of Rome who died under the reign of Marcus Aurelius. She is considered the patron saint of music and of the blind. Her feast day is November 22.

**CEDAR** Evergreen tree used in the temple and the house of King Solomon (I KINGS 5—7). Very tall cedars came from the mountains of Lebanon. The fine, fragrant wood was considered incorruptible. In religious art, cedar is a symbol of the Messiah, faithfulness, and longevity.

**CEDRON** See KIDRON.

**CELEBRANT** One who administers the mass or EUCHARIST.

**CELEBRATION** Observance of public worship or COMMUNION.

**CELEBRET** *let him celebrate* Document authorizing the holder to celebrate the EUCHARIST.

**CELESTIAL CITY** Heavenly Jerusalem (REVELATION 21).

**CELESTINE I, ST.** Pope (422–432) who fought NESTORIANISM and PELAGIANISM. He interested himself in the spiritual welfare of Ireland and Britain and was canonized. His feast day is July 27.

**CELESTINE V, ST. (1215–1296)** Ascetic pope who was imprisoned first by Charles II of Naples and then by Boniface II. Canonized in 1313, he is commemorated with a feast day May 19.

**CELESTINES** Extremely ascetic order of monks founded by Peter of Morrone who became Pope CELESTINE V. The order is now extinct.

**CELIBACY** Unmarried state. It has been commended by the ESSENES, BUDDHISTS, and certain Christian groups, although the Judeo-Christian tradition honors the marital state.

**CELIBACY OF THE CLERGY** The idea of clerical celibacy gradually evolved in the ROMAN CATHOLIC CHURCH and was con-

firmed by the Council of TRENT. There is some agitation for such celibacy in the CHURCH OF ENGLAND today; at the same time there are growing demands in Catholicism for married clergymen.

**CELL** 1. Small monastic room or building. 2. Small unit of individuals who meet for spiritual purposes. Informal agenda usually center around prayer, study, fellowship, and counsel. Sometimes called a *circle*.

**CELLA** 1. Sanctuary of a Greek or Roman temple. 2. Small Christian chapel in a cemetery, for commemoration or worship.

**CELLARER** Monastic caterer or superintendent of provisions.

**CELSUS (second century)** Roman pagan philosopher known primarily through Origen's reply to his attacks on Christianity in *Against Celsus*. Celsus denied that Jesus was divine and attacked the idea of His incarnation, miracles, and resurrection. He said that Jesus was really the son of Mary and a Roman soldier named Panthera. Celsus' book *The True Discourse* urges Christians to abandon their faith, which, he believed, undermined the government.

**CELTIC CHURCH** Organized British Christianity before the mission of AUGUSTINE in the sixth century. It apparently began in the second or third century, and was monastic and evangelistic. The Celtic Christians had a distinctive tonsure and their own method of calculating Easter.

**CELTIC CROSS** Latin cross with a ring around the intersection of the two arms. Used by the monastic community founded by COLUMBA at Iona, the Celtic cross is popular with PRESBYTERIANS.

**CELTIC RELIGION** The Celts, a large race in central and western Europe and the British Isles, were Druidic. Worshiping in the open, they sacrificed animals and people to their gods and goddesses. They also worshiped trees, spirits, and various animals. Their priests, the DRUIDS, taught them "to worship the gods, to do no evil, to exercise courage."

**CEMETERY** Area for burial. In ancient times churchyards were often cemeteries. ROMAN CATHOLICISM has its own cemeteries for the faithful.

**CENACLE** 1. A Roman dining room. 2.

The upper room where the LAST SUPPER was taken (MARK 14:15).

**CENOBITES** Members of a monastic order who live together, in contrast to hermits or ANCHORITES who live in isolation from one another.

**CENSER** Metal container holding incense for burning during worship.

**CENSORSHIP** Suppression of material thought dangerous to the government, the church, or morals. Christian countries have often practiced censorship since medieval times, but contemporary Christian thought tends to oppose censorship.

**CENSURE** Ecclesiastical penalty ranging from a reprimand or deprivation of the sacrament to EXCOMMUNICATION or removal from office.

**CENTAUR** Creature of Greek mythology, below the waist a horse and above the waist a man. The centaur often symbolized brute passion or force.

**CENTRAL CONFERENCE OF AMERICAN RABBIS** Clerical organization of REFORM JUDAISM in the United States.

**CENTURION** Commander of 100 men in the Roman army. Jesus healed a centurion's servant (MATTHEW 8:1–13); a centurion was impressed by His death (LUKE 23:47).

**CEPHAS** *rock* Name given PETER (which also means rock or stone) by JESUS (JOHN 1:42).

**CERBERUS** Greek dog or monster who guarded the gates of hell.

**CERDONIANS** GNOSTIC sect founded in the second century by the Syrian Cerdo. He rejected all the Bible except the Gospel of Luke and the epistles of Paul.

**CEREALIA** Springtime festival of the Roman goddess CERES, held in mid-April.

**CERECLOTH** Waxed cloth for the altar, or for wrapping a corpse.

**CEREMONIAL** Ritual.

**CEREMONIAL LAW** That part of the Mosaic law which has to do with rites and ceremonies, in distinction from the moral law.

**CERES** Roman counterpart of Greek Demeter, goddess of grain, worshiped with fertility rites.

**CERIDWEN** British fertility goddess.

**CERINTHIANS** Followers of CERINTHUS.

**CERINTHUS (c.100)** Religious leader of Ephesus who held GNOSTIC doctrines—for example, that the world was made by angels of whom one was the god of the Jews, and that Jesus was a naturally born mortal on whom Christ came for a time. The Apostle John is said to have left the baths when Cerinthus entered, in fear that the roof must fall on such a heretic.

**CERMAIT** Celtic god of writing.

**CERULARIUS, MICHAEL** Patriarch of Constantinople (1043–1058) who denied the claims of LEO IX to be pope and thus precipitated the GREAT SCHISM between the Eastern and Western churches.

**CHABANEL, NOËL, ST. (1613–1649)** French Jesuit missionary to the Indians of North America. He was martyred by the Iroquois Indians and canonized. His feast day is September 26.

**CHABIB, JACOB BEN SOLOMON IBN (c.1460–1516)** Spanish Jewish commentator who wrote *En Yaakob*, an annotated compilation of parts of the Babylonian TALMUD.

**CHABURAH** Jews banded together to observe the ritual laws. Each week they enjoyed a meal together.

**CHAC or CHAC-MOOL** Mayan storm god.

**CHAFER, LEWIS SPERRY (1871–1952)** American PRESBYTERIAN evangelist, founder and president of Dallas Theological Seminary. Of conservative dispensational views, he lectured widely and wrote a number of books.

**CHAIR OF ST. PETER** 1. The papal eminence. When the pope speaks *ex cathedra*, "from the chair," Catholics may not question what he says. 2. The literal chair supposed to have been used by Peter as first pope. 3. Catholic feast days observed in remembrance of Peter's high position.

**CHAITANYA (1485–c.1530)** HINDU mystic of India and founder of the sect of the CHAITANYA VAISHNAVAS. He put religious dedication to KRISHNA above ritual and accepted those of any faith as his followers. He disappeared mysteriously.

**CHAITANYA VAISHNAVAS** Followers of CHAITANYA (above), found largely in Bengal, India; they sing hymns to VISHNU and Chaitanya to the accompaniment of cymbals and drums. They are divided into Gosains (ecclesiastics), Vrikats (celibate monks and nuns), and lay disciples.

**CHAITYA** JAIN or BUDDHIST shrine.

**CHAKHAM** Jewish term for wise man.

**CHAKMA** Tribe of India with animistic faith. Members cremate their dead near running water.

**CHAKRAVARTIN** HINDU, BUDDHIST, or JAIN term for a world ruler who bears the 32 characteristics of a great person.

**CHALCEDON, COUNCIL OF** Fourth ECU-MENICAL COUNCIL in the history of the church. Held at the town of Chalcedon in Asia Minor in 451, it annulled the actions taken at the Robber Synod (see EPHESUS, ROBBER SYNOD OF), rejected EUTYCHIANISM and NESTORIANISM, and affirmed that Christ has two inseparable but distinct natures, human and divine. It also put the Eastern bishop of Constantinople on a plane equal to the pope's and gave the former jurisdiction over the Eastern Church. The ROMAN CATHOLIC CHURCH has never accepted this last feature of the Council's decrees.

**CHALCEDONY** Green, blue, or white stone anciently found near Chalcedon in Asia Minor (cf. REVELATION 21:19).

**CHALCIHUITLICUE** Aztec goddess of the waters, ruling the third hour in the day and the sixth hour in the night. She also ruled those who traveled on running waters.

**CHALDEA** Southern part of the valley of the Tigris and Euphrates Rivers.

**CHALDEANS** 1. Babylonian or later inhabitants of Chaldea. 2. NESTORIAN Christians or CATHOLICS of Mesopotamia.

**CHALDEE** Archaic term for ARAMAIC.

**CHALICE** *cup* Cup holding the wine of the EUCHARIST.

**CHALICE, MIXED** EUCHARIST chalice containing wine mixed with water.

**CHALICE VEIL** Cloth, sometimes made of silk, for covering the empty chalice in the EUCHARIST.

**CHALITZAH** *removal* Jewish ceremony freeing a man from taking his brother's childless widow as a wife (see DEUTER-ONOMY 25).

**CHALKLEY, THOMAS (1675–1741)** QUAKER trader and missionary from England to the New World.

**CHALLAH** Jewish Sabbath bread.

**CHALLONER, RICHARD (1691–1781)** English CATHOLIC ecclesiastic. A controversialist, he also translated *The Imitation of Christ*, wrote devotional works, and prepared a history of Catholic martyrs. His

*Garden of the Soul* was a popular devotional manual.

**CHALMERS, JAMES (1841–1901)** Scottish CONGREGATIONAL missionary to New Guinea. Although he resisted any attempts to force the life of the natives into a Western mold, his work prepared the way for British colonization. He was killed by armed natives at Papua.

**CHALMERS, THOMAS (1780–1847)** Scottish preacher, theologian, and philanthropist who led in the founding of the FREE CHURCH OF SCOTLAND after he failed to achieve spiritual freedom in the Established Church. He sought to refute David Hume's skeptical philosophy and attacks on Christian miracles.

**CHALUKAH** Jewish term for distribution of charitable monies among the needy in Israel.

**CHAM** 1. Variant of HAM, son of Noah. 2. Indochinese Moslem tribe which combines MOSLEM, ANIMISTIC, and HINDU rites and beliefs. Members believe each person has many souls.

**CHAMBERLAIN** 1. Cardinal who administers the property of the VATICAN. 2. Secretary-treasurer of the College of Cardinals. 3. President of the Catholic SECULAR CLERGY of a city.

**CHAMBRE ARDENTE** *burning chamber* Extraordinary court held in France in the sixteenth and seventeenth centuries to pass final judgment on heretics.

**CHAMETZ** Jewish term for bread made with leaven or for food prohibited at PASS-OVER.

**CHAMPOLLION, JEAN FRANCOIS (1790–1832)** Founder of Egyptology. He made use of the ROSETTA STONE to decipher Egyptian hieroglyphics.

**CH'AN** Chinese form of ZEN Buddhism, influenced by TAOISM.

**CHANANEEL BEN CHUSHIEL (990–1050)** Tunisian commentator on the TALMUD and Old Testament.

**CHANCE** 1. Greek goddess named Tyche or Fortune. 2. That which is unpredictable or without known cause in life. Christian theology has little or no place for chance since all things are of, through, and unto God (ROMANS 11:36).

**CHANCEL** The part of a church set apart for the clergyman and often for the choir, the altar, the baptistery, and the like. In

High Church usage, the chancel is east of the nave.

**CHANCELLOR** 1. In the CHURCH OF ENGLAND, a chancellor may be the dignitary of a cathedral or the official who presides over the bishop's court and advises the bishop on legal matters. 2. In the ROMAN CATHOLIC CHURCH, the chancellor may be the head of the papal chancery, or the priest who cares for the archives of the diocese.

**CHANCERY, APOSTOLIC or PAPAL** Vatican office which issues papal BULLS for beginning new dioceses and the like.

**CHANCERY, DIOCESAN** Department of a bishop's court which cares for diocesan documents. It is headed by an ordained chancellor.

**CHANGELING** A baby substituted by fairies for the original which they stole.

**CHANG TAO-LING (first century)** Chinese teacher credited with making TAOISM a leading faith of China.

**CHANNING, WILLIAM ELLERY (1780–1842)** American UNITARIAN leader and theologian. Coleridge said of him, "He has the love of wisdom and the wisdom of love." Many, however, did not admire his opposition to CALVINISM, TRINITARIANISM, slavery, and war. He considered Christ to be "a being distinct from the one God."

**CHANT** Ecclesiastical form of singing psalms and canticles in one voice, unaccompanied. ANGLICAN chant requires the singing of a number of words on the same note. ROMAN CATHOLIC chant or plain song proceeds on different principles and has a free rhythm. EASTERN chant is of several complex types. Jewish chanting is often antiphonal.

**CHANTAL, JANE FRANCES DE** See JANE FRANCES DE CHANTAL, ST.

**CHANTICO** Aztec goddess of hearth fire.

**CHANTRY** 1. Small chapel where masses are chanted for the soul of the founder or of someone he had designated. 2. Endowment for such a chapel.

**CHANUKAH** See HANUKKAH.

**CHAOS** In Greek myth, infinite space; source of all there is, including the gods.

**CHAPEL** Place of worship apart from a church proper.

**CHAPLAIN** Originally the custodian of sacred relics in a royal chapel, the term now applies generally to a clergyman who performs duties distinct from the ordinary ones of a parish. Thus, there are chaplains in colleges, the Army, the Navy, etc.

**CHAPLET** ROSARY.

**CHAPMAN, JOHN (1774–1845)** "Johnny Appleseed," American frontiersman holding SWEDENBORGIAN views who planted apple trees throughout Pennsylvania, Ohio, and Indiana. He was generous and brave, and kind to wild animals.

**CHAPMAN, J. WILBUR (1859–1918)** American PRESBYTERIAN evangelist and author of *The Surrendered Life* and other books.

**CHAPTER** 1. Division of a book. (The chapters and verses of the Bible are a recent addition.) 2. Division of the rule of a monastery. 3. Membership of a religious house. 4. Assembly of the members of a religious house. 5. Branch of a religious order.

**CHAPTER, LITTLE** Short lesson from the BREVIARY.

**CHAPTER HOUSE** Building where a chapter meets.

**CHARACTER** 1. In common parlance, the sum of a person's traits and habits which guide his actions. In this sense character is affected by faith and idealism or their lack. 2. In CATHOLIC theology, the indelible mark of the sacraments on the human soul.

**CHARDIN** See TEILHARD DE CHARDIN, PIERRE.

**CHARGE** 1. An exhortation to one about to undertake new duties or responsibilities. 2. A parish.

**CHARGER** Platter brought as offering to the temple (EZRA 1:9).

**CHARIOT** Two-wheeled horse-drawn war vehicle often mentioned in the Bible. It was a symbol of power (PSALM 20:7).

**CHARIS grace** Greek word for loveliness, or for God's undeserved favor—grace—toward man.

**CHARISM** Spiritual gift.

**CHARISMA gift** Greek word in the New Testament for a special gift to the Christian believers, such as prophesying, healing, or speaking in unknown tongues (cf. I CORINTHIANS 12:4–11). The plural is *charismata*.

**CHARISMATIC RENEWAL** Term for spiritual renewal among Christians through the BAPTISM OF THE HOLY SPIRIT, accompanied by the manifestation of speaking in tongues (see GLOSSOLALIA). During the latter half of the twentieth century, PROTESTANTS of many denominations experienced such renewal.

**CHARITY** This word in the KING JAMES VERSION of the Bible means self-giving love. In CATHOLIC theology charity is a divinely infused gift enabling the recipient to love God and others. The modern meaning of *charity* as "philanthropy" is far removed from the original Christian concept.

**CHARITY, ACT OF** Action expressing the supernatural love of God.

**CHARITY, BROTHERS OF** See BROTHERS OF CHARITY.

**CHARITY, SISTERS OF** See SISTERS OF CHARITY.

**CHARLEMAGNE (742–814)** First Emperor of the Holy Roman Empire. Crowned by the pope, this Frankish monarch summoned ecclesiastical councils and was to some degree supreme in both church and state. A wise and benevolent ruler and an able educator, Charlemagne opposed the image worship of the EASTERN CHURCH. He was beatified.

**CHARLES, THOMAS (1755–1814)** Welsh METHODIST churchman, a founder of the BRITISH AND FOREIGN BIBLE SOCIETY.

**CHARLES BORROMEO, ST. (1538–1584)** Italian CATHOLIC saint, ecclesiastic, and leader of the COUNTER REFORMATION. Generous and godly in his private life, as cardinal and Archbishop of Milan he reformed much of the ecclesiastical life of his see, aided the Jesuits (see SOCIETY OF JESUS), and promoted the education of the clergy. He was responsible for much of the work of the Council of TRENT and founded a Confraternity of Christian Doctrine and the order of the Oblates of the Blessed Virgin and St. Ambrose. His feast day is November 4.

**CHARLES MARTEL Charles the Hammer (c.688–741)** Ruler of the Franks in western Europe who stopped the MOSLEM invasion of Europe by routing the Saracens at the Battle of Tours in 732 and furthered the work of BONIFACE and other missionaries among the German tribes. Under him began the evolution of the feudal system including the bestowal of ecclesiastical benefices upon his supporters. In many

ways he was like his grandson Charlemagne.

**CHARM** Trinket or incantation supposed to bring good luck and ward off evil.

**CHARNEL** Burial place.

**CHARNEL HOUSE** House or vault, connected in many cases with a church, for the storage of bones or corpses. The charnel house originated in the crowded condition of medieval cemeteries where the bones of former occupants were often disinterred.

**CHARON** Greek boatman who ferried deceased souls over the river Styx into Hades.

**CHARRON, PIERRE (1541–1603)** French Catholic apologist, theologian, preacher, and philosopher. He sought to establish proofs for theism, Christianity, and ROMAN CATHOLICISM. He saw true piety as the knowledge of oneself and of God.

**CHARTERHOUSE** CARTHUSIAN monastery. One of the most famous is the Charterhouse, London, long used for a public school which since 1872 has been moved to Surrey.

**CHARTREUSE, LA GRANDE** CARTHUSIAN monastery in France, unique in producing a liqueur called chartreuse.

**CHARVAKAS** See LOKAYATAS.

**CHARYBDIS** Greek monster hurled into the sea by ZEUS for her misdeeds. She created a whirlpool near the rocks of Scylla. Thus, to pass between Scylla and Charybdis is to steer a narrow course between two equally menacing dangers.

**CHASCA** Ancient love goddess of Peru.

**CHASID, CHASSID or HASID** Hebrew term for pious or devout.

**CHASIDIM, CHASSIDIM or HASIDIM** Plural form of the above. See HASIDIM.

**CHASTISEMENT** Discipline or punishment. The New Testament indicates that seeming evils are often God's disciplinary measures with a beneficial aim (cf. HEBREWS 12:5–11).

**CHASTITY** 1. Freedom from immoral sex. 2. Among ROMAN CATHOLICS, chastity often means celibacy and avoidance of sexual pleasure. Many religions connect celibacy and spirituality.

**CHASUBLE** Sleeveless outer garment worn by priest celebrating mass. It symbolizes charity.

**CHATAN BERESHIT** Jewish male honored by being assigned to the first reading of

Genesis on the day of Rejoicing of the Law.

**CHATAN TORAH**   Jewish male honored by being assigned the last reading from Deuteronomy on the day of Rejoicing of the Law.

**CHATAT**   Jewish sin offering.

**CHÂTILLON, SÉBASTIEN**   See CASTALION, SÉBASTIEN.

**CHATTERJEE, BANKIM CHANDRA (1838–1894)**   "Ramchandra," writer of India whose song "Hail to the Mother" implies adoration of KALI, invoking destruction, and became the national anthem of India. His novels presented India as a divine motherland and aided HINDUISM there.

**CHAUMONOT, JOSEPH MARIE (1611–1693)**   French JESUIT missionary to Quebec and New York.

**CHAUNCY, CHARLES (1705–1787)**   Grandson of a scholarly clergyman and Harvard president by the same name, Chauncy was an Old Light CONGREGATIONAL theologian and liberal leader. He saw the GREAT AWAKENING in eighteenth-century New England as an outbreak of emotional extremism. Eventually he accepted UNIVERSALIST views, and opposed the establishment of an ANGLICAN bishopric in America. He was an ardent patriot in the Revolutionary War.

**CHAZARS or KHAZARS**   Turks who, under their King Bular, accepted JUDAISM in the eighth century as an effective compromise between the religious and political claims of ISLAM and CHRISTIANITY. Their regime ranked high in civilization and religious toleration.

**CHAZZAN**   Jewish CANTOR. Originally this official had various other duties.

**CHEBAR**   Canal or stream in Babylon where displaced Jews dwelt after the captivity of the fourth century B.C. Here Ezekiel had many visions.

**CHEDER room**   Jewish school or class for instruction in ritual and Hebrew.

**CHEESE SUNDAY**   Ancient designation of the Sunday in the last week before Lent, in which cheese might be eaten.

**CHELA**   Disciple of a GURU in India.

**CHELAL perfection**   Term for a Jew who returned from captivity to Jerusalem (EZRA 10:30).

**CHEMNITZ, MARTIN (1522–1586)**   German reformer who accepted and defended LUTHERAN doctrines. He took part in the ADIAPHORIST dispute, attacked Catholicism, and persuaded the Saxons and Swabians to accept the Formula of CONCORD.

**CHEMOSH**   Moabite war god before whom a Moabite king offered his son as a human sacrifice (II KINGS 3:27). Solomon built an altar for Chemosh (I KINGS 11:7). He is identified with the Babylonian god SHAMASH.

**CHENREZI**   Tibetan name of AVALOKITESVARA. The patron god of the country, he is considered to be incarnated in each DALAI LAMA.

**CHEREM ban**   Excommunication from the Jewish community. Spinoza was one thus banned because of his views.

**CHERITH**   Brook flowing into the Jordan River in the Trans-Jordan. Here Elijah hid and was miraculously fed.

**CHERRY**   Symbol of sweetness or of paradise.

**CHERUB**   Winged angelic creature which adores and serves God (PSALM 18:10; EZEKIEL 10).

**CHERUBICON**   "Cherubic Hymn" used in the EASTERN CHURCH liturgy.

**CHERUBIM**   Plural form of cherub. In the King James Bible the letter s is sometimes added to this already plural word.

**CHESTER BEATTY PAPYRI**   Scraps of papyrus found in 1931 in Egypt containing fragments of Genesis, Isaiah, Jeremiah, the Gospels, and other religious writings. Named for their purchaser, they are important in the study of the Greek text of the Scriptures.

**CHESTERTON, GILBERT KEITH (1874–1936)**   English author who made a strong case throughout his brilliant writings for medievalism, Christianity, and ROMAN CATHOLICISM—he was converted to the latter in 1922.

**CHESTNUT**   Religious symbol of chastity.

**CHETH**   Eighth letter in the Hebrew alphabet.

**CHEVERUS, JEAN LOUIS (1768–1838)**   First ROMAN CATHOLIC bishop of Boston. Popular with both PROTESTANTS and CATHOLICS, he won praise as a physician and preacher and showed courage as he ministered to victims of the yellow fever epidemic of 1798. He was made a cardinal while Archbishop of Bordeaux, France, shortly before his death.

**CHEVRA KADISHA** *holy association* Jewish guild or community group which prepares corpses for burial.

**CHIA** Moon goddess of the Muscaya Indians of North America.

**CHICAGO-LAMBETH ARTICLES** Four articles agreed upon at an EPISCOPAL convention in Chicago in 1886 and approved by the LAMBETH CONFERENCE of 1888 as enunciating the requirements of a reunited church.

**CHICAGO SCHOOL OF THEOLOGY** Theological viewpoint of Shailer MATHEWS and others of the Divinity School of the University of Chicago. Rather than accept any theology as absolute, this point of view interpreted all theology on a social, historical, and functional basis.

**CHICOMECOATL** or **CHICOMECOHUATL** Aztec maize goddess, worshiped with the sacrifice of a young girl who was flayed.

**CHILDERMAS** Old English name for the Feast of the Holy Innocents, observed December 28 in commemoration of the children slain by Herod at the birth of Christ.

**CHILDREN OF GOD** New Testament term for those redeemed by Christ and enjoying fellowship with God through faith.

**CHILDREN OF ISRAEL** Old Testament term for the Jewish people.

**CHILDREN OF THE LIGHT** An early name of the FRIENDS who were converted under the preaching of the QUAKER founder, George Fox.

**CHILDREN'S CRUSADE** After several of the CRUSADES had foundered in shame, a French peasant lad named Stephen of Cloyes gathered children from France and Germany about 1212. They followed the cross in the belief that innocent children could do what sin-stained adults could not. Some died of disease and hunger while the rest were apparently sold into slavery before they could reach the HOLY LAND.

**CHILIASM** Christian doctrine that Christ will return to earth to reign for a thousand (Greek *chilioi*) years. Compare Revelation 20:1–5, which this view interprets literally.

**CHILION** *wasting away* Son of Naomi who married the sister of Ruth (RUTH 1:2, 5).

**CHILLINGWORTH, WILLIAM (1602–1644)** English divine who after conversion to Catholicism was reconverted to the CHURCH OF ENGLAND. He proclaimed that "the Bible only is the religion of Protestants."

**CHILLUL HA-SHEM** *desecration of the name* Jewish term for desecration of the name of God.

**CHIMERA** Flame-throwing monster of Greek myth.

**CHIMERE** Long sleeveless satin garment worn by a BISHOP over his ROCHET.

**CHINA, RELIGION IN** The Chinese tend to be BUDDHIST, TAOIST, and CONFUCIANIST. Traditionally, ancestors are worshiped along with a multitude of other gods and spirits. The national worship of Confucius is not inconsistent in Chinese thought with adherence to other religions. Other religions in China include ISLAM, JUDAISM, and CHRISTIANITY. ROMAN CATHOLICS outnumber PROTESTANTS about nine to one.

**CHINA INLAND MISSION** Largest Protestant mission operating in China for some years. Founded by Hudson Taylor in 1866, it turned to other Eastern countries after the Communist conquest of the 1950's. It recently changed its name to the China Inland Overseas Missionary Fellowship.

**CHINUCH** *consecration* Jewish dedication of a new home.

**CHINVAT PERETU** Bridge in ZOROASTRIANISM over which the soul passes at death on its way to be judged. For the righteous this bridge is broad and pleasant, but for the evil it is narrow and slippery and from it the soul falls to the demons waiting below.

**CHIPPEWA INDIAN RELIGION** The Chippewa or Ojibwa Indians of North America believed in a divine force in the universe which often revealed its presence in animals. For entrance into the world beyond they joined the "Great Medicine Society" which involved elaborate picture writing and a difficult initiation.

**CHI RHO** Greek letters beginning the name of Christ, symbolizing His name and cross. They have the form $X$ and $P$.

**CHISHTI, MUIN-AL-DIN MUHAMMAD (1142–1236)** Mystic saint of India who founded a SUFI order.

**CHITTIM** See KITTIM.

**CHIVALRY** Medieval system of knighthood recognized by the church in an elaborate investiture ceremony. The knight promised to protect women and the weak and to be magnanimous in battle. He pledged loyalty to God, his master, and the mistress of his heart. Mary received special honor in the age of chivalry (the tenth through the fourteenth centuries).

**CHLISTS** See KHLYSTS.

**CHNOUMIS** Egyptian creator-god.

**CHOHAN** BUDDHIST term for exceptional spirituality.

**CHOIR** 1. Organized singers in a service of worship. 2. Class in a religious order which specializes in doing the order's particular work. 3. Portion of church where the choir sings.

**CHOIR GOWN** Robe or vestment of choir member.

**CHOIR LOFT** Elevated portion of a church where the choir sings.

**CHOIR OFFICE** Worship service conducted in the choir portion of the CHANCEL.

**CHOIR SISTERS** Nuns who must attend all choir offices.

**CHOIR STALLS** Pews where the choir sings.

**CHOKHMAH** Jewish term for wisdom.

**CHORALE** 1. Metrical hymn introduced into worship at the REFORMATION. 2. Simple hymn tune sung in unison.

**CHOREPISCOPUS** *country overseer* 1. Bishop in the early church appointed over a rural district. 2. Honorary title in the PATRIARCHATE of Antioch.

**CHORISTER** 1. Singer in a choir. 2. Choirboy. 3. Choir leader.

**CHORTENS** Tibetan memorials of BUDDHA or LAMAS.

**CHOSEN PEOPLE** 1. Term for the Jewish people, chosen by the Lord for His unfolding earthly purposes. 2. Term for Christians elect or chosen in Christ (I PETER 1:1–2; 2:9). 3. Term for Mormons.

**CHOVAH** Jewish term for religious requirement.

**CHRISM** Holy ecclesiastical oil for baptizing, blessing, etc.

**CHRISMAL or CHRISMATORY** Vessel or place for the CHRISM.

**CHRISMON** Monogram of CHI RHO, the first two Greek letters in the name of Christ. Some early Christian tombs bear the Chrismon.

**CHRISOM** White cloth thrown over a baptized child to symbolize innocence.

**CHRIST** *The Anointed One* Greek form of the Hebrew *Mashiah*, Messiah. This is the New Testament title of Jesus of Nazareth,
considered by Christians to be the Messiah of the Jewish Scriptures. To some Christ is a term for the Eternal Logos quite different from the historical Jesus, but most Christians accept the simple name Jesus Christ and see no conflict between the two names. See JESUS.

**CHRISTADELPHIANS** *brothers of Christ* American denomination founded in 1848 by John Thomas. Christadelphians believe that salvation is through Christ, who will soon return to reign from Jerusalem as capital of His Kingdom. They do not have ordained clergymen, do not accept the TRINITY, and do not participate in such civic activities as voting.

**CHRIST BEFORE PILATE** Painting by the Hungarian artist Michael Munkacsy of Christ on trial before Pilate.

**CHRISTENDOM** This is a loose term for the supposedly Christian countries of the West, as distinguished from countries where Christianity is a minority faith. Sometimes Christendom is used to mean the church or Christianity.

**CHRISTENING** Term for BAPTISM, at which a "Christian" name is often given the person baptized.

**CHRIST EVENT** Neo-orthodox term for the symbolic interpretation of Christ's life and death as revealing the eternal movement of redemption.

**CHRISTIAN** 1. One who believes in Christ and follows Him. 2. Relating to Christ or Christianity or the church.

**CHRISTIAN ACTION** 1. Lay Apostolate in the ROMAN CATHOLIC CHURCH. 2. Interdenominational movement for application of Christian principles to public life.

**CHRISTIAN AND MISSIONARY ALLIANCE** American denomination founded by A. B. Simpson in 1881. Its views are FUNDAMENTALIST, PREMILLENNIAL, and EVANGELISTIC; it recognizes Christ as Saviour, Sanctifier, Healer, and Coming Lord.

**CHRISTIAN BROTHERS** Order of the Brothers of Christian Schools, founded in 1684 by St. JOHN BAPTIST DE LA SALLE. It was the first CATHOLIC order devoted entirely to Christian education.

**CHRISTIAN BROTHERS, IRISH** Institute for Christian education founded by Edward Ignatius Rice in 1802. It conducts schools in various countries.

**CHRISTIAN CATHOLIC APOSTOLIC CHURCH**

**IN ZION** See CHRISTIAN CATHOLIC CHURCH.

**CHRISTIAN CATHOLIC CHURCH** Religious group founded in 1896 in Chicago, Illinois, by John Alexander DOWIE. It emphasizes divine healing, Scripture, SALVATION, TRINE IMMERSION, and TITHING. Its members refrain from tobacco, alcohol, and pork.

**CHRISTIAN CHURCHES (DISCIPLES OF CHRIST)** American denomination founded early in the nineteenth century by dissidents who broke away from Presbyterian, Methodist, and Baptist churches. Members observe the LORD'S SUPPER weekly and practice cooperation with other churches. The group has a congregational system of government. Sometimes uses DISCIPLES OF CHRIST and CHURCHES OF CHRIST interchangeably with full name given here.

**CHRISTIAN CHURCH OF NORTH AMERICA** American denomination resulting from a merger of the Italian Christian Churches of North America and the General Council of the Italian Pentecostal Assemblies of God.

**CHRISTIAN COMMUNITIES OF CHRIST** See DOUKHOBORS.

**CHRISTIAN CONGREGATION** American church group seeking Christian fellowship in love and emphasizing Bible study and mission work. Members do not borrow money.

**CHRISTIAN EDUCATION** Education in Christian beliefs, practices, etc. This is done in many churches locally through a church school and the pastor's work, nationally through the denomination's church school curriculum and national projects, and internationally through mission and other endeavors. From a broad point of view, Christian education involves nearly everything the church does. In addition, many parochial schools and colleges and seminaries provide such education.

**CHRISTIAN ENDEAVOR** Interdenominational youth association founded in 1881 in Portland, Maine, by Francis E. CLARK. Full name: Young People's Society of Christian Endeavor (Y.P.S.C.E.). For many years Daniel A. Poling has been an active leader of this group in the United States.

**CHRISTIAN ERA** Term for the period since the birth of Christ.

**CHRISTIAN FLAG** Banner adopted by a number of PROTESTANTS in the United States as a herald of their faith.

**CHRISTIANITY** 1. Christian character in an individual. 2. The Christian faith and gospel. 3. Christendom. 4. The sum total of Christian faith and life in the world.

**CHRISTIAN KNOWLEDGE, SOCIETY FOR PROMOTING** CHURCH OF ENGLAND organization dating from 1698 and existing to distribute Bibles and Christian literature in various languages.

**CHRISTIAN LIBRARY** Series of 50 books published by John WESLEY for the spiritual edification of his followers.

**CHRISTIAN METHODIST EPISCOPAL CHURCH** Denomination in southern United States which has METHODIST polity and Negro membership. It was established in 1870 as the Colored Methodist Episcopal Church.

**CHRISTIAN NAME** 1. First name. 2. Name assumed at baptism. When a non-Christian is converted and baptized in a non-Christian country, the new Christian name is often from the Bible.

**CHRISTIAN NATION CHURCH** Very small American denomination which forbids jesting and teaches JUSTIFICATION, SANCTIFICATION, SPIRITUAL HEALING, and the SECOND COMING.

**CHRISTIAN NURTURE** Book by Horace BUSHNELL, published in 1846, which taught that the date of conversion is less important in the life of a child of Christian parents than the process of nurture and growth. Basic principle: "That the child is to grow up as a Christian, and never know himself as being otherwise."

**CHRISTIAN RADICALS** Term applied in the late 1960's to the so-called "atheistic theologians" who popularized the idea of "the death of God." Three prominent leaders were William Hamilton, Thomas J. J. Altizer, and Paul van Buren, all PROTESTANT theological professors in the United States. They seemed to be saying that God was no longer relevant to modern man, that He had vacated the universe.

**CHRISTIAN REFORMED CHURCH** American denomination with Dutch background and Reformed principles. Like the REFORMED CHURCH IN AMERICA, from which it withdrew in 1857, it is governed by ministers and ruling elders constituting a consistory in each church, by classes, and by an annual synod. Its doctrinal standards are the Synod of DORT, the BELGIC CONFESSION, and the HEIDELBERG CATECHISM.

**CHRISTIAN SCIENCE** Religious system founded by Mary Baker EDDY. After her own healing following a serious accident through spiritual means alone, Mrs. Eddy searched for laws which underlay similar healings recorded in the Bible. She called her discovery Christian Science. The theology of Christian Science holds that God's infinite goodness is the scientific truth of being and is brought to light through prayer and Christian regeneration.

**CHRISTIAN SOCIALISM** Political philosophy based upon the attempt to substitute cooperation and the social gospel for competition and laissez faire. In the United States the Society of Christian Socialists was formed in 1889. At present Christianity in general recognizes the need for applying Christian principles not only to individual but to social concerns: poverty, labor, automation, human rights, war, etc.

**CHRISTIANS OF ST. JOHN** See MANDAEANS.

**CHRISTIANS OF ST. THOMAS** Members of the Syrian Church of India, said to have been founded by the Apostle Thomas. They have a Jacobite theology and celibate priests (see JACOBITES).

**CHRISTIAN'S SECRET OF A HAPPY LIFE** Book written by Quaker Hannah Whitall Smith, published in 1883 in the United States, outlining steps to victory and happiness in the Christian's devotional life.

**CHRISTIAN UNION** 1. Term for union of Christians and/or their churches. Christ prayed that "they all may be one" (JOHN 17:21). During the twentieth century many Protestant denominations reunited and a spirit of brotherhood increased among PROTESTANTS, CATHOLICS, and JEWS. 2. A denomination by this name was organized in 1864 in the United States. It has both male and female ministers and a congregational system of government.

**CHRISTIAN UNITY BAPTIST ASSOCIATION** Denomination originating in 1934 in North Carolina. Members practice FOOT WASHING.

**CHRISTIAN VIRTUES** Supreme Christian virtues are faith, hope, and love (I CORINTHIANS 13:13). Additional Christian virtues are listed in Galatians 5:22–23; James 2:8–14; and II Peter 1:5–7.

**CHRISTIAN YEAR** 1. Ecclesiastical calendar of the seasons and holy days of the church. Beginning with ADVENT and CHRISTMAS, the year proceeds through EPIPHANY, LENT, HOLY WEEK, EASTER, WHITSUNTIDE, and KINGDOMTIDE. 2. A collection of verse, *The Christian Year*, by John KEBLE, published in England in 1827, was popular in the nineteenth century throughout the English-speaking world.

**CHRIST IN GETHSEMANE** Famous painting by Johann Heinrich Hofmann showing Christ kneeling in prayer in the Garden of GETHSEMANE.

**CHRISTLESS** Term for being without the presence or influence of Jesus Christ.

**CHRISTLIKE** Resembling Jesus Christ in deeds, words, or spirit.

**CHRISTMAS** Derived from "Christ's Mass," the celebration of the Nativity, Christmas has won its way into the hearts of nearly all in the Western world. Although no one knows the date of Christ's birth, Christmas is generally observed on December 25. The Armenian Church observes it on January 6. Modern Christmas merrymaking owes much to German traditions, to St. NICHOLAS, and to Charles Dickens.

**CHRISTMAS EVE** The night before Christmas, on which the vigil of the nativity is kept and American children hang their stockings by the chimney.

**CHRISTMASTIDE** The "Twelve Days of Christmas" extending from Christmas through EPIPHANY Eve or Twelfth Night.

**CHRISTMAS TREE** The bringing of a green tree into the house at Christmas may have originated in the ancient Germans' sacred oak which BONIFACE replaced with a fir tree for Christ, or in Martin LUTHER's putting candles in a tree at Christmas. Prince Albert introduced this German custom to England and America.

**CHRIST MYTH** 1. Term indicating a concept of CHRIST as a source of symbolic rather than factual truth. 2. Term for a quaint German theory that JESUS originated either as an astral deity or as a projection out of the repressions of the lowest classes in the Roman Empire.

**CHRISTOCENTRIC** 1. Christ-centered, as theology or religious education. 2. This is also a technical term referring to a theology which has no place for natural revelation and holds that God has never been revealed except in Christ.

**CHRIST OF THE ANDES** Statue of Christ on the borders of Chile and Argentina beneath which are the words: "Sooner shall these mountains crumble into dust than Argentines and Chileans break the peace sworn at the feet of Christ the Redeemer."

**CHRISTOGRAM** Symbol of Christ with the first two Greek letters in His name superimposed thus: ☧

**CHRISTOLOGY** Theology of the person, work, and natures of Christ. Orthodox Christianity holds that Christ is the MESSIAH, the Son of God and Saviour. He died for the sin of the world, redeems His people forever, and is the third person of the TRINITY in two natures, fully human and fully divine.

**CHRISTOPHER, ST.** *Christ-bearer* (third century) Syrian Christian martyred in Asia Minor under the persecutions of the Emperor Decius. A legend states that he once ferried Jesus, a child holding the world in His hands, across a river. Christopher is the patron saint of travelers and ferrymen. His feast day is July 25.

**CHRISTOPHERS, THE** Organization founded by the American priest Father James Keller in 1945. It emphasizes the idea that each person has a personal responsibility to carry out a divine mission, to be a Christ-bearer, to light a candle rather than to curse the darkness. It seeks to restore human and spiritual values in government, education, labor, management, literature, entertainment, and culture.

**CHRISTOS** Greek word for anointed one, MESSIAH, or Christ.

**CHRIST SPHERE** According to the teachings of spiritism, one of the most highly exalted spheres through which a soul passes after leaving the body at death.

**CHRIST'S SANCTIFIED HOLY CHURCH** Formerly the Colored Church South, this tiny American denomination emphasizes instantaneous SANCTIFICATION and has both male and female ministers.

**CHRISTUS, PETRUS (?–c.1473)** Flemish painter of ability who executed many jewel-like scenes of Christ, the Virgin, and other religious subjects.

**CHRONICLES, I AND II** Also called PARALIPOMENON, these books record Hebrew genealogies and the reigns of David and Solomon, concluding with the BABYLONIAN CAPTIVITY. They duplicate the narratives of I and II Samuel and I and II Kings but tell the story from the viewpoint of the Southern Kingdom of Judah.

**CHRYSANTHIUS (fourth century)** Greek philosopher and NEOPLATONIST who served as high priest of Lynia.

**CHRYSOSTOM, ST. JOHN** See JOHN CHRYSOSTOM.

**CHTHONIAN** *under the earth* Term indicating relationship to spirits or gods of the world below, entered at death.

**CHUANG-TZE (fourth century)** Chinese philosopher who followed the teachings of LAO-TZE and taught them instead of those of CONFUCIUS. He was thus a founder of TAOISM.

**CHUCIUS or CHU HSI or CHU FU TZU (1130–1200)** Chinese proponent of the Confucian Sing-li philosophy which has no place for spirits or miracles but emphasizes personal righteousness. This is based on man's intelligence and spirituality.

**CHUETAS** *pork-eaters* Term of derision for Jews descended from MARANOS of Spain and Portugal who had been forced to accept Christianity in the Middle Ages but who had secretly held to their original faith.

**CHUFUT-KALE** Town of the Ukraine which was a center of KARAITE Judaism during the sixteenth, seventeenth, and eighteenth centuries.

**CHU FU TZU** See CHUCIUS.

**CHU HSI** See CHUCIUS.

**CHUMASH** *five* See PENTATEUCH.

**CHUNTOKYO** Korean religion of an impersonal God; it emphasizes repetition of the 22 words revealed in the form of a divine formula to the founder, Choi Chei Oo. He and his successor were both executed but the movement they led continued to expand.

**CHUPPAH** See HUPPAH.

**CHURCH** 1. In the New Testament particularly, the body of Christian believers.

2. This body is manifested in a particular place as a local church. Thus the one church may be said to consist of many individual churches. 3. In contemporary parlance (although never in the NEW TESTAMENT) a church is a building for worship. 4. Various sects and denominations are referred to as churches: the Church of England, the Lutheran Church, the Roman Catholic Church, the Methodist Church, etc. 5. Church often means public worship. 6. Sometimes it means religion in general, as in the phrase "church and state." 7. At times church means clergymen.

**CHURCH, RICHARD WILLIAM (1815–1890)** English ecclesiastic who was a close friend of John Henry NEWMAN and wrote the authoritative *History of the Oxford Movement* (1891).

**CHURCH AGE** The present period. Beginning with PENTECOST early in the first century, it is considered that the church will continue through the present age until Christ's reign is complete. Thereafter the body of believers will enjoy endless glory.

**CHURCH AND STATE** Term for the relationship between government and religion. This has always been a relationship of tension, and the present freedom of religion in many countries does not lessen the rivalry of church and state for supreme control of the individual who may wish to honor both.

**CHURCH ARMY** Organization of the CHURCH OF ENGLAND for evangelism and welfare work among the poor, the workers, the unemployed, delinquent individuals, soldiers, and those in need.

**CHURCHES OF CHRIST** Conservative American denomination, associated originally with the DISCIPLES OF CHRIST and still using both names interchangeably to some extent. The members do not permit musical instruments in worship, seek to abide by the doctrines of the New Testament, and practice an extreme CONGREGATIONAL form of government. They are aggressively EVANGELISTIC and have grown rapidly. Some members are known for ultraconservative political views.

**CHURCHES OF CHRIST IN CHRISTIAN UNION** American denomination which withdrew from the CHRISTIAN UNION because of its members' desire to emphasize SANCTIFICA-TION as a second definite work of grace subsequent to REGENERATION. The group holds to FUNDAMENTALISM in belief and a CONGREGATIONAL form of church government.

**CHURCHES OF GOD** In general, these are American denominations that emphasize EVANGELISM, SCRIPTURE, the TRINITY, and particularly the HOLY SPIRIT. See specific denominations.

**CHURCHES OF GOD, HOLINESS** American denomination which originated in Atlanta, Georgia, in 1914 under K. H. Burruss. Members wash one another's feet and believe in perfection and divine healing.

**CHURCHES OF GOD IN NORTH AMERICA (GENERAL ELDERSHIP)** American denomination originating about 1825 in Pennsylvania under the leadership of Rev. John Winebrenner. Members observe the SAB-BATH, practice FOOT WASHING, and believe their group to be the true church. The church government is PRESBYTERIAN in form, headed by a General Eldership.

**CHURCHES OF THE NEW JERUSALEM** Sometimes called the New Church or the Swedenborgian Church, this is a group organized in London about 1787. The first American society was organized in 1792 at Baltimore, Maryland. Members are followers of Emanuel SWEDENBORG, an eminent Swedish scientist and mystic. They believe in Jesus Christ as the only God, in beneficent and evil spirits, and in a new dispensation of the New Jerusalem into which men passed with the revelation through Swedenborg. Their ritual and government somewhat resemble the EPISCO-PALIAN.

**CHURCHGOER** One who attends church.

**CHURCH HISTORY** History of the church and of events since its inception early in the first century.

**CHURCHING OF WOMEN** Christian rite of thanksgiving, offered by a mother after birth of her child. Although "churching of women" is a British phrase, the ceremony is carried out not only in the CHURCH OF ENGLAND but also in the ROMAN and GREEK CATHOLIC CHURCHES.

**CHURCH IN THE PROVINCE OF THE WEST INDIES** ANGLICAN church of the West Indies.

**CHURCH IN WALES** ANGLICAN or Episcopal Church of Wales.

**CHURCHMAN** 1. Clergyman. 2. Church member.

**CHURCH MILITANT** Term for the church in its warfare with evil, often in contrast to the church triumphant, finally victorious.

**CHURCH MISSIONARY SOCIETY** Missionary organization of the CHURCH OF ENGLAND, founded in 1799.

**CHURCH OF CHRIST (HOLINESS) U.S.A.** American Holiness denomination founded by Rev. C. P. Jones in 1894. Members practice FOOT WASHING, baptize by IMMERSION, accept SPIRITUAL HEALING, and receive the HOLY SPIRIT. Government is by bishops.

**CHURCH OF CHRIST IN JAPAN** Merger of 15 denominations in Japan in 1941.

**CHURCH OF CHRIST, SCIENTIST** See also CHRISTIAN SCIENCE. Religious group of which the Mother Church is at Boston, Massachusetts. There are approximately 3,300 local churches or branches in 57 countries, democratically self-governed under provisions of the denomination's *Church Manual.* The church stresses SPIRITUAL HEALING as a practical element of Christian life.

**CHURCH OF CHRIST, TEMPLE LOT** MORMON body founded at Bloomington, Illinois, in 1844. The members do not practice polygamy, baptize for the dead, or accept the deity of men who have died. They plan to build a temple for the Lord's return at Independence, Missouri.

**CHURCH OF DANIEL'S BAND** American denomination founded at Marine City, Michigan, in 1893. It preaches perfect holiness and abstinence from excess.

**CHURCH OF ENGLAND** British Christianity dates from very early in the Christian era—according to tradition, from JOSEPH OF ARIMATHEA's efforts, certainly as early as the third century. It has its own special history. But the CHURCH OF ENGLAND in its present form owes much to the influence of King Henry VIII, and to the Act of Supremacy in 1534 which acknowledged the British king as its only supreme head. Thus the Church of England is established by law. Its government is EPISCOPALIAN—controlled by bishops. Its other clergymen are priests and deacons. Its worship derives from the BOOK OF COMMON PRAYER; its doctrines are from the Bible, the Thirty-Nine ARTICLES, and three creeds: the APOSTLES', the NICENE, and the ATHANASIAN.

**CHURCH OF ENGLAND IN AUSTRALIA** The ANGLICAN church of that country. Its doctrine and government are similar to those of the Church of England in England.

**CHURCH OF ENGLAND IN CANADA** Former name of the ANGLICAN CHURCH OF CANADA.

**CHURCH OF GOD** Many churches bear this name in some form. The Church of God is the specific title of a denomination organized originally by Bishop A. J. Tomlinson about 1903 (see CHURCH OF GOD OF PROPHECY). The present group by this name was organized by Bishop Tomlinson's son Homer, after the former's death in 1943. Emphasizing FUNDAMENTALIST doctrines, BAPTISM OF THE SPIRIT, SPIRITUAL HEALING, and tongue-speaking (see GLOSSOLALIA), its headquarters are in Queens Village, New York.

**CHURCH OF GOD (ABRAHAMIC FAITH)** American ADVENTIST denomination emphasizing the SECOND COMING of Christ and His literal reign over the earth during the millennium.

**CHURCH OF GOD (ANDERSON, INDIANA)** American group emphasizing New Testament Christianity, the unity of the church, personal holiness, the SECOND COMING of Christ, and God's reign at the present time. Government is CONGREGATIONAL.

**CHURCH OF GOD AND SAINTS OF CHRIST** Denomination founded in the United States in 1896 by Bishop William S. Crowdy. Members believe that Negroes are descended from the lost ten tribes of Israel, and they observe much of the Old Testament including the special feasts and the MOSAIC LAW. Heading the church is a prophet who is believed to speak directly for God and to work miracles. Members may not marry outside the church.

**CHURCH OF GOD (APOSTOLIC)** Group organized at Danville, Kentucky, by Elder Thomas J. Cox in 1896. Members wash one another's feet and use fresh grape juice and unleavened bread during communion.

**CHURCH OF GOD AS ORGANIZED BY CHRIST** American denomination organized by Rev. P. J. Kaufman in 1886. Members practice FOOT WASHING, restitution, and nonresistance. They are opposed to tobacco, jewelry, revivals, denominationalism, and cooperation between denominations.

**CHURCH OF GOD (CLEVELAND, TENNESSEE)** Denomination organized in 1886 as The Christian Union. Its theology is fundamentalist and Pentecostal, emphasizing the BAPTISM OF THE SPIRIT accompanied by speaking in tongues (see GLOSSOLALIA), salvation, SPIRITUAL HEALING, FOOT WASHING, and the SECOND COMING of Christ.

**CHURCH OF GOD IN CHRIST** American denomination founded by C. P. Jones and C. H. Mason in 1897. Emphasizes REGENERATION, JUSTIFICATION, SANCTIFICATION, SPIRITUAL HEALING, speaking in tongues (see GLOSSOLALIA), IMMERSION, the LORD'S SUPPER, and FOOT WASHING.

**CHURCH OF GOD IN CHRIST (MENNONITE)** Denomination organized by John Holdeman in 1859 in Ohio. Members may not take interest on loans, adorn themselves, or engage in the recreation or dress of the world.

**CHURCH OF GOD (NEW DUNKERS)** German BRETHREN group founded in the United States in 1848 and disbanded in 1962.

**CHURCH OF GOD OF PROPHECY** Denomination founded in North Carolina in 1903 by A. J. Tomlinson. It emphasizes REGENERATION, SANCTIFICATION, BAPTISM WITH THE HOLY SPIRIT, speaking in tongues (see GLOSSOLALIA), and the SECOND COMING of Christ.

**(ORIGINAL) CHURCH OF GOD, INC.** American Holiness body founded in 1886. It emphasizes SANTIFICATION, SPIRITUAL HEALING, and government on a New Testament basis.

**CHURCH OF GOD (SEVENTH DAY)** 1. American Adventist denomination with apparent headquarters in Salem, West Virginia, but claiming Jerusalem as its real center. Observing Saturday as the Sabbath, the church is fundamentalist and practices TITHING and FOOT WASHING. Its members may not eat pork. 2. Another denomination with headquarters in Denver, Colorado, from which the group by the same name in West Virginia divided; it has very similar doctrines. Members may not use tobacco, alcohol, narcotics, or unclean meats.

**CHURCH OF ILLUMINATION** American denomination founded in 1908 by Rev. R. Swinburne Clymer. Emphasizing the priesthood of MELCHIZEDEK and esoteric Biblical meanings, it holds to four fundamental truths: the law of action and reaction, stewardship, the Golden Rule, and the law of honesty.

**CHURCH OF INDIA, PAKISTAN, BURMA, AND CEYLON** The ANGLICAN Church of those countries, having doctrines and government similar to those of the Church of England.

**CHURCH OF IRELAND** A Calvinistic and evangelical branch of the ANGLICAN COMMUNION, with rites and government similar to the Church of England.

**CHURCH OF JESUS CHRIST** MORMON body organized by William Bickerton at Green Oak, Pennsylvania, in 1862. Sometimes called Bickertonites or the Bickerton Organization, they practice monogamy, foot washing, and the holy kiss.

**CHURCH OF JESUS CHRIST (CUTLERITES)** Tiny MORMON group founded by Alpheus Cutler in Freemont County, Iowa, in 1853. Members believe that only the church should own property.

**CHURCH OF JESUS CHRIST OF LATTER-DAY SAINTS** Largest MORMON body in the United States, with headquarters at Salt Lake City, Utah. Members accept the Scriptures of the Old and New Testaments, the BOOK OF MORMON, the Doctrine and Covenants and the Pearl of Great Price all as the Word of God. Founded by Joseph SMITH in 1830, the church is guided by the angel Moroni, a president, two high priests, patriarchs, apostles, seventies, bishops, and elders. Members believe that God has a body of flesh and bones, accept the gift of tongues and divine healing, and look forward to the SECOND COMING of Christ and the restoration of the ten lost tribes of Israel.

**CHURCH OF JESUS CHRIST OF LATTER-DAY SAINTS (STRANGITES)** Very small MORMON body organized at Burlington, Wisconsin, in 1844 by James J. STRANG. who is regarded as the only legal successor to Joseph SMITH. To the original sacred writings of Mormonism, Strange added other revelations. Members observe Saturday as their SABBATH but do not hold the doctrines of the TRINITY and of many gods.

**CHURCH OF OUR LORD JESUS CHRIST OF**

**THE APOSTOLIC FAITH, INC.** Denomination founded by R. C. Lawson in Columbus, Ohio, in 1919. Conservative beliefs are held. This church has seven bishops and a hospital.

**CHURCH OF REVELATION** Denomination founded by Janet S. Wolford in 1930 at Long Beach, California. There are several churches in the group. Membership is based on Christian love and magnetic healing is practiced.

**CHURCH OF SCOTLAND** The established church of Scotland, PRESBYTERIAN in doctrine and government (by PRESBYTERS or elders). John CALVIN's theology was brought to Scotland by John KNOX in the sixteenth century, although Scottish Christianity dates from the fourth century, and Scotland never accepted England's acquiescence to Roman Christianity. The Presbyterians fought off episcopal forms of Christianity until they became secure in 1688; thereafter they were rent by many schisms. But the Church of Scotland is the mother of Presbyterianism in many other lands today, and it has deeply influenced Protestantism.

**CHURCH OF SOUTH INDIA** Denomination resulting from the merger in 1947 of the ANGLICANS of that country with the United Church, a union of METHODISTS, PRESBYTERIANS, and CONGREGATIONALISTS. The church has fourteen bishops and its headquarters are in Madras.

**CHURCH OF THE BRETHREN** Group originating in the ANABAPTIST movement early in the eighteenth century at Schwarzenau, Germany. Driven by persecution to emigrate to Pennsylvania, the group's headquarters are now in Elgin, Illinois. Members endorse temperance, brotherhood, pacifism, and simplicity of life. Their creed is the New Testament.

**CHURCH OF THE EAST AND OF THE ASSYRIANS** American branch of a church centered in Mesopotamia and the Near East. Rites are said in ARAMAIC. It traces its origins back to the first century of the Christian era.

**CHURCH OF THE GOSPEL** American denomination whose four churches and about forty members emphasize heart-holiness.

**CHURCH OF THE LIVING GOD** Denomination founded along masonic lines in Wrightsville, Arkansas, in 1889 by William Christian. Emphases are on FOOT WASHING, IMMERSION, and the use of water and unleavened bread in communion.

**CHURCH OF THE LUTHERAN BRETHREN OF AMERICA** American group organized in Milwaukee, Wisconsin, in 1900. Members stress personal experience of salvation and worship in free rather than liturgical style.

**CHURCH OF THE NAZARENE** American Holiness denomination rooted in Civil War revivalism. Although METHODIST in doctrine and government, the church emphasizes SANCTIFICATION and SPIRITUAL HEALING. It has been called "the right wing of the holiness movement."

**CHURCH OF THE PROVINCE OF NEW ZEALAND** ANGLICAN body of that country.

**CHURCH OF THE PROVINCE OF SOUTH AFRICA** ANGLICAN church of South Africa.

**CHURCH OF THE UNITED BRETHREN IN CHRIST** American Protestant denomination instituted by Philip OTTERBEIN and Martin BOEHM in 1800. It merged with the EVANGELICAL CHURCH in 1946.

**CHURCH OF THE UNITED BRETHREN IN CHRIST (OLD CONSTITUTION)** Division of the UNITED BRETHREN IN CHRIST originating at York, Pennsylvania, in 1889. When the original denomination altered its constitution to tolerate secret societies and lodges, the Old Constitution group adhered to the original document. ARMINIAN in theology and conservative in doctrinal outlook, the group has both male and female ministers.

**CHURCH RATE** Tax once collected in England and Ireland to support the established churches.

**CHURCH SCHOOL** Denominational name for what was once called Sabbath school, Sunday school, or Bible school—weekly instruction of the young in organized classes. There is a trend at present to have church school in the middle of the week.

**CHURCH SISTERS** Women set apart by the CHURCH OF SCOTLAND for work in industrial areas.

**CHURCH SLAVIC** Ecclesiastical language, based on a ninth-century Bulgarian dialect, used in the liturgy of the EASTERN ORTHODOX CHURCH.

**CHURCH TRIUMPHANT** Theological term for the church victorious. The thought is either that the members have found triumph in heaven, or that they will share the victory of the total conquest of Christ in the future.

**CHURCH UNION** A contemporary trend, as church division and schism was a trend of so many other ages. The CHURCH OF SOUTH INDIA is a model of successful church union.

**CHURCHWARDEN** 1. In the CHURCH OF ENGLAND, a lay parish official charged with protecting the church property. 2. In the PROTESTANT EPISCOPAL CHURCH in the United States, an officer who manages temporal matters of the parish.

**CHURCH WORLD SERVICE** An agency of the NATIONAL COUNCIL OF CHURCHES for the aid of the needy in various countries.

**CHURCHYARD** Consecrated ground attached to a church, often used for burial in England.

**CHURCH YEAR** See CHRISTIAN YEAR.

**CIBORIUM** In the early church, a canopy over the altar. In the contemporary church, a vessel for communion wafers, symbolizing the LAST SUPPER.

**CID, EL** (c.1043–1099) Rodrigo Diaz de Vivar, eleventh-century Spanish champion of Christianity, according to romantic tradition. Actually, he fought both Moors and Christians.

**CIHUACOATL** Aztec goddess of childbirth.

**CIHUATETEO** Aztec spirits of women who died while giving birth to children.

**CILICIA** Province of Asia Minor in which the Apostle PAUL spent his youth.

**CIMABUE, GIOVANNI (thirteenth century)** Naturalistic painter who contributed paintings, frescoes, and mosaics to many churches. He was buried in the Cathedral of Florence.

**CINCTURE** Cord worn around the ALB or CASSOCK.

**CINTEOTL** Aztec god or goddess of maize.

**CIRCE** In Greek myth, sorceress who changed Ulysses' companions to swine.

**CIRCLE** 1. Religious symbol of eternity, or of the divine unity. 2. See CELL 2.

**CIRCUIT RIDER** Frontier preacher who traveled over an extensive circuit on horseback. Francis ASBURY and other early METHODISTS made the circuit rider an important figure in American church history, and moved the church west with the pioneers.

**CIRCUMAMBULATION** Walking around someone or something, usually three times. Circumambulation was practiced in a number of ancient religions.

**CIRCUMCISION** Ritual removal of an infant's foreskin. It has been found among Jews, Moslems, Egyptians, and peoples of Africa and Peru.

**CIRCUMCISION, FEAST OF** Festival commemorating Jesus' circumcision, celebrated January 1.

**CIRCUMINCESSION** Theological term for the interpenetration of the persons of the TRINITY.

**CISERI, ANTONIO (1821–1891)** Italian painter of many religious scenes noted for their color and composition.

**CISTERCIAN NUNS** Nuns of the CISTERCIAN ORDER, organized by St. Stephen of Citeaux in 1120, also called BERNARDINES. They lead a completely secluded life. Out of their famous convent at Port Royal, JANSENISM developed.

**CISTERCIAN ORDER** Monastic order founded in 1098 by St. Robert (Robert de Thierry, Abbot of Molesme) in Citeaux, France. The name derives from Cistercium, the Latin name of Citeaux. The Cistercians are also known as White or Grey Monks because of their habit. They emphasized simplicity of life, practicing asceticism and farming. During the twelfth century they were the most powerful order in Europe. Among their famous members were Sts. Stephen Harding and BERNARD OF CLAIRVAUX. Out of them grew the TRAPPISTS and JANSENISTS. Eventually the order acquired wealth and its influence waned.

**CISTERCIAN RULE** Severe charter guiding the Cistercians, adapted from the more lax Benedictine Rule (see BENEDICTINES).

**CISTERNS** Water reservoirs in Palestine, essential in the periods between rains. Cisterns symbolize life (ECCLESIASTES 12:6).

**CITATION** Summons to an ecclesiastical court.

**CITEAUX** French village where the CISTERCIAN ORDER originated and site of a famous Cistercian abbey.

**CITHAERON** Greek mountain range where rites of DIONYSUS and the Daedala were observed. It is also the site of several events in Greek mythology.

**CITLALLINICUE** Aztec goddess of fertility.

**CITY MISSION** Center for urban ecclesiastical work among the needy, immigrants, unemployed, etc.

**CITY OF DAVID** 1. Ancient name for Jerusalem. 2. Term for Bethlehem where David was born (LUKE 2:11).

**CITY OF GOD** 1. A name for Jerusalem (PSALM 46:4). 2. Title of a famous book by St. AUGUSTINE outlining the emergence of the divine order through the dissolution of the Roman Empire.

**CITY OF REFUGE** One of six Jewish cities where a murderer might have protection until given a trial (NUMBERS 35:9–14).

**CIVIL LAW** In the Middle Ages, secular law as opposed to the canon law of the church.

**CIVIL MARRIAGE** A marriage performed by a public official rather than by a clergyman.

**CLAIRVOYANCE** Supernormal or inexplicable perception, often claimed by mystics and spiritualists.

**CLANDESTINITY** Secrecy in marriage, long opposed by churchmen.

**CLAPHAM** Suburban area of London where the CLAPHAM SECT originated in the eighteenth century.

**CLAPHAM SECT** Group of Evangelical members of the CHURCH OF ENGLAND, including Hannah MORE and William WILBERFORCE, who sought to abolish the slave trade, improve social conditions in Great Britain and its colonies, and extend missions and Sunday schools. The "Sect" had great influence toward these ends. In 1804 the members founded the BRITISH AND FOREIGN BIBLE SOCIETY.

**CLARE, ST.** (c.1194–1253) Italian nun, born in Assisi, who founded the order of FRANCISCAN nuns, sometimes called "POOR CLARES," in admiration of St. FRANCIS. Close to him in spirit, she is a ROMAN CATHOLIC saint. Her feast day is August 12.

**CLARENDON, CONSTITUTIONS OF** Declarations of Henry II of England, in 1164, which attempted to clarify relations between church and state. Since Henry claimed jurisdiction over clerical crimes, THOMAS À BECKET, Archbishop of Canterbury, opposed the Constitutions and was murdered in the dispute.

**CLARENDON CODE** English laws adopted by Parliament 1661–1665 upholding the CHURCH OF ENGLAND and restricting the religious freedom of non-Anglicans. The laws were named for Edward Hyde, Earl of Clarendon, although he opposed them.

**CLARES, POOR** See CLARE.

**CLARETIAN** 1. Member of the Congregation of the Missionary Sons of the Immaculate Heart of Mary, instituted in 1849 by Anthony Claret. 2. Relating to the Claretians or to Blessed Anthony Claret.

**CLARI, GIOVANNI CARLO** (c. 1669–1745) Italian composer of considerable church music.

**CLARK, FRANCIS EDWARD** (1851–1927) American minister in the CONGREGATIONAL CHURCH who founded the Young People's Society of CHRISTIAN ENDEAVOR. He led this interdenominational youth work for many years and served as president of the World's Christian Endeavor Union.

**CLARKE, JAMES FREEMAN** (1810–1888) American UNITARIAN clergyman, author, and reformer. He opposed slavery, promoted woman's suffrage and temperance, and sought to lay a broad Christian foundation for moral reforms.

**CLARKE, JOHN** (1609–1676) A BAPTIST pastor and physician who helped found Rhode Island and fought for religious liberty in New England.

**CLASSICS OF CONFUCIANISM** See BOOKS.

**CLASSIS** Governing body of a group of churches in the REFORMED system, made up of clergymen and ruling elders, corresponding to PRESBYTERY in the PRESBYTERIAN churches.

**CLASS MEETING** Informal weekly church meeting, originated by John WESLEY, whereby METHODISTS keep in close touch on spiritual and ecclesiastical matters. Although unique, it serves some of the same purposes as the midweek prayer meeting in older Protestant groups and the CELL or circle in contemporary Protestantism.

**CLAUDEL, PAUL** (1868–1955) French poet of mystical power and CATHOLIC influence whose writings combine religious symbolism with metaphysical depth.

**CLEANTHES (third century B.C.)** Stoic philosopher and Greek religious poet. He held that virtue is natural but pleasure is not.

**CLEMENT** *merciful, mild* A popular name in church history; it has been borne by fourteen popes and two antipopes.

**CLEMENT I, ST. (late first century)** Christian saint and martyr who succeeded Cletus as pope, possibly 88–97 A.D. Also known as Clement of Rome, he wrote a letter to the Christians of Corinth seeking to unify the Corinthian church concerning the expulsion of several elders. Clement's feast day is November 23.

**CLEMENT VI (1291–1352)** Pierre Roger, French pope who lavishly patronized the arts and aided and protected the Jews during the Black Death. He sought the unity of the church and an end to the Hundred Years' War.

**CLEMENT VII (c.1475–1534)** Florentine pope during whose reign the CHURCH OF ENGLAND left the Church of Rome. He was a patron of Raphael, Michelangelo, and Benvenuto Cellini.

**CLEMENT XI (1649–1721)** Brilliant Italian pope who condemned certain JANSENIST doctrines with the bull *Unigenitus* in 1713. He forbade missionaries to China to accommodate their doctrines to pagan ideas.

**CLEMENT XII (1652–1740)** Italian pope who sought unity with the GREEK CHURCH and patronized the arts.

**CLEMENT XIV (1705–1774)** Italian pope who died soon after his brief *Dominus ac Redemptor* dissolved the order of the Jesuits (see SOCIETY OF JESUS) in 1773.

**CLEMENTINE EDITION** Edition of the VULGATE revised in 1592 under Pope Clement VIII.

**CLEMENTINE LITERATURE** Writings ascribed to CLEMENT I. These include two epistles to the Corinthians, two epistles on virginity, an epistle to James, *Apostolical Constitutions, Homilies,* and *Recognitions.* Only Clement's first epistle to the Corinthians is now generally attributed to his authorship.

**CLEMENT OF ALEXANDRIA (c.150–c.215)** Athens-born pagan who was converted to Christianity and contributed much to theology and knowledge of other religions. He sought to state Christian belief in terms of contemporary relevance and was later accused of heresy. He was the first Christian writer to mention BUDDHA. His writings witness to the majority of New Testament

Scriptures. Appreciative of non-Christian philosophy and religion, he held that these may have fragments of the truth while Christ is absolute truth.

**CLEMENT OF ROME** See CLEMENT I.

**CLEOPAS** One of the disciples of Jesus who, with a companion, met Him on the road to Emmaus (LUKE 24:18).

**CLERESTORY** High part of a building, above adjoining roofs, whose windows thus admit light to the main interior. Clerestories were used in Egyptian temples and Gothic cathedrals.

**CLERGY** Those ordained to carry out such religious functions as administering SACRAMENTS and preaching. In England the term is usually reserved for ANGLICAN priests.

**CLERGY, BENEFIT OF** Ancient exemption of clergymen from trial in the secular courts.

**CLERGYMAN** An ordained minister, priest, or rabbi. Originally the term meant an ordained "clerk" in the church.

**CLERGY RESERVES** Term for the portion of crown lands (one-eighth) once set aside to support PROTESTANT clergy.

**CLERIC** Clergyman (from the Latin *clericus,* priest).

**CLERICAL COLLAR** Clergyman's stiff white collar buttoned behind. It is worn always by ROMAN CATHOLIC priests and increasingly by PROTESTANT ministers.

**CLERICALISM** Preoccupation with the powers of the church and its ministry, application of religion to secular life, or the attempt to win benefits for church and clergy. Most clergymen probably favor clericalism in the second sense and reject it in the other two.

**CLERICIS LAICOS** Encyclical issued by Pope BONIFACE VIII in 1296 forbidding military taxes on clergymen on pain of excommunication.

**CLERICS REGULAR OF ST. PAUL** See BARNABITES.

**CLERK** Originally one who had taken religious orders. (Source of the words clergy and clerical.)

**CLERKENWELL** London district where MIRACLE PLAYS were enacted and the KNIGHTS HOSPITALERS had their British center.

**CLERK IN HOLY ORDERS** English priest,

deacon, or bishop, as contrasted with clerks of minor function.

**CLERKS REGULAR** Members of religious orders such as the SOCIETY OF JESUS which combine active pastoral work with monastic community life.

**CLERMONT, COUNCIL OF** Convocation of two hundred bishops, convened at Clermont in northern France by Pope Urban II, to plan the first crusade against the Saracens. It also passed other regulations such as the proscription of eating flesh in LENT.

**CLETUS** See ANACLETUS.

**CLEVELAND, GROVER (1837–1908)** President of the United States who may have been elected because a speech on behalf of his opponent denouncing "Rum, Romanism, and Rebellion" gave him additional CATHOLIC votes.

**CLIFFORD, JOHN (1836–1923)** British BAPTIST leader and first president of the BAPTIST WORLD ALLIANCE. He secured the passage of an Education Act providing nonsectarian religious education.

**CLINICAL BAPTISM** BAPTISM during illness or just before the recipient's death. This was a practice in the early church until INFANT BAPTISM replaced it.

**CLINICAL COMMUNION** Administering of the EUCHARIST to a sick person in the home.

**CLINICI** One who received CLINICAL BAPTISM.

**CLOISTER** A monastery, its walls, or the open court between monastic, church, or college buildings.

**CLOOT, CLOOTIE** Scottish term for the devil.

**CLOSE** Area by a cathedral enclosed by walls or related houses.

**CLOSED COMMUNION** Restriction of the LORD'S SUPPER to those alone who are members in good standing of the particular congregation or denomination. In actual practice this is now a rarity among PROTESTANTS.

**CLOTH, THE** Term for the clergy and their distinctive dress, "men of the cloth."

**CLOTHO** One of the three FATES, in Greek myth, who controlled human life.

**CLOTILDA, ST. (?–544)** Queen of the Franks who converted her husband King Clovis to Christianity, with him built the Church of the Holy Apostles in Paris, and

as a widow entered the Abbey of St. Martin at Tours where she cared for the poor. The feast day commemorating her as a saint is June 3.

**CLOUD** Symbol of God.

**CLOUD OF UNKNOWING** Anonymous English mystical treatise of the fourteenth century which opens with the prayer "that I may perfectly love Thee and worthily praise Thee." A guide to contemplation of the divine, it suggests that God is known not by the intellect but by "a sharp dart of love" which pierces "the cloud of unknowing."

**CLOVER** Symbol of the TRINITY.

**CLOVIS (c.466–511)** King of the Franks who married the Princess CLOTILDA and became a Christian. His conversion became an excuse to attack the Visigoths who were heretical ARIANS and unify France.

**CLUB** Symbol of betrayal in Christian art.

**CLUNIAC ORDER** CATHOLIC monastic order founded by William I of Aquitaine and the monk Berno in 910 at the Benedictine abbey of Cluny, France. Originally of a reforming character, the order was the most powerful in the church for two centuries and rapidly increased its splendor until it declined with the rise of the CISTERCIANS. It was dissolved in 1790.

**CLUNY** French religious center; site of the Abbey of Cluny, the Church of St. Marcellus, and Notre Dame Cathedral.

**C.M.S.** Abbreviation for the CHURCH MISSIONARY SOCIETY, first effective mission organization of the CHURCH OF ENGLAND.

**COADJUTOR BISHOP** See BISHOP COADJUTOR.

**COATLICUE** Aztec goddess of earth and seedtime, flowers, life and death. She wore a crown of skulls.

**COBRA** Snake whose neck expands to form a hood. In India it is regarded with religious reverence.

**COCCEIUS, JOHANNES (1603–1669)** German CALVINIST theologian who held that God and man entered into a covenant of works before the fall of Adam, followed by a covenant of grace which Christ fulfilled. He is said to have found Christ everywhere in the OLD TESTAMENT.

**COCIDIUS** Celtic god of war.

**COCK** Archaic word for rooster. Christ

warned Peter that he would deny Him thrice before the cock crowed (JOHN 13:38). Hence, the cock symbolizes watchfulness in Christian art.

**COCKATRICE** 1. In the Bible, a venomous serpent. 2. In ancient belief, a monster with an eye so evil its glance felled men.

**COCKLE** An evil-smelling plant (JOB 31:40). In religious art it is a symbol of evil.

**COCONSECRATORS** Bishops who assist the presiding bishop in the consecration of a new BISHOP.

**CODE** System of principles, ethics, or laws. Various codes of law have been noted in the Old Testament.

**CODE OF MANU** See MANU.

**CODEX** Manuscript with leaves bound in modern book form. Many important manuscripts of the Bible are in codex form (see below).

**CODEX ALEXANDRINUS** Fifth-century Greek manuscript of the Bible and the Epistles of Clement (see CLEMENTINE LITERATURE).

**CODEX AMIATINUS** Manuscript of the VULGATE Bible in Latin, dating from the early eighth century.

**CODEX BEZAE** Sixth-century manuscript in Latin and Greek of the four Gospels and part of Acts and III John. Theodore BEZA gave it to Cambridge University in 1581.

**CODEX EPHRAEMI RESCRIPTUS** Fifth-century Greek manuscript of half the New Testament and part of the Old Testament. Its name derives from the writings of Ephraem Syrus, the Scribe, which were written over the original text in the twelfth century.

**CODEX JURIS CANONICI** Contemporary canon law of the ROMAN CATHOLIC CHURCH.

**CODEX SINAITICUS** One of the most valuable parchment manuscripts of the Bible in Greek and one of the oldest manuscripts of the complete New Testament, dating from the fourth century. It was found at St. Catherine's Convent on Mt. Sinai in 1859, and contains both Testaments, apocryphal writings, the Epistle of BARNABAS, and a portion of the SHEPHERD OF HERMAS.

**CODEX VATICANUS** Fourth-century manuscript of the Bible in the VATICAN Library. The text is the most important extant for knowledge of the Greek Scriptures. It was probably inscribed in Alexandria.

**COETUS** Church assembly or governing body, particularly in the REFORMED churches.

**COFFIN** Receptacle for a corpse, often used for burial with religious rites.

**COFFIN, HENRY SLOANE (1877–1954)** American PRESBYTERIAN minister, moderator of his denomination in 1943, and a professor and president of Union Theological Seminary. He sought to make his faith relevant to the contemporary world and to intellectuals.

**COHEN or KOHEN** Hebrew word for priest or for a descendant of AARON. It is a favorite Jewish name in various forms like Kahn, Cowen, Cohn.

**COHEN, HERMANN (1842–1918)** German philosopher whose thought revolved around God but whose God is an impersonal symbol of man's individuality and victory over sin.

**COKE, THOMAS (1747–1814)** English divine who became the first bishop in METHODISM. After serving as president of the Methodist conference in Ireland he was appointed superintendent for America by John WESLEY. He opposed slavery, tried to reunite the Methodist and ANGLICAN churches, and sought to establish mission work in India.

**COLENSO, JOHN WILLIAM (1814–1883)** English bishop of Natal in South Africa. There he angered churchmen by his acceptance of native polygamy, critically examining the PENTATEUCH, and questioning the doctrine of eternal punishment. He angered the colonists by upholding the rights of the Zulus against the Boers. The metropolitan of Capetown excommunicated him but the courts upheld his bishopric and income.

**COLERIDGE, SAMUEL TAYLOR (1772–1834)** English writer who believed that CHRISTIANITY is basically an ethic and that this ethic can provide a foundation for a reunited Christendom. He struggled through rationalism and UNITARIANISM to what he called orthodoxy but Cardinal NEWMAN said that some of his ideas were often heathen and he seemed more of a PANTHEIST and FREETHINKER than a receiver of dogma. He has been called "Father of the BROAD CHURCH movement."

**COLET, JOHN** (c.1467–1519) English Catholic who questioned worldliness in the church, became the friend of ERASMUS and Thomas MORE, and introduced HUMANISM to England. He substituted the historical for the allegorical interpretation of Scripture.

**COLIGNY, GASPARD DE** (1519–1572) French HUGUENOT leader who was the first victim murdered in the BARTHOLOMEW'S DAY MASSACRE.

**COLLATION** 1. Ecclesiastical consultation. 2. A reading from the lives of the Church Fathers in a monastery. 3. A meal after such a reading, or a light meal on a fast day. 4. An ecclesiastical BENEFICE.

**COLLECT** Short opening prayer in a service of worship, said just before the EPISTLE is read.

**COLLECTAR** Medieval book of collects.

**COLLECTION** Term for the money offered in a worship service.

**COLLEGE** Group cooperating for ecclesiastical purposes.

**COLLEGE APOSTOLIC** The body of the Twelve Apostles.

**COLLEGE OF BISHOPS** BISHOPS elected by a METHODIST conference.

**COLLEGE OF CARDINALS** The body of up to seventy CARDINALS who elect and advise the pope.

**COLLEGIATE CHURCH** A church served by a group of clergymen, or a group of churches administered jointly by several ministers.

**COLLEGIUM** See SACRED COLLEGE.

**COLLOQUY** 1. Ancient term for PRESBYTERY or classis in the French Reformed Church. 2. Informal theological conference.

**COLORED CUMBERLAND PRESBYTERIAN CHURCH** Former name of the Second Cumberland Presbyterian Church in the United States.

**COLORED METHODIST EPISCOPAL CHURCH** Former name of the Christian Methodist Episcopal Church, a denomination in southern United States.

**COLORS, LITURGICAL** See BLACK, GREEN, RED, VIOLET, and WHITE.

**COLOSSAE** City of Asia Minor to which the Apostle PAUL addressed one epistle. For the first four centuries of the Chris-

tian era this area was one of extreme theological speculation and mysticism.

**COLOSSEUM** Amphitheater in Rome where gladiators fought animals and, according to tradition, Christians were devoured by wild beasts.

**COLOSSIANS** Term for the Apostle Paul's letter to the Christians of Colosse. It asserts the supremacy of Christ and warns against false speculation.

**COLPORTEUR** Distributor of religious tracts and books.

**COLUMBA, ST.** dove (521–597) "Apostle of Caledonia," missionary from Ireland to Scotland who saw that country evangelized during his lifetime. He established a church on the island of Iona and many monasteries in Scotland. He converted the kings of the Scots and the Picts, and was canonized. His feast day is June 9.

**COLUMBAN or COLUMBANUS, ST.** (c.540–615) Learned Irish saint and missionary to Europe. His adherence to Celtic usages such as the dating of EASTER aroused much opposition but he established a number of monasteries and wrote a rule for monks and some poems. His feast day is November 21.

**COLUMBINE** Symbol of the HOLY SPIRIT.

**COMENIUS, JOHN AMOS** (1592–1670) Last bishop of the BOHEMIAN BRETHREN, mystic theologian, and progressive educator. He dreamed of a church where all religions would be united in Christian love and of schools that would use divine wisdom to implant in pupils the image of Christ.

**COMFORTABLE WORDS** Passages from the New Testament (MATTHEW 11:28; JOHN 3:16; I TIMOTHY 1:15; I JOHN 2:1–2) repeated at the eucharist in the CHURCH OF ENGLAND to confirm the forgiveness of sins.

**COMFORTER** Jesus' name for the HOLY SPIRIT (JOHN 14:16). The Greek term, *Paraclete,* means Strengthener, Advocate, Defender, Helper.

**COMITY** Code of courtesy by which different denominations agree not to transgress on one another's bounds.

**COMMANDMENT KEEPERS** Negro Jewish sect in New York, also called BLACK JEWS. They observe Jewish worship patterns in synagogues and believe that Negroes are Jews from Ethiopia. The group was instituted by Rabbi Wentworth David Matthew in 1919.

**COMMANDMENTS** 1. The Ten Commandments (see DECALOGUE) given by Moses (EXODUS 20). 2. The two great commandments of love singled out by Jesus from the Old Testament as fundamental (MATTHEW 22:36–40).

**COMMANDMENTS OF THE CHURCH** Regulations prescribed by the ROMAN CATHOLIC CHURCH for all its members. They include regular attendance at mass, CONFESSION at least annually, and observance of special ecclesiastical days.

**COMMEMORATION** 1. Prayer of remembrance. 2. Recognition of a religious feast which occurs at the same date as a more important one.

**COMMENDATION OF THE SOUL** Prayers for a dying person.

**COMMENDATORY PRAYER** Prayer commending a dying person's soul to God.

**COMMENIUS** See COMENIUS, JOHN AMOS.

**COMMENTARY** Explanation, interpretation, or notes for study of Scripture.

**COMMINATION SERVICE** ANGLICAN service for the blessing of ashes in the SARUM rite.

**COMMISSARY** Church official representing a BISHOP.

**COMMISSION** 1. Command, as the Great Commission of Matthew 28:18–20 commanding the disciples to evangelize all nations (see EVANGELISM). 2. Church group with power to act. (A church committee ordinarily has power only to report back to the ecclesiastical body that created it.)

**COMMITTAL** Commitment of a corpse to the earth and its soul to God in a burial service.

**COMMIXTURE** Mixing bread and wine in the eucharist, symbolizing the RESURRECTION.

**COMMON GRACE** Theological term for the grace shared by all men, in contrast to the special grace known only by the elect.

**COMMON PRAYER, BOOK OF** See BOOK OF COMMON PRAYER.

**COMMUNICANT** One who partakes, or is entitled to partake, of the EUCHARIST.

**COMMUNICATE** To partake of communion or the EUCHARIST.

**COMMUNICATIO IDIOMATUM** *commonness*

*of the attributes* Theological doctrine that the human and divine natures of Christ are so united that the characteristics of one nature may be attributed to the other.

**COMMUNION** 1. Term for the Lord's Supper or the EUCHARIST. 2. Term for fellowship or sharing, particularly in a mystic sense. Christians have communion with Christ and with each other as members of His body.

**COMMUNION, CLOSED** See CLOSED COMMUNION.

**COMMUNION, CORPORATE** 1. Participation in the Lord's Supper or EUCHARIST with one's fellow Christians. 2. Specifically, participation by special body (society, club, or the like) as a group.

**COMMUNION, OPEN** The philosophy of inviting all believers to partake of communion or the EUCHARIST.

**COMMUNION BREAD** Bread or wafers served at communion or the EUCHARIST. Some denominations require unleavened bread.

**COMMUNION CUP** The cup of wine drunk at the SACRAMENT.

**COMMUNION IN BOTH KINDS** Serving both bread and wine to all participants in the communion SACRAMENT. This is usual in most PROTESTANT denominations; in the ROMAN CATHOLIC CHURCH it is customary, except on particular occasions, for the wine to be taken only by the priests. See UTRAQUISTS.

**COMMUNION OF SAINTS** Fellowship with other Christians through Christ (JOHN 15:1–7). CATHOLICS hold that this fellowship extends to all saints living or dead through prayer.

**COMMUNION SUNDAY** Special Sunday designated for observance of the LORD'S SUPPER.

**COMMUNION TABLE** Table or altar from which the COMMUNION elements are administered.

**COMMUNION TOKENS** Coin-like devices given those considered worthy of receiving communion. Churches in England and Scotland once used such tokens.

**COMMUNION WAFER** Thin crackerlike bread served at the EUCHARIST.

**COMMUNION WARE** Service for the COMMUNION elements.

**COMMUNISM** 1. Popularly, the atheistic political system of Russia, China, and countries under their influence. 2. Historically, an ancient ideology. The early Christians had everything in common and gave to one another according to the needs of each (ACTS 2:44–45). Many religious groups have practiced this kind of communism.

**COMMUNITY CHURCH** Generally, a congregation independent of denominational ties seeking to serve its community.

**COMPACTATA** Agreement of the Council of BASEL in 1436 pacifying the HUSSITES by various concessions, including permission for the Bohemians to take COMMUNION IN BOTH KINDS.

**COMPARATIVE ETHICS** The study of various ethical systems in the attempt to put ethics on a more scientific basis.

**COMPARATIVE RELIGION** Term for the study of various religions in a sympathetic and systematic manner. Such study shows that many religions have important elements in common and have developed along parallel lines.

**COMPASSION** This is a supreme virtue in BUDDHISM. JUDAISM and CHRISTIANITY regard compassion and mercy highly. Jesus had compassion on the multitudes (MATTHEW 15:32).

**COMPLINE or COMPLIN** Last liturgical prayer service of the day, said just before retiring by various RELIGIOUS, particularly CATHOLIC and ANGLICAN.

**COMPLUTENSIAN POLYGLOT** Bible prepared in Spain in 1502 containing the text in Hebrew, Greek, and Latin in parallel columns (with the New Testament only in Greek and Latin). The work was done by Francis Cardinal Jimenes (see JIMENEZ DE CISNEROS, FRANCISCO).

**COMPRECATION** Prayer by the saints for the rest of the church.

**COMPROMISE** Ecclesiastically, the transfer of a legal right.

**COMSTOCK, ANTHONY (1844–1915)** American Y.M.C.A. worker who organized the New York Society for the Suppression of Vice and suppressed tons of material whose perusal was considered immoral and harmful.

**COMTE, AUGUSTE (1798–1857)** French founder of the philosophy of positivism and the science of sociology. He saw man passing through the three stages of belief in the supernatural, apprehension of natural phenomena, and comprehension of scientific laws. He found sociology to be the highest science and proposed a "religion of humanity" in which humanity is worshiped as the only supreme being, great men and women are the saints, and each day in the year is a saint's day.

**COMTISM** Positivism.

**CONCELEBRATION** Celebration of the EUCHARIST simultaneously by several priests together.

**CONCEPTION, IMMACULATE** Doctrine that the Virgin MARY was herself conceived without sin, pronounced by Pope PIUS IX in 1854.

**CONCEPTUALISM** Philosophical theory that universal concepts—such as man, tree, redness—exist in the mind alone and that in reality only individual entities—specific men, trees, shades of red—exist. This position was held by ABELARD as a compromise between NOMINALISM and REALISM.

**CONCISION** Sexual mutilation or "cutting off," a term derisively applied by the Apostle PAUL to those in the church at Philippi who based salvation on the rite of CIRCUMCISION ("cutting around," PHILIPPIANS 3:2).

**CONCLAVE** 1. Secret meeting. 2. COLLEGE OF CARDINALS. 3. Room where the cardinals convene to elect a pope.

**CONCOMITANCE** Doctrine that the real presence of Christ is in either or both the bread and wine of the EUCHARIST.

**CONCORD, BOOK OF** LUTHERAN confessional writings: the APOSTLES', NICENE, and ATHANASIAN CREEDS, the AUGSBURG CONFESSION, Luther's catechisms, the SCHMALKALD ARTICLES, and the Formula of Concord (below).

**CONCORD, FORMULA OF** Last and most complete of the classical LUTHERAN confessions, drawn up in 1577 by Jakob Andreae and other theologians in an attempt to unify the church.

**CONCORDANCE** A concordance of the Bible is an index of its words, topics, or texts. Among the famous concordances to the English Bible are those of Alexander Cruden, Robert Young, John Eadie, and James Strong.

**CONCORDAT** 1. Agreement between the pope and the head of a government establishing the rights of the ROMAN CATHOLIC

CHURCH in the country concerned. 2. Civil-ecclesiastical agreement.

**CONCORDIA** Roman goddess of civic harmony.

**CONCORD OF WITTENBERG** Agreement in 1536 between LUTHERAN and ZWINGLIAN divines on the doctrine of the EUCHARIST.

**CONCUBINAGE** Living together of a man and woman without proper marriage. It was practiced among many ancient peoples, and among Christians until the Middle Ages. The development of clerical celibacy seems to have brought about considerable concubinage in place of marriage; this was condemned by the Council of TRENT.

**CONCUPISCENCE** In the New Testament this is a term for longing or yearning, often for what is forbidden. Ancient theologians applied it to sexual desire or to sensuous delight, and considered it to be a proof of human depravity. Christianity at its best finds nothing evil in the senses or sex, except when misdirected.

**CONCURRENCE** Simultaneous or consecutive occurrence of holy days in the church.

**CONCURSUS** 1. Competition for ecclesiastical appointment, as to a parish. 2. Influx of God's power into created beings in their creative activity. 3. Doctrine that before the fall man was maintained by God in spiritual perfection.

**CONDIGNITY** Theological doctrine that supernatural grace may enable a man to merit eternal life.

**CONDITIONAL ELECTION** Doctrine that God chooses men for salvation on condition of their faith or good works.

**CONDITIONAL IMMORTALITY** Doctrine that immortal life is achieved only by those who have found divine salvation.

**CONECTE, THOMAS (?–1434)** French CARMELITE monk who denounced vice in clergy and laymen and taught that the clergy might marry. After succeeding in effecting changes in the order of the English Carmelites he was burned for heresy.

**CONFERENCE** METHODIST governing body.

**CONFERENCE OF THE EVANGELICAL MENNONITE CHURCH** American body stressing nonresistance and nonconformity to the world.

**CONFESSING CHURCH** PROTESTANT movement in Nazi Germany, begun in 1933 by Martin Niemoeller, opposing Adolph Hitler's attempt to substitute government directives for conscience. It produced the BARMEN DECLARATION.

**CONFESSION** 1. Acknowledgment of sin. 2. Profession of faith. 3. Statement of belief, as by an ecclesiastical body.

**CONFESSIONAL** 1. Enclosed area where a priest listens to the confessions of sin of his penitent parishioners. 2. Term for the act or practice of confessing sins to a priest.

**CONFESSIONAL CHURCH** See CONFESSING CHURCH.

**CONFESSIONALISM** 1. Adherence to normative standards of faith. 2. Exaltation of a creed or confession of faith.

**CONFESSION OF AUGSBURG** See AUGSBURG, CONFESSION OF.

**CONFESSION OF 1967** Contemporary statement of faith drawn up by the UNITED PRESBYTERIAN CHURCH IN THE UNITED STATES OF AMERICA. It emphasizes the work of reconciliation in Christ and the ministry of reconciliation in "the whole of human life," singling out the evils of racial discrimination, war, poverty, and family disintegration. It is part of a new Book of Confessions including the WESTMINSTER CONFESSION, the APOSTLES' CREED, the NICENE CREED, the SCOTTISH CONFESSION, the Second HELVETIC CONFESSION, the HEIDELBERG CATECHISM, the SHORTER CATECHISM, and the Declaration of BARMEN.

**CONFESSIONS OF AUGUSTINE** Spiritual autobiography of St. AUGUSTINE, together with his thoughts about memory, time, and creation; for example: "Thou hast made us for Thyself, and our heart is restless until it rests in Thee." It dates from c.400 A.D.

**CONFESSOR** 1. Priest who hears confessions of sin. 2. Man who has lived a holy life and made "a good confession," as EDWARD THE CONFESSOR.

**CONFIRM** 1. To validate. 2. To strengthen spiritually. 3. To administer CONFIRMATION.

**CONFIRMAND** One who receives the rite of CONFIRMATION.

**CONFIRMATION** Consecration of a person in his or her faith. In the early church, after a candidate for membership was baptized he had hands laid upon him for the coming of the HOLY SPIRIT. In the PROTESTANT churches today confirmation often initiates young people who were baptized as infants into the full privileges of the church; but in many Protestant churches there is no such thing as confirmation. In the EASTERN CHURCH infants are confirmed immediately after baptism. In the ROMAN CATHOLIC and ANGLICAN churches, confirmation is a sacrament whereby the grace of the Holy Spirit is received in a fuller way than heretofore. In JUDAISM confirmation, like the BAR MITZVAH, consecrates both young men and maidens.

**CONFIRMATION OF BISHOPS** Ecclesiastical approval of the election of new BISHOPS.

**CONFITEOR *I confess*** A form for confession of sins, widely used in ANGLICAN and CATHOLIC churches.

**CONFORMITY** Likeness, compliance, or agreement. Christians are not to be conformed to the evil world but conformed to the image of Christ.

**CONFRATERNITY** CATHOLIC brotherhood or organization for some purpose such as education or philanthropy. Every parish must have a Confraternity of Christian Doctrine and one of the Blessed Sacrament.

**CONFRATERNITY OF UNITY** ANGLICAN society seeking reunion of the ROMAN CATHOLIC CHURCH and Anglican churches. It was founded in 1926.

**CONFUCIANISM** Principally, the ethics of CONFUCIUS and his followers, emphasizing faithfulness, justice, benevolence, intelligence, propriety, and filial piety. Confucianism also implies the cosmology of "YANG" and "YIN," government modeled along the lines of the patriarchal family, and a sacrificial system of worship. Confucianism dominated China, Japan, and Korea through most of the Christian era. Its leaders have been Confucius, MENCIUS, CHUCIUS, and Wang Yang Ming.

**CONFUCIUS (c.550–479 B.C.)** Also known as K'ung Fu-tze, "Philosopher K'ung." Born poor, he married young and started a school at the age of 22. He accepted students for the smallest fees but turned away those who were not serious or capable of learning. Appointed minister of justice in the state of Lu, he stopped crime and saw loyalty, chastity, and honesty triumph. Then he visited other states and was reviled and threatened. He finally gathered thousands of disciples and sought to teach good government by extolling the influence of good leaders and proclaiming the duties of these in five relationships. He taught the subject to obey his ruler, the wife to obey her husband, the son his father, younger brothers those older; and he insisted that friends should mutually promote virtue. He is said to have written or edited the FIVE CLASSICS of Confucianism.

**CONGÉ D'ÉLIRE *permission to choose*** Royal authorization for election of a BISHOP or ARCHBISHOP in the CHURCH OF ENGLAND.

**CONGREGATION** An assembly of those worshiping, or the entire membership of an individual church. The Hebrew and Greek words for such an assembly, *kahal* and *ekklesia,* are the basis of the word "church." In CATHOLICISM "congregation" may mean: *a.* A religious organization or association for a special purpose. *b.* A religious community. *c.* A branch of a religious order. *d.* An administrative committee of the COLLEGE OF CARDINALS. *e.* A committee of BISHOPS at a general council.

**CONGREGATIONAL** 1. Of the system of church government in which each local congregation is independent and self-governing. Congregationalism "has been implicit in Christianity from the beginning" (Frank S. Mead). Historically, however, it is rooted in the rise of the PURITANS. 2. Belonging to a CONGREGATIONAL CHURCH.

**CONGREGATIONAL CHURCH** 1. Through the SEPARATISTS and PILGRIMS, those of Congregational persuasion indelibly marked the church history of England, the Netherlands, and New England. 2. The Congregational Church in England numbers nearly half a million members. 3. The Congregationalists of Canada merged into the UNITED CHURCH OF CANADA in 1925. 4. Most of America's Congregationalists are now in the UNITED CHURCH OF CHRIST.

**CONGREGATIONAL CHRISTIAN CHURCHES (NATIONAL ASSOCIATION)** American denomination formed in 1955 when 250 Congregational Christian churches refused to join those which merged into the UNITED CHURCH OF CHRIST. There is no particular "uniformity of belief" but "acceptance of a covenant purpose to be 'the people of God.'"

**CONGREGATIONAL HOLINESS CHURCH** American Pentecostal denomination formed in 1921 by withdrawal from the Pentecostal Holiness Church. Members forsake tobacco, slang, secret societies, and all forms of worldliness.

**CONGREGATIONALISM** Church government based on the sovereignty and autonomy of the local church or congregation. Congregationalism assumes fellowship with sister churches, but permits no sovereignty of the whole as do other polities.

**CONGREGATIONALIST** Adherent to or member of CONGREGATIONALISM.

**CONGREGATIONAL METHODIST CHURCH** Group in the United States which withdrew from the Methodist Episcopal Church, South, in 1852.

**CONGREGATIONAL METHODIST CHURCH OF THE U.S.A.** Denomination which withdrew from the Methodist Episcopal Church, South, in 1852, and from which the Congregational Methodist Church is said to have withdrawn.

**CONGREGATIONAL UNION OF ENGLAND AND WALES** A union of the Congregational churches of England and Wales.

**CONGRESS** Ecclesiastical gathering for spiritual or other purposes.

**CONGRUISM** Term for belief that divine grace is adapted to or given in accordance with the merit or cooperation or good works of the recipient.

**CONJEEVERAM** City in Madras, India, sacred to HINDUS. Before the ninth century A.D. it was a center of BUDDHISM. It is now adorned with many temples.

**CONNECTICUT MISSIONARY SOCIETY** Organization originated by the CONGREGATIONALISTS of the United States in 1789 "to Christianize the heathen in North America and to support and promote Christian knowledge within the new settlements of the United States."

**CONNECTION or CONNEXION** Term for an association of Christians or churches with more unity and interrelatedness than in the CONGREGATIONAL system.

**CONNOR, RALPH (1860–1937)** Minister, missionary, and moderator of the Presbyterian Church of Canada; author of *The Sky Pilot, Black Rock,* and other popular novels. "Ralph Connor" was actually the pseudonym of Charles William Gordon.

**CONRAD OF MARBURG (c.1180–1233)** German monk who became Germany's first inquisitor in 1231. He accused Henry II of Seyn of HERESY and was himself murdered the same year.

**CONSALVI, ERCOLE (1757–1824)** Italian CARDINAL who brought about the CONCORDAT between France and the Vatican in 1801, ruled Rome wisely, and patronized the arts and music.

**CONSANGUINITY** Relationship by blood; canon law forbids the marriage of those thus related within prohibited degrees, as siblings or first cousins.

**CONSCIENCE** Sense of right and wrong; moral conviction or insight. Conscience indicates the value structure of the individual, often based upon his training and environment.

**CONSCIENCE CLAUSE** Legal provision for exemption from oath-taking and the like when the objection is based on religious conviction or conscience.

**CONSCIENCE MONEY** Payment to relieve the conscience for some ethical breach. It is often anonymous. The amount of conscience money sent the United States government necessitates a special "conscience fund."

**CONSCIENTIOUS OBJECTOR** One who refuses to give military service or objects to cooperation in a war effort from moral or religious scruples. QUAKERS, BRETHREN, DOUKHOBORS, and JEHOVAH'S WITNESSES have often been "C.O.'s."

**CONSECRATION** Setting apart from ordinary uses for holy ones in dedication to God. The VESTAL VIRGINS were consecrated to the gods. Temples, first fruits, priests, etc. were consecrated in Old Testament JUDAISM. In CATHOLICISM, consecration may apply to ordination of BISHOPS, to blessing the elements of the EUCHARIST, and in other special senses. In evangelical PROTESTANTISM, consecration generally applies to personal commitment to Christ.

**CONSENSUS PATRUM** *agreement of the Fathers* The collective agreement of the Fathers of the early centuries of the church as a basis of determining truth and heresy in doctrine.

**CONSERVATIVE AMISH MENNONITE CHURCH** Former name of the CONSERVATIVE MENNONITE CONFERENCE.

**CONSERVATIVE BAPTIST ASSOCIATION OF AMERICA** FUNDAMENTALIST association of BAPTIST churches in the United States, organized in 1947.

**CONSERVATIVE CONGREGATIONAL CHRISTIAN CONFERENCE** Organization founded in the United States in 1948 to perpetuate historic CONGREGATIONALISM. It was one of the Congregational groups which did not enter the merger in 1957–1961 that produced the UNITED CHURCH OF CHRIST.

**CONSERVATIVE DUNKERS** Another name for CHURCH OF THE BRETHREN.

**CONSERVATIVE JUDAISM** One of the three main branches of JUDAISM. Conservative Judaism stands midway between the other two branches, ORTHODOX and REFORM Judaism, seeking to conserve the fundamentals of Orthodoxy while insisting with the Reform group that the faith must find its place in the contemporary world. Conservative Jewish synagogue prayers are often in English and modern educational methods are employed in teaching.

**CONSERVATIVE MENNONITE CONFERENCE** Church founded in Pigeon, Michigan, in 1910. It holds to the Dordrecht Confession of Faith (see DORT, SYNOD OF), nonconformity, and nonresistance.

**CONSERVATISM** Religious outlook characterized by emphasis on conserving the traditions, principles, and fundamentals received from the past; the antithesis of modernism or liberalism.

**CONSIGNATORIUM** Place in early church buildings where those newly baptized were confirmed with the CHRISM. Hence it was also called the Chrismarium.

**CONSILIA EVANGELICA** *Gospel counsels* Christian "instruments of perfection"— ideals of poverty, celibacy, and obedience, the following of which is considered to bring an individual greater love and spiritual perfection. THOMAS AQUINAS explained the difference between these counsels and the duties binding all Christians.

**CONSISTORY** 1. In REFORMED and PRESBYTERIAN churches, the body governing the local congregation, consisting of the minister and ruling elders. 2. In ROMAN CATHOLICISM, the cardinals meeting in the presence of the pope.

**CONSISTORY COURT** Bishop's court to administer ecclesiastical law, in the CHURCH OF ENGLAND.

**CONSOLAMENTUM** Spiritual baptism among the CATHARI.

**CONSOLATION** 1. Comfort or alleviation of sorrow, as from the presence of God. 2. Ecclesiastical compensation for loss or sacrifice, as the evening meal of monks after prolonged labors.

**CONSTANCE, COUNCIL OF** Church council convoked by the antipope John XXIII, 1414–1418, to end the GREAT SCHISM, reform the church, and eradicate HERESY.

**CONSTANTINE I or THE GREAT (c.288–337)** First Christian emperor of Rome. According to Eusebius, while Constantine was fighting his rival Maxentius in 312, he saw in the sky a fiery cross and the words "By this sign conquer." He adopted the cross as his symbol, killed Maxentius, and issued an edict that Christianity would be tolerated throughout the Roman Empire. Constantine called together the Council of NICAEA in 325 and sought to prevent the division of the church. He promoted humanitarian reforms. In 321 he made Sunday a holiday. He was baptized on his deathbed.

**CONSTANTINOPLE** *city of Constantine* City in Turkey, once called Byzantium and now called Istanbul. Constantine the Great made it the new capital of the Roman Empire in 330. The Patriarch of Constantinople was recognized as head of the EASTERN CHURCH from the sixth century until 1453. Today he is primate of Eastern Orthodox Christians in Turkey and a number of other places. The beautiful Church of St. Sophia and many other churches and mosques make the city one of great religious interest.

**CONSTANTINOPLE, COUNCILS OF** The First Council of Constantinople in 381 reaffirmed the NICENE CREED. The Second and Third Councils, in 553 and 680 respectively, condemned certain NESTORIANS and MONOTHELITES. The Fourth Council of Constantinople in 869–870 excommunicated Photius, Patriarch of the city, and gave that patriarchate primacy in the East.

**CONSTITUTIONS OF CLARENDON** See CLARENDON, CONSTITUTIONS OF.

**CONSUBSTANTIAL** *of the same substance with* Term for the identical nature of the three persons of the TRINITY.

**CONSUBSTANTIATION** LUTHERAN doctrine of the LORD'S SUPPER, maintaining that although the bread and wine of the communion remain unchanged, the body and blood of Christ are substantially present with them.

**CONSUETUDINARY** A manual of the ritual of a religious order or cathedral.

**CONSUMMATION** Term for the fulfillment of time and the completion of God's purpose in history at the age's end.

**CONSUS** Roman god of storage, secrecy, or counsel.

**CONTEMPLATIVE LIFE** The life of prayer and meditation followed by those who live apart from the world in religious houses.

**CONTEMPLATIVE ORDERS** MONASTIC orders following the contemplative life such as CARTHUSIANS, CISTERCIANS, and CARMELITES.

**CONTINENCE** Self-restraint, particularly in sexual matters.

**CONTRITION** Sincere sorrow for sin based on pure love for God.

**CONTUMACY** Contempt for the authority of an ecclesiastical court.

**CONVENT** *coming together* 1. Technically, those living in a MONASTERY, or their dwelling place. 2. Popularly, a place where NUNS dwell.

**CONVENTICLE** Religious assembly not authorized by law, or a place where such assembly takes place.

**CONVENTICLE ACT** An English law of 1664 making illegal a meeting of more than five persons for worship other than as prescribed by the BOOK OF COMMON PRAYER.

**CONVENTION** 1. Ecclesiastical gathering. 2. In the PROTESTANT EPISCOPAL CHURCH, a legislative body. The highest body in that church is the General Convention, while the highest in a district is the Diocesan Convention.

**CONVENTUALS** 1. Branch of the order of FRANCISCANS sometimes called Black Franciscans, or, more properly, FRIARS MINOR CONVENTUAL, who desire to hold property in common and use the income as in other orders. 2. Those in an order following a rule changed from the original form. 3. Members of a convent.

**CONVERSATION** In the King James Bible this term often means conduct or way of life, as in I Peter 1:15 and Philippians 3:20.

**CONVERSI** MONASTIC lay brothers.

**CONVERSION** Change of belief, spiritual outlook, and manner of life. Such change is essential to the Christian life in evangelical PROTESTANTISM.

**CONVERT** One who has experienced a spiritual change, or has adopted a new religious belief.

**CONVICTION** In evangelical PROTESTANTISM, attainment of a sense of sin and a need of salvation through the work of the HOLY SPIRIT.

**CONVOCATION** 1. A provincial assembly of ANGLICAN clergymen, or a special assembly in the PROTESTANT EPISCOPAL CHURCH. 2. A holy assembly in ancient Israel.

**CONVULSIONARIES** Eighteenth-century French JANSENISTS who seemed to have convulsions and other symptoms like epilepsy in connection with their opposition to the papal bull *Unigenitus*.

**CONWELL, RUSSELL H. (1843–1925)** American lawyer, lecturer, and BAPTIST minister who wrote ACRES OF DIAMONDS and founded Temple University.

**CONY or CONEY** In the Bible, the rodentlike hyrax which lives among rocks.

**CONYBEARE, FREDERICK C. (1856–1924)** Armenian scholar who discovered and collated Armenian manuscripts and wrote *Myth, Magic and Morals, a Study of Christian Origins*.

**CONYBEARE, WILLIAM JOHN (1815–1857)** Scholarly vicar in the CHURCH OF ENGLAND who was coauthor with J. S. Howson of *The Life and Epistles of St. Paul*.

**COONEYITES** British followers of Edward Cooney and others in the late nineteenth century; they preached vigorously against smoking, drinking, and other extravagances.

**COOPER, ANTHONY ASHLEY** See SHAFTESBURY, SEVENTH EARL OF.

**COOPERATION** Working together: 1. There is much more cooperation among churches and religious groups now than in the past. Formal organization of this takes such shapes as the NATIONAL COUNCIL OF CHURCHES, the NATIONAL ASSOCIATION OF EVANGELICALS, and the WORLD COUNCIL OF CHURCHES. 2. Theologically, cooperation means God working with man in redemption. Classical Pauline theology finds God working alone in regeneration, since life not yet born can do nothing; but it recognizes the cooperation of God and man in sanctification, since growth in grace depends on man's appropriation of God's gifts.

**COORNHERT, DIRCK VOLCKERTSZOON (1522–1590)** Humanitarian Dutch engraver, writer, and theologian who held that the Scriptures and the APOSTLES' CREED were sufficient for Christian faith and that the HOLY SPIRIT must control one's heart. He opposed torture or death for heretics, for stating which he was put in prison and banished from the Netherlands.

**COPACATI** Inca goddess of Lake Titicaca.

**COPE** Long sleeveless cloak of rich materials, fastened at the chest with a clasp, worn in ANGLICAN and CATHOLIC churches on solemn occasions. It symbolizes dignity.

**COPERNICAN REVOLUTION** Discovery by Nicholas Copernicus in the sixteenth century that the sun, not the earth, is the center of our planetary system. The work describing this, although dedicated to Pope Paul III, was placed on the INDEX of forbidden books for many years. Copernican astronomy profoundly affected theology and was the beginning of many conflicts between the church and the emerging discoveries of science.

**COPTIC CHURCH** Native church of Egypt, dating from early in the Christian era, MONOPHYSITE and MONOTHELITE in doctrine and with many customs like those of JEWS or MOSLEMS. The Copts CIRCUMCISE their boys, pray seven times a day, and refrain from eating pork. The church is related to the Jacobite Church (see JACOBITES) and the Coptic patriarch names the Abuna (head) of the Coptic Church of Ethiopia.

**COQUEREL, ATHANASE LAURENT CHARLES (1795–1868)** Eloquent French PROTESTANT preacher with liberal theological and educational views.

**CORAL** Sea invertebrate whose skeleton builds reefs and islands. Coral, which is of various colors, is a religious symbol of protection from evil.

**CORBAN** *consecrated gift* An offering dedicated exclusively to God (LEVITICUS 1:2; MARK 7:11–13).

**CORBIE** Famous French MONASTERY near Amiens.

**CORDELIERS** FRANCISCAN monks who wore a knotted cord around the waist to pledge their strict observance of the Rule of St. Francis.

**CORE** See KORAH.

**CORELIGIONIST** Person of the same religion.

**CORINTH** City of Greece where a Christian church eventually displaced temples to APOLLO and other gods. A center of licentiousness, its name is imperishably preserved in the Apostle PAUL's two letters to the Corinthians.

**CORINTHIANS, EPISTLES TO THE** Two letters addressed by the Apostle Paul to the Christians of Corinth. They were filled with answers to the peculiar problems of the Corinthian church, ranging from immorality and drunkenness to class division, schism, and tongue-speaking. The book of I Corinthians is notable for chapter 13, on Christian love, and 15, on the resurrection.

**CORINTHIANS, THIRD EPISTLE TO THE** Apocryphal letter, falsely attributed to the Apostle Paul, which is in the canonical writings accepted by the ARMENIAN CHURCH.

**CORN** In the King James Bible, this means a cereal grain such as wheat or barley.

**CORNELIUS** Roman centurion whose conversion and baptism by Peter highlighted God's acceptance of Gentiles as well as Jews (ACTS 10, 11). According to tradition, Cornelius was the first Bishop of Caesarea.

**CORNELIUS, ST. (?–253)** Pope and saint banished and martyred by Emperor Decius of Rome. His feast day is September 16.

**CORNERSTONE** Ceremonial foundation stone of a building, often filled with religious amulets or sacrifices in ancient times. Christ is the chief cornerstone of the house of the church (MATTHEW 21:

42–44; EPHESIANS 2:20; I PETER 2:5–7).

**CORNET** White headdress of the SISTERS OF CHARITY.

**CORNICE** Top edge of a pulpit.

**CORNUCOPIA** *horn of plenty* Horn of the Greek river god Achelous which filled itself with whatever its owner asked.

**CORONATION** 1. Crowning of a king—for many years a religious occasion. 2. Crowning of a pope. 3. Crowning of Christ at His final victory over all evil. 4. Term for the death, and entrance into heaven, of a Christian.

**CORONATION OF OUR LADY** Crowning of MARY in heaven according to the fifth Glorious Mystery of the Rosary.

**CORPORAL** White linen on which the elements and vessels of the EUCHARIST rest for consecration.

**CORPORAL WORKS OF MERCY** Seven Christian duties of feeding the hungry, supplying the need of the thirsty, clothing the naked, giving shelter to the homeless, aiding the sick, ministering to prisoners, and burying the dead.

**CORPUS** Figure of Christ on a CRUCIFIX.

**CORPUS CHRISTI** CATHOLIC festival of the EUCHARIST, celebrated on the Thursday or Sunday following TRINITY SUNDAY. It was a popular medieval pageant and is often a festival of flowers.

**CORPUS IURIS CANONICI** Chief collection of canon law in the ROMAN CATHOLIC CHURCH.

**CORRECTORY** Medieval book with readings to supplement the text of the VULGATE.

**CORREGGIO (1494–1534)** Matchless Italian artist who painted many religious scenes and decorated many churches.

**CORRUPTION** Word in the King James Bible for mortality, decay, and the transient.

**CORYBANT** Attendant of CYBELE in Greek religion. The Corybantes were eunuchs who danced wildly.

**CORYBANTES** Plural of CORYBANT.

**COSMAS AND DAMIAN, STS.** Fourth-century martyrs, the saints of physicians. Their feast day is September 27.

**COSMOGONY** Term for religious or other speculation about the creation or origin of the universe.

**COSMOLOGICAL ARGUMENT** Argument seeking to prove the existence of God from the world or universe itself as a fact leading back to the "uncaused Cause."

**COTTA** Short surplice or vestment of choristers.

**COTTON, JOHN (1584–1652)** ANGLICAN vicar of St. Botolph's Church at Boston, Lincolnshire, who became a PURITAN, fled to New England, and was so popular a leader in the Massachusetts Colony that Boston, Massachusetts, was named in his honor. Through his influence Roger WILLIAMS and Anne HUTCHINSON were driven out of the theocracy. He was the grandfather of Cotton Mather.

**COUÉ, ÉMILE (1857–1926)** French psychotherapist who originated the healing thought, "Every day, and in every way, I am becoming better and better." He believed that he brought about organic changes by using imagination and autosuggestion to help his patients heal themselves. His ideas have greatly influenced psychology and religion.

**COUNCIL** Formal ecclesiastical assembly.

**COUNCIL, ECUMENICAL** See ECUMENICAL COUNCILS.

**COUNCIL, GENERAL** Another name for an ECUMENICAL COUNCIL.

**COUNCIL OF ARLES** See ARLES, SYNOD OF.

**COUNCIL OF BASEL** See BASEL, COUNCIL OF.

**COUNCIL OF CHALCEDON** See CHALCEDON, COUNCIL OF.

**COUNCIL OF CHURCHES** Group of churches associated for common purposes. See NATIONAL COUNCIL OF CHURCHES, and WORLD COUNCIL OF CHURCHES.

**COUNCIL OF CONSTANCE** See CONSTANCE, COUNCIL OF.

**COUNCIL OF CONSTANTINOPLE** See CONSTANTINOPLE, COUNCILS OF.

**COUNCIL OF EPHESUS** See EPHESUS, COUNCIL OF.

**COUNCIL OF GANGRA** See GANGRA, COUNCIL OF.

**COUNCIL OF JERUSALEM** See JERUSALEM, COUNCIL OF.

**COUNCIL OF LYONS** See LYONS and following entries.

**COUNCIL OF TRENT** See TRENT, COUNCIL OF.

**COUNCIL OF VIENNE** See VIENNE, COUNCIL OF.

**COUNCILS, VATICAN** See VATICAN COUNCIL, FIRST; VATICAN COUNCIL, SECOND.

**COUNCILS OF NICAEA** See NICAEA, FIRST COUNCIL OF, and NICAEA, SECOND COUNCIL OF.

**COUNSEL** 1. Spiritual or other guidance. 2. The divine gift of prudence. 3. Purpose or plan (as indicated in PSALM 33:11). 4. A directive of Christ (as in MATTHEW 19:21).

**COUNSELING** Individually working with a person until he sees his way through his problems. Counseling is becoming an increasing part of the church's ministry.

**COUNSELOR** 1. In PROTESTANT churches, an adviser, as in a youth group. 2. In a MORMON church, an adviser to the president.

**COUNSELS OF PERFECTION** The three MONASTIC obligations of poverty, chastity, and obedience. Since Christ's command to be perfect (MATTHEW 19:21) was considered impossible for the average person to attain, it was held that these three "counsels" made perfection a proximation.

**COUNTER REFORMATION** The ROMAN CATHOLIC response to the Protestant REFORMATION in the sixteenth century. Centered in the Council of TRENT, it sought to check the spread of Protestantism through such measures as the INQUISITION, and to strengthen the Roman Catholic Church through internal reforms and external advance in evangelism and mission work. Leaders in the Counter or Catholic Reformation were St. CAJETAN, Paul III, St. IGNATIUS OF LOYOLA, St. CHARLES BORROMEO, St. PHILIP NERI, St. THERESA OF AVILA, St. JOHN OF THE CROSS, and St. VINCENT DE PAUL.

**COUNTESS OF HUNTINGDON'S CONNEXION** Conservative Protestant group of Calvinistic Methodists in England, more sympathetic to George WHITEFIELD's theology than to John WESLEY's, although it followed the latter's evangelistic zeal.

**COURT** A judicial or a governing body in a church.

**COUVADE** Primitive ritual in which the father takes to bed for a fortnight after the birth of his child. It may root in religious tabu.

**COVENANT** 1. Sacred relationship between God and man, as in the divine covenants with NOAH, ABRAHAM, and MOSES. The designations "Old Testament" and "New Testament" indicate the Christian concept of the old covenant of works in JUDAISM being supplanted by the new covenant of grace through the work of Christ. 2. Solemn agreement between men. The marriage relationship is described as pledged by "vow and covenant."

**COVENANT CHURCHES** PROTESTANT churches, particularly in Scotland, growing out of special covenants, or stressing COVENANT THEOLOGY.

**COVENANTERS** Scottish Presbyterians who, since the sixteenth century, have pledged themselves to maintain evangelical doctrines, resist Catholicism and episcopacy, and remain true to PRESBYTERIANISM. The term applies particularly to those Scotsmen who armed themselves to defend their principles after the Restoration of 1660.

**COVENANT OF GRACE** Theological term for the arrangement between God the Father and Christ, representing His elect people, whereby Christ redeems them.

**COVENANT OF WORKS** Theological term for the arrangement between God and man during the Old Testament period, in which God had promised eternal life to man on condition of perfect obedience. Since Adam had broken the covenant of works, salvation depended on the succeeding covenant of grace.

**COVENANT THEOLOGY** System attributed to Johannes COCCEIUS as founder, elaborating the covenant of grace and that of works (see). It was espoused by PURITANS, CALVINISTS, and REFORMED PROTESTANTS, and condemned by the Council of TRENT.

**COVERDALE, MILES (1488–1569)** English AUGUSTINIAN friar who imbibed PROTESTANT doctrines and translated the first complete Bible published in England. He also edited the GREAT BIBLE of 1539 and Cranmer's Bible of 1540, and attempted to suppress religious images. Much of his life was spent fleeing persecution for HERESY.

**COVETOUSNESS** Intense desire, often mentioned in the Bible.

**COW** Sacred animal of India, revered by HINDUISM.

**COWL** Monk's hood.

**COWLEY FATHERS** Members of the Society of Mission Priests of St. John the Evangelist. This is an ANGLICAN order founded by the Rev. R. H. Meux Benson in 1865, with the usual monastic vows of poverty, chastity, and obedience. Its headquarters are at Cowley St. John near Oxford.

**COWPER, WILLIAM (1731–1800)** English poet whose work includes the hymns "God moves in a mysterious way," "Jesu, where'er thy people meet," and "Oh for a closer walk with God." With John Newton he wrote the book *Olney Hymns*, published in 1779. Throughout his life he was subject to attacks of suicidal melancholy.

**CRAIG, JOHN (c.1512–1600)** Scottish DOMINICAN who was converted to PROTESTANTISM by reading the *Institutes* of John CALVIN and became a leader of the REFORMATION. A colleague of John KNOX in Edinburgh, he was once condemned to be burned for HERESY but escaped.

**CRANACH, LUCAS (1472–1553)** German "Painter of the Reformation." A friend of Martin LUTHER, he produced warmly original woodcuts and paintings. The latter include "The Crucifixion," "St. Christopher," and "Repose in Egypt." Cranach had a son by the same name who carried on his work.

**CRANE** Religious symbol of virtue and order in MONASTICISM.

**CRANMER, THOMAS (1489–1556)** English ecclesiastic and Archbishop of Canterbury who aided Henry VIII in making the churches in England independent of Rome. To create the CHURCH OF ENGLAND, he attacked those of extreme views in either PROTESTANTISM or CATHOLICISM. He led in the renewal of the English liturgy and aided the circulation of the Bible in the English language. After persecuting and condemning certain heretical or ecclesiastical opponents, he was himself burned at the stake under Queen Mary.

**CRAOSA** ZOROASTRIAN spirit of beneficence.

**CRAPSEY, ALGERNON SIDNEY (1847–1914)** American EPISCOPAL rector expelled from the ministry for his beliefs about Christ.

**CRASHAW, RICHARD (c.1612–1649)** English CATHOLIC author of intensely religious poetry, published in the books *Steps to the Temple, The Delights of the Muses,* and *Carmen Deo Nostro.*

**CRAYER, GASPARD DE (1584–1669)** Flemish painter of many altarpieces and religious scenes. His work may be seen in many churches of Europe.

**CREATION** Divine bringing of the universe into existence. Traditional Judeo-Christian theology assumes that the act of creation was "out of nothing"; that before God created, nothing but God was.

**CREATIONISM** 1. Doctrine that at the moment of conception or birth God creates a new soul for each person born. This was maintained by JEROME and THOMAS AQUINAS. 2. Doctrine of divine creation, as opposed to PANTHEISM, EVOLUTIONISM, etc.

**CREATIVE EVOLUTION** Henri BERGSON's philosophy of spontaneous originality in nature and man.

**CREATOR** 1. A god who creates or fashions the world or mankind. 2. In the major religions, the God who is the Source of all.

**CREATURE** A being made by and dependent upon the Creator.

**CRECHE** 1. Representation of the scene at the birth of Jesus, often displayed at Christmas, showing Infant and Mother surrounded by angels, shepherds, Joseph, animals, and wise men. 2. Nursery or foundling hospital.

**CREDENCE** 1. Acceptance or belief. 2. Small table where the eucharistic elements are placed before being consecrated.

**CREDENDA** Articles of faith or things to be believed.

**CREDO** *I believe* 1. A creed. 2. The NICENE CREED.

**CREDO UT INTELLIGAM** *I believe that I may know* View of St. ANSELM and St. AUGUSTINE that faith is the basis of understanding and knowledge.

**CREED** Statement of belief. Famous Christian creeds are the APOSTLES' CREED, the NICENE CREED, and the ATHANASIAN CREED.

**CREMATION** Widespread ancient custom of disposing of corpses by burning, possibly related to belief in the purifying properties of fire. JUDAISM and CHRISTIANITY have historically preferred burial, although cremation appears to have growing acceptance in both faiths.

**CRESCAS, HASDAI BEN ABRAHAM (1340–1410)** Spanish Jewish philosopher, rabbi, and authority on Jewish law. He lost his son in the INQUISITION. Crescas sought to refute ARISTOTLE in order to free JUDAISM from his influence; he is considered to have prepared the way for the work of SPINOZA.

**CRESCENT** The new moon. 1. Symbol of the (Moslem) Ottoman Turks during the early Middle Ages. Hence, though without other support, it is a popular symbol of ISLAM. 2. Symbol of the Virgin MARY.

**CRETE** Island near Greece, site of one of the world's most ancient civilizations and religions. The Minoans worshiped in caves and sacred groves and made sacrifices. On Crete is Mt. Ida, supposed birthplace of the Greek god ZEUS. It figures in the New Testament records (ACTS 2:11; 27; TITUS).

**CRIOBOLIUM** Greek sacrifice of a ram in the cult of ATTIS and the Great Mother CYBELE. The ram's blood baptized the worshiper beneath it.

**CRISIS THEOLOGY** Term for the theology of Karl Barth and other "neo-orthodox" thinkers. Sometimes called Dialectical Theology and doubtless conditioned by the crisis of modern life in its awareness of mounting challenges, crisis theology emphasizes the three meanings of the Greek word *krisis:* separation between time and eternity, divine condemnation of human sin and imperfection, and final judgment of mankind. The neo-orthodox movement also stresses the Word of God in Christ and Scripture, the centrality of preaching in the church, the necessity of justification by faith, and the social concerns of the gospel.

**CRISPIN AND CRISPINIAN, STS. (third century)** Patron saints of leather workers and shoemakers. Their feast day is October 25.

**CRITICISM, BIBLICAL** See BIBLICAL CRITICISM; HIGHER CRITICISM; LOWER CRITICISM.

**CROCODILE** Reptile worshiped and embalmed by ancient Egyptians.

**CROMLECH** A circle of large standing stones, as at Stonehenge in England.

**CROMWELL, OLIVER (1599–1658)** English leader of the forces of Parliament and PROTESTANTISM against King Charles I. Cromwell's psalm-singing regiment of "Ironsides" were never defeated; they executed the king and made Cromwell Lord Protector. Having personally experienced conversion, Cromwell sought to win through the righteousness of his cause. During his reign England gave religious toleration to JEWS, QUAKERS, and all Christians except ROMAN CATHOLICS—an ad-

vance for that period. Offered the crown, Cromwell refused it. He said of his successes: "I have not sought these things; truly I have been called unto them by the Lord."

**CROMWELL, THOMAS (c.1485–1540)** Chief minister and vicar-general of Henry VIII of England, prominent in transforming English churches into the CHURCH OF ENGLAND. He was unpopular for suppressing monasteries, confiscating their wealth, controlling the activity of the clergy, and opposing image-worship. He had a Bible placed in every church and arranged the marriage of Henry VIII and Anne of Cleves. The king, finding Anne unattractive and his minister no longer useful, had Cromwell beheaded.

**CRONOS or CRONUS** Ancient god of Greece, probably preceding classical religion but incorporated into Greek mythology as Son of Heaven and Earth and father of ZEUS. He swallowed his own children.

**CROSBY, FANNY (1820–1915)** Blind American poet and hymn writer. Among her popular hymns were "Blessed Assurance," "Pass Me not, O Gentle Saviour," "Rescue the Perishing," "Safe in the Arms of Jesus," and "Saved by Grace."

**CROSIER or CROZIER** Bishops' staff, crook-shaped, symbolizing the pastoral function. In the EASTERN CHURCH the crosier is topped with a cross between serpents.

**CROSS** 1. Ancient instrument of execution. The victim was nailed or tied to a stake, sometimes with a crossbar, or to two stakes crossed like the letter X. 2. World-wide pre-Christian religious symbol, found in various forms (such as the Egyptian *tau* in the shape of the letter $T$ and the Eastern swastika) and possibly connected with nature worship. 3. Symbol of Christianity, commemorating Christ's death on a cross. Christian crosses are of many forms, and have been widely used in ecclesiastical rites, processions, architecture, etc.

**CROSSING** Intersection of the NAVE and TRANSEPTS in a traditionally constructed church.

**CROSSLET** Small cross.

**CROWN** Symbol of power and glory. The Jewish high priest wore a gold crown (EXODUS 28:36–7). Christ is represented in Revelation with many crowns (REVELA-

TION 19:12). The Christian looks forward to a crown (I CORINTHIANS 9:25; REVELATION 2:10). A crown is given the confirmand in the Armenian confirmation rite. Bishops and the pope wear crowns.

**CROWN OF THORNS** A crown plaited of thorns with which the soldiers mocked Christ before His crucifixion (JOHN 19:2). This crown and its thorns are religious relics and are reputed to be in various shrines and museums.

**CROWTHER, SAMUEL ADJAI (c.1809–1891)** African slave who became a missionary and first bishop of the Niger area. He translated the Bible into a number of African dialects.

**CROZIER** See CROSIER.

**CRUCIFER** Cross-bearer in an ecclesiastical procession.

**CRUCIFIX** Representation of Christ being crucified on the cross. A crucifix must hang above the altar for mass.

**CRUCIFIXION** Execution on a CROSS. Theologically, the Crucifixion refers to the death of Christ for the sin of the world.

**CRUCIFORM** Cross-shaped, as the NAVE and TRANSEPTS of many a church.

**CRUCIFY** To kill by nailing to a CROSS.

**CRUCIGER, KASPAR (1504–1548)** Associate of Martin LUTHER who helped him translate the Bible into German and preserved many of his messages in shorthand.

**CRUDEN, ALEXANDER (1701–1770)** Brilliant British bookseller and proofreader who compiled the *Complete Concordance to the Holy Scriptures,* on which many later concordances to the Bible were modeled.

**CRUET** Vessel for the wine and water of the eucharist.

**CRUGER, JOHANN (1598–1662)** German church organist and composer of many hymns and concertos. His works include "Jesu Meine Freude" and "Nun Danket Alle Gott."

**CRUSADE** Reform or evangelistic movement.

**CRUSADER** Leader in a crusade, or participant in one of the medieval Crusades.

**CRUSADES** Military expeditions undertaken by armies from western Europe during the eleventh, twelfth, and thirteenth centuries under ecclesiastical inspiration. Nine Crusades during this period went out to recover the HOLY LAND from the Saracens. In the end the MOSLEMS won. Some of these and later crusades were directed against other countries, Jews, heretics, and papal opponents.

**CRUTCHED FRIARS** Medieval order of mendicants bearing staffs with crosses, or with these emblems on their garb.

**CRUX ANSATA** Cross in the form of the ankh, the Egyptian symbol of life, with a loop above a *T*-shaped character.

**CRYPT** Burial place beneath a church floor.

**CRYPTO-CALVINISTS** Sixteenth-century followers of MELANCHTHON, outwardly LUTHERAN, suspected of secretly believing CALVINISTIC doctrines of Christ and the LORD'S SUPPER. In some parts of Europe the Crypto-Calvinists were exiled or killed.

**CRYSTAL** Colorless quartz, symbol of purity and clarity (REVELATION 21:11; 22:1).

**CU** Celtic god of healing.

**CUBIT** Bible term for a measure the length of one's forearm, about eighteen inches.

**CUDWORTH, RALPH (1617–1688)** English philosopher who criticized atheism and materialism, contending for the innateness of moral principles. The most prominent of the Cambridge Platonists, he emphasized teleology.

**CUIUS REGIO, EIUS RELIGIO** *according to his country, his religion* Principle accepted at the Peace of Augsburg giving each prince the right to choose his realm's religion.

**CULDEES** Celtic monks dating from the eighth century in Scotland and Ireland. Representing an early form of Christianity, they often married and were considered lax in discipline.

**CULPA** *fault* A fault, particularly one that must be confessed to a monastic superior.

**CULT** 1. A religious system. 2. Religious rites. 3. A sect. 4. Adoration or devotion.

**CULTUS** See CULT.

**CUMBERLAND METHODIST CHURCH** Small American denomination with 4 churches and 64 members, founded in 1950 in Tennessee.

**CUMBERLAND PRESBYTERIAN CHURCH** Denomination organized in 1810 in Tennessee by a group withdrawing from the Presbyterian Church through dissatisfaction with its doctrinal and educational standards. Most of the denomination reunited with the PRESBYTERIAN CHURCH IN THE U.S.A. in 1906, but a continuing body of the Cumberland Presbyterian Church remains active.

**CUMIN or CUMMIN**  Plant with seeds used for spice or medicine, tithed in Bible times (MATTHEW 23:23).

**CUMMINS, GEORGE DAVID (1822–1876)** PROTESTANT EPISCOPAL Bishop of Kentucky who instituted the REFORMED EPISCOPAL CHURCH in 1873.

**CUNEIFORM**  System of writing using wedge-shaped characters, probably originated in Mesopotamia as early as the fourth millennium B.C. It is important for knowledge of ancient Sumerian and other cultures and religions for it was widely used before papyrus was developed. Cuneiform inscriptions have provided archaeologists with invaluable data.

**CUP, THE**  Term for the vessel from which Jesus and the Twelve drank at the LAST SUPPER, or for the communion chalice today.

**CUPID**  Roman god of romantic love, also called EROS. He was often visualized as a wanton lad who cast his darts indiscriminately.

**CUPRA**  Etruscan fertility goddess. Two Italian towns once bore her name.

**CURATE**  1. Originally, and still in Europe, a clergyman who has "the care of souls" in a parish. 2. Usually in English-speaking countries, an assistant to a parish priest.

**CUR DEUS HOMO  Why Did God Become Man?**  Title of ANSELM's treatise on the Atonement in 1098 explaining the work of Christ as a ransom from the devil.

**CURÉ**  French parish priest.

**CURE OF SOULS**  Term for a clergyman's spiritual care of his people in the parish.

**CURETES**  Attendants on the infant ZEUS in Greek religion.

**CURETONIAN MANUSCRIPT**  See OLD SYRIAC VERSIONS.

**CURIA or CURIA ROMANA**  The body of twelve congregations, five offices, and three tribunals through which the pope governs the ROMAN CATHOLIC CHURCH.

**CURIALISM**  Acceptance of the pope as supreme head of the organized church.

**CURSE**  Imprecation invoking divine aid in destroying a person or thing. While the Old Testament Scriptures made provision for cursing, Christianity discourages the act. Blessing and cursing have been regarded as possessing special power in many religions.

**CURSILLO  little course**  CATHOLIC religious retreat with emotional overtones, originated in 1949 in Spain. A Cursillo is usually a weekend retreat from sundown Thursday to sundown Sunday in which a group of from thirty to forty Catholics live and become spiritually involved together, resulting in heightened religious and social awareness.

**CURSIVES**  Manuscripts, including those of Scripture, written in a running small-letter type of handwriting, useful in identifying date of inscription.

**CURSOR MUNDI  course of the world**  Thirteenth-century English poem outlining the history of the world from Creation to Doomsday. It is essentially a religious narrative emphasizing Bible events.

**CURSUS**  The regular course of the divine service, or directions for conducting it.

**CUSH**  Bible name for Ethiopia.

**CUSTOM**  Unwritten ecclesiastical law based on established regular usage.

**CUSTOMARY**  Book of ecclesiastical rites and rules.

**CUTHA, CUTHAH, or CUTH**  Ancient city in Mesopotamia especially devoted to the worship of NERGAL, the god of the underworld.

**CUTHBERT (c.635–687)**  Celtic Bishop of Lindisfarne and Hexham of northern England, noted for his missionary zeal.

**CUTLER, MANASSEH (1742–1823)**  American CONGREGATIONAL minister, scientist, and colonizer of Ohio. He was the first person to classify the flora of New England scientifically.

**CUTTY STOOL**  Seat or gallery in Scottish churches where those suspected of low morality had to sit in public view.

**CYBELE**  Mother-goddess of Phrygia and the Mediterranean world, patroness of fertility and public welfare. "Mother of the gods," she was worshiped in sexual orgies with wild music and dancing; her priests emasculated themselves.

**CYCLAMEN**  Modest European flower symbolizing the Virgin MARY.

**CYHIRAETH**  Celtic goddess of flowing streams.

**CYNICS**  Followers of a Greek school of ethics which held that the good life is simple and must be sought without regard for other rewards, and that pleasure is evil.

**C.Y.O.** Catholic Youth Organization, movement for ROMAN CATHOLIC young people.

**CYPRESS** Evergreen wood used in the temple of Solomon and highly prized for its fragrance, beauty, and durability. The Italian cypress symbolizes death, mourning, and immortality.

**CYPRIAN, ST. (c.200–258)** Bishop of Carthage, the first African bishop to be martyred. He was beheaded under the Roman Emperor Valerian, crying out, "Deo Gratias!" and was later proclaimed a saint. He sought to maintain the unity of the church when an attempt was made to excommunicate those who had lapsed from the faith during persecution. Cyprian favored tolerance for these, though only after penance and suitable delay. On the other hand, he insisted that heretics who wanted readmission to the church must be rebaptized. He emphasized penance and baptism as means of grace, and left the church a number of important works. His feast day is September 16.

**CYPRUS** Mediterranean island near Asia Minor to which PAUL and BARNABAS brought Christianity. Today the prevailing religion is the independent Church of Cyprus which is in communion with the EASTERN ORTHODOX CHURCHES.

**CYRIL (827–869)** Christian missionary, with his brother Methodius, to the Slavs of the Balkan region. Born in Greece, they translated the Bible into Slavonic which they used in church services—with much criticism.

**CYRIL OF ALEXANDRIA, ST. (376–444)** Bishop of Alexandria and saint, so zealous for orthodoxy that he closed Novatian churches and expelled Jews from the city. He tended toward MONOPHYSITISM and explained the Scriptures allegorically. His feast day is February 9.

**CYRIL OF JERUSALEM, ST. (c.315–386)** Saint and Bishop of Jerusalem who opposed ARIANISM and defended orthodox doctrines of the church. His addresses to CATECHUMENS are the first popular exposition of Christian doctrine.

**CYRUS II or CYRUS THE GREAT (?–529)** Persian emperor known for his leniency to the people he captured. His permission to the Jews he had captured to rebuild Jerusalem is commemorated in the Bible (EZRA 1:1–8). He praised the god MARDUK of Babylon for making him king "over the whole world."

**CZARNOBOG** Black God of the Slavs.

**CZECHOSLOVAK CHURCH** A national church of Czechoslovakia founded in 1920. When the ROMAN CATHOLIC CHURCH refused such Czech demands as marriage for the clergy, the Czechoslovak Church was formed with somewhat rationalistic doctrines and a PRESBYTERIAN form of government, but with BISHOPS.

**CZESTOCHOWA** Town in Poland to which pilgrims come from all over the world because of its monastery containing an image of the Virgin MARY believed to have been painted by St. LUKE.

# D

**D** 1. Symbol for the "D Document" prepared by the author of Deuteronomy and those editors who contributed other portions to the Scriptures with the same linguistic style, according to many modern scholars. "D" is considered to uphold monotheism and centralized worship in Jerusalem. 2. Symbol of CODEX BEZAE.

**DA-BOG** Slavonic sun god.

**DACCA** Capital of East Pakistan, noted for a number of impressive mosques and temples. It has four Christian churches.

**DA COSTA, ISAAC (1798–1860)** Jewish writer born in Amsterdam and converted to Christianity. He became a brilliant poet and a powerful Christian apologist.

**DADU (1544–1603)** Brahman Hindu who founded the DADU PANTHIS and who wrote the long poem *Bani,* venerated by them.

**DADU PANTHIS** HINDU sect of western India founded by the Brahman Dadu. Rejecting the gods and much of the system of Hinduism, the Dadu Panthi sect emphasizes monotheism and conscience; the latter is held to be the inner voice from the one God who made and upholds all things. Members wear skull caps.

**DAEMON or DAIMON** Guardian spirit or god in Greek religion. Socrates spoke often of his guiding daemon.

**DAGAN** One of the leading gods of Assyrian religion.

**DAGDA** Celtic god of agriculture and fertility.

**DAGGATUM** Jewish nomads of Morocco.

**DAGOBA or DAGABA** Monument containing BUDDHIST relics.

**DAGON** Canaanite fertility god, worshiped also in Babylonia and Phoenicia, usually in the form of a fish. He is mentioned several times in the Old Testament (cf. JUDGES 16:23–30).

**DAHLKE, PAUL (1865–1928)** German BUDDHIST ascetic and writer, founder of Europe's first VIHARA.

**DAIBUTSU Great Buddha** Gigantic Japanese statues of BUDDHA, sometimes more than fifty feet tall.

**DAIKOKU** Japanese god of riches.

**DAIMON** See DAEMON.

**DAI NICHI** Japanese term for BUDDHA as absolute reality.

**DAISY** Religious symbol of the innocence of Christ.

**DAITOKUJI** ZEN Buddhist monastery in Kyoto, Japan, founded by Daito Kokushi in 1383. It is noted for its beautiful gardens and art.

**DAITYAS** Vedic enemies of the gods.

**DAKHMA** Tower on which the PARSEES place corpses to be devoured by vultures.

**DAKINI** BUDDHIST goddess of intuition.

**DAKSHA** Goat-headed vedic god.

**DALAI LAMA** Head of Tibetan LAMAISM. The Dalai Lama is believed to be a reincarnation of previous Grand Lamas; he is reared without contact with women.

**DALE, ROBERT WILLIAM (1829–1895)** English CONGREGATIONAL minister of unusual ability as a preacher. His book *The Atonement* presents a mystical doctrine of redemption. He did much for education and religious freedom in England.

**DALETH** Fourth letter of the Hebrew alphabet.

**DALMATIA** Portion of modern Yugoslavia visited by Titus (II TIMOTHY 4:10).

**DALMATIC** Embroidered vestment with wide sleeves, worn over the alb by deacons in celebrating HIGH MASS.

**DAMASCIUS (c.480–c.540)** Last NEOPLATONIST philosopher. Born in Damascus, he spent most of his life in Greece and Persia. He held that reason leads to a God who is infinite, incomprehensible, good, powerful, and wise.

**DAMASCUS** Capital of the Syrian republic, dating from antiquity (GENESIS 14:15). Near it the Apostle Paul was converted (ACTS 9). In it the temple of ZEUS became the foundation for a Christian church, which became the Great Mosque when the MOSLEM Arabs conquered the city. This is one of the largest mosques in existence; more than 200 other mosques grace Damascus today.

**DAMASUS I, ST. (c.305–384)** Pope and saint who ruled with authority, sought out and adorned the tombs of the martyrs, and encouraged JEROME to translate the VULGATE edition of the Bible. His feast day is December 11.

**DAMASUS II** Pope who died after only 23 days in office in 1048.

**DAMBUL** Village in Ceylon visited by many pilgrims because of its cave-temples, dating from the first century B.C., one with a reclining statue of BUDDHA 47 feet in length.

**DAMIA** See BONA DEA.

**DAMIAN, PETER, ST. (c.1007–1072)** Italian church leader, reformer, and saint. At one time a CAMALDOLESE monk, he became Cardinal Bishop of Ostia and aided Alexander II against the antipope Honorius II. He opposed simony and concubinage among the priests and felt little use for the intellect in theology. His feast day is February 23.

**DAMIEN, FATHER (1840–1889)** Belgian CATHOLIC missionary to lepers in Hawaii. After greatly improving their spiritual and social conditions, he died of leprosy himself.

**DAMKINA** Babylonian goddess who was the wife of the high god EL.

**DAMNATION** Condemnation or destruction.

**DAMONA** Celtic goddess.

**DAN** 1. A son of Jacob who founded the Hebrew tribe of Dan. 2. Hebrew tribe stationed in southwestern Palestine until the Amorites drove them north. 3. City marking the northern boundary of Palestine, as "from Dan to Beersheba" (the latter marked the southern limits).

**DANAIDES** In Greek myth the fifty daughters of Danaus condemned to draw water with sieves forever in Hades.

**DANAVAS** Vedic demons.

**DANCE** The dance has long been important in religious joy and exultation. David danced before the Lord (II SAMUEL 6:14). Hinduism's SIVA is known as the Dancer. Indians of the southwestern United States dance for rain. In the Middle Ages dancing was offered before the altars of churches.

**DANCE OF DEATH** An allegory of Death leading a dance to the grave. Showing the fact of mortality, this was a common theme of literature and morality plays in the Middle Ages.

**DANCE OF SIVA** The dance of Siva in HINDUISM is believed to release his power in the universe. In turn, SIVA is honored by the dance of worshipers.

**DANCERS** Europeans in the Middle Ages and later who were seized with a frenzy and danced until they dropped, sometimes having visions of Christ and the Virgin.

**DANDELION** A symbol of Christ's suffering and death.

**DANH** Serpent god of Dahomey.

**DANIEL** 1. Hebrew taken captive with his people in Babylon who became an adviser to kings and the recipient of visions of the future, recorded in the prophecy of Daniel. 2. Prophetic book of the Old Testament giving the life and visions of the Prophet Daniel. The expression "Son of man" first occurs in this book (7:13).

**DANIEL-ROPS, HENRI (1901–1965)** Outstanding contemporary religious writer. Born Henri Jules Charles Petiot in France, he wrote books for children and adults including *Jesus and His Times* and *The History of the Church of Christ.*

**DANISH CHURCH IN NORTH AMERICA** American Lutheran denomination which merged eventually into the AMERICAN LUTHERAN CHURCH.

**DANITE** Descendant of Dan (JUDGES 13:2).

**DANTE ALIGHIERI (1265–1321)** Italian politician and writer whose works reflect medieval life. His *Divine Comedy* has contributed many additions to popular ideas of heaven, purgatory, and hell.

**DANU** 1. Irish Celtic mother of the gods. 2. Indian snake god.

**DARAMULUM** Australian deity with power to destroy one's enemies.

**DARAWIGAL** Australian spirit of evil.

**DARBY, JOHN NELSON (1800–1882)**

Clergyman of the CHURCH OF ENGLAND who became leader of a Bible-studying sect at Plymouth, later known as PLYMOUTH BRETHREN. He spoke and wrote much, wrote some hymns, and promoted dispensational theology.

**DAR-EL-JANNAH**   Paradise in ISLAM.

**DARIUS I (fifth century B.C.)**   King of Persia (521–486 B.C.) who encouraged the Jews to continue restoring their temple in Jerusalem as CYRUS had done. Also known as Darius the Great, he was contemporary with EZRA, HAGGAI, and ZECHARIAH. He appears to have been a wise statesman and a ZOROASTRIAN.

**DARIUS THE MEDE**   King of the Chaldeans who made Daniel the first of three vicegerents over his realm (DANIEL 6:1–3). This Darius is difficult to identify with known historical figures.

**DARK AGES**   Earlier name for the Middle Ages, extending from the fifth through the fourteenth centuries, because of the alleged intellectual and moral darkness of much of this period.

**DARKNESS**   Widespread religious symbol of evil.

**DARK NIGHT OF THE SOUL**   A mystic's phrase for the period of spiritual dearth that sometimes follows an exalted experience.

**DARROW, CLARENCE S. (1857–1938)**   American lawyer who fought capital punishment and FUNDAMENTALIST religion. An AGNOSTIC, he attempted to discredit literal understanding of the Bible in the Scopes case of 1925. In that trial William Jennings BRYAN prosecuted for the State of Tennessee and Darrow defended a schoolteacher charged with teaching evolution.

**DARSANA, DARSHANA, or DASSANA**   1. In HINDUISM, a system of philosophy. 2. In BUDDHISM, something splendid or the apprehension of it.

**DARSHAN** *interpreter*   Jewish preacher.

**DARU EL-BAWAR** *dwelling of destruction* MOSLEM perdition.

**DARU EL-QARAR** *dwelling of abiding* Third heaven in the paradise of ISLAM.

**DARU EL-SALAM** *dwelling of peace* Second heaven in ISLAM's paradise.

**DARWIN, CHARLES ROBERT (1809–1882)**   English originator of the hypothesis of natural selection and organic evolution.

His book *On the Origin of Species,* published in 1859, and his later works established him as a distinguished naturalist and original thinker. At first the religious world denounced Darwin's theories but today they are widely accepted with inevitable modifications. Darwin became increasingly AGNOSTIC.

**DARWINISM**   Term for the evolution of the various species as conceived by Charles DARWIN.

**DASEHRA**   Ten-day HINDU festival at the end of the rainy season.

**DASTURS**   PARSEE high priests.

**DASUS or DASYUS**   Term applied by the invading Aryans of India to the darker-skinned aboriginals. It may mean enemies, slaves, or evil demons.

**DATARY**   ROMAN CATHOLIC official who investigates the qualifications of those expected to receive papal benefices.

**DA TODI, JACOPONE (1228–1306)**   Italian FRANCISCAN monk and mystic.

**DAUGHTERS OF OUR LADY HELP OF CHRISTIANS**   Order of nuns founded by St. JOHN BOSCO to aid the SALESIANS and to do similar work.

**DAUGHTERS OF THE CROSS**   CATHOLIC sisters who aid those in schools, hospitals, prisons, and elsewhere. They wear a black habit. The order was founded in 1833 by Mère M. Therese Haze.

**DAUGHTERS OF WISDOM**   Order of nuns with gray habits founded in 1703 by St. Louis Grignion to do various good works.

**DAVID** *beloved*   Hebrew shepherd boy who became Israel's greatest king, wrote many Psalms, loved God, and led many military victories. He was a man after God's heart (I SAMUEL 13:14). The MESSIAH was a son (descendant) of David.

**DAVID, ST. (sixth century)**   Missionary and patron saint of Wales. His feast day is March 1.

**DAVIDISTS**   1. Pantheistic followers of DAVID OF DINANT in Belgium. 2. Disciples of David George. 3. UNITARIAN followers of Francis David.

**DAVID OF DINANT (twelfth century)**   Medieval Belgian PANTHEIST to whom everything was God. His doctrines were condemned in 1210 at the Council of Paris.

**DAVIDS, CAROLINE RHYS (1858–1942)**   British Pali scholar who studied the teach-

ings of BUDDHA in the PALI CANON and
wrote several books relating to Buddhism.

**DAVIDS, T. W. RHYS (1843–1922)** British
Pali scholar, first president of the BUDDHIST
SOCIETY IN GREAT BRITAIN AND IRELAND,
and author of three books on BUDDHISM.
He was the husband of Caroline Rhys
Davids.

**DAVIES, SAMUEL (1723–1761)** American
PRESBYTERIAN minister whose evangelistic
preaching was part of the GREAT AWAKEN-
ING. From 1759 to his death, he was presi-
dent of the College of New Jersey, now
Princeton University.

**DAVIES, WALFORD (1869–1941)** English
musician and organist who composed a
number of cantatas and hymns for
churches.

**DAVIS, ANDREW JACKSON (1826–1910)**
American SPIRITUALIST and author.

**DAWN** Symbol of the coming of Christ,
or of His blood.

**DAY** In the Bible, a day may be various
periods of time, from twenty-four hours to
an age.

**DAYAKA** Sponsor of a BUDDHIST monk
who provides his material needs.

**DAYAN** Hebrew term for judge in religious matters.

**DAYANANDA SARASWATI (1824–1883)**
HINDU reformer who became disillusioned
with SIVA worship, wandered for many
years as a SANNYASI, and founded the ARYA
SAMAJ, a theistic form of Hinduism.

**DAY OF THE LORD** Christ's SECOND COM-
ING (II PETER 3:10).

**DAYSMAN** Mediator or judge (JOB
9:33).

**DAYSPRING** Bible word for dawn (LUKE
1:78).

**DAY'S PSALTER** Psalm book for singing,
printed by John Day in the sixteenth century.

**DAYSTAR** Bible word for the morning star
heralding dawn. It may symbolize Lucifer
(ISAIAH 14:12) or Christ the Light-Bearer
(II PETER 1:19).

**DEACON** 1. In the New Testament, a
"servant" (Greek *diakonos*) appointed to
do charitable work and relieve the Apostles
for spiritual meditation, prayer, and
preaching. 2. In the history of the church,
various duties were added to the office of
deacon. Today the deacon may take a
minor part in the service in many churches.

In BAPTIST and CONGREGATIONAL churches,
deacons hold office comparable to that of
ELDERS in the PRESBYTERIAN system. In the
Anglican church, deacons are the lowest
ministerial order.

**DEACONATE or DIACONATE** Term for
board or order of deacons.

**DEACONESS** A woman charged with
duties similar to those of the deacon.
Phoebe was a deaconess (ROMANS 16:1).
Modern deaconesses often do visitation or
missionary work.

**DEADLY SINS** Mortal sins specified by
CATHOLICS are pride, covetousness, lust,
anger, gluttony, envy, sloth.

**DEAD SEA** Large body of water, far below sea level, into which the Jordan River
empties. Because there is no outlet, the
water has an excessive salt content and
nothing lives in or near it.

**DEAD SEA SCROLLS** Popular name for the
scrolls found in caves at Qumran northwest of the Dead Sea in 1947 and since.
These include books of the Bible and literature of ascetics who had lived in a religious community. The manuscripts date
from the time of Christ and include the
oldest Old Testament manuscripts in
existence.

**DEAE MATRES or MATRONAE** *mother goddesses* "Earth Mothers" worshiped in
Europe in pre-Christian times.

**DEAN** Official in the ANGLICAN or ROMAN
CATHOLIC CHURCH with various duties. He
may preside over a cathedral, assist a
bishop, represent a bishop pastorally, or
preside over a church court.

**DEANERY** Office or residence of a dean.

**DEARMER, PERCY (1867–1936)** Clergyman of the CHURCH OF ENGLAND who is
remembered as an outstanding hymnologist. He edited several hymnals and wrote
on various aspects of worship and the English church.

**DEATH** 1. Theologically, separation of
body and soul. 2. Spiritually, separation
from God. 3. In CHRISTIAN SCIENCE, death
is "an illusion . . . the unreal and untrue;
opposite of Life."

**DEATH OF GOD** Term popularized by
several contemporary theologians to mark
the lack of contact between the modern
world and traditional Christian faith. See
CHRISTIAN RADICALS.

**DEBENDRA NATH TAGORE (1818–1905)**

HINDU leader of the Adi Brahma Samaj. His last years were spent as a recluse.

**DEBORAH** *bee* Jewish prophetess who led her people to victory over the Canaanites, proving to be a brilliant woman judge and general (cf. JUDGES 4—5).

**DEBTS** In the Lord's Prayer this means sins or trespasses.

**DECADARY CULT** System of religion, based on a ten-day week, introduced during the French Revolution to replace Christianity.

**DECADE** Division of the ROSARY containing ten Hail Marys.

**DECALOGUE** *ten words* The Ten Commandments given man through Moses at Mt. Sinai (EXODUS 20:1–17). They cover mans duties to God and his fellow men.

**DECANI** Church singers who sit on the dean's side of the CHANCEL.

**DECAPOLIS** *ten cities* Group of ten cities leagued together, east of the Jordan (MARK 5:20).

**DECISION, VALLEY OF** Valley of the KIDRON between Jerusalem and the Mount of Olives (JOEL 3:14). MOSLEMS expect Mohammed to return to this valley at the end of the age.

**DECIUS (201–251)** Roman emperor notorious for a massive persecution of Christians. Thousands who could not prove they had sacrificed to the emperor were killed.

**DECREE** Plan or purpose. In theology the decree of God is His eternal purpose foreordaining something that is or happens.

**DECRETALS** Papal epistles formulating changes in ecclesiastical law.

**DED** Representation of a skeleton symbolizing OSIRIS in Egyptian art.

**DEDICATION** 1. Consecration, as of a church. 2. Among BAPTISTS and other PROTESTANTS of similar persuasion, children who are not baptized until maturity may be dedicated soon after birth in consecration to God.

**DEDICATION, FEAST OF** See HANUKKAH.

**DEFENDER OF THE FAITH** Title given Henry VIII by Pope LEO X after the king wrote a treatise on the SACRAMENTS disputing Luther's view.

**DEFENSELESS MENNONITE CHURCH** Former name of the Conference of the EVANGELICAL MENNONITE CHURCH.

**DE FIDE** *of the faith* Term for an article of faith which is essential, being of the very essence of Christian belief.

**DEGRADATION** Medieval removal of rights of the clergy.

**DEICIDE** Term for the murder of a god, as in the slaughter of an animal incarnating a deity.

**DEIFICATION** Elevating someone or something to the level of a god.

**DEI GRATIA** *by the grace of God* Term recognizing the power of God in earthly affairs.

**DEIL** Scottish name for the devil.

**DEISM** The philosophy or theology, common in the eighteenth century, that God created the world but does not actively participate in its affairs. Many English Deists were antagonistic to Christianity, substituting "the religion of Nature" for the revelation in the Bible and skeptical of miracles, Christ's redemption, etc.

**DEISSMANN, ADOLF (1866–1937)** German New Testament scholar who sought to show that Paul did not write formal epistles such as The Epistle to the Hebrews. Deissmann wrote a life of the Apostle and a number of Biblical studies.

**DEITY** 1. God or supernatural being with the rank of a god or goddess. 2. The rank or nature of God or a god; divinity; godhood.

**DEKANS** The name of more than thirty gods worshiped at Heliopolis in Egypt.

**DELAWARE PROPHET (eighteenth century)** American Indian prophet who inspired the Delaware Indians of Ohio to rebel under Pontiac against the white invaders in 1763.

**DELEGATE, APOSTOLIC** Representative of the pope in a land with no regular papal diplomatic relations.

**DELHI SULTANATE** The first MOHAMMEDAN empire in India, lasting through the thirteenth and fourteenth centuries.

**DELIA** Greek festival in honor of APOLLO held on the island of Delos every four years.

**DELILAH** The Philistine girl who enticed the Hebrew strong man SAMSON to tell her his secrets, as a result of which he was captured by the Philistines and blinded (JUDGES 16).

**DELITZSCH, FRANZ (1813–1890)** German LUTHERAN theologian and Old Testament scholar. He wrote many commentaries and had so mastered Jewish literature that he has been called "the Christian Talmudist." Some have called him a founder of higher criticism. Of Jewish descent, he sought the conversion of the Jews but opposed anti-Semitism.

**DELLA ROBBIA, ANDREA (1435–1525)** Florentine artist who made many medallions, altarpieces, and religious ceramics.

**DELLA ROBBIA, LUCA (c.1399–1482)** Florentine artist, uncle of Andrea (above), whose vigorous sculpture and brilliant enameled reliefs decorated many churches.

**DELMEDIGO, ELIJAH (1460–1497)** Italian Jewish teacher and philosopher who distinguished between the disciplines of philosophy and religion. His *Examination of Religion* sets forth this distinction.

**DELOS** Greek island of the Aegean with temples to ARTEMIS, APOLLO, ISIS, SERAPIS, and HERMES; a sacred forest; and the famous Sanctuary of the Bulls. Here Apollo and Artemis were born, according to Greek legend.

**DELPHI** Ancient Greek town where the DELPHIC ORACLE prophesied. Delphi was located at the foot of Mount Parnassus, and contained a sacred stone believed to mark the center of the earth.

**DELPHIC ORACLE** A Greek priestess called Pythia in Delphi's temple of APOLLO who answered the questions of visitors in cryptic utterances which were translated into verse by attendant priests. Pythia's prophesies were sometimes so carefully worded that they would fit various situations.

**DELTA** Fourth letter of the Greek alphabet with the sound of the letter *D*. The letter's triangular shape is the source of the word delta for an alluvial deposit at a river's mouth.

**DELUGE** The flood of Genesis 6—8. Accounts of a great deluge from which a few humans were saved in a boat occur among many primitive peoples. Sir Leonard Woolley found archaeological evidence of a disastrous flood about 3200 B.C. at Ur in Mesopotamia.

**DEMAS** An early Christian worker who finally abandoned the Apostle Paul (II TIMOTHY 4:10).

**DEMETER** Harvest and fertility goddess of ancient Greece. A feast called the Thesmophoria was held at Athens to honor her. Other festivals were held at Eleusis and Cos.

**DEMETRIA** A fertility rite of DEMETER.

**DEMETRIUS** A silversmith of Ephesus in Greece who incited a riot against the Apostle Paul (ACTS 19:23–41).

**DEMISSION** Relinquishment, as of the ministry of the gospel. A minister who ceases his vocation with approval of his denomination is said to demit the ministry.

**DEMIURGE** *handcraftsman* 1. Plato's name for the Creator, also used by early Christian writers. 2. GNOSTIC term for the creator of the material world, considered a much lower being than the Supreme God.

**DEMOCRACY** Government by the people. Many religious organizations are increasingly democratic; this form of government characterizes most PROTESTANT bodies. Citizens of democratic countries are often subject to a mystical belief that their form of government is peculiarly divine—just as ancient monarchies were obsessed with the divine right of kings. Obviously, democracy is a salutary forward movement in history, and in its contemporary Western form may be said to be the fruit of the Protestant REFORMATION.

**DEMOGORGON** Roman and medieval god of magic and the underworld.

**DEMON** An evil spirit. The New Testament speaks of one devil, Satan, and of many demons responsible for disease, insanity, and various kinds of evil. The Greeks considered demons to be guardian spirits (see DAEMON).

**DEMONIAC** One possessed by a demon.

**DEMONIC** Term for the evil forces in the world.

**DEMONOLATRY** Worship of demons or spirits.

**DEMONOLOGY** Study of or belief in demons, evil supernatural beings, etc.

**DEMONSTRATION** Proving or making known by presenting incontrovertible evidence. Demonstration in CHRISTIAN SCIENCE consists in exhibiting the power of immortal Mind in human life.

**DEMYTHOLOGIZATION** Term for the attempt to get at the kernel of historical and redemptive truth hidden under the myths or fictional events supposedly constituting much of New Testament history.

Popularized by the contemporary German scholar Rudolf Bultmann, it is a rather subjective process, doubtless inspired by a desire to make Christianity relevant to skeptical modern man. Erich Dinkler contends that Bultmann seeks to preserve the ultimately paradoxical truth of Christian faith. But Otto A. Piper says that the demythologization of the gospel story does violence to the message of the New Testament.

**DENARIUS** The silver denarius was a coin often used in the New Testament period and was an average day's wages.

**DENCK, HANS (c.1495–1527)** Able ANABAPTIST leader who was expelled from various German cities for his "heretical" views. A mystic, he often showed unusual Christian insight.

**DENIS, ST. (third century)** First bishop of Paris and patron saint of France, believed martyred in the Decian persecutions.

**DENNEY, JAMES (1856–1917)** Scottish PRESBYTERIAN churchman and theologian whose works concentrated on the meaning of the atonement. Beginning with liberal theological views, Denney progressed to a conservative belief in the substitutionary nature of the death of Christ.

**DE NOBILI, ROBERT (1577–1656)** Italian JESUIT missionary to India. Believed to be the first European to master the literature of India, De Nobili lived as an Indian penitent and proposed that missionaries adapt themselves to the level of the various castes. He produced many Christian writings in several languages of India and is credited with more than 100,000 converts.

**DENOMINATION** A group with certain beliefs or principles. There are more than 250 religious denominations in the United States of America alone.

**DENOMINATIONALISM** A term for continuation of the organizations, and emphasis on the divisions and distinctions, of PROTESTANTISM.

**DENTO ROKU** *Transmission of the Lamp* The earliest extant history of ZEN Buddhism.

**DEODAND** *given to God* Old English term for something which, because of having caused a death, was forfeited to the crown to be used for alms or ecclesiastical purposes.

**DEO FAVENTE** *with the favor of God*

**DEO GRATIAS** *thanks to God* Expression used in MASS and with a long history of use in the church.

**DEONTOLOGY** The science or ethics of duty or moral obligation.

**DEO VOLENTE** *God willing* A statement of submission to Providence, often abbreviated "D.V."

**DEPARTMENTAL GOD** A deity having to do with one area of life such as the hunt or the harvest.

**DE PAUL, VINCENT** See VINCENT DE PAUL, ST.

**DEPOSITION** Removal of a church official's status—in the ROMAN CATHOLIC CHURCH, depriving him of his orders forever.

**DEPOSIT OF FAITH** The body of truth given the Apostles by Christ for the guidance of the church, to be preserved continually.

**DEPRAVITY** Sinfulness or moral corruption. CALVINISM finds man totally depraved because of Adam's fall, needing the total redemption of Christ. Liberal theology emphasizes instead the innate goodness of man, based on the image of God in the creature.

**DE PROFUNDIS** *out of the depths* The title of the penitential Psalm 130, used in the Office for the Departed.

**DERVISH** *beggar* 1. MOSLEM monk or friar. 2. In Persia or Turkey, a wandering fakir.

**DE SALES, FRANCIS** See FRANCIS OF SALES, ST.

**DESCARTES, RENÉ (1596–1650)** French "father of modern philosophy," educated in a JESUIT school, who based his system of thought on the proposition "I think, therefore I am." His emphasis on intellectual foundations for philosophy marked a break with the supernaturalism of the Middle Ages. One of the first ideas one acquires outside himself, however, according to Descartes, is that of God.

**DESCENT INTO HELL** The statement in the APOSTLES' CREED that Christ "descended into hell" is often interpreted to mean that He was under the power of death until the third day after His crucifixion, during which time He visited the world of Sheol, of the dead. Some theologians, however, maintain that Christ's descent into hell consisted only in His suffering and separation from God on the Cross, and there are various other interpretations.

**DESCENT OF THE SPIRIT** 1. The coming of the Holy Spirit upon Jesus at His baptism in the Jordan. 2. The coming of the Holy Spirit upon the Disciples on the day of Pentecost, often said to mark the birthday of the church.

**DESECRATION** 1. Profanation of something sacred or holy. 2. The act of "deconsecrating" something formerly set apart for holy use.

**DESERET** The name given their territory by the MORMONS before it became the State of Utah.

**DESERET CLUBS** MORMON student groups.

**DESERT FATHERS** Early Christian monks such as St. ANTHONY who lived in the deserts of Egypt.

**DESIGN** One of St. Thomas' proofs for the existence of God is the design and organization manifest in this orderly universe.

**DE SMET, PIERRE JEAN (1801–1873)** Belgian JESUIT missionary to American Indians. He won the friendship of many Indians in the northwestern part of the present United States and labored for peace between whites and Indians, and between non-Mormons and MORMONS.

**DESTINY** 1. The goddess of Fate. 2. The predetermined course of events, attributed by many to God.

**DETERMINISM** 1. Philosophical doctrine that all events are determined by previous ones and that freedom does not actually exist. 2. Social theory that actions of a person or group are caused by such factors as environment, genetics, etc. 3. Theological term for such systems as CALVINISM and ISLAM.

**DEUCALION** Son of Prometheus, in Greek legend, who survived a great flood in an ark and later repeopled the earth by strewing about his mother's bones.

**DEUCE** Slang for the devil or hard luck.

**DEUSDEDIT, ST. (?–664)** Archbishop of Canterbury, also called Frithona, who was the first Anglo-Saxon to hold that office. His feast day is July 14.

**DEUSDEDIT, ST. (?–618)** Pope, also known as Adeodatus I, who succeeded Boniface IV. His feast day is November 8.

**DEUS MISEREATUR** *God be merciful* Title of Psalm 67, used in various church services.

**DEUS VULT** *God wills it* The slogan with which Pope Urban II inspired the First CRUSADE.

**DEUTEROCANONICAL** Term descriptive of those books of the Bible not considered to belong to the properly canonical books; the apocryphal writings are thus designated.

**DEUTERO-ISAIAH** "Second Isaiah," a name for Isaiah 40–66. Many scholars consider the style and content of these chapters so different from Isaiah 1–39 that they believe a different author wrote them. Some scholars then posit a Third Isaiah and even additional sources. Second Isaiah is believed to have come from the time of Zechariah and Haggai.

**DEUTERONOMY** *Second Law* The fifth book of the Old Testament, concluding the PENTATEUCH, generally restating the laws of Exodus. The whole Pentateuch is traditionally ascribed to Moses.

**DEUTSCH, EMMANUEL OSCAR (1829–1873)** German Jewish orientalist and Hebrew scholar. He added much to TALMUD research.

**DEUTSCHER EVANGELISCHER KIRKENBUND** Alliance of German Protestant churches, organized in 1921.

**DEVA** HINDU or BUDDHIST name for a god, or for a supernatural being.

**DEVACHAN** BUDDHIST word for heaven.

**DEVADASIS** "Brides of the gods" who serve as temple prostitutes in HINDUISM.

**DEVADATTA** A cousin and disciple of BUDDHA who finally opposed him, founded a rival monastic order, and tried to kill him.

**DEVALOKA** HINDU realm of the gods.

**DEVARIM** Jewish word for Deuteronomy.

**DEVI** 1. Siva's consort, with ten arms. 2. Any Hindu goddess.

**DEVIL, THE** From the Greek *diabolos*, "one who speaks against," this is the name of Satan the prince of evil. Modern man tends to disbelieve in both demons and the devil, but other generations were convinced of their reality. The New Testament presents the devil as a real, if immaterial, personage.

**DEVIL DANCES** Dramas in BUDDHIST

areas designed to teach ethical principles and Buddhist doctrines.

**DEVIL'S ADVOCATE** The prosecutor in canonization who questions the evidence brought forth on behalf of a candidate for sainthood.

**DEVIL WORSHIPERS** Those, often in primitive religious cults, who worship evil powers or spirits.

**DEVOTED THING** In the Old Testament, what had been captured in battle; it had to be offered to the Lord (NUMBERS 18:14).

**DEVOTEE** A religious fanatic, or an ardent ritualist.

**DEVOTION** 1. Worship, adoration. 2. A devotional service or meditation.

**DEVOTIONS** Religious exercises. These are often private, but may well mark the beginning of a public meeting.

**DEVOUT** Godly, pious, or religious.

**DEVOUT LIFE, INTRODUCTION TO THE** A work on the Christian life by Francis of Sales, showing the desirability of spiritual culture.

**DE WETTE, WILHELM MARTIN (1780–1849)** German professor of theology who sought to combine emotional feeling with scientific detachment in the approach to faith and Scripture.

**DE WOLFE, JAMES PERNETTE (1895–1966)** Episcopal bishop of Long Island. He increased the membership of his diocese and was often involved in controversy. He rebuked Bishop James A. Pike for questioning the VIRGIN BIRTH, and for several years was involved in the ouster of Dr. John Howard Melish and the Rev. William Howard Melish from a church in Brooklyn Heights.

**D.G.** Abbreviation for *Deo Gratias,* "Thanks be to God," or *Dei Gratia,* "By the grace of God."

**DHAMMA** BUDDHIST term for religion or virtue or sacred doctrine.

**DHAMMADUTA** A preacher of the teachings of BUDDHA.

**DHAMMAPADA** *The Way of Buddha's Teaching,* a famous BUDDHIST Scripture, containing such sayings as: "No happiness is higher than peace"; "Contentment is the best wealth, trust the best relationship."

**DHARANI** BUDDHIST prayer or incantation.

**DHARMA** HINDU term for religion or righteousness, or moral rights or duties.

**DHARMAKAYA** Truth personified in BUDDHA.

**DHATRI** *creator* Ancient vedic god.

**DHIKR** A ritual of MOSLEM dervishes to remember the 99 names of ALLAH.

**DHOTI** HINDU loin cloth.

**DHYANA** BUDDHIST term for intense spiritual meditation.

**DIABLERIE** Sorcery, deviltry, or demon-lore.

**DIABOLIC** Devilish or wicked.

**DIABOLISM** Devil worship or preoccupation with demonic forces.

**DIABOLOS or DIABOLUS** *he who speaks against* The devil or Satan.

**DIACONATE** See DEACONATE.

**DIACONICON** 1. Chamber in a Greek church, in the charge of the deacons, where sacred vessels are kept. It is on the south side of the APSE. 2. Deacon's portion in the liturgy of the divine service.

**DIAKONIKON** See DIACONICON.

**DIALECTIC** Originally, the method of constructing a philosophy through questions and answers, as done by Socrates. Currently, the meaning of dialectic is based on Hegel's philosophical view of life and history: proceeding from thesis to antithesis to synthesis. Involving paradox, dialectic moves beyond a thing and its opposite to a final synthetic reality.

**DIALECTICAL THEOLOGY** A term for the currently popular theological system of Karl Barth and others. Seeking to go beyond the theologies of both ritualists and mystics, it posits a "wholly other" God beyond man's limiting formulas.

**DIALOGUE** 1. A conversation between representatives of different faiths, as the ecumenical dialogue between PROTESTANTS and CATHOLICS. 2. Challenge and response in a worship service, as when the congregation responds verbally to the salutation of the officiant.

**DIALOGUE MASS** A mass in which the congregation makes the responses.

**DIALOGUE SERMON** A sermon in which two speakers alternate remarks.

**DIAMOND CUTTER or DIAMOND SUTRA** Famous sermon of BUDDHA expounding the MAHAYANA philosophy. It is part of the sacred writings of Buddhism.

**DIANA** Roman goddess of the moon, forests, and childbirth. Originally she was probably a fertility goddess. She corresponds to the Greek goddess Artemis.

**DIANA OF THE EPHESIANS** The magnificent goddess Artemis, worshiped at Ephesus in Asia Minor. The Apostle Paul antagonized her cult by his evangelism (ACTS 19).

**DIASIA** Greek religious cult in which offerings were made to a gigantic serpent and other powers of HADES as propitiation.

**DIASPORA** *dispersion* Term for the scattering of the Jewish people after the BAB-YLONIAN CAPTIVITY.

**DIATESSARON** *through four* The harmony of the four Gospels prepared by TATIAN in the second century. He wove the narratives of Matthew, Mark, Luke, and John into a single account of the life of Christ.

**DIBBUK or DYBBUK** In Jewish cabalism, the spirit of a dead person which enters the body of someone living.

**DIBELIUS, MARTIN (1883–1947)** German New Testament scholar of the "Form Criticism" school who emphasized preaching in the early church as the method by which Jesus' words were transmitted.

**DICE** Small numbered cubes used from very ancient times for games or religious purposes. Since the soldiers cast lots for Jesus' garments at the Crucifixion, dice are a symbol of the Passion.

**DICHOTOMY** Cutting in two. The Bible view of man as body and soul is a dichotomy; that of man as body, soul, and spirit is a trichotomy. An example of dichotomy in religion is ZOROASTRIANISM, which posits two supreme beings, one good and one evil.

**DICKINSON, JONATHAN (1688–1747)** American PRESBYTERIAN preacher who participated in the GREAT AWAKENING and founded the College of New Jersey—now Princeton University—at his house.

**DIDACHE** *teaching* Second-century document, *The Teaching of the Apostles*, containing ethical injunctions, directions for conducting the SACRAMENTS, and directives for BISHOPS and DEACONS. It is valuable for its information about the church soon after the New Testament period.

**DIDASCALIA APOSTOLORUM** Third-century ecclesiastical document dealing with various rites and denouncing the observ-ance of the ceremonial laws of the Old Testament.

**DIDON, HENRI (1840–1900)** Popular and brilliant French DOMINICAN preacher. He emphasized contemporary social and intellectual problems.

**DIDYMI** Massive temple of APOLLO in Miletus, Asia Minor.

**DIDYMUS** *twin* A form of the name of the Apostle THOMAS.

**DIDYMUS OF ALEXANDRIA (c.309–394)** Learned Greek theologian and head of the catechetical school of Alexandria, whose works reveal profound knowledge of the Bible.

**DIES IRAE** *Day of Wrath* Medieval Latin hymn about the Last Judgment, probably written by Thomas of Celano. It is used in the REQUIEM Mass.

**DIES LUMINUM** *day of lights* Ancient name for the day of EPIPHANY.

**DIET** A deliberative assembly.

**DIET OF WORMS** Ecclesiastical gathering at the German town of Worms to which Martin LUTHER was summoned in 1521 to reply to charges of heresy. It was here that Luther testified, "Unless I shall be convinced by the testimonies of the Scriptures or by right reasoning, I stand convinced by the Scriptures to which I have appealed, and my conscience is taken captive by the Word of God. I cannot and will not recant, for to act against conscience is neither right nor safe. On this I take my stand. I can do no other. God help me. Amen." Luther had already been excommunicated; the Edict of Worms now banned his works and opinions, and for his protection his friends kidnaped him and hid him away in a castle at Wartburg.

**DIETRICH, CHRISTIAN (1844–1919)** German PROTESTANT who served as a rector and leader in the Evangelical National Church and as president of the pietistic associations of Württemberg.

**DIETRICH OF NIEHEIM (1340–1418)** Secretary of Pope Gregory XII, called the greatest journalist of the Middle Ages because his pamphlets so clearly exposed contemporary evils. He contended that a GENERAL COUNCIL has power to depose the pope, and labored to end the GREAT SCHISM.

**DIETS OF SPIRES** German assemblies—Imperial Diets—through which Protestantism gained a firm foothold in Germany. The name *Protestant* dates from the Diet of 1529 to whose edict against religious choice LUTHERAN representatives replied, "In matters concerning the honor of God and the salvation of souls each one must on his own behalf stand before God and give account."

**DIEU AVEC NOUS** *God with us* French slogan.

**DIEU DEFEND LE DROIT** *God defends the right* French proverb.

**DIEU ET MON DROIT** *God and my right* British royal motto.

**DIFFERENCE OF RELIGION** Catholic term for a situation in which a member of the Roman Catholic Church is contemplating marriage to a non-Catholic. For many years this has been considered a DIRIMENT IMPEDIMENT to marriage.

**DIFFINITORS** Assistants to the superiors of certain monastic orders, elected by the provincial and general chapters.

**DIGAMBARAS** One of the two main sects in JAINISM. Their saints wear no clothing and they see no possibility of salvation for women.

**DIGAMY** A second marriage with legal sanctions.

**DIGGERS** Members of an English communal group who taught that "true freedom lies in the free enjoyment of the earth" and who believed that God wanted them to make the waste land fruitful rather than to speculate about heaven or hell. They flourished in 1649 but their community was soon destroyed. Their leader was Gerrard Winstanley who espoused radical social and religious views, including pantheism.

**DIGNITARY** Churchman of exalted rank.

**DIKERION** Byzantine double candlestick, used in blessing the congregation. It symbolizes the two natures of Christ.

**DIKKA** Platform in a mosque from which the service is conducted.

**DILLMANN, CHRISTIAN FRIEDRICH AUGUST (1823–1894)** German LUTHERAN theologian and scholar in Old Testament, Jewish apocalyptic, and Ethiopian literature.

**DILOWA HUTUKHTU, THE (1883–1965)** The Living Buddha of the Yellow Sect of MAHAYANA Buddhism, spiritual and temporal ruler of 900 lamas and head of three lamaseries. A distinguished BUDDHIST scholar and orientalist, he was regarded as the thirteenth reincarnation of the Buddhist saint Tilopa. The Dilowa was exiled from Mongolia in 1931 and spent his last years in the United States.

**DIME** A tenth or tithe, paid in former times as a tax to the church.

**DIMISSORY LETTER** A letter authorizing the transfer of a church member or official from one parish or diocese to another.

**DIN** Jewish word for law or judgment.

**DINAH** The daughter of Jacob and Leah, violated by Shechem, for which misdeed Dinah's brothers killed the men of Shechem (GENESIS 30:21; 34).

**DINAR** Principal gold coin in MOSLEM countries.

**DING AN SICH** *thing in itself* Philosophical term for "the thing in itself." Kant stated that it is impossible to understand a thing in itself.

**DIN ILLAHI** See AKBAR, JALAL.

**DIOCESAN** One in charge of a DIOCESE, as a bishop.

**DIOCESE** Territory of which a BISHOP has charge for ecclesiastical purposes.

**DIOCLETIAN (245–313)** Roman emperor during the last part of whose reign Christians were persecuted for fear of their power and religion.

**DIODATI, GIOVANNI (1576–1649)** Swiss PROTESTANT theologian who translated the Bible into Italian in 1603.

**DIOGNETUS, EPISTLE TO** Anonymous Christian apologetic treatise from the second or third century. Attacking pagan idolatry and Jewish ritualism, it describes Christians as the soul of the world, proclaims Christ as the revelation of God, and exhorts its readers to exhibit kindness, good works, and love. The closing portion is considered to belong to some other work.

**DIONE** In Homer, the wife of ZEUS.

**DIONYSIA** Greek festivals of DIONYSUS. They were originally of the order of fertility rites and eventually there were at least five different types. Through some of them Greek drama developed.

**DIONYSIUS AREOPAGITICUS** See DIONYSIUS THE AREOPAGITE.

**DIONYSIUS EXIGUUS (c.500–c.545)** Roman monk who, in calculating the date of Easter, devised our present method of dating events from the birth of Christ

He was also an expert in theology, canon law, and astronomy.

**DIONYSIUS OF ALEXANDRIA (c.190–c.264)** Bishop of Alexandria, also known as Dionysius the Great, who endured famine, plague, and the persecutions of Decius and Valerian. He welcomed back to the church those who had lapsed during the persecutions. In opposing SABELLIANISM he was accused of TRITHEISM although he was supported by ATHANASIUS. Rejecting CHILIASM, he questioned the common authorship of the Gospel of John and of Revelation. He had an independent mind.

**DIONYSIUS OF ROME, ST. (third century)** Bishop of Rome (259–268) who accused Dionysius of Alexandria of TRITHEISM, aided the church of Caesarea when it was attacked by barbarians, and promoted the authority of Rome as an arbiter of doctrine. He is considered a saint. His feast day is December 26.

**DIONYSIUS TELMAHARENSIS (?–848)** Monk who became patriarch of the Syrian Jacobite Church (818–848).

**DIONYSIUS THE AREOPAGITE, ST.** An Athenian converted through the influence of the Apostle Paul (ACTS 17:34). Tradition makes him the first Bishop of Athens and he is considered a saint. He is sometimes confused with St. Denis or Dionysius of Paris, and at one time was thought to be the author of certain mystical writings now attributed to DIONYSIUS THE PSEUDO-AREOPAGITE. His feast day is October 9.

**DIONYSIUS THE CARTHUSIAN (1402–1471)** Also known as Denys Ryckel or Denys van Leeuwen; a Dutch mystic, theologian, and commentator who helped inaugurate a crusade against the Turks.

**DIONYSIUS THE PSEUDO-AREOPAGITE (fiifth century)** Unknown author of ten epistles and four treatises once attributed to DIONYSIUS THE AREOPAGITE. The treatises are *The Celestial Hierarchy, The Ecclesiastical Hierarchy, Divine Names,* and *Mystical Theology.* All these writings merged Christian thought with NEOPLATONISM and profoundly influenced scholastic theology.

**DIONYSUS** Greek god of fertility, vegetation, wine, and artistic and literary inspiration, also known as BACCHUS. He is variously represented as a wine-drinking youth, a bearded man, and a goat, and was believed to take various forms and to be the son of ZEUS. He was accompanied by gay satyrs and maenads who danced about in goat-skins. See also DIONYSIA.

**DIOPHYSITE** Theological term for one who believes that two natures, divine and human, exist together in Jesus Christ.

**DIOTREPHES** An early Christian who loved positions of eminence and power (III JOHN 9).

**DIPANKARA BUDDHA** *The Luminous Buddha* A predecessor of Siddhartha Gautama (see BUDDHA) who prepared him for his unique role.

**DIPAVAMSA** *The Island Chronicle* A Pali sacred treatise of BUDDHISM relating the advent of Buddhism to Ceylon. It dates from the fourth century A.D.

**DIPTYCH** *folded* 1. A list of those for whom prayers were offered in the early church, inscribed on a two-leaved tablet. 2. An altarpiece with pictures painted on two tablets hinged together.

**DIRGE** A lament, song, or church service for the dead.

**DIRIMENT** Nullifying. A diriment impediment to marriage completely nullifies it.

**DIRONA** Celtic mother-goddess.

**DIS** Roman god of the underworld of death.

**DIS ALITER VISUM** *the gods decreed otherwise* Fatalistic expression.

**DISCALCED** *without shoes* Term for monastic orders whose members go without shoes, usually wearing sandals instead, in humility and ascetic obedience.

**DISCIPLE** 1. A follower or student. 2. A Christian. 3. A New Testament follower of Jesus. 4. An apostle.

**DISCIPLES OF CHRIST** Denomination founded by Thomas and Alexander Campbell in Washington, Pennsylvania, about 1809. See CHRISTIAN CHURCHES (DISCIPLES OF CHRIST).

**DISCIPLINA ARCANI** *discipline of the secret* Term for those "mysteries" of the Christian faith kept from CATECHUMENS in the early church. These were primarily the doctrines of the SACRAMENTS and the TRINITY, which were reserved for those who had been baptized and admitted into full membership.

**DISCIPLINE** 1. Teaching. 2. Punishment. 3. Rigorous training. 4. A scourge for penance. 5. Church law.

**DISCIPLINE, BOOK OF** A manual governing the rites and activities of a church or other religious organization.

**DISCUS** The plate on which the communion bread is placed in the EASTERN CHURCH.

**DISESTABLISHMENT** Removal of the links between religion and government which had created an Established Church.

**DISHALLOW** Violate, profane, or deconsecrate.

**DISKOS** See DISCUS.

**DISMAS or DYSMAS** Traditional name of the Penitent Thief who turned to Christ at Calvary and received His promise of paradise (LUKE 23:39–43).

**DISPATER** *Father Dis* See DIS.

**DISPENSATION** 1. Ecclesiastical exemption from a law or vow. 2. Term for God's dealing with man. 3. Conservative Protestant term for a period of history during which God deals in a special way with man.

**DISPENSATIONALISM** The belief that all history consists of seven dispensations or periods of time, in each of which God treats mankind in a different way. These dispensations are usually considered to be those of creation, conscience, human government, the patriarchs, Moses, the church, and the millennium. Because of the unique features assigned to this system of thought by such men as C. I. Scofield, the term *dispensationalism* may also refer to other FUNDAMENTALIST doctrines.

**DISPERSION** Term often applied to the scattering of the Jewish people after the BABYLONIAN CAPTIVITY.

**DISPUTATION** Ecclesiastical controversy or debate.

**DISRUPTION, THE** The schism in the CHURCH OF SCOTLAND in 1843 resulting in the formation of the FREE CHURCH.

**DISSENT** Ecclesiastically, disagreement with the doctrines of, or separation from, an established church.

**DISSENTERS** Those who "dissent" from the established religion in a country, as Presbyterians in England, Episcopalians in Scotland, or Christians in Arabia. In seventeenth-century England, a Dissenter was a Puritan or non-Anglican Protestant.

**DISSIDENT** A divisive or heretical church or person.

**DISTRIBUTION OF THE ELEMENTS** Administering communion or the EUCHARIST by giving the worshipers the bread and wine.

**DISTRICT SUPERINTENDENT** An official, particularly in the METHODIST CHURCH, who supervises ecclesiastical affairs under a bishop.

**DITAT DEUS** *God enriches* Motto of the state of Arizona.

**DITHEISM** Belief in two supreme gods, as in ZOROASTRIANISM.

**DITHYRAMB** Greek poetry or hymn honoring DIONYSUS.

**DITTHI** BUDDHIST term for a religious attitude or belief.

**DIVALI** *feast of lamps* HINDU autumn festival for the goddesses PARVATI and LAKSHMI.

**DIVALI SUNDAY** HINDU festival of lights.

**DIVES** The name of the rich man in Jesus' parable of the rich man and the beggar Lazarus (LUKE 16:19–31). The rich man was in torment after death while Lazarus enjoyed the comfort of Abraham's bosom.

**DIVINATION** Determining or foretelling future events, claimed in many religions. Divination today is associated with such practices as astrology and the study of parapsychology.

**DIVINE** 1. Godlike or related to God or religion. 2. A clergyman.

**DIVINE, FATHER (c.1870–1965)** American Negro religious leader whose racially mixed followers believed he was God. He forbade alcohol, tobacco, cosmetics, obscene language, and sex. His disciples enjoyed food, shelter, and security in a number of "Heavens" owned communally by the group. A familiar response to his messages was "Peace, Father, it's wonderful."

**DIVINE ATTRIBUTES** Such characteristics of God as omnipotence and omniscience.

**DIVINE AUTHORITY** The authority of God, as revealed in Scripture.

**DIVINE COMEDY** Dante's fourteenth-century poem describing his journeys to hell, purgatory, and paradise. He found various levels of the damned, seven stories on the mount of purgatory, and nine heavens. The work is a world classic.

**DIVINE DECREES** Theological term for the ordinances by which God is believed to carry out His purposes in the world.

**DIVINE HEALING** See FAITH HEALING and SPIRITUAL HEALING.

**DIVINE OFFICE** Daily services of prayer, required of priests, monks, and nuns in the ROMAN CATHOLIC CHURCH at the seven CANONICAL HOURS.

**DIVINE RIGHT OF KINGS** Medieval belief that kings ruled by divine plan and that all alternative forms of government were wicked.

**DIVINE SCIENCE** Religious group organized in Denver, Colorado, by Nona Lovell Brooks, her two sisters, and Mrs. Malinda Cramer in 1898. Adherents believe in Omnipresent Life, the brotherhood of man, and the power of right thinking.

**DIVINE SERVICE** 1. Public worship. 2. The choir office in ANGLICAN churches.

**DIVINITY** 1. God or a god. 2. Attribute or quality of God. 3. A supernatural being. 4. Theology.

**DIVINITY SCHOOL** Theological school or seminary.

**DIVORCE** Abolition of a marriage or separation of the marital partners, usually frowned upon by religious groups. Jewish divorce was not difficult to acquire under the Mosaic laws. Catholics hold that only death can dissolve a valid Christian marriage, while Protestants are in general more permissive.

**DIVORCEMENT** Old English term for divorce, sometimes found in the King James Bible.

**DJADID UL-ISLAM New Moslems** Marrano Jews of Persia, forced to become MOSLEMS, who secretly held to their own faith.

**DOANE, GEORGE WASHINGTON (1799–1859)** American EPISCOPAL bishop who wrote "Softly Now the Light of Day" and other hymns.

**DOCETAE or DOCETISTS** Those in the early church who believed that Christ did not have a real human body but only one that seemed real. GNOSTIC in origin, they held that matter is sinful and that the CRUCIFIXION and RESURRECTION were illusions.

**DOCETISM** Theological beliefs of the DOCETAE. For several generations Docetism troubled the church although eventually it died out.

**DOCTOR OF DIVINITY** Clergyman with an honorary degree in divinity.

**DOCTORS OF THE CHURCH** The outstanding theologians in the history of the church, including CHRYSOSTOM, ATHANA-SIUS, AUGUSTINE, JEROME, and about twenty others.

**DOCTRINE** 1. Teaching, especially religious. 2. The belief or theology of a particular religious group.

**DODDRIDGE, PHILIP (1702–1751)** English PRESBYTERIAN clergyman who wrote many hymns including "O God of Bethel" and "Awake My Soul." He also wrote *On the Rise and Progress of Religion in the Soul* and other works. He worked for the distribution of Bibles and the interchange of pulpits between ministers of the CHURCH OF ENGLAND and dissenters.

**DODONA** Town in Epirus with the oldest Greek sanctuary. It contained a tree used to forecast the future, a temple to ZEUS, and a shrine of APHRODITE. Dodona was one of the most popular oracles.

**DODS, MARCUS (1834–1909)** Scottish PRESBYTERIAN cleric, theologian, commentator, and New Testament scholar. His church once accused him of unorthodox views of inspiration but soon dropped the charge.

**DOEG** A servant of Jewish King Saul who killed the priests of Nob (I SAMUEL 21:1–9; 22:9–23). His name is given in Psalm 52.

**DOG** Religious symbol of faithfulness.

**DOGEN (1200–1253)** Founder of Soto ZEN Buddhism in Japan. He proclaimed that everything is Buddha.

**DOGMA** 1. Belief or opinion. 2. Belief authoritatively held by a religious group.

**DOGMATICS** Study of the history and meaning of Christian doctrine.

**DOGMATIC THEOLOGY** Systematic study of Christian beliefs; another expression for dogmatics.

**DO-GOODER** Contemptuous term for one who believes in practicing what he believes, or for an activist in religion, or for one who emphasizes good works. Jesus went about doing good.

**DOHNAVUR FELLOWSHIP** Mission work founded by Amy CARMICHAEL at Dohnavur in South India. The Fellowship began rescuing small girls from bondage in HINDU temples and now carries on evangelistic, vocational, medical, and other missionary enterprises.

**DOJO** BUDDHIST monastery or center in Japan.

**DOLEANTIE**  Term for the nineteenth-century struggle for reform, led by Abraham KUYPER, in the Reformed Church of Holland. It led to division of the church in the Netherlands and to worldwide interest in CALVINISM as a world and life view.

**DOLLINGER, JOHANN JOSEPH IGNAZ VON (1799–1890)**  Bavarian theologian, church historian, and leader of the OLD CATHOLICS. Dollinger sought to establish a German Catholic Church free of governmental control. For opposing the ROMAN CATHOLIC edict on papal infallibility in 1870 he was excommunicated. In the Old Catholic movement he labored for united Christianity.

**DOLMEN**  A group of gigantic stones arranged in the form of an open chamber, as a burial marker.

**DOLPHIN**  A brilliant sea mammal which often symbolized salvation and the Resurrection in Christian art.

**D.O.M.**  Abbreviation for *Deo Optimo Maximo,* "God the Best and Greatest," a Roman ascription to JUPITER eventually taken over by Christians.

**DOM**  A title for certain ecclesiastics, especially in the BENEDICTINE, CARTHUSIAN, and CISTERCIAN orders.

**DOME OF THE ROCK**  MOSLEM temple in Jerusalem believed to stand on the rock where MOHAMMED ascended to heaven. It is the site of the Jewish temple of New Testament times.

**DOMINE, DIRIGE NOS** *Lord, guide us*  Motto of London, England.

**DOMINIC, ST. (c.1170–1221)**  Spanish cleric who instituted the order of DOMINICAN monks. He preached among the ALBIGENSES in southern France, then urged the CRUSADERS against them, then brought them the INQUISITION.

**DOMINICANS**  The order of Friars Preachers or Black Friars founded by St. DOMINIC. The members dress in white with black mantles and take vows of poverty, chastity, and obedience, refraining from eating any meat.

**DOMINIE** *Master*  A minister.

**DOMINION**  Power, authority, control.

**DOMINUS AC REDEMPTOR**  Bull of Pope CLEMENT XIV in 1773 suppressing the SOCIETY OF JESUS.

**DOMINUS VOBISCUM** *the Lord be with*

*you*  Salutation of the officiating clergyman to the congregation in mass or public worship.

**DOMITIAN (51–96)**  Roman Emperor who required people to call him Lord and God, and began the persecution of Jews and Christians during which the Apostle John may have been sent to Patmos.

**DOMPELAARS**  A name by which the DUNKERS have been called.

**DOMREMY-LA-PUCELLE**  Village in France where JOAN OF ARC was born.

**DONAR**  Ancient German god of weather, crops, and marriage. His symbol was a hammer or thunderbolt.

**DONATELLO (c.1386–1466)**  Superb Italian sculptor of baptisteries, reliefs, and such statues as "David," the "Magdalene," "St. John," and "St. Mark."

**DONATION OF CONSTANTINE**  Eighth-century document granting certain territories to Pope Sylvester, used to bolster papal claims. Once thought to have been written by Constantine the Great, it is now recognized as a forgery.

**DONATISM**  Belief of the Donatists, following two ecclesiastics named Donatus, that those who had fallen away from Christian standards during the persecutions of Diocletian should be treated very severely and rebaptized before being received back into the church. Donatism was strong from the fourth through the seventh centuries.

**DONKEY**  The ass, a small animal used to carry travelers and bundles in Bible times, associated with Jesus' childhood trip to Egypt and triumphal entry into Jerusalem.

**DONNE, JOHN (1572–1631)**  Brilliant poet and cleric of the CHURCH OF ENGLAND whose sermons and poems proved powerful and profound.

**DOOMSDAY**  Day of judgment.

**DOOR**  Religious significance derives from the fact that Christ designated Himself as the door to God (JOHN 10:7).

**DOORKEEPERS**  Ancient CATHOLIC order designed to exclude unauthorized persons from mass.

**DORCAS**  Charitable Christian saint raised from the dead by Peter (ACTS 9:36–43).

**DORDRECHT, SYNOD OF**  See DORT, SYNOD OF.

**DORE, PAUL GUSTAVE (1832–1883)**

French artist who made memorable illustrations for the Bible, *Paradise Lost, The Divine Comedy,* and other works.

**DORSAL** See DOSSAL.

**DORT, SYNOD OF** An assembly of the CALVINIST churches of Europe in 1618 and 1619 at Dort or Dordrecht in the Netherlands. It denounced ARMINIANISM and emphasized five points of the REFORMED faith: man's total inability to do good without divine grace; God's unconditional election of His people; Christ's limited atonement; the Spirit's irresistible work of grace; and the eternal perseverance of the saints.

**DOSSAL** Embroidered cloth hung behind the altar in ANGLICAN churches.

**DOSTOYEVSKY, FEODOR (1821–1881)** Russian novelist of atheistic training whose imprisonment in Siberia marked a conversion to Christian faith, mirrored in the depth and insight of his writings.

**DOTHAN or DOTHAIM** City of Palestine, north of Samaria, near which Joseph was sold into slavery. A caravan route is nearby.

**DOUAI or DOUAY BIBLE** English translation of the Bible prepared for CATHOLICS at the University of Douai in France in 1568. The New Testament translation was completed at Rheims. The whole translation was revised by Bishop Challoner in the eighteenth century.

**DOUBLE FEASTS** The greater CATHOLIC feasts, at which the ANTIPHON is sung both at the beginning and the end of CANTICLES.

**DOUBLE PREDESTINATION** Term for God's prechoosing both the elect to eternal life and the damned to everlasting misery. Few predestinarians hold to more than the first type of predestination.

**DOUBT** Resistance or hesitation toward belief. The doubts of Job in the Old Testament and Thomas in the New Testament led them to a truer faith than appears possible otherwise. A clear distinction must be made between honest doubt and willful rejection of truth. As Tennyson once observed, doubt may clear the way to deeper faith. The Biblical opposite of faith is not so much doubt as pride and absorption in self.

**DOUGHERTY, DENIS J. (1865–1951)** American-born ROMAN CATHOLIC cardinal known as "dean of the Catholic hierarchy in the United States."

**DOUILLETTE padded gown** Long cloak with cuffs for outdoor wear over a CASSOCK.

**DOUKHOBORS or DUKHOBORS Spirit-fighters** Russian name for Christians of the Universal Brotherhood, a nonconformist group originating in Russia in the eighteenth century and now found mainly in Canada. Believing that God is love and love is almost all, they have little use for laws, ceremonies, war, taxes, or government. The first Doukhobors were principally peasants who devised a communal society; persecuted in nineteenth-century Russia for their refusal to support war efforts, they emigrated in large numbers to Canada whose western lands they, as excellent farmers, helped develop. But in Canada too they irritated the government because of their opposition to private property and legal regulations. They now number three groups: the Union of Doukhobors in Canada, the Christian Communities of Christ, and a militant minority, the Sons of Freedom. The latter have sometimes burned houses and schools and paraded in the nude to protest what they disliked.

**DOVE** Since the Holy Spirit descended upon Jesus like a dove (MATTHEW 3:16), the dove is traditionally a symbol of the Spirit of God, of hope, of peace, of purity, and of the church. The medieval PYX was often in the form of a dove.

**DOWIE, JOHN ALEXANDER (1847–1907)** Scottish founder of the Christian Catholic Apostolic Church in Zion in 1896 in Chicago, Illinois. In Australia he had founded the Divine Healing Association of Australia and New Zealand. He taught the healing of physical disease through prayer. As the First Apostle of the church he founded in the United States, he was accused of polygamy and peculation, and deposed in 1906. Wilbur Glenn Voliva succeeded him as head of the CHRISTIAN CATHOLIC CHURCH.

**DOWIEITES** Term for followers of John Alexander DOWIE. Many of them live in a communistic religious settlement at Zion City, Illinois.

**DOWSING** Alleged ability to find underground water or other things by holding a dowsing rod which is said to twist in the hands of one properly gifted.

**DOWSING, WILLIAM (c.1596–c.1679)** PURITAN who energetically executed Parliament's orders to abolish ornaments in English churches.

**DOXOLOGY** *speaking praise* An affirmation of praise to God, usually sung. Doxologies are used in the worship of most Christian churches.

**DOXY** Word which may mean religious opinion.

**DRACONTIUS, BLOSSIUS AEMILIUS (fifth century)** Christian poet of Carthage whose writings such as *Concerning God* reveal knowledge of both Scripture and Roman literature.

**DRAGON** Mythical monster, usually a serpent or a winged reptile breathing fire, prominent in many ancient religions—often as a symbol of evil or death, but in Greece sometimes a guardian or oracle of wisdom. Satan is symbolized by the dragon in Revelation 12. Medieval heroes like St. George were praised for slaying dragons. TAOISM regards wingless dragons as nature deities.

**DRAGONNADES** Seventeenth-century French attacks on the HUGUENOTS by mounted troops or dragoons.

**DRAMA** The first actors were priests or religious acolytes in various ancient religions such as the cult of DIONYSUS. Drama has enlivened or enlightened many religions—through miracle plays in medieval times, and through various forms, in and out of churches, used to communicate religious concepts in the present day. In the sense of conflict, growth, and climax, real drama is present in Judeo-Christian religion.

**DRAUGHT** This word in the King James Bible may mean a sewer or a catch while fishing.

**DRAVIDIAN RELIGION** The animistic religion of the dark-skinned aboriginals of southern India. Spirits and gods, mostly female, abound.

**D.R.E.** Abbreviation for Director of Religious Education, a person in many an American church who administers the local program of religious education.

**DREAMS** Long before Freud, religion re-

garded dreams as having deep significance. God spoke to Jacob, Daniel, Joseph, and many other Bible figures through dreams. On the other hand, the pagan use of dreams was forbidden in Scripture (JEREMIAH 27:9).

**DRELINCOURT, CHARLES (1565–1669)** French REFORMED cleric whose book on death was promoted for commercial purposes by Daniel Defoe in his *True Relation of the Apparition of one Mrs. Veal.* Drelincourt's *Catechism* was also popular in England.

**DREPUNG** Monastery near Lhasa in Tibet, founded in the fifteenth century. It houses thousands of Tibetan monks.

**DREW, DANIEL (1797–1879)** American speculator who before his financial ruin helped found a number of METHODIST churches and Drew Theological Seminary.

**DRIVER, SAMUEL ROLLES (1846–1914)** English Old Testament scholar whose commentaries and Biblical studies reveal personal faith combined with a critical approach. He contributed to the English REVISED VERSION of the Bible.

**DRUGS** Addiction to such drugs as heroin is very difficult to combat. One of the twentieth century's successful combatants is Rev. David Wilkerson of Brooklyn, New York, whose techniques, based on Christian commitment, have aided many former addicts. Drugs such as peyote have sometimes been used in religious rites. Late in the twentieth century there was some attempt in the United States to achieve religious experiences by the use of drugs.

**DRUIDS** Celtic priests of ancient Gaul and Britain who headed a system of divination, sacrifice, incantation, and healing. Various nature gods were worshiped, particularly in and among trees; the oak and mistletoe were considered sacred. The armies of Rome and the aggressive evangelism of Christian missionaries broke the druids' power over their subjects.

**DRUMMOND, HENRY (1786–1860)** English banker who supported laws against Catholics and Jews and organized a group in his home to study the Bible's prophecies. Out of the latter grew the CATHOLIC APOSTOLIC CHURCH, or Irvingites, in which Drummond was an apostle and eventually angel for Scotland.

**DRUMMOND, HENRY (1851–1897)** Scottish cleric who aided D. L. Moody in his British revivals. He wrote *Natural Law in the Spiritual World* and *The Greatest Thing in the World,* and was also famous as a lecturer, explorer, geologist, and theorist. In his *Ascent of Man* he argued that animals' compassion for one another aided the survival of the fittest.

**DRUNKENNESS** A condition aiding ecstasy in certain ancient religions. Protestant revulsion at drunkenness brought about prohibition of alcohol in the United States from 1919 to 1933. The New Testament church condemned drunkenness (I CORINTHIANS 6:10).

**DRUSES** People of a section of southern Syria and Lebanon who believe in one God last incarnated in Hakim, the sixth Fatimite Khalif (996–1021). They honor women, forbid tobacco and wine, and believe in reincarnation. Although they periodically massacred Christians during their history, they seem to have incorporated Christian, Jewish, and Moslem ideas into their faith. The Druses are often termed a Shiite sect. They consider Hamza ibn Ali ibn Ahmad, a mystic from Persia who became an enthusiastic disciple of Hakim, to be their founder.

**DRYAD** Greek wood nymph or tree spirit.

**DRY MASS** Shortened form of the mass popular in the Middle Ages.

**D.TH.** The degree of doctor of theology given one who does advanced study in a theological seminary.

**DUA** *today* Ancient Egyptian god.

**DUALISM** Religious or philosophical system in which there are two ultimate principles or absolutes, as in ZOROASTRIANISM and MANICHAEISM.

**DUAT** A name for the Egyptian underworld of the deceased.

**DUBNOW, SIMON (1860–1944)** Russian Jewish sociologist who wrote *The History of the Jewish People* and died at the hands of the NAZIS.

**DUBOURG, ANNE (c.1520–1559)** French law professor burned at the stake for accepting the PROTESTANT faith of the HUGUENOTS.

**DUCHAN** 1. Raised area in the Jewish temple where the priest blesses the worshipers. 2. Jewish service of blessing.

**DUCHESNE, LOUIS (1843–1922)** French CATHOLIC educator and student of church history. He was an able archaeologist and held liberal views of legendary material.

**DUCHESNE, ROSE PHILIPPINE (1769–1852)** French-born CATHOLIC nun, beatified in 1940, who conducted mission work among the Indians and the needy whites of the United States.

**DUCK RIVER BAPTISTS** Conservative Baptists of the southern United States, principally Alabama and Tennessee, who practice FOOT WASHING. They are also known as the Baptist Church of Christ.

**DUELING** A once popular way of settling disputes, roundly condemned by churchmen and others, now obsolete.

**DUFAY, GUILLAUME (c.1400–1474)** Italian canon and composer of many masses and ecclesiastical works.

**DUFF, ALEXANDER (1806–1878)** Scottish PRESBYTERIAN missionary to India who was among the first to link educational and evangelistic work in foreign missions. He helped found the University of Calcutta.

**DUHM, BERNARD (1847–1928)** German Old Testament scholar who wrote important commentaries on Isaiah, Jeremiah, and the Psalms.

**DUKES, LEOPOLD (1810–1891)** Hungarian scholar in the field of rabbinic proverbs, Jewish literature, and medieval Hebrew poets.

**DUKHOBORS** See DOUKHOBORS.

**DUKKHA** *dissatisfaction with environment* The first of the FOUR NOBLE TRUTHS of BUDDHISM.

**DULIA** ROMAN CATHOLIC term for the homage and reverence due angels and saints. It is distinguished from *latria*, due only God, and *hyperdulia*, uniquely due the Virgin Mary.

**DUNBAR, PAUL LAURENCE (1872–1906)** Negro poet of the United States, some of whose verse expresses deep religious sentiment.

**DUNKARDS** See DUNKERS.

**DUNKERS, DUNKARDS, or TUNKERS** *dippers, immersionists* Baptist-like group originating under Alexander Mack in Germany about 1708. Coming to Pennsylvania, they sought to follow the New Testament literally, emphasizing TRIPLE IMMERSION, FOOT WASHING, the holy kiss, and the anointing of the sick with oil. They opposed luxurious living, war, oaths, and legal suits. The principal groups are the CHURCH OF THE BRETHREN, the OLD GERMAN BAPTIST BRETHREN, and the BRETHREN CHURCH. See also BRETHREN.

**DUNS SCOTUS, JOHN (c.1264–1308)** Scottish-born scholastic philosopher who taught in England and Europe. He emphasized ultimate being dependent on the will of God. His name gave rise to the word dunce because of the derision of his opponents. He was the first great theologian to uphold the IMMACULATE CONCEPTION of Mary.

**DUNSTAN, ST. (c.909–988)** English Abbot of Glastonbury and Archbishop of Canterbury who reformed the English Church of his age and profoundly influenced the government during the reigns of the kings Edmund, Edred, Edgar, and Edward the Martyr. He was one of England's great saints. His feast day is May 19.

**DUOMO** *house* Italian name for a cathedral.

**DURAND or DURANDUS, GULIELMUS (c.1237–1296)** French Bishop of Mende, liturgical writer, and canon jurist whose *Mirror of Law* (*Speculum judiciale*) is a famous study of canon and civil law and whose *Rationale of the Divine Office* (*Rationale divinorum officiorum*) comprehensively expounds the origin and meaning of the liturgy.

**DURANDUS OF ST. POURCAIN (c.1270–1334)** French DOMINICAN philosopher who elevated reason above authority and opposed the views of THOMAS AQUINAS, emphasizing instead the tradition from PLATO and AUGUSTINE.

**DURER, ALBRECHT (1471–1528)** German artist famous for his "Praying Hands," "Adoration of the Magi," "Nativity," "Virgin and Child," and many other paintings and engravings. Sympathetic to Protestantism, whose influence marks his later works, he was a friend of Erasmus and admired by Martin LUTHER as "the best of men."

**DURGA** *inaccessible* A title of DEVI, the great goddess of HINDUISM and wife of SIVA. As Durga she is a fierce lady on a tiger but has a benign countenance.

**DURGA-PUJA** Important HINDU festival, honoring Durga, at the beginning of the rainy season in the fall.

**DURIE, JOHN (1596–1680)** Scottish cleric of the CHURCH OF ENGLAND who sought the union of Protestant denominations. He helped prepare the Catechisms (see LARGER CATECHISM and SHORTER CATECHISM) and the CONFESSION OF FAITH which were drawn up by the WESTMINSTER ASSEMBLY.

**DUTCH REFORMATION** Although such pre-Protestant groups as the BRETHREN OF THE COMMON LIFE were in the Netherlands in the Middle Ages, Protestantism became strong there after Luther's writings began to circulate. The New Testament was translated into Dutch in 1523, and during the sixteenth century REFORMED churches spread throughout the Netherlands.

**DUTCH REFORMED CHURCH** 1. Netherlands denomination formed in 1946 through the union of the previously existing Dutch Reformed Church with the Reformed Churches in the Netherlands. Headquarters of this group which has nearly a million members are in Baarn. 2. Popular name for the REFORMED CHURCH IN AMERICA.

**DUTY** Obligation or requirement. Moral duties, such as truthfulness and respect for human life, are often distinguished from religious duties such as church attendance, although many faiths consider both types to be binding upon their members. Liberal religion emphasizes moral and ethical duties without tying them to any specific code such as the Ten Commandments (see DECALOGUE). Conservative Christians find in the latter and in Scripture an adequate guide to duty.

**DUZZAKH** ZOROASTRIAN purgatory.

**D.V.** Abbreviation for *Deo volente,* "God willing."

**DWIGHT, HARRISON GRAY OTIS (1803–1862)** American CONGREGATIONAL missionary to the Armenians who traveled with the Rev. Eli Smith over considerable areas of Armenia.

**DWIGHT, HENRY OTIS (1843–1917)** Son of Harrison Gray Otis Dwight; a CONGREGATIONAL missionary to Turkey.

**DWIGHT, TIMOTHY (1752–1817)** American CONGREGATIONAL minister and president of Yale from 1795 to 1817. A grandson of Jonathan EDWARDS, he believed in theocracy and opposed republicanism. Through his preaching, the Second GREAT AWAKENING stirred America.

**DWIGHT, TIMOTHY (1828–1916)** Grandson of Timothy Dwight. He was professor of sacred literature and president of Yale, which he enabled to become a university. He was a member of the committee which produced the AMERICAN STANDARD VERSION of the Bible.

**DYAUS** Indo-European vedic sky god.

**DYAUS-PITAR** or **DYAUSH-PITIR** Aryan sky-father comparable to ZEUS and JUPITER.

**DYBBUK** See DIBBUK.

**DYER, MARY** (?–1660) English-born QUAKER arrested and executed in New England for visiting other Quakers in prison.

**DYKES, JOHN B.** (1823–1876) Vicar of the CHURCH OF ENGLAND who composed many hymn tunes including those for "Lead, Kindly Light," "Jesus, Lover of My Soul," "Holy, Holy, Holy," "The King of Love My Shepherd Is," and "Lead On, O King Eternal." Theologically he took a HIGH CHURCH position.

**DYLAN** Celtic sea god.

**DYNAMICS** Moral or psychological forces, the laws governing them, or the framework in which they operate.

**DYNAMISM** 1. Philosophic view of the universe as the result of force or energy of any kind. 2. Term for classifying those primitive religions which worship sacred power instead of soul or personality.

**DYOPHYSITES** Those who held that Christ has two natures, human and divine; their views were accepted at the Council of CHALCEDON in 451 and the Council of CONSTANTINOPLE in 553. Their opponents, the MONOPHYSITES, believed that Christ had only one nature.

**DYOTHELITES** Those who maintained that Christ had two separate wills, human and divine. The ECUMENICAL COUNCIL of 680 accepted their view as orthodox.

**DYSMAS** See DISMAS.

**DYU** 1. Vedic word for heaven. 2. Vedic term for a heavenly attendant of INDRA.

# E

**E** Symbol for the "Elohist" sources which lie, in the opinion of many scholars, behind various portions of the Old Testament, particularly of the Pentateuch. The Hebrew word ELOHIM is prominent in these passages. Other sources include "J," "D," and "P" (see).

**EA** Babylonian god of wisdom, magic, art, science, and fresh waters. He created mankind and the earth, and taught UTA-NAPISHTIM how to make an ark to save his family from the great flood which was to destroy much earthly life.

**EADBALD (seventh century)** Early English king of Kent who was converted to Christianity and built a church at Canterbury.

**EADMER (c.1055–1124)** English monk who wrote a history of England in the eleventh century, important for its ecclesiastical portrayal. He was named Archbishop of St. Andrew's but was never consecrated because of Scottish opposition to the English claim of spiritual authority.

**EAGLE** In Greek religion the eagle represented ZEUS, the gods, and the soul. Christian art often symbolically represents St. JOHN THE APOSTLE as an eagle. Many churches have a lectern supported by a carved eagle. The eagle may also symbolize REGENERATION and RESURRECTION.

**EAR** Christian symbol of Christ's betrayal, based on Peter's slashing off the ear of a soldier in Gethsemane (JOHN 18:10).

**EARNEST** Pledge of future benefits or blessings (cf. II CORINTHIANS 1:22).

**EARTH, THE** In Judeo-Christian thought "the earth is the Lord's." In Christian art the earth sometimes represents the church.

**EARTHY** KING JAMES BIBLE word for "earthly."

**EAST, THE** From ancient times the East has held great mystic significance. Sun-worshipers naturally bowed toward the east. After Jesus' birth "there came wise men from the east" (MATTHEW 2:1). Some CHRISTIANS face the east in worship and place the altar at the eastern end of their churches because Christ came from the East. In Christian art the East symbolizes the light of Christ. MOHAMMEDAN mosques face east so that they may look toward MECCA.

**EASTER** Festival (named from the Teutonic goddess of spring, Eostre) of the resurrection of Jesus Christ. Bitter disputes have raged over the proper date; it is celebrated on a Sunday in March or April, the date determined with reference to the first full moon after the vernal equinox. Easter and Christmas are two outstanding Christian festivals, and are both joyous occasions, particularly for children.

**EASTER CANDLE** Large ornamental candle kept lighted from EASTER EVEN to ASCENSION DAY.

**EASTER DUTY** Obligation in ANGLICAN and CATHOLIC churches to receive communion between ASH WEDNESDAY and TRINITY SUNDAY.

**EASTER EVEN** The Saturday preceding Easter.

**EASTER FAITH** Term for the resurrection-oriented faith of the early church.

**EASTER MONDAY** The day after Easter, a statute holiday in Great Britain.

**EASTERN CATHOLIC CHURCH** Ancient name for the Greek Catholic or EASTERN ORTHODOX CHURCH.

**EASTERN CHURCH** Term for the Greek, Russian, Syrian, and other non-Roman Eastern communions. See also EASTERN ORTHODOX CHURCH.

**EASTERN ORTHODOX CATHOLIC CHURCH IN AMERICA** A denomination with Russian origins, established in the United States by Bishop Raphael Hawaweeny.

Ruled by a governing synod, this is one of the numerous Eastern Orthodox churches in America.

**EASTERN ORTHODOX CHURCH** Christian community originating in eastern Europe and western Asia which split with the ROMAN CATHOLIC CHURCH early in the Christian era. It comprises one of the three principal divisions in Christianity; the other two are Protestantism and Roman Catholicism. Sometimes called the Orthodox Eastern Church, the Greek Church, or the Greek Catholic Church, Eastern Orthodoxy includes members of various nationalities, although its member churches are mainly Balkan, Russian, Syrian, Egyptian, Arabian, Armenian, and the like. There are twenty-one Orthodox branches in the United States. In the world there are approximately 175 million members of Orthodox and Eastern churches. Eastern Orthodox Christians do not acknowledge the supremacy or jurisdiction of the pope of Rome.

**EASTERN ORTHODOX EPISCOPATE** A world organization of Orthodox churches.

**EASTERN RITE CHURCHES** Catholic churches which recognize the authority of the pope and hold beliefs identical with those of the ROMAN CATHOLIC CHURCH but which follow Byzantine or other Eastern rituals. The sign of the cross is made from right to left, the priests often marry, and communion is received in both kinds (both bread and wine).

**EASTER OFFERING** Special church offering on Easter. In ancient times it was often given to the priest; today it is often devoted to the local parish.

**EASTER SEPULCHER** Recessed place in a church wall where the sacrament was anciently kept until Easter Eve.

**EASTERTIDE** The time between Easter and ASCENSION DAY, a period of forty days.

**EASTON, BURTON SCOTT (1877–1950)** American EPISCOPAL New Testament professor and exegete. He wrote outstanding commentaries on Luke and the Pastoral Epistles of Paul (see EPISTLES, PASTORAL).

**EASTWARD POSITION** The position of a clergyman who faces the east or the altar while leading divine worship. In Catholic churches today the priest often faces the congregation.

**EATING THE GOD** Primitive religious custom of eating meat, grain, baked images, etc., which symbolize the worshiper's god.

**EBAL** A mountain in Samaria known as the Mount of Cursing after Joshua built an altar on it and announced the curses that would result from breaking the MOSAIC LAW (JOSHUA 8:30–33). Today there is a church on Mt. Ebal.

**EBEDJESUS (?–1318)** NESTORIAN theologian, philosopher, and commentator on Scripture. He became Metropolitan of Armenia.

**EBED-MELECH** *servant of the king* Ethiopian eunuch who helped the prophet Jeremiah out of a dungeon (JEREMIAH 38:7–12).

**EBENEZER** *stone of help* 1. Area in Palestine where the Philistines defeated the Israelites and captured the ark of the covenant (I SAMUEL 4:1; 5:1). 2. Stone memorializing an Israelite victory over the Philistines (I SAMUEL 7:12).

**EBENEZER SOCIETY** Communal religious society formed by German pietists near Buffalo, New York, in the nineteenth century. They moved to Iowa to form the Amana Society in 1855 (see AMANA COMMUNITY).

**EBER** *one who crosses over* 1. A name for the Hebrews. 2. A descendant of Noah (GENESIS 10:21, 25) who fathered many Semitic tribes east of the Euphrates River.

**EBERHARD, JOHANN AUGUSTUS (1739–1809)** German theologian and professor of philosophy who sought to counteract atheistic moral ideas with Christian ideals and principles.

**EBERHARDT, PAUL (1876–1923)** German philosopher of religion, member of the Evangelical National Church, who interpreted the mystic principles of non-Christian religions for devotional use.

**EBERLIN, JOHANN (1470–1533)** German FRANCISCAN monk who followed Martin LUTHER and promoted clerical marriage and what were considered radical social ideas.

**EBERLIN, JOHANN ERNST (1702–1762)** German composer of a number of musical works. Most of these were for church use.

**EBIONITES** *poor men* Jewish Christians of the first six centuries who denied the deity of Jesus, although accepting Him as a prophet and Messiah, and rejected the teachings of Paul. They were ascetic, observed the Jewish law, and had some GNOSTIC tendencies.

**EBISU** Japanese god of luck and labor.

**EBLIS** MOSLEM name for the devil, condemned to wander through the world until the end of time.

**ECCARD** See ECKHART.

**ECCE HOMO** *behold the man* Pilate's words, in Latin, when presenting Jesus to the Jews (JOHN 19:5). Many paintings of Christ's judgment before Pilate bear this title. It was also the title of a popular life of Christ by John Seeley (1865).

**ECCLESIA** *assembly* A Greek word for a popular assembly, *ecclesia* was chosen to translate the Old Testament word *kahal* or *qahal* (assembly of the people of Israel) in the SEPTUAGINT. It is the New Testament word for "church."

**ECCLESIA DOCENS** *the teaching church* CATHOLIC term for clergymen.

**ECCLESIASTES** *the churchman* A book of the Old Testament's WISDOM LITERATURE, in Hebrew *Qoheleth*, "The Preacher." It emphasizes the shortness and emptiness of life on earth.

**ECCLESIASTIC** A clergyman.

**ECCLESIASTIC, ECCLESIASTICAL** Having to do with the church.

**ECCLESIASTICAL COMMISSION** Body appointed by a church group and given considerably more power than a committee.

**ECCLESIASTICAL COMMISSIONERS** The money and property managers of the CHURCH OF ENGLAND from 1835 to 1948. They were succeeded by the Church Commissioners of England.

**ECCLESIASTICAL COURTS** Church courts.

**ECCLESIASTICAL LAW** The law governing a church.

**ECCLESIASTICISM** Overconcern with the administration and interests of the church.

**ECCLESIASTICUS** *of the church* Old Testament book considered apocryphal by PROTESTANTS. Also known as *The Wisdom of Jesus the Son of Sirach*, it contains proverbs and statements in praise of wisdom and famous men.

**ECCLESIOLATRY** Undue devotion to, or worship of, the church.

**ECCLESIOLOGY** The study of church building and beautification, or of church doctrine; church policy.

**ECHO** In Greek myth, a mountain nymph able to utter only another's last words.

**ECK, JOHANN MAIER (1486–1543)** German CATHOLIC theologian who condemned LUTHER and ZWINGLI and the AUGSBURG CONFESSION. An authority in church history and canon law, Eck published the Bible in German dialect. He forced Luther to admit that church councils might err, and brought about his excommunication.

**ECKHART, JOHANNES** (c.1260–1327) "Meister Eckhart" (Eccard, Eckart, or Eckehart), German philosopher and theologian of the DOMINICAN order who had deep influence on mysticism. Some of his propositions were condemned by Pope JOHN XXII in 1329. God, he taught, is pure Being without whom nothing is. God permeates all things, particularly the human soul. Mystical experience and knowledge bring union with the divine. See also AMALRICIANS, AMALRIC OF BENA.

**ECLECTICISM** The aggregation of various elements from diverse sources in a theological or philosophical system.

**ECSTASY** Extreme, almost unendurable joy experienced by religious MYSTICS. Sometimes it is accompanied by a trance, stigmatism, levitation, or the like.

**ECTOPLASM** A semimaterial substance believed to emanate from a MEDIUM during a spiritualistic trance.

**ECUMENICAL** *of the inhabited world* Term for contact and reunion between the various separated branches of the Christian church.

**ECUMENICAL COUNCILS** Official councils representing the whole church and presided over by the pope or his representative. All Christians recognize the first four councils as ecumenical, while the Orthodox accept the first seven. Roman Catholics count twenty-one Ecumenical Councils, including the Second Vatican Council of 1962–1965.

**ECUMENICAL CREEDS** Creeds accepted by the whole church, such as the APOSTLES', ATHANASIAN, and NICENE Creeds.

**ECUMENICAL INSTITUTE** Center founded in 1946 by the WORLD COUNCIL OF CHURCHES for Christian inspiration and ecumenical studies.

**ECUMENICAL MOVEMENT** A worldwide movement toward Christian unity among all denominations, particularly vigorous in the twentieth century. Mergers of denominations, councils of churches in various localities and countries, and the formation of the WORLD COUNCIL OF CHURCHES all represent this trend. It was strengthened by the ecumenical good will of the Second VATICAN COUNCIL.

**ECUMENICAL PATRIARCH** The Patriarch of Constantinople, chief bishop of the EASTERN ORTHODOX churches. In 1964 Ecumenical Patriarch Athenagoras I embraced Pope Paul VI at Jerusalem, ending a coolness that had lasted for five centuries.

**ECUMENICS** Science or study of everything related to the worldwide church or Christian community.

**EDDAS** Old Icelandic works from the twelfth and thirteenth centuries providing much information about Norse and Icelandic mythology. The two chief works are the Elder Edda and the Younger Edda. The Frost Giants and the Dwarfs play a prominent part in the Eddas.

**EDDY, MARY BAKER (1821–1910)** Founder of CHRISTIAN SCIENCE. She wrote the movement's textbook, *Science and Health,* founded the *Journal of Christian Science,* and organized the Church of Christ, Scientist. Her writings have influenced contemporary religious emphases on health, success, and mental power.

**EDELS, SAMUEL ELIEZER (1555–1631)** Polish talmudic scholar.

**EDEN** The garden in the Near East in which Adam and Eve were placed at the beginning of human history (GENESIS 2—3). From it they were banished for eating the fruit of the tree of the knowledge of good and evil.

**EDERSHEIM, ALFRED (1825–1889)** Jewish Christian whose *Life and Times of Jesus the Messiah* was erudite and popular. Born in Austria, he entered the ministry first of the PRESBYTERIAN CHURCH and then of the CHURCH OF ENGLAND. He assembled much information about the JUDAISM of the time of Christ.

**EDESSA** Mesopotamian city, the earliest center of Syriac Christianity, which became an important religious center of the Byzantine Empire. It is now the city of Urfa, Turkey.

**EDICT OF MILAN** Proclamation of CON- STANTINE and Licinius in 313 granting toleration of Christians.

**EDICT OF NANTES** Announcement of restricted privileges for the French HUGUE- NOTS, in effect from 1598 to 1685.

**EDICT OF WORMS** Pronouncement of the Diet of Worms, Germany, in 1521, banning Martin LUTHER and his works.

**EDIFICATION** Building up of the soul and character of man—the particular goal of preaching and personal devotions in the Christian life.

**EDINBURGH** Capital of Scotland; famous for St. Giles' Cathedral which dates from the twelfth century, and for the leadership of John KNOX in establishing Scottish PRES- BYTERIANISM. A World Missionary Conference was held there in 1910. Edinburgh was also the site of the second WORLD CON- FERENCE ON FAITH AND ORDER which approved the formation of the WORLD COUN- CIL OF CHURCHES.

**EDMUND, ST. (c.840–869)** King of East Anglia, martyred in the Danish invasion of 869 for refusing as a Christian to share his kingdom with the Danish leader Inguar. He was buried at Bury St. Edmunds; many English churches are dedicated to him. His feast day is November 20.

**EDMUND, ST. (c.1170–1240)** Devout Archbishop of Canterbury whose eloquence led to his choice to preach the crusade in England in 1227. He stoutly but ineffectually resisted exploitation and insubordination within his archdiocese; a number of his rulings were overruled by the pope. His feast day is November 16.

**EDOM red** 1. Mountainous desert country, extending from the Dead Sea to Ezion- geber on the Gulf of Aqabah, inhabited by the descendants of ESAU. The country, also known as Idumaea, prospered from levies on the King's Highway which was an important trade route running north and south through Edom. Edom became part of Arabia after the time of Christ. 2. Another name for Esau.

**EDOMITES** Inhabitants of EDOM, descended from ESAU; continually at war with their neighbors, particularly the IS- RAELITES.

**EDWARD VI (1537–1553)** Precocious boy king of England and Ireland during whose short reign (1547–1553) CALVINISTIC

Protestantism made great inroads against CATHOLICISM in the realm. This was marked by the introduction of a new EUCHARIST ritual and two new BOOKS OF COMMON PRAYER; the destruction of images, altars, and relics; the reading of the Scriptures in English at HIGH MASS; the promulgation of the Forty-two ARTICLES of Religion; the placing of the GREAT BIBLE in every church; and by many other measures. Actually, Edward appears to have been completely dominated by Dudley, Duke of NORTHUMBERLAND.

**EDWARDS, JONATHAN (1703–1758)** American CONGREGATIONAL minister and theologian whose CALVINISTIC doctrines and eloquent evangelical preaching led to the GREAT AWAKENING in New England. His theology is set forth in *The Freedom of the Will*; his style of preaching, in such sermons as "Sinners in the Hands of an Angry God." He emphasized the absolute sovereignty of God and the necessity of personal Christian experience. An original philosopher, he held that ideas originate in God and that the universe exists only in the mind. He served as a missionary to Massachusetts Indians and as president of Princeton College.

**EFFECTUAL CALLING** Theological term for the leading of a person by the Holy Spirit to genuine repentance, faith, and salvation.

**EFFICACIOUS GRACE** In Christian theology, the power of God to which man's will freely consents in accepting salvation.

**EGEDE, HANS (1686–1758)** Norwegian missionary among the Eskimos of Greenland. Known as "The Apostle of Greenland," he became superintendent of the Greenland mission.

**EGEDE, PAUL (1708–1789)** Son and missionary successor of Hans EGEDE (above). He published a CATECHISM and a New Testament in the Eskimo language.

**EGERIA** Roman goddess of streams and fountains, worshiped by pregnant women.

**EGG** In Egyptian, Indian, and other religious cosmogonies, the universe derives from an egg. In Christian art, the egg is a symbol of the RESURRECTION.

**EGLON** 1. Moabite king murdered by Ehud (JUDGES 3:12–25). 2. City of Palestine near Lachish where Joshua killed five Amorite kings (JOSHUA 10). William Mat-

thew Flinders Petrie excavated it in 1890 and from its artifacts worked out a system of pottery dating.

**EGO** / Term for the person, the self, or the self-preserving drive of the mind.

**EGOISM** Ethically, the concept that action is motivated by self-interest, or that individual good is a valid standard of moral action.

**EGYPTIAN RELIGION** One of the most ancient cradles of human culture and of highly developed religion, Egypt is often mentioned in Scripture. There the children of Israel were held in bondage for two centuries, until their deliverance by Moses. Libraries could be filled with information about the ancient religions of Egypt. Great advance came when the Pharaoh IKHNATON or Akhenaton, "the world's first monotheist," in the fourteenth century B.C. substituted the worship of the one Creator-Father Aton for the other gods of the Egyptian pantheon. The advance apparently died in Egypt with Ikhnaton, but may have influenced Moses. The Egyptians firmly believed in the existence of a soul which survived the body's death in a substantial afterlife. Egyptian religion today is overwhelmingly Moslem (see ISLAM). Many of the Christians in Egypt are Copts. See COPTIC CHURCH.

**EGYPTIANS, GOSPEL ACCORDING TO THE** Apocryphal second-century gospel with an ascetic point of view.

**EHECATIL or EHECATL** Aztec wind god.

**EHUD** Israelite savior-judge who killed Eglon the king of Moab to deliver his nation from Moabite oppression (JUDGES 3).

**EIELSEN, ELLING (1804–1883)** Norwegian minister to Scandinavian immigrants in the midwestern United States, and founder of the Norwegian Evangelical Lutheran Church.

**EIELSEN SYNOD** First Norwegian synod in the United States, organized in 1846.

**EIGHT** Symbol of baptism, regeneration, and resurrection. According to one mode of reckoning, Christ was raised on the eighth day of the week.

**EIGHTEEN BENEDICTIONS** The elements in the GREAT PRAYER in synagogue worship. Originally eighteen, the number is now nineteen.

**EIKON** See ICON.

**EIKON BASILIKE** *royal image* "Spiritual autobiography" published in 1649 following the execution of Charles I of England.

**EIKONOKLASTES** *image breaker* John MILTON's reply to the *Eikon Basilike* (above), representing the Puritan dislike of Charles I.

**EILETON** Silk altar cloth in the EASTERN CHURCH.

**EILITHYIA** Greek goddess of birth.

**EINHORN, DAVID (1809–1879)** German-born leader of REFORM JUDAISM. He introduced changes in the ritual and the synagogue services, and opposed slavery during the American Civil War. For the latter he was forced out of Baltimore, Maryland.

**EINSIEDELN** Noted Swiss center of European pilgrimages. It is famous for a BENEDICTINE abbey, founded about 934, whose library holds many important manuscripts. ZWINGLI was once Einsiedeln's parish priest. A religious play entitled *The Great World Theater* is performed there each year.

**EIR** Nordic goddess of healing.

**EISAI (1141–1215)** Japanese who introduced tea and Rinzai ZEN Buddhism to Japan, both of which he brought from China.

**EISEGESIS** Interpreting a passage of Scripture according to personal notions rather than according to the original meaning (EXEGESIS).

**EISENACH** German city famous for several medieval churches and buildings. There BACH was born and LUTHER once lived.

**EISLEBEN** German town where Martin LUTHER was born, baptized, and died.

**EJACULATION** Very short prayer.

**EL** 1. Semitic name for God or for a hero or magistrate. 2. Supreme Canaanite god, father of BAAL.

**ELAMITES** Warlike people dating from 4,000 B.C. who dwelt north of the Persian Gulf. They helped Assyria and Egypt against the Israelites (ISAIAH 22:6; EZEKIEL 32:24).

**ELAT** Semitic sea goddess.

**ELDAD** One of the seventy elders selected to help Moses govern Israel. He received the Spirit and the gift of prophecy (NUMBERS 11:24–29).

**ELDAD AND MODAD** Jewish apocryphal book.

**ELDAD BEN MAHLI (ninth century)** Jewish traveler who claimed to have located the ten lost tribes of Israel.

**ELDER** A ruling official in JUDAISM and in various Christian denominations, particularly in PRESBYTERIANISM. A MORMON elder is one of the higher priests. The Greek word for elder is *presbyteros*, source of the word "priest." (See also PRESBYTER.)

**ELDER, RULING** In the PRESBYTERIAN church, an elected governing official.

**ELDER, TEACHING** In PRESBYTERIANISM, a minister. He moderates the SESSION which governs each Presbyterian congregation.

**ELEATICS** Greek philosophers of the sixth century B.C. who taught that all things are one, that the notion of many different things is illusory, and that change is impossible. Their founder was PARMENIDES.

**ELEAZAR** *God has helped* 1. The name of at least thirteen different men of the Old Testament. 2. An elderly Jew martyred for refusing to eat pork (II MACCABEES 6:18–31).

**ELECTION** Choice. The people of Israel were elected as God's special people to bring peace and salvation to the world. The New Testament asserts the divine election of Christians for redemption. The doctrine of election, historically championed by AUGUSTINE and CALVIN, has been the subject of much debate.

**ELEGABALUS** Syrian sun god.

**ELEISON** *have mercy upon us* Ecclesiastical chant or response.

**ELEMENTS** 1. Term in classical Greek philosophy and other ancient speculation for the basic constituents of the universe, as earth, air, fire, and water. 2. Ecclesiastical term for the bread and wine of the EUCHARIST.

**ELEPHANTA** Island in the Bombay harbor of India famous for its six cave-temples dedicated to SIVA. Two other caves were never completed. All the caves are impressive, containing gigantic pillars and statuary.

**ELEPHANTINE** Island near Aswan, Egypt, inhabited by a Jewish colony as early as the sixth century B.C. The Elephantine Jews had a temple, spoke ARAMAIC, and carried out various Jewish rituals. They corresponded with Jews in Palestine.

**ELEPHANTINE PAPYRI** Aramaic letters of the fifth century B.C. found at Elephantine, Egypt, 1904–1908. They described the life of the Jewish colony there at that time.

**ELEUSINIAN MYSTERIES** Ancient Greek religious festivals of the spring and fall honoring DIONYSUS and PERSEPHONE. Presumably they symbolized death, spiritual rebirth, and immortality.

**ELEUSIS** Greek city, center of the ELEUSINIAN MYSTERIES, which contained two temples, a theater, and the Telesterion, a hall of initiation.

**ELEVATION** 1. The raising of a clergyman to a higher rank. 2. The lifting up of the BLESSED SACRAMENT at the consecration in the EUCHARIST.

**ELEVATION OF THE HOST** See ELEVATION 2.

**ELEVEN, THE** Term for the twelve Apostles without Judas.

**ELF** In Teutonic myth, a small, mischievous being with supernatural powers.

**ELI** 1. The priest at Shiloh to whom young Samuel was apprenticed (I SAMUEL 3:1). 2. The first word in Aramaic of Jesus' fourth cry from the cross: "My God . . ." (MATTHEW 27:46).

**ELI, ELI, LAMA SABACHTHANI?** Jesus' cry from the cross in Aramaic, meaning "My God, my God, why hast thou forsaken me?" (MATTHEW 27:46).

**ELIAS** See ELIJAH.

**ELIEZER BEN HYRCANUS (first century)** "Eliezer the Great," a rabbinical scholar and mystic who founded a school at Lydda in Palestine.

**ELIHU** *he is my God* A friend of JOB whose words appear to form a bridge between the limitations of Job's derogatory comforters and the revelation of God Himself.

**ELIJAH or ELIAS** Hebrew prophet to Israel during the reign of wicked King Ahab. He was a forthright spokesman for God and worker of a number of miracles.

**ELIJAH BEN SOLOMON or ELIJAH WILNA (1720–1797)** Orthodox but critical talmudic scholar who opposed HASIDIC mysticism. A master of many fields of learning, he had great influence in JUDAISM.

**ELIJAH'S CHAIR or SEAT** Chair of honor on which a Jewish baby is placed before CIRCUMCISION, in recognition of the spiritual presence of Elijah.

**ELIJAH WILNA** See ELIJAH BEN SOLOMON.

**ELIMELECH** *my God is king* Husband of Naomi and father-in-law of Ruth (RUTH 1:2–3).

**ELIOT, JOHN (1604–1690)** English "Apostle to the Indians" of colonial America. A PURITAN, he converted about four thousand Indians and established them in special villages; most of them were killed in King Philip's War. Eliot translated the Bible and various religious works into the Algonquian Indian tongue.

**ELIOT, T. S. (1888–1964)** American-born poet whose later work reflected the religious hope of his ANGLO-CATHOLIC belief, as well as the desolation and despair of the twentieth century. His works include the book *The Idea of a Christian Society* and the plays *Murder in the Cathedral, The Cocktail Party, The Confidential Clerk,* and *The Elder Statesman.* His great poetic works include *The Waste Land, Ash Wednesday, Four Quartets,* and *The Rock.*

**ELIOUN** A high god of the Phoenicians.

**ELISABETH, ST.** Cousin of the Virgin MARY and mother of JOHN THE BAPTIST. Religious art often associates Elisabeth and Mary. The feast day of Elisabeth is November 5.

**ELISEUS** See ELISHA.

**ELISHA or ELISEUS** *God is salvation* Prophet to Israel who succeeded ELIJAH. A farmer's son, Elisha performed less spectacular miracles than Elijah, but they often sweetened human life. Jesus used Elisha as an example of love transcending racial barriers (LUKE 4:27).

**ELISHA BEN ABUYAH (1st–2nd century)** Known as "the Other" because of his theological nonconformity, Elisha opposed the views of contemporary rabbis and has been accused of holding GNOSTIC ideas.

**ELIZABETH I (1533–1603)** Queen of England who re-established Protestantism in England through Acts of Supremacy and Uniformity. Hence she is sometimes called the real founder of ANGLICANISM. Both PURITANS and CATHOLICS protested at the establishment of the CHURCH OF ENGLAND as the official church of that country.

**ELIZABETHAN SETTLEMENT** The establishment of the CHURCH OF ENGLAND during the reign of Queen Elizabeth.

**ELIZABETH OF HUNGARY, ST. (1207–1231)** Devout wife of Louis IV of Thuringia.

When her husband criticized her for giving bread to the poor, a miracle converted him. After his death she lost the regency because of her alleged excessive almsgiving and from then on led a life of austerity and prayer. She was a Franciscan Tertiary (see FRANCISCANS) and was canonized in 1235. Her feast day is November 19.

**ELKESAITES** Jewish-Christian group of about the first century whose members held vigorously to the MOSAIC LAW but rejected the Epistles of Paul and certain other books of the Bible. Rather ascetic, they saw redemption in baptism.

**ELLIOT, JAMES (1928–1956)** American missionary to Ecuador under PLYMOUTH BRETHREN auspices, martyred with four other young men by "stone-age" Auca Indians in 1956.

**ELLORA** Village in India famous for its 34 rock cave-temples. They are BUDDHIST, HINDU, and JAIN. The Kailasa temple, a hundred feet high, was carved from a single piece of rock and is held to be an earthly representation of Siva's palace in heaven.

**ELM** A tree symbolizing strength and dignity in religious art.

**EL MALE RACHAMIM** *Lord, full of mercy* Jewish memorial prayer for the dead.

**ELOHIM** *God; gods* Pluriform name of God common in the Old Testament.

**ELOHIST** Technical term for a writer of Scripture who favored the word ELOHIM. Also see "E."

**ELOI, ELOI** See ELI, ELI, LAMA SABACHTHANI?

**EL OLAM** *eternal God* The name of God, stressing His everlasting nature, used by Abraham at Beersheba (GENESIS 21:33).

**EL SHADDAI** A name of God in patriarchal Jewish times (EXODUS 6:3). It is believed to indicate "God Almighty," but the exact meaning is uncertain.

**ELUL** Twelfth month in the Jewish civil year.

**ELVIRA, COUNCIL OF** A church council held in Spain about 306 which decreed severe penalties for apostasy, adultery, and incontinence of the clergy.

**ELYMAS** See BAR-JESUS.

**ELYSIUM** Greek realm of happiness for the dead who have lived righteous lives.

**EMA or EMMA-O** Japanese BUDDHIST lord and judge of the afterworld.

**EMANATION** Theological term for that which comes from God. In GNOSTICISM it was believed that semidivine beings emanated from the Father, bridging the gap to earth. ". . . emanation is the denial of personality both for God and for man" (Encyclopaedia Britannica).

**EMBER DAYS** Special days of abstinence and prayer in Western churches.

**EMBLA** See ASK.

**EMBLEM** Symbol or mark, as of a saint. Typical emblems are Peter's keys, Jerome's lion, Paul's sword, and St. Andrew's transverse cross.

**EMBOLISM** A variation in the liturgy, such as *a*. insertion of a special prayer in the mass between the Lord's Prayer and breaking of the bread, *b*. change for a special occasion in the calendar.

**EMBURY, PHILIP (1728–1775)** Irish METHODIST clergyman who founded the first Methodist church in America, in New York. He also founded a Methodist society in Camden, New Jersey. See also HECK, BARBARA RUCKLE.

**EMERODS** Tumors or hemorrhoids (DEUTERONOMY 28:27; I SAMUEL 5:7).

**EMERSON, RALPH WALDO (1803–1882)** American philosopher who left the UNITARIAN ministry to devote himself to writing and lecturing. His doctrines of compensation, self-reliance, the Over-soul, and transcendentalism have profoundly influenced American thought and religion.

**EMETH** *truth or faithfulness* Hebrew word consisting of the first, middle, and last letters of the alphabet, symbolizing divine eternity.

**EMINENCE** Term of honor for Catholic CARDINALS, and for the Grand Master of the Knights of St. John of Jerusalem. See KNIGHTS HOSPITALERS.

**EMMANUEL or IMMANUEL** *God with us* The name of the Messiah in Isaiah 7:14, and a favorite Christmas name of the Christ Child. (Cf. MATTHEW 1:23.)

**EMMANUEL HOLINESS CHURCH** American Pentecostal body which withdrew from the PENTECOSTAL FIRE-BAPTIZED HOLINESS CHURCH in 1953 over theological and governmental differences.

**EMMANUEL MOVEMENT** A program of divine healing begun in 1906 with the aid of Emmanuel Church in Boston, Massachusetts. After a medical diagnosis, a patient's medical treatment was supplemented by prayer, suggestion, and encouragement, with beneficial results.

**EMMA-O**  See EMA.

**EMMAUS**  Village outside Jerusalem where Jesus appeared to two disciples the evening of His resurrection (LUKE 24:13).

**EMPEROR OF THE EASTERN MOUNTAINS** TAO god who rewards the righteous and punishes evil persons.

**EMPEROR WORSHIP**  The worship of the emperor as a god, imported by Roman emperors from the East. Refusal to grant such worship brought about the martyrdom of many Christians. Until the middle of the twentieth century, emperor worship existed in Japan.

**EMPIRICAL THEOLOGY**  The study of God on the basis of experience. Theological empiricists believe that all valid knowledge of God comes from religious experience.

**EMPIRICISM**  Philosophical theory that all knowledge is based on experience or observation. It opposes rationalism and a priori schools of epistemology.

**EMPYREAN**  Term for the highest heaven of all.

**EMSER, HIERONYMUS (1477–1527)**  German Catholic controversialist who at one time sympathized with church reform but who later opposed LUTHER and ZWINGLI. He organized a reformed ROMAN CATHOLIC church and translated the New Testament into German.

**ENCAENIA**  Festival commemorating the dedication of a church.

**ENCOUNTER, DIVINE-HUMAN**  Term for personal confrontation with God.

**ENCRATITES**  Early CHRISTIANS and GNOSTICS who abstained from wine, meat, and sex.

**ENCYCLICAL**  Letter from the pope to the bishops of the world, or to those in a particular country. An encyclical may also be any communication addressed to many people.

**ENCYCLOPEDISTS**  Eighteenth-century French scholars who prepared a multivolume encyclopedia presenting all knowledge from the viewpoint of natural morality. Since they also sought to expose religious prejudices, the work was attacked and temporarily suppressed.

**ENDIL**  Celtic sea god.

**END OF THE DAYS**  Biblical expression for the future period of judgment and eternal peace.

**ENDOGAMY**  Restriction of marriage to one's own race or religion.

**ENDOR**  Town near Nazareth visited by King Saul to learn his fate from a witch (1 SAMUEL 28:7–25).

**ENDOWMENT**  1. Ability considered to be a gift of God. 2. Gift for the maintenance of a church or other institution.

**ENELOW, HERMAN GERSON (1877–1934)** Russian-born author and rabbi who served several temples in the United States and was president of the CENTRAL CONFERENCE OF AMERICAN RABBIS from 1927 to 1929.

**ENERGUMEN**  Term for one possessed by demons in early Christian writings.

**ENFANTIN, BARTHÉLEMY PROSPER (1796–1864)**  French social reformer who became a leader of the SAINT-SIMONIANS, an eccentric religious group. Enfantin proposed that they substitute free love for "the tyranny of marriage," announced himself as the group's messiah, and began looking for a female messiah to help lead it.

**EN-GEDI** *well of the goat*  Cave on the coast of the Dead Sea where David first hid from King Saul and later spared his life (1 SAMUEL 23, 24).

**ENGLAND, CHURCH OF**  See CHURCH OF ENGLAND.

**ENGLAND, JOHN (1786–1842)**  Irish-born ROMAN CATHOLIC priest who fought for Catholic freedom in Ireland and was appointed a bishop in the United States where he won high respect and ministered especially to Negroes.

**ENGLISH LADIES**  The Institute of the Blessed Virgin Mary, founded in 1609, with houses in a number of countries. The order was approved by the pope in 1703.

**ENGLISH REVISED VERSION**  See REVISED VERSION.

**ENGO or YUAN-WU (1063–1135)**  Chinese teacher of ZEN Buddhism, noted for his comments on earlier Buddhist masters.

**ENKI**  Babylonian water god.

**ENLIGHTENMENT, THE**  The period in eighteenth-century Europe when LESSING, LOCKE, VOLTAIRE, and others sought to emancipate men from prejudice and superstition. In the process, rationalism and DEISM attracted many away from traditional forms of Christianity.

**ENLIL** One of the three great gods of Babylonian religion, Enlil was god of the earth, order, and storms. He was also known as Bel or Marduk.

**ENMESHARRA** Babylonian god of the afterlife.

**ENNEAD** The nine gods of Heliopolis in ancient Egypt: Ra, Shu, Tefnut, Geb, Nut, Osiris, Isis, Set, and Nephtys.

**ENOCH** Father of METHUSELAH who "walked with God, and he was not, for God took him" (GENESIS 5:18–24).

**ENOCH, BOOK OF** Apocryphal Jewish writing from the second and first centuries B.C., important for its record of the development of religious thought. It speaks of a final judgment by the Son of Man and is quoted in Jude 14 ff.

**ENOCH, BOOK OF THE SECRETS OF** An apocryphal book attributed to Enoch, written in Greek, in Egypt, about the time of Christ. It describes seven heavens, ten orders of angels, the seven thousand years of world history, and other marvels.

**ENOSH** See ANOSH.

**ENTELECHY** Philosophically, form as opposed to potency or matter. In CATHOLIC theology, an example of entelechy is the soul as opposed to the body.

**ENTHUSIASM** *possession by the god* Term for religious ecstasy, or for a movement associated with such ecstasy, or for a religious stance considered extravagant.

**ENURTA** Assyrian war god.

**ENVY** Resentment at another's good fortune. CATHOLIC theology considers it one of the deadly sins, an obvious violation of the commandment to love one's neighbor.

**ENZU** Babylonian moon god.

**EON** See AEON.

**EOS** Greek goddess of the dawn. For her adultery she was cursed with nymphomaniac desires for human youths.

**EOSTRE** Germanic goddess of spring from whose name the word EASTER derives.

**EPAPHRODITUS** *pleasing* A Christian of Philippi who was of great help to Paul (PHILIPPIANS 2:25, 27).

**EPARCHY** Ecclesiastical province in the EASTERN CHURCH.

**EPHAH** Biblical measure equivalent to about a bushel.

**EPHESIANS** Popular name for the epistle written by the Apostle Paul to the Christians of Ephesus in Asia Minor. It emphasizes the purpose of God to unite all things in Christ, the unity of the church, and the practical duties of Christians.

**EPHESUS** Ancient city near Smyrna in modern Turkey. Famed in the classical Greek period for its wealth and its temple to ARTEMIS, Ephesus became a cosmopolitan center of commerce. The Apostle PAUL established a church in Ephesus in which APOLLOS, PRISCILLA, and AQUILA were active. For a long period the city was a Christian center.

**EPHESUS, COUNCIL OF** This was the third ECUMENICAL COUNCIL, held in 431 to settle a controversy over the person and nature of Christ. The NESTORIANS in the church held that the Word of God indwelt the man Jesus in a union illustrated by that of a man and his wife; they emphasized the reality of Christ's manhood over against the ALEXANDRIANS who stressed His deity. The Nestorians also objected to calling Mary "Godbearer." The Alexandrians succeeded in establishing their position that Mary was the Mother of God and that Christ's divine and human natures were perfectly united in one person.

**EPHESUS, ROBBER SYNOD OF** In 449 a council of 130 bishops met at Ephesus at the call of Emperor Theodosius II to "utterly destroy NESTORIANISM." EUTYCHES, a MONOPHYSITE leader who had been deposed from his position of archimandrite in Constantinople, was cleared of heresy charges and reinstated, while Flavianus, his former bishop, and other bishops suspected of Nestorian views were deposed. The council, however, was not recognized by Leo I of Rome, who demanded another council. Eutychianism was later condemned at the Council of CHALCEDON.

**EPHOD** Sacred apron-like garment of Jewish high priests in the Old Testament period. Richly decorated, it covered the priest's chest and back and was clasped at the shoulders with onyxes. On these the names of the twelve tribes were engraved. Apparently the ephod was sometimes used for divination (NUMBERS 27:21).

**EPHPHATHA** *be opened* Jesus' command in Aramaic to a man who was deaf and dumb (MARK 7:31–37).

**EPHPHETHA** Part of the Roman Catholic rite of solemn baptism, indicating the spiritual opening of the ears of the person baptized.

**EPHRAEM THE SYRIAN, ST. (c.308–373)** Saint of Edessa, Syria, who wrote many commentaries, homilies, and hymns, and is said to have converted Syria to Christianity. In 1920 the Pope declared him a DOCTOR OF THE CHURCH. Ephraem's feast day is June 18 in the West, January 28 in the East.

**EPHRAIM** *double fruitfulness* 1. Joseph's younger son, chosen for blessing ahead of his older brother Manasseh (GENESIS 48:5–20). 2. The Jewish half-tribe descended from Manasseh. 3. The territory, extending from Jericho to the Mediterranean, given to the tribe of Manasseh. 4. The Northern Kingdom of Israel, sometimes called Manasseh after the division of the original kingdom. 5. A city north of Jerusalem in the territory of Ephraim.

**EPHRATA CLOISTERS** Christian communal community established at Ephrata, Pennsylvania, by Johann Conrad BEISSEL in 1732. The members, SEVENTH-DAY BAPTISTS and others, abstained from sexual intercourse. They were noted for their music.

**EPICLESIS** *invocation* Eastern Orthodox invocation of the Holy Spirit during COMMUNION, through which the elements become the very body and blood of Christ.

**EPICTETUS (c.60–c.138)** Greek STOIC philosopher who stressed attention to what is good within one rather than to things without. He recommended two words for peace: "endure" and "abstain," and emphasized human brotherhood.

**EPICUREANS** Greek disciples of EPICURUS who held that the gods are uninterested in human life and that therefore we may enjoy the present instead of worrying about the future.

**EPICURUS (341–270 B.C.)** Greek philosopher who founded a school at Athens. He believed that the universe is eternal and infinite, being composed of indivisible, unchangeable atoms, and that the greatest good is pleasure. But he defined pleasure in terms of peace of mind, and considered intellectual pleasures to be the greatest. The moral code he proposed was high.

**EPIKLESIS** See EPICLESIS.

**EPILEPSY** This was the disease of those described as "lunatick" in Matthew 4:24, KJV. The epileptic boy of Matthew 17:15 is said by Mark (9:17–18) and Luke (9:39) to have been possessed by an evil spirit.

**EPIMENIDES (sixth century B.C.)** Prophet and poet of Cnossos, Crete, who wrote many oracles, sayings, and other works. He may be the prophet of Crete referred to by Paul in Titus 1:12.

**EPIPHANES (second century)** Founder, with his father CARPOCRATES, of an amoral GNOSTIC sect. He wrote a book advocating communistic ownership of both property and women, and he is said by CLEMENT OF ALEXANDRIA to have been honored as a god.

**EPIPHANIUS (c.315–402)** Bishop of Constantia in Cyprus who strongly advocated monasticism and orthodox belief. He denounced ORIGEN, John of Jerusalem, and all heresy. Jerome called him "The Five-Tongued."

**EPIPHANY** *manifestation* Festival commemorating the first manifestations of Christ to the Gentiles. It is observed January 6 and is sometimes called Little Christmas or Twelfth Day. Epiphany commemorates the coming of the wise men to worship the infant Jesus, His baptism, and His first miracle, at Cana.

**EPISCOPACY** 1. Government of a church by bishops, as in the ANGLICAN, EASTERN, METHODIST, and other churches. 2. The rank or tenure of a bishop. 3. A board of bishops.

**EPISCOPAL** Having to do with bishops, or with an ANGLICAN type of church. "Episcopal" commonly denotes membership in the PROTESTANT EPISCOPAL or a similar church, or government along Anglican lines.

**EPISCOPAL CHURCH** Popular name for the PROTESTANT EPISCOPAL CHURCH.

**EPISCOPAL CHURCH IN SCOTLAND** Scottish body of ANGLICANS.

**EPISCOPALIAN** A member of an Episcopal church, or a devotee of the episcopal system.

**EPISCOPATE** A group of bishops, or a bishop's office or term.

**EPISCOPI VAGANTES** *wandering bishops* Those who have been made bishops in an irregular manner, or who have been excommunicated.

**EPISCOPIUS, SIMON (1583–1643)** Dutch

ARMINIAN leader who sought to present a practical, rather than dogmatic, type of Christianity. His views of Christ and the TRINITY were considered by his opponents to downgrade the deity of the former and to subordinate the second and third persons of the latter. See SUBORDINATIONISM.

**EPISTEMOLOGY** Theory or study of the method of knowledge, and of its limitations and validity. Epistemology is important in science, philosophy, and theology, for the method of acquiring knowledge affects the results.

**EPISTLE** 1. In Scripture, a letter, as of Paul or John. 2. In church liturgy, the reading of a lesson from one of the New Testament Epistles.

**EPISTLER** The writer of an epistle, or the reader of the Epistle in a service of worship.

**EPISTLES, CATHOLIC** The epistles of Peter, John, and Jude, and the Epistle to the Hebrews, considered to have been addressed to the church in general.

**EPISTLES, PASTORAL** Paul's epistles to individual church leaders: Titus and I and II Timothy.

**EPISTLE SIDE** In a liturgical church, the right side of the altar where the Epistle is read or sung.

**EPISTLES OF CAPTIVITY or PRISON EPISTLES** Those letters of the Apostle Paul believed to have come from his prison cell in Rome: Ephesians, Philippians, Colossians, and Philemon.

**EPITAPH** Inscription, usually on a grave or tomb, honoring one dead.

**EPITRACHELION** Long silk stole worn by Eastern priests.

**EPONA** Celtic goddess, patroness of horses; often represented holding or riding a horse.

**EPSILON** Fifth letter in the Greek alphabet, corresponding to *e*.

**EPUNAMUN** Araucanian war god.

**EQUIPROBABILISM** Ethical system advocating the choice of either course, if there are two defensible moral options before one.

**EQUIVOCATION** Technically, using words with a double meaning.

**ERASMUS, DESIDERIUS (c.1466–1536)** Renaissance humanist and theologian. Ordained a priest in the ROMAN CATHOLIC CHURCH in 1492, he edited and popular-ized such works as writings of the church fathers. He prepared a text of the New Testament which opened the way for critical Bible research, pleaded for a return to simple primitive Christianity, and won a host of friends including HENRY VIII, Thomas MORE, and Martin LUTHER. But his ability to see both sides of a question and his pleas for tolerance brought him attacks from both sides in the Protestant REFORMATION; Luther attacked him and the Catholic Church banned his books.

**ERASTIANISM** Doctrine of control of the church by the state, named for ERASTUS' supposed adherence to that view.

**ERASTUS, THOMAS (1524–1583)** Swiss physician and follower of ZWINGLI whose fame today derives from a posthumous publication, *Explicatio.* This held that sinning Christians ought to be punished by the government rather than to be excommunicated or deprived of communion by the church; Erastus feared the dominance of the church in civil affairs. In spite of the assumption of the ERASTIANS, however, Erastus never discussed the relationships between church and state as such.

**EREBUS** The son of Chaos and father of Night, Greek personification of the darkness of HADES.

**EREMITE** Obsolete word for hermit, especially for a religious recluse.

**ERETZ** Jewish word for "the land."

**ERETZ YISROEL *the land of Israel*** Jewish term for Canaan.

**ERIDU** Ancient city of Mesopotamia associated with the cult of the Babylonian God EA.

**ERIGENA, JOHANNES SCOTUS (c.815–877)** "John the Scot," medieval theologian and philosopher long suspected of heresy for his close linking of God and the world through nature. Learned and thoughtful, he emphasized the love of God as well as the importance of reason.

**ERINYES or ERINYS** Greek name for the avenging goddesses, the FURIES.

**ERIS** Greek goddess of discord or rivalry.

**ERLANGEN SCHOOL** Those theologians of the University of Erlangen, Germany, during the late nineteenth century who based theology on personal religious experience rather than on outward authority.

**ERLKING** Scandinavian king of the elves, a mischievous creature.

**ERMENSUL** See IRMENSUL.

**ERMINE** Symbol of purity in Christian art.

**EROS** 1. Greek god of passion, romance, and fertility. He was worshiped at Athens and Thespiae. Greek art usually represents him as a handsome youth or as a baby with a bow. 2. Greek word for physical love, often contrasted with "AGAPE," spiritual self-giving love.

**ERRETT, ISAAC (1820–1888)** American minister of the Disciples of Christ and first editor of the *Christian Standard.* See CHRISTIAN CHURCHES (DISCIPLES OF CHRIST).

**ERROR** Ecclesiastically, error is what does not conform to the teachings of the church. Churchmen are now less prone than in the past to regard differences as error.

**ERSKINE, EBENEZER (1680–1754)** Scottish minister who founded the Secession Church in Scotland in 1733. A noted preacher, he was deposed from the established church after maintaining the right of a congregation to choose its own minister.

**ERSKINE, JOHN (1509–1591)** Scottish reformer and friend of John KNOX and George WISHART. He helped prepare the Second Book of Discipline.

**ERSKINE, THOMAS (1788–1870)** Scottish lawyer who applied Christianity to the spiritual and moral needs of man. Proposing a mystical as against a rigid view of CALVINISM, he was widely influential in his day as a Christian thinker.

**ERUV** *mixture* Rabbinic ways of reducing the difficulties of literal observance of the Sabbath laws. For example, food was placed at the end of 2,000 paces so that the limits of a SABBATH JOURNEY could be suspended.

**ERV** Abbreviation for the English Revised Version of the Bible, published in 1885. (See REVISED VERSION.)

**ESAIAS** See ISAIAH.

**ESAR-HADDON (seventh century B.C.)** Son of Sennacherib and king of Assyria 681–668 B.C. He attacked Egypt, ravaged Syria, and captured King Manasseh of Judah (II CHRONICLES 33:11).

**ESAU** *hairy* Isaac's older son who sold his birthright to his twin brother Jacob for a meal of red lentils and lost his father's blessing through Jacob's deception. Esau is also called Edom (GENESIS 25—28; 36:1).

**ESAUGETUH EMISEE** "Lord of the wind," Creek Indian creator-god.

**ESCALANTE, SILVESTRE (eighteenth century)** Spanish FRANCISCAN missionary in the American West. He was a pioneer explorer.

**ESCALLOP** See SCALLOP.

**ESCHATOLOGY** Study of the last things. Eschatology in Christian theology involves the final coming and triumph of Christ and His Kingdom, and sometimes the resurrection and related topics.

**ESDRAELON** The ancient plain of Jezreel, near Mt. Tabor and Mt. Carmel, running from the Mediterranean Sea to the Jordan River. In ancient times, it was both a trade route and a favorite battleground; today it is a fertile area of Israel.

**ESDRAS** 1. See EZRA. 2. I and II Esdras are among the books of the APOCRYPHA according to the listing in the King James Bible; in the Western Canon the same books are III and IV Esdras. IV (or II) Esdras sets forth the visions and revelations of Ezra and is believed to date from the second century A.D.

**ESHMUN** God of healing, worshiped especially at Sidon, Phoenicia.

**ESOTERIC** Term based on the custom in the Greek MYSTERY RELIGIONS to explain advanced doctrines only to the fully initiated.

**ESOTERIC BUDDHISM** Term for the esoteric school of wisdom preceding Gautama BUDDHA. A textbook in Theosophy bears this title.

**ESSENCE** In traditional philosophy and scholastic theology, essential being or substance, opposed to ACCIDENTS (accidental, temporary, or nonessential properties of something).

**ESSENES** One of the most fascinating groups in ancient JUDAISM. An ascetic order emphasizing ritual cleansings and communal living, it is mentioned at some length by JOSEPHUS and others but never in the New Testament—although the Essenes flourished from c.200 B.C. to A.D. c.200. Some believe that Christianity grew out of Essenism. Many scholars believe the DEAD SEA SCROLLS of Qumran came from an Essene community there.

**ESTABLISHED CHURCH** A church established by the government as the official church in a country. Often this means that state taxes support the church while the government both protects and rules it to some extent. In England the established church is the Church of England.

**ESTHER** 1. The lovely Jewish girl Hadassah who was chosen by AHASUERUS (Xerxes) to become queen of Persia, and who saved her people from destruction as planned by the wicked HAMAN. 2. The Old Testament book which tells the story of Esther. God is not named in Esther and the book is never mentioned by Jesus or the New Testament writers.

**ESTHER, SCROLL OF** Ornamental scroll from which the Scripture is read in PURIM, the Jewish festival commemorating the events of the book of Esther.

**ESTRANGEMENT** Alienation, separation from God or one's fellow men: the condition of modern man.

**ESTRE** Teutonic goddess of spring.

**ETERAH** Canaanite name for the moon god EL.

**ETERNAL** Beyond time; without beginning or end; everlasting.

**ETERNAL, THE** A translation of the God of Israel, Yahweh or Jehovah, whose name seems rooted in the idea of timeless being (EXODUS 3:14–15).

**ETERNAL CITY** The name indicating the seemingly timeless glory of Rome with its two millenniums of Christian history.

**ETERNAL GENERATION** Theological term for the relation of Father and Son in the Christian TRINITY. Christ, it is held, is eternally begotten of God.

**ETERNAL LIFE** This is a term used repeatedly in the New Testament writings of John. It is not so much a concept of future or everlasting bliss as of a divine quality of life possessed by those who believe in Jesus Christ.

**ETERNAL PUNISHMENT** A New Testament expression for which the present age shows little enthusiasm. Orthodox Christians, however, take Jesus' word about the eternal punishment of the lost as seriously as they take His promise of eternal joy to the saved.

**ETERNITY** The infinite future; heaven; timelessness; immortality. Strictly, immortality is a condition of every soul, while eternity is a divine quality.

**ETHICAL CULTURE** Movement instituted by Dr. Felix ADLER in 1876 in New York City. It emphasizes the study of ethical principles, service to others, fellowship, application of ethics to all relations of life. Beliefs about metaphysical topics are held unimportant. Religious services consist of nonsectarian hymns, readings from inspiring literature, and addresses on topics of the day. Ethical societies exist in the United States, England, and Austria. Those in the United States belong to the AMERICAN ETHICAL UNION. An International Union of Ethical Societies was organized in 1896.

**ETHICS** Study of moral principles and duty.

**ETHOS** That which distinguishes one religious or other group from others, as spirit or character.

**ET INCARNATUS EST** *and he was born* Expression of the INCARNATION of Christ in the NICENE CREED.

**ET RESURREXIT** *and he rose again* Statement of the RESURRECTION in the NICENE CREED.

**ETTWEIN, JOHN (1721–1802)** German Moravian missionary in America and a leader in the MORAVIAN CHURCH in the United States. For seventeen years he was its bishop.

**ETZ CHAIM** One of the two wooden cylinders on which a scroll of the TORAH is wound.

**EUCHARIST** *thanksgiving* The SACRAMENT, also called communion, holy communion, the Lord's Supper, and the Lord's Table, which is considered the highest act of Christian worship. Instituted by Christ (see LAST SUPPER), it repeats the action in which He gave His disciples bread and wine, representing His body and blood (MARK 14:22–24).

**EUCHARISTIC CONGRESS** World gathering of ROMAN CATHOLICS over which a papal delegate presides. During it the EUCHARIST is celebrated.

**EUCHARISTIC FAST** Abstaining from food or drink between midnight and the taking of the eucharist. At present it is considered that drinking water does not violate the fast; recently the regulations have been considerably relaxed.

**EUCHARISTIC LIGHTS** Candles used only during the eucharist.

**EUCHARISTIC VESTMENTS** Items of clothing worn by the presiding official at the eucharist. They are AMICE, ALB, STOLE, MANIPLE, GIRDLE, and CHASUBLE. In Anglican services the COPE, CASSOCK, and SURPLICE may be worn.

**EUCHITES** *praying ones* Greek name for sect also known as MESSALIANS (see).

**EUCHOLOGION** Main liturgical book of the EASTERN CHURCH.

**EUCKEN, RUDOLF CHRISTOPH (1846–1926)** German philosopher who advocated a striving for the spiritual life. He wrote *The Truth of Religion, The Life of the Spirit,* and many other works.

**EUDEMONISM** Term in ethics for defining well-being and happiness as man's supreme good.

**EUGENIUS** Four popes bore this name.

**EUHEMERISM** Interpretation of religious myths as fables built up by tradition about actual historical figures and events.

**EUHEMERUS (third century B.C.)** Greek author of a romance entitled *Sacred History* in which he proposed that gods and goddesses were men and women of the past who had become deified by tradition and history.

**EULOGIA** *blessing* 1. In the Eastern churches, blessed (but not consecrated) bread distributed after communion. 2. Bread distributed after mass to catechumens and others.

**EUNAPIUS (c.347–?)** Greek historian and NEOPLATONIST philosopher whose writings show antipathy to the Christian faith.

**EUNICE** *good victory* Jewish mother of St. Timothy; she trained him in the Scriptures and faith (II TIMOTHY 1:5). She had married a Greek.

**EUNOMIANISM** See ANOMOIANS.

**EUNOMIUS (c.333–c.393)** Leader among the extreme ARIANS; studied at Alexandria and became Bishop of Cyzicus. Banished several times, Eunomius taught that there is no essential similarity between God the Father and Christ the Son and that the two were not equal. He did not baptize in the name of the Trinity but in the name of the Creator. The Father, he said, produced the Son, who created the Holy Spirit.

**EUNUCH** An emasculated male. Eunuchs were not permitted to worship in the Jewish temple, but the mystery cults of the Mediterranean had eunuch priests. Moslems used eunuchs to protect their harems.

**EUODIAS AND SYNTYCHE** Two women in the church at Philippi, both, possibly, deaconesses, who quarrelled. Paul tried to get them to settle their differences (PHILIPPIANS 4:2–3).

**EUPHEMIA, ST. (fourth century)** Patron saint of the Chalcedon Church. She was a virgin and a martyr, much honored in the EASTERN CHURCH. Her feast day is September 16.

**EUPHRATES** Longest river in southwestern Asia, extending from the highlands of Turkey through Syria and Iraq to the Persian Gulf. A river of Eden (GENESIS 2:14), it once marked a boundary of the nation of Israel (II SAMUEL 8:3). On it were the important cities of Ur, Babylon, Erech, and Carcemish. The waters of the Euphrates rocked the cradle of civilization.

**EUROPEAN BAPTIST FEDERATION** Association of the BAPTISTS of Europe.

**EUROPEAN COUNCIL OF CHURCHES** Cooperative organization of the Christian churches of eastern and western Europe, formed in 1964. The council has seven presidents.

**EUSEBIAN CANONS** A method utilizing tables ("canons") and numbers which makes it possible to locate parallel passages in all the four Gospels easily. It was worked out by EUSEBIUS OF CAESAREA.

**EUSEBIUS** Name of many leaders of the early church.

**EUSEBIUS OF CAESAREA (c.260–c.340)** "Father of church history." Probably born in Palestine, Eusebius became Bishop of Caesarea about 314 and held that position for some twenty-five years. He took a moderate position at the Council of NICAEA, evidently moving later from a semi-Arian to a more orthodox theological position. His *History of the Christian Church* provides all that is known about many leaders of the first three hundred years of Christianity. Important among his many other works are *Martyrs of Palestine, The Life of Constantine, Against Marcellus, Church Theology,* and commentaries on Isaiah and the Psalms.

**EUSEBIUS OF NICOMEDIA (?–c.342)** Greek theologian who defended ARIUS at the Council of NICAEA, maintaining even more stoutly than EUSEBIUS OF CAESAREA that Christ is not of the same substance as God the Father. Eusebius was Patriarch of Constantinople 339–342. He may have baptized the Emperor CONSTANTINE.

**EUSTATHIUS (c.280–c.335)** Bishop of Berea and Patriarch of Antioch, deposed and banished because of his opposition to ARIANISM and to EUSEBIUS OF CAESAREA at the Council of NICAEA. He was also accused of SABELLIANISM. Eustathius was an eloquent speaker.

**EUSTATHIUS (?–c.1193)** Byzantine orator, scholar, historian, and Archbishop of Salonica. He sought to reform the weaknesses in monasticism, and succeeded in getting religious freedom for the people of Salonica when it was captured by William II of Sicily.

**EUTYCHES (c.380–c.456)** Presbyter and archimandrite of Constantinople who declared that Christ's human and divine natures were so perfectly fused that only one nature remained. The "Robber Synod" of EPHESUS accepted his views, but the Council of CHALCEDON declared them heretical and he was excommunicated and died in exile.

**EUTYCHIANISM** Theological acceptance of only one nature in Christ incarnate, thus actually denying His human nature.

**EUTYCHUS fortunate** Young man who fell asleep and fell from a third-story window while St. Paul preached. Paul restored him to life (ACTS 20:7–12).

**EUYUK** Ancient Turkish village with bas-relief carvings of Hittite religion. These show scenes involving the mother-goddess CYBELE and ATTIS, who was both her husband and her son.

**EVADISME** Parisian cult centering in sex, founded by Monsieur Ganneau about 1830. The cult's name emphasizes Eve; Mary was worshiped as "God-Mother." Ganneau was also a god in the new religion.

**EVAGRIUS (c.536–600)** Syrian ecclesiastical historian whose *Ecclesiastical History* provides important information about dogma in the fifth and sixth centuries, especially about the MONOPHYSITES and NESTORIANS.

**EVANGEL good news** 1. The gospel. 2. A messenger of the gospel or of good tidings.

**EVANGELIARY** Volume containing the four GOSPELS, or portions of them.

**EVANGELICAL** 1. Having to do with the gospel, or the Gospels of the New Testament. 2. In the spirit of New Testament Christianity. 3. Protestant, as opposed to Catholic, religion. 4. Emphasizing the doctrines of sin, salvation, and saving faith. 5. A person representing the viewpoint of definitions 3 or 4.

**EVANGELICAL ALLIANCE** Association formed in London in 1846 to unify individual Christians from many denominations and countries. A number of countries now have branches.

**EVANGELICAL AND REFORMED CHURCH** American denomination in which the Evangelical Synod of North America and the Reformed Church in the United States, with Swiss and German backgrounds, united in 1934. The new denomination merged in 1957 with the CONGREGATIONAL CHRISTIAN CHURCHES—representing another previous merger—to form the UNITED CHURCH OF CHRIST.

**EVANGELICAL ASSOCIATION** See EVANGELICAL CHURCH.

**EVANGELICAL CHURCH** Denomination in the United States, founded by Jacob ALBRIGHT under the name of the Evangelical Association, which merged in 1946 with the CHURCH OF THE UNITED BRETHREN IN CHRIST to form the EVANGELICAL UNITED BRETHREN CHURCH.

**EVANGELICAL CHURCH IN GERMANY** Union of 27 regional churches, most of them LUTHERAN, in Germany in 1948.

**EVANGELICAL CONGREGATIONAL CHURCH** American denomination consisting of members of the EVANGELICAL CHURCH who withdrew from it in 1894 when it was called the Evangelical Association and never reunited. They consider themselves ARMINIAN in doctrine and METHODIST in form of government.

**EVANGELICAL COVENANT CHURCH OF AMERICA** American denomination with roots in the established church of Sweden. It emphasizes the Bible, justification by faith, the Saviourhood and Lordship of Christ, the fellowship and sacraments of the church, and individual personal freedom.

**EVANGELICAL FREE CHURCH OF AMERICA**

American denomination resulting from a merger in 1950 of the Evangelical Free Church Association and the Swedish Evangelical Free Church.

**EVANGELICAL LUTHERAN CHURCH** American denomination with Norwegian roots which merged with two other Lutheran bodies in 1960 to form the AMERICAN LUTHERAN CHURCH.

**EVANGELICAL LUTHERAN CHURCH IN AMERICA (EIELSEN SYNOD)** American denomination with Norwegian background.

**EVANGELICAL LUTHERAN JOINT SYNOD OF WISCONSIN AND OTHER STATES** Former name of the Wisconsin Evangelical Lutheran Synod, an American denomination.

**EVANGELICAL LUTHERAN SYNOD** A denomination in the United States resulting from the refusal of certain Lutherans to join a merger of Norwegian Lutheran denominations into the EVANGELICAL LUTHERAN CHURCH.

**EVANGELICAL LUTHERAN SYNODICAL CONFERENCE** Conservative Lutheran association of which the SYNOD OF EVANGELICAL LUTHERAN CHURCHES and the LUTHERAN CHURCH—MISSOURI SYNOD are the present members. Formerly two other denominations belonged to the conference.

**EVANGELICAL MENNONITE BRETHREN** American denomination with Russian Mennonite background.

**EVANGELICAL MENNONITE CHURCH** Denomination, with Russian Mennonite background, in the United States and Canada.

**EVANGELICAL METHODIST CHURCH** Fundamentalist denomination founded in the United States in 1946 in protest against modernism in the METHODIST CHURCH.

**EVANGELICAL UNION** Scottish denomination, founded by the Rev. James Morison in 1843, which merged in 1896 with the Congregational Union of Scotland.

**EVANGELICAL UNITED BRETHREN CHURCH** American denomination, formed in 1946 through the union of the UNITED BRETHREN IN CHRIST and the EVANGELICAL CHURCH. In 1967 it voted to unite with the UNITED METHODIST CHURCH.

**EVANGELICAL UNITY OF THE CZECH-MORAVIAN BRETHREN IN NORTH AMERICA** Former name of the Unity of the Brethren, a Moravian church in the United States.

**EVANGELISCHE BUND** *evangelical league* Protestant alliance formed in 1886 in Germany for the purpose of defense against Catholic power.

**EVANGELISCHE GEMEINSCHAFT** *evangelical association* Name by which the EVANGELICAL CHURCH, founded by Jacob ALBRIGHT in the United States in 1803, was known in 1816.

**EVANGELISM** Proclaiming the good news of Jesus Christ with the intention of winning disciples for Him and the Church.

**EVANGELIST** 1. A messenger of the gospel of Christ. 2. One of the four Gospel writers: Matthew, Mark, Luke, or John. 3. A professional revivalist.

**EVANGELISTIC ASSOCIATIONS** Churches existing primarily to conduct evangelistic or mission work and characterized by that purpose.

**EVE** The first woman, wife of Adam and "mother of all living" (GENESIS 3:20). Lured by a serpent, she ate fruit forbidden by God and then persuaded Adam to do likewise.

**EVENSONG** Ancient Christian worship service held at evening and still held in ANGLICAN churches.

**EVERARD, JOHN (c.1575–c.1650)** English mystic and reformer whose knowledge of Christ and the Scriptures changed his preaching, brought him into association with "the lowest of men," and often brought him into court. He was once fined a thousand pounds for "heresies." "True salvation," he said, "is in the Word of God . . . a heart illumined with the Light of God is made better by everything."

**EVERGREEN** Symbol of immortality.

**EVERLASTING, THE** God.

**EVERYMAN** Title of a medieval morality play in which Everyman finds that of all his friends only Good Deeds will accompany him beyond this life.

**EVERY MEMBER CANVASS** A solicitation of all the members in a parish for financial support. It is an annual feature in many American churches.

**EVERY MEMBER VISITATION** A campaign to visit all the members of a church, usually for spiritual or evangelistic purposes.

**EVIDENTIAL** Providing evidence; a term common in spiritualist literature for things which persuade one of the reality of the life beyond, or of the continued existence of a deceased person.

**EVIL** Harmful, immoral, unethical, bad, or corrupt; the opposite of good and right. The existence of evil is a problem in many religions.

**EVIL EYE** 1. The glance of a certain type of individual which can harm or kill, according to superstition, common in the East. 2. In Jesus' phrase, an eye fixed on evil and leading its possessor astray (MATTHEW 6:23).

**EVIL-MERODACH (?–560 B.C.) man of Marduke** Son of Nebuchadnezzar and king of Babylonia who captured King Jehoiachin of Judah but treated him kindly.

**EVIL ONE, THE** Satan, the devil, the prince of darkness.

**EVIL SPIRITS** Invisible personal agents of evil doing, recognized by many religions. Christian theology recognizes a realm of such spirits headed by Satan.

**EVOLUTION** Term for the organic development of contemporary forms of life from dissimilar previous forms. When this hypothesis was publicized by Charles Darwin in the nineteenth century, it met widespread opposition from churchmen on the grounds that it denied the Genesis account of creation. Today it is generally accepted in liberal Christian circles and opposed in fundamentalist ones. A number of conservatives accept some form of theistic evolution. All Christians agree that there can be no real conflict between the Word of God and scientific facts; the controversies occur when theories clash.

**EVOLUTIONARY ETHICS** Term for the development believed to have taken place in the growth of morality. Some birds and animals are monogamous, while many practice self-giving love and subordination of individual to family or community interests. These presage many of the ethical ideals of man, so that it is possible to hypothesize an evolution in ethics paralleling that considered to have taken place in organic life. Some philosophers believe that the next step for man must be a spiritual one.

**EWALD, GEORG HEINRICH AUGUST VON (1803–1875)** German theologian, philologist, and orientalist. His Biblical exegesis and criticism were outstanding. His *History of Israel* was particularly influential.

He popularized the Development Hypothesis of the Scriptures.

**EXALTATION OF CHRIST** 1. In the New Testament, the glorification of Christ in the Resurrection, Ascension, and thereafter. 2. In ROMAN CATHOLIC theology, events in Christ's life such as the Transfiguration and Resurrection exhibiting His deity and glory.

**EXALTATION OF THE CROSS** Festival honoring the Cross, observed September 14, "Holy Cross Day."

**EXAMINATION OF CONSCIENCE** Introspection concerning one's life in the light of one's standards. CATHOLICISM requires such an examination before confession.

**EXARCH** *commander* In the Eastern churches, a bishop's deputy, an official ranking between a metropolitan and a patriarch, or an overseer of monasteries.

**EXAUDI** Sunday after ASCENSION DAY.

**EX CATHEDRA** *from the chair* 1. With authority. 2. Term for authoritative official utterances of the pope, considered binding and infallible.

**EXCEPTIONS, THE** Catalog of English Puritans' objections to the Prayer Book of 1604, presented at the Savoy Conference in 1661.

**EXCLUSION, RIGHT OF** Privilege once claimed by the heads of certain countries to prevent the election of a pope to whom they were opposed. Pope PIUS X prohibited such a right.

**EXCLUSIVE BRETHREN** Plymouth Brethren who exclude from their fellowship all those who differ from them or have not joined their group. In contrast, the "open" Brethren admit Christians outside their group to fellowship.

**EXCOMMUNICATION** Exclusion from the privileges of a religious community. An ancient religious practice, in the medieval period it might result in the victim's being cut off from all human contact. Today it is probably used more often in the ROMAN CATHOLIC CHURCH than in any other. Major excommunication cuts the person off from all rights and rites of the church, while minor excommunication does so from the mass or from some part of it.

**EXECRATE** Curse.

**EXEGESIS** Explanation of the meaning of a portion of Scripture, or critical exposition.

**EXEGETICAL PREACHING** Preaching, popular in many PROTESTANT churches, based upon explanation of a text of the Bible with close attention to the context and some application to contemporary life.

**EXEMPLARISM** 1. The "moral influence" theory of the atonement of Christ. Its adherents hold that the principal value of Christ's death was the moral example set of self-surrender and self-giving love. 2. Philosophical theory that the world was formed according to ideas and models eternally existent in the divine mind.

**EXEMPLUM** *example* Anecdote or example in medieval preaching.

**EXEMPTION** 1. Release of one's ecclesiastical control from his normal superior to another. In practice, authority over a priest who belonged to a monastic order might be transferred from his bishop to the superior of his order. 2. Release from a spiritual obligation or from the penalty for failure to meet it.

**EXEQUATUR** The right claimed by certain rulers, but condemned by Pope PIUS IX, to decide whether or not papal decrees shall take effect in their territories.

**EXEQUY** Funeral ceremony.

**EXERCISES, SPIRITUAL** 1. Prescribed forms of prayer, meditation, etc., considered beneficial to the spiritual life. 2. Title of a small volume, written by IGNATIUS OF LOYOLA, containing prayers, self-examinations, and meditations designed to lead to union with God.

**EXETER HALL** British term for evangelical religion such as that often represented in assemblies at Exeter Hall in London in the nineteenth century.

**EXHORTATION** This has a variety of ecclesiastical meanings. In the New Testament "to exhort" means to invite, entreat, admonish, encourage, or comfort, through personal or public address. In the church, exhortation usually refers to a special type of preaching.

**EXHORTER** One licensed in the METHODIST CHURCH to hold meetings for prayer and exhortation.

**EXILARCH** *prince of the captivity* Leader of the Jewish community during the BABYLONIAN CAPTIVITY.

**EXISTENTIALISM** Term, originating with Søren Kierkegaard, for a philosophical or theological point of view which emphasizes one's individual subjective experience and grasp of existence. It is a contemporary revolt against Platonic and traditional ordering of thought based upon rational grasp of abstract principles of "essence." Its exponents may be atheistic, as Jean Paul Sartre; Catholic, as Gabriel Marcel; Protestant, as KIERKEGAARD, Karl Barth, or Paul TILLICH; or Jewish, as Martin BUBER. All to some degree emphasize subjective experience over against abstract reason, moral decision and commitment over against abstract complacency, the freedom and importance of man over against impersonal forces, and human despair and helplessness over against a self-sufficient optimism. Religious existentialism, of course, tempers such feelings of helplessness and despair with faith in a God who is the ground of meaning and hope.

**EXISTENTIAL THEOLOGY** Theology resulting from recognition of the validity of existential philosophy. Those who have produced such theology, in addition to the men named above, include Nicholas BERDYAEV, Reinhold Niebuhr, Miguel de UNAMUNO, Dietrich BONHOEFFER, and Rudolf Bultmann.

**EX NIHILO NIHIL FIT** *from nothing, nothing comes* Latin statement expressing the need for a Creator of the universe.

**EXODUS** *going out* 1. The deliverance of the children of Israel from slavery in Egypt under the leadership of Moses. 2. The Bible book detailing the story of the Exodus, second in the Pentateuch. It includes the giving of the Ten Commandments and the forty years of wandering in the desert between the people's leaving Egypt and their arrival in the promised land of Canaan.

**EXOKAMELAUKION** Veil hanging behind the head of an Eastern clergyman.

**EX OPERE OPERATO** *from the work done* Theological phrase expressing the view that the sacraments are effective from their objective nature, quite apart from the subjective attitude or character of either the administrator or the recipient.

**EXORCISM** Casting out of evil spirits with religious rites. This was done much more often in the early and medieval church than it is today.

**EXOUCONTIANS** See ANOMOIANS.

**EXPECTANT, THE CHURCH** The earthly church awaiting its triumph.

**EXPECTATION SUNDAY** The Sunday between Ascension Day and Pentecost.

**EXPIATION** Making amends or paying a penalty. As the expiation of the believer's sins, Christ has paid the debt for them.

**EXPIATION, DAY OF** See ATONEMENT, DAY OF.

**EXPLICIT FAITH** Belief in the teachings of the church, knowledge of their meaning, and ability to explain them.

**EXPOSITION** 1. Explanation of the meaning of a writing, particularly of a portion of Scripture. 2. A discourse or sermon providing such explanation.

**EXPOSITION OF THE BLESSED SACRAMENT** Open display of the sacramental Host before the people for devotion.

**EXPOSITOR** One who provides an exposition of Scripture.

**EXPOSITORY PREACHING** A type of preaching in which an extended passage of Scripture is explained and applied.

**EXPRESS** In the King James Bible, *exact* (cf. HEBREWS 1:3).

**EXSURGE, DOMINE** *arise, O Lord* Title, based on its opening words, of Pope LEO X's bull excommunicating Martin LUTHER in 1520.

**EXTERNAL EVIDENCE** One kind of data upon which textual criticism of Scripture proceeds: the various texts, manuscripts, papyri, fragments, etc. from which the true text is sought. The other principal kind of data is internal evidence: information gathered from the content of Scripture.

**EXTERNALISM** Emphasis in religion upon outward forms and rites in contrast with attention to its real meaning and value.

**EXTRASENSORY PERCEPTION** Term for the apparent ability of certain persons to acquire knowledge outside of the normal limitations of sight, sound, and time. Its connection with religion is in: *a.* the gifts of mystics, saints, and prophets of various religions in this direction; *b.* the possible proof through such perception of a spiritual world beyond the known bounds of time, space, and matter.

**EXTREME UNCTION** Sacramental anointing with holy oil of a person in imminent danger of death.

**EXULTET** Hymn sung on Easter Eve at the blessing of the paschal candle.

**EYBESCHUTZ, JONATHAN** (1690–1764) German rabbi and talmudist accused by Rabbi Jacob Emden of heresy for issuing amulets which recognized Sabbatai Sebi as Messiah.

**EYE** Symbol of the omniscience of God.

**EZECHIEL** See EZEKIEL.

**EZEKIAS** See HEZEKIAH.

**EZEKIEL** *God strengthens* One of the four MAJOR PROPHETS of the Old Testament. Carried captive into Babylon in 597 B.C., he recorded his prophecies and visions in the Bible book bearing his name. Some of his messages were carried out not in words but in actions, as when he ate a book (CH. 3). He wrote of the glory of God, the restoration of the temple, and the responsibility of the individual.

**EZION-GEBER** *backbone of a giant* Port on the Gulf of Aqabah used by King Solomon. Here enormous copper refineries have been excavated.

**EZRA** *help* Jewish priest of the fifth century B.C. who returned from Babylonia to Jerusalem during the reign of Artaxerxes and there re-established his people in their worship and life. In the Hebrew canon the books of Ezra and Nehemiah were one work.

# F

**FA** God of fate in Dahomey, Africa.

**FABER, FREDERICK WILLIAM (1814–1863)** English poet, hymn writer, and theologian. A friend of John Henry NEWMAN and a convert to CATHOLICISM, he wrote among other hymns "Faith of Our Fathers," "There's a Wideness in God's Mercy," and "Hark, Hark, My Soul!"

**FABER, JOHANNES** German DOMINICAN theologian who, after early sympathies with ERASMUS, MELANCHTHON, ZWINGLI, and LUTHER, opposed the Reformers' views and defended Catholicism. He won the title "Hammer of the Heretics" and approved the burning to death of Balthasar HÜBMAIER.

**FABER STAPULENSIS, JACOBUS (c.1455–1536)** French priest and HUMANIST who became a Bible translator and reformer. His French-language Bible appeared in 1530; commentaries on the Epistles and Gospels, in 1512 and 1523. Condemned by the Sorbonne, he was protected by Francis I. He tutored Francis' son and taught Guillaume FAREL.

**FABIAN, ST. (?–250)** Roman pope and martyr, executed by the Emperor Decius. He organized the church at Rome into seven districts, each headed by a deacon. His feast day is January 20.

**FACULTY** A special ecclesiastical permission to do something otherwise unlawful.

**FA-HIEN (fourth century)** Chinese Buddhist monk who traveled throughout India for ten years assembling information about BUDDHISM. He crossed the Gobi Desert, visited Afghanistan, saw Buddha's birthplace and other places he had lived, talked with Buddhist monks, and copied sacred books then unknown in China. During his return to China across the Bay of Bengal his life was nearly lost in a storm, but following prayer to Kuan-yin he survived.

**FAIRBAIRN, ANDREW MARTIN (1838–1912)** British CONGREGATIONAL theologian who became first principal of Mansfield College, Oxford. Influenced by acquaintance with German theologians, he adopted a liberal theological stance. He wrote a number of books. In 1883 he was chairman of the CONGREGATIONAL UNION OF ENGLAND AND WALES.

**FAIR HAVENS** Bay on the southern side of the island of Crete from which the boat taking St. Paul to Rome was caught in a nearly disastrous northeaster (ACTS 27:13–44).

**FAIRY** A supernatural being in the folklore of many countries.

**FAITH** 1. Religious belief. 2. Giving oneself to be shaped by whatever or whomever one commits himself to. Man may have no god but the true God because whatever else he deifies will demonically control and dehumanize him. 3. Creed. 4. Christian faith is allegiance to and trust in Jesus Christ as Saviour and Lord.

**FAITH, THE** The body of revelation and doctrine characterizing Christianity.

**FAITHFUL, THE** CATHOLIC term for members of their church.

**FAITH HEALING** Physical healing accompanied by an attitude of faith or suggestion. Religious, historical, and medical records are filled with examples of healing without known physical means. Jesus healed many people through faith and the early Christians were promised that "the prayer of faith shall save the sick" (JAMES 5:14, 15). See also SPIRITUAL HEALING.

**FAKIH** MOSLEM theologian.

**FAKIR** 1. A MOSLEM ascetic or monk. 2. In India, a religious wonder-worker or beggar.

**FALASHAS** Ethiopian Jews who believe themselves to be descendants either of the ten lost tribes or of Menelek, a son said to have been born to Solomon and the Queen of Sheba. They follow the Old Testament Scriptures but do not know Hebrew or the Talmud.

**FALDA** White vestment worn by the pope on solemn occasions.

**FALDSTOOL** A folding stool used by CATHOLIC bishops when not sitting upon the throne.

**FALL, THE** The descent of Adam and Eve from the innocence in which they were created to knowledge of evil, thereby, according to Romans 5:12–21, plunging the human race into a condition of sin and death. From this it is saved by Jesus Christ, the Second Adam.

**FALSE CHRISTS** "Christs" or MESSIAHS who if possible would deceive the very elect (MATTHEW 24:24).

**FALSE DECRETALS** Ecclesiastical documents, attributed to popes before Gregory I, partly spurious and partly genuine. They helped shape the supremacy of the Roman SEE over the ROMAN CATHOLIC CHURCH.

**FAMILIAR** 1. A familiar spirit consulted for advice. Such a spirit is thought to be an evil spirit or that of a dead person. 2. A domestic servant of a high ROMAN CATHOLIC dignitary. 3. In a Court of INQUISITION, the arresting official.

**FAMILISTS** Sixteenth-century religionists who founded a "family of love" in Friesland and another in England. They emphasized the "true love of Jesus Christ" and are said to have been MYSTICAL, PANTHEISTIC, and ANTINOMIAN, proclaiming love as the essence of religion. Queen Elizabeth ordered the English group put down as a damnable sect.

**FAMILY PRAYERS** or **FAMILY WORSHIP** Worship in the home, advocated by many PROTESTANTS.

**FANA** *extinction* Ultimate ecstatic condition in SUFI mysticism, marking complete union with God.

**FANATICISM** Undue religious zeal. Activity which may appear normal within a group often appears fanatical to an opponent. Genuine fanaticism is morally, intellectually, or socially unbalanced.

**FANO, IMMANUEL (1548–1620)** Italian CABALIST.

**FANON** The name of several different religious accessories in the past, a fanon to-day is usually either a MANIPLE or a short papal cape.

**FAREL, GUILLAUME (1489–1565)** Influenced by Jacobus FABER STAPULENSIS, Farel became an eloquent preacher and exponent of REFORMATION doctrines in Germany and Switzerland. He persuaded Geneva to accept these doctrines, and persuaded John CALVIN to be Geneva's principal preacher and spiritual leader. He was Calvin's lifelong associate and friend.

**FARISSOL, ABRAHAM (1451–1526)** Spanish theologian and geographer who knew Columbus, wrote several commentaries, and upheld JUDAISM against ISLAM and CHRISTIANITY.

**FARLEY, JOHN MURPHY (1842–1918)** American CATHOLIC churchman. Born in Ireland, he became Archbishop of New York and a cardinal. He solidified and strengthened his diocese.

**FARRAR, FREDERICK WILLIAM (1831–1903)** India-born ANGLICAN cleric who became Dean of Canterbury and a writer of note. His *Life of Christ* became famous. He also wrote Bible commentaries, sermons, *The Life and Works of St. Paul*, and *The Early Days of Christianity*. In *Eternal Hope* he questioned eternal punishment.

**FARSE** Interpretation of the reading from the Epistle at mass.

**FARTHING** Word in the King James Bible for the Greek *assarion*, worth about one cent (MATTHEW 10:29).

**FASSEL, HIRSCH BAR (1802–1883)** Moravian talmudist and leader of REFORM JUDAISM.

**FASTI** *permissible* Roman word for days when public business might be done without offense to the gods, or for calendars listing holy days and other special days.

**FASTING** Going without food and sometimes drink, often for religious purposes. MOSES, DAVID, JESUS, and PAUL fasted on various occasions. Fasting persists but is not common in contemporary religion, except at such occasions as the Jewish Yom Kippur.

**FASTING COMMUNION** Term for participation in communion without eating or drinking for a stated time previously.

**FAST OF AB** See AB.

**FAST OF THE FIRSTBORN** Fasting by firstborn sons on the day before PASSOVER, in commemoration of the death angel's sparing the firstborn during the plagues in Egypt.

**FATALISM** Doctrine of the determinism of all events by a supreme controlling power. The Greeks, Romans, and Germans believed in Fates or Norns who wove the web of human destiny. ISLAM grants such power to Allah. A related concept in several Oriental religions is KARMA. Calvinistic Christianity sees all events in the hand of God, although it objects to the description "fatalistic" because fate and luck have no place in its philosophy; instead, events are under the control of a sovereign God. (See CALVINISM.) Peter declared that Christ's crucifixion was "by the determinate counsel and foreknowledge of God" (ACTS 2:23), while Paul spoke of being "predestinated according to the purpose of him who worketh all things after the counsel of his own will" (EPHESIANS 1:11).

**FATA VIAM INVENIENT** *the fates will find a way* Roman proverb.

**FATE** Controlling power in life. In Roman religion "fate" was the decree of the gods.

**FATES** In Greek and Roman religion three Fates controlled human events. In the former, Clotho spun the thread of man's life, Lachesis drew it off and measured it, and Atropos cut it.

**FATHER** 1. A name for God. 2. A priest, monk, or other official in Catholic and High Anglican churches.

**FATHER DIVINE** See DIVINE, FATHER.

**FATHER DIVINE'S PEACE MISSION** American religious group founded by M. J. Divine (possibly originally George Baker), whose followers believed he was God and would care for all their needs. They lived together in communal settlements known as peace missions or heavens.

**FATHERHOOD OF GOD** Term for the relation of God to man. By creation we are God's offspring (ACTS 17:28). Through Christ we are begotten anew (I PETER 1:3). Malachi asked, "Have we not all one father? Hath not one God created us?" (2:10).

**FATHERS OF THE CHURCH** Outstanding church leaders in the six hundred years between the end of the first century and the end of the seventh. They include CLEMENT, IGNATIUS, POLYCARP, IRENAEUS,

JUSTIN MARTYR, TERTULLIAN, JOHN CHRYSOSTOM, ATHANASIUS, EUSEBIUS, AUGUSTINE, and many others.

**FATIHA** *opening* Opening chapter of the KORAN, the "chapter of praise" used as a daily prayer by MOSLEMS. It is as follows: "In the name of Allah, the Merciful, the Compassionate. Praise belongeth unto Allah the Lord of the worlds, the King of the day of judgment. Thee do we serve and of Thee do we seek help. Guide us in the straight path, the path of those to whom Thou hast been gracious, not of those with whom Thou art angered or of those who go astray."

**FATIMA (c.606–632)** Daughter of MOHAMMED, greatly honored by Moslems.

**FATIMA** Village in Portugal where three illiterate children had six visions of the Virgin Mary in 1917. A large basilica and shrine of Our Lady of Fatima mark this famous CATHOLIC place of pilgrimage.

**FATIMITES or FATIMIDS** Members of a dynasty claiming descent from Mohammed's daughter Fatima. Founded by Said ibn Husein, the dynasty dominated much of northern Africa for a time. Its power ended in 1171. A SHIITE sect, the Fatimites are said to have permitted the drinking of wine and the sharing of wives and property; however, it seems probable that they differed little doctrinally from other MOSLEMS.

**FATUA** See BONA DEA.

**FATWA** HINDU or MOSLEM term for a legal opinion, or a sentence from an expert in canon law.

**FAULHABER, MICHAEL VON (1869–1952)** German CATHOLIC archbishop and cardinal. A pacifist, he denounced NAZISM. He made contributions both to patristic studies and to such contemporary matters as female emancipation.

**FAUN** In Roman religion, mischievous god or goddess partly human and partly in the form of a goat.

**FAUNA** See BONA DEA.

**FAUNCE, WILLIAM H. P. (1859–1930)** Baptist clergyman, theologian, and educator of the United States who became president of the World Peace Foundation.

**FAUNUS** Roman counterpart of the Greek Pan; god of fruitful fields and cattle, and their protector. He was honored with festivals in February and December.

**FAUST** In German legend, a doctor who sold his soul to the devil in exchange for such benefits as magic power and youth. The legend may have originated with a sixteenth-century charlatan who was credited by Johann Gast, a Protestant minister in Basel in the sixteenth century, with making a league with Satan to get supernatural gifts.

**FAYUM GOSPEL FRAGMENT** A bit of papyrus found in Egypt in 1882 inscribed with a narrative of Peter's denial of the Lord.

**FEA** Celtic goddess of war.

**FEAR** An important element in religion, although Christianity dispels it (II TIMOTHY 1:7; ACTS 27:24; I JOHN 4:18). The "fear of the Lord" commended in Scripture might be described as godly reverence for the Almighty.

**FEASTING** Ancient and natural expression of joy and fellowship with man and God. The LORD'S SUPPER grew out of a feast among friends. The PASSOVER meal is one of the most sacred events in Judaism.

**FEAST OF BOOTHS** See BOOTHS, FEAST OF.

**FEAST OF DEDICATION** See HANUKKAH.

**FEAST OF DEVOTION** Formerly a holiday of obligation, a British feast of devotion may be that of the Purification, the Finding of the Cross, St. George, St. Joseph, St. Michael, most of the Apostles, a number of others.

**FEAST OF FOOLS** Medieval European celebration burlesquing ecclesiastical procedures. It often involved election of a Pope of Fools, a Cardinal of Numbskulls, a BOY BISHOP, etc. Sometimes an ass was brought into a church, nuns dressed like men, and other ludicrous things were done.

**FEAST OF LIGHTS** See HANUKKAH.

**FEAST OF OBLIGATION** An important day requiring Catholics to rest and worship. Different countries have different feasts of obligation. In general, the Western Church honors these days: Sundays, CHRISTMAS, CIRCUMCISION, EPIPHANY, ASCENSION, CORPUS CHRISTI, ASSUMPTION, St. Peter and St. Paul, ALL SAINTS, the IMMACULATE CONCEPTION, and ST. JOSEPH.

**FEAST OF OUR LORD** A day of worship honoring some event in the life of Christ or some mystery related to Him.

**FEAST OF TABERNACLES** One of the three great historic festivals of JUDAISM; see BOOTHS, FEAST OF.

**FEAST OF THE ASS** See FEAST OF FOOLS.

**FEAST OF THE ASSUMPTION** See ASSUMPTION, FEAST OF.

**FEAST OF TRUMPETS** Jewish New Year festival; see ROSH HASHANAH.

**FEAST OF WEEKS** See PENTECOST.

**FEBRONIANISM** Catholic movement in eighteenth-century Germany similar to GALLICANISM in France. Named after Justinus Febronius, pseudonym of Bishop Johann Nikolaus von Hontheim, it unsuccessfully attacked certain papal powers and sought to nationalize the ROMAN CATHOLIC CHURCH, as well as to bring about church reunion.

**FEDERAL COUNCIL OF EVANGELICAL FREE CHURCHES** An association of "free" denominations in England and Wales, formed in 1919. In 1940 this group became part of the FREE CHURCH FEDERAL COUNCIL.

**FEDERAL COUNCIL OF THE CHURCHES OF CHRIST IN AMERICA** An association of PROTESTANT churches in the United States, organized in 1908. In 1950 it became the NATIONAL COUNCIL OF THE CHURCHES OF CHRIST IN THE UNITED STATES OF AMERICA.

**FEDERAL THEOLOGY** A PROTESTANT theology of redemption involving the concept of Adam as federal head of mankind and Christ as head of the new creation. See COVENANT THEOLOGY.

**FEDERATED CHURCHES** American term for situations where two or more churches in a community federate with one ministry although preserving their individual doctrines, government, etc.

**FEDERATION OF COLLEGE CATHOLIC CLUBS** International ROMAN CATHOLIC association of student clubs in various colleges and universities.

**FEE, JOHN GREGG (1816–1901)** American founder of two antislavery churches and of Berea College in Kentucky. For his abolitionist views he was disinherited and driven for a time from Kentucky.

**FEEHAN, PATRICK AUGUSTINE (1829–1902)** Irish-born American Catholic cleric who became Archbishop of Chicago, where he took special care of incoming immigrants.

**FEET WASHING** See FOOT WASHING.

**FELICITY (?–203)** Girl of Carthage martyred with Perpetua; both are CATHOLIC saints. Their feast day is March 6.

**FELIX** The name of five popes and anti-popes.
**FELIX (?–c.648)** First Bishop of East Anglia in England. His feast day is March 8.
**FELIX (1127–1212)** A founder of the order of Redemptionists. Born in Valois, France, he was for a time a hermit. He established the Redemptionists to redeem Christians captured by the Saracens.
**FELIX, ANTONIUS** Procurator of Judea addressed by Paul at Caesarea (ACTS 23; 24). Felix was a cruel oppressor of the Jews during office and about A.D. 60 was recalled to Rome.
**FELL, JOHN (1625–1686)** CHURCH OF ENGLAND clergyman who while Bishop of Oxford erected many buildings and developed Oxford University Press.
**FELLOWSHIP** In the New Testament and the church, the communion or brotherhood or warm relationship of believers with one another, and a similar relationship with God through Christ.
**FELLOWSHIP, RIGHT HAND OF** Term for welcoming members or officers into their place in a church.
**FELLOWSHIP OF RECONCILIATION** International organization stressing human oneness and proclaiming love as "the effective force for overcoming evil and transforming society into a creative fellowship." With branches in twenty-five countries, it renounces war and advocates nonviolence.
**FELLOWSHIP OF ST. ALBAN AND ST. SERGIUS** Organization formed to further understanding between the churches of England and Russia.
**FENELON, FRANCOIS DE SALIGNAC DE LA MOTHE (1651–1715)** French priest, preacher, writer, and mystic. He became Archbishop of Cambrai, opposed JANSENISM, and sought to convert the HUGUENOTS. He defended a fellow mystic, Madame GUYON, until her quietism was condemned. For his own mysticism he was banished to Cambrai.
**FENG HUANG phoenix** In Chinese mythology, a bizarre creature whose appearance heralds the dawn of a day of worldwide goodness.
**FENG SHUI** See FUNG SHUI.
**FENRIR** In Germanic myth, a wolf who is an enemy of the gods.
**FENWICK, EDWARD DOMINIC (1768–1832)** American DOMINICAN clergyman who

served as a missionary in the Midwest, became first Bishop of Cincinnati, founded in Kentucky the first Dominican headquarters in America, and established Xavier University.
**FERETORY** Shrine holding the remains or relics of a saint.
**FERIA feast day** In ANGLICAN and CATHOLIC churches, a day on which there is no religious festival.
**FERID ED-DIN ATTAT pearl of the faith (?–c.1229)** Persian writer who became a SUFI, wrote several books about Sufiism, and is considered "one of the greatest mystic poets of ISLAM."
**FERMENTARIAN** One who celebrates communion with leavened bread.
**FERMENTUM leaven** Portions of bread from the Papal Mass sent to parish priests in fifth-century Rome to symbolize the unity of the faithful.
**FERN** Religious symbol of sincerity and humility.
**FERONIA** Etruscan fertility goddess.
**FERRAR, NICHOLAS (1592–1637)** CHURCH OF ENGLAND theologian who established a monastic community at Little Gidding, emphasizing ascetic devotion, religious instruction, and aid to the poor. Members bound books and produced harmonies of the Gospels. Little Gidding was raided and destroyed by the PURITANS in 1646.
**FERTILE CRESCENT** Term coined by archaeologist James Breasted for the semicircular region extending northward from Palestine through Syria and Phoenicia, eastward along the Tigris River, and southeast through Mesopotamia to the Persian Gulf. It was along this route that Abraham and many others of ancient time traveled between Palestine and the East.
**FERTILITY RITES** Religious ceremonies connected with marriage, childbirth, seedtime, and harvest. They often involved sacred prostitution. In various early religions and cults they took many different forms, some of them surviving into contemporary customs.
**FESTIVAL** Holy day or feast day. See FEASTING and following entries.
**FESTUS, PORCIUS** Governor of Judea who followed FELIX. St. Paul spoke before him on his journey to Rome (ACTS 25; 26).
**FETE-DIEU feast of God** CORPUS CHRISTI in France.

**FETISH** *charm* Object of particular devotion, believed to have saving power. Many fetishes are adopted in religious circles for psychological reasons without the knowledge or approval of spiritual leaders.

**FETISHISM** Any belief that some material object has supernatural powers. It is found in many religions.

**FETTER DIENSTAG** *Fat Tuesday* German name for SHROVE TUESDAY.

**FETTER DONNERSTAG** *Fat Thursday* German name for the Thursday before ASH WEDNESDAY.

**FEUDALISM** Medieval social and economic structure rising from the peasants through a hierarchy of nobles to the king. It was influenced by the medieval church, which had a similar hierarchic structure.

**FEUERBACH, LUDWIG ANDREAS (1804–1872)** German philosopher who held that Christianity had already long vanished from the life of man and that "it is nothing more than a fixed idea." Religion, he said, is actually consciousness of man himself; God, a projection of man's needs with no separate existence of His own. To some extent he influenced NIETZSCHE, Engels and Marx.

**FEZ** City of Morocco once noted as a MOSLEM center of learning. In it is the Karueein, Africa's largest mosque, and over a hundred other mosques. The mosque of Mulai Idris is considered to be particularly holy; the streets near it may not be used by Christians, Jews, or four-footed animals.

**FIACRE, ST. (seventh century)** Irish hermit, patron of Brie, France, who founded a monastery in that province.

**FIAT** *let it be done* Authoritative decree.

**FIAT JUSTITIA, RUAT COELUM** *let justice be done, though heaven fall* Ancient slogan.

**FIAT LUX** *let there be light* 1. Religious motto. 2. God's creative word at the beginning of the universe (GENESIS 1:3).

**FICHTE, IMMANUEL HERMANN VON (1796–1879)** German philosopher who held that God is an infinite Person who loves finite persons in whom He realizes Himself. He opposed HEGELIAN pantheism, admired SCHLEIERMACHER, and praised personal and social morality.

**FICHTE, JOHANN GOTTLIEB (1762–1814)** German philosopher whose dialectic idealism won praise from KANT and charges of atheism from others. He believed in a

moral order and emphasized doing good. To him religious symbols may be valuable but are often imperfect makeshifts; "every representation of God is a misrepresentation." Nevertheless, he taught that God is absolute Life and the moral will of the universe.

**FICINO, MARSILIO (1433–1499)** Italian philosopher and humanist whose views combined NEOPLATONIST teachings with Christianity.

**FIDEI DEFENSOR** *defender of the faith* Title of kings and inscription on coins in Great Britain. Pope Leo X awarded the title to Henry VIII for his anti-Lutheran *Defence of the Seven Sacraments.*

**FIDEISM** 1. In PROTESTANTISM, term for the doctrine that salvation and spiritual certitude rest upon faith alone rather than upon reason and doctrinal beliefs. 2. In CATHOLICISM, term for the doctrine, considered erroneous, that no truth may be acquired by reason alone, but that faith and revelation must precede reason.

**FIFTH MONARCHY MEN** PURITAN extremists in England who believed that the Kingdom of Christ—a fifth monarchy foreseen in Daniel 2 to succeed the Assyrian, Persian, Greek, and Roman empires—was at hand and tried to bring it in with armed uprisings in 1657 and 1661. Their leaders were Major General Thomas Harrison, Major General Robert Overton, Thomas Venner, and others.

**FIG** Fruit often eaten in Bible times. In religious art it often symbolizes lust and fertility.

**FIGURE** In the King James Bible, a type or representation (cf. ROMANS 5:14).

**FIGURINES** Small statues of gods, people, and animals were used in ancient religious rites throughout the Near East. An example is the use of replicas of food and servants in Egyptian tombs. (Cf. GENESIS 31:19, 34; JEREMIAH 10:4.)

**FILIOQUE** *and from the Son* Phrase in the NICENE CREED describing the procession of the Holy Ghost both from the Father and from the Son. This the Western Church accepts, but the Eastern Church rejects it.

**FINALISM** Philosophical view that there is a purpose in the universe and that events proceed toward a final end.

**FINAL PERSEVERANCE** CALVINISTIC doctrine that the redeemed will persevere in

Christian grace and can be assured of final eternal salvation. ARMINIANS reject this formulation because of their emphasis on free will.

**FINITE** Limited, determinable, or human, in contrast to infinite, limitless, unconditioned, or divine. Christian theology holds that only God is infinite.

**FINITUDE** State of being finite.

**FINNEY, CHARLES GRANDISON (1792–1875)** New England lawyer who became a sensational evangelist throughout the eastern United States, England, and Scotland. He became the first pastor of New York's Broadway Tabernacle and first professor of theology and president at Oberlin College in Ohio. His unique theological views became known as OBERLIN THEOLOGY. In them he set forth a synthesis of CALVINISM and ARMINIANISM.

**FINNIAN, ST. (c.495–579)** "Tutor of the Saints of Ireland" who founded a monastery at Moville and became patron of Ulster. His feast day is December 12.

**FINNISH APOSTOLIC LUTHERAN CHURCH OF AMERICA** See APOSTOLIC LUTHERAN CHURCH OF AMERICA.

**FINNISH EVANGELICAL LUTHERAN CHURCH** American denomination, organized in 1890, which combined with two other Lutheran bodies in 1962 to form the LUTHERAN CHURCH IN AMERICA.

**FIORETTI** *little flowers* "The Little Flowers of St. Francis," an anthology of legends about St. FRANCIS and his companions. They exhibit the childlike spirit of Francis' faith and love.

**FIQH** The canon law and theology of ISLAM, accepted by all four of its orthodox schools (the HANAFITE, MALIKITE, SHAFIITE, and HANBALITE).

**FIR TREE** In religious art, a symbol of the patient and the redeemed.

**FIRE** An ancient element in religion, often representing God and the soul. The ZOROASTRIANS worshiped fire; the fire on their altars might never go out. The perpetual fire in Roman religion was tended by the VESTAL VIRGINS. The Celts and Incas also guarded perpetual fires. Altar fires and the light of the seven-branched candlestick were important in JUDAISM's tabernacle and temple. In BUDDHISM the Three Fires of lust, hate, and illusion must be banished from the mind. The New Testament predicts the final destruction of the world by fire (II PETER 3:7). Christian art uses fire as a symbol of zeal, martyrdom, or hell.

**FIRE BAPTIZED HOLINESS CHURCH** Pentecostal group in the United States with Negro membership, headed by a bishop.

**FIRE BAPTIZED HOLINESS CHURCH (WESLEYAN)** United States Holiness group founded about 1890. Its government structure is METHODIST.

**FIRE WORSHIPERS** Erroneous name for PARSEES.

**FIRKIN** Liquid measure in the King James Bible equivalent to about eight gallons.

**FIRMAMENT** Word for the sky in the King James Bible, based on the Vulgate's *firmamentum* (cf. GENESIS 1:8).

**FIRST AND LAST** Title of Christ in Revelation 1:11.

**FIRST BOOK OF DISCIPLINE** PRESBYTERIAN service book prepared by John KNOX.

**FIRSTBORN** Among the Hebrews in the Old Testament period, the first of the flocks and crops were offered in sacrifice, and the firstborn male was offered for the priesthood. Special sanctity and privilege attended the firstborn.

**FIRST CAUSE** In Aristotelian philosophy, the ultimate cause of all; in Christian theology, God.

**FIRST DAY SABBATH** Term for Sunday as the CHRISTIAN day of rest and worship.

**FIRST ESTATE** Reference to the innocence of primeval man, before the fall.

**FIRST FRIDAY** Catholic term for the special grace promised those who receive the eucharist on the first Friday of every month for nine months. This promise is said to have been made by Christ to St. Margaret Mary ALACOQUE in the seventeenth century. ROMAN CATHOLICS, however, are warned by the church that the disposition of the heart is more essential to salvation than the day on which communion is taken.

**FIRST FRUITS** Hebrew term for the first issue of crops, animals, or people, considered especially holy. See FIRSTBORN.

**FIRSTLING** First offspring. See FIRSTBORN.

**FISH** A popular food mentioned in the New Testament, often in connection with Jesus and the disciples. The early Christians symbolized Christ by the letters in the Greek word for fish; see ACROSTIC.

**FISHER, JOHN, ST. (c.1469–1535)** English bishop and cardinal who brought ERAS-MUS to Cambridge University to lecture and advocated reforms in the church, but was against the proposals by LUTHER and others for a reformation of doctrine. Refusing to acknowledge the legitimacy of the marriage of Henry VIII to Catherine, or his claim to be supreme head of the CHURCH OF ENGLAND, Bishop Fisher was beheaded. In 1936 he was canonized. His feast day is July 9.

**FISKE, JOHN (1842–1901)** American writer and philosopher who sought to reconcile orthodox theism with the scientific findings of Herbert Spencer. He called God "the infinite and eternal Power that is manifested in every pulsation of the universe." He was a popular writer and lecturer.

**FISTULA** Golden tube through which lay participants received the eucharist wine in the Middle Ages, and through which the pope and his deacon receive it now.

**FIVE** Religious symbol of the five wounds of Christ when crucified: in His hands, feet, and side.

**FIVE ARTICLES OF ARMINIANISM** The classic five points differentiating this system from Calvinism: *a.* Election based on the divine foreknowledge of the sinner's faith; *b.* Universal atonement; *c.* Salvation only by grace; *d.* Grace necessary but not irresistible; *e.* Falling from grace possible.

**FIVE BOOKS OF MOSES** Traditionally, the first five books of the Bible, in the Pentateuch: Genesis, Exodus, Leviticus, Numbers, and Deuteronomy.

**FIVE CLASSICS** The five Scriptures of CONFUCIANISM: the books of Changes, Rites, History, Odes, and the Annals of Spring and Fall.

**FIVE HOUSES** The five schools of Chinese ZEN Buddhism at the end of the T'ang Dynasty, about 900 A.D.

**FIVE MILE ACT** English law, passed in 1665, prohibiting any Nonconformist clergyman from coming within five miles of his former parish, or of any corporate town or city. It also prevented him from teaching unless he vowed loyalty to the established order and promised nonresistance.

**FIVE POINTS OF CALVINISM** Five distinctive doctrines outlined at the Synod of DORT in 1610: total inability to do good, unconditional election, limited atonement, irresistible grace, and final perseverance of the saints.

**FIVE SCROLLS** Five short books read in the synagogue on special occasions. Esther is read at PURIM, the Song of Solomon at PASSOVER, Ruth at PENTECOST, Lamentations at the Feast of AB, and Ecclesiastes at the Feast of BOOTHS.

**FIVE YEARS MEETING OF FRIENDS** See SOCIETY OF FRIENDS (FIVE YEARS MEETING).

**FLABELLUM** Fan of ostrich plumes carried on each side of the pope in processions.

**FLAGELLANTS** Beginning in the twelfth century, processions of praying Europeans often bared their backs and lashed themselves in public penance. Such groups continued throughout the Middle Ages, particularly in times of turmoil or pestilence such as the BLACK DEATH, although they were discouraged, prohibited, and exterminated by the church. Such flagellants as Mexico's PENITENTES still exist in Latin lands.

**FLAGELLATION** Whipping for religious purposes has existed from ancient times. The Spartans flogged their children before the altars of Artemis, the Egyptians flogged themselves for the sake of Isis, initiates into the mystery religions were flogged to partake of the sufferings of their slain gods, and flogging had a part in the religions of Rome and India. Flagellation was often a method of punishment in ancient Christian monasteries, and though the flagellants were condemned, it was an approved form of penance for centuries. Self-flagellation is still required of the CISTERCIANS.

**FLAME, SACRED** See FIRE.

**FLAMENS** Highly honored Roman priests chosen to offer daily sacrifices to such gods as Jupiter, Quirinus, and Mars. Elected for life and paid well, they wore laurel wreaths and conelike white caps. The chief priest, *flamen Dialis,* was given a seat in the Senate and prevented from seeing an army or people working, from taking oaths, from touching a horse, and from leaving the city. The prisoner who met a *flamen Dialis* in the streets was pardoned of his offense.

**FLAVIUS ARRIANUS** See ARRIAN.

**FLECHE** Slender spire on the ridge of a church roof. It often intersects the TRANSEPT and NAVE.

**FLEMAL, BERTHOLET (1614–1675)** Important Flemish painter of many religious scenes. His pictures adorned many churches, and his "Mysteries of the Old and New Testaments" is in the Louvre.

**FLEMING, PAUL WILLIAM (1910–1950)** American missionary and founder of the New Tribes Mission which specializes in evangelizing inaccessible peoples.

**FLESH** 1. The body or physical aspects of man (cf. MARK 10:8). 2. The sinful element in man's life (EPHESIANS 2:3).

**FLESHHOOK** Metal fork used by a priest to handle meat at the Jewish altar of sacrifice (I CHRONICLES 28:17).

**FLESHPOT** Vessel for cooking meat, symbolizing affluence (EXODUS 16:3).

**FLETCHER, GILES (c.1585–1623)** English clergyman and poet whose work influenced and delighted John MILTON. A famous preacher whose prayers were continuous allegories, he wrote *Christ's Victorie and Triumph, in Heaven, in Earth, over and after Death* and other poems.

**FLETCHER, JOHN WILLIAM (1729–1785)** Saintly CHURCH OF ENGLAND clergyman who aided John WESLEY in his evangelistic labors, defending ARMINIANISM and attacking UNITARIANISM. Wesley called him a perfect man and VOLTAIRE said he was as perfect as Christ.

**FLEUR DE LIS** *lilyflower* Symbol of MARY, based on the symbolism of the lily. In Egypt it symbolized life and resurrection.

**FLEURY, CLAUDE (1640–1723)** Learned French church historian. A priest and confessor to King Louis XV, he wrote a twenty-volume *Church History* regarded as the first work of its kind to be organized on such a broad scale.

**FLIEDNER, THEODOR (1800–1864)** German PROTESTANT pastor who tried to get imprisoned in order to appreciate prison life; failing, he organized a prison society and many other social institutions. He established a refuge for women discharged from prison, orphanages, an insane asylum, and a deaconess house which inspired some of the work of Florence Nightingale. He founded more than a hundred

"mother houses" and philanthropic centers in many parts of the world.

**FLIGHT INTO EGYPT** Term for the trip made by Joseph, Mary, and the infant Jesus to escape Herod's slaughter of the innocents (MATTHEW 2:13–23). Many religious paintings have this as a theme.

**FLOCK** Term for a Christian congregation, based on Jesus' work as the Good Shepherd. He once said, "Fear not, little flock."

**FLOOD** See DELUGE.

**FLORA** Roman goddess of flowers.

**FLORALIA** Flora's festival, observed with amoral celebrations for six days in the spring.

**FLORENCE** City of Italy which was the heart of the Renaissance for two centuries. SAVONAROLA, MICHELANGELO, the Medici, LEONARDO DA VINCI, RAPHAEL, Machiavelli, the DELLA ROBBIAS, GIOTTO, Fra ANGELICO, and other illustrious sons added to the city's glory. It contains many beautiful churches and treasures of art.

**FLORENCE, COUNCIL OF** See COUNCIL OF FERRARA-FLORENCE.

**FLORIAN, ST. (third century)** Martyr of Austria, drowned in the persecutions of Diocletian for confessing his faith. A monastery with his name stands on the site of his supposed tomb. His aid is sought against fire. His feast day is May 4.

**FLORIGELIA** *anthologies* Collections of quotations, particularly from the Church Fathers, compiled for theological purposes.

**FLUDD, ROBERT (1574–1637)** English mystic and physician believed to have performed a number of faith healings. He has been called a pantheistic materialist and the father of FREEMASONRY. He upheld the ROSICRUCIANS.

**FLÜGEL, OTTO (1842–1921)** German pastor and philosopher who held that God is finite and neither eternal nor omnipotent.

**FLY** Symbol of evil in religious art.

**FOAKES-JACKSON, FREDERICK JOHN (1855–1941)** English scholar and author of many books in the area of church history.

**FO-ISM** Archaic name of Chinese BUDDHISM.

**FOLDED CHASUBLE** Priestly vestment rolled or pinned up for wear in penitential seasons.

**FOLK CHURCH** Term for a church coextensive with a nation, as the denominations in most countries of the modern world. This concept developed in Lutheranism's history, in which the prince of a territory decided the faith of his subjects. The ROMAN CATHOLIC CHURCH, the WORLD COUNCIL OF CHURCHES, and certain faiths such as ISLAM and BUDDHISM transcend nationalistic boundaries. No such boundaries evidently circumscribed Christ's vision of the church (MATTHEW 28:18–28).

**FONT** Baptismal container. In the church's early centuries this was often a tank. The contemporary font is often a bowl in a stone pedestal.

**FONTANA, DOMENICO (1543–1607)** Chief architect for Pope SIXTUS V; designer of many buildings in Rome and the Vatican, including the Lateran palace and the dome of St. Peter's.

**FONTREVAULT** An order of monks and nuns based on the BENEDICTINE rule, established about 1100 by Robert of Arbrissel in western France. The order had houses in England and Spain but its greatest strength was always in France.

**FOOL** One without natural or divine wisdom. The people of Israel anciently recognized wisdom as conformity with the good, righteous, commonsensical truth and will of God; therefore only the fool could say in his heart that there was no God. In some religions and cultures the fool—the simpleton or the insane person—has been endowed with saintly or supernatural qualities meriting protection and awe.

**FOOLS, FEAST OF** See FEAST OF FOOLS.

**FOOT** Symbol of service and humility. Christians are advised by St. Paul to have their feet shod with the preparation of the gospel of peace (EPHESIANS 6:15). Christ washed the disciples' feet (JOHN 13:5).

**FOOTPACE** The upper step before an altar, on which the officiant stands while celebrating the eucharist.

**FOOTSTOOL** Symbolically, the earth (ISAIAH 66:1), or the enemies of the people of God (PSALM 110:1).

**FOOT WASHING** In the East the feet are washed as a social custom, in religious rites, for cleansing, and to show hospitality. At the LAST SUPPER Christ washed the disciples' feet to show what love and service do (JOHN 13:1–17). Throughout the history of Christianity, Christians have often followed His example. In the Middle Ages kings and monks often washed the feet of the poor. Some American denominations—DUNKERS, MENNONITES, and MORAVIANS, for example—regard the washing of one another's feet as an essential church ordinance.

**FORBEARANCE** New Testament word for patience or enduring, loving mercy and kindness (cf. ROMANS 2:4).

**FOREIGNER** In every cult and culture the alien is viewed with suspicion and distrust. Israel, however, was bidden to treat the foreigner (Gentile) who lived in the land with tolerance, kindness, and charity (EXODUS 20:10; DEUTERONOMY 24:14–21; 27:19). Christ commanded love of neighbors and enemies, and willed to bring all nations into His Kingdom (MATTHEW 28:18–20).

**FOREIGN MISSIONS** Term, now becoming obsolete in many denominations, for evangelizing and aiding those in countries other than those of the missioners or missionaries. PROTESTANTISM in nineteenth-century England and America felt considerable compulsion to evangelize the whole world and complete Christ's Great Commission. Twentieth-century Protestants tend to favor the term "mission" for all Christian work at home or abroad, and to exchange fraternal workers with Christian churches in other lands rather than to unilaterally send out missionaries.

**FOREIGN MISSIONS CONFERENCE OF NORTH AMERICA** Former name of the Division of Foreign Missions of the NATIONAL COUNCIL OF THE CHURCHES OF CHRIST IN THE UNITED STATES OF AMERICA. It began officially in 1893 under the leadership of such men as Robert E. Speer and John R. MOTT, representing twenty-one foreign mission boards.

**FOREIGN MISSION SOCIETIES** Organizations in churches promoting international EVANGELISM.

**FOREKNOWLEDGE** 1. Prescience, claimed by many mystics, saints, prophets, and religious people. 2. God's knowledge of future events. CALVINISTS historically connect such divine knowledge with soteriological election and predestination, while ARMINIANS hold that the divine foreknowledge does not determine future events because of the freedom of the human will.

**FORENAME** Christian or first name of a person.

**FOREORDINATION** Theological term for the divine predetermination of the individual for eternal salvation. CALVIN wrote, ". . . eternal life is foreordained for some, and eternal damnation for others. Every man, therefore, . . . is, we say, predestined either to life or to death." PAUL wrote of God, "For whom he did foreknow, he also did predestinate to be conformed to the image of his Son" (ROMANS 8:29). ARMINIANS, LUTHERANS, CATHOLICS and others accept ordination to life but not predestination to destruction.

**FORERUNNER** One who goes before and prepares the way, as John did for Jesus (MARK 1:3–9).

**FOREST, JOHN (1471–1538)** English FRANCISCAN burned at the stake for opposing the plans of Henry VIII to divorce Catherine of Aragon and make himself head of the CHURCH OF ENGLAND.

**FORGIVENESS** Man's sense of guilt for recognized wrongdoing makes some form of divine forgiveness or removal of guilt a part of many religions. Various sacrifices were designed to appease various gods. JUDAISM and CHRISTIANITY proclaim the willingness of God to forgive sins, although in both there are ethical demands for repentance and the forgiveness of one's neighbor. The Jewish prophets emphasized the necessity for turning away from evil in receiving the forgiveness of God (ISAIAH 1:18; HOSEA 14:1, 2). Jesus stated the Father's willingness to forgive, but He also emphasized the need for men to forgive others (MATTHEW 6:12–15). The New Testament community rejoiced in the assurance of forgiveness of sin through Christ (EPHESIANS 1:7; COLOSSIANS 1:14).

**FORM** 1. According to the philosophical point of view deriving from ARISTOTLE, form is the outward pattern or arrangement which the undifferentiated matter in something finally takes, as wood takes the form of a tree or a board or a violin, depending upon the causative factors. Thus form denotes actuality while matter implies potentiality. 2. SCHOLASTIC philosophers carried this Aristotelian concept a step further to make form equivalent to essence (as opposed to incomplete substance) or perfection (as opposed to what

is potential or in process of becoming). The form of a sacrament was considered most important because a change in the form—as of the words of consecration—might change or negate the sacrament itself. 3. KANT spoke of the forms of space and time and other a priori abstractions into which we fit our experiences, although he held that things in themselves are unknowable. 4. That Christ was originally "in the form of God" (PHILIPPIANS 2:6) indicates that He had not only the appearance but also the essence and nature of God.

**FORMALISM** 1. Emphasis on ritual or outward form at the expense of reality and inner force. 2. Philosophically, stress on abstract principles of formulation rather than on concrete reality. In general, EXISTENTIALISM is a revolt against such abstraction.

**FORM CRITICISM** Term for study of the Scriptures with the intention of getting at the original data behind the sayings, legends, miracle stories, etc. which the form critics believe grew up around such data. Members of this school of criticism emphasize the role of the believing community in adapting and shaping this material into its present form. Martin DIBELIUS and Rudolf Bultmann are leaders in this approach, which has been influential in contemporary theology.

**FORMER PROPHETS** In the Hebrew canon, the books which follow the Pentateuch: Joshua through II Kings with the omission of Ruth. The title "Former Prophets" distinguishes the writers, believed to have been spokesmen for God (thus "prophets"), from the later prophets Hosea, Isaiah, etc.

**FORMER RAIN** Israelite term for the fall rains, distinguishing them from the spring or latter rains which ended the rainy season.

**FORMGESCHICHTE** *form criticism* Original German name for FORM CRITICISM.

**FORMORIANS** Pre-Celtic gods of Ireland. They became demonic powers with the establishment of the new Celtic divinities.

**FORMOSUS (c.816–896)** Excommunicated by Pope JOHN VIII after opposing him, Formosus was restored by Pope Marinus and himself became pope in 891. He crowned Arnulf of Germany emperor to the disgust of the dukes of Spoleto, who had Formosus exhumed after his death and his papacy declared a usurpation. Later he was reburied and his papacy accepted.

**FORMULA** 1. A prescribed verbal formulation in a religious ceremony. 2. A doctrinal formulation or statement.

**FORMULA OF CONCORD** See CONCORD, FORMULA OF.

**FORMULARY** Book of prayers, creeds, or ceremonies.

**FORNICATION** Sexual relations between two unmarried persons, considered a grave sin in CATHOLICISM and traditional PROTESTANTISM. Fornication in the Scriptures may symbolize the turning away from the Lord.

**FORSETI** Germanic god of justice.

**FORSYTH, PETER TAYLOR (1848–1921)** English CONGREGATIONALIST minister and theologian. His viewpoint was both evangelical and social. He saw the need of the Cross and wrote a number of books including *Positive Preaching and the Modern Mind, The Cruciality of the Cross,* and *The Christian Ethic of War.*

**FORTITUDE** Bravery combined with patience and perseverance. This virtue was considered cardinal in classical philosophy and a natural virtue in SCHOLASTIC theology. However, Christians have termed it a passive (as opposed to an active) virtue.

**FORTUNA** *fortune* Roman goddess of fortune and fertility, worshiped throughout the empire. Her symbols were a cornucopia and the rudder of a ship. Her Greek counterpart was Tyche.

**FORTUNATE ISLES** Legendary islands in the western sea where blessed souls lived in a state of paradise.

**FORTUNATUS, VENANTIUS (c.530–609)** Roman Christian poet and hymn writer, also Bishop of Poitiers. His poems filled eleven books.

**FORTUNE** See FORTUNA.

**FORTUNE-TELLERS** Those who predict the future by such means as palmistry. Many Christians associate their craft with sorcery and superstition.

**FORTY** As the number four is believed to symbolize completeness and ten, sacredness, the multiple may be taken symbolically in the Bible to indicate both completeness and sacredness. Sometimes it may also be a round number indicating about six weeks, or a rather indefinite period of extended time. The Israelites wandered for forty years in the wilderness, while Christ's temptation lasted forty days. For this reason forty may symbolize trial or testing.

**FORTY HOURS' DEVOTION** Service honoring the MASS lasting forty hours. During this period the SACRAMENT is exposed and prayers are offered.

**FORTY MARTYRS OF SEBASTE** These were forty Christian soldiers who, according to St. Basil of Caesarea, refused to worship the Roman emperor while stationed at Sebaste in Armenia. For their refusal they were placed naked in the center of a frozen lake. When one of their number recanted and crawled to safety, a soldier from the pagan guard was converted and took his place, so that the number was not diminished while the martyrs died singing hymns of praise to their Christ. They are honored in the EASTERN CHURCH with a feast day on March 9, and in the West on March 10.

**FORTY-TWO ARTICLES** See ARTICLES, FORTY-TWO.

**FORUM** Sphere of judicial authority of the ROMAN CATHOLIC CHURCH. The forum may be either internal, i.e. concerned with the spiritual good of the individual, or external—related to ecclesiastical courts and matters of public good of the church.

**FOSSARIANS or FOSSORS** *diggers* 1. Gravediggers in the early church, considered to be a lower rank of clergy. 2. Fifteenth-century hermits who worshiped in caves.

**FOSTER, GEORGE BURMAN (1858–1918)** BAPTIST minister in the United States who became Professor of the Philosophy of Religion at the University of Chicago. There he developed a naturalistic humanism which accepted the idea of God as emotionally useful although without objective validity.

**FOUCAULD, CHARLES, VICOMTE DE (1858–1916)** French TRAPPIST missionary to Sahara, slain in a desert revolt.

**FOUNDATION CEREMONIES** In ancient times buildings were often consecrated with religious ceremonies, sometimes involving the entombment of a child beneath the cornerstone. In contemporary ceremonies current literature and artifacts are sometimes buried, as in a cornerstone, for future civilizations.

**FOUNDING TOME OF 1922** Action of the Eastern churches establishing the GREEK ARCHDIOCESE OF NORTH AMERICA.

**FOUNTAIN** Symbol of *a.* the Virgin Mary; *b.* St. Clement.

**FOUQUET, JEAN (c.1415–1485)** French artist who painted Pope Eugenius IV, illuminated the Book of Hours and Josephus' *Antiquities of the Jews*, and executed other powerfully exquisite religious works.

**FOUR** Number sacred in Semitic and American Indian religions. Symbol of completeness, the earth, and the four Gospels. Also a symbol of the INTERNATIONAL CHURCH OF THE FOURSQUARE GOSPEL.

**FOUR CAUSES** ARISTOTELIAN and medieval categorization of four types of causation: material, efficient, formal, and final.

**FOUR CROWNED ONES** Four Roman martyrs, patron saints of stonecutters, whose feast day is November 8.

**FOUR CUPS OF WINE** An essential element of SEDER in PASSOVER. The drinking of the four cups of wine is obligatory in the Passover meal.

**FOUR FREEDOMS** Ideals set forth by Franklin D. Roosevelt in his message to Congress in 1941 and proclaimed in the Atlantic Charter of Roosevelt and Winston Churchill later that year. They are freedom of speech and expression, freedom of worship, freedom from want, and freedom from fear.

**FOUR HORSEMEN** The four riders of Revelation: Conquest, Violence, Famine, and Death, upon white, red, black, and pale horses, respectively (6:1–8).

**FOUR NOBLE TRUTHS** The fundamentals of BUDDHISM: *a.* Life is not possible without suffering. *b.* Suffering is caused by self-centered desire. *c.* Suffering ends with the removal of desire. *d.* The NOBLE EIGHTFOLD PATH points the way to the removal of desire. These fundamentals were proclaimed in the Buddha's first sermon: "Sorrow, the cause of sorrow, the cessation of sorrow, and the path which leads to the cessation of sorrow."

**FOUR PATHS** In BUDDHISM, four roads to salvation and freedom. The first is "entering the Stream." The second is freedom from delusion and hatred. The third is

absolute liberation from the illusion of spiritual isolation, from doubt, from ritualism, from delusion, and from hatred. The fourth road or stage is the attainment of NIRVANA through liberation from such additional fetters as ignorance, restlessness, and conceit.

**FOUR RITES OF MOSLEM LAW** Four interpretations of law among Sunnite Moslems: HANAFITE, MALIKITE, SHAFIITE, and HANBALITE.

**FOURSQUARE GOSPEL, INTERNATIONAL CHURCH OF THE** See INTERNATIONAL CHURCH OF THE FOURSQUARE GOSPEL.

**FOURTH GOSPEL** The Gospel of JOHN.

**FOUR TRUTHS OF BUDDHISM** See FOUR NOBLE TRUTHS.

**FOWLER, CHARLES HENRY (1837–1908)** American METHODIST minister and bishop who founded Nebraska Wesleyan University and two universities in China.

**FOX** In medieval sculpture, symbol of cunning and Satan.

**FOX, GEORGE (1624–1691)** English founder of the Society of FRIENDS. As a youth he forsook family and friends and set out visiting various preachers. He soon came to the conviction that supreme guidance must be found in an inward light, directly from God; he often felt impelled to speak out against various evils. This, and his denunciation of churches, clergymen, lawyers, and soldiers made him a victim of mob hatred and imprisonment many times. He built up a strong organization of Friends in Great Britain and America, and profoundly influenced history.

**FOX, MARGARET (1836–1893)** American founder, with her sisters Leah and Katherine, of modern spiritualism. Tappings in their home led to belief in communication with the world of the dead, and to psychic research.

**FOXE, JOHN (1516–1587)** CHURCH OF ENGLAND clergyman famous for writing the *Book of Martyrs* which lauded the Protestants martyred during the reign of Queen Mary. He was an ardent CALVINIST.

**FOXE'S BOOK OF MARTYRS** See FOXE, JOHN.

**FRA ANGELICO** See ANGELICO, FRA.

**FRANCESCHINI, BALDASSARE (1611–1689)** Italian painter of a number of works for churches.

**FRANCIA (c.1450–1517)** Italian goldsmith

and engraver who became one of the greatest painters of the early Bolognese school. Among his paintings are a number of the "Virgin Mary" and "The Judgment of Paris." It is said that when Francia examined Raphael's painting of St. Cecilia he became depressed and died.

**FRANCIABIGIO** (1482–1525) Originally Francesco di Cristofano, he studied under Andrea del Sarto and Albertinelli and became an outstanding painter of portraits and religious subjects. He painted "The Marriage of the Virgin" and "The Bath of Bathsheba."

**FRANCIS, ST.** See FRANCIS OF ASSISI.

**FRANCIS, SOCIETY OF ST.** Community of CHURCH OF ENGLAND friars in Dorset.

**FRANCIS BORGIA, ST.** (1510–1572) Spanish Jesuit general. A wealthy duke, he gave up his money and became a dedicated associate of St. IGNATIUS. He attracted many youths into the SOCIETY OF JESUS and established a number of missions in America. His feast day is October 10.

**FRANCISCANS** The order of Friars Minor or Grey Friars founded by St. FRANCIS OF ASSISI in 1209. There are three great divisions: Friars Minor or OBSERVANTS, Friars Minor Capuchin or CAPUCHINS, and Friars Minor Conventual or Conventuals. There is also a second women's order, the Poor Clares founded by St. Clara or CLARE with St. Francis, and a third order of TERTIARIES. The Franciscans are noted for missionary work, popular preaching, and such popular devotions as the Angelus, the Crib, and the Stations of the Cross. Among their members have been DUNS SCOTUS, WILLIAM OF OCCAM (or Ockham), St. BONAVENTURE, St. ANTHONY OF PADUA, ALEXANDER OF HALES, and Roger BACON. The Franciscans comprise the largest religious order in CATHOLICISM. They are headed by a Minister-General who resides in Rome.

**FRANCISCA ROMANA** (c.1384–1440) Founder of the OBLATES OF ST. BENEDICT. Guided by a guardian angel, she gave her life for the education and care of those in need.

**FRANCIS DE SALES** See FRANCIS OF SALES.

**FRANCIS OF ASSISI, ST.** (c.1182–1226) Originally Giovanni de Bernardone, Francis was born in Italy and acquired his name from his father's travels in France. A gay youth who served in the wars of his time, he was touched by illness, disturbed by the poverty and leprosy he met, and confronted by Christ. He felt commissioned to renounce his wealth, minister to the needy, and gather followers who would go about in imitation of Jesus, forsaking all to preach the gospel and share the love of God. Thus began the FRANCISCANS. Francis was a man of joy, humility, and devotion; he loved all creatures and called them his brothers, loved God and lived in prayer. In 1224 he received the wounds of the STIGMATA, and thereafter lived in physical suffering transcended by joy. His feast day is October 4.

**FRANCIS OF PAOLA or PAULA, ST.** (c.1416–1507) Austere founder of the hermit order of MINIMI. Later they were entitled Minim-Hermits of St. Francis of Paola. Louis XI of France called him to his deathbed and Louis' son Charles VIII made him his spiritual adviser. Born in Italy, he was canonized in 1519; his feast day is April 2.

**FRANCIS OF SALES, ST.** (1567–1622) Born in Savoy, Francis of Sales became a priest in 1591 and through his earnest preaching won back many Catholics from the influences of Calvin and Zwingli. He became Bishop of Geneva and a leader in the COUNTER REFORMATION. With Madame JANE FRANCES DE CHANTAL he founded the Order of the Visitation, an order of nuns for women of "strong souls with weak bodies." Optimistic about the possibilities of human nature, Francis of Sales was also of a mystical frame of mind. He is known for his books *Introduction to the Devout Life* and *Treatise on the Love of God.*

**FRANCIS XAVIER, ST.** (1506–1562) Spanish JESUIT missionary to the Indies, India, and Japan. With St. IGNATIUS LOYOLA and five others at the University of Paris, he took ascetic missionary vows and was ordained with them in 1537. He founded mission stations in India and an enduring church in Japan; on a mission trip to China he died. He is credited with more than 700,000 conversions, a mystical spirit, and practical wisdom. His feast day is December 3.

**FRANCK, ADOLPHE** (1809–1893) French

philosopher and author of *The Cabbalah.*

**FRANCK, SEBASTIAN (c.1499–c.1542)** German priest who became first a LUTHERAN minister and then a freethinking HUMANIST. Advocating freedom of thought and sympathetic to all religions, he was harried by both Catholics and Protestants; Luther called him a "devil's mouth."

**FRANCKE, AUGUST HERMANN (1663–1727)** German Protestant pastor, pietist, philanthropist, and professor of theology. An able preacher, he helped organize a school for Bible study, founded the Francke Institutes for the education of children, and made Halle a center of German PIETISM.

**FRANCKE, MEISTER (fifteenth century)** German painter of "Christ as the Man of Sorrows," the "Crucifixion," and other religious scenes.

**FRANK, FRANZ HERMANN REINHOLD VON (1827–1894)** German LUTHERAN theologian who emphasized the experience of REGENERATION as a basic element in Christian knowledge.

**FRANK, JAKOB (c.1726–1791)** Polish Jewish theologian and founder of the FRANKISTS. Influenced by the alleged Messiah, Sabbetai Zevi, Frank proclaimed himself Messiah and soon converted with his followers *en masse* to CATHOLICISM. The church, however, suspected his sincerity and had him imprisoned for heresy from 1760 to 1773.

**FRANK, SEBASTIAN** See FRANCK, Sebastian.

**FRANKEL, ZECHARIAS (1801–1875)** Jewish theologian and Talmudist who sought to combine Biblical criticism with faithfulness to religious tradition.

**FRANKINCENSE** An eastern incense, obtained from the resin of certain deciduous shrubs and trees, used for perfume, medicine, and embalming. It was used in religious rites by Egyptians and Jews (EXODUS 30:34) and brought by the wise men to Jesus (MATTHEW 2:11).

**FRANKISTS** Followers of Jakob FRANK. Regarding him as the Jewish Messiah, they followed him into the ROMAN CATHOLIC CHURCH in 1759 at Lvov, Poland. After his death, Frank's daughter Eve is said to have been the Frankists' "holy mistress." Later the group merged from sight in the church.

**FRANKLIN, BENJAMIN (1706–1790)** American statesman and inventor who held religious views that were moderately deistic. He was more interested in morality than in revelation although he believed in personal immortality and compared his body to an old book which he trusted would eventually be brought out in a new edition revised and corrected by its Author.

**FRANZELIN, JOHN BAPTIST (1816–1886)** Austrian theologian, an influential cardinal and JESUIT. He defended the Western view of the procession of the HOLY SPIRIT against Eastern theologians.

**FRATER** 1. Refectory, common room, or chapter house in a MONASTERY. 2. Brother or friar.

**FRATERNAL WORKER** Contemporary term for a person sent to another country to evangelize or do other church work. The older term is "foreign missionary."

**FRATERNITY** Brotherhood: the common family-like life of believers, or the spirit of kinship with others which good religion promotes.

**FRATICELLI** *little friars* 1. Spiritual FRANCISCANS who in the late fourteenth century left their order in the belief that they alone upheld the purposes of St. FRANCIS. 2. The name of several other medieval groups repressed and exterminated by the church.

**FRAVASHI** ZOROASTRIAN term for the guardian angel which helps the individual against the dark forces of AHRIMAN throughout his earthly life and at death unites with his immortal soul.

**FRAZER, JAMES GEORGE (1854–1941)** British anthropologist whose research, particularly his monumental *Golden Bough,* shows the interrelationships of comparative religions, the power of religious beliefs in human behavior and culture, and the parallel development of religion and social organizations.

**FREDERICK THE WISE (1463–1525)** Elector of Saxony who chose to save LUTHER and the REFORMATION from destruction by kidnaping the former after the Diet of Worms and hiding him at Wartburg Castle. He had founded the University of Wittenberg where LUTHER and MELANCHTHON taught, and doubtless supported German nationalism as well as educational freedom and the Protestant cause.

**FREE BAPTISTS** See FREE WILL BAPTISTS.

**FREE CATHOLIC MOVEMENT** See SOCIETY OF FREE CATHOLICS.

**FREE CHRISTIAN ZION CHURCH OF CHRIST** American Negro denomination with METHODIST doctrine and polity.

**FREE CHURCHES** Churches without government support. In Great Britain these churches' members were once called Dissenters and later Nonconformists. Several such churches emerged in Europe in the nineteenth century. They represent various PROTESTANT groups.

**FREE CHURCH FEDERAL COUNCIL** Association of Free Churches in England and Wales. Formed in 1940, it has seven million members.

**FREE CHURCH OF ENGLAND** Evangelical denomination which seceded from the CHURCH OF ENGLAND in 1844.

**FREE CHURCH OF SCOTLAND** PRESBYTERIAN group which left the established church of Scotland in 1843 and a remnant of which never reunited with any other body. Members are sometimes called "Wee Frees."

**FREE CONGREGATIONS** Nineteenth-century German movement whose members were also known as the Friends of Light. They tended to be rationalistic and politically radical. It persists today with both CATHOLIC and PROTESTANT members.

**FREEDOM** A goal of most ethics, religion, education, science, and democracy. Isaiah and the great prophets proclaimed individual freedom, and Christ offered freedom to all who would receive it.

**FREEDOM OF THE WILL** See FREE WILL.

**FREE MAGYAR REFORMED CHURCH IN AMERICA** Original name of the HUNGARIAN REFORMED CHURCH IN AMERICA, organized in 1904.

**FREEMASONRY** The institution of Free and Accepted Masons, once opposed by many churches but now accepted by most denominations. The ritual and program are of a quasi-religious nature.

**FREE METHODIST CHURCH OF NORTH AMERICA** Holiness denomination organized in New York State in 1860. Confession of sin, SALVATION, and entire SANCTIFICATION are emphasized.

**FREER LOGION** An addition to the words of Jesus in Mark 16:14. It appears in a Greek codex, dating from the fifth century, in Washington's Freer Museum.

**FREE SPIRIT, BRETHREN OF THE** See BRETHREN OF THE FREE SPIRIT.

**FREETHINKER** One who arrives at ultimate certitude by reason rather than tradition or revelation. There are various organizations of freethinkers in the world. The name originated in the eighteenth century in connection with the DEISTS but today often has anti-Christian implications.

**FREE WILL** The problem of the apparent conflict between the free will of man and the sovereign omnipotence of God has historically precipitated deep theological cleavages—between AUGUSTINIANISM and PELAGIANISM, CALVINISM and ARMINIANISM. Emphasis on the power and freedom of man seemed to detract from the majesty of God, while emphasis on His absolute predetermination of all things seemed to detract from the glory of man. The actual conflict appears to have resulted from divergent emphases and points of view. The great modern opponents of both man's freedom and God's greatness are the social systems, philosophies, scientific credos, automatized procedures, and irrationalities that leave no room for individuality and responsible choice. To this situation the Christian gospel addresses itself with resolution and hope.

**FREE WILL BAPTISTS** Denomination of Welsh origin, organized in the United States in 1727. Members are ARMINIAN in theology and practice FOOT WASHING.

**FREEWILL OFFERING** 1. A form of peace offering in the Jewish sacrificial system (LEVITICUS 7:11–16). 2. A voluntary offering in Christian churches, often made in addition to the regular offering for some special mission or benevolence.

**FRELINGHUYSEN, THEODORUS J. (1691–1748)** DUTCH REFORMED minister in Raritan, New Jersey, who launched the GREAT AWAKENING in the central colonies.

**FRENSSEN, GUSTAV (1863–1945)** German pastor and author whose books are marked by deep religious convictions.

**FRESCO** *fresh* A painting made on fresh plaster. Some of the great religious masterpieces such as Michelangelo's work on the ceiling of the SISTINE CHAPEL are frescoes. They have also been used in

Egyptian, Cretan, Minoan, Roman, and other art.

**FREUD, SIGMUND (1856–1939)** Jewish founder of PSYCHOANALYSIS whose insights have revolutionized much of modern life. While they precipitated an initial conflict with traditional religion, they are now seen to reinforce such Biblical concepts as the depths of the soul and the pervasiveness of guilt. There are remarkable parallels between psychological integration and religious conversion. Freud himself, however, called religion an "obsessional neurosis."

**FREY** Scandinavian god of spring, fertility, sun, and rain.

**FREYA** Scandinavian goddess of spring beneficence. She was the sister and wife of FREY.

**FRIAR** *brother* Monk in a mendicant order (one which has renounced all ownership of property) such as the AUGUSTINIANS, CARMELITES, DOMINICANS, and FRANCISCANS.

**FRIARS MINOR** A name for the FRANCISCANS. It is also the name of the largest branch within the Franciscans; its members are sometimes called Observants or Minorites.

**FRIARS MINOR CAPUCHINS** See CAPUCHINS.

**FRIARS MINOR CONVENTUAL** A branch of the FRANCISCANS whose rules are more relaxed than those of other Franciscans, particularly in regard to the ownership of property. They wear a black tunic and hood. See also CONVENTUALS.

**FRIARS PREACHERS** A name for the DOMINICANS.

**FRIARY** A friars' brotherhood or a MONASTERY.

**FRIDAY** Day named for the Scandinavian goddess Frigg. Friday evening begins the Jewish Sabbath and is often a time of synagogue worship. Among Christians Friday commemorates the CRUCIFIXION, and has long been a fast day in both Eastern and Western churches.

**FRIDAY, GOOD** See GOOD FRIDAY.

**FRIDAY ABSTINENCE** Refraining from meat on Fridays, commemorating the CRUCIFIXION.

**FRIEDLANDER, DAVID (1750–1834)** German leader of REFORM JUDAISM.

**FRIEDMANN, MEIR (1831–1908)** Hungarian Jewish authority on the MIDRASH. He advanced the critical study of rabbinic texts.

**FRIENDLY SOCIETIES** Associations for mutual aid in case of the illness or death of a member. An English institution, the friendly society has roots in medieval religious guilds.

**FRIENDS, SOCIETY OF** Christians, sometimes called Quakers, whose world influence seems almost in inverse ratio to their total world membership of less than two hundred thousand. Originating through the work of George FOX about 1668, the Friends emphasize divine revelation through an "Inner Light" in the individual, simple morality, and social concern. Their services of worship are simple and unstructured. The Friends have exercised a deep influence toward brotherhood, peace, and relief for the needy. Notable members include John WOOLMAN, William PENN, Elizabeth FRY, John Greenleaf WHITTIER, and Rufus JONES. Individual groups of Friends are indicated in this book under their special names.

**FRIENDS OF GOD** Fourteenth-century European mystics led by John TAULER and Heinrich SUSO. Largely DOMINICAN in leadership, they emphasized the transforming power of union with God.

**FRIENDS OF LIGHT** Another name for the FREE CONGREGATIONS of nineteenth-century Germany.

**FRIGG or FRIGGA** Scandinavian goddess of love and the home; possibly identical with FREYA.

**FRIMLA** Teutonic virgin goddess.

**FRITH, JOHN (c.1503–1533)** English associate of William TYNDALE, burned at the stake for denying that purgatory and transubstantiation were necessary doctrines.

**FROBEN, JOHANNES (c.1460–1527)** German printer and friend of ERASMUS. The latter aided him in the publication of a Greek New Testament and works by St. Ambrose, St. Jerome, and other Church Fathers.

**FROG** Symbol of uncleanness or worldliness in Christian art.

**FROMMEL, GASTON (1862–1906)** Swiss theologian who stressed man's dependence on God and obligation in conscience. He opposed subjectivism, relativism, and the subordination of religion to mere psychological considerations.

**FRONTAL** A rich hanging before a church altar.

**FRONTIER RELIGION** Term for the religion of the American frontier in the nation's westward push. Such religion was usually plain, gospel-centered Protestantism. Its preachers were often METHODIST circuit riders or BAPTIST or PRESBYTERIAN laymen with less formal education than their contemporaries elsewhere, but with no less commitment of the heart.

**FRONTLET** A passage of the Mosaic law, placed in a leather pouch, worn on the forehead in JUDAISM (EXODUS 13:9, 16).

**FRUIT** In the Bible, often a term for *a*. the results of one's actions and *b*. one's offspring.

**FRUMENTIUS** (c.300–c.360) Phoenician who was taken to Ethiopia against his will and founded the Abyssinian Church. Athanasius of Alexandria is believed to have consecrated him in 326. Known as Apostle of the Abyssinians, he is honored in the West with a feast day on October 27.

**FRY, ELIZABETH** (1780–1845) English QUAKER who reformed European prison conditions. Through her efforts men and women were separated while imprisoned, religious and other education was made available, and employment was found for those who had served their terms. Mrs. Fry, mother of a large family, also established soup kitchens for the London poor and improved conditions in hospitals and insane asylums. Her methods were widely copied.

**FUCHI** Japanese fire goddess. Fujiyama is named for her.

**FUDO** BUDDHIST god of wisdom in Japan.

**FUERST, JULIUS** (1805–1873) German Jewish scholar who prepared a Jewish and Aramaic dictionary and a German Bible.

**FUFLUNS** Etruscan god of love and wine.

**FUJIYAMA** Sacred volcanic mountain of Japan; a beautiful place of pilgrimage. See FUCHI.

**FUKUROKUJU** Japanese god of luck, wisdom, and long life.

**FULFILL** Complete, perfect. Christians regard many Old Testament prophecies as fulfilled in Christ (cf. MATTHEW 1:22). Jesus said He came not to destroy but to fulfill the law of Moses. Paul said that Jesus came in the fullness of time (GALATIANS 4:4), fulfilling the divine plan.

**FULK OF NEUILLY (twelfth century)** Popular French preacher appointed by Pope INNOCENT III to preach the Fourth CRUSADE. The result, claimed Fulk, was the enlistment of more than 200,000 crusaders.

**FULLER** Word in the King James Bible for one who fills, dyes, bleaches, or cleans cloth.

**FULLER, ANDREW** (1754–1815) British BAPTIST minister whose writings modifying extreme CALVINISM influenced William CAREY, a leader in the modern foreign mission movement.

**FULLER, THOMAS (1608–1661)** CHURCH OF ENGLAND clergyman and historian. A witty preacher, he defended the king during Oliver Cromwell's ascendancy and wrote considerably, including a history of the CRUSADES.

**FUNDAMENTAL CHURCHES OF AMERICA, INDEPENDENT** Association of undenominational American churches, emphasizing fundamental beliefs.

**FUNDAMENTALISM** Movement, prominent in the United States in the first quarter of the twentieth century, emphasizing the literal meaning of the Bible. Many denominations made response in a controversy whose leaders included on the one side such men as J. Gresham MACHEN and William Jennings BRYAN and on the other Harry Emerson Fosdick and other liberals. In general, fundamentalism holds to the items outlined in "The FUNDAMENTALS."

**FUNDAMENTAL METHODIST CHURCH, INC.** Denomination organized in the United States in 1942 in protest over the doctrines and principles of the Methodist Church from which it withdrew.

**FUNDAMENTALS, THE** Series of books published by wealthy laymen in the United States from 1910 to 1912 outlining these doctrines: the virgin birth of Christ, His physical resurrection, His imminent physical return, the substitutionary atonement, and the infallibility of the Scriptures. A reply by the Presbyterian Church to these five points was the AUBURN AFFIRMATION of 1924.

**FUNDMENTALS ASSOCIATION, WORLD CHRISTIAN** United States organization of fundamentalists founded in 1919. William B. Riley was its first president. In 1952 it united with the Slavic Gospel Association.

**FUNERAL CEREMONIES** From ancient times the awesome event of the cessation of human life has been attended by religious as well as cultic rites. Jewish funeral rites are solemn but fairly simple. Christian ceremonies emphasize Scripture reading and prayer; in the past Protestant services often featured a eulogy or sermon. There is a tendency today to simplify funeral customs and to reappraise their meaning and helpfulness to the living.

**FUNG SHUI or FENG SHUI** Chinese science of placing graves, buildings, etc. in accordance with the *Tao* or proper order of things. It is considered wrong to alter landscapes or the like, and right to conform to the harmony of nature.

**FUNK, SOLOMON (1867–1928)** Czechoslovakian Talmudist.

**FURIES** Greek goddesses of tormenting vengeance: Megaera, Tisiphone, and Alecto.

**FURLONG** About 660 feet.

**FURNESS, WILLIAM HENRY (1802–1896)** American UNITARIAN minister and prolific writer. He wrote a number of hymns and was an opponent of slavery for many years.

**FÜRST, JULIUS (1805–1873)** Distinguished German writer and Semitic scholar. He wrote several important books and advanced the study of Semitic linguistics.

**FURTADO, ABRAHAM (1756–1816)** Proponent of Jewish rights under Napoleon.

**FUSO KYO** Japanese SHINTO group founded in 1873 by Shishino Nakaba. Its polytheistic worship centers around Fujiyama ("Fuso").

**FUTSUNUSHI** Japanese god of fire or lightning.

**FUTURE LIFE** As E. Royston Pike points out, "Belief in a future life is more generally held than is belief in God or even in gods." Religious belief universally assumes the fact of such life. Christianity proclaims the assurance of that fact through the resurrection of Christ, as evidenced by His indwelling life within the believer. Again, much religion is concerned with future rewards and punishments. Christianity assures the believer that Christ has borne all his punishments and that his future is therefore one of endless blessing.

# G

**G. A.** Abbreviation for GENERAL ASSEMBLY.

**GABARS** *unbelievers* MOSLEM name for the ZOROASTRIANS of Persia.

**GABBAI** *receiver* Treasurer of a synagogue. His position is now an honorary office.

**GABBATHA** *elevation* Pavement in Jerusalem before Pilate's hall of judgment. The name was equivalent to the Greek "stone pavement." Here Pilate tried Jesus (JOHN 19:13).

**GABIROL** See IBN GABIROL, SOLOMON.

**GABRIEL** *man of God* Angel who brought messages to Daniel, Mary, and Zacharias (DANIEL 8:15 ff.; LUKE 1:19, 26, 27). The Book of Enoch lists Gabriel as one of the four great archangels. MOSLEMS hold that Gabriel dictated the KORAN to MOHAMMED. Christian tradition pictorially represents Gabriel with a lily and names him as the angel who will blow the trumpet of the last judgment.

**GAD** *fortune* 1. Son of Jacob and Zilpah who became progenitor of the tribe of Gad. 2. One of the twelve tribes of Israel. 3. Canaanite god or goddess of "Destiny" or good luck, mentioned in Isaiah 65:11 (RSV). 4. A prophet in the reign of David who wrote a history of that reign and helped organize the services of the temple (I CHRONICLES 29:29; II CHRONICLES 29:25).

**GADARA** Town on the Sea of Galilee where Jesus freed an insane man from a legion of demons who drove a herd of pigs into the sea (MARK 5:1).

**GAEA or GEA** Greek mother-goddess of all things, and daughter of Chaos. She appears also in Phoenician and Egyptian religion.

**GAINSAY** King James Bible word for "oppose" or "controvert."

**GAITER** Leg covering formerly favored by British ANGLICANS.

**GAIUS** Name of several New Testament Christians.

**GAIUS or CAIUS (late second or early third century)** Roman PRESBYTER who held that the Gospel of John and the Revelation were works of CERINTHUS rather than the Apostle JOHN.

**GALACH** Hebrew term for Christian clergyman.

**GALAHAD** The knight of King Arthur whose heart was pure, whose might was unexcelled, and who sought and found the Holy Grail (see GRAIL, HOLY).

**GALATIA** Central region of Asia Minor, named for the wild tribes of Gauls there, in which St. Paul founded a number of Christian churches.

**GALATIANS, EPISTLE TO THE** A letter from St. PAUL to the Christians of Galatia. It unequivocally states the Christian's freedom from the MOSAIC LAW and his duty to mature spiritually.

**GALBANUM** One form of Hebrew incense (EXODUS 30:34).

**GALILEAN** Inhabitant of Galilee in northern Palestine.

**GALILEE** Northern province of Palestine extending from the Jordan River to the Mediterranean Sea. Here Jesus spent most of His earthly life. From Galilee came most of His disciples; of the twelve Apostles, only Judas was a non-Galilean. In the war against Rome 150,000 Galileans gave their lives.

**GALILEE, SEA OF** Palestinian lake through which the Jordan River flows on its way to the Dead Sea. In New Testament times it was a center of boating and fishing and was, as Pliny says, "surrounded by pleasant towns."

**GALILEO (1564–1642)** Italian astronomer

and scientist who discovered mountains on the moon, spots on the sun, stars in the Milky Way, and other evidence which differed from the current interpretation of Aristotelianism and supported the findings of Copernicus. He was brought before the Roman INQUISITION, threatened with torture, and imprisoned for his discoveries and his belief that the earth revolves around the sun. Legend has it that he recanted on his knees but arose whispering, "Nevertheless it moves."

**GALL** Bitter substance which was mixed with vinegar and offered to Jesus on the cross (MATTHEW 27:34).

**GALLERY** In some churches, an elevated area to seat parishioners outside the central portion of the sanctuary.

**GALLI** Priests of ATTIS.

**GALLIA CHRISTIANA** A history of French Catholicism continually revised and carried on by BENEDICTINE scholars.

**GALLICAN ARTICLES** Demands made in 1682 by French Catholic clergymen for more freedom from papal authority. They were completely renounced by the VATICAN COUNCIL of 1870.

**GALLICAN CONFESSION** French Protestant statement of faith, drafted by John CALVIN, adopted by the Synod of Paris in 1559.

**GALLICANISM** Term for the independence of the kings and clergy of France from control by the pope. In effect it called for separation of the temporal affairs of state from the authority of the church, and creation of a self-governing national Catholic church. See GALLICAN ARTICLES.

**GALLICAN RITE** The non-Roman liturgy of the early Western Church, particularly in France before Charlemagne imposed the Roman rite.

**GALLIO (first century A.D.)** Brother of Seneca and proconsul of Achaea before whom St. Paul was brought c.53 (ACTS 18:12–17). Impartially, he "cared for none of these things." He may have been executed with Seneca by Nero.

**GALLITZIN, DEMETRIUS AUGUSTINE (1770–1840)** "Apostle of the Alleghanies," Russian Catholic missionary in the United States who founded the settlement of Loretto and won many adherents to CATHOLICISM. The Emperor of Russia disinherited him from his princely patrimony because of his religion. In Pennsylvania he was called "Father Smith."

**GALLOWAY, CHARLES B. (1849–1909)** METHODIST bishop in Mississippi who courageously promoted education and Christian race relations.

**GALUT** Jewish term for the exile from Palestine that ended Old Testament history.

**GAMAB** See BERGDAMEN RELIGION.

**GAMALIEL I (first century)** Member of the Jewish SANHEDRIN, and according to tradition its head, under whom St. Paul studied. When Peter and John were brought before the Sanhedrin he advocated tolerance on the grounds that if it were of God nothing could stop the new religion, while if it were not it would die out (ACTS 5:34–40). Gamaliel I was a grandson of the renowned HILLEL. When he died, the MISHNA laments, "purity and piety died."

**GAMALIEL II (late first century)** Grandson of Gamaliel I, also known as Gamaliel of Jabneh. He unified and strengthened the Judaism of his day, ending the division of the scribes between HILLEL and SHAMMAI.

**GAMMA** Third letter of the Greek alphabet, equivalent to the letter G. In the early church, the capital gamma Γ symbolized Christ's position as the cornerstone of the church.

**GAMMADION** Cross consisting of four capital gammas in the shape of a SWASTIKA.

**GAMPO-PA (1077–1152)** Tibetan saint who founded the KARGYUT-PA School of BUDDHISM.

**GAM ZU LE-TOVAH** *this too is for good* Proverb from the TALMUD.

**GANDHARVA** 1. Mysterious heavenly spirit or deity in vedic Hinduism. 2. Hindu adjective for a marriage based on love without wedding rites.

**GANDHI, MOHANDAS KARAMCHAND (1869–1948)** HINDU political and spiritual leader of India. Turned away from Christianity by South African racial discrimination, he gave his life to the attainment of freedom, justice, and democracy for the people of India through the power of truth and nonviolent civil resistance. He refused the title Mahatma ("Great-souled") given him by the Indian masses. When India and Pakistan became independent and fighting broke out between Hindus and MOSLEMS, Gandhi worked and fasted to restore peace. He was assassinated by a disgruntled Hindu at a prayer meeting in New Delhi. Gandhi was guided by the NEW TESTAMENT and the BHAGAVAD-GITA, asserting the oneness of man under one God. Renouncing all property, he tried to be dependent upon nothing and no one but God. "Replace greed by love," he said, "and everything will be all right."

**GANESHA or GANESH** HINDU god of wisdom and prosperity who makes and removes obstacles; oldest son of SIVA. Fat and elephant-headed, he rides on a rat and is honored by six Indian sects.

**GANGA** See GANGES.

**GANG DAYS** British term for ROGATION DAYS, based on the "BEATING THE BOUNDS" on those days.

**GANGES** Great sacred river of India; considered a HINDU god. At its juncture with the Jumna hundreds of thousands of Hindu pilgrims wash away their sins. But every inch in its 1500-mile course is considered healing and holy, and to die on the Ganges' banks means immediate access to heavenly joy.

**GANGOTRI** Hindu temple in the Himalaya Mountains at the source of the GANGES River.

**GANGRA, COUNCIL OF** Church council held about 345 at Gangra near the Black Sea. It condemned the false asceticism of EUSTATHIUS, who had attacked marriage and church attendance, and defined true asceticism.

**GANO, JOHN (1727–1804)** BAPTIST pastor who was chaplain of the Continental Army during the American Revolution.

**GANYMEDE** Handsome Greek cupbearer for ZEUS.

**GAON** *illustrious or excellency* Title of the head of one of the rabbinic academies in Sura and Pumbeditha, Babylonia, from the sixth to the eleventh centuries. The plural is *Geonim*. Later, in the twelfth century, there was a Gaon of Palestine, and still later Elijah of Vilna (see ELIJAH BEN SOLOMON) was called "The Gaon."

**GARB** Dress. The members of some re-ligious groups and the leaders of many more wear a distinctive garb.

**GARCIA MORENO, GABRIEL (1821–1875)** Devout ROMAN CATHOLIC president of Ecuador who signed a concordat in 1862 granting his church extraordinary powers over Ecuador. In 1875 liberal opponents assassinated him.

**GARDEN OF EDEN** See EDEN.

**GARDEN OF GETHSEMANE** See GETHSEMANE.

**GARDEN OF THE SOUL** ROMAN CATHOLIC devotional book, published in 1740, long popular in England.

**GARDINER, STEPHEN (c.1493–1555)** English bishop who supported Henry VIII's plans for a divorce but was imprisoned under Edward VI. He displeased English Protestants because he backed Henry's opposition to the doctrines of the REFORMATION, and displeased Catholics because he backed Henry against the pope.

**GARGOYLE** Decorated waterspout, particularly in the shape of a grotesque bird, animal, or demon common on medieval Gothic cathedrals.

**GARNETT, HENRY (1555–1606)** English JESUIT executed for taking part in the Gunpowder Plot of 1605.

**GARNIER, CHARLES (1606–1649)** French JESUIT missionary to the Huron Indians in Canada, slain by the Iroquois Indians. He is one of the Jesuit martyrs of North America, his feast day being September 26.

**GARRETT, THOMAS (1789–1871)** Pennsylvania QUAKER who used his home as a station on the Underground Railroad to help many Negroes escape from the South to liberty. For his work he was heavily fined.

**GARRETTSON, FREEBORN (1752–1827)** Citizen of Maryland who freed his slaves, became a Methodist preacher, and helped organize the METHODIST EPISCOPAL CHURCH.

**GARRISON, WILLIAM LLOYD (1805–1879)** American newspaper publisher who appealed to Christian ministers and churches to help end slavery, war, imprisonment for debt, capital punishment, and the use of alcohol and tobacco. Uncompromising and extreme, he was often mobbed and jailed, but saw American slavery abolished.

**GARSTANG, JOHN (1876–1956)** British archaeologist who excavated sites in the Sudan, Asia Minor, and Palestine, contributing much to Biblical knowledge. Among his books are *The Hittite Empire* and *Foundations of Bible History: Joshua, Judges.*

**GARUDA** HINDU lord of birds.

**GASPAR** Medieval name for one of the three Wise Men who visited the infant Jesus.

**GASPARRI, PIETRO (1852–1934)** ROMAN CATHOLIC cardinal who directed the codification of the canon law under PIUS X and was secretary of state under popes Benedict XV and Pius XI.

**GASQUET, FRANCIS AIDAN (1846–1929)** English BENEDICTINE, cardinal, and church historian. He was president of the commission for revision of the VULGATE.

**GASTER, MOSES (1856–1939)** Rumanian Jewish rabbi and scholar. A ZIONIST, he was expelled from Rumania for defending the rights of persecuted Jews and spent the rest of his life in England. In 1887 he became chief rabbi of England's SEPHARDIC communities.

**GATE** Symbol of entrance into immortal life or death.

**GATE OF HEAVEN** ROMAN CATHOLIC title for MARY.

**GATES, THEOPHILUS RANSOM (1787–1846)** PROTESTANT minister in Philadelphia, Pennsylvania, who announced that all unhappy marriages should be dissolved and all men and women should choose their mates in absolute freedom. He published a paper called *The Battle-axe* advocating these views and established a free-love community near Philadelphia for their practice.

**GATES OF HELL** Jesus' term for the forces of hell or the power of death (MATTHEW 16:18).

**GATH** *wine press* Philistine city where GOLIATH was born.

**GATHAS** Ancient portion of the Zend AVESTA of ZOROASTRIANISM. It consists of seventeen hymns with sermons and prayers and may contain ZARATHUSTRA's own teachings.

**GATHERED CHURCH** Term for the doctrine that the church is essentially a local congregation of CHRISTIAN believers, gathered together in worship and fellowship. This concept is at the opposite pole from that of the church unified under a pope or hierarchy and guaranteed by APOSTOLIC SUCCESSION. The gathered church is the local assembly of true believers, gathered out of the world around them.

**GA-TUM-DUG** Babylonian mother goddess of harvest and fertility.

**GAUDEAMUS IGITUR** *let us then be merry* University-student song drawn from and probably parodying a thirteenth-century Latin religious song.

**GAUDETE SUNDAY** Third Sunday in ADVENT, named from the first word of the INTROIT, "Rejoice."

**GAUTAMA BUDDHA** See BUDDHA.

**GAVAZZI, ALESSANDRO (1809–1889)** Italian patriot and BARNABITE monk who was exiled, became a Protestant in England, and returned to Italy to head the Free Christian Church of Italy. In 1875 he founded a theological college for this PROTESTANT denomination.

**GAYA** City of India which 300,000 HINDU Pilgrims visit each year to fulfill their holy responsibility to make offerings for their ancestors' salvation. Six miles from BUDDH GAYA, it claims more than forty sacred places. These include the grave of Kasyapa, great disciple of Buddha, the caves of Nagarjuni, and the temple of Vishnupad (Vishnu's footprint).

**GAYATRI** Daily prayer of orthodox HINDUS: "Let us meditate on the glory of Sayatri, the sun who gives us life and governs our holy rites; may he enlighten our minds" (RIG-VEDA, BOOK 3, 62:10).

**GAZA** One of the principal Philistine cities in Bible times. In it SAMSON took the lives of many Philistines when he brought their temple down on his own head.

**GEA** See GAEA.

**GEASA** Celtic religious taboos.

**GEB** Earth-mother in Egyptian religion.

**GEDALIAH** *The Lord is great* 1. Governor of Jerusalem under Nebuchadnezzar, treacherously assassinated. The day of his murder, the third of Tisri, is a Jewish fast day. 2. The name of several other Bible men.

**GEDDES, JENNY (seventeenth century)** When England's King Charles I decided to impose ANGLICAN worship on Scotland,

Jenny Geddes effectively terminated the experiment. On the Sunday of July 23, 1637, the Dean of Edinburgh had just begun to read the collect in St. Giles' Cathedral when Jenny Geddes, an herb-woman, flung her stool at his head. The congregation started to riot, the dean fled for his life, and the act "gave to the civil war in England an impulse which only ended in the overthrow of the Church and Monarchy" (A. P. STANLEY).

**GEDEON**  See GIDEON.

**GEHAZI**  Servant of Elisha who was smitten with leprosy for falsifying his master's words (II KINGS 5; 8).

**GEHENNA**  The valley of Hinnom, outside Jerusalem, where children were burned in sacrifice to Molech in the reigns of Solomon, Ahaz, and Manasseh. In New Testament times it was a garbage dump where fires perpetually burned, and became a symbol of punishment for the lost (MATTHEW 5:22; 10:28). According to the TALMUD, the fires of Gehenna purify the soul.

**GEIGER, ABRAHAM (1810–1874)**  German Jewish rabbi, orientalist, theologian, and leader of REFORM JUDAISM. He wrote *Judaism and Its History* and other books.

**GEILER VON KAISERSBERG, JOHANN (1445–1510)**  German preacher at the Cathedral of Strassburg where his bold sermons earned him the title "the German Savonarola." With vivid illustrations, racy satire, and texts not always from the Bible, he appealed for a moral reformation.

**GELASIAN SACRAMENTARY**  Early Christian prayer book attributed to Pope GELASIUS I but probably originating in Gaul in the seventh century. Upon it is based the ROMAN CATHOLIC canon of the mass in contemporary use.

**GELASIUS I (fifth century)**  Pope (492–496) during whose term the break between the Eastern and Western churches became final. He wrote a treatise on the two natures of Christ and tracts on various heresies. A saint, his feast day is November 21.

**GELBOE**  See GILBOA.

**GELILAH**  Jewish term for the binding of the scroll after reading from the TORAH.

**GELLERT, CHRISTIAN F. (1715–1769)**  German poet who wrote "Jesus Lives!" and many other hymns which set a standard for his day. Known as a moralist, he taught Goethe and inspired Bach and Beethoven. The latter set some of his hymns to music.

**GELUPA or GELUG-PA**  See YELLOW HATS.

**GEMARA learning**  Second part of the TALMUD, containing a commentary on the MISHNAH which is the first part. Authors of the Gemara were the Amoraim of the third through sixth centuries (see AMORA). The Gemara is filled with information illuminating Jewish customs and history.

**GEMATRIA**  Jewish numerology, used to determine hidden meaning of Bible words by counting the total of the numerical equivalents of each letter in a word. The CABALISTS were noted for this approach. Some Christians have also applied it to find new meanings in Scripture, although it is difficult to find religious value in such a practice.

**GEMEINSCHAFTSBEWEGUNG**  Independent movement among German Christians emphasizing Bible study, fellowship, evangelism, lay activity, and holiness. Although it works through small circles within PROTESTANT churches, often meeting in homes, there are thousands of circles and lay preachers in the movement and an organization: the *Gnadauer Verband*.

**GEMILUT CHASIDIM**  Jewish term for activities of mercy and welfare.

**GENEALOGIES**  Lists of family descent, often found in the Bible. The Gospels of Matthew and Luke provide two divergent genealogies of Jesus; some solve the problem by finding one ancestral line through Joseph and the other through Mary.

**GENERAL**  Occasional name of heads of religious orders.

**GENERAL ASSEMBLY**  Annual meeting of a PRESBYTERIAN denomination with final legislative, administrative, and judicial powers. It consists of delegates chosen from the ministers and ruling elders in each presbytery.

**GENERAL ASSOCIATION OF REGULAR BAPTIST CHURCHES**  Fellowship of conservative BAPTIST churches which withdrew from the Northern (now American) Baptist Convention in 1932. It subscribes to the New Hampshire Confession of Faith.

**GENERAL BAPTISTS**  Arminian group in

the United States, originating in the seventeenth-century flowering of Baptist churches in England and the Netherlands. FOOT WASHING is practiced in some congregations.

**GENERAL CHURCH OF THE NEW JERUSALEM** Swedenborgian denomination which separated from the General Convention of the New Jerusalem in the U.S.A. in 1890. See CHURCHES OF THE NEW JERUSALEM.

**GENERAL CONFERENCE MENNONITE CHURCH** American MENNONITE denomination considered "liberal in conduct" because its members insist on freedom from the traditional Mennonite garb.

**GENERAL CONFERENCE OF THE EVANGELICAL BAPTIST CHURCH, INC.** American group organized in 1935 out of the FREE WILL BAPTIST CHURCHES.

**GENERAL CONFESSION** 1. Comprehensive confession of all one's sins, even those previously confessed, to a confessor. This is often done when the person confessing is entering a new state of life. 2. Collective confession of sin by a congregation at worship—a practice traditional with ANGLICANS and increasingly favored in other PROTESTANT churches.

**GENERAL CONVENTION** Supreme governing body in the PROTESTANT EPISCOPAL CHURCH. Held every three years, it consists of a House of Bishops and a House of Deputies. The latter represents the various dioceses with an equal number of clergymen and laymen.

**GENERAL CONVENTION OF THE NEW JERUSALEM IN THE U.S.A.** American Swedenborgian group formed in 1817. See CHURCHES OF THE NEW JERUSALEM.

**GENERAL COUNCIL** 1. A church gathering representing all the faithful in the world; see ECUMENICAL COUNCIL. 2. American Lutheran group which withdrew from the GENERAL SYNOD in 1866. 3. Administrative body of the AMERICAN BAPTIST CONVENTION which supervises denominational work between sessions of the annual convention. 4. In PRESBYTERIANISM, an administrative body of presbytery, synod, or the GENERAL ASSEMBLY, empowered to make recommendations and to carry out such business as may be given it by the parent body.

**GENERAL COUNCIL OF THE CONGREGATIONAL CHRISTIAN CHURCHES** Advisory board of the CONGREGATIONAL CHRISTIAN CHURCHES of the United States.

**GENERAL COUNCIL OF THE ITALIAN PENTECOSTAL ASSEMBLIES OF GOD** American Pentecostal group, founded in Chicago in 1904, which merged with the Italian Christian Churches of North America in 1948 to form the CHRISTIAN CHURCH OF NORTH AMERICA.

**GENERAL JUDGMENT** Term for the last judgment.

**GENERAL MISSIONARY CONVENTION OF THE BAPTIST DENOMINATION IN THE UNITED STATES OF AMERICA FOR FOREIGN MISSIONS** One of the first national conventions of BAPTISTS in the United States. It took place in 1814.

**GENERAL PRESBYTERY** Top administrative body of American PRESBYTERIANISM from 1706 to 1716. It was succeeded by the General Synod and finally by the General Assembly.

**GENERAL SIX-PRINCIPLE BAPTISTS** The name of two different Baptist associations in the United States, both very small. Arminian in doctrine, they both base their origin on the six principles of Hebrews 6:1, 2—faith, repentance, baptism, the laying on of hands, the resurrection, and the judgment.

**GENERAL SUPERINTENDENT** Title of the highest office in many German PROTESTANT churches.

**GENERAL SUPPLICATION** A prayer for all mankind; particularly, the litany subtitled "A Prayer for All Conditions of Men" in the Anglican BOOK OF COMMON PRAYER.

**GENERAL SYNOD** 1. In REFORMED and LUTHERAN churches, the highest body, with final authority. It corresponds to the General Assembly in Presbyterian churches. 2. Predecessor to the General Assembly in the United Presbyterian Church in the U.S.A. 3. Union of Lutherans in the United States in 1820. 4. Former name of the Reformed Church in the United States which united with the Evangelical Synod of North America to form the Evangelical and Reformed Church.

**GENERAL THANKSGIVING** Prayer of thanksgiving for blessings in general, particularly in ANGLICAN churches. Such a prayer is often offered in unison by all present.

**GENERATIONISM** Variant of TRADUCIAN-ISM which holds that the soul as well as the body of a child is propagated by the parents. This is the opposite of CREATION-ISM.

**GENESIS** *origin* First book in the Bible, giving the origin of the universe, the earth, life, man, sin, redemption, civili-zation, language, and the Jewish nation. Traditionally ascribed to Moses, its author-ship is attributed by many modern critics to "J," "E," "D," "P" (see), and possibly other sources. "If the religious books of other nations make any pretensions to vie with it in antiquity, in all other respects they are immeasurably inferior" (John M'Clintock and James Strong).

**GENEVA** Swiss city, an episcopal see in the Roman Empire, where the bishops took the governing power away from the counts in 1124. Thereafter the citizens themselves fought for independence and self-government, and in 1535 eagerly ac-cepted the Protestant REFORMATION, with its emphasis on the rights of the individual. Under the leadership of Guillaume FAREL and John CALVIN, Geneva became a world center of Protestantism. In modern times it has become the center of the Interna-tional Red Cross, the League of Nations, the World Health Organization, the Inter-national Labor Organization, the WORLD COUNCIL OF CHURCHES, and other organi-zations.

**GENEVA BANDS** Two white strips hang-ing from the neck opening of a clerical gown, sometimes said to symbolize the law and the gospel.

**GENEVA BIBLE** English Bible published in Geneva in 1560, sometimes called the "BREECHES BIBLE" because of its trans-lation of Genesis 3:7. Containing CALVIN-ISTIC notes, it was long favored by the Puritans. It was the first Bible printed with chapters and verses.

**GENEVA CATECHISM** A REFORMED cate-chism published by CALVIN at GENEVA, Switzerland, in 1545. Earlier versions were issued in 1537 and 1542.

**GENEVA CONVENTION** International agreement drawn up in Geneva in 1864 and 1906 providing for civilized rules of war and humane treatment of prisoners. Observers charged that both sides violated the Convention in the Vietnamese conflict of the 1960's.

**GENEVA CROSS** Red Greek cross on a white background.

**GENEVA GOWN** Black loose-fitting aca-demic gown with full sleeves. Worn by the preachers of Geneva to emphasize the teaching rather than the priestly functions of the ministry, it is widely used among PROTESTANTS, although the Genevan PU-RITANS opposed its use by their clergy-men.

**GENEVAN ACADEMY** The Academy of Geneva, established by CALVIN and BEZA in 1559 for the training of Protestant min-isters and missionaries. Students came from throughout Europe and the Academy thus acquired international influence. It de-veloped into the University of Geneva.

**GENEVAN CATECHISM** See GENEVA CATE-CHISM.

**GENEVIEVE, ST.** (c.422–512) Pious patron saint of Paris who predicted that Attila's Huns would invade the city without suc-cess. Her feast day is January 3.

**GENIUS** In Roman religion, a guiding spirit or guardian, similar to the Greek DAEMON. This is the origin of attributing a man's powers or success to his genius.

**GENIUS FAMILIAE** Guardian spirit of a household.

**GENIUS LOCI** Tutelary spirit of a place, as a city, a state, or an institution of some kind.

**GENIZAH** Synagogue repository of sacred manuscripts or relics which have been damaged or worn out.

**GENNESARET** Fertile garden area north-west of the Sea of Galilee.

**GENTILE** 1. Jewish word for non-Jews. In the Old Testament the word for these is *goyim*, "the nations." 2. Mormon word for non-Mormons.

**GENTILE CHRISTIANITY** Term for the Christianity outside Palestine which soon took on an overwhelmingly non-Jewish tinge through the labors of PAUL and his associates in the Roman Empire.

**GENUFLECTION** The religious act of bend-ing the knee in worship, common in RO-MAN CATHOLICISM at such points in the service as the adoration of the HOST.

**GEONIM**   Plural of GAON.

**GEORGE, ST. (c.fourth century)** English martyr credited with slaying a sea monster. His feast day is April 23.

**GEORGIAN VERSION** The New Testament in the Georgian language of the Black Sea region, dating originally from the sixth century.

**GER stranger** Jewish term for a proselyte to JUDAISM.

**GERAR** Region near Gaza in Canaan where ABRAHAM and ISAAC once pitched their tents.

**GERARD (c.1040–1120)** Founder of the Knights of St. John of Jerusalem (see KNIGHTS HOSPITALERS).

**GERASA** An accurate rendering of the King James Bible's "Gadara" where Jesus healed the demon-possessed man of Perea (MARK 5:1; LUKE 8:26).

**GERBERT OF AURILLAC (?–1003)** Hardworking scholar and theologian who became the first French pope, Sylvester II.

**GERDA** Nordic goddess whose husband was FREY.

**GERHARD, JOHANN (1582–1637)** German exponent of LUTHERAN theology whose knowledge, logic, and massive grasp of detail had never previously been approached. In his day he was considered the greatest living theologian of Germany. In response to the CATHOLIC doctrine of an infallible church he expounded the infallibility of the Scriptures.

**GERHARDT, PAUL (1607–1676)** German LUTHERAN pastor and hymn writer; author of such hymns as "O Sacred Head Sore Wounded" and "The Duteous Day Now Closeth."

**GERHART, EMANUEL VOGEL (1817–1904)** American clergyman and educator of the German Reformed Church. He developed the Mercersburg theology.

**GERIZIM** Mountain in Samaria sacred to the Samaritans because they believe it was the mountain Abraham climbed to sacrifice Isaac. A colony of Samaritans in Nablus still observes the PASSOVER on this rocky mountain.

**GERLIER, PIERRE CARDINAL (1880–1965)** Influential French ROMAN CATHOLIC clergyman who promoted Catholic education, advocated the "worker priest" experiment, and became Archbishop of Lyons. He is

credited with saving a number of Jews from deportation and death during World War II.

**GERMAN BAPTIST BRETHREN** A name of the DUNKERS.

**GERMAN CATHOLICS** ROMAN CATHOLICS in Germany who followed two excommunicated priests out of their denomination in 1844.

**GERMAN EVANGELICAL LUTHERAN SYNOD** Former name of the LUTHERAN CHURCH—MISSOURI SYNOD, a large American denomination.

**GERMANUS OF AUXERRE (fifth century)** Churchman of Gaul who led his Christian British followers in the defeat of Irish and Pict enemies in Wales. A saint, his feast day is July 31.

**GERSHOM BEN JUDAH (960–c.1028)** French rabbi who revised the text of the TALMUD and MISHNAH. He called a council which forbade Jewish polygamy and prohibited divorce without the consent of the wife.

**GERSHON** The oldest son of Levi whose descendants had special duties among the Levites, particularly in music (GENESIS 46:11; EZRA 3:10).

**GERSON, JEAN CHARLIER DE (1363–1429)** Influential French churchman, theologian, and writer. He sought to promote reform and piety in the church and to end the papal schism. He opposed John HUSS and the FLAGELLANTS.

**GERSON, JOHN** See GERSON, JEAN CHARLIER DE.

**GERSONIDES or LEVI BEN GERSON (1288–1344)** Jewish commentator, astronomer, philosopher, and mathematician. His *Milchamoth Adonai (The Wars of the Lord)* sought to integrate Jewish history with knowledge from such fields as physics and astronomy, and criticized MAIMONIDES' syncretism. He wrote commentaries on the PENTATEUCH and AVERROES.

**GERTRUDE, ST. (1256–1302)** German nun and mystic whose feast day is November 15.

**GESENIUS, HEINRICH FRIEDRICH WILHELM (1786–1842)** Noted German theologian, orientalist, and Bible critic. He is credited with beginning the scientific and comparative study of Semitics apart from theological presuppositions, and prepared an outstanding *Hebrew Grammar* of enduring value.

**GETHSEMANE** *oil press* Garden where Jesus was betrayed, located across the brook KIDRON from Jerusalem. It is graced with ancient olive trees today.

**GEULINCX, ARNOLD (1624–1669)** Dutch CALVINIST theologian who propounded the philosophy of OCCASIONALISM. According to this we are only onlookers in life, since God actually performs all our actions.

**GEULLAH** Jewish term for "Redemption," a prayer following the SHEMA.

**GHANAN** Mayan harvest god.

**GHAZALI** See AL-GAZALI.

**GHAZI** MOSLEM term for a warrior champion who leads the faithful against infidels.

**GHEBERS or GHEBRES** See GABARS.

**GHEEZ NATION IN AMERICA** Religious group claiming immortality with headquarters in Jamaica, New York. The Nation considers itself a Hebraic Temple of the Melkazedek Order.

**GHETTO** 1. An area in a city where Jews were once segregated. This segregation was once voluntary but during the Middle Ages became compulsory. Abolished in 1870, it was revived in NAZI Germany. 2. Term for any area where members of a group are forced to live, as the Negro communities in many parts of the world. This kind of segregation in the United States began to weaken in the latter part of the twentieth century as legislation enforced equal education, equal employment opportunities, and fair housing.

**GHIBELLINES** Medieval opponents of the GUELPHS. They supported the emperor while the Guelphs supported the pope in the medieval struggle for supremacy.

**GHIBERTI, LORENZO (1378–1455)** Italian sculptor whose bronze gates for the baptistery of Florence were termed by Michelangelo worthy to be the gates of paradise. He served as sculptor, painter, and architect for a number of church projects.

**GHIRLANDAJO, DOMENICO (1449–1494)** Florentine painter whose work decorated many churches. He is believed to have taught MICHELANGELO.

**GHOSE, AUROBINDO (1872–1950)** Mystic philosopher and political leader in India. A nonviolent extremist, he became a student of VEDANTA and established an ASHRAM in Pondicherry.

**GHOST** Spirit or apparition.

**GHOST DANCE RELIGION** Movement among the Paiute Indians of North America. Wearing white cloaks and dancing for five successive nights, the participants entered a trancelike state in which they were believed to communicate with the ghosts of their ancestors. The dance was part of an attempt to liberate the Indian from white domination.

**GIAOUR** *infidel* Turkish term for Christians and other non-Moslems.

**GIBBON, EDWARD (1737–1794)** English historian whose *Decline and Fall of the Roman Empire* received much criticism because of his treatment of the church. In the fifteenth and sixteenth chapters he ironically analyzed the reasons for the expansion of Christianity, seeming to minimize some of its accomplishments and to magnify the failings of some of its followers. The Middle Ages he described as "the triumph of barbarism and religion." The *Decline*, now universally recognized as essentially admirable, did not hide Gibbon's ex- and anti-Christian animus.

**GIBBONS, JAMES (1834–1921)** American ROMAN CATHOLIC cardinal and archbishop whose book *The Faith of Our Fathers* was very popular in America and England. He was a friend of several American Presidents, a defender of the Canadian Knights of Labor, and instrumental in the founding of the Catholic University of America in Washington, D.C. He contended that American democracy brought many blessings to the church and openly admired the American system of the separation of church and state.

**GIBEAH** *hill* 1. The early home and later the capital of King Saul, near Jerusalem (I SAMUEL 10:26; 11:4; 14:16). 2. The name of several towns in Palestine.

**GIBEON** *hill* Hill town, five miles northwest of Jerusalem, whose inhabitants became slaves of the Israelites (JOSHUA 9—10).

**GIBIL** Babylonian god of fire.

**GIBRAN, KAHLIL (1883–1931)** Painter and poet born in Lebanon whose semimystical writings such as *The Prophet* have been very popular in the United States, where he lived for many years.

**GICHTEL, J. G.** Founder of ANGELIC BROTHERS.

**GIDEON** *hewer* Jewish farmer who was called by the Lord to deliver Israel from its enemies the Midianites and did so. He opposed the worship of BAAL, unified Israel, and refused the crown which was offered him because he believed that the Lord was the nation's king.

**GIDEONS** International organization dedicated to the placing of Bibles in hotels, schools, jails, and other institutions. The members are Christian businessmen.

**GIFFORD LECTURES** Lectures on natural theology and "the foundation of ethics" established by Adam Gifford in 1887 at the universities of Scotland. Many notable theologians and philosophers have given the lectures.

**GIFT OF TONGUES** The ability granted by the Holy Spirit to speak in "other tongues" apparently unknown to the speaker. The first instance of this is in Acts 2. Various instances of tongue-speaking have been associated with religious activity throughout history. Those who emphasize the gift today are PENTECOSTALS and believers in the BAPTISM OF THE HOLY SPIRIT which produces the gift.

**GIFTS OF THE SPIRIT** The seven graces of wisdom, understanding, counsel, fortitude, knowledge, piety, and the fear of the Lord.

**GILBERT DE LA PORREE (1076–1154)** SCHOLASTIC theologian, philosopher, and logician. To avoid pantheism he taught that the Persons of the TRINITY were alone real, that the nature of God was an abstract concept of the human mind. For this he was accused of tritheism.

**GILBERTINES** Monastic order founded by St. Gilbert of Sempringham, England, about 1148 and suppressed at the time of the REFORMATION.

**GILBOA** Rough mountain range by the plain of Esdraelon, cursed by David after Saul and his three sons were killed there in battle (II SAMUEL 1).

**GILDAS, ST. (c.516–570)** British monk whose *Fall of Britain* made him the first British historian. Feast day: January 29.

**GILEAD** *hard* Rugged grazing region, northeast of the Dead Sea, through which the Jabbok River has cut canyons to the Jordan. The land of the tribes of Gad and Manasseh, it produced a healing balm (JEREMIAH 8:22). Gilead is also the name of several Bible men.

**GILES, ST. (c.sixth century)** European hermit and abbot revered as the patron of cripples, lepers, and mendicants. His feast day is September 1.

**GILGAL** *circle* 1. Town near Jericho where Joshua pitched his first camp in Canaan and set up twelve stones for the twelve tribes (JOSHUA 4), reminiscent of STONEHENGE. 2. Several other little-known places in Palestine.

**GILGAMESH EPIC** Babylonian epic poem, discovered by George Smith in 1872 at Nineveh, recounting the story of a flood from which only a few were saved by the use of an ark made watertight with pitch. Finally the ark grounded on a mountain and sacrifices were offered to the gods. The document probably dates originally from about 2000 B.C., and may be based on much earlier traditions.

**GIMEL** Third letter in the Hebrew alphabet, equivalent to G.

**GIMLI** Hall of heaven in Nordic myth.

**GINSBURG, CHRISTIAN DAVID (1831–1914)** Polish Jewish convert to Christianity who lived most of his life in England where he published a number of studies of the MASORA.

**GINZBERG, ASHER (1856–1927)** Ukraine-born Jewish philosopher who proposed the substitution of a Jewish cultural center in Palestine for political ZIONISM. He was interested in ethics, justice, and spiritual development.

**GIOBERTO, VINCENZO (1801–1852)** Italian priest who became noted as a politician and philosopher; he sought to liberate Italy through uniting papal supremacy with political liberalism.

**GIOTTO (c.1267–1337)** Italian painter whose many religious works were filled with freshness and life. A master craftsman and architect, he is famous for "The Flight Into Egypt," "The Raising of Lazarus," "St. John the Baptist," "The Betrayal of Judas," "The Presentation in the Temple," and many other masterpieces which revolutionized European art.

**GIRALDUS CAMBRENSIS (c.1146–1223)** Welsh clergyman and historian who preached the Third CRUSADE and wrote a number of ecclesiastical treatises including lives of clerics, sermons, and poems.

**GIRDLE** In the Bible, a belt, waistband, loincloth, or ceremonial sash. In liturgical wear, a sash, waist cord, or cincture. In religious art and liturgy, a symbol of service.

**GIRGENSOHN, KARL (1875–1925)** Conservative German LUTHERAN theologian who applied the psychology of religion to Christian studies.

**GIRLING, MARY ANNE (1827–1886)** "Mother Anne," an Englishwoman who founded the SHAKER group known as CHILDREN OF GOD. She was a STIGMATIC and believed herself to be a final divine incarnation.

**GITTITH** Musical term used in the titles of Psalms 8, 81, and 84 which apparently indicates either a musical instrument derived from Gath or a Gittite melody or a vintage reference.

**GIVEN, THE** Philosophically, that which exists independently of the student or thinker. Existentialist religion emphasizes the "givenness" of concrete situations, Scripture, the church, human existence, etc., rather than absolutes and ideals.

**GIZEH, GREAT PYRAMID OF** Egyptian pyramid of Khufu or Cheops whose tunnels and measurements have been used by astrologically minded persons to chart future history. By far the largest pyramid ever constructed, covering thirteen acres, it is a marvel of engineering science and funerary architecture.

**GLADDEN, WASHINGTON (1836–1918)** American Congregational minister of liberal social and religious views. Believing that religion should be expressed in life, he is famous for the hymn "O Master, Let Me Walk With Thee."

**GLADSTONE, WILLIAM EWERT (1809–1898)** British statesman, early interested in the church, whose intellectual and political vigor united moral, social, and national interests. He wrote *The State in Its Relations With the Church* and *Church Principles* and was throughout his life deeply interested in the Bible and Christian conviction. Prime minister and leader of the Liberal Party for many years, he opposed British imperialism, promoted home rule for Ireland, and worked for social reform.

**GLAS, JOHN (1695–1773)** Scottish PRESBYTERIAN minister who decided that there is no Scriptural warrant for a national church or national covenants, that the civil magistrate has no place in the church, and that the true reformation of religion must be carried out by the Word and spirit of Christ, not by worldly forces. Deposed from the ministry, he became leader of the "Glasites" who accepted his rather narrow, pietistic views.

**GLASITES** Followers of John GLAS. Eventually their leadership passed to John Glas' son-in-law Robert Sandeman and they became known as Sandemanians.

**GLASS** Religious symbol of purity and holiness.

**GLASSITES** See GLASITES.

**GLASTONBURY** Town in Somersetshire, England, where according to legend Joseph of Arimathea preached the gospel and King Arthur reigned. It is famous for several churches and Glastonbury Abbey, which may be the oldest monastery in England.

**GLASTONBURY THORN** Hawthorn which flowered on or about Christmas Day at GLASTONBURY (see) and was believed to have grown from the staff of Joseph of Arimathea. The PURITANS nearly exterminated this species.

**GLAUCUS** Greek sea god.

**GLEBE** In British territory, land assigned to a church for its maintenance.

**GLENDALOUGH** Valley in Ireland noted for its ruins of the Seven Churches, Kevin's Cross, and Kevin's Kitchen. Kevin was a sixth-century Irish saint who founded a monastery at Glendalough, which is a leading place of pilgrimage in Ireland.

**GLOBE** In religious art, a symbol of power.

**GLORIA** *glory* 1. A DOXOLOGY beginning with the word "Glory." 2. A nimbus or aureole.

**GLORIA IN EXCELSIS** *glory in the highest* Christian hymn of praise based on the angels' Christmas song of Luke 2:14.

**GLORIA PATRI** *glory be to the Father* Brief DOXOLOGY used in many churches ascribing praise to the Father, the Son, and the Holy Ghost.

**GLORIA TIBI** *glory be to Thee* Hymn of praise sung in ANGLICAN churches before the Gospel is read.

**GLORIFY** To extol or make glorious. The Christian is promised a splendid, glorified body like that of Christ (I CORINTHIANS 15:35).

**GLORIOUS MYSTERIES** In the ROSARY: the RESURRECTION, the ASCENSION, the DESCENT OF THE SPIRIT, the ASSUMPTION, and the CORONATION OF OUR LADY.

**GLORIOUS REVOLUTION** The crowning of William and Mary at the invitation of the British Parliament in 1689. It marked the end of the "divine right of kings" in England because it acknowledged the supremacy of the people. The Declaration of Rights and Bill of Rights of 1689 excluded any CATHOLIC from the throne.

**GLORY** 1. Praise or honor. 2. The splendor or greatness of God. 3. The appearance of that splendor. 4. The blessing or joy felt in the presence of God. 5. An aureole. 6. To take just pride in.

**GLOSS** 1. A marginal note in a manuscript. 2. An interpretation, explanation, or commentary. 3. A glossary. 4. A false interpretation. 5. Any addition to an original writing, as to the original text of Scripture.

**GLOSSOLALIA** *tongue speaking* A puzzling psychological and religious phenomenon. On the Day of Pentecost the Christians were filled with the Holy Spirit and spoke in strange tongues or languages, and were accused of being drunk (ACTS 2:1–13). Glossolalia was common in worship services in the church of Corinth, and has occurred sporadically throughout religious history. In recent years renewed interest in glossolalia has produced the term "charismatic renewal."

**GLOVER, TERROT REAVELEY (1869–1943)** British Baptist who was president of the BAPTIST UNION OF GREAT BRITAIN AND IRELAND and wrote *Jesus in the Experience of Men* and other books.

**GLOVES, LITURGICAL** These are used in various ecclesiastical rites.

**GLUTTONY** Excessive eating or drinking, a capital sin.

**GNOMES** Tiny elves or spirits of mines or mountains in myth and folklore.

**GNOSIS** *knowledge* Philosophical term for absolute, exclusive spiritual knowledge, as in GNOSTICISM.

**GNOSTICISM** A religious belief in the early Christian ages arising out of mingled sources: CABALISM, the MYSTERY RELIGIONS, ZOROASTRIANISM, the religions of Babylonia and Egypt, and CHRISTIANITY. Basically dualistic, although with various forms, it held essentially to a distant God united with the evil world of matter through various AEONS; salvation was possible through esoteric knowledge (*gnosis*) of secret truths and formulae. The creator of this world, the God of the Old Testament, was an evil DEMIURGE who was the antithesis of the true God. Jesus was not God-man, for God can have nothing to do with evil matter; He did not die for our salvation but to give us knowledge. The Gnostics were either ascetic, trying to crush evil matter, or libertarian, believing that it made no difference how one treated matter. The early Christian creeds were hammered out in opposition to the teachings of Gnosticism.

**GOAT** In Christian art, a symbol of the lost, based on the reference to the goats in Matthew 25:31–46.

**GOD** 1. A supernatural being. BUDDHISM has many gods, but none are absolute. 2. An idol, or anything put in a supreme place. Thus money, popularity, sex, country, or anything else may be a person's real god. 3. In philosophy, the Absolute or Unconditioned or Ultimate Reality or First Cause. 4. In CHRISTIAN SCIENCE, "incorporeal, divine, supreme, infinite Mind, Spirit, Soul, Principle, Life, Truth, Love" (Mary Baker Eddy). 5. The infinite Spirit who created all things and has been perfectly revealed in Jesus Christ; who is the ground of our existence; who has made us for Himself and who gives Himself for our eternal blessing.

**GODAVARI** River of western India sacred to HINDUS, who have a great bathing festival there every twelve years.

**GODCHILD** A child who is sponsored at baptism by one or more adults who promise that it will be given Christian training.

**GODET, FREDERIC LOUIS (1812–1900)** Swiss Protestant theologian who was a founder of the Free Evangelical Church of Neuchatel. He wrote commentaries on many books of the New Testament. He was an able leader in conservative PROTESTANTISM and a fluent writer.

**GODFATHER** See GODPARENTS.

**GODHEAD** 1. The nature or essence of God. 2. God, or a god.

**GODHOOD** Godship; divine nature or being.

**GODLINESS** Righteousness; possession of a God-like character.

**GOD-MAN** Term for Jesus Christ as true God and true man, God incarnate in the perfect Man.

**GODMOTHER** See GODPARENTS.

**GODPARENTS** Adults who sponsor a child at baptism, promising to see that he or she is reared in the Christian faith.

**GOD'S ACRE** Ancient term for a cemetery. For many centuries Christian dead were buried near a church.

**GODSPEED** Term for safe and successful journeying, a contraction of "God speed you."

**GODWARD** Toward God.

**GOEL** *redeemer* Jewish term for the relative who had the right to purchase back property which his kinsman had sold (RUTH 4:1–12); as *goel*, Boaz also married Ruth.

**GOEL HA-DAM** *avenger of the blood* In Judaism, the next of kin to a murdered person whose duty it was to avenge him.

**GOETHE, JOHANN WOLFGANG VON (1749– 1832)** German poet and philosopher who wrote various religious poems and considered nature "the living garment of God."

**GOG AND MAGOG** Final assailants of the Kingdom of God (EZEKIEL 38; 39; REVELATION 20:8).

**GOHEI** Rods with shavings, paper strips, or strings hanging from one end, used in the AINU and SHINTO religions of Japan to ward off evil.

**GOLD** Religious symbol of something precious or divine, of light, and of idolatry.

**GOLDEN AGE** Many religions look back to a universal golden age in the past, or forward to one in the future. Christianity looks back to the garden of Paradise, and forward to a garden in the golden city of God.

**GOLDEN BOUGH** One of the great studies of comparative religion. See FRAZER, JAMES GEORGE.

**GOLDEN CALF** The image worshiped by the Israelites while Moses was on Sinai receiving the Ten Commandments (EXODUS 32).

**GOLDEN LEGEND** Book of saints' lives written by Jacob of Voragine (or Jacobus de Varagine) about 1255. Popular until the Reformation, it provides miraculous stories, feast days, and the like about many saints.

**GOLDEN ROSE** Jeweled ornament, surmounted with a rose, blessed by the pope on LAETARE SUNDAY and conferred on eminent individuals, churches, or communities.

**GOLDEN RULE** The admonition of Jesus, "Therefore all things whatsoever ye would that men should do to you, do ye even so to them: for this is the law and the prophets" (MATTHEW 7:12). In negative form it appears in Tobit (4:15) and in many religions.

**GOLDEN SEQUENCE** The WHITSUNDAY hymn, "Veni, Sancte Spiritus" (Come, Holy Spirit).

**GOLDEN TEMPLE** Unusually lovely temple, set in the center of a lake in Amritsar, India, sacred to SIKHS.

**GOLDFINCH** Symbol of Christ's suffering in Christian art.

**GOLEM** Jewish word for a creature made from clay and given life by a charm or incantation. Judah Loew, Rabbi of Prague in the sixteenth century, is often named as one who made a golem and had to destroy it.

**GOLGOTHA** *skull* Place of Jesus' crucifixion outside Jerusalem. See CALVARY.

**GOLIATH** Philistine giant, nine feet tall, slain by a stone from the sling of shepherd-boy David (I SAMUEL 17).

**GOMER** *finish* 1. A son of Japheth, possibly father of the Cimmerians (GENESIS 10:2). 2. Wife or concubine of the prophet Hosea (HOSEA 1:3).

**GOMORRAH** City destroyed with Sodom in the time of Abraham. These cities may have stood where the Dead Sea now is (GENESIS 13:10).

**GOOD** Beneficial, pleasant, adequate, moral, or right. Good has many meanings, but all of them seem related to the similar English word God in that He does all things well, righteously, adequately, and for our benefit and happiness.

**GOOD, JAMES ISAAC (1850–1924)** Minister and theologian of the German Reformed Church in the United States. President of the General Synod of his denomination 1911–1914, he wrote books on its history.

**GOOD BOOK** Term for the Bible.

**GOODELL, WILLIAM (1792–1867)** CON-GREGATIONAL missionary from the United States to Turkey, where he translated the Bible.

**GOOD FRIDAY** The Friday before Easter —good because it commemorates the Friday on which Christ died for the sin of the world.

**GOOD SAMARITAN** The man in a parable of Jesus who risked his life and went out of his way to help one wounded by thieves (LUKE 10:30–37).

**GOOD SHEPHERD** Jesus' description of Himself in John 10:11. The theme of Christ as a good shepherd carrying a lamb or leading sheep is a favorite one in contemporary Christian art.

**GOODSPEED, EDGAR JOHNSON (1871–1962)** American scholar of Greek and New Testament critic, famous for his ability and his *New Testament—An American Translation* (1923).

**GOOD THIEF** See DISMAS.

**GOOSE** In Christian art, a symbol of Martin of Tours—based on the story that his hiding place was once revealed by a goose.

**GOPHER WOOD** The wood from which Noah built the ark, possibly pine or cypress (GENESIS 6:14).

**GOPIS** KRISHNA's consorts in the Himalaya Mountains.

**GORDIN, JACOB M. (1853–1909)** Russian-born American writer of Yiddish plays with religious themes. He founded the Bible Brotherhood for Jews in 1880.

**GORDON, CHARLES WILLIAM (1860–1937)** "Ralph Connor," a PRESBYTERIAN minister and missionary in Canada who wrote such popular novels as *Black Rock* and *The Sky Pilot.*

**GORDON, GEORGE ANGIER (1853–1929)** Scottish-born CONGREGATIONAL minister in the United States who criticized Calvinism and advocated the "New Theology" of Horace BUSHNELL and the Andover theologians (see ANDOVER CONTROVERSY).

**GORDON, SAMUEL DICKEY (1859–1936)** American devotional speaker and writer whose books such as *Quiet Talks on Prayer* and *Quiet Talks on Power* had wide influence.

**GORE, CHARLES (1853–1932)** English bishop and ANGLO-CATHOLIC theologian who disturbed many by such publications as *Lux Mundi* and such propositions as that Christ erred and was subject to all human limitations while on earth. He led the socially minded Christian Social Union and founded the celibate order, the Community of the Resurrection.

**GORTON, SAMUEL (1592–1677)** English clothier who came to New England "to enjoy liberty of conscience" and was jailed and exiled for his heresies. Denying heaven, hell, and the TRINITY, he founded the Gortonites, and is remembered today as a contributor to the struggle for religious liberty.

**GOSALA (sixth century B.C.)** Mendicant of India who established a community of mendicants and founded the Ajivika sect.

**GOSHEN** 1. Region and town in Palestine (JOSHUA 10:41; 15:51). 2. Area in Egypt occupied by the Israelites during their sojourn there (EXODUS 8:22; 9:26).

**GOSPEL** *good news* 1. The good news that Christ died for our sins and lives for our blessing. 2. One of the first four books of the New Testament—Matthew, Mark, Luke, or John—tracing the life and work of Christ. 3. That part of a liturgical church service in which a portion from one of the four Gospels is read.

**GOSPEL, APOCRYPHAL** See APOCRYPHA.

**GOSPELER** 1. A reader or singer of the Gospel. 2. A gospel preacher, EVANGELICAL, PROTESTANT, or PURITAN.

**GOSPEL HYMN** Simple song expressing an evangelical truth or sentiment.

**GOSPEL OF JOHN** See JOHN, THE GOSPEL OF.

**GOSPEL OF LUKE** See LUKE.

**GOSPEL OF MARK** See MARK.

**GOSPEL OF MATTHEW** See MATTHEW.

**GOSPEL SIDE** The left side of the sanctuary, as one faces the altar in a liturgical church, where the Gospel is read or sung.

**GOSPEL SONG** See gospel hymn.

**GOTAMA** Variant of Gautama (see BUDDHA).

**GOTHIC CATHEDRAL** Magnificent church, dating from c. 1200 to 1500, with spiring arches, flying buttresses, and vaulted stone giving a feeling of infinite reaches and eternal glory.

**GOTHIC VERSION** Translation of the Bible into the Gothic language in the fourth century. Manuscripts of the Gothic Version now extant date from the fifth or sixth century.

**GOTHIC VESTMENTS** Ecclesiastical garments of medieval design, increasingly popular today.

**GOTTESFREUNDE** *friends of God* See FRIENDS OF GOD.

**GOTTHEIL, GUSTAV (1827–1903)** American rabbi, leader in REFORM JUDAISM, who founded a number of Jewish societies in the United States.

**GOTTHEIL, RICHARD J. H. (1862–1936)** British-born ZIONIST and orientalist who headed Jerusalem's American School of Archaeology 1909–1910.

**GOTTHELF, JEREMIAS** Pseudonym of Albrecht Bitzius (1797–1854), Swiss PROTESTANT pastor and writer.

**GOTTSCHALK (c.808–c.868)** Gloomily poetic German BENEDICTINE whose study of the writings of St. AUGUSTINE led him to an absolute view of predestination for which he was condemned and imprisoned.

**GOUNOD, CHARLES FRANCOIS (1818–1893)** Brilliant French composer who studied theology and produced some outstanding religious oratorios, cantatas, masses, and motets.

**GOUPIL, RENE, ST. (c.1607–1642)** French Jesuit missionary to North America who was tortured and tomahawked by American Indians. One of the Jesuit martyrs of North America, his feast day is September 26.

**GOURD** Religious symbol of resurrection.

**GOVERNMENT** According to Romans 13, a divinely ordained institution for the enhancement of good and the suppression of evil. The supreme Ruler is God, and in fact every nation is under God's law and sovereignty.

**GOVERNMENT, CHURCH** There are three basic types of church government. The CONGREGATIONAL or BAPTIST system vests ultimate power in the local congregation of gathered believers. The EPISCOPAL or CATHOLIC system vests ultimate power in one or more bishops who guide the affairs of the whole church. The PRESBYTERIAN system is a representative one, vesting power in lay elders and ministers equally; from local churches and presbyteries delegates are sent to the supremely controlling General Assembly.

**GOVERNMENTAL THEORY** A hypothesis of the atonement according to which Christ's death was a penal example, showing that the violation of law brings suffering.

**GOVINDA SINGH (1666–1708)** Guru or apostle revered by the KHALSA Sikhs.

**GOWN** Robe worn by many religious leaders.

**GOY** *nation* Jewish term for Gentile.

**GOYIM** *nations* Jewish term for the nations of the world, the Gentiles collectively.

**GOZZOLI, BENOZZO (1420–1497)** Student of Fra Angelico who became a vivacious painter of altarpieces, frescoes, and murals in many churches of Italy. In his "Journey of the Magi" he used the figures of contemporaries against an exotic background.

**GRACE** 1. Prayer at meals. 2. Ecclesiastical prayer of blessing. 3. Free, unmerited gift of God's love and favor.

**GRACE, ACTUAL** See ACTUAL GRACE.

**GRACE, MEANS OF** That which enables one to receive God's grace, as prayer, the use of Scripture, and the sacraments.

**GRACE, SANCTIFYING** The work of God in purifying, maturing, and elevating the soul or spirit.

**GRACES** The three daughters of ZEUS: Grace, Beauty, and Charm, worshiped in Greece and Rome. Originally they were probably fertility goddesses.

**GRACIAN, BALTASAR (1601–1658)** Spanish writer of satire, allegory, and philosophy; member of the SOCIETY OF JESUS. A pessimist, he is believed to have influenced NIETZSCHE and SCHOPENHAUER.

**GRADINE** Ledge behind an altar holding symbolic objects.

**GRADUAL or GRADUALE** 1. Antiphonal verses sung after the Epistle in a liturgical service of the EUCHARIST. 2. Book containing such antiphons.

**GRADUALE ROMANUM** Book with all the chants for the mass required in a year.

**GRADUAL PSALMS** The Psalms of Ascent, Psalms 120–134. They may have been sung by pilgrims making the ascent to Jerusalem, and were once part of the Roman canonical office.

**GRAF, KARL HEINRICH (1815–1869)** German orientalist and Old Testament scholar who was one of the principal founders of Old Testament criticism.

**GRAFFITI** *scratchings* Markings or drawings found by archaeologists on monuments, catacomb walls, etc. The best known graffito is a caricature of the crucified Jesus found in Rome in 1857.

**GRAIL**   Cup, chalice, or platter.

**GRAIL, HOLY**   Chalice of the LAST SUPPER, filled with the blood of Christ, sought by the knights of Arthurian legend. The legends associated with the Grail may derive from very ancient religious worship in the British Isles.

**GRANDE CHARTREUSE**   Monastery in the Alps where the CARTHUSIAN ORDER originated. Chartreuse liqueur was made by the monks.

**GRAND LAMA**   Head of the BUDDHISM of Tibet and Mongolia.

**GRANGE**   Ancient term for farm buildings belonging to a monastery.

**GRANNOS**   Celtic god of spring water.

**GRANTH** *treatise*   SIKH sacred writings containing hymns and poetic injunctions by NANAK, KABIR, and other SIKH founders.

**GRAPE**   Symbol of the blood of Christ.

**GRASSHOPPER**   Held by the infant Jesus in religious art, the grasshopper symbolizes the world dominion of Christianity.

**GRATIAN (twelfth century)**   Italian monk, probably Camaldolite (see CAMALDOLESE), who wrote the *Decretum* or *Concordia* in which papal and conciliar decrees, writings of the Fathers, and other ecclesiastical data are systematically arranged. This is the virtual basis of canon law.

**GRATIAS TIBI** *thanks be to Thee*   Ascription of praise offered after the Gospel is read.

**GRÄTZ, HEINRICH (1817–1891)**   Conservative German Jewish leader of reform in his faith. His monumental *History of the Jews* has been very influential.

**GRATZ, REBECCA (1781–1869)**   American Jewess who originated the first Jewish Sunday school in Philadelphia and whose beauty may have inspired the Rebecca in *Ivanhoe*.

**GRAVAMEN** *grievance*   Memorial in the CHURCH OF ENGLAND seeking to remedy problems or grievances.

**GRAVEDIGGERS**   See FOSSARIANS.

**GRAVEN IMAGES**   Term in the King James Bible for carved (or, at times, molten) idols or images used for worship.

**GRAY**   Religious symbol of humility, death, or immortality.

**GRAY FRIARS**   See FRANCISCANS.

**GREAT ASSEMBLY**   Jewish lawmaking body at the time of the second temple in Jerusalem.

**GREAT AWAKENING**   The religious revival in the American colonies in which Jonathan EDWARDS and George WHITEFIELD were prominent.

**GREAT BEING**   The god exalted in Comte's synthetic religion of POSITIVISM.

**GREAT BIBLE**   English Bible edited by Miles COVERDALE in 1539.

**GREAT COMMISSION**   Christ's command to evangelize the whole world.

**GREAT FRIDAY**   See GOOD FRIDAY.

**GREAT INTERCESSION**   ANGLICAN term for the prayer for the "whole state of Christ's Church."

**GREAT MOTHER**   CYBELE, Phrygian goddess of fertility. She was also called "Great Mother of the Gods."

**GREAT PRAYER**   Scottish PRESBYTERIAN term for the pastoral prayer in the church service, including adoration of God, confession of sin, petition for mercy, supplication for various needs, and general thanksgiving.

**GREAT REBELLION**   The period in English history when the PURITANS overthrew the monarchy and set up a kind of theocracy under Oliver Cromwell.

**GREAT REVIVAL**   Special term for the American revival of religion in 1800 and 1801 in states west of the Alleghenies. Such preachers as James MC GREADY and John McGee held camp meetings at which unusual physical manifestations developed among the worshipers, many conversions to Christianity took place, and eventually revivals broke out in all parts of the United States.

**GREAT SABBATH**   The Sabbath preceding PASSOVER in JUDAISM.

**GREAT SCHISM**   Division between the Eastern and Western Catholic churches, initiated by the repudiation by CERULARIUS, Patriarch of Constantinople, of the claims of Pope LEO IX as spiritual ruler of all Christendom.

**GREAT SOBOR**   RUSSIAN ORTHODOX administrative church council.

**GREAT SYNAGOGUE**   The governing council or rabbinic school of 120 scribes following the BABYLONIAN CAPTIVITY of the Jews. Exact information about this group is difficult to ascertain.

**GREAT VEHICLE** MAHAYANA, the great division of BUDDHIST doctrine in which the goal of life is renunciation of NIRVANA for the purpose of aiding men to reach it.

**GRECO, EL (c.1541–1614)** Greek icon painter whose mystic religious paintings are one of Spain's great gifts to the world. Originally Domenicos Theotocopoulos, he painted St. Jerome, St. Francis, and many scenes in the life of Christ.

**GREEK** 1. The language in which the NEW TESTAMENT was written. 2. In the New Testament, a person of Greek descent, a Jew who spoke Greek, or a Gentile Christian.

**GREEK CATHOLIC CHURCH** Popular name of the EASTERN ORTHODOX CHURCH.

**GREEK CROSS** Cross with all four arms of equal length.

**GREEK FATHERS** Church Fathers of the Eastern division such as CHRYSOSTOM, ATHANASIUS, and BASIL.

**GREEK ORTHODOX** See EASTERN ORTHODOX CHURCH.

**GREEK ORTHODOX ARCHDIOCESE OF NORTH AND SOUTH AMERICA** The Greek Orthodox churches of North and South America headed by the Patriarch of Constantinople. They conform to EASTERN ORTHODOX doctrines and government.

**GREEK RITE** Liturgy of the EASTERN ORTHODOX CHURCH.

**GREEN** Color symbolizing life, growth, initiation, and the seasons of TRINTY and EPIPHANY.

**GREEN THURSDAY** German name for MAUNDY THURSDAY. It may have originated with the custom of giving green branches to penitents who had made confession at the beginning of LENT.

**GREENWOOD, JOHN (?–1593)** English PURITAN who led the London SEPARATISTS, wrote controversial tracts against such things as formally read prayers, and was jailed and hanged.

**GREER, DAVID HUMMELL (1844–1919)** EPISCOPAL Bishop of New York whose talents helped speed the building of the Cathedral of St. John the Divine.

**GREGOIRE, HENRI (1750–1831)** French cleric and revolutionist. As a priest with JANSENIST sympathies, he supported the French Revolution but resisted all pressure to resign his office or abjure his faith. He was the first priest to take the oath under the new civil constitution, steadfastly advocated religious freedom, and often took a minority view both in politics and in his church. The Archbishop of Paris refused him the last sacrament and he died in poverty but with great popular acclaim.

**GREGORAS, NICEPHORUS (c.1295–1360)** Controversial Byzantine theologian and historian. A learned man, he wrote widely, including the *Roman History* in 37 volumes. He led negotiations for reunion of the Greek and Roman churches.

**GREGORIAN** Connected with one of the popes named Gregory.

**GREGORIANA, PONTIFICIA UNIVERSITA** University of the SOCIETY OF JESUS in Rome, founded in 1551 by St. IGNATIUS LOYOLA.

**GREGORIAN CALENDAR** Calendar now in universal use which was reformed in 1582 by Pope GREGORY XIII. The Julian Calendar previously in use had gone astray by ten days when Gregory numbered the day following October 4, 1582, as October 15, and instituted the present more accurate system of chronology. PROTESTANT countries were slow to accept it and the EASTERN ORTHODOX CHURCH did not adopt the new calendar until 1924.

**GREGORIAN CHANT** Unmetrical and unaccompanied "plainsong" music of the ROMAN CATHOLIC CHURCH. The best known type of the monodic singing of the early church, it is named for Pope GREGORY I who standardized it.

**GREGORIAN CHURCH** See ARMENIAN CHURCH.

**GREGORIAN SACRAMENTARY** The type of Roman liturgy widely accepted in the kingdom of Charlemagne and the Franks, becoming a Frankish norm.

**GREGORIAN WATER** Holy water containing salt, wine, and ashes, named for GREGORY I.

**GREGORY I (c.540–604)** "Gregory the Great," a BENEDICTINE monk and memorable pope who altered the monastic and papal systems. Born in Rome, he called the fair-haired youngsters on sale in his city's slave markets "not Angles but angels." He sent St. AUGUSTINE of Canterbury to England and consolidated the papal supremacy after being elected pope against his will. His feast day is March 12.

**GREGORY VII (c.1015–1085)** Italian BEN-EDICTINE monk originally named Hilde-brand, "greatest of the medieval popes." Condemning the evils of lay investiture and affirming the supremacy of the church over the Empire, he was defied by Henry IV, the German emperor, who declared Gregory deposed. Gregory excommuni-cated Henry, who crossed the Alps in the winter and knelt barefoot in the snow at Canossa in 1077 to receive absolution. In the unrest that followed, Rome was in-vaded and Gregory died in exile at Sa-lerno. His feast day is May 25.

**GREGORY XI (1330–1378)** Learned, sin-cere French pope who fought the doc-trines of WYCLIF, reformed the monastic orders, and moved the papal throne from Avignon back to Rome.

**GREGORY XIII (1502–1585)** Italian pope who was active in clerical education, the conversion of Protestants, and the Council of TRENT. He is probably most famous for inaugurating the GREGORIAN CALENDAR.

**GREGORY OF NAZIANZUS, ST. (c.330–c.390)** One of the four great Fathers in Eastern Christianity. A humble CAPPADOCIAN sometimes called Gregory Theologus, he became Bishop of Constantinople where he defended orthodoxy, opposed ARIAN-ISM, and revived Catholic faith. His feast day is May 9.

**GREGORY OF NYSSA, ST. (c.331–c.395)** CAPPADOCIAN churchman who became Bishop of Nyssa and one of the four great Eastern Fathers. He defended the ortho-dox faith, took part in the First Council of CONSTANTINOPLE, and wrote against APOLLINARIANS, unbelievers, and Jews. His feast day is March 9.

**GREGORY OF TOURS, ST. (538–594)** French Bishop of Tours who wrote a ten-volume *History of the Franks* and many books of biography and miracle stories. His feast day is November 17.

**GREGORY THAUMATURGUS, ST. (c.213–c.270)** "The Wonderworker," Greek Bishop of Neocaesarea to whom are at-tributed many miracles and conversions. He enthusiastically supported his friend ORIGEN. Feast day: November 17.

**GREGORY THE ILLUMINATOR, ST. (c.257–c.337)** "Apostle of Armenia," a Parthian whose preaching converted Armenia to the Christian faith, according to tradition.

He became Metropolitan of Armenia, and is considered the founder of the Armenian Church. He died a hermit on Mt. Sebuh. His feast day is September 30.

**GRELLET, STEPHEN (1773–1855)** French-born trader in America who used his prof-its to finance his travels as a QUAKER mis-sionary through western America.

**GREMIAL** Lap cloth or apron of silk used by the bishop when seated during mass or pontifical ceremonies.

**GRENFELL, WILFRED T. (1865–1940)** Eng-lish medical missionary among the fisher-men and Eskimos of Labrador. There he built schools, hospitals, cooperative stores, and many other institutions of spiritual and social service.

**GREY FRIARS** See FRANCISCANS.

**GREY MONKS** See CISTERCIAN ORDER.

**GREY NUNS** The Order of Sisters of Charity, founded by Madame d'Youville at Montreal in 1737 for the care of the ill. There are Grey Nuns in various coun-tries; those best known may be the Grey Nuns of Charity in North America.

**GRIFFIN** Mythological beast, half lion and half eagle, in religious art represent-ing *a.* Christ and *b.* Christian persecu-tions.

**GRIMKE, ANGELINA EMILY (1805–1879)** QUAKER born in Charleston, South Caro-lina, who gave her life to work for the abolition of slavery and the rights of women. She married Theodore Weld and wrote *An Appeal to the Christian Women of the South.*

**GRIMKE, SARAH MOORE (1792–1873)** QUAKER born in Charleston, South Caro-lina, who led her sister Angelina (above) into the Quaker faith and an abolitionist campaign. She began the American movement for women's rights.

**GRINNELL, JOSIAH BUSHNELL (1821–1891)** CONGREGATIONAL minister in Washington, D.C., who lost his church for preaching against slavery, went west at the advice of Horace Greeley, founded Grinnell, Iowa, and excelled in politics, business, and ag-riculture. He was a dedicated abolitionist.

**GRONINGEN SCHOOL** Members of a the-ological group whose leaders were from Groningen in the Netherlands and who combined evangelistic zeal with liberal doctrines and stress on education.

**GROOTE, GERARD (1340–1384)** "Gerard

the Great," Dutch founder of the BRETH-REN OF THE COMMON LIFE. His sermons against the sins of the day were tremendously popular but led to a ban on his preaching. A practical mystic, he may have been the original author of *The Imitation of Christ*.

**GROSSETESTE, ROBERT (c.1175–1253)** Great English churchman and philosopher of the Middle Ages. He wrote treatises on various sciences, commentaries on ARISTOTLE, and translations of important classical works. A teacher of Roger BACON and Adam Marsh, he advocated church reform and may have influenced John WYCLIF.

**GROTIUS, HUGO (1583–1645)** Statesman, humanist, jurist, and theologian of the Netherlands. His book *Concerning the Law of War and Peace* based international relationships on law and principles of statesmanship. He used the Bible to establish respect for individuals and to define the nature of just wars. His *Concerning the Truth of the Christian Religion* sets forth the essentials of religion on a nonsectarian basis. Grotius also proposed the GOVERNMENTAL THEORY of the atonement.

**GRUBER, FRANZ (1787–1863)** Austrian organist who composed the music for the Christmas hymn "Silent Night."

**GRUNDTVIG, NIKOLAI FREDERIK SEVERIN (1783–1872)** Danish LUTHERAN pastor, statesman, poet, and author of more than a thousand hymns. Offending church authorities with his frank preaching, he was expelled from the pulpit for seven years but finally became a bishop. He contributed to the understanding of the church and the sacraments, and sought to substitute the authority of the Living Word for commentary and tradition. He has been called the Danish Carlyle.

**GRUNEWALD, MATHIAS (c.1480–1528)** Masterful German painter. The realism of his depictions of the Crucifixion is powerful.

**GUARANI RELIGION** The religion of the Guarani Indians of eastern coastal South America. They believe that there are two souls at conflict within each person and once practiced cannibalism as a ritual.

**GUARDIAN ANGEL** Supernatural being assigned to care for a person.

**GUCUMATZ** Aztec serpent god and hero.

**GUECUBU** Evil being in the religion of the Araucanian Indians.

**GUELPHS** Germans or Europeans who supported the papacy against the empire-supporting GHIBELLINES in the Middle Ages.

**GUIDANCE, DIVINE** Direction by the Holy Spirit in response to faith and prayer. Jesus promised His disciples, ". . . the Spirit of truth . . . will guide you into all truth" (JOHN 16:13).

**GUIDE TO THE PERPLEXED** Medieval philosophical work by MAIMONIDES. It covers a variety of mystic, religious, and metaphysical matters.

**GUIDO D'AREZZO (c.990–1050)** Italian Benedictine monk known as the father of modern music. He devised a number of musical innovations including the names of the notes in the scale.

**GUILT** The fact or feeling of having committed a wrong and of deserving punishment. Religion through the ages with its prayers and offerings has attempted to alleviate man's universal feelings of guilt. Christianity seeks not only to relieve such feelings but also to remove the hidden power of guilt, bringing the believer the liberty of Christ.

**GUILT OFFERING** In Israel before the temple was destroyed, the guilt or trespass offering was the sacrifice of a ram along with which damages to another had to be paid (LEVITICUS 5—7:10). Damages were figured according to the loss sustained by the one injured, together with one-fifth for the priest.

**GULA** Babylonian goddess of healing.

**GUMBUM** See KUMBUM.

**GUNKEL, HERMANN (1862–1932)** German PROTESTANT theologian, critic of the Old Testament, and proponent of FORM CRITICISM.

**GUNPOWDER PLOT** Scheme of a small number of English CATHOLICS to blow up Parliament the day it opened in 1605. Planned to relieve anti-Catholic pressures in England, it actually increased them and caused Catholic–Protestant relationships to deteriorate.

**GURNEY, EDMUND (1847–1888)** One of the English founders of the Society for Psychical Research.

**GURNEY, JOSEPH JOHN (1788–1847)** English QUAKER pastor whose followers have been called Gurneyites.

**GURU** *venerable one* HINDU teacher or spiritual guide, sometimes regarded as a representative or incarnation of deity. The guru must always be obeyed absolutely.

**GUSTAV-ADOLF-VEREIN** *Gustavus Adolphus union* German society founded in memory of King Gustavus Adolphus of Sweden to aid PROTESTANTS who are in a region where they form a minority. It seeks to provide them with churches, schools, teachers, pastors, and deaconesses.

**GUSTAVUS ADOLPHUS (1594–1632)** Protestant King of Sweden who saved PROTESTANTISM in Europe by intervening in the Thirty Years War. He required his soldiers to behave like Christians, forbidding rape, torture, or looting.

**GUSTAVUS ADOLPHUS UNION** See GUSTAV-ADOLF-VEREIN.

**GUTENBERG BIBLE** First Bible printed from movable type, produced in 1456 from the printing press invented by Johann Gutenberg, in Mainz, Germany. Also known as the Mazarin Bible, its printing is sometimes attributed to Johann Fust, to whom Gutenberg lost his press, or to Peter Schoffer, Fust's partner.

**GUTHRIE, THOMAS** Eloquent Scottish preacher who advocated total abstinence, founded the Ragged Schools for poor children, and led in founding the Free Church. In 1842 he organized the Y.M.C.A. in Glasgow.

**GUYON, JEANNE MARIE BOUVIER DE LA MOTTE (1648–1717)** French mystic. A widow at 28, she became a friend of FENELON and corresponded with the Spanish Quietist, MOLINOS. Her writings were adjudged heretical and she was imprisoned in the Bastille, then confined to her son's estate. Her books include *Spiritual Torrents, Mystical Sense of Sacred Scripture,* and *Method of Prayer.* Madame Guyon advocated a quietistic, internal religion of prayer, renunciation, and striving for personal holiness.

**GWALU** Rain god of the Yoruba tribe of West Africa.

**GYMNOSOPHISTS** *nude philosophers* Greek term for HINDU philosophers who considered food and clothing to detract from thought and who lived a hermit life in the forests of India.

**GYNAECEUM** *house for women* Gallery or aisle in an Eastern church reserved for female worshipers.

# H

**H** 1. Symbol of the Holiness Code. This is a designation for the Mosaic legislation in Leviticus 17–26, in which such phrases as "for I, the Lord, am holy" are often repeated. Some critics date "H" from the time of Ezekiel. 2. Symbol for such manuscripts of the New Testament as Seidelianus II, Mutinensis, and Coislinianus, important in ascertaining the correct text. 3. Symbol for the text of the New Testament in Greek which was prepared by Westcott and Hort in 1895.

**HAAKON THE GOOD (tenth century)** King of Norway (c.935–961) who sought to bring the Christian faith into that land.

**HABAKKUK, HABACUC, or ABACUC** Eighth of the twelve MINOR PROPHETS of the Old Testament Scriptures. A resident of Judah and probably of Jerusalem, Habakkuk wrote of God's use of the Chaldeans to punish His special people, the Jews. He originated the statement, "The just shall live by faith."

**HABDALAH** Jewish rite marking the end of the SABBATH and other festivals, emphasizing the distinction between the holy day and the common day that follows it. Blessings are offered and spices savored.

**HABIRU** An aggressive people of the fourteenth century B.C. believed by some scholars to have been the Hebrews. Arad-Hiba, a king of Jerusalem about 1370 B.C., complained that the Habiru were conquering all the land.

**HABIT** 1. A physical, mental, or spiritual function acquired by repetition. Good religions encourage the formation of good habits. 2. A religious garment. Various faiths and orders wear distinctive habits.

**HABITUAL GRACE** The divine gift enabling men to do good works. Sometimes called sanctifying grace, it is received through the sacraments and is considered to bring about permanent spiritual growth.

**HACELDAMA** See ACELDAMA.

**HACHIMAN** Japanese god of war.

**HADAD** 1. See Adad. 2. Name of several Edomite kings and other persons mentioned in the Bible.

**HADADEZER** A king who fought against King David of Israel and whose followers became subjects of David after their defeat (II SAMUEL 8:3–12).

**HADADRIMMON** A name in Zechariah 12:11 apparently combining the names of two non-Jewish gods.

**HADASSAH** *myrtle* 1. Jewish name of Queen Esther (ESTHER 2:7). 2. Jewish women's ZIONIST organization founded in 1912 by Henrietta SZOLD and eleven other women. It dispenses aid for medical and social welfare, particularly through the Hadassah Medical Organization, throughout the world.

**HADES** 1. Greek word for the Hebrew Sheol, indicating the place of the dead. 2. Greek name of the ruler of the underworld of the dead.

**HADEWIJCH (thirteenth century)** Dutch nun who wrote mystic poetry of unusual power.

**HADITH** Sayings and anecdotes of MOHAMMED, transmitted by tradition, constituting the norm of orthodox ISLAM.

**HADJ, HAJ or HAJJ** A pilgrimage to MECCA, required of all MOSLEMS at least once in the life of each. The BLACK STONE is kissed and an animal offered in sacrifice.

**HADJI or HAJJI** A pilgrim, particularly one on the "HADJ" to MECCA.

**HADLAKAT NEROT** Jewish term for lighting the candles, particularly by the housewife in a home ceremony.

**HADRIAN** 1. Roman emperor (117–138) who put the Jews out of Jerusalem and ruthlessly quelled the rebellion of BAR KOKBA about 132 A.D. 2. Six different popes bear this name.

**HADRIAN IV (c.1100–1159)** Nicholas Breakspear, the only English pope in history. He brought about the execution of ARNOLD OF BRESCIA in 1155.

**HADRIAN VI (1459–1523)** Adrian Dedel, born in the Netherlands and at one time a member of the BRETHREN OF THE COMMON LIFE. He became an Inquisitor, a cardinal, and pope. He sought to quell PROTESTANTISM and to reform the CURIA.

**HADRIAN THE AFRICAN, ST. (?–709)** African monk who became head of a monastery in Canterbury, England, and founded many schools in that country. His feast day is January 9.

**HAFTARAH** *end* Reading from the Prophets in a Jewish synagogue service after reading from the Law.

**HAGAR or AGAR** *flight* Female servant of Sarah who became mother of Abraham's son Ishmael. The two were cast out into the wilderness (GENESIS 16; 21). Hagar is a symbol of the bondage of the law in Galatians 4:24.

**HAGARITES** Desert tribe with whom the Israelites warred (I CHRONICLES 5:10; BARUCH 3:23).

**HAGBAHAH** Jewish term for the elevation of the scroll of the law after the reading from it.

**HAGGADA** *narrative* 1. The narrative or literary element in the rabbinic interpretation of the OLD TESTAMENT Scriptures. 2. Imaginative Jewish exposition of the Scriptures. 3. The narration of the deliverance of the Jewish people from Egypt at the SEDER in PASSOVER.

**HAGGADIST** 1. One who studies the HAGGADA. 2. A haggadic writer.

**HAGGAI or AGGEUS** Tenth of the MINOR PROPHETS. The short book of Haggai encourages Zerubbabel and Joshua to complete the rebuilding of the temple in Jerusalem, and promises glories in the future.

**HAGIA SOPHIA** *holy wisdom* A church in Constantinople, later a MOSLEM mosque and then a museum, filled with outstanding Byzantine art and architecture. The enormous dome, once topped by a cross, now supports the Moslem crescent.

**HAGIOGRAPHA** A division of the Jewish Bible. The other divisions are the Law, constituting the five books of Moses, and the Prophets, constituting Major and Minor Prophets and certain historical books. The Hagiographa, including Psalms, Proverbs, Job, Ruth, Ecclesiastes, Esther, Daniel, Lamentations, Song of Songs, Chronicles, Ezra, and Nehemiah, constitutes the rest of the Old Testament. Also called the Writings.

**HAGIOGRAPHER** A writer of the Hagiographa, or a biographer of a saint.

**HAGIOGRAPHY** 1. A life of a saint or lives of the saints. 2. HAGIOLOGY.

**HAGIOLATRY** Invocation or veneration or worship of saints.

**HAGIOLOGY** 1. Study or history of saints or of sacred writings. 2. A catalog of saints, or literature dealing with them.

**HAGIOSCOPE** Opening in chancel wall of an ancient church to enable worshipers to view the altar.

**HAHAM** See HAKAM.

**HAI** See AI.

**HAI (939–1038)** Jewish talmudist, famed as an authority on civil and ceremonial law, who wrote commentaries on the MISHNAH and a dictionary of Jewish terms. He was principal of Pumbedita Academy in Babylonia.

**HAIL MARY** Salutation to Mary the mother of Jesus, originating in that by the angel Gabriel (LUKE 1:28).

**HAIR SHIRT** Garment woven of hair whose rough interior was very irritating. It was worn by ascetics and others seeking to mortify the flesh or do penance.

**HAJ or HAJJ** See HADJ.

**HAJJI** See HADJI.

**HAJJ OMAR (1797–1864)** African MOSLEM who began a holy war against several pagan tribes in 1848 and attempted to establish a theocracy in the Sudan.

**HAKAM** *wise one* Chief rabbi in SEPHARDIM communities, and among Palestinian Jews in talmudic times.

**HAKIM** MOSLEM term for a judge or leader.

**HAKUIN, EKAKU or HAKUIN ZENJI (1685–1768)** "The greatest Zen master of modern times" who introduced ZEN Buddhism of the RINZAI variety to his age. He was a poet, artist, and sculptor. He introduced the concept of *koan* for developing intuitive awareness.

**HALAKAH or HALACHA rule** 1. Jewish law or tradition. 2. Legal aspect of Jewish tradition, particularly of the TALMUD. Compare HAGGADA.

**HALAKAH L'MOSHEH MI SINAI law of Moses in Sinai** A law given at Sinai as one of the Ten Commandments (see DECALOGUE).

**HALBERD** Symbol of MATTHIAS, believed to have been beheaded for his Christian witness.

**HALES, JOHN (1584–1656)** "Ever-memorable" English canon who attended the Synod of DORT and expressed his breadth of religious tolerance in *Schism and Schismatics*.

**HALEVI, JUDAH or JEHUDAH HALEVY (c.1085–c.1150)** Spanish rabbi, poet, and philosopher who defended JUDAISM against ISLAM and CHRISTIANITY, proclaimed the superiority of religion over philosophy, and wrote poems and hymns of longing for the restoration of ZION.

**HALF-WAY COVENANT** Term for a decision of seventeenth-century New England CONGREGATIONALISM that the children of church adherents might be baptized, although the adherents were not full members and had not experienced personal faith. The Half-Way Covenant had few supporters after the eighteenth century's religious revivals.

**HALL, JOSEPH (1574–1656)** English prelate who lost his position and money for advocating episcopacy without prelacy, for suspected sympathies with the PURITANS, and treason. He wrote many satirical verses attacking (and attacked by) John Milton. His devotional writings were later appreciated by John WESLEY, who included in his *Christian Library* Hall's *Heaven Upon Earth*.

**HALL, ROBERT (1764–1831)** English Baptist and popular preacher who upheld the rights of the lace workers of Leicestershire.

**HALLAJ (?–922)** MOSLEM mystic who was slain at Bagdad for teaching that God is incarnate in every man and for saying, "I am Reality."

**HALLE** German city penetrated by PROTESTANTISM in 1522 and famous as a center of Protestant theology. There the first BIBLE SOCIETY was founded.

**HALLE REPORTS** Reports to his supporters in Halle, Germany by Henry Melchior Mühlenberg about his mission work in Pennsylvania in the eighteenth century.

**HALLEL praise** Term for Psalms 113–118 in which the word *Hallelujah*, "Praise ye the Lord," recurs. These Psalms are sung in the synagogue at PENTECOST, Feast of the BOOTHS, and PASSOVER.

**HALLELUJAH or ALLELUIA praise ye the Lord** Expression of praise often found in the Psalms and in some hymns and anthems.

**HALLELUJAH CHORUS** One of the great choruses and perhaps the high point of Handel's *Messiah*, an outstanding Christian oratorio.

**HALLOW** Devotional word meaning "consecrate" or "set apart."

**HALLOWEEN** Popular name for All Saint's Eve, on October 31, a time of vigil associated in the Middle Ages with the activity of ghosts and evil spirits. For centuries it has been a time of festivity, bonfires, and pranks.

**HALLOWMAS** The religious festival of ALL SAINTS' or All Hallows'.

**HALO** Circle of light, symbolizing grace or goodness, often employed in religious art to indicate Jesus and sacred figures.

**HAM** The son of Noah, cursed for spying on his drunken father's nakedness (GENESIS 9:20–25). He was the father of Cush, Mizraim, Put, and Canaan.

**HAMADRYAD** Tree spirit believed, in Greek myth, to live and die with the tree.

**HAMAN** Favored prime minister under Ahasuerus whose plot to kill the Jews in the Persian realm was foiled by Queen Esther. Haman was hanged on the gallows he had erected for Esther's cousin Mordecai (ESTHER 3–7).

**HAMANN, JOHANN GEORG (1730–1788)** German Jewish mystic who saw the Bible as the book of all knowledge, God as the foundation of reality, and faith and personal experience as the key to religion. He deeply influenced GOETHE, HEGEL, and KIERKEGAARD.

**HAMARTIOLOGY** Term in theology for the doctrine of sin.

**HAMILTON, PATRICK (c.1504–1528)** Scottish priest who accepted and expounded PROTESTANT principles and was burned at the stake in retaliation.

**HAMITE** Native of North Africa believed to have descended from Noah's son HAM.

**HAMMARSKJÖLD, DAG (1905–1961)** Secretary-General of the United Nations (1953–1961) who was not known for religious sympathies until after his death on a peace mission. His posthumous book *Markings,* based on his secret diary, reveals Hammarskjöld's constant attempt to serve God in the spirit of Jesus Christ. He wrote: "Lord—Thine the day, and I the day's."

**HAMMURABI (eighteenth century B.C.)** Babylonian king, once identified with Amraphel of Genesis 14:1, who held lofty ideals of justice and culture. During his reign (once believed to be as early as the twenty-first century B.C.) MARDUK became a great god, the Babylonian Creation Epic was begun in the AKKADIAN version, and the Code of Hammurabi was set forth.

**HAMMURABI, CODE OF** One of the greatest ancient codes of law, drawn up by HAMMURABI. Some of its provisions afford striking parallels with Bible laws and records, as in the death penalty for kidnaping (EXODUS 21:16) and the "eye for an eye" principle (EXODUS 21:24). It was an advanced attempt to legislate right relationships in business, society, and morals. The Code was found at Susa in 1901, inscribed in 3,600 lines of cuneiform on a slab of black diorite and prefaced with praise to SHAMASH the sun-god and to Hammurabi as father and shepherd of his people.

**HAMPTON COURT CONFERENCE** An assembly summoned by James I of England in 1604 to consider Puritan demands for reform in the CHURCH OF ENGLAND and to settle differences between the PURITANS and the Anglican defenders. At this conference the "King James" translation of the Bible was authorized.

**HAN** A dynasty of China, c. 202 B.C. to A.D. 220, during which the CONFUCIAN religion became the basis of government, BUDDHISM took root, the sacred books were restored, and TAOISM was strengthened.

**HANAFITE RITE** Speculative interpretation of MOSLEM law originated by ABU HANIFA.

**HANAFORD, PHOEBE ANN (1829–1921)** UNIVERSALIST woman minister, first of her sex to be ordained to clerical rights in New England.

**HANANIAH** Fifteen Bible figures bear this name, including the Hananiah cast into the fiery furnace by Nebuchadnezzar and miraculously saved (DANIEL 1:7; 3).

**HANBAL, AHMAD IBN** See AHMAD IBN HANBAL.

**HANBALITE RITE** Literal interpretation of MOSLEM law originated by AHMAD IBN HANBAL in the ninth century A.D. This is one of the four orthodox schools of Moslem law.

**HAND** Religious symbol of power or the divine will. In Michelangelo's painting of the "Creation of Adam" on the ceiling of the SISTINE CHAPEL, the hand of God is vibrant with life.

**HANDEL, GEORGE FREDERICK (1685–1759)** Christian composer, born in Germany but a permanent resident of England after 1712, who produced many religious oratorios. The most famous is *The Messiah,* although *Samson, Judas Maccabeus,* and *Israel in Egypt* are outstanding choral works.

**HAND IN A CLOUD** Symbol, in religious art, of the glory and majesty of God.

**HANDIWORK** King James Bible term for work done by hand.

**HANDMAID** King James Bible word for a female servant. The Virgin MARY identified herself at the ANNUNCIATION as "the handmaid of the Lord" (LUKE 1:38).

**HANDS, IMPOSITION OF** See LAYING ON OF HANDS.

**HANDSOME LAKE (c.1735–1815)** American Indian who advocated a new religion in some respects similar to Christianity, although it was opposed by Christian missionaries. Handsome Lake advised the Seneca and Iroquois Indians to replace their hunting and gathering activities with agriculture.

**HANIFA** See ABU HANIFA.

**HANIFITE RITE** See HANIFITE RITE.

**HANNAH** *grace* Renowned mother of Samuel (I SAMUEL 1; 2).

**HANNINGTON, JAMES (1847–1885)** Missionary of the CHURCH OF ENGLAND who sought to evangelize the natives of Uganda in Africa and was eventually consecrated Bishop of Eastern Equatorial Africa. As he was murdered with his associates on the way through Africa, he said: "I have purchased the road to Uganda with my blood." His feast day is October 29.

**HANUKKAH or CHANUKAK** *dedication* Jewish festival beginning 25 Kislev, close to the winter solstice and Christmas, commemorating the restoration to the Jewish faith (165 B.C.) of the temple in Jerusalem after its desecration by ANTIOCHUS EPIPHANES. The festival lasts eight days and is sometimes called the Feast of Lights because eight Hanukkah candles are lighted, one each day. Because the victory was won by JUDAS MACCABEUS and his band, the festival is also known as the Feast of the Maccabees.

**HANUMAN** Hindu monkey god, honored in many temples in India and Japan.

**HAOKAH** Thunder god of the Sioux, a tribe of American Indians.

**HAOMA** Sacred drink in ZOROASTRIAN religion, or the plant (rhubarb?) from which it came, or the ceremony in which it was drunk or poured on the sacred fires.

**HAP** See SERAPIS.

**HAPI** Egyptian god of the Nile, represented as a male figure with female breasts.

**HAPLOGRAPHY** Omission of letters or portions of text in copying manuscripts—a problem in Biblical studies.

**HAPOEL HAMIZRACHI** International Jewish labor organization.

**HAPPINESS** An approximation of the word "blessedness" in the Bible. In Christianity, and in the great faiths, happiness is a by-product of righteousness.

**HARA-KIRI** *belly-cutting* Ceremonial suicide in Japan.

**HARAN** 1. Brother of Abraham (GENESIS 11:26). 2. Area in Mesopotamia where Haran's father Terah died. There the Assyrian moon-god was worshiped.

**HARD SHELL BAPTISTS** Old name for Baptists in the United States who opposed benevolent societies, missionary organizations, Sunday schools, payment of salaries to ministers, and other practices they considered unorthodox.

**HARE** In religious art, a symbol of both lust and chastity.

**HAREM** *sacred* In ISLAM, a holy place forbidden to infidels, or a part of a house reserved for women.

**HARLOT** Symbol, in the Bible, of a person or a people unfaithful to the Lord.

**HARMONY OF THE GOSPELS** An arrangement of the four Gospels in parallel columns giving the life and ministry of Christ in chronological order. A very early harmony was TATIAN's *Diatessaron* in the second century.

**HARMONY SOCIETY** Communal religious society established in the United States by George Rapp. Rapp and his followers, German pietists, founded Harmony, Pennsylvania in 1805 as a center for their experiment in farming, manufacturing, and celibate living on a Christian communistic basis. They also founded New Harmony, Indiana, and Economy, Pennsylvania. The Harmony Society died out in 1906.

**HARNACK, ADOLF VON** (1851–1930) German LUTHERAN theologian and church historian. A teacher of Karl Barth, he saw Christian dogma reflecting Greek philosophy more than the teaching of Jesus, and felt that human brotherhood was more important than speculative theology or doctrinal creeds. His important works are many and include *Outlines of the History of Dogma, What Is Christianity, The Expansion of Christianity in the First Three Centuries, The Apostles' Creed, Marcion, Luke the Physician,* and *Lehrbuch der Dogmengeschichte.*

**HARNER, NEVIN C.** (1901–1951) EVANGELICAL AND REFORMED minister who was professor of Christian education in the theological seminary of his denomination, a Christian education leader in the NATIONAL COUNCIL OF CHURCHES, and executive secretary of the American Association of Theological Schools.

**HARP** Stringed instrument associated with the Hebrew Psalms and symbol of music, the Psalms, and David the King.

**HARPA-KHRUTI** *Horus the Child* A form of Horus the Egyptian sun god as a child. He became the Greek and Roman HARPOCRATES.

**HARPOCRATES** Popular Greek and Roman god of silence. His transformation from the Egyptian HARPA-KHRUTI was caused by the Egyptians' representing a child in statuary with its finger at its mouth.

**HARPY** In Greek myth, an irresistible wind; or a monstrous bird with a woman's head which was thought to symbolize, or to be able to seize, the soul of a dead person.

**HARRIS, BRAVID WASHINGTON (1896–1965)** American-born EPISCOPAL Bishop of Liberia. He served as acting director of the Foundation for Episcopal Colleges and secretary for Negro work in the Home Department of the Episcopal Church.

**HARRIS, HOWELL (1714–1773)** Founder of Calvinistic METHODISM in Wales.

**HARRIS, JAMES RENDEL (1852–1941)** English QUAKER outstanding as a scholar of Biblical literature and of the religions of the Mediterranean. He wrote *Biblical Fragments from Mount Sinai, The Magi,* and other works.

**HARRIS, THOMAS LAKE (1823–1906)** English-born mystic who organized the religious-communistic BROTHERHOOD OF THE NEW LIFE in the United States and wrote about the sexuality of angels.

**HARROWING OF HELL** Medieval term for the doctrine that after the RESURRECTION Christ descended into hell to free its captive souls and defy its powers. The name was given a thirteenth-century English poem on that subject, and the idea was popular in medieval drama.

**HART** A stag in the King James Bible (PSALM 42:1). It symbolizes fleet-footedness.

**HARTMANN, EDUARD VON (1842–1906)** German philosopher who believed that Christianity had become bankrupt in the Middle Ages, God was impersonal, the traditional Jesus was a fetish, the worship of Jesus was idolatry, Christian morality was childish, men are their own saviors, the church is dying, and a new religion is needed. For the latter he proposed a blend of Eastern religions. Hartmann's great work was *The Philosophy of the Unconscious.*

**HARUSPEX** *observer of entrails* Etruscan or Roman practitioner of divination who foretold future events and interpreted the will of the gods by studying the entrails of animals, watching the weather or the flight of birds, and similar activities. Under the Roman Empire the haruspices were salaried.

**HARUSPICES** Plural of HARUSPEX.

**HARVARD, JOHN (1607–1638)** English PURITAN who became a minister in Charles-

town, Massachusetts, and left his library and half his estate of 780 pounds to a new college which became Harvard University. It was dedicated to the education of English and Indian youth "in knowledge and godliness."

**HARVEST FESTIVALS** These have united thanksgiving for crops with religious symbolism since most ancient times. The feasts of PENTECOST and BOOTHS in Israel before the BABYLONIAN CAPTIVITY were feasts of harvest and ingathering. The Greeks worshiped the corn goddess DEMETER, the Romans the deities of produce—CERES, LIBER, and Libera. Harvest Thanksgiving in Britain and THANKSGIVING DAY in the United States are national harvest festivals with strong religious associations.

**HASE, KARL AUGUST VON (1800–1890)** German LUTHERAN theologian and church historian. He wrote a life of Christ with rationalistic views of the miracles, but sought to unite orthodoxy with idealism.

**HASIDEANS or HASIDIM** *holy ones* Strict adherents of the Jewish law, forming the center of resistance to the attempts of ANTIOCHUS IV (175–163 B.C.) to Hellenize the Jews of Palestine. When Antiochus required them to offer pagan worship and eat pork, they revolted and many were slain. Hasidean leaders were the MACCABEES. The Hasideans' spiritual successors were the PHARISEES and possibly the ESSENES.

**HASIDISM** Term for the mystical development in JUDAISM inaugurated by BAAL-SHEM TOV in eighteenth-century Poland. It emphasizes the nearness of God, fellowship with Him, and joy in worship. It is marked by cheerfulness, optimism, the use of folk music and folklore, and sometimes the cabala. Hasidism has influenced Ernst Bloch, Ravel, and Martin BUBER.

**HASMONEANS** Jewish family who led the HASIDEAN revolt against ANTIOCHUS (EPIPHANES) IV. They were Mattathias and his sons Jonathan, Simon, John, Eleazar, and Judas Maccabee. The Hasmoneans were also called MACCABEES. HEROD THE GREAT married the last Hasmonean princess, Mariamne.

**HASSOCK** Cushion for kneeling on ecclesiastical occasions.

**HASTINGS, JAMES (1852–1922)** Scottish PRESBYTERIAN minister and editor of a number of cyclopedic religious works, such as the *Dictionary of the Bible, The Encyclopedia of Religion and Ethics,* and the *Dictionary of the Apostolic Church.* In 1889 he founded the *Expository Times.* His ministry was in the FREE CHURCH.

**HASTINGS, THOMAS (1784–1872)** American hymnologist who composed a number of hymns including the music for "Rock of Ages" and the words for "Hail to the Brightness of Zion's Glad Morning."

**HATCH, EDWIN (1835–1889)** English divine and expert in early church history. His book *The Influence of Greek Ideas and Usages Upon the Christian Church* stated that Greek influence diverted Christianity from a simple emphasis on moral conduct to one on philosophy and doctrine.

**HATHOR** *house of Horus* Cow-headed mother-goddess of ancient Egypt. She was also a sky goddess, a deity of love, a guardian of men's souls, and a goddess of birth and death.

**HATI** In Egyptian religion, the biological heart as opposed to the symbolic heart.

**HATIKVAH** Israel's national anthem.

**HATTIN, HORNS OF** Double peak near the Sea of Galilee, once believed to be the setting for the SERMON ON THE MOUNT and other open-air addresses of Jesus.

**HAUCK, ALBERT (1845–1918)** German LUTHERAN theologian and church historian —particularly of the German church in the Middle Ages. He served as an editor of an encyclopedia of PROTESTANTISM.

**HAUGE, HANS NIELSEN (1771–1824)** Norwegian lay preacher imprisoned and fined by the state church for his evangelistic work. Although he was not a separatist, he condemned rationalism, called men to repentance, emphasized faith and grace, and organized societies for spiritual growth. A national revival followed him.

**HAUGEANISM** Term for a movement in the LUTHERAN Church in Norway produced by Hans Nielsen HAUGE. It emphasized conversion, personal piety, lay preaching, and spiritual brotherhood. It also resulted in new religious freedoms.

**HAURVATAT** ZOROASTRIAN spirit of perfection, one of the six immortal holy ones attending AHURA MAZDA.

**HAUSTAFEL** *house table* Term for an ancient private moral code existing in many cultures alongside public law. Such codes may be reflected in the writings of BARNABAS and POLYCARP and in such New Testament passages as Ephesians 5:20— 6:9 and I Peter 2:13—3:9.

**HAVDALAH** *separation* Jewish blessing at the close of SABBATH.

**HAVERGAL, FRANCES RIDLEY (1836–1879)** British hymn and devotional writer, famous for such hymns as "Take My Life and Let It Be" and "Lord Speak to Me That I May Speak."

**HAWK** Sacred bird of Egypt, unclean to the Hebrews (LEVITICUS 11:16).

**HAYA** *goddess of direction* Another name of the Babylonian fertility goddess Ninlil.

**HAYDN, FRANZ JOSEPH (1732–1809)** Brilliant Austrian composer whose works include *The Creation, Stabat Mater,* interludes for the *Seven Last Words of Christ,* and many musical pieces for the church.

**HAYES, PATRICK JOSEPH (1867–1938)** Archbishop of New York and American cardinal in the ROMAN CATHOLIC CHURCH. He founded the Catholic Charities of New York, interested himself in social reforms, and was greatly loved.

**HAZAEL** *God sees* Ninth-century-B.C. king of Syria who conquered Judah and murdered Benhadad (II KINGS 8—10).

**HAZOR** *enclosure* 1. City of Galilee used by King Solomon as a chariot town (I KINGS 9:15). 2. The name of several other cities of the Bible.

**HAZZAN** *officer* Synagogue official, in present times a cantor.

**HE** Fifth letter in the Hebrew alphabet.

**HEAD** In religious terminology, a symbol of the rational and intellectual factors in the makeup, sometimes opposed to those of the heart.

**HEART** In religion, often a symbol of the emotional, deep, subconscious commitments of man. In the Bible the heart often represents total personality, God's home. In religious art the heart is a symbol of love, zeal, and the compassion of Christ.

**HEART DOCTRINE** In BUDDHISM, the eternal wisdom which cannot be put in writing.

**HEART SUTRA** A short but popular Scripture of BUDDHISM, recited daily by Japanese monks.

**HEATHEN** 1. One of another religion.

2. A non-Christian. 3. One who is irreligious or opposed to accepted faith.

**HEAVEN** 1. The sky. 2. A spiritual realm of the eternal. Contemporary theologians make much of the difference between these two, although few orthodox Christians think God lives in a corner of the sky, or is "above" in a sense defined by gravity.

**HEAVEN AND HELL** Book by Emanuel SWEDENBORG, stating his doctrines in full, published in 1758.

**HEAVENLY** Spiritual, divine, beautiful, or above the earth.

**HEAVENLY CITY** The city of God, the new Jerusalem (cf. REVELATION 21:2-4).

**HEAVE OFFERING** Jewish offering lifted or tossed for the Lord and the priests. It might consist of meat, fruit, grain, oil, or cakes.

**HEBE** Goddess of youth in ancient Greek religion. ZEUS' daughter and cupbearer, she had the power to restore beauty to aged faces, and is sometimes regarded as a form of her mother HERA.

**HEBER, REGINALD (1783–1826)** Clergyman of the CHURCH OF ENGLAND who became Bishop of Calcutta and wrote many well-known hymns including "Holy, Holy, Holy," "The Son of God Goes Forth to War," and "Brightest and Best of the Sons of the Morning." His Calcutta diocese included all India.

**HEBRAISM** Attitude, spirit, or way of thinking in JUDAISM.

**HEBREW** 1. A Jew. 2. Judaism's ancient language. The Old Testament was originally written largely in Hebrew.

**HEBREWS** Popular term for the New Testament book, the Epistle to the Hebrews. Its authorship is unknown. It appears to be addressed either to all Christians or to those in a particular community and enumerates the ways in which Christ and His blessings are superior to those of JUDAISM and past revelations.

**HEBRON** *league* One of Palestine's oldest cities, c. 20 miles southwest of Jerusalem. It figured in the lives of Abraham and David, and in the CRUSADES. A mosque in it contains tombs in memory of Abraham, Isaac, Jacob, Sarah, Rebekah, and Leah. JEWS and MOSLEMS revere Hebron, and CHRISTIANS often visit it.

**HECATE** *she who works from a distance*
Greek goddess of spirits and magic. Sometimes represented with three bodies or heads, she was believed to sway heaven, the earth, and the sea or the world of the dead. To her worshipers she brought success.

**HECATOMB** *a hundred oxen* 1. Greek sacrifice of a hundred oxen at once. 2. A great act of destruction.

**HECHASID, JUDAH (thirteenth century)** Jewish leader and mystic of Regensburg, Germany. He recommended obedience, purification, prayer, and ethical righteousness as a way to God. He wrote *The Book of the Holy Ones* and *The Book of Glory*.

**HECK, BARBARA RUCKLE (1734–1805)** North American "mother of Methodism." Sailing to America with Philip Embury and others in 1760, she spurred EMBURY to preach and together they organized the first METHODIST society in the new world. She and her associates then founded the first Methodist society in Canada.

**HECKER, ISSAC THOMAS (1819–1888)** American founder of the Missionary Priests of St. Paul the Apostle, or PAULIST FATHERS. A convert from Methodism, and a friend of EMERSON and Thoreau, he was at one time a REDEMPTORIST. He held that Catholicism must adapt to American methods, founded the *Catholic World*, and led a controversial career. Some believe that LEO XIII's denunciation of Americanism was aimed at some of Father Hecker's ideas.

**HECKEWELDER, JOHN G. E. (1743–1823)** MORAVIAN missionary to American Indians. He wrote a number of books about his work and took part in United States treaties with Indians.

**HEDONISM** 1. Philosophy emphasizing pleasure as man's highest value. Greek philosophers taught either gratification or control of the desires to attain pleasure, while UTILITARIANISM sees man's goal as securing the greatest good for the greatest number. 2. Description of the pursuit of pleasure as the chief purpose of most people.

**HEGEL, GEORG WILHELM FRIEDRICH (1770–1831)** German philosopher noted for his absolute idealism and his dialectical logic of thesis, antithesis, and synthesis. His philosophy of absolute idealism substituted divine immanence for transcendence; he held that God realizes Himself through time and space. He taught that "the real is the rational and the rational is the real." His dialectical logic proceeded in terms of a thesis or concept that gives way to an opposing one, which is followed by a condition combining thesis and antithesis on a new and higher level. Hegel's influence on the modern world has been great.

**HEGELIANISM** The philosophy of HEGEL.

**HEGESIPPUS (second century)** Palestine-born Jewish Christian noted as a church historian.

**HEGIRA** *departure* The official beginning of ISLAM, through Mohammed's flight in 622 from Mecca to Medina. Moslem chronology begins from that occasion; the symbol A.H. indicates "year of the hegira."

**HEGUMEN or HEGUMENOS** *leader* Head of a small monastery in the EASTERN ORTHODOX CHURCH.

**HEHE RELIGION** The God of this Tanganyikan tribe is Nguruhe, although worship is directed principally to the spirits of ancestors. To secure their approval and avoid their curses, the head of each family places offerings on his ancestors' graves.

**HEIDELBERG CATECHISM** Confession of faith of the Reformed Church of Germany, drawn up at Heidelberg and published in 1563. It is accepted by all denominations of REFORMED background, and has been translated into many languages.

**HEILSGESCHICHTE** *history of salvation* Theological view of history as culminating in the formation and development of the people of God. European theologians widely hold this concept.

**HEIMDALLR or HEIMDAL(L)** Scandinavian watcher of the universe and god of light. He can hear grass grow and see in his sleep, and his horn will call the gods on the day of judgment.

**HEJIRA** See HEGIRA.

**HEKDESH** 1. Jewish term for something devoted to sacrifice.

**HEKHAL** Jewish name for the portion of the temple containing the golden altar. 2. Receptacle for the scrolls of the law.

**HEL or HELA** Scandinavian goddess of the world of death.

**HELEN** Daughter of Zeus whose beauty precipitated the Trojan War. She was worshiped at Sparta, Therapnae, and Dendritis, and may have been a fertility goddess.

**HELENA, ST. (c.248–c.327)** Wife of Constantius I (Chlorus) and mother of Constantine I. She was greatly honored while Constantine was Emperor. When she visited the holy land in her old age it is believed she found the Holy Sepulcher and the True Cross and founded several churches. Her feast day is August 18.

**HELIAND** *Saviour* Ninth-century Germanic poem alliteratively narrating the life of Christ.

**HELIOGABALUS** **(c.205–222)** Originally Varius Avitus Bassianus, a priest of the Syrian sun god Elegabalus who became youthful Emperor of Rome. His cruelty, superstition, and debauchery so shocked Rome that in his fourth year as emperor the Praetorian Guard threw him and his mother (who had tutored him) into the Tiber. During his reign the Christians had peace, as he was busy enjoying himself and attempting to introduce the new religion of Elegabalus.

**HELIOLATRY** Worship of the sun.

**HELIOPOLIS** *city of the sun* Egyptian city which served as a center of sun worship through the sun god RA or Re. Also called On and Beth-Shemeth.

**HELIOPOLIS COMPANY OF THE GODS** Another term for the ENNEAD, the nine great gods of Egypt.

**HELIOS** Greek sun god, known in Rome as Sol.

**HELL** In the OLD TESTAMENT Scriptures, the abode of the dead, Sheol. In the NEW TESTAMENT, Hades or GEHENNA, representing the everlasting torment of the unjust and unbelieving. Medieval theology filled hell with elaborate divisions while modern PROTESTANT theology has virtually done away with it, transferring what remains to a region of the mind. BUDDHISM has no hell as such. In CATHOLIC and MOSLEM theology, however, hell remains a genuine place of punishment, as it does in Evangelical thought.

**HELLENISM** Greek culture and religion.

**HELLENIST** 1. A Greek-speaking Jew. Those mentioned in the New Testament as Hellenists or Grecians had adapted to Greek customs (ACTS 6:1; 9:29). 2. A student of Greek language or culture.

**HELLENISTIC CHRISTIANITY** Christianity whose members and leaders were of Greek or Roman background, in contrast to the original Christianity of Palestine whose members and leaders were nearly all Jewish. St. Paul moved Christianity out of Judea into the Roman Empire and thus was the main force behind the Hellenistic type of Christianity which soon developed.

**HELLENISTIC JUDAISM** JUDAISM influenced by the prevailing Greek culture of the three centuries before Christ. This influence is represented in the apocryphal books of the Old Testament and in Christianity. A monument to Hellenistic Judaism is the SEPTUAGINT, the Greek translation of the Hebrew Bible. The great philosopher of Hellenistic Judaism was PHILO.

**HELMET** In Scripture, a symbol of salvation (ISAIAH 59:17; EPHESIANS 6:17).

**HELOISE** Nun loved by Peter ABELARD.

**HELPMEET** Bible-derived word for wife. Eve became a "help meet for" Adam (GENESIS 2:18).

**HELVETIC CONFESSION, FIRST** Confession of faith of the Swiss Reformed Church in 1536, with LUTHERAN and ZWINGLIAN elements.

**HELVETIC CONFESSION, SECOND** Confession of faith published in 1566 and accepted by many PROTESTANT churches of Europe. Drafted by Heinrich BULLINGER, it is basically Calvinistic in viewpoint. It pleads for tolerance in minor points of dispute.

**HEMACHANDRA (1089–1173)** JAIN writer of India who described the history and moral principles of his faith.

**HENDERSON, ALEXANDER (1583–1646)** Outstanding Scottish PRESBYTERIAN leader. He wrote the National Covenant of 1638, became moderator of the GENERAL ASSEMBLY, and led the fight opposing the establishment of the Anglican Church in Scotland. He was a delegate to the WESTMINSTER ASSEMBLY.

**HENGSTENBERG, ERNST WILHELM (1802–1869)** German LUTHERAN theologian and leader of orthodoxy against rationalism—the latter as represented particularly in SCHLEIERMACHER. He wrote many commentaries on the Bible.

**HENOTHEISM** Worship of one God without denying the existence of other gods.

**HENOTICON** *union* Law promulgated by the Roman emperor ZENO in 482 to settle the MONOPHYSITE dispute. Based on the NICENE CREED, it satisfied neither side and failed to end the controversy. The Western churches never accepted it, although many churches did in the East.

**HENRY, MATTHEW (1662–1714)** English PRESBYTERIAN minister and commentator. His *Exposition of the Old and New Testaments,* offering devotional remarks on every passage in the Bible, is still widely used.

**HENRY IV (1553–1610)** French HUGUENOT who became a ROMAN CATHOLIC and king of France 1589–1610. He observed "Paris is well worth a mass." Seeking to put "a chicken in every peasant's pot every Sunday," he unified and strengthened his nation. He granted religious liberty to French PROTESTANTS through the EDICT OF NANTES. In 1610 he was assassinated.

**HENRY VIII (1491–1547)** King of England during whose reign the pope's jurisdiction over the CHURCH OF ENGLAND ended. In 1521 Henry wrote a book defending the sacraments against LUTHERAN doctrines; for this Pope LEO X granted him the title "Defender of the Faith." In 1529 he sought a divorce from Catherine of Aragon in order to marry Anne Boleyn. Failing to receive the permission of Pope CLEMENT VII to do so by 1533, Henry—who had received the approval of Convocation for his authority over the English clergy—had the Archbishop of Canterbury, Thomas CRANMER, pronounce his marriage invalid and married Anne. The pope excommunicated Henry, whom Parliament made supreme head of the English church. The new ecclesiastical ruler made certain church reforms and had the English Bible set up in the churches. For opposing him Thomas MORE and John FISHER were put to death.

**HENRY OF GHENT (?–1293)** Flemish SCHOLASTIC philosopher, strongly influenced by AUGUSTINE, contemporary with Thomas Aquinas, Duns Scotus, and Bonaventure.

**HENRY OF LAUSANNE (?–c. 1145)** French preacher denounced for heresy by BERNARD OF CLAIRVAUX and Peter the Venerable, Abbot of Cluny. He was often imprisoned and probably died under arrest.

**HENRY OF UPSALA, ST. (?–1156)** English bishop and missionary to Finland where he was martyred. He is sometimes called "The Apostle of Finland." His feast day is January 20.

**HEORTOLOGY** Term relating to the origin and development of the church year, or of the ecclesiastical calendar.

**HEPATOSCOPY** Divination — forecasting the future—by studying the liver of a sacrificed animal. Babylonians, Etruscans, and other ancient people practiced hepatoscopy.

**HEPHAESTUS** Greek god of craftsmen. Originally he was a god of fire.

**HEPHZIBAH** *my pleasure is in her* 1. Wicked Manasseh's mother (II KINGS 21: 1). 2. The Lord's name for the Jerusalem of the future (ISAIAH 62:4).

**HEPTATEUCH** *seven books* The first seven books of the OLD TESTAMENT.

**HEQUET** Goddess of birth in Egypt.

**HERA** Greek queen of the gods of Olympus; wife of ZEUS. She was a fertility goddess blessing crops, guarding childbirth, and sometimes chastening husbands who strayed. She had temples at Samos and Mycenae.

**HERACLITUS** **(c.535–c.475 B.C.)** Greek philosopher who held that nothing is permanent except change. "All things flow," he said. However, the world is pervaded by reason (Logos); all life shares the universal fire or reason.

**HERBERT, GEORGE (1593–1633)** Rector in the CHURCH OF ENGLAND known principally for his enduring philosophical and Christian verse. He loved music and the church, and wrote *A Priest to the Temple,* a book of counsel for pastors.

**HERBERT OF CHERBURY, LORD (EDWARD HERBERT) (1583–1648)** English philosopher and ambassador who wrote several books providing a natural explanation for the origin of religion. He also set forth five principles which became the five fundamental truths of DEISM.

**HERES** Canaanite sun god.

**HERESIARCH** Leader in heresy.

**HERESY** Unpopular or unaccepted religious or other belief. A heresy must be measured by its deviation from an ecclesiastical or popular or conventional standard.

**HERMAS** 1. Early Roman Christian about whom little is known. 2. Second-century Roman, about whom also little is known, who wrote the "SHEPHERD OF HERMAS."

**HERMENEUTICS** In theology, the study of the principles of Bible exegesis and interpretation.

**HERMES** 1. Son of ZEUS and messenger of the gods. In the evolution of Greek religion he appears to have been a god of farmers, a guide of travelers, an inventor of musical instruments, a guide to the underworld, a patron of traders and thieves, and a god of justice. 2. Another name of the Egyptian Thoth, god of magic and wisdom.

**HERMES TRISMEGISTUS** *Hermes thrice-greatest* 1. Egyptian name of Hermes-Thoth (See HERMES 2.) 2. Title of writings from the third or fourth century containing a jumble of Neoplatonism, theosophy, and other mystic-religious elements.

**HERMETIC** 1. Mysterious or occult. 2. Referring to "HERMES TRISMEGISTUS."

**HERMETIC BOOKS** Books also described under the title "HERMES TRISMEGISTUS."

**HERMIT** Strictly, a solitary religious ascetic. The name comes from the Greek *eremos,* desert; an archaic form is "eremite."

**HERMOD** Scandinavian god who sought to ransom BALDER from hell.

**HERMON** *sacred mountain* Mountain of Syria with three snowy peaks. There the Jordan River begins. It is thought by some to have been the scene of Jesus' TRANSFIGURATION. Thirteen temples have been found on Hermon's slopes.

**HEROD** Family name of a dynasty which ruled in Palestine from c. 55 B.C. to c. A.D. 93. Its strength was the support it received from the Roman government. Its founder was ANTIPATER, an Idumean who was circumcised and accepted into JUDAISM.

**HEROD AGRIPPA I** Grandson of HEROD THE GREAT who ruled much of Palestine c. A.D. 40–44 (cf. ACTS 12:1–23).

**HEROD AGRIPPA II** Son of HEROD AGRIPPA I. Paul was brought before him on the way to Rome (ACTS 25:13—26:32).

**HEROD ANTIPAS** Ruler of Perea and

Galilee during the executions of John the Baptist and Jesus. A son of HEROD THE GREAT, he was banished by the Roman Emperor Caligula c. A.D. 39. Jesus called him a fox (LUKE 13:31, 32).

**HEROD ARCHELAUS** Son of HEROD THE GREAT who ruled Judea, Samaria, and Idumea c. 4 B.C. to A.D. 6. Dissatisfaction with his reign caused his removal from office.

**HERODIANS** First-century Jews who supported the Herod dynasty and tried to trap Jesus by questioning His political loyalties (MARK 12:13). Although they were not a religious group as such, they may have been principally SADDUCEES.

**HERODIAS** Wife of HEROD PHILIP I whom she left to marry HEROD ANTIPAS. John the Baptist's rebuke concerning this led to his death (MARK 6:17-29).

**HEROD PHILIP I** Son of HEROD THE GREAT and father of Salome. His wife Herodias married his half-brother Herod Antipas during the lifetime of John the Baptist (MARK 6:17).

**HEROD PHILIP II** Son of HEROD THE GREAT known as "Philip the Tetrarch"; during the lifetime of Jesus he ruled four countries east of the Jordan: Panias, Gaulanitis, Batanaea, and Trachonitis. He is the Philip mentioned in the Gospels (cf. MATTHEW 14:3).

**HEROD THE GREAT** Ruler of Judea when Jesus was born. He rebuilt the temple from which Jesus drove the money lenders, publicly kept the Mosaic law, and taxed the Jews heavily. He had ten wives. He murdered his wife Mariamne, her grandfather Hyrcanus, her brother Aristobulus, and his sons Aristobulus, Alexander, and Antipater. In attempting to kill the infant Jesus he murdered all the babies in Bethlehem (MATTHEW 2:16 ff.).

**HERRICK, ROBERT (1591-1674)** English clergyman who wrote some of the most spiritual and some of the most amorous poems in the language. Among the former were "His Litany to the Holy Spirit," "His Prayer for Absolution," "To His Ever-Loving God," and "A Thanksgiving to God, for His House."

**HERRMANN, WILHELM (1846-1922)** German theologian who held that the church should proclaim Jesus' moral teachings rather than such doctrines as the RESURRECTION, and that human lives must be united with the universal ethical ideal. To him the basis of religion was ethical and religious experience.

**HERRNHUT** Town in Germany founded by a colony of Moravians who had fled from persecution in Moravia to settle on the property of Count Graf von ZINZENDORF in 1722. John WESLEY made a pilgrimage to the colony in 1738.

**HERSHEF** Egyptian god represented with the head of a ram.

**HERZL, THEODOR (1860-1904)** Hungarian Jewish founder of modern political ZIONISM. Inspired by the Dreyfus affair, he devoted his life to the establishment of a Jewish fatherland, as an alternative to Jewish extinction. His body was buried in Jerusalem in 1949.

**HERZOG, JOHANN JAKOB (1805-1882)** German REFORMED theologian, a student of WALDENSIANISM and founder of the *Realencyclopädie für Protestantische Theologie und Kirche.*

**HESHBON** *reckoning* Amorite capital east of the Jordan River assigned to the Levites (JOSHUA 21:39).

**HESHVAN** Second month in the Jewish year.

**HESIOD (c. eighth century B.C.)** Greek poet who wrote a genealogy of the gods, *Theogony.* He is famed for systematizing Greek mythology.

**HESPED** Jewish term for a funeral message.

**HESTIA** Greek goddess of the home and hearth fire. In every home a hearth honored her. Her Roman counterpart was Vesta.

**HESUS** Gallic war god.

**HESYCHASTS** Fourteenth-century monks of Mt. Athos, Greece, who were said to derive spiritual blessing from sitting on the ground and contemplating their navels.

**HETERODOXY** Heretical opinion; belief contrary to accepted dogma. To combat the many heterodoxies with which it was faced and to find and sustain orthodoxy, the early church worked out the great ecumenical creeds.

**HETERONOMY** Kant's term for rule by another, the opposite of autonomy—self-rule, determining one's own course by a moral law personally established. Specifically, autonomy is direction by one's free rational will, while heteronomy is direction by pleasure, emotion, or another person.

**HETEROOUSIAN** *another being* In early church history, one such as an Arian who maintained that Christ the Son was of a different essence or substance from God the Father.

**HETZER, LUDWIG (?–1529)** Swiss ANABAPTIST who collaborated with Hans DENCK in the first Protestant translation of the Prophets of the Old Testament into German. Rejecting the sacraments, he was expelled from Augsburg and beheaded in Constance.

**HEU T'U** The goddess Earth worshiped in the state religion of ancient China.

**HEXAEMERON** *work of six days* 1. The six days of creation. 2. A commentary by AMBROSE or another on the six days of creation.

**HEXAPLA** A version of the Bible in six languages—particularly that of ORIGEN in whose *Hexapla* six columns presented the Old Testament in Hebrew and in five Greek translations. (In some portions there were as many as nine columns.)

**HEXATEUCH** The first six books of the Bible—Genesis, Exodus, Leviticus, Numbers, Deuteronomy, and Joshua. The name was given these books by Julius WELLHAUSEN to indicate their literary unity.

**HEYER, JOHN C. F. (1793–1873)** German-American LUTHERAN missionary to India, known as "Father Heyer."

**HEY-TAU** Egyptian god of Byblos who may have been identical with TAMMUZ.

**HEZEKIAH** *the Lord strengthens* King of Judah, son of Ahaz and father of Manasseh. He strengthened his country's defenses, provided Jerusalem with an extensive water system, and sought to eradicate pagan worship within Judah. Threatened by Assyria, he tried to establish a compact with Egypt which was opposed by Isaiah. When Sennacherib laid siege to Jerusalem, Hezekiah prayed and the angel of the Lord drove back the Assyrian army. (II KINGS 18—20; ISAIAH 36—39).

**H.I.A.S.** Abbreviation for Hebrew Sheltering and Immigrant Aid Society, an organization formed in 1898 to aid immigrants to America.

**HIBBERT, ROBERT (1770–1849)** British merchant who founded the Hibbert Trust which sponsors the Hibbert Lectures and publishes the *Hibbert Journal,* a liberal journal of philosophy and religion.

**HIC JACET** *here lies* Common phrase in epitaphs.

**HICKS, EDWARD (1780–1849)** American QUAKER preacher famous for his paintings of "The Peaceable Kingdom."

**HICKS, ELIAS (1748–1830)** American QUAKER preacher who often attacked slavery and opposed fixed creeds. This opposition made him the leader of the "HICKSITES" who were opposed by the "Orthodox" among the Friends in America.

**HICKSITES** The liberal branch of American Quakers (see HICKS, ELIAS).

**HIERAPOLIS** *holy city* 1. City of Asia Minor near Laodicea where there was a church in New Testament times (COLOSSIANS 4:13). There the Greeks worshiped the mother-goddess Leto and the god Apollo Lairbenos. By the fourth century, it is said, Hierapolis was "wholly Christian." 2. City of Syria in which phallic rites and self-mutilation constituted Greek forms of worship.

**HIERARCH** *sacred leader* Religious leader or authority.

**HIERARCHY** *sacred government* 1. System of government in religious affairs. 2. Government of a religious institution. 3. Power structure of a church. 4. Order of angels or other sacred beings. 5. Objects arranged in systematic order.

**HIERATIC** Priestly or consecrated.

**HIEROCRACY** Government by religious rulers or ecclesiastics.

**HIERODULE** *sacred slave* Slave attached to a Greek temple and bound to the service of a god or goddess.

**HIEROLOGY** Body of sacred knowledge or literature.

**HIEROME** See JEROME.

**HIEROMONK** Priest who was formerly a monk in the EASTERN ORTHODOX CHURCH.

**HIERONYMIAN MARTYROLOGY** Fifth-century Italian list of martyrs, attributed to St. JEROME.

**HIERONYMITES** Hermits, named after St. Jerome, who were guided by the writings of St. JEROME and St. AUGUSTINE. An important group were the Spanish Hieronymites who flourished from the fourteenth through the seventeenth centuries and were influential in government.

**HIERONYMUS** Variant of JEROME.

**HIEROPHANT** 1. One who explains religious mysteries. 2. High priest in the ELEUSINIAN MYSTERIES.

**HIERURGIA** 1. Sacred LITURGY. 2. The EUCHARIST.

**HIGGAION** Musical note or direction in Psalm 9:16.

**HIGGINSON, THOMAS WENTWORTH (1823–1911)** New England clergyman who so strongly opposed slavery that he resigned his pulpit to fight in the Civil War. There he was a colonel in a Negro regiment. Later he wrote a number of books and advocated feminine rights.

**HIGH ALTAR** Main altar in a church.

**HIGH CELEBRATION** Sung EUCHARIST or HIGH MASS.

**HIGH CHURCH** 1. EPISCOPAL or ANGLICAN church stressing tradition and ceremony more than others. 2. Anglican group emphasizing the authority of the church, its continuity with CATHOLICISM, the elevated nature of the sacraments, and apostolic succession. In some high churches Mary is venerated and "mass" is preferred as a title for the eucharist.

**HIGHER CRITICISM** Biblical criticism principally concerned with sources, writers, dates, and order of the various documents in the Bible. It seeks to apply scientific, historic, and literary principles to Scripture. Lower criticism is concerned principally with actual manuscripts and the original text of Scripture.

**HIGH MASS missa solemnis** Ordinary mass celebrated by a priest, deacon, and subdeacon, accompanied by a choir, acolytes, and incense.

**HIGH PLACE** 1. Pagan shrine, usually on a hill or elevated position (II KINGS 17:11). 2. Ancient Hebrew shrine to the Lord (I KINGS 3:2–4). 3. Region of spiritual evil (EPHESIANS 6:12).

**HIGH PRIEST** 1. Chief priest in Israel. He was custodian of the temple and represented the people before the Lord in the central sacrifices and rites. Following the exile he was also political leader of Israel. 2. President of the Melchizedek priesthood in the MORMON church.

**HILARY OF ARLES, ST. (c.403–449)** Archbishop of Arles, France. Although deprived of his powers by Pope Leo I, he was later called by the same pope, "Hilary of sacred memory," and was canonized. His feast day is May 5.

**HILARY OF POITIERS, ST. (c.315–367)** Frenchman converted from NEOPLATONISM to Christianity and made Bishop of Poitiers in 353. He vigorously supported ATHANASIUS and denounced ARIANISM, for which he was exiled for nearly four years. He wrote a twelve-volume treatise on the TRINITY, several commentaries, and some hymns; he has been termed the first Latin Christian hymn writer. He has also been called "DOCTOR OF THE CHURCH" and "Athanasius of the West." His feast day is January 14 (January 13 in England).

**HILDEBRAND** Original name of GREGORY VII.

**HILLEL (c.70 B.C.–A.D. 10)** Outstanding Jewish rabbi and scholar of his century. He was born in Babylon, became president of the SANHEDRIN in Jerusalem, founded the school Beth Hillel, and became ancestor of the patriarchs who led JUDAISM during the first four hundred years of the common era. A scholar who propounded seven rules for the exposition of Scripture, he is best known as a spiritual leader and saint. To him are attributed such sayings as these: "Judge not thy neighbor until thou art in his place"; "What is unpleasant to thyself do not to thy neighbor; this is the whole law, all else is but its interpretation." His great opponent was SHAMMAI whose interpretation of the law was much more rigid.

**HILLEL FOUNDATION** Jewish organization for college youth.

**HILLIS, NEWELL DWIGHT (1858–1929)** Popular minister of Brooklyn's Plymouth Church (Congregational).

**HILTON, WALTER (?–1396)** English mystic and AUGUSTINIAN canon. His *Scale of Perfection* reports the journey of the soul through faith and feeling to union with God.

**HINAYANA small vehicle** Doctrine that BUDDHA is a teacher for those who accept his wisdom, and that salvation is for the few. Hinayana is a school of Buddhism to be distinguished from MAHAYANA.

**HINDUISM** India's native religion and culture. One of the world's oldest religions, it has been evolving since c. 3,000 B.C. It is called Sanatana Dharma, "The Eternal Faith." It emphasizes right action, reverence for life, asceticism, transmigration of souls, the caste system. Its principal gods are BRAHMA (Creator and Giver of Life), SIVA (The Destroyer), and VISHNU (The Preserver). Siva's consort KALI, Vishnu's consort LAKSHMI, and other gods and goddesses are also revered. Hinduism's sacred writings include the RIG-VEDA, the UPANISHADS, the BHAGAVAD-GITA, the BRAHMANAS, the PURANAS, and the TANTRAS. Its priestly system is BRAHMANISM. Out of Hinduism have developed BUDDHISM, JAINISM, and SIKHISM.

**HINNOM** Steep rocky valley south of Jerusalem where children were once sacrificed to the fire god MOLECH. It became the place of refuse known as GEHENNA.

**HINSLEY, ARTHUR (1865–1943)** English ROMAN CATHOLIC missionary to Africa. He became an archbishop and a cardinal. When Italy invaded Ethiopia he criticized Pope PIUS XI, and staunchly denounced totalitarianism and fascism.

**HINUN** Iroquois Indian thunder god.

**HIPPOLYTUS, ST. (c.170–c.236)** Learned ecclesiastical writer, theologian, and martyr. Accusing Popes Zephyrinus and Calixtus I of looseness in discipline and doctrine, he made himself head of a separate church. Apparently he returned to the Roman fold before his death. He wrote several commentaries, the *Refutation of All Heresies,* and *Christ and Antichrist.* He seemed to hold that the Logos or Word developed through the incarnation, and that the Holy Spirit was not a person.

**HIRAM** *the brother is exalted (?)* 1. Name of a number of kings of Tyre, the Mediterranean port. King Hiram furnished both David and Solomon with wood and workmen for their building programs (II SAMUEL 5:11; I KINGS 9:11). Kings named Hiram or Ahiram are mentioned in inscriptions of Tiglath-Pileser and on the sarcophagus of a Phoenician King Ahiram. 2. Architect-artisan sent from Tyre by King Hiram to aid Solomon in the construction of the temple at Jerusalem (I KINGS 7:13 ff.).

**HIRANYAGARBHA** *golden germ* In Hinduism, seed or cosmic intelligence from which BRAHMA was born.

**HIRANYAKASIPU** Demon of the vedic or early Hindu period in India.

**HIRSCH, EMIL GUSTAV (1852–1923)** American rabbi, orator, philosopher, and leader in reformed JUDAISM.

**HIRSCH, MAURICE DE (1831–1896)** German Jewish banker and philanthropist who founded the Jewish Colonization Association and gave millions for education and charity.

**HIRSCH, SAMSON RAPHAEL (1808–1888)** German Jewish theologian and commentator; leader of the "Frankfort Neo-Orthodoxy."

**HISPANA CANONS** Ecclesiastical laws and decrees gathered in Spain in the sixth or seventh century. They formed a main basis of the "FALSE DECRETALS."

**HITLAHAVUT** Jewish term for the divine possession of a person.

**HITTITES** Indo-European people of Syria who flourished from the nineteenth through the thirteenth centuries B.C. Many times they are mentioned in the Hebrew Scriptures; they were one of the most important peoples in the Middle East. They incorporated many gods into their syncretistic worship, from Egypt, Assyria, Syria, and Asia Minor.

**HITZIG (1807–1875)** German theologian, philologist, and Biblical critic. He wrote commentaries on Isaiah, Jeremiah, the Minor Prophets, and the Psalms, as well as books on criticism and archaeology.

**HIVITES** People of Mt. Seir in Judea, also called Horites or Hurrians. Cave dwellers, they were peace-loving victims of the Jewish conquest of Palestine.

**HMIN** Demon of illness in Burma.

**HO** Japanese Buddhist term for DHARMA.

**HOADLY, BENJAMIN (1676–1761)** Bishop of the CHURCH OF ENGLAND and chaplain of King George I. He aroused the BANGORIAN CONTROVERSY by stating that, since Christ's Kingdom is "not of this world," His powers have not been delegated to earthly church officials. King George backed Hoadly against the other bishops of the Church of England who attacked him in a war of pamphlets. A LOW CHURCH leader, Hoadly also held that the sacrament of the EUCHARIST was no more than commemorative.

**HOBART, JOHN HENRY (1775–1830)** EPISCOPAL Bishop of New York who wrote devotional books, founded the Bible and Common Prayer Book Society of New York, and aided in the establishment of Hobart College and the General Theological Seminary.

**HOBBES, THOMAS (1588–1679)** English philosopher who attributed religion to fear and superstition although he maintained attachment to the CHURCH OF ENGLAND. Famous for such books as *Leviathan,* Hobbes denied the divine right of kings to rule, although he held that their power, derived from the people, is absolute. He appears to have been a materialist and mechanist, and his doctrines leave little room for ethical decision.

**HOBGOBLIN** Mischievous spirit or creature of medieval myth.

**HOBHOUSE, LEONARD TRELAWNEY (1864–1929)** Liberal English philosopher and sociologist who saw interrelationships among philosophy, psychology, sociology, and biological evolution. The latter, he maintained, was allied to spiritual progress in man.

**HOCKTIDE** English holiday, celebrated the second Monday and Tuesday after EASTER in the Middle Ages, when rents were due and various forms of amusement were popular. Among these was the binding of those of the opposite sex; the fee collected for their release went toward parish support.

**HOCUS-POCUS** Nonsensical or deceptive formula, as of a juggler or magician. It may have originated in imitation of the statement in the mass, "Hoc est enim Corpus Meum."

**HOD** God of night in Germanic myth.

**HODGE, CHARLES (1797–1878)** American PRESBYTERIAN churchman and theologian, famous for his three-volume *Systematic Theology.* A CALVINIST with broad sympathies, he also wrote New Testament commentaries. He led the Princeton or Old School of theology.

**HODGES, GEORGE (1856–1919)** PROTESTANT EPISCOPAL clergyman noted for preaching and applying the social gospel.

**HOFMANN, MELCHIOR (c.1498–c.1543)** German ANABAPTIST and mystic who traveled widely through Europe as a lay preacher. He denounced image worship, proclaimed the imminent end of the world, and held that only the saved should be baptized. He was banished from Denmark for his ZWINGLIAN view of communion, expelled from many cities for his alleged heresies, and finally sentenced to life imprisonment at Strassburg.

**HOG** Symbol of sensuality or evil in religious art.

**HOGAHN** Navajo Indian term for the rite or place of ceremonial cleansing.

**HOLBEIN, HANS (c.1465–1524)** Skilled German painter of many religious altarpieces, church windows, and paintings.

**HOLBEIN, HANS, THE YOUNGER (c.1497–1543)** Talented German artist who illustrated Erasmus' *Encomium Moriae,* designed initials for editions of the Bible, made many religious woodcuts, illustrated Luther's Bible, and composed many altarpieces and paintings of scenes in the life of Christ.

**HOLDEN, OLIVER (1765–1844)** American hymnologist who composed and edited a number of hymns. He wrote the tune Coronation, now wedded to "All Hail the Power of Jesus' Name," for the triumphal entry of George Washington into Boston in 1789.

**HOLIDAY** Day of rest and celebration, originally a holy day of religious significance.

**HOLIDAY OF OBLIGATION** See FEAST OF OBLIGATION.

**HOLINESS** 1. That which is religious or divine. 2. State of ethical righteousness or moral purity. The Judeo-Christian tradition finds holiness residing essentially in God, and imparted to men by His grace and love.

**HOLINESS, HIS or YOUR** 1. Title of the pope in Roman Catholicism. 2. Title of patriarchs in Eastern Orthodox churches.

**HOLINESS CHURCH** A denomination which emphasizes spiritual consecration and purity, often including a second blessing in the spiritual life following conversion.

**HOLINESS CODE** See "H."

**HOLINESS DENOMINATION** See HOLINESS CHURCH.

**HOLINESS METHODIST CHURCH** Small denomination, located principally in the western part of the United States, organized in 1911.

**HOLINESS METHODIST CHURCH, LUMBER RIVER ANNUAL CONFERENCE OF THE** Small Holiness denomination which was organized in North Carolina in 1900.

**HOLLE or HOLDA** Priestess or goddess of a Germanic lunar cult.

**HOLLY** Evergreen tree or shrub considered to house wood spirits in Germanic myth. It is a Christmas symbol in England and the United States, and in religious art is a symbol of Christ's passion.

**HOLMAN-HUNT, WILLIAM** See HUNT, WILLIAM HOLMAN.

**HOLMES, JOHN HAYNES (1879–1964)** Vigorously outspoken American clergyman and social reformer. Minister of New York City's independent Community Church for forty-two years, he opposed war and prejudice, and was a founder of the American Civil Liberties Union and of the National Association for the Advancement of Colored People. His many books include *The Affirmation of Immortality*.

**HOLOCAUST** *completely burned* Sacrifice completely consumed by fire. The SEPTUAGINT used the word *holokauston* to translate the Hebrew "burnt offering," the burning of a whole animal before the Lord.

**HOLOFERNES** Pagan general slain by the patriotess Judith (JUDITH 2–13).

**HOLY** Divine, sacred, consecrated, godly, upright. See HOLINESS. The Hebrew word for holy is *kodesh*, "set apart."

**HOLY ALLIANCE** Declaration of amity among the rulers of Russia, Prussia, and Austria in 1815. Occasioned by the religious enthusiasm of Alexander I of Russia, it proclaimed acceptance of the Christian principles of "justice, Christian charity and peace." During the nineteenth century it led to the repression of popular revolutions.

**HOLY APOSTOLIC AND CATHOLIC CHURCH OF THE EAST AND ASSYRIANS** The Church of Persia, believed to have been founded by four of Christ's Apostles and two members of the Seventy commissioned by Him. It maintains there are two natures in Christ and denies that Mary is the Mother of God. It has members in the East, Russia, and the United States.

**HOLY BIBLE** Term for the BIBLE.

**HOLY CHURCH OF NORTH CAROLINA** Original name of the UNITED HOLY CHURCH OF AMERICA, INC.

**HOLY CITY** Among the cities claiming this name are Jerusalem, Rome, Mecca, and Benares. It is also a Christian term for heaven (Cf. REVELATION 21:2).

**HOLY CLUB** Derisive contemporary term for the association of students formed by John and Charles WESLEY at Oxford University for religious purposes. The members, also called "methodists," methodically fasted, received communion, read devotional literature, and visited prisoners.

**HOLY COMMUNION** Term for communion, the Lord's Supper, or the EUCHARIST.

**HOLY DAY** Feast day; day of religious significance (see HOLIDAY).

**HOLY DAY OF OBLIGATION** See FEAST OF OBLIGATION.

**HOLY EASTERN ORTHODOX CHURCHES** See EASTERN ORTHODOX CHURCH.

**HOLY FAMILY** Christian term for the infant Jesus, Mary, and Joseph. There are many paintings of the Holy Family.

**HOLY FATHER** A title of the pope.

**HOLY FRIDAY** Term for GOOD FRIDAY, or for an Ember Week Friday.

**HOLY GHOST** Third Person of the Trinity; see HOLY SPIRIT.

**HOLY GRAIL** See GRAIL.

**HOLY INNOCENTS** Christian term for the killing of the children of Bethlehem during the attempts of Herod the Great to get rid of Jesus (MATTHEW 2:16–18).

**HOLY INNOCENTS' DAY or HOLY CHILDREN** In the Western churches, December 28, commemorating the death of the HOLY INNOCENTS.

**HOLY ISLAND** 1. Irish island of Iniscaltra containing monasteries and churches from the seventh century. 2. English island of Lindisfarne where St. Aidan founded a monastery and church in 635, and where St. Cuthbert was bishop fifty years later. Despite repeated Danish invasions, the island had monastic life for centuries, and remains of medieval ecclesiasticism are still visible.

**HOLY LAND** Term for Palestine—modern Israel and Jordan—sacred to JEWS, CHRISTIANS, and MOSLEMS. Here most of the events recorded in the Bible took place.

**HOLY MOUNTAIN** 1. Greece's Mount

Athos, sacred for its many monasteries. 2. Mount Sinai, sacred for its association with the giving of the law through Moses. 3. The Mount of Jesus' Transfiguration.

**HOLY NAME OF JESUS** Celebration of Jesus' name in CATHOLIC and some ANGLICAN churches, ordinarily on the Sunday after January 1.

**HOLY OFFICE** Once the tribunal of the INQUISITION, this ROMAN CATHOLIC office now judges heresies, examines and prohibits books, and in other ways seeks to guard the faith of the faithful.

**HOLY OF HOLIES** 1. Inner chamber of the Jewish tabernacle and temple where the high priest annually celebrated the Day of ATONEMENT. 2. Sanctuary in NESTORIAN and EASTERN ORTHODOX churches.

**HOLY ONE OF ISRAEL** Jehovah God (PSALM 71:22; 89:18; ISAIAH 30:12; 41:14).

**HOLY ORDERS** The sacrament of ordination, or grades in the church's ministry, as BISHOP, PRIEST, and DEACON.

**HOLY PLACE** 1. Court of the priests in the Jewish temple. 2. A sacred site in Palestine or elsewhere.

**HOLY ROLLERS** Derisive term for PENTECOSTALS and other Christians who tend to express their religious enthusiasm in physical action.

**HOLY ROMAN EMPIRE** The political entity roughly corresponding to central European Christendom from the crowning of Charlemagne about 800 to the end of the reign of Francis II (Francis I of Austria) in 1806. Throughout this millennium, temporal power—in principle at least—was held by the emperor while spiritual power was held by the pope.

**HOLY ROOD** Term for the holy cross of Christ.

**HOLY SATURDAY** The day preceding EASTER, commemorating the period when Jesus' body lay in the tomb.

**HOLY SCRIPTURE** Term for the BIBLE.

**HOLY SEE** The PAPACY, or its jurisdiction.

**HOLY SEPULCHER** Term for Jesus' tomb, hewn from rock and presented for His use by Joseph of Arimathea.

**HOLY SHROUD** A sheet mysteriously marked with the imprint of a human body, apparently crucified, and preserved at Turin, Italy, since 1578. Many believe it is the shroud in which Jesus' body was wrapped after the crucifixion.

**HOLY SOULS** ROMAN CATHOLIC term for the spirits of the righteous in PURGATORY.

**HOLY SPIRIT** The third Person of the TRINITY. In Christian theology there are three Persons in one Godhead: the Father, the Son, and the Holy Spirit or Holy Ghost. The term Holy Spirit occurred occasionally in pre-Christian Jewish writings but in the New Testament it refers especially to the infilling and indwelling of God in Jesus and in His followers. Special symbols of the Spirit are fire and a dove.

**HOLY SYNOD** Supreme governing body in any of the EASTERN ORTHODOX churches.

**HOLY TABLE** Term for the table or altar from which the LORD'S SUPPER or EUCHARIST is served.

**HOLY THURSDAY** Maundy Thursday, the day before Good Friday in HOLY WEEK. On Holy Thursday evening communion is often shared.

**HOLYTIDE** Period devoted to religious pursuits.

**HOLY TRINITY** See TRINITY.

**HOLY UNCTION** 1. For Protestant usage, see UNCTION. 2. In ANGLICAN usage, the rite of anointing the ill with oil, based on such passages as James 5:14, 15. 3. In CATHOLICISM, extreme unction, administered to those seriously ill or near death.

**HOLY WATER** Water blessed by a priest for religious purposes such as dedications and blessings. It contains blessed salt.

**HOLY WEEK** The week before EASTER, beginning with PALM SUNDAY. It has special significance in most churches, commemorating the last week of Jesus' life.

**HOLY WRIT** Term for Scripture or the BIBLE.

**HOLY YEAR** Year during which special indulgences are granted by the pope to those who make special pilgrimages to Rome.

**HOME, DANIEL DUNGLAS (1833–1886)** Scottish SPIRITUALIST medium who practiced levitation and gave impressive seances, believing himself to be in contact with disembodied spirits.

**HOME MISSIONS** Term for a church's work within the country of its origin; complemented by FOREIGN MISSIONS.

**HOMER** Ancient Greek poet whose *Iliad* and *Odyssey* are filled with the doings of

Zeus, Achilles, Hermes, Apollo, Aphrodite, and other gods and goddesses.

**HOMILETICS** The study or art of preaching.

**HOMILIARIUM or HOMILIARY** Medieval book of sermons and/or homilies.

**HOMILY** Sermon, or informal religious discourse sometimes contrasted with the more formal sermon.

**HOMOEANS** Party in the controversies of the early church holding that Christ was "like" (*homoios*) but not of the same substance as the Father.

**HOMOIOS** *like* Favorite word of the Homoeans who held that the Son is like but not identical with the Father in being, power, and glory.

**HOMOIOUSIOS** *of like substance* Greek word favored by the SEMI-ARIANS in the post-Nicene theological controversies. They held that Christ was of a similar but not identical substance with God.

**HOMOOUSIOS** *of the same substance* Greek word preferred by the orthodox in the ARIAN and SEMI-ARIAN disputes, since it indicates the same substance or essence in Christ and God.

**HONDO** Principal building or room in a BUDDHIST monastery in Japan.

**HONEN (c.1133–1211)** Founder of the "Pure Land" school in Japanese BUDDHISM. He proclaimed that one may attain eternal life through faith in the grace of Amida, the Buddha of limitless light.

**HOOD** 1. Ecclesiastical cowl. 2. Ornamental folded neckpiece hanging at the rear of an academic or ecclesiastical gown.

**HOOKER, RICHARD (c.1553–1600)** Clergyman of the CHURCH OF ENGLAND whose *Laws of Ecclesiastical Polity*, contending that morality is based on the law of God and that the Anglican system is a happy medium between CALVINISM and ROMAN CATHOLICISM, profoundly influenced subsequent theological and political thought. Hooker also held that government rests on the consent of the governed and that church and state are two aspects of the same government, which may well be in the hands of the king. He is one of the finest theologians of the Church of England.

**HOOKER, THOMAS (1586–1647)** PURITAN clergyman and theologian of New England. He held that people should choose their magistrates but that the choice should be according to the will of God.

**HOPE** Expectant desire. With faith and love, St. Paul classes hope among the most valuable and enduring virtues (1 CORINTHIANS 13:13).

**HOPHNI** A son of the righteous priest Eli. He committed immoral actions at the sanctuary and was slain in the battle of Aphek (1 SAMUEL 1—4).

**HOPKINS, GERARD MANLEY (1844–1889)** Gifted English JESUIT poet.

**HOPKINS, SAMUEL (1721–1803)** First New England CONGREGATIONAL clergyman to denounce slavery. He saw holiness as disinterested benevolence and expressed willingness to be damned for the glory of God.

**HOPKINSIANISM** The formulation of Jonathan Edwards' CALVINISM by Samuel HOPKINS, particularly in the latter's rigidly logical *System of Doctrines* (1793). One element in it was the belief that sin is essential to the happiness of the universe as a whole.

**HORAE** Greek and Roman goddesses of the seasons: Order, Peace, and Righteousness.

**HOREB** *mount of God* MT. SINAI.

**HORITES** See HIVITES.

**HORMISDAS, ST. (?–523)** Pope (514–523) who brought the ACACIAN SCHISM to an end, reuniting the churches of the East and West which had been separated since 484. His feast day is August 6.

**HORN** In Scripture, a symbol of prosperity and power (1 SAMUEL 2:1; PSALM 92:10).

**HORNEY, KAREN (1885–1952)** German-born psychiatrist who practiced and taught in the United States and founded the American Institute of Psychoanalysis. Although not a religious leader, she contributed great insight to the problem of neuroses and to the enlightening of the human situation.

**HORNIE** Scottish name for the DEVIL.

**HORSE** A symbol of war or conquest in the Bible, it was a symbol of lust in the religious art of the Renaissance.

**HORT, FENTON JOHN ANTHONY (1828–1892)** English scholar and expert in New Testament Greek. A friend of J. B. LIGHT-

FOOT and Charles KINGSLEY, he is best known for his collaboration with Brooke Foss WESTCOTT on an authoritative text of the Greek New Testament.

**HORTA** Etruscan fertility goddess.

**HORUS** A name of the Egyptian sun god who brought men daylight and gladness. He was sometimes represented as a falcon or as a man with the head of a hawk.

**HOSANNA O save now!** Jewish cry during processions in the Feast of BOOTHS. Those who acclaimed Jesus' triumphal entry into Jerusalem shortly before His death cried, "Hosanna!" (MARK 11:9).

**HOSEA** Prophet of Israel in the eighth century B.C. who either married a prostitute or whose wife became one. Hosea used the tragedy in the Old Testament book bearing his name, to point out God's love for His faithless people.

**HOSHAANOT** Prayers during the Jewish Feast of BOOTHS or Tabernacles.

**HOSIUS (c.255–c.357)** Leader of the orthodox against the ARIANS at the Council of NICAEA, at which he probably presided. He was Bishop of Cordoba, Spain, and supported ATHANASIUS.

**HOSPITALERS** See KNIGHTS HOSPITALERS; also BROTHERS HOSPITALERS.

**HOST** Ecclesiastically, the bread of the EUCHARIST.

**HOSTS** The powers of heaven. Jehovah was known as Lord of hosts.

**HOTEI** Japanese god of happiness and luck.

**HOUNFORT** VOODOO chapel.

**HOUNGANS** VOODOO priests.

**HOUNSI** Female assistants to VOODOO priests.

**HOURI** Black-eyed maiden who comforts the blessed in the MOSLEMS' paradise.

**HOUSE CHURCH** Church program carried out and centered in homes rather than in ecclesiastical structures. This is a contemporary return to the first-century church when there were no church buildings at all. There are ANGLICAN and CATHOLIC evangelistic programs called "house church."

**HOUSE OF DAVID** 1. Family descended from King David. Jesus was of the house and lineage of David. 2. Religious group founded in 1903 in Michigan, claiming descent from the lost tribes of Israel.

**HOUSE OF GOD** 1. Jewish term for the sanctuary of God in the tabernacle or temple. 2. Christian term for the church as a place of worship.

**HOUSE OF GOD, WHICH IS THE CHURCH OF THE LIVING GOD, THE PILLAR AND GROUND OF THE TRUTH, INC.** Small American denomination holding to "Freemason religion" and practicing TITHING and FOOT WASHING.

**HOUSE OF LIFE** Jewish term for place of interment.

**HOUSE OF ISRAEL** Jewish Negro religious group centered in Harlem, New York.

**HOUSE OF PRAYER** Negro religious group founded in the United States by Bishop Grace, PENTECOSTAL in emphasis.

**HOUSE OF THE LORD** Tiny American religious group opposing tobacco, whisky, pleasure riding, ball games, ownership of property, and the like.

**HOWARD, PETER D. (1908–1965)** British athlete and author who led MORAL REARMAMENT from 1961 to 1965.

**HOWE, JOHN (1630–1705)** English PURITAN who became chaplain to Oliver Cromwell and who sought toleration and union among different denominations.

**HOW-TOO** Chinese earth deity.

**HSUAN-TSANG (c.605–664)** Chinese BUDDHIST traveler and scholar. He translated the sacred writings of Buddhism into Chinese.

**HSUAN-WU** TAOIST god, "the Lord on high in the dark heaven."

**HSUN-TZU (third century B.C.)** Chinese TAOIST religious leader and thinker who denounced superstition and refused to accept the original goodness of man.

**HUACA** Local, animistic Inca god.

**HUAHUANTLI** Aztec god of slain soldiers.

**HUANG-PO (?–850)** Japanese Master of RINZAI Zen Buddhism.

**HUA-YEN** Chinese BUDDHIST school founded by Tu-shun and developed by Fa-tsang in the sixth and seventh centuries. It teaches universal enlightenment and harmony through the Buddha.

**HUBERT, ST. (?–727)** "Apostle of the Ardennes," believed converted by meeting a stag with a crucifix between its antlers. His feast day is November 30.

**HÜBMAIER, BALTHASAR (c.1480–1528)** German ANABAPTIST leader and an early reformer. Progressing from ZWINGLIAN to Baptistic doctrines, he held that man has free will, that baptism and the Lord's Supper are the only two sacraments, that personal faith is necessary for baptism, and that infant baptism is wrong. For his views he was tortured at Zurich and burned at the stake in Vienna.

**HUCBALD (c.840–c.930)** Flemish BENEDICTINE composer and musical reformer. He wrote *De harmonica institutione* and many lives of saints.

**HÜGEL, FRIEDRICH VON (1852–1925)** ROMAN CATHOLIC theologian and modernist. Born in Italy, he spent his life in England. He opposed too much centralization in church government, wrote a profound study of mysticism (*Mystical Element of Religion*), and sympathized with those who sought truth in all religions. Although he accepted modern methods of Biblical criticism, he rejected the doctrines officially denounced by his communion as "Modernism."

**HUGHES, HUGH PRICE (1847–1902)** Evangelical British METHODIST churchman who became first president of the NATIONAL COUNCIL OF THE EVANGELICAL FREE CHURCHES. An eloquent preacher, he opposed gambling, vivisection, profit making from alcohol, and inadequate housing for the poor.

**HUGHES, JOHN JOSEPH (1797–1864)** First ROMAN CATHOLIC Archbishop of New York City. Born in Ireland, he devoted his life to American interests and helped maintain good will toward the United States government on the part of France, Ireland, and Rome during the Civil War. He fought both Know-Nothing attacks against his church and weaknesses within the church, sought state aid for parochial schools, and helped found Fordham University.

**HUGH OF LINCOLN, ST. (c.1140–1200)** English CARTHUSIAN monk who became Bishop of Lincoln. He defended the people against the king's foresters and war taxes, and aided lepers, poor people, and Jews. Famous for his piety and charity, he was one of England's most popular saints. His feast day is November 17.

**HUGH OF ST. VICTOR (1096–1141)** AUGUSTINIAN monk and mystic of France who opposed the doctrines of ABELARD with a more orthodox dialectic. An allegorical and emotional writer, he emphasized creation, redemption, and knowledge of God. Adolf Harnack called him "the most influential theologian of the twelfth century."

**HUGUENOTS** Calvinistic French PROTESTANTS of the sixteenth and succeeding centuries. Their faith led them to espouse democracy as well as REFORMATION doctrines, and their history is one of mingled opposition from the monarchy and religion of France. They achieved freedom in 1905 through a law which separated church and state.

**HUI HAI (?–788)** ZEN Master of Chinese BUDDHISM.

**HUI-NENG (637–713)** Sixth and last Patriarch of ZEN Buddhism in China and leader in the separate establishment of the Ch'an School.

**HUITZILOPOCHTLI** War god and supreme being in Aztec religion. He was also harvest god and sun god, and war prisoners were sacrificed to him and their limbs eaten by his worshipers.

**HUIXTOCIHUATL** Aztec goddess of salt.

**HUJRAH** Room at Medina in which Mohammed's favorite wife Ayesha once lived. It now contains Mohammed's tomb and has a space for the tomb of Jesus whom MOSLEMS expect to return and die at Medina.

**HULDA or HULDE** Germanic goddess of marriage.

**HULDAH** *weasel* Shallum's wife, a prophetess consulted by King Josiah when he rediscovered the book of the law in the temple. She encouraged his religious reforms (II KINGS 22:14–20).

**HUMANISM** Philosophical or religious point of view emphasizing human values and rational thought, sometimes characterized by an antisupernaturalistic bias.

**HUMANITARIANISM** 1. Moral and ethical devotion to social progress and reform. 2. Attitude toward Christ in purely human terms; sometimes a synonym for UNITARIANISM.

**HUMAN SACRIFICE** This has been a part of religion in every land through much of man's history. Humans have sacrificed their kind to deities to atone for sin, to acquire supernatural powers, to please their gods, to secure blessings, and for various other purposes. Today human sacrifice takes place less for religious than for nationalistic purposes, although often with the blessing of religious groups.

**HUMBLE ACCESS, PRAYER OF** The prayer before that of consecration in the ANGLICAN communion service.

**HUME, DAVID (1711–1776)** Scottish philosopher, historian, and religious writer. In religion a skeptic, he held that the future is unpredictable, that the only God who can be inferred must be finite, and that religion arises out of human experience.

**HUMERAL VEIL** Silk shawl worn by the subdeacon at high mass and by a priest in processions of the sacrament or on other special occasions.

**HUMILIATI** Medieval monastic order. Founded in twelfth-century Italy, it consisted of laymen who lived at home, cared for the poor, and met on Sunday to hear one of the brethren speak. Often under suspicion, the Humiliati were finally suppressed by Pope PIUS V in 1571.

**HUMILIATION OF CHRIST** Theological term for Christ's incarnation and life as a man, in contrast with His divine exaltation later.

**HUMILITY** Cardinal religious virtue.

**HUNABKU** Supreme Mayan deity.

**HUNGARIAN REFORMED CHURCH IN AMERICA** American denomination, formerly the Free Magyar Reformed Church in America, with Hungarian background. Its theology is based on the HEIDELBERG CATECHISM and the Second HELVETIC CONFESSION.

**HUNG-JEN (605–675)** Fifth Patriarch of China's ZEN Buddhism.

**HUNT, WILLIAM HOLMAN (1827–1910)** English religious painter famous for his "Light of the World." His other paintings include "The Hireling Shepherd," "The Shadow of the Cross," "The Triumph of the Innocents," and "The Finding of the Saviour in the Temple." He sought to serve "as high priest and expounder of the excellence of the works of the Creator."

**HUNTHACA** Moon goddess of the Chibcha Indians of Colombia, South America.

**HUNTIN** Tree spirit of the Bantus of Africa.

**HUNTINGDON, SELINA HASTINGS (1707–1791)** English countess who aided George WHITEFIELD and John and Charles WESLEY in the early years of METHODISM. She made Whitefield her chaplain and built 64 chapels for the Methodist cause. Her CALVINISTIC views led to the formation of a group called "The COUNTESS OF HUNTINGDON'S CONNEXION."

**HUNTINGTON, FREDERICK DAN (1819–1904)** First PROTESTANT EPISCOPAL bishop of central New York. He had previously served in the CONGREGATIONAL and UNITARIAN denominations.

**HUNTINGTON, WILLIAM REED (1838–1909)** PROTESTANT EPISCOPAL churchman who helped found the Cathedral of St. John the Divine, proposed the LAMBETH QUADRILATERAL, and aided in revising the Order of Deaconesses.

**HUNZIGER, AUGUST WILHELM (1871–1920)** German theologian and pastor who sought to mediate between critical and orthodox theology.

**HUPFELD, HERMANN (1796–1866)** German theologian and Old Testament scholar, credited with first distinguishing between the Priestly and Elohistic sources in the Pentateuch.

**HUPPAH** *covering* Canopy or bower, sometimes made of flowers, beneath which the bride and groom stand at a Jewish wedding. The huppah may symbolize the new home.

**HUR** Hebrew who held up Moses' hands so that the Israelites might crush the Amalekites (EXODUS 17:10–12).

**HURAKAN** Wind god of the Quiche Indians of Guatemala.

**HURRIANS** See HIVITES.

**HUS, JAN** See HUSS, JOHN.

**HUSBANDMAN** Word for farmer or gardener in the King James Bible.

**HUSEIN (c.626–680)** Second son of Mohammed's daughter Fatima. Claiming the Khalifate in 679, Husein was slain in battle the next year and is considered a SHIITE saint. His tomb in Iraq is a Shiite place of pilgrimage, and the day of his death—Muharram 10—is a sacred day in Shiism.

**HUSS, JOHN (c.1369–1415)** Czech reformer also known as Jan Hus. Influenced by John WYCLIF, he accepted the Bible as his supreme authority and criticized clerical abuses. Although supported by the people, he was excommunicated, brought before the Council of CONSTANCE, and burned at the stake. The University of Prague declared him a martyr. His feast day is July 6, commemorating the day of his death.

**HUSSITES** Followers of John HUSS. See also BOHEMIAN BRETHREN.

**HUTCHINSON, ANNE (c.1600–1643)** New England religious leader. An articulate member of the Boston theocracy, she discussed the sermons with others in her home, expressing the belief that salvation is by faith alone and that the Holy Spirit dwells in every believer. Excommunicated for "traducing the ministers," Mrs. Hutchinson helped found Portsmouth, Rhode Island, and moved to Long Island where she and most of her family were killed by Indians.

**HUTTER, JACOB** See HUTTERIAN BRETHREN.

**HUTTERIAN BRETHREN or HUTTERITES** Followers of Jacob Hutter, an ANABAPTIST minister of Austria burned at the stake in the sixteenth century. Those in the United States and Canada today practice farming, hold their property in common, practice nonresistance and nonconformity to the world, and are in many ways similar to AMISH or Mennonite groups. Originally called Bruderhof.

**HUXLEY, ALDOUS LEONARD (1894–1963)** English writer who spent the last quarter-century of his life in California. A student of mysticism, psychic research, and Oriental religion, Huxley is famous for the books *Antic Hay, Point Counter Point, Brave New World, Ape and Essence,* and *The Devils of Loudon.* The latter is a study of medieval attempts to deal with witchcraft.

**HUXLEY, THOMAS HENRY (1825–1895)** Agnostic English biologist who defended Darwinian evolution and saw no relationship between human development and ethics. He held that human beings cannot understand either matter or spirit, and that one's chief duty is to enlighten ignorance and meet human needs. Although he attacked traditional Christian beliefs, he maintained that education should include the study of the Bible.

**HYACINTH** Flower symbolizing aspiration in religious art.

**HYACINTH, ST. (1185–1257)** "Apostle of the North," a Dominican monk who was a missionary to his native Poland and to Sweden, Denmark, and Norway. His feast day is August 17.

**HYACINTHE, FATHER (1827–1912)** Eloquent French preacher, Charles Loyson, who was excommunicated after calling for reform in the ROMAN CATHOLIC CHURCH and opposing the doctrine of papal infallibility. He married and founded an independent Catholic church.

**HYBRIDISM, LITURGICAL** Admixture of Eastern and Western rites and customs in a worship service.

**HYDROMANCY** Forecasting the future by observing the tides or making other use of liquids.

**HYGEIA or HYGIEIA** Greek goddess of health, daughter or wife of AESCULAPIUS.

**HYGINUS (?–c.140)** Eighth pope or bishop of Rome. During his papal term GNOSTICISM was first observed in Rome.

**HYKSOS** *rulers of foreign lands* Semitic contemporaries of the Hebrews, ruling Palestine, Syria, and Egypt c.1720–1550 B.C. Their control of these lands appears to have been at about the time Abraham and his descendants came to Palestine, through the Hebrew captivity in Egypt. The Hyksos worshiped Seth, Baal, Har, Anat, and various fertility deities. They introduced horses and chariots into Egypt, and buried infants—possibly in sacrifice —under their buildings.

**HYLIC** GNOSTIC term for those who cannot be saved.

**HYLOZOISM** Doctrine that all matter contains qualities of life.

**HYMEN** Greek god of marriage.

**HYMENAEUS** Member of the early church denounced by the Apostle Paul for having made shipwreck of his faith (I TIMOTHY 1:20).

**HYMN** Song of praise or worship. The Psalms are principally hymns to Jehovah, and many religions have utilized song in worship. In Christianity, however, hymns are almost inseparable from the spiritual life, and countless leaders of the faith have composed or utilized hymns.

**HYMNAL or HYMNBOOK** Book containing hymns for devotional use, particularly in public worship.

**HYMNARY** Medieval liturgical book containing hymns arranged according to the ecclesiastical year.

**HYMNODY** 1. Collective term for hymns and their development. 2. Art or practice of singing hymns.

**HYMNOLOGY** Study or composition of hymns.

**HYPATIA (c.370–415)** Female NEOPLATONIC philosopher of Alexandria, Egypt, noted for her intelligence and beauty. After flirting with Alexandria's pagan prefect Orestes, she was burned by a band of monks—possibly because of the jealousy of the city's archbishop Cyril.

**HYPERDULIA** Special veneration of the Blessed Virgin MARY, on a lower plane than worship of God but higher than ordinary veneration of saints.

**HYPOCRISY** *play-acting* Profanity or insincerity in religion, detested in all faiths and condemned by Jesus (cf. MATTHEW 6:2, 5; 23:13–15, 23–29).

**HYPOSTASIS** Theological term for divine substance, essence, or person. At first a confusing term because it was a synonym for the Latin *substantia*, this Greek word finally became an accepted way of indicating a Person in the Godhead.

**HYPOSTATIC UNION** Theological term for the union of Christ's two natures, human and divine, in one Person.

**HYSSOP** Shrub mentioned several times in the Bible. A reed of hyssop lifted vinegar to Jesus' parched lips at the CRUCIFIXION (JOHN 19:29). In religious art hyssop symbolizes humility, innocence, or penitence.

# I

**IACCHOS** Greek god worshiped in the Eleusinian Mysteries, possibly another name of Dionysus.

**IAHWEH** See JEHOVAH.

**I AM** American religion founded in 1930 by Mr. and Mrs. Guy Ballard at Chicago, Illinois. Its teachings, resembling a mixture of New Thought, THEOSOPHY, SPIRITISM, and other religions, were popular for several decades.

**IAMBLICHUS (?–c.330)** Principal NEOPLATONIST in Syria. He studied under PORPHYRY, wrote commentaries on PLATO and ARISTOTLE, and expounded concepts of Plato and PYTHAGORAS. His writings were popular during the Renaissance.

**IBADHIS** Sect of ISLAM with adherents in Algeria, Oman, and Zanzibar.

**IBAS (?–457)** Bishop of Edessa deposed and reinstated several times in connection with his alleged heresies, such as NESTORIANISM.

**IBIS** Storklike bird worshiped by the ancient Egyptians and sometimes mummified.

**IBLIS** In ISLAMIC teaching, the devil.

**IBN EZRA** See ABEN-EZRA.

**IBN GABIROL, SOLOMON BEN JUDAH (c.1021–c.1058)** Spanish Jewish philosopher and poet, influenced by NEOPLATONISM. His book *Fons Vitae,* "The Well of Life," relates man to the spiritual world and greatly influenced Christian thought. He was also known as Avicebron or Avencebrol. His verse has contributed to Jewish liturgy and his long philosophical work *Mekor Hayim,* "Fountain of Life," strongly influenced such Franciscan Scholastics as ALEXANDER OF HALES and DUNS SCOTUS.

**ICHABOD** *no glory* Grandson of the priest Eli, born when the ark of the covenant was captured by the Philistines and named to commemorate that inglorious event (I SAMUEL 4:17–22).

**ICHOR** According to Greek belief, the gods' substitute for blood.

**ICHTHUS** *fish* Early Christian ACROSTIC for Jesus Christ, Son of God and Saviour.

**ICON, IKON, or EIKON** *image* Religious image or painting. In the EASTERN ORTHODOX churches icons are flat paintings, bas-reliefs, or mosaics, done in a stiff and conventional manner; sculpture and statuary are prohibited.

**ICONIUM** Town in Asia Minor visited by PAUL and BARNABAS, and the center of a thriving Christian church since the third century. At one time it was the center of the sect of Mevlevi DERVISHES.

**ICONOCLASM** Image-breaking. Destructive assault on images in Christian churches was prevalent in the eighth century in the Eastern churches, and at the time of the REFORMATION in Catholic churches.

**ICONOCLASTIC CONTROVERSY** From c. 725 to 842 the combined influences of JUDAISM, ISLAM, MONOPHYSITISM, and MANICHAEISM produced conflict over images in the Eastern churches. Papal defense of images led to the schism between East and West.

**ICONOGRAPHY** Art, study, or practice of representation by images or pictures.

**ICONOSTASIS** Screen enclosing the sanctuary in an EASTERN ORTHODOX church. At the front there are usually three doors.

**ID** According to psychoanalysis, the mass of drives and life tendencies at the deepest portion of the unconscious.

**IDA** Goddess of speech in HINDUISM.

**IDEAL** Norm of value or perfection.

**IDEALISM** 1. Adherence to ideals. 2. Philosophical system emphasizing mind or spirit or an ideal world in opposition to stress on mere matter or sense experience or determinism.

**IDOL** A representation of deity, a false god, or a substitute for God. The JUDEO-CHRISTIAN God is a jealous God, tolerating no idols.

**IDOLATRY** Worship of idols. or of anything in place of God.

**IDUMAEA** See EDOM.

**IDUN** Goddess of springtime and youth in Scandinavian myth.

**IGIGI** Babylonian term for the gods in the stars above the horizon.

**IGNATIUS OF ANTIOCH, ST.** (c.35–c.107) "Theophorus" (God-bearer), Bishop of Antioch martyred by Emperor Trajan. He wrote letters to six churches, warning against DOCETISM and urging obedience to bishops. His feast day is February 1.

**IGNATIUS OF LOYOLA, ST.** (1491–1556) Spanish nobleman, converted at the age of thirty to Christian discipleship, who founded the Society of Jesus. He was general of the new order throughout his life. His *Spiritual Exercises* indicate his religious zeal and mystical inclinations. His feast day is July 31.

**IGNOSTIC** Term popularized by Rabbi Sherman Wine in 1965 to define his belief that there is no empirical evidence for the existence of God.

**IHRAM** White cotton garb of pilgrims to MECCA, worn over the left shoulder and around the hips.

**IHS or IHC** First three letters in the Greek name of Jesus, thus representing His name in religious symbolism. Other interpretations of the three letters include these: *a.* "In His Service." *b.* "In Hoc Signo" (In this sign [conquer]). *c.* "Jesus Hominum Salvator" (Jesus the Saviour of Men). *d.* "In Hoc Salus" (In this [cross] is salvation). *e.* "Jesus Habemus Socium" (We have Jesus as our Companion).

**IJMA** *agreement* "Agreement of Islam": belief that the faith and practice of the majority of Moslems are correct.

**IKH** Egyptian term for the glorious hereafter.

**IKHNATON** *the sun god is satisfied* (c.1385–c.1358 B.C.) Egyptian king who acceded to the throne as Amenhotep IV but discarded that name. He tried to replace worship of the old deities with that of ATON, a new name for the deified sun.

Chiseling the names of former gods off monuments and placing everywhere pictures of the sun's disk with rays extending down in the shape of hands, Ikhnaton gave Egyptians their first glimpse of MONOTHEISM. When he died the ancient deities returned and Ikhnaton's work seemed lost, but many attribute the concept of one supreme God to Ikhnaton's innovation. In a hymn to Aton the king wrote: "How manifold are thy works!/ They are hidden from before us,/ O God alone, whose powers no other possesseth." His wife was the beautiful Nefretete.

**ILAH** Semitic moon god.

**ILAMATECUHTLI** Aztec goddess of fertility.

**ILAT** Arabian goddess of the sun.

**ILDEFONSUS, ST.** (c.607–c.667) BENEDICTINE monk of Spain who allegorized the wanderings of the Israelites in the desert as a sort of parable of the earthly wanderings of the soul. He attended the Councils of Toledo and became Archbishop of Toledo.

**ILGEN, KARL DAVID** (1763–1834) German pastor, theologian, and orientalist.

**ILLGEN, CHRISTIAN FRIEDRICH** (1786–1844) German theologian and church historian.

**ILLIYUN** Seventh heaven in the paradise of ISLAM.

**ILLUMINATI** *enlightened* 1. Spanish mystics first mentioned in the fifteenth century. They lived in prayer and meditation, and believed they could communicate with Christ and the Virgin MARY. They were suppressed by the INQUISITION. 2. Eighteenth-century mystics of southern France. 3. ROSICRUCIANS. 4. Eighteenth-century rationalists organized along masonic lines.

**ILLUMINATION, SPIRITUAL** Reception of light that frees the spirit from darkness and imprisonment.

**ILLUMINATION OF MANUSCRIPTS** Medieval decoration of manuscripts, particularly those of the Bible, which were beautifully enlivened with color, designs, and illustrations.

**ILMAQAH** Semitic moon god.

**ILYTHYIA-LEUCOTHEA** Etruscan fertility goddess.

**IMAGE** 1. Artistic representation. Many religions require the use of images although they were forbidden in JUDAISM, unknown in the NEW TESTAMENT church, and opposed in the REFORMATION. The use of images in churches has often caused dissension (cf. the ICONOCLASTIC CONTROVERSY). 2. Spiritual similarity or revelation (cf. GENESIS 1:26, 27; ROMANS 8:29; COLOSSIANS 1:15; HEBREWS 1:3).

**IMAGO DEI** *image of God* Theological term for the image of God in which man was created (GENESIS 1:26, 27; COLOSSIANS 3:10). Christian thought holds that this image was to some extent lost in the fall of Adam but is restored in Christ.

**IMAM** *leader* Leader, teacher, khalif, or priest of ISLAM. An imam leads the faithful in prayer in a mosque on Friday.

**IMHOTEP** Egyptian god of medicine, originally a physician.

**IMITATION OF CHRIST** One of the world's most popular devotional classics, traditionally attributed to THOMAS À KEMPIS, but believed by some to have another author such as Gerard GROOTE. Dating from the fifteenth century or earlier, it summons the reader to spiritual growth through obedience and suffering.

**IMMACULATE CONCEPTION** Theological term for the sinless conception and birth of the Virgin MARY. In 1854 this teaching was proclaimed a dogma of the ROMAN CATHOLIC CHURCH. The feast of the Immaculate Conception is December 8.

**IMMANENCE** Term for the presence of God in the world, in opposition to TRANSCENDENCE.

**IMMANUEL** See EMMANUEL.

**IMMANUEL BEN SOLOMON (c.1265–c.1330)** Italian Jewish poet, satirist, and scholar. He wrote *Mehabberoth* and *Hell and Paradise*.

**IMMATERIALISM** Philosophy that no matter is independent of mind, and that external objects are of the essence of mind.

**IMMERSION** BAPTISM by completely submerging the subject in water—the BAPTIST mode. Most denominations consider this to be one of several possible methods of baptism.

**IMMERSIONISM** Belief in or practice of IMMERSION, with the implied conviction that this is the only proper method of BAPTISM.

**IMMOLATION** Sacrifice; particularly the preparation and slaughter of a sacrificial victim. In some religions the widow is immolated when her husband dies. CATHOLIC theology includes several doctrines of immolation in the mass.

**IMMORTALITY** Endless existence. Most religions from primitive to advanced have held beliefs of a survival of the soul after physical death, and the hope of immortality seems universal. CHRISTIANITY distinguishes between the immortality of all men and the special quality of eternal life granted the blessed. Jesus said, "And this is life eternal, that they might know thee the only true God, and Jesus Christ, whom thou hast sent" (JOHN 17:3).

**IMMOVABLE FEASTS** Christian days of celebration falling on a fixed day in the month, as Christmas and All Saints' Day, which are always on December 25 and November 1. Movable feasts such as EASTER vary from year to year. When the coincidence or proximity of movable and immovable feasts produces a conflict, changes are made in accordance with established rules of precedence.

**IMMUNITY** Exemption, as of a religious group or leader from civil obligation.

**IMP** Popular term for an inferior demon, or a mischievous child.

**IMPANATION** Doctrine that the body and blood of Christ are present at the EUCHARIST along with the bread and wine in hypostatic (substantial) union. Certain LUTHERANS have held this doctrine.

**IMPASSIBILITY** Doctrine that God cannot be acted upon from without, cannot internally change His emotions, and cannot experience pleasure or pain because of any external action. Apparently Greek philosophy originated this notion of God, and while orthodox Christianity maintains it, contemporary theologians and philosophers have challenged it—largely on the basis of the genuine love of God.

**IMPECCABILITY** Freedom from the taint or capability of sin, as in the case of Christ.

**IMPEDIMENT, MARITAL** Obstacle preventing an ecclesiastically proper marriage. Marital impediments may be due to civil law, church law, or various special circumstances.

**IMPLICIT FAITH** 1. Faith without reservations. 2. Belief in a dogma or doctrines even though ignorant of the details.

**IMPLICIT TRUTH** A truth contained within another explicit statement. For example, the doctrine of the pope as the successor to Peter who has always kept the CATHOLIC faith free from error is believed to have implicitly within it the doctrine of the infallibility of the pope.

**IMPOSITION OF HANDS** See LAYING ON OF HANDS.

**IMPRECATION** Curse; invocation of evil.

**IMPRECATORY PSALMS** Such Psalms as 58; 68:21–23; 109:5–19; and 137:7–9. In these God's curse or vengeance is invoked against enemies. The CHURCH OF ENGLAND now omits the reading of these passages from public worship services.

**IMPRIMATUR** *let it be printed* 1. CATHOLIC permission for the faithful to read certain works. The imprimatur is carried at the front of a book. 2. Seventeenth-century English permission for Englishmen to read books which had been declared harmless to the government or the CHURCH OF ENGLAND. This came to an end in 1695.

**IMPUTATION** Theological term for the vicarious attribution of sin, guilt, or righteousness. Through the sin of Adam, death and sin were imputed to all men (ROMANS 5:12–14). Similarly, through the work of Christ, righteousness came upon all (ROMANS 5:15–21).

**INABILITY** Theological term for man's moral helplessness because of sin. Strict CALVINISM holds to the sinner's total inability to do any real good, finding him so empowered only through Christ.

**INARI** Japanese SHINTO goddess of rice.

**INCANTATION** Verbal formula, spell, or charm used to summon or ward off evil spirits, or for other magical purposes.

**INCARDINATION** 1. Reception of a priest in a new DIOCESE. 2. Elevation of a churchman to the rank of CARDINAL.

**INCARNATION** Being made flesh; specifically, the coming of Christ into the world in the person of Jesus of Nazareth.

**INCENSE** Sweet odor of burning spice, resin, or other substance, often used in worship. It was introduced into Christian ceremony about 500 A.D.

**INCLINATION** Ecclesiastical bowing or kneeling.

**INCORPOREAL** Heavenly, spiritual, not having physical existence.

**INCUBATION** Religious term for sleeping in temples, churches, or chapels in expectation of healing or other benefit.

**INCUBUS** Nightmare, burden, or demon which lies upon someone who is sleeping.

**INCUMBENT** One who holds an office, a pastorate, or a BENEFICE.

**INDEFECTIBILITY** Theological term for the incorruptibility and freedom from failure or sin of the church, Christ, the heavenly state of believers, etc.

**INDEPENDENCY** British term for a CONGREGATIONALIST view of the church. According to this system, ultimate power is vested in the local congregation which is independent and answerable only to Christ.

**INDEPENDENT AFRICAN METHODIST EPISCOPAL CHURCH** Small American denomination originating with a group which left the African Methodist Episcopal Church in 1907.

**INDEPENDENT ASSEMBLIES OF GOD** American Pentecostal association formerly called Scandinavian Assemblies in the United States, Canada, and Other Lands.

**INDEPENDENT BAPTIST CHURCH OF AMERICA** Denomination with Swedish background, two churches, and about twenty-five members.

**INDEPENDENT CHRISTIAN CHURCHES** Association of conservative churches also affiliated, apparently, with the CHURCHES OF CHRIST or the DISCIPLES OF CHRIST. Their doctrines tend to be those of the former group.

**INDEPENDENT CHURCHES** Those churches not related to any denomination in the ordinary manner.

**INDEPENDENT FUNDAMENTAL CHURCHES OF AMERICA** Organization of fundamentalist churches in the United States, linked together since 1930.

**INDEPENDENT METHODISTS** Evangelical British denomination with independent congregations and unsalaried ministers, organized in 1806.

**INDEPENDENTS** Seventeenth-century British term for those who believed in INDEPENDENCY.

**INDETERMINISM** Philosophical doctrine allowing for human free will, in opposition to DETERMINISM.

**INDEX EXPURGATORIUS** *expurgated list* List of books which may be read by ROMAN CATHOLICS only after being amended by removal of certain passages.

**INDEX LIBRORUM PROHIBITORUM** *list of*

*forbidden books* List of books which ROMAN CATHOLICS may not read except with special permission. The first Index was made by the INQUISITION in the sixteenth century.

**INDIFFERENTISM** Doctrine that certain things or beliefs are relatively unimportant.

**INDIGENOUS CHURCH** Church native to an area, or controlled and structured by the natives of a region. The indigenous church may be the church of the future.

**INDIGITAMENTA** Roman books listing deities and prayers for various occasions.

**INDRA** Important HINDU god of war, fertility, thunder and storms. He is often represented riding an elephant.

**INDRANI** Voluptuous wife of INDRA.

**INDUCTION** 1. Appointment and placing of a clergyman in a charge or pastorate. 2. Reasoning from particular facts to general laws or principles. This is the method of classical systematic theology.

**INDULGENCE** 1. ROMAN CATHOLIC term for pardoning "the temporal punishment still due to sin after the guilt has been forgiven." Such indulgence brings the recipient merit. Martin LUTHER protested the sale and abuse of indulgences; their sale has been prohibited since 1562. 2. A grant of limited religious freedom in British history.

**INDULT** Special permission from the papal office to depart from ecclesiastical common law.

**INEFFABILIS DEUS** Papal bull of 1854 setting forth the IMMACULATE CONCEPTION.

**INEFFABLE** Inexpressible or unutterable. Through most of their history the Hebrews dared not utter the sacred TETRAGRAMMATON, transliterated as JEHOVAH or YAHWEH, for the name of the Lord.

**INFALLIBILIST** One who holds or defends the doctrine of the INFALLIBILITY OF THE POPE.

**INFALLIBILITY** Freedom from error or from the liability to err.

**INFALLIBILITY OF THE BIBLE** This is a traditional doctrine of PROTESTANTISM, based on such Scriptures as II Timothy 3:16. Many PRESBYTERIAN churches require their ruling and teaching ELDERS to affirm that the Scriptures of the Old and New Testaments are the Word of God, the only infallible rule of faith and practice.

**INFALLIBILITY OF THE CHURCH** Traditional CATHOLIC doctrine that the church is incapable of teaching anything false. While many Christians accept the authoritativeness of the church because of such Scriptures as John 14:17, 16:13, and Acts 15:28, and those in EASTERN ORTHODOX churches accept the infallibility of ecumenical councils, it is the ROMAN CATHOLIC CHURCH that emphasizes most strongly the infallibility of the church and the pope.

**INFALLIBILITY OF THE POPE** Dogma defined in the VATICAN COUNCIL of 1870 as follows: ". . . that the Roman Pontiff, when he speaks *ex cathedra*—i.e., when, in his character as Pastor and Doctor of all Christians, and in virtue of his supreme apostolic authority, he lays down that a certain doctrine concerning faith or morals is binding upon the universal Church—possesses, by the Divine assistance which was promised to him in the person of the blessed Saint Peter, that same infallibility with which the Divine Redeemer thought to endow His Church, to define its doctrine with regard to faith and morals."

**INFANT BAPTISM** Christian BAPTISM of babies or young children. Throughout most of church history infant baptism has been common. At the time of the REFORMATION, ANABAPTISTS and others began to question this practice and to limit baptism to adults, on personal confession of faith, usually by IMMERSION. Infant baptism is ordinarily administered by the sprinkling of water on the child's head.

**INFANT COMMUNION** CATHOLICISM admits infants to communion if death appears imminent.

**INFANTICIDE** In the past babies and children were sometimes killed for religious reasons in Semitic, Egyptian, Greek, and Roman cults. The druids practiced infanticide. The great world religions of JUDAISM, CHRISTIANITY, and ISLAM condemn it.

**INFANT SALVATION** CATHOLIC doctrine excludes unbaptized infants from heaven, consigning them to a *limbus infantum* where a limited degree of happiness is believed possible. John CALVIN taught the salvation of elect infants. Most religious teachers today believe in universal infant salvation. Many PROTESTANTS believe that a child is assured of salvation if he or she dies before reaching the age of moral accountability.

**INFERNO** 1. Hell. 2. In Dante's *Divine Comedy*, an enormous cone-shaped opening in the earth where sinners suffer.

**INFIDEL** 1. Unbeliever. 2. Medieval term for a non-Christian. 3. Moslem term for a non-Moslem.

**INFIDELITY** 1. Unfaithfulness or unbelief. 2. Rejection of a religion. 3. Violation of an obligation or vow, particularly in marriage. Adultery is generally considered such a violation.

**INFINITE** 1. Limitless or undetermined. 2. Term for God, based upon His character as absolute, unconditioned, and beyond normally conceivable limitations.

**INFINITY** Quality of the infinite; eternity; limitlessness.

**INFONIWOO** Formosan creator-god.

**INFRALAPSARIANISM** Branch of CALVINISTIC thought holding that in the divine mind the fall of man preceded the decrees of election and reprobation. SUPRALAPSARIANISM holds that God determined to save some and permit others to be damned before He decided to permit the fall.

**INFUSED VIRTUES** Divinely transmitted virtues such as faith and love.

**INFUSIO GRATIAE** See INFUSION OF GRACE.

**INFUSION** BAPTISM by pouring water on the head; affusion.

**INFUSION OF GRACE** Divine instilling of supernatural aid through the sacrament.

**INGATHERING, FEAST OF** See BOOTHS, FEAST OF.

**INGE, WILLIAM RALPH (1860–1954)** "Gloomy dean" of St. Paul's Cathedral, original but somewhat pessimistic in outlook. An ecclesiastic of the CHURCH OF ENGLAND, he wrote *Christian Mysticism, Lay Thoughts of a Dean, Mysticism in Religion*, and other works. He won fame as a student of mysticism and as a NEOPLATONIST. In his thought God was the "supreme value."

**INGERSOLL, ROBERT GREEN (1833–1899)** American lawyer and agnostic who won fame with attacks on the Bible and Christianity. Among his lectures were "Why I Am an Agnostic" and "Some Mistakes of Moses."

**INGLIS, CHARLES (1734–1816)** ANGLICAN rector in colonial America who became first bishop of Nova Scotia.

**INGMAN, ANTERO WILHELM (1819–1877)** LUTHERAN clergyman of Finland who took part in and led a return to renewal and Biblical theology in his country.

**INHIBITION** Prohibition of a clergyman from carrying out his ministerial duties.

**IN HIS STEPS** Influential American novel about a minister and others who tried to do what Jesus would do in various situations. Rev. Charles M. SHELDON (1857–1946) wrote it for publication in 1896.

**IN HOC SIGNO VINCES by this sign you shall conquer** Motto CONSTANTINE is said to have seen in the sky before he made the Roman Empire Christian.

**INIQUITY** Bible word for sin, injustice, or unrighteousness.

**INNANA** Babylonian mother-goddess. See ISHTAR.

**INNER-CITY CHURCH** A church in the central area of a city. Such churches, formerly often abandoned with the growth of slum conditions, now receive special attention in many denominations and have special programs for the diverse needs of their neighborhoods.

**INNER LIGHT** Mystical and QUAKER term for the direct guidance and illumination of God within the individual.

**INNER MAN** Theological term for the soul or spirit.

**INNERE MISSION** German name of the INNER MISSION.

**INNER MISSION** EVANGELICAL movement among German PROTESTANTS which combined preaching, personal evangelism, and Bible distribution with institutions and programs for the aid of poor children, needy adults, and those outside the reach of the ordinary agencies of the churches. It has produced prison reform, nursing homes, insane asylums, hospitals, and many other good works from its inception in the eighteenth century to the present time. In other Scandinavian countries a similar work has emerged, with more emphasis on evangelism.

**INNOCENCE** Freedom from impurity characterizing angels, newborn infants, and man before the fall.

**INNOCENT** Name of thirteen popes and one antipope.

**INNOCENT I, ST. (?–417)** Strong Italian

pope who denounced PELAGIUS and DONATISM, supported JOHN CHRYSOSTOM, and increased the claims of Rome to ecclesiastical supremacy. His feast day is July 28.

**INNOCENT III (c.1160–1216)** Outstanding Italian pope who organized a number of CRUSADES and summoned the twelfth LATERAN COUNCIL. He exercised authority over many countries and but for the rise of nationalism might have subjugated all Christendom to the political and spiritual supremacy of the church. He wrote: "The Lord left to Peter the governance not only of the Church but also of the whole world."

**INNOCENT X (1574–1655)** Italian pope who condemned five propositions of Jansenius' *Augustinus* (see JANSEN, Cornelius), sparking the JANSENIST controversies. He was said to be dominated by his sister-in-law Olimpia Maidalchini and during his term the prestige of the papal office tended to deteriorate.

**INNOCENT XI (1611–1689)** Saintly Italian pope who guided the church through many problems and sought genuine ecclesiastical reform. He was beatified in 1956.

**INNOCENT XII (1615–1700)** Italian pope who accomplished several reforms and repressed JANSENISM. He condemned some of the doctrines of FENELON but refused to condemn a work by Celestino Sfondrati on predestination. He was greatly admired by many.

**INNOCENTS, HOLY** See HOLY INNOCENTS.

**INNOCENTS DAY** See HOLY INNOCENTS DAY.

**INOPPORTUNISTS** Delegates to the first VATICAN COUNCIL who opposed the decree on INFALLIBILITY OF THE POPE because they considered the time inopportune for such a promulgation.

**IN PARTIBUS INFIDELIUM** *in countries of unbelievers* Former title of a ROMAN CATHOLIC bishop holding honorary office over ISLAM territory. Such a bishop is now designated a *titular bishop.*

**IN PERPETUUM** *forever.*

**IN PETTO** *in secret* Designation of CARDINALS appointed at the discretion of the pope, but not named in CONSISTORY.

**IN PLANO** *on a level* On the level of the sanctuary floor.

**INQUISITION** ROMAN CATHOLIC institu-tion for investigation and punishment of those who hold erroneous doctrines. Although JOHN CHRYSOSTOM had stated that "to put a heretic to death would be to introduce upon earth an inexpiable crime," Catholic bishops began in the Middle Ages to use the power of civil authorities to suppress heresies. In 1229 Pope Gregory IX instituted the Inquisition in southern France with the aid of DOMINICAN monks who investigated the ALBIGENSES. Soon heretics were being hunted in many countries of Europe, and FRANCISCANS were also used to ferret out misbelievers. The accused were not told who had accused them, were given no counsel, and could be tortured even though some popes opposed torture. The result might be repentance, penance, imprisonment, or burning at the stake. In 1542 the Inquisition was assigned to the Congregation of the HOLY OFFICE, which now seeks to guard the faithful from injurious books and ideas.

**INQUISITION, SPANISH** Special investigation (1478–1820) of heresy in Spain and Spanish America. Never completely approved by the papal office, and sometimes acting in defiance of the pope, it suppressed with unusual cruelty and severity heretics, Catholics who were believed insincere, and Protestants. Beginning with investigation of converted Jews and Moslems, it included even IGNATIUS OF LOYOLA, THERESA OF AVILA, and several bishops in its suspicions. Among the objects of its wrath were freemasons, blasphemers, bigamists, homosexuals, married priests, mystics, JANSENISTS, humanists, philosophers, and writers of books which had not been approved. Under the notorious inquisitor Tomas de TORQUEMADA probably two thousand victims were burned. Thirty thousand may have been killed during the whole Inquisition.

**INRI** Initials of the Latin words placed on Jesus' cross: *Jesus Nazarenus Rex Judeorum,* "Jesus of Nazareth the King of the Jews." Symbolizing Christ's royalty, these initials often appear in Christian art.

**IN SAECULA SAECULORUM** *unto ages of ages* Term for eternity.

**INSPIRATION** 1. Religious uplift. 2. Divine inbreathing to produce divine revelation, particularly in sacred Scripture. All

Scripture is inspired by God (II TIMOTHY 3:16). Theories of inspiration vary, but most CHRISTIANS accept the inspiration of the Bible as providing a trustworthy guide to moral decisions and to salvation. HINDUS, MOSLEMS, and other religionists believe in the divine inspiration of their sacred writings.

**INSTALLATION** Ecclesiastical placement of a clergyman or other church official in office.

**INSTITUTE, RELIGIOUS** Society approved by the ROMAN CATHOLIC CHURCH whose members take vows for spiritual perfection.

**INSTITUTES OF THE CHRISTIAN RELIGION** Book written by John CALVIN, published in 1536, expounding Christian doctrines in systematic form. Most influential in the REFORMATION, it emphasized the sovereign will of God and the necessity of placing prayer, Scripture, and the church in relation to His supremacy.

**INSTITUTION** Admission of a qualified applicant or new incumbent into ecclesiastical office.

**INSTITUTION, WORDS OF** Term for the words with which Christ consecrated the LAST SUPPER. They are used in the consecration of the Lord's Supper, communion or EUCHARIST in most churches. They may be found in Matthew 26:26–28; Mark 14:22–24; Luke 22:19–20; I Corinthians 11:23–25.

**INSTITUTIONAL CHURCH** Term for a church which conducts a social as well as a devotional program.

**INSUFFLATION** Breathing upon a person or thing to indicate the incoming inspiration of the Holy Spirit.

**INTELLECTUALISM** Philosophical or theological term for a theory of intellectual supremacy. When such a theory ignores the place of the will or emotions, it seems to court the danger of reaching an arid emphasis on mere logic.

**INTENTION** 1. Moral purpose. 2. Minister's purpose in "doing what the Church does" in administering the sacraments. 3. Purpose of applying the benefits from prayers, a mass, or some other devotional exercise, to a specific person or cause.

**INTERCESSION** 1. Prayer on behalf of another or of others. 2. Prayer through the saints.

**INTERCHURCH WORLD MOVEMENT** Ambitious agency for interdenominational Christian action in the United States and Canada, organized in 1918. Its failure in two years has been attributed to fears from church agencies that they would be supplanted by it, pressures resulting from its interest in the steel strike of 1919, and the lack of readiness of the public for such a program.

**INTERCOMMUNION** Participation in communion or the EUCHARIST by those of different churches. A problem since the first divisions in the church, it has been the object of increased attention in recent years. In the past ROMAN CATHOLICS have found intercommunion impossible, although with the conclusion of the Second VATICAN COUNCIL communion in fellowship and worship with other Christians began to take place in previously unheard-of ways.

**INTERDICT** Ecclesiastical exclusion from the sacraments, Christian burial, and other benefits of the church. It may be imposed only by the pope and has been directed on some historical occasions against whole countries.

**INTERIM** Edict temporarily settling disputed ecclesiastical points. The Interim of AUGSBURG in 1548 compromised in accepting transubstantiation, seven sacraments, justification by faith, clerical marriage, and other elements.

**INTERMEDIATE STATE** The state of the soul between death and the final judgment. Several religions have fairly elaborate schemes outlining such a state. PROTESTANTISM in general sees little need for such doctrines, holding that at death the individual passes immediately to his eternal destiny.

**INTERNATIONAL ASSOCIATION FOR LIBERAL CHRISTIANITY AND RELIGIOUS FREEDOM** Organization of UNITARIAN, UNIVERSALIST, and independent groups throughout the world which works for liberal religion and religious freedom.

**INTERNATIONAL BIBLE STUDENTS** Early name of the JEHOVAH'S WITNESSES.

**INTERNATIONAL CHURCH OF THE FOURSQUARE GOSPEL** American denomination originating in the work of Aimee Semple McPherson early in the twentieth century. It is FUNDAMENTALIST. PENTECOSTAL, and

MILLENARIAN. Its foursquare gospel includes salvation, sanctification, healing, and speaking in tongues.

**INTERNATIONAL CONFERENCE OF CHRISTIANS AND JEWS** Organization seeking to remove barriers and promote understanding between JEWS and CHRISTIANS.

**INTERNATIONAL CONGREGATIONAL COUNCIL** World organization of CONGREGATIONALISTS.

**INTERNATIONAL COUNCIL OF CHRISTIAN CHURCHES** FUNDAMENTALIST organization initiated by Carl McIntire of Collingswood, New Jersey, in 1948.

**INTERNATIONAL GENERAL ASSEMBLY OF SPIRITUALISTS** American organization of SPIRITUALIST churches.

**INTERNATIONAL LEAGUE FOR THE DEFENSE AND FURTHERANCE OF PROTESTANTISM** Organization of European PROTESTANTS, formed in 1923 for Protestant cooperation and defense.

**INTERNATIONAL MINISTERIAL FEDERATION** American organization, incorporated in California in 1937, representing INDEPENDENT and COMMUNITY CHURCHES.

**INTERNATIONAL MISSIONARY ALLIANCE** Former name for the foreign mission agency of the CHRISTIAN AND MISSIONARY ALLIANCE.

**INTERNATIONAL MISSIONARY COUNCIL** World organ of PROTESTANT mission activity and ecumenical relationships, formed in London in 1921. It works closely with the NATIONAL COUNCIL OF CHURCHES OF CHRIST, U.S.A., the Near East Christian Council, the Conference of Missionary Societies in Great Britain and Ireland, the WORLD COUNCIL OF CHURCHES, and many other bodies.

**INTERNATIONAL PENTECOSTAL ASSEMBLIES** American PENTECOSTAL organization with foreign mission interests.

**INTERNATIONAL RELIGIOUS CONGRESS** Quadrennial convocation of the overseers of TRIUMPH THE CHURCH AND KINGDOM OF GOD IN CHRIST.

**INTERNSHIP** Training period for a ministerial candidate or clergyman under the supervision of an ordained minister or ecclesiastical group.

**INTERNUNCIO** Papal diplomat serving between terms of nuncios, or serving a less important area than a NUNCIO.

**INTERSTICE** Period between ecclesiastical

elevation from one order or rank to another.

**INTER-VARSITY CHRISTIAN FELLOWSHIP** International organization of Christian college students for purposes of fellowship and evangelism. It originated in Great Britain.

**INTINCTION** The dipping of the consecrated bread into wine before the service of the EUCHARIST.

**INTOLERANCE** Refusal of a hearing to, or coexistence or cooperation with, those of different religious beliefs or practices from one's own.

**INTONE** To chant or recite on a single note.

**INTRA-UTERINE BAPTISM** Baptism of a fetus with water in a syringe when it is feared that the child to be born may not survive birth.

**INTROIT** *entrance* Psalm or hymn sung, played, or spoken at the beginning of mass or a service of worship.

**INTRUSION** Illegal encroachment upon others' property, or upon another's benefice or parish. Intrusion in Scotland in 1843 was a term for the placing of ministers not desired by the people of the congregations they served.

**IN TUNE WITH THE INFINITE** Inspirational-religious best seller by Ralph Waldo Trine, published in 1897, which fathered many current psychological-religious self-help notions of the twentieth century.

**INVENTION OF THE CROSS** Account of how the three crosses of Calvary were found (Latin *inventae*) by Helena, the mother of CONSTANTINE. She is said to have discovered them and miraculously learned which was Christ's during a visit to Jerusalem in 326. The feast day for this is May 3.

**INVESTITURE** Installation into ecclesiastical office, together with clothing in the proper vestments thereof.

**INVESTITURE CONTROVERSY** Medieval dispute over whether the pope or the king of a country should appoint abbots, bishops, and other churchmen to office. The high point in the conflict came when Emperor Henry IV defied Pope GREGORY VII (Hildebrand), was excommunicated, and finally knelt before the pope at Canossa to receive pardon and restoration, in 1077. The controversy was settled after a fashion in 1122 at the Concordat of Worms in a sort of stalemate. Investiture with staff and ring was returned to the pope but election of bishops and abbots in Germany must take place in the emperor's presence —only according to the law of the church. The conflict took a somewhat different form in other countries but ended in similar results.

**INVINCIBLE IGNORANCE** Ecclesiastical term for spiritual ignorance so massive that no moral effort can change it, thereby preventing the possessor from sinning.

**INVITATION** 1. Call to prayer or confession of sins in public worship. 2. Evangelistic summons to sinners to come to Christ, or to saints to receive further blessings.

**INVITATORY** Choral invitation to prayer in public worship. Psalm 95 is often used for this purpose.

**INVOCATION** 1. Prayer at the beginning of a meeting invoking the blessing of God. 2. Trinitarian formula beginning a worship service. 3. Request for the prayers of the saints. 4. Calling upon the presence of the HOLY SPIRIT at the consecration of the elements in the EUCHARIST.

**IO** Supreme Polynesian god.

**IONA** Island off the coast of western Scotland where COLUMBA established a monastery in the sixth century and Reginald founded a BENEDICTINE nunnery in the thirteenth century. The island's ecclesiastical life finally became PRESBYTERIAN. It is rich in ruins of ecclesiastical significance, and is now the center of the IONA COMMUNITY.

**IONA COMMUNITY** Religious brotherhood founded by Rev. George Macleod in 1938 on the island of Iona, Scotland. Its members are Scottish PRESBYTERIANS who live together in disciplines involving spiritual, political, and manual efforts. During the summer they rebuild the ancient BENEDICTINE abbey and during the winter they apply their faith to Scottish problems.

**IOTA** Ninth and smallest letter in the Greek alphabet, translated "jot" in the King James Bible.

**IOTA CHI (IX)** Greek letters symbolizing Jesus Christ, *IHSOUS XPISTOS.*

**IPSISSIMA VERBA** *the very words* Theological term for the presence of the very words of God in the Bible.

**IQBAL, MOHAMMED (1873–1938)** MOSLEM leader and scholar of India. He sought understanding between nations and faiths and worked for greater unity between Moslems and HINDUS. April 21, the day of his death in 1938, is a Pakistani holiday.

**IRELAND, JOHN (1838–1918)** Liberal American CATHOLIC who opposed the liquor business and political corruption, and established many Roman Catholic communities in the northwestern United States. Both as a bishop and as archbishop, he fought the employment of foreign languages in parochial schools and believed local authorities should control such schools, at least in part.

**IRENAEUS, ST. (c.130–c.202)** Church Father and Bishop of Lyons in Gaul, noted for his systematization of Christian theology and two works, *Against Heresies* and *The Demonstration of the Apostolic Preaching.* He was probably a native of Smyrna in Asia Minor, a pupil of Polycarp, and a martyr. He maintained that the Father and the Son cooperated in both revelation and redemption, and expounded the "recapitulation" theory of the life of Christ. According to this Jesus' life recapitulated the career of Adam, reversing the curse he had brought mankind by His perfect obedience. Also, "Christ made the circuit of all the stages of human life, to redeem and sanctify all" (Philip Schaff). St. Irenaeus' feast day is July 3.

**IRENE** *peace* Greek goddess of peace and daughter of ZEUS.

**IRENE (752–803)** Orphan of Athens who married Leo IV, Byzantine emperor, becoming empress after his death. When her son sought the throne she had him blinded. Irene restored images to the Eastern churches and is a saint of the GREEK CHURCH.

**IRENICS** That branch of theology which seeks Christian unity by emphasizing items of agreement and minimizing differences.

**IRIS** Flower symbolizing the Virgin MARY in religious art.

**IRISH ARTICLES** The Calvinistic statement of faith, adopted in 1615 by the Irish Episcopal Church in the form of 104 articles, which became part of the basis for the WESTMINSTER CONFESSION.

**IRMIN** Deified hero of the Germanic Saxons of western Europe.

**IRMINSUL or ERMENSUL** 1. Center of the worship of IRMIN. 2. Tree or pillar, considered to support the world, honoring IRMIN.

**IRRA** Babylonian demon with evil powers.

**IRREGULARITY** Impediment to the exercise of holy orders in ANGLICANISM and CATHOLICISM. Impediments may be illegitimacy, heresy, murder, abortion, insanity, marriage to one bound by religious vows, and other situations; they may be crimes or defects.

**IRRELIGION** Lack of religion, or opposition to it.

**IRRESISTIBLE GRACE** Theological term for that power of the HOLY SPIRIT which is not satisfied until a sinner is converted.

**IRVING, EDWARD (1792–1834)** Scottish founder of the CATHOLIC APOSTOLIC CHURCH. A friend of Thomas CARLYLE, Henry DRUMMOND, and Samuel Taylor COLERIDGE, he assisted Thomas CHALMERS in St. John's Presbyterian Church in Glasgow and became minister of a church in London. There his interest in and sermons on prophetic events drew large crowds. Becoming involved in gifts of tongues and healing, he was excommunicated by the Presbytery of London for his views of the humanity of Christ. He became a leader and angel of the Catholic Apostolic Church.

**IRVINGITES** Term for members of the CATHOLIC APOSTOLIC CHURCH.

**ISAAC _he laughs_** Abraham's second and Sarah's only son. Almost slain in his youth by Abraham as a sacrifice to Jehovah, he married Rebekah at the age of forty and fathered the twins Jacob and Esau. Isaac is one of Israel's great patriarchs, though less distinguished than Abraham or Jacob.

**ISAIAH _the Lord is salvation_** Great Hebrew prophet of the eighth century B.C. A nobleman in the Kingdom of Judah, he proclaimed the greatness and glory of the Lord during the reigns of kings Uzziah, Jotham, Ahaz, and Hezekiah. His book is the longest prophetic book in the Old Testament and his prophecies of the MESSIAH are often quoted in the New Testament. Modern scholars tend to a view of composite authorship of the book. Two manuscripts of Isaiah found among the DEAD SEA SCROLLS provide a text substantially the same as that of the MASORETES. According to tradition Isaiah was sawn asunder in the reign of MANASSEH. Also written Esaias.

**ISAIAH, ASCENSION OF** Second-century-A.D. apocalyptic work of Jewish-Christian authorship. It tells how Isaiah was sawn in half and traveled through seven heavens, learning of Christ and the church.

**ISAIAH, BOOK OF** See ISAIAH.

**ISAIAH, MARTYRDOM OF** Jewish account, dating from the first century A.D., of Isaiah's martyrdom under Hezekiah. It was incorporated into the "ASCENSION OF ISAIAH."

**ISCARIOT _man of Kerioth_** Name designating Judas who betrayed Jesus. It may indicate that Judas came from Kerioth, a town of Idumea or Moab.

**ISE CITY** Principal center of SHINTO worship in Japan. It has three temples of Ise, one of which holds a sacred mirror believed to come from the hand of the sun goddess AMATERASU-OMIKAMI. Thousands of pilgrims come to Ise City twice a year for purification ceremonies.

**ISH-BOSHETH _man of shame_** Fourth and youngest son of SAUL, also called Esh-Baal (_man of Baal,_ I CHRONICLES 8:33). He sought to rule Israel after Saul's death but was slain by two of his men (II SAMUEL 2—4).

**ISHI _my man or my husband_** Designation by which Israel might call God (HOSEA 2:16). Several Bible characters also have this name.

**ISHMAEL _may God hear_** First son of Abraham, by his concubine Hagar from Egypt. Jealousy between Hagar and Abraham's wife Sarah led to the expulsion of Hagar and Ishmael. They were saved from death by an angel and Ishmael fathered twelve desert tribes. MOSLEMS consider Ishmael their ancestor and believe that he and Hagar are buried in MECCA. Five other Bible characters bear the name _Ishmael._

**ISHTAR** Chief Babylonian and Assyrian goddess, also known as ASTARTE, ASHERAH, Ashtoreth, Ashtaroth, Anunitum, Inanna, and by similar names. She was the ancient goddess of love and fertility and was known as "lady of justice" and "queen of heaven." She was identified with the planet Venus and was probably identical with the Egyptian HATHOR, the Greek APHRODITE, the Roman VENUS, etc. Prostitution honored her at her temples at Nineveh, Akkad, and elsewhere.

**ISHVARA or ISVARA** *he who is supreme* 1. Absolute supreme being of HINDUISM. 2. Hindu term for the higher inner nature.

**ISIDORE OF SEVILLE (c.560–636)** Spanish scholar and ecclesiastic who became Archbishop of Seville. His *Encyclopedia of the Sciences* condensed much information and was influential in the Middle Ages. He was noted for his piety and charity, and sought the conversion of the Jews and the spread of his faith.

**ISIS** Mother-goddess worshiped in Egypt and other lands. The wife of OSIRIS and mother of HORUS, she was often represented with the head or horns of a cow. APULEIUS described Isis as "supreme of goddesses, ruler of the gods." J. G. FRAZER compared her worship with the later veneration of MARY in CATHOLICISM.

**ISLA, JOSE FRANCISCO DE (1703–1781)** Spanish JESUIT preacher and satirist. His works caricatured Spanish religion.

**ISLAM** *submission* [*to God*] One of the world's great monotheistic systems, the world's second largest religion with MOHAMMED as its prophet. Its adherents are called Moslems or Mohammedans, and are characterized by their submission to the will of God as they understand this. Founded in the seventh century in Arabia, it had converts from Spain to India within the middle of the eighth century. No other faith has been so successful in Africa or in Arabic-speaking lands. Islam's sacred book is the KORAN; its temples, mosques; its requirements, faith in ALLAH and in Mohammed as his prophet, prayer five times a day, adherence to the requirements of Islam, and good works. Moslems must practice prayer and fasting, give alms, and make a pilgrimage to MECCA at least once in a lifetime.

**ISLANDS OF THE BLESSED** According to ancient Greek religion, islands in the Atlantic where the blessed enjoyed life after death.

**ISM** Caustic term for a religion or cult. Each person tends to think that his own religion is normal whereas other systems of thought or worship are "isms."

**ISMAIL (?–765)** Moslem SHIITE who is regarded as the IMAM of the ISMAILI Shiites.

**ISMAIL HADJI MAULVI-MOHAMMED (1781–1831)** Moslem reformer of India who sought to purify ISLAM and establish a theocracy. He still has followers in parts of India.

**ISMAILIS or ISMAILITES** Moslem sect established by Abdallah ibn Maymun in the ninth century. He persuaded a group of SHIITES that the final IMAM (representative of God) had been eighth-century ISMAIL, and they and their successors became Ismailis. These also hold to a NEOPLATONIC or GNOSTIC view of the origin of the universe and of history, dividing the latter into seven religious epochs. There are Ismailis in India, Persia, Arabia, Egypt, and Tanzania.

**ISRAEL** 1. A name of Jacob (GENESIS 32:28; 35:10). 2. The Hebrew people. 3. The Northern Kingdom following the division of the kingdom; the Southern Kingdom was known as Judah. 4. Modern Jewish republic in Palestine. 5. Figurative name for the church, or the people of God.

**ISRAEL, MANASSEH BEN (1604–1657)** Jewish leader who sought the admission of Jews to England and other countries because he felt that they must be scattered among the nations before they could be regathered in Palestine. He founded a colony of his people in England. He was born in Portugal.

**ISRAEL BEN ELIEZER** See BAAL-SHEM-TOV.

**ISRAELI, ISAAC BEN SALOMON (c.845–c.940)** Egyptian-born Jewish thinker and physician whose knowledge of physiology provided him with sharp psychological insights.

**ISRAELITE** A member of the Old Testament people of Israel.

**ISRAELS, JOZEF (1824–1911)** Dutch Jewish painter whose work included many religious themes.

**ISRAFIL or URIEL** MOSLEM archangel and messenger of God who is to blow the trumpet at the final judgment.

**ISSACHAR** *hired worker* Ninth of Jacob's twelve sons, progenitor of the tribe of Issachar.

**ISSERLEIN, ISRAEL (1390–1460)** German Jewish authority on the TALMUD.

**ISSERLES, MOSES BEN ISRAEL (c.1520–1572)** Jewish rabbi and philosopher of Poland, noted for his commentary on the Jewish code. He was also known as Rema.

**ISTAR** See ISHTAR.

**ISVARA** See ISHVARA.

**ITALA or ITALIA VETUS** Old Latin text of the Bible preceding the VULGATE.

**ITE MISSA EST go, thou art dismissed** Words of dismissal at the end of the mass.

**I–THOU RELATIONSHIP** Martin Buber's term for the interpersonal relationship necessary for humans to communicate and relate on a fully human level. This relationship must not be degraded into one of "I–it."

**ITHURIEL** Name of an angel in MILTON's *Paradise Lost.*

**ITINERARIUM** Blessing or prayer used by clerics before beginning a journey.

**ITSUKU-SHIMA** Sacred Japanese island noted for a charming SHINTO temple, and a BUDDHIST temple dating from the ninth century.

**ITZAMNA** Beneficent Mayan moon god. A supreme deity, he was held to have created gods and men and to be lord of the heavens. He was represented as an old man with no teeth.

**ITZANAGI and ITZANAMI** Japanese heaven-father and earth-mother whose union produced all things including the gods.

**ITZLACOLIUHQUI** Aztec god of the obsidian knife.

**ITZLI** Aztec god of the stone knife.

**ITZPAPALOTL** Aztec fertility goddess.

**IUS DIVINUM divine right** Scholastic term for divinely ordained order in society and nature.

**IUS DIVINUM POSITIVIUM** That part of the divine order supernaturally revealed to man.

**IUS NATURALE natural right** That part of the divine order of the universe known to man through reason.

**IUSTITIA NATURALIS natural righteousness** Theological term for the just condition of man before Adam's fall.

**IUSTITIA ORIGINALIS original righteousness** Theological term for man's originally righteous condition, before the fall. CATHOLICISM holds that this original righteousness was the result of a special supernatural gift from God.

**IVES, ST.** See YVES.

**IVO OF CHARTRES, ST. (c.1040–c.1116)** French bishop imprisoned for speaking up against King Philip I's plan to leave his wife and marry another woman. A student of canon law, he wrote a commentary on the Psalms. His feast day is May 20 or 23.

**IVORY** Symbol of perfection and of Christ in religious art.

**IVRIT** Jewish term for the Hebrew language.

**IVY** Symbol of eternal life in religious art.

**IX** Mayan god of the west.

**IXAZALVOH** Mayan goddess of weaving.

**IXCUINA** Aztec mother-goddess.

**IXTLILTON** Aztec god of health.

**IYAR** Eighth month in the Jewish year.

**IZANAGI and IZANAMI** See ITZANAGI AND ITZANAMI.

# J

**J** Symbol for the "Jehovistic" or "Yahwistic" sources believed by many Biblical critics to have been embodied in various parts of the OLD TESTAMENT. These portions are identified by their use of the word JEHOVAH or YAHWEH, their unadorned narrative style, and their ideas (which are considered primitive and simple). Some critics subdivide "J" into "J1," "J2," etc.

**JA'ALIN** Very religious MOSLEM Arabs of the African Sudan.

**JABAL** Lamech's son, father of eastern nomads (GENESIS 4:20).

**JABBOK** River flowing from the east into the Jordan north of Jericho. There Jacob wrestled with an angel. The Jabbok has cut a canyon through the hills of the Trans-Jordan.

**JABESH-GILEAD** City east of the Jordan, south of Pella and Beth-Shan, destroyed by the Israelites when its citizens failed to come to the assembly at Mizpah (JUDGES 21). Later the men of Jabesh-Gilead were commended by David for their bravery (I SAMUEL 31:12; II SAMUEL 2:5–7).

**JABIN** Two Canaanite kings with this name were defeated respectively by Joshua and Deborah (JOSHUA 11:1; JUDGES 4; 5).

**JABLONSKI, DANIEL ERNST (1660–1741)** German Moravian theologian who sought to unite the PROTESTANTS of Germany, Switzerland, and Great Britain. He became a bishop of the MORAVIAN CHURCH and president of the Berlin Academy of Sciences, which he helped found.

**JABNEEL** *God causes to build* Village of northwestern Judea, called Jamnia in the APOCRYPHA and Yabneh or Yibna in modern Israel, which was long a center of Jewish life and learning. There the Great SANHEDRIN met after the destruction of Jerusalem. Jabneel was a bishopric in the fourth century, was held by the CRUSADERS in the Middle Ages, and now contains a school for rabbis.

**JABOTINSKY, VLADIMIR (1881–1940)** Russian Jewish leader and ZIONIST. A skilled writer and leader, he formed the Zionist Revisionist movement and sought the formation of a large Jewish state in Palestine.

**JACHIN and BOAZ** Two hollow copper pillars at the entrance to the Jewish temple near which it was the king's custom to stand (I KINGS 7:21; II KINGS 11:14). Some think they represented the pillars of cloud and of fire that guided the Israelites through the wilderness; others, that they represented sacred trees, or even the poles around which the Canaanites held fertility rites.

**JACKS, LAWRENCE PEARSALL (1860–1955)** English UNITARIAN minister who taught philosophy and edited the *Hibbert Journal* for 45 years.

**JACKSON, SAMUEL MACAULEY (1851–1912)** American PRESBYTERIAN minister and religious editor. He edited several dictionaries and encyclopedias, and was active in the American Society of Church History.

**JACKSON, SHELDON (1834–1909)** PRESBYTERIAN missionary in the western United States and Alaska. He organized schools throughout Alaska, introduced the first reindeer into that country, and carried on numerous missionary activities.

**JACOB** *supplanter or he clutches* Son of Isaac and grandson of Abraham. He connived with his mother to get the blessing his father intended for his brother Esau and later got the best of his crafty uncle Laban. At Bethel he saw a ladder or stairway reaching into heaven and by the River Jabbok wrestled with an angel. Later he traveled with his sons into Egypt where he died and was embalmed, although he was buried later in the cave of Machpelah in Palestine. Jacob's sons became the heads of the twelve tribes of Israel; another name of Jacob is Israel (GENESIS 25; 27—37; 45–50).

**JACOB, MAX (1876–1944)** French artist and writer whose conversion from the Jewish to the CATHOLIC faith is indicated in his often symbolic paintings, plays, poetry, and novels. He died in a NAZI concentration camp.

**JACOB BEN ASHER (1269–1343)** Spanish codifier of Jewish law.

**JACOB BEN JACOB MOSES OF LISSA (c.1762–1832)** Galician Jewish commentator and Talmudist.

**JACOBI, FRIEDRICH HEINRICH (1743–1819)** German philosopher who held that for consistency philosophy must rest on faith and that the things of the spirit can be known only by immediate experience. We find God as we find ourselves in Him.

**JACOBINS** DOMINICANS, so named because their first house in northern France was the Convent of St. James in the rue St. Jacques. A revolutionary group which met in the same place during the French Revolution also took the name Jacobins.

**JACOBITES** Members of the Syrian Orthodox Church of Syria, Iraq, and India. It is historically MONOPHYSITE, believing that Christ has only one nature; hence other orthodox groups consider the Jacobites heretical. Apparently established in the sixth century in Syria by Jacob Baradeus, the Jacobites claim the Apostle James as their original founder. They are divided into a number of groups some of whom have PROTESTANT tendencies and some of whom are in communion with the pope. The Jacobites' head is the patriarch of Antioch and they follow an Antiochene rite. To express the single nature of Christ they make the sign of the cross with one finger.

**JACOBS, JOSEPH (1854–1916)** Australian-born Jewish historian and scholar who lived in England and the United States.

**JACOB'S LADDER** See JACOB.

**JACOB'S WELL** Well in Samaria near Sychar (modern Nablus), 85 feet deep and a source of excellent water.

**JACOBUS DA VARAGINE (c.1230–1298)** Archbishop of Genoa, noted for his *Golden Legend* relating the lives of many saints, and himself considered a saint in Genoa. He was a DOMINICAN and a popular preacher, and was beatified in 1816.

**JACOPONE DA TODI (c.1230–1306)** Italian mystic and poet. Originally named Jacopo Benedetti, he became a FRANCISCAN and wrote many poems. One became the hymn "Stabat Mater Dolorosa"; one or more satirized Pope BONIFACE VIII, resulting in Jacopone's imprisonment for five years. He is honored at Todi with a feast day on December 25.

**JACY** Moon-god of the Tupi-Guarani Indians of Brazil.

**JADE EMPEROR** A chief god, one of the three Precious Ones in TAOISM.

**JAEL** *wild goat* Hebrew woman who killed the Canaanite general Sisera after inviting him into her tent (JUDGES 4; 5:6, 24–27).

**JAFFA** Modern name for the city of JOPPA.

**JAGANNATH or JUGGERNAUT** *lord of the world* Form in which Hindus worship VISHNU, one of their supreme gods, in Puri, Bengal, and other parts of India. At an annual festival the great 45-foot-high statue of the god, together with the statues of his brother and sister, is dragged by hundreds of pilgrims on a cart with 16 enormous wheels to a summer home. Exaggerated stories of worshipers killing themselves beneath the cart's wheels have given rise to the idea of a relentless "juggernaut."

**JAH** Abbreviation of YAHWEH or JEHOVAH, Hebrew name of the Lord.

**JAHRZEIT** Jewish term for a day honoring the memory of one deceased.

**JAHVIST or JEHOVIST** Name for author of portions of the Bible which emphasize the name YAHWEH or JEHOVAH. See "J."

**JAHWEH** See JEHOVAH or YAHWEH.

**JAIN or JAINA** Adherent of JAINISM.

**JAINISM** *religion of Jina, "The Conqueror"* Espoused by two million people of India. Although the Jains believe their faith antedates human history, it is usually traced to the sixth century B.C. Two great branches are the Svetambaras, whose monks are clothed in white, and the Digambaras, whose monks go naked as specified by the Jina Vardhamana. The first

Jina is said to have been a giant who lived 8,400,000 years; the twenty-fourth and last was Vardhamana, who was also called MAHAVIRA, "The Great Hero." The Jains believe that the universe is eternal; they practice love, moderation, and fellow-feeling, refrain from taking any life—even vegetable life—and read their scriptures daily. The latter are the teachings of Mahavira. Jainism has always been close to HINDUISM, probably beginning as a protest against it and gradually adopting many of its gods and practices.

**JAIRUS** Leader of a synagogue in Galilee whose daughter was restored to life by Jesus (MARK 5:22–43).

**JAMES** 1. The older brother of John and one of Jesus' Apostles. James and John were sons of Zebedee and were also called "Sons of Thunder" (Boanerges). A cousin of Jesus, James was slain by Herod Agrippa I. His feast day is July 25. (MATTHEW 4:21, 22; 10:2; 17:1; 20:20–29; ACTS 12:1, 2). 2. Another of the Apostles sometimes called "James the Less" or "the Younger" (MARK 15:40). A son of Alphaeus, this James is identified with the James who was the brother of Jesus. The Epistle of James has been attributed to him. His feast day is May 1. (MATTHEW 10:3; ACTS 1:13). 3. James the brother of Jesus opposed Him during His ministry (LUKE 8:19–21) but after the Resurrection was converted (I CORINTHIANS 15:7). He became leader of the Jerusalem church and was finally executed by the SANHEDRIN. The Epistle of James is commonly attributed to this James. (ACTS 15:13–34; 21:18, 19; GALATIANS 1:18, 19).

**JAMES I (1566–1625)** King of England who presided at the Hampton Court Conference (1604) to settle the differences between ANGLICANS and PURITANS. At this conference he saw the dangers in Puritanism: "No bishop, no king"; he also authorized a new translation of the Scriptures. This became the "King James" or "Authorized" Bible of 1611. (See KING JAMES VERSION.) Seeking to conciliate Anglicans, Puritans, and CATHOLICS, James succeeded in arousing suspicions and animosities through his reliance on his own ability and on the favorites he chose.

**JAMES, HENRY (1811–1882)** SWEDENBORGIAN theologian of the United States, fa-

ther of the novelist Henry James and the psychologist William James.

**JAMES, WILLIAM (1842–1910)** American psychologist and philosopher. A pragmatist and student of the psychology of religion, he is noted for the books *The Varieties of Religious Experience, The Will to Believe, The Meaning of Truth,* and *Human Immortality.* He has been termed anti-intellectual and his writings suggestive rather than systematic or final.

**JAMES, THE EPISTLE OF** This book of the New Testament has traditionally been attributed to James the Less or James the Lord's brother. Called by some "the most untheological book in the New Testament" and by LUTHER "a right strawy epistle," it emphasizes practical duties rather than doctrinal principles. It is addressed to "the twelve tribes which are scattered abroad" (1:1).

**JAMI (1414–1492)** Persian saint, poet, and SUFI philosopher.

**JAMNIA** See JABNEEL.

**JAMNIA, SYNOD OF** Rabbinical gathering at Jamnia or Jabneh in Palestine about 100 A.D. at which, according to the MISHNAH's intimations, the canon of the Jewish Scriptures was decided.

**JANE FRANCES DE CHANTAL, ST. (1572–1641)** Friend of St. FRANCIS OF SALES who with his help founded the Congregation of the VISITATION, an order of nuns, in 1610. Her feast day is August 21.

**JANSEN, CORNELIUS OTTO (1585–1638)** ROMAN CATHOLIC originator of JANSENISM. Born at Accoy in the Netherlands, he became Bishop of Ypres in Belgium which was ruled by Spain. On a visit to Spain he nearly became a victim of the Spanish INQUISITION. His antipathy to the SOCIETY OF JESUS was expressed in his posthumous *Augustinus,* representing his lifelong study of St. AUGUSTINE. In it he contended for the doctrines of predestination and irresistible grace.

**JANSENISM** Movement growing out of *Augustinus* by Cornelius Otto JANSEN. Five of the doctrines there outlined were condemned by Pope INNOCENT X in 1653. Contributors to Jansenist thought were Antoine ARNAULD and Blaise PASCAL. The movement took firm root in France where it allied itself with GALLICANISM, with a center in a convent at Port-Royal. The convent was closed and French Jansenism was silenced. But in the Netherlands Jansenism became independent of ROMAN CATHOLICISM; it has bishops in three Dutch cities today.

**JANSON, ERIC** See BISHOP HILL.

**JANSSENS, JEAN BAPTISTE (1889–1964)** Belgian Jesuit and professor of canon law. From 1946 until his death he was president general of the SOCIETY OF JESUS.

**JANUS** Roman god of doorways and beginnings. He had two faces and his temple in Rome faced both east and west. January is named for him.

**JAPHETH** *beauty* **(?)** Son of NOAH believed to have fathered the peoples of Europe and the Gentile world (GENESIS 5:32; 6:10; 10:1–5).

**JASHAR, BOOK OF** Jewish collection of verse quoted in Joshua 10:13; II Samuel 1:18–27; I Kings 8:12, 13 and possibly elsewhere in the Old Testament. The complete work has not been found.

**JASMINE** In religious art, a symbol of MARY the mother of Jesus.

**JASTROW, MARCUS (1829–1903)** American rabbi and authority on the TALMUD.

**JASTROW, MORRIS (1861–1921)** American ZIONIST and authority on Near Eastern religion and culture.

**JATAKAS** Narratives of the deeds and words of the BUDDHA in his 547 incarnations. Many are fables; some are identical with Aesop's fables. The Pali canon contains 36 jatakas.

**JAVAN** *Greece* Son of JAPHETH, ancestor of the Greeks (GENESIS 10:2, 4).

**JE** Symbol for Jehovistic-Elohistic sources in the Old Testament. See "J" and "E."

**JEBEL MUSA** *mountain of Moses* Moslem or Arabic name for Mt. Sinai, where Moses received the Ten Commandments and the law.

**JEBUS or JEBUSI** Name of Jerusalem before the time of the Hebrews.

**JEBUSITES** Canaanites who dwelt in Palestine before and during the Jewish occupation (GENESIS 10:16; 15:21; NUMBERS 13:29; JOSHUA 3:10; 9:1; 11:3; 12:8; 15:8). Apparently they were finally vanquished completely (NEHEMIAH 9:8).

**JECONIAH** See JEHOIACHIN.

**JEDIDIAH** *loved by the Lord* An early name of SOLOMON (II SAMUEL 12:24, 25).

**JEFFERS, ROBINSON (1887–1962)** Pantheistic American poet some of whose concepts derived from Greek religion of classical times. He was pessimistic about man.

**JEFFERSON, THOMAS (1743–1826)** Founding father and President of the United States who secured passage of a bill for religious freedom in 1786. A DEIST, he prepared a Bible consisting of the teachings of Jesus. He detested creeds and held that religion is best evidenced by one's daily life. But he once wrote, "I am a Christian. . . ."

**JEFFREYS, GEORGE (c.1648–1689)** Cruel English judge who sentenced Titus OATES to flogging and imprisonment for his perjury against ROMAN CATHOLICS. He was merciless toward the Puritan Richard BAXTER and many others.

**JEHOIACHIN, JECHONIAS, or JECONIAH** King of Judah carried into captivity by Nebuchadnezzar in 597 or 598 B.C. He was treated better than other captives in Babylon, and was finally freed (II KINGS 24:6—25:7).

**JEHOIADA** *the Lord knows* Jewish priest who with his wife Jehoshabeath saved the infant king Jehoash from the repeated attempts of Queen Athaliah to kill him. Jehoiada was the father of Zechariah, who was stoned to death by Joash (II KINGS 11; 12). Four other Old Testament characters are also called Jehoiada.

**JEHOIAKIM** *the Lord raises up* Last king of Judah to reign in Jerusalem. Refusing to listen to the warnings of the prophet Jeremiah, he died or was killed and was given a shameful burial shortly before Nebuchadnezzar entered the capital. He was the father of JEHOIACHIN (II KINGS 23:34; 24:6—25:30).

**JEHOSHAPHAT** *the Lord judges* King of Judah who succeeded his father, Asa. He formed an alliance with King Ahab of Israel against Ramoth-gilead and aided King Jehoram against the Moabites. He also destroyed some of the heathen worship in his land (I KINGS 22:1–51; II KINGS 3:1–14).

**JEHOVAH** One transliteration of the Jewish name for God, JHVH or IHWH, also transliterated Yahweh or Iahweh. Often translated "the Lord," Jehovah was a name so sacred to the Hebrews that it was not to be pronounced; the name Adonai was usually substituted. The meaning is suggested in Exodus 3:14, 15 and 6:2, 3, connoting pure, transcendent Being.

**JEHOVAH-JIREH** *the Lord sees* The place in the desert where Isaac was saved from the fate of human sacrifice (GENESIS 22:14).

**JEHOVAH-NISSI** *the Lord is my banner* Moses' name for the altar he erected after triumphing over the Amalekites (EXODUS 17:15).

**JEHOVAH-SHALOM** *the Lord is peace* Gideon's name for an altar at Ophrah (JUDGES 6:24).

**JEHOVAH'S WITNESSES** American religious group organized by Pastor Charles Taze RUSSELL in 1872. Its next leader was Judge Joseph Franklin RUTHERFORD. The group emphasizes the imminent destruction of worldly powers at Armageddon and the return of Christ to set up a millennial reign during which men will have a second opportunity to be saved. Members witness from door to door and have often been persecuted for refusing to fight or to salute national flags or symbols. They were formerly known as International Bible Students, and today are often called Russellites.

**JEHOVAH-TSIDKENU** *the Lord is our righteousness* Jeremiah's name for the good king he foresaw ruling Israel in the future (JEREMIAH 33:16).

**JEHOVIST** See JAHVIST.

**JEHU** *the Lord is He* 1. A supporter of King David (I CHRONICLES 12:3). 2. A prophet during the reigns of King Baasha and of JEHOSHAPHAT (I KINGS 16:1, 7; II CHRONICLES 19; 20:34). 3. A rapid chariot driver anointed by Elijah to vanquish the dynasty of Ahab. He killed the kings Jehoram and Ahaziah and Queen Jezebel (II KINGS 9; 10). 4. A Simeonite (I CHRONICLES 4:35). 5. A son of Obed in the line of Judah (I CHRONICLES 2:38).

**JENKS, BENJAMIN (1646–1724)** ANGLICAN rector in Shropshire and author of several devotional works.

**JEPHTHAE** See JEPHTHAH.

**JEPHTHAH** *he opens* Israelite judge (military leader) who celebrated a victory by giving his only daughter as a burnt offering. He finally subjugated his own countrymen, the Ephraimites (JUDGES 11; 12).

**JEREMIAH** *he whom the Lord exalts* "Weeping Prophet" of Judah a century after the time of Isaiah. He lived through the destruction of Jerusalem and the BABYLONIAN CAPTIVITY in the sixth century B.C. His prophecies, written down and arranged by his secretary Baruch, form one of the longer books of Old Testament prophecy. They are filled with dramatic symbols and include oracles against various nations.

**JEREMIAH II (1536–1595)** GREEK ORTHODOX leader who organized the RUSSIAN ORTHODOX CHURCH. He was a fine scholar and had sympathies with the humanist revolution of his age.

**JEREMIAS, JEREMIE, or JEREMY** See JEREMIAH.

**JEREMY, EPISTLE OF** Short apocryphal book attributed to the prophet JEREMIAH but probably dating from the first or second century B.C. It is in the form of a letter denouncing idolatry.

**JERICHO** *fragrant place or moon city* One of Palestine's most ancient cities, six miles northwest of the Dead Sea. Joshua conquered it for Israel, and more than a thousand years later Jesus mentioned it in the parable of the Good Samaritan (JOSHUA 6; LUKE 10:30–36).

**JEROBOAM I** First king of Israel after Solomon's kingdom was divided into northern and southern entities. After overthrowing Solomon's son Rehoboam, Jeroboam encouraged various Canaanite religions and was long known as the king who "made Israel to sin" (I KINGS 11:26—14:20).

**JEROBOAM II** Son of Joash or Jehoash and thirteenth ruler of the Northern Kingdom of Israel. The country prospered during his reign but its social and moral weaknesses were rebuked by the prophets Hosea, Amos, and Jonah the son of Amittai (II KINGS 14:16, 23–29).

**JEROME, ST. (c.347–c.420)** Church Father. Born in Dalmatia, he studied in Rome, and at Antioch had a dream or vision in which Christ told him, "You are not a Christian." He renounced his classical studies, learned Hebrew, and began to proclaim an ascetic form of Christianity. The last half of his life he spent in a monastery at Bethlehem where he wrote Biblical commentaries and made a translation of a number of Scriptures which became the basis of the VULGATE. He corresponded with AUGUSTINE and denounced ARIANISM, ORIGENISM, and PELAGIANISM. Christian art often represents Jerome with a red hat and/or with a lion. His feast day is September 30.

**JEROME OF PRAGUE (c.1370–1416)** Bohemian friend of John HUSS and advocate of the new nationalism and religious reform of his time. He accepted the teachings of John WYCLIF, attacked a bull of antipope John XXIII, and following the martyrdom of Huss was himself burned at the stake singing hymns to Mary.

**JERUBBAAL** *contender against Baal* Another name of GIDEON.

**JERUSALEM** *city of peace* (?) Palestine's holy city, sacred to Christians, Jews, and Moslems. Six thousand years old, it was ruled by Melchizedek in the time of Abraham (GENESIS 14:18), chosen for a capital by King David (II CHRONICLES 3:1), made the site of the temple by Solomon, and visited often by Jesus. Its Dome of the Rock and mosques are sacred to Moslems, and innumerable areas are loved and venerated by Christians and Jews.

**JERUSALEM, COUNCIL OF** Momentous meeting of representatives of the first churches at which it was decided that Gentiles need not keep the Jewish law or be circumcised (ACTS 15).

**JERUSALEM, SYNOD OF** Council of the EASTERN ORTHODOX CHURCH in 1672 at Bethlehem. It declared the infallibility of the church and renounced a number of Calvinistic doctrines, upholding seven SACRAMENTS, TRANSUBSTANTIATION, PURGATORY, and the APOCRYPHA. This declaration is known as the "Shield of Orthodoxy."

**JERUSALEM CROSS** Square cross with four smaller crosses in its four quarters. It is known as the Crusaders' Cross because Godfrey of Bouillon wore it after freeing Jerusalem from MOHAMMEDAN control.

**JESHURUN** *the upright one* Symbolic, tender name for Israel (DEUTERONOMY 32:15).

**JESSE** Father of King DAVID. A grandson of RUTH and BOAZ, Jesse was a prosperous herdsman and farmer. Christian art often shows Jesse as the root of the family tree of JESUS and of MARY.

**JESSE WINDOW** Medieval window, in several cathedrals, showing the genealogy of JESUS or MARY in the form of a tree beginning with JESSE.

**JESU** See JESUS.

**JESUITS** Members of the SOCIETY OF JESUS.

**JESUS** Greek form of the Hebrew name *Joshua* ("The Lord Saves") (cf. HEBREWS 4:8). It was the name divinely given the SAVIOUR and MESSIAH popularly known as Jesus Christ (LUKE 1:31). Born in Bethlehem, perhaps 6 B.C., Jesus at about the age of thirty was baptized by JOHN THE BAPTIST and soon thereafter began to teach and heal throughout Galilee, Samaria, Perea, and Judea. The first four books of the NEW TESTAMENT record His sayings, parables, conversations, good works, and miracles. After about three years He was accused of blasphemy, condemned by the SANHEDRIN, brought before Pontius PILATE, and crucified by Roman soldiers. Three days later He was seen alive by many of the disciples and after forty days He ascended into heaven, leaving behind the church. The New Testament presents Jesus as Messiah or Christ, Son of God, Saviour of the world, Mediator between God and man, Word of God, and King of kings and Lord of lords. The Christian creeds speak of Him as God of God, Light of Light, Life of Life, very God of very God, begotten, not made; yet One who became man and was born, died, and rose again for mankind.

**JESUS, SOCIETY OF** See SOCIETY OF JESUS.

**JESUS SON OF SIRACH** Popular name of the author of the book of ECCLESIASTICUS. Little is known about this author except that he probably wrote Ecclesiasticus about 180 B.C., his name in the Hebrew text is Simeon the son of Jesus the son of Eleazar the son of Sirach, and his grandson translated Ecclesiasticus into Greek about 132 B.C.

**JETHRO** *excellence* Shepherd of the Sinai desert whose sheep MOSES tended for forty years, before he led the Israelites out of Egypt. The Bible also calls Jethro Raguel, Reuel, and Hobab.

**JEUNESSE OUVRIERE CHRETIENNE** Euro-

pean organization of young factory workers, farmers, and sailors who wish to apply CATHOLICISM to daily work and life.
It was inspired in the 1920's by the encyclical *Rerum Novarum* of LEO XIII.

**JEW BISHOP** Medieval term for the leader
of a Jewish community.

**JEWESS** Female Jew. See JEWS.

**JEWISH CHRISTIANITY** Christianity as it
began in Palestine, centering in the church
at Jerusalem. Before the end of the second
century A.D., it was supplanted by GEN-
TILE Christianity.

**JEWISH SCIENCE** Religious group organized by Rabbi Morris Lichtenstein in the
United States in 1922 to offset the impact
of CHRISTIAN SCIENCE on JUDAISM.

**JEWS** Hebrews or ISRAELITES. The name
Jew derives from Judah, the Israelite tribe
whose name was transferred to the South-
ern Kingdom. Genetically Jews are of
Semitic origin, descending from Abraham.
Religiously they accept the revelation em-
bodied in the OLD TESTAMENT Scriptures;
JUDAISM is the great historic source of
MONOTHEISM and high ethical religion.

**JEZEBEL** Priestess of BAAL and ASTARTE
who became wife of King Ahab of Israel
at the time of the prophet Elijah. Notorious for her attachment to paganism and
her persecution of the Jewish prophets, she
met a shameful end (I KINGS 18; 21; II
KINGS 9).

**JEZREEL** *God sows* 1. The plain of Esdraelon which is the site of the valley of Armageddon. 2. A city near Megiddo in
the vale of Jezreel. 3. A town in Judah
where David met Ahinoam. 4. The name
of Hosea's first son.

**JEZREELITES** Abortive English religious
sect founded about 1875 by James White
or James Jezreel. He married a "Queen
Esther" and began the construction of a
temple near Chatham; this was to be the
center of Christ's millennial reign. White's
name for the group was the New and
Latter House of Israel.

**JHANA** Mystic contemplative state attained through BUDDHIST meditation.

**JHS** See IHS.

**JHVH or JHWH** See JEHOVAH.

**JIHAD** *striving* Duty of MOSLEMS to fight
non-Moslems in a holy war (KORAN 2:214,
215; 8:39–42). Today most Moslems in-

terpret this warfare spiritually, while some
look forward to a holy war with the coming of the Hidden IMAM.

**JIMENEZ DE CISNEROS, FRANCISCO (1436–
1517)** Spanish cardinal and Archbishop
of Toledo who sought to evangelize the
Moors, established clerical reforms, and
served the Spanish INQUISITION as Grand
Inquisitor of Castile. He founded the
University of Alcala and gave the church
the COMPLUTENSIAN POLYGLOT BIBLE.

**JINA** *conqueror or visitor* 1. In the Sanskrit, the BUDDHA. 2. In JAINISM, a saint.

**JINARAJADASA (1875–1953)** Ceylonese
BUDDHIST and THEOSOPHIST leader.

**JINGO (second century)** Japanese empress
whose son Hachiman became god of war.
Jingo was deified.

**JINGU or JINJA** *god house* SHINTO shrine.

**JINN** Arabian spirits or demons. In ISLAM
they may be either righteous or evil, and
may appear as animals or human beings.

**JIZO** Japanese BUDDHIST god of children
and travelers.

**JNANA** *wisdom* Sanskrit term for wisdom
or spiritual knowledge, important in BUD-
DHISM.

**JNANA-MARGA** *way of knowledge* Sanskrit term for a method of release from
the cycle of REINCARNATION, taught in
BUDDHISM, HINDUISM, and JAINISM.

**JOAB** *the Lord is father* 1. Military leader
under King David. Crafty and cruel, Joab
served David faithfully but was cursed by
the dying king and executed by Solomon.
2. Jewish craftsman (I CHRONICLES 4:14).
3. Progenitor of a family listed as returning from the BABYLONIAN CAPTIVITY
(NEHEMIAH 7:11).

**JOACHIM, ST.** Traditional father of the
Virgin MARY. His feast day is August 16.

**JOACHIMITES** Followers of JOACHIM OF
FLORIS.

**JOACHIM OF FLORIS (c.1145–1202)** Italian
mystic who established the monastery of
San Giovanni del Fiore (Floris) and
taught that great tribulation and the reign
of the ANTICHRIST would begin in 1260.
He saw all history divided into three
epochs: the age of the Father (the Old
Testament period), the age of the Son
(the current Christian era), and the age of
the Spirit (to begin after the overthrow of
the Antichrist). He wrote several com-

mentaries and had considerable influence in the thirteenth and fourteenth centuries, but certain of his views were condemned in 1215 and 1256. Dante, however, placed Joachim in Paradise.

**JOAD, CYRIL EDWIN MITCHINSON (1891–1953)** English philosopher who left his early rationalism for Christian faith. His last book was *The Recovery of Belief.*

**JOAN, POPE** Woman said by many medieval church historians to have been pope about 855 or 1100. The story was that she disguised herself as a man, ruled as pope for about two years, and finally gave birth to a child. But the investigations of a French Protestant, David Blondel, have generally convinced scholars that the whole incident was a fabrication.

**JOAN OF ARC, ST. (c.1412–1431)** French girl who in response to heavenly voices and visions led her countrymen to victory against the British invaders. "The Maid of Orleans" claimed guidance directly from God, believed herself primarily responsible to Him, and said that when she died she believed she would enter Paradise. Sold by pro-British countrymen to the English, she was brought before the INQUISITION and accused of witchcraft, heresy, and "false and diabolical" visions. Recanting under threat of torture, she later reversed her recantation and was burned at the stake while calling on Jesus. The judgment was annulled in 1456 and in 1920 she was canonized. Her feast day is May 30.

**JOASH** *the Lord gave* 1. Eighth king of Judah, saved in infancy from the assassination attempt of Queen ATHALIAH. At seven he was acknowledged as king and began religious reforms. Later in life he had the good prophet ZECHARIAH stoned and was himself killed in Jerusalem. 2. The father of GIDEON and several other Bible characters have the name JOASH.

**JOB** Wealthy patriarch of Uz in the ancient East whose goodness was tested by the loss of his health, wealth, and children. After subjection to the false comfort of several friends he gained a deeper vision of God and regained much he had lost. His story is told in the book of Job— one of the wisdom books of the OLD TESTAMENT, written in superb dramatic-poetic form.

**JOB'S COMFORTER** One who, like the friends of JOB, in seeking to comfort brings more pain and condemnation than help.

**J.O.C.** Abbreviation for the JEUNESSE OUVRIERE CHRETIENNE.

**JOCHANAN BEN ZACCAI (first century A.D.)** Jewish leader who founded a rabbinical school at Jamnia or Jabneh and sustained Jewish hope after the destruction of Jerusalem.

**JOCHEBED** *the Lord is glory* Mother of Moses (EXODUS 6:20).

**JOCISTS** Term for members of the JEUNESSE OUVRIERE CHRETIENNE.

**JOD** See YODH.

**JODL, FRIEDRICH (1848–1914)** German philosopher who proposed a religion based on nationalism and faith in self-realization.

**JODO** "Pure Land" branch of Japanese BUDDHISM founded in China in the fourth century and transferred to Japan in the twelfth. Originally emphasizing both faith and good works, it now stresses the free grace of AMITA, "Buddha of Infinite Light," and security in Paradise simply by calling upon Him. Disciples of Jodo repeat Amita's name several times a day.

**JOEL** Prophet of Judah who foresaw the coming of judgment and the outpouring of the Spirit upon mankind. (The latter was referred to by Peter on the Day of Pentecost instituting the New Testament church in its apostolic form; cf. Acts 2:17–21). Joel apparently lived after the exile and the work of Nehemiah. His book is one of the twelve among the MINOR PROPHETS of the OLD TESTAMENT.

**JOGUES, ISAAC, ST. (1607–1646)** French missionary to America from the SOCIETY OF JESUS; martyred by Mohawk Indians. His feast day is September 26.

**JOHANAN BEN ZAKKAI** See JOCHANAN BEN ZACCAI.

**JOHANNINE EPISTLES** See JOHN, THE EPISTLES OF.

**JOHANNINE GOSPEL** See JOHN, THE GOSPEL OF.

**JOHANNINE PROBLEM** Term for critical study of the differences between the Gospel of John and the other three Gospels of the New Testament. While Matthew, Mark, and Luke present very similar accounts of the life and work of Christ, John gives many anecdotes and sayings quite different from these "SYNOPTICS." It was widely held for a time that John's Gospel must come from Asia Minor in the second century, but the discovery of the DEAD SEA SCROLLS has led some scholars to return it to the country and century of Jesus. "The Johannine problem" may also refer to the question of who wrote the Gospel of John, the Epistles of John, and the Revelation.

**JOHN, ST.** See JOHN THE BAPTIST, JOHN THE APOSTLE, etc.

**JOHN I, ST.** (?–526) Pope (523–526) who was imprisoned by Theodoric and died in prison. His feast day is May 27.

**JOHN VIII** (?–882) Strong pope (872–882) who fought ecclesiastical corruption, crowned emperors, and increased papal authority. He was finally murdered through a Lateran plot.

**JOHN XII (c.938–964)** Pope (955–964) whose life and reign were marked by intrigue and scandal. He was finally murdered.

**JOHN XXII (1244–1334)** Pope (1316–1334) whose excellent administrative ability was met with many controversies. His conception of the Beatific Vision as available only after the final judgment met with strong theological resistance.

**JOHN XXIII (1881–1963)** Italian peasant's son whose warm heart and open mind were universally acclaimed. During his short term as pope (1958–1963) he doubled the size of the College of Cardinals, met many leaders of other faiths, and convened the twenty-first ECUMENICAL COUNCIL (see VATICAN COUNCIL II).

**JOHN, THE APOCALYPSE OF** See REVELATION OF ST. JOHN THE DIVINE.

**JOHN, THE EPISTLES OF** Three short letters toward the end of the New Testament traditionally attributed to the Apostle John. They are often indicated as I John, II John, and III John. Emphasizing the love of God in Christ, they show a concern for false teachings and leaders in the churches.

**JOHN, THE GOSPEL OF** The fourth Gospel in the New Testament, carrying the story of Christ from "the beginning with God" to the resurrection and His forward look "till I come" (1:1; 21:22). This Gospel gives many long discourses of Jesus and a number of extended dialogues with individuals or groups. It has been termed

"the spiritual Gospel" and conveys a unique sense of eternity.

**JOHN BAPTIST DE LA SALLE, ST. (1651–1719)** French priest and educator who founded the Institute of the Brothers of Christian Schools, dedicated to Christian education. He was called patron saint of teachers by Pope PIUS XII. His feast day is May 15.

**JOHN BOSCO, ST. (1815–1888)** Italian priest who founded the Order of St. Francis of Sales and the Daughters of Mary Auxilatrix, for boys and girls. His feast day is January 31.

**JOHN CAPISTRAN, ST. (c.1386–1456)** FRANCISCAN friar and preacher of Italy who condemned the HUSSITES and raised an army which defeated the Turks in Hungary. His feast day is March 28.

**JOHN CHRYSOSTOM, ST. (c.347–407)** "Golden-mouthed" preacher whose homilies on various books of the Bible have earned him the title "greatest of Christian expositors." An outstanding Church Father, he became patriarch of Constantinople. For opposing corruption in court and church, refusing to condemn certain heretics without a hearing, and attacking injustice, he was falsely condemned and exiled. He substituted historical and literal interpretation for the popular allegorism that often prevailed in preaching. In 1909 he was named patron of preachers by Pope PIUS X. His feast day is January 27.

**JOHN CLIMAX (c.570–649)** Abbot of Sinai whose *Ladder of Paradise*, "Climax tou Paradeisou," was a popular guide to medieval ascetic discipline. His feast day is March 30.

**JOHN MARK** See MARK.

**JOHN OF ASIA** See JOHN OF EPHESUS.

**JOHN OF DAMASCUS, ST. (c.675–c.749)** Church Father, hymn writer, and saint of the GREEK CHURCH who fought iconoclasm. His feast day is March 27.

**JOHN OF EPHESUS (c.505–c.585)** Syrian theologian and Bishop of Ephesus. A MONOPHYSITE leader, he wrote an *Ecclesiastical History* valuable for its interpretation of sixth-century events.

**JOHN OF GOD, ST.** See BROTHERS HOSPITALERS.

**JOHN OF LEIDEN** ANABAPTIST leader of Holland who eventually made himself king of a new "Zion" in which both property and wives were communally held. He and his associates were tortured and killed.

**JOHN OF NEPOMUK, ST. (fourteenth century)** Patron saint of Bohemia. His feast day is May 16.

**JOHN OF THE CROSS, ST. (c. 1542–1591)** Spanish saint and mystic who founded the order of the Discalced Carmelites with his friend St. Theresa of Avila. Suspected, imprisoned, and tortured by the hierarchy, he escaped and wrote some of the finest treatises of mysticism: *The Ascent of Mount Carmel, The Dark Night of the Soul, The Living Flame of Love,* and *The Spiritual Canticle.*

**JOHNSON, JAMES WELDON (1871–1938)** American Negro poet of deep spiritual perception. His books include *God's Trombones.*

**JOHN THE APOSTLE** Also called "the Evangelist." One of Jesus' first and most trusted disciples. A Galilean fisherman and probably quite young, John was among the few present at the return of Jairus' daughter to life, at the transfiguration, at the cross, and at the empty tomb. He is widely believed to be the disciple "whom Jesus loved" in the Gospel of John. According to tradition he escaped death in a vat of boiling oil and lived longer than any other apostle.

**JOHN THE BAPTIST** Son of Mary's cousin Elisabeth and hence a close relative of Jesus. Raised in the desert, he called all Judea to repentance and baptism—and Jesus was among those he baptized. For rebuking Herod's divorce and remarriage he was imprisoned and eventually beheaded (LUKE 1; 3).

**JONA** See JONAH.

**JONAH dove** 1. Prophet of Israel in the time of Jeroboam II, in the eighth century B.C., who foretold the enlarging of the boundaries of his country (II KINGS 14:23–25). Divinely called to preach to Nineveh, he refused but after adventures at sea he complied. The book of Jonah, which recounts the Nineveh story, ends with an enunciation of the love of God for the pagan city of Nineveh with its helpless children and "much cattle." Many believe the book to be a parable of the divine love. 2. Peter's father (JOHN 1:42, "Jona").

**JONAS** See JONAH.

**JONAS, JUSTUS (1493–1555)** German Protestant leader and friend of Martin LUTHER. He aided Luther in the translation of the German Bible, and preached Luther's funeral sermon.

**JONATHAN the Lord gave** A son of King Saul and a devoted friend of David. The latter wrote a stirring eulogy at his death in battle (I SAMUEL 13; 14; 20; 31:1, 2). Fourteen other Old Testament characters also have the name JONATHAN.

**JONES, RUFUS MATTHEW (1863–1948)** American minister and leader of the Society of FRIENDS. A humanitarian and student of mysticism, he wrote many books. His interest was in "man's inner life and the spiritual ground and foundation of the universe."

**JOPPA beauty** Mediterranean port of Palestine and Jerusalem. There Jonah embarked for Tarshish (JONAH 1:3) and Peter raised the dead Dorcas (ACTS 9). In Joshua 19:46 it is called Japho. Today it is Israel's city of Jaffa.

**JORDAN descender** 1. Winding river of Palestine, descending from the mountains of Syria through the Sea of Galilee to the Dead Sea. The Jews crossed it to enter Canaan, John the Baptist preached by it, and Jesus was baptized in it. Sacred in Christian thought, it often symbolizes the entrance into blessedness. 2. Country between modern Israel and Saudi Arabia. In it is the older part of Jerusalem.

**JORGENSEN, JENS JOHANNES (1866–1956)** Danish CATHOLIC writer, author of *Saint Francis of Assisi* and other books.

**JOROJIN** Japanese god of luck and long life.

**JOSEPH the Lord will add** 1. The patriarch Jacob's favorite son and the father of Ephraim and Manasseh, progenitors of two of Israel's twelve tribes. Joseph's youthful dreams led to his slavery in Egypt and to his eminence under the Pharaoh. Of noble spirit, Joseph helped save his family and the land of Egypt from famine. (GENESIS 30:22–24; 37—50). 2. Husband of Mary the mother of Jesus. Apparently he died during Jesus' youth. 3. A brother of Jesus (Joses, MATTHEW 13:55). 4. Several other Biblical figures bear this name.

**JOSEPH BARSABAS** Disciple who was a

candidate for the apostolate left vacant by the death of Judas (ACTS 1:23).

**JOSEPH OF ARIMATHEA** Wealthy member of the SANHEDRIN who gave his own intended sepulcher for the burial of Jesus, and rolled a stone in front of the entrance (MATTHEW 27:57–61).

**JOSEPH OF CUPERTINO, ST.** (1603–1663) Italian FRANCISCAN said to perform miracles and float in the air. His feast day is September 18.

**JOSEPH THE HYMNOGRAPHER, ST.** (c.810–886) Prolific Greek hymn writer. His feast day is April 3.

**JOSEPHUS, FLAVIUS** (37–c.95) Jewish governor of Galilee, apologist, and historian. His *Jewish War* and *Jewish Antiquities* provide important information about the Pharisees (to whom he belonged), Sadducees, and Essenes of the first century A.D., and about Jewish history after the close of the Jewish canon of the Old Testament.

**JOSHUA** *the Lord saves* 1. Jewish leader who succeeded Moses as the head of the invasion of Canaan. Under his generalship Jericho and other cities fell and the Israelites established themselves in the new land. His name sometimes appears as Jehoshua (NUMBERS 13:16), Jeshua (NEHEMIAH 8:17), and Jesus (HEBREWS 4:8). The book of Joshua tells of the conquest and settlement of Canaan, and Joshua's farewell address. 2. High priest at the time of Zerubbabel (HAGGAI 1). 3. Man of Beth-shemesh in whose field the ark of the covenant once rested (I SAMUEL 6:14). 4. A governor of Jerusalem (II KINGS 23:8).

**JOSIAH** *the Lord heals* 1. King of Judah from his eighth year, Josiah discovered the book of the law when repairing the temple and established thorough religious reforms, ousting heathen idols and priests, and centralizing all worship at Jerusalem. 2. Son of Zephaniah (ZECHARIAH 6:10).

**JOSIAS** See JOSIAH.

**JOSS** Pidgin English for a god or idol, probably a corruption of Portuguese *deos*, god.

**JOSUE** See JOSHUA.

**JOT** Smallest letter in the Hebrew alphabet. See IOTA.

**JOTUNN** Giants who often fought the gods in Norse myth.

**JO-UK** Great Creator among the Sudanese Shilluks.

**JOUVENET, JEAN BAPTISTE** (1644–1717) French religious painter, the greatest of his age. His "Miraculous Draught of Fishes" is characteristic of his work.

**JOVE** See JUPITER.

**JOVINIAN** (?–c.405) Roman monk who held that virginity is not more holy than marriage, that fasting is not more blessed than eating with thanksgiving, and that Mary's virginity was not perpetual. To crush these opinions synods were held at Rome and Milan denouncing such doctrines, and the good doctors AMBROSE, JEROME, and AUGUSTINE joined in the condemnation. Jovinian, though unmarried and poor, was banished.

**JOWETT, BENJAMIN** (1817–1893) ANGLICAN priest, Greek scholar, commentator on New Testament books, and theologian. His liberal views of the atonement and Scripture caused church controversy.

**JOY** Jubilant delight, an emotion often mentioned in the Old and New Testaments and an important part of JUDAISM and of Christian faith. Joy is a fruit of the Spirit like love, peace, and goodness (GALATIANS 5:22).

**JOYFUL MYSTERIES OF THE ROSARY, FIVE** The ANNUNCIATION, the Visit of the Virgin Mary to St. Elizabeth, the NATIVITY of our Lord, the Presentation in the Temple, and the Finding of the Boy Jesus in the Temple.

**JOYS OF MARY** These are usually listed as the ANNUNCIATION, VISITATION, NATIVITY, EPIPHANY, Finding Jesus in the Temple, RESURRECTION, and ASCENSION. The number of Mary's joys may vary from five to more than twelve.

**JUANA INES DE LA CRUZ** (1651–1695) Brilliant and dedicated Mexican nun who wrote exceptional poetry.

**JUBAL** Father of musicians (GENESIS 4:21).

**JUBE** Choir screen in French churches.

**JUBILATE** *O be joyful* Psalm 100, sung as an alternative to the BENEDICTUS at morning prayer.

**JUBILATE SUNDAY** Third Sunday after EASTER, when the INTROIT begins with the word "Jubilate."

**JUBILEE, YEAR OF** 1. Year, occurring twice each century in ancient JUDAISM, when land reverted to its former owner and slaves regained their freedom. 2. Year of special indulgence for CATHOLICS.

**JUBILEES, BOOK OF** Apocryphal Jewish book also called "The Little Genesis." An esoteric history of the world from creation to the giving of the law at Sinai, it was probably written by a strict Pharisee in the second century B.C.

**JUD or JUDAE, LEO (1482–1542)** Swiss reformer who helped translate the Zurich Bible, served as a REFORMED minister, and led in negotiations among Protestants.

**JUDA** See JUDAH.

**JUDAEA** See JUDEA.

**JUDAH** 1. Fourth son of Jacob and progenitor of the Jewish tribe of Judah—the tribe of David and Jesus. Judah was a leader among his brothers. 2. Several other Bible figures have the name JUDAH. Judas is another form of it. 3. One of Israel's twelve tribes (see 1.). 4. Name of the Southern Kingdom after the division of Solomon's kingdom. Its capital was Jerusalem.

**JUDAH BEN SAMUEL (?–1217)** German Jewish mystic who wrote the *Book of the Pious.*

**JUDAH HA-LEVI or HALEVY** See HALEVI, Judah.

**JUDAH HA-NASI** Rabbi and prince of the Jewish community in Palestine. A great-grandson of GAMALIEL I, he is also known as Judah I. He preserved and organized many Jewish traditions, and put the MISH-NAH in written form.

**JUDAISM** Religion and culture of the Jewish people, centering in devotion to the one God and brotherhood on earth. The great figures at Judaism's beginning were Abraham and Moses, but the Bible and history are filled with other important Jews. Four great branches or movements of contemporary Judaism are CONSERVA-TIVE, REFORM, ORTHODOX, and RECON-STRUCTION Judaism.

**JUDAIZERS** Early Christians who believed that all Christians must be circumcised, keep the whole law of Moses, and perform all the rites of Judaism. St. PAUL and other early church leaders condemned this as a step backward into spiritual bondage.

**JUDAS ISCARIOT** Apostle who betrayed Jesus and then committed suicide. The name Iscariot indicates that he was probably from Kerioth in Judea. Most of the other Apostles were from Galilee.

**JUDAS LIGHT** Imitation PASCHAL CANDLE.

**JUDAS MACCABEUS** *Judah the hammerer* Jewish guerrilla leader who defeated the Syrians in several battles, restored Jewish worship in the previously desecrated temple at Jerusalem, and got a pledge of religious liberty from ANTIOCHUS EPIPHANES. He was finally killed in battle. He is commemorated at HANUKKAH.

**JUDAS OF GALILEE** Leader of the revolutionary ZEALOTS, killed in a revolt in Galilee (ACTS 5:37).

**JUDE** 1. See JUDAS. 2. Apostle also named Thaddaeus or Lebbaeus and a brother of Jesus (MATTHEW 10:3; 13:55). 3. Short New Testament epistle traditionally attributed to Jesus' brother Jude. It warns against immoral actions and the loss of faith.

**JUDEA** Southern Palestine in the time of Jesus, centering around Jerusalem. About 55 miles square, it was the site of many important events in Jewish history and in the life of Christ.

**JUDEO-CHRISTIAN TRADITION** Term for the belief in one God, His revelation in Scripture, the relevancy of the moral code given at Sinai, and prophetic religion, common to the Jewish-Christian stream of religion.

**JUDETH** See JUDITH.

**JUDGE** 1. Jewish ruler in the days before there was a king—often necessarily more a military than a judicial figure. 2. Official presiding in an ecclesiastical court.

**JUDGES** Seventh book of the Old Testament, giving the history of Israel from the conquest of Canaan through the rule of various judges (leaders)—Barak, Deborah, Gideon, Jephthah, Samson, and others. It covers several hundred years.

**JUDGMENT** 1. Individual decision or interpretation. In PROTESTANTISM the right of private judgment is important. 2. Divine estimate of human life or activity. 3. Condemnation of sin accomplished by the death of Christ. 4. Final sentence of God on mankind at the final day of judgment. JUDAISM, CHRISTIANITY, and ISLAM hold to such a judgment when all men will appear before the tribunal of God. Cf. Romans 2:1–11.

**JUDICA SUNDAY** Fifth Sunday in LENT or Passion Sunday. The name derives from the INTROIT based on Psalm 43:1.

**JUDITH** *Jewess* 1. Wife of Esau (GENESIS 26:34). 2. Lovely Jewess who made Holofernes, a general of the invading Assyrians, drunk and then beheaded him to encourage her people and rout the enemy. The apocryphal book of Judith in the Old Testament relates this tale.

**JUDSON, ADONIRAM (1788–1850)** CONGREGATIONAL missionary from the United States to India who became a Baptist and labored for many years as a missionary to Burma. He translated the Bible into Burmese and was an outstanding example of missionary sacrifice and devotion. He was given splendid assistance by his three successive wives, the first two of whom died in 1826 and 1845.

**JUGGERNAUT** See JAGANNATH.

**JU-JU** West African charm or supernatural power.

**JULIAN, FLAVIUS** See JULIAN THE APOSTATE.

**JULIAN or JULIAN OF NORWICH (c.1342–c.1443)** English mystic who was probably an anchoress at Norwich. She had sixteen visions of Jesus and the Trinity, and wrote *Sixteen Revelations of Divine Love*. She saw evil as a distortion of man's will and the love of God as the answer to man's problems.

**JULIAN OF ECLANUM (c.386–454)** Bishop of Eclanum in Italy, outstanding Pelagian leader. He held that AUGUSTINE's doctrine of total depravity resulted from the evil influences of his early life, and that sin is not inherent but a result of the freedom of the human will. For his views he was deposed and banished.

**JULIAN THE APOSTATE (c.331–363)** Flavius Julian, nephew of Constantine, Roman emperor noted for championing paganism and suppressing Christianity. A just ruler, he rebuilt heathen temples and sought to remove the privileged status Constantine had granted the church.

**JULIUS I (?–352)** Pope (337–352) who assumed Roman supremacy in championing orthodoxy against ARIANISM. His feast day is April 12.

**JULIUS II (1443–1513)** Strong pope (1503–1513) who accomplished ecclesiastical reforms, encouraged mission activity, and called the Fifth LATERAN COUNCIL. He led Italian armies against the attempted dominance of Venice and France, and patronized RAPHAEL and MICHELANGELO.

**JULIUS III (1487–1555)** Pope (1550–1555) who encouraged church reform, granted new privileges to the SOCIETY OF JESUS, and supported MICHELANGELO.

**JUMADA** Name of two months in the ISLAMIC calendar, the fifth and sixth (Jumada 1 and II).

**JUMNA** River of northern India whose confluence with the GANGES marks a point of Hindu pilgrimage.

**JUMPERS** 1. Eighteenth-century Calvinistic Methodists of Wales who jumped for joy in religious ecstasy. 2. American SHAKERS who leaped with religious enthusiasm.

**JUNG, CARL GUSTAV (1875–1961)** Swiss psychiatrist and disciple of Sigmund FREUD. He emphasized the "collective unconscious" in personality, the necessity of harmonizing the unconscious with the conscious, and the importance of religious truths.

**JUNO** Roman goddess of women and the state, sister and wife of JUPITER. She was the queen of heaven and the mother of the war god MARS.

**JUPITER or JOVE** Chief deity in Roman religion. Like his Greek counterpart ZEUS, he was father in the pantheon, the king of gods and men. Probably originally an Indo-Aryan sky god, he became the Romans' protector, god of justice and oaths.

**JURAMENTADO** *bound by an oath* Moslem MORO who has sworn an oath to die killing those of the Christian faith.

**JURIEU, PIERRE (1637–1713)** French PROTESTANT theologian and REFORMED minister, sometimes a bitter controversialist.

**JURUPARI** Chief god of the Tupi-Guarani Indians in Brazil, said to have been born of a virgin.

**JUSTICE** A supreme virtue. JUDAISM holds justice to be important in the nature of God (PSALM 89:14) and a supreme duty of man (MICAH 6:8). Christian faith knows the divine justice to be satisfied by the work of Christ, received through repentance and faith. The necessity of impartial justice seems to be assumed by all men.

**JUSTIFICATION** Theological term for the way in which God counts sinful men to be righteous, through the death and resurrection of Christ received in faith. The result is a life attuned to God's will in love and trust (ROMANS 3:10; 6:5-11; 8).

**JUSTINIAN I (483-565)** Emperor at Constantinople who brought unity to the Roman Empire by codifying Roman law. To reconcile the warring MONOPHYSITES and the orthodox in the church he called the Second Council of CONSTANTINOPLE but did not accomplish his aim. He asserted the supremacy of the government over the church, built many basilicas, and persecuted pagans, ARIANS, and MONTANISTS.

**JUSTIN MARTYR (c.100-c.165)** Samaritan Christian whose two apologetic works and *Dialogue with Trypho* exhibited a mind trained in Greek thought defending Christianity against current charges. He found truth in pagans and said that Socrates and Heraclitus had been Christians, although the fullness of truth and wisdom was to be found only in Christ. He was beheaded in Rome. His feast day is April 14.

**JUSTUS, ST. (?-c.627)** Archbishop of Canterbury through whose aid Paulinus converted Northumbria to the Christian faith. Justus' feast day is November 10.

**JUSTUS OF GHENT (c.1430-c.1480)** Flemish religious painter famed for the "Adoration of the Magi," the "Crucifixion," and other works.

**JUVENTAS** Roman goddess of young men. Her Greek counterpart was HEBE.

**JUXON, WILLIAM (1582-1663)** Archbishop of Canterbury known for his fairness, character, and tolerance.

# K

**KA** Ancient Egyptian name for the spirit guardian which accompanied the soul into the future life. It appears to have been a physical extension of the dead person's earthly personality.

**KAABA or CAABA** Small building in MECCA housing the sacred BLACK STONE revered by Moslems (see ISLAM). This is the center of the pilgrimage to Mecca, and the building toward which Moslems face in prayer.

**KA-ATA-KILLA** Moon goddess worshiped in Peru before the time of the Incas.

**KABBALA or KABBALAH** See CABALA.

**KABIR (c.1488–1512)** Weaver of India acclaimed by both Hindus and Moslems. A mystic thinker, he criticized both ISLAM and HINDUISM and sought truth wherever he could find it.

**KABIR PANTHIS** *followers of Kabir* Disciples of KABIR who worship RAMA and are respected for their integrity and "Quaker-like spirit" (H. H. Wilson).

**KABUL** Mayan moon god.

**KADDISH** *holy* Jewish service of praise, particularly in commemoration of the dead.

**KADI** Moslem judge.

**KADMIS** See PARSEES.

**KAFIR** *infidel* MOHAMMEDAN term for a non-Mohammedan (see ISLAM).

**KAFTAN or CAFTAN** Long black coat often worn by European Jews.

**KAGAWA, TOYOHIKO (1888–1960)** Japanese Christian leader and social reformer. Kagawa founded the first labor union and the Kingdom of God movement in Japan, as well as schools, churches, and nurseries. He lived among Japanese slum-dwellers and was a pacifist and poet.

**KAGU-TSUCHI** Japanese fire god.

**KAHAL or QAHAL** *assembly* 1. Hebrew word in the Old Testament for the assembly of the people for religious or political reasons. In the SEPTUAGINT it was translated *ekklesia* which is the New Testament word for *church*. 2. Jewish term for self-government.

**KAHDAM-PA** BUDDHIST movement organized in the eleventh century in Tibet.

**KAILASA** HINDU paradise for worshipers of SIVA.

**KAIROS** *fullness of time* Theological term for a period when God may intervene in history, as at the birth or the second coming of Christ, or at any significant moment. "The eternal can break into the temporal; and where this happens there is a kairos" (Paul Tillich).

**KALAM** *conversation* ISLAM's scholastic theology or fundamental principles.

**KALI** *the black one* Hindu goddess of death and destruction. The wife of SIVA, she has four arms, a blood-stained face, red eyes, and a necklace of skulls. She is regarded as both creator and destroyer.

**KALKI** *time* Future, final reincarnation of VISHNU, one of Hinduism's chief gods.

**KALOGEROS** *good elder* Term for a monk in the Holy Land.

**KALPA** Sanskrit term designating the period between the beginning and the end of the universe in BUDDHISM and HINDUISM. This is the Day of Brahma, reckoned as more than four billion years.

**KALU** Babylonian priests who serve the god of the afterlife.

**KAMA** Vedic HINDU term for desire, or for the god of love.

**KAMADHENU** Sacred cow of HINDU paradise.

**KAMAKURA** Japanese city famous for its bronze statue of BUDDHA, thirty-foot statue of the mercy-goddess Kwannon (see KUAN-YIN), and many shrines. A famous Buddhist monastery, Engakuji, was founded there in 1282.

**KAMASHI** *wanton eyed* One name of the HINDU goddess Parvati, Siva's wife.

**KAMI** Japanese term for anything numinous, a supernatural being, or a deceased hero or ancestor worshiped as a deity in SHINTO.

**KAMISION** Large-sleeved robe worn by EASTERN ORTHODOX acolytes.

**KAN** Mayan god of the east.

**KANDY** City of Ceylon where there is a temple believed to house a tooth of BUDDHA, and also a Brahman temple (see BRAHMANISM). Each year the tooth is carried on the back of an elephant in a procession around the city, and each day it is worshiped by Buddhist monks.

**KANISHKA (first century A.D.)** King of Gandhara (now in West Pakistan) who promoted the dissemination of BUDDHIST faith throughout India, erected a number of Buddhist monuments, and called an important Buddhist council at Peshawar.

**KANT, IMMANUEL (1724–1804)** German philosopher who presented a weighty case for the proposition that reason can neither prove nor deny the existence of God and immortality, and that the traditional proofs of such existence are weak. Morality, however, presupposes God, and may be reduced to categorical imperatives such as these: "Act as if the maxim of thy action were to become by thy will the universal law of action"; "So act as to treat humanity, whether in thine own person or in that of any other, in every case as an end, and never as a means only." Kant's *Critique of Pure Reason* has had immense influence on philosophy, ethics, and theology.

**KANTIANISM** Philosophy of Immanuel KANT.

**KAPOTE** Black coat worn by Jews of eastern Europe.

**KAPILA** See SANKHYA.

**KARAITES, CARAITES, or QARAITES** Middle Eastern Jewish sect which apparently originated in eighth-century Persia. Its members reject rabbinic interpretations in favor of literal acceptance of Scripture, and seek to observe every detail of the MOSAIC LAW. For example, they do not permit any fires to be lighted on the Sabbath.

**KARGYUT-PA** Important division of BUDDHISM in Tibet, emphasizing silence and meditation.

**KARLI** Village in western India noted for a number of BUDDHIST temples in caves. One of them, the largest of its kind in India, is 124 feet long and 45 feet high with many elaborately carved columns.

**KARMA** *deed* Sanskrit term for what one does or makes of himself. The law of Karma is the law of cause and effect; what one does in this life affects his next incarnation, so that wrongdoers are punished with suffering and the righteous are rewarded, according to BUDDHISM and HINDUISM. In JAINISM, Karma unites soul and body, and is the cumulative effect of a person's deeds.

**KARMA-MARGA** *way of works* Sanskrit term for salvation by what one does, as offering sacrifice and making a religious pilgrimage; a tenet of HINDUISM.

**KARMATHIANS or CARMATHIANS** MOSLEMS with a pantheistic theology and communistic communities who lived in the Near East in the ninth and tenth centuries. Often at war with other Moslems, they sacked MECCA and took away the BLACK STONE about 930 A.D., returning it about 940.

**KARO, JOSEPH BEN EPHRAIM** See CARO, JOSEPH BEN EPHRAIM.

**KARTIKEYA** Ancient HINDU war god, believed to have six faces, twelve arms, and twelve legs.

**KASHERN** Yiddish term for making Jewish food KOSHER.

**KASSAPA or KASYAPA (sixth century B.C.)** Disciple of BUDDHA who acted as leader of the first Buddhist council. ZEN Buddhists consider Kassapa to be their first patriarch.

**KATHENOTHEISM** Type of theism such as vedic HINDUISM in which one god is preeminent at one time and another later.

**KATKOCHILA** Vengeful god worshiped by the Wintun Indians of western North America.

**KAVVANAH** Jewish term for a prayerful attitude.

**K.C.** Abbreviation for KNIGHTS OF COLUMBUS.

**KEBLE, JOHN (1792–1866)** ANGLICAN clergyman, hymn writer, and poet, famous for his book *The Christian Year,* popular book of poetry based on the Book of Common Prayer. Among his well-known hymns are "Sun of My Soul" and "New Every Morning Is Thy Love." When the British government sought to suppress ten bishoprics in Ireland, Keble preached a sermon of protest to which has been attributed the beginning of the OXFORD MOVEMENT.

**KEDUSHAH** *holiness* Jewish chant praising the holiness and unity of the Lord.

**KEGON** Small but influential BUDDHIST movement originating in China in the seventh century.

**KEITH, GEORGE (c.1639–1716)** Scottish QUAKER who founded an American group of Quakers called Christian Quakers. Rejected by other Quakers, he entered the ANGLICAN ministry and became one of the first missionaries of the SOCIETY FOR THE PROPAGATION OF THE GOSPEL, laboring in America 1702–1704. He then returned to a parish in England.

**KELLS, BOOK OF** Beautifully illuminated copy of the four Gospels in Latin, dating from the eighth century. It was discovered in a monastery founded by COLUMBA at Kells, Ireland.

**KELPIE** Celtic water god.

**KELPIUS, JOHANN (1673–1708)** Dutch MYSTIC who founded the Colony of the Contented of the God-loving Soul at Philadelphia, Pennsylvania, in 1694. Its members did not marry, looked for the imminent return of Christ and the millennial kingdom, and practiced Christian communism.

**KEMPE, MARGERY (c.1373–c.1438)** English MYSTIC who had visions, denounced pleasure, appeared to enjoy unusual fellowship with Christ, and described her spiritual pursuits in beautiful English.

**KEMPENER, PIETER DE (c.1503–1580)** Flemish religious painter of vivid portraiture including "The Descent From the Cross."

**KEMPIS, THOMAS À** See THOMAS À KEMPIS.

**KEN, THOMAS (1637–1711)** ANGLICAN bishop of independent mind, noted as a hymn writer. He wrote "Glory to Thee, My God, This Night" and "Praise God from Whom All Blessings Flow." He has been praised for "unstained purity and invincible fidelity to conscience."

**KENITES** Nomadic metal workers of the ancient Holy Land. Moses' wife's father was a Kenite (JUDGES 1:16) and he may have taught Moses, as Nelson Glueck believes, the skills to fashion the brazen serpent. The only unfavorable reference to the Kenites in the Bible is in an apparent curse of Balaam (NUMBERS 24:21 ff.).

**KENNEDY, CHARLES RANN (1871–1950)** English dramatist who wrote plays with strong ethical and religious overtones such as *The Servant in the House* and *The Terrible Meek.* In 1917 be became a citizen of the United States.

**KENNEDY, JOHN FITZGERALD (1917–1963)** Thirty-fifth President of the United States, the first ROMAN CATHOLIC to hold that office. During his presidency he steadfastly refused to tolerate federal aid to religious schools and convinced many that the separation of church and state is not jeopardized merely because the President is Catholic. Kennedy was the first President to enunciate the moral basis of civil rights.

**KENNICOTT, BENJAMIN (1718–1783)** ANGLICAN Bible scholar and Hebraist who collated 615 Hebrew manuscripts to show that variations in the Hebrew texts of the Old Testament are so minor as to be negligible.

**KENOSIS** *emptying* Theological term based on Philippians 2:8 in which Paul states that Christ "emptied himself" in becoming a man. A number of theologians have maintained that Christ emptied Himself of the attributes of God, while those of more orthodox mind hold that Christ emptied Himself of heavenly glory but remained divine.

**KENSIT, JOHN (1853–1902)** English Protestant controversialist.

**KENTIGERN, ST. (?–603)** British bishop and missionary to Wales and Scotland. His feast day is January 13.

**KENYON, FREDERIC GEORGE (1863–1952)** English scholar who specialized in Greek and contributed much to our knowledge of the Greek Bible and New Testament.

**KERBELA** City of Iraq whose tomb of Husein is the most important shrine of SHIITE pilgrims. Many Moslems are buried at Kerbela as this assures entrance into paradise. See also ISLAM.

**KERIDWEN** Celtic goddess of nature and inspiration.

**KERIOTH** 1. Idumaean town from which JUDAS ISCARIOT ("Man of Kerioth") may have come. 2. City of Moab which contained a temple of the god CHEMOSH.

**KERMESSE** *church mass* Once a term for a mass honoring the patron or founding of a church, kermesse now indicates a joyful celebration after a European service, or an entertainment in the United States as for charity.

**KERYGMA** *preaching* Content of proclamation of the Christian gospel.

**KESHUB CHUNDER SEN (1838–1884)** Religious reformer of India. A Hindu of high caste, he led the BRAHMA SAMAJ of India which emphasized wisdom, truth, faith, and love. In 1881 he established the Church of the New Dispensation. He injected a number of Christian elements into HINDUISM.

**KESWICK CONFERENCE** Annual gathering at Keswick in England's Lake District for the purpose of seeking a deeper Christian life. Originating in 1875, it is evangelical and undenominational. Similar Keswick conferences are held annually in the United States and Canada.

**KETHUBAH** See KETUVAH.

**KETHUBIM** See KETUVIM.

**KETTNER, FREDERICK** See BIOSOPHY.

**KETURAH** *incense* Second wife of ABRAHAM, mother of six sons who were fathers of Arab tribes.

**KETUVAH or KETHUBAH** Jewish term for marriage agreement.

**KETUVIM or KETHUBIM** Third section of the Jewish Scriptures: the Sacred Writings beginning with the Psalms and ending with the Chronicles.

**KEYS** Symbol of entrance into the kingdom of God (MATTHEW 16:19), or of St. Peter.

**KEYS, CROSSED** Special ecclesiastical symbol of St. Peter.

**KEYS, POWER OF THE** Term designating the disciplinary and papal power claimed by the ROMAN CATHOLIC CHURCH in virtue of Christ's statement to the Apostle Peter, "And I will give unto thee the keys of the kingdom of heaven" (MATTHEW 16:19). Lutherans and other Protestants view the power of the keys in a different light, usually as the power of the whole church, regarded spiritually and symbolically.

**KEYS OF THE KINGDOM** See above.

**KHADIJA or KHADIJEH** Mohammed's dearly loved wife.

**KHAIBIT** *shadow* Portion of personality, according to ancient Egyptian religion. A person's shadow somehow was a part of him.

**KHALID (?–642)** Arabian Moslem leader, called the "Sword of God" by Mohammed, who led in the conquest of Egypt and other countries for ISLAM.

**KHALIF or CALIPH** *successor, representative* A successor to MOHAMMED, representing the centralized authority of ISLAM. The KORAN names such men as Adam and David khalifs, vicegerents of God, holding both temporal and spiritual power.

**KHALIFATE** Moslem headship.

**KHALSA** *pure* SIKH military community, "Brotherhood of the Poor," evidencing MOSLEM influences.

**KHANDA-DI-PAHUL** *baptism of the sword* Term for the military aspects of SIKHISM.

**KHARIJITES** *come-outers* Separatists or seceders from ISLAM who were opposed by the SHIITES. Originally opposed to the khalifate of Ali, they held that any faithful MOSLEM might be khalif. Today there are a few Kharijites in Zanzibar and several other countries of the Near East.

**KHASM** ZOROASTRIAN spirit of evil.

**KHAZARS** See CHAZARS.

**KHENSU or KHONS** Egyptian moon god. He was worshiped principally at Thebes.

**KHEPERA or KHOPRI** Egyptian creator-god symbolized by the scarab. Khepera was another form of the sun god RA.

**KHEREBU** Term for spirits or angels in Assyrian religion. This may be the source of the Biblical cherub or cherubim; statues of winged beasts in Assyrian temples are reminiscent of the winged creatures in Ezekiel.

**KHLYSTS, CHLISTS, or KHLYSTY** *flagellants* Russian ascetics originating in the seventeenth century. They abstained from coffee, tea, and sex; and they danced, sang, and flogged themselves to receive the Holy Spirit. Their leaders were usually a "Christ" and a "Mother of God."

**KHNEMU or KHNUM** Egyptian creator-god worshiped at Elephantine. He is often represented with the head of a ram.

**KHOMIAKOFF, ALEXIS S. (1804–1860)** Russian Orthodox theologian who held that freedom and unity, separated in Protestantism and Romanism, were ideally combined in his own church.

**KHONDS** Religionists in India who until recently made regular sacrifices of young men and women to their goddess Tari Pennou.

**KHONS** See KHENSU.

**KHOPRI** See KHEPERA.

**KHORS** Germanic god of hunting and good health.

**KHOSER-ET-HASIS** Phoenician god of the sea.

**KHSHATHRA VAIRYA** ZOROASTRIAN spirit of the Desired Kingdom; one of AHURA MAZDA's six immortal attendants.

**KHUTBAH** MOSLEM sermon.

**KIBBUTZ** Collective farm or agricultural settlement in Israel.

**KIBLAH** MOSLEM term for the direction of the KAABA toward which one must bow when praying.

**KIDDERMINSTER** English town made famous by Richard BAXTER.

**KIDDUSH** *sanctification* Jewish blessing which marks the beginning of the SABBATH or other holy day.

**KIDDUSH HA-SHEM** *sanctification of the name* Jewish term for any action which glorifies God, from a righteous deed to martyrdom for the faith.

**KIDRON or CEDRON** *dark or torrent* Valley or brook between Jerusalem and the Mount of Olives, crossed by King David when retreating from Absalom's rebellion (II SAMUEL 15:23) and by Jesus before the crucifixion (JOHN 18:1).

**KIERKEGAARD, SØREN (1813–1855)** Danish theologian whose books such as *Either/Or* and *Concluding Unscientific Postscript* influenced modern existentialism, Neo-orthodoxy, and ecclesiastical re-examination. Critical of the established Lutheran Church, Kierkegaard went back to LUTHERAN principles to produce a deeper philosophy of existence and faith.

**KIHO TUMI** Principal Polynesian god in Tuamotu.

**KILHAM, ALEXANDER (1762–1798)** English clergyman—expelled from the METHODIST CHURCH for such things as proposing total separation from the CHURCH OF ENGLAND—who founded the Methodist New Connection in 1798.

**KIMHI or KIMCHI, DAVID (c.1160–c.1235)** French Jewish scholar noted for his Old Testament commentaries and Hebrew reference works.

**KIMHI or KIMCHI, JOSEPH (c.1105–1170)** Jewish scholar, father of David Kimhi and a resident of France and Spain, who simplified the study of Hebrew and wrote commentaries, poetry, and a Jewish apologetic.

**KIMHI or KIMCHI, MOSES (?–1190)** Brother of David Kimhi; he wrote a Hebrew textbook and several commentaries wrongly attributed to Abraham ibn Ezra.

**KINAH** *lamentation* Jewish dirge.

**KINDI or AL-KINDI (?–c.873)** Earliest Moslem philosopher of Arabia, "Philosopher of the Arabs," who taught the revelation, righteousness, and unity of God. His writings ranged from mathematics and medicine to astronomy and optical science, and influenced Western thought in the Middle Ages. See also ISLAM.

**KING, WILLIAM (1650–1729)** Archbishop of Dublin who supported PROTESTANT rights in Ireland.

**KINGDOM OF GOD** God's rule over the universe, a Judeo-Christian term for the Messiah's reign. According to the New Testament, the Kingdom of God begins in the heart of the believer (LUKE 17:21) but ultimately will encompass heaven and earth (MATTHEW 13). Not of this world (JOHN 18:36), the Kingdom is over all and must permeate all things. Although the church is sometimes called the Kingdom of God, the latter is greater than any earthly organization.

**KINGDOM OF HEAVEN** Term for the Kingdom of God in the Gospel according to Matthew (cf. 5:4; 13:31; 19:15; etc. with parallel passages in Mark and Luke). Matthew uses this phrase 30 times.

**KINGDOMTIDE** Season of the Christian year, designated in many churches, beginning with the Festival of Christ the King on the last Sunday of August and concluding with Thanksgiving Sunday.

**KING JAMES BIBLE or KING JAMES VERSION** The translation of the Bible resulting from a conference of English divines over which King JAMES I presided. It was published in 1611 and in England is termed the "Authorized Version," although such a designation might more accurately be given such versions of the Bible as the REVISED, AMERICAN STANDARD, REVISED STANDARD, or NEW ENGLISH BIBLE, which were authorized and executed by the churches. The King James Bible's rhythm and beauty have profoundly influenced Western literature, culture, and religion. Originally it contained the APOCRYPHA but these are omitted in modern editions.

**KINGO, THOMAS HANSEN (1634–1703)** Danish LUTHERAN bishop and hymn writer.

**KINGS** Two books of the Old Testament are known as I and II Kings, or the First and Second Books of Kings. They trace the history of Israel from the end of the reign of King David through the end of the Kingdom of Judah, perhaps 1000–560 B.C.

**KINGS, DIVINE RIGHT OF** See DIVINE RIGHT OF KINGS.

**KING'S BOOK** Term for Henry VIII's *Necessary Doctrine and Erudition for Any Christian Man*, maintaining the supremacy of the King of England.

**KING'S CONFESSION** Confession of faith asserting Protestant principles, signed by King James VI of Scotland in 1581.

**KING'S HIGHWAY** Road through Trans-Jordan in which Abraham fought with a number of kings (GENESIS 14).

**KINGSLEY, CHARLES (1819–1875)** ANGLICAN clergyman, author, and social reformer. A leader in the CHRISTIAN SOCIALIST MOVEMENT in England, he is probably best known for such books as *Water Babies* and *Westward Ho!*

**KING'S POOL** Term for the pool of Siloam (NEHEMIAH 2:14).

**KINGU** Babylonian god of evil cast out by MARDUK. From his blood EA made human beings.

**KINICH-AHAU** Mayan god of healing.

**KINO, EUSEBIO FRANCISCO (c.1644–1711)** Jesuit missionary in southwestern America (see SOCIETY OF JESUS).

**KIRK** Scottish word for church.

**KIRKLAND, SAMUEL (1741–1808)** New England missionary among the Oneida Indians.

**KIRKMAN** Scottish term for church member or ecclesiastic.

**KIRK-SESSION** Scottish term for a church's SESSION.

**KISH** 1. The father of King Saul and several other Old Testament characters bear this name (I SAMUEL 9; I CHRONICLES 8:30; 24:29; ESTHER 2:5). 2. Sumerian city, 8 miles from Babylon, whose temples and buildings reveal ancient Semitic culture. A deposit of red mud points to the Genesis deluge. One temple in Kish was built in the reign of NEBUCHADNEZZAR.

**KISHAR** Babylonian god of the earth.

**KISHI BOJIN** Goddess of children, worshiped in Japan.

**KISHON** *winding* River flowing from Galilee to the Mediterranean Sea. It trapped the Canaanite army (JUDGES 5:21), and near it Elijah killed the priests of Baal (I KINGS 18:40).

**KISLEV or KISLEU** Third month in the Jewish civil year.

**KISMET** *fate* Arabic and Moslem term for what must inevitably happen, the foreordained will of ALLAH.

**KISS** Affection or reverence expressed with the lips. Of ancient religious significance, the "holy kiss" was a part of New Testament worship (I CORINTHIANS 16:20; ROMANS 16:16). JUSTIN MARTYR refers to a continuation of the custom in the second century, and kissing has been important in various Christian liturgies.

**KISS OF PEACE** Also known as the kiss of charity, or the Pax ("Peace"), this is an ecclesiastical term for the ceremonial embrace which sometimes occurs at communion or mass in ANGLICAN and CATHOLIC churches. NESTORIANS, DUNKERS, and others may conclude a service of worship with such a kiss (ROMANS 16:16).

**KISTNA** River of India whose headwaters are regarded as holy by HINDUS, and are often visited by pilgrims.

**KISWEH** *robe* Black covering of the KAABA. A new one is made annually.

**KITCHE MANITOU** Great spirit of American Indians believed to have destroyed the earth both by flood and by fire.

**KITTEL** *shroud* White robe in which Jews are buried and which is worn by the clergy on high holy days. It symbolizes holiness and commemoration.

**KITTEL, RUDOLPH (1853–1929)** German authority on JUDAISM and editor of a widely used critical edition of the Hebrew Bible.

**KITTIM or CHITTIM** Bible name for the island of Cyprus and its inhabitants (GENESIS 10:4; EZEKIEL 27:6). It may also refer to countries north of the Mediterranean.

**KITTO, JOHN (1804–1854)** ANGLICAN missionary to Persia and Biblical scholar.

**KJV** Abbreviation for KING JAMES VERSION.

**KLAUS** Yiddish term for a place of prayer.

**KMUKAMTCH** According to Oregon's Klamath Indians, a demon who once sought to destroy the world.

**KNEELER** Bench on which to kneel in worship.

**KNEELING** Bending the knee or getting down on the knees in a gesture of submission, an ancient, universal religious custom. Kneeling is a traditional posture for prayer. In Anglican and Methodist churches communion is received as the communicant kneels.

**KNIFE** Symbol of martyrdom in religious art.

**KNIGHTS HOSPITALERS** Religious military order, also known as the Knights of St. John, Knights of Jerusalem, Knights of Malta, Hospitalers, and Order of the Hospital of St. John of Jerusalem. Apparently the order was founded during the eleventh or twelfth century, centering around a hospital erected after the CRUSADERS captured Jerusalem in 1099. The order is now devoted to hospital maintenance and works of philanthropy. It is the only order of chivalry to survive into the present age.

**KNIGHTS OF COLUMBUS** Largest Catholic fraternal order, organized in the United States in 1882. Outwardly similar to MASONRY, it is a worldwide subsidiary of the ROMAN CATHOLIC CHURCH. Members honor Christopher Columbus, encourage patriotism and benevolence, and provide Catholic information through advertisements in periodicals.

**KNIGHTS OF JERUSALEM** See KNIGHTS HOSPITALERS.

**KNIGHTS OF MALTA** Name of the Knights Hospitalers while occupying Malta. See KNIGHTS HOSPITALERS.

**KNIGHTS OF RHODES** Name of the Knights Hospitalers while in Rhodes 1309–1523. See KNIGHTS HOSPITALERS.

**KNIGHTS OF ST. JOHN** See KNIGHTS HOSPITALERS.

**KNIGHTS TEMPLARS** See TEMPLARS.

**KNOP** *knob* 1. Protuberance on a chalice for secure handling. 2. Round ornament employed in the decoration of the Jewish temple and its accessories (EXODUS 25:31; I KINGS 6:18).

**KNOT** Religious symbol of binding or restricting, universally used.

**KNOWLEDGE** Biblical term for the most intimate relationship with one of the opposite sex, or with God. God knows His people (JEREMIAH 1:5; NAHUM 1:7) and their greatest joy is to know Him (JOHN 17:3; PHILIPPIANS 3:10). GNOSTICISM made much of esoteric "knowledge," which was in sharp contrast to the knowledge of God in Christ proclaimed by the New Testament writers.

**KNOWLEDGE OF LIFE** See MANDA D'HAYYE.

**KNOW NOTHING PARTY** Political party of the United States in the 1850's which opposed ROMAN CATHOLICS and foreigners under the guise of Americanism. Its secrecy, requiring members to state that they knew nothing of its aims, led to its name. In 1854 it adopted a new name, the American Party.

**KNOX, JOHN (c.1505–1572)** Principal Protestant reformer of Scotland. He studied under John CALVIN at Geneva and made PRESBYTERIANISM the religion of Scotland. He fearlessly attacked his sovereign, Queen Mary, and after she forbade him to preach he ceased for a short time. But Mary abdicated and Knox preached at the coronation of the new king, the infant James. A man of inflexible will and a powerful preacher, he was said by Elizabeth's ambassador "in one hour to put more life in us than five hundred trumpets continually blustering in our ears."

**KOAN** Concept of ZEN Buddhism. See HAKUIN.

**KOBO-DAISHI (774–835)** Japanese founder of the SHINGON school of Buddhism about 806. The monastery he established on Mt. Koya is the center of the Shingon school. An artist and scholar, he is also known as Kukai.

**KOBOLD** Germanic earth spirit or brownie.

**KODESH CHURCH OF IMMANUEL** Inter-racial denomination in the United States, organized in 1929 by Frank Russell Killingsworth, which advocates PREMILLENNIALISM and entire SANCTIFICATION. Tobacco, alcohol, and dancing and other amusements are prohibited.

**KODESH KADASHIM** *holy of holies* Jewish term for the innermost portion of the tabernacle or temple. See HOLY OF HOLIES.

**KOGOSHUI** Ninth-century work on Japanese religion.

**KOHATH** Second son of Levi and founder of one of the great families of Levites (GENESIS 46:11; EXODUS 6:16–18). The Kohathites had special duties in connection with the temple.

**KOHELETH** *preacher* Hebrew word for a speaker, for "one who convenes an assembly" (see KAHAL), and for the author of ECCLESIASTES. Koheleth is the Hebrew title of this book; the Greek word transliterated "Ecclesiastes" means "churchman" or "leader of an assembly."

**KOHEN** See COHEN.

**KOHLER, KAUFMANN** (1843–1926) Bavarian-born American rabbi, scholar, and Reform leader (see REFORM JUDAISM).

**KOHUT, ALEXANDER** (1842–1894) Hungarian-American rabbi and Jewish scholar.

**KOINE** *common* The common Greek speech of the New Testament era, used in the New Testament. It is marked by simplicity, clarity, directness, and new words and expressions.

**KOINONIA** *fellowship* New Testament word for sharing, charity, communion, or fellowship, often indicating participation in the Christian community.

**KOJI** Disciple of ZEN Buddhism.

**KOJIKI** *record of ancient happenings* Compilation of SHINTO beliefs, creation stories, and sources—made about 712.

**KOL-BO** *all is in it* Jewish collection of all the prayers or all the laws for the year.

**KOL NIDRE** *all vows* Jewish prayer chanted at the beginning of Yom Kippur worship, asking absolution for all vows which may be made but not fulfilled. See ATONEMENT, DAY OF.

**KOMOKU** Japanese deity of the south.

**KOMORKIS** Blackfoot Indian moon deity.

**KOMPIRA** Japanese BUDDHIST god of travelers.

**KONTAKION** Book of prayers or hymns praising a saint in the EASTERN ORTHODOX CHURCH.

**KOPH** Nineteenth letter of the Hebrew alphabet.

**KORAH or CORE** Leader of a Jewish rebellion against Moses and Aaron (NUMBERS 16; 17).

**KORAN or QURAN** *recitation* Sacred book of ISLAM containing revelations of ALLAH to MOHAMMED. Its 114 chapters speak of the glory and power of God, the nature of heaven and hell, the way of Islam, and the coming end of the world. Written in Arabic and memorized by Moslems, the Koran is believed by many scholars to derive from Jewish and Christian writings.

**KOSHER** *proper* Jewish designation of that which is ceremonially appropriate, as food when it is prepared according to regulations of the faith.

**KRAUSKOPF, JOSEPH** (1858–1923) German-American rabbi, humanitarian, and leader of liberal Judaism.

**KRAUTH, CHARLES P.** (1823–1883) American LUTHERAN theologian and conservative leader. He aided in the preparation of the AMERICAN STANDARD VERSION of the Bible.

**KRIMMER MENNONITE BRETHREN CONFERENCE** American denomination which merged into the MENNONITE BRETHREN CHURCH OF NORTH AMERICA in 1960.

**KRISHNA** *black* Hindu god and avatar of VISHNU. He is represented as a dark-complexioned young man of great strength and beauty. Krishna is the most popular of all the deities of HINDUISM. The BHAGAVAD-GITA terms him very God, and his female worshipers are called "Mothers of God."

**KRISS KRINGLE** Name of Santa Claus derived from German word for Christ child (*Christkindl*).

**KROCHMAL, NACHMAN KOHEN** (1785–1840) Galician Jewish leader and scholar who sought to reconcile religion with modern knowledge and led in the establishment of CONSERVATIVE JUDAISM. He originated "cultural Zionism."

**KSHATRIYA** One of the four great HINDU castes, that of warriors and kings. BUDDHA belonged to it.

**K.T.** Abbreviation for Knights Templars. See TEMPLARS.

**KUAN-TI (?–c.219)** Chinese warrior who for many centuries after his death was worshiped by CONFUCIANS as a god of righteousness, protecting his followers from war's destruction.

**KUAN-YIN** Guardian deity in Chinese BUDDHISM. A bodhisattva according to MAHAYANA Buddhism, she is known as Kwannon in Japan.

**KUENEN, ABRAHAM (1828–1891)** Dutch Protestant theologian and Old Testament scholar. A noted Bible critic, he supported liberal trends in the DUTCH REFORMED CHURCH.

**KUKAI** See KOBO-DAISHI.

**KUKULCAN** Ancient Mayan god represented as a feathered snake.

**KULTURKAMPF** *fight for civilization* Fifteen-year struggle between Bismarck and the ROMAN CATHOLIC CHURCH for control of Germany. During it the SOCIETY OF JESUS was expelled and the schools were taken over by the state, but eventually it resulted in firmer Catholic solidarity in Germany than before.

**KUMARAJIVA (c.344–413)** Scholar of India who translated many Indian Buddhist works into Chinese and founded the MIDDLE DOCTRINE school of Chinese BUDDHISM.

**KUMBAKONAM** Town in southeastern India with many HINDU temples to which pilgrimages are made.

**KUMBUM or GUMBUM** Large BUDDHIST monastery of northeastern China known as the "Monastery of 100,000 Images." It is a favorite place of pilgrimage.

**KUNDALINI** YOGA name for the powerful serpent believed to lie at the base of the spine until it ascends to the brain. Unless this ascent is carefully guided, insanity may result.

**KUPPAH** *basket* Jewish alms container.

**KURKIL** Raven, according to Siberian Mongols, who created the world.

**KUSHTA** MANDAEAN Gnostic term for faithfulness or truth.

**KUYPER, ABRAHAM (1837–1920)** Calvinistic political and theological leader in the Netherlands. Founder of the Free Reformed Church, and of the Free University of Amsterdam, he stood for classical REFORMED doctrines and has been influential theologically in the United States and Germany.

**KWANNON** Japanese name for KUAN-YIN.

**KWEI** Chinese word for an evil spirit, commonly that of a deceased person, filling the night with danger.

**KYODAN** 1. Church of Christ in Japan (Nihon Kirisuto Kyodan), formed in 1941 by the union of 34 denominations, consisting of most of Japan's PROTESTANTS. 2. Name applied to the ROMAN CATHOLIC work in Japan in 1941 under pressure to remove foreign leaders and influence.

**KYRIALE** Service book with the chant for the ordinary of the mass in Latin.

**KYRIE ELEISON** *Lord, have mercy (upon us)* Prayer or response widely used in ROMAN CATHOLIC, GREEK CATHOLIC, ANGLICAN, LUTHERAN, and some other church services.

**KYRIOS** *Lord* Greek word for owner or god, used in the SEPTUAGINT for God or Jehovah and in the New Testament in reference to God or Christ.

# L

**LABADIE, JEAN DE (1610–1674)** French mystic and JESUIT who became a PROTESTANT and founded the LABADISTS.

**LABADISTS** Followers of Jean de LABADIE in the seventeenth and eighteenth centuries. They held property and children in common, rejected the marriage of believers with unbelievers, and believed that the Holy Spirit must be present for understanding of Scripture. They were forced out of one European community after another and eventually moved to the United States where their experiment came to an unsuccessful end.

**LABAN** *white* Brother of Isaac's wife Rebekah. A resident of Padan-aram, north of the Euphrates, he tricked his nephew Jacob and was deceived by Jacob and Rachel (GENESIS 24:29 ff.; 29—31).

**LABARUM** Monogram of the two Greek letters *chi* and *rho*, X and P, intersecting; the first two letters in the Greek word for Christ. Adopted by CONSTANTINE as a military standard, it became widespread as a Christian symbol.

**LABERTHONNIERE, LUCIEN (1860–1932)** French CATHOLIC philosopher and modernist theologian. His doctrine of the immanence of God was condemned by Pope PIUS X and his works put on the INDEX.

**LABORARE EST ORARE** *to work is to pray* Ancient CHRISTIAN motto.

**LABYRINTH** In Greek mythology the fearful minotaur was kept within a winding labyrinth. In medieval churches labyrinths inlaid in the tile floor symbolized the difficult way of the Christian, or the winding way of Jesus to the cross.

**LA CHAISE, FRANCOIS DE (1624–1709)** French JESUIT who served as confessor to Louis XIV. He was responsible for the revocation of the EDICT OF NANTES although he restrained Louis XIV's suppression of the JANSENISTS. He also admired FENELON.

**LACHELIER, JULES (1834–1918)** French philosopher who emphasized spiritual freedom and held that the religious life is intellectually supreme.

**LACHISH** City 30 miles southwest of Jerusalem often mentioned in the Old Testament. Its name today is Tell ad-Duweir.

**LACHISH LETTERS** Eighteen letters written by military officers in Lachish c.589 B.C. when NEBUCHADNEZZAR was threatening the city. They speak of YAHWEH and of a prophet who may well have been Urijah (JEREMIAH 26:20–23).

**LACHMANN, KARL (1793–1851)** German Biblical critic who first prepared a Greek text of the New Testament based on the oldest available manuscripts.

**LACHRYMATORY** Small container holding the tears of mourners.

**LACOMBE, ALBERT (1827–1916)** Canadian CATHOLIC missionary to the Cree and Blackfoot Indians. He translated the New Testament into the Cree language.

**LACORDAIRE, JEAN BAPTISTE (1802–1861)** Liberal French Catholic churchman and preacher. A DOMINICAN, he preached impressively at Notre Dame and advocated church freedom and political reform.

**LACTANTIUS (c.260–c.330)** African Christian apologist who wrote systematic treatises about the faith. He was a MILLENARIAN. His *On the Death of the Persecutors* tells of the terrible deaths of such persecutors as NERO.

**LADY, OUR** CATHOLIC designation for the Blessed Virgin Mary.

**LADY CHAPEL** Chapel dedicated to MARY and often located at the eastern end of a church, behind the high altar.

**LADY DAY** Feast of the ANNUNCIATION, March 25.

**LADY HOUSE** Chapel or niche containing a statue of Our LADY.

**LAESTADIANS** Members of a sect originating in Scandinavian Lutheranism who follow the teachings of Lars Levi Laestadius (1800–1861). They wear a special costume, oppose baptism, prefer lay preachers, and insist on coming to God through other Christians.

**LAETARE SUNDAY** Fourth Sunday in LENT, named for the first word of the INTROIT for that day.

**LA FARGE, JOHN (1880–1963)** American JESUIT author and lecturer. A founder of the National Catholic Rural Life Conference and editor of *America,* he worked for the improvement of race relations.

**LAGARDE, PAUL ANTON DE (1827–1891)** German Bible scholar and orientalist. A brilliant Biblical critic and philologist, he felt that Paul and Luther had obscured the gospel of Jesus, and that the state must help create a new church. He was anti-Semitic.

**LAG B'OMER** *thirty-third day of the omer* Jewish holiday that falls 33 days after an omer (or sheaf) of barley is brought for sacrifice on the second day of PASSOVER. It is a children's festival in Israel and in orthodox communities the only day in the month of Iyar when weddings may be solemnized.

**LAICISM** View that secular government should be totally unrelated to religion.

**LAINEZ, DIEGO (1512–1565)** Spanish ecclesiastic and theologian who helped found the SOCIETY OF JESUS and became one of its generals.

**LAIRESSE, GERARD DE (1641–1711)** Flemish religious painter.

**LAITY** Nonordained members of the church. Although historically PROTESTANTISM has given much greater place to the laity in the church than has CATHOLICISM, there is today a tendency in all churches to emphasize the ministry of the laymen, and to minimize the differences between laity and clergy.

**LAKE, KIRSOPP (1872–1946)** ANGLICAN critic and scholar of the New Testament. He was also interested in church history and archaeology. He held that the MYSTERY RELIGIONS deeply affected early Christianity.

**LAKHAME AND LAKHMU** Two of Babylonia's earliest gods.

**LAKHSMI** Ancient HINDU goddess of luck and beautiful wife of VISHNU.

**LALANDE, JEAN, ST. (?–1646)** French JESUIT martyred on a mission tour among the Mohawk Indians. His feast day is September 26.

**LALEMANT, GABRIEL (1610–1649)** French JESUIT missionary tortured to death by Iroquois Indians in Quebec. His feast day is September 26.

**LALEMANT, JEROME (1593–1673)** French JESUIT missionary among the Huron Indians of North America and director of Jesuit missions in Canada.

**LALITA VISTERA** Biography of the BUDDHA in Sanskrit, apparently dating from the fifth century A.D. It is a principal source of his life in its legendary aspects.

**LAMA** Tibetan priest, saint, or senior member of the Tibetan order of BUDDHISM.

**LAMAISM** BUDDHIST religious system of Tibet, Mongolia, and central Asia. Its strongest organization is the order of the YELLOW HAT, headed by the DALAI LAMA who also rules Tibet. In 1959 under Chinese invasion, the Dalai Lama had to flee to India and Lamaism was suppressed, but Tibet is filled with lamaseries and a large proportion of the citizens are monks or nuns.

**LAMASERY** Monastery or convent for lamas in Asian countries.

**LAMASSU** Babylonian protective spirits.

**LAMB** Biblical and Christian symbol of Christ as the Lamb of God (JOHN 1:29; REVELATION 5:12–13; 19:7–9). Catacomb drawings show a lamb with a cross.

**LAMBARENE** Village in Gabon, Africa, where Albert SCHWEITZER erected a hospital.

**LAMBETH** Borough of London where archbishops of Canterbury for centuries have maintained a London residence, called Lambeth Palace.

**LAMBETH ARTICLES** Nine Calvinistic articles of faith drawn up at Lambeth in 1595 but never formally authorized.

**LAMBETH CONFERENCES** Assemblies of ANGLICAN bishops of the world held approximately every ten years at Lambeth Palace in London. The first was held in 1867.

**LAMBETH DEGREES** Degrees in medicine, divinity, and other fields granted by the archbishop of Canterbury through an act of HENRY VIII.

**LAMBETH PALACE** London residence of the archbishop of Canterbury.

**LAMBETH QUADRILATERAL** Four articles approved by the Lambeth Conference of 1888 as essential to a reunited church. They list the Holy Scriptures, the Apostles' and Nicene Creeds, the sacraments of baptism and the Lord's Supper, and the historic episcopate.

**LAMB OF GOD** Designation of Jesus. See LAMB.

**LAMECH** 1. Father of Tubal, Jubal, and Tubal-cain, whose descendants were nomads, musicians, and metalworkers (GENESIS 4:18–24). 2. Father of Noah (GENESIS 5:25 ff.).

**LAMECH, BOOK OF** Commentary on Genesis discovered among the DEAD SEA SCROLLS.

**LAMED** Twelfth letter in the Hebrew alphabet.

**LAMED-VAV TZADDIKIM** The 36 just men in each generation through whose sufferings, according to the TALMUD, mankind is permitted to continue.

**LAMENNAIS, FELICITE ROBERT DE (1782–1854)** French thinker converted at 22 to CATHOLICISM and soon a brilliant campaigner against GALLICANISM and non-Christian philosophy. Developing liberal ideas about freedom of conscience and the press, and separation of church and state, he was condemned by Gregory XVI and excommunicated. He finally revolted into apparent pantheism and radical socialism.

**LAMENTATIONS OF JEREMIAH** Old Testament book lamenting the destruction of Jerusalem in 586 B.C. The book is in the form of poems, four of them acrostics, ascribing suffering to sin and judgment. It is read in synagogues on the feast of the Ninth of AB.

**LAMMAS** *loaf mass* English festival of wheat harvest when worshipers offered freshly made loaves in church. It occurred August 1.

**LAMP** Symbol of wisdom or piety in religious art.

**LAMY, JEAN BAPTISTE (1814–1888)** Catholic archbishop who labored tirelessly in the southwestern United States.

**LANCE** Knife in the shape of a lance used to cut the bread in Byzantine celebration of the EUCHARIST.

**LANCE, HOLY** Several relics, found through the ages, are believed to be all or part of the lance that pierced Jesus' side (JOHN 19:34). They have been found at Jerusalem, Antioch, and elsewhere. Some of these are now in St. Peter's in Rome.

**LANDMARKISM** Belief of certain BAPTISTS in four principles: *a.* The church is a local entity and there is no single invisible church. *b.* No baptism is valid except that performed by a properly ordained Baptist minister. *c.* Only members of properly constituted Baptist churches are Christians. *d.* There is an apostolic succession of true Baptist churches back to the first churches of the New Testament.

**LAND OF BEULAH** Beautiful region beyond the River of Death in *Pilgrim's Progress.*

**LANFRANC (c.1005–1089)** Italian ecclesiastic who wrote *The Body and Blood of the Lord,* renovated the monastery at Bec, and became Archbishop of Canterbury. A friend of Hildebrand (see GREGORY VII) and teacher of ANSELM, he successfully debated BERENGAR. As archbishop he strengthened and reformed the churches of England.

**LANG, ANDREW (1844–1912)** English student of religion and mythology. Scottish-born, he wrote a book about KNOX and several about Scottish history.

**LANG, COSMO GORDON (1864–1945)** Archbishop of York and of Canterbury. He fought British slum conditions and supported a movement to revise the BOOK OF COMMON PRAYER.

**LANGLAND, WILLIAM (c.1332–c.1400)** Minor English cleric who may have written the famous poem "The Vision of Piers Plowman."

**LANGTON, STEPHEN (c.1155–1228)** Archbishop of Canterbury who encouraged the English barons to make demands which ultimately produced the Magna Carta. A voluminous commentator, he divided the Bible into chapters and probably wrote the hymn "Veni, sancte spiritus" (Come Holy Spirit). H. W. C. Davis called him "perhaps the greatest of our medieval Archbishops."

**LANTERN** Religious symbol of Jesus' betrayal (JOHN 18:3).

**LAODICEA** Wealthy industrial city of Asia Minor and site of a church denounced as being lukewarm and dead (REVELATION 3:14–22). Its name today is Latakia in Turkey.

**LAODICEA, SYNOD OF** Church council which convened about 364 at Laodicea in Phrygia. It drew up a canon of Scripture (omitting Revelation), prohibited the worship of angels, dealt with the treatment of heretics, and treated of penance, liturgy, church order, and Lenten observance.

**LAOS** *people* Theological term for the body of baptized Christians.

**LAO-TZE** *old philosopher* (c.604–?B.C.) Chinese founder of TAOISM, also called Lao-tse and Lao-tzu. Little is known of his life and some scholars doubt that he ever lived. He was apparently a contemporary of, and once met, CONFUCIUS. A court librarian and mystic, Lao-tze pleaded for recognition of and surrender to the ultimate order of things—Tao.

**LAPSI** *the fallen* Theological term for "the Lapsed" who denied their faith under the early persecutions of Christians. Under the guidance of Cyprian, the church decided to readmit such persons following penance and probation. But Novatian and other leaders favored no readmittance of the lapsed and division in the church resulted.

**LARES** Roman tutelary or protective gods or spirits.

**LARGER CATECHISM** 1. Martin LUTHER'S catechism for teachers and clergymen (1529). 2. PRESBYTERIAN catechism prepared by the Westminster Assembly (1647).

**LARK** Symbol of the priesthood in religious art.

**LA SALLE, JEAN BAPTISTE DE** See JOHN BAPTIST DE LA SALLE.

**LAS CASAS, BARTOLOMÉ DE (1474–1566)** "Apostle of the Indies," Spanish missionary who opposed cruelty to the Indians of the new world and throughout his life promoted Indian rights. Working in Cuba, Peru, Guatemala, and Mexico, he succeeded in contrasting the brutality of the conquistadores with the love of Christ.

**LASCO, JOHN** See LASKI, JOHN.

**LASKI, JOHN (1499–1560)** Archbishop of Warsaw whose Calvinistic sympathies and friendship with ERASMUS led to Protestant pastorates in Holland and England. He may have influenced EDWARD VI and the 1552 BOOK OF COMMON PRAYER. He took part in the Protestant reformation in Poland.

**LASSO, ORLANDO DI (c.1532–1594)** Flemish composer of superb Renaissance music, including much in the religious field.

**LAST ADAM** The Apostle Paul's term for Christ (I CORINTHIANS 15:45).

**LAST GOSPEL** Final Gospel portion read in mass. This is usually John 1:1–14.

**LAST JUDGMENT** Final judgment of mankind, when all stand before God for approval or condemnation (cf. REVELATION 20:11–15). See also JUDGMENT.

**LAST SUPPER** Christ's PASSOVER supper with His disciples on the eve of the Crucifixion. At this time the sacrament of the EUCHARIST or communion was instituted.

**LAST THINGS** Theological term for eschatology and the final events of history, including the final judgment and the perfect reign of God.

**LATERAN** 1. Cathedral church of Rome, the basilica of St. John Lateran, possibly originating before 311 A.D. 2. The palace or group of buildings adjoining the Lateran basilica. 3. The papacy.

**LATERAN COUNCIL I** Ninth ECUMENICAL COUNCIL, forbidding ROMAN CATHOLIC clergy to have wives or concubines. It was held in 1123.

**LATERAN COUNCIL II** Tenth ECUMENICAL COUNCIL, held in 1139. It condemned ARNOLD OF BRESCIA, usury, simony, and the use of bows in fighting Christians.

**LATERAN COUNCIL III** Eleventh ECUMENICAL COUNCIL, held in 1179. It restricted the election of a pope to the college of cardinals, provided for a school for clergymen in each cathedral church, and condemned the WALDENSES and ALBIGENSES.

**LATERAN COUNCIL IV** Twelfth ECUMENICAL COUNCIL, held in 1215. It defined the EASTER DUTY, defined the meaning of the EUCHARIST as TRANSUBSTANTIATION, forbade the instituting of new religious orders, and made other important decisions.

**LATERAN COUNCIL V** Eighteenth ECUMENICAL COUNCIL, held 1512–1517. It called for church reform and book censorship, and a war against the Turks.

**LATERAN TREATY** Concordat between Italy and the VATICAN, signed in 1929, settling "the Roman Question." The Holy See recognized the Italian State; the state recognized the Vatican's independence, and ROMAN CATHOLICISM as its "sole religion." Other mutually beneficial provisions were enacted.

**LATHROP, ROSE HAWTHORNE (1851–1926)** Daughter of Nathaniel Hawthorne and founder of a community of Dominican TERTIARIES. She gave much of her life to the relief of cancer victims in the slums of New York.

**LATIMER, HUGH (c.1485–1555)** Bishop of Worcester and English reformer. Although he supported HENRY VIII in his breach with Rome, he enunciated REFORMATION doctrines in his sermons and preached against evil so clearly that he was burned at the stake with his associate Nicholas RIDLEY. His dying words were: "Be of good comfort, Master Ridley, and play the man; we shall this day light such a candle by God's grace in England as I trust shall never be put out."

**LATIN CHRISTIANITY** The ROMAN CATHOLICISM of the Latin countries.

**LATIN CHURCH** Term for the ROMAN CATHOLIC CHURCH, which has for many centuries said mass in Latin and whose pope is usually Italian.

**LATINIZE** To bring into some degree of conformity with the ROMAN CATHOLIC CHURCH.

**LATIN RITE** 1. EASTERN ORTHODOX term for Roman Catholic Christianity. 2. ROMAN CATHOLIC liturgy.

**LATITUDINARIANS** Seventeenth-century English churchmen who expressed a willingness to give up many nonessentials, and everything not specified or countenanced in the Bible, for the unity of as many Christians as possible (not including ROMAN CATHOLICS). Calling for greater "latitude" in doctrine and philosophy, they were scorned by many ANGLICANS as well as many PURITANS. Among their leaders were Tillotson, Chillingworth, Cudworth, and Whichcote.

**LATRIA** Theological term for worship which may be given only God. Compare DULIA.

**LATTER-DAY SAINTS** See CHURCH OF JESUS CHRIST OF LATTER-DAY SAINTS. See also names of specific denominations.

**LAUBACH, FRANK** See LITERACY.

**LAUD, WILLIAM (1573–1645)** Archbishop of Canterbury and HIGH CHURCHMAN who opposed PURITANISM with what he considered the Catholic heritage of the CHURCH OF ENGLAND. Supporting Charles I and the divine right of kings, he sought to Anglicanize the Church of Scotland but failed. He was accused of "Popery," imprisoned for three years in the Tower of London, and beheaded.

**LAUDA SION** SEQUENCE for CORPUS CHRISTI, composed by THOMAS AQUINAS.

**LAUDS** Second hour of the DIVINE OFFICE, the traditional morning prayer of the Western Church.

**LAURA** *alley* Group of cells for hermits.

**LAUREL** Religious symbol of victory and chastity.

**LAURENCE, ST.** See LAWRENCE, ST.

**LAUSANNE CONFERENCE** Assembly of representatives of many churches at Lausanne, Switzerland, in 1927. Unity and differences were discussed, paving the way for further discussion and cooperation.

**LAUS DEO** *praise be to God*

**LAUS PERENNIS** *endless praise* Ancient monastic custom of singing the divine praise so that it continues perpetually.

**LAUS TIBI** *praise be to Thee* Response sung after the reading of the Gospel in the sacrament of the EUCHARIST.

**LAVABO** *I will wash* Ceremony of washing the fingers of the celebrant after the offertory in the mass. The name comes from the recitation of Psalm 26:6–12 (VULGATE: 25:6–12) during the ceremony; the first word in the Latin is *Lavabo*. This may also indicate the basin of water or the towel used in the ceremony.

**LAVATER, JOHANN KASPAR (1741–1801)** Swiss PROTESTANT pastor and MYSTIC, best known for his enthusiasm for physiognomy. He interpreted the Christian faith primarily in terms of personal relationships.

**LAVATORY** Ecclesiastical term for the ritual washing of the celebrant's hands during or after the service. See LAVABO.

**LAVER** 1. Large bronze vessel used for priestly ablutions in the Jewish tabernacle. There were lavers in Solomon's temple. 2. Ecclesiastical vessel for washing. 3. Portion of a religious house set apart for ablutions.

**LAVIGERIE, CHARLES MARTIAL ALLEMAND** (1825–1892) French CATHOLIC cardinal who fed and provided for many starving orphans in Algiers and was given spiritual jurisdiction over all equatorial Africa. He evangelized many MOSLEMS, opposed slavery and the philosophy of royalism, and founded the Sahara and Sudan mission or Society of Missionaries of Africa.

**LAW** 1. Jewish term for the PENTATEUCH, or for the Scriptures. 2. Christian term for JUDAISM, or for salvation by works as opposed to salvation by grace through faith unto good works, or for the DECALOGUE, or for the Jewish ceremonial law. 3. Other meanings of law in a religious context are treated elsewhere in this book.

**LAW, ANDREW (c. 1749–1821)** Minister and composer; one of the first American hymn writers.

**LAW, CANON** See CANON LAW.

**LAW, CHURCH** See CANON LAW.

**LAW, CIVIL** See CIVIL LAW.

**LAW, MORAL** See MORAL LAW.

**LAW, MOSAIC** See MOSAIC LAW.

**LAW, NATURAL** See NATURAL LAW.

**LAW, ORAL** See ORAL LAW.

**LAW, WILLIAM (1686–1761)** ANGLICAN clergyman; "The English Mystic." Refusing to swear an oath of allegiance to George I, he was deprived of the fellowship he had been granted at Cambridge. His controversial theological writings are overshadowed by his mystical and devotional works such as his famous *Serious Call to a Devout and Holy Life*. He influenced John WESLEY and George WHITEFIELD and was himself influenced, in his later works, by Jacob BOEHME. His writings still live. His feast day is April 6.

**LAWRENCE** See BROTHER LAWRENCE.

**LAWRENCE, ST. (?–258)** Roman deacon said to have given the treasures of the church to the poor rather than hand them over to the civil authorities. For this he was martyred—according to tradition by being burned, but according to modern scholars, by being beheaded. A popular martyr and saint, he is honored with a feast day on August 10.

**LAWRENCE, WILLIAM (1850–1941)** EPISCOPAL bishop, in the United States. A liberal churchman, he founded the pension system of his denomination and wrote several biographies.

**LAWYER** KING JAMES BIBLE word for Jewish scribe or authority on the Jewish law.

**LAY** Ecclesiastical term for a church member not ordained to special office. See LAITY.

**LAY ABBOT** Layman placed in charge of an ABBEY. There were lay abbots in the medieval Western Church, and lay abbots may be named still in the Eastern Church.

**LAY BAPTISM** BAPTISM administered by a layman. In some communions this is permissible in emergencies when a clergyman cannot be present.

**LAY BROTHER** Nonordained member of a religious order. He is not bound to recite the holy office and often performs manual labor.

**LAY CLERK** Layman who leads the service of worship.

**LAY CONFESSION** Confession of one's sins to another person who is not a clergyman. ROMAN CATHOLICISM permitted this in the Middle Ages in special circumstances, as when no priest was available.

**LAYING ON OF HANDS** Imparting spiritual blessing or authority by laying the hands of one qualified, usually a bishop, on the head of the recipient in dedication, consecration, etc. In ANGLICANISM the laying on of hands is a part of confirmation, healing, blessing, and ordination. CATHOLIC practice is similar, the Catholic term being imposition of hands. Various PROTESTANT churches require the laying on of hands at ordination. Biblical precedents may be found in Genesis 48; Acts 8:17; 13:3; 19:6; I Timothy 4:14; Matthew 9:25; Mark 16:18.

**LAYMAN** See LAITY.

**LAYMEN'S ORGANIZATIONS** There are many of these in religious groups. The activity of laymen in advancing the mission of the church appears to be increasing in most denominations.

**LAY READER** ANGLICAN term for a layman licensed by a bishop to lead worship services.

**LAY RECTOR** ANGLICAN term for a layman who receives a church's rectorial TITHES, occupies the chief seat in the chancel, and must maintain and repair the chancel.

**LAY TITHES** TITHES paid not to a church but to a secular proprietor.

**LAZA** Portion of hell peopled, according to ISLAM, with Christians.

**LAZARISTS or LAZARITES** Members of the CATHOLIC order founded by St. VINCENT DE PAUL in 1625, "Congregation of Priests of the Mission." Instituted to conduct missions and retreats in France, they have seminaries, missions, and other work in many parts of the world.

**LAZARUS** 1. Friend of Jesus from Bethany, a brother of Mary and Martha. He fell sick and died; four days later he responded as Jesus called him out of the sepulcher in which his bound corpse had been placed (JOHN 11; 12). 2. In one of Jesus' parables, a poor man who enjoyed paradise while the rich man at whose steps he had begged was tormented in hell (LUKE 16:19–25).

**LAZARUS, EMMA (1849–1887)** American Jewish poetess. A spokesman for her faith, she translated several medieval Jewish poems. Her sonnet "The New Colossus" is engraved on the Statue of Liberty.

**LEA, HENRY CHARLES (1825–1909)** American historian who wrote seven volumes on the INQUISITION and other works on CATHOLICISM.

**LEAD or LEADE, JANE (1623–1704)** English MYSTIC whose followers formed the Philadelphian Society for the Advancement of Piety and Divine Philosophy. See PHILADELPHIANS. She wrote several books but believed it wrong to work for a living and died in an almshouse.

**LEAGUE, GERMAN CATHOLIC** Seventeenth-century confederation of ROMAN CATHOLIC states against the PROTESTANT UNION. This was a prelude to the Thirty Years' War.

**LEAGUE, HOLY** Sixteenth-century French CATHOLIC organization which sought to suppress PROTESTANTISM. Sparked by the activity of the HUGUENOTS, it threatened the supremacy of the king before it came to an end.

**LEAH** *gazelle* First wife of Jacob, of "tender [weak?] eyes" (GENESIS 29–30).

**LEATHER** Common writing surface in Bible times. The DEAD SEA SCROLLS were of animal skin.

**LEAVEN** Agent of fermentation used in baking in Bible times. Leaven was forbidden in certain Jewish rites and was a symbol of human corruption in Jewish theology. Jesus referred to its pervasive power in a parable (MATTHEW 13:33), comparing it to the Kingdom.

**LEBANON** Syrian mountain range whose lordly cedars provided wood for the Hebrew temple and other buildings.

**LEBBAEUS** One of the Apostles; apparently another name of the Judas who was not Iscariot.

**LECHEM HA-PANIM** *bread of His face* Twelve loaves in the Jewish sanctuary symbolizing the twelve tribes of Israel.

**LE CLERC, JEAN (1657–1736)** Swiss PROTESTANT preacher and theologian. An ARMINIAN, he insisted on scientific investigation of the origins and interpretation of the Scriptures. He denied that MOSES wrote the Pentateuch and did not believe that Ecclesiastes and certain other books were divinely inspired. He defended free thought and human reason.

**LECTERN** Church reading desk; in traditionally styled churches, opposite the pulpit. It is often in the shape of an eagle.

**LECTERN BIBLE** Bible with large type for easy public reading.

**LECTION** Bible lesson read in divine service.

**LECTIONARY** List or book of Scripture lessons for public worship, usually for the church year.

**LECTOR** *reader* One who reads the lessons in a church service. In CATHOLICISM lectors constitute a minor order. In ANGLICAN churches a lector is a layman licensed to read the Scriptures.

**LEE, ANN (1736–1784)** Founder of the SHAKERS. Attracted to the Shaking Quakers in England, she came to be accepted as God's final revelation to man and founded the first Shaker settlement in the United States at Watervliet, New York. She proclaimed perfect SANCTIFICATION and sexual abstinence. The Shaker communities she headed practiced communism, forbade marriage, and are now almost extinct.

**LEE, JESSE (1758–1816)** "Apostle of Methodism in New England." A circuit-riding preacher and assistant to Francis ASBURY, he wrote a *Short History of Methodism in America*.

**LEE, JOHN DOYLE (1812–1877)** American MORMON leader, executed for his part in the massacre at Mountain Meadows, Utah, of more than 100 pioneers bound for California.

**LEE, ROWLAND (?–1543)** English bishop who helped HENRY VIII get his divorce from Catherine of Aragon and is believed to have officiated at Henry's secret marriage to Anne Boleyn. He was one of the first in England to recognize the king as the new head of the church.

**LEGALISM** 1. Emphasis on the letter rather than the spirit of the law. 2. Belief in salvation by obedience to the law rather than by the grace of God or by faith. 3. Undue stress on legal details without balancing considerations of justice or mercy.

**LEGATE** Envoy. A papal legate is a personal representative of the pope. Papal legates may be nuncios, similar to ambassadors; *legati a latere*, sent on special temporary missions; or *legati nati*, who hold offices to which belong the status of a legate.

**LEGBA** Personal phallic god of a native of Dahomey, West Africa.

**LEGEND** Traditional story, often of religious importance but of questionable historicity. However, a legend may well be based on actual events. The word *legend* may designate the story of a saint, or a collection of lives of saints.

**LEGION** Roman division of 6,000 soldiers, mentioned several times in the New Testament (MARK 5:9; MATTHEW 26:53).

**LEIBNIZ, GOTTFRIED WILHELM (1646–1716)** German rationalist philosopher who termed this "the best of all possible worlds." He saw the universe as consisting of simple windowless monads, ultimately indivisible substances or centers of force, arranged in an ascending order culminating in the Supreme Monad, God. God is the source of all, he held, but evil is a necessary part of the world.

**LEIGHTON, ROBERT (1611–1684)** Scottish preacher and Archbishop of Glasgow who sought unsuccessfully to unite PRESBYTERIANISM and EPISCOPACY. A saintly Presbyterian, he was accused of CATHOLIC sympathies and was attacked by both Presbyterians and ANGLICANS.

**LEIPZIG INTERIM** MELANCTHON's compromise between PROTESTANTISM and CATHOLICISM. Opposed by both Protestants and the pope, it was finally abandoned.

**LEMON** Symbol of faithfulness in religious art.

**LEMUEL** Unknown king of Proverbs 31:1–9.

**LEMURES** Evil spirits of the deceased in Roman religion.

**LENT** *spring* The forty days of preparation for Easter beginning with Ash Wednesday. Traditionally marked by penance and fasting, it was relieved of the latter in 1966 by papal announcement. The only fasting now required of ROMAN CATHOLICS in Lent, apart from the usual Friday requirements, is on Ash Wednesday and Good Friday. To most PROTESTANTS Lent is less a time of privation than of consecration. Quadragesima is the Latin name for Lent.

**LEO I, ST. (c.400–461)** "Leo the Great," pope (440–461) who saved Italy from destruction by the Hun invaders. A DOCTOR OF THE CHURCH, he defined Christ in terms adopted by the Council of CHALCEDON in 451: one Person with two natures. His feast day is April 11.

**LEO III, ST. (?–816)** Pope (795–816) who crowned Charlemagne emperor and beautified Rome. His feast day is June 12.

**LEO IX, ST. (1002–1054)** German pope (1049–1054) whose advisers included Hildebrand (see GREGORY VII) and St. Peter DAMIAN. He condemned BERENGAR OF TOURS and excommunicated MICHAEL CERULARIUS; the latter's denial of Leo's claims to be pope initiated the East-West schism. A forceful reformer, he is remembered with a feast day on April 19.

**LEO X (1475–1521)** Florentine pope (1513–1521) who patronized Raphael and called the Fifth LATERAN COUNCIL. He condemned Martin LUTHER's doctrines with the bull *Exsurge Domine*, but he granted HENRY VIII of England the title

"Defender of the Faith." While he was a cardinal, SAVONAROLA was tortured and hanged. Leo was a son of Lorenzo de Medici.

**LEO XIII (1810–1903)** Pope (1878–1903) who appointed John Henry NEWMAN and James GIBBONS cardinals, ended the KULTURKAMPF, approved the philosophy of THOMAS AQUINAS, encouraged mission activity, and sought to apply Christianity to social questions. In 1899 he censured what he termed AMERICANISM. In 1900 he consecrated the human race to the Heart of Jesus.

**LEON, LUIS PONCE DE (1527–1591)** Spanish MYSTIC and poet. He was imprisoned by the INQUISITION for criticizing the VULGATE and translating the Song of Solomon.

**LEON, MOSES DE (?–1305)** Jewish cabalist, author of the *Zohar*.

**LEONARDO DA VINCI (1452–1519)** Italian inventor, scholar, and painter of outstanding religious scenes including "The Last Supper," "The Virgin of the Rocks," and "St. John the Baptist."

**LEOPARD** Symbol of evil in religious art.

**LEOPOLD III (c.1073–1136)** "Leo the Pious," patron saint of Austria who founded a number of monasteries and participated in arrangements for the Concordat of Worms.

**LESHON HA-KODESH the holy tongue** Hebrew term for Hebrew.

**LESSING, GOTTHOLD EPHRAIM (1729–1781)** German writer and philosopher who repudiated CHRISTIANITY and held that religion is basically humanitarianism. He found the same fundamental purpose in Christianity, Judaism, and Islam.

**LESSON** Portion of Scripture (or, in CATHOLICISM, of some other ecclesiastical writing) read at divine service.

**LE SUEUR, EUSTACHE (1616–1655)** French religious painter and a founder of the French Academy of Painting and Sculpture.

**LETHE** River in the Greeks' HADES which brought forgetfulness to those who drank from it.

**LETO** Mother of the Greek gods ARTEMIS and APOLLO.

**LETTERS COMMENDATORY** Letters from an ecclesiastical superior to a cleric who is traveling, asserting his integrity of doctrine and morality.

**LETTERS DIMISSORY** Letters from a bishop permitting a candidate for holy orders to be ordained in another diocese.

**LETTERS OF ORDERS** Certificate from a bishop attesting the ordination of one who has entered holy orders.

**LEUCETIOS** Celtic thunder god.

**LEUCOTHEA** Greek sea goddess.

**LEVELERS** Seventeenth-century followers of John Lilburne in England. Opposing monarchy, the privileges of the nobility, and church establishment, they demanded radical reform: toleration of all religions and of atheism; complete separation of church and state; universal male suffrage; proportional representation; a single representative body with supreme powers; complete equality before the law. The movement was attacked and its leaders tried for treason, and it had nearly disappeared by 1660.

**LEVI joined** Son of Jacob who helped his brother Simeon destroy Shechem when he raped their sister Dinah (GENESIS 34). He fathered the tribe of LEVITES and had three sons who became heads of tribes: GERSHON, KOHATH, and Merari. Levi was also a name of St. Matthew and of other Bible figures.

**LEVIATHAN** Large sea creature mentioned in the Old Testament, possibly a crocodile (JOB 41; PSALM 74:14; ISAIAH 27:1; cf. REVELATION 11:7; 12:3). It symbolized evil.

**LEVINDANTO, NIKOLAI (1896–1966)** Baptist administrator in Baltic Europe and president of the UNION OF EVANGELICAL CHRISTIANS—BAPTISTS.

**LEVIRATE MARRIAGE** Marriage to a man's brother's widow, required by the law of Moses (DEUTERONOMY 25:5–10).

**LEVITES** Descendants of LEVI, having special responsibilities in the temple worship of Israel. Their three divisions corresponded to Levi's three sons—Gershonites, Kohathites, and Merarites. A privileged religious caste, they were given special TITHES and revenues from various cities as assigned.

**LEVITICUS of Levites** Third book in the Old Testament, traditionally attributed to MOSES. It deals with the Mosaic sacrifices, priesthood, and ceremonial laws. Leviticus is in the narrower sense one of the most religious books in the Bible. Its nineteenth chapter sets forth very high moral and social obligations.

**LEVY-BRUHL, LUCIEN (1857–1939)** French philosopher who specialized in the study of primitive peoples—their modes of thought and their beliefs concerning the supernatural.

**LEWIS, CLIVE STAPLES (1898–1963)** English CHRISTIAN writer and apologist. In addition to Christian juveniles and science fiction, he wrote *Miracles, The Case for Christianity, The Screwtape Letters,* and other books. He was immensely popular in England and the United States, making Christian theology comprehensible to the masses.

**LEX TALIONIS** *law of retaliation* The "eye for an eye" rule of Exodus 21:23 ff., which placed a limit upon permissible retaliation. Considered primitive today, it set a standard at the time for justice and human respect.

**LHA** Deity or good spirit in Tibetan BUDDHISM. LHASA means "Land of the Lhas."

**LHASA** Tibet's "Forbidden City," the center of Lamaism until China's 1951 invasion. It contains a number of temples, two palaces of the DALAI LAMA, and the DREPUNG monastery—one of the world's largest monasteries. Two other important Lamaist monasteries are nearby. The Jokang temple, three stories high, contains a great jewelled image of the BUDDHA and many statues of gods and goddesses. New Year festivities in Lhasa last for fifteen days.

**LIBATION** Liquid such as wine poured out in sacrifice to a god.

**LIBER** Roman god of wine and fertility, corresponding to Greece's BACCHUS.

**LIBERAL CATHOLIC CHURCH** Religious group formed in England in 1916, combining CATHOLICISM and THEOSOPHY. Members in the United States divided into two groups in 1947.

**LIBERAL EVANGELICALISM** A trend within the Church of England's evangelical movement defending the use of modern knowledge and criticism in Christianity.

**LIBERALISM** Religious term for emphasis on the use of reason, science, and contemporary applications of doctrine, in contrast to conservatism which emphasizes faith, tradition, and dogma, without too

much concern for science or application. Religious liberalism often emphasizes human goodness and progress while conservatism stresses human inability to progress or to do good works without divine aid.

**LIBERAL RELIGION** UNITARIAN-UNIVERSALIST term for rejection of all dogma and orthodoxy and adoption of what amounts to a humanistic-agnostic philosophy of life.

**LIBER PONTIFICALIS** *papal book* Book of biographies of early popes. The first edition appeared in the sixth century, and later editions have added additional papal lives.

**LIBERTAS** Roman goddess of liberty.

**LIBERTINES** 1. Freethinkers. 2. Dissolute or morally undisciplined persons. 3. Men of the synagogue of the Libertines in Jerusalem who opposed St. Stephen (ACTS 6:9). Their name may indicate that their ancestors had been freed slaves. 4. "Perrinists" who fought John Calvin's attempts to reform Geneva. 5. Sixteenth-century ANTINOMIANS of France, Holland, and Flanders who held that good is basically the same as evil.

**LIBIDO** Psychoanalytical term for primal instinctive energy closely allied to the sexual drive.

**LIBITINA** Ancient Roman goddess of death.

**LICENSED PREACHER** One granted permission by his church to preach.

**LICENTIATE** 1. Protestant authorized to preach but not yet ordained to full ministerial status. 2. Friar empowered to hear confessions and grant absolution.

**LICH GATE** *corpse gate* Gate in a churchyard wall at which the body of the deceased is placed before the interment.

**LIDDELL, HENRY GEORGE (1811–1898)** Anglican scholar who with Robert Scott prepared the famous Greek lexicon which is still a standard reference work.

**LIDDON, HENRY PARRY (1829–1890)** Popular Anglican clergyman who had great influence and who sought to restore CATHOLIC principles to the CHURCH OF ENGLAND.

**LIEBNER, CARL THEODOR ALBERT (1806–1871)** German theologian who held that God may be known in mysticism and that Christ is the center of history.

**LIETZMANN, HANS (1875–1942)** German LUTHERAN theologian and church historian.

**LIFE** The vital principle in animate creatures which indicates a special link with God. Many religions inculcate reverence for life, and even animals kill only for food or in self-defense. The Judeo-Christian tradition maintains that life is a special gift of God, raised to its highest power only by God. Jesus claimed to be "the Life" (JOHN 14:6).

**LIFE, THE BOOK OF** 1. Heavenly list of the redeemed (PHILIPPIANS 4:3; REVELATION 21:27). 2. List of Christians in the early church (sometimes called a diptych, or Liber Vitae).

**LIFE AND ADVENT UNION** ADVENTIST group formed by John T. Walsh in the United States in 1848.

**LIFE AND WORK** Term for that part of the ecumenical movement interested particularly in the application of Christianity to social and practical life. World conferences "on Life and Work" were held at Stockholm and Oxford in 1925 and 1937, respectively.

**LIGHT** Ancient symbol of God and immortality. Christ claimed to be the light of the world (JOHN 8:12). In Christian art, light is a symbol of Christ.

**LIGHTS, FEAST OF** See HANUKKAH.

**LIGHTFOOT, JOSEPH BARBER (1828–1889)** ANGLICAN theologian, New Testament scholar, and student of the APOSTOLIC FATHERS. He helped prepare the REVISED VERSION of the New Testament (1881).

**LIGUORI, ALFONSO MARIA DE** See ALPHONSUS LIGURI.

**LILIENTHAL, MAX (1815–1882)** American leader of REFORM JUDAISM.

**LILITH** Female evil spirit in Jewish mythology. She was said to be Adam's first wife and a child-killer.

**LILLIBULLERO** Seventeenth-century English song deriding Irish Catholics.

**LILY** Flower, in Christian art symbolizing purity, immortality, and the Virgin Mary.

**LILY OF THE VALLEY** Religious symbol of both the IMMACULATE CONCEPTION and ADVENT.

**LIMBO** *edge* CATHOLIC name for the abode of souls kept from heaven through no fault of their own and therefore not consigned to hell.

**LIMBO OF CHILDREN** Eternal abode of unbaptized infants, according to ROMAN CATHOLICISM. Some earlier theologians held that it was a cheerless underground cavern but contemporary Catholicism tends to the position that it is a place of natural happiness.

**LIMBO OF THE FATHER** Term for the abode of those just men who died before the time of Christ, who opened heaven to them.

**LINDSEY, THEOPHILUS (1723–1808)** ANGLICAN clergyman who came to doubt the TRINITY, resigned his living, and became a UNITARIAN.

**LINGAM or LINGA** Representation of the male organ. Statues of the lingam, erected for religious purposes, abounded in ancient Canaan and India, and emblems of it represent the Hindu God SIVA. The lingam is worshiped throughout India, and was formerly used in the marriage ceremony.

**LINGAYATS** Hindu sect whose members worship only SIVA and always carry a stone LINGAM with them.

**LING CHOS** Ancient Tibetan mythology.

**LINUS** Friend of Paul and Timothy (II TIMOTHY 4:21). Catholic tradition names St. LINUS the first pope after St. Peter and some of the fathers identified the two Linuses as the same person.

**LINUS, ST. (first century)** Roman martyr who followed Peter on the papal throne, according to CATHOLIC tradition. His feast day is September 23.

**LION** Biblical symbol of royalty, might, and deity (GENESIS 49:9; JOB 10:16; JEREMIAH 25:30). Jesus was described as the lion of the tribe of Judah (REVELATION 5:5). A traditional symbol of royalty, in the Middle Ages the lion also symbolized John MARK. A winged lion often represents Mark today.

**LI PO (c.700–762)** TAOIST Chinese poet whose love of nature expresses that of many Japanese and Chinese.

**LIPPI, FILIPPINO (c.1457–1504)** Son of Fra Filippo LIPPI who also excelled in many religious paintings, particularly church frescoes and altarpieces.

**LIPPI, FRA FILIPPO (c.1406–1469)** Italian painter of many Christian themes. Botticelli was one of his pupils.

**LIR or LIYR** Gaelic god of the ocean.

**LISLE, GEORGE (c.1750–c.1845)** American slave who became the first Negro preacher in America, the first Negro missionary of record, and the first of his race to send missionaries back to Africa. He founded the first Negro Baptist church in Savannah, Georgia, and the first Negro Baptist church in Jamaica.

**LISSA** Goddess of Dahomey, Africa, who was mother of the sun and moon.

**LITANY** *prayer* Prayer of supplication in which the clergyman's petitions are interspersed with responses by the congregation or choir.

**LITANY DESK** Low desk at which the LITANY may be offered.

**LITANY OF LORETO** LITANY honoring the Virgin Mary.

**LITANY OF THE SAINTS** LITANY addressed to the Father, the Son, the Holy Spirit, the Virgin, and various prophets, saints, angels, and others (to the latter for intercession).

**LITERACY** Special concern of the church in the twentieth century. While literacy has been important in much modern mission work, it was especially publicized by Dr. Frank Laubach after the 1920's. The WORLD COUNCIL OF CHURCHES has a committee on World Literacy and Christian Literature.

**LITERALISM** Emphasis on the exact letter, particularly of Scripture.

**LITERATE** ANGLICAN clergyman who has no university degree.

**LITTLE OFFICE** Short service in honor of the Blessed Virgin.

**LITTLE YOM KIPPUR** Occasion such as the eve of ROSH CHODESH when part of the Yom Kippur ritual is recited (see ATONEMENT, DAY OF).

**LITURGICAL ALTAR** Ecclesiastical altar or table with no shelf or retable behind it.

**LITURGICAL COLORS** Colors used at different times in the liturgical year. They are white, red, green, purple, and black. (See each.) Purple is the common color for LENT and ADVENT, and other colors are used at other seasons.

**LITURGICAL MOVEMENT** Effort in the churches to restore lay participation in worship and activity. The RITUALIST MOVEMENT in ANGLICANISM and the Hochkirche of Germany are different phases of the trend, which was accelerated by VATICAN COUNCIL II.

**LITURGICAL PRAYER** Formal prayer or use of the CANONICAL HOURS.

**LITURGICS** Science or study of worship and liturgies.

**LITURGIST** 1. Advocate of or authority on liturgy. 2. One who conducts the liturgy in a service of prayer or worship.

**LITURGY** 1. Prescribed form for public worship. 2. The eucharistic rite (order for communion or mass).

**LIVINGSTONE, DAVID (1813–1873)** Scottish PRESBYTERIAN explorer and missionary of Africa. He opened that continent to Christianity and civilization. A tireless worker able to inspire limitless enthusiasm in others, he died in Africa and was buried in Westminster Abbey.

**LIYR** See LIR.

**L.M.S.** Abbreviation for the LONDON MISSIONARY SOCIETY.

**LO** KING JAMES BIBLE term for "Behold!"

**LOCAL PREACHER** METHODIST term for one licensed to preach in a certain place.

**LOCHNER, STEPHAN (c.1400–1451)** Distinguished German religious painter.

**LOCKE, JOHN (1632–1704)** English philosopher. Rejecting the philosophy that children have innate ideas, he emphasized the acquisition of knowledge through the senses. He stood for freedom of religion, and the natural rights of men in government. He held that God may be found through reason, which is the only sure foundation of Christianity.

**LOCULUS** 1. Niche in an altar for relics. 2. Large niche in the wall of a catacomb for Christian burial.

**LOCUM TENENS** *holding the place* Temporary rector of a parish.

**LODGE, OLIVER JOSEPH (1851–1940)** English scientist who sought to reconcile science with religion and to prove the existence of a world of departed spirits.

**LOFN** Scandinavian goddess of love.

**LOGIA** *the sayings* 1. Hypothetical early collection of the sayings of Jesus, the basis of the four Gospels. 2. Group of sayings, attributed to Jesus, discovered at the turn of the twentieth century at Oxyrhyncus, Egypt.

**LOGOS** Greek word for word, reason, or revelation. In the Gospel of John it indicates Christ as "the Word," the complete Revelation of God to man, yet eternally existent. Pre-Christian Greek philosophers had spoken of Logos as a universal, eternal, immanent force in the world. The

Jewish TARGUMS spoke of the MEMRA, "Word," as God's activity and expression. Gnosticism conceived of the Logos as a force uniting God and man.

**LÖHE, WILHELM (1808–1872)** German LUTHERAN leader and liturgist. He organized the Missouri and Iowa synods for Lutheran immigrants to America, established a theological seminary in Australia, and influenced the Lutheran liturgical movement.

**LOIS** Godly grandmother of Timothy (II TIMOTHY 1:5).

**LOISY, ALFRED (1857–1940)** French Biblical critic and Catholic MODERNIST. Rejecting the teaching that Christ instituted the church and sacraments, he was excommunicated after several of his books were banned. Thereafter he taught the history of religions and maintained that Christianity was strongly influenced in its origins by the ancient MYSTERY RELIGIONS. Loisy has been called the founder of MODERNISM in France.

**LOKA** 1. HINDU term for a portion of the universe, as the earth or heaven. The highest region is the abode of Brahma, Satyloka. 2. Hindu term for the alluring material world.

**LOKAYATAS** HINDUS who held that only matter is real, only sensual happiness counts, and there is nothing beyond the material world. There were once many Lokayatas in India but none are known today. Also called Charvakas.

**LOKESVARA** Term for BUDDHA as Lord of the World.

**LOKI** Scandinavian god of evil who caused the death of BALDER, deserted the heavenly council, and was to bring about the doom of the gods.

**LOLLARDS** *psalm singers* Disciples of John WYCLIF in fourteenth- and fifteenth-century England. Making the authority of the Bible supreme, they went over the countryside proclaiming salvation by faith and denying the validity of indulgences, pilgrimages, transubstantiation, the ecclesiastical hierarchy, and much else that was dear to Catholic Englishmen. A number of Lollards were burned at the stake during the reign of Henry IV and eventually the movement was suppressed. Also called Wycliffites.

**LOMBARD, PETER** See PETER LOMBARD.

**LONDON BUDDHIST VIHARA** Center for HINAYANA or Theravada Buddhism in London, England, opened in 1954.

**LONDON MISSIONARY SOCIETY** Organization founded in 1795 by an interdenominational group for propagating the gospel among the heathen. Still active, the Society is now supported largely by CONGREGATIONALISTS.

**LONDON YEARLY MEETING** British QUAKER group.

**LONGFELLOW, SAMUEL (1819 – 1892)** American hymn writer and UNITARIAN minister. A brother of Henry Wadsworth Longfellow, he wrote "Now on Land and Sea Descending," "God of the Earth, the Sky, the Sea!" and other hymns.

**LONGINUS** Traditional name of the Roman soldier whose spear pierced the side of Jesus.

**LONGSUFFERING** KING JAMES BIBLE word for patient endurance, an important virtue.

**LORD** 1. Master or ruler. 2. Ancient name for deity. BAAL, ALLAH, and YAHWEH all indicate Lord God. 3. Christian designation of Jesus. 4. Occasional ecclesiastical title, as of a bishop. "Rabbi" means master or teacher. (Note: While the Bible indicates various meanings of *lord*, it gives this title in a unique sense to God and to the Lord Jesus Christ.)

**LORD, OUR** Jesus Christ.

**LORD HIGH COMMISSIONER** The royal representative to the General Assembly of Scotland's established church.

**LORD OF HOSTS** Divine title used nearly 300 times in the Old Testament. It apparently indicates Jehovah's leadership of armies celestial and terrestrial in His cause.

**LORD OF MISRULE** One appointed to rule the medieval English Christmastime festivities.

**LORD'S ACRE** See GOD'S ACRE.

**LORD'S DAY** The Jewish SABBATH was a day especially set apart as holy to the Lord God. The term *Lord's Day*, however, is a special Christian term for Sunday as the day on which Christ's resurrection is honored. (Cf. REVELATION 1:10.)

**LORD'S PRAYER** The prayer given by Jesus when His disciples asked, "Lord, teach us to pray." It has been said that all its elements appear in the Hebrew KADDISH. The form in which Jesus cast them, however, produced a prayer of unique beauty and importance. Slightly different versions of the prayer occur in Matthew 6:9–13 and Luke 11:2–4. It is generally agreed that the doxology at the end of Matthew's version represents an ancient ecclesiastical response that became attached after the prayer originated.

**LORDS SPIRITUAL**  British title of bishops who sit in the House of Lords.

**LORD'S SUPPER**  The New Testament sacrament or ordinance of communion or the EUCHARIST (cf. MARK 14:17–26; I CORINTHIANS 11:23–26).

**LORD'S TABLE**  1. Synonym for the Lord's Supper or EUCHARIST (cf. I CORINTHIANS 10:21). 2. REFORMED term for the table from which communion is served. 3. Occasional ANGLICAN term for the altar.

**LORENZO, MONACO (c.1370–1425)**  Important Italian artist of the Renaissance who produced many ecclesiastical paintings.

**LORETO**  Italian town to which angels are said to have brought the house of the Virgin Mary from Nazareth in 1295. A number of miracles have been reported at the Holy House of Loreto.

**LORETTO NUNS**  Congregation of the Sisters of Loretto at the Foot of the Cross. This is a Catholic order, noted for its unusual devotion to education, founded in 1822 in Ireland by Mrs. Mary Teresa Ball.

**LOSNA**  Etruscan goddess of the moon.

**LOST BOOKS OF THE BIBLE**  Popular name for APOCRYPHA or other writings not in the canonical Scriptures.

**LOST TRIBES**  Jews carried into captivity after the fall of Israel c.722 B.C. whose descendants never returned to Palestine. Various theories have been proposed to account for the present whereabouts of the descendants of these lost tribes: e.g., that they are to be identified with the British or with the American Indians.

**LOT**  Ancient manner of determining the answer to a question. The gods might be appealed to when a stone or lot was cast on the ground, its final position indicating the answer. The Bible indicates considerable use of the lot; the Hebrew URIM AND THUMMIM may have involved sacred lots. The Apostles cast lots to determine a successor to Judas Iscariot (ACTS 1:26) and John Wesley cast lots to determine whether he should marry.

**LOT** *wrapping*  Abraham's nephew, the son of Abraham's brother Haran. He accompanied Abraham from Ur of the Chaldees to Egypt and Canaan. Offered his choice of the land, he took the rich garden-like territory near the Dead Sea; at the destruction of Sodom his wife was turned to a rocky pillar and the land of Lot became worthless. His two sons fathered the Moabites and Ammonites. (GENESIS 11— 14; 19).

**LOTS, FEAST OF**  See PURIM.

**LOTTO, LORENZO (c.1480–1556)**  Sensitive Venetian painter of numerous ecclesiastical scenes.

**LOTUS**  Flower associated in ancient Egypt with the sacred Nile and in Assyria with the sacred tree. BUDDHISTS and HINDUS regard it as highly sacred and symbolic. A prominent formula in LAMAISM is: "Ah! The jewel is indeed in the lotus!"

**LOTUS OF THE TRUE LAW**  Important scripture of MAHAYANA Buddhism dating from the second century A.D. It presents BUDDHA as eternal truth (DHARMA) and extols sainthood as conforming to the laws of reality.

**LOTZE, RUDOLF HERMANN (1817–1881)**  Theistic German philosopher who maintained that only a personal God can unite the disparate realms of fact, law, and moral values.

**LOUIS IX (1214–1270)**  A Crusader and king of France, he led a simple and prayerful personal life, and insisted that every man—whatever his station—must be treated fairly. Christians and Moslems alike recognized his worth; he has been called the "ideal medieval Christian monarch." He was canonized in 1297 and is honored with a feast day August 25.

**LOUNSBERY, G. CONSTANT (twentieth century)**  American woman who founded *Les Amis du Bouddhisme*, French Buddhist headquarters, in Paris in 1929. She wrote *Buddhist Meditation in the Southern School*.

**LOURDES**  Town in France where Our Lady of Lourdes appeared to St. BERNADETTE in 1858 and where many miraculous healings have been reported. Nearly a million visitors come to Lourdes each year.

**LOUVAIN**  Leading CATHOLIC educational center in central Belgium, famous for its university, the church of St. Peter, and other medieval churches.

**LOVE** A supreme virtue in CHRISTIANITY and JUDAISM. The latter, with Jesus, elevated the two commandments of love of God and one's neighbor. Love is greater than faith or hope (I CORINTHIANS 13:13). God is love (I JOHN 4:8). See also BENEVOLENCE 1.

**LOVE FEAST** A common early Christian term for the EUCHARIST or the Lord's Supper. It is still used occasionally.

**LOVEJOY, ELIJAH P. (1802–1837)** American PRESBYTERIAN minister, editor, and abolitionist. For printing his views against slavery, he was mobbed and slain. This greatly increased popular feeling against the slave trade.

**LOVING-KINDNESS** Old Testament word for the kindly mercies of God.

**LOW CHURCH** Anglican term for emphasis on the gospel and simple worship. Low Churchmen are relatively uninterested in elaborate ritual and accommodation of religion to scientific thought; in England they are often called Evangelicals, in contrast to High Churchmen and Broad Churchmen.

**LOWER CRITICISM** Textual criticism of the Bible. Cf. HIGHER CRITICISM.

**LOW MASS** Simplified ritual of the EUCHARIST, said but not sung.

**LOW SUNDAY** First Sunday after Easter. The name may have originated in contrast to the high nature with which Easter has been traditionally regarded.

**LOYOLA, IGNATIUS, ST.** See IGNATIUS OF LOYOLA, ST.

**LOYSON, CHARLES** See HYACINTHE, FATHER.

**L.TH.** Abbreviation for "Licentiate in Theology," the degree given by a theological seminary to a candidate for ordination to the ministry.

**LUCARIS, CYRIL (1572–1637)** Greek Patriarch of Alexandria and Constantinople in the EASTERN ORTHODOX CHURCH. He sought to merge Protestant and Orthodox principles but after his death his teachings were condemned. His *Confession of Faith*, published in 1629, is a Calvinistic interpretation of Greek Orthodox faith.

**LUCAS** See LUKE.

**LUCIAN OF SAMOSATA (c.115–c.190)** Greek satirist who presented contemporary

Christians as well-meaning but easily duped individuals who believe that "they are all brothers" and will "live forever." Christ he termed "that great man who was crucified in Palestine." Lucian also satirized Greek mythology.

**LUCIAN THE MARTYR, ST. (c.250–312)** Presbyter of Antioch and founder of Antioch's theological school. He died of hunger for refusing to eat food offered to idols. A saint, he is honored on his feast day, January 7.

**LUCIFER** *light bringer* Ancient name of the morning star Venus. In the Bible it appears to refer to Satan (LUKE 10:18).

**LUCIFER OF CAGLIARI (?–c.371)** Bishop of Cagliari, Sardinia, who violently opposed ARIANISM. In Sardinia he is considered a saint.

**LUCINA** Roman goddess of childbearing.

**LUCY, ST. (fourth century)** Virgin martyr of Sicily. Her feast day is December 13.

**LUDD or NUDD** Celtic river god.

**LUDLOW, JOHN MALCOLM FORBES (1821–1911)** French member of the CHURCH OF ENGLAND who founded CHRISTIAN SOCIALISM. He believed that the new socialist movement must be allied with the Christian faith and imbued with Christian ideals.

**LUDOLF OF SAXONY (c.1300–1377)** German monk (first DOMINICAN, then CARTHUSIAN) whose *Life of Christ* was a challenge to practice everyday application of Christianity. It was popular through the Middle Ages.

**LUG** Celtic god similar to MERCURY.

**LUKE** Christian physician who wrote the third Gospel and the Acts of the Apostles. A companion of the Apostle Paul, and one of the few Gentiles in the early church, he carefully investigated the events concerning the birth, life, death, and resurrection of Jesus (LUKE 1:1–3). The results as set forth in the Gospel of Luke probably formed, together with the Acts, a two-volume history of Christ and the early years of the church. The Gospel of Luke is particularly beautiful among New Testament writings and emphasizes Jesus' attention to Gentiles and to women. A number of events in Jesus' life and some of His parables are found nowhere but in the third Gospel.

**LULAB** *palm* Bundle of branches borne into the synagogue at the Feast of BOOTHS. Cf. Leviticus 23:40.

**LULAV** See LULAB.

**LULL, RAYMOND or LULLY, RAIMON (c.1235–c.1315)** Spanish FRANCISCAN who spent much of his life evangelizing the MOSLEMS of northern Africa. He was a profound MYSTIC and philosopher, believing that all truth could be deduced from basic principles, and was a student of cabalism. He admired AUGUSTINE and hotly opposed AVERROISM. He was stoned to death by the Moslems at Bougie. Of Christ he said: "I have but one passion in life and it is He."

**LULLISTS** Disciples of Raymond LULL. The confusion believed to inhere in Lull's mixture of faith and reason resulted in a condemnation of his doctrines by Pope GREGORY XI. Nevertheless, his followers have remained faithful to his philosophy.

**LULLY** See LULL.

**LUNA** *moon* 1. Roman moon goddess. 2. Hinged case holding the HOST during the benediction in the EUCHARIST.

**LUN-YU** *Analects* One of the nine authoritative works on CONFUCIANISM, giving Confucius' discourses on social and political matters.

**LUPERCALIA** Roman winter festival for protection and fertility. On February 15 goats and a dog were sacrificed, and youths ran about the city slapping passers-by with strips from the skins of the sacrificed animals.

**LURIA, ISAAC BEN SOLOMON (1534–1572)** Jewish MYSTIC and cabalist who had visions of the prophets, performed miracles, talked with birds, and drew the Holy Spirit by doing penance and flogging himself. His followers believed him the forerunner of the MESSIAH.

**LUST** In the New Testament, strong desire. In CATHOLICISM, excessive sexual desire, considered a deadly sin.

**LUSTRATION** Solemn ceremony of purification.

**LUSTRUM** Roman animal sacrifice made at the completion of a census to expiate the people's sins.

**LUTHARDT, CHRISTOPH ERNST (1823–1902)** LUTHERAN apologist.

**LUTHER, MARTIN (1483–1546)** German monk who inspired the Protestant Reformation. His study of Scripture and of Augustine's and other writings convinced him that man is justified by faith alone and that ecclesiastical works cannot bring peace of soul. The NINETY-FIVE THESES he drew up in protest against the INDULGENCES then being hawked through Germany were followed by other writings— *Address to the Nobility of the German Nation, Babylonian Captivity of the Church, The Freedom of a Christian Man* —which led to the threatening papal bull *Exsurge Domine* ("Arise, O Lord, . . . protect the vineyard Thou gavest Peter from the wild beast who devours it . . ."). Summoned to the Diet of WORMS, Luther refused to recant: "Unless I am convicted either by Scripture or by right reason . . . my conscience is captive to the Word of God, I neither can nor will recant anything, since it is neither right nor safe to act against conscience. I can do no other. God help me. Amen." Protected by his German friends, Luther translated the Bible into German, married a nun, organized what became LUTHERANISM, and launched the REFORMATION.

**LUTHERAN CHURCH** See names of particular denominations.

**LUTHERAN CHURCH IN AMERICA** Denomination representing the merger of the United Lutheran Church in America, the AUGUSTANA EVANGELICAL LUTHERAN CHURCH, and the FINNISH EVANGELICAL LUTHERAN CHURCH. The largest Lutheran group in the United States, it is governed by a president, a biennial convention, and the usual boards, synods, and denominational machinery.

**LUTHERAN CHURCH—MISSOURI SYNOD** Second largest Lutheran body in the United States, founded in 1847 as the German Evangelical Lutheran Synod of Missouri, Ohio, and Other States. A conservative denomination, it excels in parochial schools and education, and is strongly evangelistic.

**LUTHERANISM** Doctrine and church government originating in the work of Martin LUTHER. Lutherans, with 70 million members, constitute the largest Protestant group in the world. Lutheranism prevails in Germany, Denmark, Iceland, Norway, and Sweden, and has strong churches in most other European countries as well as in

South America, Africa, Asia, and Australia.

**LUTHERAN STUDENTS ASSOCIATION** Organization of Lutheran college students.

**LUTHERAN WORLD FEDERATION** International organization of Lutherans formed in 1947 for world relief. Its office is in Geneva, Switzerland. It meets every six years.

**LUTHER LEAGUE** Youth society in Lutheran churches.

**LUXOR** Egyptian city, site of the enormous Temple of Luxor, famous monument of antiquity. To it the Egyptians brought their divinities in the principal religious festival of Thebes. Within the temple the early Christians built churches, and the Moslems a mosque.

**LUZZATTO, MOSES HAYYIM (1707–1747)** Italian Jewish MYSTIC and author. His *Path of the Upright* has been compared to *Pilgrim's Progress*. He wrote the drama *Samson and Delilah* at 17 years of age.

**LXX** Symbol for the SEPTUAGINT.

**LYCH GATE** See LICH GATE.

**LYDIA** Merchant woman of Thyatira in Asia Minor who was the first Christian to be converted in Europe, and who opened her home to Paul (ACTS 16:14–40).

**LYON, JAMES (1735–1794)** PRESBYTERIAN minister who became one of America's first musical composers. He composed a number of Psalm tunes.

**LYONS** City of east-central France where a number of church councils and synods have been held. There the WALDENSES emerged in the twelfth century.

**LYONS, FIRST COUNCIL OF** Thirteenth ECUMENICAL COUNCIL, held in 1245, at which Emperor Frederick II was deposed.

**LYONS, SECOND COUNCIL OF** Fourteenth ECUMENICAL COUNCIL, held in 1274. It attempted church reform and a Crusade but was unsuccessful in the latter objective. It did accomplish a temporary union between Eastern and Western churches.

**LYRA, NICOLAUS DE (1270–1340)** French FRANCISCAN commentator whose literal presentation influenced Martin LUTHER.

**LYRE** Symbol of harmony and concord in religious art.

**LYSTRA** City of Galatia in Asia Minor at which Paul and Barnabas were hailed as Jupiter and Mercury (ACTS 14:6–21).

**LYTE, HENRY FRANCIS (1793–1847)** ANGLICAN cleric and hymn writer. His poems and hymns include "Abide With Me."

# M

**MA** Goddess of Asia Minor worshiped with primitive ceremonies before the time of Christ.

**MAACHAH or MAACAH** 1. City near Mt. Hermon. 2. David's wife, the mother of Absalom (II SAMUEL 3:3). 3. Absalom's daughter who married Rehoboam (I KINGS 15:2). 4. Several other men and women of the Old Testament bear this name.

**MAAHES** Nubian god with the head of a lion.

**MAAMAD** Hebrews who aided the Levites once a year in performing the sacrifices.

**MAARIB** *make evening* Jewish service of evening prayer.

**MAASER** Hebrew word for the TITHE required to be set apart for religious or philanthropic purposes.

**MAAT** Egyptian goddess of righteousness and wisdom.

**MACCABEES** Famous Jewish family which saved Judea from Syrian possession and restored Hebrew life in the second and first centuries B.C. Waging guerrilla warfare, they revolted against ANTIOCHUS EPIPHANES and established HASMONEAN rule until the time of HEROD THE GREAT. Their exploits are detailed in the apocryphal books of I and II Maccabees.

**MACCABEES, FEAST OF** See HANUKKAH.

**MACCABEUS, JUDAS** See JUDAS MACCABEUS.

**MC CLINTOCK, JOHN (1814–1870)** American METHODIST minister who became the first president of Drew Theological Seminary. With James Strong he edited the ten-volume *Cyclopaedia of Biblical, Theological, and Ecclesiastical Literature*.

**MC CLOSKEY, JOHN (1810–1885)** Cardinal who founded a number of churches and seminaries in the United States, was a central figure in the erection of St. Patrick's Cathedral in New York, and was the first American to receive the title "Sancta Maria supra Minervam."

**MC CONNELL, FRANCIS JOHN (1871–1953)** METHODIST bishop who believed in the social application of Christianity and was president of the FEDERAL COUNCIL OF CHURCHES OF CHRIST IN AMERICA.

**MACDONALD, GEORGE (1824–1905)** Scottish CONGREGATIONAL pastor who wrote a number of novels for adults and children and some profound poetry. His work combines literary power with Christian insight and sensitivity.

**MACE** Short symbolic staff borne before an ecclesiastical or other dignitary to indicate his authority.

**MACEDONIA** Country just north of Greece which PAUL evangelized after a man from it pleaded, "Come over into Macedonia and help us" (ACTS 16:9). Macedonian churches in Philippi and Thessalonica received letters from Paul (PHILIPPIANS, I AND II THESSALONIANS) which became part of the New Testament.

**MACEDONIANISM** Fourth-century heresy of those HOMOIOUSIANS who believed that the Holy Spirit had been created and was subordinate to the Father and Son. Adherents of this belief were also called PNEUMATOMACHI. The name Macedonianism derives from the belief that its founder was Macedonius, Semi-Arian bishop of Constantinople deposed in 360.

**MC GIFFERT, ARTHUR CUSHMAN (1861–1933)** American professor of church history, PRESBYTERIAN minister, and onetime president of Union Theological Seminary.

**MC GREADY, JAMES (c.1758–1817)** PRESBYTERIAN evangelist of Kentucky whose hearers began the revival which covered the southwestern United States about 1800.

**MACHA** Celtic war goddess.

**MACHEBEUF, JOSEPH P. (1812 – 1889)** French CATHOLIC missionary in the southwestern United States who was portrayed as Father Vaillant in Willa Cather's *Death Comes for the Archbishop*.

**MACHEN, J. GRESHAM (1881 – 1937)** American PRESBYTERIAN minister whose objection to liberal teaching as supported by the Presbyterian Board of Foreign Missions resulted in his suspension from the ministry. Thereafter he was instrumental in founding the ORTHODOX PRESBYTERIAN CHURCH and Westminster Theological Seminary.

**MACHZOR** *cycle* Prayer book for Jewish festivals.

**MACIP, VICENTE JUAN (c.1523–1579)** Spanish religious painter.

**MACK, ALEXANDER (1679–1735)** German REFORMED miller who founded the DUNKERS or German Baptist Brethren and led a number of them to Germantown, Pennsylvania.

**MACKAY, ALEXANDER MURDOCH (1849–1890)** Scottish EPISCOPAL missionary to Uganda, Africa, where he died of malaria. He translated the Bible into the natives' language.

**MACLAREN, ALEXANDER (1826 – 1910)** British BAPTIST preacher and expositor who presided at the first meeting of the BAPTIST WORLD ALLIANCE.

**MACLEOD, NORMAN (1812–1872)** Scottish PRESBYTERIAN cleric who served as chaplain to Queen Victoria and moderator of the CHURCH OF SCOTLAND. He was a man of broad interests and social concern, and a founder of the EVANGELICAL ALLIANCE.

**MC NABB, VINCENT (1868–1943)** English clergyman and priest of the DOMINICAN Order of preachers whose faith sustained him through great suffering.

**MC NICHOLAS, JOHN TIMOTHY (1877–1950)** Irish-born DOMINICAN who became Archbishop of Cincinnati and organized the Holy Name Society.

**MACUILXOCHITL** Aztec god of sport and dancing.

**MADHAVA ACHARYA (fourteenth century)** HINDU philosopher who wrote a commentary on the SUTRAS known as MIMAMSA Sutras.

**MADHAYAMAYANA** Middle VEHICLE branch of MAHAYANA Buddhism. It emphasizes two forms of truth, relative and absolute.

**MADHVAS** HINDUS who combine SAIVA and VAISNAVA forms of religion.

**MA. DI.** Abbreviation for *Mater Dei*, "Mother of God."

**MADONNA** *my Lady* Representation of the Virgin MARY, often holding the infant Jesus. One of the most celebrated is Raphael's "Sistine Madonna." Many other great artists have painted Madonnas.

**MADONNA LILY** White lily which often symbolized MARY in religious art.

**MAENADS** In Greek myth, "mad women" attending the god DIONYSUS, or BACCHUS.

**MAESTRO DI CAMERA** Principal chamberlain at the VATICAN.

**MAFTIR** Synagogue reader of the Scripture following the lesson from the PENTATEUCH.

**MAGDALEN, ORDERS OF ST. MARY** See MAGDALENES, 1.

**MAGDALENE, MARY** See MARY MAGDALENE.

**MAGDALENES** 1. Medieval term for religious orders some of whose members might have formerly been prostitutes. 2. Reformed prostitute.

**MAGEN DAVID** *shield of David* Six-pointed star, traced to a seal in the seventh century B.C., which is emblematic of the Jewish people.

**MAGGID** *preacher* Witty itinerant Jewish preacher.

**MAGI** *wise men or magicians* Tribe or order apparently first appearing in the ancient Akkadian culture of the Euphrates valley and thence entering Media, Persia, and ZOROASTRIANISM. Within the latter the Magi were known as wise men, astrologers, and practitioners of the occult. The "wise men [magi] from the east" of Matthew 2:1–2 may have been Zoroastrian priests from Persia. Tradition makes them three, assigns them the names Gaspar (or Caspar), Melchior, and Balthazar, and has them hail from the three continents of Asia, Europe, and Africa. The feast of EPIPHANY commemorates their visit to the Christ Child. The "Adoration of the Magi" was a favorite theme of medieval painting. The Chapel of the Three Wise Men at Cologne, Germany, claims to have their skulls.

**MAGIC** Use of words or objects to control supernatural powers. Similar to religion in its belief in a supernatural order, it contrasts sharply in its alliance with superstition, its means, and its ends. Magic makes use of incantations, secret formulae, and occult objects such as effigies; worthy religion relies on faith, hope, prayer, and love. Magic seeks to bring nature, other persons, or supernatural beings under the control of its user; good religion strives to put the worshiper at the service of God for the benefit of others. While magic and religion are often intertwined, religion tends to cast off magical elements unless it regresses into superstition.

**MAGISTERIUM** Authority or teaching office of the church.

**MAGISTER SACRI PALATII** *master of the sacred palace* Personal chaplain and theological adviser to the pope; usually a DOMINICAN.

**MAGNIFICAT** Song of Mary (LUKE 1:46–55) when she learned she was to be the mother of the Saviour. The name derives from the first word of her song in Latin. The Magnificat has been sung in the Eastern and Western churches for many centuries.

**MAGOG** 1. Son of Japheth (GENESIS 10: 2). 2. Enemy of the Kingdom of God (EZEKIEL 38–39; REVELATION 20:8). See also GOG.

**MAGUS** 1. Singular of MAGI. 2. See SIMON MAGUS.

**MAGYAR** Language of the EASTERN ORTHODOX liturgy in Hungary.

**MAHABHARATA** Great HINDU epic poem —probably the world's longest—recounting the fortunes of the descendants of Bharata and the conquest of a kingdom surrounding Delhi by the five sons of Pandu. The sixth of the eighteen books contains the BHAGAVAD-GITA. The whole work is attributed to the Indian sage Vyasa but bears the marks of many hands, and probably dates from or before the fifth century B.C.

**MAHA BODHI SOCIETY** BUDDHIST organization founded to restore the BUDDH GAYA, where Buddha found enlightenment, to Buddhist control. With headquarters at Calcutta, it has many branches.

**MAHADEVA** *the great god* Hindu name of SIVA.

**MAHADEVI** *the great goddess* Hindu name of Siva's wife PARVATI.

**MAHAKALA** *the great time* SIVA in a destructive aspect.

**MAHAMAD** Trustees ruling a Spanish synagogue.

**MAHASAMADHI** Highest spiritual state in HINDUISM. One who attains it is no longer reincarnated.

**MAHATMA** *great-souled* 1. HINDU term for one of superior spirituality. 2. Theosophical term for a "master" of great wisdom and supernatural powers.

**MAHAVAMSA** *great chronicle* Poetic BUDDHIST history of ancient Ceylon. It dates from the sixth century A.D.

**MAHAVASTU** *great story* Important Sanskrit scripture of HINAYANA Buddhism. It includes a life of Buddha, depicting his aloofness to hunger, thirst, and sex, and outlines the BODHISATTVA's ten steps to perfection.

**MAHAVIRA** *great conqueror* **(sixth century B.C.)** Rajah's son who left his wife and daughter at the age of thirty to meditate until he received enlightenment. He thereupon became a wandering preacher and founded JAINISM, in which he was considered the last of 24 great saints or TIRTHANKARAS. A contemporary of Gautama BUDDHA, Mahavira entered NIRVANA at the age of 72.

**MAHAYANA** *great vehicle* Later phase of BUDDHISM prominent in the northern countries of Korea, Japan, China, Tibet, etc. (The older Hinayana Buddhism is still prominent in such southern countries as Laos, Thailand, Ceylon, and Burma; see HINAYANA.) Mahayana Buddhism is pantheistic, interprets Buddhist doctrines spiritually, and emphasizes helping others and salvation for all. It has the world's largest collection of sacred literature. It was instituted by ASVAGHOSA and several others in the first century A.D.

**MAHDI** *the guided one* ISLAM term for the last IMAM, the redeemer who will appear at the end of this age to produce perfect righteousness throughout the world.

Several Moslems have claimed to be the Mahdi.

**MAHER-SHALAL-HASH-BAZ** *the spoil speeds, the prey hastens* Symbolic name of Isaiah's second son, indicating Israel's coming conquest by the Assyrians (ISAIAH 8:1–4).

**MAHLON** *illness* Husband of RUTH the Moabitess. See the Book of Ruth.

**MAHOMET** See MOHAMMED.

**MAHOUND** Archaic variant of MOHAMMED.

**MAHZOR** See MACHZOR.

**MAIMONIDES** **(1135–1204)** Moses ben Maimon, Jewish rabbi and philosopher considered by some the greatest Jewish thinker in history. A physician, he codified Jewish law and wrote important treatises and commentaries. His *Guide to the Perplexed* deeply influenced Christian as well as Jewish thought.

**MAISO** Creator-mother goddess worshiped by the Paressi Indians of the Bahamas.

**MAISTRE, JOSEPH DE (1754–1821)** French diplomat whose books propounded the idea that the earth should be completely controlled by the pope.

**MAITHUNA** HINDU term for copulation practiced as a religious rite.

**MAITREYA** The BUDDHA who will return to earth after six billion years. The Maitreya's statues represent him as fat and laughing, holding a bag full of happiness for mankind.

**MAJOR, JOHN (c.1469–1550)** Scottish commentator, historian, and scholastic theologian.

**MAJORISTIC CONTROVERSY** Sixteenth-century German dispute over the necessity of good works in salvation. George Major or Maier held them necessary, but his opponents denied this, maintaining that Major's thesis destroyed the doctrine of justification by faith.

**MAJOR ORDERS** Higher orders in the church, as priests and deacons, in contrast to the MINOR ORDERS.

**MAKEMIE, FRANCIS (c.1658–1708)** Scotch-Irish PRESBYTERIAN missionary to America; founder of the first presbytery in the colonies, at Philadelphia.

**MAKER, THE** Term for God as Creator.

**MALACHI** *my messenger* Last book of the Old Testament. Little is known of the author. The book, one of the MINOR PROPHETS, denounces laxness in Jewish ritual and announces the coming of the MESSIAH. "Have we not all one father?" asks Malachi. "Hath not one God created us? Why do we deal treacherously every man against his brother . . . ?" (2:10).

**MALACHIAS, MALACHIE, or MALACHY** See MALACHI.

**MALACHY, ST.** **(1094–1148)** Powerful and zealous Irish churchman, Archbishop of Armagh. His feast day is November 3.

**MALCHUS** High priest's servant whose ear St. Peter cut off at Jesus' arrest. Jesus restored it (JOHN 18:10–11).

**MALCOLM X (1925–1965)** American leader of the BLACK MUSLIMS who left that group to form the Muslim Mosque in 1964. Born Malcolm Little, he seemed torn throughout his life between the bitterness of racial hatred and the dream of brotherhood. He was shot to death on February 21, 1965.

**MALEBRANCHE, NICHOLAS (1638–1715)** French philosopher who sought to harmonize the new principles of DESCARTES with the theology of St. AUGUSTINE. The result was OCCASIONALISM and the view that men "behold all things in God."

**MALEDICTION** Curse; the opposite of benediction.

**MALIK IBN ARAS (c.713–795)** Moslem IMAM who founded the MALIKITE RITE of ISLAM.

**MALIKITE RITE** Interpretation of MOSLEM law founded by MALIK IBN ARAS.

**MALIKITES** Disciples of MALIK IBN ARAS; one of the four orthodox schools of ISLAM, influential in northern Africa.

**MALKIN** Scottish term for a familiar spirit.

**MALLEUS HAERETICORUM** *hammer of heretics* Ecclesiastical title honoring those who fiercely fought heresies and heretics.

**MALLEUS MALEFICARUM** Papal BULL of 1489 treating of witchcraft and demons.

**MALTESE CROSS** Cross with four equal arms, each arm divided into two prongs. It became the emblem of the KNIGHTS OF MALTA.

**MALVERN CONFERENCE** ANGLICAN gathering in 1941 addressed by T. S. ELIOT, Dorothy L. SAYERS, and others. It sought to apply Christianity to economics and concluded that industrial resources should not be privately controlled.

**MAMA ALLPA** Many-breasted Inca fertility goddess.

**MAMA COCHA** Inca mother of men.

**MAMALOI** VOODOO priestess.

**MAMA PACHA** Inca mother-goddess.

**MAMERTINE PRISON** Prison of ancient Rome where PETER was held, according to tradition.

**MAMMON** New Testament word for money, materialism, or reliance on wealth instead of God.

**MAN, WINGED** Ecclesiastical symbol of St. MATTHEW.

**MANA** 1. Mandaean Gnostic word for God or for the divine spirit in man (see MANDAEANS). 2. Melanesian word for a power believed to reside in ghosts, corpses, and strangely acting objects or people.

**MANANNAIN or MANANNAN** Celtic sea god with three legs.

**MANASSEH** *forgetfulness* 1. Son of Joseph from whom the "half tribe of Manasseh" was descended. (GENESIS 41:51; 48:1–22; DEUTERONOMY 3:13). 2. Exceptionally wicked king of Judah who succeeded Hezekiah and made children pass through the fire of Molech worship (II KINGS 21). Several other Bible figures bear this name.

**MANASSEH, PRAYER OF** See PRAYER OF MANASSEH.

**MANASSEH BEN ISRAEL (1604–1657)** Jewish historian and leader who persuaded Cromwell to allow Jews to enter England and wrote a book reconciling various problems in Scripture.

**MANASSES** See MANASSEH.

**MANDA** MANDAEAN word for knowledge as a means of salvation.

**MANDA D'HAYYE** *knowledge of life* MANDAEAN savior-figure.

**MANDAEANS** *knowing ones* Mesopotamian sect combining Christian, Jewish, Persian, Babylonian, and Gnostic ideas. They revere John the Baptist, immerse in running water, and look for the coming of the MANDA D'HAYYE. Jesus and Mohammed alike are considered false prophets. Their chief Scripture is the *Treasure* or "Great Book" which dates from about the seventh century; they themselves have been traced back to about the first century A.D. About 2,000 Mandaeans still survive in Iraq and Persia.

**MANDALA** Magic circle or diagram used in BUDDHIST religion.

**MANDRAKE** Narcotic plant whose root has from ancient times been considered to have supernatural powers. Reuben gave Leah mandrakes, apparently to increase ardor or fertility (GENESIS 30:14–16).

**MANES** 1. Roman term for spirits of those deceased. 2. Variant of MANI or MANICHEES.

**MANI or MANICHAEUS (c.216–276)** Babylonian who received a revelation at the age of twelve and founded Manichaeism. After making many converts he was flayed by the king of Persia, Bahram I.

**MANICHAEISM or MANICHAEANISM** Dualistic oriental religion combining pagan and Christian elements. It sees a continuing struggle between the kingdom of light and the kingdom of darkness, to be resolved after 1468 years when fire destroys the earth and the kingdom of evil. The Manichees saw women and matter as inherently evil. St. AUGUSTINE was at one time a Manichee before becoming a Christian.

**MANICHEE** Adherent of MANICHAEISM.

**MANIFESTATION** Term for SPIRITUALIST demonstration.

**MANIPLE or MANIPULE** Strip of silk worn on a cleric's left arm at MASS. Decorated with three crosses, it symbolizes good works.

**MANITO** Term of American Algonquian Indians for divine, immanent power.

**MANITOA or MANITOU** See MANITO.

**MANJUSRI** Wisdom and compassion of the BUDDHA.

**MANNA** Food divinely provided the Israelites during their desert wanderings. Various theories have been projected concerning its chemical makeup.

**MANNING, HENRY EDWARD (1808–1892)** ANGLICAN clergyman who became a CATHOLIC cardinal and Archbishop of Westminster. A prolific writer, he sympathized with the labor movement and social reforms such as slum clearance and the control of alcohol. At VATICAN COUNCIL I he vigorously supported papal infallibility.

**MANOAH** Samson's father (JUDGES 13).

**MANSE** Minister's house.

**MANTEGNA, ANDREA (1431–1506)** Brilliant Italian painter of frescoes and altar pictures with striking religious themes.

**MANTIC** Gifted with a prophet's vision; related to the occult.

**MANTILLA** Veil worn by women in church in Latin countries.

**MANTRA** HINDU or BUDDHIST hymn or incantation.

**MANTUS** Etruscan protector of the afterworld.

**MANU man** 1. HINDUISM's first man, who survived a flood and gave men a law code, the Code of Manu. On this the present laws of India are based. 2. One of a number of Hindu heroes.

**MANUALE** Medieval term for a book for administering the SACRAMENTS.

**MAOU** Sun god and creator in Dahomey, Africa, religion.

**MAOZ TZUR** HANUKKAH hymn based on the various deliverances of the Israelites from trouble.

**MARA** BUDDHIST term for the devil or death.

**MARABOUTS** Holy men of ISLAM to whom prayers are offered after their decease.

**MARAE** Holy places in the southwest Pacific.

**MARAH bitter** Oasis near Suez whose bitter waters were sweetened by Moses (EXODUS 15:23).

**MARANATHA our Lord, come** ARAMAIC expression used in the early church to indicate the Christians' longing for the imminent return of Christ.

**MARANO or MARRANO accursed** Epithet applied to Spanish Jews forced to accept Christianity but secretly retaining their native faith. The Spanish INQUISITION made them its special objects of investigation, torture, and burning.

**MARBURG COLLOQUY** Meeting assembled by Philip of Hesse in 1529 to bring about agreement between ZWINGLI and LUTHER. It succeeded in fourteen points, failed in the fifteenth—regarding Luther's doctrine of CONSUBSTANTIATION (Christ's presence in and with the sacrament of the EUCHARIST).

**MARCELLUS OF ANCYRA (?–c.374)** Bishop of Ancyra in Asia Minor who maintained that the persons of the TRINITY were emanations from God. Accused of denying the proper distinctions between the persons, he was expelled from office and his views condemned.

**MARCION (c.100–165)** Christian heretic from Asia Minor who founded a sect known as MARCIONITES, c.144 in Rome. He rejected the Old Testament, drew up his own New Testament, believed that the Old Testament Creator had nothing in common with the Father of Jesus, and held that Christ never actually became flesh. A dualist, he rejected some GNOSTIC tenets but accepted others.

**MARCIONITES** Followers of MARCION. Ascetic and dualistic, they had disappeared by the seventh century.

**MARCUS AURELIUS (121–180)** Humanitarian Roman STOIC who became emperor in the second century. A noble spirit, he was just and merciful although he persecuted the Christians. His *Meditations* show deep devotion to Stoic ideals.

**MARDI GRAS fat Tuesday** Last day before LENT; it has been celebrated with revelry in a number of Roman Catholic lands since the Middle Ages.

**MARDUK** Supreme god and creator in ancient Babylonian religion. Also known as Bel or Enlil.

**MARGARET MARY ALACOQUE** See ALACOQUE, MARGARET MARY.

**MARGARET OF NAVARRE (1492–1549)** Queen of Navarre to whose court flocked Rabelais, other literary figures, and many Protestants. A CALVINIST, she rejected Catholic doctrines of confession and indulgences.

**MARGARET OF SCOTLAND, ST. (1045–1093)** Pious Scottish queen who brought many English priests into her country and reformed many abuses in the church. Her feast day is June 10.

**MARI** Ancient city on the Euphrates in which there was a temple to ISHTAR together with a ZIGGURAT and 20,000 clay tablets of inestimable importance in understanding the twentieth century B.C.

**MARIAN** One interested in or devoted to the Virgin MARY or one of the queens named Mary.

**MARIANUS SCOTUS (c.1028–1083)** Irish monk noted for his world history *Chronicon* and his beautifully decorated Scripture commentaries.

**MARIOLATRY** Worship of the Virgin MARY.

**MARIOLOGY** Study of the place the Virgin MARY holds in theology, and of her as an individual or saint.

**MARISTS** Society of Mary founded in 1824 in France by Jean Claude Marie Colin. Ordained and lay members do educational, nursing, and evangelistic work, seeking particularly to increase devotion to the Blessed Virgin Mary. They labor in many countries, especially in Australia and the South Pacific.

**MARK or MARCUS** Young associate of the Apostle Paul. Peter called him "my son" (I PETER 5:13) and he went on missionary travels with Paul and Barnabas (ACTS 12:25; 13:1–5; 15:37–39; COLOSSIANS 4:10). Mark's mother was named Mary and was probably owner of the house in Jerusalem where the disciples took the LAST SUPPER. His full name was John Mark and to him is attributed the Gospel of Mark, which is the shortest and probably the earliest of the four Gospels. It presents Jesus in action; although it omits many of the discourses and parables in other Gospels, it provides many vivid details about Jesus' life and emphasizes the word "straightway" or "at once." Mark's symbol is a lion and he is honored with a feast day April 25.

**MARKS OF THE CHURCH** Traditional marks of the church are unity, holiness, catholicity, and apostolicity. The Protestant reformers emphasized the marks of the true preaching of the gospel, the right administration of the sacraments, and the proper exercise of discipline.

**MARNIX, PHILIP VAN (1540–1598)** Calvinistic patriot of Flanders who aided William the Silent in his attempts to free Holland from Spanish dominion. Marnix was a friend of CALVIN and BEZA, translated Scripture portions into Dutch, set the Psalms to verse, wrote theological tracts and the Dutch national anthem.

**MARONITES** UNIAT Christians originating in Lebanon. They speak Arabic, have an Antiochene liturgy and a spiritual ruler known as the patriarch of Antioch, and are in communion with the pope. They trace their origin to St. Maro in the fifth century although many scholars attribute

it to the MONOTHELITE controversies of the seventh century.

**MARPA (eleventh century)** Founder of a division of Tibetan BUDDHISM which emphasizes long periods of meditation, the KARGYUT-PA School.

**MARPRELATE CONTROVERSY** Sixteenth-century controversy between a band of PURITAN satirists and dignitaries of the CHURCH OF ENGLAND. Sparked by a series of vehement tracts against Anglican authoritarianism published under the pseudonym Martin Marprelate, the dispute aroused public indignation and Anglican rebuttal and reprisals. Summoning all his power, Archbishop John Whitgift succeeded in having the Puritans' press seized and several Puritans imprisoned. John Penry was hanged and John Udall died in prison after being pardoned.

**MARQUETTE, JACQUES (1637 – 1675)** French Jesuit explorer and missionary in North America (see SOCIETY OF JESUS). He explored the Mississippi region and founded mission centers among the Huron, Ottawa, Illinois, and Algonquian Indians.

**MARRANOS** See MARANOS.

**MARRIAGE** Relationship of husband and wife in a family unit, usually with the sanction of the prevailing religion of the culture. The marriage ceremony is traditionally a religious one. In the Judeo-Christian West, marriage is monogamous.

**MARS the shining one** Roman god of war; his counterpart in Greek religion was Ares. Surpassed in importance only by JUPITER, Mars was a god of crops in early times and was worshiped with a special procession in March, which was named after him.

**MARSDEN, SAMUEL (1764–1838)** ANGLICAN supervisor of the first Christian mission in New Zealand.

**MARS HILL** See AREOPAGUS.

**MARSHMAN, JOSHUA (1768–1837)** English BAPTIST missionary to India and Semitic scholar. He translated various Scriptures into Indian dialects and Chinese.

**MARSILIUS OF PADUA (c. 1270–1342)** Italian scholar whose tract *Defender of the Peace* maintained that the powers of both government and church derive from the people. Peter, he held, was never made head of the church, whose leaders and government are a purely human institution; the church should do little but conduct services of worship. Marsilius' ideas were influential but were roundly condemned by the church.

**MARTENSEN, HANS LASSEN (1808–1884)** Danish bishop and theologian who held that there were four elemental principles —Father, Son, Spirit, and uncreated Light—and was involved in various theological controversies.

**MARTHA, ST.** Sister of MARY and LAZARUS whose busy fingers contrasted with Mary's contemplative spirit. Cf. Luke 10:38–42; John 11; 12:2. Martha's feast day is July 29.

**MAR THOMA** The Mar Thoma Syrian Church is in southwest India and traces its founding to a mission visit of the Apostle Thomas. Once close to NESTORIANISM, this body now appears to be theologically orthodox.

**MARTIN DE PORRES** See PORRES, MARTIN DE.

**MARTINEAU, JAMES (1805–1900)** English UNITARIAN clergyman and philosopher. He opposed the materialism propounded in his day with a somewhat mystical and liberal interpretation of Christianity.

**MARTINMAS** Feast of St. MARTIN OF TOURS on November 11.

**MARTIN OF TOURS, ST. (c.316–397)** French bishop and founder of the monastery of Ligugé. Many miracles have been attributed to him. He is the patron of drinking and conviviality. His feast day is November 11.

**MARTYN, HENRY (1781–1812)** ANGLICAN missionary to India. He made a number of translations of Scriptures and his life and early death made a deep impression on the modern missionary movement.

**MARTYR** *witness* One who gives his life for his belief. It was said of the early Christians who died for their faith, "The blood of the martyrs is the seed of the church." As the twentieth century entered its final third, martyrdom continued throughout the earth.

**MARTYRIUM or MARTYRY** Church built to honor a martyr.

**MARTYROLOGY** List of martyrs, with their lives and deeds, arranged according to their anniversaries.

**MARTYRY** See MARTYRIUM.

**MARUMDA** Deity of the Pomo Indians of North America who created and sought to destroy the world.

**MARUTS** Storm gods of vedic religion, sons of RUDRA.

**MARY** 1. Mother of Jesus and wife of Joseph. Before marrying Joseph she traveled with him from Nazareth to Bethlehem where Jesus was born. Later, when Jesus was about twelve, she went with the family to Jerusalem. She seemed puzzled by some of Jesus' deeds but stood by Him at the crucifixion and later was among the disciples. In the more liturgical churches Mary is referred to as the Blessed Virgin. ROMAN CATHOLICS honor her as the principal saint; in 1964, at VATICAN COUNCIL II, she was given the title "Mother of the Church." She is honored with many feasts including these: the Immaculate Conception, the Nativity, the Annunciation, the Purification, the Visitation, and the Assumption. 2. Several other Marys in the Bible are listed below.

**MARYKNOLL FATHERS** CATHOLIC priests trained at the Catholic Foreign Mission Society of America, founded in 1911, for missionary service abroad.

**MARYKNOLL SISTERS** Nuns trained for mission work at the Catholic Foreign Mission Society of America (see MARYKNOLL FATHERS).

**MARY MAGDALENE** Woman from Mejdel by the Sea of Galilee who followed Jesus. Out of her He cast seven devils (LUKE 8:2) and she was with the faithful disciples at the crucifixion and resurrection (MARK 15:40; 16:1). Some think she had been a harlot (cf. LUKE 7; 8). She is honored with a feast day July 22.

**MARY OF BETHANY** Sister of MARTHA and LAZARUS from Bethany. Her delight in sitting at Jesus' feet while her sister Martha busied herself getting a meal indicates her loving, contemplative spirit. Some identify this Mary with MARY MAGDALENE, but with little Scriptural basis. Mary of Bethany's feast day is July 29. (Cf. LUKE 10:38–43; JOHN 11:1—12:9.)

**MARY THE MOTHER OF MARK** John Mark's mother (COLOSSIANS 4:10). In her house the Christians met after the resurrection (ACTS 12:12). See MARK.

**MASACCIO (1401–c.1428)** Original Florentine painter of many religious works including the "Expulsion from Eden," the "Crucifixion," "St. Paul," "St. Andrew," "Peter and the Tribute Money," and "Death of the Baptist."

**MASHAL**  Jewish word for an allegory.

**MASHIACH** *anointed one*  Jewish word for the MESSIAH.

**MASOLINO DA PANICALE (1383–c.1447)** Florentine painter of many religious works including the "Crucifixion" and "Madonna and Christ in Glory."

**MASORA or MASORAH** *tradition*  1. Ancient Jewish tradition as to the correct text of Scripture. 2. Marginal notes in Scripture indicating the MASORETES' interpretation.

**MASORETES**  Jewish scholars from the sixth through the eleventh centuries who vocalized and interpreted the Old Testament text.

**MASORETIC TEXT**  Text of the OLD TESTAMENT with vowels added by the MASORETES.

**MASS** *dismissal*  ROMAN CATHOLIC term for communion or EUCHARIST. See also HIGH MASS and LOW MASS.

**MASSILON, JEAN BAPTISTE (1663–1742)** Noted French preacher and Bishop of Clermont. He is remembered for his gentle persuasiveness.

**MASSORAH**  See MASORA.

**MASTER, THE**  New Testament term referring to Christ.

**MASTER OF MISRULE**  See LORD OF MISRULE.

**MASUD, SAIYUD SALAR**  See BAHREICH.

**MATER ET MAGISTRA**  Encyclical of Pope JOHN XXIII marked for its advanced social and ecumenical features.

**MATERIALISM**  Philosophy reducing all reality to what can be verified by the senses or scientific investigation. Thus it opposes IDEALISM and spiritual explanations of reality.

**MATHER, COTTON (1663–1728)**  PURITAN clergyman who wrote a history of the New England theocracy and investigated several cases of witchcraft and alleged possession by demons.

**MATHER, INCREASE (1639–1723)**  Father of Cotton Mather and PURITAN leader in New England. He was a friend of Richard BAXTER and Robert BOYLE.

**MATHER, RICHARD (1596–1669)**  Father of Increase Mather and leader of the PURITANS in Massachusetts. He was a translator of the BAY PSALM BOOK and an advocate of the HALF-WAY COVENANT.

**MATHESON, GEORGE (1842–1906)**  Blind Scottish theologian and hymn writer, noted for "O Love That Wilt Not Let Me Go."

**MATHEW, THEOBALD (1790–1856)**  CAPUCHIN monk of Ireland famous for his work in temperance and total abstinence.

**MATHEWS, BASIL JOSEPH (1879–1951)** English METHODIST churchman, professor, and author of more than forty books including *Paul the Dauntless* and *Jesus and Youth.*

**MATHEWS, SHAILER (1863–1941)**  BAPTIST theologian and New Testament professor in the United States. For four years he was president of the FEDERAL COUNCIL OF CHURCHES. He pioneered in modernistic views such as the social gospel.

**MATHS**  HINDU convents.

**MATINS**  1. Morning prayers. 2. Canonical hour or worship service with specified component elements.

**MATRIMONY**  See MARRIAGE.

**MATRONALIA**  Roman celebration in honor of JUNO, observed March 1.

**MATTHEW**  Tax collector who became one of the Twelve Apostles and wrote the First Gospel (LUKE 5:27–32). The Gospel according to Matthew is filled with Old Testament prophecies fulfilled by Christ; it lays special emphasis on the relation of the gospel to the law, and contains the only two mentions of the word *ekklesia*, "church," in the Gospels. Matthew is symbolized by a winged figure. His feast day is September 21.

**MATTHIAS, ST.** *gift of the Lord*  Apostle who replaced JUDAS (ACTS 1:23–26). His feast day is February 24.

**MATTINS**  See MATINS.

**MATUTA**  Roman goddess of dawn, mothers, and childbirth.

**MATZAH** *unleavened*  Flat unleavened bread commemorating that eaten in haste at the Jewish exodus from Egypt under Moses. The plural (and common) form is *matzoth*.

**MATZOTH**  See MATZAH.

**MAUI**  Polynesian sun god.

**MAUNDY THURSDAY**  Thursday before EASTER, traditionally observed with the EUCHARIST. On Thursday eve of Christ's last week He ate the Passover meal and instituted the LORD'S SUPPER with his disciples. The FOOT WASHING connected with that meal is also reenacted in some churches on Maundy Thursday.

**MAURICE, JOHN FREDERICK DENISON (1805–1872)** ANGLICAN writer, theologian, and leader in CHRISTIAN SOCIALISM. Although he was a BROAD CHURCHMAN he opposed the higher criticism which was becoming popular in his time.

**MAURISTS** French BENEDICTINE monks famous for their scholarship, literary works, and contributions to church history. Many of them were executed in the French Revolution and Pope Pius VII dissolved the congregation in 1818.

**MAXIMUS, ST. (c.580–662)** Greek theologian who opposed MONOTHELITISM and emphasized the Incarnate Word. His feast day is August 13.

**MAY** Month named for the Roman goddess Maia. CATHOLICISM makes May the special month of the Virgin MARY.

**MAYA illusion.** 1. HINDU term for the visible external world. 2. Name of BUDDHA's mother. 3. BUDDHIST term for the changeable world of the senses. 4. Name of South American Indians with a high culture by 1500 A.D. See MAYAN RELIGION.

**MAYAN RELIGION** Religion of the Maya Indians of Yucatan, Guatemala, and British Honduras. They worshiped the rain god Chac, the sky god Itzamna, and gods of death, the sun, maize, etc. This sometimes involved human sacrifice. The Mayas had temples erected on pyramidlike foundations, reached by steep stairways.

**MAYAN TEMPLE** See ANCIENT AND MYSTICAL ORDER OF PO-AHTUN.

**MAY DAY** May 1, observed with religious rites from ancient times in honor of fertility and the return of spring. Modern May Day festivities reflect these rites of the ancient Celts, Egyptians, Indians, and Romans.

**MAZDA** See AHURA MAZDA.

**MAZDAISM** Ancient Persian religion which grew out of ZOROASTRIANISM.

**MAZDAKISM** Communistic religious movement instituted in the fifth century A.D. in rebellion against MAZDAISM. Their founder was Mazdak, who was put to death about 529.

**MAZZAH** See MATZAH.

**M.E.** Abbreviation for METHODIST EPISCOPAL.

**MEAL OFFERING** Cereal offering incorrectly translated "meat offering" in the King James Bible. Cakes, flour, or corn were burned and eaten by the priest in Jewish sacrifice. Sometimes this was in conjunction with a peace offering or burnt offering.

**MEAN** Point or condition midway between two extremes. In ancient Greek and Asian religions, virtue was often thought of as the mean between two opposites. Temperance, for example, would be the virtue halfway between the opposite evils of total abstinence and total absorption in something.

**MEANS OF GRACE** Instrumentalities of salvation, as faith, prayer, Scripture, and the sacraments.

**MEAT OFFERING** See MEAL OFFERING.

**MECCA** Holy city of ISLAM. The capital of Hejaz, Saudi Arabia, it is the site of Mohammed's birth and the objective of holy pilgrimages for thousands of MOSLEMS every year. Even before MOHAMMED, the city was sacred; a number of deities were worshiped there until ALLAH expelled them all. Today Mecca houses the KAABA and the tombs of ISHMAEL and HAGAR.

**MECHANISM** Philosophical hypothesis that the universe is explicable in mechanical or material terms alone.

**MECHANIST** One who believes in the doctrine of MECHANISM.

**MECHILTA rules of interpretation** 1. Second-century commentary on Exodus by Rabbi Ishmael ben Elisha. 2. Third-century commentary on Exodus by Rabbi SIMON BEN YOCHAI.

**MECHITARISTS** Armenian monks whose order was inaugurated by Mechitar of Sebaste in 1701. Following the rule of St. BENEDICT, they have made contributions to literature, education, and missions.

**MEDALS** Religious emblems bearing representations of saints, holy places, symbols, or other meaningful associations. Although associated traditionally with CATHOLICISM, medals are sometimes favored by other religionists.

**MEDES** Ancient people of the Iranian area who captured Assur and Nineveh and from whom arose the prophet ZOROASTER.

Cyrus II conquered Media about 549 B.C.; thereafter for a long period the Medes and the Persians were closely linked (cf. DANIEL 5:28).

**MEDIA** Country of the MEDES, roughly equivalent to modern Iran.

**MEDIATOR** Go-between who effects reconciliation between two opposing parties. The Jewish COVENANT represented mediation between God and men; the mediator was ordinarily the priest. Christ is the mediator of God's new covenant with man (HEBREWS 8:6; 9:15; I TIMOTHY 2:5). Having atoned for our sins against God, He both represents us before God and represents Him to us.

**MEDIATRESS or MEDIATRIX** ROMAN CATHOLIC term for the Blessed Virgin MARY as one who mediates between God and man.

**MEDICINE MEN** Priests or healers, particularly among the American Indians. Sir James Frazer termed them the earliest professional class.

**MEDINA** *the city* City of central Arabia to which MOHAMMED went after being rejected by the people of Mecca. Medina contains the tombs of Mohammed, his daughter FATIMA, his wife's father ABU-BAKR, and the Khalif Omar. During Mohammed's lifetime Medina was the center of his spiritual empire.

**MEDITATION** 1. Spiritual contemplation. 2. Religious essay or discourse.

**MEDITERRANEAN** *among the lands* Sea bordering Palestine, Egypt, Greece, and other countries important in religious development. Disliked and little used by the Hebrews, the Mediterranean is seldom mentioned in the Old Testament Scriptures. In the New, however, it became the route of many voyages of Paul and his associates.

**MEDIUM** Person believed to acquire information or contact disembodied spirits through supernatural means, or in some way to induce supernormal phenomena. Mediums are important in SPIRITISM and other religions. The Hebrew Scriptures prohibited them. (Cf. EXODUS 22:18; DEUTERONOMY 18:10.)

**MEEKNESS** Virtue of self-restraint and control of temper, indicating spiritual strength, not weakness.

**MEETINGHOUSE** Building used for worship. In England the meetinghouse is a church of non-Anglicans.

**MEGIDDO** City of Palestine associated with ARMAGEDDON. There King Solomon kept his chariots and horses (I KINGS 10:26-29).

**MEGILLAH** *scroll* Hebrew word for scroll of papyrus or animal skin, particularly for the book of ESTHER.

**MEGILLOTH** Plural of MEGILLAH. It may indicate especially the five books of the Song of Solomon, Ruth, Lamentations, Ecclesiastes, and Esther.

**MEHUERET** Ancient mother-goddess of Egypt.

**MEIR** (second century) Disciple of AKIBA and rabbi noted for his wisdom and his systematization of Jewish law and teaching. He is credited with many fables. He was born and died in Asia Minor but spent most of his life in Palestine.

**MEKE MEKE** Creator worshiped on Easter Island.

**MEKILTA** See MECHILTA.

**MELANCHTHON, PHILIP** (1497-1560) German Protestant reformer whose name was originally Schwartzerd. He aided LUTHER in his German translation of the New Testament, furthered the REFORMATION through his *Loci Communes,* and composed the AUGSBURG CONFESSION of 1530. He often sought reconciliation and compromise among the disputing religious groups of his time.

**MELAVEH MALKAH** *accompanying the queen* Meal signaling the close of the Jewish SABBATH.

**MELCHITES** *royalists* Arabic-speaking Christians of the Middle East who reject MONOPHYSITE doctrines and are in communion with the pope. Their name derives from the support they originally received from the Byzantine king. They follow the BYZANTINE RITE in worship.

**MELCHIZEDEK** *king of righteousness* Mysterious king of Salem who blessed and entertained Abraham when he brought him battle spoils. Apparently a priest-king, he typifies the MESSIAH (GENESIS 14:18-20; PSALM 110; HEBREWS 5:10).

**MELIORISM** Belief that the world is either improvable or gradually growing better. George Eliot coined the word.

**MELITIANS or MELETIANS** 1. Followers of Bishop Melitius of Lycopolis, Egypt, who opposed the easy return to the church of Christians who had fallen away. These Melitians existed from the fourth to the eighth century. 2. Fourth-century followers of Bishop Melitius of Antioch, suspected of ARIAN tendencies in theology. As a result of this Melitian Schism, for a time Antioch had two competing bishops.

**MELITO, ST. (second century)** Controversial Bishop of Sardis, Asia Minor. Defending orthodox positions, he was the first Christian to list the accepted books of the OLD TESTAMENT. Christ he termed "both God and man." His feast day is April 1.

**MELKITES** See MELCHITES.

**MELVILLE, ANDREW (1545–1622)** Scottish successor to John KNOX as leader in the Protestant REFORMATION. Imprisoned in the Tower of London for opposing the episcopal system, he sarcastically defied King James I of England and was elected moderator of the PRESBYTERIAN CHURCH a number of times. A brilliant scholar and fearless churchman, he helped reconstruct Aberdeen University.

**MEM** Thirteenth letter of the Hebrew alphabet.

**MEMBER** Certified participant in a church or other organization. St. Paul likened the members of the church to members of the human body (ROMANS 12:4–5).

**MEMENTO** Prayer for the living or for the dead.

**MEMLING, HANS (c.1430–1494)** Imaginative Flemish religious painter. He executed "The Seven Joys of Mary," "The Last Judgment," "The Adoration of the Magi," and other works.

**MEMORIAL** Common designation for something given a church in memory of someone. The LORD'S SUPPER is often referred to as a memorial of the death of Christ.

**MEMORIALE RITUUM** Latin book of worship services designed for smaller parishes or fewer clergy than usual.

**MEMPHIS** Capital of ancient Egypt famed for its temple to PTAH, its deity, and the nearby pyramids. The COPTIC monastery of St. JEREMIAH once stood in Memphis.

**MEMRA** *word* Jewish word for God's work of order and creation. The SEPTUAGINT translated *memra* as "LOGOS." The Jewish TARGUMS make prominent use of the word *memra.*

**MEN, THE** Scottish term for lay leaders of emotional evangelistic meetings in the eighteenth century.

**MENAION** Book of liturgies in the GREEK CHURCH, containing prayers, hymns, and lives of saints.

**MENASSEH BEN ISRAEL** See MANASSEH BEN ISRAEL.

**MENCIUS or MENG-TSZE (third century B.C.)** Chinese disciple of CONFUCIUS and originator of a sophisticated political theory. He held that the civil ruler should provide for the peace and prosperity of his subjects, waging war only in self-defense. Government, he held, was divinely ordained and rulers responsible to God. He believed that men instinctively seek the good of others and the principles of righteousness and wisdom—although they do not always practice them. He added: "Though a man may be wicked, yet, if he adjust his thoughts, fast, and bathe, he may sacrifice to God."

**MENDELSSOHN, JAKOB LUDWIG FELIX (1809–1847)** Brilliant German composer whose works include the oratorios *Elijah* and *St. Paul.*

**MENDELSSOHN, MOSES (1729–1786)** German Jewish philosopher, grandfather of Jakob Ludwig Felix Mendelssohn (above). He advocated Jewish freedom, tolerance for all religions, and the separation of church and state. He translated the Pentateuch and the Psalms into German and sought to modernize and enlighten Jewish life.

**MENDICANTS** Members of religious orders making poverty and begging essential. Mendicant orders include the DOMINICANS, AUGUSTINIANS, FRANCISCANS, CARMELITES, and SERVITES.

**MENELAUS** King of Sparta immortalized in the *Iliad* and worshiped as a god at Therapnae.

**MENE, MENE, TEKEL, UPHARSIN *numbered, numbered, weighed, divisions*** Mysterious words appearing on the walls at Belshazzar's feast, presaging the kingdom's fall (DANIEL 5:25).

**MENG-TSZE** See MENCIUS.

**MENNONITE BRETHREN CHURCH OF NORTH AMERICA** American denomination, originating in Russia, which emphasizes mission work, Bible study, and prayer.

**MENNONITE CHURCH** Largest Mennonite

group in the United States, continuing the work of the AMISH Mennonite Church. It was established in 1683.

**MENNONITES** Christians named for MENNO SIMONS, a Dutch priest converted to Protestant belief in the sixteenth century. They stress simple worship and FOOT WASHING.

**MENNONITE WORLD CONFERENCE** International organization of Mennonites with headquarters at Goshen, Indiana.

**MENNO SIMONS (1496–1561)** Dutch priest converted to ANABAPTIST views by reading the New Testament and the writings of Martin LUTHER. Influenced by the Swiss Brethren, he rejected terms and ordinances he could not find in Scripture. He opposed religious persecution and the forcing of religious views on people. His wisdom and saintliness are now recognized; his followers are known as MENNONITES.

**MEN OF GOD** Russian sectarians also called FLAGELLANTS or KHLYSTS.

**MENOLOGION or MENOLOGY** Calendar of saints or martyrs, used liturgically.

**MENORAH** *candlestick* Seven-branched candlestick of the Jewish tabernacle and temple, or the modern HANUKKAH candelabrum.

**MENRVA** Etruscan goddess of luck and wisdom.

**MENSA** *table* Top of an altar.

**MENTAL RESERVATION** Term employed in casuistry for secretly qualifying a statement to mean something different from what is said. In the American fundamentalist-modernist controversies, conservatives accused liberals of mental reservation in stating their beliefs.

**MENTHU** Egyptian god of war symbolized as a hawk or bull.

**MEPHIBOSHETH** 1. Son of Saul killed by the Gibeonites (II SAMUEL 21:8). 2. Lame son of Jonathan honored by David (II SAMUEL 4:4; 9:1–13; 16:1–4; 19:24–30).

**MEPHISTOPHELES** Evil spirit to whom Faust sold his soul, according to German folklore. Mephistopheles was apparently an evil spirit in Akkadian religion, originally, reaching European legend through the religions of the Babylonians, the Chaldeans, and the Jewish Cabala.

**MERAB** *increase* Daughter of King Saul, also known as MICHAL (I SAMUEL 14:49; 18:17–19).

**MERARI** See LEVI.

**MERCIER, DESIRE JOSEPH (1851–1926)** Belgian cardinal and Archbishop of Malines. He interested himself in THOMIST theology and social applications of the gospel. At the German invasion of Belgium in 1914 he symbolized his country's independent spirit, proclaiming "the moral triumph of Belgium." After World War I he worked for unity between Roman Catholics and Anglicans.

**MERCURY** Roman god of commerce and business, a counterpart of the Greek HERMES.

**MERCY** Beneficence and compassion; one of the great religious values. God is characterized by mercy (PSALM 103:13) and Jesus made mercy a touchstone of the renewal of life (MATTHEW 7:1–2).

**MERCY, SISTERS OF** See SISTERS OF MERCY.

**MERCY SEAT** Cover of the ark of the covenant in the Jewish tabernacle and temple. Overlaid with gold, it held two cherubim with folded wings and downcast eyes (EXODUS 25:10–22).

**MERIT** 1. According to the New Testament, human merit is found in Christ; salvation is based on the free grace of God, "not of works, lest any man should boast" (EPHESIANS 2:8–9). 2. In medieval and Catholic theology, merit is the basis of divine rewards. 3. Buddhism sees merit as the result of selfless love.

**MERLE D'AUBIGNE, JEAN HENRI (1794–1872)** Swiss EVANGELICAL minister and church historian, famous especially for his *History of the Reformation in the Sixteenth Century*. He also wrote an eight-volume *History of the Reformation in Europe at the Time of Calvin*.

**MERODACH** Babylonian god who headed the pantheon and was patron god of Babylon.

**MERU** Center of the world in HINDU mythology; over 300,000 miles high, it is the site of the seven cities of the gods.

**MESHACH** Companion of Daniel in Babylon (DANIEL 1:7; 3:13–30).

**MESHECH** Descendant of Noah who fathered the nation of Meshech, a trading people of Asia Minor (GENESIS 10:2; EZEKIEL 27:13; 32:26). Out of Meshech came GOG.

**MESHED** Popular city of Moslem pilgrimage in Iran. Nearby the Arabic philosopher AL-GAZALI was born. A shrine in Meshed to the IMAM Riza, a Moslem martyr, includes a number of mosques.

**MESHKENIT** Egyptian goddess of childbearing.

**MESOPOTAMIA** *between the rivers* Ancient center of culture and religion referred to in Genesis 2:8–14 and 24:10. The stories of the creation and the flood, the law codes, and the forms of worship developed in Mesopotamia profoundly influenced religion.

**MESSALIANS or EUCHITES** *praying ones* Christian group which originated in the Middle East in the fourth century and held that each person's soul is attached to an evil spirit from whom the person may be freed only by praying without ceasing. The Messalians were ascetic, scorned rites and rituals, and were condemned for their heresies at the Council of EPHESUS.

**MESSIAH** *the anointed one* The deliverer long awaited by the Jews to restore the fortunes of Israel and usher in a golden age of peace and righteousness. The Greek form of the word *Messiah* is "CHRIST." The disciples of Jesus have found in Him the Messiah and hence call Him "Christ."

**MESSIANIC HOPE** Term for faith in the coming of the MESSIAH, or, occasionally, of the return of Christ.

**MESSIAS** See MESSIAH.

**METAPHYSICS** That branch of philosophy which is closest to religion, for it deals with ultimate reality and the basic questions of life and meaning. Hence the great metaphysicians such as ARISTOTLE, PLATO, DESCARTES, SPINOZA, LEIBNIZ, KANT, and HEGEL have deeply influenced religious thought.

**METATRON** In Jewish belief, a supreme angelic being.

**METEMPSYCHOSIS** Term for the TRANSMIGRATION of souls, an important teaching in Hinduism.

**METERES** Cretan mother-goddess.

**METHODISM** Term for the system of belief and church government deriving from the teachings of John and Charles WESLEY. The first Methodists emphasized regular and highly personal worship experiences, along with evangelism and deeply felt consecration. They revolutionized the social climate of England and now constitute one of the four largest groups in PROTESTANTISM.

**METHODIST CHURCH** 1. Methodists of the world. 2. Denomination formed in 1939 through the merger of three American churches—the METHODIST EPISCOPAL CHURCH, the METHODIST PROTESTANT CHURCH, and the METHODIST EPISCOPAL CHURCH, SOUTH. Long the largest Protestant denomination in the United States, the Methodist Church is governed by conferences and bishops. Its ministers are forbidden to drink or smoke, and it emphasizes total abstinence from alcoholic beverages on the part of the laity. As this is written it is completing a merger with the EVANGELICAL UNITED BRETHREN. See UNITED METHODIST CHURCH.

**METHODIST EPISCOPAL CHURCH** Early name of the METHODIST CHURCH.

**METHODIST EPISCOPAL CHURCH, SOUTH** Methodist group which split away from the METHODIST EPISCOPAL CHURCH in 1844 over slavery.

**METHODIST PROTESTANT CHURCH** American denomination which withdrew from the METHODIST EPISCOPAL CHURCH in 1830 in protest over what it considered too much government by the clergy and too little lay influence. In 1939 it reunited with its parent body.

**METHODISTS** 1. Early name for the companions of John and Charles WESLEY, who emphasized methodical prayer, Bible study, and devotional exercises. 2. Members of any of the Methodist churches.

**METHODIUS** (c.260–c.311) Greek bishop and church father apparently martyred under DIOCLETIAN. A theologian who opposed ORIGEN, he wrote a hymn to Christ and various works including Bible commentaries and a defense of the freedom of the will.

**METHODIUS** (c.825–885) Brother of CYRIL with whom he evangelized the Slavs of Moravia. The Germans in Moravia resisted his efforts, refusing to ordain his converts and opposing the introduction of Slavonic into the liturgy of the church. He translated the Bible and other works into Slavonic.

**METHUSELAH** *man of the dart* Oldest man in the Bible, reaching the age of 969 (GENESIS 5:21–27).

**METROPOLITAN** 1. A supreme ecclesiastical office in many Eastern churches. 2. An archbishop in the ROMAN CATHOLIC CHURCH who supervises two or more suffragan bishops.

**METTA** BUDDHIST term for love toward all creatures.

**METTA SUTTA** BUDDHIST poem about fellowship.

**METURGEMAN** *interpreter* Interpreters of the Scriptures into the common ARAMAIC in ancient synagogue services.

**METZTLI** Aztec moon goddess.

**MEYER, ALBERT CARDINAL (1903–1965)** Archbishop of Chicago who organized 21 new parishes and built 30 parochial schools. He advocated ecumenism and better race relations, and said that "religion cannot be separated from life."

**MEYNELL, ALICE (1847–1922)** English CATHOLIC poet who with her husband Wilfrid Meynell encouraged Francis THOMPSON. She vigorously supported various social reforms. Among many admirers of her poetry and essays were Coventry Patmore and G. K. Chesterton, who prophesied that "her fullest fame is yet to come."

**MEZUZAH** *doorpost* Parchment, on which is inscribed Deuteronomy 6:4–9 and 11:13–21, fastened to Jewish doorposts in obedience to the commands in those passages.

**MICAH** *who is like the Lord?* Jewish prophet contemporary with Isaiah. His writings form the book of Micah, sixth in the MINOR PROPHETS. He denounced the injustices and religious hypocrisy of his time, predicting correctly that unless the kingdom of Judah changed its ways, it would fall before eastern conquerors as the northern kingdom of Israel had fallen.

**MICHAEL** *who is like God?* There are several Michaels in the Old Testament Scriptures, but the most famous one is the archangel mentioned in Daniel 12:1, Revelation 12:7, and elsewhere. Michael is considered a supreme angel in CHRISTIANITY, JUDAISM, and ISLAM. He is honored in Catholicism with a feast day September 29 (November 8 in the EASTERN ORTHODOX CHURCH).

**MICHAEL CERULARIUS** See CERULARIUS, MICHAEL.

**MICHAELMAS** Feast day honoring the archangel Michael, on September 29.

**MICHAEL OF CESENA (1270–1342)** FRANCISCAN Minister General who with WILLIAM OF OCCAM and others repudiated Pope John XXII's doctrines and authority. Michael was condemned.

**MICHAL** *who is like God?* Daughter of King Saul and wife of King David, also known as MERAB.

**MICHEAS** Variant of MICAH.

**MICHELANGELO (1475–1564)** Italian artist of many talents. His sculptures of David, Bacchus, and the "Pieta," with his decoration of the ceiling of the Sistine Chapel in Rome, represent inimitable artistic heights. He directed the building of St. Peter's, wrote sonnets filled with Christian fervor, and executed sculpture, sketches, paintings, and buildings of indescribably exalted power.

**MICTLAN** Aztec name for the region of the dead.

**MICTLANCIHUATL** Aztec goddess of death.

**MICTLANTECUHTLI** Aztec god of death.

**MIDDLE DOCTRINE SCHOOL** One of India's two divisions of MAHAYANA Buddhism. It emphasizes the Middle Path of Eightfold Negation, affirming both being and nonbeing, and champions total negation in an ultimate void. The school was founded by NAGARJUNA early in the second century.

**MIDDLETON, CONYERS (1683–1750)** One of England's first radical theologians. He disputed ecclesiastical miracles and Biblical accuracy, but had "a passion for abstract truth."

**MIDDLE WAY** Buddhist term for the Noble Eightfold Path outlined in Buddha's first sermon. This is the basis of the MIDDLE DOCTRINE SCHOOL of BUDDHISM.

**MIDGARD** Earth-circling serpent in ancient Germanic myth.

**MIDIANITES** Middle Eastern people who provided Moses with a wife and met defeat at the hands of Israel under Gideon.

**MIDRASH** *explanation (plural midrashim)* Jewish commentary on Scripture which seeks to bring out a deeper meaning than lies on the surface of the text. The Midrash may refer especially to the exposition made about 1,500 years after the BABYLONIAN CAPTIVITY and exile. The two parts of the Midrash are the HALAKAH, interpreting legal points, and the HAGGADA, emphasizing folklore, lessons, parables, anecdotes, and the like.

**MIDRASH RABBAH** Jewish commentaries on the Pentateuch and Ruth, Song of Solomon, Ecclesiastes, Lamentations, and Esther.

**MIDRASH TANCHUMA** Jewish commentary on the Pentateuch arranged in liturgical form for synagogue use. It dates from the fourth century.

**MIGNE, JACQUES PAUL (1800–1875)** French religious publisher who brought out in book form the *Patrologia,* presenting all the Christian writings of the Middle Ages and other Catholic works, at popular prices.

**MIKVAH** Ritual bath in JUDAISM.

**MILAH** Jewish term for circumcision.

**MILAREPA (1038–1122)** Tibetan BUDDHIST saint and poet. A severe ascetic who wrote many hymns, he has been called "one of the most extraordinary personalities that Asia ever produced." His works are more widely read in Tibet than those of any other author.

**MILCAH counsel** 1. A title of ISHTAR. 2. A sister of Lot and wife of Abraham's brother Nahor (GENESIS 22:20). A daughter of Zelophehad (NUMBERS 26:33).

**MILIC or MILICZ (?–1374)** Bohemian churchman whose reforms presaged those of John HUSS. An eloquent preacher, he wrote several devotional works and denounced clerical vices. When he went to Rome to establish reforms in the church he was imprisoned by the INQUISITION but was finally declared innocent of heresy.

**MILITARISM** Philosophy or practice of war as an ideal way of solving various problems. While no one has discovered a satisfactory substitute for war, the horrors of modern warfare make militarism increasingly abhorrent to those of religious or humane sensitivity.

**MILK AND HONEY** Biblical symbols of prosperity and peace. Newly converted and baptized Christians in the early Christian era tasted milk and honey.

**MILLENARIANISM** Belief in the millennium of Revelation 20:5 as a literal period of 1,000 years in which Christ will reign visibly on earth.

**MILLENNIAL CHURCH** A name of the SHAKERS.

**MILLENNIAL DAWN** Series of books by Charles Taze RUSSELL, outlining his views

of sin, salvation, and the coming millennium.

**MILLENNIUM** Term for the "thousand years" specified in Revelation 20:5 as the period during which Christ reigns over the earth.

**MILLER, WILLIAM (1782–1849)** American farmer and veteran of the War of 1812 who proclaimed in 1831 that Christ would return and the world would end "about the year 1843." When that year passed the date was revised; in 1845 the ADVENTIST Church was established through Miller's influence.

**MILLERITES** Followers of William MILLER. There appears to be no credible foundation for the belief that on October 22, 1844, they donned white robes and climbed hills to await the return of Christ.

**MILLET, JEAN FRANCOIS (1814–1875)** French painter of "The Angelus," "St. Jerome," and other works.

**MILLS, JOHN (1645–1707)** ANGLICAN New Testament critic.

**MILMAN, HENRY HART (1791–1868)** ANGLICAN clergyman and church historian. His *History of the Jews* minimized the miraculous in Scripture and treated the latter from the viewpoint of historical criticism. A liberal theologian, he fought compulsory subscription by the clergy to the Thirty-nine Articles (see ARTICLES, THIRTY-NINE).

**MILTON, JOHN (1608–1674)** Anglican-Puritan poet renowned for *Paradise Lost, Paradise Regained, Samson Agonistes, Areopagitica, De Doctrina Christiana, Eikonoklastes,* and other works. He is accused of ARIAN tendencies in theology, but he was a doughty champion of human freedom and the Christian world-view.

**MIMAMSA inquiry** System of philosophy or study in HINDUISM.

**MIMBAR** Moslem pulpit (see ISLAM).

**MIN** Egyptian god of procreation, symbolized by a ram.

**MINARET** Tower on a Moslem mosque from which is sounded the call to prayer (see ISLAM).

**MINCHAH or MINHAH afternoon** Jewish ritual for daily afternoon prayer.

**MINERVA** Roman goddess of wisdom, handicrafts, professions, and arts. Her Greek counterpart was ATHENA.

**MING** Chinese word for fate or God.

**MINHAG** *custom* Jewish rite with the power of law because of established usage.

**MINHAH** See MINCHAH.

**MINIMI or MINIMS** *the least* Monastic order founded by St. FRANCIS OF PAOLA in 1453. To indicate their humility they ranked themselves below the Friars Minor (*less*). One member, Bernard Boil, became the first Vicar Apostolic in America. There are Minimi today in Spain and Italy.

**MINISTER** 1. CLERGYMAN and/or celebrant of worship, in most denominations ordained to office after fulfilling certain vows and conditions of training. 2. A minister was originally a servant, the meaning of the word in the King James Bible.

**MINISTRY** 1. Collective term for CLERGY. 2. Duties and work of a MINISTER.

**MINOR CANON** CLERGYMAN who assists in the service at a cathedral although not belonging to the cathedral chapter.

**MINORITE** Term for a FRANCISCAN.

**MINOR ORDERS** Church orders inferior to the MAJOR ORDERS. In Western churches the Minor Orders comprise ACOLYTES, LECTORS, porters, and EXORCISTS. In EASTERN ORTHODOX churches they are lectors and CANTORS.

**MINOR PROPHETS** Term for the twelve smaller books of prophecy in the Old Testament (see also MAJOR PROPHETS). The twelve books are HOSEA, JOEL, AMOS, OBADIAH, JONAH, MICAH, NAHUM, HABAKKUK, ZEPHANIAH, HAGGAI, ZECHARIAH, and MALACHI.

**MINSTER** Church or monastery.

**MINUCIUS FELIX, MARCUS (second or third century)** African Christian whose apologetic work *Octavius* is one of the earliest of its kind. It attacked paganism and defended MONOTHEISM.

**MINYAN** Minimum of ten men necessary for Jewish congregational worship.

**MIRACLE** Supernatural event in which the work of God appears to set aside or rise above the ordinary laws of nature.

**MIRACLE PLAY** Medieval drama based on events in the life of Christ, the Bible, or the lives of saints.

**MIRAJ** MOSLEM term for MOHAMMED's ascent to heaven and back.

**MIRARI VOS** Title of the papal bull of Gregory XVI denouncing the ideas of LAMENNAIS in 1832. The latter had proposed liberty of worship and freedom of the press.

**MIRIAM** Sister of Moses and Aaron. She saved the former from possible death as an infant in the bulrushes, and led the Hebrew women in a victory song after the Red Sea was crossed. (EXODUS 2:4–8; 15:20–21).

**MIRROR** Symbol of MARY as a reflection of God, based on the Wisdom of Solomon 7:26.

**MIRZA or SAYYID ALI MOHAMMED (?–1850)** See the BAB and BABISM.

**MISERERE** A title of Psalm 51, based on its first word in the Latin VULGATE.

**MISERICORD** 1. Bracket attached to a choir-stall seat, to aid those who must stand for long periods in divine worship. 2. Monastery room for those incapable of fulfilling the same duties as others in the order. 3. Religious dispensation. 4. Thin medieval dagger used for the death stroke.

**MISHNAH** *teaching* Jewish oral law containing decisions and traditions from the first century B.C. to the third century A.D. The Mishnah is the basis of the GEMARA and has six main sections: Zeraim, Moed, Nashim, Nezikin, Kodashim, and Taharot.

**MISSAL** 1. Devotional book. 2. Book of words said or sung at MASS, often in Latin.

**MISSION** 1. Purpose of the church: witnessing to Christ in word and deed. 2. Evangelistic program of preaching or teaching. 3. Church or parish financially dependent on outside resources.

**MISSIONARY** One commissioned to carry out a special task for the church, particularly in evangelism. The traditional distinction between home missionary and foreign missionary is becoming as obsolete in the modern church as the term missionary itself.

**MISSIONARY BANDS OF THE WORLD** American Holiness group which merged in 1933 into the Church of God (Holiness). See HOLINESS CHURCHES.

**MISSIONARY CHURCH ASSOCIATION** Conservative American Holiness group with virtually independent local churches.

**MISSIONS** Traditional term for the world evangelistic enterprise of the church. See also MISSION, MISSIONARY.

**MISSOURI SYNOD**   See LUTHERAN CHURCH —MISSOURI SYNOD.

**MIT BRENNENDER SORGE** *with burning anxiety*  Papal encyclical of 1937 stating the non-Christian character of German NAZISM.

**MITER or MITRE**  Headdress of Jewish high priest in Bible times.

**MITHRA or MITHRAS**  ZOROASTRIAN solar deity, worshiped as the god of wisdom and light in India and Persia, who became prominent in MITHRAISM.

**MITHRAISM**  Mystery religion originating in Persia in the second century A.D. Until the end of the third century it was popular throughout the Roman Empire. Theologically dualistic and morally rigorous, Mithraism stressed the sacred meals and baptisms common to all mystery religions. Mithra's birthday on December 25 became known eventually as that of Christ. Mithra was believed to have been born in a cave, to have been worshiped by shepherds, to have done miracles, to have ascended to heaven, and to have been a mediator between heaven and earth, providing the righteous with heavenly bliss.

**MITHRAS**  See MITHRA, MITHRAISM.

**MITLA**  Religious center of the Zapotec Indians of thirteenth-century Mexico.

**MITRA**  See MITHRA.

**MITRE**  See MITER.

**MITZVAH** *commandment*  Jewish term for religious law or duty.

**MIXCOATL**  Ancient Mexican god of fire, lightning, and hunting.

**MIYA-ZAKI-JINGU**  Japanese SHINTO shrine commemorating the Emperor Jimmu. It is at Miyazaki in Kyushu.

**MIZPAH** *watchtower*  1. Jewish shrine in the period of the Judges. 2. Place near the Jabbok River where Jacob and Laban united in the MIZPAH BENEDICTION. 3. HIVITE center near Mt. Hermon. 4. Name of several other cities of Palestine.

**MIZPAH BENEDICTION**  Term for the treaty-like benediction of Laban upon Jacob in Genesis 31:49. Although often used as a benediction in church groups, the Mizpah benediction was invoked primarily to keep the two men separate; the Lord was invoked to see that neither trespassed the boundary.

**MIZRACH** *east*  Jewish term for the custom of facing Jerusalem when praying.

**MIZRACHI**  Zionist group which merged into a world Zionist organization in 1957.

**MIZVAH**  See MITZVAH.

**MNEMOSYNE**  Greek goddess of memory.

**MOAB**  Country roughly east of the Dead Sea; home of the Moabites who often warred against the Israelites. The Jewish prophets often denounced Moab's sins (ISAIAH 15; 16; EZEKIEL 25; AMOS 2).

**MOABITES**  People of Moab. Among the more illustrious Moabites were Balak, Eglon, and Ruth the ancestress of David and Jesus. The Moabites stemmed from Lot's incest with his daughter (GENESIS 19:37).

**MOABITE STONE**  Black stone pillar with 34 lines in the Moabite language commemorating the revolt of Mesha king of Moab against Israel and Mesha's devotion to the god CHEMOSH. The stone was found at Dibon in central Moab in 1868. It mentions a number of names found in the Old Testament such as JEHOVAH and Madeba.

**MOCCUS**  Ancient Celtic god.

**MODALISM**  Ancient Christian heresy denying the orthodox view of the TRINITY. Modalists held that the persons of the Trinity were not actually distinct persons at all, but different modes or forms in which God was revealed. SABELLIUS was one of the most famous Modalists.

**MODERATISM**  Eighteenth-century movement in Scottish PRESBYTERIANISM subordinating doctrine to accommodation to the contemporary world. Favoring patronage and the supremacy of the civil courts in church matters, it gradually lost favor and disappeared.

**MODERATOR**  Presbyterian term for the official presiding at a meeting of the SESSION, PRESBYTERY, SYNOD, or GENERAL ASSEMBLY.

**MODERNISM**  Term for the tendency to emphasize the new and modern in religion, sometimes—in the judgment of conservatives—at the expense of losing the old and traditional. In 1907 Pope PIUS X condemned modernism in Catholicism, while early in the twentieth century various Protestants denounced the movement in Protestantism.

**MOFFAT, ROBERT (1795–1883)**  Pioneer Scottish missionary in South Africa, where for more than twenty years he worked to convert and aid the natives. He translated the Scriptures into the Bechuana and Sechwana languages, and persuaded his son-in-law David Livingstone to go to Africa.

**MOFFATT, JAMES (1870–1944)** British PRESBYTERIAN New Testament scholar, famous for his colloquial and fresh translation of the Bible. Among his other works he edited a seventeen-volume commentary on the New Testament.

**MOGGALLANA (fifth century B.C.)** Disciple of Gautama BUDDHA, believed to possess supernatural gifts.

**MOGUL** Moslem empire which ruled India from early in the sixteenth to the middle of the nineteenth century. Because the first emperor was Baber, descended from Timur, it might be more accurate to call the Mogul a Timurid empire.

**MOHAMMED** *praised* **(c.570–632)** Chief Prophet of Islam. Born in Mecca, he became a merchant and had four daughters by a rich widow he married. In visions the angel Gabriel communicated to him a new religion, ISLAM. His wife died when he was probably in his 40's and he married two wives, one nine years old. With his followers he waged war against his enemies and by the end of his life he ruled Arabia. Moslems consider him sinless.

**MOHAMMEDANISM** Another name for ISLAM.

**MOHAMMED IBN TUMART (c.1080–1128)** Founder of the ISLAM sect of the ALMOHADES who ruled Spain in the twelfth and thirteenth centuries. He led a holy war against those MOSLEMS who differed with his puritanical ideas.

**MOHARRAM** First month in the ISLAMIC calendar.

**MOHEL** Jewish term for the officiant at the rite of CIRCUMCISION.

**MOHENJO-DARO** Site in the Indus valley, in present-day Pakistan, where a large bath figured in ancient HINDU ablutions. It is an important city in the study of Hinduism.

**MOKSHA** *spiritual release* One of the four great goals of HINDUISM. In BUDDHISM it means practically the same thing as NIRVANA.

**MOKUGYO** *wooden fish* Japanese BUDDHIST term for a drum used in ZEN monasteries.

**MOKUSHO** Type of ZEN Buddhism stressing the perception of spiritual enlightenment through silence.

**MOLECH** or **MOLOCH** Semitic god in whose worship children were burned alive in Assyria and Canaan. Such worship is often mentioned and condemned in the Old Testament.

**MOLINA, LUIS (1535–1600)** Spanish Jesuit professor of theology who reconciled human freedom with divine predestination by stating God foreknows but does not cause men's actions. Because this "Molinism" was felt to deny divine grace, and because it differed from THOMISM, it was severely attacked.

**MOLINISM** Doctrinal system attributed to Luis MOLINA.

**MOLINOS, MIGUEL DE (c.1640–c.1697)** Spanish priest whose book *Guida Spirituale,* expounding quiet meditation as a chief spiritual exercise, gained him the reputation of founding QUIETISM. Condemned by the INQUISITION, he died in prison. His theology envisioned the believer as progressing from reliance on the church to devotion to Christ, finally fixing his trust on God alone.

**MOLOCH** See MOLECH.

**MOMUS** Greek god personifying ridicule and criticism.

**MONACHISM** See MONASTICISM.

**MONADISM** Philosophical system in which ultimate reality consists in various independent self-sufficient monads or entities. In the philosophy of LEIBNIZ these monads are established by God.

**MONAN** Creator-god in the religion of the Tupi-Guarani Indians of South America.

**MONARCHIANISM** Christian heresy of the second and third centuries denying the orthodox doctrine of the TRINITY. It was divided into two groups, ADOPTIONISTS and MODALISTS. Its central emphasis is on the supremacy of God as over against any independent "power and glory" of Jesus or the Spirit.

**MONASTERY** Dwelling of a group of MONKS.

**MONASTICISM or MONACHISM** Way of religious life in which MONKS or NUNS dwell in a community of their own, devoting themselves rather exclusively to such pursuits as prayer and self-mortification. Monasticism has played an important part in CATHOLICISM, ISLAM, BUDDHISM, and JAINISM; in some forms it has influenced JUDAISM and other religions. As a rule PROTESTANTISM has avoided this means of avoiding worldliness.

**MONERGISM** Theological term for belief in regeneration by God alone, with no human cooperation.

**MONEY** Religious symbol of Jesus' betrayal.

**MONICA or MONNICA, ST. (c.331–387)** Mother of St. AUGUSTINE OF HIPPO. His conversion he attributed to her prayers. She is considered the patron saint of Christian mothers; her feast day is May 4.

**MONIS, JUDAH (1683–1764)** Jewish Christian author of the first Hebrew grammar published in America. He always worshiped on Saturday.

**MONISM** Philosophical system explaining all reality in terms of one central unifying principle.

**MONK** One who separates from the world at large and devotes himself to religious, and often ascetic, exercises. In CATHOLICISM a monk is bound by the vows of poverty, chastity, and obedience.

**MONK, MARIA (c.1817–1850)** Canadian woman who claimed to have witnessed immorality and infanticide in the convent from which she escaped before publishing her book *Awful Disclosures.*

**MONOGAMY** Marriage to one person, the Christian ideal.

**MONOGENISM** Doctrine that all human beings began with one pair or one human type.

**MONOGRAM one letter** Symbolic representation of a name by a letter, or by two or more letters combined. A famous religious example is the *chi-rho*, appearing something like an *X* over a *P*, representing the name of Christ.

**MONOLATRY** Theological term for worship of only one god.

**MONOPHYSITISM** Belief that Christ had but one nature. The Second Council of CONSTANTINOPLE condemned this doctrine in 553, stating that Christ has two natures, divine and human, distinct but united in His person. Monophysitism existed in the fifth and sixth centuries.

**MONOTHEISM** Belief in one God. This is the doctrine of ISLAM, JUDAISM, and CHRISTIANITY.

**MONOTHELITISM** Seventh-century Christian heresy according to which Christ had only one will. The orthodox contended that He had both two natures and two wills, divine and human. Monothelitism was condemned by the Lateran Synod in 649.

**MONSIGNOR my lord** CATHOLIC title of recognition granted by the pope to outstanding clergymen.

**MONSTRANCE** Vessel in which the HOST is displayed for veneration in the MASS.

**MONTAGNA, BARTOLOMEO (c.1450–1523)** Italian religious painter. He executed many altarpieces and paintings of the MADONNA.

**MONTALEMBERT, CHARLES FORBES (1810–1870)** French political writer who sought to unite CATHOLIC beliefs with such liberal political ideas as separation of church and state and freedom for new ideas. His enthusiasm was diminished by the papal condemnation of liberalism.

**MONTANES, JUAN MARTINEZ (c.1568–1649)** Spanish religious sculptor. He executed a number of altarpieces, particularly of Christ.

**MONTANISM** Movement named for MONTANUS which emphasized speaking in tongues and abstinence from worldly practices. Prominent in the second, third, and fourth centuries, Montanism has from time to time been revived in different forms.

**MONTANUS (second century)** Phrygian Christian who began to prophesy between 156 and 172 A.D. and with the women Maximilla and Prisca proclaimed the coming of the Spirit of truth. They also held that the return of Christ was imminent.

**MONTEFIORE, CLAUDE JOSEPH (1858–1938)** Scholar and exponent of liberal or REFORM JUDAISM. His studies have aided in the understanding of the NEW TESTAMENT.

**MONTGOMERY, JAMES (1771–1854)** English MORAVIAN poet and hymn writer. Many of his hymns including "Hail to the Lord's Anointed" and "In the Hour of Trial" are still popular.

**MONTH'S MIND** REQUIEM mass celebrated

a month after the burial or death of the deceased.

**MOODY, DWIGHT LYMAN (1837–1899)** Noted American evangelist. His unschooled but simple sermons powerfully affected thousands and produced success in evangelistic campaigns throughout the United States and Great Britain.

**MOON** Object of worship in many ancient lands.

**MOONEY, EDWARD FRANCIS (1882–1958)** American archbishop and cardinal, active in labor progress and social righteousness.

**MOORE, GEORGE FOOT (1851–1931)** American PRESBYTERIAN orientalist and Bible scholar. His works included *The History of Religions* and *The Literature of the Old Testament.*

**MORAL ARGUMENT** One of the classical arguments for the existence of God, based on human moral convictions. These, it is held, presuppose a moral God and a moral order in the universe.

**MORALES, LUIS DE (c.1520–1586)** Spanish religious painter who did many versions of the "Pieta," "Ecce Homo," and other aspects of the lives of Christ and the saints.

**MORAL INFLUENCE THEORY** View of the atonement of Christ, first popularized by ABELARD, holding that the cross is essentially and example of the love of God, influencing men to a similar self-giving love.

**MORALISM** 1. Moral truth or teaching. 2. Practice of MORALITY.

**MORALITY** 1. Goodness or moral character. 2. Sexual rectitude. 3. Rightness in any area. 4. Subject of moral lessons. 5. System of morals.

**MORALITY PLAY** Medieval drama in which the characters had such names as Faith and Charity or Sloth and Vice, and the struggle for righteousness was shown in such plays as the popular *Everyman.*

**MORAL LAW** Fundamental principle of righteous conduct. Some see such a principle as the outgrowth of human logic, conscience, or experience. The Christian finds it in the word of God.

**MORAL OBLIGATION** Duty to God, a church, humanity, or the like.

**MORAL OPTIMISM** Belief in the rewards of righteous endeavor.

**MORAL PHILOSOPHY** Ethics; the science or study of morality.

**MORAL RE-ARMAMENT** Religious group founded by Frank BUCHMAN and dedicated to the goals of absolute honesty, absolute purity, absolute unselfishness, and absolute love. Beginning with individual conversion, it seeks to bring about ethical changes in social groups and in nations.

**MORALS** Moral principles or habits. Sometimes "morals" indicates merely sexual conduct.

**MORAL THEOLOGY** Study of the relationship between divine revelation and human conduct. In CATHOLICISM moral theology stresses penance and the confessional.

**MORAVIAN BRETHREN** See MORAVIANS, MORAVIAN CHURCH, and BOHEMIAN or MORAVIAN BRETHREN.

**MORAVIAN CHURCH** Name by which the Unitas Fratrum is known in the United States (see BOHEMIAN BRETHREN). Coming to America in 1734, the Moravian Church stresses "in essentials unity, in nonessentials liberty, in all things charity." It also emphasizes divine love, Biblical teaching, pacifism, the witness of the Spirit, the separation of church and state, and evangelism. There is a decennial gathering of Moravians from all parts of the world.

**MORAVIANS** Christians of Moravia and Bohemia who opposed Roman Catholic corruption early in the medieval period and were aided by John HUSS and Nicholas ZINZENDORF. The largest group is the MORAVIAN CHURCH in the United States.

**MORDECAI** Uncle and protector of Queen ESTHER. Through her influence he became prominent in the kingdom of Persia.

**MORE, HANNAH (1745–1833)** English writer who aided the founding of the Religious Tract Society and a public school system. Besides novels and dramas she wrote many religious works; she belonged to the CLAPHAM SECT.

**MORE, HENRY (1614–1687)** English philosopher and mystic who held that God governs the world through a "spirit of nature." Opposing HOBBES' materialism, he sought to establish a reasonable basis for theism through voluminous writings.

**MORE, THOMAS, ST. (1478–1535)** English CATHOLIC humanist, statesman, author, philosopher, and martyr. His *Utopia* pictures an ideal human government. Charged with treason when he opposed Henry VIII's marital schemes and assumption of headship of the church, he died affirming that "no parliament could make a law that God should not be God" and that he was "the king's good servant, but God's first." His feast day is July 9.

**MOREHOUSE, HENRY L.** (1834–1917) Baptist clergyman long active in home mission work in the United States.

**MORENU** *our teacher* Honorary Jewish title for authorities on the TALMUD.

**MORGAN, G. CAMPBELL** (1863–1945) British CONGREGATIONAL preacher who won fame as a popular Bible expositor. He wrote many books.

**MORGAN, THOMAS JEFFERSON** (1839–1902) United States Commissioner of Indian Affairs and clergyman who served as corresponding secretary of the American Baptist Home Mission Society.

**MORGENSTERN, CHRISTIAN** (1871–1914) German poet and mystic whose later writings reflected his conversion to THEOSOPHY.

**MORIAH** 1. Mountainous area where Abraham prepared to sacrifice his firstborn son Isaac (GENESIS 22:2). 2. Mountain where Solomon built the Jewish Temple (II SAMUEL 24:18 ff.; II CHRONICLES 3:1).

**MORIKE, EDUARD FRIEDRICH** (1804–1875) German minister and poet whose verse included "The Sleeping Christ Child."

**MORISCOS** Spain's native Moors converted to the CHRISTIAN faith. Those who adhered to ISLAM were known as Mudejares. The Moriscos were persecuted in the INQUISITION and finally expelled from Spain.

**MORISON, JAMES** (1816–1893) Scottish minister expelled from the United Secession Church for his views on the universal atonement of Christ. He founded the EVANGELICAL UNION.

**MORMON** 1. Compiler of the BOOK OF MORMON. 2. Unofficial name for a member of the CHURCH OF JESUS CHRIST OF LATTER-DAY SAINTS or of a similar body originating under the influence of Joseph SMITH.

**MORMON, BOOK OF** Book discovered by Joseph SMITH giving the Mormon version of American history in the centuries before the birth of Christ. The name derives from a man named Mormon who is said to have gathered the records.

**MORMONS** Members of the CHURCH OF JESUS CHRIST OF LATTER-DAY SAINTS, the REORGANIZED CHURCH OF JESUS CHRIST OF LATTER-DAY SAINTS, the CHURCH OF JESUS CHRIST, or any of the similar bodies which accept the Book of MORMON (above). Theirs is one of the indigenous American religions.

**MORNAY, PHILIPPE DE** (1549–1623) French HUGUENOT leader, writer, and statesman. His influence may be gauged by the fact that he has been termed "the Huguenot pope."

**MORO** MOSLEM of the Philippine Islands.

**MORPHEUS** Greek and Roman god of dreams.

**MORRIGU** Celtic war goddess.

**MORRISON, CHARLES CLAYTON** (1874–1966) American leader among the DISCIPLES OF CHRIST and in ecumenical circles. He wrote many books and for the greater part of his active life was editor of *The Christian Century*. A pacifist, he opposed American entrance into the world wars and led in the formation of the NATIONAL COUNCIL OF CHURCHES and the WORLD COUNCIL OF CHURCHES.

**MORRISON, NORMAN R.** (1933–1965) American QUAKER, executive secretary of the Stony Run Meeting in Baltimore, who burned himself to death in protest over the war in Vietnam.

**MORRISON, ROBERT** (1782–1834) China's first Protestant missionary. Born in Scotland, he was sent to Canton by the London Missionary Society after joining the PRESBYTERIAN CHURCH. He translated the Bible into Chinese, wrote Chinese reference works, and founded a college and a medical dispensary manned by natives.

**MORROW MASS** Medieval English term for an early MASS.

**MORS** Roman god of death.

**MORSE** Clasp or band fastening a COPE across the wearer's chest.

**MORTAL** 1. CATHOLIC term for something deserving spiritual death. 2. Earthly; related to death.

**MORTALITY** Theological term for sinfulness leading to death.

**MORTAL MIND** Term in CHRISTIAN SCIENCE for human error and delusion: "Nothing claiming to be something" (Mary Baker EDDY).

**MORTAL SIN** CATHOLIC term for deliberate sin or wilful departure from God, for which there is no remedy apart from full confession and penance.

**MORTIFICATION** Attempt to subordinate the passions and appetites to the spirit through fasting, penance, abstinence, etc.

**MORTMAIN** *dead hand* Possession of property by religious corporations or bodies.

**MORTUARY** 1. Place where dead bodies are kept until burial, as a burial establishment. 2. Gift to a clergyman from the estate of one deceased.

**MOSAIC LAW** Ancient moral and ceremonial law of the Hebrews, derived from various OLD TESTAMENT codes attributed to MOSES; especially the PENTATEUCH.

**MOSES** Jewish lawgiver and leader in the exodus from Egypt. Born and raised in Egypt, he met God at a burning bush and led the virtually enslaved ISRAELITES across the Red Sea and into the Sinai deserts. There he received the Ten Commandments and other legislation (see DECALOGUE). After forty years of wandering, the Israelites entered the land of Canaan (Palestine) at the time of Moses' death. He appeared to Christ on the Mount of Transfiguration (MATTHEW 17:3). The first five books of the Bible are traditionally ascribed to Moses.

**MOSES, APOCALYPSE OF** See APOCALYPSE OF MOSES.

**MOSES, ASSUMPTION OF** See ASSUMPTION OF MOSES.

**MOSES BEN MAIMON** See MAIMONIDES.

**MOSES BEN NACHMAN (1194–1270)** Spanish Talmudist and Jewish scholar. A physician and mystic, he wrote a commentary on the PENTATEUCH and defended his faith against CHRISTIANITY.

**MOSHEIM, JOHANN LORENZ VON (c.1694–1755)** German LUTHERAN church historian, scholar, and theologian. He is noted for his *Institutes of Ecclesiastical History.*

**MOSLEM** Adherent of ISLAM or Mohammedanism.

**MOSLEM CALENDAR** Lunar calendar with 354 or 355 days. The twelve months have Moslem names.

**MOSQUE** Building for Moslem worship. A typical mosque has a fountain in the center and minarets from which the faithful are called to prayer. The mosque may also have a courtyard, a pulpit, a school, and a niche indicating the direction of Mecca.

**MOST CATHOLIC** Title of the king of Spain.

**MOST CHRISTIAN** Title of the king of France.

**MOST HIGH** Title sometimes given God.

**MOST REVEREND** Title often given an ARCHBISHOP.

**MOST SACRED** Title of the king of England.

**MOT** Phoenician god of death.

**MOTET** Originally, a liturgical choral composition, usually without accompaniment.

**MOTHER CHURCH** Cathedral church, or a church sponsoring other churches or missions.

**MOTHER-GODDESS** Ancient deity in many lands, symbolizing fertility and life.

**MOTHER HOUSE** Center of a religious order with branch houses.

**MOTHERING SUNDAY** Fourth Sunday in LENT. The name may derive from the Epistle for the day, referring to "Jerusalem . . . the mother of us all" (GALATIANS 4:26).

**MOTHER OF GOD** Title of the Virgin MARY in her role as mother of Christ, God incarnate. This is essentially a CATHOLIC term.

**MOTHER OF THE CHURCH** Title given the Virgin MARY at VATICAN COUNCIL II in 1964.

**MOTHER'S DAY** Second Sunday in May, long observed in American churches as a day of honor for mothers. The day is now designated the Festival of the Christian Home by the NATIONAL COUNCIL OF CHURCHES.

**MOTT, JOHN RALEIGH (1865–1955)** American METHODIST churchman who was active in the YOUNG MEN'S CHRISTIAN ASSOCIATION, the WORLD COUNCIL OF CHURCHES, and mission recruitment. He labored for the goal, "The Evangelization of the World in Our Generation," and directed many young people toward the foreign mission field.

**MOTU PROPRIO** *of his own accord* Papal letter written on the pope's own initiative and bearing his personal signature.

**MOTZI** Jewish term for a benediction on food.

**MOULE, HANDLEY CARR GLYN (1841–1920)** ANGLICAN commentator and EVANGELICAL leader. He was Bishop of Durham.

**MOULTON, WILLIAM F. (1835–1898)** English METHODIST clergyman and authority on New Testament Greek. He translated Winer's *Grammar of New Testament Greek* and prepared a Greek New Testament concordance.

**MOUNT OF OLIVES** Hilly area east of Jerusalem. There Ezekiel (11:23) saw God. Zechariah announced that it would eventually split (14:4). There Jesus was praying when he was arrested on the eve of the CRUCIFIXION (MATTHEW 26:30; 47–56).

**MOVABLE FEAST** Ecclesiastical festival whose date varies according to the date of EASTER.

**MOZARABIC LITURGY** Ancient Spanish liturgy, preserved at Toledo since 1500 but dating back many centuries before that. In the MASS the HOST is divided into nine parts, of which seven are arranged in the shape of the cross.

**MOZARABS** Term by which the Christians were known while Spain was under ISLAM rule. Their liturgy is the MOZARABIC.

**MOZETTA** Cape with a small hood whose color—violet, red, or black—indicates the rank of the ecclesiastical official wearing it.

**M.R.** Letters symbolizing the Virgin MARY.

**M.R.A.** Abbreviation for MORAL RE-ARMAMENT.

**MT. REV.** Abbreviation for MOST REVEREND.

**MUCHI (thirteenth century)** Skillful Japanese ZEN artist.

**MUCKERS** Popular name for the followers of Johann Schonherr and Johann Wilhelm Ebel in nineteenth-century Germany. Their religion appears to have consisted chiefly of THEOSOPHY.

**MUDEJAR** 1. Medieval Moslem-Christian architecture of Spain. 2. A Moor in Spain who adhered to ISLAM.

**MUDRA** Gestures used in BUDDHIST magic and devotional rites.

**MUELLER, GEORGE** See George MÜLLER.

**MUENZER, THOMAS (1489–1525)** German ANABAPTIST leader, beheaded after leading the abortive PEASANTS' WAR which LUTHER denounced.

**MUFTI** Lawyer and exponent of MOSLEM canon law.

**MUGGLETON, LODOWICKE (1609–1698)** English religious innovator who with John Reeve claimed to be the two witnesses of Revelation 11:3. They denied the Trinitarian doctrine and held that Eve was the spirit of evil.

**MUGGLETONIANS** Disciples of Lodowicke MUGGLETON from the seventeenth to the nineteenth century in England.

**MUHAMMAD** See MOHAMMED.

**MUHARRAM** *sacred* First month in the ISLAMIC calendar.

**MUHLENBERG, HEINRICH MELCHIOR (1711–1787)** "Patriarch of Lutheranism in America." Ordained in Germany, he organized LUTHERAN congregations through the British colonies, establishing America's first Lutheran synod in 1748.

**MUHLENBERG, WILLIAM AUGUSTUS (1796–1877)** EPISCOPAL leader and hymn writer. He founded an industrial community in New York State, a "church village" named St. Johnland. He established the first Episcopal school in the United States and its first order of Episcopal deaconesses.

**MUJTAHID** Moslem teacher, particularly in SHIISM.

**MUKDAM** Jewish SEPHARDIC official.

**MUKTI** Term for salvation in Indian HINDUISM.

**MULLA** Learned official of ISLAM and teacher of the law.

**MÜLLER, GEORGE (1805–1898)** Prussian-born Christian and philanthropist in England who established a number of orphanages by faith and maintained them through prayer.

**MÜLLER, MAX (1823–1900)** British orientalist and student of comparative religions, particularly those of the East.

**MULLINS, EDGAR Y. (1860–1928)** Theologian and president of the Southern Baptist Theological Seminary at Louisville, Kentucky.

**MUMBO JUMBO** Evil spirit worshiped or feared in the western Sudan, Africa.

**MUMMIFICATION** Preservation of the body after death. Dating from before 3,000 B.C. in Egypt, it apparently was connected from early times with religious ritual and the belief in life after death.

**MUNDATORY** White linen used to wipe the vessels after the EUCHARIST or MASS.

**MUNDELEIN, GEORGE WILLIAM (1872–1939)** American cardinal and Archbishop of Chicago. He worked for various phases of social justice and was an early critic of NAZISM. Mundelein, Illinois, is named for him.

**MUNK, KAJ (1898–1944)** Danish minister whose dramas such as *The Word* inspired faith and moral resolve.

**MUNKACSY, MICHAEL VON (1844–1900)** Hungarian painter famous for such paintings as "Ecce Homo" and "Christ Before Pilate." His real name was Michael Leo Lieb.

**MUNSEE PROPHET** American Indian who sought to inspire those of his race, particularly the Delaware Indians, to resist white aggression.

**MÜNSTER, SEBASTIAN (1489–1552)** German FRANCISCAN monk who became one of the Protestant scholars of the REFORMATION. He was editor of the first Bible to be prepared by a German in Hebrew. A LUTHERAN, he became court preacher at Heidelberg.

**MUNT** Egyptian god of war.

**MUNZER, THOMAS (c.1489–1525)** German ANABAPTIST reformer. He preached social as well as spiritual reform, advocated common ownership of property, denounced Martin LUTHER, and claimed to be under the direct inspiration of the Holy Spirit. At the end of the PEASANTS' WAR he was beheaded.

**MURATORI, LUDOVICO ANTONIO (1672–1750)** Italian priest and scholar known as the "father of Italian history." He discovered the MURATORIAN CANON in 1740.

**MURATORIAN CANON** Oldest extant list of NEW TESTAMENT books. It is believed to have been written in the second century A.D. and is in Latin. It contains all the present New Testament writings except Hebrews, James, the epistles of Peter, and one epistle of John.

**MURIGEN** Irish water goddess.

**MURILLO, BARTOLOMÉ ESTEBAN (1617–1682)** One of Spain's greatest painters, famed for such religious works as the "Vision of St. Anthony," "Birth of the Virgin," "Moses," and "The Miracle of the Loaves and Fishes."

**MURJITES or MURJIYAH postponers** Early MOSLEM opponents of the KHARIJITES. They said that ALLAH could decide which Moslems were worthy, and emphasized the importance of human faith as well as of divine predestination.

**MURNER, THOMAS (1475–1537)** German FRANCISCAN monk who satirized not only the PROTESTANTS but even his own order and the follies of his time.

**MURRAIN** Plague or curse.

**MURRAY, JOHN (1741–1815)** British founder of the UNIVERSALIST CHURCH in the United States. During the Revolution he was chaplain of the troops of Rhode Island. He popularized the doctrines of universal salvation and UNITARIAN theology.

**MURUGAN** Supreme deity of the Tamils of southern India.

**MUSAPH or MUSSAF** Additional service of prayer following the usual morning service in a Jewish synagogue.

**MUSES** Greek gods of the arts. Originally they appear to have been water nymphs with mystic powers, dwelling in springs or fountains.

**MUSLEM or MUSLIM** See MOSLEM.

**MUSLIM LEAGUE** Political organization formed to protect Moslem rights in India. Through its influence Pakistan became an independent state.

**MUSSULMAN** Archaic term for MOSLEM.

**MUSTARD** Plant used by Jesus to symbolize the power of faith and the growth of the Kingdom of God (MATTHEW 17:20; LUKE 13:19).

**MUTAZILITES dissenters** Ancient Moslem sect emphasizing Allah's righteousness and awards or punishments for men based upon their lives. From the eighth through the tenth centuries, the Mutazilites, sometimes described as freethinkers, questioned ISLAM orthodoxy regarding the KORAN, the nature of ALLAH, and similar matters. They dissipated after the tenth century, merging with the SHIITES.

**MUTIAN, KONRAD (1471–1526)** German HUMANIST who sought ecclesiastical reform but balked at Luther's thoroughgoing measures.

**MUTILATION** Wounding or removal of some part of the body. Mutilation had religious sanction in many older religions but is now, it is hoped, on the decline.

**MWARI** Supreme deity of the Mtwaras of Rhodesia, Africa.

**MYERS, FREDERIC WILLIAM HENRY (1843–**

**1901)** English author of the poem *St. Paul* and other works. He helped found the Society for Psychical Research and investigated the whole realm of spiritism and survival after death.

**MYLITTA** Babylonian goddess of birth and fertility.

**MYOSHINJI** Important temple of ZEN Buddhism at Kyoto, Japan.

**MYRRH** Bush in Palestine providing gum used in perfume, cosmetics, anointing oil, and embalming. In wine it apparently relieved pain (MARK 15:23).

**MYRTLE** Beautiful shrub of Palestine symbolizing love to the Greek pagans and Gentile conversion to the later Christians.

**MYSTAGOGUE** Interpreter of mysteries, as the ELEUSINIAN MYSTERIES.

**MYSTAGOGY** Teaching during initiation into a mystery religion.

**MYSTERIES** 1. Religious teachings considered above human reason. 2. MYSTERY RELIGIONS.

**MYSTERY PLAY** See MIRACLE PLAY.

**MYSTERY RELIGIONS** Secret cults in pre-Christian Greek and Roman culture, as well as in areas of Egypt and Asia. Candidates were usually initiated in a baptism of blood, taught secret lore, and permitted to view symbolic religious drama; in the typical service this was followed by a sacred meal. The mystery religions included the ORPHIC, ELEUSINIAN, MITHRAIC, and those of ISIS, CYBELE, ATTIS, and SABAZIOS. In the Asian mysteries the rites might involve sacred prostitution or emasculation.

**MYSTIC** One who communes directly with God, or follows a mystical way of life.

**MYSTICAL BODY** The Church considered as the body of Christ (cf. ROMANS 12).

**MYSTICAL ROSE** Characterization of the Virgin MARY (cf. ECCLESIASTICUS 24:18).

**MYSTICAL SCHOOL** Sect of ancient Chinese BUDDHISM known in Japan as SHINGON. It viewed right action, right speech, and right thought as manifestations of the Sun Buddha.

**MYSTICISM** Religious emphasis on communion with God without the intermediate stages or means often thought essential. It may stress visions, meditation, ecstasy, or a sense of oneness with the divine. BUDDHISM has been called a religion of mysticism. Medieval Christianity produced such great mystics as John TAULER, Meister ECKHART, Jan RUYSBROECK, THOMAS À KEMPIS, and St. BONAVENTURA. Later mystics included St. JOHN OF THE CROSS, St. THERESA, Madame GUYON, and St. FRANCIS OF SALES. Protestant mystics include George FOX, Jacob BOEHME, William LAW, John WOOLMAN, and Emanuel SWEDENBORG. Jewish mysticism is represented by interest in the CABALA and HASIDISM.

**MYSTICS OF ST. VICTOR** Religious school centered in the abbey of St. Victor outside Paris. Teachers there such as PETER LOMBARD and HUGH OF ST. VICTOR spread Christian mysticism throughout Europe during the medieval period.

**MYTH** 1. Fiction symbolizing or accepted as religious fact. 2. Poetry or prose embodying profound religious truth. 3. Collective legends or myths.

**MYTHOLOGY** 1. Body of myths. 2. Study or science of myth.

# N

**NAAMAH** *pleasant* 1. Daughter of Lamech and sister of Tubal-cain (GENESIS 4:22). 2. Mother of King Rehoboam of Israel (I KINGS 14:21; II CHRONICLES 12:13). 3. Town of Judah or Arabia from which Job's friend Zophar came (JOB 2:11; JOSHUA 15:41).

**NAAMAN** *pleasant* 1. Grandson of Benjamin and forefather of the Naamites (GENESIS 46:21; NUMBERS 26:38–40). 2. Captain of the Syrian army of Benhadad, miraculously cured of leprosy by the prophet Elisha when he washed in the Jordan River (II KINGS 5:1–15).

**NAASENES** GNOSTICS who worshiped serpents to show their enmity to the God of the Old Testament (cf. GENESIS 3:14, 15). Like most Gnostics, they saw Jehovah as their opponent.

**NABAL** *fool* Israelite shepherd whose life was saved from King David's threatened attack by his wife Abigail, whom David married after Nabal's death (I SAMUEL 25:1–42).

**NABI** Hebrew and Arabic term for prophet (one who speaks on behalf of God, through divine revelation).

**NABOTH** Jewish vineyard owner stoned to death for refusing to allow King Ahab to take his property. This brought the divine curse through Elijah on Naboth and his descendants (I KINGS 21; II KINGS 9:21–26).

**NABU** See NEBO.

**NABUCHODONOSOR** See NEBUCHADNEZZAR.

**N.A.E.** Abbreviation for NATIONAL ASSOCIATION OF EVANGELICALS.

**NAGARJUNA (c. second century)** BUDDHIST philosopher, magician, and saint of India. He is said to have seized the sacred writings from the oceanic serpents.

He has been called the father of MAHAYANA Buddhism.

**NAHMANIDES (1194–c.1270)** Spanish mystic and Jewish scholar; author of several commentaries.

**NAHUM** *comfort* Hebrew prophet who foretold the fall of Nineveh. His prophecy is the seventh of the MINOR PROPHETS.

**NAIADS** Greek divinities inhabiting rivers and other waters.

**NAILS** Artistic symbol of Christ's crucifixion.

**NAIN** Village near Nazareth in Galilee. A boy from Nain was brought back from death by Jesus (LUKE 7:11–17).

**NAKAYAMA, OMIKI SAN (1798–1887)** Japanese founder of the church of TENRI KYO. Mrs. Nakayama is said to have healed the sick; her writings—the sacred literature of Tenri Kyo—indicate that mind may profoundly influence matter.

**NAMAM** HINDU symbol of VISHNU, consisting of three lines suggesting a trident.

**NAME** Descriptive title or characterization identifying a person or thing. In primitive religion the name was of great importance; because it was often identified with the person himself, it was usually kept secret from strangers or enemies. In Scripture the name is often practically synonymous with the person. The name of God was sacred because God was supreme and holy.

**NAME DAY** Day commemorating one's baptism or patron saint.

**NAMTAR** Babylonian evil spirit.

**NANA** Goddess of the city of Erech in ancient Sumer.

**NANAK (1469–1538)** Founder of SIKHISM. Born a HINDU, he had a MOSLEM teacher when a child; the religion he fathered blended both faiths. He traveled widely and was admired by both Hindus and Moslems.

**NANDA**  Hindu goddess-consort of SIVA.

**NANDA DEVI**  Mountain in India nearly 26,000 feet high at the top of which Nanda, wife of SIVA, is believed by HINDUS to dwell.

**NANDI**  Sacred white bull whose statue guards each HINDU temple of SIVA.

**NANNA**  Scandinavian wife of BALDER and daughter of Nef, symbolizing mental and physical perfection.

**NANNAR**  Moon god whose temple dominated ancient Ur in Mesopotamia.

**NANTES, EDICT OF**  See EDICT OF NANTES.

**NAOMI** *pleasant*  Jewish widow of Elimelech and mother-in-law of Ruth. To her Ruth made the famous promise, "Entreat me not to leave thee . . . for whither thou goest, I will go" (RUTH 1:16).

**NAOS**  Center of a Greek temple containing an idol of the temple's patron god or goddess.

**NAPHTALI** *wrestlings*  Son of Jacob and Rachel, and ancestor of the Hebrew tribe of that name. It became part of the Northern Kingdom of Israel.

**NARA**  City of Japan famous for its BUDDHIST images, temples, and monasteries, for the SHINTO shrine of Kasuga, and for nearby Mt. Kasuga which is considered to be a dwelling place of the gods. Among Nara's sculptures are a trinity in bronze and an image of Buddha 53½ feet high.

**NARAKA**  Hinduism's hell in which the wicked suffer until they have atoned for their sins.

**NARAYANA**  A title of VISHNU or BRAHMA, referring to the primal egg from which Brahma was born.

**NARBADA**  River of central India whose sanctity is surpassed only by that of the Ganges. On it are a number of special centers of HINDU pilgrimage, and a journey along its course and back brings special merit.

**NARCISSUS**  Son of the river god Cephissus, in Greek myth; falling in love with his own reflection, he became a flower. The latter symbolizes self-love in art, but may indicate the Christian love which transcends self-love.

**NARTHEX**  Vestibule or portico of a church, originally a place for CATECHU-MENS and others not admitted to the sanctuary proper.

**NASHVILLE**  City of Tennessee which serves as a center of PROTESTANT religious publishing in the United States.

**NASI** *prince*  Jewish title for the president of the SANHEDRIN, and later for the leader of the community.

**NASIK**  Town of Bombay, India, famed as a center of religious pilgrimage. Sacred to HINDUS as the place where RAMA was exiled and near BUDDHIST and JAIN caves. The former date back as far as the third century B.C.

**NAT**  Burmese name for the spirit associated with a tree, a body of water, a house, and the like. Nats are worshiped in local shrines.

**NATA**  The "Noah" of Aztec myth. Nata and his wife Nena made a boat for refuge during a great flood.

**NATHAN** *given*  1. Hebrew prophet who used a parable of the theft of a beloved ewe lamb to condemn King David's infamous love affair with Bathsheba. Nathan helped anoint Solomon king and wrote a chronicle of the lives of David and Solomon. (II SAMUEL 7; 12; I KINGS 1:8–45; I CHRONICLES 29:29). 2. A son of King David (II SAMUEL 5:14). 3. The name of several other Bible characters.

**NATHANAEL** *God gave*  Disciple of Jesus, probably the same as BARTHOLOMEW. (JOHN 1:45–51; 21:2).

**NATICK**  Massachusetts town founded by John ELIOT as a settlement for Christian Indians.

**NATION, CARRY (1846–1911)**  American opponent of alcohol who felt called of God to destroy saloons with her hatchet. She also fought tobacco, corsets, and fraternal organizations.

**NATIONAL ASSOCIATION OF EVANGELICALS**  Organization of evangelical Christians organized in the United States in 1942. Opposed to the NATIONAL COUNCIL OF CHURCHES OF CHRIST IN THE U.S.A., it lists about thirty denominations and various other organizations in its membership.

**NATIONAL BAPTIST CONVENTION OF AMERICA**  Negro church organized in the United States in 1880.

**NATIONAL BAPTIST CONVENTION, U.S.A., INC.**  American church of more than five million Negro BAPTISTS; it originated in 1880.

**NATIONAL BAPTIST EVANGELICAL LIFE AND SOUL SAVING ASSEMBLY OF U.S.A.** EVANGELICAL Negro Baptist organization founded in 1920.

**NATIONAL CATHOLIC WELFARE CONFERENCE** American organization coordinating CATHOLIC work in such fields as education and social welfare, and directing three national councils: those of Catholic Men, Catholic Women, and Catholic Youth.

**NATIONAL CHURCH LEAGUE** Evangelical organization in the CHURCH OF ENGLAND formed to promote REFORMATION principles.

**NATIONAL CONFERENCE OF CHRISTIANS AND JEWS** Organization formed in New York City in 1928 to promote mutual understanding and respect. Out of it grew the INTERNATIONAL CONFERENCE OF CHRISTIANS AND JEWS, and WORLD BROTHERHOOD, with similar aims.

**NATIONAL COUNCIL OF JEWISH WOMEN** American organization of Jewish women devoted to aiding immigrants, young people, and the aged.

**NATIONAL COUNCIL OF THE CHURCHES OF CHRIST IN THE UNITED STATES OF AMERICA** Cooperative organization of about thirty-three denominations representing more than forty million members. Formed in 1950 as a successor to the FEDERAL COUNCIL OF CHURCHES, the National Council also represents a merger of various other PROTESTANT agencies. Its four main divisions are those of Christian Education, Christian Life and Work, Home Missions, and Foreign Missions.

**NATIONAL COUNCIL OF YOUNG ISRAEL** Jewish group interested in maintaining and promoting the traditions and values of JUDAISM.

**NATIONAL DAVID SPIRITUAL TEMPLE OF CHRIST CHURCH UNION (INC.), U.S.A.** Group founded in the United States in 1932, emphasizing the gifts and guidance of the Holy Ghost. Officials are apostles or archbishops, bishops, overseers, elders, pastors, prophets, prophetesses, deacons, missionaries, evangelists, teachers, and divine healers.

**NATIONAL EVANGELICAL LUTHERAN CHURCH** Denomination formed in the United States in 1898 by Lutherans with a Finnish background. It merged with the LUTHERAN CHURCH—MISSOURI SYNOD in 1964.

**NATIONAL PRIMITIVE BAPTIST CONVENTION OF THE U.S.A.** Negro denomination which opposes "all forms of church organization."

**NATIONAL SOCIETY** British organization founded in 1811 for religious instruction within the CHURCH OF ENGLAND.

**NATIONAL SPIRITUAL ALLIANCE OF THE U.S.A.** SPIRITUALIST body established in 1913.

**NATIONAL SPIRITUALIST ASSOCIATION OF CHURCHES** American group described by Frank S. Mead as "the orthodox body of American Spiritualism." It considers Spiritualism to be a science, a philosophy, and a religion (see SPIRITISM).

**NATIVE AMERICAN CHURCH** United States Indian sect which uses peyote—a non-habit-forming cactus with hallucinatory effects—for religious purposes.

**NATIVITY** 1. Ecclesiastical term for the birth of Jesus. 2. See CHRISTMAS.

**NATIVITY OF ST. JOHN THE BAPTIST** Festival commemorating the birth of JOHN THE BAPTIST on June 24; one of the earliest church feasts.

**NATIVITY OF THE BLESSED VIRGIN** Festival of the birth of MARY the Mother of Jesus, on September 8.

**NATURALISM** Philosophical system explaining all reality in terms of the material and "natural," denying validity to teleology or the supernatural.

**NATURAL LAW** System of ethical principles considered to be inherent in human nature, summed up by SCHOLASTICISM as: "Do good and avoid evil." PROTESTANTISM and modern thought have veered away from the concept of a universal natural law.

**NATURAL RELIGION** Religion discoverable by human reason—basically, belief in a Creator, human responsibility, and an immortal destiny proportioned to one's earthly actions. Such religion does not require divine revelation or grace.

**NATURE** 1. Essence or essential character of something. 2. The force controlling the universe, or the universe—often personified or deified.

**NATURE WORSHIP** Worship of nature, or of some part or force of nature. This is considered to have been a basic part of primitive religion.

**NAVAJO or NAVAHO RELIGION** Complex system of rites, myths, and worship of many gods and supernatural beings. The Navajo creator-god was Ahsonnutli.

**NAVARETTE, JUAN FERNANDEZ (1526–1579)** Spanish religious painter of "The Baptism," "The Nativity," "The Burial of St. Lawrence," and other works.

**NAVE** Central part of a church, for the use of the laymen. It extends from the vestibule to the CHANCEL. Strictly, however, it includes only the central aisle.

**NAYLER, JAMES (c.1618–1660)** English PURITAN who became a QUAKER and then came to the conviction that he was a re-incarnation of Christ. His followers hailed him as "Lord God of Sabaoth." Tried by Parliament, he was branded in the forehead, his tongue was bored through, and he was whipped through the streets and jailed.

**NAZARENE** 1. Term for Christ (cf. MATTHEW 2:23). 2. Term for one from NAZARETH.

**NAZARENES** 1. Early term for CHRISTIANS (cf. ACTS 24:5). 2. Jewish Christians of Syria during the first few centuries of the Christian era. They made use of an ARAMAIC Gospel known as the Gospel According to the Hebrews. 3. Group of nineteenth-century German artists who specialized in Christian themes.

**NAZARETH** Village near the Sea of Galilee where Jesus spent His youth and early manhood. It is today a center of Christian pilgrimage, with many shrines.

**NAZARITE or NAZIRITE** *consecrated* Hebrew who abstained from wine, unclean food, or contact with dead bodies, and vowed never to cut his hair. Notable Nazarites were SAMUEL, SAMSON, and JOHN THE BAPTIST. Nazarite vows were known to the Apostle Paul (ACTS 18:18; 21:20–30).

**NAZISM** Term for the pseudoreligious ideology of Germany, personified in Adolf Hitler, which brought on World War II. Ethically nihilistic, it glorified and practically deified the German race and nation, expressing such absolute contempt for Jews and Negroes that it finally slaughtered millions of Jews and degraded countless others. It revived the paganism of ancient Europe and sought to control Christianity by establishing what it called the German Christian Church. Notable opponents of the latter were Martin Niemoeller and Dietrich BONHOEFFER.

**N.C.C.** Abbreviation for the NATIONAL COUNCIL OF CHURCHES.

**NEAL, DANIEL (1678–1743)** PURITAN preacher and historian.

**NEALE, JOHN MASON (1818–1866)** English clergyman (HIGH CHURCHMAN), hymnologist, hymn writer, and historian. He translated many Latin and Greek hymns including "Jerusalem the Golden" and wrote many hymns and books.

**NEANDER, JOACHIM (1650–1680)** German PIETIST and hymn writer. Among his hymns is "Praise to the Lord, the Almighty."

**NEANDER, JOHANN AUGUST WILHELM (1789–1850)** Jewish Christian theologian and church historian of Germany. He helped make German LUTHERANISM more simple, joyful, and informal. Among his famous works are a *Life of Christ* and a nine-volume *General History of the Christian Religion and Church.*

**NEAR EAST** The lands in the vicinity of the eastern Mediterranean: Palestine, Asia Minor, etc. Here such religions as JUDAISM and CHRISTIANITY developed; here the earlier religions of the Hittites, Canaanites, and Phoenicians spread until replaced by the higher faiths that succeeded them.

**NEB** Abbreviation for NEW ENGLISH BIBLE.

**NEBIIM** *prophets* Jewish term for the Scriptures following the Pentateuch: "The Prophets."

**NEBO** 1. Babylonian god of righteousness and wisdom (also called Nabu), patron of culture in the town of Borsippa. 2. Mountain where Moses died and was buried just before the Israelites entered the land of Canaan. It is in Moab east of Jericho.

**NEBUCHADNEZZAR or NEBUCHADREZZAR** *Nebo, guard the borders* Able king of Babylonia during the first half of the sixth century B.C. He invaded Judah and deported the citizens on three different occasions. Much is related about Nebuchadnezzar in the prophecy of DANIEL.

**NECESSITARIANISM** See DETERMINISM.

**NECROLOGY** Roll of the deceased for whom prayers may be offered, as on ALL SAINTS' DAY.

**NECROMANCY** Divination by communication with spirits of the dead, or any kind of magic.

**NECTAR** Drink of the gods in Greek myth. See also AMBROSIA.

**NEED-FIRE** New fire used in ancient times to bring good fortune or remove a curse.

**NEFERTUM or NEFERTEM** Bearded Egyptian god, symbolized by the lotus, and a form of the sun god RA.

**NEGATION** Philosophical term for non-existence or privation.

**NEGATIVISM** Skepticism or denial of the observable world.

**NEGEB or NEGEV the dry** Southern Palestine, extending from Judea to Ezion-Geber, occupied by Edomites in Old Testament times. In the Christian era a number of monasteries and churches were built there. Today the Negeb belongs to the state of Israel.

**NEGINAH** Hebrew word for music, song, or musical instrument, often occurring in the Psalms. The plural is *neginoth*.

**NEGRO CHURCHES** The United States has six Negro denominations with nine million members. Most American Negroes belong to the NATIONAL BAPTIST CONVENTION OF U.S.A., INC., the NATIONAL BAPTIST CONVENTION OF AMERICA, the AFRICAN METHODIST EPISCOPAL CHURCH, and the Episcopal Zion Church. During the 1960's Negro churches in the southern United States often served as the center for civil rights demonstrations, and were sometimes burned for it.

**NEHEMIAH or NEHEMIAS comfort of the Lord** Wealthy cupbearer of King Artaxerxes of Persia who returned to Judea and rebuilt the walls of ruined Jerusalem despite heavy opposition. The book of Nehemiah tells his story.

**NEHUSHTAN brazen** Name of the bronze serpent erected by Moses to save the Israelites from a plague of serpents. When it became an object of worship it was destroyed by King Hezekiah (NUMBERS 21:8, 9; II KINGS 18:4).

**NEILAH closing** Final service of the Day of ATONEMENT, concluding with the sevenfold declaration "The Lord is God."

**NEITH** See NET.

**NEKHEBIT** Egyptian goddess who guarded Upper Egypt.

**NEKHEN** Egyptian goddess of law.

**NEMBUTSU** BUDDHIST prayer assuring entrance into Paradise.

**NEMESIS** Greek goddess of retribution, or of luck. She was the daughter of Night.

**NEMESIUS (fourth century)** Bishop of Emesa in Syria and Christian thinker. His volume *On Human Nature*, dealing with the immortality of the soul, has been said (apparently mistakenly) to foreshadow the discovery that the blood circulates throughout the body.

**NEMI** Lake in central Italy near which stood a temple and a grove sacred to the goddess DIANA.

**NEMON** Celtic war goddess.

**NEMU** New Guinea gods who created men but were destroyed by a deluge.

**NEO-CATHOLIC** Term for ANGLICANS or PROTESTANTS favorable to CATHOLIC theology or liturgy.

**NEO-ORTHODOXY** 1. Movement in PROTESTANTISM, reacting against both fundamentalism and liberalism, in which the Reformation doctrines are given an existential twist. It emphasizes the Word of God and the divine-human encounter, but puts modern content into these terms. 2. Movement in JUDAISM seeking to revive traditional rites.

**NEOPHYTE** New Christian MONK, NUN, or PRIEST; novice.

**NEOPLATONISM** Philosophical system growing out of various pagan ideas woven together by PLOTINUS. Based largely on Plato's thought, it emphasized the unity of God and the supremacy of the spiritual world. But it related God to the physical universe through various emanations, and made matter unreal. The emanations of Mind and World Soul formed with the divine Unity a kind of trinity. Plotinus taught that the human soul must seek the ecstasy of union with God through mystic contemplation. Neoplatonism had considerable influence on St. AUGUSTINE and on medieval Christian theology.

**NEOSCHOLASTICISM** Modern CATHOLIC revival of interest in SCHOLASTICISM, seeking to free its basic truths from misleading and unscientific accretions. LEO XIII encouraged such an effort in his encyclical *Aeterni Patris.*

**NEO-THOMISM** Recent renewal of study of the theology and philosophy of St. THOMAS AQUINAS.

**NEPHESH** *soul* Hebrew word for breath or soul, occurring often in the Old Testament.

**NEPHILIM** Giant offspring of the union between the sons of God and the daughters of men (GENESIS 6:4).

**NEPHTHYS** Egyptian mother goddess, daughter of RA and sister of ISIS and OSIRIS.

**NEPTUNE** Roman god of fresh water, eventually identified with the Greek sea god, Poseidon.

**NEREUS** Greek sea god, in mythology a kindly old man.

**NERGAL** Ancient Babylonian god of death, war, the underworld, and the malevolent power of the sun.

**NERI, PHILIP, ST. (1515–1595)** Italian clergyman and saint. Beginning works of charity and mercy as a youth, he so influenced the people of Rome that a great religious revival ensued. He founded the Oratorians in 1575; these were secular priests organized in a community or Congregation. See ORATORY OF ST. PHILIP NERI. His feast day is May 26.

**NERO (37–68)** Roman emperor who was Caesar during an important part of St. Paul's life. Both PAUL and PETER may have been martyred in Nero's reign. Tacitus states that Nero blamed and punished the Christians for the fire that destroyed much of Rome in the year 64, accusing them of hatred of the human race. The emperor had murdered his adopted son Britannicus, his mother, and his wife. After his death, applauded throughout Rome, many Christians feared he would return as the ANTICHRIST.

**NER TAMID** *perpetual light* Lamp continually burning in the synagogue before the Hebrew ark which holds the sacred scrolls.

**NERTHUS** Scandinavian mother-goddess, also known as Hertha, in whose honor slaves were sometimes drowned.

**NESTORIAN CHURCH** Eastern Christian church with members in India, Iraq, Iran, and the United States. Following NESTORIUS, they hold that Jesus had two natures and two persons; they honor Nestorius and the Virgin MARY but refuse Mary the title "Mother of God." Nestorian priests may marry but their bishops may not.

**NESTORIANISM** Doctrinal development in fifth-century Christianity holding that Jesus had two persons as well as two natures combined in one flesh. Arising out of Nestorius' refusal to call Mary the Mother of God, it was rejected by the Councils of EPHESUS and CHALCEDON.

**NESTORIUS (?–c.451)** Syrian patriarch of Constantinople. Although he was vigorous at suppressing heresies in his diocese, his statement "that God should be born of a human being is impossible," and his refusal to honor MARY as Mother of God, led to his own deposition for heresy. For more about Nestorius' ideas and influence, see above.

**NET or NEITH** Egyptian goddess of war.

**NE TEMERE** Decree announced by Pope PIUS X in 1907 placing special restrictions on a mixed marriage. The non-Catholic must rear the children in the CATHOLIC faith and may not interfere with the religion of the spouse.

**NETER** Early Egyptian name for the creator-god.

**NETHERLANDS REFORMED CONGREGATIONS** Tiny American Reformed church with Dutch roots.

**NEUMANN, JOHN NEPOMUCENE (1811–1860)** American bishop; the first Roman Catholic priest to be beatified by the ROMAN CATHOLIC CHURCH. The beatification took place in 1963.

**NEVELAH** Jewish term for a non-Kosher animal (see KOSHER).

**NEVIN, JOHN WILLIAMSON (1803–1886)** American theologian who taught at the Western Theological Seminary of the Presbyterian Church and the German Reformed Church Seminary. Proposing the real mystical presence of Christ in the EUCHARIST, he is known as originator (with Philip SCHAFF) of the Mercersburg theology.

**NEW AND LATTER HOUSE OF ISRAEL** See JEZREELITES.

**NEW APOSTOLIC CHURCH OF NORTH AMERICA** American branch of the New Apostolic Church, related to the Catholic Apostolic Church of England. It emphasizes the gifts of the Spirit including divers tongues and three sacraments: BAPTISM, COMMUNION, and Holy Sealing. The latter indicates the receiving of the HOLY SPIRIT.

**NEW BIRTH**  Christian term for conversion and the impartation of spiritual life. Jesus told Nicodemus, "Except a man be born again, he cannot see the kingdom of God" (JOHN 3:3). Men are born again "by the word of God" (I PETER 1:23).

**NEW CHURCH**  Term for the CHURCHES OF THE NEW JERUSALEM arising from the influence of Emanuel SWEDENBORG.

**NEW CONGREGATIONAL METHODIST CHURCH**  Tiny United States denomination which withdrew from the METHODIST EPISCOPAL CHURCH in 1881. Members practice FOOT WASHING.

**NEW COVENANT**  1. See NEW TESTAMENT. 2. A new relationship between God and man, predicted by the prophets Isaiah (55:3) and Jeremiah (31:33, 34). This new agreement Christians find perfectly revealed in Jesus Christ, "the mediator of a better covenant" (HEBREWS 8:6). The new and better covenant (HEBREWS 8:1—9:28) succeeds the old covenants of law and works, made with Israel, as a relationship of divine grace received through faith "unto good works." It is a covenant with all who believe.

**NEW ENGLAND THEOLOGY**  Term for the movement in New England in the latter part of the eighteenth century and the first half of the nineteenth century to tie CALVINISM to human reason and experience. In the process, PURITAN theology was "shorn of the essential features of Calvinism" (C. A. Beckwith). Among the leaders of the movement were Samuel HOPKINS, Timothy DWIGHT, and Nathaniel W. Taylor.

**NEW ENGLISH BIBLE**  New translation of the Scriptures prepared by the churches of Great Britain during the second half of the twentieth century. The New Testament was published in 1961. The translation, in bold and vigorous English, was the first completely new one undertaken by a group of churches in the English-speaking world since the Authorized or KING JAMES VERSION.

**NEW JERUSALEM**  Christian term for the church or heaven. It was popularized by the medieval hymn "Jerusalem the Golden."

**NEW JERUSALEM CHURCH**  See CHURCHES OF THE NEW JERUSALEM.

**NEW LEARNING**  The doctrines of the Protestant Reformers and Renaissance leaders, introduced into England in the sixteenth century.

**NEW LIGHTS**  Term for the proponents of revival in American churches during the eighteenth and nineteenth centuries.

**NEWMAN, JOHN HENRY (1801–1890)**  Evangelical leader of the CHURCH OF ENGLAND who converted to CATHOLICISM and wrote voluminously. Among his best known works are the *Apologia pro vita sua, The Idea of a University,* and the hymn "Lead, Kindly Light." In the Church of England he worked for reconciliation of the Roman Catholic and Anglican creeds, and led the OXFORD MOVEMENT. In the Roman Catholic Church he was a priest of the ORATORY OF ST. PHILIP OF NERI and a cardinal. Hundreds of Protestants became Catholics through Newman's influence.

**NEWMAN CLUB**  ROMAN CATHOLIC organization for college youth.

**NEW MORALITY**  Twentieth-century term for an attempt, popularized by such men as John Robinson and Douglas A. Rhymes, to base moral conduct on love alone. Such critics of the movement as Robert E. Fitch stated that love "had to be pinned down to earth with the specifics of principle" and that moral laws are not yet obsolete.

**NEW ROME**  Fourth-century term for Constantinople as the eastern capital of Christendom.

**NEW SCHOOL**  Term for that part of American PRESBYTERIANISM in mid-nineteenth century which favored liberal positions in theology, church government, and social issues such as slavery.

**NEW SIDE**  The more active and liberal wing of American PRESBYTERIANISM in the eighteenth century. It favored the revival known as the GREAT AWAKENING.

**NEW TESTAMENT**  That portion of the Bible added by Christians to the Jewish Scriptures (commonly called the OLD TESTAMENT). It consists of four GOSPELS, 22 EPISTLES, and the REVELATION. For the background of the term New Testament, see NEW COVENANT.

**NEW THEOLOGY** Term for several different theological movements, principally in the United States, during the nineteenth and twentieth centuries. Most of these were attempts to reconcile traditional Christianity with contemporary trends in science, sociology, and similar areas. The new theology of the 1960's sought to state theological concepts in terms acceptable to those schooled in modern disciplines and ways of thinking. Some of its proponents seemed to deny such doctrines as the transcendence of God.

**NEW THOUGHT** American religious movement, apparently deriving from Phineas P. Quimby of Maine, emphasizing "the divinity of man and his infinite possibilities . . . the Indwelling Presence which is our source of Inspiration, Power, Health and Prosperity." Groups are now found in many parts of the world. An influential book stating the principles of New Thought is Ralph Waldo Trine's *In Tune With the Infinite.*

**NEWTON, ISAAC (1642–1727)** Brilliant English scientist who saw God as the Supreme Being whose power upholds the universe and whose laws produce its beauty and order.

**NEWTON, JOHN (1725–1807)** English slave trader who, influenced by George WHITEFIELD and William COWPER, became a devout CALVINIST, a rector in the CHURCH OF ENGLAND, and a hymn writer. Among his famous hymns are "Glorious Things of Thee Are Spoken" and "How Sweet the Name of Jesus Sounds."

**NEW YEAR FESTIVAL** Beginning of the year, marked with special rites in many religions. In JUDAISM the ROSH HASHANAH is the Day of Memorial and Day of Judgment. In CHRISTENDOM New Year's Day marks the feast of the Circumcision of Christ. In PROTESTANTISM New Year's has often been a time of meditation and of Watch Night Services, beginning the new year with prayer and worship.

**NGURUHE** God in the HEHE RELIGION.

**NICAEA, FIRST COUNCIL OF** Church council held in 325 at Nicaea, Bithynia, in Asia Minor. Called by CONSTANTINE, it was the church's first ECUMENICAL COUNCIL and produced an early version of the NICENE CREED to settle the problem of ARIANISM. It unequivocally stated the deity of Christ and established other reforms. Its great accomplishment, however, was the use of the word *homoousios* to indicate that the Son is of the same nature as the Father.

**NICAEA, SECOND COUNCIL OF** ECUMENICAL COUNCIL convened in 787 to bring the ICONOCLASTIC CONTROVERSY to an end. It made the judgment that images should be venerated but not adored or worshiped. It also enacted various ecclesiastical and disciplinary measures.

**NICANOR** *victor* 1. General defeated by the Maccabees (I MACCABEES 7:26–32). 2. One of the first deacons in the church (ACTS 6:5). 3. Gate in the Jewish temple of the New Testament era.

**NICENE or NICAEAN** Having to do with the Creed or the Councils of Nicaea.

**NICENE COUNCILS** See NICAEA, FIRST COUNCIL OF; NICAEA, SECOND COUNCIL OF.

**NICENE CREED** 1. Creed drawn up at the First Council of NICAEA to defend Christian orthodoxy against ARIANISM. It is fairly short and states that Christ is identical in nature with God. 2. Creed sometimes termed the Niceno-Constantinopolitan Creed, approved at the Council of CHALCEDON in 451. It elaborates on the glory and deity of God the Son and God the Holy Spirit.

**NICENO-CONSTANTINOPOLITAN CREED** See NICENE CREED, 2.

**NICEPHORUS (c.758–829)** Historian, patriarch and saint of Eastern Christendom. Attending the Second Council of NICAEA, he fought ICONOCLASM and was exiled for his stand. His feast day is March 13.

**NICHANT** Destroying god of the Gros Ventre tribe of Algonquin Indians.

**NICHE** Recess in the wall of a church or temple for a statue, as of a patron saint.

**NICHIREN (1222–1282)** Japanese BUDDHIST leader and reformer. He denounced ZEN Buddhism and held that the eternal Buddha should be considered sovereign and supreme. He founded the Buddhist sect called NICHIREN.

**NICHIREN** Buddhist sect founded by NICHIREN. Its central Scripture is the Lotus of the True Law and it tends to be rather intolerant of other approaches.

**NICHOLAS, ST. (fourth century)** Churchman and bishop of Asia Minor whose charity and good deeds are legendary. The patron saint of Greece, Sicily, Russia, youths, and sailors, he is the original of today's SANTA CLAUS. Nicholas' feast day is December 6.

**NICHOLAS I (c.825–867)** Strong pope, also known as Nicholas the Great, who upheld the right of bishops to appeal to the VATICAN and was known for his efforts at righteousness and charity. He defended Christian unity and Christian marriage, strengthening and adorning the papal office. His feast day is November 13.

**NICHOLAS OF CUSA (c.1400–1464)** German philosopher and cardinal, learned in many fields. Something of a mystic, he opposed the blanket condemnation of the HUSSITES and established various reforms. He held that in God all contradictions are resolved.

**NICK, OLD** Slang term for the devil.

**NICODEMUS** *conqueror of the people* Pharisee who talked with Jesus by night and aided in His burial (JOHN 3:1–21; 19: 39 ff.).

**NICODEMUS, GOSPEL OF** Apocryphal work consisting of the Acts of Pilate and the Descent of Christ into the Underworld. It dates from the fourth century.

**NICOLAITANS** Persons in the churches of Asia Minor at Ephesus and Pergamum who were rebuked for teaching the Christians to eat food offered to idols and to commit fornication (REVELATION 2:6, 14, 15).

**NICOLAS** One of the first Christian deacons (ACTS 6:5).

**NICOLL, WILLIAM ROBERTSON (1851–1923)** Scottish PRESBYTERIAN minister who edited the *Expositor* and the *British Weekly*.

**NIDDAH** Jewish term for a female who is ceremonially uncleansed.

**NIDDUI** Excommunication in JUDAISM.

**NIEBUHR, H. RICHARD (1894–1962)** American clergyman of the EVANGELICAL AND REFORMED CHURCH and theologian; a brother of Reinhold Niebuhr. He taught theology and ethics at Yale University.

**NIETZSCHE, FRIEDRICH WILHELM (1844–1900)** German philosopher who held that "God is dead" and that Christianity represents "slave morality." He lamented Jewish and Christian decadence and saw hope only in the rise of a "superman" who would rise above the common herd through "the will to power." Nietzsche died insane.

**NIFLHEIM** Abode of the dead in Germanic myth.

**NIGGUN** Chant in Jewish services of worship.

**NIGHT THOUGHTS** Book by Edward YOUNG published in England in 1742 and containing religious reflections in blank verse.

**NIHILIANISM** Term for the medieval belief of some that the human nature of Christ was an illusion.

**NIHILISM** 1. Philosophy of political revolution and social destruction. 2. Philosophical doctrine denying real existence, a real basis of morality, or a real foundation of truth.

**NIHIL OBSTAT** *nothing hinders* Formula of approbation from the official censor in books considered acceptable for ROMAN CATHOLICS.

**NIHON KIRISUTO KYODAN** See KYODAN.

**NIHONGI** Ancient chronicles of SHINTOISM, completed c.720 A.D.

**NIKE** *victory* Greek goddess of victory; sometimes identified with ATHENA.

**NIKKAL** Sumerian goddess of the sun.

**NIKON (1605–1681)** RUSSIAN ORTHODOX cleric and reformer who supported separation between the church and the state. He founded the monastery of the New Jerusalem and eventually became patriarch of Moscow, although he was deposed and banished for a time.

**NILE** Great river of northern Africa considered so sacred in ancient Egypt that it was worshiped as a god.

**NIL SINE NUMINE** *nothing without the will of God* Motto of the state of Colorado.

**NIMAVATS or NIMBARKAS** HINDU sect apparently named for Nimbarka, a twelfth-century GURU of India. Adherents worship KRISHNA and RADHA.

**NIMBUS** Luminous circle often surrounding the head of a saint or deity in religious art. See HALO.

**NIMROD** Famous hunter and builder descended from Noah (GENESIS 10:8–12). The statement in Genesis that he built cities in Assyria seems to be confirmed by discoveries of the name NIMROD in various tells or mounds of Mesopotamia.

**NINE** Religious symbol of angels or, in BAHAISM, of perfection.

**NINE, THE** Term for the MUSES.

**NINELLA** Ancient Mesopotamian goddess.

**NINETY-FIVE THESES** Form in which Martin LUTHER stated the principles which guided the Protestant REFORMATION. The theses stated that repentance applies to one's whole life, that the true treasure of the church is the gospel of God's grace, that the pope has no "power of the keys," and that any true Christian partakes of all the benefits of Christ without letters of pardon or payment for indulgences.

**NINEVEH** Capital of the ancient Assyrian empire. It was feared and hated by the Jewish people, and scorned by such prophets as Nahum. Jonah's preaching led to Nineveh's repentance. (Cf. GENESIS 10:9–11; ISAIAH 8:4; JONAH 1–4; NAHUM 2:8; 3:7; MATTHEW 12:41.)

**NINGAL** Babylonian sun goddess.

**NINGIRSU** Babylonian water god. Also see NINIB.

**NINIAN, SAINT (c.360–432)** "Apostle of Scotland" to whom many churches have been dedicated and whose tomb at Whithorn was a medieval shrine. His feast day is September 16.

**NINIB or NINURTA** Babylonian-Assyrian god of war, healing, and the sun. One of his shrines was at Nippur. At Girsu he was worshiped as NINGURSU.

**NINURTA** See NINIB.

**NIORD, NJORTH or NJORD** Scandinavian god of fertility or of the seas, patron of sailors and fishermen.

**NIORT** City of France inhabited by many HUGUENOTS in the REFORMATION period.

**NIPPON SEI KO KWAI or SEIKOKAI** The ANGLICAN church of Japan.

**NIPPUR** Babylonian city where ENLIL or BEL had his chief shrine. The temple of Inanna in Nippur, 4,000 years old, has yielded many important cuneiform tablets. Among others at Nippur are records of the creation and fall of man and of the deluge.

**NIRAYA** BUDDHIST term for the way to hell.

**NIRMALINS** SIKHS who give all their time to the study of the ADI GRANTH and their other sacred writings.

**NIRVANA** 1. In BUDDHISM, the perfect state of salvation in which one has escaped the rigors of existence and the flames of passion. 2. In HINDUISM, final union with BRAHMA and release from earthly life.

**NISAN or ABIB** First month of the Jewish ecclesiastical year, corresponding to March or April. (Cf. TISHRI.)

**NISHMAT breath** Jewish prayer beginning, "The breath of every living creature shall praise Thee."

**NISROCH** God of Nineveh in whose temple Sennacherib was killed (II KINGS 19: 37).

**NITZSCH, KARL IMMANUEL (1787–1868)** German LUTHERAN churchman and theologian. He opposed rationalism with an emphasis on Christian experience and held that religion is "life, direct consciousness, feeling." He furthered practical theology and aided the Evangelical Union of the Prussian Churches.

**NIVARANA** BUDDHIST term for the things which cloud faith and vision.

**NIVEDITA, SISTER** See Margaret NOBLE.

**NIX or NIXIE** Scandinavian water spirit. Often evil, it sometimes appeared in a form half human and half fish, like a mermaid or merman.

**NJORTH, or NJORD** See NIORD.

**NOACHIAN** Adjectival reference to NOAH.

**NOAH rest** Son of Lamech and builder of the ark which preserved his family from the deluge which drowned mankind. The ark also preserved birds and animals from the flood. After the flood was over, Noah made wine and became drunk. He was later revered as a hero of faith. (GENESIS 6—10; HEBREWS 11:7).

**NOB height** Priests' city near Jerusalem. King Saul ordered all its inhabitants killed (I SAMUEL 21:1—22:23).

**NOBLE, MARGARET (1866–1911)** English woman who became a convert to VEDANTA Hinduism through the influence of VIVEKANANDA. She founded the Nivedita Girls' School, wrote a number of books about HINDUISM, and was known as Sister Nivedita.

**NOBLE EIGHTFOLD PATH** Buddhist route to NIRVANA or Enlightenment through right views, right aims, right words, right deeds, right living, self-control, intellectual alertness, and contemplation.

**NOCTURN** 1. In the ancient church, a service of prayer held at night. 2. In modern CATHOLICISM, the night office of matins, or one of the three divisions of matins (see CANONICAL HOURS).

**NOD** Country east of Eden to which Cain fled after killing Abel (GENESIS 4:16).

**NODENS** Celtic god of ancient Britain.

**NOEL** *Christmas* 1. French word for CHRISTMAS; the Yule season. 2. Christmas carol. 3. Jubilant expression of Christmas joy.

**NOLO EPISCOPARE** *I do not wish to become bishop* Latin expression of reluctance or unwillingness to be made a BISHOP.

**NOMINALISM** Philosophical theory of reality, popular in the Middle Ages. It holds that universals or abstract ideas are mere names without basis in actual fact.

**NOMINATIO REGIA** Ancient term for the right claimed by kings to nominate those holding certain offices in the church.

**NOMISM** The grounding of conduct on moral law; or the defining of religion as conformity to a legal code. One opposite of nomism is ANTINOMIANISM.

**NOMOCANON** EASTERN ORTHODOX arrangement of ecclesiastical laws by topic, alphabetically.

**NON** See NUN.

**NON ABBIAMO BISOGNO** Papal bull directed against fascism in 1931.

**NON-CHRISTIAN** Term for a person or thing not considered Christian.

**NONCONFORMIST** British term for one who does not accept the doctrines or government of the CHURCH OF ENGLAND. Most non-Anglican Protestants in England are considered to be Nonconformists.

**NONCONFORMITY** Historically, the religious movement occasioned by the Act of Uniformity in 1662 which required all English clergymen to be ordained in and give allegiance to the CHURCH OF ENGLAND.

**NONES** Ninth and last of the "little hours" in the Divine Office, originally held at 3 P.M. It is now often recited after the principal mass, about noon. (See CANONICAL HOURS.)

**NON EXPEDIT** *it is not expedient* Papal decree of 1868 forbidding CATHOLICS from participating in civil elections. The purpose was to resist the absorption of papal territory by the civil government of Italy.

**NONJURORS** English clergy who refused to swear allegiance to William and Mary or their successors. Believing in the divine right of kings, the nonjurors held that James II was still their rightful sovereign. Many of them were of high intellect and character.

**NONLITURGICAL** Not having or emphasizing the interest in LITURGY of liturgical churches and churchmen.

**NONRESISTANCE** Philosophy of seeking certain objectives without physically resisting those opposing change. Adherents of this philosophy take Jesus' counsel to "resist not evil" (MATTHEW 5:39) quite literally and generally oppose all war and violence. Nonresistance gained GANDHI the independence of India, and aided civil rights progress in the southern United States.

**NONVIOLENCE** Dedication to peaceful achievement of political or social gains. It is often linked with NONRESISTANCE.

**NORBERT, ST.** (c. 1080–1134) French churchman who founded the Order of the PREMONSTRATENSIANS in 1119. In 1127 he became Archbishop of Magdeburg. His feast day is June 6.

**NORITO** Japanese SHINTO prayers for blessing and prosperity.

**NORNS** Scandinavian fates controlling individual fortunes and often portrayed as the Past, the Present, and the Future. Their dwelling is beside the Spring of Fate.

**NORTH AFRICAN CHURCH** Christian community of northern Africa, powerful until the invasions of Vandals and Moslems.

**NORTH AMERICAN BAPTIST ASSOCIATION** Fundamentalist American Baptist group enthusiastically supporting mission activity and opposing open communion, unions of churches, liberalism, and the like.

**NORTH AMERICAN BAPTIST GENERAL CONFERENCE** Baptist organization with German roots, stressing missions and other good works.

**NORTH AMERICAN CATHOLIC CHURCH** American church originating in the OLD CATHOLIC churches of Europe. Although acknowledging the supremacy of the pope, it has fellowship with the EASTERN ORTHODOX CHURCH, its priests may marry, and its officers are elected by local congregations.

**NORTH END** Position for celebrating the

EUCHARIST endorsed by certain evangelicals in the CHURCH OF ENGLAND, and required in the CHURCH OF IRELAND. Based in part on the BOOK OF COMMON PRAYER, it appears to be adopted principally to rule out any mediatorial or sacerdotal quality of the celebrant.

**NORTHUMBERLAND, JOHN DUDLEY, DUKE OF (c.1502–1553)** English statesman who, through his vast influence upon Edward VI, did much to advance the cause of PROTESTANTISM in England though his own purposes were apparently more political than religious.

**NORTIA** Etruscan goddess of luck.

**NOSAIRIS** MOSLEMS of the Middle East who believe in the TRANSMIGRATION of souls and certain CHRISTIAN doctrines.

**NOSTRADAMUS (1503–1566)** French Jewish physician and astrologer whose book of prophecies in verse, *Centuries,* has been believed by some to have accurately forecast future events.

**NOTKER BALBULUS (c.840–912)** German monk who composed a life of CHARLEMAGNE and liturgical sequences, and compiled a martyrology.

**NOTKER LABEO (c.950–1022)** German monk famous for translating the Psalms and other great works into Old High German.

**NOTRE DAME** *our Lady* Name of several French cathedrals, particularly of the famed Notre Dame de Paris built in 1163.

**NOUMENON** Philosophical-metaphysical term for a thing in itself, as opposed to a phenomenon (a thing as it is perceived).

**NOUS** Philosophical term for reason, mind, or Infinite Mind.

**NOVALIS (1772–1801)** Pseudonym of Friedrich Leopold, Freiherr von Hardenberg, mystical German poet who wrote *Hymns to the Night* and *Devotional Songs* (a volume of hymns).

**NOVATIAN (third century)** Roman priest who became the first antipope and the first Roman Christian to produce a quantity of writing in Latin. Opposing readmission to the church of those who had lapsed from the faith during persecution, he found himself excommunicated in 251. His defense of the TRINITY was found to point toward ARIANISM.

**NOVATIANISTS** Followers of NOVATIAN.

They eventually merged with the DONATISTS and were considered heretical.

**NOVENA** Nine days of ROMAN CATHOLIC devotion, sometimes accomplishing special grace or indulgence.

**NOVICE** New member of a religious order, considered to be on probation for at least a year. Ordinarily the novice must first have been a POSTULANT.

**NOVITIATE** 1. State of being a novice. 2. Place where novices reside.

**NOX** Roman goddess of night.

**NOYES, ALFRED (1880–1958)** English poet whose later work reflected the CATHOLICISM to which he converted in 1925.

**NOYES, JOHN HUMPHREY (1811–1886)** American founder of the ONEIDA COMMUNITY, a communistic religious community in which all things including love were shared by all. His ideas derived in large part from a type of religious perfectionism according to which perfect love must be expressed physically as well as spiritually.

**N.T.** Abbreviation for the NEW TESTAMENT.

**NU** Thirteenth letter of the Greek alphabet.

**NUDD** See LUDD.

**NUMBERS** Fourth book of the Bible. Its title derives from the numbering of the Hebrew people recorded therein (1—4; 26). Traditionally ascribed to Moses, the book recounts the wandering of the Jews on the way to the land of Canaan. It emphasizes the character and faith of Moses and the guidance of the Lord.

**NUMEN** In Roman religion, a guiding or presiding spirit believed to dwell in individuals and objects.

**NUMERICAL SYMBOLISM** Various numerals have religious significance. Scripture is filled with examples of such numerals. See individual numbers in this volume, as THREE, SEVEN, etc.

**NUMINOUS** Metaphysical term for the sacred, mysterious nature of ultimate reality. Rudolph OTTO coined this term.

**NUN** 1. Woman who has taken the MONASTIC vows of poverty, chastity, and obedience. 2. Joshua's father (JOSHUA 1: 1). 3. Fourteenth letter in the Hebrew alphabet. 4. Egyptian father-god and husband of NUT.

**NUNC DIMITTIS** *now lettest thou* Opening Latin words and title of the song of Simeon welcoming the Christ child (LUKE 2:29–32). It has been much used in ROMAN CATHOLIC and ANGLICAN worship.

**NUNCIO** Permanent papal representative with official ambassadorial status.

**NUPTIAL MASS** MASS following a wedding and conferring Christian blessing on those married.

**NUREMBERG DECLARATION** German CATHOLIC manifesto of 1870 protesting the papal claims of VATICAN COUNCIL I.

**NURRUNDERE** Creator-god of the Narrinyeri tribe of Australia.

**NURTURE** In religious circles, term for education and growth of a spiritual nature.

**NUSACH** Jewish term for liturgical music in synagogue services.

**NUSKU** Babylonian god of fire.

**NUT** Egyptian mother-goddess personifying the sky. One of the supreme triad, and mother of the universe, she was the wife of Nun or Nu or Geb and mother of Osiris and Isis.

**NYANATILOKA, MAHA THERA (1878–1957)** German BUDDHIST scholar and translator of many Buddhist works. He founded Island Hermitage in Ceylon.

**NYIMGMA-PA** Ancient school of Tibetan BUDDHISM founded by PADMA SAMBHAVA, possibly in the eighth century.

**NYMPH** Beautiful female divinity in Greek and Roman religion, associated with a tree, a river, a pool, or some other natural object. There were thousands of nymphs in the sea and elsewhere.

**NYSSA** City of Asia Minor where DIONYSUS was worshiped and GREGORY OF NYSSA lived.

# O

**OAK** Tree often connected with important events of the Bible (GENESIS 13:18; 35:4, 8; JUDGES 6:11, 19; 9:6; II SAMUEL 18:9, 14). In religious art an oak may symbolize strength, endurance, and faith.

**OANNES** Babylonian god of wisdom, in form part human and part fish.

**OATES, TITUS (1649–1705)** Clergyman of the CHURCH OF ENGLAND who became notorious for his perjury in connection with the so-called POPISH PLOT. His apparent fabrications produced anti-Catholic hysteria and the death of more than thirty individuals.

**OATH** Invocation of God or supernatural powers to support a statement or promise. Jesus discouraged the use of oaths (MATTHEW 5:33–37) and such Christian bodies as QUAKERS and MENNONITES forbid them.

**OBADIAH, ABDA, or ABDIAS** *servant of the Lord* Hebrew prophet about whom little is known. The book that bears his name is the shortest in the OLD TESTAMENT; it denounces Israel's enemy Edom and predicts the final triumph of Israel and the Lord.

**OBAKU-SHU** Small Japanese sect of ZEN Buddhists, founded by Ingen in 1654.

**OBATALLA** Heavenly god of the Yoruba tribe of West Africa.

**OBEAH** Charm or magic favored among some American Negroes, as in the British West Indies.

**OBEDIENCE** Submission to the will of another. Obedience is one of the three MONASTIC VOWS commonly required in religious orders.

**OBELISK** Narrow four-sided monument—in ancient Egypt commonly erected in honor of the sun god.

**OBERAMMERGAU** German town famous for the PASSION PLAYS regularly enacted there—originally in thanksgiving for the ending of a dire plague in 1633.

**OBERLIN, JEAN FREDERIC (1740–1826)** LUTHERAN clergyman whose program of community renewal in France inspired similar movements in many parts of the world. Oberlin College in Ohio was named in his honor.

**OBERLIN THEOLOGY** Distinctive theology traced to Charles G. FINNEY while president of Oberlin College, Oberlin, Ohio. Characterized by both CALVINIST and ARMINIAN elements, the Oberlin theology stresses perfect obedience to the will of God.

**OBI** Snake god of West African tribes, related to American Negro sorcery (see OBEAH).

**OBLATE** 1. Religiously dedicated. 2. One dedicated to the ROMAN CATHOLIC CHURCH although not under monastic vows.

**OBLATION** Religious offering, as in the EUCHARIST service.

**OBSCURANTISM** Opposition to intellectual progress—often alleged of certain groups because of their religious ideas.

**OBSERVANTS or OBSERVANTINES** Reforming FRANCISCANS who held to literal observance of the original rule of St. Francis. They eventually became the Order of Friars Minor.

**OCCAM, WILLIAM OF** See WILLIAM OF OCCAM.

**OCCASIONALISM** Philosophical system holding that the only cause of a change in mind or matter—when there seems to be an interaction between the two—is the causality of God. GEULINCX, MALEBRANCHE, and LOTZE favored occasionalism.

**OCCOM, SAMSON (1723–1792)** American

Indian teacher and minister who helped begin Dartmouth College.

**OCCULT** Mysterious, magical, or supernatural.

**OCCULTISM** 1. Belief in magic, spiritism, or the supernatural. 2. Experimentation in ALCHEMY, ASTROLOGY, THEOSOPHY, or the like.

**OCEAN GROVE** Town in New Jersey governed by METHODISTS, through the Ocean Grove Camp Meeting Association, and stressing religious activities.

**OCEANIDS** Greek ocean nymphs.

**OCEANUS** 1. Greek god of the ocean. 2. River circling the earth, according to Greek mythology.

**OCHINO, BERNARDINO (1487–1564)** Italian CAPUCHIN friar and eloquent preacher who became a PROTESTANT reformer. Endangered by the INQUISITION, he was welcomed by John CALVIN at Geneva. But later he repudiated predestination and was accused of favoring polygamy, hence was driven from Switzerland by the Calvinists. Charles V said that Ochino could make the stones weep.

**OCKHAM** See WILLIAM OF OCCAM.

**O'CONNELL, DANIEL (1775–1847)** Irish statesman who founded the Catholic Association and led in accomplishing the Catholic Emancipation Act.

**O'CONNELL, WILLIAM HENRY (1859–1944)** American cardinal and hymn writer.

**OCTAVE** Week or eighth day after a Christian festival.

**OD** Archaic English word for God.

**ODES OF SOLOMON** Pseudepigraphical book containing forty-two psalms, dating from the first or second century A.D. These psalms may have originated as baptismal hymns.

**ODIN** See WODEN.

**OECOLAMPADIUS, JOHN (1482–1531)** German PROTESTANT Reformer who eventually sided with ZWINGLI against LUTHER in the disputes on the EUCHARIST. Of Christian salvation he stated: "Our salvation is of God; our perdition, of ourselves."

**OECUMENICAL** See ECUMENICAL.

**OFFERING** 1. Anything offered, as to God. 2. In church services, the money received for ecclesiastical purposes.

**OFFERTORY** 1. Music sung or played during the collection of the OFFERING in a church service. 2. Consecration of the bread and wine in the EUCHARIST or communion service.

**OFFICE** Church service or rite.

**OFFICE HYMNS** HYMNS in the monastic office of worship, introduced into the Roman liturgy in the thirteenth century.

**OFFICIANT** Clergyman who leads a service of worship, or directs an ecclesiastical ceremony.

**OG** King of Bashan defeated by the Hebrew people at Edrei (DEUTERONOMY 3:1–13).

**OHARAI** Japanese rite of purification from the sins of the people or their rulers.

**OIL** Liquid often used for religious purposes, as anointing. The prophets, priests, and kings of JUDAISM were anointed with oil. In CHRISTIAN use, oil may be employed for the anointing of the sick, those being confirmed, and those about to be baptized. Oil often symbolizes the HOLY SPIRIT, or divine grace.

**OLAF, ST. (995–1030)** King and patron saint of Norway. The cruelty of his reign was soon forgotten and his shrine at Trondheim was a popular medieval place of pilgrimage. His feast day is July 29.

**OLAF TRYGGVESSON (c.969–1000)** King of Norway who sought to make his country Christian by every means in his power.

**OLAH** Jewish term for the ancient burnt offering of the temple sacrifices.

**OLCOTT, HENRY STEEL (c.1830–1907)** American agriculturist who aided Madame BLAVATSKY in founding the Theosophical Society.

**OLD ADAM** Term for the demonic element in human nature.

**OLD BELIEVERS** RUSSIAN ORTHODOX Christians who were excommunicated in 1667 for resisting liturgical reforms. They crossed themselves with two fingers and never shaved.

**OLD CATHOLICS** 1. Dutch Catholics who separated from the ROMAN CATHOLIC CHURCH in 1724 in support of JANSENISM. 2. European Catholics who refused to accept the doctrine of papal INFALLIBILITY enunciated at the VATICAN COUNCIL of 1870. 3. Catholics who accept the Declaration of UTRECHT, drawn up in 1889, rejecting papal infallibility, the Immaculate Conception, and other Roman Catholic doctrines. 4. Several other religious groups term themselves Old Catholics.

**OLD GERMAN BAPTIST BRETHREN (OLD ORDER DUNKERS)** American Dunkers who withdrew from the CHURCH OF THE BRETHREN in 1881. They stress closed communion, plain dress, and total abstinence from alcoholic beverages.

**OLD HUNDREDTH** Psalm 100, or the tune to which it is often sung in PROTESTANT churches.

**OLD LIGHTS** New England CONGREGATIONALISTS who opposed revival during the GREAT AWAKENING of colonial times.

**OLD MAN** New Testament term for the unregenerate principle with which the new nature of the Christian often struggles.

**OLD NICK** Colloquial term for Satan.

**OLD ORDER AMISH MENNONITE CHURCH** American Mennonite group founded about 1865. Members do not wear buttons or gay clothing, and worship in homes instead of churches.

**OLD ORDER BRETHREN** Tiny branch of River Brethren in the United States. Their worship services are usually held in members' homes.

**OLD ORDER DUNKERS** See OLD GERMAN BAPTIST BRETHREN.

**OLD ORDER (WISLER) MENNONITE CHURCH** American Mennonite group organized by Bishop Jacob Wisler in 1870.

**OLD ROMAN CREED** Early form of the APOSTLES' CREED, used in the Church of Rome from the late second century.

**OLD SCHOOL** Conservative wing of the United States' Presbyterian Church, formed in 1838; out of this wing came the southern division of American Presbyterians, the PRESBYTERIAN CHURCH IN THE UNITED STATES.

**OLD SIDE** Term for American PRESBYTERIANS in the eighteenth century who emphasized education and church discipline over against evangelism and revivalism associated with the GREAT AWAKENING.

**OLD SYRIAC VERSIONS** Ancient Syriac translations of the New Testament: the Sinaitic and the Curetonian.

**OLD TESTAMENT** The 39 books or writings which form the Jewish Scriptures and which with the 29 writings of the New Testament form the Christian Bible. The three principal divisions of the Old Testament are the Law, or PENTATEUCH, the PROPHETS, and the Writings, or HAGIOGRAPHA.

**OLIER, JEAN JACQUES** See SULPICIANS.

**OLIVE** In religious thought, symbol of peace and reconciliation.

**OLIVES, MOUNT OF** See MOUNT OF OLIVES.

**OLIVET** See MOUNT OF OLIVES.

**OLIVETAN (c. 1506–1538)** Cousin of John CALVIN, Bible scholar, and Protestant reformer. With Calvin he translated the Bible into French.

**OLIVETANS** Branch of the BENEDICTINE Order whose members followed their rule with strict faithfulness. They probably originated the Benedictine Reform.

**OLORUN** Leading god of the Yorubas of West Africa.

**OLYMPIAN** Greek god living on Mt. Olympus.

**OLYMPUS** Greek mountain range believed inhabited by the gods: ZEUS, ATHENA, MARS, etc.

**OM** Sacred affirmation of HINDUISM, symbolizing the TRIMURTI, the Hindu triad of deities, or BRAHMA.

**OMACATL** Aztec god of joy and happiness.

**OMECIUATL** Aztec goddess.

**OMEGA** Last letter in the Greek alphabet, symbolizing the end. Alpha, the first letter, symbolizes the beginning. (Cf. REVELATION 1:8.)

**OMEI** Sacred mountain peak of Szechwan, China. On it are many BUDDHIST shrines.

**OMEN** Token of some impending event; in divination, a clue to the future. Greek and Roman religion provided an important place for the finding and interpretation of omens.

**OMER** See LAG BA-OMER.

**OMETECUHTLI** Aztec creator.

**OMICLE** Phoenician mother-goddess.

**OMNIPOTENCE** Infinite power, a characteristic of God.

**OMNIPRESENCE** Divine attribute by which God is everywhere.

**OMNISCIENCE** Divine knowledge of everyone and everything.

**OMPHALOS** *navel* Greek and Roman stone, shaped like a navel, with religious usage. The omphalos at Delphi was thought to mark the center of the world.

**OMRI (ninth century B.C.)** King of Israel who strengthened the economy and the defense of his country. Named on Assyrian records, he was the father of AHAB. (Cf. I KINGS 16:16–28; 20:34.)

**OMUMBOROMBONGA** Tree which produced both human beings and animals, according to the Damara tribe of South Africa.

**ON** See HELIOPOLIS.

**ONAN** Son of Judah struck dead because he deprived his brother's widow of the seed to which she was entitled (GENESIS 38; 46:12).

**ONE** Symbol of unity or uniqueness.

**ONE AND THE MANY, THE** Philosophical phrase indicating the dialectic tension between universals and particulars, or between the ideal unity and the concrete differentia of the universe.

**ONEIDA COMMUNITY** Community founded by John H. NOYES at Oneida, New York, in 1848. Members practiced "complex marriage" and "Bible communism"; each was considered married to all, everything was held in common, and parenthood was planned on scientifically advanced eugenic lines. In 1880 the community broke up from outside pressures and internal unrest. It was succeeded by the company called Oneida Community, Ltd.

**ONESIMUS** *useful* Slave of New Testament Christian named Philemon. The Epistle to Philemon from St. Paul urged him to receive back and forgive his runaway slave. (Cf. PHILEMON; COLOSSIANS 4:7–12.)

**ONE THOUSAND** Religious symbol of eternity (cf. REVELATION 20:6).

**ONKELOS (c.100–130)** Jewish teacher to whom is attributed the ARAMAIC version of the PENTATEUCH.

**ONNION** Snake god of the Huron Indians of North America.

**ONTOLOGICAL ARGUMENT** Case for the existence of God based on the idea of a perfect Being. Such an idea, St. ANSELM argued, required God to exist, for without existence a being could not be perfect. The ontological argument has had several different forms and has been severely criticized by Kant and other philosophers.

**ONTOLOGISM** Philosophical-metaphysical system based on the idea of absolute Being. All knowledge, according to this system, depends on the divine Being and truth.

**ONTOLOGY** Science or philosophy of being. Ontology played an important part in the theology of Paul TILLICH, who saw God as the "ground" of all existence.

**OONAWIEH UNGGI** Wind god of the Cherokee Indians of North America.

**OOST, JACOB VAN (1601–1671)** Flemish religious painter noted for his "Descent from the Cross."

**OPEN BIBLE STANDARD CHURCHES, INC.** American denomination with PENTECOSTAL doctrines and affiliations.

**OPEN COMMUNION** Term for inviting all Christians present to participate in the Lord's Supper or EUCHARIST. The opposite practice, inviting only those of the same group to participate, is called CLOSED COMMUNION.

**OPHIANS or OPHITES** *serpent-disciples* Second-century GNOSTICS, notorious for their licentiousness, who revered Cain, the Sodomites, and the serpent of Eden. They saw Satan as good and the Old Testament God as an evil power.

**OPHIR** Area of southern Arabia from which King Solomon brought gold and precious cargo (I KINGS 9:26–28; ISAIAH 13:12).

**OPUS DEI** *work of God* 1. BENEDICTINE expression of the concept that prayer is one's primary duty to God. 2. CATHOLIC lay society, founded in 1928 by Msgr. Jose Maqia Escriva de Balaguer, with world headquarters in Rome. With many professional people among its members, it seeks "to spread the life of evangelic perfection . . . especially among the intellectuals."

**OPUS OPERATUM** *the act done* CATHOLIC term indicating the inherent efficacy of a SACRAMENT, regardless of the merit of the administrator or recipient.

**ORACLE** 1. Divine revelation. In Greek religion such revelation might be granted through a priest or priestess at an oracular shrine. 2. Thing or person considered the medium of divine revelation. 3. Place of divine revelation, as the Jewish temple or a Greek shrine. 4. Wise utterance (cf. PROVERBS 31:1).

**ORANGE** Symbol of generosity and purity in religious art.

**ORANGE ASSOCIATION** Group founded in 1795 to defend and promote PROTESTANTISM in Ireland. Its name derived from William, Prince of Orange, and its members were called Orangemen.

**ORANGEMEN** See ORANGE ASSOCIATION.

**ORANS** Figure in the attitude of prayer found in early Christian catacombs.

**ORA PRO NOBIS** *pray for us* Portion of a litany to the Virgin MARY.

**ORATIO** Sermon or prayer.

**ORATORIANS** See ORATORY OF ST. PHILIP NERI.

**ORATORIO** Dramatic and elaborate musical composition with soloists, chorus, and orchestra. Famous Christian oratorios have been composed by Bach, Handel, Mendelssohn, and other musicians. A noted contemporary oratorio is Honegger's *King David*.

**ORATORY** Ecclesiastical term for a place of prayer.

**ORATORY, FRENCH** CATHOLIC organization, founded in 1611 by Pierre de Berulle, for the education and rehabilitation of priests. It is the French Congregation or division of the ORATORY OF ST. PHILIP NERI.

**ORATORY OF ST. PHILIP NERI** Community of secular ROMAN CATHOLIC priests founded by St. Philip NERI in 1564 in Rome. Its purpose is to bring men to God. It exists in many countries; its members are often called Oratorians.

**ORCUS** Greek god of the world of the deceased.

**ORDAIN** 1. Consecrate to the CHRISTIAN ministry or priesthood. 2. Establish or predestine by divine decree.

**ORDEAL** Ancient manner of determining the guilt or innocence of one accused. If the accused withstood fire, drowning, or trial by combat without excessive injury, he or she was adjudged innocent; God was expected to protect the innocent.

**ORDER** Religious institute or community.

**ORDER OF SALVATION** Order in which REGENERATION, JUSTIFICATION, SANCTIFICATION, and other steps in the process of salvation take place. Much theological controversy has arisen over the correct order.

**ORDERS, HOLY** See HOLY ORDERS.

**ORDINAL** 1. Manual for conduct of divine services. 2. Book of regulations and orders of service for the ordination of deacons, priests, and bishops.

**ORDINANCE** 1. Religious rite. BAPTISTS consider baptism and the Lord's Supper to be ordinances rather than sacraments. 2. Rite for administration of a SACRAMENT. 3. Divine decree.

**ORDINAND** One being ordained to the clerical profession, or preparing for such ordination.

**ORDINARY** 1. BISHOP or ARCHBISHOP in the exercise of his permanent jurisdiction, or clergyman with ordinary jurisdiction. 2. Portions of the MASS which do not change.

**ORDINATION** Setting apart to the ministry or holy orders.

**ORDO** CATHOLIC calendar of feasts and offices.

**ORDO SALUTIS** *order of salvation* See ORDER OF SALVATION.

**ORGAN** Musical instrument often used in Christian worship. In religious art the organ may symbolize divine praise, or St. Cecilia.

**ORGIES** Greek and Roman rites honoring BACCHUS or other deities with revelry and abandon.

**ORIENTATION** 1. Placing of a church so that the celebrant at the altar may face east, or that the altar may be on the eastward side. 2. Facing east in a worship service.

**ORIGEN (c.185–c.254)** Theologian and philosopher ranking with St. AUGUSTINE in ability and importance. Born in Egypt, he replaced Clement as head of the catechetical school of Alexandria when he was eighteen years old. He became an ascetic, founded a theological school at Caesarea in Palestine, and gained a reputation as a devotional writer, interpreter and critic of Scripture, and Christian thinker. Author of numerous scholarly works, he brought new insights to theology and apologetics, buttressing Christian doctrine with massive knowledge of Greek and Gnostic thought.

**(ORIGINAL) CHURCH OF GOD, INC.** American Holiness body founded in 1886. It emphasizes SANCTIFICATION, spiritual healing, and government on a New Testament basis.

**ORIGINAL RIGHTEOUSNESS** Theological

term for the perfectly righteous condition of man in Eden before the fall. According to CATHOLIC theology, this original righteousness included happiness and immortal life.

**ORIGINAL SIN** Theological term for man's congenital depravity, inherited or acquired from Adam's disobedience in the garden of Eden. Thus, original sin differs from specific acts of sin, which may result from this depraved condition.

**ORISHAKO** God of the harvest, according to the Yoruba tribe of West Africa.

**ORISON** 1. Archaic word for prayer. 2. Ecclesiastical term for an anthem in the form of a prayer sung at the close of a service of worship.

**ORKO** Basque thunder god.

**ORMAZD or ORMUZD** See AHURA MAZDA.

**ORO** Polynesian war god.

**OROSIUS, PAULUS (c.385–420)** Spanish theologian and historian. His *History Against the Pagans* was highly esteemed in the medieval period.

**ORPAH** Daughter-in-law of Naomi who returned to her own country, unlike her sister-in-law Ruth, who accompanied Naomi to Israel (RUTH 1).

**ORPHIC MYSTERIES** Greek mystery religion originating about the seventh century B.C. It was based on legends attributed to the musician Orpheus—also a legendary figure—involving the death of Dionysus Zagreus and the advent of human beings who had both divine and evil characteristics. The rites of the Orphic mysteries included asceticism, initiation, and a monastic fellowship designed to lift the soul completely to the divine level.

**ORPHREY** Embroidered band on ecclesiastical vestments.

**ORTHODOX** 1. Characterized by "right opinion" in religion; nonheretical. 2. Relating to the GREEK ORTHODOX churches.

**ORTHODOX CHURCHES** See EASTERN ORTHODOX CHURCH.

**ORTHODOX JUDAISM** Traditional JUDAISM, accepting all the laws and rituals of the faith. Orthodox Judaism includes a great many Jewish people.

**ORTHODOX LUTHERAN CONFERENCE** LUTHERAN group whose members withdrew in 1951 from the LUTHERAN CHURCH—MISSOURI SYNOD because they felt the latter had begun to depart from the true faith.

**ORTHODOX PRESBYTERIAN CHURCH** PRESBYTERIAN body founded in 1936, under the influence of J. Gresham Machen, in an attempt to hold fast the beliefs considered abandoned by the PRESBYTERIAN CHURCH IN THE U.S.A.—from which the Orthodox Presbyterians withdrew.

**ORTHODOXY** Proper, approved, or accepted doctrine. In Christian circles orthodoxy sometimes indicates adherence to TRINITARIANISM.

**OSEAS or OSEE** See HOSEA.

**OSIANDER, ANDREAS (1498–1552)** Controversial German reformer who held that Christ infused righteousness into the believer in JUSTIFICATION. The accepted Lutheran view was that such righteousness was imputed to the believer's account in the act of justification but not imparted or infused.

**OSIRIS** Egyptian god of the afterlife, known as "god of gods, king of kings, lord of lords . . . everlasting." Believed to have ruled ancient Egypt, Osiris may have originally been a predynastic king.

**OSTENSORIUM** Term for MONSTRANCE.

**OSTIARY** 1. Church doorkeeper. 2. Member of the lowest of the minor orders in CATHOLICISM.

**OSWALD, ST. (c.605–641)** King of Northumbria who was converted to Christianity and helped establish Lindisfarne as a monastery. A martyr, he is honored on a feast day August 5.

**OSWALD, ST. (?–992)** Archbishop of York who sought to reform the clergy and founded many monasteries. His feast day is February 28.

**O.T.** Abbreviation for OLD TESTAMENT.

**OTTERBEIN, PHILIP WILLIAM (1726–1813)** American Protestant leader and a founder of the CHURCH OF THE UNITED BRETHREN IN CHRIST.

**OTTO, RUDOLF (1869–1937)** German PROTESTANT theologian whose book *Idea of the Holy* gave contemporary religion a new concept of the NUMINOUS. Otto stressed the uniqueness of Christianity and Scripture.

**OUR FATHER** Term for the LORD'S PRAYER.

**OUR LADY** Term for the Virgin MARY as a patron saint.

**OUSIA** *being* Greek word prominent in the fourth-century controversies over the relationship of Christ to God the Father. Orthodox believers held that He was "of the same substance" or "of the same being" or "essence" as the Father, while others denied this.

**OVERBECK, JOHANN FRIEDRICH (1789–1896)** German religious painter who was said to have revived Christian art in the nineteenth century. A saintly man, he is remembered for such paintings as "Christ's Agony in the Garden" and the "Triumph of Religion in the Arts."

**OVERSOUL** EMERSON's term for the divine spirit which seems to indwell mankind, or the ideal spiritual reality.

**OVERTURE** PRESBYTERIAN term for the formal submission of a proposal or communication from a presbytery to the general assembly, or vice versa.

**OWEN, JOHN (1616–1683)** English PURITAN scholar and preacher. A controversial CALVINIST, he was admired for his piety, balance, and work for religious freedom.

**OWL** In religious art, symbol of wisdom, solitude, and evil.

**OX** Religious symbol of service.

**OX, WINGED** Christian symbol of St. LUKE.

**OXFORD CONFERENCE** World gathering of PROTESTANTS in 1937 at Oxford, England. At this conference the WORLD COUNCIL OF CHURCHES became a reality.

**OXFORD GROUP** Religious movement originated by Frank N. D. BUCHMAN. The group emphasized personal conversion, often through group involvement and witnessing, and the application of Christian principles to social and international problems. See also MORAL RE-ARMAMENT.

**OXFORD MOVEMENT** Nineteenth-century movement within the CHURCH OF ENGLAND designed to offset the decline and dangers with which religion was then confronted. Such leaders as John Henry NEWMAN, E. B. PUSEY, and John KEBLE sought to return to ancient Christian beliefs and practices—thus bridging the gap between ANGLICANISM and CATHOLICISM. An original emphasis on ritual has been followed by a contemporary interest within this movement in the application of religious faith to social and practical concerns.

**OXNAM, GARFIELD BROMLEY (1891–1963)** METHODIST bishop of the United States whose liberal views made him a controversial figure. Among his books were *Preaching in a Revolutionary Age* and *I Protest*.

**OXYRHYNCHUS** Egyptian site where many papyri from as early as the first century B.C. have been found since 1897. These have thrown new light on many NEW TESTAMENT passages.

**OXYRHYNCHUS PAPYRI** Fragments found at OXYRHYNCHUS. Certain hitherto unknown sayings of Jesus among these fragments created worldwide interest.

**OYOMEI** Chinese and Japanese religious movement, emphasizing intuitive insight, prominent in the fifteenth century.

**OZANAM, ANTOINE FREDERIC (1813–1853)** French CATHOLIC historian and scholar who helped found the SOCIETY OF ST. VINCENT DE PAUL. He held that the church must adapt to the new conditions of the modern world.

# P

**P**  Symbol for the Priestly Code believed by many scholars to lie behind much of the material in the first six books of the OLD TESTAMENT. It usually emphasizes priestly and ritual activity, and is considered to embody a later addition to Scripture than the other sources.

**PACE-AISLE**  Walkway behind the altar in a cathedral.

**PACHECO, FRANCISCO** (c.1564–1654) Able Spanish religious painter.

**PACHOMIUS, ST.** (c.290–346) Egyptian founder of community MONASTICISM. He established nine monasteries and two convents. His feast day is May 14.

**PACIFISM**  Opposition to war—a tenet of QUAKERS, MENNONITES, and many contemporary CHRISTIANS. BUDDHISM and JAINISM also tend toward pacifism.

**PADMA SAMBHAVA (eighth century)**  Buddhist teacher of Swat, adjoining Kashmir, who introduced BUDDHISM to Tibet.

**PADRE** *father*  Term for priest, clergyman, or chaplain.

**PAEAN**  1. Song of praise or prayer associated in Greek religion with the worship of ARTEMIS or APOLLO. 2. Greek physician to the gods.

**PAEDOBAPTISM**  See INFANT BAPTISM.

**PAEZ, PEDRO** (1564–1622) Spanish JESUIT missionary to India and Abyssinia.

**PAGAN**  1. Heathen, irreligious, or non-Christian. 2. City of Burma important for its BUDDHIST temples. In the eleventh century it had thousands of such temples and sacred centers.

**PAGODA**  Eastern shrine in the form of a tower—pyramidal, square, hexagonal, or octagonal—often with a number of stories. A pagoda often indicates a BUDDHIST temple.

**PAINE, THOMAS** (1737–1809) English QUAKER who became an American found-

ing father. Although his book *The Age of Reason* and his criticism of what he regarded as superstition led many to consider him irreligious, Paine held Deist views, lauding morality and natural religion. He once said, ". . . my religion is to do good."

**PALAEMON**  Greek sea god.

**PALESTINE**  The ancient land of Canaan, now divided between Israel and Jordan, where most of the events of the Bible took place. There, east of the Mediterranean, Abraham wandered, David reigned, the Jewish prophets proclaimed the message of God, and Jesus lived and died. In Palestine are the Jordan River, the Sea of Galilee and the Dead Sea, the valley of Armageddon, Jacob's well, the villages of Bethlehem and Nazareth, and the cities of Jericho, Joppa, Caesarea, Tyre, Sidon, and Jerusalem.

**PALESTRINA, GIOVANNI PIERLUIGI DA** (c.1525–1594) Italian composer of many works for the church. Known as "the first Catholic Church musician," he had great influence on the development of sacred music.

**PALETTE**  In religious art, symbol of St. LUKE.

**PALEY, WILLIAM** (1743–1805) ANGLICAN apologist, theologian, and philosopher who sought to buttress Christian evidences logically from nature. In such books as *Natural Theology* and *The Evidences of Christianity* he elaborated on the argument that a fine watch presupposes a skillful watchmaker.

**PALI CANON**  Sacred body of writing of the HINAYANA or Theravada school of BUDDHISM. Pali was an ancient vedic dialect and is no longer spoken.

**PALIMPSEST**  Parchment whose original writing has been replaced with a later inscription. A number of Biblical manuscripts are palimpsests.

**PALINGENESIS** 1. Doctrine of REINCARNATION, or the transmigration of souls from the deceased to the newly born. 2. Doctrine of rebirth or of BAPTISM.

**PALL** Covering for a coffin, an altar, or the EUCHARIST.

**PALLADIAN** Relating to Pallas ATHENA, Greek goddess of wisdom.

**PALLADIUM** Greek statue of Pallas ATHENA, considered to have fallen from heaven.

**PALLADIUS, ST. (?–c.430)** Irish missionary and bishop. His feast day is July 7.

**PALLAS** Name of several Greek characters, particularly Pallas ATHENA, goddess of wisdom.

**PALLIUM** White circular band, marked with six purple crosses and with two strips hanging from it, worn by the POPE and certain BISHOPS and ARCHBISHOPS. It indicates the power and authority of the pontifical office.

**PALM** Symbol of victory and triumph (cf. REVELATION 7:9; JOHN 12:13).

**PALMER** Pilgrim who carried a palm to indicate that he had visited the HOLY LAND.

**PALMER, GEORGE HERBERT (1842–1933)** American philosopher who actively influenced religious teaching.

**PALM SUNDAY** The Sunday before EASTER, commemorating Jesus' triumphal entry into Jerusalem during which palm branches were waved and strewn before Him (JOHN 12:13). Palm branches are often used today in connection with church services on Palm Sunday.

**PALSY** Term for paralysis in the King James Bible.

**PAN** Greek god of fertility and flocks, famous for his love affairs and his merry piping. See also FAUNUS.

**PANACEA SOCIETY** English religious group which emphasized the writings of Joanna SOUTHCOTT, a perfect future age, and divine healing.

**PANATHENAEA** Greek festival honoring ATHENA. Probably held in August, it featured contests, war games, and sacrifices.

**PANCAKE DAY** See SHROVE TUESDAY.

**PANCHARATRAS** HINDU sect emphasizing YOGA doctrines. It seems to have originated in about the eighth century.

**PANCHEN LAMA** Next to the highest lama in Tibetan BUDDHISM. He is a REINCARNATION of the Buddha of Light, AMITABHA.

**PAN-CHRISTIANITY** View of Christianity as consisting of all branches—PROTESTANT, CATHOLIC, EASTERN ORTHODOX—and as requiring unity and tolerance.

**PANCOSMISM** Philosophical explanation of all things on the basis of cosmic forces, without the need for God.

**PANDEMONIUM** Satan's palace and capital in Milton's *Paradise Lost*.

**PANDHARPUR** City of India annually visited by many pilgrims to the HINDU festivals at the temple of VISHNU.

**PANENTHEISM** Belief that all things exist within God, who permeates the whole universe.

**PANNONHALMA** BENEDICTINE abbey of Hungary, near Gyor, serving as a central point for the Benedictines of that country.

**PANPSYCHISM** Belief that everything in the universe contains some form of intelligence, sensitivity, or psychical element. A similar belief underlay ANIMISM and the Stoics' HYLOZOISM—making life inseparable from matter itself.

**PANTHEISM** Belief that God is everything in the universe and that everything which exists constitutes God. Hindu BRAHMANISM, STOICISM, NEOPLATONISM, and some forms of mysticism have embraced pantheism. AVERROES, Johannes ECKHART, Jakob BOEHME, and Friedrich SCHLEIERMACHER all attached some form of pantheism to their religious beliefs.

**PANTHEON** *all the gods* 1. All the deities of a country. 2. Roman temple to all the gods, erected in 27 B.C.

**PAPA** *father* 1. Italian name for the pope. 2. EASTERN ORTHODOX name for a priest. 3. Mother-goddess in the mythology of Mangaia Island, Polynesia.

**PAPACY** 1. System of church government in which the POPE holds supreme power and authority. This is the system of polity in the ROMAN CATHOLIC CHURCH. 2. Office of the pope. 3. Papal succession, or all the popes collectively. 4. Reign of a particular pope.

**PAPALIN** Archaic term for a ROMAN CATHOLIC.

**PAPAL MASS** Pontifical high mass which the pope sings and in which the gospel and epistle are sung in both Latin and Greek.

**PAPALOI** voodoo term for a priest.

**PAPIAS (c.60–c.130)** Church Father and Bishop of Hierapolis whose *Expositions of the Oracles of the Lord,* quoted by Eusebius and Irenaeus, states: "Mark became the interpreter of Peter and he wrote down accurately, though not in order, as much as he remembered of the sayings and doings of Christ. . . . Mark made no mistake. . . ."

**PAPIST** Derogatory term for a ROMAN CATHOLIC (who must accept the papacy).

**PAPYRI** Manuscripts written on scrolls made from the Egyptian papyrus, a water plant. Many Biblical books were written on papyri, and many copies of the Scriptures are on them.

**PAPYROLOGY** Study or science of papyrus manuscripts. It deals with their discovery, classification, and value, and is especially important for knowledge of the NEW TESTAMENT.

**PARABLE** Short story conveying a spiritual truth through a narrative of a familiar experience. Jesus used many parables in His teaching; famous ones are those of the Lost Sheep, the Prodigal Son, the Rich Man and Lazarus, the Sower, and the Good Samaritan.

**PARACLETE** Name for the HOLY SPIRIT based on the Greek *parakletos*—helper, advocate, or intercessor.

**PARADISE** 1. Heaven, or a place of heavenly bliss in which the souls of the righteous await heaven. Jesus promised the penitent thief, "This day shalt thou be with me in paradise" (LUKE 23:43). 2. GARDEN OF EDEN.

**PARADISE LOST** Famous epic poem by John MILTON describing Satan's temptation of Adam and its consequences in heaven, hell, and earth. It was written about 1667.

**PARADOX** Seeming contradiction based on the tension between two apparently opposite facts, tenets, or situations. Contemporary neo-orthodoxy makes much of such paradoxes as the temporal embracing the eternal and faith seeming to contradict reason.

**PARALIPOMENON** *of the things omitted* Name in the VULGATE and the DOUAI BIBLE for I and II CHRONICLES.

**PARALLELISM** Repetition of similar or antithetical thoughts in successive phrases—a characteristic of much Hebrew poetry, particularly in the Psalms.

**PARAMATMAN** HINDU term for the sovereign soul or spirit of the world.

**PARAMENTS** Ornamental ecclesiastical hangings or garments.

**PARAMITAS** BUDDHIST stages of perfection including love, patience, wisdom, kindness, and virtue.

**PARAN** Wilderness near Sinai where Hagar and Ishmael fled and Israel wandered (GENESIS 21:21; NUMBERS 12:16).

**PARAPSYCHOLOGY** Study of phenomena related to thought transference, knowledge of the future, and the like through experiments in extrasensory perception. F. W. H. MYERS, Whately Carrington, and J. B. Rhine did pioneer work in this area.

**PARASHAH or PARSHA** Division of the TORAH read in the synagogue.

**PARAVRITTI** BUDDHIST term for the religious experience of conversion.

**PARAY-LE-MONIAL** French place of pilgrimage where St. Margaret Mary had a vision of Christ and established the cultus of the Sacred Heart of Jesus (see ALACOQUE, MARGARET MARY).

**PARCAE** The three FATES, important in ancient Roman religion.

**PARCHMENT** Animal skin on which manuscripts were often written through the Middle Ages. Many ancient Scriptures first appeared on parchment.

**PARDON** Exemption from the penalty for sin or wrongdoing. The Christian's pardon, achieved for him by Christ, is received through faith in Him. Jesus took pains to link our forgiveness by God with our spirit of pardon toward others (MATTHEW 18:21–35).

**PARDONER** Medieval hawker of indulgences, granting remission of temporal punishment—usually that in purgatory—while raising money for ecclesiastical projects. Pardoners' abuses led to LUTHER'S break with the ROMAN CATHOLIC CHURCH and to the Council of TRENT'S abolition of the granting of indulgences for offerings.

**PARENTALIA** February period of sacrifice in honor of one's deceased ancestors, observed in ancient Roman religion.

**PARENTHESIS** Dispensationalist term for the present age, considered a parenthesis in God's plan for human history.

**PARISH** Area or group of people under the spiritual care of a pastor or priest.

**PARISHIONER** Member of a PARISH.

**PARJANYA** VEDIC storm god.

**PARKER, JOSEPH (1830–1902)** Eloquent British CONGREGATIONAL minister, temperance leader, and author. His *People's Bible* ran to twenty-five volumes.

**PARKER, MATTHEW (1504–1575)** Archbishop of Canterbury in England. He helped prepare the BISHOPS' BIBLE and revised the Thirty-nine ARTICLES of the CHURCH OF ENGLAND.

**PARKER, THEODORE (1810–1860)** American UNITARIAN minister, reformer, and theologian. Believing that working for God was more important than believing in Jesus' miracles, he fought slavery and the liquor industry, and labored for prison reform and female education.

**PARKHURST, CHARLES H. (1842–1933)** American CONGREGATIONAL minister who exposed social corruption in New York City and helped oust the Tammany government of the city.

**PARMENIDES (sixth century B.C.)** Greek founder of ELEATIC SCHOOL of philosophy.

**PARNAS** *steward* Lay president of a synagogue congregation.

**PARNASSUS** Sacred mountain of ancient Greece. There APOLLO and the MUSES were worshiped.

**PAROCHIAL** Connected with or confined to a PARISH.

**PAROCHIAL SCHOOL** School—often elementary—supported by a parish or controlled by a religious group.

**PAROKHET** Curtain before the ark in a synagogue.

**PAROUSIA** *appearance* Greek word indicating the SECOND COMING of Christ to the earth. Eventually, according to the New Testament, He will return in power and glory, and all men will recognize His authority.

**PARSEES or PARSIS** ZOROASTRIANS of India. The name Parsee indicates their origin in Persia, from which they are believed to have been expelled in the eighth century A.D. The Parsees' God is AHURA MAZDA or Ormazd, and his prophet is ZOROASTER or Zarathustra. The Parsees reverence fire and believe in angels, immortality, and the ultimate conquest of evil and the devil (AHRIMAN). They have high moral and educational standards. Their Scripture is the AVESTA. There are two divisions in Parseeism, the Kadmis and the Shahanshahis.

**PARSHA** See PARASHAH.

**PARSIS** See PARSEES.

**PARSON** Clergyman. The name derives from the old English respect for the rector as the "personage" or "ecclesiastical person" who symbolized the church in a local situation.

**PARSONAGE** 1. Minister's residence. 2. That which supports a parson or rector, according to English ecclesiastical law.

**PARTHENOGENESIS** Reproduction without male fertilization, as in certain bees, fleas, aphids, and other forms of life. The relationship between parthenogenesis and the VIRGIN BIRTH, though sometimes the former is cited to defend the latter, seems far-fetched.

**PARTHENON** Beautiful temple of Athens dedicated to ATHENA. Built in the fifth century B.C., it contained a colossal statue of the goddess and was an architectural triumph. At one time the Parthenon served as a church, and later as a mosque.

**PARTICULAR BAPTISTS** English Baptists with Calvinistic doctrines. In 1891 they united with the General Baptists, who held to Arminian theology, to form the BAPTIST UNION OF GREAT BRITAIN AND IRELAND.

**PARTICULARISM** Theological term for a scheme of salvation such as that of CALVINISM in which particular individuals are singled out for eternal redemption and others are passed by.

**PARTRIDGE** Henlike game bird symbolizing both truth and falsehood in religious art.

**PARVATI** Lovely HINDU goddess and mate of SIVA. Also known as Kamashi.

**PARVIS** 1. Court or porch in front of a cathedral or church. 2. Room built on such a court or portico.

**PASCAL, BLAISE (1623–1662)** French theologian, philosopher, mathematician, and scientist. Early influenced by JANSENISM, Pascal attacked SOCIETY OF JESUS doctrines and sought to make a defensible case for essential Christianity. He emphasized personal experience: "The heart has its reasons, which reason does not know." His *Pensees*, published posthumously from his notes, emphasize personal decision and faith in Christ as Saviour.

**PASCENDI** Encyclical of Pope PIUS X, issued in 1907, denouncing the errors of MODERNISM, described as an antisupernatural and agnostic "synthesis of all heresies."

**PASCH** European term for PASSOVER and EASTER.

**PASCHAL** Relating to PASSOVER or EASTER.

**PASCHAL CANDLE** Large candle lighted throughout the EASTER season in ROMAN CATHOLIC churches.

**PASCHAL LAMB** Lamb sacrificed at the first PASSOVER and thereafter in commemoration of that event (EXODUS 12:3–14). The lamb had to be perfect and one year old. In contemporary JUDAISM it is symbolized by a roasted shankbone at the SEDER meal.

**PASCHAL SEASON** Time of PASSOVER or EASTER week.

**PASSION, THE** Christian term for the agony and death of Christ.

**PASSIONFLOWER** Tropical American flower whose features are taken to represent the sufferings and crucifixion of Christ.

**PASSIONISTS** Popular name for the Congregation of Discalced Clerks of the Most Holy Cross and Passion of our Lord Jesus Christ. Founded in 1720 by St. PAUL OF THE CROSS, this order emphasizes contemplation and seeks to honor Christ's Passion among the faithful. Passionists wear black garments and heart-shaped badges symbolizing the Passion.

**PASSION PLAY** Religious drama built around Christ's Passion. Probably the most famous passion play today is that of OBERAMMERGAU.

**PASSION SUNDAY** Fifth Sunday in LENT, marking especially the suffering and crucifixion of Jesus.

**PASSIONTIDE** Concluding two weeks of LENT.

**PASSION WEEK** Week from PASSION SUNDAY to PALM SUNDAY.

**PASSOVER** 1. The PASCHAL LAMB sacrificed when the angel of death "passed over" the Hebrews, smiting the firstborn in Egyptian households (EXODUS 12). 2. Important Jewish festival commemorating the nation's deliverance from Egyptian slavery at the time of Moses. Lasting eight days, it begins in the spring on Nisan 14 and is celebrated with ceremonial meals filled with symbolism.

**PASTOR** *shepherd* Clergyman in charge of a congregation of believers; minister or priest.

**PASTORAL EPISTLES** The letters of PAUL the Apostle to TIMOTHY and TITUS. They are characterized as pastoral because they are not written to churches, as were St. Paul's other epistles, but to individuals, and emphasize the requirements of the pastoral office.

**PASTORAL LETTER** 1. In nonliturgical churches, a letter from the minister to the congregation. 2. In liturgical churches, a letter from the bishop or House of Bishops, addressed to all within the jurisdiction of the writer or writers.

**PASTORAL PRAYER** The "long prayer" in many PROTESTANT services, combining adoration, confession, supplication, thanksgiving, and intercession.

**PASTORAL THEOLOGY** Study of the minister's duties as pastor, preacher, and church administrator.

**PASTORATE** Length, place, or nature of a minister's duties in a particular parish.

**PASTORIUM** Minister's residence.

**PASUPATI** HINDU Lord of the creatures.

**PATAN** City of Nepal containing a number of shrines sacred to BUDDHISTS.

**PATANJALI (second century B.C.)** HINDU author of the *Yoga Sutras* and a founder of YOGA philosophy.

**PATEN** Metal plate, usually silver or gold, from which the bread is dispensed during the EUCHARIST.

**PATERESSA** GREEK ORTHODOX bishop's staff.

**PATERNOSTER** *our Father* Term for the LORD'S PRAYER, or for the rosary bead on which the Lord's Prayer is recited.

**PATIMOKKHA or PRATIMOKSHA** *words of unburdening* The 227 regulations governing the life of BUDDHIST monks, regularly recited along with confession of any violations. It is part of the "VINAYAPITAKA," one of Buddhism's three great sacred writings.

**PATINIT, JOACHIM DE (c.1475–1524)** Flemish painter of landscapes and religious themes—"St. Jerome," "The Temptation of St. Anthony," "The Baptism of Christ," "The Flight into Egypt," "St. John of Patmos."

**PATMORE, COVENTRY KERSEY DIGHTON (1823–1896)** English CATHOLIC poet, converted in 1864. He wrote some enduring verse.

**PATMOS** Mediterranean island near Miletus, Asia Minor, where the writer of the Revelation was imprisoned (cf. REVELATION 1:9). In 1088 the Monastery of St. John was founded there, and it now owns about half the island.

**PATON, JOHN GIBSON (1824–1907)** REFORMED PRESBYTERIAN missionary from Scotland to the New Hebrides, where he had many trials and experienced many accomplishments.

**PATRIARCH** 1. One of the Fathers of JUDAISM—Abraham, Isaac, and Jacob. 2. The Bishop of Rome, Antioch, Alexandria, Jerusalem, or Constantinople, with jurisdiction over ecclesiastics in his territory in the EASTERN ORTHODOX CHURCH. 4. High dignitary in the ROMAN CATHOLIC CHURCH. 5. A high MORMON priest. 6. BUDDHA or one of Buddhism's twenty-seven other famous leaders.

**PATRIARCHATE** Spiritual territory or office of a PATRIARCH.

**PATRICK, ST. (c.389–461)** Son of a Christian deacon, possibly in Wales, captured by Irish invaders and held a slave in Ireland through his youth. Having escaped to Gaul, he became a bishop and spent many years as a missionary in Ireland. To him are attributed many conversions and miracles. His feast day is March 17.

**PATRIMONY OF ST. PETER** Temporal dominion or territory of the VATICAN and the ROMAN CATHOLIC CHURCH.

**PATRIPASSIANISM** Third-century doctrine, considered heretical, that God the Father suffered in the Passion of Christ.

**PATRISTIC LITERATURE** Writings of CLEMENT, POLYCARP, IGNATIUS, JUSTIN MARTYR, ORIGEN, and other leaders in the first several centuries of the church.

**PATRISTICS** Study of the fathers of the early church and their writings.

**PATROLOGY** 1. Handbook of patristic writings. 2. Same as PATRISTICS.

**PATRON** 1. Deity or saint guarding a person, group, place, or institution. 2. In England, one with the power of filling a benefice.

**PATRON SAINT** Saint considered the special intercessor and guardian of a church, city, country, individual, group, occupation, or institution.

**PATTESON, JOHN C. (1827–1871)** English founder of the Melanesian Mission and Bishop of Melanesia in the South Pacific, where he was martyred. His feast day is September 20.

**PATTISON, ANDREW SETH PRINGLE-** See PRINGLE-PATTISON, ANDREW SETH.

**PAUL, ST.** Jewish Pharisee, born at Tarsus in Asia Minor, who became one of Christianity's greatest leaders. Often called "the Apostle to the Gentiles," Paul was harassing Christians about four years after the CRUCIFIXION when he beheld Christ and was converted. Thereafter he took the new faith into the cities of many parts of the Roman Empire. The letters he wrote in the process constitute a major part of the NEW TESTAMENT. Tradition indicates that Paul was martyred in Rome while Nero was emperor. The Apostle's three great missionary journeys, faith, and noble life are detailed in the Acts of the Apostles and the fourteen Pauline Epistles.

**PAULA, ST. (347–404)** Roman widow who founded a Christian community in Rome and aided St. JEROME in various ways. When he established two monasteries in Bethlehem, St. Paula headed that for women. Her feast day is January 26.

**PAULA, ST. (1416–1507)** See FRANCIS OF PAOLA.

**PAULICIANS** Dualistic Christian sect whose members flourished in Syria and Armenia from the third through the twelfth centuries. They considered matter to be evil, rejected the Old Testament, and honored the Gospels and the epistles of Paul. They also rejected images, baptism, communion, monasticism, and veneration of the cross.

**PAULINE** Related to or referring to the Apostle PAUL.

**PAULINE EPISTLES** New Testament letters ascribed to St. Paul: Romans, I and II Corinthians, Galatians, Ephesians, Philippians, Colossians, I and II Thessalonians, I and II Timothy, Titus, and Philemon.

**PAULIST FATHERS** Popular name of the Society of Missionary Priests of St. Paul the Apostle, instituted by Isaac Hecker in

1858. An American organization, the Society is evangelistic in purpose. Paulist discipline is based on the rule of the REDEMPTORISTS.

**PAUL OF SAMOSATA (third century)** Bishop of Antioch (260–272) whose denial of the TRINITY and contention that Jesus was an ordinary man possessed by the LOGOS or Word of God led to his excommunication. Some hold that the PAULICIANS sprang from his views.

**PAUL OF THE CROSS (1694–1775)** Italian founder of the PASSIONISTS. His feast day is April 28.

**PAX** 1. Roman goddess of peace. 2. Christian kiss of peace (ROMANS 16:16). 3. (Pax Brede or Osculatorium) Small plate with a religious representation on the face, kissed by participants at MASS.

**PAX ROMANA** World organization of CATHOLIC students. In Europe it is called the International Movement of Catholic Students.

**PAX VOBISCUM** *peace be with you* Ecclesiastical salutation.

**PAYNE, FRANCIS (1870–1954)** English BUDDHIST who founded the London Buddhist League and was long active in Buddhist endeavors.

**PAYNE, PETER (c.1380–1455)** English LOLLARD who became a follower of John HUSS and narrowly escaped condemnation for heresy. He became a Hussite spokesman.

**PAYNIM** Old English term for heathen or MOSLEM.

**PAZMANY, PETER (1570–1637)** Hungarian cardinal and leader in the COUNTER REFORMATION.

**P.B.** Abbreviation for presiding bishop, or prayer book.

**PE** Seventeenth letter of the Hebrew alphabet.

**P.E.** Abbreviation for PROTESTANT EPISCOPAL.

**PEACE** Ancient Jewish and early Christian word for complete spiritual, social, and personal well-being, used both as a greeting and as a farewell.

**PEACE MISSION MOVEMENT** Institution founded by Father DIVINE.

**PEACE OFFERING** Ancient Jewish sacrifice in which the blood was poured out as a libation, the fat burned on the altar, and the meat eaten by the offerer and his friends.

**PEACOCK** Religious symbol of pride and immortality.

**PEAKE, ARTHUR SAMUEL (1865–1929)** English METHODIST scholar and Biblical critic.

**PEARL** Religious symbol of blessing and salvation. In the EASTERN ORTHODOX churches a portion of the EUCHARIST is called a pearl.

**PEASANTS' REVOLT** Sixteenth-century German revolution sparked by the Reformers' talk of freedom and spiritual equality. Although Ulrich ZWINGLI helped begin the revolt, it was condemned by Martin LUTHER and ruthlessly crushed. Perhaps 100,000 peasants were murdered.

**PECAUT, FELIX (1827–1898)** A founder of Switzerland's Free Church, of liberal and antisupernatural views.

**PECCADILLO** *little sin* Minor sin or offense.

**PECTORAL CROSS** Cross suspended by a chain around a bishop's, abbot's, or cardinal's neck and worn over the breast.

**PECULIAR PEOPLE** Term for several religious groups, particularly the "Plumstead Peculiars" organized in London in 1838. These practice faith healing and discourage dependence on medicine or physicians.

**P.E.C.U.S.A.** Abbreviation for the Protestant Episcopal Church in the United States of America.

**PEDOBAPTISM** See INFANT BAPTISM.

**PELAGIANISM** Doctrinal system stemming from the views of PELAGIUS. It is based upon the natural ability of man to do good, the natural innocence of man, the primacy of the human will in achieving salvation, and the possibility of sinless perfection. Opposed to Augustine's doctrines of predestination and original sin, Pelagianism was popular with some in the fifth century and later but was condemned by the Council of EPHESUS in 431.

**PELAGIUS (c.360–c.420)** British theologian and monk who visited Rome and sought to refute the doctrines of AUGUSTINE with PELAGIANISM. One of his favorite sayings: "If I ought, I can."

**PELE** Hawaiian goddess of fire and the volcano.

**PELICAN** In medieval symbolism and religious art, a type of the love of Christ and the church. It was anciently supposed that the pelican pierced its breast to feed its offspring with its own blood.

**PENANCE** 1. Term for Christian repentance or penitence. 2. Act indicating repentance or sorrow for sin. 3. CATHOLIC sacrament involving contrition, confession, satisfaction, and absolution. The Council of TRENT traces the sacrament to Jesus' words in John 20:19–23.

**PENATES** Roman gods of the storeroom or household.

**PENITENTES** See BROTHERS PENITENT.

**PENITENTIAL** Book of directions for the conduct of hearing confessions and assigning penance.

**PENITENTIAL ORDERS** CATHOLIC religious orders emphasizing penance or asceticism and such objectives as evangelism and care of the ill.

**PENITENTIAL PSALMS** Psalms 6, 32, 38, 51, 102, 130, and 143, considered especially appropriate for penitential use in ANGLICAN and CATHOLIC liturgies.

**PENITENTS** 1. Christians doing public penance in ancient churches. 2. CATHOLIC congregations emphasizing penance and works of mercy.

**PENITENT THIEF** See DISMAS.

**PENN, WILLIAM (1644–1718)** English QUAKER who established the commonwealth of Pennsylvania and made outstanding progress in just and friendly relationships with American Indians. An itinerant preacher, he fought for religious freedom and tolerance. He wrote *Primitive Christianity*; *No Cross, No Crown*; *The Fruits of Solitude*; and other works.

**PENTAGRAM** Five-pointed star, symbolizing the five wounds of Christ and sometimes believed to protect against sorcery.

**PENTATEUCH** *five books* First five books of the Bible—Genesis, Exodus, Leviticus, Numbers, Deuteronomy—traditionally attributed to Moses and constituting the Jewish LAW or TORAH. Hebrew term for Pentateuch is *Chumash* or *Humash*.

**PENTECOST** *fiftieth* 1. Feast of Weeks, celebrated seven weeks after PASSOVER in recognition of the grain harvest and its ingathering. It is a joyous Jewish festival. 2. In Christendom, seventh Sunday after EASTER, commemorating the bestowal of the Holy Spirit upon the church at Pentecost in Jerusalem (ACTS 2). Another name for the day is Whitsunday.

**PENTECOSTAL ASSEMBLIES OF THE WORLD, INC.** American Pentecostal group governed by bishops and elders. It permits divorce in some circumstances.

**PENTECOSTAL BODIES** Churches or religious groups emphasizing the baptism of the HOLY SPIRIT as at Pentecost, usually in association with the gift of tongues (see GLOSSOLALIA), faith healing, and fundamentalist beliefs.

**PENTECOSTAL CHURCH OF CHRIST** Very small American Pentecostal group.

**PENTECOSTAL CHURCH OF GOD OF AMERICA, INC.** Pentecostal group holding annual meetings of its districts and a general convention every two years.

**PENTECOSTAL FELLOWSHIP OF NORTH AMERICA** Association of Pentecostal bodies of North America.

**PENTECOSTAL FIRE-BAPTIZED HOLINESS CHURCH** Small American Pentecostal group emphasizing holiness, emotion, premillennialism, and simplicity of life.

**PENTECOSTAL FREE-WILL BAPTIST CHURCH, INC.** American denomination emphasizing Baptist and Pentecostal doctrines.

**PENTECOSTAL HOLINESS CHURCH** American Pentecostal group with emphasis on three experiences: SALVATION, SANCTIFICATION, and Spirit baptism. See BAPTISM OF THE HOLY SPIRIT. Government is along METHODIST lines.

**PENTACOSTALISM** Religious movement originating largely in the twentieth century in its present form but finding its source in the baptism of the Holy Spirit at Pentecost. There are perhaps two million Pentecostals in the world. See PENTECOSTAL BODIES.

**PENTECOSTAL WORLD CONFERENCE** World conference of Pentecostal churches held every three years.

**PENUEL** *face of God* Site on the Jabbok River, east of the Jordan, where Jacob wrestled all night with an angel of God and received his blessing (GENESIS 32:30–31).

**PEOPLE'S METHODIST CHURCH** Tiny METHODIST denomination in North Carolina, U.S.A.

**PEOR** *opening* Mountain in Moab where Balaam blessed Israel when seeking to curse that nation (NUMBERS 23:28).

**PERCHTA** Slavic fertility goddess.

**PER DIEM** *by the day* Protestant term for a stated fee as for conducting a worship service.

**PERDITION** Loss and damnation of an immortal soul.

**PERE** *father* French term for a priest.

**PERFECTIONISM** Theological term for belief in the necessity and possibility of sinless perfection for the Christian believer in this life. It is often associated with the baptism of the HOLY SPIRIT.

**PERI** Persian term for fairy, elf, or demon.

**PERICOPE** Scripture selection for use in a church service, as for the text of a sermon.

**PERKUNAS or PEROUN** Baltic thunder god.

**PEROUN** See PERKUNAS.

**PERPETUA, ST.** (?–203) Woman of Carthage martyred with FELICITY for their Christian faith. Their feast day is March 6.

**PERPETUAL ADORATION** Ceaseless worship of the BLESSED SACRAMENT, accomplished through the continual presence of one or more persons at the altar. It is maintained at Spain's Lugo Cathedral and in certain CATHOLIC congregations.

**PERPETUAL DEACON** A deacon who does not intend to advance to the office of the priest; a permanent deacon.

**PERPETUAL VIRGINITY** See VIRGINITY, PERPETUAL.

**PERSECUTION** An unfortunate by-product of much religious zeal. Happily, it is less common today than in the past.

**PERSEPHONE** Greek goddess of spring and fertility, wife of PLUTO, and queen of HADES.

**PERSEVERANCE** Theological term for endurance in the Christian life. CALVINISM historically maintains that God assures the final perseverance of the saints whom He has chosen for redemption.

**PERSON** Individual entity. In struggling with the relationship of Father, Son, and Spirit, early Christian theologians adopted the Latin word for mask or individual character in a play—*persona*—to distinguish each. Thus Christian orthodoxy arrived at a formulation of one God in three persons.

**PERSONALISM** Philosophical or theological emphasis on persons as the supreme realities and values. Contemporary theology is strongly influenced by personalist thinkers.

**PERTH, ARTICLES OF** Five articles forced upon the CHURCH OF SCOTLAND by James I in 1618. They required confirmation, kneeling at the Lord's Supper, and other traditionally un-Presbyterian observances.

**PERUGINO, PIETRO** (c.1446–1524) Italian painter of "The Crucifixion," "Christ Giving the Keys to St. Peter," "The Adoration of the Holy Child," "Pieta," "The Preparation for the Tomb," and other works. Their devotional appeal made them long popular.

**PESACH or PESAH** Jewish term for the PASSOVER, or the PASCHAL LAMB.

**PESHA** Jewish term for a deliberate sin.

**PESHITTA or PESHITTO** Official and oldest Syriac version of Scripture. It omits the Catholic Epistles and the Revelation. Originally dating from as early as the second century, its present form appears to date from a fifth-century revision.

**PETAVIUS, DIONYSIUS** (1583–1652) Theologian, historian, and philologist of the SOCIETY OF JESUS who recognized the limitations of certain Church Fathers.

**PETER, ST.** Spokesman and leader of the Twelve Apostles, called by Jesus from the fishing business. Originally known as Simon, he was renamed Peter or Cephas (*rock* or *stone*). After the CRUCIFIXION he was a leader in the church (ACTS 1:15–26; 2:14–40; 3—5; 8:14–25; 12:1–3; 15:1–35; GALATIANS 2:7–9, 11). Jesus once told him, "Thou art Peter, and upon this rock I will build my church" (MATTHEW 16:18). CATHOLICS count Peter the first pope and honor him and St. Paul with a feast day June 29.

**PETER, ACTS OF** See ACTS OF ST. PETER.

**PETER, APOCALYPSE OF** See APOCALYPSE OF PETER.

**PETER, EPISTLES OF** Two short NEW TESTAMENT letters from the Apostle Peter. Both emphasize the hope of the return of Christ and the necessity of persevering in spite of apostasy and persecution. The

Second Epistle includes most of the Epistle of Jude.

**PETER, GOSPEL OF** Second-century apocryphal work attributed to St. Peter. It has DOCETIC and heretical overtones.

**PETER CANISIUS, ST.** (1521–1597) Eloquent Jesuit preacher and theologian (see SOCIETY OF JESUS). Powerfully and charismatically he opposed LUTHERANISM and proclaimed the CATHOLIC faith. His feast day is April 27.

**PETER CLAVER, ST.** (1581–1654) Spanish JESUIT "Apostle of the Negroes" in Colombia, South America. Often opposed, he worked unsparingly for the spiritual and material benefit of perhaps a third of a million slaves from West Africa. His feast day is September 9.

**PETER DAMIAN** See DAMIAN, PETER.

**PETER LOMBARD** (c.1100–c.1160) Lombardy-born theologian and Bishop of Paris, known as "Master of the Sentences." An outstanding Schoolman (see SCHOLASTICS), he collected patristic sayings in a work entitled *The Sentences*. His formulation of the seven sacraments is a high point in CATHOLIC theology.

**PETER OF AMIENS** See PETER THE HERMIT.

**PETER'S PENCE** Lay contributions gathered throughout the world for papal support. At one time it took the form of a tax.

**PETER THE HERMIT** (c.1050–1115) Eloquent French preacher of the First CRUSADE. A Crusade leader, he founded the AUGUSTINIAN monastery of Neufmoutier and became its prior.

**PETIOT, HENRI** See DANIEL-ROPS, HENRI.

**PETITION** 1. Prayer or request. 2. Form of prayer requesting special favors.

**PETRA** *rock* Ancient city of Jordan, also called Sela, between the Dead Sea and the Gulf of Aqabah. It was the capital of the Nabateans throughout the time of Christ and long an Arabian religious center; its chief deities were Dhushara and Allat. By the fourth century Petra was a CHRISTIAN center, and in the seventh it fell to the MOSLEMS. The tombs and inscriptions on the rose-red cliff walls around it are an impressive sight.

**PETRARCH, FRANCESCO** (1304–1374) Italian humanist poet whose works such as *Contempt for the World* expressed the tension between spiritual and sensuous appeals. A religious note is implicit in a number of his poems. He admired St. Augustine as well as Cicero and Seneca.

**PETROBRUSIANS** Twelfth-century heretics who followed Peter de Bruys, a defrocked priest, in opposing infant baptism, the mass, the veneration of images and the cross, the authority of the church, and the celibacy of the clergy. They sought a completely spiritual faith.

**PEW** Bench for worshipers in a church, or compartment containing worshipers' seats.

**PEYOTE** Cactus whose root is ingested, with hallucinatory and sensory effects, by Indians of the American Southwest in their religious ceremonies.

**PEYOTISM** Religious use of peyote by American Indians. Although experts agree that peyote is not addictive, Christian missionaries have strongly opposed its use for religious purposes.

**PFLEIDERER, OTTO** (1839–1908) German PROTESTANT theologian and New Testament critic.

**PHALLICISM** Worship of the generative powers or organ, common in many ancient religions. Phallic worship has been found in Canaanite, Greek, Roman, Hindu, Shinto, and American Indian religions.

**PHARAOH** *the great house* Ancient Egyptian title of the king. Egyptian pharaohs were in contact with Abraham, Joseph, and Moses, and are mentioned during later periods of Hebrew history (cf. GENESIS 12: 14–20; 41:37–57; EXODUS 1—5; II CHRONICLES 10:2; 12:2–9; 14:9–15; JEREMIAH 43:6–13).

**PHARISEES** *separated ones* Those in JUDAISM during the first century of the Christian era who sought to apply the TORAH to contemporary conditions and to preserve the Jewish faith by exalting strict adherence to Jewish law. The TALMUD and the NEW TESTAMENT record criticism of Pharisaism that had lost touch with the common people and emphasized the letter rather than the spirit of the law. Nicodemus and St. Paul were outstanding Pharisees of the New Testament. The Pharisees' chief opponents were the SADDUCEES.

**PHIDIAS** (c.500–c.432 B.C.) Greek sculptor of the majestic "Athena Parthenos" of

Athens, the "Athena Lemnia" of the Acropolis, and "Zeus" at Olympia.

**PHILADELPHIA brotherly love** City of Asia Minor in which the Christians were accused of being spiritually lukewarm (REVELATION 3:7–13).

**PHILADELPHIANS** Seventeenth-century Londoners with goals of mystical insight and brotherly love. Leaders were Jane LEAD and Francis Lee.

**PHILANTHROPY love for mankind** Form of practical religion consisting of good will and charity.

**PHILEMON** Christian of Colossae in Asia Minor to whom St. Paul addressed an epistle urging forgiveness for the runaway slave Onesimus. This epistle is one of Paul's shortest.

**PHILIP, ST. horse lover** Member of the Twelve Apostles who led Nathanael to Jesus (JOHN 1:45 ff.). According to tradition he was martyred in Phrygia. His feast day is May 1.

**PHILIP, ST.** One of the deacons chosen to aid in caring for the widows supported by the early church. He brought the gospel to Samaria and (indirectly) Ethiopia (ACTS 6:5; 8:25–40). His feast day is June 6.

**PHILIP NERI** See NERI, PHILIP.

**PHILIPPI** Macedonian city where St. Paul preached for the first time in Europe (ACTS 16:12).

**PHILIPPIANS, EPISTLE TO THE** Letter from St. Paul to the Christians of Philippi. It exhorts them to follow Christ's example, avoiding legalism, pride, and worldliness.

**PHILIPPISTS** Term for the sixteenth-century followers of Philip MELANCHTHON. Their faith was a mixture of LUTHERAN, CALVINISTIC, and CATHOLIC doctrines.

**PHILISTINES** Cretan invaders of Palestine, long holding the land along the Mediterranean coast. SAMSON, SAUL, and DAVID warred against them. Their principal god was DAGON.

**PHILO (c.20 B.C.–A.D. c.50)** Jewish philosopher of Alexandria who interpreted Scripture in terms of Greek thought. Allegorizing the Bible, he saw the LOGOS as the creative power of God through whom God is known to man. Philo's influence was great on both JEWISH and CATHOLIC theology.

**PHILOSOPHY love of wisdom** Study of ultimate reality, involving logic, ethics, and a credible world view. Necessarily, it often borders on religious concerns.

**PHILOSOPHY OF RELIGION** Study of religion and its validity, implications, and relationships.

**PHOEBUS** Greek name for the god APOLLO.

**PHOENIX** Bird which according to ancient legend burned itself alive after five centuries, and from whose ashes a new phoenix arose. In Egypt the phoenix symbolized the sun; in Christian art, the resurrection.

**PHOTIUS (c.820–891)** Greek theologian, scholar, and Patriarch of Constantinople. He and Pope NICHOLAS I excommunicated each other, following involved controversies. In the EASTERN ORTHODOX churches he is considered a saint; his feast day is February 6.

**PHYLACTERY amulet** Small leather box containing Scripture verses (EXODUS 13:1–10; 13:11–16; DEUTERONOMY 6:4–9; 11:13–21). In literal obedience to the command in Deuteronomy 6:8, one box is worn on the forehead and one on the left arm by orthodox Jews. (Cf. MATTHEW 23:5.)

**PIARISTS** Catholic order founded by St. Joseph Calasanctius in 1597 for education of youth. The Piarists form an order of Clerics Regular.

**PICARDS** Fifteenth-century Flemish Christians who went nude to recover Adamic innocence.

**PICKETT, CLARENCE E. (1884–1965)** American QUAKER leader and humanitarian. He founded the AMERICAN FRIENDS SERVICE COMMITTEE, won the Nobel Peace Prize in 1947, and wrote fifty books. Active on the Committee for a Sane Nuclear Policy, he served various humane causes.

**PICO DELLA MIRANDOLA, GIOVANNI (1463–1494)** Italian humanist and philosopher, of devout Christian belief. Admiring beauty and truth wherever he found it, he sought to reconcile Greek philosophy and Christian theology, and seriously studied the CABALA.

**PIERIA** Ancient Macedonian site sacred to the MUSES.

**PIETA pity** Representation of MARY mourning the dead body of Christ, which she holds on her lap. Probably the most famous Pieta is MICHELANGELO's sculpture.

**PIETISM** PROTESTANT religious current emphasizing personal devotions, Bible study, evangelism, and the like. Largely inspired by the LUTHERAN Philipp SPENER in seventeenth-century Germany, it also influenced the Moravians and Methodism.

**PIETY** Devout religious faithfulness.

**PILAN** Supreme deity of the Araucanian Indians of South America.

**PILATE, PONTIUS** Roman governor of Judea and nearby territories during the public ministry of Christ. Presiding at the latter's trial, he left the decision of crucifixion to the people and washed his hands of guilt. He is honored in the COPTIC CHURCH as a martyr, with a feast day June 25.

**PILGRIM** 1. Traveler to a holy place or shrine. 2. PURITAN settler in New England in the seventeenth century.

**PILGRIMAGE** Journey to a shrine as an act of religious devotion.

**PILGRIMAGE OF GRACE** Movement in northern England in 1536 and 1537 on the part of ROMAN CATHOLICS protesting the suppression of monasteries and the abolition of papal supremacy. Rigid suppression of the protesters and execution of their leaders ended the protest.

**PILGRIM HOLINESS CHURCH** American denomination resulting from a merger of Pentecostal and Holiness groups with the International Apostolic Holiness Union, founded by Rev. Martin Wells Knapp in 1897.

**PILGRIM'S PROGRESS** Christian allegory written by John BUNYAN, an unschooled English tinker with deep spiritual perception. The story takes Christian through the Slough of Despond and past Vanity Fair and other places to the Heavenly City.

**PILGRIMS' WAY** Ancient English road followed by medieval pilgrims to the tomb of THOMAS À BECKET at Canterbury.

**PILLAR** Religious symbol of support (GALATIANS 2:9).

**PILLAR OF FIRE, THE** Holiness group founded in the United States by Mrs. Alma White in 1901. It was originally called the Pentecostal Union.

**PILLAR SAINT** Recluse in the early church

who lived on top of a pillar. A famous example was SIMEON STYLITES.

**PILPUL** *judgment* Jewish term for dialectic study of the TORAH and TALMUD. It involves detailed study of a particular text and comprehension of all its implications.

**PILTZINTECUHTLI** Aztec sun god.

**PINDA** Food offered to ancestral spirits in India.

**PINKSTER** Colloquial term for WHITSUNTIDE in American communities of Dutch origin.

**PIPAL** India's sacred BO TREE.

**PIR** Teacher of religion in ISLAM.

**PISCINA** *basin* Niche in a church wall for washing the utensils and the celebrant's hands after MASS.

**PISGAH** Mountain in Palestine northeast of the Dead Sea. From it Moses viewed the land of promise before his death (DEUTERONOMY 34:1–3).

**PIT, THE** Term in the Psalms and elsewhere for hell or the afterworld.

**PITAKA** *basket* BUDDHIST term for a collection of sacred writings. Buddhist Scripture contains three Pitakas, the Tripitaka, in the PALI CANON. They are the Abhidhammapitaka, Vinayapitaka, and Suttapitaka.

**PITCH** Tar or asphalt used to calk Noah's ark and the basket in which the baby Moses floated. In religious art pitch symbolizes evil.

**PITRIS** Ancestral spirits venerated in India.

**PIUS II (1405–1464)** Aeneas Sylvius, Sienese pope who united the Christian world against the threat of Turkish conquests. He wrote several commentaries.

**PIUS IV (1499–1565)** Milanese pope who reconvened the Council of TRENT in 1562 and reestablished the INQUISITION.

**PIUS V, ST. (1504–1572)** Italian pope trained as a DOMINICAN. He executed the decrees of the Council of TRENT, establishing the COUNTER REFORMATION, promoting the INQUISITION, and seeking reform in the church. His feast day is May 5.

**PIUS IX (1792–1878)** Italian pope who defined the IMMACULATE CONCEPTION of the Virgin Mary and issued the Syllabus of Errors, condemning modernism and liberalism.

**PIUS X, ST. (1835–1914)** Italian pope who condemned the French separation of church and state, religious modernism, and World War I. He urged the faithful to take daily COMMUNION and proposed the codification of the new canon law. His feast day is September 3.

**PIUS XI (1857–1939)** Italian pope who denounced Italian Fascism, National Socialism (see NAZISM), and COMMUNISM. Encouraging the social application of Christianity, he correctly saw all forms of totalitarianism as affronts to the sovereignty of Christ. He favored indigenous religious forms of Christianity and furthered understanding between the Eastern and Western churches.

**PIUS XII (1876–1958)** Italian pope, Eugenio Pacelli, who sought to prevent and limit World War II, opposed Communist attacks on religion, and prepared the way for the liturgical reforms and social concerns of contemporary CATHOLICISM. In 1950 he defined the ASSUMPTION of the Virgin Mary.

**PIYYUT** Jewish liturgical poem with a religious theme or motif, recited on special days or read for devotional purposes.

**PLACEBO** *I will please* Title of vespers for the dead, based on the Latin of Psalm 116:9.

**PLACET** *it pleases* 1. Ecclesiastical affirmation of assent. 2. State sanction of religious measures.

**PLAGUES, TEN** Series of catastrophes harassing the people of Egypt until the Israelites were permitted to depart in the Exodus (EXODUS 7—12).

**PLAIN SONG** Ancient ecclesiastical melody, sung in unison with free rhythm. It is often synonymous with GREGORIAN CHANT and is sometimes called plain chant.

**PLANETA** Term for the CHASUBLE.

**PLANE TREE** Broad-leaved tree symbolizing the grace of Christ in religious art.

**PLATO (427–347 B.C.)** Greek philosopher with unparalleled insight. The highest realities, he taught, are the good, the beautiful, the true, and the just. Through the *Socratic Dialogues* and other works he encouraged the questioning of all assumptions in order to find truth and reality. He saw God as the supreme Soul who fashions the world after a model in the divine Mind; time as "a moving image of eternity." Few men have influenced Western Christendom as has Plato.

**PLENARY COUNCIL** Church council of the bishops and archbishops in a specified region, presided over by a legate from the VATICAN.

**PLENARY INDULGENCE** Remission of all the temporal punishment for one's sins. The other type of indulgence, partial, remits only a part of the punishment for sin.

**PLOTINUS (c.205–270)** Egyptian philosopher and mystic who fathered the chief form of NEOPLATONISM. He traveled to Persia to study Eastern thought and founded his own philosophical school in Rome. It influenced Christianity through Plotinus' interpretation of the ideas of Plato and other Greek thinkers.

**PLOUGH MONDAY** British term for the first Monday after Epiphany, a time of prayer for agriculture.

**PLUMSTEAD PECULIARS** See PECULIAR PEOPLE.

**PLURALISM** Philosophy of many ultimate principles or realities. William JAMES, DESCARTES and others held this view.

**PLURALITY** Ecclesiastical term for the holding of several offices or benefices by one person. This was prohibited in England by the Pluralities Act of 1838.

**PLUTO** Greek god of fertility and the world of the dead.

**PLUTUS** Greek god of wealth.

**PLYMOUTH BRETHREN** PROTESTANT group originating in Dublin about 1827 and in Plymouth, England, about 1830. Early leaders were John Nelson Darby, J. G. Bellett, Samuel P. Tregelles, and A. N. Groves. Schism soon occurred; today there are eight divisions in the United States alone. Members practice "breaking of bread" every Sunday, call their groups *assemblies* and their buildings *chapels,* expect the imminent premillennial return of Christ, evangelize earnestly, and emphasize the priesthood of all believers. They have no ordained clergy and no planned order of worship; the Holy Spirit is considered in charge, and any male Christian may participate in the service.

**PNEUMA** *spirit* Greek word for spirit, human or divine.

**PNEUMATOMACHI** Followers of Macedonius, a Bishop of Constantinople in the fourth century, who held that the Holy Spirit was subordinate to God the Father and God the Son. They were condemned as heretical by Pope DAMASUS in 374 and suppressed out of existence soon after.

**POGROM** *destruction* Russian term for the massacre of a Jewish or other community.

**POIMENICS** Term for pastoral theology: study of the care of souls by the Christian pastor.

**POINTING** 1. Marking of Hebrew letters to indicate the vowels. 2. Marking of the Psalms in ANGLICAN worship to indicate pauses, in singing or reading.

**POLE, REGINALD (1500–1558)** Archbishop of Canterbury in England and cardinal. Putting the pope before the king, he found Henry VIII attempting to eradicate his family; his mother was executed in 1541. When war erupted between Spain and the Vatican, Pole fell victim of the enmity of Pope Paul IV. But he was always devout and sincere, and refused to countenance the killing of heretics.

**POLEMICS** Study of theological discussion or controversy for the rebuttal of error.

**POLISH NATIONAL CATHOLIC CHURCH OF AMERICA** Church founded in Pennsylvania in 1897. Polish in background, the group emphasizes Scripture, tradition, and the first four ECUMENICAL COUNCILS in the history of the church. Seven SACRAMENTS are accepted and two types of confession, private and general. Leadership is through a prime bishop, bishops, and an annual church council.

**POLITY** Government and discipline of a religious group. Four main types of polity are congregational, republican, aristocratic, and monarchical; examples of each are the BAPTIST, PRESBYTERIAN, ANGLICAN, and ROMAN CATHOLIC CHURCHES.

**POLTERGEIST** Phenomenon involving noises or movements with no known physical cause. Spiritism attributes such phenomena to the influence of spirits, while parapsychology seeks possible psychical or unknown causes.

**POLYCARP, ST. (c.70–c.155)** Greek bishop and Church Father who fought heresy and was burned to death for his faith at Smyrna in Asia Minor. His feast day is January 26.

**POLYGLOT BIBLE** A Bible with several versions in different languages in parallel columns. Origen's *Hexapla*, in Hebrew and five Greek versions, was the first.

**POLYTHEISM** Belief in a number of gods.

**POMEGRANATE** In religious art, a symbol of spring, the Resurrection, and the church.

**PONTIFEX** 1. In Roman religion, a priest. 2. In the church, a bishop or pope.

**PONTIFEX MAXIMUS** *supreme pathfinder* 1. Chief priest in Roman religion. 2. The pope.

**PONTIFF** 1. In Roman religion, a priest belonging to the highest priestly advisory group, the Pontifical College. 2. Catholic bishop or, usually, the pope.

**PONTIFICAL** 1. Papal or episcopal. 2. Book of rites or offices to be performed by a pontiff or bishop. 3. Vestments of a prelate celebrating PONTIFICAL MASS.

**PONTIFICAL MASS** Special high mass usually celebrated by a cardinal, bishop, abbot, or one of certain other prelates at the throne or FALDSTOOL.

**PONTIFICALS or PONTIFICALIA** Insignia and pontifical vestments of a bishop, cardinal, or abbot.

**PONTIFICATE** Office of a pontiff.

**PONTIUS PILATE** See PILATE, PONTIUS.

**PONTUS** Greek or Phoenician sea god.

**POOR CLARES** See CLARES.

**POPE** *father* 1. EASTERN ORTHODOX priest. 2. Title of the Bishop of Rome, the head and supreme pontiff of the ROMAN CATHOLIC CHURCH.

**POPISH PLOT** Supposed Catholic plot against England's King Charles II, apparently invented by Titus OATES.

**POPPY** In religious art, a symbol of sleep and of Christ's Passion.

**PORENTIUS or POREVIT** Slavonic god with five heads.

**PORPHYRY (c.232–303)** NEOPLATONIST philosopher who denounced Christianity and the church and claimed there were contradictions in the Gospels. He was a disciple of PLOTINUS.

**PORRES, ST. MARTIN DE (1579–1639)** Peruvian DOMINICAN who became the first American Negro to be canonized. His feast day is November 5.

**PORT-ROYAL** French site of a women's abbey founded in 1204 near Paris. Its nuns were originally BENEDICTINE, and later, CISTERCIAN. In the seventeenth century it became a center of JANSENISM and was destroyed.

**PORTUNUS** Roman god of portals and harbors.

**POSEIDON** Greek god of water and the ocean.

**POSITIVISM** Philosophy emphasizing physical facts and rejecting metaphysical considerations. A religion called Positivism was invented by Auguste Comte in the nineteenth century. It had no god but humanity, and a priesthood of philosophers.

**POSTCOMMUNION** Prayer after the communion of the priest in the mass, or the final prayer in the EUCHARIST.

**POSTLUDE** Music concluding a worship service in many churches.

**POSTMILLENARIANISM** See POSTMILLENNIALISM.

**POSTMILLENNIALISM** Belief that Christ will return after a thousand years of Christian triumph, peace, and blessing. See also AMILLENNIALISM and PREMILLENNIALISM.

**POSTULANT** Candidate for entrance into a religious order or for clerical ordination.

**POTIPHAR** Egyptian official who employed Joseph and then imprisoned him on his wife's accusation (GENESIS 37:36; 39).

**POTIPHERAH** Egyptian priest of the sun god RE at On. He was the father of Joseph's wife Asenath (GENESIS 41:45, 50).

**POTTER'S FIELD** Area near Jerusalem where Judas died (ACTS 1:18, 19). Apparently the poor were buried there.

**POVERTY** Renunciation of wealth, required in various religious orders.

**POWWOW** American Indian ceremony for conjuring, or an Indian medicine man.

**P.P.** Abbreviation for parish priest.

**PRAEMUNIRE** English laws protecting the king from papal authority.

**PRAJAPATI** HINDU "Lord of creatures" who made the world; BRAHMA or one of his ten sons.

**PRAJNA** BUDDHIST word for divine wisdom.

**PRAKRITI** Fundamental substance of visible things, according to the HINDU Sankhya philosophy and the BUDDHIST faith.

**PRAPATTI-MARGA** HINDU term for salvation through submission to the divine grace and love.

**PRATIMOKSHA** See PATIMOKKHA.

**PRATYEKA BUDDHA** Solitary Buddhist wise man who attains NIRVANA.

**PRAYER** Fellowship with God, often involving adoration, praise, thanksgiving, petition, confession, repentance, meditation, and dedication. Prayer is a central element in most forms of religion. Christian prayer is addressed to the God revealed in the Bible, in the name and spirit of Jesus Christ, that His perfect will may be carried out and His love, righteousness, and justice may prevail.

**PRAYER MEETING** Midweek prayer service held in many PROTESTANT churches of the United States in the nineteenth and early twentieth centuries, often with considerable lay participation. By the latter half of the twentieth century the prayer meeting was as extinct in many churches as the Sunday evening worship service.

**PRAYER OF MANASSES** Apocryphal book of the Old Testament dating from perhaps 200 A.D. Jews, Catholics, and Protestants all reject it from the canon.

**PRAYER SHAWL** White shawl with fringes or tassels worn over the head or shoulders of a Jewish male during prayer.

**PRAYER WHEEL** Cylinder employed by Tibetan Lamaists or Buddhists for invocation or meditation. Strips of paper inscribed with a prayer formula are attached to the wheel which is turned with a handle, wind, or falling water.

**PRAYING INDIANS** Term for North American Indians converted to Christianity.

**PREACH** Originally to preach meant to proclaim the good news of Jesus Christ. The term has degenerated into a synonym for merely preaching a sermon or for offering moralistic advice.

**PREACHER** Clergyman; one who preaches.

**PREACHING OF PETER** Second-century tract ascribed to St. Peter. It was one of the earliest Christian apologetics.

**PREADAMITES** 1. Human beings believed by some to have existed on earth before Adam. 2. Those who believe in such preadamites; in particular, seventeenth-century followers of the views of Isaac La

Peyrere, who wrote a book about people before Adam.

**PREBEND** ANGLICAN term for an endowment supporting a priest, or a BENEFICE.

**PREBENDARY** ANGLICAN canon who holds a PREBEND or BENEFICE providing income in compensation for his work.

**PRECENTOR** Clergyman directing the choir or choral services in an Anglican service.

**PRECEPT** Law or rule for behavior.

**PRECIOUS BLOOD** The blood of Christ poured out for the salvation of sinners. The ROMAN CATHOLIC CHURCH celebrates a feast of the Most Precious Blood on July 1.

**PRECISIAN** Archaic term for a PURITAN.

**PREDELLA** 1. Platform on the highest step to the altar, where the celebrant administers mass. 2. Lowest portion of the REREDOS.

**PREDESTINATION** Theological term for the eternal purpose of God by which whatever He has decreed takes place. St. AUGUSTINE and John CALVIN linked predestination to the election of certain individuals to salvation, and the sovereign grace which brings them to glory.

**PRE-EXISTENCE** Term for the existence of Christ before the Incarnation, or for the existence of the individual previous to his present incarnation on earth. BUDDHISM and HINDUISM hold forms of the latter belief.

**PREFACE** Introduction to the central portion of the EUCHARIST, beginning with the "Sursum Corda" and ending with the "Sanctus."

**PRELACY** 1. The ANGLICAN or episcopal system of church government—by prelates such as bishops. 2. Office of a prelate.

**PRELATE** High church official such as a bishop.

**PRELUDE** Music before the worship service in many churches.

**PREMILLENARIAN** One who believes in the imminent return of Christ, to be followed by a thousand years of peace during which He reigns over the earth.

**PREMILLENNIALISM** Belief of PREMILLENARIANS. Most fundamentalists incline to premillennialism.

**PREMONSTRATENSIAN CANONS** Religious order founded by St. NORBERT in France in 1120, also called the Canons Regular of Premontre. Members are active in missions and education.

**PREPARATION DAYS** The days before Jewish festivals and holy days such as the Sabbath.

**PREPARATORY SERVICE** Worship service, once prominent in PRESBYTERIAN churches, designed to prepare communicant members for the reception of the Lord's Supper.

**PRESBYTER** *elder* 1. Ancient synagogue leader, called an elder. 2. Ruling official in the New Testament church (cf. ACTS 14:23). 3. Member of the governing board of a PRESBYTERIAN congregation. 4. Priest. (See also ELDER.)

**PRESBYTERIAN** 1. Member of a PRESBYTERIAN CHURCH. 2 Relating to a Presbyterian church, PRESBYTERY, or government by PRESBYTERS (elders).

**PRESBYTERIAN CHURCH** 1. Congregation governed by elders elected by the people and accepting the authority of the PRESBYTERY, the Scriptures, and the REFORMED system of doctrine. 2. Denomination consisting of congregations holding the above views.

**PRESBYTERIAN CHURCH IN THE UNITED STATES** Presbyterian denomination of the southern United States, originating in opposition to northern antislavery pressures and taking a moderate stance on theological and social issues.

**PRESBYTERIAN CHURCH IN THE U.S.A.** Former name of the UNITED PRESBYTERIAN CHURCH IN THE U.S.A.

**PRESBYTERIANISM** Adherence to Presbyterian doctrines, polity, history, or all three. See PRESBYTERIAN CHURCH and names of various Presbyterian denominations.

**PRESBYTERY** 1. Alliance of the Presbyterian churches in an area in a strong self-governing unit, through the ministers and elders of the churches involved. The presbytery oversees the district, governs worship, ordains ministers, receives and dismisses them, and serves as a court of the church. 2. Place at the eastern portion of a church or cathedral reserved for clergymen of high rank, or for officiating priests. 3. Priest's residence.

**PRESTER JOHN** Legendary Asian priest and king about whom various legends circulated in the Middle Ages. Epistles believed to have been from him or about him also circulated.

**PRETA** BUDDHIST term for a spirit help-lessly awaiting a new body.

**PREVENIENCE** Theological term for the prior acts of God which result in man's salvation.

**PREVENIENT GRACE** Divine favor which precedes human response to God's love and brings about salvation.

**PRIAPUS** Greek god of fertility and good luck.

**PRIDE** Excessive love of one's own superiority, chief of the seven deadly sins emphasized in medieval Christianity. Pride is considered by many theologians to be the supreme sin.

**PRIE-DIEU** *pray God* Private kneeling desk.

**PRIEST** One who represents the people before God and God before men. In most faiths a priest is ordained or authorized to perform specific religious duties.

**PRIESTLEY, JOSEPH (1733–1804)** PRESBY-TERIAN minister and scientist whose increasingly liberal views led him to found the Unitarian Society in England and to establish the first UNITARIAN church in America. He sympathized with the French Revolution, opposed slavery, and discovered oxygen.

**PRIESTLY CODE** See "P."

**PRIMATE** Chief bishop of a territory.

**PRIME** First canonical hour, celebrated at 6 A.M.

**PRIMER** Devotional book for laymen in the Middle Ages. Primers were later used in New England and elsewhere to teach children such subjects as reading and spelling.

**PRIMITIVE ADVENT CHRISTIAN CHURCH** Very small ADVENTIST church in West Virginia.

**PRIMITIVE BAPTISTS** Very conservative, exclusive Baptists in the United States who oppose missionary societies, Sunday schools, and institutionalized religion.

**PRIMITIVE METHODIST CHURCH** Methodist Church organized in England in 1811 in enthusiasm for CAMP MEETINGS and unorthodox evangelistic methods. In 1932 it merged into England's present METHODIST CHURCH.

**PRIMITIVE METHODIST CHURCH, U.S.A.** American denomination carrying on the principles of England's PRIMITIVE METHODIST CHURCH.

**PRIMUS** Presiding bishop in the Scottish Episcopal Church.

**PRINCE OF DARKNESS** Term for the devil.

**PRINCE OF PEACE** Isaiah's term for the MESSIAH (ISAIAH 9:6), and a common Christian designation for Jesus.

**PRINGLE-PATTISON, ANDREW SETH (1856–1931)** Scottish philosopher who saw God as the origin of human individuation and wrote many philosophical works. Among these were *Man's Place in the Cosmos*, *The Idea of Immortality*, and *Studies in the Philosophy of Religion*.

**PRIOR** Superior of a MONASTERY, or an abbot's deputy.

**PRIORESS** Superior or deputy head of a house of NUNS.

**PRIORY** Religious house, ranking below an abbey, over which a prior or prioress presides.

**PRISCILLA, or PRISCA, ST.** New Testament Christian woman who with her husband Aquila aided St. Paul and Apollos (ACTS 18:2, 18, 26; ROMANS 16:3). Her feast day is July 8.

**PRISCILLIANISM** Spanish heresy of the fourth and fifth centuries apparently originating in the GNOSTIC teachings of one Priscillian. Adherents were accused of dualism and various aberrations.

**PRITHIVI** The earth, a member of the divine pantheon and an attendant of Indra in vedic mythology.

**PROBABILIORISM** Term in CATHOLIC theology for choice of an action when one is in a dilemma between liberty and obedience to a law. Probabiliorism favors such obedience unless the theological opinion favoring liberty is more probable.

**PROBABILISM** Term in CATHOLIC theology for moral choice between liberty and obedience to law. The reverse of PROBABILIORISM, probabilism holds that even though theological opinion favoring such obedience is more probable, one may choose liberty on good authority or if it seems wise and safe. (See also EQUIPROBABILISM.)

**PROCESSION** Ecclesiastical march.

**PROCESSIONAL** 1. March of the choir into the chancel at the beginning of a worship service. Sometimes it includes the clergy. 2. Hymn sung in such a processional. 3. Book of music and litanies for ecclesiastical processions.

**PROCESSIONAL CROSS** Cross leading an ecclesiastical procession.

**PROCESSIONAL HYMN** Hymn sung during the procession of the choir into the chancel during a processional.

**PROCESSION OF THE HOLY GHOST** Theological term for the coming of the Holy Spirit from the Father and the Son (cf. JOHN 15:26). According to the Constantinopolitan Creed, the Holy Spirit "proceedeth from the Father." At a council in Toledo, Spain, in 447, the Spirit was stated to proceed also from the Son. The CAPPADOCIAN FATHERS first developed the doctrine of the procession of the Holy Ghost on a rather extensive scale.

**PRODIGAL SON, THE** Wayward son in one of Jesus' parables (LUKE 15:11–32). After leaving home and leading a dissolute life, he became hungry and returned to his father, who gave him a warm welcome.

**PROFANATION** Desecration of something sacred.

**PROFESSION** Formal entrance into a religious order.

**PROFESSION OF FAITH** Public statement of faith of a person becoming a member of a church.

**PROGRESSIVE DUNKERS** See BRETHREN CHURCH.

**PROGRESSIVE SPIRITUAL CHURCH** Spiritualist group in the United States; it has four sacraments: baptism, marriage, spiritual communion, and the funeral.

**PROHIBITION** 1. Something forbidden, as by ecclesiastical decree. 2. American movement against the use of alcoholic beverages; it culminated in the Eighteenth Amendment which forbade the manufacture and sale of such beverages. The movement was inspired to a great extent by PROTESTANT churches and workers.

**PROMISED LAND** Canaan or Palestine, promised to Abraham and his seed, and accepted by the Hebrew people as God's special gift.

**PROMOTOR FIDEI** *promoter of the faith* Official of the Congregation of Rites who carefully examines the evidence for a candidate's beatification or canonization. A popular title is "Devil's Advocate."

**PROPAGANDA** CATHOLIC term for the propagation of the faith.

**PROPAGANDA, SACRED CONGREGATION OF** CATHOLIC organization also known as the Sacred Congregation for the Spreading of the Faith. Established by Pope Gregory XV in 1622, it is devoted to world missionary enterprises.

**PROPER** Portion of a worship service especially appointed for a particular day or season. The rest of the service does not ordinarily vary.

**PROPHECY** Divinely inspired utterance; the message of a PROPHET. While prophecy popularly means foretelling future events, the emphasis in Biblical prophecy is on the enunciation and interpretation of the will of God. In some cases this was accompanied on the part of the Biblical messengers by revelation of things to come.

**PROPHET** 1. Messenger of God who proclaims His will for men. 2. One of the Hebrew spokesmen for God such as Amos, Isaiah, Jeremiah, or Hosea. 3. In the early church, one who spoke by divine inspiration (I CORINTHIANS 14:4, 22; ACTS 11: 27; 15:32; 21:10). 4. One of the Old Testament books included in the Former or Latter Prophets such as Joshua, Judges, Isaiah, Jeremiah, etc. 5. In Islam, Mohammed is known as the Prophet.

**PROPHETESS** Female PROPHET.

**PROPHETIC** Relating to a PROPHET, or to prophecy.

**PROPHETISM** Belief in divine revelation through PROPHETS.

**PROPHETS, FORMER** OLD TESTAMENT writings known as Joshua, Judges, I and II Samuel, and I and II Kings.

**PROPHETS, LATTER** OLD TESTAMENT writings of Isaiah, Jeremiah, Ezekiel, Hosea, Joel, Amos, Obadiah, Jonah, Micah, Nahum, Habakkuk, Zephaniah, Haggai, Zechariah, and Malachi.

**PROPHETS, MAJOR** The Jewish prophets Isaiah, Jeremiah, Ezekiel, and Daniel. (The Hebrew Scriptures do not include Daniel among the Prophets.)

**PROPHETS, MINOR** The Jewish prophets whose writings were quite short compared to those of the Major PROPHETS. They are Amos, Hosea, Micah, Zephaniah, Nahum, Habakkuk, Haggai, Zechariah, Malachi, Obadiah, Joel, and Jonah.

**PROPITIATION** Theological term for the appeasement of the wrath of God through sacrifice, prayer, or in some other way. According to the New Testament, guilt is removed and broken relationships with God restored only by the sacrifice of Christ, received in faith and obedience. God has set forth Christ "to be a propitiation through faith in his blood, to declare his righteousness for the remission of sins that are past" (ROMANS 3:25).

**PROSE** Hymn without regular meter, also known as a sequence, sung or spoken in the mass.

**PROSELYTE** Convert from another faith or sect. Originally this word applied to converts from other faiths to Judaism.

**PROSTITUTION, RELIGIOUS** Term for sexual relationships associated with Hinduism and many ancient religions. The Judeo-Christian Scriptures sternly discountenance such rites.

**PROTESTANT** Originally, one who joined the German protest against the suppression of religious freedom of the Diet of SPEYER in 1529. Today a Protestant is generally considered to be a non-Catholic Christian, or a member of a Baptist, Methodist, Presbyterian, or similar religious group.

**PROTESTANT CONFERENCE (LUTHERAN)** Evangelical LUTHERAN group centering in Wisconsin.

**PROTESTANTENVEREIN** German society of Protestants who banded together in 1863 for mutual concerns and progress.

**PROTESTANT EPISCOPAL CHURCH** Principal ANGLICAN denomination in the United States, established by the Church of England in the seventeenth century but now autonomous although in communion with the See of Canterbury. Its doctrinal standards and government are similar to those of the CHURCH OF ENGLAND, but laymen have a greater part in polity and administration.

**PROTESTANTISM** Doctrines and churches of non-Catholic Christianity, emphasizing the priesthood of all believers, the authority of the Bible, justification by faith, preaching, and the two sacraments or ordinances of baptism and communion.

**PROTESTANT REFORMED** British term for the religion of the CHURCH OF ENGLAND.

**PROTESTANT REFORMED CHURCHES IN AMERICA** Small denomination in Grand Rapids, Michigan, which withdrew from the Christian Reformed Church in 1926.

**PROTESTANT UNION** 1. Seventeenth-century league of German Protestants who banded together for mutual defense. 2. Sixteenth-century French Huguenot alliance.

**PROTEUS** Greek sea god and prophet.

**PROTEVANGELIUM** Apocryphal Book of James, narrating the writer's conception of the birth and early life of the Virgin Mary.

**PROTHONOTARY** 1. Member of the College of Prothonotaries Apostolic in the ROMAN CATHOLIC CHURCH, expected to sign encyclicals and perform other duties. 2. Honorary Catholic title. 3. Chief secretary to the chief patriarch in the EASTERN ORTHODOX CHURCH.

**PROTOCOLS OF THE WISE MEN OF ZION** Forgery employed by Hitler and other anti-Semites to stir up hatred against the Jews. The book presents a supposed international Jewish plot against the world.

**PROTOMARTYR** *first martyr* 1. Title of St. STEPHEN, first martyr in the church (ACTS 7:60). 2. First martyr of a country, as St. ALBAN of England.

**PROTONOTARY** See PROTHONOTARY.

**PROTOPOPE** *first father* High priestly rank in the EASTERN ORTHODOX CHURCH, comparable to that of dean in Western churches.

**PROVERBS** Old Testament book containing wise sayings attributed to Solomon, Agur, Lemuel, and others. An example of the Bible's wisdom literature, it praises industry, morality, wisdom, good etiquette, temperance, righteousness, charity, and other virtues.

**PROVIDENCE** 1. Sustaining and governing care of God. 2. God in His sovereign and guiding relationships to men.

**PROVINCE** Area under a single ecclesiastical jurisdiction, as of an archbishop.

**PROVINCIAL** Superior of a religious order, having administrative duties but responsible to the superior-general.

**PROVOOST, SAMUEL (1742–1815)** Chaplain of the Continental Congress and first EPISCOPAL Bishop of New York.

**PROVOST** 1. Cathedral dean or chapter head. 2. Person with supreme authority in a religious community or church.

**PRUDENCE** Cardinal virtue of wise self-regulation, avoiding all excess and folly.

**PSALM** Song of praise and worship.

**PSALMODY** Study or practice of the use of psalms.

**PSALMS** Old Testament book containing 150 poems and songs employed in Hebrew worship. Known as the Psalms of David; individual psalms are also attributed to Moses, Solomon, and others. Portions of the Psalms are quoted throughout the New Testament and the book has been most influential in both JUDAISM and CHRISTIANITY.

**PSALMS OF SOLOMON** Pseudepigraphic Hebrew work, mistakenly attributed to Solomon, containing eighteen psalms.

**PSALTER** The Old Testament book of Psalms, or a book containing psalms, often with music.

**PSALTERY** Stringed musical instrument used in Hebrew worship.

**PSEUDEPIGRAPHA** *false headings* Writings wrongly attributed to worthies such as Enoch, Moses, Solomon, etc. They are both Jewish and Christian. Examples of Christian epigrapha are the Gospel of Peter, the Gospel of Thomas, the Apocalypse of Peter, and the Ascension of Isaiah.

**PSEUDO-DIONYSIUS** A name of DIONYSIUS THE PSEUDO-AREOPAGITE.

**PSEUDO-ISIDORIAN DECRETALS** Ninth-century group of letters spuriously ascribed to early popes with a preface mistakenly believed to be by Isidore of Seville. See FALSE DECRETALS.

**PSEUDO-MESSIAHS** Persons falsely claiming to be MESSIAH. There have been a number in Jewish and Christian history.

**PSI** 1. Greek letter representing the sound *ps.* 2. Term for psychical phenomena.

**PSYCHE** 1. Greek personification of the soul. 2. Soul, mind, life, or self.

**PSYCHEDELIC** Adjective indicating the "hallucinogenic" drugs alleged to produce psychic and religious experiences.

**PSYCHIANA** American religious movement founded and headed by Frank B. Robinson in the twentieth century. It emphasized "the God-power" and "the God-law" which could bring disciples healing, peace, and prosperity.

**PSYCHIATRY** Study and treatment of mental disorders. Through the work of Sigmund Freud and others it has become one of the most revolutionary forces in the understanding of human personality.

**PSYCHIC** Relating to the soul, the mind, or the occult.

**PSYCHIC RESEARCH** Study of such phenomena as telepathy and clairvoyance. Societies for such study in England and America have produced impressive results. See also PARAPSYCHOLOGY.

**PSYCHOLOGY** Study of the mind and mental phenomena.

**PSYCHOLOGY OF RELIGION** Study of the relationship between psychology and religion, with emphasis on religious consciousness and experience.

**PTAH** Egyptian creator-god, a chief deity of Memphis and patron of artisans.

**PUBLICANS** Tax collectors of New Testament times, generally despised. Jesus was a friend of publicans and extolled one of them in a parable (LUKE 18:9–14).

**PUCK** Mischievous or malevolent spirit in Germanic and British folklore.

**PUJA** 1. HINDU term for religious respect or worship. 2. BUDDHIST term for a gesture of religious reverence, as of elevating clasped hands.

**PULPIT** Platform, often with enclosed sides and usually with a desk or stand for reading, from which the sermon is preached in most churches.

**PUNCHAU** Inca sun god.

**PUNDIT** Learned HINDU teacher.

**PURANAS** Eighteen epic works of the religious literature of India, honoring various deities in verse. The Puranas are among the sacred writings of HINDUISM.

**PURCELL, HENRY (1659–1695)** English composer of ecclesiastical and other music of enduring merit. Organist at Westminster Abbey, he wrote some outstanding anthems.

**PURE LAND SCHOOL** School of MAHAYANA Buddhism emphasizing faith in AMIDA, the Buddha of Infinite Light, as a way to birth in the "Pure Land" paradise.

**PURGATORY** According to Catholic teaching, a place, state, or period of temporal punishment in which venial sins may be expiated and the soul purified in preparation for heaven. Souls in Purgatory may be aided by the prayers and sacrifices of the faithful on earth.

**PURI** Town in India housing a huge image of JUGGERNAUT which is carried in a long procession every summer.

**PURIFICATION** In many religions, removal

of guilt or impurity by various means. In JUDAISM, *purification* refers to the preparation of a corpse for burial.

**PURIFICATOR** Small white linen cloth used to cleanse and dry the chalice after the EUCHARIST.

**PURIM** Jewish festival, celebrated in the spring on ADAR 14, commemorating Jewish deliverance from a threatened massacre (ESTHER 3:7; 9:24, 26). It is a time of joy and carnival.

**PURITANS** English PROTESTANTS who sought to purify the CHURCH OF ENGLAND of what they considered to be CATHOLIC influences, and finally separated from it. Becoming prominent at the time of Queen Elizabeth I, they were generally CALVINISTIC in doctrine and a majority were PRESBYTERIANS. A number emigrated to New England in the seventeenth century; there many of them were CONGREGATIONALISTS. The Puritans included John MILTON, Thomas Cartwright, Oliver CROMWELL, Richard BAXTER, Thomas HOOKER, John COTTON, Roger WILLIAMS, John ROBINSON, John Smith, and Cotton and Increase MATHER. Their influence on English and American religious and political life has been profound.

**PUROHITA** HINDU priest.

**PURPLE** Color signifying royalty in Bible times (JUDGES 8:26; ESTHER 1:6; MARK 15:17, 20). In liturgical use it symbolizes penitence and is used in LENT, in ADVENT, and on ROGATION DAYS and EMBER DAYS.

**PURUSHA** Sanskrit term for spirit, soul, Brahma, or God, in HINDU and BUDDHIST religion.

**PURVEY, JOHN (c.1353–c.1428)** Follower of John WYCLIF who revised the Bible which had been translated by Wyclif and

Nicholas of Hereford into the first thorough English translation. A LOLLARD, Purvey was prohibited from preaching and imprisoned.

**PUSA** Chinese word for the Buddhist BODHISATTVA, whose wisdom and loving compassion make him a candidate for Buddhahood.

**PUSEY, EDWARD BOUVERIE (1800–1882)** HIGH CHURCH leader in the Church of England's OXFORD MOVEMENT. He held to the real presence of Christ in the EUCHARIST, advocated private confession and absolution, and maintained that hell is everlasting. He sought grounds for eventual reunion of the churches of England and Rome.

**PUSHAN** Vedic sun god and patron of roads and travelers.

**PYRAMID TEXTS** Inscriptions found inside five pyramids near Memphis, Egypt, forming what has been termed the earliest collection of religious literature.

**PYROMANCY** Divination with the use of fire.

**PYTHAGOREANS** Greek members of a brotherhood founded by the philosopher Pythagoras, who lived in the sixth century B.C. The Pythagoreans had mystic inclinations and a passion for numbers—which they believed the true essence of all things. They believed in immortality and the transmigration of souls, and held high moral standards.

**PYTHIA** Greek prophetess of APOLLO at Delphi. See DELPHIC ORACLE.

**PYTHONESS** Woman in Greek religion believed to possess the spirit of divination.

**PYX or PIX** Vessel in which the communion sacrament is reserved or taken to the sick.

# Q

**Q** Symbol of the document which, it is theorized, is the source of much material in the Gospels of Matthew and Luke not found in the Gospel of Mark. According to a widely accepted hypothesis, "Q" is a written collection, probably in Greek, of sayings of Jesus which were worked into the Gospels of Luke and Matthew. The German scholar Adolph HARNACK first proposed this theory of "Q."

**QADARITES** MOSLEMS who believe that humans have the ability to act autonomously and are not completely subservient to the will of ALLAH. Their founder, Abd al-Qadir al-Jilani, was a mystic and ascetic to whom miracles were attributed.

**QADESH or QEDESHET** Syrian goddess who appears to have been worshiped in Egypt as a manifestation of HATHOR.

**QADI** MOSLEM leader who settles religious questions.

**QADIRIYA** See QADARITES.

**QARAITES** See KARAITES.

**QASISHA** Priest in the ASSYRIAN CHURCH of the East.

**QEDESHET** See QADESH.

**QUADRAGESIMA** The Latin name for LENT; specifically, its first four Sundays.

**QUADRAGESIMA SUNDAY** First Sunday in the season of LENT.

**QUADRAGESIMO ANNO** Papal encyclical of 1931, from Pope PIUS XI, emphasizing Christian principles in the social order.

**QUADRATUS, ST. (second century)** Earliest known apologist for the Christian faith. His feast day is May 26.

**QUAHOOTZE** War god of the American Nootka Indians.

**QUAKER** Originally a term of contempt for one of the FRIENDS. It was used either to indicate the depth of Quaker emotion, or because the Friends bade their hearers tremble at the word of God.

**QUAKER MEETING** Friends' worship service, in which there may be extended periods of silence. See FRIENDS, SOCIETY OF.

**QUAMTA** Supreme deity of the Kaffir tribe of Africa.

**QUARLES, FRANCIS (1592–1644)** English religious poet. He published several books including one of Scripture paraphrases, *Divine Fancies*.

**QUARTODECIMANS** Second-century Christians who insisted on observing EASTER on the same day as the Jewish PASSOVER.

**QUASIMODO SUNDAY** The Sunday after EASTER.

**QUEEN OF HEAVEN** 1. The Babylonian goddess ISHTAR whose worship Jeremiah denounced (JEREMIAH 44:17–19, 25). 2. A title of the Virgin MARY.

**QUESNEL, PASQUIER (1634–1719)** French adherent of JANSENISM who wrote a commentary on the New Testament and saw his doctrines condemned by the Roman Catholic Church. He held that the grace of God is vital to salvation and that it is irresistible.

**QUETZAL** Striking Central American bird worshiped by the Aztecs and Mayas.

**QUETZALCOATL** *feathered serpent* White-skinned Aztec god who departed after teaching many things. The Aztecs thought the invasion of Cortez in 1519 represented their god's return.

**QUICK** Word in the KING JAMES BIBLE for "living."

**QUICUNQUE VULT** *whosoever wishes* A name and the opening words of the ATHANASIAN CREED.

**QUIET DAY** Term for a day devoted to quiet religious contemplation or other spiritual exercises.

**QUIETISM** Religious movement originating with the Spanish priest Miguel de

MOLINOS in the seventeenth century. Madame GUYON and Francois FENELON supported it. It advocated total cessation of human effort and submission to God in complete passivity. It extolled pure faith, pure love, and pure prayer—concentrating so completely on God that nothing is left in the soul but consciousness of His presence. Its doctrines were condemned by Pope INNOCENT XI.

**QUIMBY, PHINEAS P. (1802–1866)** New England mesmerist and faith healer whose patients included Mary Baker EDDY. It is difficult to state with precision what his influence on her may have been.

**QUINDENA** Fifteenth day after an ecclesiastical festival.

**QUINQUAGESIMA** 1. The fifty days before EASTER. 2. The Sunday before LENT begins.

**QUIRINIUS** Roman governor of Syria during a census and taxation of the Roman Empire (LUKE 2:2).

**QUIRINUS** With Jupiter and Mars, one of the three principal deities of ancient Roman religion.

**QUMRAN** Village near the Dead Sea in Jordan, in whose caves the DEAD SEA SCROLLS were discovered. About a century before the time of Christ Qumran was the center of a community of the men who inscribed and hid the Scrolls.

**QUOTIDIAN** *daily* Ecclesiastic who labors daily, or the fee for such daily service.

**QUO VADIS?** *whither goest thou?* Question raised by PETER, according to legend, when he fled from persecution at Rome and met Christ going toward that capital. When Christ replied that he was bound for Rome to be re-crucified, Peter was shamed and returned himself to be martyred.

**QURAN** See KORAN.

**QUTB** MOSLEM word for an outstanding saint or spirit directing earthly affairs.

**QUTB MINAR** Very ancient MOSLEM minaret, nearly 250 feet high, near New Delhi in India.

# R

**R.** Abbreviation for "Response" in worship services and prayer books.

**RA or RE** The sun or sun god in ancient Egyptian religion. Its principal deity, Ra was usually represented with a solar disk over his head. Sometimes he had a falcon's head; sometimes he was a cat or a lion. He was considered to be creator of the world and all things in it, and Lord of heaven and earth.

**RAB or RABBAN** See RABBI.

**RABANUS MAURUS, ST. (c.776–856)** Learned German theologian and scholar. Monk, abbot, and Archbishop of Mainz, he evangelized Germany and has been termed the nation's preceptor. He wrote commentaries on various portions of the Bible and a mystical exposition of the universe. His veneration as a saint is recognized by a feast day February 4.

**RABAT** Clerical collar, bands, vest, or waistcoat.

**RABBI, RAB or RABBAN** *my master* Jewish teacher or clergyman.

**RABBINIC** Term for the language of Jewish exposition and talmudic study in the early Middle Ages.

**RABBINISM** Term for post-Biblical and talmudic JUDAISM, sometimes used derogatorily.

**RABBONI** *my great master* Title of respect sometimes given Jesus (MARK 10:51 RSV; JOHN 20:16).

**RABIA** Third month in the ISLAMIC calendar.

**RABIA AL-ADAWIYA (?–801)** Middle Eastern woman regarded as a saint and founder of SUFISM.

**RACA** New Testament word expressing contempt (MATTHEW 5:22; JAMES 2:20).

**RACE SUPREMACY** Belief that one race is somehow superior to another, or destined to guide another. The Apostle Peter confessed that he had once believed in racial supremacy, but, as he said, "God hath shewed me that I should not call any man common or unclean" (ACTS 10:28).

**RACHEL** *ewe* Jacob's favorite wife and Joseph's doting mother (GENESIS 29—33; 35). Rachel's tomb is said to be on the road between Jerusalem and Bethlehem. She is honored by JEWS, CHRISTIANS, and MOSLEMS.

**RACISM** See RACE SUPREMACY.

**RADEWYN, FLORENTIUS** See BRETHREN OF THE COMMON LIFE.

**RADHA** Special mistress of Hinduism's amorous god KRISHNA.

**RADIN, PAUL (1883–1959)** American authority on the religion and philosophy of primitive human beings. Born in Poland, he made extensive studies of the Winnebago Indians of Wisconsin and Nebraska.

**RAGNAROK** Term for the "twilight of the gods" and the end of the age in Scandinavian mythology.

**RAHAB** *broad* 1. Harlot of Jericho who aided the Jewish scouts that spied on the city; she was saved from destruction and became an ancestress of Jesus (JOSHUA 2:1–24; MATTHEW 1:5). 2. Symbolic name for Egypt (ISAIAH 30:7). 3. Dragon who fought the Lord before the creation (PSALM 89:10).

**RAHULA (sixth century B.C.)** Son of BUDDHA, who became one of Buddhism's twelve Elders.

**RAIDEN** Japanese god of thunder and storm.

**RAIKES, ROBERT (1735–1811)** English publisher and benefactor who opened the first Sunday school to teach slum children to read and write. Although this innovation was opposed by religious conservatives, Raikes is now honored as the founder of the Sunday school.

**RAINBOW** Symbol of divine pardon and of the throne of God. (Cf. GENESIS 9:12–17; REVELATION 4:3.)

**RAJ** Slavic term for heaven.

**RAJAB** Seventh month in the ISLAMIC calendar.

**RAKSHAS or RAKSHASAS** HINDU demons with destructive powers.

**RAM** Religious symbol of sacrifice and triumph. Ancient Babylonian altars were supported by statues of rams apparently caught in thickets, reminiscent of the ram whose death became a substitute for that of Abraham's son Isaac (GENESIS 22:13). Rams' horns, used as trumpets, encouraged the fall of Jericho (JOSHUA 6:5).

**RAMA** Name of an important incarnation of VISHNU in Hindu religion.

**RAMACHANDRA** See RAMAYANA.

**RAMADAN** Ninth month in the ISLAMIC calendar. In it all able-bodied persons are expected to abstain from eating and drinking during daylight, as a willing sacrifice to ALLAH. Orthodox Moslems observe Ramadan in January; BLACK MUSLIMS, in December.

**RAMAKRISHNA (1836–1886)** HINDU priest of Kali who studied YOGA, ISLAM, and CHRISTIANITY, and concluded that God may be found through all religions or none, provided that one seeks to realize His presence through mystical union and charity.

**RAMAKRISHNA MOVEMENT** Religious movement inspired by the teachings of RAMAKRISHNA. The Ramakrishna Mission or VEDANTA SOCIETY and the monastic order Ramakrishna Math carry these teachings to the world. The whole movement is a neo-Hindu renaissance.

**RAMANANDA (fifteenth century)** HINDU ascetic who exalted RAMA and sought followers from any faith or caste. He emphasized devotion to the god Rama and human brotherhood.

**RAMANANDIS** Followers of the teachings of RAMANANDA.

**RAMANUJA (twelfth century)** Teacher of India who founded the HINDU sect of Ramanujas or Sri Vaishnavas. His religious philosophy made room for individual souls, who become separated from BRAHMA or VISHNU (considered identical) by unbelief and reunited through loving devotion.

**RAMANUJAS** Followers of the doctrines of RAMANUJA.

**RAMAYANA** One of Hinduism's two great epics. Written in Sanskrit, probably in the third century B.C., it is a long narrative about RAMA, also called Ramachandra.

**RAMMAN** See ADAD.

**RAM MOHAN ROY (1774–1833)** Religious leader of India. Originally a Hindu, he studied Buddhism and Christianity and after becoming affluent in the service of the East India Company he founded the BRAHMA SAMAJ, a theistic religion modeled somewhat on UNITARIAN or DEISTIC lines, with a HINDU basis. He also founded Atmiya Sabha. A reformer, he opposed caste discrimination and idolatry and inspired the abolition of suttee—the sacrifice of the widow on her husband's funeral pyre. Also written Rammohun Roy.

**RANJIT SINGH** See SINGH, RANJIT.

**RANSOM THEORY** Early theory of the ATONEMENT; such Church Fathers as ORIGEN and AUGUSTINE held that Christ died to ransom human souls from the power of Satan. This theory was supplanted by various other views of the Atonement.

**RANTERS** 1. Seventeenth-century English individuals who believed that God was in the world and Christ was in them without benefit of the clergy, the creeds, or the Scriptures. They were suppressed and denounced as immoral, radical, fanatic, antinomian, and pantheistic. 2. Derogatory term for nineteenth-century PRIMITIVE METHODISTS OF ENGLAND.

**RAPHAEL God heals** Archangel listed in the apocryphal books of Tobit and Enoch as a healer and hearer of prayer. Milton included Raphael among the leading figures of *Paradise Lost*. Raphael's feast day is October 24.

**RAPHAEL SANZIO (1483–1520)** Superb Italian painter of the "Sistine Madonna," the "Transfiguration," the "Crucifixion," the "Coronation of the Virgin," "St. Peter Released from Prison," the "Agony in the Garden," the "Temptation of Eve," the "Triumph of Religion," and many other masterpieces. He designed several churches and some tapestries. He died on Good Friday at the age of 37. He has been called "almost without a rival."

**RAPP, JOHANN GEORG (1757–1847)** German mystic who founded the HARMONY

SOCIETY in the United States. This was a communistic Christian settlement whose members practiced celibacy and considered BAPTISM and the EUCHARIST to be evil.

**RAPPITES** Followers of Johann Georg RAPP.

**RASHDALL, HASTINGS (1858–1924)** English theologian and philosopher. Emphasizing the importance of human reason and character in religious thought, he opposed both mysticism and modernism. He wrote *The Theory of Good and Evil* and *The Idea of Atonement in Christian Theology.*

**RASHI (1040–1105)** Outstanding medieval scholar. A French Jew named Rabbi Solomon ben Isaac ("Rashi" is a sort of acrostic based on his initials), he wrote two commentaries, on the BIBLE and the TALMUD. It was said of him that "his lips were the seat of wisdom"; Martin LUTHER is believed to have been influenced by his work.

**RASHNU** ZOROASTRIAN spirit of truth who judges the dead.

**RASKOLNIKI** *schismatics* Russian "Old Believers" who left the Russian Church in 1661 because of liturgical changes made by Patriarch NIKON. They opposed tobacco, favored an eight-pointed cross, and crossed themselves with only two fingers.

**RAS SHAMRA** Syrian city famous for the discovery, from 1929 to 1936, of hundreds of clay tablets dating from the fourteenth century B.C. These "Ras Shamra Tablets" illumine many Old Testament passages and mention such gods as Baal, Dagon, El, Asherat, Anath, Mot, and Koshar. Many parallels are found in them to Hebrew literature, customs, and religious modes.

**RASTAFARIANS** Natives of Jamaica who believe that Haile Selassie is God incarnate and that he will come as the Messiah to take them to an African paradise.

**RAT** Symbol of evil in religious art.

**RATI** HINDU wife of the love god Kama.

**RATIONALISM** 1. In philosophy, the belief that truth may be attained through human reason. Rationalism exalts the supremacy of reason and emphasizes deductive logic. 2. In religion, the subordination of experience and revelation to human reason. Religious rationalism is usu-ally antisupernatural, opposing equally the claims of churches, clergy, creeds, scriptures, and mystics—except as such claims square with rationalistic conclusions.

**RATRAMNUS (?–c.868)** French monk who taught double predestination, attacked the theology of Eastern Christianity, and maintained his own views of the EUCHARIST. He held that the HOST is not identical with the body of Christ but symbolized both Christ and Christians.

**RAUSCHENBUSCH, WALTER (1861–1919)** Baptist clergyman in the United States who popularized the concerns of the SOCIAL GOSPEL. Among his books were *Christianity and the Social Crisis, Christianizing the Social Order, The Social Principles of Jesus,* and *A Theology for the Social Gospel.* He preached, lectured, and taught at German Baptist Theological Seminary and Rochester Theological Seminary.

**RAVEN** In religious art, symbol not only of Satan but also of St. Paul the Hermit, St. Anthony Abbot, and St. Vincent. Although included among the unclean birds of the Old Testament, ravens fed the prophet Elijah and are mentioned as objects of God's care (DEUTERONOMY 14:14; I KINGS 17:4; PSALM 147:9; LUKE 12:24).

**R.C.** Abbreviation for ROMAN CATHOLIC or REFORMED CHURCH.

**RE** See RA.

**READER** 1. One appointed to read or sing portions of the service in ANGLICAN or CATHOLIC worship. 2. One who reads the lessons in CHRISTIAN SCIENCE worship. 3. Nineteenth-century Swedish Lutherans who read the Scriptures in private homes.

**READING DESK** Pulpit desk or LECTERN.

**REALISM** 1. Philosophical doctrine that universals—abstract categories or concepts —exist independently of the human mind. NOMINALISM, to which realism has been historically opposed, holds that such universals do not exist in reality but are merely useful names for concepts and categories of things. Early SCHOLASTICISM favored realism of this type but later veered toward nominalism. 2. Belief in a real external universe apart from human consciousness. 3. Term for emphasis on scientific facts and pragmatic "workability."

**REAL PRESENCE** Theological term for the true presence of the body and blood of

Christ in the sacrament of the EUCHARIST or holy communion. This is the CATHOLIC, ANGLICAN, and LUTHERAN doctrine; many Christians believe that Christ is truly present in the Lord's Supper, although spiritually rather than physically.

**REBEKAH**  Wife of the Hebrew patriarch Isaac. Mother of Esau and Jacob, she favored the second against the elder. (GENESIS 24—27.) She is believed to be buried in a mosque at Hebron.

**RECAPITULATION**  Theological view of IRENAEUS that Christ passed through every phase of human life, from birth to death, recapitulating each that He might save human beings in every phase.

**RECESSIONAL**  Procession of choir and clergy out of the chancel after a church service, usually to the accompaniment of a hymn.

**RECHABITES**  Ascetic Jewish group founded by Jehonadab (II KINGS 10) and commended by Jeremiah (JEREMIAH 35: 2–19). They lived in tents and abstained from wine.

**RECOLLECTION**  Term in religious literature for meditation and concentration on God and prayer.

**RECONCILIATION**  Restoration of fellowship. Reconciliation between God and man was sought through the Hebrew offerings and sacrifices. Christ's work was "a ministry of reconciliation" (II CORINTHIANS 5: 20). Christ Himself taught the importance of reconciliation with one's enemies before coming to God (MATTHEW 5:23, 24).

**RECONSTRUCTIONISM**  Twentieth-century Jewish movement inaugurated by Mordecai M. Kaplan. It seeks to unify JUDAISM and to revitalize its cultural, political, artistic, and spiritual life.

**RECTOR**  ANGLICAN or EPISCOPAL clergyman who has charge of a church or parish.

**RECTORY**  Residence of a rector.

**RECUSANT**  Term for a ROMAN CATHOLIC in sixteenth- and seventeenth-century England who refused to attend ANGLICAN church services.

**RED**  In religious art, a symbol of the Holy Spirit, love, hate, activity, power, zeal, and martyrdom. It is the color of the PENTECOST season in church liturgy, and of martyrs' festivals.

**REDACTION**  Critical term for the "editing" widely believed to have been done

in the preparation of many writings of the Bible.

**REDACTOR**  In Biblical criticism, term for an editor who pieced together, adapted, and unified many original literary strands into the final composite document. The redactor has a vital part in Old Testament documentary criticism.

**REDEEM**  Save, rescue, deliver, or regain possession. The Jewish Scriptures record the redemption of the people of God by His mighty acts. Christians see these acts culminating in the redemption of the world through Jesus Christ. Peter reminds his readers that they "were not redeemed with corruptible things, as silver and gold," but "with the precious blood of Christ" (I PETER 1:18, 19).

**REDEEMER**  1. One who buys back something for another, as Boaz redeemed the ancestral possessions of Ruth (RUTH 4: 1–6). 2. God, the Redeemer of His people (cf. DEUTERONOMY 13:5; ISAIAH 63: 16). 3. Christ, the Redeemer of all who trust and follow Him.

**REDEMPTION**  See REDEEM.

**REDEMPTORISTINES**  Religious congregation of contemplative nuns who intercede for sinners and the objectives of the Redemptionists. This "Order of the Holy Redeemer" was founded in 1731 and approved in 1750.

**REDEMPTORISTS**  "Congregation of the Most Holy Redeemer" founded in 1732 by St. ALPHONSUS LIGUORI and approved in 1749. Members labor particularly for the poor.

**RED HAT**  Flat-crowned red hat with fifteen tassels worn by a cardinal.

**RED LETTER BIBLE**  Bible in which the words of Jesus are printed in red.

**RED LETTER DAY**  Festival or saint's day, printed in red in liturgical calendars.

**RED MASS**  VOTIVE MASS of the Holy Ghost, offered for judges, synods, councils of the church, etc.

**RED SEA**  Gulf between the Arabian peninsula and Egypt. Apparently its northern portion was crossed by the Hebrews in the exodus from Egypt (EXODUS 14—15).

**REEB, JAMES J. (1926–1965)**  UNITARIAN minister clubbed to death in Selma, Alabama, for his devotion to the rights of American Negroes.

**REED**  Religious symbol of Christ's Passion. At His trial a reed was mockingly placed in His hand, and at Calvary a vinegar-filled sponge was offered Him on a reed (MATTHEW 27:29, 48).

**REFECTORY** Dining room in a MONAS-TERY, CONVENT, or theological SEMINARY.

**REFORMATION** Religious revolution and renewal, from the fourteenth to the seventeenth centuries, affecting all of Christendom. Beginning with the LOLLARDS and such men as John HUSS and John WYCLIF, the Reformation is most clearly identified with the revolt of Martin LUTHER in Germany but was also brought about by John CALVIN and Ulrich ZWINGLI in Switzerland, John KNOX in Scotland, the PURITANS in England, the HUGUENOTS in France, and many others. It centered in a questioning of the authority of the ROMAN CATHOLIC CHURCH and an emphasis on liberty of conscience, personal devotions, and study of Scripture. Out of it grew modern PROT-ESTANTISM. The Catholic response produced the COUNTER REFORMATION.

**REFORMATION, CATHOLIC** See COUNTER REFORMATION.

**REFORMATION DAY** October 31, celebrating the nailing of Martin LUTHER's NINETY-FIVE THESES to the door of a Wittenberg Church on that day in 1517. This precipitated the Protestant REFORMATION.

**REFORMATION SUNDAY** Last Sunday in October, celebrated in many PROTESTANT churches in memory of the Protestant REFORMATION and its great principles.

**REFORMED** Term for Protestantism with CALVINISTIC theology, often with a PRESBY-TERIAN type of government.

**REFORMED CHURCH** See REFORMED; also, names of particular churches.

**REFORMED CHURCH IN AMERICA** American denomination with roots in the Reformed Church of the Netherlands and its creedal and governmental structure. It is governed by consistories, classes, synods, and a general synod.

**REFORMED CHURCH OF FRANCE** French denomination including the former Evangelical Free Churches, the Reformed Evangelical Church, and the Evangelical Methodist Church.

**REFORMED EPISCOPAL CHURCH** American denomination formed in 1873 by a withdrawal from the PROTESTANT EPISCOPAL CHURCH. It tends toward a conservative and evangelical theology.

**REFORMED MENNONITE CHURCH** Tiny American denomination which stresses nonresistance and strict MENNONITE discipline.

**REFORMED METHODIST UNION EPISCOPAL CHURCH** American denomination which originated in 1885 in a withdrawal from the AFRICAN METHODIST EPISCOPAL CHURCH.

**REFORMED NEW CONGREGATIONAL METH-ODIST CHURCH** Small denomination founded in the United States in 1916.

**REFORMED PRESBYTERIAN CHURCH** Scottish denomination whose members are called CAMERONIANS.

**REFORMED PRESBYTERIAN CHURCH EVAN-GELICAL SYNOD** American denomination resulting from a merger in 1965 of the Evangelical Presbyterian Church and the Reformed Presbyterian Church in North America (General Synod).

**REFORMED PRESBYTERIAN CHURCH OF NORTH AMERICA (OLD SCHOOL)** American denomination with roots in COVE-NANTER Scotland. It seeks a Constitutional amendment recognizing God, Christ, and the Holy Scriptures.

**REFORMED ZION UNION APOSTOLIC CHURCH** American denomination founded in 1869 by Elder James R. Howell. A Negro church, it is METHODIST in doctrine and government.

**REFORMER** In church history, one of the leaders in the Protestant REFORMATION such as LUTHER or CALVIN.

**REFORM JUDAISM** Jewish movement emphasizing the ethical laws of Scripture and contemporary forms of worship. Other Jewish laws and certain orthodox practices are rejected or minimized. Reform Judaism is one of modern Judaism's three great divisions. (See also CONSERVATIVE JUDAISM and ORTHODOX JUDAISM.)

**REFRESHMENT SUNDAY** Fourth Sunday in LENT, providing a break in Lenten fasting in England.

**REGENERATION** Theological term for the spiritual new birth promised in the New Testament (JOHN 3:4, 7; I PETER 1:3, 23). The believer is begotten of God by the Holy Spirit, justified by faith, sanctified, and prepared for eternal glory. "Regeneration is a vital step in the natural development of the spiritual life" (Herbert A. Youtz).

**REGINA COELI** *Queen of Heaven* 1. Title of the Blessed Virgin MARY. 2. Name of a hymn and antiphon addressed to the Virgin Mary, used during the EASTER season in CATHOLIC churches.

**REGNUM** Papal tiara or triple crown.

**REGULAR BAPTISTS** American group of Baptists who emphasize the total depravity of man, the saving grace of God, and the sacrifice of Christ whose benefits are made available through faith.

**REGULAR CLERGY** Clergymen who are members of a religious community and are bound by vows of poverty, chastity, and obedience.

**REGULARS** See REGULAR CLERGY.

**REHOBOAM** Son of Solomon who became first king of the Southern Kingdom, Judah, after the division of the Hebrew Kingdom into two parts. Rejecting the suggestions of his older counselors to treat the people leniently after Solomon's death, he provoked the rebellion that divided the land and ended in the Jewish captivity. (1 KINGS 12; 14:21–31).

**REIMARUS, HERMANN SAMUEL (1694–1768)** German philosopher, Biblical critic, and religionist. His *Apologie* denied miracles and revelation and championed a naturalistic type of deism. A professor of Hebrew and Oriental languages, Reimarus questioned the historicity of a number of events recorded in Scripture.

**REIMS** French city where JOAN OF ARC induced the coronation of Charles VII. It is famous for its importance in church history—it is the center of an archbishopric—and for the Cathedral of Notre Dame and the tomb of St. Remigius.

**REINCARNATION** Doctrine that after a person dies his soul may return to life in a new body or form. See TRANSMIGRATION.

**RELATIVISM** The point of view that since anything must be described in terms of something else, and measured accordingly, everything is relative, and reality must be considered in subjective terms. In the religious field this may produce moral nihilism and spiritual confusion. The Christian acknowledges temporal relativity but trusts in an eternal God who is the source of absolute values and standards.

**RELEASE, YEAR OF** Hebrew term for every seventh year, in which slaves were freed (EXODUS 21:2–6).

**RELIC** Object of religious veneration, as a bone of a martyr.

**RELIEF CHURCH** Scottish denomination which united with the Secession Church in 1847 to produce the UNITED PRESBYTERIAN CHURCH.

**RELIGIEUX** French term for a RELIGIOUS or nun.

**RELIGION** Religion is difficult to define; even the origin of the word is disputed. It has to do, however, with God or gods or the ultimate values of life, depending upon one's point of view. It may be thought of in terms of worship, belief, morality, or religious group. The Epistle of James defines pure religion as: "To visit the fatherless and widows in their affliction, and to keep [oneself] unspotted from the world" (1:27).

**RELIGIOUS** 1. Member of a religious institute, congregation, or order. 2. Pious, godly, or having to do with religion.

**RELIGIOUS SOCIETY OF FRIENDS (CONSERVATIVE)** Conservative American Quaker group. (See FRIENDS, SOCIETY OF.)

**RELIGIOUS SOCIETY OF FRIENDS (GENERAL CONFERENCE)** American Quaker group founded in 1900 to further the religious and social concerns of the Friends. (See FRIENDS, SOCIETY OF.)

**RELIGIOUS SOCIETY OF FRIENDS KANSAS YEARLY MEETING** American Quaker group with headquarters in Wichita, Kansas. (See FRIENDS, SOCIETY OF.)

**RELIQUARY** Shrine or receptacle for RELICS.

**REMA** See ISSERLES, MOSES BEN ISRAEL.

**REMONSTRANCE, THE** ARMINIAN doctrinal statement drawn up in 1610, setting forth the non-Calvinistic Protestant view of such matters as PREDESTINATION and the extent of the ATONEMENT.

**REMONSTRANTS** Dutch Protestant ministers who signed the REMONSTRANCE of 1610. Remonstrants in the Netherlands today have a number of strong churches.

**RENAN, JOSEPH ERNEST (1823–1892)** French theologian and philosopher who rejected supernatural elements in religion and even in Christ. He wrote a *Life of*

*Jesus, St. Paul,* the *History of Israel,* and *Studies in Religious History.*

**RENENIT** Egyptian goddess of birth.

**REORGANIZED CHURCH OF JESUS CHRIST OF LATTER DAY SAINTS** MORMON church with headquarters in Independence, Missouri. It differs from other Mormons on several points including polygamy (which it never accepted) and the nature of God. It followed the son of Joseph SMITH rather than Brigham YOUNG when the latter led many other Mormons farther west.

**REPENTANCE** Abhorrence of one's sin accompanied by a radical turning toward God. The Bible says much about repentance, which has also been termed the other side of faith.

**REPROBATE** Theological term for one depraved, condemned, or lost.

**REPROBATION** Term for divine condemnation of sinners.

**REQUIEM** *rest* Mass for the dead, invoking eternal rest for their souls.

**REREDOS** Decoration or screen behind and above an altar.

**RERET** Hippopotamus goddess worshiped in ancient Egypt.

**RERUM NOVARUM** *of new things* Encyclical issued by Pope LEO XIII in 1891 stating the concern of the church for working men, their families, and their place in society.

**RESCRIPT** Papal reply to a question about judicial or ethical matters.

**RESERVED SACRAMENT or RESERVATION** Communion bread set aside for those sick and dying.

**RESERVED SINS** Sins especially set apart to be dealt with by a bishop.

**RESH** Twentieth letter in the Hebrew alphabet.

**RESHEP or RESHEPH** Canaanite god of fire and lightning.

**RESHPU** See RESHEP.

**RESPONSA** Answers to questions about Jewish matters, given by eminent rabbis and scholars of the TALMUD.

**RESPONSE** Liturgical statement said or sung by choir and congregation in reply to a statement by the worship leader. Hebrew worship had a number of responses, and they are often used in Christian worship.

**RESPONSORY** Liturgical chants and versicles, based on synagogue worship but used in Christian worship. The priest and congregation and choir alternate in these liturgical responses.

**REST** The Ten Commandments (see DECALOGUE) require worshipers to rest on the SABBATH. Adequate rest for all is an important Christian concern. Rest is found in the Lord (PSALM 37:7; 132:14; HEBREWS 4:9).

**RESTITUTION** 1. Restoration or reparation to one who has been wronged. In Jewish and Christian religion this was an important step for a wrongdoer to take. 2. Divine restoration of all things to their pristine order and purpose (cf. ACTS 3:21). This is usually connected with the return and triumph of Christ.

**RESURRECTION** Return to life of those who have died. Belief in resurrection characterizes Jews, Moslems, Catholics, Protestants, and some other religious groups; Greek religion, on the other hand, included a concept of immortality but not resurrection. The former implies survival after death, a belief held in many religions. Resurrection connotes a return to life, often in connection with the physical body. Christians particularly emphasize the resurrection because Christ rose from the tomb three days after His crucifixion. Christ's resurrection assures that of believers (I CORINTHIANS 15:49).

**RETABLE** Shelf or set of panels behind the altar in a liturgical church.

**RETREAT** Period of spiritual renewal in which a group withdraws from the usual pressures of the world and seeks direction and peace through faith and meditation.

**REUBEN** *behold a son* Jacob's oldest son. When the brothers of Joseph planned to destroy him, Reuben pleaded for leniency and planned to rescue him (GENESIS 29:32; 37:22, 29, 30). Reuben became progenitor of the Hebrew tribe of that name. The tribe of Reuben on at least one occasion failed to help the other tribes of Israel (JUDGES 5:15–17).

**REUCHLIN, JOHANN (1455–1522)** German CHRISTIAN humanist and student of Hebrew and JUDAISM. After defending the right of the Jews to possess books he was accused of heresy and narrowly escaped destruction.

**REUSCH, FRANZ HEINRICH (1823–1900)** OLD CATHOLIC theologian who protested the doctrine of papal infallibility and the inability of Roman Catholic priests to marry. He wrote many books on the Old Testament and church history.

**REUSS, EDOUARD GUILLAUME EUGENE (1804–1891)** German PROTESTANT theologian who wrote a number of important religious works and edited the works of John CALVIN. He was one of the first to apply historical criticism to the study of the Bible.

**REV.** Abbreviation for REVEREND.

**REVELATION** 1. What God makes known to men, as in Scripture. 2. The REVELATION OF ST. JOHN (see below).

**REVELATIONIST** 1. A person who accepts the Genesis account of the creation of the universe. 2. Term for the writer of the REVELATION OF ST. JOHN.

**REVELATION OF ST. JOHN** The last book in the New Testament, often called simply "Revelation" or "The Book of Revelation," and sometimes called "The Apocalypse." The John to whom it is attributed has been indentified by some with the Apostle John and by others with a "John the Elder" of Asia Minor. A striking book, the Revelation presents seven letters and various messages from Jesus Christ. The book is filled with visions of heaven, the future, and mystic figures. In times of change it assures the reader of the eternal Kingdom of God and the ultimate triumph of Christ and His followers.

**REVELATOR** 1. Term for the author of the REVELATION OF ST. JOHN. 2. Term for one who reveals something.

**REVERENCE** 1. Respect or honor, sometimes mingled with awe. 2. Term of honor with which a clergyman is sometimes addressed. 3. Term for bowing in worship.

**REVEREND** Title of respect commonly accorded clergymen.

**REVISED STANDARD VERSION** Revision of the King James Bible by scholars commissioned by the churches of the United States, published in 1952.

**REVISED VERSION** 1. Revision of the English Bible produced by British and American scholars 1880–1890. Now sometimes called the "English Revised Version" to distinguish it from the American REVISED STANDARD VERSION. 2. Any revised version of the Scriptures.

**REVIVAL** Spiritual renewal. In common parlance revival means a professional and often emotional search for converts. Revival, however, need be neither excessively emotional in nature nor professionally organized. Some of the most effective movements of Christian revival seem to have ignited and spread spontaneously, with enduring and valuable results.

**REVIVALIST** Evangelist or leader of a revival.

**RHABDOMANCY** The practice of divination with the use of rods.

**RHADAMANTHUS** Greek judge of the dead.

**RHEA** Cretan and Greek fertility goddess.

**RHEIMS** See REIMS.

**RHODA** *rose* Young woman who met St. Peter, liberated from prison, at the door of a home where the inhabitants were praying for his release. They could not believe her message (ACTS 12:13).

**RICCI, MATTEO (1552–1610)** Italian JESUIT missionary to China. His conversions and writings in Chinese laid the foundation for later Catholic missionary endeavors there.

**RICE, LUTHER (1783–1836)** American educator and Baptist missionary.

**RICHARD OF CHICHESTER, ST. (1197–1253)** Deeply spiritual Bishop of Chichester, England. Also a good administrator, he was famed for his courage and charity. Many cures have been attributed to his shrine, which Henry VIII destroyed. He prayed: "May I know Thee more clearly, love Thee more dearly, and follow Thee more nearly." His feast day is April 3.

**RICHARD OF ST. VICTOR (?–1173)** British-born mystic and theologian who became prior of the abbey of St. Victor in France. He wrote a number of exegetical books on Scripture and the doctrine of the TRINITY. He listed six steps to spiritual contemplation; beginning with a study of art and nature, he proceeded to spiritual ecstasy.

**RIDDELS** Curtains at both ends of an altar.

**RIDLEY or RIDGLEY, NICHOLAS (c.1500–1555)** English bishop burned to death with LATIMER and CRANMER for his PROTESTANT leanings and his support of Lady Jane Grey against the princesses Elizabeth and Mary. After Mary became queen, Ridley was proclaimed a heretic, excommunicated, and martyred. During his ministry Ridley helped prepare the BOOK OF COMMON PRAYER and preached on social righteousness.

**RIGHTEOUSNESS** What is right, just, and good. For JUDAISM righteousness means "right conduct and behaviour, namely to carry out what God in His revelation and commandments has shown to be right and good. Righteousness is not so much a state or condition as a continual activity" (Hugh Schonfield). Throughout the Bible righteousness is a primary characteristic of God; Job ascribed righteousness to his Maker (36:3), David was assured that "he leadeth me in the paths of righteousness" (PSALM 23:3), and St. Paul proclaimed the righteousness of God and of faith (ROMANS 1:17; 9:30). The CHRISTIAN is granted the righteousness of Christ, and seeks to bring about personal and social righteousness in all his relationships.

**RIGHTEOUSNESS, ORIGINAL** See ORIGINAL RIGHTEOUSNESS.

**RIGHTS, CIVIL** The rights to which a citizen of a democracy is entitled by birth, such as the right to vote. In the 1960's the members and leaders of many churches and synagogues in the United States joined the movement to see that Negroes were granted their full civil rights.

**RIGHTS, HUMAN** The rights of man, as for example the right to freedom under just laws. Religion at its best is increasingly concerned with such rights.

**RIG-VEDA** Oldest collection of sacred writings in HINDUISM. Containing 1,028 hymns in ten books, it is one of ancient Vedic Hinduism's most important Scriptures.

**RIMMON** *thunderer* Important Syrian god worshiped by the captain Naaman (II KINGS 5:18).

**RING** Circlet, usually of precious metal, often fraught with religious significance. The ephod of the Hebrew high priests bore rings. In ancient Greece rings often were thought to have magic powers. Today Catholic bishops and nuns have special rings, as does the pope. Christian and Jewish weddings often employ a ring to symbolize the enduring and precious nature of love.

**RINZAI (?–867)** Chinese master of Zen Buddhism who originated the school of

Rinzai Buddhism (see ZEN). His words are important in Zen Buddhism.

**RINZAI ROKU** Sayings of RINZAI.

**RISHI** HINDU sage or seer.

**RISHUT** Hebrew term for evil.

**RITA** Ancient HINDU word for order or righteousness.

**RITE** Religious ceremony or ritual or liturgy.

**RITSCHL, ALBRECHT (1822–1889)** German LUTHERAN theologian who emphasized the unique experience of faith, the centrality of the Christian community, the revelation of God in Christ, and the importance of ethics. He wrote a *History of Pietism, The Christian Doctrine of Justification and Reconciliation,* and other works.

**RITSCHLIANISM** Term for the theology growing out of the concepts of Albrecht RITSCHL. Among its emphases are the historical Jesus, moral and social religion, freedom for the individual in his religious quest, and the importance of value judgments.

**RITUAL** Religious ceremony or its verbal form.

**RITUALISM** 1. Emphasis on religious ceremony. 2. Movement attempting to make ANGLICAN worship more Catholic.

**RIVER BRETHREN** European Mennonites and Anabaptists who fled to the United States in the seventeenth century and settled by the Susquehanna River in Pennsylvania, led by John and Jacob Engle. Today they are divided into BRETHREN IN CHRIST, Old Order Brethren, and the United Zion Church. Members practice FOOT WASHING and TRINE IMMERSION.

**RIVERS, FOUR** The four rivers of paradise (GENESIS 2:10–14), in religious art sometimes symbolizing the four Gospels.

**ROBBER SYNOD** See EPHESUS, ROBBER SYNOD OF.

**ROBE** Garb worn by members and/or clergy of various religious groups. In Christian art the robe symbolizes the passion of Christ.

**ROBERTS, BENJAMIN TITUS (1823–1893)** American minister of the METHODIST EPISCOPAL CHURCH who helped found the FREE METHODIST CHURCH OF NORTH AMERICA.

**ROBERTSON, FREDERICK WILLIAM (1816–1853)** Eloquent minister of the CHURCH

OF ENGLAND. Famed as "Robertson of Brighton," he was popular with the working classes and admired by many. He helped turn the attention of the church to the needs and currents of the world.

**ROBINSON, FRANK B. (1886–1948)** American founder of PSYCHIANA. A Baptist preacher's son, he intrigued millions with the claim, "I talked with God . . . actually and literally! So can you!"

**ROBINSON, JOHN (c.1576–1625)** English PURITAN pastor who encouraged the PILGRIM emigration to New England. He wrote a number of theological works.

**ROCHET** White surplice-like vestment with close-fitting sleeves. The Anglican rochet has loose sleeves.

**ROCK** Religious symbol of St. PETER or of Christ.

**ROCKEFELLER, JOHN D. (1839–1937)** American businessman and philanthropist who gave much of his wealth to such causes as the BAPTIST Church and the YOUNG MEN'S CHRISTIAN ASSOCIATION.

**ROGATION** Ecclesiastical term for litany or prayer.

**ROGATION DAYS** Special days of prayer before planting crops or before ASCENSION DAY.

**ROGATION SUNDAY** Sunday before ASCENSION DAY.

**ROLLE OF HAMPOLE, RICHARD (c.1300–c.1349)** English hermit whose works such as the book *The Fire of Love* made him noted as a mystic. His feast day is September 29.

**ROMAN** Term for ROMAN CATHOLIC.

**ROMAN CATHOLIC CHURCH** Church whose members accept traditional Catholic doctrines and liturgy and the headship of the pope of Rome. A title more acceptable to Catholics is the "Holy Catholic and Apostolic Church." With nearly a billion members, it is the world's largest religious group. It claims St. PETER as its first pope and some of the world's greatest historical figures as its members. Although it has had something of a reputation for uniformity and changelessness, the twentieth century brought marked openness to discussion, flexibility, ecumenicity, and adaptation to the new age.

**ROMAN COLLAR** Stiff clerical collar fastened at the back of the neck.

**ROMAN CURIA** See CURIA.

**ROMANIAN ORTHODOX EPISCOPATE OF AMERICA** American body of Eastern Orthodox Christians originally related to the Romanian Orthodox Patriarchate but now under the jurisdiction of the Russian Orthodox Greek Catholic Church of America. It has five deaneries and an episcopal polity.

**ROMAN RITE** Typical CATHOLIC liturgy, the most widely used rite in the world.

**ROMANS** Popular term for the letter of St. PAUL to the Christians of Rome, forming the sixth book in the New Testament. The letter is Paul's longest and most systematically developed, presenting the doctrines of sin, grace, justification, sanctification, and Christian duty in clear and logical form. The Apostle wrote it from Corinth about 58 A.D. It played an important part in the lives of such diverse figures as AUGUSTINE, LUTHER, CALVIN, WESLEY, and BARTH.

**ROME** "Eternal City" whose bishopric eventually became the supreme one in the CATHOLIC CHURCH. Its traditions, shrines, architecture, art, and the VATICAN make it an outstanding center of world pilgrimage.

**ROOD** Cross or CRUCIFIX.

**ROOD SCREEN** Arch, screen, or latticework separating the nave and chancel of a church. Early Protestants opposed rood screens as posing an unnecessary division between clergy and people.

**ROPE** Religious symbol of Judas' betrayal of Christ. After the betrayal Judas hanged himself (MATTHEW 27:5).

**ROSARY** *rose garden* 1. String of beads used by CATHOLICS in prayer. Each set of beads suggests a mystery, the object of meditation while prayers are said. 2. String of beads used by MOSLEMS or BUDDHISTS in prayer and meditation.

**ROSE** In Roman religion, a symbol of victory. In Christian art, a symbol of martyrdom, or of purity.

**ROSE OF LIMA, ST. (1586–1617)** DOMINICAN nun of Peru who was the first saint canonized in the Americas (1671). Her feast day is August 30. She is the Patroness of South America and the Philippines.

**ROSE OF SHARON** The lover in the Song

of Solomon (2:1) who symbolizes Christ in mystic devotional thought.

**ROSETTA STONE** Basalt slab found near Rosetta, Egypt, in 1799, and now in the British Museum. The three languages with which it is inscribed proved a key to ancient Egyptian hieroglyphics.

**ROSE WINDOW** Round window suggesting a rose, found in a number of churches.

**ROSH CHODESH** *head of the month* The New Moon marking the beginning of a Jewish month—an occasion for thanksgiving and prayer.

**ROSH HASHANAH** *head of the year* Jewish New Year observed as a day of judgment and memorial. Also called the Feast of Trumpets, it summons the people to repentance with the use of a shofar, a ram's horn. Rosh Hashanah occurs on the first of Tishri, in the fall of the year.

**ROSHI** Japanese term for the ZEN master of a Buddhist monastery.

**ROSICRUCIANS** Members of esoteric groups who trace secret wisdom to ancient times. Claiming Isaac Newton, Francis Bacon, and Benjamin Franklin as members, the Rosicrucians emphasize occult knowledge, mystic writings, and such symbols as the cross, rose, and pyramid. There are several Rosicrucian orders in the United States, and groups in various parts of the world.

**ROSMINIANS** "Fathers of the Institute of Charity," founded by Antonio Rosmini-Serbati in 1828. Its members stress sanctification and works of charity.

**ROTHE, RICHARD (1799–1867)** German LUTHERAN whose *Theological Ethics* stressed the close connection of faith and morality. He saw the mission of Protestantism as freeing religion from ecclesiasticism.

**ROUALT, GEORGES (1871–1958)** Outstanding French artist whose religious as well as secular works are unique in the twentieth century.

**ROUEN** French city noted as the home of Notre Dame Cathedral and other churches. Long an ecclesiastical center, Rouen was the place where JOAN OF ARC was burned at the stake in 1431.

**ROUNDER** Term at one time applied to METHODIST circuit riders, or preachers with churches on a circuit.

**ROUNDHEAD** Term for a PURITAN, whose hair in the seventeenth century was cut short, unlike the curls of the Cavaliers.

**ROUSSEAU, JEAN JACQUES (1712–1778)** French philosopher whose ideas deeply affected later society and education. At one time a CALVINIST and then a CATHOLIC, Rousseau became a DEIST and enunciated a natural religion which elevated sentiment above revelation or reason.

**ROWNTREE, JOSEPH (1836–1925)** British Quaker businessman who labored for such reforms as temperance, adult education, and more just working conditions. See FRIENDS, SOCIETY OF.

**ROY, RAMMOHUN** See RAM MOHAN ROY.

**ROYCE, JOSIAH (1855–1916)** American philosopher who saw an absolute Mind in the universe and propounded absolute idealism. Christianity he defined in terms of "loyalty to the Beloved Community." He wrote *The World and the Individual, The Religious Aspect of Philosophy, The Philosophy of Loyalty,* and other works.

**ROYDEN, AGNES MAUDE (1876–1956)** English woman preacher who served ANGLICAN and CONGREGATIONAL churches and promoted social hygiene.

**RSV** See REVISED STANDARD VERSION.

**RUACH** *spirit* Hebrew word for spirit of man or God.

**RUACH HA-KODESH** *the holy Spirit* Hebrew term for the divine Spirit which is the source of human life and inspiration.

**RUBENS, PETER PAUL (1577–1640)** Flemish painter whose unique creations include such famous religious works as "Descent From the Cross," "The Assumption," "The Holy Family," "Return of the Holy Family from Egypt," "The Circumcision," "The Crowning With Thorns," and "The Crucifixion."

**RUBRIC** Rule or ritual for the conduct of a worship service, as of the MASS.

**RUDRA** *howler* Ancient HINDU storm god, later identified to some extent at least with SIVA.

**RULE, CARPENTER'S** Symbol of St. Thomas in Christian art.

**RULE OF FAITH** Creed or standard by which orthodoxy is tested.

**RUMI, JALAL ED-DIN (1207–1273)** Persian SUFI poet who founded the Maulawi sect of whirling dervishes and is honored as a saint.

**RUMINA** Roman goddess of nursing mothers.

**RURAL DEAN** ANGLICAN or EPISCOPAL priest who heads a group of parishes as dean.

**RUSSELL, CHARLES TAZE (1852–1916)** American founder of JEHOVAH'S WITNESSES. He established the Watch Tower Bible and Tract Society and the magazine *The Watchtower*.

**RUSSELLITES** Somewhat derogatory term for JEHOVAH'S WITNESSES.

**RUSSIAN ORTHODOX CHURCH** EASTERN ORTHODOX church of Russia. Once controlled by the government, it became independent in the Russian revolution. In 1961 it entered the WORLD COUNCIL OF CHURCHES.

**RUTH** Moabite woman who married a Hebrew and thus became an ancestress of David and Christ. The Book of Ruth tells of her loyalty to her Jewish mother-in-law and her love for Boaz, whom she married after her first husband died.

**RUTHENIAN RITE** Byzantine liturgy used in the Ruthenian Catholic Church of the Balkan countries.

**RUTHERFORD, JOSEPH FRANKLIN (1869–1942)** American lawyer and judge who became leader of the JEHOVAH'S WITNESSES following the death of Charles Taze RUSSELL. He was imprisoned in 1918 for supporting conscientious objectors in their protest against participation in World War I. He was a prolific writer and traveled widely.

**RUTHERFORD, SAMUEL (1600–1661)** Scottish CALVINIST minister who attended the WESTMINSTER ASSEMBLY and wrote *Lex Rex*, putting law above the king. He attacked "pretended liberty of conscience" on the grounds that tolerance contradicts Scripture. He also wrote a number of devotional works.

**RUYSBROECK, JAN VAN (1293–1381)** Flemish priest and AUGUSTINIAN monk who headed a group which grew into the BRETHREN OF THE COMMON LIFE. A noted mystic, he was beatified in 1908.

**RV** See REVISED VERSION.

**RYOBU-SHINTO** Japanese term for Buddhist SHINTOISM.

# S

**S.** Abbreviation for saint, Sabbath, Sunday, or society. It is also a symbol for *Seir*, representing a document or narrative which some scholars believe underlay portions of the Book of Genesis.

**SAADI** See SADI.

**SAADIA BEN JOSEPH (882–942)** Outstanding Jewish scholar who headed the Jewish Academy at Sura in Babylonia. Born in Egypt, he studied various philosophies and religions and maintained that truth and religion may never ultimately conflict. He prepared the first Hebrew dictionary and prayer book.

**SABAISTS** Babylonians who particularly revered JOHN THE BAPTIST and mixed Christianity with several other religious systems.

**SABAOTH, JEHOVAH Lord of hosts** Old Testament title of God as the Conquering One (PSALM 89:6–8; cf. JAMES 5:4).

**SABATIER, AUGUSTE (1839–1901)** French PROTESTANT theologian who evolved a theory of "critical symbolism" from the viewpoint that dogmatic theology symbolizes religious experience. He was influenced by Ritschl and SCHLEIERMACHER and wrote such works as *Religions of Authority and the Religion of the Spirit, The Apostle Paul,* and *Outlines of a Philosophy of Religion.*

**SABATIER, PAUL (1858–1928)** French CALVINIST pastor, historian, and student of the life of St. FRANCIS OF ASSISI, of whom he wrote a biography. He also studied and sympathized with the MODERNIST movement in CATHOLICISM. He was a younger brother of Auguste SABATIER.

**SABAZIOS** Ancient Phrygian god.

**SABBATAI ZEVI (1626–1676)** Middle Eastern Jewish religious leader and mystic. Having announced that he was the MES-

SIAH, he gathered many followers known as Sabbateans.

**SABBATARIAN** A Sabbath-keeper, or a proponent of strict SABBATH observance.

**SABBATEANS** See SABBATAI ZEVI.

**SABBATH rest** 1. Day or period of rest. 2. Jewish holy day. The seventh day in the week, it has traditionally been a day of rest, worship, and joy. 3. Jewish seventh year, set apart as sacred. Every seventh year the land was to "rest" from cultivation. 4. Sunday, regarded by many Christians as a Sabbath, the observance of which fulfills the fourth commandment.

**SABBATH DAY'S JOURNEY** Two thousand cubits, slightly more than half a mile, the distance considered permissible for one to travel without breaking the Sabbath (JOSHUA 3:4; cf. ACTS 1:12).

**SABBATH OF SABBATHS** Jewish name for Yom Kippur, the day of ATONEMENT.

**SABBATH SCHOOL** 1. Religious school with classes on the Sabbath. 2. Term used by some PROTESTANTS for Sunday school or church school.

**SABBATICAL YEAR** Seventh year. See SABBATH 3.

**SABBATINE PRIVILEGE** CATHOLIC term for the Virgin MARY's freeing from PURGATORY, particularly on Saturdays or Sabbaths (Our Lady's day), those who had been especially devoted to her, according to an apocryphal papal bull of 1322.

**SABELLIANISM** Heresy originating in the doctrines of SABELLIUS. In place of the traditional view of the TRINITY, Sabellianism held that the one God appeared in three different modes: as Father and Creator, as Son and Redeemer, and as Holy Spirit and Life-giver.

**SABELLIUS (third century)** Egyptian or Libyan Christian priest excommunicated for his "modalism." Little is known about him except the heresy he fathered (see SABELLIANISM).

**SABORAIM** Jewish scholars who redacted the Babylonian TALMUD in the sixth century. The singular form is *sabora*.

**SACERDOTAL** *priestly* Relating to priests or the priesthood.

**SACERDOTALISM** 1. The priesthood. 2. Elaborate devotion to the ceremonies and forms of the priesthood. 3. Belief in ordination as the channel of special priestly powers.

**SACKCLOTH** Rough cloth worn as a sign of mourning or repentance (GENESIS 37: 34; JEREMIAH 4:8; LUKE 10:13).

**SACRAL** *sacred* Related to religious ceremonies.

**SACRAMENT** *something consecrated or holy* Traditionally, a CHRISTIAN ordinance manifesting an inward, spiritual grace by an outward, visible sign or symbol. CATHOLICS recognize seven sacraments; Protestants, but two: BAPTISM and holy COMMUNION. The latter, or the eucharistic HOST, is sometimes also called "the Sacrament." BAPTISTS do not use the term sacrament. QUAKERS, the SALVATION ARMY, and certain other groups do not employ any sacraments.

**SACRAMENTAL** 1. Sacrament-like object or ceremony, such as the sign of the cross. 2. Relating to a sacrament.

**SACRAMENTARY** Catholic liturgical book containing some but not all parts of the mass for the church year.

**SACRE-COEUR** *sacred heart* Paris BASILICA devoted to the Sacred Heart of Jesus.

**SACRED** Holy or consecrated.

**SACRED BABOON** Baboon worshiped in ancient Egypt.

**SACRED COLLEGE** The seventy cardinals, constituting the Collegium, who elect the pope and serve as his privy council.

**SACRED HEART** Worship of Jesus' heart of flesh, considered to be directed to Jesus Himself. Throughout ROMAN CATHOLICISM, the Friday after octave of CORPUS CHRISTI marks a feast of the Sacred Heart.

**SACRED ORDERS** The three CATHOLIC orders of the priesthood, DIACONATE, and SUBDIACONATE.

**SACRED THREAD** Thin cord worn around the left shoulder and right side of HINDUS of the three higher castes, to mark their "twice born" status.

**SACRED VESSELS** 1. Candlesticks, dishes, and other furnishings of the Hebrew temple or the synagogue. 2. COMMUNION vessels.

**SACRIFICE** Something offered to God or a deity. Most religions include some form of sacrifice. Ancient JUDAISM stressed various sacrifices of animals, birds, and grain, but these were discontinued after the destruction of the temple. CHRISTIANS regard Christ as their sacrifice (I CORINTHIANS 5:7; HEBREWS 9:26), and are constrained to offer themselves as a sacrifice to serve God (ROMANS 12:1, 2).

**SACRILEGE** Theft, desecration, or irreverent treatment of something sacred.

**SACRING** Ecclesiastical term for CONSECRATION.

**SACRING BELL** Small bell rung during the SANCTUS and at other parts of the mass, and sometimes called the sanctus bell.

**SACRISTAN or SACRIST** Sexton, or church official in charge of the SACRISTY.

**SACRISTY** Room in or adjoining a church where the vestments, sacred vessels, and the like are kept.

**SADDHARMA PUNDARIKA** *lotus of the true law* Important Buddhist scripture, originating in second-century India, presenting BUDDHA as a transcendental, eternal being. It exalts right living and salvation by the grace of the cosmic saviors.

**SADDUCEES** Aristocratic Jews who formed a priestly party during the time of Jesus. They were opponents of the PHARISEES and did not believe in a life after death, in angels, or in the MESSIAH. A conservative group, they were not as popular as the Pharisees.

**SAD-EL** *field of God* Ancient Semitic term for heaven.

**SADHANA** HINDU term for union with the Infinite.

**SADHU** *holy* HINDU saint or ascetic.

**SADI (1184–1291)** Persian MOSLEM poet, a SUFI of deep religious belief. His tomb, enclosed in a garden, is still venerated.

**SAFAR** Second month in the MOSLEM year.

**SAFED** Town in northern Israel which was the residence of a number of Jewish scholars from the fifteenth century on.

**SAFFRON** Orange-yellow, the color of the robe of a saint or religious teacher in India.

**SAGALELLI, GERHARD** See APOSTOLIC BRETHREN.

**SAHIJA** HINDU term for passion without lust, as practiced by Hindu gods and goddesses.

**SAHU** Ancient Egyptian term for the form one takes in the afterlife.

**SAINT** 1. In the New Testament, a believer in Christ (EPHESIANS 1:1). 2. In certain religions, and in popular parlance, one of exceptional consecration or virtue. 3. In certain religious bodies, a member of the group.

**SAINT** For the names of various saints listed in this book, see the individual's name. St. Francis, for example, is listed under FRANCIS.

**SAINT BARTHOLOMEW'S DAY MASSACRE** See BARTHOLOMEW'S DAY MASSACRE, St.

**SAINT JOHN THE DIVINE, CATHEDRAL OF** Enormous EPISCOPAL church in New York City, begun in 1892.

**SAINT MARK'S CHURCH** Impressive church in Venice, in the form of a Greek cross, covered with splendid mosaics.

**SAINT PATRICK'S CATHEDRAL** Largest CATHOLIC church in America, on Fifth Avenue in New York City. It is a Gothic structure in the form of a Roman cross.

**SAINT PATRICK'S DAY** March 17, on which St. PATRICK is remembered.

**SAINT PAUL'S CATHEDRAL** Baroque church in London begun and completed by Sir Christopher Wren (1675–1710). There had been much earlier churches on the site, dating from c.607.

**SAINT PETER'S CHURCH** Christendom's largest church. The first church on the site was built by CONSTANTINE early in the fourth century. The present structure dates from the sixteenth century. In it more than 130 popes, including St. Peter, are believed to be buried.

**SAINTS' DAYS** Days commemorating the saints, as ALL SAINTS' DAY.

**SAINT-SIMONIANS** Followers of Claude Henri Saint-Simon (1760–1825), a French social reformer, who mixed his goals of social progress with religious overtones and pantheism. See also ENFANTIN, BARTHÉLEMY PROSPER.

**SAIVISM** Worship of the HINDU god SIVA. Some Saivists are ascetic while some are sexually licentious, worshiping Siva's symbol, the LINGAM.

**SAKTAS** Hindus who worship the female principle (SAKTI) of a god. See SAKTISM.

**SAKTI or SHAKTI** HINDU term for a god's female principle, incarnated in his consort, embodying his creative energy; also for creative or sexual power or the worship of such power.

**SAKTISM** HINDU worship of the SAKTI. This may be accomplished when a lovely girl is venerated or enjoyed by a group of SAKTAS, with appropriate ceremonies.

**SAKYA MUNI** Title for Gautama BUDDHA as "Sage of the Sakyas," indicating the clan to which he belonged.

**SALAAM** *peace* MOSLEM greeting meaning "Allah's peace and blessing be with you." The form may be "Salaam aleykum."

**SALAGRAMA** Black stone symbolizing VISHNU in HINDUISM.

**SALEM** *peace* 1. Old Testament city apparently the same as the later Jerusalem (GENESIS 14:18; PSALM 76:2). 2. Ancient name for the planet Venus.

**SALESIANS** Society of St. FRANCIS OF SALES, founded by St. JOHN BOSCO in 1859. It seeks to aid, educate, and evangelize the poor in various countries.

**SALIAN PRIESTS** Priests of the war god MARS in Roman religion.

**SALOME** *peace* 1. Female disciple of Jesus who stood by Jesus' cross and visited His tomb (MATTHEW 27:56; MARK 16:1). 2. Daughter of Herodias who danced before HEROD ANTIPAS, her grand uncle, to accomplish the beheading of John the Baptist (MARK 6:16–28).

**SALT** Symbol of brotherhood among Easterners. In the TALMUD salt symbolizes the pricelessness of the TORAH. In Jesus' sayings it may indicate various symbolic and actual values of salt. He told His disciples, "Ye are the salt of the earth" (MATTHEW 5:13). In Christendom salt may symbolize protection, wisdom, and excellence.

**SALT LAKE CITY** Capital of Utah and Mormon center, founded by Brigham YOUNG in 1847.

**SALT SEA** See DEAD SEA.

**SALUTATION** Greeting, as at the beginning of a church service.

**SALVATION** Condition of being saved from sin and destruction. The Jewish Scriptures associate salvation with the nation's deliverance from her enemies, and the hope of immortal life. Various religions offer various means and goals of salvation. Christianity finds sin so pervasive and deep that nothing but the grace of God in Jesus Christ, applied through faith, can bring men salvation.

**SALVATION ARMY**  Christian organization founded by William BOOTH about 1865. Utilizing military structure and uniforms, the Army has always concentrated on aiding the poor and needy masses, combining spiritual and social emphases. It is highly respected in all parts of the world.

**SALVE REGINA** *Hail, Queen*  One of the oldest and most popular hymns to the Virgin MARY. Dating from the eleventh century, it is used at vespers and after low mass.

**SAMADHI**  Final stage on the path to NIRVANA and union with God in BUDDHISM and HINDUISM.

**SAMAEL** *God's venom*  Jewish name for the angel of hell and death.

**SAMARIA**  1. Central Palestine, in the Old Testament corresponding to the land held successively by the tribes of EPHRAIM and MANASSEH and by the Northern Kingdom of Israel. In the New Testament period Samaria occupied roughly the same territory, lying between Judea and Galilee. 2. City near Nablus which served as capital of the Northern Kingdom. It was built by King OMRI in the ninth century B.C. A tradition places the grave of JOHN THE BAPTIST in this city.

**SAMARITAN PENTATEUCH**  Hebrew version of the first five books of the Bible, accepted by the SAMARITANS. It may date from the fourth century B.C.

**SAMARITANS**  Inhabitants of Samaria who have descended from non-Jewish colonists settled there about 722 B.C. (II KINGS 17:24). They worshiped at their own temple on Mt. Gerizim. They and the Jews had no dealings with and no tolerance for one another in the time of Jesus. A few Samaritans still live at Nablus and Jaffa in Israel.

**SAMAS**  Ancient Semitic sun god.

**SAMA-VEDA**  Third Hindu VEDA or scripture. It consists of sacrificial chants and hymns.

**SAMBODHI**  Wisdom important to spiritual advance in BUDDHISM.

**SAMECH**  Fifteenth letter of the Hebrew alphabet.

**SAMHAIN**  Ancient Celtic festival, marked by sacrifices and magic rites, celebrating harvest and the new year. It was held about the time of November.

**SAMKHAT**  Babylonian goddess of happiness.

**SAMSARA**  HINDU term for the wheel of life, with births and deaths and the transmigration of souls.

**SAMSON** *sun*  Old Testament judge and hero of great strength. He won many victories against the Hebrews' enemies, the Philistines, but lost his power when he told his secret to Delilah and she cut his locks. Finally he died in destroying many Philistines (JUDGES 13—16).

**SAMUEL** *name of God*  Last of the Hebrew judges and first of the prophets following Moses. Trained to be a priest, Samuel proved an able leader. He anointed Saul as Israel's first king, and later anointed David when Saul proved unworthy of the office. After his death Samuel apparently appeared to Saul through the mediumship of a witch at Endor (I SAMUEL 1—7; 13; 15; 19; 25:1; 28:8-19).

**SAMUEL, I AND II**  Two books of the Old Testament (originally one) relating the history of Israel under the prophet Samuel and the kings Saul and David.

**SAMURAI**  Japanese knights or warriors of the feudal era. They followed a high code of chivalry, loyalty, and honor.

**SANBENITO**  Yellow garment decorated with a red cross, designed for penitents who admitted to heresy in the Spanish INQUISITION.

**SANCHI**  Area in Bhopal, India, where a number of noted BUDDHIST shrines and burial mounds are located.

**SANCTIFICATION**  Act, process, or experience of consecration, purification, making something holy, or being made holy. Ancient religions often involved some form of sanctification in the sense of setting persons or objects apart for sacred purposes. In the Christian faith sanctification is a work of the Holy Spirit whereby the believer is enabled more fully to manifest the character and do the work of a child of God.

**SANCTIFY**  Consecrate or make holy. See SANCTIFICATION.

**SANCTION** Influence producing or principle validating moral action.

**SANCTITY** Sacredness, holiness, or saintliness.

**SANCTUARY** 1. Sacred place, as a temple or church. 2. Portion of a church containing the altar. 3. Immunity from punishment, based upon the medieval custom of protecting criminals who took refuge in churches.

**SANCTUM SANCTORUM** *holy of holies* Latin term for the most holy place in the Hebrew temple or elsewhere.

**SANCTUS** *holy* Hymn beginning "Holy, holy, holy, Lord God of hosts" sung during the EUCHARIST or mass.

**SANCTUS BELL** See SACRING BELL.

**SANDAY, WILLIAM (1843–1920)** ANGLICAN canon, theologian, and NEW TESTAMENT scholar. He wrote important books on the life of Christ, the Gospels, Romans, and Biblical inspiration. He encouraged the use of modern principles of Bible study.

**SANDEK** *godfather* Jewish term for the godfather who holds a child while it is being circumcised.

**SANDEMANIANS** Eighteenth-century Scottish followers of Robert Sandeman and John GLAS. They were also known as GLASITES.

**SANGHA** Buddhist term for assembly, or for the order of monks believed to have been founded by Gautama BUDDHA.

**SANGHAKAMMA** Buddhist term for the council of the SANGHA.

**SANGYAS** *Buddha* Name of the BUDDHA in Tibet.

**SANHEDRIN** Court in Jerusalem governing Jewish religious and political life during and before the New Testament era. Under Roman domination, of course, the supreme political power was the Empire. The Great Sanhedrin had 71 members presided over by a prince or high priest. Jesus, Peter, John, and Paul all appeared before this tribunal at one time or another (MATTHEW 26:59; ACTS 4:5–21; 22:30). Nicodemus and Joseph of Arimathaea were members of the Sanhedrin (JOHN 7:50–52; 19:38).

**SAN JUAN CAPISTRANO** California town to which it is said the swallows come each year on St. Joseph's Day in the spring, departing on the anniversary of St. John Capistran's death in the fall.

**SANKARA (c.788–850)** Hindu theologian of India. A BRAHMAN, he expounded VEDANTA Hinduism and wrote an important commentary on the Vedanta-sutras and on the BHAGAVAD-GITA. He held that BRAHMA creates and destroys all things, and that man finds true wisdom within his own soul. Everything outside of Brahma is illusion or *maya*.

**SANKEY, IRA DAVID (1840–1908)** American hymn writer and song leader who shared the ministry of D. L. MOODY.

**SANKHYA** Ancient religious philosophy of India founded by Kapila about six hundred years B.C. According to it there are two eternal substances: soul and matter. Although Kapila is said to have denied that God exists, some forms of Sankhya appear to be theistic.

**SANNYASI** HINDU term for ascetic and saint.

**SANSKRIT** Ancient language of the Hindus of India, in which the VEDAS are written.

**SANTA CLAUS** Mysterious and jolly giftgiver in the American folklore of Christmas. The name originated in a corruption of the name of St. NICHOLAS.

**SANTA SOPHIA** Famous building in Constantinople. See HAGIA SOPHIA.

**SANTAYANA, GEORGE (1863–1952)** Spanish-born American philosopher. Styling himself a materialist, he declared that "Religions are the great fairy tales of the conscience."

**SANUSI** MOSLEM brotherhood prevalent in northern Africa.

**SAN-ZEN** Dialog form of indoctrination of a student by a ZEN master.

**SAOSHYANT** ZOROASTRIAN prophet and savior to be born of a virgin to Zoroaster at the end of the present age.

**SARACENS** Medieval term for the MOSLEMS against whom many of the CRUSADES were fought.

**SARAH, SARA or SARAI** *princess (?)* Abraham's wife and Isaac's mother. A beautiful woman, she was twice sought by foreign kings. She gave birth to Isaac in her old age and lived 127 years.

**SARASVATI** HINDU goddess of education.

**SARASWATI, DAYANANDA** See DAYANANDA SARASWATI.

**SARDIS** Ancient center of the worship of ARTEMIS in Asia Minor. In New Testament times it had a Christian church (REVELATION 3:1–4).

**SARDIUS** Ruby or ruby-like gem contained in the breastplate of the Hebrew high priest and in the walls of the New Jerusalem in St. John's vision (REVELATION 21:20).

**SARDONYX** Onyx in the walls of the New Jerusalem (REVELATION 21:20).

**SARNATH** Buddhist holy place near Benares, India. There Gautama BUDDHA once preached.

**SARTO, ANDREA DEL (1486–1531)** Italian religious painter. He portrayed "The Annunciation," "The Procession of the Magi," "The Holy Family," "The Deposition From the Cross," and many other subjects.

**SARUM RITE** Liturgy used at Sarum or Salisbury Cathedral in England before the REFORMATION. Dating from the Middle Ages, it has been adopted in various parts of England.

**SATAN** *adversary* Jewish and Christian name for the directing agent or principle of evil. The TALMUD and the SCRIPTURES regard him as having been a mighty angel who fell from heaven through pride and rebellion.

**SATANISM** Satan-worship, a travesty of Christianity apparently practiced at times by enemies of the latter.

**SATARUPA** Female aspect of BRAHMA. According to some, Satarupa is his wife or daughter.

**SATISFACTION** 1. Compensation or payment to God satisfying the demands of His justice. ANSELM and others have held that the atonement of Christ is a vicarious satisfaction of this kind. Christ, in this view, paid the debt caused by men's sin. 2. PENANCE.

**SATNAMIS** HINDU ascetics said to partake of strange ceremonies.

**SATORI** Important period of awareness in ZEN training, heralding an advance toward NIRVANA.

**SATTYALOKA** Supreme heaven in HINDUISM.

**SATURN** Roman god of agriculture, planting, and harvest.

**SATURNALIA** Roman time of peace, feasting, and gift-exchanging, in honor of SATURN. It was originally held in December.

The word SATURNALIA today indicates a licentious feast.

**SATURNIANS** Second-century GNOSTICS who followed Saturninus, a Syrian teacher, rejecting meat and marriage.

**SATYA** *truth* BUDDHIST term for truth.

**SATYAGRAHA** *truth-grasping* Ghandilike method of achieving reforms through persistent nonviolent noncooperation. It originated in India in 1919.

**ŞATYR** In Greek mythology, a woods creature half human and half goat, fond of drinking, dancing, making music, and sex.

**SAUL** 1. The Hebrews' first king, anointed by Samuel to unite the people against the Philistines. Saul's spirit of pride and rebellion caused the crown to pass to King David. 2. Variant of PAUL. St. Paul was originally known as Saul of Tarsus.

**SAVE** Rescue or redeem. Christians are saved from spiritual destruction and granted eternal life through Christ.

**SAVING FAITH** Faith which saves. Deeper than mere intellectual assent or historical faith, saving faith is a commitment of the whole person to Jesus Christ for time and eternity, and a personal trust in Him. Such faith saves from sin and death.

**SAVIOR or SAVIOUR** 1. One who saves. 2. *Saviour*, capitalized, is applied specifically to Jesus Christ, "the Saviour of all men" (I TIMOTHY 4:10), "the Saviour of the world" (I JOHN 4:14).

**SAVITRI** Sun god in ancient HINDUISM; one of the twelve ADITYAS.

**SAVONAROLA, GIROLAMO (1452–1498)** Eloquent Italian DOMINICAN preacher and reformer. He correctly prophesied the death of Lorenzo the Magnificent and the death date of Innocent VIII. A man of personal purity and severe denunciation of evil, he and two of his followers were tortured, strangled, and burned.

**SAVOY DECLARATION** CONGREGATIONALIST statement of faith drawn up at the Savoy Palace in London in 1658. It is similar to the WESTMINSTER CONFESSION OF FAITH, except that it refuses to accept the supremacy of the state over the church, and it sets forth the individual congregation as the center of ecclesiastical power.

**SAW** Religious symbol of Joseph, the carpenter who acted as Jesus' father.

**SAXON CONFESSION** Statement of faith similar to the AUGSBURG CONFESSION, prepared for the Council of TRENT in 1551 by Philip MELANCHTHON. It stressed forgiveness of sins on the basis of faith and defined the church as a spiritual fellowship.

**SAYBROOK PLATFORM** CONGREGATIONAL-IST statement adopted by Connecticut churches in 1708. It provided for supervision of individual congregations by county "Consociations" similar to presbyteries in the PRESBYTERIAN system.

**SAYERS, DOROTHY L. (1893–1957)** English writer of detective fiction and religious works such as *Creed or Chaos?* The latter works included prose, poetry, and drama.

**SAYID** *prince* Descendant of MOHAMMED through his cousin Ali and his daughter Fatima.

**SAYYID ALI MOHAMMAD** See the BAB and BABISM.

**SCALA SANCTA** *holy stairs* Stairway in Rome said to have been used by Jesus after His trial and to have been brought from Jerusalem by St. HELENA. Pilgrims often go up the stairs on their knees.

**SCALES** In religious art, a symbol of justice, the archangel Michael, and the martyrdom of SIMON ZELOTES.

**SCALLOP** Medieval pilgrims to the tomb of St. James wore a scallop shell on their caps. The scallop was known as "St. James' shell." Thus the scallop shell became a symbol of pilgrimage.

**SCAPEGOAT** Goat upon which the sins of the Jewish people were symbolically laid in Old Testament times. The goat was sent into the desert and pushed off a cliff.

**SCAPULAR** Long band of cloth worn over the shoulders and hanging down at front and back. It is the garb of certain monastic orders such as that of St. BENEDICT.

**SCARAB** Beetle associated with immortality in Egyptian religion.

**SCHAFF, PHILIP (1819–1893)** Swiss-born theologian and church historian in the United States. He wrote *The Creeds of Christendom, History of the Christian Church,* and other important works. He was a man of both evangelical zeal and critical insight.

**SCHECHTER, SOLOMON (1847–1915)** Jewish scholar who was born in Rumania and did notable work in England and America. He lectured on the TALMUD at Cambridge University, became president of New York's Jewish Theological Seminary, and founded the UNITED SYNAGOGUE OF AMERICA. Among his important writings are *Studies in Judaism, Some Aspects of Rabbinic Theology,* and *A Glimpse of the Social Life of the Jews.*

**SCHIN** Twenty-first letter of the Hebrew alphabet.

**SCHISM** Division or separation, especially from a church or religious body; breach of unity among people of the same faith.

**SCHLATTER, ADOLF (1852–1939)** European PROTESTANT theologian and New Testament scholar who based his theology on independent exegesis of the Bible text. He opposed both philosophical and idealistic perversions of the original gospel message.

**SCHLEIERMACHER, FRIEDRICH DANIEL ERNST (1768–1834)** German PROTESTANT theologian, minister, and philosopher. He identified religion with feeling and intuition rather than dogma; creeds he saw as expressions of personal experience. He felt that dogma was a kind of incrustation on Christianity, and opposed both orthodoxy and rationalism. He wrote *The Christian Faith* and other works. Schleiermacher has probably been one of the most important influences on contemporary Protestantism.

**SCHMALKALD ARTICLES** Statement of faith drawn up by Martin LUTHER and other German reformers at Schmalkald, a republic of Germany, in 1537. It labeled the pope as antichrist and the mass as "the greatest and most horrible abomination."

**SCHMALKALD LEAGUE** Alliance of German Protestant princes from 1531 to 1547, uniting REFORMED and LUTHERAN interests against those of the ROMAN CATHOLIC princes and principalities.

**SCHOLA CANTORUM** *school of singers* School for training singers to aid Christian worship. Pope GREGORY I is said to have founded the first such school.

**SCHOLASTICISM** Christian theology and philosophy of the Middle Ages, often characterized by opposing schools of interpretation and speculation. These included NOMINALISM VS. REALISM, AUGUSTINIANISM and AVERROISM VS. ARISTOTELIANISM, and other movements which sought to work out a Christian view of reality, of reason, of the natural world, of the sacraments, and of ethics. Among the great Scholastics were John Scotus ERIGENA, St. ANSELM, Peter ABELARD, St. THOMAS AQUINAS, St. BONAVENTURE, WILLIAM OF OCCAM, and DUNS SCOTUS.

**SCHOLASTICS** The great divines of SCHO-LASTICISM.

**SCHOLIA** Marginal notes on manuscripts, often made by medieval scholars on texts of Scripture.

**SCHOOLMEN** See SCHOLASTICS.

**SCHOPENHAUER, ARTHUR (1788–1860)** German philosopher who saw the central force in the universe as a blind will to live. Apparently influenced by BUDDHISM and HINDUISM, he idealized the cessation of all desire. Although he was a pessimist, Schopenhauer idealized compassion in which one attempts to relieve another's pain.

**SCHWABACH ARTICLES** LUTHERAN statement of faith drawn up by Martin LUTHER and others in 1529. They represent the first common German Protestant confession of faith, and form the basis of the first part of the AUGSBURG CONFESSION.

**SCHWEITZER, ALBERT (1875–1965)** Humanitarian, organist, musicologist, philosopher, theologian, and surgeon who gave most of his adult life to the natives of Lambarene in French Equatorial Africa. He wrote a life of Bach, *The Quest of the Historical Jesus, Paul and His Interpreters, The Philosophy of Civilization,* and other important works. His guiding ethic was "reverence for life." In his hospital at Lambarene he cared for hundreds of patients and maintained a village for lepers, all in simple fashion. He believed that anyone might become "a simple channel of the power of Jesus."

**SCHWENKFELD, KASPER VON (1490–1561)** German MYSTIC and religious reformer whose differences from orthodox Protestants led to his persecution and condemnation. He emphasized fellowship with God, the guidance of the Holy Spirit, and the reading of Scripture, but his disparagement of the sacraments, justification by faith, and the visible ordinances of the church led to his denunciation by LUTHER as a heretic.

**SCHWENKFELDERS** Followers of Kaspar von SCHWENKFELD. Under persecution they scattered, and exist today only as the Schwenkfelder Church in the United States. They have five congregations near Philadelphia, Pennsylvania.

**SCIENCE AND HEALTH WITH KEY TO THE SCRIPTURES** Book by Mary Baker EDDY constituting the only textbook of CHRISTIAN SCIENCE considered authoritative.

**SCIENTISM** Commitment to science as the only guide to ultimate truth.

**SCILLITAN MARTYRS** Group of seven men and five women martyred in Scillium, North Africa, by Saturninus for their refusal to renounce Christianity about 180 A.D. (See SATURNIANS.) *The Acts of the Scillitan Martyrs* proves that Christianity had gained a foothold in northern Africa in the second century.

**SCIOMANCY** Term for seeking information from the spirits of those deceased.

**SCONE, STONE OF** "Stone of Destiny" marking Celtic coronations at Scone, an ancient Scottish center of worship. The stone, believed by some to have been that on which Joseph slept at Bethel, was removed to WESTMINSTER ABBEY in the thirteenth century.

**SCORPION** Religious symbol of evil and treachery.

**SCOTISM** Philosophical-theological views of DUNS SCOTUS.

**SCOTLAND, CHURCH OF** See CHURCH OF SCOTLAND.

**SCOTUS, DUNS** See DUNS SCOTUS, JOHN.

**SCOTTISH or SCOTS CONFESSION** Statement of faith drawn up by John KNOX and other clergymen and adopted by the parliament of Scotland in 1560. Like the WESTMINSTER CONFESSION OF FAITH, it emphasizes the election and sovereignty of God and states that the civil magistrate must guide the church.

**SCOURGE** Symbol of the Passion of Christ.

**SCREEN** Partition in a church, often dividing the NAVE from the CHANCEL.

**SCRIBES or SOFERIM** Jewish scholars who copied Bible manuscripts and interpreted and taught the Scriptures. Jesus was sometimes in conflict with them, as He was with other Jewish groups. There were many great scribes in Jewish history.

**SCRIPTORIUM** Portion of a monastery where manuscripts were copied in the Middle Ages.

**SCRIPTURE** 1. Sacred writing. 2. BIBLE, or a portion of it.

**SCROLL** Manuscript wound in a roll. Many Scriptures were originally written on scrolls.

**SCROLL OF THE LAW** Scroll in the synagogue containing the five books of Moses, the Law or PENTATEUCH.

**SCROLLS, DEAD SEA** See DEAD SEA SCROLLS.

**SCRUPLE** Doubt concerning the rightness of an action—sometimes on an inadequate basis.

**SCRUTINY** 1. Examination of candidates for church membership or for the ordained ministry. 2. Election of a pope by ballot.

**SCUDDER, HENRY MARTYN (1822–1895)** American missionary to Japan under the auspices of the REFORMED church. He was born in Ceylon.

**SCUDDER, IDA S. (1870–1960)** Medical missionary to India and founder of the Vellore Christian Medical College and Hospital. This was the first accredited Christian medical college in India and was supported interdenominationally. "Dr. Ida" was a member of the REFORMED CHURCH IN AMERICA.

**SCYTHE** Symbol of death in religious art.

**SEA** In the Bible, a body of water. In such passages as Daniel 7:2 the sea apparently symbolizes humanity.

**SEABURY, SAMUEL (1729–1796)** First bishop of the Protestant Episcopal Church in America. A loyalist in the American revolution, he served at various times as physician, priest, and army chaplain. Unable to take the Anglican oath of allegiance when the United States became independent of England, he was consecrated by the Scottish Episcopal Church at Aberdeen.

**SEAGRAVE, GORDON S. (1896–1965)** "Burma Surgeon" who spent his life giving medical aid to the people of Burma. An American Baptist, he was honored in 1961 by President John F. Kennedy as "a symbol to the entire world of the American tradition of humanitarian service abroad." He once wrote: "All I wanted was plenty of jungle and thousands of sick people to treat, preferably with surgery."

**SEAL** Hard implement designed to make an impression on clay or wax, or the impression thus made. Seals have had wide use in authenticating religious documents.

The sacraments of BAPTISM and EUCHARIST seal or permanently impress those receiving them.

**SEAL OF CONFESSION** Secrecy imposed upon one who hears confession, which must be kept in inviolate confidence. Here CATHOLIC doctrine requires the seal of secrecy to be maintained despite the gravest arguments advanced for breaking it.

**SEAL OF SOLOMON** Six-pointed Star of David (symbolizing Israel) decorating early synagogues.

**SEASON** Special religious period such as ADVENT or LENT.

**SEB** Egyptian deity also named Geb: the earth as an object of worship.

**SE-BAPTISTS** Seventeenth-century followers of John SMYTH, a PROTESTANT leader who baptized himself.

**SEBASTE, MARTYRS OF** See FORTY MARTYRS OF SEBASTE.

**SEBAT or SHEBAT** Eleventh month in the Jewish ecclesiastical year, occurring about the time of January.

**SEBASTIAN, ST. (third century)** Christian martyr of Rome persecuted by DIOCLETIAN; he was shot by arrows. His feast day is January 20.

**SEBEK** Egyptian god with the head of a crocodile.

**SECOND ADAM** Theological term for Christ, based on such Scriptures as Romans 5:1–14 and I Corinthians 15:45.

**SECOND ADVENT** Theological term for the return of Christ. See SECOND COMING.

**SECOND BIRTH** Theological term for REGENERATION or the process of being spiritually reborn.

**SECOND BLESSING** Term used in Holiness churches for sanctification as a second definite work of grace, received by faith like justification, in which the believer is lifted into a higher life above the failures of sin.

**SECOND COMING or SECOND ADVENT** According to Acts 1:11, when Jesus ascended into heaven two angels said, "This same Jesus, which is taken up from you into heaven, shall so come in like manner as ye have seen him go into heaven." According to the APOSTLES' CREED Christ will return from heaven "to judge the quick and the dead."

**SECOND MAN** Christ in contrast to the first man Adam (I CORINTHIANS 15:47).

**SECRET SOCIETY** Organization with quasi-religious rites, oaths, and the like.

**SECT** Religious denomination; term often applied to a group which dissents from an established church.

**SECTARIANISM** 1. Zealous attachment to a sect. 2. Presence of divergent religious groups in a place or epoch.

**SECTARY** British term for a nonconformist or sectarian.

**SECULAR CLERGY** Clergymen who are not attached to religious orders but live "in the world," often as priests of parishes.

**SECULARISM** 1. Immersion in the world and disregard of God or the supernatural. 2. Belief in the separation of religion from government, education, and the like.

**SECULAR PRIESTS** Priests working outside monasticism. See SECULAR CLERGY.

**SEDER** *order* Order of service for the Jewish PASSOVER celebration. Seder is also a synonym for Passover.

**SEDE VACANTE** *the seat being empty* Ecclesiastical term for a vacancy in an EPISCOPAL see or DIOCESE.

**SEDILIA** *seats* Seats for the celebrants of the EUCHARIST or mass. There are usually three, on the south or epistle side of the CHANCEL.

**SEDNA** Eskimo goddess of water creatures and polar bears.

**SEE** Ecclesiastical term for the seat or throne of a bishop or the pope.

**SEE, APOSTOLIC or HOLY** Seat of papal authority: the VATICAN.

**SEEKERS** Seventeenth-century English Christians, often considered radical or heretical, who sought to worship God in spirit. They believed the visible church to be largely under the control of ANTICHRIST and opposed religious coercion. Their leader Bartholomew LEGATE was burned for heresy in 1612.

**SEER** Prophet; one who "sees" more than other men. In later Jewish history distinction was made between the seer who was known for his visions and the prophet who was recognized as a speaker and truth-teller.

**SEGOMO** Celtic war god.

**SEKER** Egyptian god of the afterlife.

**SEKHEM** Term for soul in ancient Egyptian religion.

**SELAH** Word in the Hebrew Psalms of undetermined liturgical significance.

**SELENE** Greek moon goddess.

**SELF-REALIZATION FELLOWSHIP** Religious group with headquarters on Mount Washington, California, founded in 1925 by Paramhansa Yogananda. A "sect for the space age," it encourages yoga, meditation, and a vegetarian diet, and teaches the unity of truth behind all religious experience.

**SELICHOT or SELIHOT** *pardon* Jewish prayers of penitence, offered especially in the period before ROSH HASHANAH.

**SELMA** City in Alabama where Protestants, Catholics, Jews, and the nonreligious provided a demonstration of moral concern for justice and righteousness in 1965.

**SELWYN, GEORGE AUGUSTUS (1809–1878)** ANGLICAN missionary to and first bishop of New Zealand; later Bishop of Lichfield, England.

**SEM** See SHEM.

**SEMI-ARIANISM** Fourth-century movement propounding a theological position between ARIANISM and orthodoxy. Its adherents held that Christ is like God in substance, but not identical.

**SEMICHAH** *laying on of hands* Jewish term for ordination of a RABBI.

**SEMINARY** Training school for clergymen. Protestant seminaries for this purpose are usually referred to as theological seminaries.

**SEMI-PELAGIANISM** Theological movement in the fourth and fifth centuries between AUGUSTINIANISM and PELAGIANISM. Accepting the necessity of divine grace in regeneration, adherents of semi-Pelagianism taught a cooperation of such grace with the human will. While Augustine had held that God's grace preceded regeneration, the various semi-Pelagian theologians (as they are termed) made the divine grace subsequent.

**SEMITES** Middle Eastern peoples believed to have descended from Noah's son Shem. Jews, Arabs, Babylonians, Assyrians, and various peoples of Palestine are among those considered Semitic.

**SEMITIC** Of or related to the SEMITES.

**SEMITICS** Study of Semitic languages such as Hebrew and Arabic.

**SEMLER, JOHANN SALOMO (1725–1791)** German LUTHERAN theologian and Bible critic. His historical and rational principles of Biblical study profoundly influenced later study of Scripture.

**SENGAI (1750–1837)** Japanese painter and poet, a BUDDHIST abbot of insight and humor.

**SENGEN** Japanese goddess of Fujiyama.

**SENG-T'SAN (?–606)** ZEN Buddhist patriarch of China.

**SENNACHERIB (?–681 B.C.)** Assyrian monarch who made many military conquests. He invaded Judah while Hezekiah was king, and his armies were routed by a miraculous plague (II KINGS 18; 19). A prism inscribed by Sennacherib tells how he captured 200,150 people and besieged the capital: "Hezekiah the Jew . . . like a caged bird I shut in Jerusalem his royal city."

**SENTENCES** Book by Peter LOMBARD. A topical arrangement of the sayings of St. AUGUSTINE and other Church Fathers, it was "the most commented upon book of the Middle Ages" (Stephen C. Tornay).

**SENUSI or SENUSSI** See SANUSI.

**SENZAR** Secret language of BUDDHISM and THEOSOPHY.

**SEPARATE BAPTISTS** Baptists who accept no creeds and reject CALVINISM, having separated from other Baptists in the eighteenth century. They accept three ordinances: BAPTISM, the LORD'S SUPPER, and FOOT WASHING.

**SEPARATISTS** British term for Protestants who separated from the CHURCH OF ENGLAND in the sixteenth and seventeenth centuries. Thus the Separatists included the PILGRIMS, BAPTISTS, QUAKERS, and PRESBYTERIANS.

**SEPHARDIM** Jews from Spain and Portugal. When driven out of their adopted lands they maintained their distinctive rites and organizations. (Cf. ASHKENAZIM.)

**SEPT** The dog star Sirius, one of the deities of ancient Egypt.

**SEPTUAGESIMA** *seventieth* Third Sunday before LENT, about seventy days before EASTER.

**SEPTUAGINT** *seventy* Greek translation of the OLD TESTAMENT Scriptures, sometimes abbreviated as *LXX*. According to tradition 72 scholars made this translation in about seventy days. Somehow material was added in the process of translation that was not in the accepted Hebrew version. The ROMAN CATHOLIC Old Testament is based on the Septuagint, with its additional "APOCRYPHA," while PROTESTANT and JEWISH versions of the Old Testament adhere to the Hebrew text. Some New Testament quotations of Old Testament books follow the Septuagint, while others follow the Hebrew form.

**SEQUENCE** Hymn sung between the GRADUAL and the GOSPEL in certain church services.

**SERAPH** Six-winged angel who praises and glorifies God (ISAIAH 6). Seraphim (the plural form) are considered the highest order of angels.

**SERAPHIM** See SERAPH.

**SERAPION, ST. (fourth century)** Egyptian bishop and friend of St. ATHANASIUS. He supported Athanasius in the latter's controversies and wrote or compiled an elaborate prayer book. His feast day is March 21.

**SERAPIS or HAP** God of healing and the afterlife, symbolized as a bull and worshiped in the ancient religions of Egypt, Greece, and Rome.

**SERBIAN EASTERN ORTHODOX CHURCH** EASTERN ORTHODOX CHURCH of Serbia, Yugoslavia. There is a Diocese of the United States and Canada with headquarters at Libertyville, Illinois.

**SERIOUS CALL TO A DEVOUT AND HOLY LIFE** Devotional book by William LAW.

**SERMON** Religious address or discourse. The popular conception of a sermon as a condemnatory harangue is far removed from the New Testament conception of preaching as sharing incredibly good news from God.

**SERMON ON THE MOUNT** Jesus' discourse recorded in Matthew 5—7. It presents the BEATITUDES, the LORD'S PRAYER, and a spiritual interpretation of Old Testament laws. It has been called "The Constitution of the Kingdom of Heaven."

**SERPENT** Animal regarded with reverence and awe in many ancient religions. In the Bible the serpent symbolizes the devil and evil. See also SNAKE WORSHIP.

**SERVANTS OF MARY** See SERVITES.

**SERVANT SONGS** Passages in the book of Isaiah concerning the Servant of Jehovah. They are Isaiah 42:1–4; 49:1-6; 50:4-9; and 52:13—53:12.

**SERVER** Assistant to the celebrant at the EUCHARIST or mass. He is usually a lay person.

**SERVETUS, MICHAEL (1511–1553)** Spanish theologian and physician who discovered the circulation of the blood through the pulmonary system. His views of the TRINITY and of the nature of Christ led to his condemnation by both CATHOLICS and PROTESTANTS. He was burned to death in Geneva while crying to Jesus.

**SERVICE** Something done for another. Good religion calls for service to God and man. A service of worship is a public act of devotion and praise to God.

**SERVITES** Religious order founded in 1240 at Florence, sometimes called the Servants of Mary. Wearing long black cloaks and hoods, the members practice devotion to the Sorrowful Virgin, preach, conduct missions, and seek to elevate human souls.

**SERVUS SERVORUM DEI** *servant of the servants of God* Papal title.

**SESHA** Ancient HINDU serpent god.

**SESHETA** Goddess of books in ancient Egypt.

**SESSHIN** Japanese term for concentrated BUDDHIST meditation. It may occupy a period of a week in a monastery.

**SESSHU (1420–1506)** Outstanding ZEN Buddhist artist and priest of Japan.

**SESSION** Board of ELDERS governing a PRESBYTERIAN church. Members are lay ruling elders and a teaching elder, the minister.

**SET** See SUT.

**SETCHO (980–1052)** ZEN Buddhist master of China.

**SETH** Third son of Adam and Eve (GENESIS 4:25–26). He fathered many children.

**SETON, ELIZABETH ANN (1774–1821)** New York widow who became a nun and founded the Sisters of Charity or Daughters of Charity, St. Joseph's College, and America's first Catholic free school (the latter at Emmitsburg, Maryland). She was beatified in 1963.

**SEVEN** Number sometimes symbolizing completeness or perfection. Its sacredness was honored in Jewish and American Indian religion. Seven appears often in the Bible. In religious art seven may symbolize God, the Holy Spirit, grace, or charity.

**SEVEN CHURCHES OF ASIA** The seven Christian churches listed in Revelation 2—3. They were Ephesus, Smyrna, Pergamum, Thyatira, Sardis, Philadelphia, and Laodicea in Asia Minor.

**SEVEN DEADLY SINS** Capital sins of pride, covetousness, lust, anger, gluttony, envy, and sloth.

**SEVEN GIFTS OF THE HOLY SPIRIT** Attributes of the Spirit listed in Isaiah 11:2. They are wisdom, understanding, counsel, fortitude, knowledge, piety, and fear of the Lord. They have been mentioned in a confirmation prayer dating from ancient church history.

**SEVEN LAST WORDS** Seven sayings of Jesus from the cross before His death.

**SEVEN PENITENTIAL PSALMS** Psalms 6, 32, 38, 51, 102, 130, and 142. They have been used in LENT for many years.

**SEVEN SORROWS OF MARY** The Blessed Virgin's sorrows at the prophecy of Simeon, at the flight into Egypt, at the absence of Jesus in the temple, at finding Him going to the cross, on standing at the cross, at the descent of Jesus from the cross, and at His burial in the sepulcher. The Seven Sorrows are honored on the Friday after Passion Sunday and on September 15.

**SEVENTH-DAY ADVENTISTS** Christians who worship on Saturday and emphasize the imminent return of Christ. Regarding the Ten Commandments (see DECALOGUE) as an ethical norm, they proclaim salvation by the grace of God through the atonement of Christ. They tithe—giving one tenth of their money to the church—and practice IMMERSION and FOOT WASHING. They stress religious liberty but discourage personal use of tobacco or alcohol.

**SEVENTH DAY BAPTISTS** Baptists who observe Saturday as their Sabbath. A number came from England to America, organizing in 1672.

**SEVENTH DAY BAPTISTS (GERMAN, 1728)** Monastic community at Ephrata, Pennsylvania, founded in 1732 by Peter Becker, who also established the DUNKERS. They practice FOOT WASHING and TRINE IMMERSION.

**SEVENTH HEAVEN** MOSLEM and CABALISTIC term for the highest and most blessed spiritual abode.

**SEVENTY, THE** Seventy disciples sent out by Jesus to heal and proclaim the coming of the Kingdom of God (LUKE 10:1–20).

**SEVENTY WEEKS, THE** Period revealed to Daniel (9:20–27)—no doubt 490 years—during which sin was to end, the Most

Holy anointed, and everlasting righteousness brought in. Some relate this period to the profanation of the temple by ANTIOCHUS EPIPHANES in 166 B.C.; others, to the advent of Christ.

**SEVEN VIRTUES** Faith, hope, love, prudence, justice, self control, and fortitude.

**SEVEN WORDS** Jesus' seven sayings from the cross.

**SEX** Difference and/or relationships between men and women, with which religion has often been concerned. The Old Testament sets forth careful standards of sex relationships, as does the New. Contemporary religion often assumes a positive and permissive attitude toward sex relationships.

**SEXAGESIMA** *sixtieth* Second Sunday before LENT, about sixty days before EASTER.

**SEXT** The "little hour" of the Divine Office to be said at noon. See CANONICAL HOURS.

**SEXTON** Church officer or caretaker with various duties.

**SHABAN** Eighth month in the Moslem year. See ISLAM.

**SHABBAT** *Sabbath* Hebrew term for SABBATH.

**SHABBAT HA-GADOL** *Great Sabbath* Sabbath before the PASSOVER in JUDAISM.

**SHABERON** In Tibetan BUDDHISM, one of superior discipleship.

**SHACHARIT** *dawn* Jewish term for morning devotions.

**SHADDAI, EL** See EL SHADDAI.

**SHAFIITE RITE** Interpretation of Moslem canon law founded by Mohammed ibn Idris ash-Shafii in the eighth century. It emphasizes the KORAN and SUNNA, and is particularly strong in Indonesia. See ISLAM.

**SHAFTESBURY, ANTHONY ASHLEY COOPER, SEVENTH EARL OF (1801–1885)** Evangelical English nobleman who fought for better conditions in the slums and among laborers—including women and young children. He succeeded in getting workingmen a ten-hour day, in improving tenements and the care of the insane, and in accomplishing many other social gains. He also interested himself in such causes as the Y.M.C.A. and the BRITISH AND FOREIGN BIBLE SOCIETY.

**SHAHADA** Moslem confession of faith. See ISLAM.

**SHAHANSHAHIS** See PARSEES.

**SHAIKH or SHEIKH** *elder* Moslem religious leader. See ISLAM.

**SHAITAN** Moslem name for SATAN. See ISLAM.

**SHAKERS** Popular name for the Millennial Church, or the United Society of Believers in Christ's Second Appearing, which began in England about 1747. An early leader was Mother Ann (LEE), who was considered to represent the divine female principle as Jesus did the male. Members visibly trembled when under divine inspiration. Their worship often involved marching and dancing. Practicing celibacy, they were nearly extinct by the middle of the twentieth century.

**SHAKESPEARE, JOHN HOWARD (1857–1928)** English BAPTIST clergyman who organized the Baptist Union and founded the BAPTIST WORLD ALLIANCE.

**SHAKTI** See SAKTI.

**SHALOM ALEICHEM** *peace be with you* Jewish salutation.

**SHAMAN** Priest, healer, or medium among primitive peoples. He often works in a state of religious ecstasy.

**SHAMASH or CHEMOSH** Leading sun god in Assyrian and Babylonian religion, identified with beneficence, justice, and order.

**SHAMMAI (first century B.C.)** Jewish rabbi whose rigid interpretation of the TORAH was perpetuated in the School of Shammai. Shammai's moderate, more liberal contemporary HILLEL also left a school which prevailed over Shammai's toward the end of the first century A.D.

**SHAMMASH** *servant* Synagogue officer with duties similar to those of an Anglican BEADLE.

**SHANGO** Thunder deity of the West African tribe, Yoruba.

**SHANG-TI** *the lord above* Chinese term for the Emperor, God, or "the Lord of heaven" in TAOISM or CONFUCIANISM.

**SHARI'A** Moslem term for the divine law or way of life. See ISLAM.

**SHARON** *plain* Fertile plain near Jaffa in Palestine. Men lived there 4,000 years B.C.

**SHASTRA** 1. BUDDHIST commentary on a SUTRA. 2. Sacred HINDU textbook.

**SHAWNEE PROPHET (c.1775–1838)** American Indian who proclaimed a divinely inspired message of Indian culture and unity. At one time many Indians rallied to his call.

**SHEAR-JASHUB** *a remnant will return* Son of the prophet Isaiah. His name indicates the certainty of the return of a remnant of the Hebrews after the exile in Babylon. (ISAIAH 7:3).

**SHEBA** 1. Name of several Bible personages. 2. Area of southern Arabia from which a queen came to visit Solomon (I KINGS 10). According to Ethiopian legend the visit produced the first king of Ethiopia; through Solomon all the kings of that land bear the title "Lion of the Tribe of Judah."

**SHEBAT** See SEBAT.

**SHECHITA or SHEHITA** *ritual slaughter* Jewish term for the killing of animals with the minimum of pain and the maximum draining of blood, according to precise rabbinic laws.

**SHEDD, WILLIAM G. T. (1820–1894)** American PRESBYTERIAN theologian and seminary professor. He wrote a three-volume *Dogmatic Theology.*

**SHE ELOT U-TESHUBOT or -TESHUVOT** *queries and responses* Term for rabbinical decisions on various matters in the form of questions and answers. These decisions form a considerable body of Jewish literature.

**SHEEP** Common animal of the Middle East, in Biblical literature often symbolizing foolishness, helplessness, meekness, and the need for redemption and guidance.

**SHEER THURSDAY** A name for MAUNDY THURSDAY. The "sheer" probably relates to the absolution received on that day in some churches.

**SHEHITA** See SHECHITA.

**SHEIKH** See SHAIKH.

**SHEKINAH** *dwelling* Hebrew term for the presence of God. The Shekinah in the Temple indicated His presence there. Sometimes Shekinah is a substitute for the name of God in Jewish writings.

**SHELAMIM** Ancient Jewish peace offerings.

**SHELDON, CHARLES M. (1857–1946)** American CONGREGATIONAL minister and author. He served as editor of *Christian Herald* and wrote the novel *In His Steps.*

**SHELL** Instrument and symbol of BAPTISM. See also SCALLOP.

**SHEM** Noah's oldest son, loyal to Noah during the latter's drunkenness. He fathered Semitic peoples such as the Jews, the Arabs, and the Aramaeans.

**SHEMA** *hear* Jewish term for an affirmation of MONOTHEISM drawn from Deuteronomy 6:4–6; 11:13–21; Numbers 15:37–41. It is to be recited morning and evening.

**SHEMONEH ESREH** *eighteen* Portion of the liturgy of the synagogue originally consisting of 18 benedictions. It now has 19 benedictions; it is recited standing. It is also called AMIDAH and Tefillah.

**SHEN** 1. Chinese term for great good spirits. 2. Egyptian symbol of immortality.

**SHEOL** Hebrew term for the grave, hell, or the world of the dead.

**SHEPHELAH** *lowland* Low hills lying along the western coast of Palestine, constituting a natural area of defense against any maritime enemies.

**SHEPHERD** Symbol of a pastor, religious leader, or Christ. He said, "I am the good shepherd" (JOHN 10:11).

**SHEPHERD OF HERMAS** Book of apocalyptic visions, parables, and "mandates" dating from late in the first or early in the second century A.D. The title derives from the fact that Christ appeared to Hermas as a Shepherd.

**SHEPPARD, HUGH RICHARD LAWRIE (1880–1937)** Charismatic ANGLICAN vicar and popular Christian leader. He became Dean of Canterbury and Canon of St. Paul's, and founded the Peace Pledge Union. He was a vigorous social reformer and pacifist.

**SHESMU** Executioner of the wicked, in Egyptian religious folklore.

**SHEVAT** See SEBAT.

**SHEWBREAD** Term in the King James Bible for the twelve loaves of bread, the "Bread of the Presence," put in the holy place of the Jewish tabernacle and temple. (Cf. LEVITICUS 24:5–9.) Only the priests might eat this holy bread.

**SHIAHS** See SHIITES.

**SHICHI FUKUJIN** Japanese term for seven deities of fortune and chance.

**SHIISM** One of the two great divisions of ISLAM. The Shiites hold that Mohammed's son-in-law Ali should have been the Prophet's successor and accordingly they reject the first three Khalifs of Moslem history. They also reject the SUNNA. (The Sunnites constitute the other great division of Islam.)

**SHIITES or SHIAHS** Adherents of SHIISM (above).

**SHILOH** Town in central Palestine where the Levites had their sanctuary for a time. There the prophets Samuel, Eli, and Ahijah lived.

**SHIN** *true sect* BUDDHIST sect founded or chiefly influenced by SHINRAN SHONIN. The Shin school is one of the largest Buddhist groups in modern Japan.

**SHINGON** Buddhist "School of the True Word" in Japan, founded in 806. It has been described as a mystical pantheism. It brought together SHINTO and BUDDHISM.

**SHINRAN SHONIN (c.1173–1262)** Japanese founder of SHIN. A monk who broke his vows in order to marry, he emphasized faith in AMIDA and wrote hundreds of hymns.

**SHINTO** Ancient Japanese religion. Its chief emphasis is on reverence toward and worship of ancestors and certain nature deities. State Shinto was Japan's official religion until General Douglas MacArthur required the separation of Japanese religion and political life. Sect Shinto or Shrine Shinto is the popular form of Shinto, with many divisions.

**SHIP** Ancient symbol of the church. As Noah's ark carried those within it safely through the flood, the church was seen as an ark of safety from sin and the world. This conception is rapidly changing today.

**SHITTAH or SHITTIM** Hebrew term for wood used in the tabernacle; probably ACACIA.

**SHIVA** 1. Jewish term for seven days of mourning. 2. Also variant of SIVA.

**SHOBOGENZO** *eye of the true law* Noted work of ZEN Buddhism.

**SHODOKA** ZEN Buddhist poem popular in the East.

**SHOEMAKER, SAMUEL M. (1893–1963)** PROTESTANT EPISCOPAL clergyman, rector of churches in New York City and Pittsburgh. He wrote *How to Become a Christian* and other books, and was an influential leader in the application of Christian faith to personal and social problems.

**SHOFAR** Trumpet made from a ram's horn, blown in Jewish services on New Year's Day and the Day of ATONEMENT.

In pre-Christian times the shofar was blown on various occasions.

**SHONEY** Ancient Celtic sea god.

**SHONIN** Japanese term for a superior BUDDHIST monk.

**SHOPHAR** See SHOFAR.

**SHORTER CATECHISM** Popular term for PRESBYTERIAN catechism in the form of questions and answers covering the entire body of Christian theology, drawn up at the WESTMINSTER ASSEMBLY for those "of weaker capacity." The Shorter Catechism, written in 1647, begins with the question, "What is the chief end of man?" The answer is: "Man's chief end is to glorify God and to enjoy Him forever."

**SHOWBREAD** See Shewbread.

**SHRADDHA** HINDU ceremony offering gifts to the souls of dead members of the family. It is accompanied by chants in a complex rite.

**SHRIFT** Confession or absolution.

**SHRINE** Holy place, as a church, a receptacle of the relics of a holy person, or the tomb of a saint.

**SHRIVE** To hear a confession of sin, require a penance, or absolve from guilt.

**SHROVE MONDAY** Monday before LENT, designated for special pre-Lenten confession.

**SHROVE SUNDAY** Sunday before LENT, a special time to confess.

**SHROVETIDE** The day or three days immediately before LENT, set apart for confession of sins.

**SHROVE TUESDAY** The day immediately before LENT, designated as a special time for confession. In some countries it is a day of merrymaking or carnival; cf. MARDI GRAS and Pancake Day.

**SHRUTI or SRUTI** Hindu sacred writings, including the BRAHMANAS and the UPANISHADS, believed divinely inspired in the highest sense.

**SHU** Egyptian god of the atmosphere.

**SHULCHAN ARUKH** *prepared table* Joseph CARO's codification and digest of Jewish law.

**SHWE DAGON** Elegant Burmese BUDDHIST temple.

**SIBYL** Ancient Greek prophetess.

**SIBYLLINE ORACLES** Group of Jewish and Christian oracles prepared in imitation of the Sibylline Books of Greece. Dating from the second century B.C. through the third century A.D., they forecast a number of events.

**SIDDHA** *perfected one* One of the eighty-four "Perfected Ones" of BUDDHISM.

**SIDDHARTHA** *the one whose purpose is achieved* Given name of Gautama BUDDHA.

**SIDDHI** BUDDHIST term for powers of the spirit, often believed attained through intense spiritual discipline.

**SIDDUR** *order* Jewish prayer book for daily use.

**SIDON** City of Palestine on the Mediterranean coast. It was an ancient Phoenician city and later an important seaport, often mentioned in the Bible.

**SIDONIUS, ST.** See APOLLINARIS SIDONIUS.

**SIFRA** Jewish commentary on Leviticus.

**SIGER DE BRABANT** (c.1235–c.1282) French canon, theologian, and philosopher who led the Averroist movement of his day. Denying a time of creation, he held that a statement might be true in theology but false in philosophy, and vice versa. Cf. AVERROES.

**SIGMA** Greek letter equivalent to *s*.

**SIGN OF THE CROSS** Tracing the cross in outline with a motion of the hand. The sign of the cross is often employed in prayer, baptism, confirmation, and blessings. Its use dates from the second century.

**SIKHISM** Religion of India founded by NANAK in the sixteenth century. Originally attempting to mediate between HINDUISM and ISLAM, Sikhism opposed polytheism, idolatry, caste, and ascetic practices. Its sacred book of writings is called the GRANTH and contains the writings of Nanak and others. Today there are more than six million Sikhs in India. Those of the KHALSA, a military caste, carry daggers and do not cut their hair.

**SIKKHA** BUDDHIST term for the training of novitiates.

**SILAS** Companion of St. Paul on several of his early journeys. Another form of his name seems to have been Silvanus. He apparently aided Paul and Peter in the writing of several epistles (cf. ACTS 15:22–18:5; II CORINTHIANS 1:19; II THESSALONIANS 1:1; I PETER 5:12).

**SILENCE** Condition of quiet often useful in worship.

**SILENCE, ARGUMENT FROM** Contention that an author is ignorant of anything about which he does not write. At times used to discredit orthodox Christianity, the argument was attacked by the Anglican theologian, Joseph Barber LIGHTFOOT.

**SILENT PRAYER** Inaudible prayer. Some churches allow for a period of silent prayer amid their services.

**SILENUS** Minor Greek deity of forests.

**SILOAM** Pool in Jerusalem fed by a conduit cut by the engineers of King Hezekiah when threatened by siege. To this pool the sick were brought in the time of Jesus. (II CHRONICLES 32:4–8, 30; LUKE 13:4; JOHN 9:7–11).

**SILVANUS** Variant of SILAS (see).

**SILVER** Representation of purity in religious symbolism.

**SILVER, ABBA HILLEL** (1893–1963) Lithuanian-born rabbi and ZIONIST. An American leader of world JUDAISM, he proclaimed his faith as "an ancient faith adapted to modern times." Author of several books, he helped further the restoration of the state of Israel.

**SIMCHAT TORAH** *rejoicing of the Law* Last day of the Feast of Booths. It includes a joyful procession concluding the annual reading of the TORAH.

**SIMEON** 1. Jacob's second son, progenitor of the Hebrew tribe of that name. 2. Just old man who blessed Jesus during His presentation in the temple (LUKE 2:22–34). 3. Form of the name of Simon Peter (ACTS 15:14, KJV). 4. Simeon Niger, a member of the church of Antioch (ACTS 13:1).

**SIMEON, CHARLES** (1759–1836) Evangelical ANGLICAN leader. He was a founder of the CHURCH MISSIONARY SOCIETY and a supporter of various evangelical and missionary enterprises.

**SIMEON BEN YOCHAI** See SIMON BEN YOCHAI.

**SIMEON STYLITES, ST.** (c.390–c.459) First of the Christian saints to live atop a pillar. He spent over thirty-five years on one near Antioch, Syria. His presence there startled Christians, converted pagans, and produced many more ascetics who lived on top of pillars (STYLITES).

**SIMHATH TORAH** See SIMCHAT TORAH.

**SIMON** 1. A name of St. PETER (see). 2. Relative of Jesus (MATTHEW 13:55). 3. Leper at whose home in Bethany Jesus was anointed by an unnamed woman (MARK 14:3). 4. Jewish leader who entertained Jesus (LUKE 7:36–50). 5. Father of Judas (JOHN 6:71). 6. Native of Cyrene, Africa, who carried Jesus' cross (MARK 15:21). 7. Citizen of Joppa who entertained St. Peter while he had a revolutionary vision (ACTS 9:43 ff.).

**SIMON, RICHARD (1638–1712)** French theologian and Biblical scholar who questioned the Mosaic authorship of the PENTATEUCH and established many modern principles of criticism, particularly of the Old Testament. Although a champion of orthodox CATHOLICISM, he was attacked by both Protestants and Catholics for his critical ventures.

**SIMON or SIMEON BEN YOCHAI (second century)** Palestinian rabbi noted as an interpreter of the Law. He founded an academy and has been named as the author of the *Zohar,* a cabalistic work.

**SIMON MAGUS** Sorcerer known as "the Power of God which is called Great" who tried to buy the power of the Holy Spirit with money. (Cf. ACTS 8:9–24.)

**SIMON OF CYRENE** See SIMON 6.

**SIMON OF TRENT, BLESSED LITTLE (1472–1475)** Child for whose death most of the Jews of Trent were tortured to death. In 1965 the ROMAN CATHOLIC CHURCH acknowledged the Jews' innocence of Simon's death and withdrew the status of martyr from Little Simon.

**SIMONS, MENNO** See MENNO SIMONS.

**SIMON ZELOTES, ST.** One of the Twelve Apostles chosen by Jesus. Also known as Simon, Simon the Zealot, and Simon the Canaanite, he may have been a member of the nationalistic party of ZEALOTS (MATTHEW 10:4; MARK 3:18; LUKE 6:15). His feast day is October 28.

**SIMONY** Purchase of sacred things, particularly church appointments, with mere money. The name comes from the attempt of SIMON MAGUS to buy the power of the Spirit.

**SIMPSON, A. B. (1843–1919)** Founder of the CHRISTIAN AND MISSIONARY ALLIANCE. Originally a PRESBYTERIAN minister, he wrote and edited religious publications and encouraged much evangelistic and mission work.

**SIMPSON, MATTHEW (1811–1884)** American bishop of the METHODIST CHURCH, first president of DePauw University, and antislavery leader.

**SIN** Violation of the divine will. St. AUGUSTINE defined it as "any thought, word, or deed opposed to the law of God." Ethically, sin is that which is immoral. The word, however, is basically a religious one and holds meaning in relation to God; sin is closely identified with pride and unbelief—both negative reactions toward the Deity. While various forms of theism recognize sin, Christianity has historically recognized it as fundamentally spoiling the soul and character of man. "The wages of sin is death, but the gift of God is eternal life through Jesus Christ our Lord" (ROMANS 6:23). The only hope for man and the only Saviour from sin is Christ, through whom man re-enters full communion with God. The Christian is promised, "Sin shall not have dominion over you" (ROMANS 6:14).

**SIN** 1. Desert area through which the Hebrews journeyed after the exodus from Egypt (EXODUS 16:1). 2. Babylonian moon god, known as "Lord of knowledge."

**SINA** Moon goddess of the people of Polynesia.

**SINAI** Peninsula of eastern Egypt through which the Israelites traveled after leaving Egypt, and mountain therein where Moses received the Ten Commandments. The latter, called Jebel Musa ("Mount of Moses"), is the site of the monastery of St. Catherine where the CODEX SINAITICUS was discovered in the nineteenth century. Some scholars, however, believe that the original Mt. Sinai is another mountain such as Mt. Seir, Jebel Serbal, or Jebel Hellal.

**SINAITIC MANUSCRIPT** See OLD SYRIAC VERSIONS.

**SINECURE** Ecclesiastical office without pastoral responsibilities for the "cure of souls."

**SINGH lion** Name taken by each Sikh. See SIKHISM.

**SINGH, GOVIND or GOBIND (1666–1708)** Tenth and last guru (leader) of the SIKHS. He founded the militant KHALSA sect and the baptism of the sword, and established the Sikh custom of wearing a turban, carrying a dagger, and not cutting the hair.

**SINGH, RANJIT (1780–1839)** Greatest

Sikh leader. A militant believer in SIKHISM, he sought to establish a Sikh state. The one he founded eventually fell to the British.

**SINGH, SADHU SUNDAR** See SUNDAR SINGH.

**SIN OFFERING** Offering to God made to free the worshiper from defilement. In the Old Testament there were provisions for guilt and trespass offerings for both moral and ceremonial transgressions. Sin offerings might be made by a layman, a ruler, the high priest, or the entire community.

**SINURC** Persian lord of eternal life.

**SION** 1. Variant of MT. HERMON (see). 2. See MT. ZION.

**SIRACH** 1. Father of the "Jesus ben Sirach" who wrote the book of ECCLE-SIASTICUS. 2. A name for Ecclesiasticus.

**SIRACH, JESUS BEN** See JESUS SON OF SIRACH.

**SIREN** Greek sea nymph who lured sailors to their doom.

**SISTER** Member of a women's religious order.

**SISTERHOOD** Community of women united in a religious order or faith. There are many sisterhoods in CATHOLICISM.

**SISTERS OF CHARITY** Catholicism has a number of women's religious orders with this name. The first order was founded by St. VINCENT DE PAUL in 1634. Members wear peasant-like blue-gray gowns and seek to aid the needy in various ways. Other orders of the Sisters of Charity were founded by Mgr. Marechaux, Canon E. J. Triest, Mary Aikenhead, Mgr. Zwissen, and Mme. Mole de Champlatreux.

**SISTERS OF MERCY** 1. CATHOLIC women's organization founded by Catherine Mc-Auley in Ireland in 1827. Its purpose is to help women in various ways, with education, charity, hostels, hospitals, and training schools. Many of the sisters teach in parochial schools. 2. Term for various ANGLICAN women's orders engaged in nursing or the like.

**SISTINE** Adjectival reference to popes named Sixtus.

**SISTINE CHAPEL** Main chapel in the VAT-ICAN. The pope's private chapel, it was built by Pope SIXTUS IV and is used for the election of new popes and for important papal rites. The "Last Judgment"

by Michelangelo and other great works adorn it.

**SISTINE MADONNA** "Sublimest lyric of the art of Catholicity" (J. A. Symonds). It is a painting by Raphael for the Church of St. Sixtus (San Sisto) and shows the Virgin and Child with St. Barbara and St. Sixtus II.

**SISTRUM** Musical instrument used in the worship of Isis in ancient Egypt.

**SITA** VEDIC goddess of agriculture.

**SITALA** HINDU goddess of smallpox.

**SITTARS** Members of a HINDU sect in India with quietistic, kindly attitudes.

**SIVA or SHIVA** Hindu god of creative power, as well as destruction; symbolized by the LINGAM. With VISHNU and BRAHMA he forms the supreme triad in HINDUISM.

**SIVAN** Ninth month in the Jewish civil year.

**SIX** Symbol of creation and of man in religious symbolism.

**SIX ARTICLES** Decree issued by England's King Henry VIII in 1539 upholding such doctrines as TRANSUBSTANTIATION and clerical celibacy against REFORMED or LU-THERAN doctrines and practices. Vigorously protested, it was not rigidly enforced.

**SIX HUNDRED SIXTY-SIX** "Number of a man" concealing the name of the beast (one like a lamb in appearance but speaking like a dragon) who is to be allied with another beast against God and the church (REVELATION 13:11–18). The numerical value of the Hebrew letters in the words "Nero Caesar" is 666. Various other names have been suggested as fulfilling the same value.

**SIX POINTS** Principles adopted by the English Church Union in 1875 for the restoration of such features in the CHURCH OF ENGLAND as the eastward position, eucharistic vestments, the mixed chalice, altar lights, unleavened bread in the eucharist, and incense.

**SIXTUS IV (1414–1484)** FRANCISCAN general and pope who furthered the arts and letters. He built the SISTINE CHAPEL, enlarged the Vatican Library, and instituted the Sistine Choir. He agreed to the Spanish INQUISITION but welcomed the Jews expelled from Spain. He also sought to improve the quality of ecclesiastical music through legislation.

**SIXTUS V (1521–1590)** Priest, friend of St.

IGNATIUS LOYOLA, cardinal, and able pope. A giant of the COUNTER REFORMATION, he beautified Rome and filled the papal treasury. He issued a definitive edition of the VULGATE, built the Vatican Library and the Lateran Palace, and reformed the college of cardinals.

**SIYAMA SAMAGAMA** BUDDHIST sect founded in the eighteenth century in Ceylon.

**S.J.** Abbreviation for the SOCIETY OF JESUS.

**SJOFNA** Germanic love goddess.

**SKANDA** HINDU god of war and son of SIVA.

**SKANDHA or KHANDHA** BUDDHIST term for one of the five elements or activities of human personality, or of existence. These elements are form, sensation, consciousness, perception, and emotion.

**SKELETON** Symbol of death in religious art.

**SKEPTIC** Doubter, disbeliever, or one who questions or criticizes accepted beliefs.

**SKOPTSI or SKOPTSY** *eunuchs* Russians who emasculated themselves (at least in theory) in reaction to the licentious antinomianism of some of the KHLYSTS. They denigrated sex and practiced flagellation. Early leaders were Akulina Ivanovna and Blochin, known as Mother of God and Christ. Oppressed in Russia, they formed several ascetic communities in Rumania.

**SKULL** Symbol of mortality.

**SKY PILOT** Idiomatic term for minister or missionary.

**SLESSOR, MARY (1848–1915)** UNITED PRESBYTERIAN missionary from Scotland to West Africa. She brought such practices as witchcraft and slavery to an end on the Calabar coast.

**SMARTAS** HINDU disciples of SANKARA. They believe that BRAHMA, creator and destroyer of all, is both immanent and transcendent, and take an intellectual approach to religion.

**SMITH, GEORGE ADAM (1856–1942)** Scottish Old Testament scholar famous for his commentaries *The Twelve Prophets, The Book of Isaiah, Historical Geography of the Holy Land,* and other works.

**SMITH, GIPSY (1860–1947)** British EVANGELIST and gypsy's son. He conducted evangelistic work through much of the English-speaking world and South Africa.

**SMITH, HENRY PRESERVED (1847–1927)** Liberal PRESBYTERIAN and CONGREGATIONALIST commentator and OLD TESTAMENT scholar.

**SMITH, JOSEPH (1805–1844)** New Englander who dug up sacred revelations on gold tablets at Palmyra, New York, in 1827; these formed the basis of Mormonism and of the CHURCH OF JESUS CHRIST OF LATTER-DAY SAINTS. Driven west, he was killed by a mob at Carthage, Illinois, after declaring himself a candidate for President of the United States.

**SMITH, WILLIAM ROBERTSON (1846–1894)** Scottish theologian and Old Testament scholar. Author of *The Prophets of Israel, The Religion of the Semites,* and other works and a commanding scholar, he lost his professorship at the Free Church College in Aberdeen for popularizing and elaborating on the ideas of Julius WELLHAUSEN.

**SMITHFIELD** Portion of London where three hundred PROTESTANTS were burned during the reign of Queen Mary Tudor.

**SMOKE** Religious symbol of mortality and the vanity of life.

**SMRITI** HINDU term for such sacred literature as the PURANAS and TANTRAS, in contrast to the directly inspired "SHRUTI" or "sruti."

**SMYRNA** Turkish city which held a church from New Testament times. It was a city of wealth, located near ancient Ephesus. There POLYCARP (Bishop of Smyrna) was martyred about 155 A.D. Smyrna became an archiepiscopal see of the GREEK ORTHODOX CHURCH and has a rich if tragic history.

**SMYTH or SMITH, JOHN (c.1554–1612)** English BAPTIST known as "the Se-Baptist" (self-baptizer) because after determining the errors in infant baptism he baptized himself. He instituted a Baptist church in Amsterdam, called the Brethren of the Separation of the Second English Church at Amsterdam.

**SMYTH, NEWMAN (1843–1925)** CONGREGATIONALIST minister and leader of New England's NEW THEOLOGY of the late nineteenth and early twentieth centuries.

**SNAIL** Religious symbol of sloth and sinfulness.

**SNAKE WORSHIP** Snakes were often the objects of worship or veneration in ancient religions; cf. SERPENT. In the southern United States, Christian cults sometimes practice snake handling in attempted fulfillment of Mark 16:18.

**SNÖTRA** Nordic goddess of good manners.

**SNOW, LORENZO (1814–1901)** American MORMON leader. He translated the BOOK OF MORMON into Italian and became an apostle, president of the Twelve Apostles, and president of the CHURCH OF JESUS CHRIST OF LATTER-DAY SAINTS.

**SOCIAL BRETHREN** Group formed in 1867 in Illinois. Their churches, found in the Midwest, hold to traditional Protestant doctrines but they maintain that ministers are not called "for political speeches."

**SOCIAL GOSPEL** Term for application of the Christian gospel ("good news") to every social area: business, government, economics; and to family, community, national, and international problems. Pioneers of the social gospel include Washington GLADDEN, William Ellery CHANNING, Joseph PARKER, Walter RAUSCHENBUSCH, Harry Emerson Fosdick, and Reinhold Niebuhr.

**SOCIETY** CONGREGATIONAL term for the parish which controls the church buildings and pastor's salary.

**SOCIETY FOR PROMOTING CHRISTIAN KNOWLEDGE** British organization founded in 1698 with various missionary and educational aims. It publishes important religious works.

**SOCIETY FOR THE PROPAGATION OF THE GOSPEL IN FOREIGN PARTS** ANGLICAN body organized to aid the mission program of the SOCIETY FOR PROMOTING CHRISTIAN KNOWLEDGE. It carries out a global missionary work.

**SOCIETY OF FREE CATHOLICS** British organization, active in the early twentieth century, uniting Protestants who share Catholic empathy and emphases.

**SOCIETY OF FRIENDS** See FRIENDS, SOCIETY OF.

**SOCIETY OF FRIENDS (FIVE YEARS MEETING)** Largest group of QUAKERS in the United States, representing the union of a number of such groups in 1902. See also FRIENDS, SOCIETY OF.

**SOCIETY OF JESUS** Religious order founded by IGNATIUS LOYOLA in Paris in 1534. It has a military framework, adding to the usual vows of chastity, poverty, and obedience one of missionary activity. FRANCIS XAVIER was one of its famous missionaries. Outstanding in education and in its publications, it has often been the object of suspicion for alleged political intrigues and casuistical rules of ethics. Its members are known as Jesuits.

**SOCIETY OF MARY** See MARISTS.

**SOCIETY OF ST. FRANCIS** ANGLICAN community of friars specializing in caring for destitute men.

**SOCINIANISM** Religious movement, dating from the sixteenth century, which interpreted Christianity along rationalistic lines. The doctrines of the TRINITY, Scripture, and the sacraments were so altered that the group was persecuted as heretical. Out of Socinianism came UNITARIANISM and liberal Protestant theology.

**SOCINUS, FAUSTUS (1539–1604)** Italian CATHOLIC who with his uncle Laelius Socinus (below) founded SOCINIANISM and a number of anti-Trinitarian groups.

**SOCINUS, LAELIUS (1525–1562)** An Italian originally known as Lelio Sozini or Sozzini. Repelled by the burning of SERVETUS, he became a founder of SOCINIANISM. His writings were often employed by his nephew Faustus Socinus (above) in establishing the new movement.

**SODALITY** CATHOLIC guild or CONFRATERNITY organized for religious purposes.

**SODERBLOM, NATHAN (1866–1931)** Archbishop of Upsala and Swedish theologian, religious historian, and ecumenical leader. A primate of the Lutheran Church of Sweden, he won the Nobel Peace Prize in 1930 and was active in the ecumenical Stockholm Conference of 1925. Author of several books, he wrote in *The Living God:* "I know that God lives; I can prove it through the history of religions." He defended RITSCHLIANISM, higher criticism, and liberal theology, and maintained that God's revelation is through history as well as through Scripture and church.

**SODOM** Wicked city destroyed in the time of Abraham and Lot, perhaps 1900 B.C. Evidence places its remains beneath the southern end of the Dead Sea, which inundated it after an earthquake.

**SODOMY** Unnatural sex relations, named from the practices in the city of SODOM.

**SOFER** *scribe* See SCRIBES.

**SOKA GAKKAI** "True Buddhism," one of the fastest-growing new religions in Japan. Its adherents chant the prayer, "I am the Supreme Power." Founded in 1930 by Tsunesaburo Makiguchi, it is fiercely evangelistic and intolerant.

**SOL** Roman sun god.

**SOLA FIDES** *faith alone* Term for the Protestant doctrine, derived principally from Luther, of JUSTIFICATION BY FAITH, stressing the love of God as the source of redemption. See SOLIFIDIANISM.

**SOLA GRATIA** *grace alone* Theological term for the exclusivity of the grace of God as the final cause of salvation. This is a PAULINE, AUGUSTINIAN, PROTESTANT emphasis.

**SOLA SCRIPTURA** *Scripture alone* Term for the concept that the Bible alone is the ultimate authority of faith and life.

**SOLDAN** Medieval term for the ruler of a MOSLEM country; sultan.

**SOLEMN** Performed with religious sanction or tradition.

**SOLEMN LEAGUE AND COVENANT** Agreement between England and Scotland in 1634 providing for the removal of "popery" from the CHURCH OF ENGLAND and the preservation of the CHURCH OF SCOTLAND along Protestant lines.

**SOLEMN MASS** High mass sung with the aid of deacon and subdeacon.

**SOLIFIDIANISM** Lutheran doctrine of justification by faith alone. LUTHER translated Romans 3:28, "A man is justified by faith alone." See SOLA FIDES.

**SOL INVICTUS** *invincible sun* Roman title for the sun god MITHRA.

**SOLOMON** *peaceable* Israel's third king, whose reign was characterized by peace and affluence. A son of David and Bathsheba, also called Jedidah ("loved by the Lord"), Solomon sought divine wisdom early in his reign and has been considered the author of such "Wisdom" writings as Proverbs and Ecclesiastes. He built the first temple in Jerusalem. In his old age he had many wives and concubines and tolerated heathen religions (I KINGS 1—11).

**SOLOMON, ODES OF** See ODES OF SOLOMON.

**SOLOMON, PSALMS OF** See PSALMS OF SOLOMON.

**SOLOMON, SONG OF** See SONG OF SONGS.

**SOLOMON, WISDOM OF** See WISDOM OF SOLOMON.

**SOLOMON BAR ISAAC (1040–1105)** Noted Jewish commentator also known as RASHI.

**SOLOVIEFF, VLADIMIR (1853–1900)** Russian poet, philosopher, and theologian. He urged the reunion of the Eastern and Western churches, had visions of SOPHIA (divine Wisdom), and predicted the imminent coming of ANTICHRIST in 1899. A devout MYSTIC, he influenced Russian intellectuals toward Christian faith.

**SOMA** 1. Greek term for the body. 2. Intoxicating drink of India. 3. HINDU god of the moon and stars.

**SONG OF DEGREES or ASCENTS** One of the Psalms sung on pilgrimages to Jerusalem: Psalms 120—134.

**SONG OF MOSES** Eloquent poetic work detailing the Lord's deliverance of the Hebrews (DEUTERONOMY 32:1–43).

**SONG OF OUR SYRIAN GUEST** Study of the Twenty-third Psalm by William Allen Knight, first published by Pilgrim Press in 1903.

**SONG OF SOLOMON** See SONG OF SONGS.

**SONG OF SONGS** The Song of Solomon, or Canticles, a group of poetic verses about a lover and his beloved. Attributed to SOLOMON from ancient times, the book exalts human love and has often been taken as a symbol of divine love for the people of God.

**SONG OF THE THREE CHILDREN** Apocryphal book of the Old Testament giving the prayer of AZARIAH as a portion of the narrative in Daniel of the youths thrown into a fiery furnace.

**SONGS OF ASCENT** See SONG OF DEGREES.

**SONS OF FREEDOM** Militant DOUKHOBORS who at times parade naked and burn buildings to protest such requirements of the Canadian government as compulsory education and service by conscientious objectors.

**SOPHER or SOPHERIM** See SCRIBES.

**SOPHIA** Greek word for WISDOM, worshiped by GNOSTICS and revered in various religious developments.

**SOPHISTS** Greek teachers who seemed to be more interested in persuasion than in wisdom, and more relativistic than truth-seeking.

**SOPHONIAS** Variant of ZEPHANIAH (see).

**SORROWS OF MARY** See SEVEN SORROWS OF MARY.

**SORTILEGE** WITCHCRAFT or DIVINATION.

**SOSIPATER** Relative of Paul who brought greetings to the Roman Christians (ROMANS 16:21).

**SOSTHENES** 1. Christian who sent greetings to the Corinthian brethren (I CORINTHIANS 1:1). 2. Synagogue leader beaten at Corinth when Paul was accused of blasphemy (ACTS 18:8, 12–17).

**SOTERIOLOGY** Theological term for the doctrine of SALVATION.

**SOTO** A division of Zen Buddhism. See ZEN.

**SOUBIROS, MARIE BERNARDE** See BERNADETTE of Lourdes.

**SOUL** Spiritual, immortal part of man. Although some theologians distinguish between soul and spirit (and the two words differ in the New Testament), the Bible tends to use the two terms interchangeably. We are to love God with all our heart and soul and might (DEUTERONOMY 6:5). When God breathed upon the first man, he became a living soul (GENESIS 2:7). Jesus taught that the soul is worth more than the whole visible world (MATTHEW 16:26).

**SOUTHCOTT, JOANNA (1750–1814)** Englishwoman who wrote voluminously, claiming to be a prophetess and the future mother of Christ announced in Revelation 12. She died before the expected Christchild could be born. A box alleged to contain her prophecies was opened in 1927 and only a lottery ticket was found therein. During her lifetime she had many disciples and undertook to seal 144,000 of them as the elect.

**SOUTHERN BAPTIST CONVENTION** Large group especially strong in the southern United States. In 1845 the Southern Baptists withdrew from the General Missionary Convention and ever since have increased in zeal and size. Their theological stance tends to be warmly conservative. There are congregations throughout the United States.

**SOUTHERN METHODIST CHURCH** American denomination consisting of members of the former Methodist Episcopal Church, South, which refused to merge with the Methodist Church, and of the former Methodist Protestant Church. Conservative theologically and otherwise, it holds that "holy writ teaches the separation of peoples."

**SOUTHERN PRESBYTERIAN CHURCH** Popular term for the PRESBYTERIAN CHURCH IN THE UNITED STATES.

**SOUTH INDIA, CHURCH OF** See CHURCH OF SOUTH INDIA.

**SOUTHWELL, ROBERT (c.1561–1595)** English CATHOLIC poet and martyr. A JESUIT, he was sent on a mission from Rome to England, tortured as a traitor and spy, and hanged. His verse is vivid and expresses deep Christian feeling.

**SOVEREIGNTY** Theological term for the supremacy and omnipotence of God.

**SOZOMEN (c.400–c.443)** Middle Eastern church historian, originally Salmaninius Hermias Sozomenus. Much of his historical writing was based on that of a contemporary historian, Socrates Scholasticus.

**SPALATIN, GEORG (1484–1545)** German reformer influenced by Martin LUTHER. He wrote a history of the Protestant Reformation, *Annales Reformationis.* He also translated works of the reformers.

**SPANGENBERG, AUGUST GOTTLIEB (1704–1792)** Prussian-born Moravian bishop. He led Moravian work in Europe and America and was an associate of Nicholas ZINZENDORF.

**SPARROW** Symbol of divine providence (cf. MATTHEW 10:29).

**S.P.C.K.** Abbreviation for the SOCIETY FOR PROMOTING CHRISTIAN KNOWLEDGE.

**SPEAKING IN TONGUES** See GLOSSOLALIA.

**SPEAR** Symbol of the CRUCIFIXION.

**SPECIAL INTENTION** Performance of a rite with a specific purpose, as of carrying out the original intention of the ceremony.

**SPELL** Formula, complex of activities, or incantation designed to produce magical power, as to bewitch someone.

**SPENER, PHILIPP JAKOB (1635–1705)** German LUTHERAN pietist. As a minister he held "schools of piety" for Bible study and Christian fellowship and sought to renew the spiritual life of the laymen. He became the founder of modern PIETISM in Germany and much of Europe.

**SPENTA ARMAITI** Spirit of beneficent devotion in ZOROASTRIANISM.

**SPENTA MAINYU** *holy spirit* ZOROASTRIAN title for the supreme being AHURA MAZDA.

**SPEYER, FIRST DIET OF** Conference in Speyer, Germany, in 1526 which granted each prince power to determine the religion of his area.

**SPEYER, SECOND DIET OF** Conference summoned by the German Charles V in 1529 at which CATHOLICS voted to end toleration of LUTHERANS. Thereupon a Protestant minority made a protest (*protestatio*) and thereafter those sympathizing with Luther's doctrines were called PROTESTANTS.

**SPIDER** Symbol of evil in Christian art.

**SPIKENARD** Aromatic perfume used to anoint Jesus' feet (JOHN 12:3).

**SPINOZA, BARUCH (1632–1677)** Dutch Jew whose philosophical ideas led to his condemnation by PROTESTANTS, CATHOLICS, and JEWS. He ground lenses for a living and developed a philosophy of a single universal substance he called God. All things are expressions of this one reality, he held, and man finds happiness in doing God's will—or obeying natural law—and loving God intellectually. Thus Spinoza is considered a pantheist and rationalist, although his ethical insights were profound. He advocated freedom of thought and state control of religion.

**SPINOZISM** Thought system of Spinoza, emphasizing the unity of all reality (perceived as thought and extension or mind and matter).

**SPIRE** Steeple or slender tower, as of a church.

**SPIRES, DIETS OF** See SPEYER, FIRST DIET OF; SPEYER, SECOND DIET OF.

**SPIRIT** 1. Life, as opposed to inanimate matter. 2. The human soul, or the intellectual and moral portion thereof. 3. Noncorporeal being, as an angel or a personality surviving death. 4. Purpose or real quality or meaning. 5. God. 6. The Holy Spirit.

**SPIRIT, HOLY** See HOLY SPIRIT.

**SPIRIT BAPTISM** See BAPTISM OF THE HOLY SPIRIT.

**SPIRITISM or SPIRITUALISM** 1. Belief in communication between living persons and entities of the spirit world, usually through the medium of "mediums." 2. Philosophy of idealism, or belief in spirit as the only reality.

**SPIRITUAL** 1. Of or relating to or characterized by spirit or God or faith or the highest reality. 2. Religious song of Negro origin. 3. FRANCISCAN friar believing in rigorous adherence to the original rule of St. FRANCIS. Cf. FRATICELLI.

**SPIRITUAL EXERCISES** Work by St. IGNATIUS LOYOLA, consisting of devotional meditations, the use of which is required for entrance into CATHOLIC orders.

**SPIRITUAL HEALING** Term for healing by or with faith, prayer, and the like. Interest in spiritual healing as a ministry of the church increased in the twentieth century. See also FAITH HEALING.

**SPIRITUALISM** See SPIRITISM.

**SPIRITUALISTS** Persons or members of religious organizations believing in SPIRITISM. American organizations of this type include the NATIONAL SPIRITUAL ALLIANCE OF THE U.S.A., the NATIONAL SPIRITUALIST ASSOCIATION OF CHURCHES, the INTERNATIONAL GENERAL ASSEMBLY OF SPIRITUALISTS, and the PROGRESSIVE SPIRITUAL CHURCH.

**SPIRITUAL WIVES** Women considered to be spiritual mates of men regardless of ordinary legal marital ties. Spiritual wives have been taken in various religious groups, often of the perfectionist variety.

**SPONGE** Symbol of the CRUCIFIXION (cf. MARK 15:36).

**SPONSOR** One who vouches for another at baptism or confirmation, as a godparent.

**SPRITE** Spirit, ghost, elf, or the like.

**SPURGEON, CHARLES HADDON (1834–1892)** Eloquent English BAPTIST preacher, long a pastor of London's Metropolitan Tabernacle. A conservative Calvinist, he wrote many books; his sermons have been sold widely throughout the world.

**SPY WEDNESDAY** Wednesday after PALM SUNDAY, named for Judas' betrayal of Jesus on that day.

**SQUARE** Symbol of the earth in religious motifs.

**SRADDHA** See SHRADDHA.

**SRAOSHA** ZOROASTRIAN spirit of truth and obedience.

**SRI** *good fortune* A name of Vishnu's mate, in HINDUISM.

**SRI VAISHNAVAS** See RAMANUJA.

**SRONG TSAN GAMPO (seventh century)** King of Tibet, converted to BUDDHISM by his two wives, who brought that faith officially into Tibet. He founded LHASA and translated many Buddhist writings into Tibetan.

**SRUTI** See SHRUTI.

**STABAT MATER** *the Mother was standing* Ancient Latin hymn based on Mary's sorrows during the PASSION. It is often used in HOLY WEEK and at the STATIONS OF THE CROSS.

**STABILITY** Monastic vow to remain with one's chosen monastery throughout life.

**STAFF** Symbol of religious pilgrimage, and of St. CHRISTOPHER, St. JEROME, and St. JOHN THE BAPTIST.

**STAG** Symbol of aspiration or hope, and of St. Eustace, St. HUBERT, St. RAPHAEL, and St. Julian the Hospitaler.

**STAINER, JOHN (1840–1901)** English organist and composer of such works as the oratorio *The Crucifixion* and the anthem "Lead, Kindly Light." He also composed a number of hymn tunes.

**STALL** Permanent seat for clergy in a church CHOIR or CHANCEL.

**STANLEY, ARTHUR PENRHYN (1815–1881)** ANGLICAN clergyman and BROAD CHURCH spokesman. He supported liberal causes, contributed to the knowledge of church history, and often found himself engaged in controversy. He wrote many books.

**STANLEY, HENRY MORTON (1841–1904)** English-American explorer who found David LIVINGSTONE in Africa in 1871.

**STAR** Symbol of divine guidance and care.

**STAR OF BETHLEHEM** The mysterious light which guided the "wise men from the east" to the infant Jesus (MATTHEW 2).

**STAR OF DAVID** Six-pointed star symbolizing Israel.

**STATED CLERK** Permanent officer with secretarial and other responsibilities in the PRESBYTERIAN CHURCH.

**STATION** 1. Older METHODIST term for a fixed pastorate. 2. Representation of the Passion (see STATIONS OF THE CROSS). 3. Stated CATHOLIC fast.

**STATIONS OF THE CROSS** Series of representations of the passion, death, and burial of Christ. There are fourteen of these, beginning with Christ's condemnation before Pilate and concluding with the placing of the body in the sepulcher. Usually stationed around the interior of a church,

they are used in CATHOLIC ceremonies in LENT.

**STAUFFER MENNONITE CHURCH** Small denomination founded by Jacob Stauffer in Pennsylvania in 1845. Doctrines are conservative, and, of course, MENNONITE; German is used in the services.

**STAUPITZ, JOHANN VON (?–1524)** German AUGUSTINIAN vicar-general who counseled and influenced Martin LUTHER in his spiritual pilgrimage toward the REFORMATION. Later, however, Staupitz stated Lutheranism to be heretical.

**STAVKIRKE** Uniquely structured medieval church buildings in central Europe. Their architecture somewhat suggests that of pagodas.

**S.T.D.** Abbreviation for the theological degree of Doctor of Sacred Theology. Some theological seminaries confer this degree upon their graduates.

**STEEPLE** Church tower.

**STEINER, RUDOLF (1861–1925)** German student of occultism and founder of ANTHROPOSOPHY, a "spiritual science."

**STEPHEN, POPE** Nine popes bear the name of Stephen. The first reigned in the third century and the ninth in the eleventh.

**STEPHEN, ST.** *crown* First martyr and one of the first seven deacons in the church. He was stoned to death after accusing the Jewish nation of turning against God and killing His Son, Jesus. His death apparently influenced the conversion of St. Paul (ACTS 6:5—8:2). Feast days honoring Stephen are August 3 and December 26. He has been called the patron saint of horses.

**STEVENS, ABEL (1815–1897)** American METHODIST minister, author, and historian.

**STEWARDSHIP** Ecclesiastical term for the devout investment of money, time, ability, etc., in worthy causes. In the Bible a steward was the supervisor of a household or estate. The children of God deem Him the source of all that they have, seek to hold it in trust for Him, and desire to be good stewards "of the grace of God" (I PETER 4:10).

**STHANAKAVASIS** JAINS who do not accept the worship of idols. Their founder was Lonka Sa; their origin, in the fifteenth century.

**STHIBEL** Yiddish term for a place of prayer.

**STIGMATA** *marks* Marks reminiscent of the five wounds of Christ, sometimes appearing on the bodies of devout persons. These marks, sometimes in the form of bleeding wounds, may be accompanied by paranormal manifestations. A number of stigmatics have been canonized.

**STIGMATIC** One who produces stigmata on his body.

**STIPEND** ANGLICAN term for offerings for or support of pastors and clergymen.

**STOCKHOLM CONFERENCE** World assembly of concerned Christian leaders in 1925 for consideration of world peace, economic justice, and similar issues. It met in Stockholm, Sweden, as the Universal Christian Conference on Life and Work.

**STOICISM** Greek philosophical school, founded by ZENO toward the end of the fourth century B.C., based on the ultimacy of nature and the necessity of living in harmony with natural law. The world is material, according to Stoicism, but it is pervaded by divine energy (fire, spirit, or Logos); man must subject his passions to reason and the laws of nature. Hence, the Stoic in popular thought lives above pain or pleasure. Famous Stoics were EPICTETUS and Seneca.

**STOLE** Long band worn around the neck in certain ecclesiastical rites and costumes. Stoles are commonly worn by deacons, priests, and bishops.

**STONE** Symbol of ultimate foundations, or of divine judgment.

**STONE, BARTON WARREN (1772–1844)** Kentucky preacher who helped form a religious group called simply Christians. Some of these became DISCIPLES OF CHRIST; others, members of the CHRISTIAN CHURCH.

**STOOL OF REPENTANCE** High stool on which grievous sinners had to sit, in ancient Presbyterian Scotland.

**STORCH, NICHOLAS** See ABECEDARIANS.

**STORK** Religious symbol of purity, prudence, piety, and Christ's Annunciation.

**STOUP** Vessel for holy water placed near the front of CATHOLIC and certain ANGLICAN churches.

**STRACHAN, JOHN (1778–1867)** ANGLICAN bishop and educator in Canada.

**STRACHAN, R. KENNETH (1910–1965)** General director of the Latin American Mission, an interdenominational evangelical missionary agency.

**STRANG, JAMES JESSE (1813–1856)** MORMON leader in Wisconsin and Michigan. He was excommunicated by the majority of Mormons, but acclaimed by many who crowned him king. Continually attacked by non-Mormons, he was finally assassinated.

**STRAUSS, DAVID FRIEDRICH (1808–1874)** German philosopher and theologian who denied the supernatural aspects of the life of Christ and finally became an evolutionary pantheist.

**STRAW DAY** British term for St. Stephen's Day.

**STREET, GEORGE EDMUND (1824–1881)** Architect of many English churches, specializing in Gothic forms.

**STREETER, BURNETT HILLMAN (1874–1937)** English New Testament scholar and theologian. He studied the sources of the four Gospels, emphasizing the priority of Mark, "Q," and "Proto-Luke." An active Christian, he was alert to various contemporary needs and movements.

**STRIBOG** Slavic god of winter.

**STRINDBERG, JOHAN AUGUST (1849–1912)** Powerful Swedish writer, converted late in life to Swedenborgianism. See CHURCHES OF THE NEW JERUSALEM.

**STRITCH, SAMUEL ALPHONSUS (1887–1958)** American CATHOLIC archbishop and cardinal. He administered Catholic mission work in various parts of the world, and helped organize the NATIONAL CATHOLIC WELFARE CONFERENCE.

**STRONG, AUGUSTUS HOPKINS (1836–1921)** BAPTIST theologian and educator in the United States, noted for his famous *Systematic Theology*.

**STRYPE, JOHN (1643–1737)** English historian of the REFORMATION and biographer of a number of churchmen.

**STUART, JANET ERSKINE (1857–1914)** English CATHOLIC writer and superior general of the Society of the Sacred Heart.

**STUDD, C. T. (1862–1931)** English missionary who helped inspire the Student Volunteer Movement. He served as a missionary in China, India, and Africa, and organized the World Evangelization Crusade.

**STUDDERT-KENNEDY, GEOFFREY ANKETELL (1883–1929)** Charismatic ANGLICAN clergyman and World War I chaplain (called

"Woodbine Willie" by the soldiers). He was a gifted poet and a champion of social righteousness.

**STUDENT CHRISTIAN MOVEMENT** World organization seeking fellowship among all Christian students and promoting world-wide missionary activity. It was organized in 1895 under the influence of John R. MOTT.

**STUDITES** See ACOEMETI.

**STUNDISTS** Russian Christians whose name derives from their giving of designated hours (*stunden*) for Bible study and prayer.

**STUPA or TOPE mound** BUDDHIST or JAIN shrine, often in the form of a mound.

**STYLITE** Hermit who lived on top of a pillar in the early centuries of the church. A famous stylite was SIMEON STYLITES, who is said to have lived for more than thirty years atop a pillar that was eventually at least sixty feet high.

**STYX** River surrounding the land of the dead, in Greek myth.

**SUAREZ, FRANCISCO (1548–1589)** Spanish JESUIT philosopher and theologian whose religious teachings held to a middle ground between THOMISM and MOLINISM. He held that the right of kings derives from the people, all of whom are equal before God. He has been called "The teacher of Europe, as also of the whole world."

**SUBDEACON** Church official whose rank is below that of DEACON.

**SUBDEAN** A kind of vice-dean in an ANGLICAN cathedral.

**SUBDIACONATE** Order of SUBDEACONS.

**SUBLAPSARIANISM** CALVINIST doctrine that God foresaw evil before He elected some to salvation.

**SUBMERSION** See IMMERSION.

**SUBORDINATIONISM** Theological tenet that the Son is subordinate to the Father, or the Holy Spirit subordinate to Father and Son. It was condemned by the Councils of NICAEA and CONSTANTINOPLE.

**SUBSTANCE** 1. In medieval theology, essence, or underlying reality or inmost nature. 2. In CHRISTIAN SCIENCE, Spirit.

**SUBSTITUTIONARY ATONEMENT** Concept of the death of Christ as a substitute for the death of sinners, so that those who believe in Him may have eternal life.

**SUCCAH** See SUKKAH.

**SUCCOTH** 1. City of Palestine (GENESIS 33:17). 2. Variant of SUKKOTH.

**SUCCOTH-BENOTH** Babylonian deity mentioned in II Kings 17:30.

**SUCCUBUS** Demon believed to tempt men in their sleep.

**SUCEAVA** Rumanian city noted for its churches and shrines.

**SUDDEN SCHOOL** School of ZEN Buddhism emphasizing the suddenness of spiritual perception and of enlightenment.

**SUDRA** Hindu or Indian of the lowest caste. Sudras do the most menial tasks.

**SUFFERING DAY** Term for GOOD FRIDAY.

**SUFFRAGAN** Subordinate or assistant.

**SUFFRAGAN BISHOP** BISHOP who assists a diocesan bishop. Also, a bishop under an ARCHBISHOP.

**SUFFRAGE** Supplicatory or intercessory prayer.

**SUFIS** Members of a mystic movement or order in ISLAM. Sufism is particularly strong in Persia, where it is conjoined with much symbolism.

**SUKHA** BUDDHIST term for joy.

**SUKHAVATI** BUDDHIST paradise.

**SUKKAH booth** Little leafy booth made for SUKKOTH (below) by Jewish families.

**SUKKOTH booths** See BOOTHS, FEAST OF.

**SULLIVAN, ARTHUR S. (1842–1900)** English composer noted for his "Onward, Christians Soldiers" and other hymns, anthems, and oratorios—as well as for his collaboration in the Gilbert and Sullivan operas.

**SULPICIANS** Religious congregation founded by Jean Jacques Olier in 1642 and noted for its interest in theological education.

**SULTAN** Moslem ruler or prince. See ISLAM.

**SUMER** Ancient land near the Persian Gulf from whose city Ur Abraham came. It had a high culture three thousand years B.C., and its epics of creation and the like antedate the writing of Genesis.

**SUMMA** Theological compendium, often used as a textbook in the Middle Ages.

**SUMMA CONTRA GENTILES** Work by St. THOMAS AQUINAS defending natural theology against Arabian attacks.

**SUMMANUS** Etruscan thunder god.

**SUMMA THEOLOGICA** A theological treatise, particularly the famous one by St. THOMAS AQUINAS expounding dogmatic theology. This treats theology in relation to God, man, Christ, and the church; it is one of the finest theological works in the history of the church and the outstanding one of the Middle Ages.

**SUMMUM BONUM** *highest good* The supreme value in ethics or theology, often defined as the BEATIFIC VISION.

**SUMPTUARY LAW** Civil law based on religious considerations.

**SUN** An object of worship in various religions, the sun is sometimes a symbol of Christ in religious art and thought.

**SUNDAR SINGH, SADHU (1889–c.1929)** Sikh-born native of India, converted to Christianity after seeing a vision of Jesus. After preaching to thousands and writing several books, he disappeared into Tibet in 1929. He dressed as a Sadhu or holy man to gain attention from his hearers; sometimes he is called "Apostle of the Bleeding Feet."

**SUNDAY** First day of the week, once identified with sun worship as the name evidences. The early Christians often met on the first day of the week, and under CONSTANTINE Sunday became the official Christian day of worship. The PURITANS first identified Sunday with the (Christian) SABBATH.

**SUNDAY, WILLIAM ASHLEY (1863–1935)** American baseball player whose evangelistic work as "Billy Sunday" sometimes produced sensational results.

**SUNDAY SCHOOL** School for religious instruction, often held on Sunday morning. The first Sunday schools were organized by Robert RAIKES late in the eighteenth century to educate poor children in England. During the next century Sunday schools blossomed throughout Protestantism, particularly in the United States. Today the Sunday school is often termed the church school.

**SUNG, JOHN (1902–1944)** First Chinese to be elected to Phi Beta Kappa, Greek-letter society in the United States. A dramatic preacher of bluff and uncompromising but powerful personality, Sung evangelized in Formosa, Indonesia, Malaya, Thailand, and the Philippines. By some he is considered the greatest Christian evangelist produced by China.

**SUNNA** *tradition* Moslem term for "the Way of the Prophet," the doctrine and practice of orthodox ISLAM. Also, the traditional or oral record of the sayings of MOHAMMED or of "the custom of the Community."

**SUNNITES** Members of the main group in ISLAM. Orthodox Moslems, the Sunnites hold strictly to the KORAN and accept the SUNNA as of equal authority. They hold that the first four khalifs were Mohammed's legitimate successors, in the proper order. (Shiite Moslems maintain that the fourth khalif ought to have been the first.) The four schools among which all Sunnites are divided are the rites of the HANAFITES, the HANBALITES, the MALIKITES, and the SHAFIITES.

**SUPAY** Inca god of the lower world.

**SUPEREGO** The conscience, according to psychoanalytic theory.

**SUPEREROGATION** In CATHOLIC theology, works of supererogation were those performed beyond the requirements of salvation; thus, such works produced merits which might be put to a common account in the church.

**SUPERINTENDENT** 1. Leader of a Sunday school or church school. 2. Official in charge of certain parishes in some denominations.

**SUPERIOR** Head of a religious order, or one ecclesiastically superior to others. The head of a convent is often known as a "mother superior."

**SUPERNAL** Heavenly.

**SUPERNATURAL** Beyond or above the natural; miraculous.

**SUPER-PERSONAL** Term applied by C. S. Lewis and others to the personal or TRINITARIAN nature of God.

**SUPERSTITION** Irrational belief or practice bordering on the supernatural or religious.

**SUPPER, THE LAST** See LAST SUPPER.

**SUPPLICATION** Earnest entreaty in prayer.

**SUPRALAPSARIANISM** Theological doctrine, held by some CALVINISTS, that God willed to elect some to salvation before He gave thought to the fall of man.

**SUPREME BEING** Common term for God.

**SURA** 1. Chapter of the KORAN. 2. Ancient HINDU word for an evil god.

**SURPLICE** White liturgical garment with wide sleeves, worn over the CASSOCK.

**SURSUM CORDA** *lift up your hearts* Response preceding the preface in the EUCHARIST or mass.

**SURT** Nordic fire god.

**SURYA** HINDU sun god.

**SUSANNA** Apocryphal book relating the attempts of two elders to seduce a noble Jewess, their subsequent attempts to have her falsely condemned, and her deliverance through the help of an eloquent champion named Daniel.

**SUSA-NO-O** Japanese SHINTO god of evil and storm.

**SUSO, HENRY (1295–1366)** German MYSTIC associated with Meister ECKHART, whom he defended, and Johannes TAULER. In 1831 Suso was beatified.

**SUS'SISTINNAKO** Creator-god of the Sia Indian tribe.

**SUT or SUTEKH or SET** 1. Ancient Semitic demon. 2. Ancient Egyptian god of darkness and evil.

**SUTRAS** Religious writings or sayings of BUDDHISM or HINDUISM.

**SUTTA or SUTRA** Dialogue or saying attributed to BUDDHA.

**SUTTAPITAKA** One of the three divisions of BUDDHIST scripture. See PITAKA.

**SUTTEE** Cremation of a HINDU widow on her husband's funeral pyre. This practice is now forbidden by law.

**SUWA** Arabian sun goddess.

**SVAROG** *heaven* Slavic term for heaven.

**SVETAMBARAS** Adherents of JAINISM who dress in white.

**SWALLOW** In Christian art of the Renaissance, a symbol of Christ's INCARNATION and RESURRECTION.

**SWARGA** Ancient HINDU term for heaven.

**SWASTIKA** Ancient religious symbol, often indicating good fortune, the sun, or the four quarters of the earth. In Nazi Germany it became an antireligious symbol.

**SWEDENBORG, EMANUEL (1688–1772)** Swedish scientist and philosopher whose mystical insight led to the birth of Swedenborgianism. He interpreted Scripture allegorically and had intense spiritual visions.

**SWEDENBORGIANS** Adherents of the teachings of Emanuel SWEDENBORG. See also CHURCHES OF THE NEW JERUSALEM.

**SWINE** Animals whose meat was considered unclean by many ancient religions, by the Mosaic law, and by MOSLEMS and ADVENTISTS.

**SWORD** Ecclesiastical symbol of Scripture, martyrdom, and such martyrs as Paul, Agnes, and Peter Martyr.

**SYLLABUS OF ERRORS** Eighty theses denounced as erroneous in the encyclical "Quanta Cura" issued by Pope PIUS IX in 1864. The errors are listed under headings including Modern Liberalism; Pantheism, Naturalism and Absolute Rationalism; and Socialism, Communism, secret societies, Bible societies and liberal-clerical societies.

**SYLVESTRINES** Monastic CATHOLIC order stressing poverty, founded by St. Sylvester Gozzolini in 1231.

**SYMBOL** 1. Creed. 2. Visible representation of a religious truth or reality. 3. A conventional sign, letter, or character used instead of an abbreviation to stand for a word, phrase, or title, especially for historical documents.

**SYMBOLICS** Theological study of Christian creeds.

**SYMBOLISM** Study and use of symbols in religion.

**SYMBOLIST** In Christian theology, one who regards the communion elements as merely symbolic, or one who advocates the use of symbols in worship.

**SYMEON** See SIMEON or SIMON.

**SYNAGOGUE** Jewish assembly for worship, or worship center. Existing since the Babylonian exile in the sixth century B.C., the synagogue has long been the Jewish community's social and religious focus.

**SYNCRETISM** Fusion of different philosophies or religions.

**SYNCRETISTIC CONTROVERSY** Seventeenth-century debate over the proposal of Georg CALIXTUS that the REFORMED and LUTHERAN churches be reconciled with each other and with the CATHOLIC CHURCH.

**SYNERGISM** Doctrine of MELANCHTHON and others that God and man cooperate in the work of regeneration.

**SYNOD** 1. Church council such as the Synod of DORT. 2. In several communions, representative body of a diocese or province. 3. In PRESBYTERIANISM, an ecclesiastical gathering midway between PRESBYTERY and GENERAL ASSEMBLY.

**SYNOD OF ARLES** See ARLES, SYNOD OF.

**SYNOD OF BETHLEHEM**   See JERUSALEM, SYNOD OF.

**SYNOD OF DORT**   See DORT, SYNOD OF.

**SYNOD OF EVANGELICAL LUTHERAN CHURCHES**   Denomination established in Pennsylvania in 1902, sympathetic to the program of the LUTHERAN CHURCH—MISSOURI SYNOD.

**SYNOD OF JERUSALEM**   See JERUSALEM, SYNOD OF.

**SYNOPTIC GOSPELS**   Term for the Gospels of Matthew, Mark, and Luke, which are similar in many respects.

**SYNOPTIC PROBLEM**   Question of the origin, chronology, and various differences, similarities, and relationships of the three Gospels of Matthew, Mark, and Luke.

**SYRACUSE**   Important Greek city of Sicily containing a temple of APOLLO and a temple of ATHENA.

**SYRIA**   Country north of Israel which often figured in ancient Jewish history, although the name of Syria as such never appears in the Hebrew Scriptures. The land came under early Christian influence.

Today the majority of the people are MOSLEMS.

**SYRIAN ANTIOCHIAN ORTHODOX CHURCH**   American denomination consisting of members of EASTERN ORTHODOX churches of Syria and other nearby countries who emigrated to the United States.

**SYRIAN CATHOLICS**   Christians of Syria descended from the Syrian Jacobites or MONOPHYSITES.

**SYRIAN JACOBITE CHURCH**   See JACOBITES.

**SYRIAN ORTHODOX CHURCH OF ANTIOCH**   EASTERN ORTHODOX diocese with headquarters in Hackensack, New Jersey.

**SYSTEMATIC THEOLOGY**   Study of God and His relationships to man and the universe. Standard classical divisions are revelation, God, man, sin, Christ, salvation, the church, and eschatology.

**SZOLD, HENRIETTA (1860–1945)**   American Jewish leader and editor. She founded HADASSAH, translated a number of Jewish works into English, and did social work among many in need.

# T

**T** Letter sometimes imbued with mystic significance because of its resemblance to a cross, sometimes regarded as a symbol of God because of the Greek word for God *Theos*.

**TAANIT** Jewish word for a fast or fast day.

**TABB, JOHN BANISTER (1845–1909)** American CATHOLIC poet, teacher, and priest. Though the poet was blind, his poems often suggest the presence of God in nature.

**TABERNACLE** *tent* 1. Worship center enshrined in a tent by the Israelites before they built the temple. The Book of Exodus details the structure of this "tent of meeting" above which appeared a pillar of cloud indicating the presence of God. 2. Receptacle in CATHOLIC churches for the RESERVED SACRAMENT.

**TABERNACLES, FEAST OF** See BOOTHS, FEAST OF.

**TABLE, THE LORD'S** PROTESTANT term for the LORD'S SUPPER or for the table from which it is served.

**TABLES OF THE LAW** Stone tablets on which the Ten Commandments were originally engraved (see DECALOGUE).

**TABOO** Set apart or forbidden, often in connection with religious custom or worship.

**TABORITES** Extreme group of HUSSITES in the fifteenth century. Their name originates in Bohemia's city Tabor where John HUSS once preached.

**TAGORE, RABINDRANATH (1861–1941)** Educator and writer of India whose mystical beliefs were expressed in his essays, poems, dramas, fiction, and other works.

**TAI** Chinese mountain long honored in TAOISM and BUDDHISM.

**TAISHA** Japanese town noted for its BUDDHIST and SHINTO shrines.

**TAIZE** French religious community of PROTESTANTS with ecumenical sympathies.

**TAKEMIKADZUCHI** Japanese storm god.

**TALAPOIN** BUDDHIST monk.

**TALISMAN** Amulet, charm, or figure used in superstitious observance.

**TALITHA CUMI** *little girl, get up* Jesus' words to a stricken child in Mark 5:41. They were in ARAMAIC.

**TALLITH** 1. Jewish prayer shawl with fringed corners. It is worn by Jewish males at morning synagogue services and on the Day of ATONEMENT. 2. Orthodox Jewish undergarment.

**TALMUD** *instruction* Body of Jewish literature containing the MISHNAH (text) and GEMARA (commentary)—although sometimes the Talmud indicates the Gemara only. The principal version is the Babylonian Talmud; an important early version was the Jerusalem Talmud.

**TALMUD TORAH** Jewish elementary school.

**TAMARISK** Palestinian shrub with many religious associations (cf. GENESIS 21:33; I SAMUEL 22:6).

**TAMMUZ** 1. Babylonian nature god. 2. Tenth month in the Jewish civil year.

**TANG** Chinese dynasty during which BUDDHISM flourished, 618–907.

**TANGALOA** Polynesian sky god.

**TANIT** Sky goddess of ancient Carthage.

**TANNAIM** *teachers* Rabbinical scholars who contributed to the MISHNAH. They flourished in the first two centuries A.D.

**TANTALUS** Greek god condemned to endless torture for his misdeeds.

**TANTRAS** Religious writings of the SAKTAS of India who worship the male-female relationships or powers of their deities.

**TANTRISM** Erotic HINDU and BUDDHIST movement originating about the sixth century in India.

**TAO** *order or way* Chinese term for the ultimate principles governing the universe. In BUDDHISM *Tao* has several special meanings.

**TAOISM** Philosophy and religion whose origin is attributed to LAO-TZE in the fifth century B.C. Some date his book *Tao-teh-ching* which outlines the basic principles of Taoism in the third century B.C. It advocates submission to the laws of the universe, humility, patience, temperance, submissiveness to those in authority, kindliness, beneficence, and religious devotion. Eventually Taoism incorporated into itself the worship of a number of gods and certain features of BUDDHISM. Today there are probably fifty million Taoists in the world.

**TAO-SHENG (?–434)** Chinese BUDDHIST who held that anyone might reach Buddhahood.

**TAO-TEH-CHING** Basic Scripture of TAOISM, traditionally attributed to LAO-TZE in the fifth century B.C.

**TAPAS** *heat or fervor* Sufferings and austerities important in HINDUISM but renounced by Gautama BUDDHA in his quest for enlightenment.

**TARAHUMARA INDIANS** Mexican Indians whose religion involves the use of PEYOTE.

**TARGUM** *translation* Paraphrase of the Jewish Scriptures in ARAMAIC. Beginning with the oral translations or paraphrases that became necessary during the public reading of Scripture in the BABYLONIAN CAPTIVITY, the targums were eventually put into writing.

**TARSHISH** Old Testament name for a city or country distant from Palestine, perhaps Spain or one of its cities, or for ships that plied the Mediterranean in pre-Christian times.

**TARSUS** City of Asia Minor where St. PAUL was born. It was also the site of a STOIC school; eventually it became the see of a number of successive bishops.

**TARTARUS** Greek place of punishment for the wicked dead.

**TASHI LAMA** See PANCHEN LAMA.

**TASHI LUMPO** Tibetan monastery where the PANCHEN LAMA dwells.

**TASHLICH** Jewish rite of symbolically washing away sins by casting them into living water on ROSH HASHANAH. (Cf. MICAH 7:18–20.)

**TATIAN (second century)** Syrian Christian apologist who became a GNOSTIC, founding the ENCRATITE sect.

**TATUMEN** Creator in Egyptian religion.

**TAU** Twenty-second letter of the Hebrew alphabet.

**TAUERET** Egyptian goddess of childbirth.

**TAUHID** 1. Term in ISLAM for the divine oneness. 2. SUFI term for the unity of life, both human and divine.

**TAULER, JOHANNES (c.1300–1361)** German DOMINICAN who became acquainted with Henry SUSO and Meister ECKHART and through their influence became an important MYSTIC. An eloquent preacher, he exhorted men to commit themselves completely to God and stressed the presence of the Spirit within the soul.

**TAUROBOLIUM** Baptism by blood in the MYSTERY RELIGIONS.

**TAWHIRI** Polynesian storm god.

**TAYLOR, JAMES HUDSON (1832–1905)** American medical missionary to China and founder of the CHINA INLAND MISSION.

**TAYLOR, JEREMY (1613–1667)** ANGLICAN theologian, bishop, and writer. Author of *The Rule and Exercise of Holy Living, The Rule and Exercise of Holy Dying, The Great Exemplar,* and other important devotional works, he was known as "the glory of the English pulpit."

**TAYLOR, JOHN (1808–1887)** British-born American leader of the CHURCH OF JESUS CHRIST OF LATTER-DAY SAINTS. In 1880 he became its president.

**TEACHER OF RIGHTEOUSNESS** Obscure figure mentioned in the DEAD SEA SCROLLS, to some minds prefiguring Jesus.

**TEACHING OF THE TWELVE APOSTLES** See DIDACHE.

**TEBET** Fourth month of the Jewish civil year.

**TE DEUM** *Thee, O God* Latin hymn beginning "We praise Thee, O God." It has often been ascribed to St. AMBROSE or St. AUGUSTINE, but may well be the work of St. Niceta in the fourth century.

**TEFILLAH** See SHEMONEH ESREH.

**TEFILLIN** *phylacteries* See PHYLACTERIES.

**TEH** Practical aspect of TAOISM.

**TE IGITUR** *Thee, therefore* Opening words of the canon of the MASS.

**TEILHARD DE CHARDIN, PIERRE (1882–1955)** French philosopher and paleontologist, member of the SOCIETY OF JESUS, who wrote *The Divine Milieu, The Phenomenon of Man,* and other works. He expounded a mystical interpretation of theistic evolution in which man ascends toward God.

**TEKOA** Desert and town south of Bethlehem whence the prophet AMOS came.

**TEL-EL-AMARNA** Ancient Egyptian city at whose site more than 350 "Tel-el-Amarna" tablets have been found. These vividly portray conditions in Palestine about 1400 B.C., naming Jerusalem, Tyre, and other cities there. They also mention the Habiru —quite possibly the Hebrews.

**TELEOLOGICAL ARGUMENT** Classical attempt to prove the existence of God on the grounds that natural processes are directed toward a preordained purpose, evidencing a wise Creator.

**TELEPATHY** Term for instant thought transference, posited by some to explain SPIRITIST and other similar phenomena.

**TELL** Mound caused by rise and fall of successive cities, affording rich archaeological evidence. Tells in the HOLY LAND provide considerable knowledge of Semitic religion and Old Testament events.

**TELL-EL-AMARNA** See TEL-EL-AMARNA.

**TELLUS** Roman fertility goddess.

**TEMPE, VALE OF** Valley near Mount Olympus sacred to APOLLO.

**TEMPERANCE** Cardinal virtue in CATHOLIC morality. "Temperance" in the New Testament is better translated "self-control."

**TEMPERANCE MOVEMENT** Nineteenth-century movement, backed by many churches, which advocated total abstinence from and prohibition of alcoholic beverages.

**TEMPLARS** Knight Templars, Knights of the Temple of Solomon, or Poor Knights of Christ. Initially a military order, founded by Godfrey of Bouillon about 1118, the Templars became a Catholic religious order. It was dissolved early in the fourteenth century.

**TEMPLE** Place of worship. The outstanding temple in history is that built by King Solomon in Jerusalem, twice rebuilt and finally razed in the destruction of the city in 70 A.D.

**TEMPLE, WILLIAM (1881–1944)** ANGLICAN clergyman who became Archbishop of York and of Canterbury. A friend of labor, he helped found the WORLD COUNCIL OF CHURCHES.

**TEMPLE EMANU-EL** Jewish synagogue in New York City whose REFORMED Jewish congregation is the United States' oldest.

**TEMPORALITIES** Property held by British clergy.

**TEMPORAL POWER** Theological term for the realm of government as opposed to that of the church or of God.

**TEMPTATION** Testing, or enticement to sin. According to Scripture, God tests the believer while Satan tempts him.

**TEMPTER** Term for Satan or the devil.

**TEN** Symbol of completeness and of the Ten Commandments (see DECALOGUE).

**TENACH** Jewish term for the Law, the Prophets, and the Writings constituting the Scriptures. *Tenach* is actually an acrostic based on the initial Hebrew letters of these three groups of writings.

**TEN ARTICLES** See ARTICLES, TEN.

**TEN COMMANDMENTS** See DECALOGUE.

**TENDAI** School of BUDDHISM founded in the sixth century and put substantially in its present form by Saicho or Dengyo Daishi early in the ninth century. It seeks to provide a philosophical basis for the unity of all reality in the teachings of Gautama BUDDHA.

**TENEBRAE** *darkness* CATHOLIC service for Wednesday, Thursday, and Friday of HOLY WEEK during which fourteen candles are extinguished one by one. The darkness indicates the death and burial of Christ.

**TENNENT, GILBERT (1703–1764)** PRESBYTERIAN minister of the United States who took a leading part in the GREAT AWAKENING of the eighteenth century and in the NEW SIDE movement in his denomination.

**TENNYSON, ALFRED (1809–1892)** English poet whose work expressed both religious doubts and yearnings for faith, and convictions about God, immortality, and a supreme moral order.

**TENRI KYO** Japanese school of SHINTO which expresses confidence that elimination of negative attitudes brings peace of mind, success, and longevity.

**TENT OF MEETING** Term for the ancient Jewish TABERNACLE.

**TEN TRIBES** The ten northern tribes of Israel—REUBEN, ISSACHAR, ZEBULUN, GAD, ASHER, DAN, NAPHTALI, EPHRAIM, MANASSEH, and part of the tribe of BENJAMIN —which separated from the two southern tribes of JUDAH and a portion of Benjamin following the reign of Solomon.

**TEOCALLI** Ancient pyramid-shaped Mexican temples.

**TERAH moon** Abraham's father (GENESIS 11:24).

**TERAPHIM wicked things** Jewish household gods or idols, probably used for oracular purposes (GENESIS 31:19, 30).

**TERCE or TIERCE** Third hour in the CATHOLIC Divine Office, recited about nine A.M.

**TERESA** See THERESA.

**TERMA revelations** Esoteric Tibetan BUDDHIST Scriptures.

**TERMAGANT** Idol in ancient Christian morality plays supposed to represent an ISLAMIC deity.

**TERMINUS** Roman god of boundary lines.

**TERRITORIALISM** Doctrine that the ruler of a territory should determine the faith of the people.

**TERSTEEGEN, GERHARD (1697–1769)** German REFORMED mystic, poet, and hymn writer. He gave his money to the poor and translated books by Madame GUYON, LABADIE, and other QUIETIST writers.

**TERTIARY** Member of a "third" order—usually, a layman connected with a CATHOLIC order. Though not bound by vow, tertiaries observe the rules of their order.

**TERTULLIAN (c.160–c.220)** Roman apologist for Christianity and first theologian to write in Latin. Known as the father of ecclesiastical Latin, he originated the statement "The blood of the martyrs is the seed of the church." He finally became a MONTANIST.

**TESHUB** Hittite storm god.

**TESTAMENT** 1. Greek word (*diatheke*) for covenant (HEBREWS 9:1, 4). Term for a division of the Bible. The Hebrew Scriptures are known as the OLD TESTAMENT, the Christian writings as the NEW TESTAMENT.

**TESTAMENTS OF THE TWELVE PATRIARCHS** Spurious work purporting to give deathbed messages from the twelve sons of Jacob to their descendants. Probably it originated in the second century B.C.

**TESTIMONY** 1. Divine law (EXODUS 25:16). 2. Scripture. 3. Personal witness to what the Lord has done.

**TETH** Ninth letter of the Hebrew alphabet.

**TETRAGRAMMATON** The four letters of the Hebrew word YHWH or JHVH, commonly translated as the Lord, JEHOVAH, or YAHWEH. Because of its sacred character it was rarely pronounced.

**TETRAPOLITAN CONFESSION** Sixteenth-century REFORMED confession of faith based on the AUGSBURG CONFESSION. It sought to maintain PROTESTANT unity in Germany.

**TETZEL, JOHANN (c.1465–1519)** German DOMINICAN friar who debated INDULGENCES with Martin LUTHER. Tetzel promised his hearers that money for an indulgence would release a soul from the torment of PURGATORY—contrary to the approved teaching of CATHOLICISM.

**TEUTATES** Ancient Gallic war god.

**TEUTONIC KNIGHTS** German religious order formed about 1190 to help fight in the third CRUSADE, and to aid the ill and wounded. Today it is a strictly religious, educational, and humanitarian order.

**TEVETH** See TEBET.

**TEXT** 1. Original form of a writing, as of Scripture. 2. Particular form of such a writing, as the MASORETIC TEXT of the OLD TESTAMENT. 3. Portion of Scripture from which a sermon is drawn.

**TEXTUAL CRITICISM** Study of a writing in the attempt to recover its original form. (Cf. BIBLICAL CRITICISM; HIGHER CRITICISM; LOWER CRITICISM.)

**TEZCATLIPOCA** Supreme Aztec god.

**THADDAEUS** One of Jesus' Twelve Apostles, apparently identical with Lebbaeus or Judas son of James (MATTHEW 10:3; MARK 3:18; LUKE 6:16; ACTS 1:13).

**THAGS or THUGS** Members of a secret religious order of India who secretly strangled certain individuals in honor of DURGA, KALI, or Kevi until suppressed by the British about 1830.

**THALNA** Etruscan mother-goddess.

**THAMMUZ** See TAMMUZ.

**THANKA** Paintings of Tibetan deities.

**THANKSGIVING** Offering of gratitude to God for His gifts and blessings.

**THANKSGIVING DAY** Holiday in the United States commemorating the time in 1621 when the Pilgrims of the Plymouth Colony proclaimed such a day, in gratitude to God for an abundant harvest. It is observed the fourth Thursday in November.

**THARGELIA** Greek sacrifice in honor of Apollo.

**THARSHISH** See TARSHISH.

**TH.D.** Abbreviation for the degree of Doctor of Theology, granted those completing advanced study in a special theological area.

**THEANTHROPISM** 1. Term for anthropomorphism—attributing human characteristics to God. 2. Theological term for the union of two natures—those of God and man—in Jesus Christ.

**THEARCHY** Government by God, or in the name of deity.

**THEATINES** CATHOLIC monastic order founded by St. CAJETAN and John Peter Caraffa in 1524 for the purpose of ecclesiastical reform. Although important in the COUNTER REFORMATION, the order never spread very far geographically.

**THEBAID** "Cradle of Christian monasticism" in the upper part of the valley of the Nile. In this district around Thebes, many monks worshiped God in solitude.

**THEISM** Belief in God, or in gods. Sometimes theism is used synonymously with MONOTHEISM of the Judeo-Christian tradition.

**THEMIS** Greek goddess of justice.

**THEOCRACY** Government by or in the name of God.

**THEODICY** Theological term for a formal attempt to justify God's temporary toleration of evil.

**THEODORE OF MOPSUESTIA (c.350–428)** Syrian exegete, bishop, and theologian. He preferred the historical rather than the allegorical interpretation of Scripture. Although considered orthodox in his lifetime, he was condemned at the Councils of EPHESUS and CONSTANTINOPLE.

**THEODORET (c.393–c.458)** Syrian theologian and biographer whose views were less extreme than those of his teacher THEODORE OF MOPSUESTIA.

**THEOLOGIA GERMANICA** Anonymous fourteenth-century work commending complete commitment to God and His love.

**THEOLOGICAL SEMINARY** School for clergymen, usually on the postcollegiate level.

**THEOLOGICAL VIRTUES** Faith, hope, and love.

**THEOLOGY** Study of God or religion.

**THEOPASCHITES** Early Christians who believed that God suffered during Jesus' crucifixion. To orthodox theology, such belief was heretical.

**THEOPATHY** Mystical feeling or ecstasy in relation to experiencing the presence of the divine.

**THEOPHANY** Manifestation of God.

**THEOPHILUS** Unknown person, probably a Roman official, addressed in the superscriptions of the Gospel of Luke and the Acts of the Apostles.

**THEOSOPHY** 1. Intuitive knowledge of God. 2. Religious movement founded by Madame Helena Petrovna BLAVATSKY in 1875. Such principles in it as REINCARNATION and PANTHEISM seem primarily HINDU and BUDDHIST. It encourages human brotherhood and religious study.

**THEOTOKOS God-bearer** EASTERN ORTHODOX term for MARY as Mother of God.

**THERAPEUTAE** Recluses in first-century Egypt who held that salvation is achieved through mystical knowledge of God.

**THERAVADA** See HINAYANA.

**THERESA OF AVILA, ST. (1515–1582)** Spanish CARMELITE nun and mystic who had many supernatural visions and founded the sisterhood of Discalced Carmelites in 1562. She wrote *The Way of Perfection* and other important mystical works.

**THERESA OF LISIEUX, ST. (1873–1897)** French CARMELITE nun and mystic also known as "Theresa of the Child Jesus" and "The Little Flower of Jesus." Many miracles were attributed to her. Her early death was caused by tuberculosis.

**THERIOLATRY** Ancient worship of animals.

**THESES OF MARTIN LUTHER** See NINETY-FIVE THESES OF LUTHER.

**THESMOPHORIA** Greek fertility rite performed each fall.

**THESSALONIANS, I AND II** Epistles of St. Paul to the Christians of Thessalonica or Salonika in Macedonia. They emphasize salvation and the return of Christ.

**THEURGY** Art or science of manipulating a supernatural power through certain rites or deeds.

**THIRD ORDER** Lay order. (Cf. TERTIARY.)

**THIRTEEN** Symbol of betrayal and bad luck.

**THIRTEEN ARTICLES OF FAITH** 1. Statements formulated by Moses MAIMONIDES in the twelfth century, sometimes considered "the nearest approach to a Jewish

Creed" (Hugh Schonfield). 2. ANGLICAN statement. See ARTICLES, THIRTEEN.

**THIRTY-NINE ARTICLES** See ARTICLES, THIRTY-NINE.

**THISTLE** In religious art, symbol of sorrow and of Christ's sufferings.

**THOLUCK, FRIEDRICH A. G. (1799–1877)** German PROTESTANT minister and mediating theologian. His personal piety was accompanied by a somewhat rationalistic view of Scripture.

**THOMAS, ST.** Apostle also called Didymus ("The Twin"). The Gospel of John records his doubts of Jesus' resurrection (20:24–29; 21:2). He was also a man of loyalty and courage (JOHN 11:8, 16). According to tradition he became a missionary to India or Parthia. His feast day is December 21.

**THOMAS À BECKET, ST. (c.1118–1170)** Archbishop of Canterbury who, although previous to his induction a friend of King Henry II, became a staunchly independent and capable church leader. For a time he fled to France. Reconciled with Henry, he returned in 1170 but was murdered that year in Canterbury cathedral by a band of supporters of the king. Thomas became a very popular saint. His feast day is that of his death: December 29.

**THOMAS À KEMPIS (c.1380–1471)** German monk and mystic. Educated in the Netherlands by the BRETHREN OF THE COMMON LIFE, he became an AUGUSTINIAN priest. *The Imitation of Christ* is usually attributed to him.

**THOMAS AQUINAS, ST. (c.1225–1274)** Italian theologian and philosopher and outstanding SCHOLASTIC. Often called the "Angelic Doctor," he produced a profound analysis of Christian theology in his brilliant *Summa Theologica*. Another outstanding work was his *Summa contra Gentiles*. Upon the logical foundations of ARISTOTLE he built a Christian interpretation of nature, law, ethics, and revelation.

**THOMAS CHRISTIANS** Christians of South India who trace their origin to the missionary visit of the Apostle THOMAS. Their tradition is JACOBITE.

**THOMISM** Theology of St. THOMAS AQUINAS, viewed as a system of thought.

**THOMPSON, FRANCIS (1859–1907)** English CATHOLIC poet noted for the poem "The Hound of Heaven" and other works. He was a friend of Wilfrid and Alice MEYNELL.

**THOR** Scandinavian storm god.

**THORN** Religious symbol of grief and trouble.

**THORVALDSEN, ALBERT BERTEL (1770–1844)** Danish sculptor of Christ and the Apostles, and other religious subjects.

**THOTH or HERMES** Egyptian god of wisdom, magic, and the arts.

**THREE** Religious symbol of the TRINITY, of deity, and of the three days of Jesus' death.

**THREE GEMS** 1. JAIN basis of salvation: right knowledge, right conception, and right conduct. 2. The BUDDHA, the DHAMMA, and the SANGHA in BUDDHISM.

**THREE HOLY CHILDREN** Shadrach, Meshach, and Abednego, Daniel's compatriots thrown into a furnace for refusing to put the emperor above their God. *The Song of the Three Children* is an apocryphal addition to the book of Daniel relating the song these three youths sang after their rescue.

**THREE HOURS** The three hours Christ hung on the cross—from noon until three o'clock on Good Friday—or a three-hour GOOD FRIDAY service commemorating that event.

**THREE KINGS** The "wise men from the east" who came to adore the infant Jesus. Scripture does not give the wise men's number. See MAGI.

**THUGS** See THAGS.

**THUMMIM** See URIM AND THUMMIM.

**THUNAR** Ancient Anglo-Saxon storm god.

**THUNDER, SONS OF** Name for the Apostles St. James and St. John (MARK 3:17). Perhaps their temperament was reminiscent of thunder and storm (LUKE 9:52–56).

**THURIBLE** Metal censer for the burning of incense in certain ecclesiastical ceremonies.

**THURIFER** Carrier of the THURIBLE in a service.

**THYATIRA** Town in Asia Minor with a Jewish colony and a church. To the latter Christ addressed a letter (REVELATION 2).

**TIAMAT** Babylonian dragon which produced chaos before succumbing to MAR-

DUK, in an ancient epic of creation. From Tiamat's body the world was then made.

**TIARA** Triple papal crown symbolizing the pope's authority over three realms: purgatory, the spiritual world, and the temporal scene.

**TIBERIAS** 1. Town on the Sea of Galilee long known for its Jewish settlement. There MAIMONIDES was buried. 2. Another name for the Sea of Galilee.

**TIBERIUS** The Roman emperor designated as Caesar in the four GOSPELS. Although disliked by many Romans for his economy in government, he produced a generally excellent administration.

**TIEN** Chinese term for heaven or the infinite.

**TIERCE** See TERCE.

**T'IET-T'AI** Chinese BUDDHIST school corresponding to the Japanese school called TENDAI.

**TILLICH, PAUL JOHANNES (1886–1965)** German-born theologian and philosopher who profoundly influenced contemporary religious thought. A LUTHERAN, he left Germany in 1933 after futilely protesting Hitler's actions. The rest of his life was spent teaching at Union Theological Seminary in New York and at Harvard University. Tillich held God to be the Ground of all being and faith to be "ultimate concern." He saw religion as "the state of being concerned about one's own being and being universally."

**TIMOTHEUS** See TIMOTHY.

**TIMOTHY** *God-honorer* Youth of Jewish-Gentile descent who mightily aided the Apostle Paul in his work. Paul called him his "fellow laborer" and "beloved son." Timothy went with Paul on his second missionary journey and led the Ephesus church. There, according to tradition, he was bishop and was stoned to death. His feast day is January 24.

**TIMOTHY, I AND II** Two New Testament epistles from St. PAUL to St. TIMOTHY. The Book of I Timothy emphasizes such aspects of church life as prayer and duties of members and clergy; II Timothy forecasts future apostasy and suffering, counseling faithfulness to Christ.

**TINA** Etruscan god of lightning and fire.

**TINDAL, WILLIAM** See TYNDALE, WILLIAM.

**TINTORETTO (1518–1594)** Gifted Italian painter of "The Last Judgment," "The Last Supper," "The Crucifixion," "Paradise," "The Miracle of the Loaves and Fishes," and many other works.

**TIPITAKA** Pali term for the Three Baskets of the Law, the Pali canon of BUDDHIST Scripture.

**TIPPET** Long broad black scarf worn by ANGLICAN clergymen in choir.

**TIRAWA** See ATIUS-TIRAWA.

**TIRTHANKARA** A great JAINIST saint or holy man.

**TISCHENDORF, CONSTANTIN VON (1815–1874)** German NEW TESTAMENT critic who discovered the CODEX SINAITICUS, one of the oldest complete manuscripts of the Bible in Greek, at Mt. Sinai in 1844. His work on the Greek text of the New Testament is of lasting value.

**TISHA B'AB** Ninth day of Ab, Jewish fast day commemorating the destruction of the temple.

**TISHAH B'AV** See TISHA B'AB.

**TISHBITE** Term identifying the prophet ELIJAH as a native of Tishbe (I KINGS 17:1).

**TISHRI** First month in the Jewish civil calendar (cf. NISAN). The New Year celebration of ROSH HASHANAH occurs on the first day.

**TITAN** 1. Primeval Greek deity. 2. Latin name for the Greek sun god Helios.

**TITANESS** Primeval Greek goddess.

**TITHE** *tenth* Old English term for a tenth. The Israelites set aside tithes of their produce or possessions for God. Other ancient peoples gave tithes to their rulers. In the Middle Ages tithes were customarily collected for the church. Today many Christians tithe on a voluntary basis, giving their tithes to their churches or to what they deem the Lord's work.

**TITIAN (c.1490–1576)** Venetian painter whose "Pieta," "Pesaro Altarpiece," "Christ Crowned with Thorns," "Madonna of the Cherries," "Assumption of the Virgin," and other works show his talented handling of religious themes.

**TITLE** 1. Parish or church headed by a CARDINAL. 2. Ecclesiastical position with maintenance of the clergyman guaranteed. 3. Ecclesiastical or other appellation of rank or office.

**TITULAR** 1. Relating to a title. 2. Holding a title from a parish or the like which is no longer active. 3. Person holding such a title. 4. Honorary. 5. Patron saint.

**TITUS** First-century friend and associate of the Apostle PAUL. A Greek convert, he took charge of the church of Crete and according to tradition was its bishop. Paul's Epistle to Titus is one of the Apostle's many letters; it outlines the qualifications of elders and the behavior to be expected from Christians.

**TIW, TIU, or TYR** Scandinavian god of war and sports.

**TLALOC** Aztec god of rain.

**TLAZOLTEOTL** Aztec earth goddess.

**TLOQUE NAHUAQUE** Aztec creator-god.

**TOBIAS** 1. Variant of TOBIT (see). 2. A son of TOBIT.

**TOBIT** Righteous Jew whose son Tobias frustrated the demon Asmodeus by use of a powerful incense. The book of Tobias is an apocryphal book of the Old Testament, probably dating from the second century B.C.

**TODAH** Jewish term for a thank offering.

**TODAIJI** BUDDHIST temple at Nara, Japan, containing an immense statue of Buddha.

**TOHI** Quiche Indian fire god.

**TOKENS, COMMUNION** Metal or cardboard objects issued to those in good standing in certain Scottish PRESBYTERIAN churches before admission is given to the LORD'S SUPPER.

**TOLERATION** Permission for the propagation and practice of beliefs or rites differing from the established religion or belief.

**TOLERATION ACT** Act of the English Parliament in 1689 granting conditional religious freedom to various Protestant groups. Roman Catholics, Unitarians, and those who could not subscribe to the Thirty-nine ARTICLES were excluded from toleration.

**TOLSTADIUS, ERIK (1693–1759)** Swedish PROTESTANT preacher and pietist leader.

**TOLSTOY, LEO (1828–1910)** Russian novelist whose works present a unique moral and religious point of view. He extolled Christian love and passive nonresistance, finding the SERMON ON THE MOUNT a supreme guide to the spiritual life. He was excommunicated by the RUSSIAN ORTHODOX CHURCH.

**TONACATACUHTLI** Creator in Aztec religion.

**TONATIUH** Aztec sun deity.

**TONGUES** See GLOSSOLALIA.

**TONSURE** Shaving of the head, in whole or in part, to indicate religious office.

**TOPE** See STUPA.

**TOPHETH or TOPHET** High place near Jerusalem in the valley of Hinnom where children were once burned in sacrifice to the god MOLECH. Its name *Ge Hinnom* became Gehenna or Hell (II KINGS 23:10; ISAIAH 30:33; JEREMIAH 7:31–33; 19:6, 11–15).

**TOPLADY, AUGUSTUS MONTAGUE (1740–1778)** English Calvinist hymn writer and ANGLICAN clergyman. He wrote "Rock of Ages" and other hymns as well as several volumes on CALVINISM.

**TORAH or TORA** *instruction* 1. The five books of Moses often known as the Law or the PENTATEUCH. 2. Divine revelation, as all Scripture or all authoritative Jewish writings.

**TORCH** Symbol of wisdom, Christ, or His Passion.

**TORII** Gate to a SHINTO temple.

**TORNARSUK** Supreme Eskimo god.

**TORQUEMADA, JUAN DE (1388–1468)** Important Spanish theologian and uncle of Tomas de TORQUEMADA. His *Summa de Ecclesia* upheld papal infallibility.

**TORQUEMADA, TOMAS DE (1420–1498)** Cruel inquisitor general of the Spanish INQUISITION. Thousands of victims were burned at his hands and in 1492 the Jews were driven from Spain through his influence.

**TORTURE** Concomitant of various forms of religion through the ages. Although torture customarily accompanied the judicial process through the Middle Ages, JUDAISM prohibited it and it is out of keeping with the ideals of most religions. During the twentieth century torture was often accepted as an accompaniment of war.

**TOSAFOT** *additions* Commentaries on, or additions to, the TALMUD, made by rabbis in the twelfth and thirteenth centuries.

**TOSAN RYOKAI (807–869)** Japanese religionist sometimes called the real founder of the Soto ZEN school of Buddhism.

**TOSEFTA, TOSIFTA, or TOSEPHTA** *supplement* Collection of Jewish tradition much like the MISHNA but not a part of it. It has six divisions and dates from the second or third century.

**TOTAL DEPRAVITY** Theological term for man's condition following Adam's fall. This, according to orthodox Christian doctrine, imparted to all men a bent toward evil and an inability to do good apart from divine grace. CALVINISM holds to a thoroughgoing total depravity which makes election and predestination necessities for salvation.

**TOTEM** Object of religious or superstitious awe, believed to possess a blood relationship with a particular family grouping.

**TOTEMISM** Belief in or acceptance of the totem system.

**TOU MU** Chinese sky goddess.

**TOURO, JUDAH (1775–1854)** American patriot, philanthropist, and businessman of the Jewish faith.

**TOURS** French city, famous as an educational center in the Middle Ages. The Basilica of St. Martin contains the body of Tours' fourth-century bishop, St. MARTIN OF TOURS.

**TOY, CRAWFORD HOWELL (1836–1919)** Southern Baptist clergyman and theological professor who taught Biblical literature and Semitic languages at Harvard. He wrote studies of the relationship of CHRISTIANITY to JUDAISM and other religions.

**TRACT** 1. Pamphlet with a religious or evangelistic message. 2. Polemical treatise issued for political, moral, or religious purposes. 3. Scripture portion sung before the GOSPEL at mass.

**TRACTARIANISM** Nineteenth-century movement in the CHURCH OF ENGLAND involving the OXFORD MOVEMENT. The name derives from the *Tracts for the Times*, issued by John Henry Newman and others, promoting the CATHOLIC aspects of the Church of England.

**TRACTS FOR THE TIMES** See TRACTARIANISM.

**TRADITION** 1. Rites, beliefs, or values handed down from the past in religion. 2. Oral transmission of information, as of divine revelation. 3. Unwritten law or religious matter. Some tradition ascribes unwritten legislation to Moses; other tradition ascribes unwritten religious instruction to Christ or others. In Christendom, Catholics usually value such noninscribed material more than Protestants.

**TRADITIONALISM** 1. Religious point of view subordinating all else to tradition, or emphasizing tradition. 2. Nineteenth-century view according to which knowledge of God derives from His original primitive revelation, transmitted by tradition to later generations. The VATICAN COUNCIL of 1870 banned contemporary forms of this view.

**TRADITORS** Christians of the second or third century who gave up their copies of the Scriptures to their persecutors. The traditors were scorned by other Christians.

**TRADUCIANISM** Belief that the soul of an infant is procreated or transmitted to the child by the parents in the act of propagation. Modified forms of traducianism are less crude.

**TRAHERNE, THOMAS (c. 1636–1674)** English clergyman and religious poet. Author of *Christian Ethics* and other prose works, he is also noted for his metaphysical verse with its joyous sense of the presence and love of God.

**TRANSCENDENCE** Theological term for the exaltation of God above the universe and for His distinctness from it. Cf. IMMANENCE.

**TRANSCENDENTALISM** 1. Nineteenth-century New England philosophy, growing out of UNITARIANISM, emphasizing spiritual values and the importance of the individual. 2. Philosophical movement stressing the ultimate and the a priori.

**TRANSEPT** Portion of a Gothic-type church extending out at right angles to the central portion or nave, the whole suggesting the shape of a cross.

**TRANSFIGURATION** Occasion when Jesus' face and clothing glistened as He communed on a mountaintop with Moses and Elijah (MARK 9:2–13). The event was witnessed by James, John, and Peter; the latter's experience is reflected in II Peter 1:16–18. The Feast of the Transfiguration is celebrated on August 6.

**TRANSGRESSION** Term for sin or violation of moral law, often used in the Bible.

**TRANSLATION** 1. Ancient term for the manner in which Enoch went to be with God (GENESIS 5:24). 2. Removal of a bishop or the remains of a saint from one area to another. 3. Postponement of an ecclesiastical festival when there is a conflict with a more important festival. 4. Process or result of transferring something verbal from one language to another. The Bible has been translated countless times.

**TRANSMIGRATION** Removal of a soul from one body to another. This is approximately identical with REINCARNATION or metempsychosis. Transmigration of souls has been accepted in various religions, including BUDDHISM and HINDUISM.

**TRANSUBSTANTIATION** Doctrine that the bread and wine of the communion or EUCHARIST are transformed into the very body and blood of Christ, although retaining the outward appearance of mere bread and wine. A CATHOLIC doctrine, transubstantiation assumes a change in the substance but not in the "accidents" or "species" or portions observable by the human senses.

**TRAPA** Tibetan term for a BUDDHIST monk.

**TRAPPISTINES** CATHOLIC nuns forming a female division of the TRAPPISTS.

**TRAPPISTS** CATHOLIC monks of the order of Reformed Cistercians. Their name reflects the reform introduced at La Trappe in France in 1664. The order stresses silence, manual labor, abstention from meat, community life, and liturgical worship.

**TREACLE BIBLE** Miles COVERDALE's Bible of 1539, which translates Jeremiah 8:22 as follows: "There is no more treacle in Gilead."

**TREASURY OF MERITS** Catholic term for the "supererogatory" merits of Christ and the saints, from which merits are dispensed under certain conditions to those in need of them.

**TREE** Religious symbol of life and of death. Trees figured prominently in ancient religion. Canaanites in Old Testament times worshiped at sacred groves.

**TREFOIL** Three-leaved symbol of the TRINITY.

**TRENCH, RICHARD CHENEVIX (1807–1886)** ANGLICAN philologist, New Testament scholar, and poet who became Archbishop of Dublin. He is noted for his books *Study of Words, Synonyms of the New Testament, Notes on the Parables of Our Lord,* and *Notes on the Miracles of Our Lord.*

**TRENDEL** Top with four sides played with by Jewish children at HANUKKAH.

**TRENT, COUNCIL OF** Nineteenth ECUMENICAL COUNCIL, held at Trent in Italy from 1545 to 1563. Convened by Paul III, it concluded under Pius IV. It affirmed the authority of tradition, the authority of the text of the VULGATE, the institution and necessity of seven sacraments, and the use of divine grace in enabling the sinner to work out his own salvation. It reformed certain abuses but in the main hardened the cleavage between PROTESTANTISM and CATHOLICISM, becoming the principal instrument of the COUNTER REFORMATION.

**TRENTAL** Thirty masses for the repose of the soul of one who is deceased.

**TRESPASS** Term for sin or transgression, often used in the Bible and ecclesiastical formulas.

**TRESPASS OFFERING** Ancient Jewish offering, usually of a ram, to atone for one's sin against another.

**TRIAD** See TRINITY. Theophilus of Antioch said that "God and His Word and His Wisdom" constituted a Triad.

**TRIANGLE** Symbol of the TRINITY.

**TRIBES** Term for the tribes of Israel, descending from Jacob's twelve sons: Reuben, Simeon, Levi, Judah, Issachar, Zebulun, Joseph, Benjamin, Gad, Asher, Dan, and Naphtali. The actual tribes included Joseph's sons Ephraim and Manasseh.

**TRICHOTOMY** Theological term for conception of man as a tripartite entity: body, soul, and spirit. St. Paul wrote, "I pray God your whole spirit and soul and body be preserved blameless" (I THESSALONIANS 5:23). In other New Testament passages, however, spirit and soul seem practically synonymous. See DICHOTOMY.

**TRIDENTINE** Related to Trent or the Council of TRENT.

**TRIDENTINE PROFESSION OF FAITH** Statement of faith formulated by Pope PIUS IV in accordance with the requirements of the Council of TRENT.

**TRIDUUM** *three days* Three days set apart for devotion preparatory to celebrating an ecclesiastical feast or seeking the aid of a saint.

**TRIDUUM SACRUM** *three holy days* Last three days of HOLY WEEK: Maundy Thursday, Good Friday, and Holy Saturday.

**TRIFORIUM** Gallery with three openings above the AISLE of a church.

**TRIMURTI** *triple form* HINDU Trinity, consisting of the deities BRAHMA, VISHNU, and SIVA. Brahma is the Creator, Siva the Destroyer, and Vishnu the Preserver.

**TRINE IMMERSION** Triple inundation in water in BAPTISM. Several EASTERN ORTHODOX churches and some PROTESTANTS baptize in this way.

**TRINITARIAN** One who believes in the Christian doctrine of the TRINITY.

**TRINITARIANS** Members of the Order of the Most Holy Trinity, founded in 1198 in Rome. Their original purpose was to ransom Christian captives from unbelievers. Today they devote themselves to nursing, teaching, and the like.

**TRINITY** Term for the orthodox Christian conception of God as one being in three Persons: Father, Son, and Holy Spirit. Not susceptible of simple explanation, the doctrine of the Trinity envisions the same divine Being in the God of creation, the Jesus of history, and the Spirit within believers.

**TRINITY SUNDAY** Sunday after PENTECOST, set apart to honor the TRINITY.

**TRIPITAKA** *three baskets* BUDDHIST Scriptures. See also PITAKA.

**TRIPTYCH** Altar picture in three panels.

**TRIRATNA** BUDDHIST triad (see THREE GEMS 2). The three elements are commonly stated as the Buddha, the word of truth, and the order of monks.

**TRISAGION** *thrice holy* Ancient Christian liturgy beginning "Holy God, holy and mighty, holy and immortal. . . ."

**TRITHEISM** Heretical conception of the persons of the TRINITY as three distinct gods.

**TRITO-ISAIAH** Author of the third portion of the book of Isaiah—someone, according to many Old Testament scholars, considerably later than the authors of the first or second portions.

**TRITON** Greek demigod of the sea.

**TRIUMPH THE CHURCH AND KINGDOM OF GOD IN CHRIST** American denomination begun in 1902 in Georgia. Doctrines include instantaneous sanctification and baptism by fire.

**TRIUNE** Three in one. The adjective often refers to the Trinitarian nature of God.

**TROAS** City of Asia Minor where St. PAUL envisioned a Macedonian who led him to bring the gospel to Macedonia and Europe.

**TROELTSCH, ERNST (1865–1923)** German philosopher and theologian whose many works probed the interrelationships of culture, history, and Christian thought. He emphasized nonskeptical relativism and syntheses of culture.

**TROLL** Man-like, cave-dwelling, supernatural being, important in certain ancient Scandinavian legends and myths.

**TROLLOPE, ANTHONY (1815–1882)** English novelist whose books chronicled life among the clergy of his day.

**TROPOLOGY** Figurative interpretation of the Scriptures.

**TRUCE OF GOD** Medieval ecclesiastical proscription of warfare from Thursday night to Monday morning and on certain religious days.

**TRUMBULL, CHARLES G. (1872–1941)** Conservative American Christian editor and author.

**TRUMPETS, FEAST OF** See FEAST OF TRUMPETS.

**TRUSTEE** One holding property in trust. American church property is usually maintained and administered by a board of trustees.

**TRUTH** That which squares with reality. Jesus Christ is the Truth (JOHN 14:6) because ultimate reality is revealed in Him.

**TSONG-KHA-PA (1357–1419)** Tibetan BUDDHIST reformer who founded the order of the GELUPA (Virtuous Ones), sometimes called Yellow Hats. His reforms, designed to restore primitive Buddhism, affected various schools of the faith.

**TSUKI-YUMI** Japanese moon deity.

**TUAT** A name for the world of the deceased in Egyptian religion.

**TUATHA DE DANANN** Ancient Irish gods led by Lug and Lir. They were nature deities with various powers.

**TUBAL-CAIN** Ancient metalsmith (GENESIS 4:22).

**TÜBINGEN SCHOOL** Theological movement, founded by F. C. BAUR of the Theological Seminary at Tübingen University. The school interpreted Christianity on the basis of an early conflict between Paul and Peter and their respective followers. The books of the New Testament were considered to have reflected the opposing views of the Petrine and Pauline camps more than actual history.

**TULASI** Sacred HINDU shrub believed to possess healing and redemptive powers.

**TULCHAN BISHOPS** Scottish PRESBYTERIAN term for the bishops temporarily introduced into their church in the sixteenth century.

**TULSI DAS (1532–1623)** Popular HINDU poet.

**TUNICLE** Subdeacon's outer garment.

**TUNKERS** See DUNKERS.

**TURAN** Etruscan mother-goddess.

**TUSHITA or TUSITA** BUDDHIST term for heaven.

**TUTELARY DEITY** God or goddess considered to guard someone or something.

**TVASTRI** Vedic god renowned as an artificer and giver of life.

**TWELFTH NIGHT** EPIPHANY Eve, twelve days after Christmas. In the Middle Ages it concluded the Christmas season.

**TWELLS, HENRY (1823–1900)** ANGLICAN rector and hymn writer. He was honorary canon of Peterborough.

**TWELVE** Symbol of the Apostles, the tribes of Israel, and the church.

**TWELVE PRINCIPLES OF BUDDHISM** List of Buddhist principles drawn up by the Buddhist Society in 1945 and widely disseminated.

**TWELVE TRIBES OF ISRAEL** See TRIBES.

**TWENTY-FIVE ARTICLES** See ARTICLES, TWENTY-FIVE.

**TWO** Religious symbol of the two natures of Christ and of various dualisms.

**TWO-SEED-IN-THE-SPIRIT PREDESTINARIAN BAPTISTS** Very small group of BAPTISTS founded in the southern United States by Daniel Parker late in the eighteenth century.

**TYCHE** Greek goddess of fortune.

**TYNDALE, WILLIAM (c.1494–1536)** English reformer and translator of the Bible into his native tongue. An advocate of religious freedom, he published several versions of the New Testament and had begun work on the Old when he was burned at the stake. His vigorous translations profoundly influenced subsequent English versions of Scripture. He advocated the doctrines of justification by faith and the authority of Scripture.

**TYPE** Theological term for that which foreshadows a divine fulfillment. The Israelites' slavery in Egypt typified man's bondage in sin, while Moses' deliverance typified Christ's redemption. Although some types are indicated in the New Testament, certain religionists seem to see more types than evidence can substantiate.

**TYPICON** EASTERN ORTHODOX liturgical book.

**TYPOLOGY** Study of the types in Scripture or Christian doctrine, and their fulfillment.

**TYRE** Phoenician city on the western coast of Palestine, mentioned a number of times in the Bible. A great Christian cathedral was built there in the fourth century; the city now contains the Mosque el-Kebir.

**TYRELL, GEORGE (1861–1909)** Irish CATHOLIC theologian whose growing suspicion of orthodox theology led to his reputation as a MODERNIST and his excommunication. He finally wrote of Christianity as a prelude to a universal religion.

**TZADDI** Eighteenth letter of the Hebrew alphabet.

**TZADDIK** Jewish term for a wise man or a pious or saintly person.

**TZITZIT** See ZIZITH.

# U

**UBASTET** See BAST.

**UBIQUITARIANISM** Lutheran doctrine that the human nature of Christ is present everywhere by virtue of its union with the divine nature.

**UBIQUITY** Theological term for the divine omnipresence.

**UCCELLO, PAOLO (c.1396–1475)** Realistic Italian painter of many religious scenes.

**U.C.M.** See UNIVERSITY CHRISTIAN MOVEMENT.

**UDASINS** SIKH ascetics of India, founded by Sri Chand.

**UKRAINIAN ORTHODOX CHURCHES** EASTERN ORTHODOX churches of the Ukraine. Ukrainian emigrants to America brought with them the Ukrainian Orthodox Church of the U.S.A. and the Ukrainian Orthodox Church of America. They also support the Holy Ukrainian Autocephalic Orthodox Church in Exile.

**ULAMA** Moslem scholars learned in canon law and Moslem tradition. See ISLAM.

**ULFILAS (c.311–383)** Christian missionary among the Goths and Visigoths of central Europe. He translated the Bible into Gothic and made the Goths ARIANS for centuries.

**ULTIMATE, THE** Philosophical term for the infinite or God.

**ULTRAMONTANISM** CATHOLIC movement emphasizing stronger papal authority and power. Ultramontanist influence came to a climax in the nineteenth century; the twentieth's VATICAN COUNCIL II marked the beginning of decentralization of ecclesiastical power and of other tendencies opposed to rigid Ultramontanism.

**UMA** Hindu deity, wife of SIVA.

**UNAM SANCTAM** Papal encyclical of 1302 stating that there is "neither salvation nor remission of sins" outside the "One Holy Catholic and Apostolic Church," and that temporal power is subordinate to the spiritual power of the pope and the church.

**UNAMUNO, MIGUEL DE (1864–1936)** Spanish writer and philosopher whose thought shows profound Christian insights. He was greatly influenced by Søren Kierkegaard.

**UNA SANCTA** *one holy* Two marks of the church, often indicating the four marks of unity, holiness, apostolicity, and catholicity.

**UNBELIEF** Failure to believe in God.

**UNCONDITIONED, THE** Philosophical term for the absolute or infinite.

**UNCONSCIOUS, THE** Portion of the mind below the level of consciousness, possibly corresponding in some respects to the Biblical term "heart." Psychiatry finds the key to many mental problems in the unconscious.

**UNCTION** 1. Anointing, as with oil. 2. Anointing of the Spirit, resulting in a charismatic power or winsomeness.

**UNDERCROFT** Crypt or other underground chamber beneath a church.

**UNDERHILL, EVELYN (1875–1941)** English mystic and author. An Anglican, she wrote *Mysticism, The Path of Eternal Wisdom, The Mystic Way,* and other books on mysticism; she translated *The Cloud of Unknowing* and other works. She was noted as a worship leader and a pacifist. Her married name was Mrs. Stuart Moore.

**UNDINE** Female water spirit in medieval myth.

**UNFROCK** Popular term for removing a clergyman from his ministerial office and functions.

**UNIAT CHURCHES** EASTERN ORTHODOX churches which are in communion with the ROMAN CATHOLIC CHURCH and accept its authority. However, they retain their own distinctive rites and canon law. Uniat churches include Copts, Ruthenians, and Catholics of the ARMENIAN RITE and of the BYZANTINE RITE in a number of countries of the Middle East. There are about nine million Uniats in the world.

**UNIATE** Variant of Uniat. See UNIAT CHURCHES.

**UNICORN** Mythical one-horned beast sometimes symbolizing chastity in religious art.

**UNIFORMITY, ACTS OF** British legislation of the sixteenth and seventeenth centuries which sought to establish uniform faith and worship throughout England and Ireland. Through the fourth Act, of 1662, "the Established Church forced from her fellowship much of the strongest religious leadership of the age" (Peter G. Mode).

**UNIGENITUS** *only begotten* 1. Latin term indicating the unique status of Christ as the only begotten Son of God, eternally existing in a filial relationship with God the Father. 2. Papal encyclical of 1343 stating the efficacy of indulgences through papal dispensation of the treasury of merit. 3. Papal bull of 1713 condemning Pasquier QUESNEL and JANSENISM.

**UNIO MYSTICA** *mystic union* Latin term for the union of the human soul with the divine Spirit.

**UNION AMERICAN METHODIST EPISCOPAL CHURCH** American Negro denomination founded in Delaware in 1805. Its original name was the Union Church of Africans.

**UNION OF AMERICAN HEBREW CONGREGATIONS** Central organization of synagogues of REFORM JUDAISM, organized in 1873 by Isaac M. WISE.

**UNION OF DOUKHOBORS IN CANADA** Association of DOUKHOBORS, united in 1945.

**UNION OF EVANGELICAL CHRISTIANS—BAPTISTS** Largest PROTESTANT organization in Soviet Russia.

**UNION OF ORTHODOX JEWISH CONGREGATIONS OF AMERICA** Organization of synagogues representing ORTHODOX JUDAISM in North America.

**UNITARIAN** 1. Believer in one God but not in the TRINITY. 2. Member of Unitarian religious group.

**UNITARIANISM** Religious movement dating in its contemporary form from the sixteenth century. In general it opposes creedal restrictions and favors free inquiry and humanitarian goals.

**UNITARIAN UNIVERSALIST ASSOCIATION**

American denomination formed in 1961 by the merger of the Unitarian and Universalist churches. It emphasizes the search for truth, the Judeo-Christian heritage, the worth of the individual, and world brotherhood.

**UNITAS FRATRUM** *society of brethren* Latin name of the BOHEMIAN BRETHREN.

**UNITED BAPTISTS** Denomination in southern United States holding three ORDINANCES: BAPTISM, the LORD'S SUPPER, and FOOT WASHING.

**UNITED BRETHREN** See CHURCH OF THE UNITED BRETHREN IN CHRIST. Also see EVANGELICAL UNITED BRETHREN CHURCH, the UNITED CHRISTIAN CHURCH, and the CHURCH OF THE UNITED BRETHREN IN CHRIST (OLD CONSTITUTION).

**UNITED CHRISTIAN CHURCH** American denomination formed in the late nineteenth century through the influence of George W. Hoffman and others. ORDINANCES are BAPTISM, the LORD'S SUPPER, and FOOT WASHING.

**UNITED CHURCH BOARD FOR WORLD MINISTRIES** See AMERICAN BOARD OF COMMISSIONERS FOR FOREIGN MISSIONS.

**UNITED CHURCH OF CANADA** Canadian denomination resulting from a merger in 1925 of CONGREGATIONALIST, METHODIST, and PRESBYTERIAN churches.

**UNITED CHURCH OF CHRIST** American denomination resulting from a 1957 union of the EVANGELICAL AND REFORMED CHURCH and the CONGREGATIONAL CHRISTIAN CHURCHES. Emphases include congregational independence, church unity, and the progress of knowledge, justice, peace, and brotherhood.

**UNITED FREE CHURCH OF SCOTLAND** Scottish PRESBYTERIAN church which united with the Established Church of Scotland in 1929.

**UNITED FREE WILL BAPTIST CHURCH** American Negro denomination organized in 1901. ORDINANCES are BAPTISM, the LORD'S SUPPER, and FOOT WASHING. Doctrines incline to ARMINIANISM.

**UNITED HOLY CHURCH OF AMERICA, INC.** American Negro denomination organized in 1886. Doctrines are PENTECOSTAL.

**UNITED METHODIST CHURCH** American denomination uniting the METHODIST CHURCH and the EVANGELICAL UNITED BRETHREN CHURCH in 1968.

**UNITED MISSIONARY CHURCH** American

denomination formerly known as the Mennonite Brethren in Christ Church. Doctrines are fundamentalist, Holiness, and Arminian.

**UNITED PENTECOSTAL CHURCH, INC.** American Pentecostal denomination resulting from a church merger in 1945.

**UNITED PRESBYTERIAN CHURCH** Scottish denomination, formed in 1847, which entered the United Free Church of Scotland in 1900.

**UNITED PRESBYTERIAN CHURCH IN THE U.S.A.** American denomination resulting from the 1958 merger of the UNITED PRESBYTERIAN CHURCH OF NORTH AMERICA and the PRESBYTERIAN CHURCH IN THE U.S.A. It brings to its Calvinistic heritage an emphasis on social concerns and Christian education.

**UNITED PRESBYTERIAN CHURCH OF NORTH AMERICA** Denomination formed in the United States in 1858, which merged with the PRESBYTERIAN CHURCH IN THE U.S.A. in 1958. It emphasized psalm-singing and conservative Presbyterian doctrines.

**UNITED SYNAGOGUE OF AMERICA** Organization of United States Jewish congregations representing CONSERVATIVE JUDAISM.

**UNITED WESLEYAN METHODIST CHURCH OF AMERICA** Small American denomination with a background in the British West Indies. It was founded in 1905.

**UNITED ZION CHURCH** American denomination organized in 1855. ORDINANCES are TRINE IMMERSION, the LORD'S SUPPER, and FOOT WASHING. Women in this church are veiled.

**UNITY** Religious movement begun by Charles and Myrtle Fillmore in 1889. Headquarters of the Unity School of Christianity are at Lee's Summit, Missouri. The movement stresses positive thought, prayer, and faith as guides to health, happiness, and prosperity.

**UNIVERSALISM** 1. Belief that all human beings will eventually be saved. 2. Religious system emphasizing the universal fatherhood of God and universal salvation.

**UNIVERSALIST CHURCH OF AMERICA** North American denomination committed to an emphasis on the final reconciliation of all men with God. In 1961 it became part of the UNITARIAN UNIVERSALIST ASSOCIATION.

**UNIVERSITY CHRISTIAN MOVEMENT** Organization of PROTESTANT, ROMAN CATHOLIC, ANGLICAN, and EASTERN ORTHODOX youth groups on American college campuses.

**UNKEI (c.1150–1220)** Magnificent Japanese sculptor of many figures for BUDDHIST temples.

**UNLEAVENED BREAD** Bread made without yeast, necessary for the Jewish PASSOVER and often used in Christian services of the EUCHARIST.

**UNPARDONABLE SIN** Theological term for a sin which God cannot or will not pardon. Such passages of the Bible as Mark 3:28–30 and Hebrews 6:4–6, while often adduced to substantiate such a sin, may well be interpreted from the point of view that the prime unpardonable sin is failure to seek the divine mercy. The sin indicated in such passages as Matthew 12:24–32 is generally construed to be the ascription to the devil of what has been done by the Holy Spirit.

**UPANISHADS** Philosophic portion of the HINDU Scriptures dating from the sixth century B.C. or before. There are thirteen Upanishads. The authors were Hindu or vedic wise men.

**UPPER ROOM, THE** Room in which Jesus and His disciples took the LAST SUPPER together. It was a large, furnished, second-floor room in Jerusalem (LUKE 22:12).

**UPSILON** Greek letter corresponding to the letter *u*.

**UPUAUT** Egyptian wolf god.

**UR** Ancient city of Mesopotamia from which Abraham came (GENESIS 11:28, 31). It contained the temples of Ninhursag, Ningal, Enummah, and a moon god. At Ur have also been found remains of statues suggesting a ram caught in a thicket (cf. GENESIS 22:13).

**URANUS** Greek god of the sky or heaven.

**URBAN VIII (1568–1644)** Italian pope (1623–1644) who encouraged ecclesiastical reform, condemned JANSENISM, and beautified Rome.

**URBANUS** Canaanite god, father of EL.

**URBI ET ORBI** *to the city and to the world* Papal blessing pronounced from the balcony of St. Peter's.

**URD** Scandinavian personification of fate.

**URI or URIAS** See URIAH.

**URIAH** *the Lord is light* Jewish Hittite slain by King David to acquire Uriah's wife Bath-sheba (II SAMUEL 11, 12; MATTHEW 1:6).

**URIEL** One of four archangels in Jewish apocryphal writings. An angel by this name appears in the book of Enoch, in II Esdras, and in Milton's *Paradise Lost*.

**URIM AND THUMMIM** Objects of unknown nature attached to the breastplate of the Jewish high priest and used somehow in divination up to the time of King Solomon. (EXODUS 28:30; I SAMUEL 14:41.)

**URSINUS, ZACHARIAS (1534–1583)** German theologian and reformer who framed the HEIDELBERG CATECHISM with Kaspar Olevianus. Although of Calvinistic inclination, Ursinus once said: "We are not baptized in the name of Luther, or Zwingli, or of any other, but of Christ alone."

**URSULA, ST. (c. third century)** British Christian virgin martyred, according to tradition, with 11,000 other virgins by pagan Huns at Cologne. Her feast day is October 21.

**URSULINES** Members of the oldest and largest CATHOLIC order of teaching nuns. Founded in 1535 by St. ANGELA MERICI, the order's purposes are to educate girls and women, to evangelize, and to aid those in need. The garb is black. In addition to the original order, there are several other groups of Ursulines.

**USE** Ecclesiastical term for a particular religious rite.

**USHAS** Vedic goddess of the morning.

**USHEBTI** Egyptian statue of a dead person believed to perform the deceased's duties in the afterlife.

**USHER** One who conducts people to their seats in a church or elsewhere. Church ushers usually take up the offerings in a service of worship.

**USSHER, JAMES (1581–1656)** ANGLICAN Archbishop of Armagh, Ireland, admired for his learning. The chronology in many Bibles, including the creation of the world in 4004 B.C., is Ussher's work.

**USURY** Lending of money at interest, particularly at exorbitant rates. Ancient Jewish and medieval Christian law forbade usury.

**UTA-NAPISHTIM** Gentleman in Babylonian legend who, like the Bible's NOAH, escaped a universal flood by building a boat.

**UTHRA** Divine beings in the MANDAEAN religion, emanating from the Great Mana which is the supreme godhead.

**UTILITARIANISM** 1. Philosophy of morality based on the attempt to bring the greatest good or happiness to the greatest number of people. 2. Attitude basing ethics on usefulness or pleasure.

**UTNAPISHTIM** See UTA-NAPISHTIM.

**UTOPIA *nowhere*** Ideal place where all evil has been disposed of and happiness reigns. Although Sir Thomas MORE coined the word in the sixteenth century with an imaginary account of such a place, utopias have often been connected with religion. St. AUGUSTINE's *City of God* might be described as a utopia. Scripture speaks of a perfect age before the fall of man and a future state without blemish.

**UTRAQUISTS** Fifteenth-century believers that laymen should receive the holy communion in both kinds (*sub utraque specie*), bread and wine. The HUSSITES were in general Utraquists.

**UTRECHT** Dutch city noted since the seventh century as an important episcopal see. It contains a fourteenth-century cathedral. In the seventeenth century it was a center of JANSENISM.

**UTRECHT, DECLARATION OF** Confession of faith of the OLD CATHOLIC CHURCH. It was formulated in 1889 at Utrecht in the Netherlands.

**UZ** 1. Country of the patriarch JOB, possibly Arabia or Edom. 2. Name of several Bible personages.

**UZZA** Ancient Arabian goddess, worshiped as the planet Venus or the acacia tree.

**UZZIAH *the Lord is my strength*** King of Judah in the first half of the eighth century B.C. (also known as Azariah). Though his reign was prosperous, it included a great earthquake (AMOS 1:1) and Uzziah became a leper for interfering with the duties of the priesthood. Isaiah's ministry began in the year Uzziah died (ISAIAH 6:1). Cf. II Chronicles 26.

**UZZIEL *my strength is God*** 1. Jewish founder of a group of Levites known as the Uzzielites (EXODUS 6:18, 22; NUMBERS 3:19, 30; I CHRONICLES 15:10). 2. Musician in the orchestra of King David (I CHRONICLES 25:4). 3. Several other Bible personages bear this name.

# V

**V.** Abbreviation for versicle or verse.

**VÁC** Vedic goddess of speech and wife of BRAHMA.

**VACATION SCHOOL** Instruction period, usually two weeks long, held by many American churches during the summer vacation period to teach the Bible or religion. Other common names are Daily Vacation Bible School, Vacation Bible School, and Vacation Church School.

**VACHASPATI MISRA (ninth century)** BRAHMAN philosopher and HINDU theologian.

**VAGANTES** *wanderers* Medieval priests not attached to specific parishes or monasteries and roving from place to place. Some of the Vagantes were minstrels.

**VAHANA** *vehicle* Animal specially related to a HINDU god, as the bull to Siva.

**VAIKUNTHA** HINDU paradise.

**VAINAMOINEN** Finnish god of music.

**VAIROCANA or VAIROCHANA** Buddha of infinite light of MAHAYANA Buddhism. He is sometimes identified with the sun.

**VAISESHIKA** HINDU philosophical system in which the invisible power of Adrishta seems to replace the gods.

**VAISNAVISM** HINDU worship of VISHNU as the supreme God.

**VAISYA** Member of the HINDU caste of farmers and merchants.

**VAJRAYNA** Special school of BUDDHISM in India and Tibet.

**VALDES, ALFONSO DE (c.1490–1532)** Humanistic Spanish satirist who sometimes ridiculed the church.

**VALDES, JUAN DE (c.1500–1540)** Spanish reformer who believed in JUSTIFICATION by faith alone. A twin brother of Alfonso de VALDES, Juan never left the CATHOLIC CHURCH but influenced a number of followers to do so. He translated and made commentaries on several parts of the Bible.

**VALENTINE, ST.** Several saints bear this name. The best candidate for commemoration February 14 (St. Valentine's feast day) is probably a Roman priest beheaded by Claudius about 270 A.D. He may have been a physician.

**VALENTINIANS** Second-century GNOSTIC followers of a theologian of Alexandria named Valentinus.

**VALHALLA** Norse heaven for those killed in battle.

**VALKYRIES** Maidens in Norse mythology who conducted the dead in battle to VALHALLA.

**VALLOMBROSANS** BENEDICTINE monks of the Vallombrosan Order, founded about 1036 by St. John Gualbert. Their mother house is in Vallombrosa, Italy. Austere and contemplative, the order has produced a number of noted writers, artists, and scientists.

**VAN DYCK, ANTHONY (1599–1641)** Strong religious painter of Flemish school.

**VAN DYCK, CORNELIUS VAN ALEN (1818–1895)** American CONGREGATIONAL missionary to Syria. He translated the Bible into Arabic.

**VAN DYKE, HENRY (1852–1933)** American PRESBYTERIAN minister and author, famous for *The Story of the Other Wise Man* and certain poems and hymns.

**VANINI, LUCILIO (c.1585–1619)** Italian thinker whose tongue was excised and his body burned because of his liberal views.

**VANIR** Ancient Norse gods of weather, trade, wealth, etc.

**VANITY** Word often used in Scripture for emptiness, worthlessness, or nothingness.

**VANITY FAIR** John Bunyan's allegorical name for this world in *Pilgrim's Progress*.

**VARDHAMANA** Alternate name for MAHAVIRA, a founder of JAINISM.

**VARIETIES OF RELIGIOUS EXPERIENCE** Noted book by William JAMES, an American professor of psychology and philosophy. *The Varieties of Religious Experi-*

*ence,* originally Gifford Lectures, illustrates various types of religion.

**VARI-MA-TE-TAKERE** Polynesian mother-goddess.

**VARUNA** HINDUISM's supreme god and creator.

**VASHTI** Ahasuerus' queen before ESTHER.

**VASTOSH-PATI** Vedic god of homes and sacred ceremonies.

**VASUDEVA** See VISHNU.

**VATA** HINDU wind god.

**VATICAN** Official residence of the pope in Rome. It is a palace near St. Peter's Cathedral, on the lower part of the Vatican Hill. Sometimes "the Vatican" indicates the papacy or CATHOLICISM.

**VATICAN CITY** Sovereign state of about a hundred acres in Rome, ruled by the pope.

**VATICAN COUNCIL, FIRST (1869–1870)** Twentieth ECUMENICAL COUNCIL of the ROMAN CATHOLIC CHURCH, convened by Pope PIUS IX. The Council proclaimed the infallibility of the pope "when speaking ex cathedra for the definition of doctrines concerning faith and morals." It also enacted decrees concerning religious orders, clerical education, the election of bishops, and various other matters.

**VATICAN COUNCIL, SECOND (1962–1965)** Twenty-first ECUMENICAL COUNCIL of the Roman Catholic Church, convened by Pope JOHN XXIII. It approved documents strengthening the role of bishops, absolving the Jews of the responsibility for the crucifixion of Christ, expressing good will toward Moslems and atheists, reforming Catholic liturgy and garb, and seeking to adjust the church more completely to the contemporary world. It emphasized the importance of Scripture and Bible study. It furthered the possibility of eventual ecumenical reunion. Some observers felt that the Council markedly lessened tensions between Catholics and other groups.

**VATICANUS** Roman deity from which the Vatican Hill in Rome was named.

**VAU** See WAW.

**VAUDOIS** See WALDENSIAN CHURCH.

**VAUGHAN, HENRY (1622–1695)** English physician and poet whose verse was of metaphysical moment. He was influenced by George HERBERT.

**VAUGHAN, HERBERT (1832–1903)** English CATHOLIC clergyman, Archbishop of West-

minster, and cardinal. Strong but kindly, he interested himself especially in education and in the welfare of American Negroes.

**VAYU** Vedic wind god.

**VEADAR** Month in the Jewish calendar which falls between Adar and Nisan on leap years.

**VEDANTA** *end of the sacred lore* HINDU philosophy interpreting the last part of the VEDAS and their purpose. According to Vedanta only BRAHMA is real; the world is illusion. Salvation is reached through realizing this. Vedanta also indicates a group of six Hindu philosophical systems, and may indicate certain UPANISHADS.

**VEDANTA SOCIETY** United States religious group based on the authority of the VEDAS.

**VEDAS** *sacred knowledge* Oldest and most sacred scriptures of HINDUISM, written in Vedic Sanskrit. They consist of more than a hundred books of prayers, hymns, and formulas for worship, grouped into four collections: RIG-VEDA, YAJUR-VEDA, SAMA-VEDA, and Atharva-Veda. The term *veda* is also used in the singular as a collective noun.

**VEDIC RELIGION** Pre-Hindu religion of the Aryans of India, based on that of the VEDAS, particularly the RIG-VEDA. Vedic gods included Dyaus, Prithivi, Indra, Varuna, Soma, and Agni.

**VEGETARIANISM** Practice of certain religious groups including HINDUS, BUDDHISTS, and SEVENTH-DAY ADVENTISTS.

**VEHICLE** Buddhist term for a way of salvation. The major Buddhist vehicles are MAHAYANA, "The Great Vehicle"; HINAYANA, "The Lesser Vehicle"; and MADHAYAMAYANA, "The Middle Vehicle."

**VEIL** Head covering often used in religious garb. The veil's symbolic meaning is that of chastity and purity.

**VENDIDAD** Priestly code of ZOROASTRIANISM, specifying religious rites of various kinds.

**VENERABLE** 1. ANGLICAN title for an archdeacon. 2. CATHOLIC title for one who has reached a particular point in the process of beatification. 3. Title of honor for one of unusual sanctity, as the Venerable BEDE.

**VENERATION** In CATHOLICISM, worship offered the saints. It is of a different quality from the worship offered God.

**VENIAL SIN** Minor sin, the result of which

is not deprivation of God's sanctifying grace. Venial sins need not be confessed before one takes COMMUNION.

**VENI, CREATOR** *come, Creator* Ninth-century hymn to the Holy Spirit, widely used in Christian worship.

**VENI SANCTE SPIRITUS** *come, Holy Spirit* Thirteenth-century hymn known as the SEQUENCE in ANGLICAN worship.

**VENITE** *O come* Latin version of Psalm 95, often used at MATINS.

**VENI, VENI EMMANUEL** *come, O come, Emmanuel* Eighteenth-century ADVENT hymn.

**VENN, HENRY (1725–1797)** Evangelical ANGLICAN clergyman and author of *The Complete Duty of Man.*

**VENUS** Roman goddess of love, beauty, fertility, and vegetation.

**VERETHAGHNA** ZOROASTRIAN war god.

**VERGER** 1. Caretaker of a church. 2. One who attends a dignitary or heads a procession in Anglican worship.

**VERMIGLI, PIETRO MARTIRE (1500–1562)** "Peter Martyr," Italian reformer. Son of a disciple of SAVONAROLA, Vermigli became an AUGUSTINIAN, studied the Bible, and was impressed by the writings of ZWINGLI and BUCER. Forced to flee his country, he married a nun and taught theology at Strassburg. At various times, he visited England and taught at Zurich, deeply influencing the growing Protestant REFORMATION.

**VERONICA** Handkerchief or veil with which St. Veronica wiped Jesus' face during His Passion.

**VERONICA, ST.** Woman who, according to legend, wiped Jesus' bleeding face with a handkerchief or veil. A veil in Rome containing an image of a human face is said to be St. Veronica's veil. Although Veronica is not included in official lists of Catholic saints, her feast day is July 12.

**VERROCCHIO, ANDREA DEL (1435–1488)** Skillful Italian sculptor of *David* and other works, and painter of "The Madonna and Child," "The Baptism of Christ," and "Crucifixion With Saints."

**VERSE** Short portion of a hymn, or of a chapter of the Bible, or of certain other writings.

**VERSICLE** Short statement in a worship service followed by a congregational or choral response. Example: "The Lord be with you" followed by the response, "And with thy spirit."

**VERSION** Translation, as of the Bible. Among famous versions of Scripture are the DOUAI VERSION, the Authorized or KING JAMES VERSION, the REVISED STANDARD VERSION, and the NEW ENGLISH BIBLE.

**VERTUMNUS** Roman god of vegetation and the seasons.

**VERY, JONES (1813–1880)** Mystical American poet.

**VESPERS** Afternoon or evening service or EVENSONG in ANGLICAN and CATHOLIC worship. Vespers is the CANONICAL HOUR next to the last.

**VESTA** Roman goddess of the hearth and of cooking. Counterpart of Greek Hestia.

**VESTAL VIRGINS** Roman girls who tended the sacred flame in temples to VESTA. They were very highly honored but could never marry; if they lost their virginity they were buried alive.

**VESTMENT** Article of clothing worn by religious officiant. Ecclesiastical vestments tend to be garments of the past.

**VESTRY** 1. Board governing the temporal affairs of a parish. 2. Robing room adjoining a sanctuary; sacristy.

**VESTRYMAN** Member of a VESTRY.

**VEVE** Esoteric VOODOO drawing.

**VIA DOLOROSA** *sorrowful way* Path Jesus took through Jerusalem from Pilate's tribunal to Calvary. Along it now are fourteen STATIONS OF THE CROSS.

**VIANNEY, SAINT JEAN-BAPTISTE (1786–1859)** French CATHOLIC priest who attracted thousands by his simplicity, dedication, and love. He is credited with performing many miracles. His feast day is August 8.

**VIATICUM** *provision for travel* Administration of holy COMMUNION to one expected to die soon. It is considered a spiritual provision for the journey to heaven.

**VIBERT, JEHAN GEORGES (1840–1902)** French artist who often satirized the clergy and the church.

**VICAR** 1. Priest or incumbent of a parish. 2. Clergyman who serves as the deputy or substitute for another.

**VICAR APOSTOLIC** Prelate appointed by the pope to administer a vacant diocese, or to serve where there is no canonical see.

**VICAR FORANE** CATHOLIC clergyman given limited jurisdiction within a diocese.

**VICAR-GENERAL** 1. Bishop's deputy in the CATHOLIC CHURCH. 2. Lay deputy of the archbishop of York or of Canterbury, in the CHURCH OF ENGLAND.

**VICARIOUS ATONEMENT** Belief that Christ died as a substitute for sinners, who are saved when they receive Him and His work in faith. See ATONEMENT.

**VICAR OF JESUS CHRIST** CATHOLIC title of the pope, who is considered to be Christ's deputy on earth.

**VICTORIA, THOMAS LUIS DE (c.1548–1611)** Spanish composer of many sacred works: cantatas, masses, and music for many hymns. His compositions have mystical overtones.

**VICTORINES** Members of the CATHOLIC religious order founded in 1108 at the abbey of St. Victor in France. PETER LOMBARD was a Victorine. The order ended with the French Revolution.

**VIDAR or VIDHAR** Scandinavian god of forests and silence.

**VIDDUI** *confession* Jewish term for confession of sins.

**VIDHAR** See VIDAR.

**VIDHI** Sacred saying or law.

**VIDYA** *knowledge* Term for knowledge in Sivaism.

**VIENNE, COUNCIL OF (1311–1312)** Fifteenth ECUMENICAL COUNCIL. Held at Vienne in France, it called for the suppression of the Knights TEMPLARS, condemned BEGHARD heresies, and issued various decrees.

**VIGIL** *watch* Service of prayer and devotion the night before an ecclesiastical feast.

**VIGNOLA, GIACOMO DA (1507–1573)** Papal architect and designer for churches. Church architecture owes much to his creativity.

**VIHARA** *shrine* BUDDHIST shrine or monastery; term used especially in Ceylon.

**VIKKUACH** *debate* Jewish term for medieval discussion between Jew and Christian.

**VILMAR, AUGUST F. C. (1800–1860)** German LUTHERAN theologian who upheld orthodox against critical rationalism.

**VINAYAPITAKA** One of three divisions of Buddhist scripture. See also PITAKA.

**VINCENT, JOHN HEYL (1832–1920)** American METHODIST bishop who interested himself in education and improved church school techniques.

**VINCENT DE PAUL, ST. (c.1580–1660)** French founder of the LAZARISTS (Vincentians) and the SISTERS OF CHARITY. A priest who greatly aided the poor, he inspired the creation of the Society of St. Vincent de Paul for humanitarian purposes. His feast day is July 19.

**VINCENT FERRER, ST. (c.1350–1419)** Popular DOMINICAN preacher who helped end the papal schism of his time. Austere and ascetic, he called thousands to repentance. His feast day is April 5.

**VINCENT OF BEAUVAIS (c.1190–1264)** French DOMINICAN scholar who composed encyclopedic works of secular and sacred knowledge.

**VINCENT OF LERINS, ST. (fifth century)** Ecclesiastical writer and monk of Lerins, Gaul. The Vincentian Canon is part of his famous *Commonitorium*. He considered the Bible to be the ultimate spiritual authority and formulated this test of Christian truth: "That which is believed everywhere, always, and by all."

**VINE** Religious symbol of the church as an organic unity centered in Christ. Cf. JOHN 15:1–7.

**VINE, ALFRED HENRY (1845–1917)** English METHODIST minister, poet, and hymn writer.

**VINEGAR** The vinegar given Jesus at Calvary (MARK 15:36) was apparently a sour wine used by Roman soldiers.

**VINEGAR BIBLE** English Bible (1717) which misprinted the parable of the vineyard in Luke 20 as "The Parable of the Vinegar."

**VINET, ALEXANDRE RODOLPHE (1797–1847)** Swiss REFORMED historian and theologian. A warm evangelical, he opposed rationalism and creedal hairsplitting. His emphasis was on conscience and good deeds as opposed to formality and mere dogma, and on personal experience in religion, religious freedom, and the separation of church and state.

**VIOLET** In religious symbolism violet often represents truth, humility, and love. See also PURPLE.

**VIRACOCHA** Ancient Inca god who created human beings.

**VIRBIUS** Roman deity whose priestly representative secured office by murdering his predecessor.

**VIRGIN BIRTH** Doctrine that Jesus was

conceived supernaturally, by the power of the Holy Spirit upon the Virgin Mary (MATTHEW 1:18; LUKE 1:35) and without a human father.

**VIRGINITY** From ancient times various religions have had a peculiar interest in virginity; see VESTAL VIRGINS. Many Christian groups have long considered virginity to be an unusually holy condition. While St. Paul likened the church to a chaste virgin (II CORINTHIANS 11:2), the New Testament does not particularly exalt virginity above the marital state.

**VIRGINITY, PERPETUAL** Doctrine that Mary the mother of Jesus, although she married Joseph, remained a virgin throughout her life. Few Protestants share this view.

**VIRGIN MARY, THE** A title of Jesus' mother MARY.

**VIRTUALISM** Doctrine that virtue or power from Christ is received in the EUCHARIST although the bread and wine remain bread and wine. John CALVIN formulated this view rather clearly. Cf. TRANSUBSTANTIATION.

**VIRTUES** PLATO and the Greek STOICS enumerated four cardinal virtues: prudence, justice, fortitude, and self-control. To these, medieval theologians added the three Christian virtues of faith, hope, and love, to complete the qualities of the ideal person.

**VISHNU** Second of HINDUISM's three supreme deities. He is considered to have been incarnated as RAMA, KRISHNA, BUDDHA, and others, and has had multitudes of worshipers in these forms. Vishnu is the preserver of the universe. His consort is LAKSHMI or SRI. Also called Vasudeva.

**VISHNUISM or VAISNAVISM** Indian worship of VISHNU or of one of his incarnations. A great exposition of Vishnuism may be found in the famous BHAGAVAD-GITA.

**VISION** Glimpse of the divine or supernatural.

**VISITATION** 1. Divine bringing of blessing or punishment. 2. St. Mary's visit to St. Elisabeth before the birth of John the Baptist. 3. CATHOLIC feast commemorating Mary's visit to Elisabeth, observed on July 2, and known as the Visitation of Our Lady. 4. Ecclesiastical visit.

**VISITATION, CONGREGATION OF THE** Female religious order founded by St.

FRANCIS OF SALES and St. JANE FRANCES DE CHANTAL in 1610. Members wear a black habit. The order's purposes are religious contemplation and female education. A noted member was St. Margaret Mary ALACOQUE.

**VISITATION OF OUR LADY** See VISITATION, 3.

**VISPERED** *all the principal ones* Second part of the Zend AVESTA of ZOROASTRIANISM. It contains prayers to the spirits associated with AHURA MAZDA or Ormazd.

**VISVA-KARMA** *all-powerful* HINDU term for the Creator.

**VISVESVARA** *Lord of all* A title of SIVA.

**VITAL, HAYIM (1543–1620)** Jewish mystic and cabalist who wrote the gigantic *Tree of Life.*

**VITORIA, FRANCISCO DE (c.1485–1546)** Spanish theologian often considered to be the father of international law. He criticized the Spanish conquest of South American lands and held that the only just war consists in righting a wrong.

**VITRINGA, CAMPEGIUS (c.1659–1722)** Dutch REFORMED Biblical exegete whose two-volume commentary on Isaiah was highly praised by GESENIUS.

**VITUS, ST. (c. fourth century)** Sicilian martyr invoked against hydrophobia, St. Vitus' Dance, and other diseases. His feast day is June 15.

**VIVEKANANDA (1863–1902)** HINDU Bengali of India, originally named Narendra Nath Datta, who expounded the beliefs of RAMAKRISHNA and founded the Ramakrishna Mission. He founded several VEDANTA SOCIETIES in the United States and wrote extensively.

**VLADIMIR, ST. (956–1015)** Russian duke who was converted to Greek Orthodoxy and forced his subjects in Kiev to become Christians. He built many monasteries and churches. His feast day is July 15.

**VOCATION** Call to serve God, in one's work, life, or religious ministry.

**VOHU MANAH** ZOROASTRIAN spirit of wisdom.

**VOID** Buddhist term for a doctrine or reality difficult to express, but apparently indicating nothingness or the infinite or absolute.

**VOLOS** Serbian cattle god.

**VOLTAIRE, FRANÇOIS MARIE AROUET DE (1694–1778)** French writer and philosopher whose JESUIT education did not prevent his severe strictures against the Christianity he knew. He was a brilliant pessimist who advocated religious tolerance and freedom of thought. A DEIST, he built a temple and made a final statement: "I die adoring God."

**VOLTUMNA** Etruscan mother-goddess.

**VOLUNTEERS OF AMERICA** American religious organization founded by General Ballington BOOTH, son of the founder of the SALVATION ARMY, and his wife Maud in 1896. Its purpose and organization are similar to the Salvation Army, in which General Ballington Booth had been commander in Australia and the United States.

**VONDEL, JOOST VAN DEN (1587–1679)** CATHOLIC poet and dramatist of the Netherlands. Much of his work contains the theme of religious renunciation.

**VOODOO or VOODOOISM** Religion brought to the West Indies by African Negroes. In America sacrifices of an animal or a child and worship of pagan deities were soon combined with Christian elements. Magic, superstition, sorcery, and moonlight dances play an important part in Voodoo.

**VORTUMNUS** See VERTUMNUS.

**VOTARESS** Female votary.

**VOTARY** One consecrated by a vow.

**VOTIVE MASS** MASS for a special purpose such as a papal election or a wedding.

**VOTIVE OFFERING** Offering of gratitude or devotion to God or a saint.

**VOW** Solemn promise to the deity to do something considered important.

**VOWS OF RELIGION** Promises of a member of a CATHOLIC religious institute requiring poverty, chastity, and obedience. Some orders require a fourth vow.

**VOYSEY, CHARLES (1828–1912)** English founder of the Theistic Church. Once an ANGLICAN, he was deprived of his priesthood for heresy.

**VRIHASPATI** Vedic tutor of the gods.

**VULCAN** Roman god of fire and metal work.

**VULGATE common** Latin version of the Bible translated by St. JEROME over the turn of the fourth century. At first attacked, the Vulgate gradually won its way into the heart of Catholicism and became the official version of the ROMAN CATHOLIC CHURCH at the Council of TRENT. In 1908 Pope PIUS X appointed a commission to revise the text of the Vulgate.

# W

**WACHTNACHT** *watch night* Jewish term for the night preceding a CIRCUMCISION.

**WAFER** Thin crackerlike piece of bread used in the EUCHARIST in CATHOLIC and ANGLICAN churches.

**WAHABIS** Members of a MOSLEM sect founded in the eighteenth century by Mohammed ibn Abd al-Wahab. A reform movement, it interprets the KORAN literally and encourages sexual purity and a life of austerity. Ostentation, liquor, tobacco, hashish, usury, idolatry, and pilgrimages to the tombs of saints were originally forbidden, although time has liberalized some of Wahab's restrictions.

**WAILING WALL** Portion of the western wall of Jerusalem where for centuries pious Jews lamented the loss of the city and temple.

**WAKE** 1. Twenty-four-hour-long festival, honoring the patron saint of a church, observed in ancient England. 2. Vigil in the presence of a corpse, perhaps originating in Celtic superstition.

**WALBURGA or WALPURGA, ST. (c.710–779)** English missionary to Germany. Her name survives in the German witches' sabbath, Walpurgisnacht, which falls on the eve of May Day. According to some authorities, this is St. Walburga's feast day, which may account for the association. More commonly, her feast day is considered to be February 25.

**WALDENSES** Followers of Peter WALDO. Originating in medieval France, they held the Bible to be the supreme spiritual authority and condemned the mass, the papacy, and other things they did not find therein; they proclaimed the literal meaning of the words of Christ and renounced sex and private property. Through the Middle Ages they were continually persecuted.

**WALDENSIAN CHURCH or VAUDOIS** French PROTESTANT group with simple Biblical and Calvinistic principles. Members claim apostolic origin.

**WALDENSTROM, PAUL PETER (1838–1917)** Swedish pastor and evangelistic leader whose views of the love of God and the atonement of Christ produced considerable controversy. He was a leader in revival and foreign mission work.

**WALDO, PETER (c.1140–1217)** Wealthy merchant of Lyons, France, who gave away all his possessions to preach the literal gospel of Christ. Forbidden to preach without ecclesiastical permission, Waldo replied that he must obey God rather than men. He was excommunicated, traveled widely, and died in Bohemia. His followers, traveling in pairs, were called WALDENSES or Waldensians.

**WALI or WELI** Moslem term for ALLAH, saints, and guardian angels.

**WALLACE, LEWIS (1827–1905)** American lawyer, general of the army, and writer—noted for his religious novel *Ben Hur.*

**WALLIN, JOHAN OLOF (1779–1839)** Swedish archbishop and prolific hymn writer.

**WALPURGISNACHT** See St. WALBURGA.

**WALTHER, KARL F. W. (1811–1887)** German immigrant to the United States who founded the LUTHERAN CHURCH—MISSOURI SYNOD in 1847. A powerful leader, he wrote a number of theological works and was professor of theology at Concordia Theological Seminary.

**WANDERING JEW** Legendary Jew said to have mocked Jesus on his way to Calvary and to have been condemned to wander throughout time about the earth. The legend has of course no factual basis.

**WAR** Violent armed conflict denounced in principle, except on a just basis, by most religious groups. Jesus warned, "All they that take the sword shall perish with the sword" (MATTHEW 26:52) and the Scriptures extol the blessings of peace and justice. In specific wars, however, churches and religious groups usually support the national or cultural group within whose bounds they exist.

**WARD, JOHN (1781–1837)** Irish mystic who proclaimed many divine revelations and announced that he was the messiah to be born of Joanna SOUTHCOTT.

**WARD, MARY (1585–1645)** Founder in 1609 of the Institute of the Blessed Virgin Mary, a religious order organized on Jesuit lines.

**WARD, WILFRID PHILIP (1856–1916)** Son of William George WARD, and biographer of Cardinal Newman, Cardinal Wiseman, and his father.

**WARD, WILLIAM GEORGE (1812–1882)** ANGLICAN theologian who became a member of the OXFORD MOVEMENT and a CATHOLIC layman and apologist. He fiercely and powerfully espoused papal infallibility and similar doctrines.

**WARDEN** 1. Head of an ecclesiastical institution. 2. Official entrusted with the temporal affairs or the protection of property in a parish.

**WARE, HENRY (1764–1845)** American CONGREGATIONAL minister who aided in the organization of UNITARIANISM as a distinct religious group.

**WARFIELD, BENJAMIN BRECKINRIDGE (1851–1921)** Conservative American PRESBYTERIAN theologian. He tenaciously expounded the principles of historic CALVINISM and the authority of Scripture.

**WARS OF RELIGION** Sixteenth-century wars of the HUGUENOTS for religious freedom. They began in 1562 and ended with the EDICT OF NANTES in 1598.

**WAT** BUDDHIST monastery or temple in Siam.

**WATER** Religious symbol of purification and life.

**WATTS, ISAAC (1674–1748)** Independent English theologian, minister, and author of several hundred hymns. These include "Jesus Shall Reign," "O God, Our Help in Ages Past," "When I Survey the Wondrous Cross," "There Is a Land of Pure Delight," and "Joy to the World." Before Isaac Watts, Protestant singing had been restricted to the Psalms. To him we owe our present use of hymns in the church.

**WAVE OFFERINGS** Portions of the peace offerings in ancient Jewish sacrifices. Bread and boiled meat were waved before the Lord and eaten by the priests (LEVITICUS 7:30–34; 23:10–20).

**WAW or VAU** Sixth letter in the Hebrew alphabet.

**WAY** Term for a means of finding God. Christ said, "I am the way" (JOHN 14:6).

**WEBER, MAX (1864–1920)** German economist and sociologist who formulated the thesis that capitalism is intimately related to PROTESTANTISM. Familiar with the social and religious history of China and India, he held that the individualistic emphasis and the austere outlook of the Protestant faith—and of CALVINISM in particular—account for the fact that capitalism is a unique product of the Protestant West. Weber's books include *General Economic History* and *The Protestant Ethic and the Spirit of Capitalism*.

**WEDDING** Ceremony beginning a marriage, often a religious affair. According to the JUDEO-CHRISTIAN tradition, weddings should take place in the presence of God.

**WEE FREES** Popular name of members of the Free Church of Scotland, an independently minded PRESBYTERIAN denomination.

**WEEKS, FEAST OF** See FEAST OF WEEKS.

**WEEMS, MASON LOCKS (1759–1825)** American EPISCOPAL parson whose biography of George Washington originated the story of Washington's boyhood attack on a cherry tree with his hatchet.

**WEHU RACHUM and He, being merciful** Jewish prayers, stressing the mercy of the Lord, recited in services on Monday and Thursday.

**WEIGEL, GUSTAVE A. (1906–1964)** Liberal American JESUIT. A theologian and church leader, he pioneered in the attempt to create Catholic–Protestant dialogue and was considered an authority on relationships between church and state.

**WEIGEL, VALENTIN (1533–1588)** German LUTHERAN pastor who studied the writings of Paracelsus and DIONYSIUS THE AREOPAGITE, became a mystical writer, and denounced Bibliolaters.

**WEIL, SIMONE (1909–1943)** French Jewish mystic who became a Roman Catholic and wrote many essays with spiritual overtones.

**WEISS, JOHANNES (1863–1914)** German New Testament scholar and theologian. He discovered form criticism and wrote a commentary on First Corinthians and studies of primitive Christianity.

**WEIZMANN, CHAIM (1874–1952)** Zionist leader, scientist, and first president of Israel. He aided in the formation of Hebrew University and founded the Weizmann Institute of Science.

**WELD, THEODORE D. (1803–1895)** American abolitionist who put the antislavery movement on strong Christian foundations.

**WELI** See WALI.

**WELLHAUSEN, JULIUS (1844–1918)** German Old Testament scholar, a Protestant, who made critical studies of both the Old Testament and the New Testament. He saw in the first the gradual evolution of Hebrew religion, and in the second, the priority of Mark among the Gospels.

**WELL OF THE STAR** Well near Bethlehem said to have reflected the light of the star sought by the wise men (see MAGI) as they came to worship Jesus.

**WELLS, BLESSED SWITHIN (c.1536–1591)** English CATHOLIC teacher martyred for his faith.

**WELSH CALVINISTIC METHODISTS** Welsh Protestant church founded about 1735. It is PRESBYTERIAN in doctrine and government.

**WENCESLAS, ST. (c.907–929)** Bohemian king, noted for his Christian zeal, assassinated by his brother. Regarded as a martyr with a feast day September 28, Wenceslas' name is widely known through the Christmas carol "Good King Wenceslas."

**W'EN-CH'UNG or WEN TSCH'ANG** Chinese TAOIST god of literature.

**WESEL, JOHN OF (c.1420–1489)** Dutch member of the BRETHREN OF THE COMMON LIFE who anticipated LUTHER with his substitution of the Bible for church councils as the ultimate spiritual authority. He attacked fasting, indulgences, ritualism, and transubstantiation. Forced to recant, he was imprisoned in a monastery where he died.

**WESLEY, CHARLES (1707–1788)** English Methodist leader, hymn writer, and brother of John WESLEY. One of the first METHO-

DISTS, he is said to have composed more than five thousand hymns including "Love Divine," "Jesus, Lover of My Soul" and "Hark! the Herald Angels Sing."

**WESLEY, JOHN (1703–1791)** English founder of METHODISM. An Anglican clergyman, he found his heart being strangely warmed in 1738 while listening to the reading of a comment by LUTHER on Romans. He became a preacher to multitudes and is credited with saving England from the throes of revolution through the changes Methodism produced in the nation's life. Although he never left the CHURCH OF ENGLAND, he inspired the organization of Methodist churches in various areas. "The world is my parish," he is reported to have said.

**WESLEYAN METHODIST CHURCH** Early name of the METHODIST CHURCH in England.

**WESLEYAN METHODIST CHURCH OF AMERICA** Denomination founded in the United States in 1843. It emphasizes personal holiness, entire sanctification as a second definite work of grace, and abstention from tobacco, alcohol, and secret societies. At present the Wesleyan Methodist Church is contemplating union with the FREE METHODIST CHURCH OF NORTH AMERICA.

**WESLEYAN REFORM UNION** Small English denomination founded in 1849.

**WESLEY CLUBS** METHODIST organizations for young people of college age.

**WESSEL, JOHANN** See WESEL, JOHN OF.

**WEST, BENJAMIN (1738–1820)** American painter of many religious themes. A QUAKER, he spent most of his life in England.

**WESTCOTT, BROOKE FOSS (1825–1901)** ANGLICAN bishop who wrote important commentaries on New Testament books and contributed much to Biblical understanding. As a bishop he interested himself in social problems while as a theologian he emphasized the person and work of Christ. An outstanding achievement was his preparation, together with Fenton John Anthony HORT, of a critical edition of the Greek New Testament.

**WESTERMARCK, EDWARD A. (1862–1939)** Finnish anthropologist and professor of philosophy who wrote widely on marriage and morality.

**WESTERN CHURCH** Term for Christianity

in Europe and America, or for ROMAN CATHOLICISM as opposed to EASTERN ORTHODOXY.

**WESTERN TEXT** Rugged early form of the Greek text of the New Testament, named by WESTCOTT and HORT. Important light on the probable original meaning of many passages is supplied by this text.

**WESTMINSTER ABBEY** Ancient London church dating back to at least the middle of the eleventh century. There the great of England are buried.

**WESTMINISTER ASSEMBLY** PROTESTANT convocation at Westminster Abbey from 1643 to 1647. It produced the WESTMINSTER CONFESSION OF FAITH, the LARGER CATECHISM, and the SHORTER CATECHISM which have been normative for PRESBYTERIANISM for centuries. Delegates were 30 laymen and 121 clergymen, including Anglicans, Presbyterians, and Independents.

**WESTMINSTER CONFESSION OF FAITH** Creedal statement produced at the WESTMINSTER ASSEMBLY, 1643–1647. It emphasizes the authority of Scripture, the sovereignty of God, the sinfulness of man, and the redemption of Christ. It is the basis of the doctrine of most PRESBYTERIAN and CONGREGATIONAL churches, and has deeply influenced Protestantism.

**WESTMINSTER FELLOWSHIP** PRESBYTERIAN youth organization.

**WEYDEN, ROGER VAN DER (c.1400–1464)** Brilliant Flemish painter whose works include "Virgin and Child With Saints," "Adoration of the Magi," "St. Luke Painting the Virgin," "The Crucifixion," "The Descent From the Cross," and "The Last Judgment."

**WEYMOUTH, R. F. (1822–1902)** English BAPTIST headmaster of Mill Hill School noted for his *New Testament in Modern Speech* published in 1903.

**WHALE** Religious symbol of evil and Satan. Interestingly, the book of Jonah does not mention a whale; it does speak of a great fish which swallowed Jonah.

**WHEAT** Symbol of communion or blessing in religious art. Ripe wheat may symbolize maturity or the imminence of death.

**WHEEL** Symbol of St. CATHERINE OF ALEXANDRIA, who according to tradition was tortured while tied to a wheel.

**WHEELOCK, ELEAZAR (1711–1779)** American CONGREGATIONAL minister who founded Dartmouth College and served as its first president. He also founded a school for Indians.

**WHEEL OF LIFE** HINDU and BUDDHIST conception of reincarnation as an endless cycle of birth, death, rebirth, death, rebirth, etc. Escape comes only by salvation through buddhahood, union with the infinite, or the like.

**WHIPPLE, HENRY BENJAMIN (1822–1901)** First EPISCOPAL Bishop of Minnesota and co-founder of the Seabury Divinity School.

**WHITBY, SYNOD OF** English ecclesiastical gathering which settled on the date of Easter reckoned by the Roman as opposed to that calculated by the Irish Church. The date was 664 or 663.

**WHITE** Religious symbol of light, joy, purity, innocence, and holiness. It often represents Christ, St. Mary, and nonmartyred saints. White is used in many churches at Christmastide and Eastertide, on Trinity Sunday, and at communion, weddings, and special festivals.

**WHITE, ANDREW DICKSON (1832–1918)** American EPISCOPAL diplomat who worked for the founding and served as the first president of Cornell University. His *History of the Warfare of Science With Theology in Christendom* expounded his conviction that knowledge is furthered through liberty and stifled through religious oppression.

**WHITE, BOUCK (1874–1951)** Social-minded CONGREGATIONAL minister who founded New York City's Church of the Social Revolution.

**WHITE, ELLEN GOULD HARMON (1827–1915)** SEVENTH-DAY ADVENTIST leader in the United States whose writings are still widely influential.

**WHITE, WILLIAM (1748–1836)** ANGLICAN clergyman whose pamphlet entitled *The Case of the Episcopal Churches in the United States* and diligent effort helped establish the PROTESTANT EPISCOPAL CHURCH in the United States. He became Episcopal Bishop of Pennsylvania.

**WHITE FATHERS** Popular name of the Society of Missionaries of Africa, a CATHOLIC organization of white-garbed missionaries in North Africa and Central Africa founded in 1868.

**WHITEFIELD, GEORGE (1714–1770)** METH-

ODIST evangelist of Calvinist persuasion who with John and Charles Wesley led the eighteenth century's English revival. In America he was prominent in that century's GREAT AWAKENING.

**WHITE FRIARS**  Friars of the order of the CARMELITES.

**WHITEHEAD, ALFRED NORTH (1861–1947)** English philosopher who conceived God as limited and gradually developing. His philosophy emphasized God, change, and individuality. Among his works are *Religion in the Making* and *Essays in Science and Philosophy*.

**WHITE LADIES**  Term for several religious orders: Magdalens, Cistercian nuns, and Sisters of the Presentation of Mary.

**WHITE MONKS**  Popular name for white-garbed CISTERCIANS.

**WHITE SUPREMACY**  Pseudoscientific notion that one race, the white, is inherently superior to another, the colored. While sometimes cloaking itself in religion, the idea of race supremacy is fundamentally irreligious.

**WHITMAN, MARCUS (1802–1847)**  American PROTESTANT missionary and pioneer of the Oregon Trail, murdered by Cayuse Indians.

**WHITMAN, WALT (1819–1892)**  American poet whose free-swinging verse contains many profoundly religious insights.

**WHITSUNDAY**  "White Sunday" or PENTECOST, Christian festival on the seventh Sunday after EASTER.

**WHITSUNTIDE**  Day of PENTECOST and the first two or six days that follow.

**WHITTIER, JOHN GREENLEAF (1807–1892)** QUAKER poet of New England who wrote many hymns including "Dear Lord and Father of Mankind." His verse reveals devout faith and a strong sense of social righteousness.

**WHORE OF BABYLON**  Figure in Revelation 17, often identified in Reformation days as the pope or ROMAN CATHOLICISM.

**WIDOWS**  Women who had lost their husbands were the objects of special solicitude in both JUDAISM and CHRISTIANITY in ancient times. (Cf. DEUTERONOMY 16:11; 26:12, ACTS 6:1; I TIMOTHY 5:3–16.) For centuries the church has continued this special care for widows and orphans.

**WILBERFORCE, WILLIAM (1759–1833)**  English philanthropist and statesman who sought both evangelical and social progress. An ANGLICAN layman, he led the Evangelical Party, opposed the wars of England against the United States and France in the late eighteenth century, fought a successful campaign against the British slave trade, and championed foreign missions. He belonged to the CLAPHAM SECT, and helped found the BRITISH AND FOREIGN BIBLE SOCIETY and the CHURCH MISSIONARY SOCIETY. He also supported Catholic emancipation and many other reforms.

**WILBUR, JOHN (1774–1856)**  American QUAKER who opposed the teachings of Elias HICKS and Joseph John GURNEY. These men proclaimed an evangelical Quaker faith with emphasis on the work of salvation and the authority of Scripture. Wilbur and his followers held to the earlier principles of silently waiting before God for the breaking forth of the inner light. The "Wilburites," breaking away in 1845, became the Religious Society of Friends (Conservative).

**WILFRID, ST. (634–709)**  Noble English archbishop who led the church in England to follow Roman rather than Celtic practices, including the Western calculation of the date of Easter. He championed culture, education, and the evangelization of the Frisians. His feast day is October 12.

**WILKINSON, JEMIMA (1752–1819)**  New England religious fanatic who founded several churches, as well as the colony of Jerusalem near Penn Yan, New York. The latter became a center of her disciples, who considered her a messiah.

**WILLARD, FRANCES ELIZABETH CAROLINE (1839–1898)**  American educator who became a cofounder of the WOMAN'S CHRISTIAN TEMPERANCE UNION. She was energetic in the causes of total abstinence and woman suffrage.

**WILLIAM DE LA MARE (thirteenth century)** English FRANCISCAN who disputed the theology of THOMAS AQUINAS.

**WILLIAM OF OCCAM (c.1300–c.1349)** Medieval Franciscan SCHOLASTIC renowned for his philosophy. A leader in the school of NOMINALISM, he denied the common doctrine of universals and abstraction, holding that only specific individual things exist. He traced the basis of morality and of existence itself to the will of God. This led to his contention that knowledge is reached through intuition and that reason can neither prove nor disprove things of faith. He denied the pope's temporal authority. For a time he was imprisoned for his beliefs.

**WILLIAMS, GEORGE (1821–1905)** English merchant who held prayer meetings for his fellow workers and founded the YOUNG MEN'S CHRISTIAN ASSOCIATION in 1844.

**WILLIAMS, ROGER (c.1604–1683)** English ANGLICAN clergyman who became first a PURITAN and then a BAPTIST leader. After voicing his belief in religious liberty he was banished from the Massachusetts colony and went to Rhode Island, where he founded a new colony. This became a haven from religious oppression; those "distrest in conscience" found a welcome in Rhode Island. Williams sought to live in peace with the Indians and succeeded until the beginning of King Philip's War.

**WILLIBRORD, ST. (c.658–739)** English missionary to the Frisians. A BENEDICTINE, he became archbishop of the Frisians. His feast day is November 7.

**WILLOW** Symbol of the Christian gospel.

**WIND** Symbol of the Holy Spirit. In the two languages of the Bible, Hebrew and Greek, the words for wind and spirit are often identical.

**WINE** Symbol of abundance, joy, and the sacrificial blood of Christ.

**WINEPRESS** Symbol of the wrath of God.

**WINER, JOHANN GEORG BENEDIKT (1789–1858)** German PROTESTANT theologian renowned for his *Grammar of New Testament Greek* (1822), long a standard reference work.

**WINES, ENOCH COBB (1806–1879)** American minister who sparked the reform of many prisons and reformatories.

**WINGS** Symbol of celestial mission.

**WINTHROP, JOHN (1588–1649)** Governor of New England's Massachusetts colony. He helped shape its theocracy and fought the heresies of Anne HUTCHINSON, who was considered a pillar of ANTINOMIANISM.

**WISDOM** Important religious element. The Bible emphasizes the wisdom of God and the necessity of wisdom in man. GNOSTICISM deified Wisdom as an object of worship.

**WISDOM LITERATURE** Term for the OLD TESTAMENT books of JOB, PROVERBS, ECCLESIASTES (and in the CATHOLIC canon, ECCLESIASTICUS and the WISDOM OF SOLOMON). These books emphasize what might be called common sense: true wisdom in business, in the home, in amusement, etc.

**WISDOM OF JESUS THE SON OF SIRACH** See ECCLESIASTICUS.

**WISDOM OF SOLOMON** Apocryphal book of the Old Testament extolling righteousness, wisdom, and the rewards and punishments of God. Examples of the latter are taken from Jewish history.

**WISE, ISAAC MAYER (1819–1900)** Bohemian-born rabbi who established REFORM JUDAISM in America. He founded the UNION OF AMERICAN HEBREW CONGREGATIONS, the CENTRAL CONFERENCE OF AMERICAN RABBIS, and the Hebrew Union College. A controversial writer, he edited *The American Israelite* and was the author of *The Essence of Judaism, History of the Israelitish Nation,* and other works.

**WISE, JOHN (1652–1725)** American CONGREGATIONAL minister who labored hard for democracy in both church and state. While upholding traditional Congregationalism he had to oppose the plan of Increase and Cotton MATHER to set groups of clergymen over the churches.

**WISE, STEPHEN SAMUEL (1874–1949)** Rabbi who came to the United States from Hungary and founded the Jewish Institute of Religion and the Free Synagogue of New York. He was a leader in REFORM JUDAISM, ZIONISM, and international Jewish work.

**WISEMAN, NICHOLAS PATRICK STEPHEN (1802–1865)** English cardinal and Archbishop of Westminster who lessened tensions both within and relating to the ROMAN CATHOLIC CHURCH. He sympathized with the OXFORD MOVEMENT.

**WISE MEN** See MAGI.

**WISHART, GEORGE (c.1513–1546)** Scottish PROTESTANT reformer who converted John KNOX. A preacher of REFORMATION doctrines, he was arrested for heresy and burned at the stake.

**WITCH** Female magician considered to have supernatural powers.

**WITCHCRAFT** Practice of magic through diabolical possession. Witchcraft was condemned in ancient JUDAISM and the ancient CHRISTIAN CHURCH.

**WITCH DOCTOR** African priest who heals and reverses spells by locating the witch or enemy who caused his client's misfortune.

**WITCHES' SABBATH** Orgy of witches, demons, and the like, usually at midnight.

**WITHERSPOON, JOHN (1723–1794)** Scottish-born PRESBYTERIAN minister who signed the American Declaration of Independence. He was a president of the College of New Jersey, a leader in the Presbyterian Church, and a worker for the independence of the Thirteen Colonies.

**WITNESS** 1. One who has personal knowledge. A Christian witness knows what God has done for him and can testify to that fact. 2. Attestation. Christian witness is the certification of God's mighty acts of redemption.

**WITTENBERG** German city known as "the cradle of the Reformation." There Martin LUTHER posted his NINETY-FIVE THESES, burned the papal encyclical which denounced him, and preached justification by faith. There he lived and was buried. There too lies Philip MELANCHTHON (who also preached in that town). There the first Lutheran Bible was printed.

**WITTENBERG, CONCORD OF** Agreement in 1536 between Martin LUTHER, Philip MELANCHTHON, and Martin BUCER and their followers about the doctrine of the EUCHARIST. The concord accepted basically Lutheran views, but the Zwinglian churches did not accept them.

**WIZARD** Sorcerer, magician, or male practitioner of witchcraft—reputed to have supernatural powers.

**W.I.Z.O.** Abbreviation for WOMEN'S INTERNATIONAL ZIONIST ORGANIZATION.

**WODEN or ODIN** Supreme Scandinavian god, master of war, storms, winds, agriculture, poetry, learning, earth, and heaven. He was creator of men, the earth, and the sky. His consort was FRIGGA or FREYA and his children THOR, BALDER, and TIW. Also written Wodan, Wotan, or Odhin.

**WOES, SEVEN MESSIANIC** Sevenfold condemnation of religious leaders by Jesus, recorded in Matthew 23.

**WOES OF THE MESSIAH** Term for the time of troubles indicated in the New Testament before the end of the age (MATTHEW 24; II TIMOTHY 3).

**WOLFF, CHRISTIAN (1679–1754)** German philosopher who devised a thoroughly rationalistic view of God; this so offended the German pietists that for a time Wolff was exiled. He wrote treatises on ethics, natural theology, logic, and various other fields of thought.

**WOLSEY, THOMAS (c.1474–1530)** English CATHOLIC cardinal who controlled much of England's power during the earlier years of King Henry VIII. Failing, however, to win papal approval of Henry's divorce from Catherine of Aragon, he was charged with treason. Wolsey sought to be pope and strengthened the interests of England.

**WOMAN'S CHRISTIAN TEMPERANCE UNION** Organization founded in the United States in 1874 to battle prostitution, the double sex standard, and the sale and use of alcoholic beverages. Many Christian women have been active in it.

**WOMEN'S GALLERY** Portion of synagogue sometimes reserved for women.

**WOMEN'S INTERNATIONAL ZIONIST ORGANIZATION** International Jewish women's group seeking the interests of the state of Israel.

**WON** School of BUDDHISM in Korea founded about 1916. Somewhat related to ZEN Buddhism, Won emphasizes both the social and the spiritual aspects of the faith.

**WOODPECKER** Symbol of Satan in medieval art.

**WOOL** Biblical symbol of purity.

**WOOLLEY, CHARLES LEONARD (1880–1960)** English archaeologist who did considerable excavation in the Near East. His works include *Digging Up the Past* and *Excavations at Ur*.

**WOOLMAN, JOHN (1720–1772)** American QUAKER preacher, humanitarian, and mystic. He intensely opposed slavery and is noted for his *Journal*, a spiritual autobiography published in 1774.

**WORCESTER, ELWOOD (c.1862 – 1940)** American EPISCOPAL rector and professor of psychology who helped begin the EMMANUEL MOVEMENT, a ministry relating medical and spiritual healing, and wrote several books in this area. These include *Religion and Medicine, The Christian Religion as a Healing Power*, and *Body, Mind, and Spirit*.

**WORCESTER, NOAH (1758–1837)** CONGREGATIONAL minister of New England who wrote able critiques of the policy of warfare and labored for peace. He wrote extensively on behalf of peace and helped found several peace societies.

**WORD** 1. Means of communication between personalities. Cf. LOGOS. 2. Scripture as the divine revelation written. 3. Christ as God's supreme revelation (cf. JOHN 1:1). 4. Preaching of the message of God, as in the gospel.

**WORDS, SEVEN LAST** The seven sayings of Jesus from the cross.

**WORDS OF INSTITUTION** The words used by Jesus in instituting the LORD'S SUPPER (cf. I CORINTHIANS 11:23-25).

**WORDSWORTH, WILLIAM (1770-1850)** English poet whose works impart a sense of the presence of God in nature and everyday life. His *Ecclesiastical Sonnets* sketch the history of the church in Great Britain to the seventeenth century.

**WORKS** New Testament term for demonstrable activity. Jesus' works evidenced His divine mission (JOHN 20:30, 31). Believers demonstrate their faith by their works (MATTHEW 5:16; JAMES 2:14-26). But human works result from the inner spirit, and are the result, not the cause, of divine grace (ROMANS 4:1-5; 8:7-8; EPHESIANS 2:8-9).

**WORKS OF MERCY** Theological term for deeds done from a spirit of love. Many religious orders emphasize the doing of works of mercy.

**WORLD** 1. Earth or universe created by God and inherently good. 2. System and course of the present age, so filled with and distorted by sin that Christians are bade not to love it (I JOHN 2:15-17; 5:4). Contemporary theology is taking a new look at the world; reversing the ancient religious retreat from secularism, it poses ways and means of penetrating the world for spiritual conquest.

**WORLD BROTHERHOOD** Organization formed in Paris in 1950 to promote international understanding, particularly among CHRISTIANS and JEWS.

**WORLD CONFERENCE OF PENTECOSTAL CHURCHES** Former name of PENTECOSTAL WORLD CONFERENCE.

**WORLD CONFERENCE OF MENNONITES** See MENNONITE WORLD CONFERENCE.

**WORLD CONFERENCE ON FAITH AND ORDER** World conference to which all Christian churches in the world were invited in 1910 by the PROTESTANT EPISCOPAL CHURCH of the United States. Conferences were held in response in 1920, 1927, and 1937.

**WORLD CONVENTION OF THE CHURCHES OF CHRIST (DISCIPLES)** International organization of CHRISTIAN CHURCHES or DISCIPLES OF CHRIST. Headquarters are in New York City.

**WORLD COUNCIL OF CHRISTIAN EDUCATION AND SUNDAY SCHOOL ASSOCIATION** International organization of church schools originally known as the World's Sunday School Association. Headquarters are in London and New York.

**WORLD COUNCIL OF CHURCHES** International fellowship of churches. Constituted in the Netherlands in 1948 with representatives from 150 denominations, both PROTESTANT and ORTHODOX, it now includes more than 200 religious groups. Members profess to "accept our Lord Jesus Christ as God and Saviour." Assemblies are held every six or seven years. Administration is through a 90-member central committee; headquarters are in Geneva, Switzerland. There are six presidents.

**WORLD FEDERATION OF LUTHERANS** International LUTHERAN organization.

**WORLD FELLOWSHIP OF BUDDHISTS** International BUDDHIST organization founded in 1950 in Ceylon. It has called together several world conferences of Buddhists.

**WORLD JAIN MISSION** International JAIN organization with headquarters in Lucknow, India.

**WORLD JEWISH CONGRESS** International association of Jewish communities formed in 1936. Administration is through an executive committee; there is a general council which meets every year and a plenary session which meets every three years.

**WORLDLINESS** Theological term emphasizing an interest in the physical world which crowds out spiritual concerns.

**WORLD METHODIST COUNCIL** International METHODIST organization, formed in 1881, with headquarters at Lake Junaluska, North Carolina. It periodically convenes conferences of Methodist churches from various parts of the world.

**WORLD MUSLIM LEAGUE** Supreme religious grouping in ISLAM, founded in 1962. It is governed by 23 grand IMAMS who are leading MOSLEM teachers of the world.

**WORLD OF EMANATION** Supreme world of the four between this world and the highest heaven, according to CABALISM.

**WORLD SOUL** Term in HINDUISM and other Eastern religions for the spirit of the universe, as BRAHMA, the creative principle, or the animating spirit in nature.

**WORLD TO COME** JUDEO-CHRISTIAN concept of the messianic age which is to follow the present age of imperfection and evil.

**WORLD WITHOUT END** Liturgical term for eternity concluding the GLORIA PATRI.

**WORMS** German city with an ancient Jewish settlement and an independent history. There Pope GREGORY VII was deposed. Worms is probably most famous, however, for the Diet of Worms in 1521 (see below).

**WORMS, DIET OF** Imperial assembly held at Worms, Germany, in 1521 to hear the charges against Martin LUTHER, who had been excommunicated by Pope LEO X. Refusing to recant, Luther was condemned in the EDICT OF WORMS.

**WORSHIP** Religious homage or reverence toward the deity, or (sometimes) toward saints or religious objects. Worship may be public or private, formal or informal. It is an important part of vital religion.

**WORSHIP CENTER** Altar or area serving as a focus of worship.

**WORSHIP, ORDER OF** Sequence of elements in a program of public worship. In most American churches the order of worship is printed or mimeographed in a bulletin for all members of the congregation.

**WOUNDS, FIVE SACRED** 1. Wounds in Jesus' feet, hands, and side. 2. CATHOLIC feast or devotion commemorating Jesus' wounds.

**WOTAN** See WODEN.

**WOVOKA (c.1858–1932)** American Indian prophet of the GHOST DANCE RELIGION. His call for pacifistic quietism among North American Indians stirred many of them.

**WRATH OF GOD** Biblical term for God's attitude toward sin and evil. His perfect justice, holiness, and love will not rest until all evil and sin are destroyed, and His wrath is against those who refuse to do His will. (PSALM 2:5; MATTHEW 3:7; ROMANS 1:18; REVELATION 11:18; 14:10; 16:19.)

**WREN, CHRISTOPHER (1632–1723)** Skilled English architect who designed more than fifty churches in London, including the noted St. Paul's Cathedral.

**WRITINGS** Jewish term for that division of Old Testament Scripture following the Law and the Prophets. The Writings include the Psalms, Proverbs, Job, the Song of Solomon, Ruth, Lamentations, Ecclesiastes, Esther, Ezra, Nehemiah, and I and II Chronicles.

**WROE, JOHN (1782–1863)** English founder of the Christian Israelites.

**WURTEMBERG CONFESSION** PROTESTANT statement of faith prepared by Johann Brenz in 1552 for consideration by the Council of TRENT.

**WU-TAO-TZU (c.700–760)** Outstanding BUDDHIST painter of China.

**WU-WEI** TAOIST term for harmonious conformity to the divine order of things.

**WYCLIF or WYCLIFFE, JOHN (c.1329–1384)** English rector whose criticism of wrongs he found in the church led to his fame as a reformer and his condemnation as a heretic. He attacked indulgences, penances, and transubstantiation, asserting the authority of the Bible against the decisions of the church. His followers produced the WYCLIF BIBLE, and his work foreshadowed the Protestant Reformation. In 1428 his remains were exhumed and burned by order of the Council of CONSTANCE.

**WYCLIF BIBLE** Popular term for one of the first translations of the whole Bible into English. This was actually brought about by Wyclif's followers, particularly by Nicholas Hereford and John PURVEY.

**WYCLIFFITES** Followers of John WYCLIF. See LOLLARDS.

**WYTTENBACH, THOMAS (1472–1526)** Swiss reformer and teacher of ZWINGLI.

# X

**X** English letter identical in appearance with the Greek letter *chi* and therefore often a symbol of Christ (from *Christos*).

**XAVIER, FRANCIS, ST.** See FRANCIS XAVIER, ST.

**XAVIERIAN BROTHERS** Lay CATHOLIC congregation of teaching brothers, organized in 1839 by Brother Francis-Xavier Ryken. Its main purpose is religious education, St. FRANCIS XAVIER its patron saint.

**XENOPHANES (c.570–c.480 B.C.)** Greek philosopher who rejected ancient conceptions of many gods in favor of one eternal Creator.

**XILONEN** Goddess of green corn among the Aztecs and the Mexicans of the twelfth century.

**XIMENES DE CISNEROS, FRANCISCO** See JIMINEZ DE CISNEROS, FRANCISCO.

**XIPE** Aztec god who lived in human flesh.

**XIUHTECUHTLI** Aztec god of fire and the hearth.

**XOCHIPILLI** Aztec "Lord of the Flowers," god of play, dance, love, and joy.

**XOCHIQUETZAL** Aztec goddess of flowers and pleasure.

**XP** Symbolic representation of Christ, based on the identification of these two letters with the two Greek letters *chi* and *rho*, the first two letters in *Christos*.

**XYLOLATERS** *wood-worshipers* Term used by the ICONOCLASTS to describe EASTERN ORTHODOX Christians who revered images and statues.

# Y

YACATECUTLI   Aztec god of travelers.

YAD *hand*   Pointer used in synagogue services in the reading of the TORAH.

YAGHUTH   Ancient Arabian deity.

YAHRZEIT   Jewish term for yearly commemoration of the death of a parent or close relative.

YAHWEH   Jewish name for the Lord, based on the four letters *yodh, he, waw,* and *he.* It is sometimes transliterated as "JEHOVAH."

YAHWISM   1. Use of the name *Yahweh* or *Jehovah.* 2. Worship of YAHWEH or JEHOVAH.

YAHWIST   Term in Biblical criticism for a writer of Scripture who is seemingly addicted to excessive use of the name "YAHWEH" or "JEHOVAH."

YAJUR-VEDA   Second VEDA, consisting of prayers, hymns, and magical formulae. It was important in Vedic religion.

YAKSHA   HINDU nature deities.

YAMA   Lord of death in BUDDHISM and HINDUISM.

YAMIM NORAIM *days of solemnity*   Jewish term for ROSH HASHANAH and Yom Kippur (see ATONEMENT, DAY OF) or for the ten days including these. They are days of reverence, prayer, and penitence.

YAMM   Ancient Babylonian god of the sea.

YANG   Active male principle of the universe in TAOISM. The passive female principle is YIN.

YANTRA   Symbolic diagram used for meditation or for magical purposes in BUDDHISM and HINDUISM. See also MANTRA.

YARMULKE   Jewish skullcap.

YASHT   ZOROASTRIAN hymn praising a deity or an angelic being.

YASNA   Liturgical book in the sacred writings of ZOROASTRIANISM.

YATI   JAIN ascetic.

YAZATAS   ZOROASTRIAN deities of lower rank than AHURA MAZDAH and his angelic host.

YELLOW   In religious symbolism, color of degradation, deceit, and treachery. A golden yellow, however, is a symbol of divinity.

YELLOW HATS   Popular term for the Tibetan order of BUDDHISM, Gelupa or Gelug-pa (Virtuous Ones). Its members sometimes wear yellow hats.

YEMAJA   Water goddess in the religion of the Yoruba tribe of West Africa.

YEMEN   MOSLEM state in southern Arabia. Natives are of Arabian and Jewish descent.

YENGISHIKI   Oldest written record of SHINTO ritual. It was compiled in the tenth century.

YEN LI-PEN (?–c.673)   Chinese painter who executed many TAOIST and BUDDHIST themes.

YESHIVA   Higher Jewish school for rabbinical and talmudic study.

YESHIVA-BACHUR   Student of the TALMUD.

YEW   Religious symbol of immortality.

YEW SUNDAY   Name for PALM SUNDAY in the Middle Ages, since yew was often substituted for palm branches in festivities on that day.

YEZIDIS   Middle Eastern people whose religion appears to be a mixture of ZOROASTRIAN and other elements. Called Devil-Worshipers by the Moslems, they believe the universe is under the control of Malak Ta'us who is symbolized by a peacock. Their religious rites include baptisms, dancing, the singing of hymns, and the offering of sacrifices. They revere Sheikh 'Adi ben Musafir, a SUFI mystic of the twelfth century who is generally considered the founder of Yezidi religion. They trace their origin, however, to artificial conception from the seed of Adam.

**YGGDRASILL** Ash tree of Scandinavian myth with roots in the world below and evergreen branches reaching into both earth and ASGARD (the dwelling of the gods). It is to be destroyed in the twilight of the gods.

**YHWH** Transliteration of the four letters of the ineffably sacred name of YAHWEH or JEHOVAH.

**YIDAM** Protective aspect of God venerated by Tibetan BUDDHISTS.

**YIDDISH** Jewish language based on medieval German with many elements of Hebrew and other languages. Written in Hebrew characters, it has been the medium of much Jewish literature.

**YIGDAL** Synagogue hymn comprising thirteen articles of Jewish faith formulated by MAIMONIDES.

**YIH-KING** *book of changes* Canonical Chinese work on CONFUCIANISM dating from the twelfth century B.C. It includes many mystical diagrams.

**YIN** TAOIST symbol of the negative, the passive, the female, the dark and the dead. See also YANG.

**YIZKOR** *may He remember* Prayers for the deceased said on special Jewish holy days.

**Y.M.C.A.** Abbreviation for YOUNG MEN'S CHRISTIAN ASSOCIATION.

**Y.M.H.A.** Abbreviation for YOUNG MEN'S HEBREW ASSOCIATION.

**YMIR** Giant in Scandinavian myth slain by WODEN. From his flesh and bones the gods fashioned the earth, sea, and heaven.

**YODH or JOD** Tenth letter in the Hebrew alphabet. In religious symbolism the yodh, which slightly resembles a comma, may represent the name of the Lord when enclosed in a circle or triangle.

**YOGA** *yoke or union* HINDU philosophy or discipline designed to bring about union with the World Soul through physical and mental exercises. It involves specified postures, breathing exercises, and concentration.

**YOGACARA** Idealistic school of MAHAYANA Buddhism. Founded in the fifth century by Asanga and Vasubandhu, it distinguishes the true and false elements of existence. Knowledge of true existence leads to NIRVANA.

**YOGI** HINDU ascetic, or practitioner of YOGA. Yogis are known to possess extraordinary physical powers and have been credited with performing miraculous feats.

**YOKE** Wooden bar uniting two animals such as oxen for plowing or pulling a load. The Jewish prophets spoke of a yoke as a symbol of bondage or subjection (cf. JEREMIAH 28:4, 10). Jesus made the yoke a symbol of His way (MATTHEW 11:29-30). Hence, the yoke is often a token of Christian discipleship.

**YOKEFELLOW** St. Paul's term for an unknown fellow worker (PHILIPPIANS 4:3).

**YOM KIPPUR** *day of atonement* See ATONEMENT, DAY OF.

**YOB TOM or YOM TOV** *good day* Jewish term for a religious festival.

**YORK** English town which had a Christian community as early as the third or fourth century. It was the home of Alcuin and St. Paulinus; its archbishop is the primate of the Church of England, and its archbishops have included Thomas of York, Thomas Wolsey, and William Temple. York is the locale of the Fountains Abbey, the Abbey of St. Mary, the Cathedral of St. Peter, and the Monastery of Bolton.

**YORK USE** Ancient Catholic rite used in northern England and named for the diocese of YORK.

**YOUNG, BRIGHAM (1801–1877)** American Mormon leader and missionary. He led the Latter-Day Saints west, became governor of Utah and president of the CHURCH OF JESUS CHRIST OF LATTER-DAY SAINTS, married twenty-seven wives, and fathered fifty-six children. He shepherded his church through numerous problems and violent attacks and established it securely as one of the strong native religions of the United States.

**YOUNG, EDWARD (1683–1765)** ANGLICAN rector and poet, famous for the book-length poem *Night Thoughts* and other works.

**YOUNG, PATRICK (1584–1652)** English clergyman who published several important scholarly works including annotations on the CODEX ALEXANDRINUS and a first edition of the *First Epistle to the Corinthians* by St. CLEMENT OF ROME.

**YOUNG, ROBERT (1822–1888)** Scottish PRESBYTERIAN minister and missionary to

India who published numerous scholarly works. One of the most famous of these is his *Analytical Concordance* to the Bible.

**YOUNG, WILLIAM (1749–1815)** English statesman and poet.

**YOUNG LIFE** Aggressive yet conservative Christian group dedicated to evangelizing high school and college youth. It was founded in the United States by Jim Rayburn in 1937.

**YOUNG MEN'S CHRISTIAN ASSOCIATION** Youth organization founded by George WILLIAMS in London in 1844. Formed to aid young men physically, mentally, and spiritually, it long emphasized Bible study and interdenominational PROTESTANT Christianity. Today its program is more ecumenical and directed more toward social service.

**YOUNG MEN'S HEBREW ASSOCIATION** Youth organization dedicated to a social and cultural program for Jewish young people, particularly boys and young men.

**YOUNG WOMEN'S CHRISTIAN ASSOCIATION** Counterpart of the Young Men's Christian Association for young women, organized in 1877 in England.

**YOUNG WOMEN'S HEBREW ASSOCIATION** Counterpart of the Young Men's Hebrew Association for young women.

**YOUTH FELLOWSHIP** Common term for the program of Christian fellowship and training for young people in many PROTESTANT churches.

**YOUTH FOR CHRIST** Nondenominational fundamentalist organization formed in Chicago in 1944 by Torrey Johnson, George Beverly Shea, and Douglas Fisher to evangelize young people. "Youth for Christ" rallies have been held throughout the world.

**YOVEL** Jewish term for the Year of JUBILEE.

**Y.P.S.C.E.** See CHRISTIAN ENDEAVOR.

**YRSLM** Ancient form of the name of JERUSALEM.

**YUAN-WU** See ENGO.

**YUGA** One of the four ages of the world according to HINDUISM.

**YUH-HWANG-SHANGTE** TAOIST term for the Creator-Savior.

**YULE** 1. Scandinavian festival in honor of WODEN or Odin and his companions, held in mid-January. 2. Ancient British name for November, December, or January. 3. Christmas.

**YUM KAAX** Mayan fertility deity.

**YUN-KANG** Caves near Peking containing a multitude of BUDDHIST images from as early as the fifth century.

**YVES, ST. (c.1253–1303)** Priest and lawyer of Brittany, noted for his concern for those in need, who became the patron saint of lawyers. His feast day is May 19.

**Y.W.C.A.** Abbreviation for the YOUNG WOMEN'S CHRISTIAN ASSOCIATION.

**Y.W.H.A.** Abbreviation for the YOUNG WOMEN'S HEBREW ASSOCIATION.

# Z

**ZABUL** *prince* A title of the ancient god BAAL.

**ZACCARIA, ANTONIO MARIA** See BARNA-BITES.

**ZACCHAEUS** *pure* Tax collector of Jericho, who climbed a tree to see Jesus and became a disciple (LUKE 19:1–10).

**ZACHARIAH** *the Lord remembers* 1. King of Israel who inherited the throne from his father Jeroboam II and was murdered six months later (II KINGS 15:8–12). 2. Variant of ZECHARIAH.

**ZACHARIAS, ST.** 1. Priest of the Jewish temple in Jerusalem to whom the angel Gabriel revealed that he was to become the father of JOHN THE BAPTIST. "The Benedictus," his song of praise when John was circumcised, is a beautiful prophecy of the imminence of the Messiah's triumph (LUKE 1:5–80). St. Zacharias' feast day is November 5. 2. Greek pope (741–752) who denounced ICONOCLASM, supported the missionary activity of St. BONIFACE, and strengthened papal authority. His feast day is March 22.

**ZACHARIE or ZACHARY** Variants of ZACHARIAS or ZECHARIAH.

**ZACUTO, MOSES (1625–1697)** Amsterdam-born Jewish commentator and expert on the CABALA.

**ZADDICK, JOSEPH IBN (1080–1147)** Spanish talmudist, poet, scholar, and judge. He is noted for his *Microcosm*, a Neoplatonic philosophical treatise, and other works.

**ZADOK** *righteous* 1. Jewish war veteran and high priest who founded an exclusive priestly family (I KINGS 1:7—2:35; I CHRONICLES 12:28; 24:2–3; EZEKIEL 40:46; EZRA 7:2). 2. The name of several other Old Testament figures.

**ZAHN, THEODOR (1838–1933)** German PROTESTANT theologian and New Testament scholar. He wrote important commentaries on NEW TESTAMENT books and on patristic literature. Extremely erudite, he helped buttress the historicity of much of the New Testament.

**ZAIN or ZAYIN** Seventh letter in the Hebrew alphabet, comparable to the letter *z*.

**ZAKAT** MOSLEM tax on behalf of the needy and poor.

**ZARATHUSTRA** See ZOROASTER.

**ZAYIN** See ZAIN.

**ZAZEN** *Zen-sitting* Japanese word for meditation in ZEN Buddhism. A preferred position is the lotus posture in which the subject sits with the sole of each foot turned up on his opposite thigh.

**ZEAL** Ardent fervor in doing something, particularly from religious motives. Cf. Psalm 69:9; John 2:17.

**ZEALOTS** Jewish revolutionaries of the first century A.D. who sought to establish the messianic Kingdom by force. One of Jesus' Apostles was Simon the Zealot (LUKE 6:15; ACTS 1:13).

**ZEBEDEE** *given by the Lord* Well-to-do fisherman and father of the Apostles James and John (MATTHEW 4:21; 20:20; 26:37; MARK 1:19–20; 15:40).

**ZEBULUN** *dwelling* Son of Jacob from whom one of the twelve tribes of Israel descended. Zebulunites aided Barak and Deborah in the war with Sisera, and Gideon in the defeat of the Midianites.

**ZECHARIAH** *the Lord remembers* 1. Jewish prophet contemporary with HAGGAI. Like the latter, he urged his fellow citizens to rebuild the temple about 520 B.C. The book of Zechariah, constituting the eleventh book of the MINOR PROPHETS, contains visions and messages relating to this rebuilding. 2. Variant of ZACHARIAH.

3. Name of nearly thirty other Bible figures.

**ZEDEKIAH** *the righteousness of the Lord* 1. Son of Joash, also known at Mattaniah, who reigned as Judah's last king about 597–586 B.C. A contemporary of Jeremiah and Ezekiel, Zedekiah was carried captive with his people when Nebuchadnezzar captured Jerusalem and brought the Kingdom of Judah to an end. 2. False prophet in the court of King Ahab (I KINGS 22: 24). 3. False prophet burned to death in Babylon (JEREMIAH 29:31). 4. Son of Hananiah and prince of Judah during the reign of Jehoiakim (JEREMIAH 36:12).

**ZEISBERGER, DAVID (1721–1808)** MORAVIAN missionary among the Indians of North America. He prepared a grammar and a dictionary for the Indians.

**ZEITGEIST** *spirit of the time* Term for the intellectual and moral climate of opinion at a given time.

**ZEKENIM** *elders* Term for Jewish leaders.

**ZELOTES** A name of Simon the Zealot. See ZEALOTS.

**ZEMIROT** Jewish songs sung at SABBATH meals.

**ZEM-ZEM** Name of the sacred well at MECCA said to have saved the lives of ISHMAEL and his mother HAGAR when driven away by ABRAHAM.

**ZEN** Contemplative school of BUDDHISM, developed in China and Japan, that became popular in Japan in the fourteenth century and gained adherents in the United States in the latter part of the twentieth century. Known as CH'AN in China, this sect reacted against the intellectual emphasis of the Buddhism of India by stressing meditation, physical training, and mystic intuition. The disciple of Zen discovers reality by looking within. Two main divisions of Zen are Rinzai (brought to Japan in the twelfth century by the Japanese monk EISAI) and Soto (founded in the thirteenth century by Eisai's pupil Dogen). Soto emphasizes "ZAZEN" while Rinzai emphasizes the riddle or nonsense statement as a way to spiritual enlightenment.

**ZEND AVESTA** *interpretation of the sacred text* ZOROASTRIAN scripture. See AVESTA.

**ZENDO** ZEN building for spiritual contemplation.

**ZEN-JI** A ZEN teacher.

**ZENKO-JI** Site of a number of seventh-century BUDDHIST buildings in the vicinity of Nagano, Japan.

**ZENO (fifth century)** Roman emperor of the East about 474 to 491. Through his "HENOTIKON," he sought to end the division caused by the MONOPHYSITES, but instead caused a worse one.

**ZENRIN JUSHU** Compilation of BUDDHIST, TAOIST, and CONFUCIAN writings studied by scholars of Rinzai ZEN Buddhism.

**ZEPHANIAH** *the Lord has hidden* 1. Prophet of royal blood, contemporary with JEREMIAH and JOSIAH, who prophesied during the latter's reign in Judah. The book by his name, ninth of the MINOR PROPHETS, warns of the coming judgment of God but also speaks of His love and care. 2. A Kohathite (I CHRONICLES 6:33, 36). See KOHATH. 3. Priest and contemporary of Jeremiah slain by Nebuchadnezzar (JEREMIAH 21:1; 52:24–27). 4. Father of Josiah and contemporary of ZERUBBABEL (ZECHARIAH 6:10, 14).

**ZERUBBABEL** *born in Babylon* Prince of Judah, contemporary with ZECHARIAH and HAGGAI, who led the rebuilding of the temple in Jerusalem in the sixth century B.C. He is among those listed in the genealogies of Jesus. (EZRA 2:2; 3:2, 8; 5:1–2; ZECHARIAH 4:9–10; MATTHEW 1:12, 13.)

**ZERVAN** *time* Father of AHURA MAZDAH and AHRIMAN in ZOROASTRIANISM.

**ZERVAN AKARANA** *time eternal* Another name for ZERVAN, apparently the ultimate reality or first cause in ZOROASTRIANISM.

**ZETHEUS** Son of Zeus. See AMPHION.

**ZEUS** *God* Supreme god in Greek religion. The god of the heavens, the elements, and justice, Zeus punished wrongdoers and upheld ancient morality. His Roman counterpart was JUPITER, "Father Zeus."

**ZIEGENBALG, BARTHOLOMAUS (1683–1719)** German missionary to India, one of the first in PROTESTANTISM. He translated the New Testament into Tamil.

**ZIV** Early name of the Jewish month Iyar, the eighth month.

**ZIGGURAT** Ancient Sumerian temple, pyramidal in form with an outside stairway ascending in a spiral ramp to the top. Reminiscent of the tower of Babel (GENESIS 11:3 ff.), the ziggurat had a house for the god at the top. Important ziggurats have been found at Uruk and Ur.

**ZILPAH** Handmaiden of Leah who bore Leah's husband two sons, Asher and Gad (GENESIS 29:24; 30:9–13; 35:26; 37:2).

**ZIMRI** Jewish general who killed King Elah of Israel and reigned for seven days. He was succeeded by Omri who attacked him in turn (I KINGS 16:8–19).

**ZIN** Desert region of Sinai where the ISRAELITES wandered on their exodus from Egypt.

**ZINZENDORF, NIKOLAUS LUDWIG (1700–1760)** German nobleman under whose guidance and aid the MORAVIAN BRETHREN developed. He became a bishop, influenced John WESLEY, and established Moravian settlements in Pennsylvania. His theology emphasized personal love for and devotion to Christ, and "religion of the heart."

**ZION** 1. Part of Jerusalem called the City of David (II SAMUEL 5:7). 2. Jerusalem, or the temple area (PSALM 2:6; 9:11; 137:1). 3. The Promised Land of JUDAISM. 4. The city of God or heaven (Hebrews 12:22). 5. City in Illinois founded by John Alexander DOWIE as the center of the CHRISTIAN CATHOLIC CHURCH.

**ZIONIDES** Jewish songs lamenting the loss of ZION.

**ZIONISM** Jewish movement begun to establish an autonomous Jewish state in Palestine. Today it supports a variety of activities including immigration to Israel.

**ZIONITES** Term for members of CHRISTIAN CATHOLIC CHURCH.

**ZIPPORAH** *sparrow* Moses's Midianite wife (EXODUS 2:16–22).

**ZIZITH or TZITZITH** Tassels at the corners of the Jewish TALLITH or prayer shawl.

**ZOAR** City to which Lot and his daughters fled upon the destruction of Sodom (GENESIS 14:2, 8; 19:19–29).

**ZOHAR** Cabalistic book allegorically interpreting the PENTATEUCH. Attributed to Rabbi SIMON BEN YOCHAI, it was prepared by Moses de Leon in the thirteenth century.

**ZOMBI** Reanimated VOODOO corpse, or the supernatural power which so reanimates it, or a Voodoo snake god.

**ZOROASTER (sixth century B.C.)** Persian founder of ZOROASTRIANISM. Also called Zarathustra, he was a prophet and religious leader whose visions led to the gradual spread of the Zoroastrian faith. See also PARSEES.

**ZOROASTRIANISM** Dualistic religion of Persia founded by ZOROASTER. Its sacred writings compose the Zend AVESTA. Its doctrines revolve around the interaction between the good god AHURA MAZDAH or Ormazd and the evil spirit AHRIMAN or Angra Mainyu. These are forever in conflict, as are the angelic hosts who follow each and the People of Righteousness who are opposed by the People of Falsehood. Three great commandments in Zoroastrianism are to think good thoughts, to speak good words, and to perform good deeds. Those who do this will inherit eternal rewards while the wicked will meet their doom in a horrible abyss. See also PARSEES.

**ZOROBABEL** See ZERUBBABEL.

**ZOSIMUS, ST. (fifth century)** Greek bishop of Rome 417–418. Several of his ventures had to be abandoned. His feast day is December 26.

**ZOSIMUS (fifth century)** Greek historian whose works, though polemically anti-Christian, preserve valuable information relating to the church in the first four centuries.

**ZOTZILAHA CHIMALMAN** Mayan bat god.

**ZU** Babylonian storm god.

**ZUCCARO, FEDERIGO (1542–1609)** Italian painter who decorated cathedrals in Florence and Rome.

**ZUCCARO, TADDEO (1529–1566)** Italian painter to Popes JULIUS III and Paul IV. With his brother Federigo (above) he painted frescoes in the VATICAN.

**ZUCCHETTO** Small skullcap worn by CATHOLIC clergymen during mass.

**ZUGOT** *pairs* Head of the SANHEDRIN and his assistant, or two representative teachers, through the time of HILLEL.

**ZULHIJYAH** Month of pilgrimage in the MOSLEM calendar.

**ZUMARRAGE, JUAN DE (1468–1548)** Spanish FRANCISCAN who became the first bishop of Mexico. He prepared some of the first books printed in America.

**ZUNZ, LEOPOLD (1794–1886)** Leader in JUDAISM who helped modernize the doctrines and worship of his faith.

**ZURBARAN, FRANCISCO DE (1598–1664)** Distinguished Spanish painter of many religious scenes including "The Crucifixion,"

"Virgin and Child with St. John," and "St. Francis."

**ZURICH** Canton of Switzerland with an autonomous history. It became a bastion of PROTESTANTISM during the REFORMATION.

**ZURICH CONSENSUS** Theological statement, drafted by John CALVIN and Heinrich BULLINGER, which united Swiss Protestants.

**ZWEMER, SAMUEL M. (1867–1952)** American missionary to Moslems in various parts of the world under the REFORMED CHURCH. A leader in the Student Volunteer Movement which inspired many young people to become missionaries, he wrote many books and edited *The Moslem World*.

**ZWICKAU PROPHETS** ANABAPTISTS who set up a religious community in Saxony in the sixteenth century. Led by Thomas MÜNZER, they moved to Wittenberg where their movement was destroyed by Martin LUTHER in 1522.

**ZWINGLI, ULRICH (1484–1531)** Swiss PROTESTANT reformer. Ordained a priest in 1506, he became a friend of ERASMUS and a student of Scripture. Through his influence priests began to marry, the mass was transformed into a feast commemorating the death of Christ, and monasticism began to disintegrate. Theologically more radical than LUTHER, Zwingli heavily stressed the authority of the Bible and the commemorative nature of communion. To him the sacraments conveyed no divine grace; they merely symbolized it. He was killed in a war between Zurich and the other Swiss cantons in 1531.

**ZWINGLIANISM** Term for the theology or sacramental tenets of Ulrich ZWINGLI.

**ZYGOMALAS, JOHN (1498–1578)** Greek Orthodox ecclesiastic who proposed union between the PROTESTANT and GREEK ORTHODOX churches.